Standard Basque

MW00339447

Standard Basque

A Progressive Grammar

Volume 1: The Grammar

Rudolf P. G. de Rijk

The MIT Press
Cambridge, Massachusetts
London, England

This book was set in Times New Roman and Syntax on 3B2 by Asco Typesetters, Hong Kong, and was printed and bound in the United States.

Library of Congress Cataloging-in-Publication Data

Rijk, Rudolf P. G. de.
Standard Basque : a progressive grammar / Rudolf P. G. de Rijk.
p. cm. — (Current studies in linguistics; 44)
Vol. 2: by Rudolf P. G. de Rijk and Armand De Coene.
Includes bibliographical references and index.
ISBN 978-0-262-04242-0 (hardcover : alk. paper), 978-0-262-54654-6 (paperback)
1. Basque language—Grammar. 2. Basque language—Textbooks for foreign speakers—English. I. De Coene, Armand. II. Title.
PH5031.R54 2008
499′.9282421—dc22 2007010132

This book is dedicated to the Basque people

The bertsolari Lazkao-txiki to the Dutch guest, from a recording made August 1965 in Ormaiztegi (in the Goierri dialect of southern Guipuzcoa):

Baldin zuk ontzat artu badezu / Euskalerriko egona,
Gauz auxe eskatutzen dizut gaur / zu holandatar gizona:
Zabaldu zazu emengo berri / naiz txarra eta naiz ona.
Esan izkuntza zar bat badala / ia galduan dagona.
. . . .
Baldin zu bizi bazera eta / zartu eta emen izan,
Emen mintzoa galdu liteke, / oraintxen dijuan gixan.
Emen ezjakin gazterik bada, / zuk gazte aieri esan:
Ni gazterik etorritakuan / olaintxen itzegiten zan.

Translation:
If you have found your stay in the Basque country pleasant,
Then I ask of you today, man from Holland, this:
Make known the news from here, be it bad or good.
Say that there is an old language that is almost lost.
. . . .
If you live long and are here in your old age,
Our language may be lost, the way things are going.
If there are unknowing youths here, tell those young people:
When I came here as a young man, people used to speak in this way.

Contents

Map of the Basque Country

Foreword

Rudolf de Rijk of the Netherlands was a linguist much loved and respected by all his Basque colleagues—loved because of his frequent visits to the Basque Country, where he would seek out his numerous Basque-speaking friends and ply them with questions and suggestions about examples drawn from literature and conversation; and respected because all of us saw that he was a great specialist in Basque, an expert in both its synchronic and diachronic development. As such, he was constantly called upon to direct dissertations, deliver papers, and participate in academic committees, meetings, and seminars, while at the same time teaching and sharing his research in numerous works published over the 25 years preceding his death in 2003.

Rudolf de Rijk was a great lover of languages and spoke several with ease and fluency. First of course was his mother tongue, Dutch, but his Ph.D. thesis, "Studies in Basque Syntax: Relative Clauses" (MIT, 1972b), written under the direction of our late mutual friend Ken Hale, attests to his command of English, and he also wrote often in French, a language he especially admired because of its sound and grace. Then, too, in Chinese restaurants he would occasionally launch into explanations on the similarities and differences between Cantonese and Mandarin based on the characters he read in the menu. But these were only some of the languages that he was skilled in—apart of course from Basque, which he spoke with manifest ease.

He devoted many hours of patient study to Basque, to its phonology, to its syntax, and to its literature. For years he taught the secrets of this language to the young people who had the privilege of being his students in the Netherlands. And during those same years he was a teacher and guide for Basque linguists as well. He was always under the impression that he was learning from us, but what was really happening was exactly the opposite. Every doubt or question that he so tentatively raised would spark in us the discovery of aspects of our language that not only had remained unexplained until that moment, but that no one had even thought to explore in any published grammar. For this reason, Rudolf de Rijk became a point of reference for Basque linguists.

The book now published by MIT Press is an exceptional piece of scholarship, a magnificent descriptive grammar of Basque or *Euskara* (the name by which we who live in the

Basque Country refer to our language when speaking either in Basque or Spanish). *Standard Basque: A Progressive Grammar* can be said to be de Rijk's life's work, the one he devoted most of his time to, particularly since the 1980s, until illness finally took over and kept him from completing it with the care and attention characteristic of all his writings. It is because of this devotion that it is a great work, and an unfinished one—unfinished at least in the way he would have wanted.

Fortunately, Rudolf de Rijk had poured his greatest energies into this project, and most of its main chapters were finished by the time of his death. So these pages encapsulate many years of endeavor—too many perhaps by today's normal standards. He began by writing the first chapters in Dutch and ended up with a grammar in English, having reworked and rewritten those early chapters. But there were others for which no English version existed. Thanks, however, to the patient and painstaking efforts of his widow, Virgina de Rijk, and his former student Fleur Veraart, these were meticulously recovered and incorporated separately (see "The Unfinished Chapters," p. 779) following the chapters originally written in English. Thus this publication is much more complete than it might have been.

What Rudolf de Rijk presents here is a descriptive grammar, complete with well-explained examples, of the Basque spoken at the end of the 20th century. When we say Basque in general like this, however, it should be noted that within this language there are numerous dialects, all quite distinct—so much so in fact that if we compare the two that are furthest apart geographically, we find that a speaker in the easternmost area of the Basque Country (Zuberoa or the Soule region in France) will have great difficulties in communicating with a Basque speaker in the westernmost region (Bizkaia, in Spain)—serious difficulties indeed, unless they are both literate in this language. As speakers learn to read and write in Basque, such communication problems gradually lessen and disappear, because the terms and constructions of neighboring dialects become much more intelligible.

Literature in Basque has existed since the 16th century, in particular books and works of a religious nature. The Catholic Church was the institution most interested in preserving the language both in written texts and in its teachings. In many places, the only "educated" Basque that native speakers heard was the language used by Catholic priests on Sunday. This was especially the case in the Spanish Basque Country, where the largest number of Basque speakers can be found. The facts that there were so many different dialects and that the speech community was further divided by the border between Spain and France meant that unification of the written language proved nearly impossible in centuries past. Writers naturally used their own dialect and, in the absence of a common system, even their own spelling in transcribing Basque words, based on French or Spanish conventions. Consequently, a single sound ended up being written in various ways. However, the concern on the part of Basque authors to make their writing comprehensible to all speakers has existed down through the centuries, particularly when undertaking a work of certain importance.

It was with a view to resolving this problem that the Royal Academy of the Basque Language (Euskaltzaindia in Basque) was founded in 1919, thanks to the combined effort—in actions dating back to the middle of the 19th century—on the part not only of Basque experts from within Spain and France but also of foreign specialists interested in our language. In this regard, Rudolf de Rijk was carrying on a well-established tradition, of which he himself was perhaps the best-known exponent in recent times. One of the main objectives of the new academy was to promote the birth of a standard literary language—a single orthographic and morphological code or system following common guidelines that could be used by all Basque writers, regardless of their dialect of origin. Much time was to pass, however, before this wish could be fulfilled, because a consensus could never be reached on any of the different models proposed over the years. The moment of unification, based on the morphological features of the central dialects (the differences between dialects being more of a phonetic-morphological nature than a matter of syntax), occurred finally at the end of the 1960s at the height of the Franco dictatorship. Under the guidance of the eminent linguist Luis Michelena (Koldo Mitxelena in Basque), the academy proposed, at a congress held in the Arantzazu monastery, a set of basic guidelines to resolve spelling, morphology, and certain lexical aspects of the language in a systematic way. Those were momentous times. A process of this kind is never easy, but on top of the intrinsic difficulties involved, there was the challenge of trying to carry on the business of an academy such as Euskaltzaindia, whose stated mission was to safeguard a language prohibited under the dictatorship.

The objective did not appear readily attainable. It would be necessary to convince people who used the language naturally in both speech and writing—but in their own dialect—to suddenly abandon that habit and begin to use other, different forms. Not many years ago, Gabriel García Márquez proposed a set of spelling changes for Spanish, and there have also been attempts to introduce changes in the spelling of French and English. There is no need to recall here the commotion raised whenever such a change is suggested. However, all such proposals pale in comparison to the one put forward by the Basque Academy back in 1968 to unify literary Basque. It meant attempting to achieve in just a few decades what other languages had resolved gradually over centuries. Moreover, it meant going from habitual use of the language in rural areas and restricted environments only to generalized use in schools, literature, the media, and so on. Naturally many writers felt, as they began to struggle with the new standard dialect, that what flowed from their pen was an artificial language that no longer reflected their own voice. For this reason, enormous tensions arose at first, and there were writers who refused to follow the new guidelines.

As things turned out, however, success came in just a few months, thanks primarily to two key factors. Professor Koldo Mitxelena (a long-time acquaintance of Rudolf de Rijk's) held the chair of Indo-European Linguistics at the University of Salamanca and enjoyed solid prestige among Spanish and Basque linguists. He had also taught at the

Sorbonne in Paris, at the invitation of Professor André Martinet. His enormous erudition and vast knowledge of Basque, comparative linguistics, and classical and ancient languages were such that few were foolish enough to gainsay him. His Ph.D. thesis on historical Basque phonetics (*Fonética Histórica Vasca*) is still, after so many years, one of the finest studies on Basque ever published and one that has marked the training of several generations of new linguists educated in Basque universities, particularly the University of the Basque Country. It was through the efforts of Mitxelena that Basque studies finally took their rightful place alongside other university course offerings. And it was Mitxelena who wrote the project for unified literary Basque that was debated and finally accepted by the Royal Academy of the Basque Language.

The other main factor contributing to the success of the model proposed by Euskaltzaindia was its widespread acceptance among the youngest, most active, and most creative Basque writers, who harbored no doubts about the wisdom of the proposal. Those years began to see more publications in Basque than ever before, with novels, poetry, and other genres finally moving into the front, ranking ahead of religious texts. There was also great demand for textbooks written in Basque, as more and more families enrolled their children in schools where all subjects were taught in this language. In the years since then, the triumph of the standard model (*Euskara Batua* or Unified Basque) has been absolute, although still today, at the beginning of the 21st century, it is far from being a perfected, finished model.

In the years since 1968, the original proposal has been honed, and Euskaltzaindia continues to work on standardizing various aspects of the language that are not sufficiently fixed. However, thanks to phenomena such as the burgeoning of Basque literature in the 1990s (e.g., Bernardo Atxaga, whose books are translated into dozens of languages), the emergence of mass media in Basque (television, radio, newspapers, and magazines), and the introduction of the language at all levels of education from nursery to university (with dozens of majors available entirely in Basque), today "educated" Basque is spoken by nearly all members of the speech community, although at a cost that cannot be ignored. For one thing, the language is losing some of its vividness and subtlety. By this I do not mean merely the gradual disappearance of dialectical differences, in particular those that have been least studied (the "tone" or "music" of each dialect), but the fact that the standard dialect often presents a somewhat dull, colorless photograph of the language, giving the impression it has lost its richness of expression. For another, the language continues to suffer the effects of diglossia because of the overriding importance of Spanish and French, and it is being altered accordingly. In addition to the internal, dialectical division of the language that has always existed, today, as a result of political factors, the "state-based" external division giving rise to differences depending on whether the language is spoken in Spain or in France is more apparent than ever.

Against this background then, Rudolf de Rijk has left us a grammar of the Basque spoken at the end of the 20th century, of the language more or less common now to all

Basques and used in teaching, the media, and literature. That is, in contrast to other magnificent grammars written in languages other than Basque (e.g., the grammar of Lafitte, first published in 1944, written in French), this is a grammar of the unified standard language.

It is not of course the first grammar of the Basque language—indeed, many have been published over the course of history. Euskaltzaindia's Committee on Grammar has devoted more than 25 years to this subject and has published six volumes of a descriptive grammar (*Euskal Gramatika. Lehen Urratsak*). But these books are being written in Basque by a broad team of linguists and presuppose a high degree of knowledge of the language on the part of readers. *Euskal Gramatika* is a grammar written for people who already know the language, although it does provide abundant information on dialects and speech forms that some readers might be totally unfamiliar with, depending on where they live.

There are also other Basque grammars written in English. Most recently, in 2003 Mouton de Gruyter brought out an excellent grammar edited by José Ignacio Hualde and Jon Ortiz de Urbina entitled *A Grammar of Basque*, but the approach is quite different from de Rijk's, for the work presented here is in many respects unique. First, particularly through the examples, but also in the text itself, it provides a wealth of information on the dialects, even though its main objective is to give readers having no prior knowledge of Basque sufficient, reliable, and detailed information on the standard version of the language. But the author saw it as a work halfway between a traditional grammar and a method for learning Basque—a grammar because of the abundant information on morphology, syntax, phrases, and the like explained with numerous examples drawn from a broad array of writers from different periods (for which purpose, by the way, he had to devise a somewhat unified spelling system). De Rijk presents a problem and then, little by little, as though working in concentric circles, probes deeper and deeper into different aspects of the language. Occasionally he seems to be proposing simple solutions for problems whose complexity appears obvious. But this is easily explained. De Rijk was not only a superb linguist, but one who had spent years investigating these very problems, examining and experiencing them deeply and thoroughly. Moreover, he had already published studies on some of these, including relative constructions (chapter 19) or the partitive (chapter 13), to name just two.

Rudolf de Rijk had his own students in mind when years ago he began to write those first lines on Basque grammar in Dutch. And this becomes obvious in the text. One can see it, for example, in the structure of the book. Each chapter consists of a presentation setting out in detail the problem being addressed and contains abundant examples, vocabulary, and information on verb morphology. De Rijk dwells patiently and meticulously on all the possible morphological variants for the case in hand in order to provide the reader with adequate information. He then systematically ends each chapter with translation exercises from Basque to English and vice versa. It is for these reasons that we say that the work often strikes us as being both a traditional grammar and a language-learning method—exactly the brilliant kind of work that would have pleased his thesis director, Ken Hale.

De Rijk refused to have glosses included in his text explaining the examples. He was not convinced they would provide enough extra information to make the text any easier to follow, and he also feared that their inclusion would further lengthen a book that was already overly long. Therefore, they have been added separately, trusting that the decision will meet with a positive response. The work done in this regard by Armand De Coene is exemplary—there is no other word for it. The inclusion of these glosses and the chapters translated from the original Dutch (and not, therefore, revised in their final version by the author) has added to the comprehensiveness of this great work.

What the reader has now is a grammar written by a man with vast knowledge of the language he wished to describe. He had a thorough firsthand knowledge of the different grammars already written on this language; he had delved into the literature of dozens of Basque authors; he was well versed in the new approaches to linguistic analysis developed as a result of the research begun in and around MIT; he had taught this language to people living far from the Basque Country and was therefore well aware of the problems that this language poses for people learning it abroad; he had discussed the language at length with Basque linguists; and he was a person singularly endowed with a great deal of common sense and with the kind of teaching skill that enabled him to get his points across with few words. Clearly, such a combination of knowledge, skill, and talent is rarely found. For these reasons, he was made an honorary member of the Royal Academy of the Basque Language and awarded a doctor of letters degree, honoris causa, by the University of the Basque Country. The honor was ours, Rudolf. *Eskerrik asko*, thank you very much indeed.

Pello Salaburu
Professor of Basque Philology
University of the Basque Country

Acknowledgments

My husband Rudolf de Rijk would have relished this opportunity to express his gratitude to the many people who helped him through the years in his continuing study of the Basque language. It is with mixed feelings of both pleasure and sadness that I now attempt to do this for him.

This book is the culmination of a collaboration between Rudolf and many others that began over 40 years ago and continued to within weeks of his death in 2003. He first came across the Basque language when he saw the "Aita Mari" monument in San Sebastian in 1957. A local resident, the late Gregorio Iraola, explained to him what it meant and in what language it was written. His interest aroused, Rudolf returned to the Basque Country in the summer of 1959 with the express intention of learning Basque. He settled himself in Azpeitia, where—as he told me later—he greatly enjoyed the generous hospitality of the Bar Victor, where he received so much help from one and all in learning the language. Already in that summer, and continuing in later years, he made his way around the Basque provinces, learning the various dialects. But it was here in this particular area of Guipuzcoa that he concentrated his efforts in the beginning.

The welcome and hospitality he received in Azpeitia, Régil, and Gabiria, and from families such as the Etxaides in San Sebastian, the Garmendias of Ormaiztegi and Beasain, and the continuing friendship and encouragement of Iraola—all so willing to help a young Dutch student—made a deep impression on him.

He considered this grammar to be a collaborative work that would not have been possible without the active help of these and other Basque friends and colleagues, who not only served as informants but also stimulated his thinking in discussions while they worked together trying to unravel the intricacies of the Basque language.

In addition to those (e.g., I. Laka, X. Artiagoitia, the late J. Basterrechea) to whom he has already expressed his indebtedness in various sections of the grammar and in his published writings, he would have wanted to elaborate on the great influence of the late Koldo Mitxelena, Yon Etxaide, and Nemesio Etxaniz. He would certainly have mentioned how in recent years he benefited from regular consultation with the following: Xabier Altzibar, Miren Azkarate, Arantzazu Elordieta, Patxi Goenaga, Mari Pilar Lasarte, Beñat

Oihartzabal, Pello Salaburu, Felipe Yurramendi, and Koldo Zuazo. There are perhaps others whose names I have not mentioned, and I apologize for the oversight. My excuse is that I am handicapped in that I was not actively involved in his work until the last months of his life, and we never discussed this matter before his death.

He profited also from comments from non-Basque linguists who saw earlier versions of this grammar. Both E. Wayles Browne and the late Kenneth Hale regularly received new chapters from him as they were written. At a later stage of the work, Henk Schultink also commented on the chapters.

That Rudolf was able to devote most of his professional life to the study of Basque was due first to a 1975–1977 grant (Project 39–37) from ZWO, at that time the Dutch foundation for the advancement of pure research, and thereafter to his faculty position at the University of Leiden—first in the department of comparative linguistics, and after his retirement in 2002, for an all too brief period in the general linguistics department and the University of Leiden Center for Linguistics. The grammar developed in these years out of his government-financed research into the Basque dialects and his experience teaching Basque to his Dutch students.

It was not without sacrifice that Rudolf devoted so many years to the writing of this grammar. A natural polymath, he had to discipline himself to concentrate on this one task, deferring the pursuit of his multiple interests to a future that never came. Rudolf hoped that in writing this grammar he would be able to give back something of value to the Basque people. By sharing his hard-won insights into Basque he would not only help lay the groundwork for future investigation but also give an impetus to a new wave of linguistic interest in this singular language.

For myself, in preparing Rudolf's grammar for publication, I have greatly benefited from the goodwill Rudolf generated. Not only from his Basque friends and colleagues, but also here in the Netherlands I have received a plenitude of help and support.

From Leiden University, Lisa Cheng and the late Jan Kooij immediately offered help. They assigned me one of their students as an assistant and provided the first computer to enter my house. Lisa remained supportive and gave valuable advice throughout the period of manuscript preparation. Stella Gryllia, my student assistant, was my main helper in the beginning, and her knowledge of both computers and linguistics has been absolutely invaluable. But most of all, her enthusiastic involvement has given me the greatest pleasure, and I am happy to acknowledge her help.

Two friends from Rudolf's chess club, Wim van Vugt and Ton van Garderen, helped me acquire my own computer and gave technical and moral support. Ton also helped me later with some laborious manuscript preparation. They and other Dutch friends helped me understand better the nuances of the Dutch language in the period I was engaged in translating. I thank here also Cor Berben, Theo Mol, my sister-in-law Suzanne de Rijk, Roelie Wilms, and especially Wim van der Wurff. Besides his helping Armand De Coene in preparing the glosses, he aided me tremendously in explaining and helping me translate Dutch linguistic terminology.

While verifying the citations for the many example sentences in the grammar, I called on Pruden Garzia and his staff at the Azkue library of the Basque Academy for help in obtaining photocopies. Maider Etxaide, Arantzazu Elordieta, Bram Jagersma, and Henrike Olasolo all helped me in locating sources. Henrike also helped me even more by advising me on my translations of Basque sentences in the unfinished chapters. Also, Basque colleagues of Rudolf's helped me understand what was happening in Basque when I was translating his Dutch chapters. I am very grateful to Patxi Goenaga, Pello Salaburu, Beñat Oihartzabal, and Itziar Laka, who all took time to answer my questions. Of course, I take full responsibility for the resulting text.

In the final phases of preparing the manuscript for the publisher my daughter Joyce Jacobsen and her husband Bill Boyd came to my aid, providing me with material and technical assistance at their home in Connecticut, and then helping me transfer the weighty manuscript copies to Cambridge, where I finally met Tom Stone of The MIT Press. As senior acquisitions editor, he and Jay Keyser were instrumental in securing this grammar for the MIT Press.

The production team responsible for bringing this project to a successful conclusion deserves my fullest respect. I thank MIT Press's linguistic consultant Anne Mark for her preliminary work on the manuscript. I am very grateful to Peggy M. Gordon and her associates, in particular copy editor Peter Reinhart, for their thoughtful care and expertise in dealing with a complex manuscript. It has been a pleasure working with them.

Were it not for the appearance in my life of Fleur Veraart and the fruitful collaboration that evolved, this grammar would be very different (see "The Unfinished Chapters," p. 779). Besides the magnificent work she did in her translations, she and her husband David McKay also helped me with my own translations. I cannot but think how very pleased Rudolf would have been by this generous and expert help from his former student whom he had encouraged to go on to study linguistics at MIT.

To Armand De Coene, who took on the monumental task of preparing the glosses for the almost four thousand example sentences, I can only express my greatest admiration and thankfulness. He has fully achieved what my husband expected of his brilliant friend and former student. Because of his knowledge of Basque and his familiarity with the manuscript, his input in all aspects in the preparation of the grammar for publication, and especially his collaboration in preparing the Selected Index of Basque Formatives and Words, was absolutely invaluable.

E. Wayles Browne, a dear friend of Rudolf's since their student days, has been involved in the entire project from the very beginning. He received and commented on all chapters of the grammar throughout the years of its development. He was someone I could turn to whenever I needed help in things linguistic. His encouragement and support gave me the courage to continue when I despaired of my efforts in understanding what I was attempting to translate. And it was Wayles who brought this grammar to the attention of Jay Keyser, whose advice and support led to its being published by the MIT Press.

But of all who have worked to see this grammar published, no one has worked harder and with such effect as our dear friend Pello Salaburu. When he learned of Rudolf's fatal illness, he called at once to offer whatever help he could give. It was he who came in our time of great despair and assured Rudolf that his magnum opus would be published; he was not to worry. And, to the surprise of his doctors who had predicted that he could expect no more than three months to live, Rudolf found new strength to continue work on the grammar, the last three chapters being written in the last nine months of his life. It was Pello who took photocopies of the typewritten manuscript and personally made an electronic version with only the partial help of an assistant, Eurydice Arregi, and his wife Carmen Gamarra. And it was he who, after Rudolf's death, gave unstintingly of his advice and expertise and who facilitated the publication of the grammar by obtaining financial support from the Basque government, for which I thank him, his colleague Xabier Aizpurua, general manager of the University of the Basque Country, and Lorea Bilbao, who so ably assisted them.

The Department of Culture of the Basque government contributed generously to support the publication of this book. That this government saw fit to render this aid is an instance again of the generosity that was always shown Rudolf in all his years in the Basque Country. Words are lacking for the gratitude I feel.

Although the grammar as published falls short of what Rudolf had envisaged but was unable to bring to conclusion, all of us involved in this project are nonetheless confident that this publication will justify his hope that his life's work will foster new research and thus become a legacy of consequence to the Basque people.

Virginia de Rijk–Chan
Amsterdam
June 2007

1 Introduction; Orthography and Pronunciation; the Basque Noun Phrase

1.1 Basque Dialects and Euskara Batua

Basque is the original language of the Basque Country, a region of some 20,000 square kilometers partly under French and partly under Spanish rule.

The extent of the Basque Country in modern times is shown on the map on page xvi, which also outlines the traditional seven Basque provinces: Biscay, Alava, Guipuzcoa, Navarra, Labourd, Low Navarra, and Soule. The latter three are administratively part of the French "département des Pyrénées Atlantiques" and will be designated henceforth as "the Northern Provinces."

Not all of the Basque Country has preserved the Basque language. Almost all of Alava as well as a great part of Navarra now lack native speakers. In many other areas throughout the Basque Country native speakers constitute a minority among speakers of the local Romance language: Spanish, French, or Béarnese, depending on the area. The greatest density of Basque speakers is reached in the province of Guipuzcoa and the adjacent zones of Biscay. All in all, the number of native or near-native speakers can be estimated at about a half million.

Nowadays all adult speakers of Basque are bilingual. Moreover, there are many indications that a sizable portion of the population must have been bilingual since time immemorial, going back to Roman and perhaps pre-Roman periods. Bilingualism, then, has been a paramount factor in the Basque sociolinguistic situation for a long time.

Another important factor of long standing, however, has been the extreme local diversity within Basque itself. No fewer than eight dialects were distinguished by the first fieldworker in Basque dialectology, Prince Louis Lucien Bonaparte (1813–1891), Napoleon's nephew. Although his understanding of the concept of dialect is no longer ours, his famous map, "Carte des sept provinces basques, montrant la délimitation actuelle de l'euscara et sa division en dialectes, sous-dialectes et variétés" (London 1863), still forms the basis of contemporary Basque dialectology work.

The eight dialects are

1. Biscayan
2. Guipuzcoan
3. Northern High Navarrese
4. Southern High Navarrese
5. Labourdin (including Baztanese)
6. Western Low Navarrese (including Aezcoan)
7. Eastern Low Navarrese (including Salazarese)
8. Souletin (including the now extinct Roncalese)

Not surprisingly, dialect boundaries coincide only very roughly with provincial limits. Thus Biscayan is spoken not just in Biscay but also in a substantial part of western Guipuzcoa and in the Basque-speaking area of Alava directly south of Biscay. Needless to say, the dialects are by no means uniform within their geographic extensions. This is true even of the subdialects set up by Bonaparte and others. Between neighboring localities in the same subdialect region, phonetic, phonemic, and even morphological differences are quite commonplace and frequently commented upon by native speakers.

No supradialectal written language tradition has evolved in the past, let alone a spoken standard. The reason for this lack is not hard to find. The conditioning factors needed for any of the dialects to achieve supremacy were quite simply lacking. Indeed, there was no unchallenged cultural focus for the whole of the Basque Country, and, for various historical reasons, Basque was never used as a language of administration, so governmental authority failed to lend its prestige to any form of Basque. In fact, the higher classes of the population tended to adopt Castilian (or, in the Northern Provinces, French) for all uses outside the immediate family, or even rejected Basque altogether.

When it comes to our own time, the Basque language situation cannot be discussed, however briefly, without mention of the role of *Euskaltzaindia*, an academy of Basque scholars founded in 1919 with the aim of guarding and investigating the Basque language. In 1976 this Basque academy was accorded official status by King Juan Carlos of Spain, and it has since been denominated "Real Academia de la Lengua Vasca, Euskaltzaindia."

Within this body, since its founding days, there has been an ever growing perception of an urgent need: for Basque to survive at all in the modern world, the introduction of a standard language for written communication is an absolute necessity.

In the first decade of Euskaltzaindia's existence, mere lip service was paid to this issue, but in 1933 its first president, the learned Biscayan priest and prolific author R. M. de Azkue, made the first real effort in this direction. His detailed proposal, however, based on the Guipuzcoan dialect, which was accordingly called *Gipuzkera Osotua* ('Guipuzcoan made complete'), found little support outside Guipuzcoa. Shortly afterward, in 1936, the Spanish Civil War intervened with its dire consequences for all aspects of Basque life and culture. The academy itself led a precarious existence, and it was not until the end of the 1960s that the intellectual climate in the Basque Country became ripe for a renewed attempt at linguistic unification—eagerly desired by some and strongly feared by others.

Realizing by 1968 that there was an influential group of young Basque writers ready to put into practice whatever linguistic norms it would issue, the Basque Academy decided, after much discussion, to go ahead with its project to create a new shared form, *Euskara Batua* ('Unified Basque'), to be used as a written standard for the entire Basque Country.

Filling in the features of this new form has been a gradual process, carried out by the academy under the guidance and supervision of a linguistic scholar of world repute, Koldo Mitxelena (1915–1987)—Luis Michelena to the world at large—now universally acknowledged as the father of Euskara Batua.

Noting that dialectal differences diminish the further one goes back in time, Mitxelena, in his continuous effort to create a type of Basque agreeable to all native speakers, quite naturally favored older forms of speech. Thus, studying the classic Basque authors, above all the most admired Pedro de Axular (1556–1644), came to be seen as an important tool for the creation of the new literary language Basque society was waiting for.

Euskara Batua, unlike the earlier Gipuzkera Osotua, was not conceived as a more elegant version of any of the traditional dialects, not even that of Axular. All the same, it has seemed a natural and commendable policy to prefer central dialect features to those of peripheral dialects. As a result, Euskara Batua conforms most closely to Guipuzcoan, despite the liberal use of the phoneme /h/, unknown in that dialect. The Guipuzcoan affinity of Batua is particularly visible in its morphology. Indeed it was decided without much opposition to adopt in Batua the nominal and verbal morphology of northern Guipuzcoa, modified, to be sure, with some important characteristics shared by all dialects east of Guipuzcoa. These non-Guipuzcoan traits are few in number but high in frequency, as they include the ergative plural form as *-ek* rather than *-ak*, the past tense of the copula as *zen* rather than *zan*, and the relative form of the copula as *den* rather than *dan*. On the lexical level, the influence of the Biscayan dialect is also very noticeable, especially in the more technical vocabulary.

It has taken considerable time for Euskara Batua to become widely accepted, and even now acceptance is not wholly complete. But there is no doubt that the battle has been won. More than 90 percent of what has been published in Basque over the past decade is couched in Batua. It is the only form of Basque used by the "Autonomous Basque Government" as well as by Euskal Telebista (Basque television). Clearly, Basque culture from now on will be inseparably linked with the fate of this new standard language.

Although many matters of detail are not yet codified, it is this language that will constitute the subject of the present book.

As a consequence of this somewhat normative orientation, all sentences used as examples have been normalized with respect to both orthography and morphology, even when taken from Basque authors cited by name who utilized their own dialects.

1.2 Spelling and Pronunciation

1.2.1 Vowels and Diphthongs

Basque has a five-vowel system not unlike that of Castilian Spanish, with the low vowel /a/, the mid vowels /e/ and /o/, and the high vowels /i/ and /u/.

There is no distinctive vowel length. The vowels are generally pronounced rather short, but they can be subject to expressive lengthening, thereby conveying intensity of feeling on the part of the speaker: *beti jaaten, ta edaaten* . . . (Bartolomé, 15) 'always éáting and drínking . . .'.

The pronunciation of a vowel, especially a mid vowel, is often affected by the consonants following it. Thus the mid vowels /e/ and /o/, while usually open, become semiclosed before an adjacent nasal in the same syllable and fully closed before an adjacent nasal belonging to the next syllable.

For the Guipuzcoan dialect, the Spanish phonetician T. Navarro Tomás (1925) presents a detailed account of the pronunciation of the vowels in various contexts. His results are summarized in Jungemann 1956, 295–296.

In the absence of a native Basque speaker, the advice to pronounce the following examples as if they were Spanish words should not lead the reader too far astray.

/a/	ama	mother
	alaba	daughter
	sagar	apple
	sarri	often
/e/	seme	son
	emakume	woman
	eder	beautiful
	egun	day
/o/	on	good
	gona	skirt
	oso	whole, very
	gorri	red
/i/	gizon	man
	ijito	gypsy
	zuri	white
	min	pain
/u/	buru	head
	mutil	boy
	zeru	sky, heaven
	musu	kiss

In addition to these pure vowels, there are six diphthongs, all falling, with /u/ or /i/ as the second element. Their pronunciations follow directly from those of the contributing vowels.

/au/	gau	night
	jaun	sir, lord
/eu/	euskara	Basque language
	euri	rain
/ai/	bai	yes
	aita	father
/ei/	sei	six
	hogei	twenty
/oi/	oin	foot
	goi	above
/ui/	muin	medulla, marrow
	fruitu	fruit

1.2.2 Consonants

1.2.2.1 Plosives

There are only bilabial, dental, and velar plosives in Basque. They can be either voiceless (/p/, /t/, /k/) or voiced (/b/, /d/, /g/). In syllable-final position all plosives are pronounced voiceless and spelled accordingly.

In intervocalic position—often also after /l/ and /r/—voiced plosives are pronounced as the corresponding fricatives. This change is not indicated in the orthography, which lacks the corresponding symbols. For the pronunciation of the following examples, Spanish can again be a reasonable guide.

/p/	polit	pretty
	piper	pepper
	lepo	neck
	premia	need
/b/	behi	cow
	alaba	daughter
	garbi	clean
	brontze	bronze

[*N.B.* The letter *v*, occurring only in recent loans, has the same pronunciation as /b/: *vanpiro* 'vampire', *vodka* 'vodka'.]

/t/	toki	place, spot
	mutil	boy

	bat	one
	tresna	tool
/d/	diru	money
	ardo	wine
	eder	beautiful
	droga	drug
/k/	ke	smoke
	leku	place
	malko	tear
	klera	chalk
/g/	gorri	red
	sagu	mouse
	argi	light
	grina	passion

It should be noted here that combinations of the type plosive plus liquid—excluding, however, **tl*, **dl*—are the only initial clusters permitted in Basque. Except for their presence in onomatopoeia and interjections (*plast!* 'smack!'), they occur exclusively in loanwords. Despite the relative rarity of such clusters, they are not felt as foreign to the language, since many of these loans have become fully naturalized, such as those mentioned in this section.

1.2.2.2 Nasals

There are two nasal phonemes in Basque: bilabial /m/ and /n/, normally alveolar, unlike /t/ and /d/, which are dental.

A palatal nasal *n* occurs phonetically but has no independent status: sometimes it is an allophone of /n/ (see section 1.2.4), sometimes an expressive counterpart to it (see section 1.2.5).

At the end of a syllable, only /n/ occurs, never /m/. With a plosive following, the point of articulation of /n/ totally assimilates to that of the plosive: /nb/ sounds like *mb* and /ng/ like *ŋg*.

Mitxelena, in his unsurpassed *Fonética Histórica Vasca*—henceforth abbreviated as *FHV*—(Michelena 1977, chap. 13), has shown that there is evidence that /m/ did not exist in an earlier stage of Basque. Particularly, many intervocalic *m*'s may have originated as realizations of /nb/. Some examples follow:

/m/	seme	son (from *sembe*, attested in Aquitanian inscriptions)
	mehe	thin (from **bene*)
	min	pain
	horma	wall
	malmutz	sly

/n/	nagusi	boss
	lan	work
	anaia	brother
	arnasa	breath
	zenbat	how much, how many
	handi	big, great (also in frequent use: *haundi*)
	hanka	leg

[*N.B.* Vowels in contact with a nasal nasalize for at least a part of their duration. The Souletin dialect shows distinctive nasalization on vowels as a result of the loss of intervocalic nasal consonants. The other dialects must have gone through a similar stage, for which there is ample documentary evidence in the case of Biscayan. (See *FHV*, section 1.2.)]

1.2.2.3 Liquids

The three Basque liquids (/l/, /r/, and /R/) share the following properties:

1. They are normally realized as apico-alveolars; that is, they are pronounced with the tip of the tongue against the upper alveolar ridge.
2. They are always voiced.
3. They are never syllabic.

For the lateral /l/, the main body of the tongue is held toward the middle of the palate, which gives Basque /l/ an acoustic quality intermediate between the clear Castilian /l/ and the darker /l/ of most forms of English.

Before a dental consonant, /l/ has an apico-dental rather than an apico-alveolar realization. Examples:

lo	sleep
nola	how
hil	dead
plater	plate
elkar	each other
zaldi	horse

The remaining liquids are vibrants: weak /r/ and strong /R/. Weak /r/ is phonetically identical to Castilian *r*, as in Spanish *pero* 'but'; strong /R/ to Castilian *rr*, as in Spanish *perro* 'dog'. Thus J. Harris's definition of Spanish /r/ as "a voiced apico-alveolar single flap" (Harris 1969, section 2.6.1) applies equally well to Basque /r/. Having the same tongue position as weak /r/, strong /R/ consists in a trill made up of three or more flaps in rapid succession.

Just as in Spanish, weak /r/ and strong /R/ are distinguished only in intervocalic position, where strong /R/ is written as *-rr-*. A vibrant in other positions must be deemed an archiphoneme in Prague School parlance. Written *r*, it is commonly realized as a weak trill, consisting of just two flaps.

In Basque, vibrants cannot begin a word: *Erroma* 'Rome', *Erramun* 'Ramon', *errege* 'king', *arrazoi* 'reason'. Some, but not all, Romance neighbors share this peculiarity; Gascon and Aragonese do, Castilian and Galician do not.

Despite this restriction, vibrants are rather frequent in Basque. Some examples:

zuri	white
berri	new
bart	last night
erbi	hare
sorgin	witch
urte	year
zahar	old

As stated previously, /R/ and /r/ do not contrast in final position, where they are pronounced identically and spelled as a single *r*. Suppose now that a suffix beginning with a vowel follows a word ending in *r*. Obviously, the originally final position then turns into an intervocalic one, in which the contrast between the two vibrants is no longer neutralized.

As an example, we can take the comparative suffix *-ago* 'more'. With *eder* 'beautiful', we get *ederrago* 'more beautiful'. What we observe here is this: to be able to pronounce and write such derived forms correctly, one has to know something not indicated by the standard orthography, namely, whether a word-final *r* is weak or strong. Fortunately, the number of words with a final weak *r* is so small that we can state the following rule: Final *r* is always strong, except in the following words:

zer	what
ezer	anything
nor	who
inor	anyone
hor	dog (a very rare word)
paper	paper
plater	plate
plazer	pleasure
ur	water
zur	wood

1.2.2.4 Sibilants and Affricates

Basque has three sibilants: dorso-alveolar /z/, apico-alveolar /s/, and dorso-palatal /x/. In all Basque dialects apart from Souletin and Eastern Low Navarrese, all sibilants are voiceless, except when immediately followed by a nasal or lateral.

Dorso-alveolar /z/ sounds not unlike an English *s*, but even more like a sharp *s* in French. The constriction of the vocal tract required for the sibilant arises when the blade of the tongue is kept close to the back part of the upper alveolar ridge. The tip of the tongue is held downward, often touching the lower teeth or alveolar ridge. Examples are

zu you
gizon man
apaiz priest
zer what
ezti honey
ez no, not

The sibilant spelled *s* sounds rather similar to the *s* of central Castilian Spanish. Its articulation is apico-alveolar: the tongue does not vibrate, but is otherwise in the same position as for the Basque *r*. The needed constriction is accordingly brought about by holding the tip of the tongue up against the upper alveolar ridge. The area of contact is somewhat broader than for a Castilian *s*, so that Basque *s* tends to give a slightly palatal impression, without ever becoming a true palatal.

A clarification by Martin Joos (1952, 223; 1957, 372) may be welcome: "The apical articulation has the tongue tip raised, and the tip itself makes the sibilant squeeze. Thus apical [ṣ] articulation leaves a resonance chamber under the tongue-tip and behind the lower incisors; but dorsal [s̱] has this same space filled up by the tongue. Therefore the [ṣ] has a lower resonance and sounds rather 'blunt', somewhat like [š], while the [s̱] has a higher resonance and sounds relatively 'sharp'."

Here are some examples:

su fire
oso whole, very
asko much, many
esne milk (in certain dialects *ezne*)
arras totally, very

The sibilant /x/ is a palatal, or rather palato-alveolar, fricative similar to English *sh* or French *ch*, except that the position of the tongue is a shade more to the back and there is no rounding of the lips. Examples are

xede goal, purpose
xaboi soap
xume puny, paltry, common
axola care
toxa pouch

Each of the three sibilants has a corresponding affricate, represented in writing by a combination of *t* and the sibilant: *tz*, *ts*, *tx*.

Despite this spelling convention, they are not to be analyzed as clusters, but rather as a fortis articulation of the sibilants, that is, phonologically strengthened sibilants. With some rare exceptions in the Souletin and Eastern Low Navarrese dialects, Basque affricates are always voiceless.

/tz/ is a dorso-alveolar affricate, sounding like *z* in German *Zahn* 'tooth':

ametz Pyrenean (muricated) oak
hotz cold
atzo yesterday
beltz black
hartz bear
antz likeness

/ts/ is an apico-alveolar affricate, ending like Basque /s/:

amets dream
hots sound, noise
atso old hag
saltsa sauce
intsusa elder (*Sambucus nigra*)

/tx/ is a palatal affricate, ending like Basque /x/. It is unaspirated, but otherwise similar to English *ch*:

etxe house
itxura appearance
txar bad
txiki small
txori bird

[*N.B.* Of these three affricates, only /tx/ can occur in word-initial position.]

1.2.2.5 Other Fricatives: /f/ and /j/

/f/ is a labiodental fricative, quite similar to English *f*. Basque /f/ is severely restricted in distribution: it occurs only at the beginning of a syllable. In some areas, /p/ is substituted for /f/ in some—or even most—words. Examples:

fede faith, religion
falta lack, fault
froga proof
afari evening meal
alfer lazy, useless

/j/ is pronounced differently in different dialects. In Euskara Batua two pronunciations are commonly encountered: a semivocalic pronunciation (like *y* in English), spread by

Basque television and recommended by the Basque Academy, and a velar pronunciation (like the Spanish jota or the *ch* of Scottish *loch*), taken over from the Guipuzcoan dialect. Examples:

jaun sir, Lord
jende folk, people
joko game, play
moja nun

[*N.B.* The distribution of /j/ is even more restricted than that of /f/. It only occurs at the beginning of a syllable and does not enter into clusters. Even medial clusters are avoided: the loan word *aljebra* is much less common than *algebra*.]

1.2.2.6 The Letter *h*

While there are good reasons to assume that during the first millennium of our era all Basque dialects had a phoneme /h/ (*FHV*, sec. 11.3–4), only the dialects north of the Pyrenean border have been able to maintain it. We quote from Bonaparte (1869, xv, fn. 3):

L'*h*, à l'exception d'une seule commune, n'existe pas en Espagne, pas même dans les sous-dialectes qui au point de vue linguistique appartiennent à la France. En effet, on n'entend ce son ni dans le roncalais, qui est une subdivision du souletin; ni dans le salazarais, qui fait partie du bas-navarrais oriental; ni dans l'aezcoan, qui appartient au bas-navarrais occidental. C'est donc le pays, plutôt que le dialecte, qui détermine l'absence de l'*h*.

[The *h*, with the exception of a single parish, does not exist in Spain, not even in the subdialects that from a linguistic point of view belong to France. Indeed one does not hear this sound, not in Roncalese, which is a subdivision of Souletin, nor in Salazarese, which belongs to Eastern Low Navarrese, nor in Aezcoan, which belongs to Western Low Navarrese. Thus it is the country, rather than the dialect, that determines the absence of the *h*.] (All translations of quoted material are the author's unless stated otherwise. Here, by V. de Rijk–Chan [VdR].)

As Bonaparte goes on to observe, /h/ is also absent in the southwestern region of Labourd, including St. Jean de Luz, Urrugne, and Biriatou, but not Ascain or Guéthary. In the dialects where it is found, /h/ is pronounced as in standard English. It always requires a following vowel, and unless word-initial, must be preceded by one of these: a vowel, a nasal (but never *m*), or a liquid. Moreover, voiceless plosives can be aspirated in certain positions—commonly at the beginning of the first or second syllable.

Turning now to Euskara Batua, by far the most controversial decision taken by the Basque Academy in standardizing Basque orthography was the inclusion of the letter *h*. Accordance between two or more dialects served as a guideline; those *h*'s occurring only in Souletin were to be discarded. As a concession to the non-*h* dialects, postconsonantal *h*'s were banned, leaving only word-initial or intervocalic ones. Examples: *hiru* 'three'; *bihotz* 'heart'; *zahar* 'old'.

Quite a number of minimal pairs can be listed, where the presence of *h* distinguishes words that would otherwise be homonyms:

ahate	duck	ate	door
hala	thus	ala	or
har	worm	ar	male
haran	valley	aran	plum
sehi	servant	sei	six

(For more examples, see *FHV*, section 11.5.)

The disappearance of /h/ in the pronunciation of all but the northern dialects has caused a displacement of syllable boundaries, or even coalescence of vowels, with the result that standard spelling and what must be called standard pronunciation are sometimes rather at variance:

leiho	window	Usual pronunciation	leyo
mahai	table	Usual pronunciation	mai
mahats	grape	Usual pronunciation	mats
mehe	thin	Usual pronunciation	me

1.2.3 Accentuation

In his interesting article "Tone and Stress in Basque: A Preliminary Study," J. I. Hualde aptly states: "The Basque speaking domain encompasses a surprising variety of accentual systems. These systems range from some that are quite similar to the ones found in the neighboring Romance languages to others that are very different in their nature from anything found in Romance" (Hualde 1986, 867).

Simplifying Mitxelena's fourfold classification (Michelena 1972b), Hualde (1986) distinguishes only two accentual types in his essay: a Western, or Tonal, type, and an Eastern, or Stress, type. Where does Euskara Batua fit into this dichotomy?

Reluctant to regulate on matters of pronunciation, the Basque Academy has not issued any directives regarding accentuation. Strictly speaking then, there is no prescribed accentuation in Euskara Batua. Yet, because the majority of native speakers of Basque follow the Western system, we will describe its character here very briefly.

For this purpose, we must rely mainly on Basterrechea's (1974, 1975) careful, if atheoretic, study on accentuation in his native Guernican dialect. The Western accentual system, obtaining in nearly all of Guipuzcoa and Biscay, is a tonal system characterized by two distinctive patterns of intonation, henceforth called *tonemes*. The domain of intonation is not the word as such but the phonological phrase, that is, a syntactic unit pronounced without a pause.

The first, or normal, toneme consists of a rather flat sequence of syllables, in which the initial one has a slightly lower pitch and the final one a slightly higher pitch than the others. Observers accustomed to a stress system tend to interpret this tonal contour as a main stress on the second and a secondary stress on the last syllable of the phrase.

The second, or anormal, toneme contrasts with the first merely in that the last two syllables are pronounced with a marked decrease in pitch and intensity. Here the pitch contrasts stand out much more clearly than in the first toneme, which was therefore described as "rather flat."

In short phrases, that is, three syllables or less, this toneme tends to give an impression of initial stress, provided both the final and the penultimate syllables are lowered. This is not always the case, as the intonation of anormal three-syllable phrases is subject to some variation: either high-low-low (older generation in Guernica) or low-high-low (younger generation in Guernica).

Phonological phrases based on a plural noun always carry the second toneme. Phonological phrases based on a singular noun follow the first toneme, except when the head noun belongs to a marked class of nouns. Suffixes also play an important role, as the presence of certain suffixes requires the second toneme, regardless of the head noun.

1.2.4 Automatic Palatalization

In the western part of Labourd, an extensive portion of Navarra, all of Guipuzcoa, and nearly all of Biscay, the following rule of pronunciation obtains: After the vowel *i*, intervocalic /1/ and /n/ are realized as palatals.

We may speak here of "palatalization" as long as we realize that we are dealing not with a superimposed secondary articulation as in Russian but rather with a change in primary articulation.

Whereas older spelling systems marked this change by writing *ñ* for palatal *n* and *ll* for palatal *l* in the Spanish fashion, the new orthography for Euskara Batua ignores it, as the alternation is purely contextual and therefore nonphonemic.

Some examples with palatal *l*, sounding like Spanish *ll* in *llano* 'plain': *ile* 'hair', *pila* 'pile', *ilun* 'dark', *zilar* 'silver'.

An interesting exception is the loanword *lili* 'lily', 'flower' (and its derivatives, such as *lilitxo* 'harlot'), where the intervocalic *l* remains strictly nonpalatal. Some examples with palatal *n*, sounding like *ny* in English *canyon*: *inor* 'anyone', *grina* 'passion', *pinu* 'pine'. In the loanword *minutu* 'minute' some speakers palatalize the *n*, but most do not.

The semivowel [y] of the diphthongs *ai, ei, oi, ui* likewise palatalize an adjacent *1* or *n* followed by a vowel. This palatalization, in fact, happens in a much wider area than the one brought about by vocalic [i]. Now included are Soule, all of Guipuzcoa and Biscay, and nearly all of Navarra (but not, e.g., Roncal).

A few regions, High Soule for example, even palatalize *n* and *l* in the absence of a following vowel.

After palatalization, the semivowel [y] is usually absorbed by the palatal consonant, as can be seen from the older spellings of such words. Examples: *maila* 'degree', 'level', *teilatu* 'roof', *oilo* 'chicken', *baina* 'but', *keinu* 'gesture', *soinu* 'music'. Older spelling: *malla, tellatu, ollo, baña, keñu, soñu.*

More details about these palatalizations can be found in *FHV*, section 10.12–14, and A. M. Echaide 1976.

In certain regions of Guipuzcoa and Biscay, intervocalic /t/ also is palatalized after vocalic [i] and, especially, semivocalic [y]. Palatalized *t* may then become indistinguishable from the affricate *tx*, so that *aita* 'father' sounds as [*atxa*]. We do not recommend this pronunciation, as it is far from general and apt to be viewed as substandard.

1.2.5 Expressive Palatalization

Basque nominals, that is, nouns, adjectives, and adverbs, can enter into a process called "expressive palatalization," connoting smallness in nouns and mitigation in adjectives and adverbs. The smallness evoked is seldom factual (in that case a diminutive suffix is preferred); it rather serves to express a strong emotional content, be it negative, when contempt is signaled, or positive, when affection or sentimental attachment is conveyed. This explains why expressive palatalization is extensively utilized in the formation of pet names and nicknames.

Onomastics aside, the importance of expressive palatalization in general speech varies according to region. In many areas it is rarely used except in talking to young children. Women, and of course children, use it more than men.

The details of this palatalization process are as follows: In a word containing one or more sibilants, their palatalization is all that is required. In other words, all *z* and *s* turn into *x*, all *tz* and *ts* into *tx*. Examples are

gizon	man	gixon	little fellow, little squirt
zoro	crazy, insane	xoro	silly, foolish
gozo	sweet	goxo	nice and sweet, tasty, delicious
seme	son	xeme	sonny
bildots	lamb	bildotx	lambkin
beltz	black	beltx	black and pretty, blackie

In the absence of a sibilant, the dentals *t*, *d*, *n*, and *l* become eligible for palatalization. This expressive palatalization of dentals is indicated in the standard orthography by a doubling of the consonant: *tt*, *dd*, *ll*, except for *n* which receives instead a tilde sign (*ñ*).

In the northern dialects, *tt* and *dd* are pronounced like the initial consonants of the English words *tune* and *duke*, respectively; in the Guipuzcoan and Biscayan dialects *tt* is often (but not always) pronounced the same as *tx*, and *dd* is not in use. Some examples are

lapur	thief, robber	llapur	rogue, rascal
liburu	book	lliburu	booklet, pamphlet
tontor	peak	ttonttor	hump
tanta	drop	ttantta	droplet, wee bit
eder	beautiful	edder	lovely, very pretty
labur	short	llabur	quite short, shortish
nabar	piebald, gray	ñabar	gray and pretty, grayish
mando	mule	manddo	little mule, little hybrid

The vibrants /R/ and /r/, being dentals, may be expected to also allow expressive palatalization. Yet this rarely occurs. We observe it only in the eastern dialects, with examples in Baztanese, Salazarese, and, especially, Souletin and Roncalese. Among those are *bello* 'warmish', 'lukewarm' from *bero* 'hot', and *holli* 'yellowish', 'blond' from *hori* 'yellow'.

Palatalization of velars, resulting in *tt* or *tx*, is much less common than that of dentals. One of the rare examples is Baztanese *ttottoriko*, expressive variant of *kokoriko* 'crouched'. The word *ttotta* 'brandy', used in Guipuzcoa and Labourd, no doubt originated as an expressive variant of the loanword *gota* 'drop'. Another case where etymology, rather than synchronic relationship, is involved, is that of the adjective *txume* 'lowly', 'common', 'simple', a High Navarrese form (also Roncalese), softened to *xume* in the Northern Provinces, whence the Batua form. In all probability, *txume* arose as an expressive variant of *kume* 'young of an animal', now mostly restricted to compounds, the independent form today being *ume*.

It sometimes happens that the palatal variant loses its expressive character and becomes the normal designation for its referent. Then the nonpalatal variant takes on an augmentative connotation, usually unfavorable. This semantic development has phonological consequences, at least in Guipuzcoan and Biscayan. There, initial *x* has turned into an affricate *tx*, except for words felt to be expressive. Accordingly, we have *zezen* 'bull' and *xexen* 'nice little bull', but *zerri* 'swine' and *txerri* 'pig', the latter form having lost the expressive character it once had.

Instead of becoming an augmentative, the nonpalatal form may also fall into disuse or assume a quite different meaning. The word for bird, *txori* (northern form *xori*), must have once been an expressive variant of *zori*. This form still exists, but it no longer denotes 'bird'. It now means 'fate' or 'luck', as in the compounds *zorion* 'good luck', 'happiness' and *zorigaitz* or *zoritxar* 'bad luck', 'unhappiness', a change of meaning pointing to the well-known practice of divination by flight of birds. The original forms *guti* and *tiki* have disappeared in most areas in favor of their palatal variants *gutxi* 'few', *txiki* 'small', and the original form *etse* of *etxe* 'house' survives only in a few zones of Biscay.

For more details on expressive palatalization we refer the reader to chapter 10 of Michelena's *FHV*, from which nearly all examples in this section have been taken. It should be mentioned here that Basque also employs diminutive suffixes: *-txo*, *-tto*, and *-ño*, all having low pitch. Of these synonymous suffixes, Guipuzcoan and Biscayan only use *-txo*. Examples are *saguño* 'little mouse', *haurtto* 'little child', *semetxo* 'little son', *amatxo* 'Mummy', and *aitatxo* 'Daddy'.

A last remark. Whereas the sound of *ñ* and *ll* also arise from automatic palatalization, the use of the letters *ñ* and *ll* in Euskara Batua is limited to expressive forms. There is one important exception, however: place names. Examples are *Oñati* 'Oñate', *Iruñea* 'Pamplona', *Mallabia* 'Mallavia', and *Sunbilla* 'Sumbilla'.

1.2.6 A Touch of Phonology: Six Sandhi Rules

Mainly for future reference, we will list some sandhi rules governing the behavior of consonants in close succession. We will state them informally, as a formulation in terms of distinctive features would be unnecessarily technical. A slightly less general form of some of these rules can be found in G. N'Diaye's (1970) treatise.

Sandhi rule 1
When two plosives meet, the first drops, and the second is or becomes voiceless. (N'Diaye, 5.3.2.)

Sandhi rule 2
When a sibilant follows a plosive, the plosive drops, and the sibilant turns into the corresponding affricate. (Cf. N'Diaye, 5.3.3.)

Sandhi rule 3
When a plosive follows an affricate, the affricate turns into a sibilant, and a voiced plosive becomes voiceless. (Cf. N'Diaye, 5.3.4.)

Sandhi rule 4
When a voiced plosive follows a sibilant, it becomes voiceless, except in very slow careful pronunciation.

Sandhi rule 5
In the central dialects, a sibilant turns into an affricate when following a liquid or a nasal. (Cf. N'Diaye, 5.3.5.)

Sandhi rule 6
When a plosive follows a nasal, there is a strong tendency for the plosive to become voiced.

We should make clear that these rules apply both within a word (internal sandhi) and between words (external sandhi) as long as there is no intervening pause. Thus, *emaiok bat* 'give him one' comes out as [emayopat], and *hil zen* 'he died' as [hiltzen].

In a sequence of two identical plosives, only the second one is realized, in accordance with rule 1. As N'Diaye has observed, this statement is true of Basque consonants in general. Consonant gemination is totally foreign to Basque as we know it.

At first sight, the behavior of sibilants may appear to refute this claim, as the affricate *tz* in *etzen* 'he wasn't', resulting from *ez* 'not' and *zen* 'he was', looks suspiciously like a realization of a geminate sibilant *zz*. The appearance of this affricate, however, must be considered a morphophonemic property of the negation morpheme *ez* (note its emphatic form *ezetz*), not a direct result of normal phonological processes. Nowhere else does a sequence of sibilants produce an affricate. There are no affricates in the pronunciation of *ni naiz zure aita* 'I am your father' or in that of *ardoaz zaletu dira* 'they have grown fond of wine'.

Many examples of sandhi phenomena can be found throughout this grammar. We will return to these rules in chapter 31, where we discuss the morphophonology of compounds.

1.3 Introducing the Basque Noun Phrase

1.3.1 The Definite and Indefinite Articles

The numeral *bat* 'one' serves as an indefinite article. It invariably follows the noun, forming with it one phonological phrase; yet it is written separately:

gizon bat	one man, a man
alaba bat	one daughter, a daughter

Basque also has a definite article: *a*. It likewise follows the noun and forms with it one phonological phrase. But, unlike *bat*, it is written together with the noun, being always considered a suffix:

gizona	the man
emakumea	the woman
alaba	the daughter

We note that with nouns ending in *a* only one *a* is pronounced and written. Thus, *alaba* is ambiguously 'daughter' or 'the daughter'. This ambiguity is due to the operation of the *a*-Elision Rule, to be stated as follows:

***a*-Elision Rule:** The vowel *a* is elided before any following vowel, unless a word boundary intervenes.

Although the *a*-Elision Rule is common to all dialects, some dialects have found a way to avoid the ambiguity of *alaba*. In Biscayan, a Vowel Dissimilation Rule precedes *a*-Elision, so that we get *alaba* 'daughter' and *alabea* (or *alabia*, *alabie*, *alabí*) 'the daughter' (see de Rijk 1970). In Souletin, whose accentual system is based on stress, Stress Assignment precedes *a*-Elision, so that *alába* is 'daughter' and *alabá* 'the daughter'.

Because the definite article is a suffix beginning with a vowel, our discussion at the end of section 1.2.2.3 about weak and strong *r* yields the key to the following contrasts:

paper bat	a piece of paper	papera	the paper
piper bat	a pepper	piperra	the pepper
zur bat	a piece of wood	zura	the (piece of) wood
txakur bat	a dog	txakurra	the dog
ur asko	much water	ura	the water
ur asko	many hazelnuts	urra	the hazelnut

The indefinite article has a plural form *batzuk* (northern dialects also *batzu*), and the definite article has a plural form *-ak* (derived from **-ag* with final devoicing, as we shall find in section 2.2.1):

gizon batzuk	some men	gizonak	the men
emakume batzuk	some women	emakumeak	the women
alaba batzuk	some daughters	alabak	the daughters

Observe that Basque nouns do not have gender; they all take the same form of the article—in sharp contrast to the surrounding Romance languages, whose nouns are either masculine or feminine.

1.3.2 Adjectives and Their Syntax

In Basque, adjectives always follow the noun they modify. (The exceptions adduced by P. Lafitte in his *Grammaire basque* [1962, section 267] do not involve adjectives at all, but are in fact nominal compounds: *Euskal Herria* 'the Basque Country', *giristino legea* 'the Christian law', *frantses bandera* 'the French flag', *gaixo gizona* 'the poor miserable man'.)

Articles appear but once in a noun phrase—at the very end:

emakume ona	the good woman
liburu gorria	the red book
gizon gaztea	the young man

txakur txiki bat	a small dog
etxe berri bat	a new house
sorgin eder bat	a beautiful witch

More than one adjective is allowed in a noun phrase:

etxe gorri handi berria	the new big red house
ontzi berri zuri eder handi bat	a big beautiful white new boat

Note that the distance of the adjectives to the head noun in Basque is the same as in the English gloss, although the linear order is reversed.

In Basque, the combination of any adjective and an article makes up a complete noun phrase. Such nounless noun phrases have a twofold interpretation. They can bear a generic meaning:

ona	whatever is good	on bat	one instance of whatever is good
ederra	whatever is beautiful	eder bat	one instance of whatever is beautiful
berria	whatever is new	berri bat	one instance of whatever is new

They can also bear a context-dependent meaning, in which the noun phrase will be interpreted with regard to a specific category of referents to be inferred from the surrounding discourse. In this reading, we may assume the head of the noun phrase to be an empty pronoun $\emptyset$, whose function corresponds to that of the pronoun *one* in the English glosses:

ona	the good one	on bat	a good one
ederra	the beautiful one	eder bat	a beautiful one
berria	the new one	berri bat	a new one

We see no need to assume a category change from adjective to noun in these constructions. A process of that type looks somewhat more applicable to a minor subclass of adjectives that do appear to be changeable into nouns. But even there, a simple statement that these adjectives happen to be paired in the lexicon with semantically related homonymous nouns seems preferable. Typical examples are

berri	new	berri	news
on	good	on	good, goodness, goods
gaitz	evil (obs., now: difficult)	gaitz	evil, harm, illness
bero	hot, warm	bero	heat, warmth
hotz	cold	hotz	cold, coldness
argi	clear, bright	argi	light, brightness
ilun	dark	ilun	dark, darkness (also *ilunbe*)
isil	silent, quiet	isil	silence (also *isiltasun*)
huts	empty	huts	void, emptiness, mistake
bete	full	bete	fullness
gose	hungry	gose	hunger
egarri	thirsty	egarri	thirst

As a result of Romance influence (*J'ai faim/soif*; *qu'ei hami/set*; *tengo hambre/sed*; but *affamé/assoiffé*; *ahamàt/assecàt*; *hambriento/sediento*), the use of *gose* and *egarri* as adjectives is no longer common. These words still appear frequently as nouns, but in the adjectival function derived forms are employed, each derivate with its own shade of meaning: *gosetsu*, *goseti*, *gosebera* 'hungry', and *egartsu*, *egarti*, *egarbera* 'thirsty' (suffixes: *-tsu* 'abundance', *-ti* 'tendency', *-bera* 'inclination').

It has occasionally been maintained that there is no clear-cut distinction between nouns and adjectives in Basque. This is quite clearly an exaggeration. Although it is true that there are syntactic similarities between adjectives and nouns (for which see also section 1.3.3), and also that any adjective can behave as a noun, no noun can behave as an adjective (unless it starts out as one). For a detailed discussion of this and other issues, see R. Lafon 1964.

Adjectives can be modified by adverbs of degree. The adverb *samar* 'somewhat' follows the adjective: *liburu on samarra* 'the somewhat good book', *etxe handi samar bat* 'a somewhat large house'. Most other adverbs of degree precede the adjective. We mention here *oso* 'very' and its synonyms *txit, guztiz, arras, biziki*. Their syntactic properties will be treated in section 11.2.1. Examples are *oso eder* 'very beautiful', *txit on* 'very good', *guztiz argi* 'very clear', and *biziki hotz* 'very cold'.

1.3.3 Nominal Predicates

To form nominal predicates, Basque makes use of a copulative verb *izan*, also used independently in the meaning 'to be', 'to exist'. We introduce here only the third-person forms of the present tense: *da* '(he, she, it) is', and *dira* '(they) are'. Unless it has an impersonal or sentential subject, a nominal predicate formed with this copula requires the definite article

-a (or its plural *-ak*), no matter whether the predicate is a noun, adjective, or noun phrase of any kind whatsoever. Examples:

(1) Ama sorgina da eta alabak ere sorginak dira.
Mother is a witch and the daughters are witches too.

(2) Sorgina polita da eta ijitoak ere politak dira.
The witch is pretty and the gypsies are pretty too.

(3) Ama emakume ederra da eta alabak ere emakume ederrak dira.
Mother is a beautiful woman and the daughters are beautiful women too.

Negative predicates are formed by putting the word *ez* ('not', 'no') right in front of the copula:

(4) Ama ez da sorgina eta alabak ere ez dira sorginak.
Mother isn't a witch and the daughters aren't witches either.

(5) Sorgina ez da polita eta ijitoak ere ez dira politak.
The witch isn't pretty and the gypsies aren't pretty either.

(6) Ama ez da emakume ederra eta alabak ere ez dira emakume ederrak.
Mother isn't a beautiful woman and the daughters aren't beautiful women either.

Observe that the positive copula ends the nominal predicate, whereas the negative copula introduces it:

(7) Etxea berria da baina eliza ez da berria.
The house is new but the church isn't new.

The word *ere* 'also', 'too', 'either' can survive unaided only in the presence of a verb—*dira* in the preceding examples. Otherwise it must be reinforced by an immediately following *bai* 'yes' in positive clauses, or *ez* 'no', 'not' in negative ones: *Ama ere bai.* 'Mother too.'; *Ijitoa ere ez.* 'Not the gypsy either.'

Instead of a following *bai* or *ez*, a preceding *baita* or *ezta* may be used, where *-ta* is a reduced form of the conjunction *eta* 'and': *Baita ama ere.* 'Also Mother'.; *Ezta ijitoa ere.* 'Nor the gypsy'.

1.4 Vocabulary

Carefully chosen to serve as examples, clarifications, and occasionally refinements of grammatical statements, illustrative sentences of increasing complexity, often taken from Basque literature, ancient and modern, are a vital feature of this work. Because the unusual characteristics of Basque grammar make the expedient of interlinear translation much too awkward to be practical, the reader is urged to build up a modest vocabulary of the more common Basque words. For this purpose, each chapter contains a vocabulary section of words and expressions to be memorized. Many of these will occur in the translation exercises at the end of the chapter, and they will often be taken for granted in subsequent chapters.

1.4.1 Nouns

adiskide	friend (male or female)	jabe	owner
aita	father	jaun	sir (*Jauna* 'the Lord')
alaba	daughter	kafe	coffee
ama	mother	katu	cat
andre	lady	ke	smoke
apaiz	priest	lan	work
ardo	wine	liburu	book
argi	light, daylight	lore	flower
begi	eye	mendi	mountain
behi	cow	mutil	boy
bihotz	heart	nagusi	boss
buru	head	neskatxa	girl
diru	money	ogi	(loaf of) bread
egun	day	oilo	chicken
eliza	church	oin	foot
emakume	woman	sagar	apple
emazte	wife	sagu	mouse
esku	hand	seme	son
etsai	enemy	sorgin	witch
etxe	house	su	fire
gau	night	txakur	dog
gizon	man	txerri	pig
gona	skirt	ur	water
haur	child	urte	year
ibai	river	zaldi	horse
ijito	gypsy	zezen	bull
izar	star	zur	wood

1.4.2 Adjectives

argi	clear, bright	eder	beautiful
beltz	black	garbi	clean, pure
bero	hot, warm	garesti	expensive
berri	new	gorri	red
bete	full	goxo	tasty, delicious

gozo	sweet	maite	dear, beloved
handi	big, large, great	merke	cheap
hotz	cold	on	good
ilun	dark	polit	pretty
isil	silent, quiet	txar	bad
itsusi	ugly	txiki	small, little
labur	short	zahar	old
luze	long	zuri	white

1.4.3 Other Words

aski	enough
asko	many, much
bai	yes
baina	but
da	(he, she, it) is
dira	(they) are
ere	also, even
eta	and
ez	not, no
gaur	today
gutxi	few
hemen	here
inor	anybody
nor	who
oso	whole, very
txit	very
zenbat	how many, how much
zer	what
zerbait	something

1.5 Exercises

1.5.1 Translate into English

1. Sua gorria da, eta kea beltza.
2. Sua gorria eta kea beltza da.
3. Alaba ederra da, baina ama oso ederra.
4. Gaua iluna da, eguna ez.
5. Gaur egun iluna da.

6. Emakumeak politak dira, baina gizonak itsusiak.
7. Apaiza eta ijitoa adiskideak dira.
8. Nor da hemen nagusia?
9. Etxe asko zuriak dira.
10. Apaizak eta sorginak ez dira etsaiak.
11. Gona gorria ez da itsusia.
12. Sagar zaharrak merkeak dira hemen, baina kafe ona oso garestia.

1.5.2 Translate into Basque

1. The red wine is good. (Translate "black wine"; *ardo gorria* is 'rosé wine'.)
2. It is expensive wine.
3. The witch and the gypsies are friends.
4. The woman and the priest are not enemies either.
5. The chicken is small but very tasty.
6. Many churches are cold and dark.
7. The hands are hot, but the feet cold.
8. The new book is expensive, but the old one cheap.
9. What is the work, and who (is) the boss?
10. How much is the money?
11. The witches are friends, and the gypsies are also friends.
12. The day is short, and the year (is) too.

2 More about the Basque Noun Phrase

2.1 Numerals

2.1.1 Cardinals

1	bat	one
2	bi	two
3	hiru(r)	three
4	lau(r)	four
5	bost	five
6	sei	six
7	zazpi	seven
8	zortzi	eight
9	bederatzi	nine
10	hamar	ten
11	hamaika	eleven
12	hamabi	twelve
13	hamahiru(r)	thirteen
14	hamalau(r)	fourteen
15	hamabost	fifteen
16	hamasei	sixteen
17	hamazazpi	seventeen
18	hemezortzi (or *hamazortzi*)	eighteen
19	hemeretzi	nineteen
20	hogei	twenty
21	hogeita bat	twenty-one
22	hogeita bi	twenty-two
30	hogeita hamar	thirty
31	hogeita hamaika	thirty-one
40	berrogei	forty

41	berrogeita bat	forty-one
50	berrogeita hamar	fifty
60	hirurogei	sixty
70	hirurogeita hamar	seventy
80	laurogei	eighty
90	laurogeita hamar	ninety
99	laurogeita hemeretzi	ninety-nine
100	ehun	one hundred
101	ehun eta bat	one hundred and one
199	ehun eta laurogeita hemeretzi	one hundred ninety-nine
200	berrehun	two hundred
300	hirurehun (or *hiru ehun*)	three hundred
400	laurehun (or *lau ehun*)	four hundred
500	bostehun (or *bost ehun*)	five hundred
600	seiehun (or *sei ehun*)	six hundred
700	zazpiehun (or *zazpi ehun*)	seven hundred
800	zortziehun (or *zortzi ehun*)	eight hundred
900	bederatziehun (or *bederatzi ehun*)	nine hundred
1,000	mila (*hamar ehun* is obsolete)	one thousand
1,100	mila eta ehun	eleven hundred
1,200	mila eta berrehun	twelve hundred
2,000	bi mila	two thousand
10,000	hamar mila	ten thousand
100,000	ehun mila	one hundred thousand
1,000,000	milioi bat	one million
1,000,000,000	miliar bat (or *mila milioi*)	one billion

Observations

1. As we saw in section 1.3.1, *bat* also serves as an indefinite article. The ambiguity is dispelled by intonation: used as an article, *bat* will be integrated into the intonation pattern of its overall noun phrase, and as a final element it usually carries a low pitch; used as a numeral, it will have a high pitch of its own.
2. The final weak *r* of *hirur* and *laur* is always dropped before a consonant or a word boundary, even in writing.
3. The prefix *berr-* of *berrogei* 'forty' and *berrehun* 'two hundred' can be related to the adjective *berri* 'new'. Compare *berriz* 'again'.
4. The suffix *-ta* of *hogeita*, *berrogeita*, and so on derives from the conjunction *eta* 'and' which is pronounced *ta* after a vowel (or sonorant). As the southern dialects do not sound the *h*, *berrogeita hamar* is usually pronounced *berrogeitamar*, and it can be found written that way also.

5. The conjunction *eta* 'and' is used after *mila*, where it is pronounced *ta*, as well as after *ehun* and its compounds, where it is pronounced *da*. Note, however, that after *mila*, *eta* is dropped whenever there is another *eta* following *ehun* or its compounds: *zortziehun eta berrogeita hamazazpi* '857', *ehun eta berrogeita bi mila eta zortziehun* '142,800', but *ehun eta berrogeita bi mila zortziehun eta berrogeita hamazazpi* '142,857'. Moreover, when the numeral serves to express a price or a historical date, *eta* is always omitted after *mila*: *lau mila bostehun pezeta* '4,500 pesetas'; *mila bederatziehun* '(the year) 1900'. (An alternative expression, *hemeretziehun* 'nineteen hundred', is found in certain dialects but is not common in Batua.)
6. Phone numbers are usually spoken digit by digit. The word for 'zero' is *huts* or *zero*. Thus, the phone number 283 014 is pronounced *bi-zortzi-hiru-huts-bat-lau*.
7. The vigesimal system of the Basque numerals is strikingly similar to that of Celtic. Even *bostogei* for '100' is attested (*borzogei* in Darricarrère's dictionary, n.d.). The expected form for 120, *seiogei*, is attested in the sixteenth century (Acts 1:15, Lz), but it is now quite obsolete.
8. Cardinals always stand before the noun, with the exception of *bat* 'one', which, like the article *-a*, comes after the noun, and *bi* 'two', which can take either position:

etxe eder bat	a beautiful house
etxe eder bi	two beautiful houses
bi etxe eder	two beautiful houses
hiru etxe eder	three beautiful houses
lau etxe eder	four beautiful houses

[*N.B.* In the Biscayan dialect, *bi* is always postponed, in the northern dialects hardly ever. Note the eastern idiom *esker mila* 'a thousand thanks', in Batua much less common than the regular construction *mila esker*, or the compound form *milesker*.]

9. The numeral *hamaika* 'eleven' also means 'a lot'. In this sense, the diminutive form *hamaikatxo* is also used. Thus: *hamaika apaiz* 'eleven priests' or 'a lot of priests'; *hamaikatxo apaiz* 'quite a few priests'.
10. Nouns and adjectives do not distinguish between singular and plural. Articles (and also demonstratives), however, do. Accordingly,

ehun etxe eder	one hundred beautiful houses
ehun etxe ederrak	the hundred beautiful houses

11. A cardinal followed by a definite article makes up a complete noun phrase, just as an adjective does (section 1.3.2). Since only a context-dependent reading is possible here, we again assume the presence of an underlying pronoun:

bata	the one
biak	the two (of them), both (of them)

hirurak	the three (of them)
laurak	the four (of them)

It is important to realize that the cardinals maintain their status in this construction; they do not turn into nouns here.

12. Genuine cardinals are used only to count. They can, however, nominalize, in order to serve as names for figures. When *hirur* and *laur* turn into nouns, they invariably lose their final *r*. Other numerals show no formal change: *bata* 'the 1', *bia* 'the 2', *hirua* 'the 3', *laua* 'the 4', *bosta* 'the 5', and so on. (But *hamahirua* 'the 13'.) Contrast, therefore, *hirurak* 'the three' and *hiruak* 'the threes', *laurak* 'the four' and *lauak* 'the fours'.

13. Followed by the indefinite article *bat*, nominalized numerals express approximate quantities:

hiru bat haur	about three children
lau bat urte	about four years
hamar bat egun	about ten days

14. There is an interrogative cardinal *zenbat*: *Zenbat haur*? 'How many children?'.

2.1.2 Ordinals

Ordinals are formed by putting the suffix *-garren* after the corresponding cardinal. There is just one exception: the ordinal corresponding to *bat* is suppletive. The word for 'first' is *lehen*, which also means 'formerly'. The word *azken* 'last' (also used as a noun meaning 'end') also behaves like an ordinal in some ways.

Ordinals occur inside noun phrases, immediately preceding the head noun. With the noun *aldi* 'time':

lehen aldia	the first time
bigarren aldia	the second time
hirugarren aldia	the third time
laugarren aldia	the fourth time
bosgarren aldia	the fifth time
hogeita batgarren aldia	the twenty-first time
azken aldia	the last time

Note the elision of *t* in *bosgarren* (pronounced: *boskarren*), and observe that, although *batgarren* does not exist, *hogeita batgarren* (pronounced *hogeitabakarren*) does; likewise *berrogeita batgarren*, *hirurogeita batgarren*, and so on.

Instead of a full noun, a zero pronoun may occur, in which event the article directly follows the ordinal:

lehena	the first (one)
bigarrena	the second (one)

hirugarrena the third (one)
laugarrena the fourth (one)
azkena the last (one)

As *lehena* can also mean 'the former one' and *azkena* 'the end', nonambiguous forms are sometimes preferred: *lehenengoa* (or *lehenbizikoa*) and *azkenengoa*. Here *-en* is the superlative marker (see section 26.5.1), and *-go* is an allomorph (after *n*) of the linking morpheme *-ko* to be discussed in section 5.1.

Except for *azken*, all ordinals have adjunctive forms in *-ko* (realized as *-go* following the *n* of *-garren*) which may substitute for them in all contexts: *lehengo liburua*, or unambiguously, *lehenengo liburua*, for *lehen liburua* 'the first book'; *zazpigarrengo liburua* for *zazpigarren liburua* 'the seventh book'. For *azken liburua* 'the last (or latest) book', we have *azkenengo liburua* or *azkeneko liburua*, the latter form being derived from the noun *azken* 'end'.

Whenever the head of the noun phrase is a proper noun, ordinals are placed after it, contrary to the general rule given previously:

Karlos bosgarrena	Charles V
Jon hogeita hirugarrena	John XXIII
Santxo laugarrena Azkarra	Sancho IV, the Wise

When ordinals are written as figures, *-garren* may be abbreviated as *gn.* or, even shorter, as a simple period. Thus, *hamalaugarren* can be written as *14 garren* (in two words), *14gn.* (one word) or *14.*; *hamalaugarrena* as *14 garrena, 14gna* (no period), or *14.a* (cf. *EGLU* I, 209).

Years can be designated either by cardinals or by ordinals:

Mila bederatziehun eta laurogeita lau: 1984 (when used alone)
Mila bederatziehun eta laurogeita laua: 1984 (when used in a sentence)
Mila bederatziehun eta laurogeita laugarrena: 1984 (always with the article *-a*)

We see that the use of the term *urte* 'year' is not necessary here. If *urte* is used, however, the cardinal form requires the linking morpheme *-ko* (section 5.1):

Mila bederatziehun eta laurogeita lauko urtea: The year 1984.
Mila bederatziehun eta laurogeita laugarren urtea: The year 1984.

[*N.B.* These expressions can be written as *1984eko urtea, 1984.urtea.*]

Since the noun meaning 'story', 'floor', *bizitza* (also *goi*, or the Spanish loan *piso*), is often left out, ordinals, when definite, can denote the stories of a building: *bigarrena* 'the second story', *hirugarrena* 'the third story'.

There is an interrogative ordinal *zenbatgarren* in common use:

Zenbatgarren emaztea da? 'What number wife is she?'

In accordance with the observation just made, *zenbatgarrena*? 'the how many-th?' can also mean 'which story?', 'which floor?'.

2.1.3 Collective Nouns

The collective suffix *-kote*, borrowed into Batua from the Biscayan dialect, combines with a low numeral n ($2 \leq n \leq 8$) to form a noun denoting a group of n similar objects, often—but not necessarily—animate:

bikote	couple, pair, duo
hirukote	trio, triad, threesome
laukote	quartet, foursome
boskote	quintet, fivesome
seikote	sextet
zazpikote	septet
zortzikote	octet

The nature of the group can be specified by means of a preceding noun, which then enters into a compound relation with the *-kote* formation:

ijito hirukotea	the gypsy trio
neskamutil bikotea	the boy-girl couple

A frequent synonym of *bikote* is the Romance loan *pare*, which in combination with *bat* can also be used to indicate a small quantity: 'a couple of', that is, 'a few'.

zezen parea	the pair of bulls
zezen pare bat	a couple of bulls, a few bulls

2.1.4 Multiplicative Suffixes: *-koitz* and *-kun*

The suffix *-koitz* combines with any cardinal n to form an adjective meaning 'consisting of n similar parts':

bakoitz	*single, *unique
bikoitz	double, twofold, ambiguous
hirukoitz	triple, threefold, doubly ambiguous
laukoitz	quadruple, fourfold
boskoitz	quintuple, fivefold
...	...
anizkoitz	multiple, manifold (from the word *anitz* 'many')

In arithmetic, *anizkoitz* can be utilized as a noun: *Hamabi hiruren anizkoitza da*. 'Twelve is a multiple of three.'

[*N.B.* The meanings listed for *bakoitz* are now totally obsolete. Nowadays the adjective *bakoitz* has but a single meaning: 'each'. (To be sure, the outdated meaning was once used by Mitxelena in a ceremonial speech before the Basque Academy: *mintzabide zehatz eta bakoitz* 'a precise and unique system of speech' [*MEIG* IV, 111]. This usage must be deemed a deliberate archaism occasioned by the austere academic setting. The only other example in Mitxelena's works is *forma bakar eta bakoitz gisa* [*MEIG* VI, 128].)]

The suffix -*kun* combines with any cardinal *n* to form an adjective with a double meaning: '*n* times as much' or 'consisting of *n* similar parts'.

bakun	single, simple
bikun	double, twofold
hirukun	triple, threefold
laukun	quadruple, fourfold
boskun	quintuple, fivefold
. . .	. . .
anizkun	multiple, manifold

Some of these adjectives have been used as nouns, with appropriate meanings: *hamarkun* 'decade', 'decalogue'; *hamalaukun* 'sonnet'.

This suffix -*kun*, introduced into Batua from the northern dialects, has rather a literary flavor. Colloquially, the Spanish loan *doble* is employed instead of *bikun*.

Basque, furthermore, has fractional numerals, which will be discussed in section 2.5, and distributive numerals, to be treated in chapter 30.

2.2 Case Endings

To show the grammatical function of a noun phrase within a sentence, Basque makes use of case endings the way English uses prepositions.

2.2.1 The Basic System

There are two quite different systems of case endings in Basque. This chapter will deal with what we will call "the basic system" consisting of the "basic case endings." The second system, that of the "locative case endings," therefore called the "locative system," will be set forth in chapter 3. Often in this book, the term "case ending" will be used without any further qualification. When that happens, the statement in question is intended to apply to the case endings of either system.

The first thing to note at this point is that Basque has three number categories: indefinite, definite singular, and definite plural. Any noun phrase fitted with a case ending must be morphologically marked for one of these categories.

To show the interaction of number and case in the basic system, we will start out with the dative case, which has the ending -*(r)i*. By putting parentheses around the *r* we mean to indicate that the ending is -*ri* after a vowel, and -*i* after a consonant.

As a first example, we choose the word *gizon* 'man':

Indefinite	gizoni	to men
Definite singular	gizonari	to the man (cf. *gizona* 'the man')
Definite plural	gizonei	to the men (cf. *gizonak* 'the men')

In the basic system, the plural forms are always characterized by a vowel *e* immediately following the noun stem. After this *e*, the case ending appears, but without the expected *r*. It is commonly assumed that this system derives from a purely agglutinative structure by the obligatory deletion of weak intervocalic consonants in a weakly accentuated ending. Thus, the postulated source of *gizonei* is a sequence **gizon-ag-eri*, where *-eri* is an older form of the dative ending and *-ag* is the plural marker, which, in word-final position, will be devoiced to *-ak*.

Our second example, the word *ijito* 'gypsy', ends in a vowel. Accordingly, the *r* of *-(r)i* is preserved in the indefinite form:

Indefinite	ijitori	to gypsies
Definite singular	ijitoari	to the gypsy
Definite plural	ijitoei	to the gypsies

Diphthongs also count as vowels. Therefore, with the noun *etsai* 'enemy' we have

Indefinite	(bi) etsairi	to (two) enemies
Definite singular	etsaiari	to the enemy
Definite plural	etsaiei	to the enemies

Similarly, with *sakristau* 'sexton',

Indefinite	(bi) sakristauri	to (two) sextons
Definite singular	sakristauari	to the sexton
Definite plural	sakristauei	to the sextons

Some other case endings of the basic system are

Ergative	*-k*	(to be discussed in section 9.2.1)
Genitive	*-(r)en*	'of'
Sociative	*-(r)ekin*	'with'
Instrumental	*-z*	'by means of', 'about', and so on (See chapter 27.)

Taking again *gizon* 'man' as an example, we have

	Indefinite	Singular	Plural
Ergative	gizonek	gizonak	gizonek
Genitive	gizonen	gizonaren	gizonen
Dative	gizoni	gizonari	gizonei
Sociative	gizonekin	gizonarekin	gizonekin
Instrumental	gizonez	gizonaz	gizonez

Between the purely consonantal endings *-k* (ergative) and *-z* (instrumental) and an adjacent consonant, a vowel *e* is intercalated for the sake of euphony. This process, named *e*-epenthesis, never occurs after vowels, except in the instrumental form of monosyllabic stems ending in a dipthong, such as *gau* 'night' and *dei* 'call', with indefinite instrumentals *gauez* 'by night' and *deiez* 'by call', 'calling'. We may note that the word *lau* 'plane' and also 'plain' still betrays its origin from Latin *planum* by acting as a bisyllabic stem: *hitz lauz* 'by plain word', that is, 'in prose'. By way of further illustration, we now give the paradigm of the word *etsai* 'enemy':

	Indefinite	Singular	Plural
Ergative	etsaik	etsaiak	etsaiek
Genitive	etsairen	etsaiaren	etsaien
Dative	etsairi	etsaiari	etsaiei
Sociative	etsairekin	etsaiarekin	etsaiekin
Instrumental	etsaiz	etsaiaz	etsaiez

Nouns ending in *a* show the effects of the obligatory *a*-Elision Rule of section 1.3.1 in all their definite forms. Thus the paradigm of *alaba* 'daughter' runs as follows:

	Indefinite	Singular	Plural
Ergative	alabak	alabak	alabek
Genitive	alabaren	alabaren	alaben
Dative	alabari	alabari	alabei
Sociative	alabarekin	alabarekin	alabekin
Instrumental	alabaz	alabaz	alabez

In contrast to *a*, stem-final *e* does not drop before a vowel—even another *e*—in Batua, as shown by the plural forms of *seme* 'son': *semeek, semeen, semeei, semeekin, semeez.*

Two other basic case endings do not follow the noun directly but are joined to it via the genitive—such forms being nonetheless written as one word. These are

Benefactive	*-tzat* (also *-tzako* or *-tako*)	'for'
Motivational	*-gatik*	'because of', 'in spite of'

With the motivational, the use of the genitive is optional, except in the plural. With the benefactive, however, leaving out the genitive is not possible, for it would change the meaning of the ending *-tzat* to that of the prolative, to be studied in section 17.8. Again taking as an example the noun *gizon* 'man', we get the following forms:

Indefinite	(lau) gizonentzat (gizonentzako, gizonendako)	'for (four) men'
	(lau) gizonengatik *or* (lau) gizongatik	'because of (four) men'
Singular	gizonarentzat (gizonarentzako, gizonarendako)	'for the man'
	gizonarengatik *or* gizonagatik	'because of the man'

Plural	gizonentzat (gizonentzako, gizonendako)	'for the men'
	gizonengatik	'because of the men'

According to a near general rule of Basque phonology, a nonaffricate obstruent (i.e., *p*, *t*, *k*) becomes voiced after a nasal. Hence the change of *-tako* to *-dako* after the *n* of the genitive.

The interrogative pronoun *zer* 'what' gives rise to the combinations *zergatik* 'why' and *zertako* 'for what'. Here, the genitive is not used in Batua; the forms *zerengatik* and *zerendako* are dialectal (Navarrese and Souletin).

2.2.2 The Syntactic Status of Basque Case Endings

Our use of the term "case ending" has one disadvantage: it misleadingly conjures up dreary visions of the rather tiresome declension paradigms in the classical Indo-European tongues. This connotation is unfortunate, all the more as Basque case endings, from a syntactic point of view, stand midway between the classical case markers and the familiar prepositions of English and many modern Indo-European languages. To see this point, let us compare the Basque case system with that of a language like Latin.

In a Latin noun phrase, the case marking is distributed over each of its members: each of the three words in the phrase *sacerdoti seni bono* 'to the good old priest' shows a dative case ending. Not so in Basque. In the Basque translation *apaiz zahar onari*, the dative ending appears but once, at the very end of the noun phrase.

This example also points to another difference between Basque and Latin. The morphology of Latin case marking is by no means uniform. There are no less than five declension types called "declensions," resulting in quite different forms for the same case value. In our example, the adjectives *senex* 'old' and *bonus* 'good' belong to different declensions, so that the dative form of *senex* ends in *-i* and that of *bonus* in *-o*. In contrast, Basque has no need for declension types. The case endings have exactly the same shape for all nouns, discounting just one exception: personal pronouns show an older form of the genitive ending: *-re* instead of *-ren*. (See section 6.1.3.)

Differences of this sort with respect to the classical case paradigm lead to the following question: Rather than equating the Basque endings with the case markers of Latin and similar languages, would it not be preferable to equate them with prepositions, familiar to us from English and a host of other tongues? After all, from a structural point of view Basque noun phrases can be seen to be perfect mirror images of their English counterparts. If *apaiz zahar on-a-ri* has the order 1-2-3-4-5, its English counterpart *to the good old priest* shows the order 5-4-3-2-1, the exact reverse of the Basque one. Replacing the term "preposition" with "postposition" seems therefore all we have to do in order to fit the Basque situation to perfection.

Yet, while there is a lot to be said for this approach, there are certain facts it fails to account for. Between English prepositions on the one hand and Basque case endings on the other, there is an important difference in syntactic behavior, over and above linear order.

Prepositions enjoy, syntactically speaking, a certain degree of independence. Although they presuppose in some sense a directly following noun phrase, they are not unconditionally tied down to it in their manifestation. Not so, however, with Basque case endings. They stand or fall by the material presence of an accompanying noun phrase. When the latter is deleted, as happens for instance in relative clause formation (chapter 19), the case ending must vanish with it.

Coordination phenomena likewise illustrate the difference obtaining between prepositions and case endings. Conjoined prepositions are quite common. We have in English: *(Did you mean) with or about the priests? For and because of the witch.* In Basque, conjoined case endings are excluded. The noun involved must be repeated in full, or at the very least, resumed by a pronoun. Thus: *apaizekin ala apaizez? sorginarentzat eta sorginarengatik*. Or: *sorginarentzat eta harengatik* 'for the witch and because of her'.

In short, Basque case endings are not words but bound morphemes. In this grammar, the term "postposition" will be reserved for certain morphemes that do reach word status, such as *alde* 'in favor of', 'pro', 'for' and *kontra* 'against' (see section 4.1.3.11). To denote the Basque case endings as well as the noun phrases they mark, we shall use Latin-based designations: genitive, dative, sociative, benefactive, and so on. We do so, not because we consider Basque nominal structure similar in any significant way to that of Latin, but solely to keep to a well-established custom that does no serious harm provided one is careful not to read too much into it.

2.3 Definite and Indefinite

2.3.1 The Use of the Definite Form

When asked what the Basque word is for 'fire', any Basque speaker—unless he happens to be a Souletin—will answer "*sua*." Likewise for 'black': "*beltza*."

The normal or unmarked form of a noun or adjective is for him the definite form, the form carrying the article *-a*. Consequently, this article occurs with a much greater frequency than the definite article in English. Lest the Basque use of the article *-a* be a continual stumbling block for the English reader, we now go on to present a survey of the main conditions under which it is used in contrast to the definite article in English.

1. In forms of address, provided they are not proper nouns:

Jaun-andreak,	Ladies and gentlemen,
Irakurle maiteak,	Dear readers,
Egun on, jauna.	Good morning, sir.
Arratsalde on, andrea.	Good afternoon, madam.
Gabon, andereñoa.	Good evening (*or* night), miss.
Agur, adiskidea.	Goodbye (*or* Hello), friend.
Ez, gizona.	No, man.

Bai, emakumea.	Yes, woman.
Ixo, txakurra.	Quiet, dog.

In the singular, the employment of the definite article, while preferred, is not strictly obligatory as long as the noun phrase ends in a vowel, *n*, or *l*. The word *jaun* 'sir', 'lord', however, always takes the article when used in addressing, the word *gizon* 'man' nearly always.

2. In appositions and titles:

Altube jauna	Mr. Altube
Goenaga andrea	Mrs. Goenaga
Mitxelena irakaslea	Prof. Mitxelena
Etxegarai alkatea	Mayor Etxegarai
Jon Aita santua	Pope John
Lizardi olerkaria	Poet Lizardi (*or* Lizardi the poet)

[*N.B.* As a rule, the title follows the name.]

3. In inscriptions, letterings, and headings:

Bigarren liburua	Second book
Hirugarren kapitulua	Third chapter
Laugarren atala	Fourth part
Ipuin onak	Good Tales
Liburutegia	Library
Jatetxea	Restaurant
Barrenkalea	Inner Street
Norabide bakarra	One-way traffic
Arriskua	Danger

4. With names of days, months, seasons, or points of the compass:

(1) a. Astelehena eta asteartea egun txarrak dira.
Monday and Tuesday are bad days.
b. Uztaila eta abuztua beroak dira.
July and August are warm.
c. Negua eta udaberria ez dira beroak.
Winter and spring are not warm.

5. With themes of generic judgments:

(2) a. Eztia gozoa da.
Honey is sweet.
b. Apaiz isilak onak dira.
Silent priests are good.

[*N.B.* The form of (2b) is ambiguous. It can also be descriptive: 'The silent priests are good'.]

6. In exclamations of various types:

Bai liburu ederra! What a magnificent book!
Bai hotza! How cold!

Hau (da) eguna! This is some day! (*Hau*: 'this')
Haiek urteak! Those were some years! (*Haiek*: 'those')

Zer emakumea! What a woman!
Zer polita! How pretty!

Gauaren iluna! How dark the night!
Ardoaren goxoa! How tasty the wine!

[*N.B.* Note the idiomatic use of the genitive in these exclamations. Literally, "The dark of the night!", "The tasty(ness) of the wine!".]

7. In nominal predicates, provided the copulative verb *izan* is present (cf. section 1.3.3):

(3) a. Miren sorgina da.
Mary is a witch.
b. Miren ederra da.
Mary is beautiful.
c. Miren sorgin ederra da.
Mary is a beautiful witch.

As we shall see in section 18.2.2, the article need not appear when the subject of the predicate involved is impersonal or sentential.

An important remark to end this section: In this grammar, conforming to general practice, we will call *-a* "the definite article." The appropriateness of this designation, however, could well be challenged. As we have just observed, the distribution of *-a* differs markedly from that of the definite article in English. The same holds true for its semantic import. In a conservative form of Basque, the statement expressing 'He saw a gypsy today' will use the phrase *ijitoa* and not *ijito bat*, which in this context would only mean 'one gypsy'. In Basque, therefore, the presence of the definite article does not necessarily render the noun phrase definite in the semantic sense of the term. The student is advised to keep this fact in mind.

2.3.2 The Use of the Indefinite Form

In Basque, the appearance of the indefinite or bare form of a noun phrase (i.e., occurring without an article of any kind) must be justified on the basis of specific grammatic conditions. Semantic indefiniteness by itself is not enough. The indefinite form is possible only under one of the following circumstances:

1. With unmodified proper nouns, as well as kinship terms in the ascending line—which in daily parlance tend to function as proper nouns. The term "proper noun" subsumes a variety of names: place names, first names, surnames, nicknames, and so on. In our examples throughout this book, we will often make use of the following first names: *Jon* 'John', *Miren* 'Mary', *Nekane* 'Dolores', *Patxi* 'Frank', *Pello* 'Pete'.

Kinship terms apt to occur without an article are *aita* 'father', *ama* 'mother', *aitona* 'grandfather', *amona* 'grandmother', *osaba* 'uncle', *izeba* 'aunt', *aitabitxi* 'godfather', *amabitxi* 'godmother', and also all corresponding diminutives: *aitatxo* 'daddy', *amatxo* 'mommy', and so on.

The word *errege* 'king', as long as it denotes the speaker's own king, must be treated as a proper noun, and hence does not take the article: *erregeri* 'to the king'.

Kristo 'Christ' (or *Jesukristo* 'Jesus Christ') is a proper name, but the term *Jaungoiko* (or *Jainko*) is not, and it is thus required to take the article *-a*: *Jaungoikoa* (or *Jainkoa*) 'God'.

Needless to say, the article *-a* makes its appearance as soon as the proper name is accompanied by an adjective: *Patxi azkarra* 'smart Frank', *Miren maitea* 'dear Mary', *izeba lodia* 'fat aunt', *errege ona* 'the good king'.

2. In wishing formulas with the adjective *on* 'good':

Arratsalde on!	Good afternoon!
Bidaldi on!	A good trip!
Egun on!	Good morning! (Lit. 'A good day', but not used after lunchtime.)
Gau on!	Good evening! Good night! (More common is the contraction *Gabon*.)
Suerte on!	Good luck!
Urteberri on!	Happy New Year!

3. In set phrases with either the instrumental or a locative ending (cf. chapter 3), to be thought of as adverbs. As instrumental adverbs will be treated more fully in chapter 27, we can limit ourselves to the presentation of a few examples.

a. Expressing means or medium of conveyance:

bidez	by road (*liburuen bidez* 'through books'; *Pelloren bidez* 'through Pete')
itsasoz	by sea
mendiz	through the mountains
oinez	on foot
trenez	by train
zaldiz	on horseback

b. Involving the use of bodily organs:

ahoz	with the mouth, orally
begiz	with the eye, visually

bihotzez	with the heart, cordially, sincerely
eskuz	with the hand

c. Expressing emotions:

beldurrez	with fear, fearfully
gogoz	with interest, gladly
lotsaz	with shame, bashfully
pozez	with pleasure, happily

d. Various others:

egiaz	in truth, truthfully, really
gezurrez	falsely
nahiz	deliberately
nekez	with effort, barely, hardly

4. With cardinal numerals and the noun phrases they govern (i.e., are in construction with). Note the difference in meaning between the definite and the indefinite forms:

baten	of one	bataren	of the one
biren	of two	bien	of the two
seiren	of six	seien	of the six
zazpiren	of seven	zazpien	of the seven

With *hirur* 'three' and *laur* 'four' the definite form in Batua ought to be *hiruren*, *lauren*. In actual fact, the final weak *r* of *hirur* and *laur* is often ignored in accordance with the general practice of most dialects. The "new" definite forms *hiruen* 'of the three', *lauen* 'of the four' thus contrast with the indefinite forms *hiruren* 'of three', *lauren* 'of four'. For *bost* and *hamar*, of course, the ambiguity cannot be removed: *bosten* 'of five', 'of the five'; *hamarren* 'of ten', 'of the ten'. With an accompanying noun we have

etxe baten	of one (a) house	etxe bataren	of the one house
bi etxeren	of two houses	bi etxeen	of the two houses
hiru etxeren	of three houses	hiru etxeen	of the three houses
lau etxeren	of four houses	lau etxeen	of the four houses

5. With noun phrases governed by an expression of quantity or measure:

litro bat esne	one liter of milk
bi kilo sagar gorri	two kilos of red apples
hirurehun gramo gatz	three hundred grams of salt
baso bat ardo beltz	a glass of red wine
ahokada bat ke	a mouthful of smoke (here the suffix *-kada* [section 33.1.13] indicates a measure)

[*N.B.* In contrast to English, Basque admits no possessive form in such phrases.]

6. With interrogative pronouns and the noun phrases they govern. Thus the interrogatives *nor* 'who', *zer* 'what', *zein* 'which', and *zenbat* 'how many' are restricted to the indefinite form of the case endings:

nori	to whom	noren	whose	norekin	with whom
zeri	to what	zeren	of what	zerekin	with what
zeini	to which	zeinen	of which	zeinekin	with which
zenbati	to how many	zenbaten	of how many	zenbatekin	with how many

The pronouns *nor* and *zer* do not allow *e*-epenthesis: the ergative forms are *nork, zerk*. (Compare *zeinek* and *zenbatek* with *e*-epenthesis.) A homonym of the pronoun *zer* is the noninterrogative noun *zer* 'whatchacallit', 'thingummy'; its definite form *zera* is also used as a hesitation particle. The pronouns *zer*, *zein*, and *zenbat* may govern noun phrases. These are always indefinite:

zer berri?	what news?
zein apaizi?	to which priest?
zenbat ijitori?	to how many gypsies?
zein adiskideren liburua?	which friend's book?
zenbat nagusiren dirua?	the money of how many bosses?

[*N.B.* Interrogative *nolako* 'what kind of' is exceptional in that it nearly always combines with the definite form: *nolako liburua*? 'what kind of book?'. It can also itself take the definite article: *Nolakoa da?* 'What kind of thing is it?' or 'What kind of person is he/she?'. But the indefinite form is used with cardinals higher than *bat*: *nolako hiru umeri?* 'to what kind of three children?'.]

7. With indefinite pronouns and the noun phrases they govern. As indefinite pronouns will be discussed at length in chapter 28, a minimum of examples will suffice:

norbait	somebody	norbaiti	to somebody
inor	anybody	inori	to anybody
edonor	ánybody, everybody	edonori	to ánybody, to everybody
nornahi	ánybody, everybody	nornahiri	to ánybody, to everybody
zerbait	something	zerbaiti	to something
ezer	anything	ezeri	to anything
edozer	ánything, everything	edozeri	to ánything, to everything
zernahi	ánything, everything	zernahiri	to ánything, to everything
edozein	ány whatsoever	edozeini	to ány whatsoever
zeinnahi	ány whatsoever	zeinnahiri	to ány whatsoever

For example, *edozein andre* 'ány lady', *edozein andreri* 'to ány lady' (*zeinnahi andreri*).

[*N.B.* Adjectives combined with *norbait* or *zerbait* take the definite form: *zerbait beroa* 'something warm', *norbait jakintsua* 'somebody learned' (cf. *EGLU* I, 92). Exceptions, however, are not frowned upon: *zerbait maitagarri* (*MEIG* VIII, 77; *MIH*, 273) 'something lovable'.]

8. With indefinite quantifier expressions and the noun phrases they govern. Here we have in mind words and phrases such as the following:

gutxi	few, little (also: *gutti*)	sorgin gutxi(rekin)	(with) few witches
asko	a lot, many, much	adiskide asko(rekin)	(with) many friends
anitz	a lot, many, much	anitz katu(rekin)	(with) many cats
franko	quite a few	apaiz franko(rekin)	(with) quite a few priests
aski	enough	aski diru(rekin)	(with) enough money
nahikoa	enough	nahikoa esne(rekin)	(with) enough milk
doi	sufficient	doi itzal(ekin)	(with) enough shade
pixka bat	a little	ogi pixka bat(ekin)	(with) a little bread
apur bat	a little	gazta apur bat(ekin)	(with) a little cheese
doi bat	a little	doi bat argi(rekin)	(with) a little light
makina bat	a lot of	makina bat ijito(rekin)	(with) a lot of gypsies
gehiago	more	jende gehiago(rekin)	(with) more people
gehiegi	too many, too much	txakur gehiegi(rekin)	(with) too many dogs

We must note that *gutxi*, *asko*, *pixka bat*, *apur bat*, *gehiago*, and *gehiegi* always follow the noun they modify, while *nahikoa*, *doi* (except when used as an adjective 'scanty'), *doi bat*, and *makina bat* always precede it. The words *anitz*, *franko*, and *aski* can take either slot, with *anitz* preferring prenominal and *franko* postnominal position. Some further examples:

lore gorri polit gutxi	few pretty red flowers
etxe zuri haundi gehiago	more big white houses
aski liburu eder	enough beautiful books
nahikoa ardo beltz	enough red wine
makina bat atso itsusi	a lot of ugly old women
anitz esker bero	many warm thanks
esker bero anitz	many warm thanks

The quantifier *franko* can also function as an adverb (possibly an instance of quantifier float)—a property it shares with some adjectives: *ugari* 'abundant', *urri* 'scant', *eskas* 'meager', 'inadequate'. In these instances, *franko* is no longer part of the noun phrase quantified, so that the latter must now assume the definite form: *apaiza franko* or *apaizak franko* 'quite a few priests'. The adjectives listed in this subsection behave in the same way; compare *gari ugari* 'abundant wheat', *sari urri* 'scant reward', *diru eskas* 'meager money' with *garia ugari* 'wheat in abundance', *saria urri* 'reward in scantiness', *dirua eskas* 'money in shortage'.

To our main list of quantifiers we should add all words meaning 'so many', 'so much': *hainbeste, horrenbeste, honenbeste, hainbat, horrenbat, honenbat*—for example, *hainbeste andreri* or *hainbat andreri* 'to so many ladies'; *hainbeste nekerekin* or *hainbat nekerekin* 'with so much effort'; *hainbeste aldiz* or *hainbat aldiz* 'so many times'.

Basque has several terms for plural 'some'; the most common one being *batzuk*, declined as a definite plural: *batzuk, batzuek, batzuen, batzuei, batzuekin, batzuez.*

A more elevated style of Batua has borrowed indefinite *batzu* from the northern dialects; this is declined *batzu, batzuk, batzuren, batzuri, batzurekin, batzuz.*

Only slightly less common than *batzuk, zenbait* invariably renders its noun phrase indefinite. When used inside a larger noun phrase, *batzuk* and *batzu* always follow the noun or adjective, while *zenbait* usually precedes the noun:

etxe handi batzuk (batzu), zenbait etxe handi	some big houses
etxe handi batzuei (batzuri), zenbait etxe handiri	to some big houses
etxe handi batzuekin (batzurekin), zenbait etxe handirekin	with some big houses
etxe handi batzuentzat (batzurentzat), zenbait etxe handirentzat	for some big houses

Although interchangeable in many contexts, *batzuk* and *zenbait* are not quite synonymous. When *some* might be replaced by *a few* in English, *batzuk* is used; when *some* might be replaced by *certain, zenbait.*

Both terms can be used substantively to refer to persons as well as to things. In this use their semantic difference is most noticeable: *batzuk*: 'some', 'a few', 'some people', 'a few people'; *zenbait*: 'some', 'certain', 'some people', 'certain people'—for example, *batzuen etxeak* 'a few people's houses'; *zenbaiten etxeak* 'certain people's houses'.

[*N.B.* Noun phrases with *batzuk* take plural verb forms; noun phrases with *zenbait* take singular or plural.]

9. In a genitive noun phrase followed by *bat* or *batzu(k)*. This construction, translatable by the English expression *some . . . or other*, emphasizes the indefinite character of the genitivized noun phrase:

katuren bat	some cat or other
hotsen bat	some sound or other
nagusiren batzuk	some bosses or other
alkate gazteren batzuk	some young mayors or other

With cardinal numbers this construction is quite common:

zortziren bat sorgin	eight or so witches
hogeiren bat urte	twenty or so years

The reader may recall here a shorter alternative involving nominalized numerals: *zortzi bat sorgin, hogei bat urte* (see observation 13 of section 2.1.1). This alternative is not available for *bat*—a pronoun more than a numeral—in the current expression *baten bat* 'someone or other', 'something or other'. There is also a plural form *batzuren batzu(k)* 'some persons or other', 'some specimens or other', although the spoken language prefers *baten batzuk*.

10. With certain bare nouns accompanying the verbs *izan* 'to be' (see section 7.5), **edun* 'to have' (see section 13.4.2), *egin* 'to do', 'to make' (see section 13.3), *eman* 'to give' (see section 15.6.6), and *hartu* 'to take', 'to receive' (see section 13.4.1).

Which nouns enter this construction is a largely unpredictable, hence lexical, matter. These noun-verb combinations are usually translatable by a single verb in English. As numerous instances are given in the chapters cited, a small sample will do here:

With the verb *izan* 'to be': *beldur izan* 'to be afraid', from *beldur* 'fear'; *bizi izan* 'to live', from *bizi* 'life'.
With the verb **edun* 'to have': *nahi *edun* 'to want', from *nahi* 'will'; *uste *edun* 'to think (so)', from *uste* 'opinion'.
With the verb *egin* 'to do', 'to make': *barre egin* 'to laugh', from *barre* 'laughter'; *lan egin* 'to work', from *lan* 'work'.
With the verb *eman* 'to give': *hitz eman* 'to promise', from *hitz* 'word'; *musu eman* 'to kiss', from *musu* 'kiss'.
With the verb *hartu* 'to take', 'to receive': *min hartu* 'to be hurt', from *min* 'pain'; *su hartu* 'to catch fire', from *su* 'fire'.

It is tempting here to speak of incorporation of the noun into the verb, as this would account for the restriction to bare nouns—nouns without any modifier or determiner. The objection that the noun and the verb need not be adjacent in surface structure is by no means fatal; witness the verb-particle combinations in English, or, better still, the separable verb prefixes in German.

11. In noun phrases functioning as subject complements or object complements. Noun phrases indicating an office, title, or function frequently serve as subject or object complements, which, in Basque, admit no determiner of any kind. Examples are

morroi joan	to go into service as a farmhand
neskame sartu	to enter service as a maid
apaiz egon	to serve (in some area) as a priest
lehendakari izendatu	to designate as president
lagun eraman	to take along as a companion

12. In predicate adjectives with an impersonal or sentential subject. For examples see section 18.2.2.

2.4 Syntax and Nature of the Genitive

With rare exceptions the genitive phrase precedes the noun phrase it modifies:

sorginaren etxea	the witch's house
lur askoren jabea	the owner of a lot of land
lau ijitoen hamar oiloak	the ten chickens of the four gypsies

To predicate possession, genitive phrases are used in combination with the copulative verb *izan* 'to be'. Just like predicate adjectives (section 1.3.3), such genitives must take the article *-a* or its plural *-ak*:

Dirua apaizarena da.	The money is the priest's.
Etxea alabena da.	The house is the daughters'.
Oiloak ijitoarenak dira.	The chickens are the gypsy's.
Txakurra norena da?	Whose is the dog? (i.e., To whom does the dog belong?)
Txakurra ez da inorena.	The dog is nobody's.
Zein apaizena da umea?	Which priest's is the child?

Genitive noun phrases may also carry the article (in fact, the complete determiner system) when they are not in predicate position:

katuarena	the one of the cat
ijitoena	the one of the gypsies
apaizarenak	the ones of the priest
sorginenak	the ones of the witches

As the reference of such noun phrases depends on the context, we must postulate an underlying zero pronoun ∅ as head of the noun phrase: *katuaren ∅-a*. (This approach, of course, is exactly parallel to our treatment of substantivized adjectives in section 1.3.2.) Since such genitive phrases are genuine noun phrases, they again admit all case endings, including the genitive:

katuarenarekin	with the one of the cat
ijitoenarentzat	for the one of the gypsies
apaizarenenak	the ones of the ones of the priest
sorginenena	the one of the ones of the witches

The following examples will help make the meaning clear:

ijitoaren adiskideen oiloak eta apaizarenenak
the chickens of the friends of the gypsy and the ones of the ones of the priest

apaizen adiskideen liburuekin eta sorginenenekin
with the books of the friends of the priests and with the ones of the ones of the witches

This kind of recursion is known, misleadingly, as "hyperdeclension" ("*surdéclinaison*").

Comparing the genitive with the other cases in Basque, we find it to be different in at least three important respects:

1. No verb in Basque selects genitive noun phrases or even admits them as complement. (Clearly, the zero alternant of benefactive *-tzat*, found in the Souletin dialect, is not to be identified with the genitive.)
2. Unlike any other oblique noun phrase, genitives can be followed by determiners, as has been noted previously.
3. Genitive noun phrases can modify other noun phrases directly—again in contrast to all other oblique cases (cf. section 5.1).

All this leads to the conclusion that the Basque genitive is adjectival in nature, as represented by the following formula:

$[_A$ NP $[_A$-*ren*]]

That is, as Mitxelena has recognized (*MEIG* VI, 177), *-ren* is not a flexional but a derivational morpheme, albeit a somewhat unusual one in that it operates not on a lexical category such as N, but on the maximal projection of N, the syntactic category NP.

We must stipulate that adjectives having this internal structure precede their noun instead of following it. This construction, however, is nothing unusual; the same must be done for adjectives in *-tar* (section 6.6) as well as for ordinals in *-garren* (section 2.1.2), both undoubtedly adjectival.

2.5 Fractionals

Fractional numerals in Basque are homonymous with the indefinite genitive of the corresponding cardinals. Only the first three are irregular:

erdi bat	one-half
heren bat	one-third
laurden bat	one-fourth
bosten bat	one-fifth
seiren bat	one-sixth
zazpiren bat	one-seventh
zortziren bat	one-eighth
bederatziren bat	one-ninth
hamarren bat	one-tenth (also 'a tithe')
. . .	. . .
ehunen bat	one-hundredth
milaren bat	one-thousandth
miloiren bat	one-millionth

Fractional numerals are basically nouns:

liburuaren erdia	half of the book (also 'the middle of the book')
bidearen bi herenak	two-thirds of the way (Ax., 71)
hiru bosten	3/5
diruaren hiru bostenak	three-fifths of the money
bekatuen hamarrena	a tenth (part) of the sins

Yet, fractionals, especially *erdi* 'half' and *laurden* 'quarter', can also occur in adjectival position, thus following a noun not in the genitive case:

pitxar erdi ardo	a half pitcher of wine
ordu erdi bat	a half hour, half an hour
Bilbo erdia	half Bilbao
ordu laurden bat	a quarter of an hour
kilo laurden bat	a quarter of a kilo

Hence also:

hiru ordu laurden	three-quarters of an hour
hiru miloi laurden	three-quarters of a million

Theoretically, the morphologically regular forms (*bosten, seiren*, etc.) give rise to ambiguity when they are followed by *bat*: *ehunen bat* 'one-hundredth', but also 'a hundred or so' (section 2.3.2, item 9). The presence of a noun, however, will dispel the ambiguity:

ogi seiren bat	one-sixth of a loaf
seiren bat ogi	six loaves or so
miloi zortziren bat	one-eighth of a million
zortziren bat miloi	eight million or so

Among the fractionals, only *erdi* can modify adjectives: *erdi huts* 'half empty', *erdi bete* 'half full', *erdi zoro* 'half crazy', *erdi ustel* 'half rotten'.

2.6 Expressive Adjectives

After making the acquaintance of a collective suffix *-kote* in section 2.1.3, we would like to wind up this chapter discussing a different suffix of the same form: the suffix *-kote* creating expressive forms of adjectives. The suffix must be called nonproductive as it occurs in no more than a dozen words, many of which are quite uncommon:

beltz	black	belzkote	swarthy
gizen	fat	gizenkote	plump, fatty
handi	tall, big	handikote	burly, hulky, hulk
lodi	thick, bulky	lodikote	chubby

motz	short	mozkote	dumpy, shorty
on	good	onkote	meek, (too) good-natured
sendo	robust	sendokote	hefty, sturdy, husky
zabal	wide, broad	zabalkote	broadish, quite broad
zahar	old	zaharkote	oldish, decrepit
zakar	rough, coarse	zakarrote	quite rough, very coarse

(Note the dissimilatory loss of *k* in the last example.)

As the translations intend to show, such expressive adjectives are quite colloquial and usually refer to persons or their bodily features: *aurpegi zabalkote* 'very broad face' (Azkue, *DVEF* II, 399).

The suffix *-kote* also operates on a few nouns. Thus: *gizakote* 'big hefty fellow' from *gizon* 'man'; *zaldikote* 'strong draft horse' from *zaldi* 'horse'.

2.7 Vocabulary

aho	mouth	ilargi	moon
aitona	grandfather	izeba	aunt
alkate	mayor	kale	street
amona	grandmother	lo	sleep
anitz	many, much	lotsa	shame
apur bat	a little, a bit	nahikoa	enough
arratsalde	afternoon	negu	winter
arrisku	danger	odol	blood
bakoitz	each	ordu	hour, time
baso	glass (for drinking)	osaba	uncle
bekatu	sin	pixka bat	a little, a bit
beldur	fear	poz	joy
bide	way, road	sari	reward, prize
egia	truth	sendo	robust, healthy, strong
eguzki	sun	uda	summer
errege	king	ugari	abundant
gauez	by night	ume	kid, child
gazte	young, youngster	zergatik	why

(The reader is advised to also review the vocabulary given in section 1.4 before beginning the following exercises.)

2.8 Exercises

2.8.1 Translate into English

1. Bi ijitoak adiskide zaharrak dira.
2. Sorginaren alabaren mila oiloak beltzak dira.
3. Pelloren adiskidearen semearen etxea handi eta ederra da.
4. Sagarrak Jonentzat dira, ogia Koldorentzat eta dirua Patxirentzat.
5. Aita behi gutxiren jabea da, baina txerri askorena.
6. Anitz umeren amak sorginak dira.
7. Etxe zuria hamaika emakumerentzat da.
8. Askoren etxea ez da inorena.
9. Zaldi zuriak norenak dira?
10. Zergatik ez da ona nagusiaren adiskidearen lana?
11. Eguzkiaren argia egunez eta ilargiarena gauez merke eta ugariak dira.
12. Alkatearen semeen zalditxoak onak baina ijitoarenak txarrak dira.

2.8.2 Translate into Basque

1. The ten houses are new.
2. The little boy's white horse is expensive.
3. The fear of the red women is great.
4. Four boys and five girls are nine children.
5. Many witches are young and pretty.
6. Few ladies are silent.
7. The new house is for the big daughter of the mayor's friend.
8. For whom is the money and for whom not?
9. A little money is not enough.
10. Which book belongs to (is of) the old priest?
11. Nobody is the owner of a hundred thousand books.
12. Whose is the dog, and whose (is) the horse?

3 The System of Locative Case Endings

3.1 Introductory Remarks

The basic system of case endings analyzed in chapter 2 does not apply to the full set of Basque cases. It leaves out the locative ones, locative here taken in a broad sense to include not only the inessive case marked by *-an*, but also the elative marked by *-tik* (also serving as an ablative) and the allative marked by *-ra* with its derivatives the terminal *-raino* (*-ra* + suffix *-ino*, historically *-gino* or *-dino*) and the tendential *-rantz* (*-ra* + suffix *-antz* 'likeness'). These five cases are all ruled by the same morphological system, henceforth "the locative system."

Previous grammars are wont to include here the linking morpheme *-ko*, often called the "locative genitive." The reasons why we deem this assignment a fundamental mistake will be found in section 5.1 devoted to this morpheme.

The locative system differs from the basic system on at least two counts. Indeed, the contrasts are so striking that one finds it hard to escape the impression that the two systems are rooted in differing chronological stages of the language.

It is true that, like the basic system, the locative system scrupulously observes the definite/indefiniteness distinction, resulting in the same three number paradigms as we had in chapter 2: definite singular, definite plural, indefinite. However, as we will soon see, it realizes this distinction in a very different fashion, marked out by a total absence of the definite article *-a*. As all scholars are agreed that this article developed out of a demonstrative pronoun at some relatively late period, a likely conclusion would seem to be that the locative system antedates this development and is therefore in some way more archaic than the basic system, which does involve the article *-a*.

Equally noteworthy within the locative system is the role of the feature "animate." In fact, the system can be said to discriminate against animate noun phrases inasmuch as it does not allow them to take locative endings directly, but only through the mediation of an intervening morpheme *-gan* or *baita*, as will be shown in section 3.6.

For the present, we restrict our attention to inanimate noun phrases, using mainly the following nouns: *herri* 'village', *eliza* 'church', *ibai* 'river', *arau* 'rule', 'norm', *oin* 'foot'.

3.2 The Definite Singular Locative Paradigm for Common Nouns

Inessive	herrian	at the village, in the village
Elative	herritik	out of the village, from the village
Allative	herrira	to the village
Terminal	herriraino	as far as the village, up to the village
Tendential	herrirantz	toward the village
Inessive	elizan	at the church, in the church
Elative	elizatik	from the church
Allative	elizara	to the church
Terminal	elizaraino	as far as the church, up to the church
Tendential	elizarantz	toward the church
Inessive	ibaian	at the river, in the river
Elative	ibaitik	from the river
Allative	ibaira	to the river
Terminal	ibairaino	as far as the river, down to the river
Tendential	ibairantz	toward the river
Inessive	arauan	in the rule
Elative	arautik	from the rule
Allative	araura	to the rule, according to the rule
Terminal	arauraino	as far as the rule
Tendential	araurantz	toward the rule
Inessive	oinean	at the foot, on the foot, in the foot
Elative	oinetik	from the foot
Allative	oinera	to the foot
Terminal	oineraino	up to the foot, down to the foot
Tendential	oinerantz	toward the foot

These paradigms plainly demonstrate what I have intimated in my introductory remarks: in spite of their definiteness, there is no trace of a definite article at all. The locative endings are attached directly to the bare noun.

Note that in the inessive form of stems ending in *-a*, the expected cluster *-aan* (still maintained in older Biscayan) simplifies to *-an*: *elizan* (older Biscayan *eleisaan*).

With stems ending in a consonant an epenthetic vowel *e* appears before all locative endings, including inessive *-an*, presumably derived from an earlier form *-gan*. From a diachronic and perhaps even synchronic point of view, we may speak of three phonological processes applying in the following order: first, *e*-epenthesis; then, intervocalic *g* deletion; and last, cluster simplification (obligatory only for *aa*).

There are two lexical exceptions to this paradigm. First, the noun *gau* 'night', which behaves here as if it ended in a consonant: *gauean* 'in the night', *gauetik* 'from the night on', *gauera* 'to the night', *gaueraino* 'until the night', *gauerantz* 'toward the night'.

Second, the noun *goi* 'height', 'top' (also used as an adjective with the meaning 'elevated', 'highest') loses its final *i* in the allative, terminal, and tendential forms, resulting in the following paradigm:

Inessive	goian	on top, above, up, upstairs
Elative	goitik	from the top, from above, from upstairs
Allative	gorato	the top, up (motion), upstairs (motion)
Terminal	goraino	as far as the top, up to the top
Tendential	gorantz	toward the top, upward

The noun *behe* 'bottom', 'lower floor' declines regularly. Note the expressions:

goitik behera	from top to bottom, down
behetik gora	from bottom to top, up

It is worth pointing out that the allative forms *behera* 'down' and *gora* 'up' can act as postpositions. The noun phrase that they govern takes the inessive, elative, or instrumental case, depending on the meaning of the construction.

If surface contact is maintained throughout the motion, the inessive case obtains:

kalean behera	down the street
mendian gora	up the mountain

If the motion results in separation, the elative case is in order:

dorretik behera	down the tower
herritik gora	above the village

Also, for example, with age limits:

zazpi urtetik behera	below seven (years of age)
hogei urtetik gora	above twenty (years of age) (*MEIG* V, 131)

In describing a spatial arrangement definable without regard to any motion that may take place, the instrumental case can be used. Typical examples are

buruz behera	with the head down, upside down, reverse
buruz gora	with the head raised, upside up, sloping up
ahoz behera	face down, on one's belly, forward
ahoz gora	face up, on one's back, backward

The numeral *bat* usually conforms to this definite singular paradigm:

etxe batean	in one house, in a house	batean	in one, together, sudden
etxe batetik	from one house, from a house	batetik	from one, from one place

etxe batera	to one house, to a house	batera	to one, jointly
etxe bateraino	as far as one house	bateraino	up to one
etxe baterantz	toward one house	baterantz	toward one

To end this section, two more remarks about the elative case. Aside from its meaning 'starting point', *-tik* carries the related meaning 'transit point', so that it also conveys 'through', 'by way of', 'via'. Incidentally, the same is true for the Latin ablative case: *Romam venit Albanis montibus* 'He came to Rome via the Alban mountains'.

As far as intonation is concerned, in contrast to all other locative endings, the elative *-tik* (from older *-tika*) must have low pitch and hence cannot show contrastive stress. (The terminal ending *-raino* has low pitch on its final syllable only.)

3.3 The Definite Plural Locative Paradigm

Using the same examples as in section 3.2, we get

Inessive	herrietan	at the villages, in the villages
Elative	herrietatik	from the villages, through the villages
Allative	herrietara	to the villages
Terminal	herrietaraino	as far as the villages
Tendential	herrietarantz	toward the villages
Inessive	elizetan	at the churches, in the churches
Elative	elizetatik	from the churches, through the churches
Allative	elizetara	to the churches
Terminal	elizetaraino	as far as the churches
Tendential	elizetarantz	toward the churches
Inessive	ibaietan	at the rivers, in the rivers
Elative	ibaietatik	from the rivers
Allative	ibaietara	to the rivers
Terminal	ibaietaraino	as far as the rivers
Tendential	ibaietarantz	toward the rivers
Inessive	arauetan	in the rules
Elative	arauetatik	from the rules, through the rules
Allative	arauetara	to the rules, according to the rules
Terminal	arauetaraino	as far as the rules
Tendential	arauetarantz	toward the rules
Inessive	oinetan	at the feet, on the feet, in the feet
Elative	oinetatik	from the feet
Allative	oinetara	to the feet
Terminal	oinetaraino	as far as the feet, down to the feet
Tendential	oinetarantz	toward the feet

Evidently, then, the definite plural is characterized in the locative system by the presence of a segment *-eta-* between the stem and the endings. These are the same as in the singular, except for one optional feature borrowed from the eastern dialects (i.e., the northern dialects and High Navarrese): the form *-tik* may be replaced by *-rik*. Thus *-etatik* has a free variant *-etarik*: *etxeetatik* or *etxeetarik* 'from the houses'.

For stems ending in *-a*, contact with *-eta-* results in the loss of this vowel: *elizetan* 'in the churches'. Other vowel combinations, including $e + e$, are maintained: *etxeetan* 'in the houses', *ahoetan* 'in the mouths', *suetan* 'in the fires'.

3.4 The Indefinite Locative Paradigm

We will again use the same examples as before, putting them, however, into a suitable noun-phrase frame, to account for the occurrence of the indefinite form. (See section 2.3.2.)

Inessive	hainbeste herritan	in so many villages
Elative	hainbeste herritatik	from so many villages
Allative	hainbeste herritara	to so many villages
Terminal	hainbeste herritaraino	up to so many villages
Tendential	hainbeste herritarantz	toward so many villages
Inessive	zenbait elizatan	in certain churches
Elative	zenbait elizatatik	from certain churches
Allative	zenbait elizatara	to certain churches
Terminal	zenbait elizataraino	up to/as far as certain churches
Tendential	zenbait elizatarantz	toward certain churches
Inessive	zein ibaitan?	in which river?
Elative	zein ibaitatik?	from which river?
Allative	zein ibaitara?	to which river?
Terminal	zein ibaitaraino?	up to/as far as which river?
Tendential	zein ibaitarantz?	toward which river?
Inessive	bi arautan	in two rules
Elative	bi arautatik	from two rules
Allative	bi arautara	to two rules, according to two rules
Terminal	bi arautaraino	as far as two rules
Tendential	bi arautarantz	toward two rules
Inessive	lau oinetan	in four feet, on four feet
Elative	lau oinetatik	from four feet
Allative	lau oinetara	to four feet
Terminal	lau oinetaraino	up to four feet
Tendential	lau oinetarantz	toward four feet

The semantic category of indefiniteness, which is shown in the basic system by nothing more than the absence of the definite article, is seen to be explicitly indicated in the locative system by means of an indefinite marker *-ta-* preceding the case endings. When this marker *-ta-* is added to a stem ending in a consonant or to the stem *gau* meaning 'night' (from **gab*), *e*-epenthesis takes place, with the result that the formal distinction between the indefinite and the definite plural is erased: *lau oinetan* 'in the four feet' or 'in four feet', *bi gauetan* 'in the two nights' or 'in two nights'.

Just as in the definite plural, the case endings themselves are unchanged, again with the proviso that the ending *-tik* may be replaced by *-rik*: *zein etxetatik* or *zein etxetarik* 'from which house?'.

Exceptionally, *e*-epenthesis does not apply to pronouns ending in a weak *r*, that is, not to *zer* 'what', *ezer* 'anything', *edozer* 'anything whatsoever', *zer edo zer* 'something'. The paradigms of *zer* and *ezer* are given as illustrations:

zertan	in what	ezertan	in anything
zertatik	from what	ezertatik	from anything
zertara	to what	ezertara	to anything
zertaraino	as far as what	ezertaraino	as far as anything
zertarantz	toward what	ezertarantz	toward anything

The pronouns *zein* 'which', *zenbat* 'how many', and *zenbait* 'some' decline regularly:

zeinetan	in which	zenbatetan	in how many, for how much
zeinetatik	from which	zenbatetatik	from how many
zeinetara	to which	zenbatetarato	how many, to how much
zeinetaraino	as far as which	zenbatetaraino	up to how many/how much
zeinetarantz	toward which	zenbatetarantz	toward how many

[*N.B.* The English distinction between (*how*) *many* and (*how*) *much* is not made in Basque.]

The locative stem *no-* of the terms *non* 'where', *inon* 'anywhere', *edonon* 'wheresoever' or 'everywhere'—in the south usually pronounced *nun*, *inun*, *edonun*—dispenses with *-ta-*, so that the inessive form has *-n* only. Besides, the elative forms are irregular in being based on the inessive, instead of on the stem:

non	where	inon	anywhere
nondik	from where	inondik	from anywhere
nora	to where	inora	to anywhere
noraino	up to where	inoraino	up to anywhere
norantz	in what direction	inorantz	in any direction

[*N.B.* The interrogative phrase *nondik nora* 'from where to where' possesses the additional meanings 'what for', 'why', 'how'; the negative phrase *inondik inora ez* 'from nowhere to nowhere' has the force of the English expression *by no means.*]

3.4.1 The Declension of Cardinal Numbers

Cardinal numbers, whether in isolation or as part of an indefinite noun phrase, are declined in accordance with this indefinite paradigm. The numeral *bat* 'one', however, forms an exception. As mentioned in section 3.2, it usually follows the definite paradigm, in conformity with the practice of the southern dialects: *batean, batetik, batera, bateraino, baterantz.* Is this practice due to analogical pressure from the definite article onto the definite one?

Owing to the optional ellipsis of the noun *aldi* 'turn', 'time' in inessive contexts (see section 20.3.1), inessive forms of numerals have the additional meaning 'so many times'. Likewise, allative forms of the numerals have the additional meaning 'in so many ways'. Some examples may be welcome:

Inessive		*Allative*	
batean	in one, at the same time	batera	to one, jointly, together
bitan	in two, (in) two times	bitara	to two, in two ways
hirutan	in three, (in) three times	hirutara	to three, in three ways
askotan	in many, (in) many times	askotara	to many, in many ways
gutxitan	in few, (in) few times	gutxitara	to few, in few ways
zenbatetan	in how many (times)	zenbatetara	to how many, in how many ways

[*N.B.* Distinguish: *bitan* 'in two (times)' and *bietan* 'in the two (times)', *bitara* 'to two' or 'in two ways' and *bietara* 'to the two' or 'in the two ways'.]

3.4.2 Use of the Indefinite Form in the Locative System

Generally speaking, the point taken in section 2.3.2 to the effect that indefinite forms occur only under specific syntactic conditions remains valid in the locative system also. It is for this reason that quite a few English locative phrases without an overt article correspond to definite singular phrases in Basque. Some examples are

esku	hand	eskuan	in hand
etxe	house	etxean	at home
itsaso	sea	itsasoan	at sea
jolas	play	jolasean	at play
lan	work	lanean	at work
lur	earth	lurrean	on earth
negu	winter	neguan	in winter
ohe	bed	ohean	in bed
otoitz	prayer	otoitzean	in prayer
uda	summer	udan	in summer
zeru	heaven	zeruan	in heaven

There is nonetheless one situation where a purely semantic criterion suffices to license the indefinite form of a noun. This is seen when the noun occurs in a locative noun phrase and the object it denotes is immaterial or otherwise lacking clearly definable boundaries. The following examples should make this point sufficiently clear:

amets	dream	ametsetan	in a dream, in dreaming
argi	light	argitan	in the light, openly
auzi	lawsuit, dispute	auzitan	in dispute, at issue
begi	eye	begitan	in view
bero	heat, hot	berotan	in the heat
diru	money	dirutan	in money, converted into money
eguzki	sun	eguzkitan	in the sun
gar	flame	garretan	in flames, aflame
ilargi	moon	ilargitan	in the moonlight
ilun	darkness, dark	ilunetan	in the dark
izerdi	sweat	izerditan	in a sweat, sweating
ke	smoke	ketan	in smoke, fuming
lo	sleep	lotan	asleep, sleeping
odol	blood	odoletan	bleeding, covered in blood
su	fire	sutan	on fire, burning, raging
ur	water	uretan	in water
zati	part, piece	zatitan	in parts, in pieces

To refer to a period of life, indefinite inessives can be used:

gazte	young, youngster	gaztetan	as a youngster, in one's youth
haur	child	haurretan	as a child, in one's childhood
txiki	small, little	txikitan	as a small child, in early childhood
ume	small kid	umetan	as a small kid, in early childhood
zahar	old	zaharretan	as an old person, in old age

Allative indefinites occur under the same condition as inessive ones:

argi	light	argitara	to light, into the open
auzi	lawsuit, trial	auzitara	to trial, to court
buru	head, end	burutara	to a head, to an end
eskuin	right hand	eskuinetara	to the right
ezker	left hand	ezkerretara	to the left
lo	sleep	lotara	to sleep
meza	Mass	mezatara	to Mass
nahi	will	nahitara	at will, deliberately
su	fire	sutara	into the fire
ur	water	uretara	into the water

Similarly for elative indefinites: *lotatik* 'from one's sleep', *sutatik* 'out of the fire', *uretatik* 'out of the water', and several others.

Obviously, as soon as the noun has a concrete reference, a definite form will be in order:

auzian	at the trial, in the issue at hand
ahora	to the mouth
etxetik	from home

The distinction, however, can be quite subtle: thus we get indefinite *haizetan* 'in the wind', but definite *airean* 'in the air'.

3.5 The Declension of Place Names

Place names are declined following the indefinite declension, but without the insertion of -*ta*-. Therefore, the main difference with the definite declension is in the shape of the inessive ending: -*n* instead of -*an*. A further difference is that *e*-epenthesis after a consonantal stem is not obligatory for elative -*tik* or allative -*ra*. It is obligatory, however, for the other three locative case endings.

With the elative ending -*tik*, as a matter of fact, there is a strong tendency in Batua not to apply *e*-epenthesis, although with the ending -*ra* it is customarily applied. When the elative -*tik* follows an *l* or an *n* without epenthesis, its *t* turns into *d* because of a widespread phonological rule voicing all stops in this position. Hence we get *Madrildik* or *Madriletik* 'from Madrid', *Irundik* or *Irunetik* 'from Irun'.

When the allative -*ra* follows any consonant without epenthesis, its *r* is elided, so that the allative ending appears as -*a*. Hence we get *Madrila* or *Madrilera* 'to Madrid', *Iruna* or *Irunera* 'to Irun', *Parisa* or *Parisera* 'to Paris'.

Some example paradigms:

Bilbon	in Bilbao	Gernikan	in Guernica
Bilbotik	from Bilbao	Gernikatik	from Guernica
Bilbora	to Bilbao	Gernikara	to Guernica
Bilboraino	as far as Bilbao	Gernikaraino	as far as Guernica
Bilborantz	toward Bilbao	Gernikarantz	toward Guernica

[*N.B. Gernika* is not accented on the first syllable!]

Irunen	in Irun	Madrilen	in Madrid
Irundik (Irunetik)	from Irun	Madrildik (Madriletik)	from Madrid
Irunera (Iruna)	to Irun	Madrilera (Madrila)	to Madrid
Iruneraino	as far as Irun	Madrileraino	as far as Madrid
Irunerantz	toward Irun	Madrilerantz	toward Madrid

Eibarren	in Eibar	Zarautzen	in Zarauz
Eibartik (Eibarretik)	from Eibar	Zarauztik (Zarautzetik)	from Zarauz
Eibarrera (Eibarra)	to Eibar	Zarautzera (Zarautza)	to Zarauz

Eibarreraino	as far as Eibar	Zarautzeraino	as far as Zarauz
Eibarrerantz	toward Eibar	Zarautzerantz	toward Zarauz
Gazteizen	in Vitoria	Parisen	in Paris
Gazteiztik (Gazteizetik)	from Vitoria	Paristik (Parisetik)	from Paris
Gazteizera (Gazteiza)	to Vitoria	Parisera (Parisa)	to Paris
Gazteizeraino	as far as Vitoria	Pariseraino	as far as Paris
Gazteizerantz	toward Vitoria	Pariserantz	toward Paris

Where *e*-epenthesis does not apply, the sandhi rules of section 1.2.6 will operate. Thus, in *Zarauztik* the consonant cluster *tz* + *t* has turned into *zt*, in accordance with sandhi rule 3.

Some Basque place names invariably co-occur with the article *-a*. (Compare the American place names *the Middle West, the Bronx*.) Some examples are

Azkoitia	Azcoitia	Ermua	Ermua
Azpeitia	Azpeitia	Hondarribia	Fuenterrabia
Basaburua	Basaburua	Iruñea	Pamplona
Batikanoa	The Vatican	Mallabia	Mallavia
Bizkaia	Biscay	Mañaria	Mañaria
Deustua	Deusto	Zokoa	Socoa

When such place names are combined with a following adjective, the article *a* hops over onto it in the usual fashion: *Batikano madarikatua* 'the accursed Vatican', *Azpeiti maitea* 'dear Azpeitia', *Bizkai ederra* 'beautiful Biscay'.

In fact, these place names are declined exactly like common nouns. The article *a* must disappear in front of the locative endings, and the inessive ending is not *-n* but *-an*:

Bizkaian	in Biscay	Iruñean	in Pamplona
Bizkaitik	from Biscay	Iruñetik	from Pamplona
Bizkaira	to Biscay	Iruñera	to Pamplona
Bizkairaino	as far as Biscay	Iruñeraino	as far as Pamplona
Bizkairantz	toward Biscay	Iruñerantz	toward Pamplona

We should not forget that in the majority of place names ending in *-a* this *a* is not the article, but part of the word itself. Such an *a* is called organic.

With the sole exception of *Batikanoa* 'the Vatican', names of countries and regions situated outside of the Basque Country have organic *-a*. The following listing is far from exhaustive:

Andaluzia	Andalucia
Errusia	Russia
Eskozia	Scotland
Espainia	Spain

Frantzia	France
Galizia	Galicia
Grezia	Greece
Japonia	Japan
Katalunia	Catalonia
Polonia	Poland
Suedia	Sweden
Suitza	Switzerland
Turkia	Turkey
Txekia	Czech Republic

Other place names with organic *-a* are

Aezkoa	Aezcoa	Gipuzkoa	Guipuzcoa
Baiona	Bayonne	Hendaia	Hendaye
Bidasoa	Bidasoa (river)	Leioa	Lejona
Donostia	San Sebastian	Nafarroa	Navarra
Errenteria	Renteria	Ordizia	Villafranca de Oria
Getaria	Guetaria, Guéthary	Zuberoa	Soule

Organic *-a*, of course, stays present throughout the declension:

Donostian	in San Sebastian	Nafarroan	in Navarra
Donostiatik	from San Sebastian	Nafarroatik	from Navarra
Donostiara	to San Sebastian	Nafarroara	to Navarra
Donostiaraino	as far as San Sebastian	Nafarroaraino	as far as Navarra
Donostiarantz	toward San Sebastian	Nafarroarantz	toward Navarra

Some geographical names always occur in the definite plural; English examples are *the Netherlands* and *the Rockies.* A good example in Basque is *Amerikak* 'America', literally: 'the Americas', that is, North and South. Its (definite) declension is perfectly regular:

Inessive	Ameriketan	in America
Elative	Ameriketatik	from America
Allative	Ameriketara	to America
Terminal	Ameriketaraino	as far as America
Tendential	Ameriketarantz	toward America

Naturally, *Iparramerika* 'North America' and *Hegoamerika* 'South America' are singular.

Inasmuch as the form *-rik* for the elative is ruled out in the definite singular paradigm, its occurrence after vocalic stems in the Souletin dialect (*Maulerik* 'from Mauléon') supports my assignment of the place name declension to the indefinite paradigm in spite of its uncharacteristic morphology. Later, section 16.8.1 will provide further support.

3.6 The Locative Paradigm for Animate Noun Phrases

Characteristic of the locative paradigm for animate noun phrases is the ending *-gan* in the inessive, and combinations of *-gan* with the usual endings *-tik* (or its variant *-rik*), *-ra*, *-raino*, and *-rantz* in the other cases. Between the segment *gan* and these endings no *e*-epenthesis obtains. Since *-tik* turns into *-dik* after the *n* of *-gan*, while the *r* of the other endings simply disappears in this context, the full endings are as follows:

-gan	at, in
-gandik (or *-ganik*)	from
-gana	to
-ganaino	as far as, up to
-ganantz	toward

These endings are attached to the noun stem through the intermediary of the genitive case. It is this case form that expresses the number distinction: definite singular, definite plural, indefinite; the animate locative endings themselves remain invariable. In the definite singular forms the genitive may optionally be left out, with the locative endings then added directly onto the definite form of the noun phrase.

In the indefinite paradigm, the genitive is optional only for stems ending in a vowel. In these, the endings can be added directly to the stem. In the definite plural, the genitive must not be omitted in Batua, although it can be omitted in the Biscayan dialect, resulting in such forms as *gizonakana*, from *gizonak* + *gana*. As examples we take the nouns *herri* 'population', 'nation', and *mutil* 'boy'. Thus:

Definite singular

herriarengan	in the population, in the nation (also *herriagan*)
herriarengandik	from the population, from the nation (also *herriagandik*)
herriarengana	to the population, to the nation (also *herriagana*)
herriarenganaino	up to the population, up to the nation (also *herriaganaino*)
herriarenganantz	toward the population, toward the nation (also *herriaganantz*)
mutilarengan	in the boy, at the boy (also *mutilagan*)
mutilarengandik	from the boy (also *mutilagandik*)
mutilarengana	to the boy (also *mutilagana*)
mutilarenganaino	as far as the boy, up to the boy (also *mutilaganaino*)
mutilarenganantz	toward the boy (also *mutilaganantz*)

Definite plural

herriengan	in the populations, in the nations
herriengandik	from the populations, from the nations
herriengana	to the populations, to the nations
herrienganaino	all the way to the populations, all the way to the nations
herrienganantz	toward the populations, toward the nations

mutilengan	in the boys
mutilengandik	from the boys
mutilengana	to the boys
mutilenganaino	all the way to the boys, as far as the boys
mutilenganantz	toward the boys

Indefinite

anitz herrirengan	in many populations/nations (*anitz herrigan*)
anitz herrirengandik	from many populations/nations (*anitz herrigandik*)
anitz herrirengana	to many populations/nations (*anitz herrigana*)
anitz herrirenganaino	all the way to many populations/nations (*anitz herriganaino*)
anitz herrirenganantz	toward many populations/nations (*anitz herriganantz*)

zenbait mutilengan	in certain boys
zenbait mutilengandik	from certain boys
zenbait mutilengana	to certain boys
zenbait mutilenganaino	as far as certain boys
zenbait mutilenganantz	toward certain boys

In the plural, animate noun phrases may follow the inanimate paradigm of section 3.3, particularly when a collective sense is intended: *mutiletan* 'among the boys' as opposed to *mutilengan* 'in (each of) the boys'. Likewise: *emakumeetarik* 'from (among) the women' (collective sense) as opposed to *emakumeengan* 'from the women' (individual sense). (The collective connotation is not found in the northern dialects, which, in the plural, virtually always employ the inanimate forms.)

Equivalent to the *-gan*-based paradigm is a construction involving the form *baita* borrowed into Batua from the northern dialects. The declension is as follows: inessive: *baitan*; elative: *baitatik* or *baitarik*; allative: *baitara*; terminal: *baitaraino*. (A tendential form does not exist.)

Like *-gan*, *baita* combines with the genitive form of the noun phrase it belongs to, but unlike *-gan*, it is written as a separate word. Again like *-gan*, in the case of singular noun phrases, proper names, or pronouns, the genitive may optionally be left out, the absolutive form being used instead. For proper names the absolutive form seems to be preferred to the genitive, although the latter is possible.

mutilaren baitan	in the boy, at the boy (also *mutila baitan*)
mutilaren baitatik	from the boy (also *mutila baitatik*)
mutilaren baitara	to the boy (also *mutila baitara*)
mutilaren baitaraino	as far as the boy (also *mutila baitaraino*)

mutilen baitan	in the boys, at the boys
mutilen baitatik	from the boys (also *mutilen baitarik*)
mutilen baitara	to the boys
mutilen baitaraino	as far as the boys

mutil askoren baitan	in many boys, at many boys
mutil askoren baitatik	from many boys
mutil askoren baitara	to many boys
mutil askoren baitaraino	as far as many boys
Pello baitan	in Pete, at Pete (also *Pelloren baitan*)
Pello baitatik	from Pete (also *Pelloren baitatik*)
Pello baitara	to Pete (also *Pelloren baitara*)
Pello baitaraino	as far as Pete (also *Pelloren baitaraino*)

[*N.B.* The Labourdin dialect presents house names of the type *Pello baita*. In the absence of any indication that *baita* ever existed as a noun meaning 'house' in Basque, I conclude that these represent back formations from *Pello baitan* 'at Pete', in the Labourdin dialect also used for 'at Pete's'; compare French *chez*.]

The concepts "animate" and "inanimate" that we have used denote grammatical categories, not biological ones. The boundaries of these categories are culture-specific and liable to individual variation. In Basque, on the one hand, plants and the smaller animals belong to the inanimate category, as do the terms *arima* 'soul', *gorputz* 'body', and *izpiritu* 'spirit'. On the other hand, words like *eguzki* 'sun', *ilargi* 'moon', and *euskara* 'the Basque language' may occasionally be personified and then take the animate forms: *eguzkiagandik* 'from the sun', *euskaragana* 'to the Basque language'.

3.7 Temporal Use of Locatives

In Basque, as in most languages, locative forms apply to the time dimension as well. In fact, unless they are adverbs, time expressions in Basque require a locative ending, usually the inessive: *neguan* 'in winter', *egun batean* 'one day' (here the northern dialects use the instrumental *egun batez*), *igandean* 'on Sunday', *igande batean* 'on a Sunday', *igandeetan* 'on Sundays' (note the definite plural form here). Cases other than the inessive occur too: *igandetik* 'since Sunday', *igandetik igandera* 'from Sunday to Sunday', *iganderaino* 'up to Sunday'.

3.8 Derivational Morphology

3.8.1 Derivational Suffixes

A striking characteristic of Basque is its richness in the area of derivational morphology—almost exclusively suffixal in nature. Derivation is largely nominal: nouns and adjectives make up the overwhelming majority of derived forms.

Over and above the normal phonological processes, such as the sandhi rules of section 1.2.6, more restricted rules, also applicable to compounds, may operate on the last syllable of a derivational base. These rules will be described in detail in chapter 31, but two of them need to be mentioned forthwith: Major Apocope, by which a vocalic base of more than two syllables loses its final vowel; and Minor Apocope, turning a final vowel of a two-syllable base into *a*, except for a high vowel, which drops altogether. (To this change of *e* and *o* into *a* the word apophony has sometimes been applied, a term we would much rather avoid.)

Derivational suffixes can be divided into those that induce apocope and those that do not. Moreover, Minor Apocope seems to be a minor rule: there are many vocalic bases counting two syllables that are never affected. For that matter, even Major Apocope has its exceptions.

For practical as well as pedagogical reasons the decision has been taken to spread the discussion of derivational morphology over the various chapters of this book rather than concentrating all of it into one lengthy and, of necessity, tedious chapter. This way, the learner encounters the array of derivational processes in bite-size portions with no risk of overload. He is thus enabled to gradually build up a useful vocabulary as he progresses through the grammar. The drawbacks this policy entails are minimal, especially since the index will include a list of derivational suffixes treated.

In this chapter we start with a rather simple example, the suffix *-tegi*.

3.8.2 The Suffix *-tegi*

The productive suffix *-tegi*, reputedly borrowed from Celtic, can be attached to a noun *N*, or somewhat less frequently, to a verb radical *V*.

If *N* is a noun, *N-tegi* denotes a container destined to house N, where N may be animate or inanimate.
If *V* is a verb radical, *V-tegi* denotes a place expressly destined for the process or activity given by the verb.

In some dialects *tegi* can be employed as an independent noun with the meaning ‘stable’, ‘shed’. In those dialects then, we ought to speak of compounding rather than of derivation.

In the following list of examples we can observe many instances of base-final vowel change brought about by Minor Apocope. In colloquial speech, these changes are very often ignored: thus *ohetegi* ‘bedroom’ and *oilotegi* ‘chicken coop’.

Following are examples with nouns:

abere	animal, cattle	abeltegi	stable, sheepfold, zoo
ale	grain	aletegi	barn, granary
apaiz	priest	apaiztegi	presbytery
apaizgai	seminarian	apaizgaitegi	seminary
arau	rule	arautegi	set of rules, code of laws
ardi	sheep	artegi	sheepfold
ardo	wine	ardandegi	tavern, bar, pub (also *ardotegi*)
arma	weapon	armategi	armory

arrain	fish	arrandegi	fish market, fish shop
auzi	trial, lawsuit	auzitegi	court of law, tribunal
auzo	neighbor	auzotegi	neighborhood, vicinity
behi	cow	behitegi	stable, cowshed
belar	grass, hay	belartegi	hay barn
bihi	grain	bihitegi	granary
bitxi	jewel	bitxitegi	locket, jewel case, jewelry shop, jewel house
diru	money	dirutegi	treasury
edari	drink	edaritegi	bar, tavern, pub, cantina
egun	day	egutegi	calendar
egur	firewood	egurtegi	woodshed
eri	sick, patient	eritegi	infirmary, hospital
erle	bee	erlategi	apiary, beehive
gaixo	sick, patient	gaixotegi	infirmary, hospital
garau	grain	garautegi	granary
gezur	lie	gezurtegi	tattling corner, bunch of lies, liar
haragi	flesh, meat	harategi	butcher shop
haur	child	haurtegi	nursery, kindergarten, child-care center
hauts	ash, ashes	haustegi	urn, ashtray
hezur	bone	hezurtegi	ossuary
hitz	word	hiztegi	dictionary, vocabulary
ikatz	coal	ikaztegi	coal shed
izar	star	izartegi	firmament, starry sky
izen	name	izendegi	catalog, list of names
judu	Jew	judutegi	Jewish ghetto
kafe	coffee	kafetegi	coffee shop
lan	work	lantegi	workshop, factory
lapur	thief	lapurtegi	thieves' den
lasto	straw	lastategi	straw loft
liburu	book	liburutegi	library, bookcase
lore	flower	lorategi	flower garden, anthology
maleta	suitcase	maletegi	luggage counter/compartment
ohe	bed	ohategi	bedroom, alcove
ohoin	thief	ohointegi	thieves' den
ohol	board, plank	oholdegi	timber yard, lumberyard
oilo	chicken	oilategi	chicken coop, poultry house
ontzi	vessel, container	ontzitegi	cupboard, closet
ordu	hour	ordutegi	schedule
oski	shoe	oskitegi	shoe store
sagardo	cider	sagardotegi	cider shop

simaur	manure	simaurtegi	manure pit
su	fire	sutegi	fireplace, forge, furnace
ume	kid, child	umetegi	nursery, child-care center
ur	water	urtegi	cistern, pond
urde	male pig	urdandegi	pigsty
uso	pigeon, dove	usategi	dovecote
zakur	dog	zakurtegi	doghouse, kennel
zaldi	horse	zalditegi	stable (also *zaltegi*)
zapata	shoe	zapategi	shoe store
zerri	pig	zerritegi	pigsty
zoro	crazy	zorotegi	madhouse

[*N.B.* The forms *maletegi* and *zapategi* can be explained by the effects of Major Apocope: *malet* + *tegi* and *zapat* + *tegi*.]

With verb radicals (see section 7.2.2) the examples are less numerous:

aitortu	to confess	aitortegi	confessional
amildu	to hurl downward	amildegi	precipice, chasm, ravine
bildu	to gather	biltegi	storehouse
bizar egin	to shave	bizartegi	barbershop
bizi izan	to live	bizitegi	residence, dwelling
erakutsi	to show	erakustegi	showroom, showcase, shop window
erre	to burn	erretegi	grillroom, incineration plant
ikasi	to learn	ikastegi	learning center
irakatsi	to teach	irakastegi	teaching center, college, classroom
laboratu	to work, to elaborate	laborategi	laboratory
lehortu	to dry	lehortegi	drying place
otoitz egin	to pray	otoiztegi	oratory
saldu	to sell	saltegi	store, shop
sendatu	to heal, to cure	sendategi	sanatorium, clinic

3.9 The Diminutive Suffix *-xka*

As we saw in section 1.2.5, diminutives in Basque are formed by means of the suffix *-txo* (or *tto*, *no*), which can be attached to almost any noun. There is in Batua also a nonproductive diminutive suffix shaped *-xka* (variant form *-ska*), borrowed from the northern dialects. It combines with a few dozen nouns. The main examples are

abere	animal	aberexka	small animal, insect, bug
adar	horn, branch	adaxka	small horn, small branch, twig
ate	door, gate	atexka	small door, small gate

bide	road	bidexka	small road, short trail, path
buru	head	buruxka	small head, ear of grain, gleanings
deabru	devil	deabruxka	little devil
etxe	house	etxexka	small house, cottage
gudu	battle, war	guduxka	skirmish, fray, scuffle
gurdi	cart, wagon	gurdixka	small cart
herri	village	herrixka	small village, hamlet
hiri	town, city	hirixka	small town, small city
ibai	river	ibaixka	streamlet, rivulet
ibar	valley	ibarxka	small valley
leiho	window	leihoxka	small window, skylight
liburu	book	liburuxka	small book, booklet
mendi	mountain	mendixka	small mountain, hill
mordo	bunch, group	mordoxka	small bunch, small group
ontzi	vessel, ship	ontzixka	small ship, little boat
orga	cart	orgaxka	small cart
sarde	pitchfork	sardexka	table fork
zaldi	horse	zaldixka	pony, foal, filly
zubi	bridge	zubixka	small bridge, footbridge, gangway
zuhaitz	tree	zuhaixka	little tree, bush

Unlike *-txo*, *-xka* also combines with adjectives, where it indicates a weaker or vaguer form of the property in question: *aberats* 'rich', *aberaxka* 'fairly rich'. Its most frequent use in Batua is with color adjectives:

arre	gray	arrexka	grayish
beltz	black	belxka	blackish
berde	green	berdexka	greenish
gorri	red	gorrixka	reddish, ruddy
hori	yellow	horixka	yellowish
more	purple	morexka	purplish
urdin	blue, gray	urdinxka	bluish, grayish
zuri	white	zurixka	whitish

3.10 Terms for 'sister' and 'brother'

Basque contains two words for 'sister', *arreba* and *ahizpa*. An interesting meaning distinction obtains between them, which is meticulously observed:

ahizpa	a female person's sister
arreba	a male person's sister

The Biscayan dialect insists on the same distinction for 'brother' too:

neba a female person's brother
anaia a male person's brother

The other dialects do not use the word *neba*. In Batua, the use of *neba* is at most optional, so that the term *anaia* can serve for all types of brothers.

3.11 Vocabulary

ahizpa	sister (see section 3.10)	Jainko	God
anaia	brother	Jaungoiko	God
arreba	sister (see section 3.10)	jende	people (singular noun)
askotan	many times, often	lantegi	workshop, factory
asto	donkey, ass	lege	law
ate	door, gate	leiho	window
auzi	trial, lawsuit, issue	leku	location, site, post
auzo	neighbor, neighborhood	lur	earth, ground, soil
behin	once	mahai	table
berriz	again, once more	more	purple
beti	always	neke	effort, tiredness, toil
bihar	tomorrow	non	where
deabru	devil	ohe	bed
eguraldi	weather	ohitura	custom, habit
fede	trust, faith, confidence	oilategi	chicken coop
gaztelu	castle	orain	now
gela	room	pago	beech tree
gurutze	cross	toki	place
gutxitan	few times, rarely	txoko	nice little corner
hiri	city, town	urdin	blue, gray (of hair)
igande	Sunday	urre	gold
ile	hair	zeru	sky, heaven
indar	power, strength, force	zilar	silver
ingeles	Englishman	zoko	hiding corner, spot
inon	anywhere	zubi	bridge
itsaso	sea	zulo	hole, den, lair

3.12 Exercises

3.12.1 Translate into English

1. Elizatik neskatxa politengana.
2. Gaur etxetik elizara eta bihar berriz elizatik etxera.
3. Ijitoengandik apaizarengana eta berriz apaizarengandik ijitoengana.
4. Liburu ederretarik herriarenganaino.
5. Nondik nora beti auzitara?
6. Sorginaren katu beltza zergatik da apaizaren oilategian?
7. Elizetan saguak eta etxeetan katuak dira beti.
8. Orain lantegi zaharretan da diru gutxi.
9. Eliza berri ederretan ez da jende asko.
10. Hiru neskatxa polit dira apaiz berriaren eliza txikian.
11. Alkatearen arreba ederra amaren adiskide baten ahizpa da.
12. Lurretik zerurantz eta gizonengandik Jaungoikoarenganantz.

3.12.2 Translate into Basque

1. Today from Navarra up to Biscay and tomorrow by way of Hendaye to Paris.
2. From the Vatican to the churches and again from the churches to the Vatican.
3. From many towns and villages to few people.
4. From whom to whom? From the ugly boy to the pretty girl.
5. In whose house are always witches?
6. In what direction is it now?
7. In how many castles are books and flowers?
8. The old man and the young girl are in America.
9. In certain villages there are many mice and few cats.
10. Today there is nobody in the workshop. (Translate "Today there isn't anybody . . .")
11. On Sundays there are few people in the big cities.
12. Why now from father's sister to mother's sister?

4 The Syntax of Location Nouns

4.1 Introduction

As the reader will have noticed, the Basque inessive (endings *-an*, *-n*, *-gan*) does not always translate into English in the same way. Quite a variety of English prepositions are called upon to lend their services: *leihoan* 'at the window', *kalean* 'in the street', *mahaian* 'on the table', *atean* 'by the door', *mutiletan* 'among the boys'.

Conversely, although the English prepositional phrases *at the door*, *by the door*, *in the door*, and *on the door* are far from being all synonymous, they are, nonetheless, all apt to be represented by the same Basque inessive: *atean*.

Generally speaking, there are no case endings or postpositions in Basque to correspond to spatial prepositions in English, such as *above*, *before*, *behind*, *between*, *on*, *over*, *under*, and so on. (I am aware of only one possible exception: the loanword *kontra* 'against', as in *hormaren kontra* 'against the wall', section 4.1.3.11.)

4.1.1 Location Nouns

Whenever a precise specification of a spatial relationship is required, Basque draws upon a resource called "location noun," a type of noun analogous to such English nouns as *back*, *bottom*, *front*, *rear*, *side*, *top*, and the like.

In the absence of more or less exceptional circumstances to be delved into before long, most location nouns govern the genitive. In other words, the noun phrase connected to them is required to be in the genitive case. Syntactically, the structure is therefore identical to that of other genitive constructions: the governed noun phrase must precede the location noun and cannot be separated from it by intervening constituents. Still, as we will see in chapter 15, a pronominal governee can and must be deleted under certain conditions.

4.1.2 The Syntax of *aurre* and *atze*, 'front' and 'back'

In this section, we will explore the behavior of the prototypical location nouns *aurre* 'front(side)' and *atze* 'back(side)', originally from *aur* 'face' and *atz* 'track', the final *e* having crept in from the locative forms. All other location nouns and their separate properties will be examined more briefly in the next section (4.1.3). An inherent property of location nouns is that they express a spatial relationship; hence their reference is always relative to some contextually given object X.

Applying this specifically to *aurre* and *atze*, we can state their meaning more precisely as follows:

aurrea	the frontside of X (as viewed from the outside), the space in front of X
atzea	the backside of X (as viewed from the outside), the space behind X

Thus:

etxe zuriaren aurrea	the frontside of the white house (seen from outside the house), (or also) the space in front of the white house
eliza handiaren atzea	the backside of the big church (seen from outside the church), (or also) the space behind the big church

Therefore:

etxe zuriaren aurrean	in front of the white house
eliza handiaren atzean	behind the big church

[*N.B.* When used with a noun phrase denoting one or more persons, the meaning of *aurre* weakens to 'presence':

aita eta amaren aurrean	in the presence of father and mother
emakumeen aurrean	in the presence of the women]

While the genitive-based construction illustrated here is always correct, an alternative form is sometimes available. If the governed noun phrase is inanimate and head-final—that is, it ends in a noun rather than in an adjective or a numeral—a type of compound construction can be used:

etxe aurrean	in front of the house
ispilu aurrean	in front of the mirror
mendi atzean	behind the mountain
leiho atzean	behind the window
Jonen begi aurrean	before John's eyes
Mirenen ate atzean	behind Mary's door
Yolandaren jauregitxo aurrean	in front of Yolanda's villa (Oñatibia, 37)
Pilatosen etxe aurrera	(to) in front of Pilate's house (*Pas Sant* 131)

As shown by these examples, preceding modifiers do not block the construction. Even a preceding relative clause is possible: *Feldman bizi den etxe aurrean* 'before the house where Feldman lives' (Garate, *NY* 159).

With animate noun phrases the compound construction is generally excluded. In particular, no compounds occur based on personal pronouns or personal proper nouns. An exception must be made, however, for semantically indefinite expressions of the following cast:

lagun aurrean	in the presence of companions
testigu aurrean	before witnesses
neska atzean	after girls, chasing girls
Also:	
errege aurrean	before the king

What we are mostly dealing with here is a type of syntactic compounding in which the members of the compound remain morphologically intact. It is only when the governed noun phrase consists of a single inanimate noun that syntactic compounding may give way to lexical compounding. If that option is chosen, the final syllable of the governed noun can be affected by special phonological rules applying to lexical compounds, as was hinted at in section 3.8.1.

In particular, the Major Apocope rule mentioned in 3.8.1 regularly deletes the final vowel of words containing more than two syllables. Taking *itsaso* 'sea' or *eliza* 'church' as examples, we get

itsas aurrean	in front of the sea
eliz atzean	behind the church

In some instances, consonants too can change:

afari	evening meal, supper	afalaurrean	before supper
bazkari	midday meal, lunch	bazkalaurrean	before lunch
gosari	breakfast	gosalaurrean	before breakfast
atari	doorway	atalaurrean	before the doorway

Application of the Minor Apocope rule (see section 3.8.1) before a location noun is quite rare and lends the text an archaic flavor. Thus a stylistically marked *betaurrean* 'before the eyes' can be employed instead of the unmarked *begi aurrean*.

Note on spelling: Location nouns are written separately from the preceding noun even in lexical compounds, except when a consonantal change has taken place: *itsas aurrean* 'in front of the sea', but *afalaurrean* 'before supper'.

A location noun can take any locative ending, not just the inessive one:

mendi atzean	behind the mountain
mendi atzetik	from behind the mountain
mendi atzera	(to) behind the mountain
mendi atzeraino	all the way to behind the mountain
mendi atzerantz	toward behind the mountain

When the governed noun phrase designates a moving object (or at least an object normally conceived of as moving), instead of the inessive, the elative may be used on the location noun:

zezen gorriaren aurretik	in front of the red bull
zaldi zuriaren atzetik	behind the white horse
trenaren atzetik (korritu)	(to run) after the train
neska baten atzetik (ibili)	(to chase) after a girl

In all of these examples, however, the inessive case could have been used without, it seems, any difference in meaning. Thus, the phrases *neska baten atzetik ibili* and *neska baten atzean ibili* can both be used for the literal meaning 'to walk behind a girl' and for the metaphorical one 'to chase after a girl'. Similarly, 'to chase after money' can be either *diru atzean ibili* or *diru atzetik ibili.*

A governed noun phrase need not be overtly expressed when its reference is clear from the rest of the sentence, the context, or the situation. Moreover, the various case forms of location nouns can be self-supporting, without any governed noun phrase at all either present or understood. Used that way, they correspond to various spatial adverbs or particles in English.

By way of illustration we offer the paradigms of *aurre* and *atze* together with some English equivalents. The choice between them depends, of course, on the sentence in question. The first translation given corresponds to the case of an understood governed noun phrase, the others to that of independent use:

aurrean	in front of X, in (the) front, up front, ahead, present
aurretik	away from X, away from here, before, beforehand, in advance
aurrera	(to) in front of X, to the fore, forward, ahead
aurrerantz	toward the front of X, forward, advancing

[*N.B.* In the meaning 'beforehand', 'previously' the indefinite instrumental *aurrez* also occurs. As an answer to a knock on the door, *Aurrera!* is the situational equivalent of English *Come in!* (cf. Spanish *Adelante!*).]

atzean	behind X, at the back, in the rear, behind
atzetik	from behind X, from the back, from the rear, from behind, behind
atzera	(to) behind X, to the back, to the rear, backward, back
atzerantz	toward the back of X, backward, retreating

[*N.B.* When *backward* means 'in reverse', it is usually rendered by the expression *atzetik aurrera*, literally 'from back to front'.]

Independently used *atzera* can serve to indicate a return to a previous state: *atzera bihurtu* 'to turn back', *atzera bildu* 'to gather back', *atzera ekarri* 'to bring back', *atzera eman* 'to give back', *atzera erosi* 'to buy back', *atzera eskatu* 'to ask back', *atzera ikasi* 'to relearn', *atzera irabazi* 'to gain back', *atzera itzuli* 'to return back', *atzera izkutatu* 'to hide back', *atzera joan* 'to go back', *atzera saldu* 'to sell back', *atzera sartu* 'to enter back'.

A slightly different meaning of *atzera* is seen in *atzera deitu* 'to call back', *atzera erantzun* 'to answer back', *atzera esan* 'to reply'.

Independent *atzera* is sometimes used to express mere reiteration, corresponding to *again*, *anew*, or *once more* in English. In this meaning *berriz* or *berriro* is perhaps more common. Pleonastic *atzera berriz* also occurs.

4.1.2.1 Northern *aitzin* and *gibel*

Neither *aurre* nor *atze* is used in the northern dialects. These dialects make use instead of *aitzin* 'frontside' and *gibel* 'liver', 'backside', employed in very much the same way as *aurre* and *atze*:

gizonen aitzinean	before (the) men
begi(en) aitzinean	before the eyes
gerla(ren) aitzinean	before the war
etxe(aren) gibelean	behind the house
Jonen gibelean	behind John

The allative forms are *aitzina* or *aitzinera*, *gibela* or *gibelera*. The latter two terms share all the meanings of *atzera*. In independent use *aitzina* is much more common than *aitzinera*.

Etymologically an inessive form (of *aitzi*, now sometimes used as a postposition meaning 'against'), *aitzin* itself may occur instead of *aitzinean*:

negu aitzin	before the winter
joan aitzin	before going

4.1.2.2 Biscayan *oste*

Typical of the Biscayan dialect is the form *oste* 'backside', 'behind', used as a synonym of *atze*—equally common there. Thus:

etxe ostera	(to) behind the house
mendi ostean	behind the mountain
nekearen ostean	after the effort, after the suffering
bazkalostean	after lunch
etorri ostean	after coming

The allative *ostera* has every meaning of *atzera* ('backward', 'back', 'once more', 'again') and a few more in addition: 'besides' (when constructed with a preceding instrumental noun phrase), 'on the other hand', 'however'.

All these forms are employed and accepted in Euskara Batua.

4.1.3 Other Location Nouns

We will briefly survey the remaining location nouns. Unless otherwise indicated, the general system studied in section 4.1.2 applies to these also.

4.1.3.1 The Pair *gain* 'upper part' and *azpi* 'lower part'

An important spatial opposition is expressed by the word pair *gain* 'upper part', 'top' and *azpi* 'lower part', 'bottom'. The latter term will be discussed first, as its use is by far the simpler of the two.

Some typical uses of *azpi* follow:

lurraren azpian	under the earth, below (the) ground
eguzkiaren azpian	under the sun
komunismoaren azpian	under communism
ohe azpitik	from under the bed
belaun azpiraino	down to below the knee

With inanimate noun phrases, there is an alternative phrasing that makes use of a suffix *-pe*, to be treated in section 32.3.3: *lurpean* 'under the earth', 'buried'; *eguzkipean* 'under the sun'; *oinpean* 'under the foot', 'underfoot'; and so on.

About *azpi*, nothing more needs to be said except that it shows the same type of metaphorical use found for English *under*: *legeen azpian* 'under the laws', *zigorraren azpian* 'under the punishment', *aitzaki ederren azpian* 'under fine pretexts'.

Constructions based on *gain* serve for 'on' as well as for 'over':

asto baten gainean	on top of a donkey, on a donkey
liburuen gainean	on top of the books, on the books, over the books
hiriaren gainean	over the city, above the city
belar gainean	on the grass
mahai gainetik	from (on) the table
Jonen buruaren gainetik	over John's head

Like *azpi*, *gain* is often employed in a nonspatial, metaphoric sense, corresponding to English metaphorical uses of *upon*, *over*, and *above*. In such metaphoric uses, the uninflected form *gain* tends to occur, especially in formal style: *gizonaren gain* 'upon (the) man', 'above (the) man', '(hanging) over (the) man'.

In particular, uninflected *gain*, in construction with an animate noun phrase in the genitive, may express accountability. This concept is to be taken here in a rather broad sense, the several shades of meaning being covered by such English translations as *up to*, *on*, *at the expense of*, and so on: *alkatearen gain* 'up to the mayor', 'on the mayor'.

The inessive form *gainean* is often used to signal the topic of a verb of saying; that is, *gainean* can serve as the equivalent of English *about*, a function for which the literary style prefers the instrumental case ending. Thus: *emakumearen gainean* 'about the woman' (*emakumeaz*); *ijito batzuen gainean* 'about some gypsies' (*ijito batzuez*); *Jesu-Kristoren gainean* 'about Jesus Christ' (*Jesu-Kristoz*).

There is also the option of using the instrumental of *buru* governing the dative, a construction originally meaning 'facing': *emakumeari buruz* 'facing the woman', 'about the woman', *Joni buruz* 'facing John', 'about John'.

When constructed with a preceding noun phrase in the instrumental, the allative *gainera*, as well as *gain* itself, acquires the meaning 'in addition to...': *diruaz gainera* (or *diruaz gain*) 'in addition to the money'; *Patxiz gainera* (or *Patxiz gain*) 'in addition to Frank'. Used independently, *gainera* signifies 'besides'.

Note, finally, the use of the instrumental in construction with elative *gainetik*, as in *bost milaz gainetik* 'over five thousand', *oroz gain* 'above all'.

4.1.3.2 The Spatial Opposites *barren* 'inside' and *kanpo* 'outside'

A third spatial opposition is that between *barren* 'inside', 'interior' (also 'inner self') and *kanpo* 'outside', 'exterior' (obviously borrowed from Spanish *campo* 'field'). The declension of *barren* is regular, with the sole provision that before the endings *-tik* and *-ra* *e*-epenthesis may or may not occur: *barrendik* or *barrenetik*, *barrena* or *barrenera*; but always *barreneraino* and *barrenerantz*. Examples are

gela txikiaren barrenean	inside the small room
eliz barrenean	inside the church, within the church
zortzi egunen barrenean	within eight days
mendi baten barrenera	(to) inside a mountain
mahuka barrendik	from inside the sleeve, down the sleeve

The allative *barrena* (or its northern variant *barna*, but not *barrenera*) following an inessive noun phrase serves to express the meaning 'through' or 'throughout'. (Compare the phrases *kalean gora* 'up the street' and *kalean behera* 'down the street' [cited in section 3.2].) Representative examples are

munduan barrena	through the world, throughout the world
oihanean barrena	through the forest
liburuan barrena	throughout the book
kaleetan barrena	through the streets
hezurretan barrena	through the bones

In this construction the adverbs *zehar* 'across' or *gaindi* 'over' may substitute for *barrena*: *Nafarroa osoan zehar* 'through the whole of Navarra', *urtean zehar* 'throughout the year', *urteetan zehar* 'through the years', *etxean gaindi* 'through the house', *Zuberoan gaindi* 'through Soule'.

Synonymous with *barren* are *barne* (*barnean*, *barnetik*, *barna* or *barnera*) and *barru* (*barruan*, *barrutik*, *barrura*). Uninflected *barru* can occur in time adverbials without the need for a preceding genitive: *hiru egun barru* 'within three days'. The regular *hiru egunen barruan* is also possible in the same meaning.

The opposite of *barren*, *kanpo*, displays a vastly different behavior from that of the other location nouns treated so far. It does not follow the system set out in section 4.1.2, since it hardly ever governs the genitive case, but rather the elative or the instrumental. Moreover, the compound construction is not available for *kanpo* or its synonyms. The noun *kanpo* itself can remain uninflected, or else can take an inessive or allative ending. The allative case can occur even when no motion is implied. Thus the phrase meaning 'outside the city' can be rendered in no less than seven ways, of which the first two appear to be, in Euskara Batua, the most common: *hiritik kanpora, hiritik kanpoan, hiritik kanpo, hiriaz kanpora, hiriaz kanpoan, hiriaz kanpo, hiriaz kanpotik*.

The noun *landa*, commonly used in the meaning 'field', functions in the eastern dialects (and in Euskara Batua) as a location noun analogous to *kanpo*. Like the latter, it governs either the elative or the instrumental case. But in contrast to *kanpo*, *landa* shows a clear semantic differentiation between these two case frames. In its more concrete sense, 'outside', *landa* always governs the elative, but when used in its less concrete sense, 'apart from', 'besides', 'except (for)', the instrumental case frame is required. Thus *hiritik landa* means 'outside the city', whereas *hiriaz landa*, *hiriaz landan*, or *hiriaz landara* must be translated 'apart from the city', 'besides the city', or 'except (for) the city'. In construction with an instrumental noun phrase, *kanpo* can also assume this meaning: *Mirenez kanpo* 'except for Miren', *zenbait kasuz kanpoan* 'except for certain cases', *Etxaidez kanpora* 'apart from Etxaide' (*MEIG* II, 50). Whenever a preceding elative noun phrase admits a temporal interpretation, *landa(n)* (but not *kanpo*) carries the meaning 'after': *lanetik landa* 'after work'.

The meaning 'outside' can also be conveyed by the location noun *ate* 'door', governing the elative or the instrumental. The traditional constructions are *elizatik atean* or *elizaz atetik* 'outside the church', but, propagated by Azkue's dictionary (1905–1906), *elizatik ate* and *elizaz ate* are also occasionally found in that meaning.

Much more common than those, however, is an etymologically related postposition *at* governing only the elative case. It can be employed in contexts of motion as well as nonmotion: *elizatik at* (*izan*) '(to be) outside the church', *elizatik at (bota)* '(to throw) out of the church', *etxetik at* (*bidali*) '(to send) out of the house'.

In independent use, *kanpo*, *landa*, and *ate* must carry the case endings imposed by the context and cannot be used bare: *kanpoan, landan, atean* 'outside'; *kanpotik, landatik, atetik* 'from outside'; *kanpora, landara, atera* '(to) outside'; *kanporantz, landarantz, aterantz* 'outward'; *kanporaino, landaraino, ateraino* 'all the way out'.

4.1.3.3 The Location Noun *alde* 'side'

The location noun *alde* 'side' (amply provided with secondary senses: 'difference', 'region', 'support', and many others) occurs quite frequently in all varieties of Basque. It follows the system of section 4.1.2 and typically serves to express lateral location (with respect to the referent of the governed noun phrase). Often, however, *alde* indicates nothing more than proximity, or, by metaphoric extension, comparison. The inessive *aldean*, when used alone, can also mean 'right near', 'close by'. A few examples must suffice:

ohearen aldean	beside the bed, next to the bed, in comparison to the bed
eliz aldean	beside the church, next to the church
amaren aldean	beside mother, next to mother, in comparison to mother
aitaren aldetik	from father's side, on the part of father
etxe aldera	to the side of the house, toward the house

Uninflected *alde* functions as a postposition governing the genitive and translating 'in favor of', 'for', 'pro', 'on behalf of':

ijitoen alde	in favor of the gypsies, on behalf of the gypsies
sozialismoaren alde	in favor of socialism, for socialism
alde ala kontra	for or against

The meaning of the nouns *saihets* and *albo*, originally 'side of the body', has been extended to 'side in general'. Correspondingly, they are used as location nouns with the exact meaning of *alde*: *neskatxaren saihetsean*, *neskatxaren alboan* 'beside the girl', 'next to the girl', 'in comparison to the girl'. Unlike *alde*, *saihets* and *albo* do not appear as postpositions, although the uninflected form *albo* is occasionally used instead of *alboan*: *aitaren albo* 'at father's side', 'next to father'.

4.1.3.4 Nearness Expressed by *aldamen* and *ondo*

The location noun *aldamen* with the meaning 'nearness', 'vicinity' serves to translate the English preposition *near*. *Aldamen* does not allow the compound construction and invariably governs the genitive:

etxearen aldamenean	near the house
astoaren aldamenera	(to) near the donkey
otso baten aldamenetik	away from (near) a wolf

[*N.B.* The inessive form *aldamenean* frequently occurs alone as an adverb meaning 'near at hand', 'nearby'.]

The location noun *ondo* indicates contiguity: adjacency in space or succession in time. Adjacency is often weakened to mere nearness:

eliz ondoan	next to the church, near the church
sutondoan	near the fire (irregular compound of *su* 'fire')
amaren ondoan	at mother's side, near mother
amonaren ondora	to grandmother's side, (to) near grandmother
aitaren ondotik	away from father's side, away from father

A context of motion actualizes the fundamental meaning of *ondo*, a location noun basically denoting the position of being next in line. In such a context, *ondoan* and its motional variant *ondotik* are to be translated into English as *behind* or *after*: *aitaren ondotik* 'behind father', *diruaren ondotik* 'after money'. The fact that time itself is conceived as forward motion explains why, in a temporal context, *ondoan* and *ondotik* acquire the meaning 'after':

gerlaren ondoan	after the war
afal ondoan	after supper
bazkal ondoan	after lunch
hil ondoan	after dying

Aldamenean, too, can occur in a temporal context, but, lacking the fundamental meaning characteristic of *ondo*, it always retains its usual sense 'near': *mende-mugaren aldamenean* (*MEIG* VI, 48) 'near the turn of the century'.

4.1.3.5 The Location Noun *inguru* 'around'

The location noun *inguru* (borrowed from the late Latin phrase *in gyrum* 'in a circle') means 'circumference', 'periphery', but also 'vicinity', and, in the plural, 'surroundings': *hiriaren inguruak* 'the outskirts of a city'. Constructions with *inguru* seem to correspond to all uses of the English preposition *around*:

gazteluaren inguruan	around the castle, in the vicinity of the castle
ibaiaren inguruan	to the vicinity of the river
euskararen inguruan	around Basque, about Basque
sorginen inguruan	around the witches, about the witches

Just like English *around*, *inguruan* (and also uninflected *inguru*) can mean 'approximately'. In that meaning, there is never a genitive on the preceding noun phrase: *bostehun sorgin inguru(an)* 'around five hundred witches'.

4.1.3.6 The Location Noun *arte* 'gap', 'interval'

The location noun *arte* meaning 'gap', 'crevice', 'interval', 'opportunity' helps to express the concept 'between' or 'among'. *Arte* follows the system explained in section 4.1.2 in that it optionally governs the genitive. Some typical examples are

tenplearen eta aldarearen artean (Mt 23:35; Lz)	between the temple and the altar
Gazteiz eta Bilbo artean	between Vitoria and Bilbao
hiru ibairen artera	(to) between three rivers
itsuen artetik	from among the blind
zakurren artean	among the dogs, among dogs
zakur artean	among dogs
jende artean	among the people
esku artean	between the hands, in hand
malko artean	between tears, in tears, tearfully

In a temporal context, uninflected *arte* (formerly also inessive *artean*) serves to express a time limit. Its translation depends on the character of the verb phrase in the clause: *as long as* in a stative context (including continuous or habitual action), *until*, otherwise. Temporal *arte*, whether inflected or not, governs the nominative and never the genitive, characteristic of the spatial use of *arte*. The compound form, detectable by the absence of article, however, does occur when its conditions are met. *Arte* itself never governs the allative; examples such as *Baionara arte* 'until Bayonne', *heriotzera arte* 'until death', *igandera arte* 'until Sunday' are readily explained as due to an intervening abstract verb of motion with the sense of *heldu* 'to arrive'. Illustrations of the temporal use of *arte* and *artean* are

munduaren azkena arte	until the end of the world
goizetik arrats artean	from the morning until the evening
1893garren urtea arte	until the year 1893
1893garren urte arte	until the year 1893
goiz arte	until the morning
bazkal arte	until lunch

Note also the common phrases: *noiz arte* 'until when', *atzo arte* 'until yesterday', *gaur arte* 'until today', *orain arte* 'until now', *ordu arte* 'until then'.

The following phrases are used as greetings: *aurki arte* 'see you shortly' ('until shortly'), *bihar arte* 'see you tomorrow' ('until tomorrow'), *gero arte* 'see you later' ('until later'), *laster arte* 'see you soon' ('until soon'), *sarri arte* 'see you soon' ('until soon'), *hurren arte* 'see you next time' ('until next time').

The inessive *artean* used alone can mean 'still (at the time)'. More about *arte* and *artean* can be found in section 20.4.5.

4.1.3.7 The Noun *erdi* 'middle', 'half'

The noun *erdi* with the meaning 'middle' or 'center' as well as 'half' regularly functions as a location noun, as in the following examples:

egunaren erdian	in the middle of the day
hiriaren erdian	in the middle of the city, in the center of the city
itsasoaren erdian	in the middle of the sea
itsas erdian	in the middle of the sea
otsoen erdira	into the midst of wolves
lagunen erditik	from out of the midst of his fellows

[*N.B.* Cf. section 32.5.3.]

4.1.3.8 Some Uses of the Noun *pare*

The noun *pare*, meaning 'pair' and also 'counterpart' or 'likeness', can serve as a location noun referring to the 'opposite side':

eliza ederraren pare	across from the beautiful church
etxe parean	across from the house
ijitoen parean	across from the gypsies, in comparison to the gypsies

As we observe in the last example, *parean*, when constructed with the genitive, can also mean 'in comparison to . . .'. Furthermore, the uninflected form *pare* functions as a postposition meaning 'like', as in *zilar finaren pare da pilotaria* (beginning of Etxahun-Iruri's song "Laida pilotaria") 'a ballplayer is like pure silver'. Other examples are *asto baten pare* 'like a donkey', *ur garbiaren pare* (*MEIG* VII, 153) 'like clean water', *deabruaren pare* 'like the devil' (see section 26.1.6).

4.1.3.9 Some Location Nouns Indicating 'edge'

The location noun *bazter* means 'corner', 'fringe', 'margin', 'edge':

bidearen bazterrean	on the shoulder of the road, at the edge of the road
itsas bazterrera	to the shore of the sea
munduaren bazterreraino	to as far as the edge of the world

Almost synonymous to *bazter* is *ertz* 'edge', 'hem', 'margin', 'shore', 'bank':

gona gorriaren ertzean	on the hem of the red skirt
ibai handiaren ertzera	to the bank of the big river
itsas ertzean	at the seashore, at the coast

The noun *hegi* has the same meaning as *ertz*, in addition to that of 'mountain ridge': *itsas hegian* 'at the coast', *su hegian* 'at the edge of the fire'.

4.1.3.10 To Indicate 'right (side)', 'left (side)'

Obvious location nouns are *eskuin* 'right side', 'right hand' and *ezker* 'left side', 'left hand':

Jainkoaren eskuinean	at the right hand of God
zubiaren ezkerrera	to the left side of the bridge

While these definite forms are traditional and still in common use, the indefinite forms *eskuinetan* and *ezkerretan* are also quite frequent. In independent use, the indefinite forms seem to be preferred: *eskuinetara* (*eskuinera*) 'to the right', *ezkerretara* (*ezkerrera*) 'to the left'. Note, therefore, *zubitik ezkerretara* 'from the bridge to the left', rather than *zubitik ezkerrera*.

4.1.3.11 Other Indicators of Position

It is not clear whether *buru* 'head' should be considered a location noun meaning 'end' in such expressions as *bidearen buruan* 'at the end of the road', *hamar urteren buruan* 'at the end of ten years', *denboren bururaino* 'to the end of time'.

Despite the existence of such seemingly inflected forms as *kontran* and *kontrara*, *kontra* is usually thought of as a postposition governing the genitive, not as a location noun. Its meaning is 'against', in an oppositional as well as in a spatial sense:

apaizen kontra	against (the) priests
hotzaren kontra	against the cold
harriren baten kontra (Mt 4:6; *Lau Eb.*)	against some stone
hormaren kontra	against the wall

In the spatial sense, *kontra* governs the dative in the northern dialects: *hormari kontra* 'against the wall', *amari kontra* '(leaning) against mother'. In some expressions *kontra* governs the instrumental: *gogoz kontra* 'against the will', 'reluctantly'.

4.2 Telling Time

The noun *ordu* has a double meaning: as a mass noun, it means 'time' in a general sense; as a count noun, 'hour'. (The northern dialects have *tenore* for 'time' and *oren* for 'hour'.) Ellipsis of *ordu* is a frequent phenomenon in Basque syntax. Deletion of the mass noun *ordu* will be studied in section 20.2. Deletion of the count noun *ordu* is applied in the process of telling time. In naming hours the word *ordu* will always be omitted, except for *ordu bata* 'one o'clock', and optionally, (*ordu*) *biak* 'two o'clock'. As a result, hours are named by the definite plural form of the corresponding cardinals, exactly as in Spanish: *hirurak* 'three o'clock', *laurak* 'four o'clock', compare Spanish *las tres*, *las cuatro*. For convenience, a complete paradigm follows, including also the frequently used inessive forms (cf. *EGLU* I, 193–194):

Ze(r) ordu da?	What time is it?	Ze(r) ordutan?	At what time?
Ordu bata da.	It is one o'clock.	Ordu batean.	At one o'clock.
(Ordu) biak dira.	It is two o'clock.	(Ordu) bietan.	At two o'clock.
Hirurak dira.	It is three o'clock.	Hiruretan.	At three o'clock.
Laurak dira.	It is four o'clock.	Lauretan.	At four o'clock.
Bostak dira.	It is five o'clock.	Bostetan.	At five o'clock.
Seiak dira.	It is six o'clock.	Seietan.	At six o'clock.
Zazpiak dira.	It is seven o'clock.	Zazpietan.	At seven o'clock.
Zortziak dira.	It is eight o'clock.	Zortzietan.	At eight o'clock.
Bederatziak dira.	It is nine o'clock.	Bederatzietan.	At nine o'clock.
Hamarrak dira.	It is ten o'clock.	Hamarretan.	At ten o'clock.
Hamaikak dira.	It is eleven o'clock.	Hamaiketan.	At eleven o'clock.
Hamabiak dira.	It is twelve o'clock.	Hamabietan.	At twelve o'clock.

Instead of *hamabiak* 'twelve o'clock', one often uses *eguerdi* 'noon' (lit. 'midday') or *gauerdi* 'midnight'. With these nouns the article is optional: *eguerdi da* or *eguerdia da* 'it is noon'; *eguerditan* or *eguerdian* 'at noon'. Similarly for *gauerdi* 'midnight' (*EGLU* I, 194).

Half hours are expressed by means of the noun *erdi* 'half', preceded by the conjunction *eta* 'and', here usually pronounced *t.* The plural ending is transferred from the cardinal to *erdi*, a natural thing to happen, since *erdi* is the last element of the noun phrase:

ordu bata eta erdiak	half past one	ordu bata eta erdietan	at half past one
(ordu) bi eta erdiak	half past two	(ordu) bi eta erdietan	at half past two
hiru eta erdiak	half past three	hiru eta erdietan	at half past three
lau eta erdiak	half past four	lau eta erdietan	at half past four
hamabi eta erdiak	half past twelve	hamabi eta erdietan	at half past twelve

[*N.B.* In the northern form of Batua, where *oren* is used, we find the plural form *orenak*: *hiru orenak eta erdiak* 'half past three', *hiru orenak eta erdietan* 'at half past three'.]

Quarter hours are called *ordu laurden*, where *laurden* means 'fourth' (cf. section 2.5). Here too, in telling time, *ordu* is left out. Just how the remaining *laurden* 'quarter' figures in time indications of the type 'a quarter past' differs according to dialect and has not yet been fully standardized. To simplify matters, we will focus on a particular pattern, widespread in Guipuzcoa and Biscay (cf. J. Basterrechea 1981, II, 24ff). In it, the word *laurden* behaves exactly like *erdi*:

ordu bat(a) eta laurdenak	a quarter past one
(ordu) bi eta laurdenak	a quarter past two
hiru eta laurdenak	a quarter past three

The corresponding inessives are invariably plural:

ordu bat(a) eta laurdenetan at a quarter past one

[*N.B.* A pattern with a pleonastic plural on the cardinal (*hirurak eta laurdenak*) also exists in spoken usage (*EGLU* I, 194), but is condemned by the grammarian P. Salaburu (1985, 290).]

In the northern dialects, a different pattern prevails: *hirurak eta laurden*, apparently modeled on the French idiom (cf. *trois heures et quart*).

Time indications of the type 'a quarter to ...' make use of the comparative *gutxiago* 'less' of *gutxi* 'few' (see section 26.4.5). Instead of *gutxiago*, *gutxi* itself may occur:

ordu bata laurden gutxi(ago)	a quarter to one
(ordu) biak laurden gutxi(ago)	a quarter to two
hirurak laurden gutxi(ago)	a quarter to three

As *gutxi* and *gutxiago* are indefinite quantifiers (cf. section 2.3.2, item 8), the corresponding inessives require the indefinite ending *-tan*:

ordu bata laurden gutxi(ago)tan	at a quarter to one
(ordu) biak laurden gutxi(ago)tan	at a quarter to two
hirurak laurden gutxi(ago)tan	at a quarter to three

More exact indications of time present no problem:

hirurak eta bost	five past three	hirurak eta bostean	at five past three
hirurak eta hamar	ten past three	hirurak eta hamarrean	at ten past three
hirurak eta hogei	twenty past three	hirurak eta hogeian	at twenty past three
laurak hogei gutxi(ago)	twenty to four	laurak hogei gutxi(ago)tan	at twenty to four
laurak hamar gutxi(ago)	ten to four	laurak hamar gutxi(ago)tan	at ten to four
laurak bost gutxi(ago)	five to four	laurak bost gutxi(ago)tan	at five to four

Even more precise specifications can be readily constructed:

hirurak eta hemezortzian	at eighteen minutes past three
laurak hogeita zazpi gutxi(ago)tan	at twenty-seven minutes to four

Time intervals are usually indicated with the help of *arte* or *artean* of section 4.1.3.6:

lauretatik seiak arte	from four to six o'clock
zazpi eta erdietatik hamar eta erdiak arte	from half past seven to half past ten
lau eta laurdenetatik seiak laurden gutxi arte	from a quarter past four to a quarter to six

Instead of *arte*, the allative case is not uncommon: *lauretatik seietara* 'from four to six o'clock'. This usage is slightly frowned upon by the grammarians of the Basque Academy (*EGLU* I, 195).

As we will see in section 26.4.4, anteriority with respect to a given time is often signified by the use of the comparative phrase *baino lehen(ago)* 'earlier than' directly following the time specification. A much less common alternative is the use of the elative form *aurretik* of the location noun *aurre* 'front', or, in the northern dialects, uninflected *aitzin*:

hamar eta erdiak baino lehen(ago)	earlier than half past ten, before half past ten
hamar eta erdiak aurretik	before half past ten
hamar eta erdiak aitzin	before half past ten

Posteriority with respect to a given time is often expressed by *ondoren*, based on the location noun *ondo*, and less often by the elative *ondotik* or the inessive *ondoan*. An alternative way makes use of *gero* 'later' preceded by a time expression in the instrumental:

seiak laurden gutxi(ago) ondoren	after a quarter to six
seiak laurden gutxi(ago)z gero	after a quarter to six

Note also the use of the allative forms *aurrera* and *aitzina* (see section 4.1.2), as in *seiak laurden gutxi(ago)tatik aurrera* (or: *aitzina*) 'from a quarter to six on'.

A translation of *around* in the meaning 'approximately' is furnished by the inessive location noun *aldean* or by the location noun *inguru*, either uninflected, definite, or inessive.

(Note also the more colloquial idioms *hor nonbait* and *nonbait han* to be mentioned in section 28.1.6.3.)

hirurak aldean (also *hirurak aldera*)	around three o'clock
Hirurak inguru(a) dira.	It is around three o'clock.

The opposite characteristic, utter precision, is sometimes expressed by reduplication:

eguerdi-erditan	at noon exactly
hamabi-hamabietan	at exactly twelve o'clock

[*N.B.* For a fuller treatment of reduplication, see chapter 32.]

4.3 Compounds with *arte*

The location noun *arte* meaning 'gap', 'interval', 'opportunity' occurs as a second member of a fair number of compound nouns. Such a compound, *N-arte*, denotes primarily a gap, stretch, or interval between two or more N's, but it can also be used more generally to refer to an ambiance or milieu composed of N's. (The meaning of *gogarte*, namely, 'meditation', does not seem to clearly fit either characterization.)

Regarding phonology, note that only those nouns that constitute an exception to the Minor Apocope rule (cf. section 3.8.1) preserve their final *e* or *o* when entering into a compound with *arte*. Those that do undergo this rule must drop the resulting vowel *a* before the initial *a* of *arte*. A basic final *a*, of course, also disappears. After a preserved final *i*, *arte* may occasionally change to *tarte*, presumably an older form of *arte*.

aldi	time, turn	aldarte	phase, mood, opportunity
anaia	brother	anaiarte	brotherhood, fraternity
apaiz	priest	apaizarte	clergy, priesthood
aste	week	astearte	Tuesday, midweek
baso	woods, vacant land	basarte	wilds, wilderness, woodland
begi	eye	begitarte	brow, face, countenance
beso	arm	besarte	bosom
bi	two	bitarte	interval, period, interstice
bide	road	bidarte	junction
esku	hand	eskuarte	resource, reach
etxe	house	etxarte	courtyard
gizon	man	gizarte	society (*giza-*: allomorph of *gizon*)
gogo	mind, desire, intention	gogarte	meditation, reflection, thought
haitz	rock	haitzarte	gorge, canyon, gully
huts	emptyness	hutsarte	(empty) space, void, empty hour
ibai	river	ibaiarte	delta
itsaso	sea	itsasarte	strait, inlet, cove

jende	people	jendarte	public
lagun	companion, fellow	lagunarte	company, club, association
lan	work	lanarte	break, vacation
lerro	line	lerroarte	space between lines
mendi	mountain	mendi(t)arte	valley, mountain pass
oihal	cloth, fabric	oihalarte	interlining, interior lining
senide	sibling, relative	senitarte	kinfolk, relations
txola	bundle	txolarte	spare time, opportunity
ur	water	uharte	island (see section 31.2.1, rule 1)

4.4 The Augmentative Suffix *-tzar*

Any count noun admits an augmentative form constructed with the fully productive suffix *-tzar*, dialectally *-zar* (a homonym of *zar*, contracted form of the adjective *zahar* 'old').

Augmentatives merely denote a larger size than is deemed normal and are by no means necessarily pejorative. Still, when applied to human beings and some of their body parts, the purely augmentative sense of *-tzar* may give way to a depreciative meaning. Hence the frequent use of *astotzar*, *mandatzar*, *sugetzar*, *urdetzar*, and so on as terms of abuse. The similarity of the suffix *-tzar* to the adjective *txar* 'bad' may play a role here, as well as a commonly felt association of big size with big nuisance. Some examples will illustrate these points:

abere	animal, head of cattle	aberetzar	large animal, beast
andre	lady	andretzar	tramp, prostitute
anka	leg	ankatzar	big leg, thick leg
arrain	fish	arraintzar	huge fish, sea monster
arratoi	rat	arratoitzar	big rat
asto	donkey	astotzar	large ass, stupid ass
basurde	wild boar	basurdetzar	large wild boar
behi	cow	behitzar	large cow
buru	head	burutzar	large head, fathead, pighead
eme	female	ematzar	prostitute, whore
esku	hand	eskutzar	burly hand
etxe	house	etxetzar	large house
euli	fly	eulitzar	large fly
gizon	man	gizatzar	big man, giant, brute, cad (*gizontzar*)
idi	ox	iditzar	large ox (older form: *itzar*)
kamioi	truck	kamioitzar	large truck
katu	cat	katutzar	large cat, huge cat
liburu	book	liburutzar	large book, hefty book

mailu	hammer	mailutzar	heavy hammer, sledge hammer
mando	mule	mandatzar	large mule, monstrous man (*mandotzar*)
mutil	boy	mutiltzar	hefty boy
neska	maiden, girl	neskatzar	bad girl, prostitute
sardina	sardine	sardintzar	big sardine, herring
suge	snake	sugetzar	large snake, slick operator
urde	male pig	urdetzar	large pig, big swine, hog
zakur	large dog	zakurtzar	huge dog
zaldi	horse	zalditzar	big horse, percheron
zezen	bull	zezentzar	large bull

4.5 Vocabulary

4.5.1 Principal Location Nouns

aldamen	vicinity, side
alde	side, region
arte	gap, interval, stretch
atze	rear, backside, back part
aurre	front, front side, front part
azpi	bottom, lower part
barren	inside, inner part, interior
barru	inside, inner part, interior
erdi	middle, center
eskuin	right side, right hand (also adjectival: right-handed)
ezker	left side, left hand (also adjectival: left-handed)
gain	top, upper part, surface
inguru	periphery
kanpo	outside, exterior
ondo	proximity, nearness

4.5.2 Other Words

afari	supper
arrain	fish
arratoi	rat
atso	old woman, old hag
atzo	yesterday
azken	end, last
bazkari	main meal, lunch
belar	grass, herb

belaun	knee
berriz	again
beso	arm
bezero	customer
burdina	iron
eraztun	ring
errota	mill
ezpata	sword
gainera	moreover
gerla	war (also *gerra*)
goiz	morning, early
gosari	breakfast
harri	stone
hartz	bear
heriotza	death
hezur	bone
horma	wall
ispilu	mirror
itsu	blind
jai	festivity, legal holiday
kontra	against
mahuka	sleeve
malko	tear
min	pain
muga	limit, border
mundu	world
negar	crying, tear
oihan	forest
otso	wolf
talde	group
tren	train
zapata	shoe

4.6 Exercises

4.6.1 Translate into English

1. Lantegi handiaren atzean bi etxe zuri eder dira.
2. Nor da ur azpian eta nor belar gainean?
3. Hiri zaharraren barrenean etxe polit asko dira.

4. Mahai txikien azpian ez da ezer ere.
5. Amonaren eraztuna alkatearen oin azpian da.
6. Zaldi baten gainean dira hiru atso itsusi.
7. Sorginaz kanpo ez da inor kanpoa.
8. Zenbat bezero itsu dira horma zuriaren atzean?
9. Gaztelu beltzaren inguruan katutzar asko eta lore gutxi dira.
10. Arrisku handia da errota zaharraren eta eliza berriaren artean.
11. Zeren gainean dira lege berriak?
12. Jaiak sei eta erdietatik bederatziak laurden gutxi arte dira.

4.6.2 Translate into Basque

1. In front of the white house is an old mill.
2. Between the two large cities is a long road.
3. Behind which mountain is the enemy?
4. The pain is inside the bones.
5. What is under the red table?
6. Outside the big cities are wolves and bears.
7. Except for ten ladies, nobody is inside.
8. Who is near Father, and who (is) near Mother?
9. On top of the pretty shoes is a little mirror.
10. How many swords are there inside the customer's big sleeve?
11. At what time is supper today?
12. At exactly ten o'clock.

5 The Grammar of Adnominal Forms

5.1 The Linking Morpheme *-ko*

In English, prepositional phrases freely function as modifiers of noun phrases, as shown by the following examples:

(1) a. the tables for the customers
 b. ties with the enemy
 c. bread from heaven
 d. evil from man
 e. the road from Bilbao to San Sebastian
 f. the impulse toward mathematics
 g. women against war

It is important to realize that this is a distributional fact about English, by no means a language universal.

Indeed, in both the Romance and the Semitic languages, such combined phrases are possible only with certain prepositions. Thus in French we get *de l'eau-de-vie avec du sucre* 'brandy with sugar', but instead of **les livres sur la table* 'the books on the table', one must say, *les livres qui sont sur la table* 'the books that are on the table'. Similar facts can be adduced from the other Romance languages and from the Semitic languages as well.

In fact, in quite a few of the world's languages, structures of the type [$_{NP}$ NP PP] are excluded altogether. Such is the case, for instance, in older Hungarian, Japanese, Quechua, Turkish, and Basque.

In all these languages, expressions of this sort are never found in normal speech or writing, although they are allowed to occur in the telegraphic style of chapter headings, inscriptions, newspaper headlines, and the like.

Whenever the need arises for a functional equivalent of an English expression of the type shown in (1), special measures have to be taken, ranging from the use of an intervening relative clause, often in participial form, to the obligatory insertion of a genitivoid linking morpheme, such as the Japanese genitive marker *no*. Among these languages Basque is exceptionally fortunate in having at its disposal a special—that is, otherwise unemployed—suffix *-ko* (carrying a low tone), converting postpositional phrases into adjectival ones. It was most likely borrowed from an older Indo-European language, quite possibly some early form of Celtic.

Basque phrases ending with this linking morpheme *-ko* will henceforth be called "adnominal" phrases, following the Spanish usage of Michelena's *Diccionario General Vasco (DGV)*.

We are now able to translate the English phrases under examples (1a–g) into Basque as follows:

(2) a. bezeroentzako mahaiak (Oñatibia, 36)
    b. etsaiarekiko loturak
    c. zerutikako ogia (Jn 6:31; Dv, *JKBO*)
    d. gizonagandikako gaitza (*MEIG* II, 101)
    e. Bilbotik Donostiarako bidea (Cf. Garate, *Alaba* 9)
    f. matematiketaranzko bultzada (*MEIG* VI, 93 = *MIH* 195)
    g. gerlaren kontrako emakumeak

The linking suffix *-ko* does not allow *e*-epenthesis in the standard language. Therefore, various phonological changes can be observed in examples (2a–g). According to our sandhi rule 1 in section 1.2.6. the final *t* of *-tzat* drops before the *k* of *-ko*, hence the resulting form *-tzako* of (2a). The final *n* of *-(r)ekin* likewise disappears before *-ko*, which explains the form *-(r)ekiko* of (2b), although in a few local dialects the form *-(r)ekingo* is also found. The elative ending *-tik* is derived from an older form *-tika*, hence the result *-tikako* of (2c) and *-gandikako* of (2d). The shorter form *-tiko*, however, attested as early as 1571, is considered equally acceptable. Finally, the adnominal form of the tendential *-rantz* is *-ranzko*, following sandhi rule 3 of section 1.2.6.

Although so far no example of an adnominal instrumental phrase has been adduced, they are in fact extremely common. For one thing, because Basque lacks the category of material adjectives, adnominal instrumentals step in to fill this need:

altzairu	steel	altzairuzko ezpata	the steel sword
burdina	iron	burdinazko atea	the iron door
larru	hide, leather	larruzko zapatak	the leather shoes
lur	earth	lurrezko ontzia	the earthen vessel
urre	gold	urrezko eraztuna	the golden ring
zilar	silver	zilarrezko platera	the silver plate
zur	wood	zurezko zubia	the wooden bridge

Furthermore, given the fact that the Basque instrumental case serves to express a great variety of semantic relations (analyzed in chapter 27), it is only natural that many English adjectives correspond to adnominal instrumentals in Basque.

A few common examples will illustrate this point sufficiently:

ahoz	by mouth	ahozko	oral
beharrez	by necessity	beharrezko	necessary, indispensable, obligatory
diruz	with money	diruzko	monetary, financial
dudaz	in doubt	dudazko	doubtful
egiaz	in truth, really	egiazko	true, real, genuine
errukiz	with compassion	errukizko	compassionate
euskaraz	in Basque	euskarazko	Basque (referring to language only)
gezurrez	with lies, lyingly	gezurrezko	false, unreal
itxuraz	in appearance	itxurazko	apparent, fake, decent, proper
legez	by law, legally	legezko	legal, lawful
ohituraz	by custom	ohiturazko	customary, traditional
premiaz	in need, by need	premiazko	indispensable, necessary
presaz	in a hurry, hastily	presazko	urgent, hasty
zalantzaz	in doubt, in hesitation	zalantzazko	doubtful, dubious
zentzuz	by the senses, by common sense	zentzuzko	sensory, sensible, reasonable

Adnominals have the status of morphologically marked adjectival phrases. Like several other types of marked adjectives, they prefer to occupy prenominal position, although the standard postnominal adjective position is also open to them. Thus one readily encounters such phrases as *bailara negarrezko* 'valley of tears', *ama errukizko* 'compassionate mother', and *zezen suzko* 'bull of fire' (a wooden bull filled with fireworks).

5.2 Postposition Deletion

The analysis of adnominals presents an interesting complication because certain case endings appear to be dispensable if they are followed by the linking morpheme *-ko*. This phenomenon will be referred to as *Postposition Deletion*, although it should be noted that what is actually deleted is not lexical postpositions but rather morphological inflections on certain postpositional phrases.

Only five grammatical cases participate in this process: the inessive, elative, and allative of the locative system, and the sociative and instrumental of the basic system. We must deal with these cases one by one.

5.2.1 Inessive Deletion

By far the most common application of Postposition Deletion involves the inessive. This deletion is strictly obligatory in all present-day varieties of Basque, except Souletin. Some examples are

mendiko herria	the village on the mountain
ibaiko arrainak	the fish in the river
Bilboko eguraldia	the weather in Bilbao

buruko mina	the pain in the head, the headache
udako lorea	the flower in summer, the summer flower

Adnominal forms of location nouns are especially frequent. They can occur either with a preceding complement: *etxe aurreko pagoa* 'the beech tree in front of the house'; or without: *aurreko pagoa* 'the beech tree in front'. Their underlying case form is nearly always inessive. Further examples are

aldameneko herria	the adjacent village, the village nearby
aldeko bidea	the lateral road, the road nearby
arteko ibaia	the river in between
atzeko atea	the door in the back, the back door
azpiko lurra	the soil underneath
barreneko poza	the joy inside, the inner joy
barruko ardoa	the wine inside
erdiko kalea	the street in the middle, the street in the center
eskuineko begia	the eye on the right-hand side, the right eye
ezkerreko oina	the foot on the left-hand side, the left foot
gaineko liburua	the book on top, the topmost book
inguruko loreak	the surrounding flowers
kanpoko txakurra	the dog outside (also 'the dog from outside')
ondoko hiria	the city nearby

Time adverbs (*gaur* 'today', *bihar* 'tomorrow', *orain* 'now', *sekula* 'ever', etc.) are properly thought of as being underlying inessives. Note that for certain time adverbs the inessive ending is optionally present: *luzaro* or *luzaroan* 'for a long time', *antzina* or *antzinan* 'a long time ago', *sekula* or *sekulan* 'ever', and so on.

Moreover, the inessive ending always shows up in compounds such as *gaurbiharretan* 'today and/or tomorrow'. It is thus hardly surprising to see that time adverbs possess adnominal forms:

aspaldi	long ago	aspaldiko adiskidea	a friend of long ago, an old friend
atzo	yesterday	atzoko apaizak	yesterday's priests
aurten	this year	aurtengo uzta	this year's harvest
behin	once	behingo bekatua	a nonrecurrent sin
beti	always	betiko ametsa	an eternal dream
bihar	tomorrow	biharko sorginak	tomorrow's witches
egun	today	egungo eguna	today's day, this day
gaur	today	gaurko emakumeak	today's women
gero	later	geroko nekeak	the future efforts
iaz	last year	iazko ardoa	last year's wine
lehen	before	lenengo bideak	the ways of the past

orain	now	oraingo neskatxak	the girls of the present
sekula	ever	sekulako agurrak	greetings for ever

[*N.B. Sekulako* has also acquired an idiomatic meaning 'extreme', usually applied negatively: 'horrible', 'outrageous', but sometimes positively: 'fantastic'.]

5.2.2 Elative Deletion

Without being strictly obligatory, Elative Deletion before *-ko* has become so well established that phrases to which it has not been applied have begun to sound clumsy or pedantic.

A good example is the formula *nire bihotzeko agur beroa* 'a warm goodbye from my heart', sometimes used in concluding a letter. The heavier version without Elative Deletion, *nire bihotzetiko agur beroa*, can also be found (cf. S. Onaindia, *Eskutitzak* 118, 161).

In this area, the various Basque New Testament versions provide valuable data. For present-day Batua, the optional character of Elative Deletion is brought out by the contradictory evidence of two modern Batua versions: *IB* (1980) almost invariably applies Elative Deletion; *EAB* (1983) hardly ever does so. Thus, *IB* has *Dabiden etxeko Jose* 'Joseph from the house of David' (Lk 1:27), *zeruko ogia* 'bread from heaven' (Jn 6:31), but *zerutikako ikuspena* 'the vision from heaven' (Acts 26:19), and again, *zeruko hura* 'the one from heaven' (1 Cor 15:48). *EAB* has *Dabiden jatorriko gizon bat* 'a man from the lineage of David' (Lk 1:27), but *zerutiko ogia* 'bread from heaven' (Jn 6:31), *zerutiko ikuskaria* 'the vision from heaven' (Acts 26:19), *zerutikako hura* 'the one from heaven' (1 Cor 15:48).

The Biscayan version of Kerexeta employs both *-tiko* and *-ko*: *Dabiden etxeko gizon bat, zerutiko ogia, zerutiko ikuspena, zerukoa*, while the northern versions, *JKBO* (1974) and *Biblia* (1983), follow Duvoisin (1858) in having an unreduced *-tikako* throughout.

The oldest Basque New Testament version, that of Leizarraga (1571), prefers *-tiko* in three of the four texts but has plain *zerukoa* in 1 Cor 15:48.

Still in a historical vein, we may note that the Labourdin grammarian Pierre d'Urte, writing toward the end of the 17th century, seems to look upon *zerutikako* and *zeruko* as more or less synonymous: "du ciel, *cerucoa* ou *ceruticacoa*" (*Grammaire cantabrique* 52); "*Caelestis*: *çerucoa, ceruetacoa, ceruticacoa, ceruetaricacoa*" (*Dictionarium latino cantabricum* IV, 24).

5.2.3 Allative Deletion

Deletion of the allative *-ra* before *-ko* seems to be slightly less common than its retention, at least in most contexts. A clear instance of it is furnished by the designation for 'prayer book'. For this, either *elizarako liburua* or *elizako liburua* 'church book' can be used.

For another example we again turn to the New Testament versions. Translating the Greek *hodon thalassēs* or the Latin *via maris* of Mt 4:15, both Leizarraga and Duvoisin make use of *itsasorako bidea* 'the road to the sea', whereas Echenique and *JKBO* employ *itsasoko bidea*. The Batua version *IB*, like *Lau Eb.*, utilizes the compound *itsas bidea*; the other Batua version *EAB* has *itsas ondoko bidea*.

To recapitulate what we have learned so far: a phrase like *Bilboko trenak* is triply ambiguous. Depending on which case ending has been deleted, it can mean 'the trains in Bilbao', 'the trains from Bilbao', or 'the trains to Bilbao'. Incidentally, if we gloss *Bilboko trenak* as 'the Bilbao trains', the same will be true of the English gloss.

Before taking leave of the allative case, we must discuss an important meaning extension of the unreduced form *-rako*. From a semantic point of view, allatives and destinatives are not very far apart. Thus a phrase like *Bilborako trena* 'the train to Bilbao' also admits the translation 'the train for Bilbao'. With this as a starting point, *-rako* has evolved beyond its original status as an adnominal allative, turning into a case ending in its own right, a "locative destinative" for adverbial as well as adnominal use: *bai arimarako eta bai gorputzerako* 'for the soul as well as for the body' (Azkue, *DVEF* II, 193). A rather neat division of labor seems to have developed: the basic destinative *-(r)entzat* being used mainly with animate noun phrases; the locative destinative *-rako* being reserved for inanimate ones: *haurrentzat* (*erosi*) '(to buy) for the children', *etxerako* (*erosi*) '(to buy) for the house'.

The locative destinative can also be used in a temporal context: *egun gutxirako* 'for (i.e., during) a few days' (Heb 12:10; *IB*—in Greek: *pros oligas hēmeras*).

No reduced forms exist for the remaining locative cases, either for the adnominal terminal (*izarretarainoko prezioak* 'prices as high as the stars') or for the adnominal tendential (*matematiketaranzko bultzada* 'the impulse toward mathematics', *MEIG* VI, 93).

5.2.4 Sociative Deletion

Sociative Deletion appears to be semantically conditioned in that its application depends on the nature of the meaning relationship between the head of the sociative modifier and that of the modified noun phrase. When this relationship is inalienable, or has a permanent character, the sociative ending will be deleted. But when the relationship is felt to be contingent rather than intrinsic, the case ending must remain, in which event the full ending *-(r)ekiko* will show up on the modifying phrase. Obligatory Sociative Deletion accounts for the presence of *-ko* in many expressions corresponding to the Latin *genetivus qualitatis*, for example, *mulier magni ingenii* 'a woman of great ability', rendered in Basque by *dohain handiko emakumea*, derived from an underlying sociative **dohain handiekiko emakumea*.

Further examples of obligatory Sociative Deletion are

sudur handiko gizona	a man with a big nose
bihotz oneko emakumea	a woman with a kind heart
hogei urteko neskatxa	a girl of twenty (lit. with twenty years)
hamar laguneko taldea	a group with ten members
soinu txarreko pianoa	a piano with a bad sound

Yet we find *begi berdeekiko moja* 'the nun with the green eyes' (Atxaga, *Z.H.* 127).

The unquestionable permanence of the relation between an object and its name will easily account for the form *izeneko* in the phrase *Zakeo izeneko gizon bat* 'a man with the name Zacchaeus' (Lk 19:2; *IB*, *EAB*, *Lau Eb.*, Ker.).

This example is especially noteworthy because of the existence of a further rule of *izen*-deletion applying in front of *-ko*. As we will see in section 5.2.6, the linking morpheme *-ko* rarely follows animate nouns, and never once personal names. Accordingly, *izen*-deletion is restricted to inanimate contexts, that is, place names and other geographical names. Thus *Baiona izeneko hiria* 'the city with the name Bayonne' will turn into *Baionako hiria* by the rule of *izen*-deletion.

This fact affords us a general explanation as to why geographical names used as appositions (*Donostia hiria*, *Deba ibaia*, *Ernio mendia*) optionally take the adnominal form: *Donostiako hiria* 'the city of San Sebastian', *Debako ibaia* 'the Deba river', *Ernioko mendia* 'the Ernio mountain'.

The somewhat vague manner in which the semantic condition on the rule of Sociative Deletion has been formulated may lead to problems in trying to decide whether it is met or not in a given instance. One therefore anticipates the existence of borderline cases in which there is some measure of uncertainty about the contingent character of the relevant meaning relation. In these cases, it can be expected that different speakers will opt for different solutions.

A good case in point may be the relation between emotions and their bearer. The renowned writer Orixe once wrote

(3) a. Ez da bihotzaldi handiekiko poeta (*Euskal Esnalea* XVII, 1927, 192).
He is not a poet with great emotions (i.e., who expresses great emotions).

Most other speakers, however, would prefer the following version, guided, no doubt, by the intimate character of the relationship between persons and their emotions:

(3) b. Ez da bihotzaldi handiko poeta.
He is not a poet with great emotions.

Another matter of interest is the relation between clothes and their wearer. According to *EGLU* I, *E* 54, both (4a) and (4b) are possible:

(4) a. Jantzi gorriarekiko gaztea
The young person with the red suit
b. Jantzi gorriko gaztea
The young person with the red suit

[*N.B.* Many speakers, however, prefer the use of the suffix *-dun* to either version: *jantzi gorridun gaztea*. (For this suffix, see section 19.8.)]

It should be noted finally that *-(r)ekiko*, just like *-rako*, has begun a life of its own as a case ending with various meanings, of which 'concerning' and 'toward' are the most common. (For a more detailed study, see de Rijk 1993.)

5.2.5 Instrumental Deletion

Only in the northern dialects has the instrumental ending *-z* retained sufficient vitality to count as a genuine and regular case. In Guipuzcoan and Biscayan the ending has survived but is largely idiomatic in its occurrence, being restricted, more often than not, to the indefinite form. (For details, see chapter 27.)

It follows that we must turn to the northern dialects to hunt for examples of Instrumental Deletion, and after finding some, it will be our task to decide which of those are likely to be accepted into Batua usage.

It must at once be admitted that Instrumental Deletion is a somewhat rare phenomenon: in most of its uses, the instrumental ending *-z* can never be deleted before *-ko*. There are no phrases like **urreko eraztuna* instead of *urrezko eraztuna* 'the golden ring', nor will anyone say **arrazoiko* or **zentzuko* instead of *arrazoizko* 'rational' and *zentzuzko* 'sensible'.

Yet clear instances of Instrumental Deletion are not very hard to detect. To start with an example found in Leizarraga's New Testament Version (1571)—and thus of mere historical interest—the synonymy of *alliantzazko arkha* (Rv 11:19) and *alliantzako arkha* (Heb 9:4), both meaning 'ark of the covenant', shows either that the otherwise closely similar dialects of the two translators of these passages differed with respect to Instrumental Deletion, or that the application of this rule was optional in the dialect of the translator responsible for both of them.

A less arcane example can be discovered looking at derivatives formed with the suffix *-garri* to be analyzed in chapter 14. As we will find there, these sometimes function as nouns, but also, and more frequently, as adjectives. To take a concrete example, the noun *harri* 'stone', serving also as a verb radical with the sense 'to astonish', has a derivative *harrigarri*, which means 'object of wonder', 'marvel' as a noun and 'astounding' as an adjective. Synonymous with the adjective is the adnominal instrumental *harrigarrizko*. Now, in Duvoisin's unpublished dictionary, a form *harrigarriko* appears (*DRA* 5, 1953), a form we find used by the later Souletin authors Lhande (Lh. 615) and Mirande (*Pr*. 225). Other specimens created in this fashion could be cited: *izugarriko* 'terrible', *ikaragarriko* 'horrible', and so on. Yet such forms, for which Instrumental Deletion is clearly responsible, are, even in the northern dialects, quite rare as compared to those with their instrumental ending retained. In the other dialects, adnominal *-garrizko*, but never *-garriko*, occurs as a convenient alternative to adjectival *-garri*. In his normative Batua dictionary, Sarasola includes *harrigarrizko* (*E.H.* 355) but omits *harrigarriko*, a decision I would consider amply justified.

Another example, *gaitzeko* 'enormous', derived by way of *gaitzezko* from the noun *gaitz* 'evil', has enjoyed a sufficiently wide circulation to be accepted by Sarasola into Batua, still described, however, as a northern localism (*E.H.* 293).

Furthermore, frequency adverbs, such as *egunero* 'every day', are likely to have an underlying instrumental case, visible in synonyms of the form *egun oroz*. Therefore, Instrumental Deletion is required by their adnominal forms: *eguneroko* and *egun oroko* 'daily'.

Apart from a few scattered instances of this sort, the main reason warranting Instrumental Deletion as a rule of Batua has to do with the generation of some *genetivus qualitatis* constructions. Northern users of Batua will employ the instrumental in preference to the sociative in such phrases as *indar handiz* 'with great strength', but they too make use of the adnominal phrase *indar handiko* 'of great strength'. For such speakers then Instrumental Deletion should be available in Batua as in their own dialects.

We may add that the common expression *zorioneko* 'fortunate' (often used highly ironically: 'deuced') may be derived from *zorionezko* for some, especially northern, speakers and from inessive *zorionean* + *ko* for others. Note that the Latin adjective *beati* of Lk 12:37 was rendered *zorionezkoak* by Duvoisin (1858) and *zorionekoak* by both *IB* (1980) and *EAB* (1983).

5.2.6 Echoes of the Locative System

Adnominal forms based on an indefinite or plural postpositional phrase will carry the number indicators *-ta-* or *-eta-*, provided the postposition deleted belongs to the locative system:

zein herritako ohitura?	the custom of which village?
lantegietako mutilak	the boys from the workshops

But when the postposition deleted belongs to the basic system, the use of these number markers is not indicated:

ehun urteko atsoa	an old woman of a hundred years old
hogei haurreko taldea	a group of twenty children

For inessive animate adnominals one might anticipate the ending *-gango*, composed of *-gan* and *-ko*. Such forms are indeed attested in previous centuries: *ni gango uste ona* 'the trust in me' (Mendiburu, *Ot. Gai.* III, 207); *nigango aitetasuna* '(your) fatherhood in me' (Añibarro, *E.L.* 147), but have now become entirely obsolete. Instead the alternative *baitako* (cf. section 3.6) must be used, or else the plain genitive, if possible:

Miren baitako uste ona	the trust in Mary (*uste* 'opinion', *uste on* 'trust')
Miren baitako indarra	the strength in Mary
Mirenen indarra	Mary's strength

In the actual presence of a locative ending, however, animate adnominals do exhibit the morpheme *-gan-*:

gizonagandikako gaitza (*MEIG* II, 101)	evil proceeding from man
Jainkoaganako bidea (Ax. 485)	the road to God

An alternative to *-gan-*, the word *baita*, does not block Postposition Deletion:

gizona baita(ti)ko gaitza	evil proceeding from man
Jainkoa baita(ra)ko bidea	the road to God

5.3 Similarities between Adnominals and Genitives

As the preceding section has shown, the linking morpheme *-ko* has at least one property in common with the case endings of the locative system: it shares with them an affinity for the number markers *-ta-* and *-eta-*. Solely for this reason, traditional grammars of Basque are wont to include *-ko* among the locative cases, sometimes describing it as a "locative genitive" (most recently in the grammar of the Basque Academy: "Lekugenitiboa," *EGLU* I, 347).

Misleading though this description is, there exist nonetheless obvious similarities between adnominals and genitives. They both serve an adjectival function and can be represented by analogous schemata (cf. section 2.4):

(5) a. $[_A$ NP $[_A$ *-ren*]] NP
 b. $[_A$ PP $[_A$ *-ko*]] NP

As Mitxelena clearly recognized (*MEIG* VI, 177), both *-ren* and *-ko* are derivational rather than inflectional. Yet as a derivational device, they are a trifle unusual inasmuch as they operate on syntactic categories, namely NP and PP, not lexical ones such as N or P.

If the approach advocated here is correct, a rather important corollary remains to be pointed out. It surely can be no accident that there are no adnominals corresponding to dative—or, for that matter, ergative—noun phrases. What one finds instead are genitives. Accepting the schemata (5a,b) forces us to claim that datives as well as ergatives are case-marked NPs rather than PPs. I can see no grounds at all for doubting this conclusion, particularly since the way verbal agreement operates in Basque provides independent support for it (cf. section 15.1).

Given the operation of Postposition Deletion, schemata (5a,b) lead us to expect a very similar, even identical, syntactic distribution of the morphemes *-ren* and *-ko*. This prediction is indeed largely borne out, as we can see from these four observations:

1. Both genitives and adnominals normally precede the noun phrase they modify, but, exceptionally, may also follow it.

Regular order	etxearen jabea	the owner of the house
	etxeko alaba	the daughter of the house
Exceptional order	Aita gurea	our father (For the genitive *gure*, see section 6.1.3.)
	Ama errukizkoa	the compassionate mother

2. Genitive phrases and adnominal phrases both admit the definite article—in fact, they both allow the complete determiner system. Such phrases are to be thought of as modifiers to a pronoun:

elizarena(rekin)	(with) the one of the church
elizakoa(rekin)	(with) the one of (from or in) the church

Similarly:

etxeko bat	one of the house
etxekoa	the one of the house, that of the house
etxekoak	those of the house

Given these constructions, it is not surprising that *etxeko* has been lexicalized as a noun meaning 'member of the household'. Likewise, from *auzo* 'neighborhood', we have *auzoko* 'neighbor'.

3. Together with the copula *izan* 'to be', both genitives and adnominals can occur as nominal predicates. They will then carry the definite article *-a(k)*:

Liburuak haurrarenak dira.	The books are the child's.
Arrainak itsasokoak dira.	The fish are from the sea.
Mahaia zurezkoa da.	The table is wooden (made of wood).
Norena da haurra?	Whose is the child?
Nongoa da emakumea?	Where is the woman from?

4. Hyperdeclension (cf. section 2.4) can occur for both genitives and adnominals:

alkatearen alabaren dirua eta apaizarenarena	the money of the daughter of the mayor and that of the one of the priest
Loiolako elizako aldarea eta Burgoskokoa	the altar of the church of Loyola and that of the one of Burgos

Iteration of *-ko* is already attested in Harriet's 1741 *Gramatica escuaraz eta francesez* (pp. 459–461): *egungoco* 'de celui d'aujourd'hui' (of that of today); *atçococo* 'de celui d'hier' (of that of yesterday); *herenegungoco* 'de celui d'avant hier' (of that of the day before yesterday); *biharcoco* 'de celui de demain' (of that of tomorrow); *ondococo* 'de celui d'après' (of that of the one after); *aitçinecoco* 'de celui de devant' (of that of the one before).

While some native speakers find the preceding example unobjectionable, many users of the language, including the grammarian P. Lafitte (*Grammaire basque*, 1962, sec. 146) and the eminent scholar K. Mitxelena (*MEIG* VI, 177; Michelena 1985, 138) deny the iterability of *-ko*, though not that of *-(r)en*. These speakers feel compelled to repeat *elizako* in the second conjunct, being unable to proceed beyond the stage shown by *Loiolako elizako aldarea eta Burgosko elizakoa* 'the altar of the church of Loyola and that of the church of Burgos'.

This unexpected asymmetry between genitives and adnominals demands an explanation. Is the problem perhaps phonological rather than syntactic? But why should sequences of *-ko* be forbidden by the phonology? Could it be a tonal constraint operative in the western dialects only? However, a simple output constraint that disallows adjacent syllables bearing each an obligatory tonal descent would not work; for, while it would effectively block all sequences of *-ko*, it would also, unfortunately, reject such perfectly acceptable sequences as *-tiko* and *-rainoko*.

A plausible nonphonological explanation has been suggested by Kenneth L. Hale (oral communication, October 1990). He conjectured that the absence of an overt article renders sequences of *-ko* altogether too hard to process and hence unacceptable, in contrast to an iterated genitive where the repeated article *-a* furnishes enough of a clue to the underlying syntactic structure. If this explanation is correct, *-ko* sequences must count as fully grammatical, although unacceptable to many speakers at the level of performance.

5.4 Hints for Translating English Possessive Phrases into Basque

English possessives—a term subsuming two types of English genitives: prepositional (*the possession of the possessor*) and postpositional (*the possessor's possession*)—clearly represent a wide array of semantic relations. For the translation of these possessives into Basque careful analysis is needed, as Basque will use either the genitive in *-(r)en* or the adnominal in *-ko*, depending on the nature of the meaning relation in question. A few hints should prove to be helpful:

1. When the possessor is animate, only the genitive is eligible:

Mother's skirt	amaren gona
Father's pants	aitaren prakak
the strength of ten horses	hamar zaldiren indarra

The reason adnominals are banned here lies in the unavailability of the form *-gango*, as we observed in section 5.2.6. This constraint explains the otherwise puzzling asymmetry in Duvoisin's translation of the Vulgate phrase *fructus ventris tui, et fructus terrae tuae, fructusque iumentorum tuorum* (Dt 28:4): *zure sabeleko fruituak, zure lurreko fruituak, zure azienden fruituak*, where *azienda* 'head of cattle' is animate and hence must take the genitive, in contrast to *sabel* 'belly' and *lur* 'soil'.

A phrase like *haurreko egunak* 'the days of childhood' constitutes no exception, since the underlying inessive *haurrean*, meaning 'in childhood' is, unlike *haurrengan*, clearly inanimate.

Yet one type of genuine exceptions must be recognized. It consists of expressions based on *-(r)ekin* or *-z* deletion, such as

bostehun laguneko herria	a village of five hundred inhabitants
hamabi mutileko taldea	a group of twelve boys

2. When the possessor denotes the material or content the possession is made of, filled with, overwhelmed by, or inspired by, then the adnominal instrumental must be used:

a skirt of a beautiful black fabric	oihal beltz ederrezko gona (cf. *P.Ad.* 33)
a beautiful statue of stone	harrizko irudi eder bat (Lafitte, *Murtuts* 12)

a heart of gold	urrezko bihotza
a sea of blood	odolezko itsasoa
the fire of love	amodiozko sua (Argaiñaratz, *Dev. B.* 30)
the bread of tears	negarrezko ogia (Ps 79:6; Dv; *Imit.* I, 21.6; SP, Chourio)
a shout of joy	pozezko oihua
a tale of hatred	gorrotozko ipuina

3. When the English preposition *of* could be replaced by another one, such as *at*, *on*, *in*, *to*, *from*, or *for*, without any great difference in meaning, Basque will require the adnominal. In such cases the connection between the possessor and the possession lacks the character of an intrinsic relation. Rather, the possessor specifies a local or temporal frame for the possession, or indicates its origin, distance, or some other accidental property. Examples:

the weather of (in) Bilbao	Bilboko eguraldia
the furniture of (in) the house	etxeko erredizak
the hair of (on) the head	buruko ilea
the months of (in) the winter	neguko hilak
the custom of (in) the village	herriko ohitura
the boss of (in) the workshop	lantegiko nagusia
the smoke of (from) the house	etxeko kea
half a day's job (for half a day)	egun erdiko lana
the rent of (for) two months	bi hileko errenta
the man of (for) the year	urteko gizona

4. When there is an intrinsic, natural (i.e., nonfortuitous) relation between the possessor and the possession, the genitive is the appropriate translation form. A typical example of this kind of relation is the *genetivus objectivus*, that is, the relation between an agent and the object involved in this agent's action, such as that obtaining between a creator and the creation achieved, an observer and the observation performed, and so on.

A few examples will serve to illustrate this point:

the owner of the workshop	lantegiaren jabea
the author of the book	liburuaren egilea (*egile* 'maker')
the receiver of the money	diruaren hartzailea
the finder of the ring	eraztunaren aurkitzailea
the light of the sun	eguzkiaren argia
the smoke of the fire	suaren kea
the shadow of the mountain	mendiaren itzala
the smell of the wine	ardoaren usaina
the honor of the village	herriaren ohorea
the name of the house	etxearen izena
the buyer of the coffee shop	kafetegiaren eroslea

(Note that the naming relation as such provides an intrinsic connection, although the relationship between a particular name and a particular object is fortuitous.)

Observe furthermore the difference between *errotaren lana* 'the work of the mill' (i.e., 'work done by the mill itself') and *errotako lana* 'the work in the mill'; *gauaren beldurra* 'the fear of the night' and *gaueko beldurra* 'the nighttime fear'. The grammarian P. Goenaga also mentions an interesting example: *Elizaren isiltasuna* 'the silence of the Church' versus *elizako isiltasuna* 'the silence in the church' (see Goenaga 1981, 157; cf. Lafon 1965, 145–146). The difference between *etxeko jauna* 'the lord of the house' and *etxearen jabea* 'the owner of the house' was already discussed in the first Basque grammar ever written, the 17th-century *Grammaire de la langue basque* by Silvain Pouvreau:

> On ne dit pas *Etxearen jauna*, le maître de la maison, mais *Etxeko jauna*, et de là vient *Etxekoa*, domestique. On dit pourtant, *Etxearen jabea*, le possesseur de la maison, et non pas *etxeko jabea*. (Chap. 2, sec. 3; spelling modernized.)

> [One does not say *Etxearen jauna*, 'the lord of the house', but *Etxeko jauna*, and hence *Etxekoa*, '(the) domestic'. (Literally, 'the one/that of the house'; see section 5.3.) Yet, one says *Etxearen jabea*, 'the owner of the house', and not *etxeko jabea*. (trans VdR)]

All too obviously, the meager hints dealt out here do not even begin to exhaust the subject. It may hearten the reader to learn that there are plenty of instances in which Basque speakers will disagree or allow either construction. Thus the relation between a house and its roof, a door and its key, or a church and its lightning rod may either be considered intrinsic, in which case we get the genitive—*etxearen teilatua, atearen giltza, elizaren tximistorratza* (so López Mendizabal, 170)—or else viewed as a matter of mere location, with the resulting authorization of the adnominal—*etxeko teilatua, ateko giltza, elizako tximistorratza* (*tximist* 'lightning', *orratz* 'needle').

Except for the minor detail that in *ateko giltza* postpositions other than just the inessive could be hiding—with the allative *-ra* as a likely candidate—the following observation reported as hearsay by Mitxelena neatly agrees with the theory set forth in this chapter: "The difference between *atearen giltza* and *ateko giltza*, both translated as 'the key of the door', is that the former phrase is somehow related to the clause *ateak giltza du* 'the door has a key', while the latter has to do with *giltza atean da* (or *dago*) 'the key is in the door'" (translated from Michelena 1972a, 312).

The hesitations experienced by modern speakers are reflected in Bible translations, beginning with Leizarraga's New Testament Version of 1571. Illustrations are not hard to find:

In the 19th century Uriarte translated the Vulgate phrase *tectum tabernaculi* 'the roof of the tabernacle' in Ex 36:14 as *tabernaculoaren tellatua*, but his Labourdin contemporary Duvoisin wrote *tabernakleko hegaztegia*, while using the genitive *gela baten hegaztegitik* to translate *a tecto thalami* 'from the roof of a cell' in Ez 40:13.

Two modern Batua versions of the New Testament, the Roman Catholic *IB* (1980) and the ecumenical *EAB* (1983), differ in their rendering of the phrase 'the keys of the Kingdom of Heaven' occurring in Mt 16:19: *IB* has *zeruetako erreinuaren giltzak* and *EAB Jainkoaren* (sic) *erreinuko giltzak*. Sticking to keys, we turn to 'the key of knowledge' in Lk 11:52 and find that Duvoisin gives *jakitateko gakhoa*, while most other translations use the genitive: *jakintzaren giltza* (*IB*). *EAB* takes advantage of a circumlocution: *ezagupenaren ateko giltza* 'the key of the door of knowledge'. Note that for *clavem abyssi* 'the key of the abyss' all translations use the adnominal form, for example, *leizeko giltza* (Rv 20:1; *EAB*, *IB*).

Furthermore, to translate the phrase 'the fruit of the tree' occurring in Gn 3:3, some Basque authors use the genitive: *zuhaitzaren fruitua*, others the adnominal: *zuhaitzeko fruitua*. For 'the fruit of the womb' (Gn 30:2; Lk 1:42 and various Catholic prayers), every single writer uses the adnominal *sabeleko fruitua*, except I. M. Manzisidor once in his book *Jesukristoren Bizitza*, where we read *zure sabelaren frutua* 'your womb's fruit' (p. 55).

For one more example of hesitation we turn to Añibarro's word list *Voces Bascongadas*, which dates from the beginning of the 19th century. On page 131 of Villasante's edition we read, "POTENCIAS DE EL ALMA: *arimaren o* [i.e., *or*] *arimaco almenac*."

5.5 Historical and Bibliographical Comments

The preceding sections have shown the rule, or rather rules, of Postposition Deletion to be central to an adequate understanding of the nature of the linking morpheme *-ko*. A brief account of the discovery of these rules is therefore appropriate, the more so as it will amount to something of an annotated bibliography.

As R. Trask (see later in this section) has observed, we must turn first of all to P. Lhande's well-known *Dictionnaire basque-français*, published in installments from 1926 to 1938. The wording of the entry *-ko* on page 614 plainly shows full awareness of the underlying inessive: "*-KO* C. suffixe relatif qui affecte: 1° l'inessif: *etxen*, à la maison, *etxenko*, qui est à la maison; *burutan*, en tête, *burutako*, qui est en tête; *buruan*, à la tête, *buruko*, qui est à la tête; *buruetan*, dans les têtes, *buruetako*, qui est dans les têtes;—2° l'adlatif. ..." [*-KO* C. (common to the three dialects Labourdin, Low Navarrese, and Souletin) relative suffix that affects (1) the inessive: *etxen* 'at home', *etxenko* 'who is at home'; *burutan* '(literally) in head', *burutako* 'which is (literally) in head'; *buruan* 'in/at the head', *buruko* 'which is in/at the head'; *buruetan* 'in the heads', *buruetako* 'which is in the heads'; (2) the allative.... (trans. VdR)] [*N.B.* The form *etxenko* is exclusively Souletin, never used in Batua.]

It is unclear, though, whether this entry should be attributed to Lhande himself or to his later editors P. Lafitte and Ph. Aranart. At any rate, Lafitte, in his epoch-making *Grammaire basque* of 1944, displays some perspicacity in speaking of "le génitif locatif en *-ko*" (1962, sec. 146) and translating *hiriko eliza* as 'l'église de la ville (qui est *dans* la ville ['which is *in* the town'])' (1962, sec. 147).

Yet neither Lafitte nor anybody else at the time seemed interested in developing the insight lurking behind this formulation. In a noteworthy article (Lafon 1965), one of Lafitte's most assiduous readers, the French bascologist R. Lafon (1899–1974), diligently provides a wealth of material on the use of what he once designates with remarkable aptness as "le génitif adnominal" yet remains totally unaware of any syntactic linkage with the inessive case. Characterizing the difference between the genitive and the adnominal in purely semantic terms clearly appears to be his central aim. Lafon's painstaking efforts in this direction, however, cannot be deemed very successful, or even moderately satisfactory, when judged by today's standards. As was the case with many a scholar of his generation, his unrelenting concentration on semantics led to a virtual exclusion of syntax, thereby precluding a correct appraisal of the type of linguistic structure represented by the adnominal.

In clear contrast, a Basque scholar of the next generation, K. Mitxelena (1914–1987), albeit considering himself first of all a phonologist and a lexicographer, had a mind eminently open to the more abstract point of view of syntax, as is attested by the fact that it was he who introduced generative grammar into the Basque Country as well as into Spain. It is thus no accident that we can trace the first explicit recognition of a rule of inessive deletion before *-ko* to a linguistics course taught by Mitxelena—more precisely, to the fourth of a series of lectures given in San Sebastian in the summer of 1970. These lectures, delivered in Spanish, have never been published. What we do have is a Basque version made on the basis of the original tape recordings. This version was revised by the author and appeared as a small book under the title *Zenbait Hitzaldi* ('Some Lectures'; 1972c).

After 1970 the concept of a deleted inessive played an essential role in his essay "Egunak eta egun-izenak" (Mitxelena 1971). The diachronic perspective broached here was again taken up in Michelena 1972a.

Here one shortcoming of Mitxelena's analysis needs to be pointed out. Inasmuch as his approach treats the adnominal as a concomitant of the inessive, Mitxelena was forced to admit defeat when faced with examples unrelated to the inessive, such as those corresponding to the Latin *genetivus qualitatis*. (See Michelena 1972a, 314 [or 305].)

Some years later a student of Mitxelena's, P. Goenaga, in his book *Gramatika bideetan* ('On the roads of grammar'), written in 1978 (revised edition 1980), treats adnominals as transformationally reduced versions of various types of relative clauses (pp. 73, 112–114; in the revised edition pp. 95, 133–135; see also p. 291). Two main types are recognized: one based on adverbials such as *Bilborako trena* 'the train to Bilbao' and one based on noun phrases, such as *bihotz oneko neska* 'a good-hearted girl' (lit. 'a girl of good heart'), which he derives from the relative clause *bihotz ona duen neska* 'a girl who has a good heart'.

This same approach is adhered to in a later, more elaborate, discussion of these topics in Goenaga 1981. One of the interesting observations made in this paper is that the two phrases *etxe oneko neska* 'a girl of a good house' and *bihotz oneko neska* 'a good-hearted girl', superficially similar though they are, require in fact quite different grammatical analyses.

An American scholar, T. H. Wilbur, also proposed to derive adnominals from reduced relatives: *ateko giltza* 'the key of the door' from *atean dagoen giltza* 'the key that is in the door', but failed to consider the *genetivus qualitatis* examples (Wilbur 1979b, 94, 158).

The problem posed by these examples was tackled a few years later by R. L. Trask in his Pamplona lecture of September 1984 (Trask 1985b). Although I must disagree with its final conclusion, this masterly exposition, short as it is, has certainly helped a great deal to clarify matters. The main problem addressed is the same as was faced by Goenaga: what is the origin of the numerous *-ko* phrases that do not admit a locative interpretation? Trask's proposed solution is quite different from Goenaga's and starts from the none too elegant assumption that we are dealing with two homonymous adjectivizers corresponding to Goenaga's two types of *-ko* phrases: one, a purely syntactic tool transformationally attached to postpositional phrases à la Goenaga; the other, a derivational suffix selecting a class of noun phrases.

It must be noted that Trask's characterization of this class as those NPs equipped with the internal structure of N-bar is clearly erroneous: witness the free occurrence of numerals and quantifiers (*lagun askoko taldea* 'a group of many members'), incompatible with N-bar structure.

The unitarian counterclaim that all adnominals in Basque are based on postpositional phrases originated with the present author, who has maintained that Goenaga's second type of *-ko* phrases consists of just those adnominals in which an underlying basic—that is, nonlocative—case ending has been deleted. This position was first defended in my contribution to the 1987 II Basque World Congress (de Rijk 1988), and further explored in my essay "Basque Hospitality and the Suffix *-ko*" (de Rijk 1993).

A. Eguzkitza 1993 contains some useful background information. Without offering any syntactic explanation, Basterrechea 1989 briefly provides examples showing that certain types of adnominals, such as *lau hankako mahai bat* 'a table with four legs', take neither the indefinite marker *-ta-* nor the plural marker *-eta-*. Since these markers are a prerogative of the locative-based type of adnominals, their absence is only to be expected with the basic ones, that is, those formed after deletion of an underlying basic postposition (sociative or instrumental), a type to which all of Basterrechea's examples can be seen to belong.

5.6 The Frequency Suffix *-ero*

The suffix *-ero*, a weakened form of the quantifier *oro* 'every', creates adverbs of frequency. It can be attached to any noun—or, occasionally, noun phrase—defining a recurrent pattern of time. These words include not just genuine period nouns like *urte* 'year' or *egun* 'day', but also nouns denoting a regularly recurring activity, like *jai* 'holiday', 'festivity' or *otordu* 'meal'.

From the phonological point of view it may be observed that nouns ending in *a* or *e* lose these vowels before the *e* of *-ero*.

Examples are

aldi	turn, time	aldiero	every turn, every time
arrats	evening	arratsero	every evening
arratsalde	afternoon	arratsaldero	every afternoon
aste	week	astero	every week, weekly
egun	day	egunero	every day, daily
gau	night	gauero	every night, nightly
goiz	morning	goizero	every morning
hil	month	hilero	every month, monthly
hilabete	month	hilabetero	every month, monthly
igande	Sunday	igandero	every Sunday
ilunabar	sundown	ilunabarrero	every sundown
minutu	minute	minutuero	every minute
ordu	hour	orduero	every hour, hourly
ordu erdi	half hour	ordu erdiero	every half hour
ordu laurden	quarter of an hour	ordu laurdenero	every quarter of an hour
otordu	meal	otorduero	at every meal
une	moment	unero	every moment
urte	year	urtero	every year

The word *noizero* 'how often' deserves separate mention, as it is based on an adverb (*noiz* 'when') rather than a noun. Equally worth stating is the fact that the suffix *-ero* is not restricted to nouns, but can occur with fuller noun phrases too: *lau hilabetero* 'every four months', *ia hamar minutuero* (Atxaga, *Obab.* 62) 'almost every ten minutes'. The assumption made in section 5.2.5 that derivatives with the suffix *-ero* have the syntactic status of instrumentals explains the existence of adnominal forms. Thus we get *eguneroko ogia* 'the daily bread', *asteroko berriak* 'the weekly news'.

Some of these adnominals have been widely used as nouns denoting periodicals. Modern Batua prefers the suffix *-kari*:

eguneroko	daily paper	(egunkari)
asteroko	weekly magazine	(astekari)
hileroko	monthly journal	(hilabetekari)
urteroko	annual publication	(urtekari)

[*N.B.* Speakers from the northern dialects have kept the unreduced form *oro* even as a suffix. Hence *egunoro, hiloro*, and so on. In the Souletin dialect, the use of *oro* as a full-fledged quantifier is still common: *egun oroz* 'every day', *hil oroz* 'every month'. Batua accepts all three forms: *astero, asteoro, aste oroz* 'every week'. For more about *oro*, see section 28.3.]

5.7 The Four Seasons of the Year

The four seasons (*urtaro*) are

udaberri	spring	udaberrian	in spring
uda	summer	udan	in summer
udazken	autumn	udazkenean	in autumn
negu	winter	neguan	in winter

Note the use of the definite forms, in contrast to English (cf. section 2.3.1).

Since *udaberri* and *udazken* literally mean 'new summer' and 'end of summer', the conclusion can be drawn that in former times not more than two seasons were distinguished: *uda* and *negu*, summer and winter.

5.8 The Months of the Year

Based as they are on agricultural life, which differs from place to place depending on local conditions, the names of the months vary a great deal from dialect to dialect. Not only are there several names for the same month, but the same name can be used for distinct months in different areas. Thus the term *garagarril* 'Barley month' means 'June' in Guipuzkoa but 'July' in Biscay; *urri* 'Scarcity' is used for 'September', 'October', or both, according to region; *agor* 'Drought', mostly employed for 'September', means 'August' in certain localities and 'October' in Larraun.

Within the Basque Academy, the issue of standardization was first raised in 1961 (Villasante 1962), to be finally settled nearly a decade later (see the official list published on page 107 of *Euskera*, n.s., 16, 1971). The official Batua designations read as follows:

urtarril	January	urtarrilean	in January
otsail	February	otsailean	in February
martxo	March	martxoan	in March
apiril	April	apirilean	in April
maiatz	May	maiatzean	in May
ekain	June	ekainean	in June
uztail	July	uztailean	in July
abuztu	August	abuztuan	in August
irail	September	irailean	in September
urri	October	urrian	in October
azaro	November	azaroan	in November
abendu	December	abenduan	in December

Although listed here without their article, these terms always occur in the definite form (section 2.3.1): *urtarrila* 'January', *otsaila* 'February', and so on.

For etymological explications, see chapter 5 in J. Caro Baroja 1973; for *urtarril*, cf. *FHV*, p. 513. Turning now to matters of syntax, I wish to draw attention to an interesting contrast between the genitive and the adnominal in the following noun phrases:

ekainaren bigarren eguna	the second day of June
ekaineko bigarren astea	the second week of June

This contrast is easily understood inasmuch as a month, quite literally, consists of days (intrinsic relation, see section 5.4, item 4), but in no way consists of weeks.

Dates can be given as follows (cf. *EGLU* I, 196):

maiatzaren lehena	the first of May
uztailaren zazpian	on the seventh of July
1995eko otsailaren bosta	the fifth of February 1995
1996ko irailaren lauean	on the fourth of September 1996

[*N.B.* The latter two dates can be written as *1995eko.2.5a* and *1996ko.9.4ean*.]

5.9 The Days of the Week

The standardization of the terms for the days of the week (*astegun*) presented much less of a problem. True enough, here too dialectal diversity is considerable. By way of illustration, we include in parentheses the characteristic Biscayan names, even though these are rarely, if at all, utilized in Batua.

However, a natural solution imposed itself: adoption of the widely known terms shared by the two central dialects Guipuzcoan and Labourdin:

astelehen	Monday	(Bisc. *ilen*)
astearte	Tuesday	(Bisc. *martitzen*)
asteazken	Wednesday	(Bisc. *eguazten*)
ostegun	Thursday	(Bisc. *eguen*)
ostiral	Friday	(Bisc. *bariku*)
larunbat	Saturday	(Bisc. *zapatu*)
igande	Sunday	(Bisc. *domeka*)

(The phonological variants *ortzegun* and *ortzirale*, typical of Labourdin and the other northern dialects, are equally acceptable.)

[*Reminder: Larunbatean* 'on Saturday' (definite form, see section 2.3.1); *larunbatetan* 'on Saturdays'; *larunbatero* 'every Saturday'.]

From the meanings of the original three items (*astelehen* 'first of the week'; *astearte* 'middle of the week'; *asteazken* 'end of the week') the inference seems warranted that the ancient Basques used to work with weeklike periods of three days, just as the Celts appear to have done. On the etymology of the remaining terms, see chapter 6 of J. Caro Baroja 1973, and also Mitxelena 1971.

5.10 Vocabulary

agur	greeting, hello, goodbye
argal	weak
arima	soul
arrazoi	reason
auzoko	neighbor, nearby
balio	value, worth
errenta	rent
erruki	compassion
etxeko	member of the household
gaitz	evil, illness, fault
gorroto	hatred, hate
haize	wind
harrigarri	astounding, surprising
ipuin	tale, story
irudi	image, picture, statue
itzal	shadow, shade, respect
itzulpen	translation
izugarri	frightful, terrible
jantzi	clothing, dress, suit
larru	skin, hide, leather
leize	abyss, chasm, gorge
libera	franc
lotura	tie, link, connection
oihal	cloth, fabric, curtain
oihu	shout, scream
praka	pants, trousers
sudur	nose
usain	smell, odor
zen	(he, she, it) was
ziren	(they) were

[*N.B.* Note also the words given in section 5.6, such as *egun* 'day' and *aste* 'week'.]

5.11 Exercises

5.11.1 Translate into English

1. Non dira atzoko adiskide onak?
2. Ohe gaineko hiru neskatxak nor dira?

3. Aurreko atea burdinazkoa eta atzekoa zurezkoa zen.
4. Mirenen praka berriak balio gutxikoak dira.
5. Ondoko gaztelu zaharraren inguruan leize izugarriak dira.
6. Zilarra itsasoko sorginarena zen, eta urrea mendikoarena.
7. Harrizko zubia sendoa zen, baina zurezkoa txit argala.
8. Eliz barruko irudiak politak ziren eta kanpokoak itsusiak.
9. Auzokoekiko loturak oso sendoak ziren hemen.
10. Euskaratiko itzulpen berriak oso ederrak dira askotan.
11. Gorrotozko hitzak gutxitan dira arrazoizkoak.
12. Itxurazko munduari eta gezurrezko adiskideei agur!

5.11.2 Translate into Basque

1. The story from Bayonne was frightful.
2. Why is the wind from the sea cold?
3. The smell of today's supper is delicious.
4. The new bridges in Bilbao are not wooden ones.
5. The houses in the villages are beautiful, those on the mountain (are) not.
6. The fabric of Pete's suit is cheap, but not bad.
7. The compassion of the cat was surprising, not the fear of the rat.
8. Books in Basque are always expensive here.
9. The shadow of the cross on top of the mountain was astounding.
10. The whole year's rent is two hundred thousand francs.
11. The danger of sleep near the abyss is clear.
12. The table on the left and the mirror on the right belong to an old friend of Father's.

6 Personal Pronouns; Synthetic Conjugation of Intransitive Verbs

6.1 Personal Pronouns

6.1.1 Inventory of Personal Pronouns

Genuine pronouns are confined to the first and second persons, that is, those directly participating in the speech act. The need for third-person pronouns is filled in Basque by independent demonstratives: *hau, hori, hura*, for which see section 9.6.

There are five personal pronouns in Basque: three singular in meaning and two plural: *ni* 'I', *hi* 'you' (encoding "Solidarity," see section 6.1.2), *zu* 'you', *gu* 'we', *zuek* 'you' (plural reference).

It is generally agreed among grammarians that this system goes back to an earlier one consisting of only four elements: singular *ni* and *hi*; plural *gu* and *zu*. In particular, there is abundant evidence—part of which can be found in *DRA* (9:4067–4068)—to show the present plural form *zuek* to be a relatively late addition to the language, despite its presence in all dialects and its early attestation (1545).

Since modern English has but one second-person pronoun to offer us, glossing the three Basque forms causes a slight problem, especially when paradigms are to be displayed. However, the use of diacritic marks provides an expedient solution: henceforth, the notation 'yoú' will serve as an English gloss for the Basque pronoun *hi*, while 'yoû' will do duty glossing the plural pronoun *zuek*, the unadorned form 'you' being left to stand for the pragmatically unmarked singular pronoun *zu*.

6.1.2 Pragmatics of the Two Modes of Address: *zu* and *hi*

Traditionally, the pronoun *zu* is said to be polite, the pronoun *hi* familiar. And true enough, a standard analysis along the lines of R. Brown and A. Gilman's 1960 seminal paper "The Pronouns of Power and Solidarity" does seem to afford a first approximation to the sociolinguistics of pronominal address in Basque. Here, too, inequality of "Power" gives rise to asymmetrical forms of address: one-sided *hi* downward from above, and one-sided *zu* upward from below.

Actually, in view of the firmly egalitarian ethic of traditional Basque society, such asymmetry is quite rare. Even between employer and employee mutual *zu* prevails, or, more rarely, mutual *hi*. Only within the family context does the power dimension play a significant role: parents will address their teenage children with *hi* but not vice versa.

The other dimension introduced by Brown and Gilman, "Solidarity," will serve very nicely to elucidate the symmetrical use of the pronoun *hi*, on the understanding, however, that its definition be tailored to the Basque cultural situation. Here indeed solidarity must be conceived of as an objective social reality: psychological factors play very little part in it. Thus friendship is neither a necessary nor a sufficient condition for the use of mutual *hi*. The kind of solidarity that is relevant consists, above all, in being subject to similar living conditions: children raised in the same family, hamlet, or neighborhood, workers on the same farm or in the same factory, and so on. Age differences strongly hamper solidarity: a gap of 15 years or more is known to virtually block the use of *hi* between adults.

This idiocratic concept of solidarity may help explain some of the rather striking divergencies found between the use of *tu* in Romance and that of *hi* in Basque:

1. The alleged familiar form *hi* is never used by adults to small children, not even by their own parents. Traditional lullabies nicely illustrate this: the baby in the cradle is invariably addressed as *zu*. The critical age for the subsequent transition from *zu* to *hi* varies a great deal; it ranges from roughly six to as much as 15 years of age. We may note that, however much affection may obtain between young children and the surrounding adults, there is but little solidarity, at least in the sense defined in this section.
2. Aside from rare individual exceptions, spouses never use *hi* to each other, although they may well have done so before marrying. Apparently, the vastly different role patterns assumed in marriage are felt to preclude solidarity between husband and wife.

Although in a few urban and semiurban areas the pronoun *hi* has fallen out of active use, in most of the Basque-speaking territory this form is being kept very much alive. Its general survival is all the more remarkable as mastering the corresponding morphology is no mean task, as we will see in chapter 29. A constant feature of the Basque language in all its dialects consists in the obligatory use of allocutive verb forms: any conjugated main verb, be it first, second, or third person, must change to a different form as soon as the utterance is directed to someone requiring the use of *hi*.

Against this background it is fair to conclude that the traditional conception of *zu* as a polite form and *hi* as a familiar form is far from adequate, if only for the reason that it suggests more conformity with the neighboring Romance practices than is in fact the case. In this grammar, therefore, an altogether different characterization is being proposed. Our advice to the reader is to view *zu* as the normal, pragmatically unmarked, form of address, and *hi* as a marked substitute, encoding the feature "Solidarity," as it is defined by the social realities of local Basque culture.

A more extensive study of the modes of address in Basque can be found in the writings of J. Alberdi Larizgoitia (e.g., 1986a, 1986b, 1995 [in English]), especially his now-published doctoral dissertation (1996), and a small article by myself (de Rijk 1991).

6.1.3 Declension of Personal Pronouns

Compared to that of other nouns, the declension of personal pronouns presents a few particularities, such as a genitive in *-re* instead of *-ren*, and the insertion of a segment *-ta-* in the instrumental. The following chart also shows the reflexive; its use will be explained in section 6.1.4.

Meaning (cf. section 6.1.1)	Absolutive	Ergative	Dative	Genitive	Reflexive	Sociative	Instrumental
I	ni	nik	niri	nire	neure	nirekin	nitaz
yoú	hi	hik	hiri	hire	heure	hirekin	hitaz
we	gu	guk	guri	gure	geure	gurekin	gutaz
you	zu	zuk	zuri	zure	zeure	zurekin	zutaz
yoû	zuek	zuek	zuei	zuen	zeuen	zuekin	zuetaz

Comments

1. For the dative, genitive, and sociative of the first person singular, the standard language presents two additional variants: *neri, nere, nerekin* of Guipuzcoan origin, and *eni, ene, enekin*, pertaining to the northern dialects. In southern speech, only the form *ene* has survived, its use being, moreover, restricted to exclamations: *ene ama!* 'oh, Mother!', *ene Jainkoa!* 'oh, my God!', or simply *ene!* 'good heavens!', *ai ene!* 'oh, my!'.
2. Inasmuch as traditional Basque culture emphasizes the family unit rather than the individual, the plural form *gure* 'our' is often used where English speakers would prefer the singular: *gure etxea* 'my house', *gure semea* 'my son', *gure emaztea* 'my wife', *gure senarra* 'my husband'.
3. Just as in the general nominal paradigm of section 2.2.1, the benefactive *-tzat* and the motivational *-gatik* are based on the genitive. Thus: *guretzat* 'for us', *zuregatik* 'because of you'. With the motivational, the absolutive form may replace the genitive, except for *zuek*: *nigatik* 'because of me', *gugatik* 'because of us', *zugatik* 'because of you', but only *zuengatik* 'because of yoû'.
4. The locative paradigm of personal pronouns is a muster of regularity. Note that all personal pronouns are animate noun phrases and need therefore the segment *-gan* (see section 3.6): *niregan* or *nigan* 'in me', *zuregana* or *zugana* 'to you', *guregandik* (*gureganik*) or *gugandik* (*guganik*) 'from us', and so on.

5. Given that personal pronouns are animate, the use of their genitive forms is obligatory with location nouns (see section 4.1.2): *gure aurrean* 'in front of us', *zure atzetik* 'after you', *nire ondoan* 'near me'.
6. The instrumental ending *-z* here occurs in an amplified form *-taz*, with dialectal variants *-tzaz* or *-zaz*. This long form of the instrumental is, in fact, typical of pronouns in general. It is found with all demonstratives (except for a few idiomatic combinations, see section 9.6.1), with the interrogative pronouns *nor* 'who', *zer* 'what', and *zein* 'which', and also with the corresponding indefinite pronouns. The indefinite pronouns ending in *-bait* (*norbait* 'somebody', *zerbait* 'something', and *zenbait* 'some') indifferently take the long or the short instrumental ending. When *asko* 'much', *gutxi* 'little', and *oro* 'all' function as pronouns, they can, but need not, take the long form: *askoz* or *askotaz* 'by much' 'by far'; *gutxiz* or *gutxitaz* 'by little'; *oroz* or *orotaz* 'by all'.

6.1.4 The Reflexive

The reflexive has the same general meaning as the genitive but adds a touch of insistence very roughly similar to that expressed by the English adjective *own*: *geure etxea* 'our own house'.

Its use—nowadays optional—is subject to Linschmann's constraint: the minimal clause S containing the reflexive form must include a noun phrase NP coreferential with the possessor. This crucial NP does not need to be overtly realized; sometimes its presence is merely understood, that is, implied by the verb form.

A noun phrase that is part of a larger phrase within S cannot trigger the reflexive: *ni eta nire emaztea* 'I and my wife' (not: **ni eta neure emaztea*); *hi eta hire etxea* 'yoú and yoúr house' (taken from Acts 16:31 in Leizarraga's NT version, where the reflexive is obligatory unless blocked by Linschmann's constraint).

A coreferential NP contained within a PP must be discounted for the same reason. Therefore, only absolutive (nominative), ergative, or dative NPs are able to trigger the reflexive within their S, since all other case forms are PPs rather than NPs, as we have seen in section 5.3.

The appellation "Linschmann's constraint" finds its justification in a passage from Schuchardt's preface to the 1900 re-edition of Leizarraga's Basque books of 1571: "Linschmann has made the discovery that *ene*, *hire* are used nonreflexively, *neure*, *eure* reflexively" (p. cxvii). The same result was rediscovered more than 50 years later by G. Aresti, a Basque writer from Bilbao (Kintana 1971). My formulation of the constraint is basically that of Sarasola (1980).

6.1.5 The Quasi Pronoun *bera*

The stem *ber* acts an an adjective meaning 'same': *andre bera* 'the same lady', *liburu berak* 'the same books'. Like all adjectives *ber* can be used substantively: *bera* 'the same one', which also admits the translation 'he himself', and in the plural: *berak* 'the same ones' and also 'they themselves'. This anaphoric noun phrase *bera* occurs with considerable frequency, for it serves as a convenient counterpart to third-person pronouns of other languages. To be so used, however, its referent must have been mentioned shortly before in the same discourse; otherwise, purely deictic forms have to be employed, that is, demonstrative pronouns, as mentioned in section 6.1.1.

The genitive form of the quasi pronoun *bera* is *bere*, an obvious assimilation to the pronominal declension displayed in section 6.1.3. The genitive of the plural form *berak* is *beren*, a form in which both declensions coincide. Thus *mutil beraren liburua* 'the book of the same boy', but *bere liburua* 'his (own) book'.

All other case forms of the quasi pronoun *bera* are built in accordance with the definite paradigm of sections 2.2.1 and 3.6: *berari, berekin* (colloquially also *berakin*), *beraz, beregan* or *beragan*, and so on; likewise for the plural *berak*: *berei, berekin, berez, berengan*, and so on.

The binding domains of the Basque pronouns, and especially of *bera* and its genitive *bere*, have been extensively discussed by the French linguist G. Rebuschi in a series of articles (see section 6.1.7). His study revealed a great deal of systematic variation between dialects. Whereas the northern dialects require *bere* to be bound in the same sentence in which it occurs—in certain areas of Low Navarra even in its own minimal clause—the southern dialects are frankly more liberal in allowing *bere* to be bound by a noun phrase occurring in a previous utterance within the same discourse, possibly spoken by a different interlocutor. For the standard Batua, the more liberal system must be accepted as the norm, given the fact that its users are predominantly from the southern dialects.

6.1.6 A Deferential Mode of Address: *berori*

The form *berori* consists of two morphemes: the demonstrative pronoun *hori* of the second degree of deixis—the one that points to the sphere of the addressee—preceded by *ber* 'same'. It therefore amounts to 'that same person which you are'. This term, not quite as deferential as the English expression *Your Lordship*, always requires a third-person verb form. It has been traditionally used by farmers to address priests, monks, doctors, and other dignitaries. Its use appears to be quite rapidly disappearing, the unmarked second-person pronoun *zu* taking its place. The plural form corresponding to *berori* is *beroriek*, which is also fading out.

6.1.7 Bibliographical Note on the Binding Properties of *bera* and *bere*

Most of the basic facts can be found in a brief nontechnical discussion devoted to the matter in the grammar of the Basque Academy (*EGLU* I, sec. 2.3.6).

More recently, an important source of information is the *Diccionario General Vasco*; note, for instance, its lemma *bere*, featuring a brief survey of the grammatical tradition concerning its use as well as many interesting examples (*DGV* IV, 741ff). Technical treatments of binding in Basque within Chomsky's GB theory have been contributed by P.

Salaburu (1986), and, especially, G. Rebuschi (1985, 1986, 1988b, 1989). As to contributions written in English, we can cite the following articles: Rebuschi 1990 (originally written in 1984), 1988a, 1991, 1992.

6.2 Synthetic Conjugation of Intransitive Verbs

6.2.1 Introduction: Synthetic and Periphrastic Conjugations

The vast majority of Basque verbs present only a periphrastic conjugation, consisting of a small set of nonfinite verb forms combined with a conjugated auxiliary verb.

A few frequently used verbs are exceptional in having also synthetic, that is, single-word, finite forms. Henceforth, such verbs will be referred to as strong. In Basque as it is currently spoken, one finds only about two dozen strong verbs. There used to be more, but even in the 16th century their number did not exceed 50, as evidenced by Leizarraga's New Testament translation of 1571 and several other texts of that period.

In today's literary language, the use of synthetic verb forms functions as an indicator of style in the following sense: the loftier the style, the more synthetic forms will appear in the text. Thus, in the realm of modern poetry in particular, many an author seems to revel in creating verb forms that are wholly unprecedented.

Transitive and intransitive verbs display sharply different morphologies in Basque. For this reason our present analysis will start with the simpler intransitives, leaving transitives to be dealt with later in chapters 9 and 10.

Given that the auxiliaries involved in the periphrastic conjugation are, of necessity, strong verbs, it appears appropriate to treat the synthetic conjugation first. The periphrastic conjugation of intransitives will then be taken up in the next chapter.

6.2.2 Intransitive Verb Morphology: The Indicative

In Batua there are ten intransitive strong verbs. Four of these require a dative noun phrase; they will be discussed in chapter 15. The remaining six verbs are *joan* 'to go'; *etorri* 'to come'; *ibili* 'to walk', 'to function'; *etzan* 'to lie down'; *egon* 'to stay', 'to be situated'; *izan* 'to be' (verb of existence, also serving as a copula for noun phrases, including, of course, adjectives).

[*N.B.* In the northern dialects, *egon* means 'to stay put', 'to remain', whereas in the south *egon* serves as a counterpart to the Spanish verb *estar* and means 'to be in a certain place, state, or condition'. In the north the verb *izan* is often used where the south prefers *egon*: 'to be ill' is *eri izan* in the north, and *eri egon* or *gaixo egon* in the south. Batua usage combines these two systems in a more or less eclectic fashion.]

The customary citation form of a Basque verb is that of its perfect participle. Thus the dictionary entry *joan* actually means 'gone' rather than 'go'. Most perfect participles are characterized by a final suffix *-i* or *-tu*, removal of which yields the radical form of the verb, used in the periphrastic forms belonging to moods other than the indicative or the conditional.

Except for derived verbs and late borrowings, all nonfinite verb forms share an initial prefix, which, although etymologically *e-*, has sometimes been altered to *i-*, *j-*, or ∅ by phonological processes: *i-bil-i* from **e-bil-i*, *joan* from **e-oan*, *izan* from **e-izan*, and so on. Henceforth, verbs with this prefix will be called "canonical" verbs. To get from the perfect participle of a Basque verb to its morphological stem, we must strip off its prefix as well as its suffix. Moreover, verbs having a perfect participle ending in *-n* will drop this final consonant in the stem form. Applying these steps to the six verbs under discussion produces the following stems: *-oa-*, *-torr-*, *-bil-*, *-tza-*, *-go-*, *-iza-*.

We are now ready to study the morphology of the finite verb. Restricting ourselves in these early chapters to the indicative mood, we only have two synthetic tense paradigms to deal with: past and nonpast, or past and present in the traditional terminology. All other tenses are periphrastic: they require the intervention of an auxiliary verb.

An insightful analysis of Basque verbal morphology can be given starting with two base forms: a present base consisting of the present tense marker *da* (no doubt related to the ancient Basque adverb *dan* 'now' reconstructed in my 1992 article "'Nunc' Vasconice") followed by the verb stem, and a past base consisting of the past tense marker *ze-* (or *e-* in the Biscayan dialect) again followed by the verb stem.

In accordance with regular phonological rules of Basque, the *a* of *da-* elides before a vocalic stem, whereas the *e* of *ze-* drops before a high vowel while turning into *i* before a nonhigh vowel.

The base forms for our six verbs are as follows:

Verb	Stem	Present Base	Past Base
joan	-oa-	doa	zihoa
etorri	-torr-	dator(r)	zetor(r)
ibili	-bil-	dabil	zebil
etzan	-tza-	datza	zetza
egon	-go-	dago	zego
izan	-iza-	daiza	zitza

Note that the form *zihoa* has undergone *h*-insertion, a phonological rule breaking up a sequence of three vowels into two syllables. Also, the second *z* of **ziza* has undergone a process of dissimilation whereby it was strengthened to the corresponding affricate, resulting in the form *zitza*.

With a third-person singular as subject, the present base itself will serve as a finite verb form. Thus the base form *doa* translates as 'he is going', 'she is going', or 'it is going'.

The sole exception is the verb *izan* 'to be'. The expected form **daiz* (from **daiza* by a minor rule called Final Vowel Truncation) was nowhere attested before the celebrated grammarian R. M. Azkue used it systematically in his *Euskal izkindea* (*Gramática eúskara*) of 1891, a work he came to regard at a later date as a youthful lapse. The later Azkue made exclusive use of *da*, the only documented form for this meaning in the whole history of Basque. This form, of course, is nothing other than the bare present tense marker and, morphologically speaking, not a form of the verb *izan* at all.

When we turn to the past tense, matters are slightly more complex. Except for Aezcoan and a few High Navarrese enclaves, all past tense forms in Basque must end in *-n*. More precisely, past tense forms are characterized by a final past tense suffix, shaped *-en* (in Biscayan and Southern Guipuzcoan *-an*) after a stem-final *i*, *o*, or *u*, and *-n* elsewhere. With consonant-final stems, *e*-epenthesis will automatically apply, so that the corresponding past tense forms will show final *-en* in all dialects.

With this in mind, we can state the following: With a third-person singular as subject, the past base followed by the past tense suffix will serve as a past tense finite verb form. Thus we expect the following six third-person past tense forms: *zihoan*, *zetorren*, *zebilen*, *zetzan*, *zegoen* (western dialect form: *zegoan*), **zitzan*. Here again the verb *izan* 'to be' constitutes the only exception.The expected form **zitzan*, even though used by Azkue in its Biscayan form *itzan* in his work *Euskal izkindea*, seems never to have existed in this meaning in any dialect of the language. Instead the western dialects, Biscayan and Guipuzcoan, make use of *zan*; the eastern dialects, including Batua, of *zen*: 'he was', 'she was', 'it was', 'there was'. The regular base form *zitza*, however, does underlie certain other past tense forms, as we will find in section 15.3.1.

To construct the third-person plural forms, we must add a pluralizer to the third-person singular. There are no less than eight different pluralizers, although only five occur with intransitive verbs. The evidence in chapter 15 suggests that the suffix *-z* is the unmarked pluralizer; yet, of our six verbs, only two take it. As illustrated in the following list, the other four select each their own pluralizer:

joan 'to go' — Pluralizer: suffix *-z*.
doaz 'they are going', *zihoazen* 'they were going'.

etorri 'to come' — Pluralizer: suffix *-z*.
datoz 'they are coming', *zetozen* 'they were coming'.
Note that the stem-final *r* elides before the pluralizer *-z*.

ibili 'to walk' — Pluralizer: suffix *-tza*.
dabiltza 'they are walking', *zebiltzan* 'they were walking'.

etzan 'to lie down' — Pluralizer: prefix *u-* (found with this verb only).
dautza 'they are lying down', *zeutzan* 'they were lying down'.

egon 'to stay' — Pluralizer: suffix *-de*, causing the weak intervocalic *g* of the preceding syllable to elide, after which the stem *-go-* ends up as *-u-*.
daude 'they are staying', *zeuden* 'they were staying'.

izan 'to be'	Pluralizer: infix *-ir-*, often replacing the stem. *dira* 'they are', *ziren* 'they were'.

Next we must see what happens when the subject of the verb is a personal pronoun. Here too the base forms provide a convenient starting point. The personal paradigm of the present tense can be described as follows: the initial consonant of the present base is replaced by that of the personal pronoun involved, which, if plural, also induces the characteristic pluralizer of the verb. As verbal morphology has remained largely unchanged since the days that *zu* had a plural reference, the pluralizer will occur with *zu* 'you' as well as with *gu* 'we' and *zuek* 'yoû' (plural). With the latter pronoun, however, an additional plural marker *-te* must be suffixed to the verb form.

In the past tense the same process applies to the past base, with the final past tense suffix added at the end. One further change differentiates the past tense even more from the present: the initial syllable of past personal forms acquires a nasal closure, by which *e* or *i* becomes *en* or *in*. This device serves to remove the homonymy that would otherwise arise between second-person forms like *zentozen* 'you were coming' and third-person plural forms like *zetozen* 'they were coming'.

Why this particular homonymy proved intolerable remains unclear. After all, some languages do tolerate ambiguities of this sort. Thus the imperfect of classical Hebrew displays systematic homonymy between the second- and third-person feminine plural forms. Even more mysterious is the availability of nasal insertion as a remedial device. My conjecture would be that it might originally represent a past tense marking on the pronoun incorporated into the finite verb, explaining thereby its absence in the third-person forms. The preceding description has made the following fact clear: each verbal paradigm consists of seven forms: one for each personal pronoun *ni*, *hi*, *gu*, *zu*, and *zuek*, as well as two third-person forms, singular and plural. Moreover, these seven forms are always distinct.

Inasmuch as this section is devoted to the broad outlines of the intransitive conjugation, some fine details of the morphology of a few individual verbs have not been mentioned. These will be commented on in the next section, where all the paradigms will be shown in full detail.

6.2.3 Intransitive Verb Paradigms

As we noted in section 6.2.2, a third-person verb form like *doa* equally serves to translate 'he is going', 'she is going', or 'it is going'. More generally, no third-person verb form in Basque shows sexual differentiation. Neither do demonstrative pronouns, nor any pronoun or anaphor in Basque whatsoever. This being so, for brevity's sake, in translating paradigms we will use only the English pronoun *he*, yet understanding thereby 'he, she, or it, as the case may be'.

At this point we also remind the reader of our glossing convention explained in section 6.1.1 regarding the distinction between *you*, *yoú*, and *yoû*.

The verb *joan* 'to go':

Etxera noa.	I am going home. (or: to the house)
Etxera hoa.	Yoú are going home.
Etxera doa.	He is going home.
Etxera goaz.	We are going home.
Etxera zoaz.	You are going home.
Etxera zoazte.	Yoû are going home.
Etxera doaz.	They are going home.
Etxera nindoan.	I was going home.
Etxera hindoan.	Yoú were going home.
Etxera zihoan.	He was going home.
Etxera gindoazen.	We were going home.
Etxera zindoazen.	You were going home.
Etxera zindoazten.	Yoû were going home.
Etxera zihoazen.	They were going home.

Observe that the *h* of *zihoan*, when following a nasal, turns into a voiced stop homorganic with the nasal. In the southern dialects, this *h* turns into *j* or drops altogether.

In unpolished Batua, instead of the forms *noa*, *doa*, *zoaz*, *zoazte*, *doaz*, one may encounter *nihoa*, *dihoa*, *zihoaz*, *zihoazte*, *dihoaz*, Batua spellings for the Guipuzcoan variant forms *nijoa*, *dijoa*, *zijoaz*, *zijoazte*, *dijoaz*.

In the past tense one may find *j* instead of *d*, again in imitation of Guipuzcoan: *ninjoan* or *nijoan* instead of *nindoan*, and so on.

J. Basterrechea (1981, I, 123) has observed that the verb *joan* is exceptional within the western accentuation system in that its finite forms follow the anormal toneme and do not admit a high tone under any circumstance.

The verb *etorri* 'to come':

Bilbotik nator.	I am coming from Bilbao.
Bilbotik hator.	Yoú are coming from Bilbao.
Bilbotik dator.	He is coming from Bilbao.
Bilbotik gatoz.	We are coming from Bilbao.
Bilbotik zatoz.	You are coming from Bilbao.
Bilbotik zatozte.	Yoû are coming from Bilbao.
Bilbotik datoz.	They are coming from Bilbao.
Bilbotik nentorren.	I was coming from Bilbao.
Bilbotik hentorren.	Yoú were coming from Bilbao.
Bilbotik zetorren.	He was coming from Bilbao.
Bilbotik gentozen.	We were coming from Bilbao.

Bilbotik zentozen. You were coming from Bilbao.
Bilbotik zentozten. Yoû were coming from Bilbao.
Bilbotik zetozen. They were coming from Bilbao.

Here, the only peculiarity is the elision of the stem-final *r* when followed by the pluralizer -*z*.

The verb *ibili* 'to walk':

Mirenekin nabil. I am walking with Mary.
Mirenekin habil. Yoú are walking with Mary.
Mirenekin dabil. He is walking with Mary.
Mirenekin gabiltza. We are walking with Mary.
Mirenekin zabiltza. You are walking with Mary.
Mirenekin zabiltzate. Yoû are walking with Mary.
Mirenekin dabiltza. They are walking with Mary.

Mirenekin nenbilen. I was walking with Mary.
Mirenekin henbilen. Yoú were walking with Mary.
Mirenekin zebilen. He was walking with Mary.
Mirenekin genbiltzan. We were walking with Mary.
Mirenekin zenbiltzan. You were walking with Mary.
Mirenekin zenbiltzaten. Yoû were walking with Mary.
Mirenekin zebiltzan. They were walking with Mary.

This paradigm is completely regular, granted the form -*tza* of the pluralizer, also found with some transitive verbs.

The verb *etzan* 'to lie down', 'to lie':

Lurrean natza. I am lying down on the ground.
Lurrean hatza. Yoú are lying down on the ground.
Lurrean datza. He is lying down on the ground.
Lurrean gautza. We are lying down on the ground.
Lurrean zautza. You are lying down on the ground.
Lurrean zautzate. Yoû are lying down on the ground.
Lurrean dautza. They are lying down on the ground.

Lurrean nentzan. I was lying down on the ground.
Lurrean hentzan. Yoú were lying down on the ground.
Lurrean zetzan. He was lying down on the ground.
Lurrean geuntzan. We were lying down on the ground.
Lurrean zeuntzan. You were lying down on the ground.
Lurrean zeuntzaten. Yoû were lying down on the ground.
Lurrean zeutzan. They were lying down on the ground.

The irregular *geuntzan* and *zeuntzan* derive from the regular forms **genutzan* and **zenutzan* through the historical rule of intervocalic *n*-elision (see *FHV*, chap. 15) followed by a later restoration of the nasal: *genutzan* > *gẽũtzan* > *geuntzan*. Similarly for *zeutzan*.

In Batua, but not, for instance, in the Souletin dialect, the literal meaning of *etzan* exemplified in the preceding list is quite obsolete and found only in the loftiest style, if at all. It is commonly employed in a figurative sense only, so that its use is restricted to the third-person forms: *Hortxe datza arazoa* 'That is just where the problem lies' (*EGLU* II, 409). The expression *lo etzan* 'to lie asleep' was still used by the Guipuzcoan author Lardizabal in 1855 (*TB* 207). Today's equivalent is *lo egon* 'to be asleep'.

The verb *egon* 'to stay', 'to be (situated)':

Etxean nago.	I am at home. (or: in the house)
Etxean hago.	Yoú are at home.
Etxean dago.	He is at home.
Etxean gaude.	We are at home.
Etxean zaude.	You are at home.
Etxean zaudete.	Yoû are at home.
Etxean daude.	They are at home.
Etxean nengoen.	I was at home.
Etxean hengoen.	Yoú were at home.
Etxean zegoen.	He was at home.
Etxean geunden.	We were at home.
Etxean zeunden.	You were at home.
Etxean zeundeten.	Yoû were at home.
Etxean zeuden.	They were at home.

The expected regular form *dagode* instead of *daude* is documented in 19th-century Labourdin (e.g., Duvoisin, *Lab.* 315).

The past tense forms *geunden* and *zeunden* must have originated from an older **genuden* and **zenuden*. Relating these to the expected **gengoden* and **zengoden* seems to require postulating an even older four-syllable form **genegoden*, **zenegoden*.

The verb *izan* 'to be':

Sendoa naiz.	I am strong. (In some dialects: healthy)
Sendoa haiz.	Yoú are strong.
Sendoa da.	He is strong.
Sendoak gara.	We are strong.
Sendoa zara.	You are strong.
Sendoak zarete.	Yoû are strong.
Sendoak dira.	They are strong.

Sendoa nintzen.	I was strong.
Sendoa hintzen.	Yoú were strong.
Sendoa zen.	He was strong.
Sendoak ginen.	We were strong.
Sendoa zinen.	You were strong.
Sendoak zineten.	Yoû were strong.
Sendoak ziren.	They were strong.

As already noted in section 6.2.2, the third-person forms *da*, *dira*, *zen*, and *ziren* were not originally part of the paradigm. The forms *naiz* and *haiz* are related to the base **daiza* through a historical rule of Final Vowel Truncation and can therefore be considered regular.

This Batua paradigm, officially accepted by the Basque Academy in 1973, reflects the Labourdin dialect, except for the latter's use of the newer forms *gare* and *zare*, which replaced the old forms *gara* and *zara*, still surviving in the Biscayan dialect. Literary Guipuzcoan employs the following forms: *naiz*, *aiz*, *da*, *gera*, *zera*, *zerate*, *dira*. In the past tense: *nintzan*, *intzan*, *zan*, *ginan*, *zinan*, *zinaten*, *ziran*.

6.3 Deictic Location Words

6.3.1 Demonstrative Adverbs

Like demonstrative pronouns (see section 9.6.1), demonstrative adverbs in Basque exhibit a three-way contrast:

First degree: *hemen* 'here', designates a location near the speaker.
Second degree: *hor* 'there', designates a location near the addressee.
Third degree: *han* 'over there', designates a location removed from both the speaker and the addressee.

These adverbs only allow locative case endings (section 3.1), no basic ones (section 2.2.1). Paradigms are as follows:

hemen: here	*hor*: there	*han*: over there
hemendik: from here	*hortik*: from there	*handik*: from over there
hona: here, hither	*horra*: there, thither	*hara*: (to) over there
honaino: up to here, hitherto	*horraino*: up to there, thitherto	*haraino*: up to over there
honantz: hitherward	*horrantz*: thitherward	*harantz*: thitherward

Note the compound expressions: *han-hemen* 'here and there'; *hara-hona* 'hither and thither', 'there and back'; *harantz-honantz* 'to and fro'.

The tendential forms *honantz* and *harantz*, when governing an elative noun phrase, express the spatial concepts 'this side of...' and 'beyond', respectively: *ibaitik honantz* 'this side of the river', *gure elizatik harantz* 'beyond our church'. With unmodified nouns, the indefinite instrumental may substitute for the elative: *mendiz honantz* 'on this side of the mountains', *mendiz harantz* 'beyond the mountains'.

The basic forms of the paradigm *hemen*, *hor*, and *han* are syntactically inessives, as shown by their being found in construction with *barrena*, *zehar*, and *gaindi* (cf. section 4.1.3):

hemen barrena (zehar, gaindi)	through here, along here, around here
hor barrena (zehar, gaindi)	through there, along there, around there
han barrena (zehar, gaindi)	through over there, along there, around there

Note also (cf. section 3.2): *hemen behera* 'down here', *hor behere* 'down there', *hemen gora* 'up here', *hor gora* 'up there', *han gora* 'up there'.

All forms in the paradigm admit the linking morpheme *-ko*, producing adnominal phrases:

hemengo eguraldia	the weather here
horko nagusia	the boss there
hango alkatea	the mayor (of) over there
mendiz honanzko jendea	the people on this side of the mountains
mendiz haranzko jendea	the people beyond the mountains

[*N.B.* Note the use of *harako* in *harako apaiz bat* 'a certain priest'.]

6.3.2 Presentatives

The allative adverbs *hona* '(to) here', *horra* '(to) there', and *hara* '(to) over there' frequently act as presentatives, rather similar to the French terms *voici* and *voilà*, that is, without the intervention of a copula. As English lacks a precise equivalent of this construction, our translations have to be only approximative:

(1) a. Hona Etxahun bera, present da zurekin. (From the song "Otxalde eta Etxahun," *Kantuz* 67)
Look, here is Etxahun himself, he is here present with you.
b. Hona Jainkoaren Bildotsa. (Jn 1:29; Lz)
Behold the Lamb of God.
c. Horra sei bertso kale-garbitzaileari ... (From the song "Zaldi baten bizitza," Bilintx, 63)
Look, six stanzas to the street-cleaner ...
d. ... eta hara zaldi zuri bat. (Rv 19:11; EAB)
... and there is (or: *was*) a white horse.

[*N.B.* In their presentative use, the meaning distinction between *hona*, *horra*, and *hara* is often blurred to the point of nonexistence. Thus in the passage cited in (1d) (from Rv

19:11), Duvoisin gives *hara*, while Uriarte has *horra* in his Biscayan and *hona* in his Guipuzcoan version.]

For reasons of rhythm and style, presentatives are often found accompanied by the corresponding inessives, to wit, *hemen*, *hor*, *han*:

(2) a. Hona hemen lapiko galanta eta pitxer bete ardo. (Mogel, *P.Ab.* 55)
Here you have a nice stew and a pitcher of wine.
b. Horra hor nire mutila. (From the song "Basatxoritxo," Arratia I, 137; cf. Jn 19:26)
There is my boy.
c. Hara han zure Jauna. (From a poem by Arrese Beitia, *Ama E.* 433)
There is your Lord.

[*N.B.* It is indicative of the blurring of the meaning distinctions already alluded to, that the phrases *hara hor* and *hara hemen* are also widespread.]

The form *hara* can be used to introduce a reply: *Hara, Jauna,...* 'Look here, sir,...'. Spoken with an exclamatory high tone on the final syllable, *Hara!* can occur by itself as an interjection meaning 'Well, there you are!', 'That's exactly it!'.

6.4 Complex Locatives

Animate noun phrases X admit the ending *-(r)enean*, which has the meaning 'at X's home':

alkatearenean at the mayor's
Pellorenean at Pete's
Andresenean at Andrew's

This ending is readily analyzable. The initial part *-(r)en* represents the genitive; which explains why personal pronouns take *-rean* instead of *-renean*:

gurean at our home
zurean at your home (but *zuenean* 'at yoûr home')

The final part of the ending *-an* is identical with the inessive suffix and can be replaced by other locative endings:

amonarenetik from Grandmother's
osabarenera to Uncle's

These morphological considerations, together with the meaning encoded by the ending as a whole, prompt us to assume the existence of a synchronic rule deleting the noun *etxe* (or a near synonym of it) in any environment where it both follows a genitive and precedes a locative. After the deletion of the understood noun, *e*-epenthesis applies where needed, even before the seemingly vocalic suffix *-an* (see section 3.2). Thus we get *noren etxean?* ⇒ *noren* + *an?* ⇒ *norenean?* 'at whose home?'. Similarly, *zure etxeraino* ⇒ *zure* + *raino* ⇒ *zureraino* 'as far as your home'. (Contrast: *zureganaino* 'as far as you'.)

Note that English too seems to have an analogous deletion rule, since the phrase *at Pete's* must be understood as *at Pete's home*.

In the provinces of Guipuzcoa and Biscay, houses often bear names of the type *Pellorenea, Andresenea, Gurenea*. In view of the fact that the shape of the inessive ending for place names is *-n* (section 3.5), these are clearly back-formations based on the inessive forms *Pellorenean, Andresenean*, and *Gurean*, similar to *Pello baita* from *Pello baitan* in the Labourdin dialect (section 3.6).

I should add that the explanation offered here for the suffixes *-(r)enean* and *-(r)enea* appears to be generally accepted. It was already expounded, though quite succinctly, by the famous Basque grammarian R. M. de Azkue in his *Morfología vasca* (1923–1925, I, sec. 28).

6.5 The Period Suffix *-te*

The suffix *-te* combines with some nouns X and a few adjectives Y to form nouns with the meaning 'a prolonged period characterized by X or Y-ness'.

This suffix, now no longer productive, differs slightly in meaning with the productive compounds of the noun *aldi* 'time', 'turn' discussed in chapter 20, which may denote a period of any length, including brief ones denoted by such English terms as "bout" or "fit."

The following list of examples is nearly exhaustive:

agor	sterile, arid	agorte	sterile period, drought
antzina	former times	antzinate	olden times, antiquity
bake	peace	bakete	period of peace, peacetime
berde	green, raw, rough	berdate	period of rough weather
bero	hot, warm	berote	hot spell, heat wave
busti	wet	bustite	wet season, rain period
ekaitz	storm	ekaizte	stormy season, stormy period
elur	snow	elurte	snow season, snowfall
eskas	scanty, scarce	eskaste	time of scarcity, dearth
euri	rain	eurite	rain period, rainy season
frantses	Frenchman, French	frantseste	Napoleonic war
gaitz	evil, harm, ailment	gaitzete	time of calamity, plague
gerla	war	gerlate	time of war, lengthy war
gerra	war	gerrate	time of war, lengthy war
gose	hunger	gosete	famine

guda	battle, war	gudate	campaign, time of war, war
haize	wind	haizete	windy season, gale
harri	stone, hailstone	harrite	hail season, hail spell
hotz	cold	hozte	cold spell, cold wave, cold season
idor	arid, barren	idorte	penury, drought
izotz	frost, ice	izozte	frost season, frost
izurri	epidemic, plague	izurrite	pestilence, plague
lehor	dry	lehorte	drought
min	pain	minte	pestilence
negu	winter	negute	winter season, long winter
su	fire	sute	conflagration, riot, commotion
uda	summer	udate	summer season, long summer
ur	water	urte	high water, flood
urri	scarce, rare	urrite	time of scarcity, dearth

6.6 A Suffix Denoting Origin: *-tar*

Despite some metaphoric extensions not altogether easy to classify, the central meaning of the nominal suffix *-tar* still remains 'originating from', 'native of'. It is, accordingly, fully productive with geographic names, especially those of cities, districts, provinces, and countries: *paristar* 'Parisian', *londrestar* 'Londoner', *bizkaitar* 'Biscayan', *txinatar* 'Chinese'.

Nouns derived with this suffix freely combine with other animate nouns, acting either as a first or as a second component of a bipartite compound:

erromatar soldadua the Roman soldier
soldadu erromatarra the Roman soldier

Proper names, however, never follow *-tar* forms. Only the following order is possible:

Miren bilbotarra the Mary (originally) from Bilbao

Given the meaning of the suffix *-tar*, inanimate noun phrases as a rule do not take *-tar* forms as modifiers. Adnominal forms are used instead:

Erromako ohitura the Roman custom

[*N.B.* Standard Basque tends to follow Spanish orthographic conventions in not capitalizing forms derived from geographic names (except with the linking morpheme -*ko*); compare Spanish *vizcaíno* from *Vizcaya*.]

When the suffix *-tar* follows a stem ending in a consonant, the regular phonological rules from section 1.2.6 apply as expected: affricates simplify to sibilants before *-tar* (sandhi rule 3), and *-tar* itself turns into *-dar* after *n* or *l* (sandhi rule 6), except in the case of Souletin place names, as in the following examples:

Zarautz	Zarauz	zarauztar	native of Zarauz
Baztan	Baztan	baztandar	native of Baztan, Baztanese
Brasil	Brazil	brasildar	native of Brazil, Brazilian
Madril	Madrid	madrildar	native of Madrid
Portugal	Portugal	portugaldar	Portuguese

The suffix *-tar* has as its allomorphs *-ar* and *-iar*. These forms are restricted to geographic names, the variant *-iar*, moreover, being strictly limited to names of countries.

In order to specify the precise distribution of these allomorphs, it is convenient to separate place names situated inside the Basque Country from those situated elsewhere. For the latter, the distribution can be stated with relative ease:

Allomorphy Rule The allomorph *-tar* occurs in combination with

1. Consonant-final names.
2. Trisyllabic names ending in a diphthong or a sequence of two vowels not ending in *a*.
3. All names shorter than three syllables.

All other names, that is, trisyllabic names ending in a single vowel or vowel + *a*, as well as all longer names ending in a vowel, take *-ar*, before which form stem-final *a* or *o* is dropped.

Examples with *-tar*:

Erroma	Rome	erromatar	Roman
Kuba	Cuba	kubatar	Cuban
Malta	Malta	maltar	Maltese (from **maltatar* by haplology)
Peru	Peru	perutar	Peruvian
Portugal	Portugal	portugaldar	Portuguese
Txile	Chile	txiletar	Chilean
Txina	China	txinatar	Chinese

[*N.B.* Apparently, the prothetic vowel *e-* of *Erroma* is not counted as a syllable. The form *batikandar* 'man from the Vatican' results from an application of the Major Apocope Rule (section 3.8.1) to the stem *Batikano* of *Batikanoa* 'the Vatican'.]

Examples with *-ar*:

Amerika	America	amerikar	American (also: *amerikano*)
Errusia	Russia	errusiar	Russian
Espainia	Spain	espainiar	Spaniard
Frantzia	France	frantziar	Frenchman (also: *frantses*)
Holanda	Holland	holandar	Dutchman
Japonia	Japan	japoniar	Japanese
Mexiko	Mexico	mexikar	Mexican
Polonia	Poland	poloniar	Pole

Suedia	Sweden	suediar	Swede
Suitza	Switzerland	suitzar	Swiss
Turkia	Turkey	turkiar	Turk

Contemporary usage in newspapers and television shows the Allomorphy Rule to be overruled by a semantic rule: Countries situated in North Africa or Asia, except for the Pacific and the Far East, take the suffix *-iar* regardless of phonological form.

Examples with *-iar*:

Afghanistan	Afghanistan	afghaniar	Afghan
Egipto	Egypt	egiptiar	Egyptian
Iran	Iran	iraniar	Iranian
Irak	Iraq	irakiar	Iraqi
Israel	Israel	israeliar	Israeli (also: *israeldar*)
Libano	Lebanon	libaniar	Lebanese
Laos	Laos	laosiar	Laotian
Maroko	Morocco	marokiar	Moroccan
Nepal	Nepal	nepaliar	Nepalese
Pakistan	Pakistan	pakistaniar	Pakistani
Sudan	Sudan	sudaniar	Sudanese
Txad	Chad	txadiar	Chadian
Yemen	Yemen	yemeniar	Yemenite

(Data from X. Mendiguren, "*Estatu Izenak.*" *Mendiguren*, however, writes *Iraqiar*, *Marokkiar*, *Egyptiar*.)

As we now turn to place names of the Basque Country itself, the Allomorphy Rule given remains quite useful as a general guideline. But its predictions occasionally fail as a result of accidents of linguistic history and dialectal variation, as the form utilized by the population in or near the locality in question has understandably been chosen for the standard language.

For example, consider two phonologically similar names, both ending in the article *-a*: *Mañaria* and *Mallabia*, denoting two Biscayan districts very near to each other. The former is regular, *mañariar*, but the latter irregular, *mallabitar*. Other instances of unexpected *-tar* are

Elantxobe	Elanchove	elantxobetar	native of Elanchove
Hiriburu	St. Pierre d'Irube	hiriburutar	native of St. Pierre d'Irube
Mondragoe	Mondragon	mondragoetar	native of Mondragon
Portugalete	Portugalete	portugaletetar	native of Portugalete

A final *-e*, often, but not always, epenthetical in origin (*FHV* 6.5), will be dropped before *-tar*, unless preceded by a plosive:

Donibane	St. Jean	donibandar	native of St. Jean
Mugerre	Mouguerre	mugertar	native of Mouguerre
Uztaritze	Ustaritz	uztariztar	native of Ustaritz

[*N.B.* Names ending in *-de* drop their final *e* and take *-ar*:

Aldude	the Aldudes	aldudar	native of the Aldudes
Garde	Garde	gardar	native of Garde]

The main deviation from the Allomorphy Rule found in Basque place names consists in bisyllabic names taking *-ar* instead of *-tar*.

True enough, a fair number of bisyllabic names ending in a vowel follow the rule in taking the form *-tar*, such as *Axpe*, *Bera* (*Vera de Bidasoa*), *Ea*, *Erbi*, *Erro*, *Getxo* (*Guecho*), *Itza* (*Iza*), *Jugo*, *Jutsi* (*Juxue*), *Latse*, *Murga*, *Oro*, *Sara* (*Sare*), *Uba*.

Yet many more take the form *-ar*, contrary to the rule. Examples include *Aia* (*Aya*), *Alli*, *Allo*, *Burgi* (*Burgui*), *Busto* (*El Busto*), *Deba* (*Deva*), *Dima*, *Elo* (*Monreal*), *Esa* (*Yesa*), *Fika* (*Fica*), *Intza* (*Inza*), *Kanbo* (*Cambo*), *Lana*, *Lasa* (*Lasse*), *Lerga*, *Leza*, *Lezo*, *Luxo* (*Lujo*), *Oko* (*Oco*), *Oltza* (*Olza*), *Sesma*, *Zalla*, *Zare* (*Sada de Sangüesa*), *Zaro* (*Çaro*), *Zollo* (*Sojo*), *Zuia* (*Zuya*). (Data from J. L. Lizundia and H. Knörr 1976, and K. Mitxelena 1978.)

The suffix *-tar* is not restricted to geographic names. In fact, it may combine with any noun that can be thought of as defining a location. Such common nouns do not induce allomorphy: the form *-ar* does not appear. We do find, of course, the phonologically conditioned variant *-dar*, appearing after *n* and *l*.

The most common examples are

atzerri	foreign country	atzerritar	foreigner
baserri	farmhouse	baserritar	farmer
baso	wilderness, woods	basotar	forest dweller, savage
eremu	desert	eremutar	desert dweller, hermit
hego	south wind, south	hegotar	southerner
herri	village, township	herritar	inhabitant, native
hiri	city	hiritar	city dweller
ifernu	hell	ifernutar	hellish being, devil
ipar	north wind, north	ipartar	northerner
itsaso	sea	itsastar	seafarer, coastlander
kale	street	kaletar	nonfarmer
kanpo	outside	kanpotar	outsider, foreigner
lur	earth, ground	lurtar	terrestrial being
mendebal	west wind, west	mendebaldar	westerner, occidental
mendi	mountain	menditar	mountain dweller
muga	border	mugatar	border resident

mundu	world	mundutar	earthling
zelai	plain, prairie	zelaitar	plain dweller
zeru	heaven	zerutar	celestial being

Furthermore, the suffix *-tar* can be joined to family names. The resulting form may refer either to the whole clan of that name or just to the family unit:

Mogeldarrak	the Moguels
Gabikagogeaskoetxeatarrak	the Gavicagogeascoecheas

Use of *-tar* when stating one's full name, for example, *Magunagoikoetxea-tar Peru*, a custom very much in vogue in certain circles influenced by Sabino de Arana y Goiri early last century, has now been abandoned in favor of the general European fashion: *Peru Magunagoikoetxea*.

The same suffix *-tar* also serves to define religious orders:

beneditar	Benedictine
dominikar	Dominican
frantziskotar	Franciscan
karmeldar	Carmelite
pasiotar	Passionist

But

jesulagun Jesuit (also *jesuita*)

To conclude this section, we wish to draw attention to a non–locally oriented, more or less figurative, use of *-tar*. Of the following examples, all part of the standard language, some are quite old (*goiztar*, Garibay, from 1591; *zuretar*, Oihenarte, from 1657), others of more recent vintage:

afari	supper	afaldar	supper guest
apaiz	priest	apaiztar	supporter of the clergy, clerical
bazkari	lunch	bazkaldar	luncheon guest
berandu	late	berandutar	latecomer, late bloomer
eliza	church	eliztar	parishioner, pious person
eskuin	right-hand side	eskuindar	rightist, right-winger
gau	night	gautar	night owl, nocturnal being
goi	height	goitar	highlander, lofty person
goiz	early	goiztar	early bird, precocious person
gu	we, us	gutar	supporter of our clan or party
gure	our	guretar	supporter of our clan or party
mahai	table	mahaitar	table guest
zure	your	zuretar	fan of yours, supporter of your party
zuen	yoûr	zuentar	supporter of yoûr party

[*N.B.* While the normal term for 'rightist' remains *eskuindar*, the corresponding form for 'leftist', *ezkertar* from *ezker* 'left-hand side', although attested, has been discarded in favor of *ezkertiar*, which makes use of the suffix *-tiar* discussed in section 6.7.]

[*N.B.* At the time of writing this section, I had not as yet had access to Artiagoitia 2002; a perusal of this insightful study would have led to substantial improvements.]

6.7 The Propensity Suffix *-tiar*

Stemming from the northern dialects, the suffix *-tiar* combines with a few nouns, adjectives, and adverbs to create human nouns indicating a disposition to whatever is expressed by the base term. Its meaning is thus very similar to that of the suffix *-tar* when used in a figurative way. The yield of the suffix *-tiar* in the predominantly southern-oriented standard language is rather low. Of the possible examples that follow, only *ezkertiar* 'leftist' occurs with some frequency in everyday speech:

bake	peace	baketiar	pacifist, peace lover
berant	late (also *berandu*)	berantiar	latecomer, late bloomer
eliza	church	elizatiar	parishioner, pious person
errege	king	erregetiar	royalist
etxe	house	etxetiar	domestic, tenant farmer
ezker	left-hand side	ezkertiar	leftist, left-winger
gero	later	gerotiar	procrastinator
goiz	early	goiztiar	early bird, precocious person
Jainkoa	God	jainkotiar	devout person

6.8 Vocabulary

aldi	turn, time
aldiz	in turn, on the contrary, however
amerikar	American
bart	last night
baserritar	farmer
benetan	really, truly, truthfully
beraz	thus, so, therefore
bizkaitar	Biscayan
donostiar	native of San Sebastian
Euskal Herria	the Basque Country
gipuzkoar	Guipuzcoan
herenegun	(on) the day before yesterday
herrixka	hamlet

kilometro	kilometer
soldadu	soldier

6.9 Exercises

6.9.1 Translate into English

1. Horra hor Euskal Herriko mendi maiteak!
2. Zergatik dator hona zure osaba donostiarra?
3. Gure alaba bizkaitar apaiz gazte batekin kalean dabil.
4. Hemendik itsasoraino zenbat kilometro daude?
5. Hara, neskatxa, inor ere ez dabil hemen barrena.
6. Herenegun zure semeen artetik nor zegoen Mirenenean?
7. Atzo neure etxera nindoan, ez zurera.
8. Zuen herriko eliza zaharreko arratoi haundiak orain gure etxeetaraino datoz.
9. Beraz, zure amerikar adiskidea orain etxe zurian dago.
10. Hemengo nagusiaren behi beltzak errotarantz doaz soldadu gorriekin.
11. Bart hiru mutil eder zure atzetik zebiltzan.
12. Orduan hiri itsusi batean nengoen, orain, aldiz, herrixka benetan polit batean nago.

6.9.2 Translate into Basque

1. Who am I?
2. Where am I?
3. Where were many farmers going yesterday?
4. I am going now to my father's.
5. When are the Altunas coming to our place?
6. Why is nobody coming here today? (Translate: ... not... anybody...)
7. The day before yesterday we were walking to Guernica with a Biscayan friend.
8. Whose books are lying on the small table there?
9. Your father and my mother are standing there behind the front door. (Translate: ... the door in front...)
10. Look, here is a Guipuzcoan priest and a Biscayan witch.
11. The witch is walking over the river toward her sister.
12. The girls over here are astonishing, those over there, however, really frightful.

7 Periphrastic Conjugation of Intransitive Verbs

7.1 Inventory of Intransitive Verbs

7.1.1 Definitions of Intransitivity

In section 6.2, where we had a mere handful of verbs to discuss, the concept of intransitivity was taken for granted. It is now time to point out that there are at least three different notions of intransitivity to reckon with: logical intransitivity, syntactic intransitivity, and morphological intransitivity.

Logical intransitivity is based solely on argument structure: a verb is logically intransitive if and only if it represents a unitary predicate, that is, a predicate admitting no more than a single argument.

The much weaker notion of syntactic intransitivity is tied in with case considerations: a verb is syntactically intransitive if and only if its internal (i.e., nonsubject) arguments are all realized as oblique noun phrases, that is, noun phrases that do not acquire their case from the verb.

By virtue of these definitions, all logically intransitive verbs are at the same time syntactically intransitive, but the converse is unlikely to hold in any human language.

Morphological intransitivity can be defined only in languages where a morphological property within the verbal system correlates with syntactic intransitivity.

Thus in Basque a verb will be termed morphologically intransitive if and only if its basic periphrastic conjugation makes use of the auxiliary verb *izan* 'to be'. Since a perfect correlation between syntactic and morphological intransitivity would render the latter notion next to pointless, we may mention that, although morphological intransitivity empirically entails syntactic intransitivity in Basque, the reverse is by no means the case. As we will find in section 12.2.1, there are even logically intransitive verbs that are not morphologically intransitive.

In this book the term "intransitive," if left unmodified, will stand for morphologically intransitive. The same is true for "transitive," which we take to be the negation of intransitive.

Our discussion then leads up to the following conclusion: In Basque, any intransitive verb is syntactically intransitive, whereas a transitive verb need not be syntactically transitive.

7.1.2 Strictly Intransitive Verbs

The most striking fact about intransitive verbs in Basque is that there are so few of them. Fewer than 20 verbs are limited to intransitive use. Such strictly intransitive verbs can be divided into three groups:

1. Verbs of motion or state

abiatu	to set out, to depart
egon	to be situated, to stay
erori	to fall
etorri	to come
ibili	to walk
igan	to ascend
irten	to come out
jaiki	to get up, to rise
jausi	to fall

2. Verbs of appearance and disappearance

desagertu	to disappear
gertatu	to happen
jaio	to be born

Note that the subject arguments of the verbs under 1 and 2 are semantically themes, so that we are dealing with unaccusative verbs in the sense of Pullum (1988) and Perlmutter (1978).

3. Miscellaneous verbs where the subject argument appears to be an agent rather than a theme—that is, unergative verbs in the sense of Pullum and Perlmutter:

aritu	to be occupied (with objects in the inessive: *lanean aritu* 'to be working', or in the instrumental: *ijitoez aritu* 'to discuss gypsies')
atrebitu	to dare
ausartu	to dare
baliatu	to utilize (requiring an object in the instrumental)

In older Basque the number of such verbs may have been even smaller, as several of the now strictly intransitive verbs formerly used to allow transitive uses:

ausartu	to encourage
etorri	to bring

ibili	to use
joan	to take away (still so used in the northern dialects)

7.1.3 Semi-intransitive Verbs

The great majority of verbs in Basque admit both transitive and intransitive uses; that is, they admit both the intransitive auxiliary *izan* 'to be' and the transitive auxiliary **edun* 'to have'.

For many such verbs the intransitive construction depicts a change of state or position of the theme without regard to a possible agent responsible for the change. This constitutes the inchoative, or anticausative, use of the verb, clearly an instance of an unaccusative structure. The transitive use of the verb then denotes the same action, but, in addition, imputes it to the intervention of an agent, expressed as the grammatical subject of the verb in a way to be clarified in chapter 9.

For quite a few of these verbs the intransitive use seems so basic and common as to foster the impression that it represents in some way the unmarked option. These we might assume to be listed in the lexicon as intransitive, yet allowing a zero causative affix to account for the transitive use.

I will henceforth call such verbs semi-intransitive. True enough, in the absence of operational criteria, our attempted definition remains sorely unsatisfactory. Yet banishing these verbs for that reason would exclude from the discussion most of the verbs traditionally labeled intransitive.

Although exhaustive listing is clearly out of the question, we can classify the semi-intransitive verbs into the following five groups:

1. Verbs of motion or state

atera	to go out(doors)
bihurtu	to go back, to become
eseri	to sit down
etzan	to lie down
gelditu	to stop, to remain
geratu	to remain
heldu	to arrive
igaro	to pass by
igo	to go up
iritsi	to arrive
itzuli	to go back
jaitsi	to go down
jauzi	to jump
sartu	to go in

2. Verbs of appearance and disappearance

agertu	to appear
esnatu	to wake up
hil	to die
sortu	to arise

3. Verbs of emotion

harritu	to be surprised
haserretu	to get angry
ikaratu	to tremble with fear
izutu	to be frightened
jostatu	to have fun
lotsatu	to be ashamed
nazkatu	to be disgusted
poztu	to be glad

4. Aspectual verbs

amaitu	to be completed
bukatu	to end
hasi	to begin

5. Miscellaneous verbs where the subject argument appears to be an agent rather than a patient or theme—unergative verbs in the sense of Pullum and Perlmutter:

ezkondu	to get married
mintzatu	to talk, to speak
solastatu	to converse

As for the verb *izan* 'to be', although its finite forms are all intransitive, it must count as semi-intransitive in the western dialects (including Batua) because its nonfinite forms allow a transitive use, namely, 'to have'. In the eastern dialects, however, *izan* is strictly intransitive, as there the meaning of 'to have' is always expressed by another verb: *ukan*.

Apart from this rather special instance, the meaning of the transitive use of a semi-intransitive is quite transparent: direct causation of the intransitive meaning. See further section 12.4 for a more elaborate discussion of these matters.

It is not just strictly intransitive verbs that are rare in Basque. Even when all semi-intransitives are taken into account, the total set of intransitives is still much less numerous than the corresponding set in English or French.

One reason is that a substantial subgroup of intransitive verbs present in many languages is not found in Basque. There are but few verbs denoting bodily activities of the type 'to sleep', 'to laugh', 'to cry', 'to cough'. Acts of this kind are expressed instead by a transitive construction consisting of the verb *egin* ('to make' or 'to do') together with an object noun in the indefinite form: *lo egin* 'to sleep', *barre egin* 'to laugh', *negar egin* 'to cry', *eztul egin* 'to cough'. Acts of communication are often expressed the same way: *hitz egin* 'to speak', *hots egin* 'to call', *oihu egin* 'to shout', *uko egin* 'to deny'.

In fact, many single-agent verbs—that is, unergative rather than unaccusative verbs—are rendered by the transitive *egin* pattern in Basque: *barau egin* 'to fast', *lan egin* 'to work', *piper egin* 'to play hooky', *zotz egin* 'to draw lots'. See sections 13.3ff. for a fuller discussion of this syntactic pattern.

7.1.4 Bibliographical Comments

Nearly all intransitive verbs in Basque are unaccusative, although, as we have noted, some exceptions do exist, for example, *ausartu* 'to dare', *baliatu* 'to make use of', *mintzatu* 'to speak'. This intriguing fact coupled with the language's ergative system of case marking (to be explained in section 9.2.1) has given rise to some interesting theoretical speculation. The clearest presentation of these matters is found in the work of Beth C. Levin, who first noticed the overwhelming prevalence of unaccusative verbs in Basque, a detail that had hitherto escaped the attention of native grammarians. The main references are Levin 1983a, 1983b, 1989, and Levin and Rappaport Hovav 1995.

7.2 Participles and Other Nonfinite Verb Forms

Note that sections 7.2 and 7.3 apply to all verbs, transitive and intransitive.

7.2.1 The Perfect Participle

The perfect participle, the citation form of the verb, is adjectival in nature; witness such examples as *neska eroria* 'the fallen maiden', *ipuin gertatu bat* 'a tale that happened'.

With few exceptions, perfect participles carry one of the two perfect participle suffixes: *-i* or *-tu*, the latter turning into *-du* after *n* or *l*. No difference in meaning can be detected between these two. To all appearances, the *-i* suffix is the more ancient one, whereas the *-tu* suffix is commonly assumed to be of Latin ancestry. While the former has long ceased to be productive, the latter is still very much so, as section 7.4 will amply demonstrate.

Any verb-final segment *tu* or *du* invariably embodies the perfect participle suffix. The same applies to a verb-final *i*, unless it is preceded by a plosive, in which case the vowel belongs to the verb as such—at least in Batua, though not necessarily in Souletin.

7.2.2 The Radical and Its Uses

Not bearing tense or aspect markers, the radical is the shortest nonfinite form of the verb, and it consists of the perfect participle stripped of its suffix. Thus the radicals of the verbs *egon*, *eseri*, *gertatu*, *heldu*, *hil*, *ibili*, and *jaiki* are *egon*, *eser*, *gerta*, *hel*, *hil*, *ibil*, and *jaiki*, respectively.

The radical plays no part in the indicative mood. Rather, it is the form taken by the main verb in the periphrastic conjugations belonging to the imperative, subjunctive, and potential moods. The radical also appears in certain nonfinite clauses, namely, those based on a wh-complementizer: *Nor honaino etor?* 'Who would come all the way here?', *Zergatík herrira jaits?* 'Why go down to the village?'.

Furthermore, the radical occurs in stage directions (cf. *EGLU* II, 27), indubitably an instance of an elliptic subjunctive, the ordinary tensed subjunctive also being found in that function.

Both the Guipuzcoan and the Biscayan dialects have lost this radical form. Speakers of these dialects substitute the perfect participle, often even when intending to apply the standards of Batua. Written Batua, however, mostly observes the distinction between the two forms, which is still very much alive in the eastern and especially the northern dialects.

7.2.3 The Verbal Noun: Form and Function

The verbal noun results from adding the nominalizer *-tze* to the radical, except with verbs ending in *n*, which receive the suffix *-te*, eliding the nasal in the process. A small number of verbs borrowed from the northern dialects take *-ite* instead of *-te*: *igan* 'to ascend', *iragan* (and *igaran*) 'to pass', *ukan* 'to have'. Thus the verbal nouns of *egon*, *ibili*, *igan*, *igo*, and *jaiki* are *egote*, *ibiltze*, *igaite*, *igotze*, and *jaikitze*.

With radicals ending in a sibilant or affricate a sandhi rule will operate turning the initial affricate *tz* of *-tze* into *t*. Moreover, according to sandhi rule 3 of section 1.2.6, an affricate immediately preceding this plosive simplifies to the corresponding sibilant. Hence, the verbal nouns of *hasi* 'to begin', *jaitsi* 'to go down', and *jauzi* 'to jump' come out as *haste*, *jaiste*, and *jauzte*.

The verb *etsi* 'to give up' yields regular *este* in compounds, but *etsitze* otherwise. The allomorphic distribution of *-te* versus *-tze* in Batua reflects that of the central dialects, which seem to have expanded the use of *-tze* at the expense of *-te*. Both Biscayan and Souletin show *erorte, ibilte* instead of *erortze, ibiltze*.

Historically, I would assume with Azkue that the nominalizer was initially identical with the period suffix *-te* discussed in section 6.5, added directly onto the perfect participle, not the radical. If so, the allomorph *-tze* can be explained as a phonetic development of earlier *-tute*. (Cf. Azkue 1923–1925, 522, and pace Michelena in *FHV*, 18.2, p. 346.)

Firmly established as it is, the term "verbal noun," due to canon Inchauspe (1858), is actually a dangerous misnomer. What is nominalized is not the verb but rather the whole clause containing it. As an illustration, consider

(1) Ez da ona gizona bakarrik egotea.
   It is not good for a man to stay alone.

The grammatical subject of example (1) is the nominalized clause *gizona bakarrik egotea* 'for a man to stay alone'. The form *egotea* 'staying' by itself is not a constituent at all here, let alone a noun phrase, as can be seen from the following formula:

$[_{NP}\ [_{S}\ Z \ldots V]$ *-tze*] *-a*

The contrast between examples (2a) and (2b) is then readily explained:

(2) a. Zu hemen ibiltzea ona da.
It is good that you walk here.
b. Zure hemengo ibilera ona da.
Your walking here is good.

The absolutive (i.e., nominative) form *zu* as well as the bare adverb *hemen* in (2a) are licensed by the verb radical *ibil* governing them. But in (2b) the verb radical *ibil*, hidden as it is inside the deverbal noun *ibilera*, is no longer able to govern anything, so that *zu* and *hemen* can only survive as adjuncts to this noun, and hence must be in the genitive and adnominal forms, respectively. (The noun-forming suffix *-era* with the basic meaning 'manner' will be discussed in section 26.9.2.)

Since they are noun phrases, nominalized clauses accept most of the case endings introduced in chapters 2 and 3, except, for semantic reasons, benefactive *-(r)entzat* 'for' and tendential *-rantz* 'toward' (cf. *EGLU* II, 98). A few examples will illustrate the point: *asko ibiltzeaz* 'by walking a lot'; *hemen ibiltzean* 'in walking here'; *mina beti ibiltzetik dator* 'the pain comes from always walking'; *mendian ibiltzera goaz* 'we are going to walk in the mountains', a construction taken up again in section 16.5.6.

In the same way as inessive noun phrases (see section 5.2.1), nominalized clauses in the inessive case may underlie adnominals: *gaur hemen ibiltzeko poz handia* 'the great joy of walking here today'; *ongi hiltzeko bidea* 'the way (method) of dying well'.

It is worth noting that the adnominal form of a nominalized clause serves as a purpose clause when used without any accompanying noun phrase: *hemen ibiltzeko* 'in order to walk here', *ongi hiltzeko* 'in order to die well', *ona izateko* 'in order to be good'. As the corresponding interrogative is *zertarako* 'what for', such adnominals can be argued to be based on the allative form of the verbal noun, with obligatory deletion of the allative case ending (see section 5.2.3), a conclusion also acceptable on semantic grounds.

The nominalized clause is often used to describe a fact; incidentally, Basque has no native term for this concept: *Pello atzo zubitik ibaira erortzea* 'the fact that Pete fell off the bridge into the river yesterday'. This factive interpretation, however, is by no means the only one. Indeed, whereas *zu ibiltzea* is frequently factive, *zure ibiltzea* 'your walking' most often refers to a manner of walking. Furthermore, the nominalized clause also acts as a nonfinite complement to a variety of nonfactive verbs, such as *debekatu* 'to forbid', *erabaki* 'to decide', *ahaztu* 'to forget'.

7.2.4 The Imperfect Participle

The imperfect participle consists of the verbal noun combined with a suffix *-n*, most likely to be identified with the original shape of the inessive case ending before intercalation of *(g)a* or *(g)an* changed it to *-an*. As we saw in section 3.5, place names still require the form *-n*. In this connection it is interesting to observe that in the Biscayan dialect of Ceánuri it is the modern inessive ending *-an* that serves as the imperfect participle suffix (*FHV* 5.2, n. 5, p. 111). Furthermore, their use as gerunds may also suggest that imperfect participles are in fact inessive phrases.

As will be apparent from section 7.3.1, the role that the imperfect participle plays within the periphrastic verb system of Basque is comparable—but by no means identical (cf. section 7.3.2, item 5)—to that played by the present participle within the English verbal system. Yet this partial analogy should not mislead the reader into ascribing to the Basque participle all, or even most, of the syntactic behavior of its English counterpart. Inasmuch as the Basque form has inessive status, its character is strictly adverbial. Thus, unlike the English present participle, the Basque imperfect participle form never occurs in a nominal or adjectival function. Accordingly, English phrases like "the coming week" must be rendered by means of a relative clause: *datorren astea* (cf. chapter 19).

7.2.5 The Future Participle

The stylistically unmarked form of the future participle in Batua consists of the verb followed by a suffix *-ko*, whose *k* turns into *g* after *n* but not after *l*. Thus: *etorriko*, *gertatuko*, *hilko*, *joango*.

In the stylistically marked form, a suffix *-(r)en* (i.e., *-ren* after a vowel, *-en* after a consonant) appears instead of *-ko*: *etorriren*, *gertaturen*, *hilen*, *joanen*. The *ko* form and the *-(r)en* form are entirely synonymous, but in the spoken language the latter is restricted to the eastern dialects and therefore less commonly used in Batua.

Although in the absence of historical evidence the genesis of these forms remains unclear in detail, the coincidence of the suffixes with the adnominal and the genitive endings can hardly be an accident.

7.3 The Indicative Mood

The Basque verbal paradigm accommodates five moods: indicative, conditional, subjunctive, imperative, and potential. Our discussion here will be confined to the indicative, leaving the other moods for later chapters: 17, 21, 22, and 24.

7.3.1 The Array of Indicative Tenses

The periphrastic tenses of the indicative mood consist of combinations of a participle of the main verb with a conjugated auxiliary verb, which, for intransitive verbs, is always *izan* 'to be'. Using an imperfect participle yields an imperfect tense; selecting a perfect participle produces a perfect tense; while a future participle will give rise to a future tense.

The auxiliary used will be either present or past, according to the time frame set by the utterance or its context.

As a result, we are faced with a total of six major tenses:

1. The present imperfect: Imperfect participle + present tense auxiliary

Ibaira erortzen da.	He is falling into the river.
Seietan jaikitzen zara.	You are getting up at six o' clock.
Etxean gelditzen naiz.	I am staying home.

2. The past imperfect: Imperfect participle + past tense auxiliary

Ibaira erortzen zen.	He was falling into the river.
Seietan jaikitzen zinen.	You were getting up at six o' clock.
Etxean gelditzen nintzen.	I was staying home.

3. The present perfect: Perfect participle + present tense auxiliary

Ibaira erori da.	He has fallen into the river.
Seietan jaiki zara.	You have gotten up at six o' clock.
Etxean gelditu naiz.	I have stayed home.

4. The past perfect: Perfect participle + past tense auxiliary

Ibaira erori zen.	He fell into the river.
Seietan jaiki zinen.	You got up at six o' clock.
Etxean gelditu nintzen.	I stayed home.

5. The (present) future: Future participle + present tense auxiliary

Ibaira eroriko da.	He will fall into the river.
Seietan jaikiko zara.	You will get up at six o' clock.
Etxean geldituko naiz.	I will stay home.

6. The past future: Future participle + past tense auxiliary

Ibaira eroriko zen.	He was going to fall into the river.
Seietan jaikiko zinen.	You were going to get up at six o'clock.
Etxean geldituko nintzen.	I was going to stay home.

[*N.B.* As will be obvious from section 7.3.2, the English translations cited here are only makeshift, offering one possibility among often equally plausible alternatives.]

7.3.2 Use of the Tenses

1. The tense used to convey timeless truths is the simple present if existent, otherwise the present imperfect:

(3) a. Berri txarra korrika dabil.
Bad news travels fast. (Lit. "walks runningly")

b. Gatza uretan urtzen da.
   Salt dissolves in water.

2. The present tenses occur when the time frame of the utterance (sometimes expressed by an overt time adverbial, but often merely implicit in the speaker's mind) includes the present moment; otherwise, a past tense will appear.

Hence, certain time adverbials, such as *orain* 'now', *gaur* 'today', *egun* 'today', and *aurten* 'this year', require a present tense in the clause, whereas certain others, such as *atzo* 'yesterday', *herenegun* 'the day before yesterday', *iaz* or *igaz* 'last year', *behinola* 'at one time', and *aspaldi* 'long ago', call for a past tense. Note, however, that *aspaldian* and *aspalditik*, both meaning 'for a long time', usually take the present tense.

A seeming paradox confirms this approach to tense assignment: Mary's birth, described in (4a) by means of the past perfect, is likely to have occurred long after Gloria's, stated in the present perfect, brought on by the use of the time adverb *aurten* in (4b):

(4) a. Miren atzo jaio zen.
    Mary was born yesterday.
  b. Aintzane aurten jaio da.
    Gloria was born this year.

The notion "relevance for the current moment," often mentioned in discussions of perfect tenses, fails to discriminate between (4a) and (4b), as both births may very well be equally relevant to the present.

One adverb, *bart* 'last night' behaves somewhat specially, as the authors of *EGLU* (cf. I, part 3: 2.2.2.2) noticed. The English sentence 'You came late last night' is translated, at least into the central dialects, in two different ways depending on the time of arrival:

If before midnight:

(5) a. Bart berandu etorri zinen.

If after midnight:

(5) b. Bart berandu etorri zara.

Therefore, *bart* is like *goizean* 'in the morning' in its failure to adequately pin down the time reference of the utterance. Compare the following:

(6) a. Goizean berandu etorri zinen.
    You came late that morning.
  b. Goizean berandu etorri zara.
    You came late this morning.

Obviously, it is not the adverb *bart* or *goizean* that determines the tense of these utterances, but rather the understanding of the event as having occurred today or earlier than today. In other words, just in case the utterance itself lacks a time adverbial precise enough to determine the choice of tense, convention steps in and constrains the speaker to take a stand on whether or not 'today' will be an appropriate time frame.

Note that no claim is put forward here to the effect that *bart* and *goizean* are syntactically similar. They are indeed quite different. As a shifter, *bart* belongs to the deictic system and therefore cannot co-occur with adverbs like *atzo* and *gaur*, whereas *goizean*, not being deictic, does allow them: *atzo goizean* 'yesterday morning', *gaur goizean* 'this morning'. Granted, however, that tense selection has a conceptual rather than a syntactic basis, the distributional disparity between *bart* and *goizean* appears wholly irrelevant.

To round off this topic, I should add that a sequence-of-tenses rule functions in Basque much in the same way as it does in Spanish. (See, e.g., Comrie 1985, 106–107.) A discussion of these matters, as well as of the related problems of indirect speech, would lead us too far afield, in spite of their obvious relevance for the choice of tenses in subordinate clauses. As a matter of fact, even the apparent main clauses of represented speech or thought in the so-called "style indirect libre" show clear violations of normal tense selection: *Orain aitona zen* 'He was now a grandfather'.

3. The present perfect in Basque is often held to serve a double function: that of a genuine perfect denoting a past event with present relevance, on the one hand, and that of a proximate past designating an event that happened earlier today regardless of any current relevance, on the other. This dichotomy, helpful as it may be to the learner, ought not to be singled out as a primary characteristic, inasmuch as its overall validity can be seen to follow from the general nature of tense assignment in Basque.

Basically, the present perfect amounts to a present tense referring to a completed event. Accordingly, the time adverbial associated with the clause—often merely understood—must embrace the present together with some prior moment. A prototypical example of this type of adverbial is *gaur* 'today', and it is in fact the privileged status which, as noted earlier, Basque linguistic convention grants this adverb that accounts for the proximate past reading frequently evinced by the Basque present perfect.

Another interesting time adverbial in this connection is *arestian* 'a short while ago'. While, strictly speaking, not containing the present moment, it does extend arbitrarily close to it, and hence counts as including it. Thus it almost invariably necessitates the present perfect. The adverb *artemein* 'a while ago', 'recently' is farther removed from the present and thus, as a rule, combines with a past tense. Its etymological source *aurten behin* 'once this year', however, still requires the present perfect.

4. The choice between past perfect and past imperfect depends on aspect. The normal past tense form is past perfect:

(7) Miren elizara joan zen atzo.
    Yesterday Mary went to church.

The past imperfect denotes durative, iterative, or habitual action:

Durative

(8) Haizea loreen petaloekin jostatzen zen. (Atxaga, *Obab.* 377)
The wind was playing with the flower petals.

Iterative

(9) Egunero herrira jaisten zen.
Every day he went down to the village.

Habitual

(10) a. Oso gutxitan Donostiara joaten zen.
He went very seldom to San Sebastian.
b. Hire anaiaren kontra mintzatzen hintzen. (Ps 49:20; Dv)
Yoú were (forever) talking against yoúr brother.

Thus the past imperfect tends to occur with adverbials of frequency or duration, such as *askotan* 'often', *beti* 'always', *egunero* 'every day', *gehienetan* 'mostly', *gutxitan* 'seldom', *maiz* 'often', *sarritan* 'often', and *usu* 'often'. Compare the following:

(11) a. Atzo zubitik erori zen.
Yesterday, he fell off the bridge.
b. Sarritan zubitik erortzen zen.
He often fell off the bridge.

In its semantic behavior the Basque imperfect has a great deal in common with the imperfects of Spanish, French, and the other Romance tongues. However, a typical use of the imperfect in Romance as well as in many other languages, namely, that of setting the background to another event, is not found in Basque. Thus, whereas Spanish employs the imperfect tense in the first clause of the sentence "Se despertaba cuando entré" ('He was waking up when I came in'), Basque avoids the corresponding form *esnatzen zen* but makes use of *esnatzen ari zen*, applying the progressive gerund form with *ari izan*, for which see section 16.5.1.1 (cf. *EGLU* II, 424).

5. For those verbs maintaining a synthetic conjugation in everyday use (cf. section 6.2.1), a clear difference in meaning obtains between the simple present or past and the corresponding periphrastic imperfect. Contrary to what happens in English, the simple tenses denote momentary or ongoing activity, the periphrastic imperfect being reserved for the expression of habitual or iterative action.

(12) a. Seietan etortzen da.
He (usually) comes at six o'clock.
b. Seietan etortzen zen.
He (usually) came at six o'clock.
c. Seietan dator.
He is coming at six o'clock.

d. Seietan zetorren.
He was coming at six 'o clock.

(13) a. Liburutegian egoten da.
He (usually) sits in the library.
b. Liburutegian egoten zen.
He (usually) sat in the library.
c. Liburutegian dago.
He is sitting in the library.
d. Liburutegian zegoen.
He was sitting in the library.

(14) a. Andre Madalen mozkorra izaten da.
Lady Magdalen is usually drunk.
b. Andre Madalen mozkorra izaten zen.
Lady Magdalen was usually drunk.
c. Andre Madalen mozkorra da.
Lady Magdalen is drunk.
d. Andre Madalen mozkorra zen.
Lady Magdalen was drunk.

6. As there are no obligatory distinctions of relative tense in Basque, the past perfect corresponds not only to the English past tense but equally to the English pluperfect. After all, any action, state, or event denoted by the pluperfect is represented as accomplished prior to a reference point located in the past, thus falling a fortiori into the domain of the past perfect. Some examples are

(15) a. Manolo gelditu zen artean ezkongai. (*LBB* 54)
Manuel had remained a bachelor at the time.
b. Oraindik ez zen Jesus herrian sartu. (Jn 11:30; *IB*)
Jesus had not yet entered the village.
c. Iluna zen, eta oraindik Jesus ez zen iritsi. (Jn 6:17; *IB*)
It was dark, and Jesus had not yet arrived.

Possibly under the influence of the surrounding Romance languages, all keeping a separate pluperfect, Basque too has developed the means to unambiguously express this tense. It does so by combining the past perfect of the auxiliary verb with the perfect participle of the main verb.

(16) a. Lazaro erori izan zen eritasun handi batean. (Larréguy II, 202)
Lazarus had fallen into a serious illness.
b. Jesus ez zen artean herrira heldu izan. (Jn 11:30; Ker.)
Jesus had not, at the time, arrived in the village.

Another device to force a pluperfect reading consists in emphasizing the adjectival character of the perfect participle by suffixing the article to it. Thus, in examples (15a,b,c), instead of using *izan*, the northern dialects prefer the forms *gelditua*, *sartua*, *iritsia*. To be sure, this preference is also an option in the standard language. (More examples of the use of these forms can be found in the discussion of them in section 25.2.3.)

7. As in English, the present tense often depicts future events:

(17) a. Berehala noa zuengana. (Garate, *Esku* 127)
I am coming to yoû at once.
b. Bihar dator Kattalin. (*EGLU* II, 405)
Cathy is coming tomorrow.
c. Bihar ezkontzen da emakume polit batekin. (Cf. Echebarria, *Eib*. 175)
Tomorrow he is getting married to a pretty woman.

8. Proposals and requests regularly take the form of queries couched in the present future tense:

(18) a. Taberna batera joango gara? (*EGLU* II, 421)
Shall we go to a pub?
b. Jaitsiko naiz zurekin?
Shall I go down with you?

(19) a. Eseriko zara? (*EGLU* II, 421)
Do you want to sit down?
b. Etorriko zara nirekin?
Do you want to come with me?

9. As in many languages, the future tenses in Basque can express a high degree of probability with reference to a present or past situation:

(20) a. Liburutegian egongo dira orain.
They'll be in the library now.
b. Liburutegian egongo ziren atzo.
They'll have been in the library yesterday.

(21) a. Ez da orain etxean egongo.
He won't be home now.
b. Ez zen atzo etxean egongo.
He won't have been home yesterday.

Note also the expressive force of the future tense in exclamations:

(22) Ene! Jesus! Ez da egia izango! (*TOE* II, 242)
My! Jesus! It can't be true!

10. In most spoken dialects of Basque as well as in Batua, the past future tense is often found in the apodosis of a conditional sentence: (*Ni geldituko banintz,*) Miren joango zen. '(If I were to stay,) Mary would go.' This usage is frowned upon by normative grammarians, and indeed both in the written language and in the higher styles of the spoken language a special form belonging to the conditional mood will appear instead: *Miren joango litzateke* 'Mary would go'. (See chapter 17.)
11. Purist grammarians disapprove of all modal uses of the past future, insisting that it be employed in a temporal sense only. In that vein, most of the "correct" instances of the past future would be due to the sequence-of-tenses rule, that is, examples such as "I knew that Mary would go."
12. The future tenses do not clearly distinguish between events that will happen and events that will have happened in the future. Thus, in many contexts, *ibaira eroriko da* must be translated as 'he will have fallen into the river', and *ibaira eroriko zen* as 'he would have fallen into the river'.

When necessary, the Basque tense system calls upon the future tenses of the auxiliary verb *izan* to provide unambiguous forms for this meaning, but in actual fact native speakers very seldom feel compelled to use such constructs.

In theory then our paradigm of section 7.3.1 could be completed in the following way:

[7.] The present future perfect: Perfect participle + future tense auxiliary

Ordurako ibaira erori izango da.	By then he will have fallen into the river.
Seietan jaiki izango zara.	You will have gotten up at six o'clock.
Sarri etxean gelditu izango naiz.	I will have stayed home often.

[8.] The past future perfect: Perfect participle + past future tense auxiliary

Ordurako ibaira erori izango zen.	By then he would have fallen into the river.
Seietan jaiki izango zinen.	You would have gotten up at six o'clock.
Sarri etxean gelditu izango nintzen.	I would have stayed home often.

13. Although infrequent in Batua, there exists a habitual perfect with past and present forms, serving to denote a habit or tendency lasting up to a specific point in time. It consists of a combination of the perfect participle—in Biscayan the imperfect participle—of the main verb with a perfect tense form of the auxiliary *izan* 'to be':

(23) a. Pello beti berandu iritsi izan da.
So far, Pete has always arrived late.
b. Gure etsaiak hegoaldetik etorri izan ziren.
So far, our enemies had come from the south.

Except in its Biscayan form, the habitual past perfect is homonymous with the pluperfect; see examples (16a) and (16b).

14. Tense forms where the main participle is combined with a periphrastic tense form of the auxiliary are called hyperperiphrastic. The five hyperperiphrastic tenses accepted into

Batua usage have already been dealt with: the pluperfect, the present as well as the past future perfect, and the habitual perfect, which can be either present or past. These tenses are mostly avoided in conversation. They are held to be relatively late calques on certain Romance compound tense forms, and, as such, of at most marginal interest.

7.3.3 The Time Adverbs *oraindik* and *artean* Denoting 'still'

To express that something is 'still', or, in negative environments, '(not) yet' the case, Basque employs *oraindik*, elative of *orain* 'now', or else an eastern form, *oraino*. However, for events set in the past, written Batua prefers *artean*, inessive form of *arte* 'interval', discussed in section 4.1.3.6. Compare

(24) a. Oraindik hemen dago; bere emaztea ez da oraindik itzuli.
He is still here; his wife has not yet returned.
b. Artean etxean zegoen; bere ama ez zen artean hil.
He was still at home; his mother had not yet died.

7.4 Morphologically Derived Intransitives

7.4.1 The Magic Suffix -*tu*

The Basque language owes much of the smooth flexibility that ensures its continued survival as a medium of culture to the remarkable ease with which members of sundry lexical categories can be turned into verbs. Indeed, all adjectives and nouns, some adverbs, and many allative postpositional phrases can and often do function as verb radicals. This process entails no phonological change, except for one small class of forms: nouns and adjectives ending in a mid vowel (i.e., *e* or *o*) change this vowel into *a*, provided the same change occurs in other productive derivations as well. (Cf. the Minor Apocope rule of section 3.8.1.)

To form perfect participles from these derived radicals, the suffix -*tu* is used without exception, allowing, of course, for the appearance of the voiced variant -*du* after *n* and *l* (cf. section 7.2.1). This then is what prompted the grammarian Azkue to proclaim: "Le suffixe verbal -*tu* est un des plus féconds qui se puisse concevoir dans une langue." (The verbal suffix -*tu* is one of the most productive ones conceivable in a language.) (Azkue 1905–1906, I, p. xviii)

All verbs derived by means of -*tu* have a double use: inchoative when used intransitively and causative when used transitively. In this chapter our attention will be focused on the intransitive use; the transitive use will be taken up later in section 12.3.

7.4.2 Deadjectival Intransitives

To any adjective *X* corresponds an intransitive verb *X-tu* with the meaning 'to become X', or 'to become more X'. A few common examples will suffice here:

aberats	rich	aberastu	to get rich
ero	insane	erotu	to go insane
gaiso	ill	gaisotu	to fall ill
gorri	red	gorritu	to redden, to blush
handi	big	handitu	to swell, to grow up, to increase
ilun	dark	ilundu	to darken, to get dark
isil	silent	isildu	to become quiet, to shut up
mozkor	drunk	mozkortu	to get drunk
on	good	ondu	to improve, to ripen
sendo	robust, healthy	sendatu	to get well, to heal
ugari	abundant	ugaritu	to proliferate (also: *ugaldu*)
zahar	old	zahartu	to grow old
zoro	crazy	zoratu	to go crazy
zuri	white	zuritu	to whiten, to turn pale

Note that *sendo* and *zoro* (but not *ero* and *gaiso*) are subject to the Minor Apocope rule. The derived verbs *askotu* 'to increase' and *gutxitu* 'to decrease' are also worth citing, although the quantifiers *asko* 'much' and *gutxi* 'few' may not be, strictly speaking, adjectives.

7.4.3 Deadverbal Intransitives

Mostly, adverbs referring to a situation or state can serve as verb radicals:

berandu	(too) late	berandutu	to get (too) late
hurbil	nearby	hurbildu	to come close
urrun	far away	urrundu	to move away

Included are all adverbs formed with the suffix *-ka* (see section 33.1.11), some of which may express a dynamic situation:

gainezka	overflowingly	gainezkatu	to overflow
lasterka	in a rush	lasterkatu	to run, to hurry
txandaka	by turns	txandakatu	to alternate

Adverbs of manner—typically carrying the suffix *-ki*—do not qualify. The apparent exceptions *ongitu* 'to get better' and *gaizkitu* 'to get worse' may actually be denominals from the nouns *ongi* 'good' and *gaizki* 'evil'.

7.4.4 Denominal Intransitives

In principle, any noun *X* can be made into the radical of a verb *X-tu* with the meaning 'to become X' or 'to become more X', but in some cases the meaning relation is less straightforward, as in *saiatu* 'to try'. Here are some illustrations:

adiskide	friend	adiskidetu	to become friends
alargun	widow, widower	alargundu	to become widowed

ama	mother	amatu	to become pregnant
bat	one	batu	to become one, to unite
etsai	enemy	etsaitu	to become enemies
mintzo	voice, speech	mintzatu	to speak (lit. 'to become voice')
molde	mould, form, manner	moldatu	to adapt, to manage, to get along
neke	effort, fatigue	nekatu	to exert oneself, to get tired
saio	attempt, essay	saiatu	to try, to attempt
udazken	autumn	udazkendu	to become autumn

In particular, nouns denoting a physiological or psychological state give rise to some useful inchoatives:

ardura	care, interest	arduratu	to care, to be interested
asper	boredom	aspertu	to get bored
beldur	fear	beldurtu	to get afraid
damu	repentance	damutu	to repent
dolu	mourning	dolutu	to mourn
egarri	thirst	egarritu	to get thirsty
gose	hunger	gosetu	to get hungry
grina	passion	grinatu	to get excited
haserre	anger	haserretu	to get angry
ikara	tremor	ikaratu	to tremble, to shiver
izu	fright	izutu	to become frightened, to take fright
kezka	worry	kezkatu	to worry
lotsa	shame	lotsatu	to feel ashamed
poz	joy	poztu	to feel happy, to rejoice
zorabio	dizziness	zorabiatu	to feel dizzy, to become dazed

[*N.B.* Still utilized by Oihenarte (17th century) and Harriet (18th century), the inchoative *lotu* 'to fall asleep' from the noun *lo* 'sleep', has long given way to *lokartu*, presumably because of its homonymy with the verb *lotu* 'to tie' (radical *lot*).]

Morphological complexity does not inhibit the occurrence of the suffix *-tu*: *hiritartu* 'to adapt to city life' with *-tar* (section 6.6); *euskaldundu* 'to become Basque speaking' with *-dun* (section 19.8); *sentikortu* 'to become touchy', with *-kor* (section 23.8).

7.4.5 Deallatival Intransitives

Any noun *N* in the allative case can serve as a verb radical meaning 'to move to N'. This will yield verbs ending in *-atu, -ratu, -taratu, -etaratu, -ganatu*. Examples are

aitzina	forward	aitzinatu	to move forward, to progress
aldera	to the side, toward	alderatu	to move closer, to approach
atera	to the door	ateratu	to go outdoors, to go out

atzera	backward	atzeratu	to move back, to regress
aurrera	forward	aurreratu	to move forward, to progress
batera	together	bateratu	to come together, to unite
behera	downward	beheratu	to move down, to decrease, to descend
bidera	to the (right) road	bideratu	to get on the right track
burura	to the head	bururatu	to come to mind
etxera	to the house, home	etxeratu	to come home, to go home
gogora	to the mind	gogoratu	to come to mind
gora	up	goratu	to move up
hondora	to the bottom	hondoratu	to sink, to reach bottom
kalera	to the street	kaleratu	to go out on the street
kanpora	out	kanporatu	to go outside
lotara	to sleep	lotaratu	to go to sleep
lurrera	to the ground	lurreratu	to fall on the ground, to moor
mahaira	to the table	mahairatu	to go to the table
mundura	into the world	munduratu	to come into the world
ohera	to bed	oheratu	to go to bed
ondora	to the proximity	ondoratu	to go near, to approach
plazara	to the forum	plazaratu	to perform in public
zuregana	to you	zureganatu	to come to you

Even the interrogative forms *nora* 'to where' and *zertara* 'to what' can be made to function as verb radicals: *noratzen zara?* 'where are you going?' (Pouvreau, see *DGV* XII, 903); *Horra zertaratu zen erregea.* 'That is what the king came to.' (Cf. J. B. Etcheberry, *Orotarik* 22).

7.4.6 Complex Intransitives

Apart from the somewhat unusual participation of postpositional phrases of the form $N + ra$, all examples cited so far belong to the garden-variety type of derivation, which takes lexical items, here nouns and adjectives, as starting points. Most contemporary speakers do indeed impose just this restriction. Others, however, accept and occasionally produce derived verbs based on more complex phrases:

1. Coordinated nouns: *su eta gartu* 'to get all in a flame' (*DRA* 8, 3432).
2. Complex adjectival phrases: *geroago eta zabalagotu* 'to become more and more widespread' (Ibiñagabeitia, in *OrOm* 276).
3. Allatives with genitive complement: *bere baitaratu* 'to come to himself' (Joannategi, *SBi* 12, 82, 293; Barbier, *Lég.* 69; Lafitte, *Murtuts* 24; many more in *DGV* III, 718); *gure baitaratu* 'to come to us' (SP, Dv, see *DGV* III, 718); *bere herriratu* 'to go to his village' (Etxaide, *16 Seme* 17); *bere basetxeratu* 'to go to his farmhouse' (Ibiñagabeitia, in *OrOm* 114); *zure erreinuratu* 'to come into your kingdom' (*TB* 135; Lk 23:42; *Lau Eb.*); *haren*

eskuetaratu 'to fall into his hands' (*TB* 93–94); *Turkoen eskuetaratu* 'to fall into the hands of the Turks' (Joannategi, *SBi* 351); *gure "Orixe" ren eskuetaratu* 'to get into the hands of our "Orixe"' (M. Lekuona, in *OrOm* 209); *aitaren alboratu* 'to come close to father' (Zaitegi, *Sof.* 137).
4. Allatives modified by a relative clause: *hain barrenki maitatu izan zuen Jainkoaganatu* 'to go to God, whom he had loved so deeply' (Ibiñagabeitia, in *OrOm* 116).

Note that all examples involve premodification; postmodification appears totally out of the question. As Artiagoitia (1994, 24) has noticed, *etxe berriratu* 'to go to the new house' is impossible. Therefore, putative verb radicals must be head-final. For a similar restriction elsewhere, see section 4.1.2.

7.4.7 Amorphous Deallatival Intransitives

While phrases of the type *etxeratu naiz* 'I have come home' are current in the spoken as well as the written language, there is a more literary variant without the suffix *-tu*: *etxera naiz*, still understood but rarely used in everyday speech. Similarly, *etxeratuko naiz* 'I will (have) come home' has the literary variant *etxerako naiz*.

One might explain these forms, which we will call "amorphous," by the intervention of an abstract verb of motion such as *heldu* 'to arrive', but positing an optional zero allomorph of the perfect participle suffix *-tu* is also feasible, and it allows us to account for the fact that the syntactic constraints on the *-tu*-less forms appear to be the same as those governing the corresponding *-tu* forms.

Whereas nowadays amorphous deallatives are highly marked and belong to an archaizing literary style, they must have been commonplace in the past; witness such relic forms as *atera* 'to go outdoors', even now more common than its regular variant *ateratu*.

7.5 Bare Nouns Governed by *izan* 'to be'

As we may recall from section 2.3.1, item 7, a noun occurring as a predicate with the verb *izan* 'to be' normally requires the definite article: *Miren sorgina da* 'Mary is a witch'. We will now look into some exceptions, already alluded to in section 2.3.2, item 10.

When states, expressed by an adjective, a stative adverb, or less frequently a noun, are to be linked to a subject, the verb *egon* normally appears as the linking verb: *bare nago* 'I am calm', *gaiso dago* 'he is sick', *bero dago* 'it is hot', *lasai gaude* 'we are unworried', *lo daude* 'they are asleep'.

However, a limited class of nouns denoting a state, mostly psychological or physiological in nature, allows the verb *izan* to serve as a copula to form predicates and yet rejects the definite article. Here is a membership list of this class:

ahalke	shame	ahalke izan	to be ashamed
beldur	fear	beldur izan	to be afraid (with genitive comp.)

bero	heat	bero izan	to be hot, to feel hot
bizi	life	bizi izan	to be alive, to live
egarri	thirst	egarri izan	to be thirsty
eri	illness	eri izan	to be ill
falta	lack	falta izan	to be missing or lacking
gai	material, matter	gai izan	to be suited, to be worthy
gose	hunger	gose izan	to be hungry
haserre	anger	haserre izan	to be angry
herabe	shyness, repugnance	herabe izan	to be shy, to shirk from
hotz	cold	hotz izan	to be cold, to feel cold
ikara	trembling	ikara izan	to be trembling, to feel frightened
izu	fright	izu izan	to be frightened, to feel frightened
izerdi	sweat	izerdi izan	to be sweating
logale	sleepiness	logale izan	to be sleepy
lotsa	shame	lotsa izan	to be ashamed
mintzo	voice, speech	mintzo izan	to speak
nagi	laziness	nagi izan	to be lazy, to feel lazy

[*N.B.* For many of these, other expressions are sometimes preferred in spoken Batua, such as *gose nago*, *goserik nago*, *goseak nago*, for which see chapter 25.]

There is, at least in principle, an aspectual difference between these copular phrases and the corresponding inchoative verbs of section 7.4.4:

Guztiz egarri naiz.	I am very thirsty.
Gauero egarri izaten naiz.	Every night I am thirsty.
Askotan egarri izan naiz.	I have often been thirsty.
Poliki-poliki egarritzen naiz.	Bit by bit I am getting thirsty.
Azkenean ni ere egarritu naiz.	Finally I too have gotten thirsty.
Oso beldur gara.	We are very much afraid.
Gauero beldur izaten gara.	Every night we are afraid.
Askotan beldur izan gara.	We have often been afraid.
Gero eta gehiago beldurtzen gara.	We are getting more and more afraid.
Beldurtu nintzen burutik behatzetara.	I got scared from head to toes.

(For *gero eta gehiago* 'more and more', literally: 'later and more', see section 26.4.8.)

For many speakers, especially in eastern Guipuzcoa, the aspectual distinction becomes a little blurred, inasmuch as they allow habitual state forms such as *egarri izaten* and *beldur izaten* to be shortened to *egarritzen* and *beldurtzen*.

Moreover, some *-tu* verbs have lost their inchoative value because of their lexical meaning. Thus, intransitive *faltatu* does not mean 'to become missing' as one might expect, but 'to be missing or lacking', which is also the meaning of *falta izan*.

7.6 The Expression *bizi izan* 'to live'

A morphological peculiarity makes *bizi izan* look rather like a verb: its habitual form *bizi izaten* is nearly always shortened to *bizitzen*, and its future *bizi izango* to *biziko*. Note, however, that *bizi da* does not mean 'he has lived' but 'he lives', showing that the form *bizi* is indeed not a verb.

There is only one other expression on our list in section 7.5 with this property: *falta izan* 'to be missing or lacking', which displays *faltatzen* and *faltako* as optional variants of *falta izaten* and *falta izango*. As mentioned earlier, speakers from eastern Guipuzcoa allow *beldurtzen* and *gosetzen* to take the place of *beldur izaten* and *gose izaten*. They do not, however, make use of *goseko* or *beldurko* instead of *gose izango* or *beldur izango*.

Just like its English equivalent 'to live', *bizi izan* shares the "ambiguity" of its Spanish counterpart *vivir* in meaning 'to reside' as well as 'to be alive':

(25) a. Gizona ez da ogiz bakarrik bizi. (Mt 4:4; *IB, EAB*)
A man does not live on bread alone.
b. Behin bizi gara soilik. (Txill., *Let*. 107)
We only live once.
c. Oraino bizi haiz enetzat. (Ax. 430)
Yoú are still alive for me. (For *oraino*, see section 7.3.3.)

(26) a. Ni Azpilen bizi naiz. (Irigoyen, 96)
I live in Azpil.
b. Ni Crotona kalearen ondoan bizi izan nintzen bost urtean. (Garate, *NY* 83)
I had lived near Crotona Street for five years.
c. Gu Donostian bizitzea harrigarria zen.
It was astounding that we lived in San Sebastian.

7.7. Diminutive Adjectives in *-xko*

Whereas nouns regularly allow diminutive forms on the basis of the suffix *-txo* (*-tto* or *no*), adjectives and adverbs do not have productive diminutives in Batua. However, a nonproductive suffix has been borrowed from the northern dialects for this purpose: *-xko* (variant form *-sko*), adding the qualification 'rather' to the meaning of the adjective or adverb.

Although *belxko* 'rather black' and *zurixko* 'rather white' do exist, color adjectives prefer *-xka*, the nonproductive diminutive suffix mostly used for nouns that was already discussed in section 3.9.

The following examples are attested:

aberats	rich	aberaxko	rather rich
anitz	many, much	anixko	rather many, rather much
apal	low, humble	apalxko	rather low, rather humble
aspaldi	long ago	aspaldixko	rather long ago

arin	light, not heavy, quickly	arinxko	rather light, rather quickly
beltz	black	belxko	rather black
bero	hot, warm	beroxko	rather hot, rather warm
berri	new	berrixko	rather new
ero	demented, crazy	eroxko	rather crazy
handi	big, great	handixko	rather big, rather great
harro	proud, arrogant	harroxko	rather proud, rather arrogant
hotz	cold, chilly	hoxko	rather cold, rather chílly
gora	high	goraxko	rather high
gutxi	few	gutxixko	rather few
idor	arid, dry	idorxko	rather arid, rather dry
ilun	dark	ilunxko	rather dark
luze	long	luzexko	rather long
motel	weak, tasteless	motelxko	rather weak, rather tasteless
on	good	onxko	rather good
ongi	well	ongixko	rather well
urrun	far	urrunxko	rather far
urruti	far	urrutixko	rather far
zabal	wide	zabalxko	rather wide
zahar	old	zaharxko	rather old
zoro	crazy, silly	zoroxko	rather crazy, rather silly
zozo	stupid	zozoxko	rather stupid
zuri	white	zurixko	rather white

7.8 Vocabulary

7.8.1 Intransitive Verbs

abiatu	to set out, to depart
aritu	to be occupied, to be working
atera	to go outdoors, to go out, to come out, to result
erori	to fall, to fall down, to fall out
eseri	to sit down, to sit
esnatu	to wake up
etorri	to come
ezkondu	to get married
gelditu	to stay, to remain, to stop, to end up
geratu	to remain, to stop, to end up
gertatu	to happen, to chance to be
harritu	to be surprised, to be astonished
heldu	to arrive, to ripen

hil	to die
ibili	to walk, to hang out, to act, to function
igaro	to pass, to pass by
igo	to go up, to rise, to climb
iritsi	to arrive
irten	to go out, to exit, to leave
itzuli	to return, to go back, to come back
jaiki	to get up, to rise, to rise up
jaio	to be born
jaitsi	to go down, to come down, to descend
jausi	to fall
mintzatu	to speak
poztu	to be glad, to rejoice
sartu	to come in, to go in, to enter

[*N.B.* The goal of motion verbs such as *atera*, *erori*, *etorri*, *heldu*, *ibili*, *igaro*, *igo*, *iritsi*, *itzuli*, and *jaitsi* is indicated by the allative case *-ra* or, sometimes, the terminal *-raino*. Only the verb *sartu* 'to go in' takes instead the inessive case *-an*. The point of transit or departure is expressed by means of the elative case *-tik*, as in *zubitik igaro nintzen* 'I passed by the bridge', which is vague as to whether the bridge was in fact crossed or not.]

7.8.2 Other Words

aspalditik	since long, for a long time
azkenean	in the end, finally
berandu	late, too late
berehala	at once, immediately
egarri	thirst
gose	hunger
haserre	anger
laster	fast, quick, quickly, soon
orduan	then, at that time, in that case
ostatu	hotel, inn
taberna	pub
teilatu	roof

7.9 Exercises

7.9.1 Translate into English

1. Atera da deabrua zure alabarengandik. (Mk 7.29; *EAB*)
2. Aspalditik ni ez naiz etxetik atera, eta zu ere ez.

3. Harritzen naiz zu oraindik oso neskatxa gazteekin ibiltzeaz.
4. Noiz ezkonduko zara nirekin?
5. Ni hil arte ez haiz hi gurean sartuko.
6. Bilboko zein ostatutan gelditzen zarete gaur?
7. Eguerditik honaino zenbat ordu igaro dira?
8. Emakumea haserre gorrian irten zen lantegitik eta berehala Bilboratu.
9. Gu atzo arratsaldean leizera ez jaustea benetan harrigarria zen.
10. Bilbora itzuli arte, ez ginen ez gose ez egarri.
11. Orduan zure tabernako zakur haundien beldur ginen.
12. Azkenean oso berandu Donostiaratu zen gure amona bere oiloekin.

7.9.2 Translate into Basque

1. Which lady has lain down on my bed with her golden hair?
2. The witches went up at once to the roof of the castle.
3. Our books have now fallen off the table into the water.
4. Fast trains always depart late from here.
5. We woke up every morning at quarter to six.
6. We will arrive in San Sebastian at half past ten in the morning.
7. It was good that you then came down from the mountain.
8. A lot happened today in our village pub.
9. How many priests are living still in your little house?
10. I was very angry with you this morning.
11. Pete will have been walking behind our girls last night.
12. The pain comes from still being hungry.

8 Modal Particles; Topic; Focus and Constituent Order

8.1 Modal Particles

8.1.1 Sentence Modality Expressed by Proclitics to the Finite Verb

There is a set of five mutually exclusive particles denoting sentence modality: reportative *omen* (*ei* in Biscayan), inferential *bide*, optative *ahal*, interrogative *al*, and dubitative *ote* (*ete* in Biscayan).

Although written separately, they normally function as proclitics to the finite verb; that is, they precede it and make up one phonological word with it. For *bide*, *ahal*, and *al*, this option is, in fact, the only one. The other two, *omen* and *ote*, also show up in elliptic constructions without a finite verb or, perhaps under the influence of northern usage, may occasionally follow the verb.

Note the obligatory application of sandhi rule 5 of section 1.2.6 after *omen*, *ahal*, and *al*. Forms like *omen zen*, *ahal zegoen*, and *al zetorren* are pronounced as *omentzen*, *ahaltzegoen*, and *altzetorren*, a purely automatic change, not indicated by the orthography.

8.1.2 Reportative *omen*

Cognate to the noun *omen* 'repute', 'rumor', the sentence particle *omen* conveys that the speaker has to rely on hearsay and cannot personally vouch for the truth of his statement. Accordingly, with folktales and legends as traditionally told, *omen* occurs in virtually every descriptive main clause. Its use introduces a shade of doubt. A speaker certain of his facts will not employ *omen*, even when not himself a witness to the events reported.

The particle *omen* may be rendered in English by an introductory "They say that..." or "It is said that..." or, again, by adverbs like "reportedly" and "allegedly," although in many contexts, like storytelling, it would be overly pedantic to do so, since English usage does not insist on the systematic expression of this modality. Here are some typical examples:

(1) a. Lenago Jentilbaratzan Jentilak bizi izaten omen ziren. (JMB, *Mundo* I, 37)
They say that formerly there used to be heathens living at Jentilbaratza.

b. Gure ama eta bere ahizpa Sarako leizera joan omen ziren ongarriketara. (JMB, *Mundo* IV, 110)
(It is said that) My mother (section 6.1.3, item 2) and her sister had gone to the cavern at Sara looking for manure.
c. Etxeko alaba oso polita omen da.
The daughter of the house is said to be very pretty.

While most speakers south of the Pyrenees accept *omen* only in its canonical preverbal position, northern speakers also allow it to appear elsewhere in the sentence, especially at the very end. For this option to be realized, however, the canonical site must be somehow unavailable—for example, when already filled by a different particle such as completive *bait-*, when separated from *omen* by a major syntactic boundary (often indicated by a comma), or when the clause containing *omen* lacks a finite verb altogether. Southern speakers, under these circumstances, will use other lexical expressions, such as *dirudienez* 'as it seems':

(2) a. Azkenean Miren, semearengatik omen/dirudienez, itzuli zen etxera.
At the end, for the sake of her son as rumor has it, Mary returned home.
b. Nekane Parisera joan zen, eta ez bakarrik, omen/dirudienez.
Dolores went to Paris, and not alone, it seems.
c. Nor etorri da? Apezpikua, omen.
Who has come? The bishop, it seems.

8.1.3 Inferential *bide*

Historically derived from the noun *bide* '(right) way' (cf. *bide da* 'it is just'), the sentence particle *bide* signals that certain facts known to the speaker lead him to infer the truth of his statement. Hence, a clause containing *bide* can in principle always be accompanied by another clause stating the grounds for the inference, even though in practice this rarely happens. The closest English translation of *bide* is thus the epistemic modal *must* (*surely*):

(3) a. Aberatsa bide zara.
You must surely be rich.
b. Ijitoak gaur Donostiara joan bide dira.
The gypsies must have gone today to San Sebastian.
c. Apaiza ez bide zen berehala etorri.
The priest must surely not have come at once.
d. Oinazearen beldur izanen bide zen Theresa samurra. (Mirande, *HaurB* 73)
Frail Theresa would surely be afraid of pain.

Inferences being what they are, the use of *bide* also hints at the possibility of error, so that it is compatible with adverbs of uncertainty such as *nonbait* 'apparently':

(4) Orduan nonbait giro hotza bide zen. (JMB, *ELG* 16)
At that time there was apparently a cold climate.

8.1.4 Optative *ahal*

A homonym to the noun *ahal* 'power', the preverbal proclitic *ahal* with its characteristic rising intonation conveys a strong wish on the part of the speaker. It is therefore a frequent component of blessings and curses. The English locution "I do hope that ..." (or "I just hope that ...") provides a close semantic equivalent in most cases, a fact that translators may keep in mind, as no other lexical item in Basque distinguishes between 'hope' and 'expectation'. A few examples will suffice as illustration:

(5) a. Laster etxeratuko ahal dira!
I do hope they will come home soon!
b. Ez ahal da oinez etorriko! (*EGLU* II, 456)
I do hope he won't come on foot!
c. Itoko ahal haiz!
I do hope yoú drown!

In virtue of its meaning, the particle *ahal* generally co-occurs with the future tense, but other tenses are possible:

(6) a. Garaiz etorri ahal gara!
I do hope we have come on time!
b. Jaungoikoa gutaz errukitzen ahal da! (*TOE* I, 302)
I do hope God has pity on us!

8.1.5 Interrogative *al*

There are two ways of marking an utterance as a yes-or-no question in Batua. The most common strategy is to apply a rising sentence-final pitch to what would otherwise be a normal declarative sentence. Instead of this rising pitch, however, a preverbal proclitic *al* may appear, a reduced form of *ahal*, originally borrowed from the Guipuzcoan dialect. (In the Low Navarrese and Souletin dialects a postverbal clitic *-a* is used instead.) The use of *al* is restricted to direct yes-or-no questions in Batua, although some speakers of the Guipuzcoan dialect also use it in embedded questions. Examples:

(7) a. Laster etorriko al da? (*LBB* 81)
Will he come soon?
b. Maiz joaten al zara Parisa? (*MEIG* I, 65)
Are you going to Paris often?
c. Ez al da iritsi ordua? (Atxaga, *Behi* 13)
Has the time not arrived?
d. Inor gelditzen al da elizan? (*LBB* 170)
Is there anybody remaining in the church?

A question with *al* can be rhetorical:

(8) a. Gure nagusia al haiz hi?
Are yoú our boss?
b. Ez al zara nitaz fidatzen? (*TOE* II, 270)
Don't you trust me?

A divergent, noninterrogative, use of *al* is found in certain exclamations:

(9) a. Etorri al haiz, seme! (*EGLU* II, 514)
So you've come, son!
b. Hemen al zaude!
So you're here!

8.1.6 Dubitative *ote*

The particle *ote*, for which I would like to suggest a Late Latin etymology *aut ne* 'or not' (cf. *FHV* 18.2, p. 346), adds an element of speculation to questions of all types. Although Azkue held it to be untranslatable (1905–1906, II, 143), its core use translates quite well into English as "I wonder" (cf. Saltarelli 1988, 29), or, in some contexts, "one wonders." Indeed, an utterance containing *ote*: *Alkatea hil ote da?* only differs in illocutionary force from an utterance containing *al*: *Alkatea hil al da?* 'Has the mayor died?'. The latter constitutes an act of asking, the former an act of wondering.

This view of *ote* squares nicely with the observation that *ote* questions are typically addressed to oneself just as much as to one's interlocutor, in contrast to regular questions, which tend to have a well-defined addressee. Thus: *Sartuko ote naiz?* (*LBB* 107) 'Shall I go in?'.

Thus, in a sense, Mitxelena is right in asserting that *ote* questions do not ask anything, but he overstates his case when he adds that they expect no answer but merely serve to express the speaker's anxiety (*MEIG* VI, 166). To be sure, *ote*, like *al*, may occur in purely rhetorical questions:

(10) a. Ni ote naiz neure anaiaren zaina? (Gn 4:9; Dv)
Am I my brother's keeper?
b. Profeten arteko ote da Saul ere? (1 Sm 10:11; Dv)
Is Saul also among the prophets (one wonders)?
c. Ez ote zen Chomsky aspaldi jaio? (*MEIG* VIII, 173)
Was Chomsky not born a long time ago?
d. Zergatik nire semea ez ote dator? (*TZ* II, 147)
Why isn't my son coming, I wonder?

Nonetheless, the presence of *ote* does not necessarily render a question merely rhetorical—as is witnessed by the large number of *ote* questions that appear in the context of interviews, including those conducted by Mitxelena himself. What happens is that expressions of wonder, though not technically questions, do activate a conversational maxim: "If you happen to know something relevant, please tell me." Hence the interrogative effect observed:

(11) a. Izan ote da euskal eskolarik pinturan? (*MEIG* I, 67)
Has there been a Basque school in painting, I wonder?

(For the partitive ending *-rik* in *eskolarik*, see section 13.1.2.)

b. Kaltegarri ote da artistarentzat erretratugintzan aritzea? (*MEIG* I, 68)
Is it harmful for the artist to engage in portraiting, I wonder?

The particle *ote* also occurs in wh-questions:

(12) a. Nor ote da gizon hau? (Atxaga, *Obab.* 257)
Who is this man, I wonder? (For *hau* 'this', see section 9.6.1.)
b. Zer ote da gazte izatea. (*TOE* II, 361)
I wonder what it is to be young.
c. Non ote dabiltza gure Malen eta Xalbador? (*TOE* II, 281)
Where are our Maggie and Xalbador hanging out, I wonder?
d. Nora joango ote naiz? (*LBB* 158)
Wherever shall I go?

Unlike *al*, the particle *ote* appears in embedded questions quite freely (see section 18.1.2). Just like *omen*, *ote* is allowed to persist when its canonical preverbal position is inaccessible or nonexistent. By far the most common examples are elliptic constructions:

(13) a. Purrustada latzak ere ez dira falta. Neurriz gainekoak ote? (*MEIG* VIII, 157)
Harsh grumblings are not lacking either. Excessive, one wonders?
b. Bere alaba Ameriketara joan zen. Zergatik ote?
His daughter went to America. Why was that, I wonder?

8.1.7 Bibliographical Note on Proclitics

For a further discussion on the syntax of these particles, see de Rijk 1972c, Mujika 1988, and the exposition in the grammar of the Basque Academy (*EGLU* II, chap. 16, pp. 485–516) or its summary in *EGL*, sec. 19.3.2, pp. 441–446.

8.2 Syntax of Negation

8.2.1 Autonomy of Negation

The structure of sentence negation in Basque differs from the corresponding profile in English in quite an interesting way. To see this difference, let us look at a conjoined sentence where the second predicate is a negated version of the first. This second predicate, we note, can—and usually will—be completely deleted in Basque with only the negative *ez* remaining, whereas English grammar requires the auxiliary verb to remain as well:

(14) a. Miren itsusia da, baina Karmen ez.
Mary is ugly, but Carmen isn't. (or: is not.)
b. Miren ohera doa, baina Karmen ez.
Mary is going to bed, but Carmen isn't. (or: is not.)

Observe the contrast with constituent negation, which operates the same way in both languages, the negative morpheme introducing the negated constituent:

(15) a. Miren da itsusia, ez Karmen.
Mary is ugly, not Carmen.
b. Miren doa ohera, ez Karmen.
Mary is going to bed, not Carmen.

With sentence negation present in both conjuncts, we find the same disparity between Basque and English as in (14a,b):

(16) a. Miren ez da polita, eta Karmen ere ez.
Mary isn't pretty, and Carmen isn't either.
b. Miren ez doa ohera, eta Karmen ere ez.
Mary isn't going to bed, and Carmen isn't either.

These facts strongly support what we may call the autonomy of Basque negation. In Basque, negation appears independent of inflection, in contrast to the situation in English. The Basque scholar Itziar Laka, who first addressed these issues (see section 8.2.4), phrases it more technically: In Basque D-structure, negation dominates inflection (i.e., the tense phrase), while the exact reverse holds true in English.

Another contrast between Basque and English, also noticed by Itziar Laka, provides some more support for this conception. Unlike English, Basque allows negative polarity items in sentence-initial position:

(17) a. Ezer ez dator. (also: *Ez dator ezer.*)
Nothing is coming. (lit.: *Anything isn't coming.)
b. Inor ez doa. (also: *Ez doa inor.*)
Nobody is going. (lit.: *Anybody isn't going.)

The most plausible explanation here appears to be that Basque negation is fundamentally sentence-initial, while English negation, being tied in with inflection, is sentence-internal and, therefore, unable to govern the subject position.

8.2.2 Auxiliary Attraction

Consider some typical affirmative statements:

(18) a. Miren itsusia da.
Mary is ugly.

b. Miren ohera doa.
Mary is going to bed.
c. Miren bihar etorriko da.
Mary will come tomorrow.

Their denials will read as follows:

(19) a. Ez da Miren itsusia.
Mary isn't ugly.
b. Ez doa Miren ohera.
Mary isn't going to bed.
c. Ez da Miren bihar etorriko.
Mary won't come tomorrow.

Or, alternatively, with the subject marked as an emphatic sentence topic:

(20) a. Miren ez da itsusia.
Mary isn't ugly.
b. Miren ez doa ohera.
Mary isn't going to bed.
c. Miren ez da bihar etorriko.
Mary won't come tomorrow.

Sentences (19a,b,c) and (20a,b,c) illustrate a general characteristic of sentence negation in Basque: When there is a finite verb form in a negative sentence, nothing can come between it and the negative morpheme *ez* that precedes it.

Modal particles (section 8.1) constitute an apparent exception; compare examples (3c), (5b), (7c), and (8b). Actually, such particles have been incorporated into the verb, which, therefore, remains adjacent to the negation marker *ez*.

Furthermore, the word order in (19a,b,c), when compared to that in the corresponding affirmatives (18a,b,c), suggests that it is the finite verb (usually an auxiliary) that is moved from its original position and then adjoined to the negation marker. It follows that a negated verb, perhaps combined with a focus constituent (section 8.6.2), lays claim to clause-initial position, so that it can be preceded at most by a dislocated or preposed constituent, such as an emphatic adverbial or topic.

The necessity of Auxiliary Attraction, as we will henceforth call this process, arises from the Tense C-Command Condition, a universal constraint proposed by Itziar Laka (1990) to the effect that in surface syntax (technically at S-Structure) all propositional operators of a tensed clause must be c-commanded by tense.

As we saw in section 8.2.1, in Basque, sentence negation, a propositional operator par excellence, starts out dominating tense. Therefore, the only way for tense to c-command negation will be for the former to give up its original position and adjoin itself to the latter.

8.2.3 Sandhi Rules Involving *ez*

Although mostly written as a separate item, the negation *ez* combines with a following finite verb to form one phonological word. Accordingly, we find some sandhi rules affecting the pronunciation:

Rule A Voiced plosives following *ez* turn voiceless (cf. sandhi rule 4 of section 1.2.6): *ez da* > *ezta*; *ez doa* > *eztoa*; *ez gara* > *ezkara*.

Rule B An initial sibilant *z* coalesces with the final *z* of *ez* into an affricate *-tz*: *ez zen* > *etzen*; *ez zara* > *etzara*; *ez ziren* > *etziren*.

Rule C Except for slow or emphatic speech, the *z* in *ez* drops before *n*, *l*, or *h*: *ez naiz* > *enaiz*; *ez habil* > *ehabil*; *ez litzateke* > *elitzateke*.

Spellings corresponding to these pronunciations—especially for rules A and B, much less so for rule C—are often met with in older texts and occasionally in modern writings. This book will follow the 1971 recommendation of the Basque Academy to separate in writing *ez* from the following verb, so that these purely automatic modifications will not be indicated in the standard orthography.

8.2.4 Bibliographical Note on Negation

The treatment of negation presented here is based on the work of the Basque linguist Itziar Laka (1990, 1991). In my article of 1969, concerned with constituent order, a rule of Auxiliary Movement was introduced and discussed, but the analysis was marred by the incorrect assumption that negation in Basque originates in pre-auxiliary position.

8.3 Syntax of Emphatic Assertion

In older forms of Basque, an affirmative particle *ba* could occur, the syntax of which completely paralleled that of the negation marker *ez*:

(21) a. Jon bada etorri.
John has (so) come.
b. Jon ez da etorri.
John hasn't come.

This use of *ba* survives in parts of Biscay and among children elsewhere as well, but only in the context of a rebuttal of a negative statement, hence with the force of a double negative:

(22) a. Ez zara Aizkorrira igo!
You didn't climb Mount Aizkorri!
b. Banaiz igo!
I did so climb!

Like *ez*, the particle *ba* combines with the following finite verb into one phonological word. The combination is written as one word following the practice of the Basque Academy, in contrast to the quite parallel case of the negation marker *ez*.

With a synthetic verb form not contained in a periphrastic construction, affirmative *ba* appears in all varieties of Basque in great abundance. In this context, however, use of *ba* has been grammaticalized in Batua and almost all contemporary dialects, as will be discussed in section 8.6.1.

8.4 Relative Order of Participle and Auxiliary

With some important exceptions to be noted in later chapters, in many types of subordinate clauses, the auxiliary must be clause-final and immediately follow its corresponding participle.

Restricting ourselves now to main clauses, we can posit three rules.

Rule 1 Except in negative clauses and emphatic assertions, the auxiliary follows its corresponding participle. Moreover, it follows it immediately: Nothing intervenes between the two, granted, of course, that the auxiliary may incorporate modal proclitics.

(23) a. Gure alkatea zure ostatuan geldituko omen da jaietan.
Our mayor will allegedly stay in your hotel during the festivities.
b. Joan al da azkenean Karmen ijitoengana?
Has Carmen finally gone to the gypsies?
c. Zer gertatu ote da gaur hemen?
What has happened here today, I wonder?

[*N.B.* For the northern dialects and the Batua usage influenced by these, Rule 1 describes the unmarked order commonly followed in ordinary conversation. In a narrative context, deviations from this order in which the auxiliary precedes the participle are possible, but never obligatory. In the southern dialects, Rule 1 is faithfully adhered to in all contexts, except only in versification (Osa 1990, 232).]

Rule 2 In negative clauses and emphatic assertions, the auxiliary precedes its participle. We recall from section 8.2.2 that the auxiliary must adjoin to the negative morpheme *ez*, or to the emphatic particle *ba* in the case of emphatic assertion:

(24) a. Gure herrira ez al zara inoiz etorriko?
Won't you ever come to our village?
b. Zergatik ez zinen ezkondu gure Mirenekin?
Why didn't you marry our Mary?
c. Miren ez omen da mintzatuko soldadu zahar batekin.
Mary, they say, isn't going to talk with an old soldier.

d. Karmen bada etxeratu.
   Carmen hás come home.

The negation *ez* can be canceled by an ensuing affirmative particle *ba* or, more rarely, its full form *bada*. The resulting statement, which is characterized by an exclamatory intonation, conveys surprise or even dismay. Here the negated auxiliary may either precede or follow the participle:

(25) a. Ijito batekin ez da ba ezkontzen Miren!
        Mary is getting married to a gypsy!
     b. Ijito batekin ezkontzen ez da ba Miren!
        Mary is getting married to a gypsy!

(26) a. Bart gure haurtxoa ez zen ba erori mahaitik!
        Last night our baby fell from the table!
     b. Bart gure haurtxoa erori ez zen ba mahaitik!
        Last night our baby fell from the table!

Sometimes the surprise conveyed by a canceled negation is directed not so much at the state of affairs expressed by the sentence but rather at the fact of the matter coming up at all:

(27) a. Pello ez da ba etorriko!
        You bet Pete will come!
     b. Pello etorriko ez da ba!
        You bet Pete will come!

Canceled negations also show up in rhetorical questions:

(28) a. Nola ez naiz ba geldituko Donostian?
        How should I not stay in San Sebastian?
     b. Nola geldituko ez naiz ba Donostian?
        How should I not stay in San Sebastian?

In genuine negative questions only the first order is found, at least nowadays:

(29) a. Zergatik ez zen geldítu Karmen Donostian?
        Why didn't Carmen stay in San Sebastian?
     b. *Zergatik gelditu ez zen Karmen Donostian?
        Why didn't Carmen stay in San Sebastian?

[*N.B.* Up to the end of the 19th century, many varieties of Basque retained a stylistic rule of VP Preposing: ... *eta Tomas ageri ez zen* (*TB* 152) '... and Thomas did not appear.' In those varieties, (29b), although stylistically marked, was a perfectly fine sentence.]

Rule 3 Whenever the auxiliary precedes the participle, any number of constituents can be positioned in between:

(30) a. Ez da Patxi bihar gurekin mendira igoko.
Frank isn't going to climb the mountain with us tomorrow.
b. Bai, ez naiz inorekin inora inoiz joango.
Yes, I will never go anywhere with anybody.
c. Karmen bada askotan hona etortzen.
Carmen does often come here.

[*N.B.* The largest number of words intercalated to date between a negated auxiliary and its corresponding participle in spontaneous writing is 24. The record holder is none other than Mitxelena, the father of Euskara Batua. Although the reader cannot at this point be expected to understand the example, I will quote it for curiosity's sake. It is taken from Mitxelena's address to the Ninth Congress of Eusko-Ikaskuntza, held in 1983.]

(31) Nik neronek ezagutu dut gaztetan gure artean nabari zen halako susmo txarra *ez ote zuten* azken finean hangoek, guk, hain garbiak ginelarik ere (eta batzuek, noski, besteak baino garbiago), idazten genuen baino hobeki, modu jatorragoan, ez hain modu "dorphean," *idazten*. (*MEIG* VI, 58)
I myself in my youth have recognized a certain suspicion that was manifest among us as to whether those over there weren't writing better, in a purer fashion, not in such a "heavy" fashion, than we ourselves were writing, we being so puristic (some, of course, more so than others).

8.5 Topic

In section 8.2.2 the notion of sentence topic cropped up. A full discussion of this key notion will not be attempted, as this would require a monograph in itself.

A few orientating remarks, however, can be offered for the convenience of the reader. I take the sentence topic, hereafter simply topic, to be that constituent of the sentence the referent of which the speaker intends his utterance to be about.

It is thus a pragmatic notion, connected with a concrete utterance as uttered by a particular speaker to a particular audience in a particular situation.

Successive utterances in a connected discourse or conversation often show coreferential topics. Accordingly, topics are frequently realized as anaphoric pronouns, in Basque most commonly a zero form, as will be seen in chapters 9 and 15.

It is often claimed that a topic noun phrase embodies information known to both speaker and hearer, and hence must be grammatically definite. This, however, is not necessarily the case. A sentence may very well introduce its own topic, not previously known to the hearer. This topic will then be an indefinite noun phrase, to wit, of the specific variety.

Moreover, even when the topic represents old information, shared by speaker and listener alike, the corresponding noun phrase may still be indefinite, indeed nonspecific, provided we are dealing with a set of referents, instead of an individual. Thus a partitive noun phrase (section 13.1.2) can count as a topic.

A topic is by no means a necessary part of an utterance. It is lacking, for instance, in a class of statements known as presentationals.

When present, a topic has psychological reality, not just for the speaker, but also for the hearer. Psycholinguistic evidence seems to indicate that the hearer normally processes the sentence starting from its topic and, moreover, will use the mental representation of the topic's referent as a peg to store the contents of the utterance in his memory.

It is therefore essential that the hearer should be able to recognize the topic of any utterance he is faced with. Usually the prior discourse coupled with its situational setting suffices to reveal the topic's identity. When that is the case, the topic needs no special marking in Basque and can occur in virtually any position within the sentence. When, however, circumstances and context do not enable the hearer to identify the topic, a careful speaker will endeavor to encode this information into the structure of the utterance.

Languages differ widely in the range of devices employed for this purpose, as their nature can be phonological, mostly involving stress or tone; morphological, that is, invoking a lexical topic marker; or again, syntactic.

For a syntactic identification to be possible, the topic must stand out in some way from the remaining parts of the sentence, which make up the "comment." The saliency it thus needs can be conferred upon the topic by applying to it some syntactic process that is "marked" in a Praguean sense, as Davison (1984) has argued. In many languages, including Basque, the most common process meeting this description is Topic Fronting, by which a topic is lifted out of its clause and moved to a topic slot in front of the sentence. It is noteworthy that in Basque a noun phrase thus fronted will retain the case marking that matches its original function inside the clause. As an illustration, consider these examples:

(32) a. Pello pozik ezkonduko da Karmenekin.
Pete will gladly marry Carmen.
b. Karmenekin Pello pozik ezkonduko da.
Carmen, Pete will gladly marry.

Context permitting, *Karmenekin* could be topic in example (32a), but must be so in (32b).

A preposed topic tends to be followed by a slight pause, indicated by a comma. Fronted topics will henceforth be called "emphatic" topics. More interesting examples of fronted topics will be found in the treatment of embedded clauses in section 18.7.

8.6 Focus

8.6.1 Focus in Positive Clauses

The theory outlined here, which relates word order to focus, goes back to work published in 1920—and, in an augmented version, 1929—by the Biscayan scholar S. Altube, the first Basque grammarian to study focus in commendable detail.

It has been repeatedly pointed out by native critics that its validity is restricted to one use of language, namely, conversation. In other—and, one might say, less central—uses of language, such as storytelling and similar pursuits, quite often special effects of style are achieved by breaking Altube's rules. This observation, often adduced as invalidating to some extent Altube's analysis, in fact rather supports it. Obviously, if special effects can be achieved by breaking them, those rules of necessity must first be part and parcel of the linguistic competence of the speaker.

This preliminary out of the way, we will open our discussion with an English example. Pronounced with a normal, rather flat, intonation, the sentence "Grandmother is going to Bilbao tomorrow" may serve to answer any of the following inquiries (among others):

a. Who is going to Bilbao tomorrow? (Requires, perhaps, some stress on *Grandmother*.)
b. When is Grandmother going to Bilbao?
c. Where is Grandmother going tomorrow?

In Basque, unlike English, the order of constituents makes it perfectly clear which particular inquiry the speaker has in mind:

(33) a. Amona joango da bihar Bilbora.
(Nor joango da bihar Bilbora?—Amona.)
b. Amona bihar joango da Bilbora.
(Amona noiz joango da Bilbora?—Bihar.)
c. Amona Bilbora joango da bihar.
(Amona nora joango da bihar?—Bilbora.)

Each of these sentences highlights a different constituent, which the speaker represents as embodying the relatively most important piece of information at the moment, that is, the "point" of his utterance. In (33a) this is the subject *amona* 'Grandmother', in (33b) the time adverb *bihar* 'tomorrow', and in (33c) the directional adjunct *Bilbora* 'to Bilbao'.

This type of highlighted constituent, known in Spanish publications in the wake of Azkue's *Gramática eúskara* of 1891 as "el elemento inquirido," accurately fits the description of what we nowadays refer to as "focus," either "selective" or "completive."

We speak of selective focus when the required piece of information is anticipated to be a member of a small finite set of known alternatives, and of completive focus in all other cases. Thus, in example (34a) the focus phrase *Gipuzkoara* 'to Guipuzcoa' may be either completive or selective. It will be the latter if questions like (34b) or (34c) are to be taken as the underlying inquiry:

(34) a. Gipuzkoara joango naiz.
I will go to Guipuzcoa.
b. Nora joango zara, Gipuzkoara ala Bizkaira?
Where will you go, to Guipuzcoa or to Biscay?

c. Gipuzkoara ala Bizkaira joango zara?
   Will you go to Guipuzcoa or to Biscay?

More than one constituent can be focus in a single clause. Example (35a) instantiates such multiple focus, provided the underlying inquiry has the form of (35b):

(35) a. Amona bihar Bilbora joango da.
   Grandmother will go to Bilbao tomorrow.
b. Amona noiz nora joango da?
   When will Grandmother go where?

It is by no means to be assumed that a nonfocus constituent may relate only information already known to the hearer, or presupposed to be such by the speaker. What happens is merely that any nonfocus item carries a content held by the speaker to be less essential to the communication than that contributed by the focus. The speaker creates, as it were, an information peak. It should be added that this information peak coincides with an intonation peak. Indeed, the focused phrase stands out phonetically by being realized on a somewhat higher pitch than the remaining parts of the Basque sentence, maintaining, however, the same tonal stress pattern (cf. section 1.2.3) that it would show outside of focus.

An examination of examples like (33a,b,c) establishes the main fact about focus in Basque, generally cited as Altube's Law: the focused constituent immediately precedes the verbal phrase. Accordingly, the position immediately in front of the verb, whether periphrastic (*joango da*) or synthetic (*doa*), will be styled "focus position."

In the northern dialects, as G. Rebuschi (1983) has argued, the focus is always placed in front of the finite verb, that is, *da* rather than *joango da*. This interesting detail, however, will not be elaborated on here, inasmuch as our discussion is geared to the southern variety of Euskara Batua.

As first pointed out on page 105 of de Rijk 1978, the syntax of Basque focus is more than a matter of word order; it also involves constituent structure. No adverb whatsoever can be intercalated between focus and verb, not even a harmless sentence adverb like *noski* 'of course'. Nor is there room, before the articulation of the verb, for any hesitation or pause to follow the focus (cf. Michelena 1976, 149). All this goes to show that focus and verb together form a tightly knit surface constituent, a verb phrase of sorts, albeit deprived of the usual complements, unless, of course, one or more of those happen to be focus.

Needless to say, it is still possible for a phrase to immediately precede a verb without the two forming a single constituent. This, however, only happens when the clause involved lacks focus, that is, when it is unconnected in the mind of the speaker to any particular enquiry expressable as a wh-question.

Strictly speaking, focus has been defined only for statements, that is, declarative sentences. Yet, since the focus indicates what was being looked for—*elemento inquirido*—one naturally expects its properties to carry over to the wh-items in wh-questions. This is indeed what we find. Interrogative phrases in Basque, while not necessarily clause-initial, must appear in focus position in all finite clauses, positive as well as negative:

(36) a. Zubitik ibaira nor erori zen atzo?
Who fell yesterday from the bridge into the river?
b. Gaur zer gertatu da gure elizan?
What happened today in our church?
c. Zenbat sorgin igaro dira gaur zure aurretik?
How many witches passed you today?

(37) a. Nor ez da inoiz Madrilen izan?
Who has never been to Madrid?
b. Zergatik ez dira Pello eta Karmen ostatuan gelditzen?
Why are Pete and Carmen not staying at the inn?
c. Zenbat alaba ez dira oraindik ezkondu?
How many daughters have not married yet?

For some reason, nonfinite clauses are not subject to this constraint:

(38) a. Nora, ordea, zurekin joan?
Where, however, to go with you?
b. Zergatik gaur mendira igo?
Why go up to the mountains today?

We now give some examples to show how a proper understanding of focus is a sine qua non for a correct interpretation of even the simplest Basque sentence:

(39) a. Jainkoa ona da.
God is good.
b. Jainkoa da ona. (Lk 18:19; *Lau Eb.*)
It is God who is good.

Sentence (39a), with the adjective *ona* 'good' as focus, answers the question *Jainkoa nolakoa da?* 'How is God?' by ascribing to God the quality of goodness. Sentence (39b), where *Jainkoa* 'God' is focus, answers a very different question: *Nor da ona?* 'Who is good?', and so fits the communicative intent of the text in Lk 18:19.

To take an example of a different cast:

(40) a. Zu alkatea al zara?
Are you a mayor?
b. Zu al zara alkatea?
Are you the mayor?

Sentence (40a) displays the word order of the question *Zu zer zara?* 'What are you?' and thus has *alkatea* as focus. Its most likely meaning is therefore 'Are you a mayor?'. Sentence

(40b) shares its word order with the question *Nor da alkatea?* 'Who is the mayor?', and thus has *zu* 'you' as focus. Hence its most likely meaning: 'Are you the mayor?'.

At times it is quite clearly the action expressed by the verb that is the focus of interest within the sentence. To choose an example of the simplest kind, for *the snow* to be the focus of the utterance "The snow has melted," this statement would have to be conceived of as an answer to the question "What has melted?" There are no doubt some circumstances in which this assumption might be correct, but in general a far more likely question to be relevant here is "What has happened to the snow?", which makes *the snow* topic rather than focus.

In instances of this sort, the verb will be regarded as focus, and quite justifiably so, as Basque grammar treats it in precisely the same fashion it does nominal or adverbial focus: the focused verb is required to be in focus position.

To achieve this purpose, the grammar introduces into the sentence a dummy verb *egin*, which represents the regular Basque counterpart of the English verb *to do*, or, when used with an intransitive auxiliary, *to become*. It is then in focus position before this verbal dummy that the focused verb finds its rightful place. The verb in focus naturally assumes its unmarked form, the perfect participle, while the dummy verb *egin* is periphrastically conjugated the same way the focused verb would be outside of focus.

A few examples will illustrate the procedure:

(41) a. Elurra urtu egin da.
The snow has melted.
b. Nekane nekatu egiten zen.
Dolores was getting tired.
c. Mutilak lotsatu egin ziren neskatxen aurrean.
The boys felt ashamed in front of the girls.
d. Erori egin al da? (Atxaga, *Obab.* 266)
Did he fall?
e. Ia hil egin naiz.
I almost died.

As soon as any constituent other than the verb carries focus, the dummy verb *egin* no longer appears:

(42) a. Elurra oraintxe urtu da.
The snow has just now melted.
b. Nekane agudo nekatzen zen.
Dolores was getting tired quickly.
c. Mutilak zeharo lotsatu ziren neskatxen aurrean.
The boys felt totally ashamed in front of the girls.
d. Ibaira erori al da?
Did he fall into the river?

e. Ia zuregatik hil naiz.
   I almost died because of you.

So far only half of the story of verbal focus has been told, since we can see that the procedure that we have detailed applies solely to periphrastically conjugated verbs. What about focus on a synthetic verb form?

To answer this question, we must first reveal a vital fact, to wit: Any synthetic verb form in Basque is by nature syntactically incomplete and remains ungrammatical until completed in some fashion. One way to complete it is by means of a preceding focus:

(43) a. Amona doa gaur Bilbora.
   Grándmother is going today to Bilbao.
b. Amona gaur doa Bilbora.
   Grandmother is going to Bilbao todáy.
c. Amona Bilbora doa gaur.
   Grandmother is going today to Bilbáo.

Whenever a positive clause has no nominal or adverbial focus, its synthetic verb form must be completed in the only remaining way: by adding the affirmative particle *ba-*, treated already in section 8.3, as a prefix to the verbal form. Some examples are

(44) a. Norbait badoa gaur Bilbora.
   Somebody is going today to Bilbao.
b. Badoa ala ez doa?
   Is he going or is he not going?
c. Bazatoz ala bazoaz?
   Are you coming or are you going?

On account of its origin as an affirmative particle, *ba-* does not appear in negative clauses. Nor is there need for that, since the negation marker *ez* suffices to complete the synthetic verb form: *Ez doa.* 'He is not going.' This actually may be the prime reason, not mentioned in section 8.2.2, why *ez* has to be adjacent to the finite verb. In front of modal proclitics, the prefix *ba-* is represented in writing as a separate word:

(45) a. Behin ba omen zen errege bat.
   Once upon a time there was a king.
b. Ba ote dator Karmen?
   Is Carmen coming, I wonder?
c. Etxeko andrea ba al da etxean?
   Is the lady of the house at home?

Synthetic verbs, unlike their periphrastic colleagues, do not distinguish between verbal focus, as in example (44c), and no focus at all, as in (45a). In Batua, at least in its southern variety, affirmative *ba-* appears in either case. Only some subdialects of Biscayan are able to mark verbal focus by placing the unmarked form of the verb immediately in front of the synthetic verb form: *Ibili nabil* 'I walk'. Another example is

(46) Etorri zatoz, ala joan zoaz? (Arejita, *Eusk. Josk.* 18)
Are you coming, or are you going?

At this point, the following contrast scarcely calls for explanation:

(47) a. Bada ardoa.
There is wine.
b. Ardoa da.
It is wine.

In example (47b), the bare form *da* shows that the preceding noun *ardoa* must be focus. The pertinent inquiry is therefore *Zer da?* 'What is it?'. Hence the meaning 'It is wine'. Similarly,

(48) a. Ni banaiz.
I am. (I exist.)
b. Ni naiz.
It's me.

And, using an adjective, like *zahar* 'old':

(49) a. Ni zaharra naiz.
I am old.
b. Ni naiz zaharra.
I am the one who is old.
c. Ni banaiz zaharra. (Only in dialects with emphatic *ba-*; cf. section 8.3.)
I ám old.

While it is quite true that no adverb can appear between the focus and the following verb, a slight complication arises owing to the ability of certain adverbs to occur as a final part of the focus noun phrase. As an example, consider sentence (50):

(50) Gaur zaharrak bakarrik doaz elizara.

Now, when only *bakarrik* 'alone' bears focus intonation, the sentence means 'Today, old people are going to church alone.' A more likely interpretation, however, results when focus intonation is given to the phrase *zaharrak bakarrik* 'old people alone', namely, 'Today, old people alone are going to church.'

Connective adverbs, such as *aldiz* 'on the contrary', *bederen* 'at least', *berriz* 'on the other hand', *behintzat* 'at least', and *ordea* 'however', neither are able to bear focus themselves, nor can be part of a noun phrase. For that reason, such adverbs are focus blockers when they occur in front of the verb:

(51) a. Orain, behintzat, bazatoz.
Now, at least, you are coming.
b. Apaizak, ordea, badoaz.
The priests, however, are going.

Although being a postclitic tied to a preceding noun phrase, the particle *ere* in the sense 'also' acts as a focus blocker too, but does so strictly by virtue of its meaning: "Who is coming? *Also the witches. Where are they hanging out? *Here too." Note that in negative clauses where it means '(not) even' *ere* does not block focus. In positive clauses, however, a synthetic verb form must start with the prefix *ba-* whenever it immediately follows *ere*:

(52) a. Sorginak ere badatoz.
The witches too are coming.
b. Hemen ere badabiltza.
They are hanging out here too.

Summarizing:

(53) a. Nor dator ijitoarekin? Karmen dator (ijitoarekin).
Who is coming with the gypsy? Carmen is coming (with the gypsy).
b. Norekin dator Karmen? Ijitoarekin dator (Karmen).
With whom is Carmen coming? She (Carmen) is coming with the gypsy.
c. Zer gertatzen da? Badator Karmen ijitoarekin.
What is happening? Carmen is coming with the gypsy.
d. Eta Karmen, zer? Karmen badator ijitoarekin.
And what about Carmen? She (Carmen) is coming with the gypsy.

[*N.B.* In example (53d), there is no focus, only topic and comment (section 8.5).]

8.6.2 Focus and Quasi Focus in Negative Clauses

Defined as that constituent in the sentence which matches the wh-item in the pragmatically pertinent question, focus shows the same behavior in negative clauses as in positive ones: it immediately precedes the first member of the finite verb complex:

(54) a. Nor ez da etorri?
Who hasn't come?
b. Miren ez da etorri.
Mary hasn't come.

(55) a. Zergatik ez doaz gaur ahizpak elizara?
Why aren't the sisters going to church today?
b. Elurrarengatik ez doaz gaur ahizpak elizara.
The sisters aren't going to church today because of the snow.

(56) a. Noiz ez da Patxi laneratzen?
When doesn't Frank go to work?
b. Igandeetan ez da Patxi laneratzen.
Frank doesn't go to work on Sundays.

As in positive clauses, the verb itself may be focus ("What didn't happen?"), in which case the dummy verb *egin* appears, again just as in positive clauses:

(57) Itsasora erori ziren sorginak, baina ito ez zen egin inor.
The witches fell into the sea, but nobody actually drowned.

Actually, negative clauses bearing focus are quite rare. Indeed, most negative clauses are not mentally linked up with negative questions at all, but are simply denials of positive statements and, therefore, given our definition, do not contain focus.

What they may have is an informationally prominent constituent to be labeled quasi focus, which is in fact the focus of the positive statement denied by the speaker. Focus and quasi focus display quite dissimilar properties in Basque. Five points of difference can be noted here:

1. Since a speaker may decide to make the focus of an assertion into the topic of his denial of that assertion, quasi focus, unlike focus, can function as sentence topic.
2. As noticed in the previous section, the particle *ere* blocks focus, but does not block quasi focus.
3. The intensifying suffix *-xe* (see section 26.8) frequently occurs with focus constituents, but never with quasi focus.
4. Emphatic personal pronouns (see section 28.2.5.1) occur as either topic or focus but never as quasi focus.
5. Quasi focus, unless topicalized, appears in postauxiliary position instead of in the preauxiliary position characteristic of focus.

For clauses with a periphrastically conjugated verb there is a canonical quasi-focus site: the position immediately in front of the participle.

The reason is not far to seek. Auxiliary Attraction—alone responsible for the divergent word order of positive and negative clauses (section 8.2.2)—merely moves the finite verb to the posttopic position, leaving everything else unchanged. In particular, the position immediately in front of the participle remains unaffected. This, however, is the focus site of the positive clause, and hence the quasi-focus site of the negative one. Our deduction is confirmed by the facts:

(58) a. Amona ez da gaur Bilbora joango, Gazteizera baizik.
Grandmother won't go today to Bilbao, but to Vitoria.

But not:

(58) b. *Amona ez da gaur Bilbora joango, bihar baizik.
Grandmother won't go today to Bilbao, but tomorrow.

Rather:

(58) c. Amona ez da gaur joango Bilbora, bihar baizik.
Grandmother won't go to Bilbao today, but tomorrow.

Similarly, to take an attested example from the Labourdin dialect:

(59) Ez zarete, alabaina, zuek mintzatzen, baina Izpiritu saindua. (Mk 13:11; Dv)
Yoû are not speaking, however, but the Holy Spirit.

Of course, verbal quasi focus is also possible. It is characterized by the presence of the dummy verb *egin*, inherited from the corresponding positive assertion:

(60) Oraindik ez naiz Balantzategiko ikuiluan sartu ere egin! (Atxaga, *Behi* 60)
I have not even *gone* yet into the cowshed of Balantzategui!

With respect to a synthetically conjugated verb, there is no well-defined quasi-focus position. We saw in section 8.2.2 that Auxiliary Attraction—which applies to any conjugated verb, not just to auxiliaries—forces the verb to move forward to join the negation marker *ez*. In doing so, the verb can leap over any number of sentence constituents (cf. example 31), thereby causing the original preverbal focus site to become undetectable in the absence of a fixed landmark like a participle. Example (61) represents just one of various possibilities:

(61) Aita ez dator oinez gaur etxera, autobusez baizik.
Father is not coming home today on foot, but by bus.

8.6.3 Bibliographical Note on Focus and Constituent Order

The literature on Basque focus is too plentiful for this survey to be other than highly selective. My choice consists of the following authors, arranged according to the chronology of their contributions:

P. P. Astarloa, *Apología de la lengua bascongada*, Madrid, 1803.

Astarloa's discussion on pages 179–187 of the "orden de movilidad" in the placement of words "en los conceptos bascongados" make Astarloa a pioneer of word-order studies and a precursor of Altube. See also pages 520–527 and pages 766–773 of his *Discursos filosóficos sobre la lengua primitiva*, posthumously published, Bilbao, 1883.

R. M. Azkue, *Euskal-izkindea* (*Gramática eúskara*), Bilbao, 1891.

Azkue correctly understood the nature of focus, for which he coined the phrase "elemento inquirido," explaining it in terms of the interrogative elements of implicit questions. Yet he assigned it the wrong sentence position: sentence-initial instead of preverbal.

M. Lekuona, "Métrica vasca," Vitoria, 1918.

In note 1 of this inaugural lecture we find a clear statement of what is now known as Altube's law: "la palabra principal de una oración es la inmediata anterior al verbo, ..." (p. 39).

S. Altube, *De sintaxis euskérica*, San Sebastian, 1920.
———, *Erderismos*, Bermeo, 1929.

The classic study on Basque focus, which, despite the criticisms that have been leveled at it, deservedly remains the basis of all later work.

P. Lafitte, *Grammaire basque*, Bayonne, 1944 (2nd edition, 1962).

Chapter 6 contains a short but influential exposition of constituent order in the northern dialects based on the concept "mot de valeur" (also "terme requis"), in which he distinguishes primary, secondary, and tertiary focus.

R. P. G. de Rijk, "Is Basque an SOV Language?" *FLV* 1 (1969): 319–351.
———, "Topic Fronting, Focus Positioning and the Nature of the Verb Phrase in Basque," pp. 81–112 in F. Jansen (ed.), *Studies on Fronting*, Lisse, 1978 (= *DLV* 183–201).
———, "Focus and Quasifocus in Basque Negative Statements," (1996a) in *DLV* 421–433.

The first article's final section (pp. 342–349) constitutes the first discussion of Basque focus in English. Dealing with Basque topic and focus from the point of view of generative semantics, the second article leads up to the claim that Basque has no verb phrase other than a derived one made up of focus and verb. The third article introduces quasi focus as a concept distinct from focus in the study of negative clauses.

F. Donzeaud, "The Expression of Focus in Basque," *ASJU* 6 (1972): 35–45.

A somewhat sketchy discussion of Basque focus aiming toward an interpretive rule of Focus Assignment à la Jackendoff 1973.

K. Mitxelena, "Galdegaia eta Mintzagaia Euskaraz," pp. 57–81 in *Euskal linguistika eta literatura: bide berriak*, Bilbao, 1981.

A medley of syntactic observations culled from older Basque texts, part of which relates to topic and focus.

G. Rebuschi, "A Note on Focalization in Basque," *Journal of Basque Studies* 4 (1983): 29–42.

A generative account of some of the differences between the northern and southern dialects, concentrating on the use of focus-related *ba-* and that of the dummy verb *egin*.

B. Oihartzabal, "Le préfixe *ba* d'assertion positive en basque," *Bulletin du Musée Basque* 102 (1983): 161–190.
———, "Behako bat ezezko esaldieri," *Euskera* 30 (1985): 103–115.

Insightful observations by a native linguist, first on the use of affirmative *ba-*, and then on the expression of focus in negative clauses, mostly with regard to the northern dialects.

J. M. Ortiz de Urbina, "Empty Categories and Focus in Basque," *Studies in the Linguistic Sciences*, 13 (1983): 133–156.

S. Tamura, "Hitzen ordena erabakitzeko faktoreak," *Euskera* 30 (1985): 71–101.

A comparative study of word order and its pragmatic conditioning in Basque and Japanese.

P. Salaburu, "El movimiento de las frases-QU y el foco en vasco," *FLV* 21 (1989): 7–26.

A lucid lecture on Basque focus movement and configurationality in a GB framework.

E. Osa, *Euskararen hitzordena komunikazio zereginaren arauera*, Leioa, 1990.
———, "Esapidearen gramatika funtzionala (egokitasunaren teoriarako)," *ASJU* 27 (1993): 395–448.

The first item is an excellently written, well-reasoned doctoral dissertation (directed by P. Goenaga) concerned with informational structure and its realization in Basque syntax, in which the author strongly advocates a text- or discourse-oriented approach to word order. Its width of coverage and its critical tone toward earlier work make for rewarding reading. The second item, a posthumous article whose title translates as "Functional Grammar of the Sentence for the Theory of Relevance," surveys the literature dealing with functional grammar and pragmatics, with the aim of establishing the specific features of "relevance" in Basque.

8.7 The Suffix of Abundance *-tsu*

Oddly reminiscent of Latin *-ōsus*, the adjectival suffix *-tsu* (from earlier *-zu*, according to Mitxelena) productively combines with—mostly inanimate—common nouns *N*, which it turns into adjectives meaning 'rich in N' or 'full of N'. (A double exception—animate base and deviant meaning—is *adiskidetsu* 'friendly' of recent origin [1933]; the few other animates attested bear the expected meaning: *haurtsu*, *jendetsu*, *umetsu*.)

Some count nouns allow a distinction between an intensive and an extensive sense in their derivatives: *maldatsu* (and its synonym *aldapatsu*) from *malda* (or *aldapa*) 'slope', can mean either 'steep' (intensive sense) or 'hilly' (extensive sense).

Here as elsewhere, a derivational base can be a bound form: while the free form *maite* is an adjective with the meaning 'dear', 'beloved', as the first member of a compound *maite-* functions like a noun meaning 'love': *maitemin* 'lovesickness', literally 'love pain'; whence also the derivative *maitetsu* 'loving'. The noun *doha-*, base of *dohatsu* 'fortunate' is likewise bound, ocurring, for example, in *dohakabe* 'misfortune'.

Some common examples are

adin	age	adintsu	aged
ahal	power	ahaltsu	powerful, mighty
amore	affection	amoltsu	affectionate
ardura	care, diligence	arduratsu	careful, diligent
argi	light	argitsu	bright, lustrous, luminous
arrisku	danger, risk	arriskutsu	dangerous, risky
atsegin	pleasure	atsegintsu	pleasurable, nice, delightful
atsekabe	sorrow, suffering	atsekabetsu	sorrowful, sad, painful
ausardia	boldness	ausarditsu	bold (also: *ausartsu*)
balio	value, worth	baliotsu	valuable, precious
behar	necessity	behartsu	poor
berri	news	berritsu	talkative, gossipy
buru	head	burutsu	ingenious
diru	money	dirutsu	rich
doha	bliss	dohatsu	blissful, fortunate, happy
erabaki	decision	erabakitsu	determined, resolute
erruki	compassion	errukitsu	compassionate
euri	rain	euritsu	rainy
gar	flame, ardor	gartsu	flamy, ardent, fervent
garrantzi	importance	garrantzitsu	important
gorroto	hatred	gorrototsu	hateful, rancorous
gozo	sweetness, sweet	gozatsu	sweet, delightful
grina	passion, tendency	grinatsu	passionate, nervous, excited
gupida	pity, compassion	gupidatsu	merciful, compassionate
haize	wind	haizetsu	windy, boastful
hari	thread	haritsu	thready, stringy, fibrous
haur	child	haurtsu	with many children
herra	rancor, resentment	herratsu	rancorous, resentful
hodei	cloud	hodeitsu	cloudy
ile	hair	iletsu	hairy
indar	strength	indartsu	strong
itzal	shadow, shade, respect	itzaltsu	shadowy, sad, respectful, venerable
jende	people	jendetsu	crowded, populous
ke	smoke	ketsu	smoky
kemen	energy, vigor	kementsu	energetic, vigorous
koipe	grease	koipetsu	greasy

lan	work	lantsu	busy, active
lohi	mud	lohitsu	muddy
maite	love	maitetsu	loving, tender
mami	substance	mamitsu	substantial, juicy
mendi	mountain	menditsu	mountainous
muki	snot	mukitsu	snotty
nahigabe	sorrow, suffering	nahigabetsu	sorrowful, sad
neke	effort	neketsu	laborious, hard
neurri	measure	neurritsu	sober, moderate
odol	blood	odoltsu	bloody
ordu	time, hour	ordutsu	timely, punctual
osasun	health	osasuntsu	healthy
ospe	fame	ospatsu	famous (also: *ospetsu*)
pozoi	poison	pozoitsu	poisonous, venomous
premia	need	premiatsu	needful, necessary
sats	muck, filth	satsu	filthy, mucky
seta	stubborness	setatsu	stubborn, persistent
su	fire	sutsu	fiery, fervent, enthusiastic
tema	obstinacy	tematsu	obstinate
ume	offspring, child	umetsu	with a lot of offspring
ur	water, juice	urtsu	watery, juicy
urte	year	urtetsu	long-lived, aged
usain	smell, odor	usaintsu	smelly, odoriferous, aromatic
zarata	noise	zaratatsu	noisy
zorion	happiness	zoriontsu	happy

8.8 Vocabulary

amorratu	rabid, mad
behintzat	at least
bestela	otherwise
bete	filled, full
bikain	excellent
dantza	dance
edo	or
elur	snow
gauerdi	midnight
lehenago	formerly
ongi	well
saiatu	to try, to attempt

txakur	dog
zakur	big dog
zoratu	to turn crazy

[*N.B.* If necessary, refer back to section 7.8.]

8.9 Exercises

8.9.1 Translate into English

1. Eguzkiaren barrua oso beroa omen da.
2. Itsas ondoko jendea beldurrez betea bide zegoen.
3. Zure nagusiaren txakur amorratua laster hilko ahal da!
4. Ez al da orain arte inon ezer gertatu?
5. Noiz itzuliko ote zara zure emazte bikainarengana?
6. Zergatik ez ote zen inor gelditzen sorgin gazteen ostatuan?
7. Elurra oraindik zuri izateaz nor ez da harritzen?
8. Ez gara zu eta ni ijitoen tabernan inoiz sartuko.
9. Lotsatu egiten gara amerikar batzuen soinura herri osoa dantzan ikustea.
10. Esnatu egin zarete azkenean?
11. Saiatu, behintzat, egingo gara.
12. Ni ez naiz gertatuarengatik itzuli itsasora.

8.9.2 Translate into Basque

1. Once there was a pretty witch from San Sebastian, and she got married to a black soldier.
2. Mary will surely not stay in my ugly old house.
3. The old gypsy's friend must surely not have woken up at five o'clock.
4. I do hope nobody will stay until midnight.
5. Who will speak in the hotel on Sunday, I wonder?
6. There was somebody here; or else I have turned crazy.
7. Was it you, I wonder?
8. A girl from Bermeo spoke well about you.
9. From what bridge did your son fall yesterday morning?
10. Formerly the mayors of our village used to be bad, but not now.
11. My brother seldom comes to our home, and my sister never at all.
12. It is a long way, but we will arrive.

9 Synthetic Present of Transitive Verbs; Ergativity; Demonstratives

9.1 Synthetic Present of Transitive Verbs

The following transitive verbs are strong; that is to say, they admit a synthetic (i.e., single-word) conjugation:

Perfect Participle	Stem	Present Base	Meaning
eduki	-uka	dauka	to hold, to contain, to have
*edun	-u-	du	to have
egin	-gi-	dagi	to do, to make, to accomplish
ekarri	-karr-	dakar	to bring
entzun	-ntzu-	dantzu	to hear
erabili	-rabil-	darabil	to use, to handle, to treat, to stir
erakarri	-rakarr-	darakar	to cause to be brought, to attract
erakutsi	-rakutsa-	darakutsa	to show, to exhibit, to teach
eraman	-rama-	darama	to carry, to lead, to bear
eroan	-roa-	daroa	to carry, to drive, to bear
ezagutu	-zagu-	dazagu	to recognize, to acknowledge
ikusi	-kus-	dakus	to see, to view, to visit
*ion	-io-	dio	to say
irakin	-iraki-	diraki	to boil
iraun	-irau-	dirau	to last, to endure
irudi	-irudi-	dirudi	to resemble, to seem
jakin	-ki-	daki	to know
jardun	-ihardu-	dihardu	to be busy with, to engage in

Comments

1. Just as in the case of intransitive verbs (cf. section 6.2.2), the third-person singular form is identical to the present base consisting of the verbal stem prefixed with the present tense

marker *da-*. Before a stem with an initial vowel, the *a* of *da-* elides: *du, dihardu, diraki, dirau, dirudi*. The apparent exception *dauka* goes back to an earlier *daduka* (a form still used in poetry and lofty style) from the stem *-duka-* of *eduki*. Likewise, the general Biscayan form *dau* instead of *du* is based on a former **dadu*, from the stem *-du-* of the verb **edun*.
2. The nonfinite forms of **ion*, an unattested hypothetical construct, are borrowed from its synonym *esan* 'to say'. Similarly, when in the early 17th century the nonfinite forms of **edun* were becoming obsolete, the southern dialects adopted those of another auxiliary verb, *izan*, whose nonfinite forms are therefore ambiguous between the senses 'to be' and 'to have'. The northern dialects resorted instead to the nonfinite forms of a close synonym *ukan* (*ukaiten, ukanen*, never **ukango*). In present Batua either option is permissible.
3. Notice that the verbs *iraun* 'to last', *irakin* 'to boil', and *jardun* 'to be busy' do not take grammatical objects and are thus syntactically intransitive (cf. section 7.1.1). They are, however, morphologically transitive.
4. Imperative aside (see chapter 22), use of the synthetic forms of the verbs *egin* 'to do', *entzun* 'to hear', *erakarri* 'to attract', *erakutsi* 'to show', *ezagutu* 'to be acquainted with', *ikusi* 'to see', *irakin* 'to boil', and *iraun* 'to last' tends to be confined to the loftier registers of the written language (cf. section 6.2.1).

Next, let us look at the conjugation of the transitive verb *ekarri* 'to bring', comparing it with that of the intransitive verb *etorri* 'to come':

nator	I am coming	nakar	he/she/it is bringing me
hator	yoú are coming	hakar	he/she/it is bringing yoú
dator	he is coming	dakar	he/she/it is bringing him/her/it
gatoz	we are coming	gakartza	he/she/it is bringing us
zatoz	you are coming	zakartza	he/she/it is bringing you
zatozte	yoû are coming	zakarzte	he/she/it is bringing yoû
datoz	they are coming	dakartza	he/she/it is bringing them

With regard to morphology, we notice that the pluralizer is not *-z* but *-tza* for this transitive paradigm. The double pluralizer corresponding to *zuek* 'yoû', however, is the same: *-zte*.

With regard to meaning, it is striking that *nakar* does not mean 'I am bringing', like *nator* 'I am coming', but rather 'he/she/it is bringing me'. Thus, in the present tense form of a transitive verb, it is the direct object, not the subject, that is marked by the well-known person prefixes resulting from the substitution of the initial consonant of a personal pronoun for the initial *d* in the present tense marker *da* (cf. section 6.2.2).

The subject of a transitive verb, however, also plays a part in verbal morphology. It is marked by a person suffix located toward the end of the verb form. Apart from complementizers, only the past tense suffix *-n* follows the subject marker, except for the verb **ion*, where the object pluralizer *-z* follows all person markers.

The subject person suffixes are shaped as follows:

First-person singular	-da
Second-person singular "familiar" feminine	-na (with lowered pitch)
Second-person singular "familiar" unmarked	-ga
Third-person singular	-∅ (i.e., non-marked)
First-person plural	-gu
Second-person singular	-zu
Second-person plural	-zue (with lowered pitch on *e*)
Third-person plural	-te (with lowered pitch)

In word-final position the suffixes ending in *a* (*-da*, *-ga*, *-na*) lose their *a* vowel, except for *-na* when preceded by a consonant. Since voiced obstruants (except nasals) are not allowed in final position, the resulting *-d* or *-g* turns into *-t* or *-k* by the final devoicing rule.

Concerning the suffix *-ga*, it should be added, for later reference, that the *g* elides whenever the *a* does not, so that the suffix surfaces as either *-k* or *-a-*.

Note that while there is no gender contrast in the third person, there is such in the second person "familiar," but only in the pronominal suffixes, not when the second person is indicated by a prefix or a pronoun. Interestingly, a woman talking to herself regularly uses the suffix *-ga*, from which it follows that this suffix is unmarked for gender, rather than being marked for male gender, as is generally assumed.

To facilitate the translation of Basque verb forms, the conventions of section 6.1.1 will be extended to make use of the gloss 'yoù' to denote a "familiarly" (see section 6.1.2) addressed female. Thus, in the second person, four forms are to be distinguished: 'yoû' for the plural *zuek*, 'you' for the unmarked singular *zu*, 'yoù' for the solidarity form *hi* with the suffix *-na*, and 'yoú' for the *hi* in the absence of this suffix.

For brevity's sake, when translating a paradigm, I will put *he* for any third-person singular subject (instead of *he/she/it*), and *it* for any third-person singular object (instead of *him/her/it/∅*).

Now, for the verbs *ekarri* 'to bring' and *eraman* 'to carry' the following paradigm results:

dakart	I am bringing it	daramat	I am carrying it
dakark	yoú are bringing it	daramak	yoú are carrying it
dakarna	yoù are bringing it	daraman	yoù are carrying it
dakar	he is bringing it	darama	he is carrying it
dakargu	we are bringing it	daramagu	we are carrying it
dakarzu	you are bringing it	daramazu	you are carrying it
dakarzue	yoû are bringing it	daramazue	yoû are carrying it
dakarte	they are bringing it	daramate	they are carrying it

The forms shown presuppose a third-person singular direct object. When instead a plural object is involved, an object pluralizer will be included in the verb form. The exact shape depends on the verb:

1. The verb **edun* employs a prefix *it-* directly in front of the stem *-u-*.
2. The verb *eduki* employs an infix *-z-* placed inside the stem *-uka-*.
3. The verb **ion* employs a suffix *-z* positioned after the subject marker.
4. The verbs of knowing and perceiving—*verba sapiendi* and *sentiendi*—*entzun*, *erakutsi*, *ezagutu*, *ikusi*, and *jakin*, employ a suffix *-zki* directly following the stem.
5. All other verbs (*egin*, *ekarri*, *erabili*, *erakarri*, *eraman*, *eroan*) employ a suffix *-tza* directly following the stem.

Thus, for the verbs *ekarri* and *eraman* with a third-person plural object, we get

dakartzat	I am bringing them	daramatzat	I am carrying them
dakartzak	yoú are bringing them	daramatzak	yoú are carrying them
dakartzan	yoù are bringing them	daramatzan	yoù are carrying them
dakartza	he is bringing them	daramatza	he is carrying them
dakartzagu	we are bringing them	daramatzagu	we are carrying them
dakartzazu	you are bringing them	daramatzazu	you are carrying them
dakartzazue	yoû are bringing them	daramatzazue	yoû are carrying them
dakartzate	they are bringing them	daramatzate	they are carrying them

The rare synthetic forms of the verb *erakarri* are patterned on those of *ekarri*: *darakart* 'I attract it', *darakartzat* 'I attract them', and so on.

For the reader's convenience, paradigms will now be given for all other verbs mentioned, with the exception of *eduki* 'to hold' and **edun* 'to have', which will be left for the end of this section.

First, we will view the remaining verbs taking the object pluralizer *-tza*: *egin* 'to make', *erabili* 'to use', and *eroan* 'to drive', 'to bear':

dagit	I am making it	dagitzat	I am making them
dagik	yoú are making it	dagitzak	yoú are making them
dagin	yoù are making it	dagitzan	yoù are making them
dagi	he is making it	dagitza	he is making them
dagigu	we are making it	dagitzagu	we are making them
dagizu	you are making it	dagitzazu	you are making them
dagizue	yoû are making it	dagitzazue	yoû are making them
dagite	they are making it	dagitzate	they are making them

darabilt	I am using it	darabiltzat	I am using them
darabilk	yoú are using it	darabiltzak	yoú are using them
darabilna	yoù are using it	darabiltzan	yoù are using them
darabil	he is using it	darabiltza	he is using them

darabilgu	we are using it	darabiltzagu	we are using them
darabilzu	you are using it	darabiltzazu	you are using them
darabilzue	yoû are using it	darabiltzazue	yoû are using them
darabilte	they are using it	darabiltzate	they are using them

daroat	I am driving it	daroatzat	I am driving them
daroak	yoú are driving it	daroatzak	yoú are driving them
daroan	yoù are driving it	daroatzan	yoù are driving them
daroa	he is driving it	daroatza	he is driving them
daroagu	we are driving it	daroatzagu	we are driving them
daroazu	you are driving it	daroatzazu	you are driving them
daroazue	yoû are driving it	daroatzazue	yoû are driving them
daroate	they are driving it	daroatzate	they are driving them

We will now look at the five verbs that take the object pluralizer *-zki*: *entzun* 'to hear', *erakutsi* 'to show', *ezagutu* 'to recognize', *ikusi* 'to see', and *jakin* 'to know':

dantzut	I hear it	dantzuzkit	I hear them
dantzuk	yoú hear it	dantzuzkik	yoú hear them
dantzun	yoù hear it	dantzuzkin	yoù hear them
dantzu	he hears it	dantzuzki	he hears them
dantzagu	we hear it	dantzuzkigu	we hear them
dantzuzu	you hear it	dantzuzkizu	you hear them
dantzuzue	yoû hear it	dantzuzkizue	yoû hear them
dantzute	they hear it	dantzuzkite	they hear them

darakutsat	I am showing it	darakuskit	I am showing them
darakutsak	yoú are showing it	darakuskik	yoú are showing them
darakutsan	yoù are showing it	darakuskin	yoù are showing them
darakutsa	he is showing it	darakuski	he is showing them
darakutsagu	we are showing it	darakuskigu	we are showing them
darakutsazu	you are showing it	darakuskizu	you are showing them
darakutsazue	yoû are showing it	darakuskizue	yoû are showing them
darakutsate	they are showing it	darakuskite	they are showing them

[*N.B.* Observe that the plural object forms of *erakutsi* are based on an apocopated stem *-rakuts-* instead of the singular stem *-rakutsa-*. The now stem-final *s* coalesces with the suffix *-zki* producing *-ski*, explicable via an intermediate stage *-tski*.]

dazagut	I recognize it	dazaguzkit	I recognize them
dazaguk	yoú recognize it	dazaguzkik	yoú recognize them
dazagun	yoù recognize it	dazaguzkin	yoù recognize them
dazagu	he recognizes it	dazaguzki	he recognizes them
dazagugu	we recognize it	dazaguzkigu	we recognize them

dazaguzu	you recognize it	dazaguzkizu	you recognize them
dazaguzue	yoû recognize it	dazaguzkizue	yoû recognize them
dazagute	they recognize it	dazaguzkite	they recognize them

[*N.B.* The intervocalic *g* of the stem *-zagu-* can be dropped: *dazaut* instead of *dazagut*, and so on.]

dakust	I see it	dakuskit	I see them
dakusk	yoú see it	dakuskik	yoú see them
dakusna	yoù see it	dakuskin	yoù see them
dakus	he sees it	dakuski	he sees them
dakusku	we see it	dakuskigu	we see them
dakutsu	you see it	dakuskizu	you see them
dakutsue	yoû see it	dakuskizue	yoû see them
dakuste	they see it	dakuskite	they see them

[*N.B.* Note that the stem-final *s* devoices the *g* of *gu* and that the combination *s* + *z* in *kus* + *zu* produces the affricate *ts*. Similarly, in the plural object forms *-kus* + *zki-* turns into *-kuski-* through an intermediate stage **-kutski-*.

The singular object forms may take a lengthened stem *-kusa-*, whence the alternative forms *dakusat*, *dakusak*, *dakusan*, *dakusa*, *dakusagu*, *dakusazu*, *dakusazue*, and *dakusate*.]

dakit	I know it	dakizkit	I know them
dakik	yoú know it	dakizkik	yoú know them
dakin	yoù know it	dakizkin	yoù know them
daki	he knows it	dakizki	he knows them
dakigu	we know it	dakizkigu	we know them
dakizu	you know it	dakizkizu	you know them
dakizue	yoû know it	dakizkizue	yoû know them
dakite	they know it	dakizkite	they know them

Noteworthy is the verb **ion*, whose object pluralizer *-z* follows the personal endings:

diot	I am saying it	diodaz	I am saying them
diok	yoú are saying it	dioaz	yoú are saying them
dion	yoù are saying it	dionaz	yoù are saying them
dio	he is saying it	dioz	he is saying them
diogu	we are saying it	dioguz	we are saying them
diozu	you are saying it	diozuz	you are saying them
diozue	yoû are saying it	diozuez	yoû are saying them
diote	they are saying it	diotez	they are saying them

[*N.B.* Note that the plural object paradigm of **ion* shows the full forms of the person endings *-da*, *-ga*, and *-na*, now no longer word-final. *Dioaz* results from intervocalic *g* deletion before *a*.]

The verbs *irakin* 'to boil', *iraun* 'to last', *irudi* 'to seem', and *jardun* 'to be occupied', which do not admit direct objects, present no more than one paradigm each:

dirakit	I am boiling
dirakik	yoú are boiling
dirakin	yoù are boiling
diraki	he is boiling
dirakigu	we are boiling
dirakizu	you are boiling
dirakizue	yoû are boiling
dirakite	they are boiling

diraut	I last
dirauk	yoú last
diraun	yoù last
dirau	he lasts
diraugu	we last
dirauzu	you last
dirauzue	yoû last
diraute	they last

dirudit	I seem
dirudik	yoú seem
dirudin	yoù seem
dirudi	he seems
dirudigu	we seem
dirudizu	you seem
dirudizue	yoû seem
dirudite	they seem

dihardut	I am occupied
diharduk	yoú are occupied
dihardun	yoù are occupied
dihardu	he is occupied
dihardugu	we are occupied
diharduzu	you are occupied
diharduzue	yoû are occupied
dihardute	they are occupied

[*N.B.* All stems with initial *i* have lowered pitch on their final syllable.]

Direct objects in the first or second person have thus far remained outside of consideration. Yet these are frequently encountered, except, of course, with **ion* 'to say', *jakin* 'to know', and the four syntactic intransitives that we have cited. In the presence of such objects many verbs resort to periphrastic forms. But the verbs *eduki* 'to hold', **edun* 'to have', *ekarri* 'to bring', *erabili* 'to use', *eraman* 'to carry', and, in highly archaic usage, *ezagutu* 'to recognize', do possess direct-object forms for the first and second person, derived by substituting the first consonant (*n*, *h*, *g*, *z*) of the corresponding personal pronoun for the *d* in the present tense marker *da-*, as we have seen at the beginning of this section.

With *gu* 'us' or *zu* 'you' as direct object, the same object pluralizer appears as in the third-person forms. With *zuek* 'yoû' as direct object, however, the object pluralizer is *-zte*, regardless of its shape for the other persons (except for *eduki*).

For the verbs *eduki* 'to hold' and **edun* 'to have', full paradigms will be given shortly. As to the others, considering the regularity of the system and the actual rarity of the forms, it will be sufficient to illustrate the pattern by means of a few examples:

hakart	I am bringing yoú ('yoú' can be male or female)
zakartzat	I am bringing you
zakarztet	I am bringing yoû
zakartzate	they are bringing you
zakarztete	they are bringing yoû
narabilk	yoú are using me
narabilna	yoù are using me
zarabiltza	he is using you
zarabilzte	he is using yoû
zarabilztete	they are using yoû
garamatzak	yoú are carrying us
garamatzan	yoù are carrying us
haramagu	we are carrying yoú ('yoú' can be male or female)
zaramatzagu	we are carrying you
zaramaztegu	we are carrying yoû
hazagugu	we recognize yoú ('yoú' can be male or female)
nazaguzu	you recognize me
gazaguzki	he recognizes us
zazaguzki	he recognizes you
zazaguzte	he recognizes yoû

Note that as far as Basque morphology is concerned, subject and obiect must have disjoint reference. There are no forms like **gakartzat* 'I am bringing us' or **narabilgu* 'we are using me'.

The extremely common verb *eduki* or *euki* with the meanings 'to hold', 'to contain', 'to possess', and 'to have' (cf. Spanish *tener*) uses as object pluralizer an infix *-z-* within the stem *-uka-*. Consequently, the object pluralizer for *zuek* 'yoû' is not shaped *-zte*, as for all other verbs, but -*te* combined with the infix -*z*- inside the stem. Apart from that, the paradigm is quite regular.

The verb is translated here as 'to possess', in order to bring out its relationship to the verb **edun* 'to have', with which it is often interchangeable.

daukat	I possess it	dauzkat	I possess them
daukak	yoú possess it	dauzkak	yoú possess them
daukan	yoù possess it	dauzkan	yoù possess them
dauka	he possesses it	dauzka	he possesses them
daukagu	we possess it	dauzkagu	we possess them
daukazu	you possess it	dauzkazu	you possess them
daukazue	yoû possess it	dauzkazue	yoû possess them
daukate	they possess it	dauzkate	they possess them
naukak	yoú possess me	gauzkak	yoú possess us
naukan	yoù possess me	gauzkan	yoù possess us
nauka	he possesses me	gauzka	he possesses us
naukazu	you possess me	gauzkazu	you possess us
naukazue	yoû possess me	gauzkazue	yoû possess us
naukate	they possess me	gauzkate	they possess us
haukat	I possess yoú	zauzkat	I possess you
hauka	he possesses yoú	zauzka	he possesses you
haukagu	we possess yoú	zauzkagu	we possess you
haukate	they possess yoú	zauzkate	they possess you

zauzkatet	I possess yoû
zauzkate	he possesses yoû
zauzkategu	we possess yoû
zauzkatete	they possess yoû

The verb **edun* 'to have', also serving as an auxiliary verb for the periphrastic conjugation of all transitive verbs, uses as object pluralizer the prefix *it*-. Accordingly, the object pluralizer for *zuek* 'yoû' is the suffix -*te* combined with the prefix *it*- in front of the verb stem -*u*-. However, this suffix acquires the shape -*tze*, because in this verb the sequence -*tute* always turns into -*tuzte*, possibly a doubly marked plural. These considerations taken into account, the paradigm is surprisingly regular:

dut	I have it	ditut	I have them
duk	yoú have it	dituk	yoú have them
dun	yoù have it	ditun	yoù have them
du	he has it	ditu	he has them
dugu	we have it	ditugu	we have them
duzu	you have it	dituzu	you have them

duzue	yoû have it	dituzue	yoû have them
dute	they have it	dituzte	they have them
nauk	yoú have me	gaituk	yoú have us
naun	yoù have me	gaitun	yoù have us
nau	he has me	gaitu	he has us
nauzu	you have me	gaituzu	you have us
nauzue	yoû have me	gaituzue	yoû have us
naute	they have me	gaituzte	they have us
haut	I have yoú	zaitut	I have you
hau	he has yoú	zaitu	he has you
haugu	we have yoú	zaitugu	we have you
haute	they have yoú	zaituzte	they have you

zaituztet	I have yoû
zaituzte	he has yoû
zaituztegu	we have yoû
zaituztete	they have yoû (or *zaituzte*)

9.2 Ergativity

9.2.1 The Ergative Case

A basic property of Basque is brought out by the following sentences:

(1) a. Peru dator.
Peter is coming.
b. Peru dakar.
He is bringing Peter.
c. Peruk dakar.
Peter is bringing him (or *her*, or *it*).

(2) a. Arantxa dauka.
He has Arantxa.
b. Arantxak dauka.
Arantxa has him (or *her*, or *it*).

(3) a. Nor dator? Peru.
Who is coming? Peter.
b. Nor dakar? Peru.
Who is he bringing? Peter.
c. Nork dakar? Peruk.
Who is bringing him? Peter.

(4) a. Nor dauka? Arantxa.
Who does he have? Arantxa.
b. Nork dauka? Arantxak.
Who has him? Arantxa.

The Basque language has no accusative case, no special form for the direct object of a verb (like English *him* as against *he*); it has an ergative case, a special form for the subject—which may or may not be a semantic agent—of a transitive verb. Basque is therefore classified as a morphologically ergative language, which is generally defined as a language wherein the subject of an intransitive predicate and the (direct) object of a transitive verb share a morphological trait not shared by the subject of a transitive predicate. This shared morphological trait may be realized either directly on the noun phrases involved—with case marking being the prime example—or else within the verbal morphology by means of agreement markers referring to subject and/or object. Constituent order, too, may play a role.

In Basque, the shared morphological trait is simply the zero case marking common to the subject of an intransitive predicate and the (direct) object of a transitive verb, in contrast to the different—ergative—case marking on the subject of a transitive predicate.

Basque verb morphology is also ergative, at least in the present tense. As we have seen in section 9.1, one and the same set of prefixes is used to refer to an intransitive subject as well as to a transitive object, whereas suffixes are used for the transitive subject. In the past tense morphology, however, matters are less clear-cut, as we will see in section 10.1.

In Basque, ergative case marking affects nouns and pronouns alike (in contrast to many Australian and Papuan languages), occurs in both embedded and main clauses (unlike in the Mayan languages), and is not sensitive to tense or aspect distinctions (contrary to what happens in certain languages, such as Burushaski, Georgian, Hindi, or Tibetan).

Inasmuch as the category of morphologically unmarked noun phrases seems to be irrelevant in the functioning of such syntactic processes as reflexivization, reciprocalization, equi-NP deletion, and subject raising, and plays no part in determining pronominal reference in conjoined clauses, Basque, like the vast majority of ergative languages in the world, is not syntactically ergative. On the other hand, whether or not Basque is syntactically accusative must as yet be left open, as it is unclear to what extent Basque syntax requires a notion of grammatical subject that is distinct from sentence topic and independent of morphological case.

The only complicating factor in Basque ergativity is the existence of syntactically intransitive verbs that take ergative subjects. Some theoreticians have been tempted to conclude that Basque is not technically ergative at all, being instead a language whose case marking directly reflects the distinction set up in relational grammar between unaccusative and unergative verbs. Only the latter would take genuine subjects, which are marked by the ergative case, whereas the former would take initial objects functioning as surface subjects while keeping their object case marking.

This theory neatly explains certain facts, such as the relative rarity of intransitives in Basque (cf. section 7.1.3), but at a heavy price: the distinction between the two basic verb classes comes to seem totally ad hoc, that is, lacking any basis in universal grammar or semantics. Indeed, active verbs like *ausartu* 'to dare', *baliatu* 'to make use', and *mintzatu* 'to speak' act as unaccusatives; and, vice versa, standard examples of unaccusatives, such as *izarniatu* 'to shine', *distiratu* 'to glitter', the patient verb *irakin* 'to boil', and the durative verb *iraun* 'to last', 'to subsist', clearly function as unergatives under this theory.

Be that as it may, I have no qualms in adopting ergative terminology to describe the structure of Basque. Accordingly, the case taken by the subjects of most transitive verbs will be named the ergative case, while the morphologically unmarked case form common to the direct object of transitive verbs and the subject of most intransitive verbs will be styled the absolutive case. The classical designation "nominative" does not properly fit either case, and should best be reserved for languages that, unlike Basque, show a nominative-accusative contrast in their case forms. "Ergative," of course, is a modern term (first coined by A. Dirr in 1912 [Dixon 1994, 3 fn.]), not used by native Basque grammarians until quite recently. For this case, the term "active" (also "agent") was traditionally resorted to, a usage going back to the earliest Basque grammarian, A. Oihenart, who spoke of *nominativus activus* or *casus agendi* versus *nominativus passivus* in his *Notitia utriusque Vasconiae* of 1638 (Oihenart 1992, 58–61). Still in the 17th century, S. Pouvreau translated those terms into French as *nominatif substantif ou passif* and *nominatif actif* (*Les petites oeuvres basques*, 1892, 3).

As already noted in section 2.2.1, the ergative in Basque is characterized by a basic ending *-k*. Naturally, *e*-epenthesis will apply whenever this ending immediately follows a consonant, for example, after the proper name *Miren*:

(5) a. Peruk eta Mirenek ogia dakarte.
   Peter and Mary are bringing the bread.
 b. Mutil batek arrain bat dakar.
   There is a boy bringing a fish.

Whereas combining the ergative ending *-k* with the singular article *-a*, not surprisingly, results in the form *-ak*, combining it with the plural article *-ak* produces the form *-ek* (from **-ag-e-k*) in the standard language as well as in the northern dialects. The southern dialects, Guipuzcoan and Biscayan, use *-ak* (from **-aga-k*) in the definite form of the ergative plural. Thus we get

(6) a. Gizona dator.
   The man is coming.
 b. Gizonak datoz.
   The men are coming.
 c. Gizonak dakar.
   The man is bringing it.

d. Gizonek dakarte.
   The men are bringing it.

In the dialects of Biscay and the greater part of Guipuzcoa, there is an appreciable difference in intonation between the ergative singular *gizonak* and the plural *gizonak*, the former taking the normal toneme and the latter the anormal one (cf. section 1.2.3).

9.2.2 Historical and Bibliographical Note on Ergativity

Earlier scholarship in the area of ergativity was quite literally obsessed by the passivity thesis of the Basque verb. It stands to reason that obligatory passivization of transitive clauses provides a plausible account of the origin of ergative systems in various languages of the world. Despite a complete lack of positive evidence—there being no collateral function for the ergative case, nothing precludes postulating a comparable development for Basque as well. Unfortunately, in debating this thesis, first voiced by F. Müller (1888, III, II, 18) and sealed shortly after with the authority of H. Schuchardt (1893, 2), synchrony and diachrony were rarely kept separate.

In the otherwise excellent dissertation *Le système du verbe basque au XVI*[e] *siècle* published in 1943 by the French scholar R. Lafon (1899–1974), the form *dut* is regularly translated as "il est eu par moi," a practice that culminates in the presentation of "en vue il est eu par lui" as a "literal interpretation" of *ikusten du* 'he sees him'. Later on, Lafon repudiated the passive theory. In his monumental contribution "Basque" to *Current Trends in Linguistics* (1972, vol. 9), he wrote: "I ceased to translate the verb forms of the 2nd class with the passive forms in French, for this procedure, which Schuchardt had followed and recommended because of his 'passive conception' of the transitive verb in Basque, appeared unjustified to me" (p. 1763). And on page 1765: "It is incorrect to state that, in principle, what is not active is passive. One has only to consider those languages where it is the middle voice, and not the passive, which is opposed to the active."

Starting in the late 1970s, more modern concerns involving typological considerations or issues of universal grammar begin to be mirrored in the literature on Basque ergativity. The following list of publications is fairly representative, albeit by no means exhaustive. The order of citation is chronological: Zytsar 1977, 1978 (Spanish version of 1977 article); Rebuschi 1978; Wilbur 1979a; Brettschneider 1979; Heath 1981; Levin 1983a, 1983b; Bossong 1984 (in which the thesis is argued that Basque syntax is "neutral," neither ergative nor accusative); Ortiz de Urbina 1989 (see chap. 1); and Laka 1993 (in which she uses Basque data to refine Chomsky's [1992] theory of case assignment).

For background reading on ergativity in general, the 1994 monograph by the world's leading expert in this field, R. M. W. Dixon, is highly recommended. For a different perspective, see G. A. Klimov 1973, to be read in combination with the review of B. Comrie (1976). Also Comrie 1978, which includes examples from Basque, makes profitable reading.

9.3 Use of Synthetic Forms of Transitive Verbs

9.3.1 Synthetic Verb Forms in Common Use

In everyday spoken language, only ten of the verbs treated in this chapter display synthetic forms. These are **edun*, *eduki*, **ion*, *jakin*, *ekarri*, *erabili*, *eraman*, *eroan*, *jardun*, and *irudi*. I will discuss them in that order.

Unlike Spanish *haber*, to which it is similar in being an auxiliary for the conjugation of transitive verbs, **edun* 'to have' can be freely used to express possession of all types, alienable as well as inalienable:

(7) a. Nik baditut mila ardi. (From Souletin song "Maiteak biloa hori," Riezu, 63)
I have one thousand sheep.
b. Badut andrea, badut semea, badut alaba ere nik. (Elzb. *Po.* 196)
I have a wife, I have a son, I have a daughter too.
c. Arrosatxoak bost hosto ditu, krabelintxoak hamabi. (From the Guipuzcoan song "Donostiako iru damatxo," *Xaramela* 94)
The (little) rose has five leaves, the (little) carnation twelve.
d. Midasek astabelarriak ditu. (J. B. Aguirre, *Erak.* III, 491)
Midas has donkey's ears.
e. Zer duzu? (Atxaga, *Obab.* 241)
What is the matter with you? (Lit. 'What have you [got]?')

The traditional meaning of *eduki* is 'to hold', 'to retain', 'to contain'. Under the influence of the Spanish verb *tener* of similar meaning, the southern dialects, including Batua, regularly use it in the sense 'to have':

(8) a. Neure andreak atorra zaharra . . . zazpi astean soinean dauka. (From the Guipzcoan song "Neure Andrea," *Xaramela* 236)
My wife keeps an old shirt on her body for seven weeks.
b. Zuk hor dauzkazu bi autore: Lizardi eta Agirre Asteasukoa. (*MEIG* VII, 133)
You have two authors there: Lizardi and Aguirre from Asteasu.

The verb **ion* 'to say' has nothing but synthetic forms:

(9) a. Joera berriez zer diozu? (*MEIG* I, 66)
What do you say about the new trends?
b. Gezurrak diodaz? (Mogel, *C.O.* 133)
Am I telling lies?

Synthetic forms of the verb *jakin* 'to know' are extremely common:

(10) a. Nik ez dakit zer esan. (*MEIG* VIII, 109)
I don't know what to say.
b. Egia inork ez daki.
Nobody knows the truth.

c. Ba al dakizu euskaraz?
Do you know (how to speak) Basque?

As its meaning matches that of French *savoir* or German *wissen*, the verb *jakin* disallows animate noun phrases as direct objects. These, however, may occur as genitive complements to the indefinite noun *berri* 'news', resulting in a noun phrase which may then serve as the object of *jakin*:

(10) d. Nork ez daki gure artean aita Plazido Mujikaren berri? (*MEIG* I, 89)
Who among us doesn't know of Father Plácido Mujica?

The verb *ekarri* means 'to bring' and, hence, 'to carry', 'to produce', 'to cause':

(11) a. Zerk zakartza hona?
What brings you here?
b. Lanak lana dakar. (Cf. Amuriza, *Hil ala bizi* 77)
Work brings work.
c. Orduko geldiak dakar oraingo lehia. (*MEIG* IX, 59)
It is the stagnation of that time which causes the hurry of this time.

The verb *erabili*, originally a causative of *ibili* 'to walk', shows quite a wide range of meanings: 'to use', 'to handle', 'to treat', 'to carry', 'to move', 'to stir', 'to plot'. Here are some examples:

(12) a. Ikastetxean euskarazko liburuak darabiltzagu.
At school, we use Basque books.
b. Urak darabil errota. (*E.H.* 222; *E.H.M.* 299)
The water moves the mill.
c. Zerbait badarabilzu zuk hor barruan. (Agirre, *Kres.* 41)
You are brooding over something there inside.
d. Zer darabilzu buru horretan? (Atxaga, *Obab.* 297)
What are you brooding over in that head (of yours)?

[*N.B.* A common way of expressing 'to think about', 'to consider' is *gogoan erabili*, literally 'to stir in the mind':

(12) e. Zer darabilzu gogoan?
What are you thinking about?]

The verb *eraman* means 'to carry (off)', 'to lead', 'to wear', 'to bear', 'to spend time':

(13) a. Sua eta egurra badaramatzagu. (Gn 22:7)
We are carrying the fire and the wood.
b. Geuregan daramagu heriotza. (*MEIG* I, 193)
We carry death within ourselves.
c. Mirenek gaur minigona darama.
Mary is wearing a miniskirt today.

d. Luisek bere logelarantz zaramatza. (Oñederra, 79)
   Louis is leading you toward his bedroom.
e. Hamar egun daramatzat hemen. (Atxaga, *Ziut.* 42)
   I have (now) spent ten days here.

The verb *eroan* substitutes for *eraman* in Biscay and parts of Soule. In Batua, it is mostly used in the meanings 'to lead', 'to conduct', 'to drive'.

(14) a. Bideak nora daroa?
   Where does the road lead?
b. Jonek orain automobil ona daroa.
   John is now driving a good car.

The verb *jardun* means 'to be busy with' and also 'to talk':

(15) a. Zertan diharduzu? Nire lanean dihardut.
   What are you busy with? I am busy with my work.
b. Zertaz diharduzue? Eguraldiaz dihardugu.
   What are yoû talking about? We are talking about the weather.

The verb *irudi* means 'to be similar to' or, in other words, 'to seem':

(16) a. Tresnak jabea dirudi. (proverb: Garate, *Atsot.* 12,436)
   The tool is like the master.
b. Zure gerriak palmera bat dirudi. (Sg 7:8; Ker.)
   Your waist is like a palm tree.
c. Buenos Airesko berriek ez dirudite onak. (*TOE* II, 90)
   The reports from Buenos Aires don't seem good.
d. Heure etxe-barruan atzerritarra dirudik. (*G.* 117)
   Inside your own house, yoú seem a foreigner.
e. Maite, Salomonen gurdiaren behorra dirudizu. (Sg 1:9; Ker.)
   Dear, you are like the mare of Solomon's chariot.

[*N.B.* Of this verb, many speakers use only third-person forms. For the remaining persons, they use periphrastic forms of the verb *eman* 'to give': *ematen dut* instead of *dirudit, ematen duk* instead of *dirudik*, and so on.]

9.3.2 Synthetic Verb Forms Restricted to Literary Style

The eight remaining verbs have been included in this chapter because the student might encounter their synthetic forms in his readings, especially where texts from older periods are involved. These forms no longer occur in the spoken form of any dialect and are exceedingly rare even in contemporary literary prose. Examples will be given for five of the verbs: *iraun*, *ezagutu*, *entzun*, *ikusi*, and *egin*.

The verb *iraun* 'to last', 'to hold out' constitutes a borderline case, in that quite a few speakers still feel comfortable using its synthetic forms for the third person:

(17) a. Sarajevok zutik dirau. (*EHM* 1142)
Sarajevo remains erect.
b. Tortoken irlan udak hamabi hilabete dirau. (Atxaga, *Obab.* 293)
On the island of turtles the summer lasts twelve months.
c. Hark leial dirau. (2 Tm 2:13) (For *hark* see section 9.6.1.)
He remains loyal.
d. Zure leialtasunak belaunaldiz-belaunaldi dirau. (Ps 119:90)
Your loyalty lasts from generation to generation.
e. Zuk, ordea, Jauna, badirauzu beti. (Ps 101:13; Dv)
You, however, O Lord, last forever.

The verb *ezagutu* means 'to know' in the sense of 'to be acquainted with' and furthermore 'to recognize' and 'to acknowledge'. In the spoken language only periphrastic forms occur, despite the citations from Garate's novel:

(18) a. Gainerakoa ongi dazaguzu. (Garate, *Esku* 44)
The rest you know (very) well.
b. Badazaguzu kafetetxe hori, ez da? (Garate, *Esku* 122)
You know that coffeehouse, don't you?
c. Jainkoak badazaguzki zuen bihotzak. (Lk 16:15; Lz)
God knows yoûr hearts.
d. Nondik nazaguk? (Jn 1:48; Lz)
Whence knowest thou me? (i.e., From where do yoú know me?)

Synthetic forms of *entzun* 'to hear' were still heard in 19th-century Biscayan:

(19) a. Zer dantzut? (Mogel, *P.Ab.* 61)
What do I hear?
b. Ez dantzu ezer. (Mogel, *P.Ab.* 72)
She hears nothing.
c. Peru, ez dantzuzu zuk? (Mogel, *P.Ab.* 81)
Pete, don't you hear it?

Synthetic forms of the verb *ikusi* 'to see', very rare nowadays and highly literary, were abundantly used up to the 19th century:

(20) a. Sua eta egurra dakuskit. (*TZ* I, 49)
I see the fire and the wood.
b. Jainkoak badakuski . . . gauza guztiak. (Duhalde, 203)
God sees all things . . . (For *guzti* 'all', see section 10.5.)
c. Nire begiak zer dakus? (*LBB* 241)
What does my eye see?
d. Guk gauza bat dakusagu garbi. (Garate, *Musk.* 68)
We see one thing clearly. (For *garbi* 'clearly', see section 11.1.4.)

Curiously enough, the synthetic conjugation of so common a verb as *egin* 'to do', 'to make' has become obsolete in all dialects. The following examples are all highly literary:

(21) a. Askotan dagit hau. (Orixe, *Aitork*. 297)
I often do this.
b. Galde dagit, Aita; ez aitor. (Orixe, *Aitork*. 321)
I am asking, Father; not affirming. (From *galde egin* 'to ask', cf. sect. 13.3.3.)
c. Zin dagit Jaun biziarengatik. (Ru 3:13)
I swear (it) by the living Lord. (From *zin egin* 'to swear', section 13.3.3.)
d. Haien aurrean dar-dar dagi lurrak. (Jl 2:10)
Before them earth trembles. (From *dar-dar egin* 'to tremble'.)

9.4 Number Agreement

As we noted in section 9.1, the finite verb agrees in number both with its subject and its object:

(22) a. Andreak liburua dakar.
The lady is bringing the book.
b. Andreek liburua dakarte.
The ladies are bringing the book.
c. Andreak liburuak dakartza.
The lady is bringing the books.
d. Andreek liburuak dakartzate.
The ladies are bringing the books.

Noun phrases quantified by the operators *asko* 'many', *anitz* 'many', *franko* 'quite a few', *gutxi* 'few', *zenbait* 'some', and also *honenbeste*, *horrenbeste*, *hainbeste*, *honenbat*, *horrenbat*, and *hainbat*, all meaning 'so many', may be considered either plural or singular, even when headed by a count noun:

(23) a. Andre asko dator.
Many ladies are coming.
b. Andre asko datoz.
Many ladies are coming.

(24) a. Andreak liburu asko dakar.
The lady is bringing many books.
b. Andreak liburu asko dakartza.
The lady is bringing many books.

In the Souletin dialect, but not in Batua, the same situation obtains for indefinite noun phrases quantified by numerals, such as *hamar liburu* 'ten books', as opposed to *hamar liburuak* 'the ten books', which invariably counts as plural.

9.5 Multi-pro-drop

In Latin and most of its descendants, subject personal pronouns are usually left out, since their recoverability is ensured by a sufficiently rich system of subject-verb agreement. Such languages are known as pro-drop languages: subject pronouns can be freely dropped, as in Spanish *amas* 'you love' versus *tu aimes* in French, a non-pro-drop language. Inasmuch as it involves objects as well as subjects, agreement in Basque is even more extensive than it is in Latin. Accordingly, Basque personal pronouns freely drop both as subjects and as objects of the finite verb. Even indirect object pronouns are regularly dropped, as will be seen in chapter 15.

The pro-drop rule operates under a pragmatic constraint: emphatic topic pronouns and pronouns in focus do not delete but keep their position in front of the sentence or verb complex.

Furthermore, pro-drop in Basque is never obligatory. Pronouns may be retained for stylistic reasons, in which event they will be located after the finite verb. Given the rule of multi-pro-drop, many finite verb forms, say, *zaramatzat*, suffice to express a full state of affairs, in the following example: 'I am carrying you'.

Yet, as we noted in section 8.6.1, such forms cannot constitute a complete sentence by themselves. As long as there is no explicit pronoun to serve as focus, they need to be completed by the nonfocus prefix *ba-*. Thus we get

(25) a. Bazaramatzat.
I am carrying you.
b. Nik zaramatzat.
I am carrying you.
c. Zu zaramatzat.
I am carrying *you*.

Negative verb forms need no further completion:

(25) d. Ez zaramatzat
I am not carrying you.

9.6 Demonstrative Pronouns: Declension and Use

9.6.1 Demonstrative Pronouns: Basic Case Forms

Like the demonstrative adverbs (*hemen, hor, han*) introduced in section 6.3.1, demonstrative pronouns in Basque display a three-way contrast:

First degree: *hau* 'this', related or near to the speaker in space or time.
Second degree: *hori* 'that', related or near to the addressee in space or time.
Third degree: *hura* 'yon', removed from both speaker and addressee in space or time.

[*N.B.* Instead of *hura*, the Biscayan dialect makes use of the more archaic *(h)a*, presumed to be the origin of the article *a* common to all dialects.]

[*Note*: Since English "yon" is obsolete, I will use 'that', or if need be, 'thàt' as a translation for *hura*.]

The singular case forms of these three pronouns are based on an oblique stem different from the absolutive: *hon-*, *horr-*, *har-*. With this fact taken into account, the declension paradigm is perfectly regular:

	Singular		
Absolutive	hau	hori	hura
Ergative	honek	horrek	hark
Dative	honi	horri	hari
Genitive	honen	horren	haren
Sociative	honekin	horrekin	harekin
Instrumental	honetaz	horretaz	hartaz

[*N.B.* The Guipuzcoan form *hortaz*, without the epenthetic vowel, occurs in Batua as an adverb with the meaning 'therefore'.]

Archaic instrumental forms *honez*, *horrez*, and *harez*, lacking the segment *-ta-* characteristic of pronouns (see section 6.1.3), survive in a few set expressions. Thus their use is obligatory in construction with *aurrera* 'forward': *honez aurrera* 'from now on' (more commonly with the elative: *hemendik aurrera*) and *harez aurrera* 'from then on' (more commonly: *handik aurrera*).

Use of the archaic forms is optional in combination with *gain* 'top' or *gainera*, as in *honez gain* (or *honetaz gain*) or *honez gainera* (or *honetaz gainera*), all meaning 'in addition to this', 'moreover' (cf. section 4.1.3). Likewise for combinations with *ostean* 'behind': *honez ostean* (or *honetaz ostean*) 'aside from this', 'besides'.

As we saw in section 2.2.1, the benefactive *-tzat* 'for' and the motivational *-gatik* 'because of', 'in spite of' combine with the genitive: *honentzat*, *horrentzat*, *harentzat*, and *honengatik*, *horrengatik*, *harengatik*. With the latter ending, the *n* of the genitive is optional, hence also *honegatik*, *horregatik*, *haregatik*. The form *hargatik*, without epenthesis, can be used with inanimates—*arrazoi hargatik* 'for that reason'—and also occurs as an independent adverb with the meaning 'yet', 'nevertheless'.

Unlike nouns and adjectives, demonstratives discriminate between singular and plural. The plural has no special oblique stem. The plural case endings, *-ek* (both ergative and absolutive), *-ei*, *-en*, *-ekin*, and *-etaz*, are added directly to the absolutive singular, except for *hura*, which has a plural stem *hai-* based on *ha-*:

Plural			
Absolutive	hauek	horiek	haiek
Ergative	hauek	horiek	haiek
Dative	hauei	horiei	haiei
Genitive	hauen	horien	haien
Sociative	hauekin	horiekin	haiekin
Instrumental	hauetaz	horietaz	haietaz

Unlike the article *-a*, which has an absolutive plural *-ak* and an ergative plural *-ek*, plural demonstratives, in Batua as in nearly all dialects, have only one form for the absolutive and the ergative. Only the Souletin dialect distinguishes the absolutive plural (*hoík, hórik, húrak*) from the ergative plural (*hoiék, horiék, haiék* or *hek*).

Again, the benefactive and the motivational are regularly based on the genitive: *hauentzat, horientzat, haientzat* and *hauengatik, horiengatik, haiengatik*.

9.6.2 Demonstrative Pronouns: Locative Case Forms

In the singular paradigm, the locative cases are based on the oblique stem enlarged with a suffix *-ta* requiring epenthesis. The forms based on *har-* are exceptional in dispensing with the epenthetic vowel. The endings are the usual ones seen in section 3.2.1:

Singular			
Absolutive	hau	hori	hura
Inessive	honetan	horretan	hartan
Elative	honetatik	horretatik	hartatik
Allative	honetara	horretara	hartara
Terminal	honetaraino	horretaraino	hartaraino
Tendential	honetarantz	horretarantz	hartarantz

The plural paradigm is based on the plural stem augmented with the suffix *-eta*:

Plural			
Absolutive	hauek	horiek	haiek
Inessive	hauetan	horietan	haietan
Elative	hauetatik	horietatik	haietatik
Allative	hauetara	horietara	haietara
Terminal	hauetaraino	horietaraino	haietaraino
Tendential	hauetarantz	horietarantz	haietarantz

[*N.B.* The form *hauetan* can be found in the meaning 'in these parts', that is, 'here in this area'. As noted in section 3.3, the endings *-tatik* and *-etatik* have a northern variant *-tarik* and *-etarik*, frequently used in Batua, even in the south.]

A reminder of the linking morpheme discussed in chapter 5 may be relevant at this point:

herri honetako ohitura	the custom of this village
aste hauetako lana	the work of these weeks
etxe horietako teilatuak	the roofs of those houses

When the demonstrative pronoun refers to an animate being or modifies an animate noun phrase, in accord with section 3.6, either the morpheme *-gan* or the word *baita* will appear following the genitive form of the demonstrative:

emakume honengan	in this woman
andre horren baitan	in that lady, at that lady's
apaiz horiengana	to those priests
sorgin haien baitatik	from those witches

9.6.3 Syntax and Use of the Demonstratives

Demonstratives appear either as independent nominals or else as modifiers occupying the endmost position within a noun phrase and, accordingly, taking charge of the case endings:

(26) a. Ijito aberats honek arrosa eder hauek neskatxa polit horrentzat dakartza.
This rich gypsy is bringing these beautiful roses for that pretty girl.
b. Honek hauek horrentzat dakartza.
He/she (here) is bringing these for him/her (there).

In emotive utterances, even proper names can be modified by a demonstrative:

(27) Zer dio Itziar honek?
What is this Itziar saying?

Demonstratives are perfectly compatible with possessives and genitive complements:

(28) Gure seme hauek ezkonduko dira alkatearen alaba horiekin.
These sons of ours will marry those daughters of the mayor.

Demonstratives may denote statements or words that are part of the speaker's own discourse. Then, the first-degree pronouns can be cataphoric, that is, referring to something still to follow (subsequent-discourse deixis). The second-degree pronouns must be anaphoric, that is, referring to something already expressed by the speaker or perhaps by someone else (prior-discourse deixis):

(29) a. Hau bakarrik diot: Aurrera!
I only say this: Forward!
b. Huts hori honetan datza: . . . (*MEIG* I, 243)
That mistake (anaph.) lies in this (cataph.): . . .

c. Gutxi gara. Hori da arazoa.
We are few. That is the problem.

[*N.B.* The phrase *hau da* 'this is' is used like English *i.e.* or *to wit.*]

The nearness to the speaker signaled by the first-degree pronouns may encompass identity; that is, the pronoun can be used with reference to the speaker himself: *alargun gaixo hau* 'this poor widow' is also the only way to express 'I, poor widow':

(30) Alargun gaixo hau ez doa inora.
This poor widow isn't going anywhere. (That is, I, poor widow, am not going anywhere.)

Well attested in older literature, first-person agreement (here: *ez noa*) is no longer observed in modern usage, though it is still acceptable to some speakers.

Similarly, second-degree pronouns may refer to the addressee of the utterance. Thus *deabru zahar hori* 'that old devil' can mean 'you old devil', and *asto hori* 'that donkey' can have the force of 'you ass'. When integrated within a sentence, such phrases bear the appropriate case marker and show second-person agreement with the verb:

(31) Zer darabilk hemen lapur zital horrek? (*P.Ab.* 89)
What are yoú up to here, you nasty thief?

Finally, the three demonstratives serve as equivalents for the third-person pronouns found in many other languages. In the southern variety of Batua, they suffer the competition of *bera* (plural: *berak* or *eurak*), employed whenever the speaker expects the hearer to be aware of a previous mention of the referent intended (see section 6.1.5):

(32) a. Honek ez daki ezer.
He/she doesn't know anything.
b. Haiek horrengan fede osoa daukate.
They have full faith in him/her.
c. Horiengana ez da inor joango orain.
Nobody now will go to them.

9.7 The Behavioral Suffix *-ti*

The adjectival suffix *-ti* (bearing low tone) combines with a fair number of nouns to form adjectives descriptive of the habitual behavior of an animate being, usually human. Like all adjectives, but perhaps more frequently so, they can be used as substantives: *gezurti* 'mendacious' can be used as a noun with the meaning '(habitual) liar'. Examples follow:

adur	slaver, drool	adurti	slavering, drooling
amets	dream	amesti	dreamy
ardura	care, responsíbility	ardurati	careful, responsible

axola	care, concern	axolati	careful, attentive
bakar	single, alone	bakarti	solitary, reclusive
barre	laughter	barreti	cheerful, full of smiles
baso	wilderness, forest	basati	savage, wild, fierce
bekaitz	envy	bekaizti	envious
beldur	fear	beldurti	fearful, cowardly
bihotz	heart	bihozti	affectionate
birao	curse, blasphemy	biraoti	prone to cursing, blasphemous
buru	head	buruti	headstrong, stubborn
egarri	thirst	egarti	thirsty
egia	truth	egiati	truthful
gaixo	ill(ness)	gaixoti	sickly
gerla	war	gerlati	warlike, hawkish
gezur	lie	gezurti	mendacious, liar
gose	hunger	goseti	famished, hungry
haserre	anger	haserreti	quick-tempered, irascible
herabe	diffidence, timidity	herabeti	diffident, shy, timid
ikara	trembling, shiver	ikarati	timorous, frightened
itxura	appearance	itxurati	hypocritical
izu	fright	izuti	jumpy, nervy, frightened
kezka	worry	kezkati	worrying, uneasy
liskar	quarrel	liskarti	quarrelsome
lo	sleep	loti	sleepy, sleepyhead
lotsa	shame	lotsati	bashful, shy, timid
maite	love	maitati	loving, devoted
negar	crying, tear	negarti	weepy, cryish, crybaby
neke	fatigue, effort	nekati	weary
ohar	observation, remark	oharti	observant
ohe	bed	oheti	sickly, sleepyhead
(p)uzker	fart	(p)uzkerti	flatulent
seta	stubbornness	setati	stubborn, pigheaded
sukar	fever	sukarti	feverish
tema	obstinacy	temati	obstinate

9.8 Vocabulary

alargun	widow, widower	atzerritar	foreigner, foreign
ardi	sheep	belarri	ear
arrosa	rose	bihozti	affectionate
atorra	(woman's) shirt	bizitza	life

euri	rain	latz	rough
gauza	thing	lehia	diligence, haste
gerri	waist	leial	loyal
gezurti	mendacious, liar	lodi	thick
gurdi	cart, coach, wagon	lotsati	bashful, shy, timid
heriotza	death	ordea	however
hosto	leaf	soin	shoulder, body
irla	island	tresna	tool
izen	name	zital	vile, nasty, base, infamous
joera	inclination, trend	zorrotz	sharp
krabelin	carnation	zutik	standing, upright, erect

[*N.B.* The citation forms of the verbs discussed in section 9.1 ought to be committed to memory also but are not repeated here.]

9.9 Exercises

9.9.1 Translate into English

1. Itsasoko haize honek euria dakar.
2. Zer ordutan dakartzazue tresna berri horiek gaur?
3. Noren gurdia daramazu gaztelu handi hartara?
4. Gauza haietaz zer diozu eta zer diote adiskide leial horiek?
5. Baserritar hauek gerri lodiak eta esku latzak dituzte.
6. Gure mutil lotsatiek ez dakite sorgin gazte haien berri.
7. Joera gaiztoek heriotzara daroate.
8. Ez dakit belarriko min zorrotz hau nola eraman.
9. Gazteluak ez dirudite gure etxe zahar hauek.
10. Nola zarabiltza bizitzak?
11. Urte honetan gau eta egun dihardugu lanean.
12. Ez zazaguzkit zeure izenaz.

9.9.2 Translate into Basque

1. Who knows Basque?
2. What is bringing you here?
3. What are you bringing here?
4. Are you taking your sheep outside in this cold?

5. This excellent lady is not wearing yesterday's old shoes.
6. I use those thick books of yours every day.
7. Are you taking me to those foreign widows?
8. Those young widows lead a rough life.
9. This pretty lady has red carnations under her shirt.
10. Who does not know that vile liar?
11. This young person doesn't know Mary's name.
12. They seem (to be) loyal and affectionate people.

10 Synthetic Past of Transitive Verbs; Universal Quantifiers

10.1 Past Tense Morphology of Transitive Verbs

The same verbs that allow synthetic forms for the present tense also admit them for the past tense, as shown in the following chart:

Perfect Participle	Stem	Past Base	Third-Person Form	Meaning
eduki	-uka-	zeuka-	zeukan	he held, he had
*edun	-u-	zu-	zuen	he had
egin	-gi-	zegi-	zegien	he did, he made
ekarri	-karr-	zekarr-	zekarren	he brought
entzun	-ntzu-	zentzu-	zentzuen	he heard
erabili	-rabil-	zerabil-	zerabilen	he used
erakarri	-rakarr-	zerakarr-	zerakarren	he attracted
erakutsi	-rakutsa-	zerakutsa-	zerakutsan	he showed
eraman	-rama-	zerama-	zeraman	he carried
eroan	-roa-	zeroa-	zeroan	he drove
ezagutu	-zagu-	zezagu-	zezaguen	he recognized
ikusi	-kus-	zekus-	zekusan	he saw
*ion	-io-	zio-	zioen	he said
irakin	-iraki-	ziraki-	zirakien	he boiled
iraun	-irau-	zirau-	zirauen	he lasted
irudi	-irudi-	zirudi-	zirudien	he seemed
jakin	-ki-	zeki-	zekien	he knew
jardun	-ihardu-	zihardu-	ziharduen	he was busy with

Comments

1. As for intransitive verbs (cf. section 6.2.2), the past base consists of the verb stem preceded by the past tense marker *ze*-, whose *e* elides before a vowel. The exceptional form

zeuka- (instead of **zuka-*) derives from an older *zeduka*, based on an earlier stem form *-duka-*.
2. As stated in section 6.2.2, the third-person singular past tense form consists of the past base together with an additional past tense suffix shaped *-n*, except when it directly follows a verb stem not ending in *a-*, in which case an intervening vowel *-e-* appears. Thus: *zekarren*, *zekien*, but *zeraman*, *zeukan*.

In discussing past tense morphology, it will be convenient to start with those forms that show either a first- or a second-person direct object. With these, as in the present tense, there are object prefixes that substitute for the tense marker *ze-*. They are the usual *n-*, *h-*, *g-*, and *z-*, augmented, however, with an unexplained formative *-inde-* borrowed from the northern dialects. (In the southern dialects, this formative is *-en-*.)

It will be remembered from section 9.1 that the object prefixes *g-* and *z-* require an object pluralizer, whose shape depends on the verb stem—and thus remains the same in all tenses. The object marker for *zuek* 'yoû' is invariably *-zte*, with the sole exception of the verb *eduki* 'to hold'.

The pluralizer *-tza*, and also *-tze* can be followed directly by the past tense suffix *-n*, whereas the pluralizer *-zki* needs a vowel *e* after it before the *-n* can be added.

To illustrate all this, I will use as examples the verb *ekarri* 'to bring' with its object pluralizer *-tza* and the verb *ezagutu* 'to recognize' with its object pluralizer *-zki* even though synthetic forms of this verb are no longer part of the spoken language.

nindekarran	yoú brought me	nindezaguan	yoú recognized me
nindekarnan	yoù brought me	nindezagunan	yoù recognized me
nindekarren	he brought me	nindezaguen	he recognized me
nindekarzun	you brought me	nindezaguzun	you recognized me
nindekarzuen	yoû brought me	nindezaguzuen	yoû recognized me
nindekarten	they brought me	nindezaguten	they recognized me
hindekardan	I brought yoú	hindezagudan	I recognized yoú
hindekarren	he brought yoú	hindezaguen	he recognized yoú
hindekargun	we brought yoú	hindezagugun	we recognized yoú
hindekarten	they brought yoú	hindezaguten	they recognized yoú
gindekartzaan	yoú brought us	gindezaguzkian	yoú recognized us
gindekartzanan	yoù brought us	gindezaguzkinan	yoù recognized us
gindekartzan	he brought us	gindezaguzkien	he recognized us
gindekartzazun	you brought us	gindezaguzkizun	you recognized us
gindekartzazuen	yoû brought us	gindezaguzkizuen	yoû recognized us
gindekartzaten	they brought us	gindezaguzkiten	they recognized us
zindekartzadan	I brought you	zindezaguzkidan	I recognized you
zindekartzan	he brought you	zindezaguzkien	he recognized you

zindekartzagun	we brought you	zindezaguzkigun	we recognized you
zindekartzaten	they brought you	zindezaguzkiten	they recognized you
zindekarztedan	I brought yoû	zindezaguztedan	I recognized yoû
zindekarzten	he brought yoû	zindezaguzten	he recognized yoû
zindekarztegun	we brought yoû	zindezaguztegun	we recognized yoû
zindekarzteten	they brought yoû	zindezaguzteten	they recognized yoû

[*N.B.* As in the present tense, the intervocalic *g* of the stem *-zagu-* may be elided.]

The verbs *erabili*, *erakarri*, *eraman*, and *eroan* are conjugated just like *ekarri*. The paradigms of the verbs *eduki* and **edun* will be given in full at the end of this section.

We now turn to the past tense forms with a third person as direct object. Here, a surprise awaits us. All of a sudden, the person prefixes refer to the ergative subject, while the direct object is left without marking, except for the pluralizer suffix when plural. It is here that we are witnessing that breach of morphological ergativity hinted at in section 9.2.1. As we will find in section 10.2, this breach has no syntactic repercussions.

Using again the verbs *ekarri* and *ezagutu*, the paradigm we are discussing runs as follows:

nekarren	I brought it (him/her)	nezaguen	I recognized it (him/her)
hekarren	yoú brought it	hezaguen	yoú recognized it
zekarren	he brought it	zezaguen	he recognized it
genekarren	we brought it	genezaguen	we recognized it
zenekarren	you brought it	zenezaguen	you recognized it
zenekarten	yoû brought it	zenezaguten	yoû recognized it
zekarten	they brought it	zezaguten	they recognized it
nekartzan	I brought them	nezaguzkien	I recognized them
hekartzan	yoú brought them	hezaguzkien	yoú recognized them
zekartzan	he brought them	zezaguzkien	he recognized them
genekartzan	we brought them	genezaguzkien	we recognized them
zenekartzan	you brought them	zenezaguzkien	you recognized them
zenekartzaten	yoû brought them	zenezaguzkiten	yoû recognized them
zekartzaten	they brought them	zezaguzkiten	they recognized them

Note that there is no distinction of gender in the second-person familiar forms here, as this contrast is tied to the use of the suffixes *-ga* and *-na*.

The paradigms just given show that in the absence of a first- or second-person direct object, the subject marking of transitive verbs in the past tense parallels that of intransitives. In both, the initial consonant of the past base (i.e., *z*) is replaced by that of the subject pronoun, whether ergative or absolutive. Still, there is a morphological difference between the two. In the intransitive paradigm, replacement of the initial *z* also brings about the appearance of a pre-stem nasal formative *-n-*, whereas in the transitive paradigm this formative is followed by *e* and appears in the plural subject forms only. Compare the following:

nentorren	I came	nekarren	I brought
hentorren	yoú came	hekarren	yoú brought
gentozen	we came	genekarren	we brought
zentozen	you came	zenekarren	you brought
zentozten	yoû came	zenekarten	yoû brought

Furthermore, plural marking for subjects is quite different for transitive and intransitive verbs. Whereas the latter mark plurality of the subject by means of a suffix *-z*, the former use a suffix *-te* instead. Moreover, while the suffix *-z* occurs in all four plural forms (see sections 6.1.1 and 6.2.2), the suffix *-te* only appears in the third-person plural and with *zuek*, as follows:

zetorren	he came	zekarren	he brought
zetozen	they came	zekarten	they brought
gentozen	we came	genekarren	we brought

As a further illustration, I now present the paradigms of the verbs *eraman*, *egin*, *erabili*, and *eroan*, all taking the object pluralizer *-tza*. Only third-person direct object forms will be shown:

neraman	I carried it	neramatzan	I carried them
heraman	yoú carried it	heramatzan	yoú carried them
zeraman	he carried it	zeramatzan	he carried them
generaman	we carried it	generamatzan	we carried them
zeneraman	you carried it	zeneramatzan	you carried them
zeneramaten	yoû carried it	zeneramatzaten	yoû carried them
zeramaten	they carried it	zeramatzaten	they carried them
negien	I made it	negitzan	I made them
hegien	yoú made it	hegitzan	yoú made them
zegien	he made it	zegitzan	he made them
genegien	we made it	gerregitzan	we made them
zenegien	you made it	zenegitzan	you made them
zenegiten	yoû made it	zenegitzaten	yoû made them
zegiten	they made it	zegitzaten	they made them
nerabilen	I used it	nerabiltzan	I used them
herabilen	yoú used it	herabiltzan	yoú used them
zerabilen	he used it	zerabiltzan	he used them
generabilen	we used it	generabiltzan	we used them

zenerabilen	you used it	zenerabiltzan	you used them
zenerabilten	yoû used it	zenerabiltzaten	yoû used them
zerabilten	they used it	zerabiltzaten	they used them

neroan	I drove it	neroatzan	I drove them
heroan	yoú drove it	heroatzan	yoú drove them
zeroan	he drove it	zeroatzan	he drove them
generoan	we drove it	generoatzan	we drove them
zeneroan	you drove it	zeneroatzan	you drove them
zeneroaten	yoû drove it	zeneroatzaten	yoû drove them
zeroaten	they drove it	zeroatzaten	they drove them

Corresponding paradigms will now be given for the four remaining verbs using the object pluralizer *-zki*, to wit, *entzun*, *erakutsi*, *ikusi*, and *jakin*:

nentzuen	I heard it	nentzuzkien	I heard them
hentzuen	yoú heard it	hentzuzkien	yoú heard them
zentzuen	he heard it	zentzuzkien	he heard them
genentzuen	we heard it	genentzuzkien	we heard them
zenentzuen	you heard it	zenentzuzkien	you heard them
zenentzuten	yoû heard it	zenentzuzkiten	yoû heard them
zentzuten	they heard it	zentzuzkiten	they heard them

nerakutsan	I showed it	nerakuskien	I showed them
herakutsan	yoú showed it	herakuskien	yoú showed them
zerakutsan	he showed it	zerakuskien	he showed them
generakutsan	we showed it	generakuskien	we showed them
zenerakutsan	you showed it	zenerakuskien	you showed them
zenerakutsaten	yoû showed it	zenerakuskiten	yoû showed them
zerakutsaten	they showed it	zerakuskiten	they showed them

[*N.B.* As in the present tense, the plural object forms of *erakutsi* are based on an apocopated stem *-rakuts-*, whose final *ts* coalesces with the *z* of *-zki* producing a plural stem *-rakuski-*, as the affricate *ts* turns into a fricative before a stop. Similarly, in the verb *ikusi*, the combination of *-kus-* and *-zki* results in *-kuski*.]

The singular object forms of the verh *ikusi* require the augmented stem *-kusa-* in the past tense. Recall that in the present tense use of this stem is merely optional.

nekusan	I saw it	nekuskien	I saw them
hekusan	yoú saw it	hekuskien	yoú saw them
zekusan	he saw it	zekuskien	he saw them
genekusan	we saw it	genekuskien	we saw them
zenekusan	you saw it	zenekuskien	you saw them

zenekusaten	yoû saw it	zenekuskiten	yoû saw them
zekusaten	they saw it	zekuskiten	they saw them
nekien	I knew it	nekizkien	I knew them
hekien	yoú knew it	hekizkien	yoú knew them
zekien	he knew it	zekizkien	he knew them
genekien	we knew it	genekizkien	we knew them
zenekien	you knew it	zenekizkien	you knew them
zenekiten	yoû knew it	zenekizkiten	yoû knew them
zekiten	they knew it	zekizkiten	they knew them

The verb **ion* 'to say' takes an object pluralizer *-za*, apocopating to *-z* in word-final position—for example, past tense *niozan* 'I said them', but present tense *diodaz* 'I say them':

nioen	I said it	niozan	I said them
hioen	yoú said it	hiozan	yoú said them
zioen	he said it	ziozan	he said them
genioen	we said it	geniozan	we said them
zenioen	you said it	zeniozan	you said them
zenioten	yoû said it	zeniozaten	yoû said them
zioten	they said it	ziozaten	they said them

No objects are taken by the verbs *jardun*, *irakin*, *iraun*, and *irudi*:

niharduen	I was occupied	nirakien	I boiled
hiharduen	yoú were occupied	hirakien	yoú boiled
ziharduen	he was occupied	zirakien	he boiled
geniharduen	we were occupied	genirakien	we boiled
zeniharduen	you were occupied	zenirakien	you boiled
zeniharduten	yoû were occupied	zenirakiten	yoû boiled
ziharduten	they were occupied	zirakiten	they boiled
nirauen	I lasted	nirudien	I seemed
hirauen	yoú lasted	hirudien	yoú seemed
zirauen	he lasted	zirudien	he seemed
genirauen	we lasted	genirudien	we seemed
zenirauen	you lasted	zenirudien	you seemed
zenirauten	yoû lasted	zeniruditen	yoû seemed
zirauten	they lasted	ziruditen	they seemed

I now present the complete past tense paradigm of the verb *eduki* 'to hold', 'to contain', 'to possess'. As seen in the present tense, this verb uses an infix *-z-* within its stem *-uka-* as an object pluralizer. Perhaps as a result of haplology (*-indu-* from **-indedu-*), the final *e* of the formative *-inde-* always elides before the stem *-uka-*. The forms with a third-person direct object do not show elision of *e*, since they continue older forms derived from the stem *-duka*: *neukan*, *zeukan*, *geneukan*, and so on deriving from *nedukan*, *zedukan*, *genedukan*, and so on, forms still abundantly used in versification and lofty style.

(besoetan) neukan	I held him/her/it (in the arms)
(besoetan) heukan	yoú held him/her/it (in the arms)
(besoetan) zeukan	he held him/her/it (in the arms)
(besoetan) geneukan	we held him/her/it (in the arms)
(besoetan) zeneukan	you held him/her/it (in the arms)
(besoetan) zeneukaten	yoû held him/her/it (in the arms)
(besoetan) zeukaten	they held him/her/it (in the arms)

(besoetan) neuzkan	I held them (in the arms)
(besoetan) heuzkan	yoú held them (in the arms)
(besoetan) zeuzkan	he held them (in the arms)
(besoetan) geneuzkan	we held them (in the arms)
(besoetan) zeneuzkan	you held them (in the arms)
(besoetan) zeneuzkaten	yoû held them (in the arms)
(besoetan) zeuzkaten	they held them (in the arms)

nindukaan	yoú held me	ginduzkaan	yoú held us
nindukanan	yoù held me	ginduzkanan	yoù held us
nindukan	he held me	ginduzkan	he held us
nindukazun	you held me	ginduzkazun	you held us
nindukazuen	yoû held me	ginduzkazuen	yoû held us
nindukaten	they held me	ginduzkaten	they held us

hindukadan	I held yoú	zinduzkadan	I held you
hindukan	he held yoú	zinduzkan	he held you
hindukagun	we held yoú	zinduzkagun	we held you
hindukaten	they held yoú	zinduzkaten	they held you

(besoetan) zinduzkatedan	I held yoû (in the arms)
(besoetan) zinduzkaten	he held yoû (in the arms)
(besoetan) zinduzkategun	we held yoû (in the arms)
(besoetan) zinduzkateten	they held yoû (in the arms)

We now arrive at the most important verb of all, **edun*, expressing possession and also acting as auxiliary for the periphrastic conjugation of all transitive verbs. Here too we find the same properties in the past tense as we did in the present: stem *-u-* and a prefix *it-* as object pluralizer. The object marker for *zuek* 'yoû' is the usual suffix *-zte*, used in combination with the pluralizer prefix *it-*.

Forms indicating a first- or second-person plural object start with *gintu-* or *zintu-*, syncopations of the expected **ginditu-* or **zinditu-*. Last, any expected sequence *-*tute-* surfaces as *-tuzte*, while a sequence *-dute-* remains unaltered. Therefore we have

nuen	I had it	nituen	I had them
huen	yoú had it	hituen	yoú had them
zuen	he had it	zituen	he had them
genuen	we had it	genituen	we had them
zenuen	you had it	zenituen	you had them
zenuten	yoû had it	zenituzten	yoû had them
zuten	they had it	zituzten	they had them
ninduan	yoú had me	gintuan	yoú had us
nindunan	yoù had me	gintunan	yoù had us
ninduen	he had me	gintuen	he had us
ninduzun	you had me	gintuzun	you had us
ninduzuen	yoû had me	gintuzuen	yoû had us
ninduten	they had me	gintuzten	they had us
hindudan	I had yoú	zintudan	I had you
hinduen	he had yoú	zintuen	he had you
hindugun	we had yoú	zintugun	we had you
hinduten	they had yoú	zintuzten	they had you
zintuztedan	I had yoû		
zintuzten	he had yoû		
zintuztegun	we had yoû		
zintuzteten	they had yoû		

10.2 Syntax of Past Tense Verbs

Despite the clear breach of morphological ergativity displayed by some of the past tense verb forms, there is not the slightest difference in syntactic behavior between sentences in the past tense and those in other tenses including the present.

Thus all examples given in section 9.3 could be switched to the past tense without any concomitant change in either case marking or word order. Conversely, substituting present tense verb forms will turn any past tense sentence into a present tense one:

(1) a. Gizon batek bi seme zituen. (Lk 15:11)
A (certain) man had two sons.
b. Bi seme zituen gizon batek. (Lk 15:11; *Lau Eb.*)
A (certain) man had two sons.
c. Gizon batek bazituen bi seme. (Lk 15:11; *JKBO*, Dv)
A (certain) man had two sons.

(2) a. Alargunak hogei urteko alaba zeukan. (Garate, *Alaba* 39)
The widow had a twenty-year-old daughter.
b. Bazeukaten han kazetalariek gai ederra. (Garate, *Alaba* 85)
The journalists had a fine topic there.

(3) a. Aideak kanpo-usai gozoa zekarren. (*LBB* 24)
The air brought a sweet smell of the fields.
b. Laugarren alaba honek bazekarren akatsen bat. (*LBB* 19)
This fourth daughter carried some fault or other.

(4) a. Mikolas eta Erromanak etxe eta seme-alabekin nahikoa arazo zerabilten. (*LBB* 56)
Mikolas and Romana experienced plenty of worries with the house and the children.
b. Gogoeta hauek zerabiltzan Jon Bidart detektibeak. (Garate, *E.E.* 8)
Detective Jon Bidart nourished these thoughts.

(5) a. Mutilak trumoia zeraman bere barruan. (*LBB* 15)
The boy carried thunder inside him.
b. Gizonak ereinotz-usaia zeraman, andreak alkanfor-usaia. (*G.* 70)
The man carried a laurel smell, the lady a camphor smell.
c. Bi deabruk suzko leize batera ninderamaten. (Lapitze, 217)
Two devils led me to a cave of fire.

(6) a. Inork ez omen zekien ezer. (Garate, *Iz.B.* 28)
Nobody knew anything.
b. Baina zuk, Maya, bazenekien nire berri. (Lertxundi, *Aise* 57)
But you, Maya, knew about me.

(7) a. Eta isilak baietza zirudien. (Lertxundi, *Aise* 98)
And the silence seemed assent.
b. Sorginkeria edo zeruko laguntza zirudien kontu hark. (*LBB* 19)
And that venture seemed witchcraft or help from heaven.

10.3 Periphrastic Conjugation of Transitive Verbs

10.3.1 The Transitive Auxiliary

The periphrastic conjugation of transitive verbs follows the same pattern described in section 7.3.1 for intransitives; the only difference is in the choice of auxiliary: transitive **edun* 'to have' instead of intransitive *izan* 'to be':

(8) a. Jonek etxea saltzen du.
John is selling the house.
b. Jonek etxea saldu du.
John has sold the house.

c. Jonek etxea salduko du.
   John will sell the house.

(9) a. Mirenek sorginak gorrotatzen ditu.
   Mary hates (the) witches.
 b. Mirenek sorginak gorrotatu ditu.
   Mary has hated (the) witches.
 c. Mirenek sorginak gorrotatuko ditu.
   Mary will hate (the) witches.

10.3.2 Synthetic Tenses versus Periphrastic Tenses

Just as we saw in section 7.3.2, item 5, for intransitive verbs, periphrastic imperfect tenses of the few verbs possessing commonly used synthetic forms (see section 9.3.1) express habitual or iterative action only:

(10) a. Mirenek minigona gorri-gorria darama.
   Mary is wearing a bright red miniskirt.
 b. Mirenek beti minigona gorri-gorria eramaten du.
   Mary always wears a bright red miniskirt.

(11) a. Jonek txapel beltza zeraman atzo.
   John wore a black beret yesterday.
 b. Jonek egun haietan txapel beltza eramaten zuen.
   John (usually) wore a black beret those days.

The same is true for the verb **edun* 'to have' when used as a main verb. Remember that its imperfect participle in southern Batua is *izaten*, just like that of *izan*:

(12) a. Gure alabak ez zuen diru asko.
   Our (my) daughter did not have much money.
 b. Gure alabak ez zuen diru asko izaten. (Garate, *Esku* 158)
   Our (my) daughter did not usually have much money.

Since the verb **ion* 'to say' lacks periphrastic forms altogether, its habitual aspect is expressed by the synonymous verb *esan*:

(13) a. Hori aitonak zioen. (or, alternatively, *esan zuen*)
   That's what Grandfather said. (*hori* is topic, *aitona* focus)
 b. Hori aitonak esaten du.
   That's what Grandfather (always) says.
 c. Hori aitonak esaten zuen.
   That's what Grandfather used to say.

Periphrastic forms of the stative verb *jakin* 'to know' do not have a habitual, but an inchoative meaning: 'to get to know', 'to find out':

(14) a. Asko dakigu.
We know a lot.
b. Asko jakiten dugu.
We are finding out a lot.
c. Asko jakin dugu.
We have found out a lot.

As far as the other stative verb in this class, *irudi* 'to seem', is concerned, it is like **ion* in lacking periphrastic forms. In contrast, its near synonym *iruditu* is intransitive and has no synthetic forms. Later chapters will have more to say about these two verbs.

10.4 The Substantival Quantifier *dena* 'all'

The oldest universal quantifier in Basque is *oro*, still commonly used in the Navarrese and Souletin dialects. Its somewhat limited role in present-day Batua will be taken up in section 28.3. Its duty has been taken over by *dena* (dialectally *dana*), originally a free relative clause: 'what there is', an etymology that has ceased to be relevant, as *dena* is now used in all tenses and persons, singular as well as plural (*denak*).

There is, in fact, an interesting correlation between number and animacy: except when used appositively, singular *dena* refers to inanimates only, whereas plural *denak* refers to either animates or inanimates, with a definite slant toward the former. To simplify slightly, English *everything* corresponds to *dena*; English *everybody* to *denak*, requiring, of course, a plural verb form:

(15) a. Dena iritsi da orain.
Everything has now arrived.
b. Denak iritsi dira orain.
Everybody has now arrived. (In context also: All the things have arrived.)

(16) a. Orain dena ikusten dut.
I now see everything.
b. Orain denak ikusten ditut.
I now see everybody. (In context also: I now see all the things.)

Dena can be reduplicated to make it more emphatic: *den-dena* 'absolutely everything', *den-denak* 'absolutely everybody'.

Since Basque speakers identify the final *a* of *dena* as the definite article (which it is, historically speaking), *dena* is morphologically definite, and, accordingly, follows the regular definite declension pattern with the usual singular versus plural contrast. Only in the instrumental case do the singular and the plural coincide, and they do so on account of the insertion of the formative *-ta-*, characteristic of the instrumental of pronouns: *denetaz* (sg) 'about everything', *denetaz* (pl) 'about everybody'.

Notice that there is a three-way contrast in the locative cases—for example, in the inessive: *denean* 'in everything', *denetan* 'in all things', *denengan* 'in everybody'.

Etymologically a noun phrase, *dena* remains so for most speakers of Batua. Sarasola's earlier explicit warning from 1985 that *dena* must appear alone, unaccompanied by a noun phrase (*HLEH* 255), took issue with a sizable minority of speakers mostly in Guipuzcoa (cf. *DGV* VI, 106) who feel free to make adjectival use of *dena*, producing examples such as *nire bizi eta poz dena* (*LBB* 365) 'all my life and joy', *bihotz dena* 'the whole heart', *itsaso zabal dena* 'the whole wide sea', and *urte denean* 'during the whole year'. But see his later *E.H.* (p. 183), from 1996.

Appositive use of *dena*, however, is fully acceptable to everyone: *bihotza dena* 'the whole heart', *gauza eder hauek denak* 'all these beautiful things', *Bizkaian denean* 'in all of Biscay', *haientzat denentzat* 'for them all'.

As we can see from those examples, it is quite usual for appositive *dena* to immediately follow the noun phrase to be modified. This construction, however, is by no means obligatory:

(17) Bordalegiko txakurrek ez dute denek entzungo. (Amuriza, *Emea* 55)
The dogs at Bordalegi won't all hear it.

The noun phrase modified by the apposition *dena* may just be a pronoun:

(18) a. Zu zara gure denen ama. (also: *gu denen ama*)
You are the mother of us all.
b. Egia al zen hura dena? (Garate, *Esku* 183)
Was all that the truth?

The pronoun thus modified may even be a zero pronoun implicit in the sentence:

(19) a. Denak etorri zarete.
Yoû have all come.
b. Denak harrapatu gaituzte.
They have caught us all.

[*N.B.* As will be explained in section 19.7, plural *denak* or *denek* is usually changed to *denok* whenever its reference includes a first or a second person, that is, *I* or *you*.]

When *dena* stands in apposition to a singular noun phrase, its meaning 'all' can also be paraphrased as 'completely', 'totally':

(20) a. Hona beraz liburu bat, dena euskaraz. (Barbier, *Sup.* 41)
Here then is a book, all in Basque.
b. Negarrez urtu naiz dena. (*LBB* 376)
I am all dissolved into tears. (Lit. "all melted by tears")

Some idiomatic expressions with *dena* are

denetan (also *denean*)	in all parts, everywhere
denetara (also *denera*)	in all, in total
denetara ere	at any rate, in any case
denen artean	between all, all (working) together

[*N.B.* An extensive discussion of the diachronic evolution of *dena* as well as its contemporary use is offered in *DGV* VI (pp. 97ff.).]

10.5 The Adjectival Quantifier *guzti* 'all'

In construction with singular count nouns, the adjective *guzti* (variant form *guzi*) indicates totality and, as a rule, is interchangeable with *oso* 'whole'. In this use, it typically combines with nouns denoting periods of time, sets, or readily divisible objects:

egun guztia	the whole day (*egun osoa*)
Euskadi guztia	the whole Basque Country (*Euskadi osoa*)
liburu guztia	the whole book (*liburu osoa*)
mundu guztia	the whole world (*mundu osoa*)

[*N.B.* The expression *mundu guztia* is also idiomatic for 'everybody' (cf. French *tout le monde*), a sense not present in *mundu osoa*.]

Combined with mass nouns or plurals, *guzti* indicates universality, that is, the concept 'all':

lore eder guztiak	all beautiful flowers
emakume aberats guztiak	all rich women
ostatuko ardo guztia	all the wine in the inn
munduko diru guztia	all the money in the world
min guztia	all pain
neke guztia	all effort

As Saltarelli (1988, 81) notes, *guzti*, like other quantifiers, is incompatible with numerals. Phrases like **sei gizon guztiak* 'all six men' do not occur in Basque.

The quantifier adjective *guzti* must follow all other adjectives, and, like them, it can be reduplicated for the sake of emphasis: *gau guzti-guztia* 'absolutely all night', *sorgin guzti-guztiak* 'absolutely all witches'.

When *guzti* is to be combined with a demonstrative noun phrase, it can do so either as an apposition or as an adjectival modifier internal to the noun phrase.

The appositive variant represents the older system once common to all dialects and, for that reason, preferred by the Basque Academy (cf. its decree dated November 28, 1994). In this system, the quantifier appears in its definite form *guztia* (or its plural *guztiak*), which functions as an apposition to the immediately preceding demonstrative noun phrase, both components being declined separately:

etxe hau guztia	this whole house	etxe honetan guztian	in this whole house
etxe hori guztia	that whole house	etxe horretan guztian	in that whole house
etxe hura guztia	yon whole house	etxe hartan guztian	in yon whole house
etxe hauek guztiak	all these houses	etxe hauetan guztietan	in all these houses
etxe horiek guztiak	all those houses	etxe horietan guztietan	in all those houses
etxe haiek guztiak	all thòse houses	etxe haietan guztietan	in all thòse houses

The adjectival variant, dating from the latter half of the 18th century, is found exclusively in the southern dialects, where it is, however, quite current:

jende guzti hau	all these people	jende guzti honekin	with all these people
jende guzti hori	all those people	jende guzti horrekin	with all those people
jende guzti hura	all thòse people	jende guzti harekin	with all thòse people
katu guzti hauek	all these cats	katu guzti hauekin	with all these cats
katu guzti horiek	all those cats	katu guzti horiekin	with all those cats
katu guzti haiek	all thòse cats	katu guzti haiekin	with all thòse cats

It may happen that the demonstrative noun phrase modified by *guzti* reduces to the demonstrative pronoun itself. Here too, both the older appositive system and the younger adjectival construction are found, so that the corresponding paradigms are obtained from those displayed previously simply by leaving all the nouns out: *hau guztia* or *guzti hau* 'all this', *honetan guztian* or *guzti honetan* 'in all this', and similarly for the five other forms.

An extreme instance of ellipsis is for *guzti* to modify a zero pronoun, in which event only the appositive system obtains: *guztia* 'it all' or 'all of it'; *guztiak* 'they all' or 'all of them'. We can therefore contrast

(21) a. Denek gorrotatzen naute.
Everybody hates me.
b. Guztiek gorrotatzen naute.
They all hate me.

Many speakers, especially in the western area, have lost this rather subtle distinction between *dena* and *guztia*. Whereas the *Elizen Arteko Biblia* has most correctly *dena huskeria da* (Eccl 1:2) 'everything is emptiness' and also *denak du bere sasoia* (Eccl 3:1) 'everything has its season', Kerexeta's Biscayan version reads *guztia da huskeria* and *guztiak dauko bere unea*.

Some idiomatic expressions with *guzti* are

guztira (or: *guztitara*)	in all, in total
guztiz	wholly, completely, very

guztiz gain	above all (cf. Spanish *sobre todo*)
guztiarekin ere (or: *guztiaz ere*)	nevertheless (cf. Spanish *con todo*)
hala eta guztiz ere	nonetheless
. . . eta guzti	. . . and all

For example,

(22) Jantzi eta guzti sartu zen ibaian. (*E.H.* 340)
He went into the river clothes and all.

10.6 The Propensity Suffix *-koi*

The adjectival suffix *-koi* (with low tone) was analyzed by Azkue as the stem *ohi* meaning 'custom' preceded by an "epenthetic" *k* (Azkue, 1923–1925, I, 145). This obvious etymology was accepted by Mitxelena, who, however, pointed out that *k*, instead of being epenthetic, represents the ancient initial of *ohi*, subsequently lost in word-initial position: "*ohi* comes from **kohí* and *-(k)oi* from **-kóhi*" (*FHV*, sec. 21.5). This suffix combines with a variety of nouns to form adjectives denoting a liking or inclination to whatever is expressed by the noun. On account of this meaning, these adjectives are prototypically applied to animate, or even human, beings, although exceptions are possible. Thus the adjective *herrikoi* 'folksy' is mainly applied to cultural creations, such as music, dances, speech, writings, and so on.

With the same semantic impact, the suffix *-koi* can be added to reflexive possessives (cf. section 6.1.4) and to a few allative phrases, listed at the end of this section.

The suffix is not productive. In southern usage, except for *elizkoi*, *etxekoi*, and *herrikoi*, *-koi* derivatives are restricted to the written language, occurring but rarely even there. The main examples are

abere	animal	aberekoi	fond of animals, zoophile
alderdi	side, party	alderdikoi	partial, biased
ama	mother	amakoi	fond of mother, mama's boy/girl
amets	dream	ameskoi	dreamy, moony
andre	lady	andrekoi	fond of the ladies, skirt-chasing
ardo	wine	ardankoi	fond of wine
barren	inside, interior	barrenkoi	inward-looking, introverted
buru	head, self	burukoi	headstrong, egoistic, brainy
diru	money	dirukoi	avaricious, money-hungry, greedy
eliza	church	elizkoi	devout, churchgoing, religious
eme	female	emakoi	fond of women, skirt-chasing
etxe	house	etxekoi	home-loving, homey
gizarte	society	gizartekoi	sociable
gizon	man	gizakoi	fond of men, man-crazy

haragi	meat, flesh	haragikoi	carnally inclined, carnal, lascivious
haserre	anger	haserrekoi	irascible, short-tempered
haur	child	haurkoi	fond of children
herri	people	herrikoi	folksy
irri	laugh	irrikoi	quick to laugh
lagun	companion	lagunkoi	companionable
lur	earth	lurkoi	earthly, mundane
mundu	world	mundukoi	worldly, mundane
odol	blood	odolkoi	bloodthirsty, sanguinary
oldar	impulse	oldarkoi	impulsive, impetuous
sabel	belly	sabelkoi	gluttonous
seme	son, child	semekoi	fond of (your own) children
su	fire	sukoi	inflammable, fond of fire
sumin	irritation	suminkoi	irritable, huffish, touchy
zintzur	throat	zintzurkoi	voracious, gluttonous

[*N.B.* The rather specialized meaning 'carnal', 'lascivious' of *haragikoi* reflects the ecclesiastic monopoly of Basque literature up to well into the 20th century. The term for 'fond of meat' is *haragizale*; see section 10.7.1.]

Not many adjectives are based on allative phrases:

atzera	backward	atzerakoi	backward, reactionary
aurrera	forward	aurrerakoi	progressive, advanced
eskura	to the hand	eskurakoi	manageable, docile, obedient
mendira	to the mountain	mendirakoi	fond of hiking in the mountains

The suffix *-koi* combines with the reflexives of section 6.1.4 to express the concept 'egoistic'. Depending on whose ego is involved, an appropriate choice must be made between *neurekoi*, *heurekoi*, *berekoi*, *geurekoi*, *zeurekoi*, *zeuenkoi*, and *berenkoi*.

10.7 Compounds with *zale*

10.7.1 The Fondness Parasuffix *zale*

Compounds with the adjective *zale* 'fond' as their rightmost member fill the void left by the nonproductivity of the suffix *-koi* studied in section 10.6.

The adjective *zale* takes genitival complements, as in example (23):

(23) Ez naiz ohitura horien zalea.
I am not fond of those customs.

Substantival use of this adjective is of course possible, and, in fact, so frequent that Sarasola (*E.H.* 768) grants it a double subcategorization: adjective as well as noun. Used as a noun, it may be translated as *devotee*, *fancier*, or *fan* (including the fans of a soccer team).

This adjective, now, is a typical example of a parasuffix—if by that term, coined by Luis M. Múgica (1978), we mean a free morpheme occurring as the final member in a large number of useful compounds.

The following list, to which any number of examples could be added, provides ample evidence for *zale* to qualify:

aberri	fatherland	abertzale	patriotic, patriot
ama	mother	amazale	fond of mother, mother's child
andre	lady	andrezale	fond of the ladies, womanizer
ardo	wine	ardozale	fond of wine, wine lover
arrain	fish	arrainzale	fond of fish, fish lover
atsegin	pleasure	atseginzale	fond of pleasure, pleasure seeker
diru	money	diruzale	fond of money, money lover
droga	drug	drogazale	fond of drugs, drug addict
egia	truth	egiazale	veracious, truth lover
errege	king	erregezale	royalist, royalist republican
errepublika	republic	errepublikazale	republican
euskara	Basque language	euskaltzale	fond of Basque, bascophile
ezti	honey, sweet	eztizale	fond of sweets, sweet tooth
gozo	sweet, candy	gozozale	fond of sweets, sweet tooth
haragi	meat, flesh	haragizale	fond of meat, meat lover, carnivore
liburu	book	liburuzale	fond of books, bibliophile
mendi	mountain	mendizale	fond of mountains, mountain hiker
musika	music	musikazale	fond of music, music lover
mutil	boy	mutilzale	fond of boys, flirt
neska	maiden	neskazale	fond of girls, skirt chaser
ogi	bread	ogizale	fond of bread, bread lover
ur	water	urzale	fond of water, water lover, teetotaler

[*N.B.* All compounds with *zale*, like *zale* itself, are adjectives as well as nouns.]

Also proper nouns can enter into compounds with *zale*:

(24) a. Jon oso Mirenzalea da.
John is very fond of Mary.
b. Gure irakaslea Kafka eta Atxagazale amorratua da.
Our teacher is a raging fan of Kafka and Atxaga.

Even nouns accompanied by an adjective can combine with *zale*:

(25) Andre horiek guztiak pintura berrizaleak dira.
All those ladies are fond of modern painting.

All compounds with *zale* can be used predicatively as well as attributively:

(26) a. Pello oso neskazalea da.
Pete is very fond of girls.
b. Pello mutilzahar neskazalea da.
Pete is an old bachelor fond of girls.

10.7.2 The Trade Suffix *-zale*

Some trades can be designated by means of the nominal suffix *-zale* added to certain nouns denoting things relevant to the trade:

arrain	fish	arrantzale	fisherman
atun	tuna fish	atunzale	tuna fisher
esne	milk	esnezale	milkman
kamioi	truck	kamioizale	truck driver
karta	card, letter	kartazale	postman, mailman
taxi	taxicab	taxizale	taxi driver
txerri	pig	txerrizale	pig trader

[*N.B.* This suffix is not productive in Batua.]

10.8 Vocabulary

arazo	problem
arratsalde	afternoon
barkatu	to forgive
behin ere (ez)	never
berri	news, new
bilera	gathering, assembly, reunion, meeting
egunkari	newspaper, diary
erosi	to buy
erraz	easy, easily
esan	to say, to tell
giltza	key
gorrotatu	to hate
guraso	parent
haragi	meat, flesh
harrapatu	to catch
igaro	to pass, to spend (time)
inoiz . . . ez	never
kendu	to take away
korbata	tie
lapur	thief
ordu	hour, time
saldu	to sell
senar	husband
zarata	noise

10.9 Exercises

10.9.1 Translate into English

1. Arazo guztien giltza eskuan neukan aspalditik.
2. Nitaz eta nire arazoez zer ote zenioten?

3. Guztia aurretik ba al zenekien?
4. Gau guztian lanean niharduen atzo, bai eta nire senarrak ere.
5. Denei dena kentzea lapur handi baten lana da.
6. Atzoko bilera zaratatsuak arratsalde guztian zirauen.
7. Egia esan, zuk ordu asko igarotzen zenituen etxetik kanpo.
8. Egun hartan guztian, mendiko hartz haragizalea zenirudien.
9. Guztiek zekiten alargunaren arazoen berri.
10. Urte hartan, nire adiskide guztienean ikusten zintudan.
11. Gurasoenganako haserre bizia zeraman mutil hark barruan.
12. Denei barkatzea ez da erraza.

10.9.2 Translate into Basque

1. Who brought you here, husband and all?
2. A thief carried us on his white horse.
3. It seemed a dream.
4. Who will catch all the thieves in Bilbao?
5. Our newspaper brought little news yesterday.
6. Your friend was wearing a red tie the whole year.
7. Everybody brought something for the young widow.
8. The witches carried us to your beautiful house.
9. The whole day you held me in the arms.
10. I did not know anything about that.
11. I never hated all gypsies.
12. All the money in the world won't buy me.

11 Adverbs of Manner and Degree

11.1 Manner Adverbs

Not counting such minor classes as degree adverbs, time adverbs, and location and directional adverbs, we find that Basque grammar distinguishes two major categories of adverbs: "stative" adverbs, frequently marked by the stative suffix *-(r)ik* (for which see section 25.5.2), on the one hand, and manner adverbs, characterizing the way something is being done or happens, on the other.

We may note that adjectives and manner adverbs are distinct categories in Basque, for, although quite a few adjectives also appear as manner adverbs, many others can do so only with the help of a derivational suffix. Standard Basque presents no less than five adverbializing suffixes: *-to*, *-ro*, *-ki*, and the combined forms *-roki* and *-kiro*, all strictly synonymous, but each having its own distributional restrictions.

11.1.1 The Adverbializer *-to*

Distributionally, the suffix *-to* is by far the most limited of all the adverbializers. Aside from the adverb *ondo* 'well', derived from *on* 'good' and *-to*, and its comparative form *hobeto* 'better', both used profusely in the southern variety of Batua, *-to* occurs only in Biscayan, and even there with barely a dozen adjectives. Of these adverbs, *ederto* 'nicely', *txarto* 'badly', and *polito* 'handsomely' may occasionally be encountered in a Batua text, with the effect of lending it a Biscayan touch.

Based on this suffix *-to* is the Guipuzcoan adverb *osotoro* 'completely', also found in Batua, although for this meaning *osoro* and *osoki* are much more common.

11.1.2 The Adverbializer *-ro*

Once common to all dialects of Basque, the adverbializer *-ro* now belongs exclusively to the south. This suffix can be added directly only to adjectives ending in a vowel, with Minor Apocope (section 3.8.1) applying to any stem ending in *-e*: *emaro*, *luzaro*, *zeharo*, and so on. With *o* stems, however, apocope is considered merely dialectal.

As to adjectives ending in a consonant, they also admit the suffix *-ro* but require the presence of an intervening morpheme *-ki-* (no doubt identical to the adverbializer *-ki* of section 11.1.3), thus forestalling the need for an epenthetic vowel. Accordingly, from the adjective *epel* 'lukewarm' we get the adverb *epelkiro* 'halfheartedly', and from *samur* 'tender', *samurkiro* 'tenderly'.

Even in southern Batua, where it is most firmly entrenched, use of *-ro* now tends to give way to that of *-ki*, judged, it would seem, to have more literary prestige. Yet, the following adverbs formed with *-ro* are still widely accepted by speakers in Guipuzcoa and Biscay, and can be freely used in Batua, spoken as well as written:

argi	clear, bright	argiro	clearly
berri	new	berriro	again, newly, recently
bizi	living, keen, intense	biziro	lively, keenly, intensely, highly
egoki	fitting, suitable, proper	egokiro	suitably, properly
eme	female, gentle	emaro	gently, patiently, slowly
ezti	sweet, soft	eztiro	sweetly, softly
garbi	clean, clear, pure	garbiro	clearly, frankly
geldi	quiet, slack	geldiro	quietly, slowly
gozo	delicious, sweet	gozoro	pleasantly, sweetly
handi	big, great	handiro	on a grand scale, greatly
luze	long	luzaro	for a long time, at length
maite	beloved, dear	maitaro	lovingly
nagi	lazy	nagiro	lazily
nagus	principal, main	nagusiro	principally, mainly
naro	abundant, lavish	naroro	abundantly, lavishly
oso	whole, complete	osoro	wholly, completely
sendo	firm, solid	sendoro	firmly, solidly
ugari	abundant, copious	ugariro	abundantly, copiously
zehe	minute	zeharo	minutely, precisely, totally
zintzo	dutiful, honest	zintzoro	dutifully, honestly

[*N.B.* In practice there is little or no difference in meaning between the time adverb *beti* 'always' and its derived manner adverb *betiro* 'eternally'.]

There are but very few examples of the suffix *-ro* adverbializing nouns:

adiskide	friend	adiskidero	in a friendly way
asti	leisure	astiro	leisurely, slowly
opa	wish	oparo	abundantly (also *abundant*)

[*N.B.* As Azkue has pointed out (1923–1925, I, 241; II, 418), historically *astiro* may very well have been derived from the now obsolete adjective *asti* 'indolent', 'slow'.]

An enlarged form *-roki* of the suffix *-ro* originated in the eastern dialects and can occur in Batua, where it is, however, far from common. Attested examples are *argiroki* 'lucidly'; *astiroki* 'unhurriedly'; *berriroki* 'anew', 'newly'; *biziroki* 'keenly'; *handiroki* 'greatly'; *maitaroki* 'lovingly'; and *osoroki* 'completely'.

As compared to the scarcity of the items just cited, a similar formation, *gaingiroki* 'superficially', is quite current in Batua, partly on account of its use by the classical Navarrese-born author Axular (Ax. 20, 189). Its structure is that of a *-roki* derivation of the noun *gain* 'upper surface', where the second syllable *-gi-* derives from the intervening morpheme *-ki-* by voicing assimilation. Interestingly, the shorter form *gaingiro* is a mere Gipuzcoan localism with a different meaning: 'superbly', 'on top of it all'; not an alternative to *gaingiroki*. (For the northern lexicographer Duvoisin, *gaingiro* is an adjective meaning "superficial, in a moral sense"; cf. *DGV* VIII, 171.)

11.1.3 The Adverbializer *-ki*

Any adjective semantically compatible with the noun *era* 'manner' can be made into a manner adverb by combining it with the suffix *-ki*, sometimes subject to Major Apocope (see section 3.8.1): *itsuski* 'grossly' from *itsusi* 'ugly', but *nagusiki* 'mainly' from *nagusi* 'principal'.

In contrast to the other adverbializer *-ro, -ki* is always added directly to the stem, and, moreover, does not induce Minor Apocope. Compare *maiteki* 'lovingly' to *maitaro*. The shape of this suffix is invariably *-ki*, even when following *l* or *n*, with the sole exception of *ongi* 'well', derived from *on* 'good'. (The rather special case of *gaingiroki* 'superficially' of section 11.1.2 may be disregarded here.)

The following list displays commonly used adverbs where the ending *-ki* cannot be dropped if these are to function as manner adverbs (cf. section 11.1.4).

As we will note in section 25.5.1, several of the adjectives (*alai*, *apain*, *harro*, etc.) can, however, act as stative adverbs.

alai	merry, cheerful	alaiki	merrily, cheerfully
amoltsu	amiable, loving	amoltsuki	amiably, lovingly
anker	cruel	ankerki	cruelly
apain	elegant	apainki	elegantly
ausart	daring, bold	ausarki	daringly, boldly, abundantly
baldan	rude, rough	baldanki	rudely, roughly
baldar	clumsy, ponderous	baldarki	clumsily
berezi	special	bereziki	specially
bero	warm	beroki	warmly
bortitz	firm, tough, harsh	bortizki	firmly, forcibly, harshly
demokratiko	democratic	demokratikoki	democratically
doilor	mean, vile	doilorki	meanly, villainously

dorpe	heavy, harsh	dorpeki	heavily, harshly
eder	beautiful	ederki	beautifully, nicely, very well
eme	female, gentle	emeki	gently, patiently, slowly
epel	lukewarm	epelki	halfheartedly
ergel	idiotic, foolish	ergelki	foolishly, stupidly
ero	insane, crazy	eroki	insanely, crazily
ezti	sweet	eztiki	sweetly
faltsu	false	faltsuki	falsely
gaizto	wicked, vicious	gaiztoki	wickedly, viciously
harro	proud, arrogant	harroki	proudly, arrogantly
hotz	cold, cool	hozki	coldly, coolly
ideal	ideal	idealki	ideally
itsu	blind	itsuki	blindly
itsusi	ugly	itsuski	grossly, crudely, terribly
latz	rough, harsh	lazki	harshly, rudely
leial	loyal	leialki	loyally
lizun	lewd	lizunki	lewdly
lotsagabe	shameless, brazen	lotsagabeki	shamelessly, brazenly
maite	dear, beloved	maiteki	lovingly
nabarmen	notable, patent	nabarmenki	patently, ostentatiously
nagusi	principal	nagusiki	mainly
normal	normal	normalki	normally
on	good	ongi	well
oso	whole, complete	osoki	wholly, completely
polit	pretty	poliki	nicely, slowly
prestu	honest, honorable	prestuki	honorably, nobly
samin	bitter	saminki	bitterly
samur	tender, sensitive	samurki	tenderly
serios	serious	serioski	seriously
soil	bald, bare, mere	soilki	merely, only
sutsu	fiery, ardent	sutsuki	fervently, ardently
trakets	clumsy	trakeski	clumsily
txar	bad	txarki	badly
xehe	minute, small	xeheki	minutely, in detail
zital	nasty, vile, mean	zitalki	nastily, vilely, meanly

[*N.B.* The adverb *txarki* 'badly' is little used in Batua. Its place is taken by *gaizki*, derived from the adjective *gaitz*, which, however, has changed its former meaning 'bad' to 'difficult' (and also 'tremendous'), so that we are faced with a typical case of suppletion: *txar* 'bad', *gaizki* 'badly'.]

In view of their adjectival nature, perfect participles too may be expected to give rise to manner adverbs in *-ki*. This development has occurred, however, only in the northern dialects. A small number of those adverbs have found their way into Batua:

deliberatu	decided	deliberatuki	deliberately
itsutu	blinded	itsutuki	blindly
izendatu	named	izendatuki	specifically
lehiatu	hurried	lehiatuki	hurriedly
markatu	marked	markatuki	emphatically, markedly
ohartu	noticed	ohartuki	consciously

Examples with the suffix *-ki* adverbializing nouns are extremely rare. Only two need mentioning:

anaia	brother	anaiki	brotherly, fraternally
gizon	man	gizonki	humanly, manly, bravely

Manner adverbs based on the instrumental case form of an adjective or noun are more numerous:

bidez	in right, rightfully	bidezki	rightly, legitimately
dolorez	in sorrow, anxious	dolorezki	painfully, anxiously
egiaz	in truth	egiazki	truthfully, really, truly
handiz	on a large scale	handizki	greatly, specially
luzaz	for long	luzazki	for a long time
ohorez	in honor, with honor	ohorezki	honorably, nobly
zentzuz	in reason, with prudence	zentzuzki	judiciously

[*N.B.* Without *-ki*, such instrumental forms describe either a state or a manner: *zentzuz jokatu* 'to act with prudence'.]

Finally, we may note the existence of an augmented form of the suffix: *-kiro*, virtually restricted to bisyllabic adjectives. It co-occurs not only with consonantal stems, producing adverbs such as *apainkiro*, *ausarkiro*, *bortizkiro*, *ederkiro*, and *epelkiro*, which were analyzed in section 11.1.2 as belonging to the adverbializer *-ro*, but also with vocalic stems, where no intervening *-ki* is required for the sake of euphony: *emekiro*, *handikiro*, *harrokiro*, *osokiro*, and so on.

11.1.4 Adjectives Used as Manner Adverbs

Many adjectives allow a zero adverbializer; that is, they are able to act as manner adverbs themselves. No semantic characterization as to which adjectives behave in this way is at present available. We may notice that all adjectives referring to quantity seem to be included; witness *eskas* and *urri*, both meaning 'scant' as well as 'scantily', and their antonyms *jori*, *naro*, *oparo*, and *ugari*, all meaning 'abundant' as well as 'abundantly'. Yet such generalizations are apt to be spurious, and the property in question may well be purely lexically governed, the more so as there are substantial differences between dialects: southern varieties accepting considerably more adverbial adjectives than northern ones do.

Thus, from the point of view of the interdialectal standard, we may speak of an optional use of the adverbializer *-ki* (or *-ro*) with certain adjectives, with a tendency of the northern dialects to keep it and a preference of the southern ones to drop it. Some adjectives, however, never take *-ki* although used as adverbs: *bapo* 'splendid' (not used in the north), *egoki* 'suitable' (for euphonic reasons, but cf. *egokiro*), *laster* 'fast', where *lasterki*, while found in dictionaries, is exceedingly rare, even in the north. Also *zoli* 'keen' or 'keenly'.

The most common adverbial adjectives are as follows:

aldrebes	wrong, backward	aldrebes(ki)	wrongly, the other way round
alfer	idle, useless, lazy	alfer(ki)	in vain, idly, fruitlessly
apal	low, humble	apal(ki)	soft, softly, humbly
apropos	appropriate	apropos(ki)	appropriately, intentionally
argi	clear	argi(ki)	clearly
arin	light, quick	arin(ki)	lightly, quickly
artez	straight	artez(ki)	straight, straightforwardly
azkar	vigorous, rapid, clever	azkar(ki)	vigorously, rapidly, fast
bapo	splendid	bapo	splendidly
berdin	equal	berdin(ki)	equally
biguin	soft	biguin(ki)	softly
bikain	superb, magnificent	bikain(ki)	superbly, magnificently
bizi	alive, quick, strong	bizi(ki)	lively, quickly, strongly
bizkor	brisk, spry, quick	bizkor(ki)	briskly, quickly
dotore	fashionable, elegant	dotore(ki)	fashionably, elegantly
egoki	fitting, suitable	egoki(ro)	suitably, conveniently
eragabe	irregular, immoderate	eragabe(ki)	irregularly, immoderately
eroso	comfortable, easy	eroso(ki)	comfortably, easily
erraz	easy	erraz(ki)	easily
garbi	clean	garbi(ki)	frankly, clearly
garratz	sour, stern, severe	garratz(ki)	sourly, sternly, severely
gogor	hard, rigid, rigorous	gogor(ki)	harshly, rigidly, rigorously
gozo	delicious, sweet	gozo(ki)	pleasantly, sweetly
jator	proper, authentic	jator(ki)	properly, correctly
labur	brief, short	labur(ki)	briefly
larri	big, grave, tight	larri(ki)	broadly, gravely, seriously
lasai	loose, carefree, calm	lasai(ki)	freely, tranquilly, calmly
laster	rapid, quick	laster	rapidly, quickly, fast, soon
leun	smooth	leun(ki)	smoothly

luze	long	luze(ki)	at length
makur	crooked	makur(ki)	crookedly, wrongly
motel	faltering	motel(ki)	falteringly
ozen	loud, sonorous	ozen(ki)	loudly, sonorously
sakon	deep, profound	sakon(ki)	deeply, profoundly
sendo	firm, solid	sendo(ki)	firmly, solidly, strongly
txukun	tidy, neat	txukun(ki)	tidily, neatly
zalu	quick, agile	zalu(ki)	quickly, fast
zehatz	precise	zehatz(ki)	precisely
zintzo	dutiful, decent	zintzo(ki)	dutifully, decently, civilly
zoli	keen, vigorous	zoli	keenly, vigorously
zoro	foolish	zoro(ki)	foolishly
zorrotz	sharp, rigorous	zorrotz(ki)	sharply, strictly, rigorously
zuhur	cautious, wise	zuhur(ki)	cautiously, wisely
zuzen	upright, straight	zuzen(ki)	directly, straightly

11.1.5 Syntax of Manner Adverbs

In principle, a manner adverb can occur anywhere in its clause, as long as it does not precede the topic. But in an overwhelming majority of instances, a manner adverb, even when not particularly prominent from a pragmatic point of view, will be treated as the focus of its clause and occupy the corresponding position right in front of the verbal complex. The following examples are typical:

(1) a. Ongi etorri! (Often found on doormats in the Basque Country)
Welcome! (Literally: Well come!)
b. Ondo ibili! (Customarily said to a parting traveler)
Good journey! (Literally: Walk well!)
c. Gizona eta gizartea ederki ezagutzen zituen. (*MEIG* II, 41)
He knew man and society very well.
d. Ene bihotza azkar zebilen. (Haranburu, *Itsas.* 113)
My heart was beating fast.
e. Oso zintzo portatu gara. (Atxaga, *Obab.* 355)
We have behaved very civilly.
f. Dena garbi zekusan. (Mk 8:25; Olab.)
He saw everything clearly.
g. Organoaren notak ozenki hedatzen ziren katedralean. (Txill., *Exkixu* 223)
The notes of the organ were expanding resoundingly through the cathedral.

In negative clauses, manner adverbs will usually function as quasi focus (cf. section 8.6.2), standing in front of the verbal participle, if there is one:

(1) h. Ez naiz oso ongi oroitzen. (*MEIG* I, 160)
I don't remember very well.
i. Ez duzu oso erraz barkatzen. (Garate, *Iz.B.* 29)
You don't forgive very easily.

Focushood may be claimed by another constituent, in which case the manner adverb will usually be relegated to after the verb:

(2) a. Zer egin dut zehatz? (Txill., *Let.* 114)
What have I done exactly?
b. Orain ikusten dut garbi. (Atxaga, *Obab.* 64)
I clearly see it now.
c. Bestela, zuregana joango naiz laster. (Rv 2:16)
Or else, I will quickly come to you.
d. Eseri egin da haundikiro. (Garate, *Hades* 7)
He majestically seated himself.

Finally, it is quite possible for a sentence to have no preverbal focus at all, despite the presence of a manner adverb:

(3) Gero, urteen buruan, gauzak lasaitu ziren astiro eta poliki. (*MEIG* VII, 36–37)
Later on, as the years went by, things eased down slowly and gradually.

11.1.6 Deictic Manner Adverbs

Whereas modern English has but a single deictic manner adverb (so), Basque distinguishes here too three degrees of deixis:

honela, corresponding to *era honetara* (or *era honetan*) 'in this way'
horrela, corresponding to *era horretara* (or *era horretan*) 'in that way'
hala, corresponding to *era hartara* (or *era hartan*) 'in thàt (yon) way'

Following are some examples:

(4) a. Honela ez goaz inora. (*E.H.* 387)
This way we are going nowhere.
b. Horrela ez zoaz inora.
That way you are going nowhere.
c. Hala ez doa inora.
Thàt way he is going nowhere.

(5) a. Lehen hala, orain horrela, gero ez jakin nola. (Proverb, in López Mendizabal, 251)
First thàt way, now that way, afterward there is no knowing how.
b. Hala dirudi.
So it seems.

In terms of synchronic morphology, these adverbs consist of the oblique stem of a singular demonstrative, followed by a special manner suffix *-la*, also found in *bestela* 'otherwise' and *nola* 'how'.

Given, however, that the suffix *-la* represents the original shape of the allative case ending (now turned into *-ra* because of its invariable intervocalic occurrence), it is natural to assume that a straightforward Basque equivalent of the French gloss "à la manière de ceci/cela" was instrumental in creating these adverbs through deletion or nonlexicalization of the head noun meaning 'manner': *honen* ERA-*la* > **honen* + *la* > **honella* > *honela*.

The view that *-la* is a case ending rather than a derivational suffix finds some additional support in that those deictic adverbs, unlike other manner adverbs, can be turned into adnominals by means of the linking morpheme *-ko*, just as if they were postpositional phrases:

(6) Nolako liburua? Honelako/horrelako/halako liburua.
What kind of book? This/that/thàt kind of book.

In the spoken language this threefold system tends to give way to a twofold one, with the contracted form *hola* serving for both *honela* and *horrela*. The Basque Academy, however, strongly opposes the use of *hola* in the standard language, except as part of the expression *hala-hola* (or its variants *hola-hala*, *hola-hola*) meaning 'so-so', that is, 'not very well'. The corresponding adnominal is also current: *hala-holako* 'mediocre'.

11.2 Degree Adverbs

Adverbs used to express the extent or intensity of a property, state, or action are called degree adverbs. They occur in combination with gradable adjectives, adverbs, verbs, or even nouns denoting gradable concepts, such as *adiskide* 'friend'.

Degree adverbs do not form a morphological category of their own. They arise from manner adverbs meaning 'strongly' or 'completely', and also from quantifiers, such as those signifying 'much' (*agitz*, *anitz*, *asko*), 'so much' (*honenbeste*, *horrenbeste*, *hainbeste*), 'enough' (*aski*, *franko*, *nahikoa*), and 'a little bit' (*pixka bat*, etc.).

Only the by now slightly dated adverb *txit* 'very' remains without known etymology. For the sake of convenience, degree adverbs will be divided into three groups. Section 11.2.1 deals with intensifiers, that is, adverbs concerned with the higher points of the scale. Section 11.2.2 discusses the deictic adverbs *honen*, *horren*, and *hain*, corresponding to English *so* when used as an adverb of degree, while section 11.2.3 is devoted to the remaining adverbs.

11.2.1 Intensifiers

In contrast to the neighboring Romance languages where the intensifier normally used with verbs is a quantifier (*mucho*, *beaucoup*) not used with adjectives or adverbs, Basque intensifiers are used across all categories: *oso eder* 'very beautiful', *oso ederki* 'very nicely', *oso adiskide* 'great friends', *oso poztu* 'to rejoice greatly'. True enough, in combination with verbs, *asko* 'much' is a lot more common than *oso* in southern Batua, a fact no doubt accountable to Spanish influence. Yet the across-the-board regularity still holds for *oso* as well as for *asko*. For, on the one hand, *oso poztu* remains possible even in spoken Batua, and, on the other hand, *eder asko* and *ederki asko* are also coming into use.

In the northern dialects, all intensifiers, quantifier based or not, can be used across the board: *anitz eder*, *anitz ederki*, and *anitz poztu*, and *biziki eder*, *biziki ederki*, and *biziki poztu*.

Although *oso* (originally an adjective meaning 'whole' or 'complete', and still used in that sense) is by far the most frequent intensifier in the southern variety of Batua, there are numerous synonyms, most of them literary, but some fairly colloquial, such as *izugarri* 'terribly' and *ikaragarri* 'horribly'. (For *-garri*, see section 14.7ff.)

Among the more literary intensifiers we may mention *hagitz* (Navarrese in origin and meaning 'much' as well as 'loudly'), *txit* (a frequent intensifier in 19th-century Guipuzcoan), and *guztiz* (instrumental form of *guzti* 'all', occurs as an intensifier in all dialects).

Furthermore, quite a few manner adverbs are prone to lose their individual meaning and fade into degree adverbs with roughly the force of *oso* 'very'. Some common examples are

arras	totally (originally from the northern dialects, now also in southern Batua)
arrunt	totally (common in the north, highly literary in the south)
biziki	lively, strongly (very common in northern usage)
biziro	lively, keenly (mildly literary in southern Batua)
erabat	completely, totally (tends to be rather stronger than *oso*)
ikaragarri	horribly, frightfully (colloquial, in the north: *ikaragarriki*)
itsuski	grossly (colloquial, little used in the south)
izugarri	terribly (somewhat colloquial, in the north: *izigarriki*)
osoki	wholly, completely (not used in the south)
osoro	wholly, completely (highly literary in the south, not used in the north)
zeharo	exactly, totally (mildly literary)

When we turn to the syntactic properties of intensifiers, five observations seem to be relevant:

1. All intensifiers, except for *asko*, normally precede the constituent they modify: *oso bero* 'very hot', *oso gaizki* 'very badly', *txit gora* 'very high', *txit ondo* 'very well'; but *polit asko(a)* 'very pretty', *ederki asko* 'very nicely'.

When modifying a verb phrase, intensifiers tend to be focus, and thus, very often, directly precede the verb: *oso harritu* 'to be greatly astonished', *txit poztu* 'to rejoice greatly', *asko aurreratu* 'to progress greatly'. When not in focus, the adverb does not need to precede the verb:

(7) a. Nabarmendu egin haiz zeharo. (Atxaga, *Obab.* 209)
You have made quite a scene.
b. Yolanda, zoratu al haiz zeharo? (*LBB* 151)
Yolanda, have you gone quite crazy?
c. Sutu da biziro Erko zintzoa. (*MEIG* III, 46)
Honest Erko has gotten very angry.

2. When an intensifier modifies an adjective modifying a noun phrase, by far the most common order is for the intensifier to precede the noun: *oso mutil ona* 'a very nice boy', *txit poz handia* 'a very great joy', *izugarri liburu ederra* 'a terribly beautiful book', *biziki euskara garbian* 'in a very pure Basque'. (This order is already found in Etxepare writing in 1545: *guziz gauza emea* [*LVP* III-52] 'a very soft thing'.) Placement of the intensifier between the noun and the adjective requires considerable emphasis on the adverb and is therefore much less common: *gauza oso txarra* (Garate, *Ald.* 32) 'a véry bad thing', *borroka izugarri latza* (2 Sm 2:17) 'a térribly fierce struggle'.
3. When part of the predicate of a predicative clause, an intensifier can bear focus and hence occupy the focus site directly in front of the copula. We can call this practice *focus extraction*, since the intensifier ends up separated from the noun phrase it modifies. While not all speakers can make use of this construction, attested examples are plentiful:

(8) a. Zuzenez irabaztea oso da bidezkoa. (Munita, 106)
To justly earn it is móst legitimate.
b. Ona dirudi. Oso da ona, etxekoia eta maratza. (*G.* 36)
She seems nice. She's véry nice, home loving and hardworking.
c. Paula oso zen emakume itxurazkoa eta maitagarria. (*G.* 171)
Paula was a móst good-looking and lovable woman.
d. Eta hura ere anitz zen ederra. (1 Kgs 1:6; Dv)
And he also was a véry handsome man.

4. An intensifier may undergo extraposition; that is, it can be pulled out of its dependent canonical position to a location following the verb, usually at the very end of the clause. This device enables the speaker to focus on the predicate as such, regardless of any degree of intensity, and still express this intensity as well:

(9) a. Inspektorearen erantzuna azkarra izan zen oso. (Atxaga, *Obab.* 44)
The inspector's reply was very quíck.
b. Baina orain bestela da oso. (Atxaga, *Obab.* 218)
But now he is very dífferent.
c. Gaur gaiztoa ikusten haut oso. (M. D. Agirre)
I see that you are very náughty today.
d. Gure Miren alaba ona izan da beti oso.
Our Mary has always been a very góod daughter.

e. Joxepa goibel zegoen oso. (Zapirain, *M.* 207)
Joxepa was very míserable.

For many—albeit not all—speakers, there must be at least a slight pause preceding the intensifier, so that the adverb takes on the character of an afterthought:

(10) a. Gure Miren alaba ona izan da beti, oso.
Our Mary has always been a good daughter, very much so.
b. . . . eta ezagutza mingarria da, oso. (Mintegi, 15)
. . . and a painful acquaintance it is, very much so.
c. Bizia, bai, baina mingarria ere bai, oso. (Mintegi, 19)
Vivid, yes, but painful too, very much so.

5. *Saltarelli's constraint*: As Saltarelli has noted (1988, 81), a great many speakers have a constraint against combining intensifiers—often, in fact, any adverb of degree, with the possible exception of *samar*—with adjectival demonstratives. For those speakers, both *oso gauza on hauek* and *gauza oso on hauek* 'these very good things' are ruled out, as mentioned in *EGLU* I, 299.

Inquiry has revealed, however, that by no means all native speakers obey this constraint. In this vein, it may be mentioned by way of curiosity that the outstanding Basque litterateur Orixe (Nikolas Ormaetxea, 1888–1961) violated it even twice in one noun phrase. Translating the Latin noun phrase *iste ordo pulcherrimus rerum valde bonarum* from St. Augustine's *Confessions* (13.35), he wrote, *gauza oso on hauen burubide txit eder hau* 'this very beautiful order of these very good things' (Orixe, *Aitork.* 422). Furthermore, on the same page, Orixe does not hesitate to insert a demonstrative where the original Latin text does not have one. As a translation of *post opera tua bona valde*, he offers *zure lan oso on haien ondotik* 'after those very good works of yours'.

We end this section with a remark on the use of *asko* as a modifier of nouns: The quantifier *asko* quite commonly occurs as an intensifier with nouns denoting sensations: *min asko* 'much pain', *beldur asko* 'much fear', *bero asko* 'much heat'. Careful speakers, mostly of an older generation, however, reject this use of *asko*, insisting that *min asko* can signify only 'many pains', whereas *min handia* 'great pain' is the correct expression for 'much pain'. The same is true of *beldur handia* 'great fear', *bero handia* 'great heat', and *asti handia* 'a lot of (free) time'. But 'little pain' is *min gutxi*, not **min txiki*; likewise *asti gutxi* 'little spare time'.

11.2.2 Deictic Adverbs of Degree

Deictic degree adverbs, like deictic manner adverbs, are based on the demonstrative pronouns. More precisely, they seem to coincide with the genitive singular form of those pronouns: *honen*, *horren*, *hain*, except for the last, whose older form *haen*, however, points to its likely origin as a contraction of the genitive *haren*, taken for granted by Mitxelena in *FHV* (section 7.4, p. 141).

It may be noted in this connection that the English demonstratives *this* and *that* can also serve as adverbs, in exact correspondence with Basque *honen* and *horren*:

(11) a. Zergatik jaiki gara honen goiz?
Why did we get up this early?
b. Nora zoaz horren apain?
Where are you going that elegantly?

The more distant form *hain* is pragmatically unmarked: to be used when neither *honen* nor *horren* is called for, and, at times, even as a substitute for those:

(11) c. Hain isila da! (*TOE* II, 241)
He is so uncommunicative!

[*N.B.* The phrase *hain gutxi* 'so little' is an old and now largely outmoded way of expressing 'no more than', 'not either' (cf. Spanish *tampoco*).]

An interrogative counterpart to the three deictic adverbs is worth noting: *zeinen*, genitive form of *zein* 'which'. Besides its interrogative use, as in *zeinen beroa?* 'how warm?', it also appears in exclamations: *zeinen ederra!* 'how beautiful!', *zeinen neskatxa polita!* 'what a pretty girl!', *zeinen ederki!* 'how nicely!'

A great deal more common in this function, however, is the form *zein* itself: *zein ederra!* 'how beautiful!', *zein neskatxa polita!* 'what a pretty girl!', *zein ederki!* 'how nicely!'

In contrast to English, where *so* turns into *such* in the presence of a noun, *honen*, *horren*, and *hain* are invariable, just like other adverbs of degree: *hain ederki* 'so nicely', *hain ederra* 'so beautiful', *hain neskatxa polita* 'such a pretty girl'. (Already in Etxepare: *hain biaje bortitzean* [*LVP* I-96] 'on such a hard journey'.)

In most respects, the syntactic behavior of these deictic adverbs resembles that of intensifiers. Like the vast majority of those, the deictics are always preposed, as illustrated by the preceding examples. Except in the presence of strong emphasis on *hain*, when *emakume háin ederra* is acceptable, the normal word order is *hain emakume ederra* 'such a beautiful woman', in complete parallelism to the intensifier pattern.

Another similarity is that focus extraction can apply to the deictic adverbs also:

(12) Jose hain zen mutil ona!
Joseph was súch a good boy!

Moreover, when applied to the deictic adverbs, Saltarelli's constraint has the same partial validity as was noted for intensifiers: Noun phrases such as *honen etxe eder hau*, *horren etxe eder hori*, *hain etxe eder hura* 'this so beautiful a house' and so on are readily accepted by some native speakers but categorically rejected by others.

Deictic degree adverbs, however, differ from intensifiers in two ways: they cannot undergo extraposition, and they have lost the capacity for modifying verbs.

While older usage in all dialects allowed certain verbs to combine with *honen*, *horren*, or *hain* (see *DGV* I, 350), nowadays the deictic quantifiers *honenbeste*, *horrenbeste*, or *hainbeste* must be used instead:

(13) Ni ez naiz hainbeste harritzen.
I am not so much surprised.

Deictic adverbs of degree, then, no longer evince the across-the-board distributional regularity that is still characteristic of intensifiers.

11.2.3 Other Adverbs of Degree

All quantifiers signifying 'enough' are able to function as adverbs of degree across all categories. Of such quantifiers, there are three in Batua: *aski*, *franko*, and *nahikoa*, a substantivized form of the adjective *nahiko* 'sufficient'.

Used as adverbs, they indicate a degree somewhat less than *oso* 'very', but still quite adequate, much in the vein of English *rather* or *pretty*.

These adverbs, like the intensifiers, all precede the constituent they modify—again, barring the case of a verb phrase with a focus different from the adverb. Thus: *aski etxe handia* 'a pretty big house', *aski itsusia* 'pretty ugly', *aski ongi* 'rather well', *aski harritzen naiz* or *harritzen naiz aski* 'I am rather surprised', *franko liburu merkea* 'a pretty cheap book', *nahikoa emakume aberatsa* 'a pretty rich woman', *nahikoa polita* 'rather pretty', *nahikoa ondo* 'rather well'.

Observe that postponed *aski* is a quantifier only, not an adverb of degree. Distinguish therefore *aski goiz* 'pretty early', *aski maiz* 'pretty often', *aski ongi* 'rather well', *aski segur* 'pretty sure' from *goiz aski* 'early enough', *maiz aski* 'often enough', *ongi aski* 'well enough', *segur aski* 'sure enough'.

[*N.B.* As was stated in section 2.3.2, item 8, the quantifier *aski* indifferently precedes or follows the noun it modifies. Therefore, preposed *aski* can be a quantifier rather than an adverb, provided there is a noun following. This accounts for phrases such as *aski aldiz* 'often enough', literally 'for enough times'.]

A lesser degree than that indicated by *aski* and its equivalents is signified by *samar*—originally a noun meaning 'splinter', 'mote'—following either an adjective, automatically adopting its article and case ending, or an adverb.

Used that way, it translates into English as 'fairly' or 'somewhat', often having the connotation 'not quite adequate'. Thus: *esku garbi samarra* 'a fairly clean hand', *on samarra* 'fairly good', *urruti samar* 'fairly far', *ongi samar* 'fairly well'.

In contrast to *aski* and its synonyms, *samar* does not obey Saltarelli's constraint: *liburu lodi samar hau* 'this fairly thick book', *hiri handi samar hartan* 'in that fairly large city'.

With perfect participles ending in *-tu* (or *-du*) acting as adjectival predicatives, a suffix *-xe* signifying 'somewhat' can be employed instead of *samar*: *ahaztuxe(a)* 'somewhat forgotten', *handituxe(a)* 'somewhat enlarged', 'somewhat grown up', *minduxe(a)* 'somewhat hurt', *nekatuxe(a)* 'somewhat tired', *zahartuxe(a)* 'somewhat aged'.

The palatalized variant *xamar* (cf. section 1.2.5) may be used to express a still lesser degree than *samar*. Whether or not an occurring *xamar* is in fact employed in contrast to *samar*, however, is hard to tell, since in the usage of a majority of speakers palatalized *xamar* has wholly ousted nonpalatal *samar*.

As *samar* (or *xamar*) never modifies verbs, the corresponding degree is expressed in that combination by means of the quantifier *pixka bat* 'a bit' or one of its synonyms *apur bat*, *doi bat*, *pitin bat*, or *poxi bat*. Thus: *pixka bat harritu* 'to be somewhat surprised', *apur bat ulertu* 'to understand somewhat', *doi bat itzuli* 'to turn somewhat', *pitin bat azaldu* 'to explain somewhat', *poxi bat argitu* 'to clarify somewhat'.

Note that these quantifier expressions, either bare or with a suitable case ending, can also indicate a short duration. Thus, choosing the most currently used example, *pixka bat*, *pixka batean*, *pixka batez*, *pixka baterako*, and *pixka batentzat* can all mean 'for a moment'.

[*N.B.* The phrase *pixka bat* is often pronounced, and sometimes written, *pixkat*.]

The lowest possible degree or duration is indicated by the diminutive form of the quantifiers mentioned, except for the northern one *doi bat*, which instead undergoes reduplication. Therefore, *pixkatxo bat*, *apurtxo bat*, *doi-doi bat*, *pitintxo bat*, and *poxino bat* are all used to express the meaning 'a little bit'.

Careful speakers avoid combining *pixka(txo) bat* and its synonyms with adjectives or adverbs, a practice regularly indulged in by many speakers heavily influenced by French or Spanish. Thus, rather than *pixka bat nekatua* 'a bit tired', *apur bat beroa* 'a bit warm', *pixka bat gaiztoki* 'a little viciously', and *apur bat hozki* 'a little coolly', a more polished style of Batua prefers *nekatu samarra* or *nekatuxea* for 'a bit tired', *bero samarra* for 'a bit warm', *gaiztoki samar* for 'a bit viciously', and *hozki samar* for 'a bit coolly'.

11.3 Operators of Approximation: *ia, kasik, abantzu*

The operators *ia*, *kasik*, and *abantzu* (the latter restricted to the northern dialects) function in much the same way as English *almost*, indicating approximation to a target from below.

The scope of these operators must extend to a full phrase. This can be a noun phrase: *ia ehun kilo sagar* 'almost a hundred kilograms of apples', *ia dena* 'almost everything', *ia denak* 'almost everybody'; a postpositional phrase: *ia lehenengo hilabetetik* 'almost from the first month', *ia Bilboraino* 'almost as far as Bilbao'; a verb phrase: *ia jautsi* 'to almost fall', *ia bukatu* 'to almost finish it'; or even an entire clause, as in the idiomatic expression *ia gureak egin du* (*Xenp.* 410) 'we are almost done for', *ia ez dut ezagutu aita* (Garate, *Esku* 46) 'I have hardly known my father'.

Given that any operator must be adjacent to its scope, *ia*, *kasik*, and *abantzu* must occur at the very beginning of the phrase they operate on, or else at the very end of it.

In practice, the phrase-initial position is by far the most common, it being virtually the only case in which operator and scope form a single intonational unit. Much more rarely, the final position is exploited, in which event scope and operator tend to remain independent intonational units.

Thus we have *ia Bizkai osoan* 'in almost all of Biscay', *kasik mundu guztian* 'in almost the whole world', with the alternatives *Bizkai osoan, ia* and *mundu guztian, kasik*, but not **Bizkai ia osoan*, **mundu kasik guztian*.

With a short adverb serving as scope, the final option is not available for *ia*: *ia beti* 'almost always', never **beti ia*.

With the more substantial *kasik*, however, partisans can be found of either *kasik beti* (*E.H.* 475) or *beti kasik*:

(14) Jakin ukan du beti kasik non zen egia. (Arradoy, *S. Fran.* 300)
He has known almost always where the truth was.

Ia and *kasik* can be reduplicated for the sake of emphasis:

(15) a. Ia-ia erori nintzen. (Ps 73:2)
I had almost fallen. (Or: I very nearly fell.)
b. Hurbildu ziren eta bi ontziak ia-ia hondoratzeraino bete zituzten. (Lk 5:7)
They drew near and filled the two boats almost to the point of sinking.

It goes without saying that indefinite pronouns or adverbs in negative sentences can be acted on by the operators *ia*, *kasik*, or *abantzu*:

(16) a. Ez zen ia inor etorri.
Almost nobody came.
b. Jonek ez du ia ezer egin.
John has done almost nothing.
c. Ia inon ez dut aurkitu.
I have found it almost nowhere.
d. Ia inoiz ez gara etxetik ateratzen.
We almost never go out of the house.

What is interesting, however, is that these sentences have idiomatic equivalents in which the quantifier *gutxi* replaces both *ia* and the negation *ez*:

(17) a. Inor gutxi etorri zen.
Almost nobody came.
b. Jonek ezer gutxi egin du.
John has done almost nothing.

c. Inon gutxitan aurkitu dut.
I have found it almost nowhere.
d. Inoiz gutxitan etxetik ateratzen gara.
We almost never go out of the house.

Note that the expressions with *gutxi* have the status of compounds, so that only *gutxi*, as the final member, receives the case endings: *ezer gutxirengatik* 'on account of almost nothing', *inor gutxirentzat* 'for almost nobody'.

At this point, another construction needs to be mentioned that also bypasses the use of the regular operators *ia*, *kasik*, and *abantzu*. The adverb *hurran* 'near' or 'next' as well as its superlative form *hurren* 'nearest' or 'next' (cf. *hurren arte* 'be seeing you', lit. 'until next [time]'), can assume the meaning 'nearly': *hurren beti* 'nearly always'. In Batua as used in the south, however, *hurran* and *hurren* take on this meaning only when they follow a perfect participle:

(18) a. Nire lana bukatu hurran dut.
I have nearly finished my work.
b. Etxea saldu hurren zuen.
He had nearly sold the house. (Or: he nearly sold the house.)
c. Hil hurren da. (Also: hil hurrena da.)
He is close to dying.

11.4 Some Sentence Adverbs of Modality: Translations of 'perhaps'

In Batua the sentence modality expressed in English by *maybe* or *perhaps* is usually signified by one of the adverbs *agian*, *apika*, or *beharbada*, the latter term historically deriving from the phrase *behar bada* 'if need be' (see section 17.1). Less frequently used synonyms are *ausaz*, *menturaz*, and *onenean*, a verbatim translation of the Spanish phrase *a lo mejor*, literally 'at best', but now employed in the plain sense 'perhaps'.

As to the location these adverbs occupy within the sentence, considerable freedom obtains. While initial position is clearly favored, placement at the very end of the clause is by no means rare. Nor do these positions exhaust the range of possibilities. Adverbs of modality, indeed, may occur at the boundaries of any immediate constituent of the clause to which they belong; that is, Basque sentence adverbs are transportable in the sense of Keyser 1968.

Not even sentence adverbs, however, can intervene between the focus—and, in a negative clause, quasi focus—and the adjacent verb, since these combine into a single constituent (see section 8.6.1).

Sentences (19a–d) serve to illustrate the various options, with *Zugarramurdira* 'to Zugarramurdi' taken as focus and *Donostiara* 'to San Sebastian' as quasi focus, while *agian* 'perhaps' stands for any of the adverbs under discussion:

(19) a. (Agian) sorginak (agian) bihar (agian) Zugarramurdira joango dira (agian).
Perhaps the witches will go to Zugarramurdi tomorrow.
b. (Agian) sorginak (agian) Zugarramurdira joango dira (agian) bihar (agian).
Perhaps the witches will go to Zugarramurdi tomorrow.
c. (Agian) sorginak (agian) ez dira (agian) bihar (agian) Donostiara etorriko (agian).
Perhaps the witches won't come to San Sebastian tomorrow.
d. (Agian) sorginak (agian) ez dira (agian) Donostiara etorriko (agian) bihar (agian).
Perhaps the witches won't come to San Sebastian tomorrow.

To round off this section, some examples quoted from literary texts may be helpful. The following are examples showing initial placement, either absolute or preceded by a conjunction:

(20) a. Agian bigarren ezkontza batek arinduko du zuen alarguntzaren dolua. (Larréguy I, 244)
Perhaps a second marriage will alleviate the grief of yoùr widowhood.
b. Agian, ez da hori neskaren izena. (Urretabizkaia, *Sat.* 29)
Perhaps that is not the maiden's name.
c. Gainera, agian lan lasai bat topatuko duzu. (Urretabizkaia, *Sat.* 98)
Furthermore, perhaps you will find an easy job.
d. Eta, beharbada, nigandik aldegiteko zoaz gaur. (Txill., *Let.* 113)
And, perhaps, you are going off today in order to run away from me.
e. Menturaz zuretzat dauka dekreto hau: ... (Mogel, *Sermoi.* 12 = Arejita, 282)
Perhaps he has for you this decree ...

These are examples of clause-final placement:

(21) a. Ero baten antza ote dut agian ...? (Txill., *Let.* 97)
Do I have the looks of a lunatic perhaps ...?
b. Hori, ordea, Europa zaharreko jokabide horietako bat izango da, beharbada. (*MEIG* II, 141 = *MIH* 339)
That, however, will be perhaps one of those ways of conduct of the old Europe.
c. Istiluren bat zuten han behean, apika. (Garate, *E.E.* 20)
They had some kind of trouble there below, perhaps.
d. Bekatu asko genituen, apika, baina nork bereak. (*MEIG* VIII, 130 = *MIH* 207)
We had a lot of sins, perhaps, but each of us his own.

These are examples of intra-clausal placement:

(22) a. Hiru aste ez dira, agian, ezer itsasoan. (Urretabizkaia, *Sat.* 74)
Three weeks are, perhaps, nothing at sea.
b. Hori ez da, beharbada, gizontasun prestua. (*MEIG* VII, 159 = *MIH* 124)
That is not, perhaps, proper courtesy.

c. Hemendik hamar urtetara, agian, gaurkoa egun gogoragarri bat izango da. (Urretabizkaia, *Sat.* 111)
Ten years hence, perhaps, the present one will be a memorable day.
d. Orduko, beharbada, aberastuko naiz loteriekin. (Izeta, *Dirua* 64)
By that time, perhaps, I will get rich with the lotteries.
e. Bakezaleen bilerak ere ez dira, ausaz, aski. (*MEIG* I, 195)
The meetings of the pacifists aren't, perhaps, sufficient either.

11.5 The Determiner *beste* 'other'

The determiner *beste* (northwestern variant *bertze*) with the meaning 'other' acts in many ways like an adjectival modifier; yet, invariably preceding the head noun, it shuns the canonical adjective site, which is postnominal: *beste arrazoi bat* 'another reason', *beste arrazoia* 'the other reason'.

A semantic peculiarity *beste* shares with Spanish *otro* may be noted in passing: more clearly so than English *other*, Basque *beste* combines the sense of 'additional' with its basic meaning 'different': *beste lau arrainzopa* 'four more servings of fish soup', *beste kafe bat* 'one more coffee', *beste bat* 'one more'.

We now face the task of specifying the position of *beste* vis-à-vis other preposed determiners and modifiers. In an attempt to do so, the *DGV* states that it can be preceded by quantifiers, such as *zenbait* 'several' and *anitz* 'many', as well as by predeterminers like *zer* 'what', *zein* 'which', and also *edozein*, *zein-nahi*, and *zernahi*, all signifying 'any whatsoever'.

With all dialects and periods lumped together, this statement may well be correct; with Batua being our sole concern, it will have to be amended.

Only *zer* 'what' and *zein* 'which' readily precede *beste*, while *edozein*, *zein-nahi*, *zernahi* 'any', and *anitz* 'many' very seldom do so, and *zenbait* 'several' never at all. We have indeed *ze(r) beste berri?* or *beste ze(r) berri?* for 'what other news?' and *zein beste arrazoi?* (*MEIG* IX, 77) or *beste zein arrazoi?* for 'which other reason'. But, for 'any other lady' we get *beste edozein andre*, with some speakers hesitantly accepting *edozein beste andre*. Similarly, for 'in many other books' we find *beste anitz liburutan*, with, at most, reluctant acceptance of *anitz beste liburutan*. Finally, for 'in several other houses' we get *beste zenbait etxetan*, with universal rejection of *zenbait beste etxetan*, although constructions of this very type are attested in early texts: *cembeit berce afflictione motaz* (Leizarraga, *Ins.* A 7 r) 'through several other kinds of affliction'.

The *DGV* states further that adnominal or genitival modifiers are placed indiscriminately either before or after *beste* with no difference in meaning.

Here again Batua, like most contemporary dialects, applies a much stricter system. True enough, adnominals may sometimes intervene between *beste* and its head noun, but only as long as there is no danger of ambiguity. Hence, we get *beste honelako hitzak* or *honelako beste hitzak* 'other such words'; *beste bere gisako arima bakar bat* (*MEIG* I, 151) or *bere gisako beste arima bakar bat* 'another lonely soul like himself'; *beste Bilboko apaizak* or *Bilboko beste apaizak* 'the other priests of Bilbao'; but only *hiriko beste apaizak* 'the other priests of the city', with *beste hiriko apaizak* having as its sole meaning 'the priests of the other city'.

Genitival modifiers of the head noun never follow *beste*, even when there is not the slightest danger of ambiguity, as in *gure beste semea* 'our other son', where the unaccepted alternative **beste gure semea* would have done just as well.

Thus *ijitoaren beste alabak* denotes 'the other daughters of the gypsy', while *beste ijitoaren alabak* has as its sole denotation 'the daughters of the other gypsy'.

However, cardinal numerals other than *bat* and *bi* as well as all ordinals always occur following *beste*:

beste bost etxe	five other houses
beste bost etxeak	the five other houses
beste mila arrazoi (*MEIG* V, 21)	a thousand other reasons
beste bigarren saria	the other second prize

Beste may co-occur with interrogative, and also with indefinite, pronouns:

beste nor	who else
beste zer	what else
beste non	where else
beste noiz	when else
beste nola	how else
beste inor	anyone else
beste ezer	anything else
beste inon	anywhere else
beste inoiz	any other time
beste inola	any other way
beste norbait	someone else
beste zerbait	something else
beste nonbait	somewhere else
beste noizbait	some other time
beste nolabait	some other way

A noun phrase, occasionally in the instrumental but usually in the absolutive case, directly preceding *beste*, indicates the starting point of the deviation implied:

(23) a. Zutaz beste inork ba al daki berri hau? (Garate, *Esku* 25)
Does anyone else besides you know this piece of news?
b. Zu beste inork ba al daki berri hau?
Does anyone else besides you know this piece of news?

The ability of Basque noun phrases to allow zero heads accounts for the following phrases:

beste bat	another one, another
beste batzuk	some other ones, some others
bestea	the other one, the other
besteak	the other ones, the others
beste hau (*hori*, *hura*)	this (that, thàt) other one
beste hauek (*horiek*, *haiek*)	these (those, thòse) other ones
beste lau	four other ones, four others
beste laurak	the four other ones, the four others
beste asko	many other things, much else, many others
beste guztia	everything else
beste guztiak	all the others, all others

A noun phrase in the instrumental case, placed directly in front of *beste*, specifies the starting point implied:

Mirenez beste bat	someone other than Mary
gutaz beste batzuk	some people other than us
Mirenez beste guztiak	all but Mary
Mirenez besteak	all others except Mary

Confusingly, instead of the instrumental case, the negative morpheme *ez* can be used:

Miren ez beste bat	someone other than Mary
gu ez beste batzuk	some people other than us
Miren ez beste guztiak	all but Mary
Miren ez besteak	all but Mary
bost ez besteak	all but five

Leaving the determined forms we have been concerned with so far (*bestea*, *beste bat*), we must now turn to the use of *beste* as an indefinite pronoun taking indefinite case endings (*bestek*, *besteri*, *besteren*, *besterekin*, *bestetaz*, *bestetan*, *bestetatik*, *bestetara*, etc.), except in the absolutive case, which only allows determined forms: *beste bat* 'another' or *beste batzuk* 'some others', never just *beste* (*EGLU* I, 103). Since the indefinite declension does not distinguish number, only the context can help decide whether a form like *besterentzat* must be rendered as 'for someone else' or 'for others'.

A few examples will serve as illustration:

(24) a. Gure Jainkoak daki hori, eta zuk ere bai, eta ez bestek. (Materre, 296)
Our God knows that, and you too, and no one else.

b. Ba al daki bestek? (*G.* 283)
Does anyone else know?

c. Izen ona besteri kentzea ez da ongi.
It is not good to take away his good reputation from someone (else).
d. Besteren buruko zorria dakusa eta ez bere lepoko xerria. (Oihenarte, *Prov*. 96)
He sees the louse on someone else's head and not the scrofula on his own neck.
e. Auzia bestetan datza. (*MEIG* VI, 174)
The dispute lies somewhere else.
f. Orain, ordea, haizeak bestetara garamatza. (*MEIG* VIII, 119)
Now, however, the wind leads us elsewhere.

When used as a predeterminer, *beste* may remain indefinite and thus call for the indefinite declension.

beste ijitori	to another gypsy, to other gypsies
beste hiritan	in another city, in other cities

In addition, there are, of course, the forms cited earlier in this section:

beste ijito bati	to another gypsy
beste hiri batean	in another city
beste ijitoari	to the other gypsy
beste hirian	in the other city
beste ijitoei	to the other gypsies
beste hirietan	in the other cities

Finally, a few idiomatic expressions involving *beste* may be worth noting here:

bestera	otherwise, on the contrary
bere gogoaz bestera	contrary to his wish, reluctantly
beste orduz (bestorduz)	in other times
bestalde	other side, on the other hand, furthermore
batez beste	on the average
besteak beste	among other things, among others
beste hariko ezpala	a fiber of another thread (i.e., another kettle of fish)

[*N.B.* For the reciprocal *batak bestea* 'each other', see section 15.8.2.]

11.6 The Manner Adverb *bestela* 'otherwise'

Derived from *beste* 'other' is the manner adverb *bestela* 'otherwise' (cf. section 11.1.6):

(25) a. Honela, hala, bestela ote da? (Zaitegi, *Plat*. 134)
Is it this way, that way, another way, I wonder?
b. Bihar bestela pentsatuko du. (Aresti, 60)
Tomorrow he will think otherwise.

Note the role of the instrumental case here: *atzoz bestela* 'in another way than yesterday'. Just like *otherwise* in English, *bestela* developed also into a conjunction meaning 'or else'.

(26) a. Nahasmendura goaz bestela, ez batasunera. (*MEIG* VII, 151 = *MIH* 113)
Otherwise we are heading for confusion, not unity.
b. Etorri azkar, bestela etxean utziko haut.
Come quickly, or else I will leave yoú at home.

An additional meaning of the conjunction *bestela* is 'on the other hand' or 'furthermore' in which sense it is often followed by the particle *ere* 'even', 'also': *bestela ere*.

The adnominal form of *bestela*, *bestelako*, fulfills the same function as the adjective *different* in English. The starting point of the divergence can be clarified by a noun phrase in the instrumental or elative case: *hitaz bestelako nagusia* 'a boss different from yoú', *harengandik oso bestelakoa* 'very different from him'.

11.7 The Parasuffix *gai* Denoting 'matter'

The noun *gai* refers to matter in the widest sense: 'material', 'substance', 'theme', and, with respect to animates: 'candidate', as in *kanposanturako gaia* (Garate, *E.E.* 98) 'a candidate for the graveyard'.

Interestingly, the case ending *-gatik* happens to be based on this noun, as evidenced by the Biscayan variant form *-gaitik*.

The noun *gai* appears as a final member in a great many compound nouns, thus qualifying as a parasuffix (see section 10.7.1). Compounds with a verb radical V as a first member signify 'something to be V-ed'. A few exceptions, like *gozagai* 'sweetener', *osagai* 'component', and *sendagai* 'medicine', all present variants in *-kai* and may be based instead on the suffix *-kari*. The main examples of such compounds are

aditu	to understand	adigai	concept
ageri izan	to be manifest	agerkai	document (by voicing dissimilation)
aldatu	to change	aldagai	variable
aztertu	to investigate	aztergai	object of investigation
egin	to do	egingai	project
erakutsi	to show	erakusgai	muster, sample
erre	to burn	erregai	fuel
ezkondu	to get married	ezkongai	unmarried person
galdetu	to ask	galdegai	focus of inquiry
gozatu	to sweeten	gozagai	sweetener, sop
hautatu	to elect	hautagai	candidate for election
hornitu	to supply	hornigai	provision, supply

idatzi	to write	idazgai	theme of writing
ikasi	to learn	ikasgai	lesson
ikertu	to research	ikergai	object of research
ikusi	to see	ikusgai	sight, curiosity
irakatsi	to teach	irakasgai	subject for teaching
irakurri	to read	irakurgai	reading matter
jakin	to know	jakingai	piece of information, curiosity
jan	to eat	jangai	food item
lehertu	to burst	lehergai	explosive
mintzatu	to speak	mintzagai	topic
osatu	to complete	osagai	component
saldu	to sell	salgai	merchandise, wares
salerosi	to trade	salerosgai	commodity, merchandise, wares
sendatu	to heal, to cure	sendagai	medicine, medication
sinetsi	to believe	sinesgai	article of faith, tenet, dogma

[*N.B.* Note the phrase: *salgai dago* 'it is for sale'.]

As to compounds with a noun as a first member, because of the convenient vagueness of *gai*, quite a profusion of instances could be exhibited, ranging from utterly concrete examples like *gonagai* 'material for skirts' to such abstract ones as *maitasun gai* 'matter of love': *maitasun gaietan* (*TOE* I, 68) 'in matters of love'. Forgoing this rather futile exercise, I will confine myself to the presentation of a small subset in which compounds with *gai* refer to an anticipated future:

aita	father	aitagai	future father (-in-law), postulant
ama	mother	amagai	mother-to-be, future mother-in-law
andre	lady	andregai	future wife, fiancée
apaiz	priest	apaizgai	future priest, seminarian
azti	diviner, wizard	aztigai	future diviner, sorcerer's apprentice
ehiza	hunting, piece of game	ehizagai	fair game
emazte	wife	emaztegai	future wife, fiancée
errain	daughter-in-law	erraingai	future daughter-in-law
errege	king	erregegai	future king, heir to the throne
jabe	owner	jabegai	future owner, heir
lege	law	legegai	draft of law, bill
liburu	book	liburugai	draft of a book
nagusi	boss	nagusigai	future boss
senar	husband	senargai	future husband, fiancé
suhi	son-in-law	suhigai	future son-in-law

11.8 Vocabulary

agian	maybe, perhaps	ikasgai	lesson
amagai	mother-to-be	irakasle	teacher
andregai	fiancée	irakurri	to read
apika	perhaps	itsuki	blindly
arrantzale	fisherman	modu	manner
azaldu	to explain, to appear	nonbait	somewhere, apparently
beharbada	perhaps	ondo	well, good
behin	one time, once	portatu	to behave
behin ere . . . ez	not even once, never	sakon	deep, profound
biziro	keenly, greatly, very much	salgai	merchandise, object for sale
ederki	nicely, very well	senargai	fiancé
gai	material, matter, theme	ulertu	to understand
gaizki	badly	zeharo	exactly, totally, completely
guztiz	wholly, intensely, very	zozo	silly, stupid

11.9 Exercises

11.9.1 Translate into English

1. Ez al zaitut beste nonbait ikusi?
2. Ni ez beste bat izango zen.
3. Honelako liburuak ez dituzu, apika, behin ere irakurri.
4. Aspalditik inor gutxi etortzen da gure bileretara.
5. Nire gelatik ederki asko ikusten dut zubi zaharra.
6. Honelako gurasoek ezer gutxi dakite beren haurrez.
7. Arazo haiek guztiak sakonki aztertu zituen apaiz gazte honek.
8. Zure senargaiak zeharo gorrotatzen nau, eta ez dakit zergatik.
9. Gure irakasleak ikasgai guztia argi eta garbi azaldu du, guk erraz ulertzeko moduan.
10. Amagai batentzat ez da ondo horren laster ibiltzea.
11. Zure andregaia ikusteak biziro pozten nau.
12. Horrelako gaietan itsuki sartzeak arrisku handi samarrak ekartzen ditu ia beti.

11.9.2 Translate into Basque

1. I have learned my lesson rather well.
2. Almost nobody reads such silly books.

3. All children but one came home late.
4. Why did you behave so badly last night?
5. Those apples of yours are really terribly tasty.
6. Your fiancé seems totally different from you.
7. Such a pretty house is very rarely for sale.
8. Perhaps almost nothing will happen here.
9. Today my husband very nearly lost the keys to our house.
10. On such a beautiful day the children have perhaps gone down to the sea.
11. Almost all fishermen understand all these matters very well.
12. The fishermen of today easily catch a lot of fish.

12 Transitivity

12.1 Some Meaning Classes of Transitive Verbs

So far we have been dealing with a fairly small subset of transitive verbs: those that allow synthetic forms. The time has come to acquaint the reader with a much larger sample of commonly used transitives, so as to lay the foundation for our analysis of their syntactic behavior, a central concern of this grammar, to be broached in this chapter.

For the sake of convenience, our sample of verbs will be split up into semantic categories, many of which will be referred to later on in this work. Needless to say, there is not the slightest claim to exhaustiveness, neither in the categories chosen, nor in the listing of their members.

12.1.1 Prototypical Transitives: Verbs of Effective Action

These verbs depict a situation where a willful agent performs some action perceptibly affecting some already existing being or object, referred to as the *patient*. The agent is encoded as the ergative subject, and the patient as the absolutive object of the verb. An important subcategory form the verbs of change of state, such as *egosi* 'to cook', *hautsi* 'to break', and *iriki* 'to open'. Only a few of them will be listed here, as they will receive full attention in section 12.4.2. Examples of prototypical transitives are

astindu	to shake, to shake up, to shake off
atxilotu	to arrest
ebaki	to cut
eraso	to attack
eten	to break off, to cut, to interrupt
garaitu	to overcome, to triumph, to prevail
harrapatu	to catch
hunkitu	to affect, to touch
jo	to hit, to strike, to knock
konpondu	to repair, to settle, to fix

lotu	to tie, to bind
moztu	to cut, to trim, to shear
ukitu	to touch
zigortu	to punish, to whip
ziztatu	to prick, to sting
zulatu	to bore a hole into, to tunnel, to transfix, to pierce

12.1.2 Verbs of Motion and Rest

The agent by his action causes the patient to move, attempts to do so, or impedes motion. The main examples can be found in section 12.4.3 and need not be listed here.

12.1.3 Verbs of Obtaining or Transfer

The absolutive object encodes the theme, that is, the object obtained or transferred. Examples are

bidali	to send
ebatsi	to steal
eman	to give
erosi	to buy
eskuratu	to obtain, to get
hartu	to take, to receive
igorri	to send
kendu	to take away, to remove, to subtract
lapurtu	to steal, to rob
lortu	to acquire, to obtain, to achieve
ordaindu	to compensate, to repay, to pay
ostu	to steal
pagatu	to pay
saldu	to sell
utzi	to leave, to abandon, to let

12.1.4 Verbs of Production (*Verba Creandi*)

The referent of the direct object is brought into being by the agent's action.

antolatu	to arrange, to organize, to mend
asmatu	to invent, to guess right
egin	to make, to do
eho	to weave
ekoitzi	to produce
eratu	to form, to put in order
idatzi	to write

moldatu to shape, to form, to mold
prestatu to prepare, to arrange
sortu to conceive, to generate, to beget, to originate

[*N.B.* Used intransitively, *moldatu* means 'to manage': *moldatuko gara* 'we will manage'.]

For the concept of 'building', Basque makes use of verbs with the primary meaning 'to raise', 'to lift up': *altxatu*, *eraiki*, *jaso*.

12.1.5 Verbs of Destruction

By the agent's action the referent of the direct object is destroyed. Examples are

birrindu to destroy, to crush
borratu to wipe off, to wipe out
desegin to undo
erre to burn up
ezeztatu to nullify, to cancel, to undo
hondatu to sink, to ruin
suntsitu to destroy
triskatu to devastate
urtu to melt
xahutu to spend, to waste, to liquidate
xehatu to pulverize, to crush

An interesting subset of the verbs of destruction form the verbs of consumption. Their ergative subject must be animate. Examples are

edan to drink
hurrupatu to gulp up
irentsi to swallow
jan to eat
xurgatu to suck up, to absorb
zurrupatu to slurp

Furthermore,

afaldu to have for supper
bazkaldu to have for lunch
gosaldu to have for breakfast

The latter three are often used absolutely, that is, without any direct object: 'to have supper', 'to have lunch', 'to have breakfast'. In that use, they are intransitive in most of the eastern dialect area, but remain morphologically transitive in Guipuzcoa and Biscay, and therefore in the southern standard: *afaldu dut* 'I have had supper'.

12.1.6 Verbs of Ordering, Requesting, and Advising (*Verba Petendi*)

The following verbs all share an endeavor on the part of the subject for the addressee to either perform or refrain from performing a certain action:

agindu	to order, to command
aholkatu	to advise
arrendu	to implore
debekatu	to forbid
eragotzi	to impede, to prevent, to forbid
erregutu	to request, to pray
eskatu	to ask for, to beg
galarazi	to forbid, to prevent
gomendatu	to recommend
gonbidatu	to invite
iradoki	to suggest
manatu	to order
otoiztu	to pray, to beseech
sustatu	to encourage

When the subject's endeavors are directed at performing the action himself, the verb is called a conative. These, in Basque, are intransitive:

ahalegindu	to do one's best
lehiatu	to endeavor, to hasten, to compete
saiatu	to try

[*N.B.* The transitive verb *probatu* 'to taste', 'to try on', 'to try out' does not qualify as a conative in our sense.]

12.1.7 Verbs of Communication (*Verba Dicendi*)

A typical communication verb allows for a direct object that denotes the message transmitted. Verbs like *mintzatu* 'to speak', which is either intransitive or has a direct object referring to the addressee, are therefore omitted. Here are some examples:

aipatu	to mention
erantzun	to answer
esan	to say
idatzi	to write
ihardetsi	to answer (northern, or highly literary)
*ion	to say
irakurri	to read
kantatu	to sing

kontatu	to tell
salatu	to denounce
ukatu	to deny, to refuse
xuxurlatu	to whisper

Manner-of-speaking verbs, such as *xuxurlatu* 'to whisper', are conspicuously rare in Basque. Instead, as will be clear from sections 13.3.2 and 13.3.3, the language favors combinations of suitable bare nouns with the verb *egin* 'to make': *oihu egin* 'to shout', *zin egin* 'to swear'.

12.1.8 Verbs of Cogitation (*Verba Cogitandi*)

hausnartu	to ruminate
pentsatu	to think

More authentic than these single verbs, certain phrasal expressions are quite common:

buruan erabili	to revolve in the head
gogoan erabili	to revolve in the mind
gogoeta egin	to meditate, to think (lit. 'to make thought')

12.1.9 Verbs of Cognition (*Verba Sapiendi*)

ahantzi	to forget (northern, or slightly literary)
ahaztu	to forget
asmatu	to figure out, to invent
atzendu	to nearly forget, to forget
ezagutu	to be acquainted, to recognize, to acknowledge
gogoratu	to recall, to remind
ikasi	to learn
irakatsi	to teach
jakin	to know
oroitu	to remember

These verbs form a rather motley crowd, inasmuch as their ergative subjects bear different thematic roles depending on the verb denoting possessing, acquiring, losing, or imparting knowledge. Besides their shared connection to cognition, an additional reason for grouping these verbs together is that they all take identical complement structures.

Verbs of forgetting and remembering can be used transitively with an absolutive object, as well as intransitively with an instrumental object. Thus, for 'You have forgotten me quickly', we have *Laster ahaztu nauzu* or *Laster ahaztu zara nitaz*. And for 'I recall that (very) well', *Hori ongi gogoratzen dut* or *Horretaz ongi gogoratzen naiz*.

12.1.10 Verbs of Perception (*Verba Sentiendi*)

The ergative subject of verbs of perception has the role of an experiencer; the object denotes the source of the experience. This object bears the absolutive case, unless noted otherwise. The principal examples are

aditu	to understand, to listen, to hear, to smell
entzun	to hear
hauteman	to notice
ikusi	to see, to experience
konturatu	to realize
nabaritu	to notice, to perceive, to feel
ohartu	to note, to notice, to realize
sentitu	to feel, to feel sorry about
usaindu	to smell

[*N.B.* Noises can be heard; people only indirectly. Therefore, animate objects of *entzun* 'to hear' are usually found in the dative case: *norbaiti entzun* 'to hear somebody'.]

Note that the verbs *konturatu* and *ohartu* are intransitive and take instrumental objects *zerbaitetaz konturatu* (*ohartu*) 'to realize something'. In northern usage, *ohartu* may take a dative object instead: *zerbaiti ohartu* 'to notice something'.

A somewhat atypical example of a perception verb is *aurkitu* 'to find', with its Biscayan synonym *idoro* and its northern equivalents *ediren* and *kausitu*.

12.1.11 Emotive Verbs

With emotive verbs, it is the direct object that fills the role of experiencer, while the ergative subject denotes the cause of the emotion experienced. Examples are

aspertu	to bore
atsekabetu	to distress
harritu	to astonish, to surprise
haserretu	to anger
izutu	to frighten
kezkatu	to worry
lotsatu	to embarrass, to make ashamed
nahigabetu	to upset
poztu	to cheer up, to delight

All these verbs can also be used intransitively, with little difference in meaning. The shift from an ergative subject to an instrumental or, more commonly, sociative object may suggest that its referent merely focalizes the emotion rather than causes it:

(1) a. Gure alabek kezkatzen naute bere jokabide zoroarekin.
Our daughters worry me with their crazy behavior.

b. Gure alabez (or *alabekin*) kezkatzen naiz.
I worry about our daughters.

(2) a. Harritu egiten zuen bere adiskidearen portaerak.
His friend's conduct astonished him.
b. Harritu egiten zen bere adiskidearen portaerarekin. (Atxaga, *Gizona* 19)
He was astonished at his friend's conduct.

In section 12.4.1, changes in transitivity of this type will be seen to fit into a general process named the anticausative alternation.

12.2 Preliminary Remarks on Transitivity

12.2.1 Morphological versus Syntactic Transitivity

In section 7.1.1 transitivity was taken to be the negation of intransitivity. This, in turn, was defined in morphological terms: a verb is intransitive if and only if its periphrastic conjugation employs the auxiliary verb *izan* 'to be'.

Since there are, from a syntactic point of view, merely two auxiliary verbs in Basque, it follows that a verb will be transitive if and only if its periphrastic conjugation employs the auxiliary verb **edun* 'to have'.

Ideally, such morphologically transitive verbs should also be syntactically transitive; that is, they ought to take absolutive objects and ergative subjects. Now, while this conclusion holds true for a vast majority of transitive verbs, including by definition all prototypical ones (cf. section 12.1.1), some challenging exceptions have to be noted.

For one thing, there are transitive verbs that disallow absolutive objects, admitting, at most, oblique ones. Thus, *jarraitu* 'to follow' takes dative objects only, *dimititu* 'to resign' elative ones, *dudatu* 'to doubt' instrumental ones, and *jardun* 'to be occupied with (work or talk)' inessive or instrumental ones, respectively.

(3) a. Bere kargutik dimititu zuen.
He resigned his office.
b. Zertaz dudatzen duzu?
What do you doubt?
c. Aitzurrean jardun al duzue? (Etxaniz, *Antz.* 78)
Have you been busy digging with a hoe?

Some transitive verbs are, in fact, logically intransitive, admitting no object of any kind. Examples are *iraun* 'to last' and *irakin* 'to boil' (i.e., 'to be on the boil'), as well as many verbs denoting the emission of light or sound: *izarniatu* 'to twinkle', *durundatu* 'to clang', *distiratu* 'to glitter', and *argitu* in the meaning 'to shine':

(4) a. Euskarak noiz arte iraungo du?
Until when will Basque last?

b. Esneak irakin du.
The milk has boiled.
c. Zilarrak distiratzen du.
Silver glitters.
d. Eguzkiak argitzen du.
The sun is shining.

Furthermore, for many speakers, the verb *atertu* 'to stop raining', although morphologically transitive, must do not only without an object, but also without a subject:

(5) a. Atertu du.
It has stopped raining.

[*N.B.* Just once, the 17th-century author J. Etxeberri Ziburukoa did provide *atertu* with a subject: *zu* 'you', referring to God (*Man.* II, 147).]

Some speakers, however, allow *euria* 'the rain' as a direct object of *atertu*:

(5) b. Joan da negua, atertu du euria. (Sg 2:11)
The winter has gone, it has stopped raining.

The status of *atertu* has changed even more for those speakers who use it in the more general sense 'to run dry' or even 'to cease'. They may even make it intransitive:

(5) c. Haren negarra ez zen atertu. (Mirande, *HaurB.* 44)
Her crying had not ceased.

As a matter of fact, most weather expressions are subjectless, although many of them do show objects. For expressions with *egin* 'to make', see section 13.2.5.

12.2.2 Indefinite Object Deletion

Given that pro-drop in Basque extends to object pronouns (cf. section 9.5), we have

(6) a. Garbitzen du.
He is cleaning it. (or: *him/her*)
b. Ezagutzen du.
He recognizes it. (or: *him/her*)

With verbs denoting an action aimed at the very agent performing it (cf. Saksena 1980), another interpretation is available for this type of sentence:

(7) a. Jaten du.
He is eating. (or: *He eats.*)
b. Irakurtzen du.
He is reading. (or: *He reads.*)

In order to account for these examples, we may postulate an implicit direct object typical of the activity in question: some kind of food in (7a), some kind of text in (7b).

The domain that the implicit object is to be selected from can be narrowed down by an elative phrase:

(8) a. Gure ogitik jaten du.
He is eating from our bread.
b. Bibliatik irakurtzen du.
He is reading from the Bible.

In these examples, the absence of a direct object is not due to anaphoric deletion as in (6a,b), but to another process, traditionally, if somewhat inadequately, named indefinite object deletion.

In Basque, unlike in Greenlandic, morphological transitivity is not affected by this process in any way. More in general, barring the behavior shown by the *afaldu* class of verbs in (parts of) the eastern dialects as mentioned in section 12.1.5, the transitivity of a Basque verb never fluctuates as long as its subject retains the same thematic role.

12.3 Morphologically Derived Transitives

Any verb derived by means of the magic suffix *-tu* will display a twofold use, occurring sometimes as an intransitive inchoative, sometimes as a transitive causative. The former use has been studied in section 7.4; the latter will be focused on here.

To begin with, one important fact should be recalled from section 7.4.1: the radical form of a derived verb coincides with its derivational base, except in cases of Minor Apocope. Thus the radical of *aberastu* is *aberats*, and that of *zorroztu* is *zorrotz*; that of *askatu*, however, is *aska*, even though the verb is derived from the adjective *aske*.

12.3.1 Deadjectival Transitives

To any adjective *X* corresponds a transitive verb *X-tu* with the meaning 'to make object O X', or 'to make object O more X'. Some very common examples are

aberats	rich	aberastu	to enrich
apain	elegant	apaindu	to adorn
argi	bright, clear	argitu	to brighten, to clarify
arin	light	arindu	to lighten, to relieve
aske	free	askatu	to free, to liberate
beltz	black	beztu	to blacken, to defame
berdin	equal	berdindu	to equalize, to level
bero	warm, hot	berotu	to heat, to heat up
berri	new	berritu	to renew
bizi	alive, quick	bizitu	to enliven
eder	beautiful	edertu	to embellish
egoki	suitable	egokit	to adapt, to adjust

erraz	easy	erraztu	to facilitate
garbi	clean	garbitu	to clean, to wash
gozo	sweet	gozatu	to sweeten
handi	big, great	handitu	to enlarge, to increase
hotz	cold, cool	hoztu	to cool
huts	empty	hustu	to empty
labur	short	laburtu	to shorten
larri	tight	larritu	to alarm, to worry
luze	long	luzatu	to lengthen, to extend, to postpone
motz	short	moztu	to cut off, to shear, to trim
oso	complete, whole	osatu	to complete, to heal
samin	bitter	samindu	to embitter
sendo	firm, solid	sendotu	to strengthen, to fortify
sendo	healthy	sendatu	to cure
txiki	small, little	txikitu	to cut into pieces, to make small
txukun	neat, tidy	txukundu	to tidy up, to retouch
xehe	minute, small	xehatu	to pulverize, to shred
zorrotz	sharp	zorroztu	to sharpen
zuri	white	zuritu	to whitewash, to peel, to excuse
zuzen	straight	zuzendu	to straighten, to correct, to direct

[*N.B.* Recent forms such as *antiklerikaldu* 'to make anticlerical' (Urruzuno, *E.Z.* 48) show the continuing productivity of the suffix *-tu* with adjectives.]

Adnominals too can be converted into verbs:

etxeko	of the house	etxekotu	to domesticate
gaurko	of today	gaurkotu	to update, to modernize
herriko	of the country	herrikotu	to naturalize

Even possessive pronouns can be converted into verbs. Thus the notion 'to appropriate' is variously expressed as *neuretu*, *heuretu*, *beretu*, *geuretu*, *zeuretu*, *zeundu*, or *berendu*, according to who it is that obtains ownership.

12.3.2 Deadverbal Transitives

Generally, adverbs referring to a situation or state can turn into verb radicals:

berandu	late	berandutu	to postpone
esna	awake	esnatu	to wake up
hurbil	nearby	hurbildu	to place nearer
urrun	far away	urrundu	to move away

Adverbs formed with the iterative suffix *-ka* (see section 33.1.11) are especially suitable, since they tend to depict a "dynamic" state. Here are some examples:

apurka	in small amounts	apurkatu	to crumble, to shred
banaka	one by one	banakatu	to divide, to distribute
eskuka	touching with the hands	eskukatu	to feel with the hands, to paw
eztenka	stingingly, stinging	eztenkatu	to sting, to prick
horzka	bitingly, with the teeth	horzkatu	to bite
musuka	kissing	musukatu	to cover with kisses
sailka	in groups	sailkatu	to classify
zatika	piecemeal, in pieces	zatikatu	to break up, to split up
zirika	prodding	zirikatu	to prod, to provoke, to challenge

12.3.3 Denominal Transitives

While the meaning of deadjectival verbs is, as just shown, rigorously causative, that of denominal verbs is not so clearly predictable. Their meaning seems to cover a wide variety of senses, many of which fit the description "causative" extremely loosely, if at all. Such semantic variety may at first appear bewildering, but a closer look at the data reveals that five meaning templates are in fact sufficient to account for them all.

Let X denote the referent of the base nominal, E that of the ergative subject, and O that of the absolutive object. The meaning of the *X-tu* verb will then conform to one out of five possible patterns:

1. E turns O into X.
2. E causes O to have X, where X is something that can be experienced.
3. E produces or obtains O, which is an instantiation of X.
4. E uses X on O in the appropriate manner.
5. E experiences X toward O.

We will review these patterns one by one.

1. *E turns O into X.* Here the label *causative* seems to fit quite well. Some common examples are

adiskide	friend	adiskidetu	to befriend
anaia	brother	anaitu	to make like brothers
apur	crumb, fragment	apurtu	to crumble, to break into pieces
azal	surface	azaldu	to bring to the surface, to explain
bat	one	batu	to unite
bazter	edge, margin	baztertu	to put aside, to disregard
etsai	enemy	etsaitu	to antagonize
nor	who	nortu	to personify
pila	pile	pilatu	to pile up
puska	shred, piece	puskatu	to break into pieces
saihets	side	saihestu	to leave aside, to avoid

zati	part, piece	zatitu	to divide
zer	what	zertu	to specify, to concretize

To explain the examples *nortu* 'to personify' and *zertu* 'to concretize', one must be aware that the interrogatives *nor* 'who' and *zer* 'what' can also assume the meaning 'somebody' and 'something' in certain contexts, especially as bound morphemes. The verb *zertu* can also have a different meaning, namely, 'to do you know what', and is used when the speaker cannot hit on the proper verb to employ or for some reason wishes not to make use of it. Taken in that sense, *zertu* does not fit this pattern.

2. *E causes O to have X, where X is something that can be experienced.* There are many derived verbs following this pattern. Among them are

agur	greeting	agurtu	to greet
argi	light	argitu	to illuminate
arma	weapon	armatu	to arm
atsegin	pleasure	atsegindu	to delight, to please
atsekabe	displeasure, sorrow	atsekabetu	to distress, to sadden
bake	peace	baketu	to pacify
behar	need, necessity	behartu	to force, to compel
beldur	fear	beldurtu	to frighten
bortxa	violence, coercion	bortxatu	to force, to rape
dei	call	deitu	to call
egarri	thirst	egarritu	to make thirsty
era	manner, form	eratu	to form, to put in order
ferra	horseshoe	ferratu	to shoe
froga	proof	frogatu	to prove
gose	hunger	gosetu	to make hungry
indar	force	indartu	to strengthen
inguru	environment, surroundings	inguratu	to surround
itxura	appearance, shape	itxuratu	to shape, to feign
izu	fright, terror	izutu	to terrify
kezka	worry	kezkatu	to worry
lagun	companion, mate	lagundu	to accompany, to help
laztan	caress, kiss	laztandu	to caress, to kiss
lohi	mud, filth	lohitu	to soil, to stain
min	pain	mindu	to hurt, to offend
molde	mold, form	moldatu	to shape, to form
neke	effort, fatigue	nekatu	to tire out, to bother
ohore	honor	ohoratu	to honor
pena	grief, sorrow	penatu	to grieve, to distress
poz	joy	poztu	to rejoice, to gladden

pozoi	poison	pozoitu	to poison
sari	reward, prize	saritu	to reward, to award a prize
tankera	shape, style	tankeratu	to shape, to condition
toles	fold, pleat	tolestu	to fold, to pleat
zain	guard, custodian	zaindu	to guard, to watch, to protect
zauri	wound	zauritu	to wound
zorabio	dizziness	zorabiatu	to make dizzy
zorion	happiness	zoriondu	to make happy
zulo	hole	zulatu	to pierce, to perforate

3. *E produces or obtains O, which is an instantiation of X.* Some common verbs accounted for by this template are

aholku	advice	aholkatu	to advise
asmo	purpose, plan	asmatu	to invent, to devise
aukera	choice	aukeratu	to choose
dantza	dance	dantzatu	to dance
erregu	request, prayer	erregutu	to request, to pray
eske	petition	eskatu	to ask for, to petition, to beg
galde	question	galdetu	to ask
joko	play, game	jokatu	to play
zor	debt	zortu	to owe

Historically, the verb *eskertu* 'to thank' may very well have arisen in conformity with this pattern. Assuming one of the various meanings of *esker*, namely, 'favor', to be basic, the derived verb *eskertu* must have meant 'to acknowledge as a favor', a notion much akin to its present meaning.

An interesting subpattern is that where O is identical to X, and therefore unavailable to the syntax. The template then simplifies to "E produces or obtains X."

This will account for the derived verbs of emission, which combine morphological transitivity with logical intransitivity:

argi	light	argitu	to shine
burrunba	humming, buzzing	burrunbatu	to hum, to buzz
dirdira	radiance, gleam	dirdiratu	to gleam
distira	sparkle, glittering	distiratu	to sparkle, to glitter
durunda	clang, din	durundatu	to clang, to resound

[*N.B.* In its meaning 'to illuminate' *argitu* is syntactically transitive and belongs to pattern 2.]

4. *E uses X on O in the appropriate manner.* For this pattern to apply, X must be a tool or a potential tool. Some examples follow:

aitzur	spade, hoe	aitzurtu	to spade, to hoe
bahe	sieve, winnow	bahetu	to sift, to winnow
erratz	broom	erraztu	to sweep
giltza	key	giltzatu	to lock
golde	plow	goldatu	to plow
iltze	nail	iltzatu	to nail, to nail down
orrazi	comb	orraztu	to comb
zerra	saw	zerratu	to saw
zigor	whip, punishment	zigortu	to whip, to punish

5. *E experiences X toward O.* This pattern will apply whenever X is an emotion directed toward a person or object:

arbuio	contempt	arbuiatu	to despise
desira	desire	desiratu	to desire
gorroto	hatred, hate	gorrotatu	to hate
gutizia	craving	gutiziatu	to crave, to covet
hastio	loathing	hastiatu	to loathe, to detest
higuin	disgust	higuin	to detest
maite-	love	maitatu	to love
narda	aversion	nardatu	to loathe, to detest
nazka	aversion	nazkatu	to loathe, to detest

12.3.4 Deallatival Transitives

Any noun *N* in the allative case can serve as a transitive verb radical with the meaning 'to take to N'. This will yield verbs ending in *-atu*, *-ratu*, *-taratu*, *-etaratu*, and *-ganatu*. The following list contains the most important examples:

ahora	to the mouth	ahoratu	to raise to the mouth
aitzina	forward, ahead	aitzinatu	to advance, to promote
albora	to the side	alboratu	to put closer, to put aside
aldera	to the side	alderatu	to put closer, to compare, to put aside
argitara	into the light	argitaratu	to publish, to bring to light
atera	to the door	ateratu	to take out, to extract
atzera	backward	atzeratu	to push back, to postpone
aurpegira	to the face	aurpegiratu	to throw to the face, to reproach
aurrera	forward, ahead	aurreratu	to advance, to lend, to save (money)
azpira	to below	azpiratu	to subdue, to defeat, to dominate
bazterrera	to the edge	bazterreratu	to put out of the way, to exclude
batera	together	bateratu	to join, to unite, to unify
begira	to the eye	begiratu	to look at, to watch
behera	downward	beheratu	to lower, to depreciate
bidera	to the road	bideratu	to channel, to guide

bizkarrera	onto the back	bizkarreratu	to load onto one's back, to blame
burura	to the head	bururatu	to bring to a head, to finish
erdira	to the center/half	erdiratu	to put in the middle, to split (halve)
eskura	into the hand	eskuratu	to lay hands on, to obtain, to get
etxera	homeward	etxeratu	to bring home, to take home
gainera	to the top	gaineratu	to put on top, to add
gibela	backward	gibelatu	to set back, to restrain, to delay
gogora	to the mind	gogoratu	to bring to mind, to remind
gora	up, upward	goratu	to elevate, to exalt, to praise
hobira	to the grave	hobiratu	to carry to the grave, to bury
hondora	to the bottom	hondoratu	to sink, to destroy
kalera	to the street	kaleratu	to put out on the street
kanpora	out, outward	kanporatu	to bring out, to expel
lepora	onto the neck	leporatu	to shoulder, to foist upon
lurrera	to the ground	lurreratu	to pull down, to tear down
mundura	into the world	munduratu	to bring into the world
oinpera	to under the foot	oinperatu	to trample, to oppress
ondora	to the vicinity	ondoratu	to bring near
urrutira	to far away	urrutiratu	to remove far away
zokora	to the corner	zokoratu	to put away, to put aside
zuregana	to you	zureganatu	to bring to you

[*N.B.* Even the interrogative verb *noratu* 'to take where' derived from *nora* 'to where' is attested: *haurra noratzen zuten ikusteko* (*TZ* I, 106) 'in order to see where they took the child'.]

12.3.5 Complex Transitives

For most speakers, derived verb radicals must be single lexical items or, at most, allative nouns, as was the case in all the examples presented so far. Other native speakers, however, produce or accept more complex verb radicals, used transitively as well as intransitively. Since the latter use has already been dealt with in section 7.4.6, it now remains to illustrate the transitive use.

All instances I have encountered involve allative bases, most of them containing a genitival modifier: *etsaien eskuetaratu* (*TB* 113) 'to deliver into the hands of the enemies', *deabruaren sareperatu* (Bartolomé, 131) 'to gather under the devil's net', *gizagaiso haren bizkarreratu* (F. Arrese, *Dic.* 96; *DRA* 3, 1035) 'to load onto the back of the poor wretch', *bere bizkarreratu* (*MEIG* IV, 73) 'to load on his back', *bere etxeratu* (L.E. *Kop.* 84) 'to take to his home', and *bere baitaratu* (many examples listed in *DGV* III, 718) 'to come to oneself'. Examples with a slightly different structure include *beste munduratu* (Etxaide, *Alos* 21) 'to send to the other world', and *bidez besteratu* (Etxaide, *Gor*[1] 297, *Gor*[2] 299) 'to sidetrack'.

Artiagoitia's (1994) constraint requiring a derivational base to be head-final appears to hold for transitive bases just as it does for intransitive ones (cf. section 7.4.6). The only counterexample I am aware of occurs in the 16th-century poet Etxepare: *Zerk andere-hantu du?* (*LVP* VII-10) 'What has turned her into a fine lady?', where *andere handi* 'fine lady' seems to act as a derivational base without being head-final.

12.3.6 Amorphous Deallatival Transitives

Except for an isolated example such as *atera* 'to take out', the use of a zero allomorph for *-tu*, as in *argitara* (*MEIG* VII, 158) or *lepora* (*MEIG* IX, 97) for *argitaratu* 'to publish' or *leporatu* 'to shoulder', nowadays represents a highly marked stylistic device, whether used in transitive or intransitive sentences (cf. section 7.4.7). In times past this usage seems to have been considerably more common, perhaps normal. For example, the works of F. Lardizabal (1806–1855) present numerous examples of the type *mundura zuen* (*TZ* I, 219) 'she brought into the world', and going back all the way to Leizarraga's New Testament version of 1571, we find several examples even of complex amorphous deallatival transitives: *Gentilen eskuetarako dute* (Mk 10:33) 'they will deliver him into the hands of the Gentiles'; *bere staturako ditu gauza guztiak* (Mt 17:11, repeated in Mk 9:12, with a similar phrase in Acts 1:6) 'he will turn all things to their (pristine) state'.

12.4 The Anticausative Alternation

12.4.1 External versus Internal Causes

Our first aim in this section is to tie together the two categories of *-tu* verbs, the inchoatives and the causatives, hitherto studied separately. In a vast majority of instances, we find the transitive sentences depicting a change of state brought about by an external cause encoded by the ergative subject, while the intransitive sentences likewise depict a state, but without mention of cause. To see this point, let us look at some examples:

(9) a. Ate-hotsak esnatu nau. (Etxaniz, *Antz.* 121)
The sound of the door woke me up.
b. Zortzietan esnatu naiz.
I woke up at eight o'clock.

(10) a. Mirenek sendatu du Patxi.
Mary has cured Frank.
b. Patxi sendatu da.
Frank has recovered.

(11) a. Norbaitek atea zabaldu zuen.
Somebody opened the door.
b. Bat-batean ate guztiak zabaldu ziren eta guztien kateak erori. (Acts 16:26; *JKBO*)
Suddenly all doors opened and everybody's chains fell off.

(12) a. Jauna, zuk niri oinak garbitu? (Jn 13:6)
Lord, you washing my feet?
b. Garbitu nintzen eta ikusi egiten dut. (Jn 9:15)
I washed (myself) and I see.

(13) a. Aldare hori puskatuko du eta bere gaineko hautsak zabalduko ditu.
He will break that altar to pieces, and the ashes on top of it he will scatter.
b. Aldare hori puskatuko da eta bere gaineko hautsak zabalduko dira. (*TZ* II, 58)
That altar will break to pieces, and the ashes on top of it will scatter.

Note that the theme, by which we mean the entity undergoing the change, is uniformly expressed by the absolutive case form, whether the clause is transitive or intransitive. Actually, the same phenomenon can be observed in English, with the verb *to break* as a paramount example. There it is known as the anticausative (or simply causative) alternation, a topic to which B. Levin and M. Rappaport Hovav have devoted chapter 3 of their monograph entitled *Unaccusativity* (1995), a truly admirable work to which this and the following sections owe a considerable debt.

In Basque, a closer investigation reveals that this alternation is by no means restricted to derived *-tu* verbs. Quite independent of morphology, it is conditioned by the meaning class of the verb. In short, the alternation is found with emotive verbs, as made clear by our discussion in section 12.1.11; quite generally with verbs denoting a change of state, including the borderline cases of production and destruction; and, finally, with verbs of motion, where it is, however, less general. It will be convenient to deal with the last two verb classes in separate sections. For both verb classes, the distinction between an external cause and an internal one will be the governing factor in the alternation. By internal cause is meant a cause consisting of tendencies internal to the theme. Whether such tendencies, in the event of an animate theme, are or are not subject to some form of control is immaterial to the definition.

12.4.2 Verbs of Change of State

When using a verb denoting either production or destruction, change of state or its maintenance, the speaker is forced to choose between two options. He must represent the event either as tied to some external cause, in which case this cause will have to be expressed as an ergative argument of a transitive verb, or else as arising spontaneously, or, at most, due to a cause internal to the theme, in which case the verb will be intransitive. Characteristically, Basque makes use of the same verb in both instances, the only difference being in the choice of auxiliary: **edun* 'to have' or *izan* 'to be'.

Verbs describing no change sustained by the theme itself except for its location belong to the class of verbs of motion and rest, to be discussed in section 12.4.3.

A small but fairly representative list of the verbs we are concerned with will now be provided, in order to study the relation between their transitive and intransitive senses:

Verb	Transitive Sense	Intransitive Sense
agertu	to manifest, to reveal, to show	to appear, to be published
aldatu	to alter, to change	to vary, to change
amaitu	to finish, to end	to be finished, to end
bete	to fill, to fulfill	to fill, to be fulfilled
bihurtu	to turn into	to turn into
bukatu	to finish, to end	to be finished, to end, to end up
busti	to soak, to wet, to moisten	to soak, to grow moist, to become wet
desegin	to undo, to demolish	to get undone, to fall apart
egin	to make, to do	to become
egosi	to cook, to digest	to boil, to cook, to be digested
erantzi	to undress, to take off	to undress (oneself)
erre	to burn, to bake, to smoke	to burn, to be consumed
esnatu	to wake up, to stir up	to wake up, to become alert
estali	to cover, to cover up	to cover oneself, to become covered
eten	to break off, to interrupt	to break (off), to be interrupted
galdu	to ruin, to lose	to be ruined, to be lost
hautsi	to break	to break
hazi	to bring up, to grow	to grow
hil	to kill	to die
hondatu	to destroy, to squander, to sink	to sink, to collapse
ito	to choke, to drown	to suffocate, to choke, to drown
itzali	to put out, to turn off	to go out, to fade away
jantzi	to dress, to put on	to dress oneself
orraztu	to comb	to comb oneself
prestatu	to prepare, to make ready	to prepare oneself, to get ready
sortu	to beget, to conceive, to generate	to arise, to be born
suntsitu	to destroy, to annihilate	to be destroyed, to vanish

We will end this section with a few more examples illustrating the alternation, although there should be little need for them at this point.

(14) a. Nork ez ditu ateak itxi?
Who has not closed the gates?
b. Haren ateak ez dira arratsean itxiko. (Rv 21:25)
Its gates will not close in the evening.

(15) a. Kristau bihurtuko nauzu. (Acts 26:28)
You will turn me into a christian.
b. Bertsolari bihurtu al zarete? (Etxaniz, *Antz*. 43)
Have you turned into bards?

(16) a. Amak haurra janzten du.
Mother is dressing the child.
b. Haurra janzten da.
The child is dressing.

(17) a. Ardoak galdu gaitu.
Wine has ruined us.
b. Basoan galdu gara.
We have gotten lost in the woods.

(18) a. Hiri osoa suntsituko ote duzu bost horiengatik? (Gn 18:28)
Will you destroy the whole city because of those five, I wonder?
b. Hilko naiz, baina ez naiz osoro suntsituko. (*MEIG* VIII, 64)
I will die, but I will not vanish totally.

12.4.3 Verbs of Motion and Rest

No less than when dealing with a change of state, a speaker faced with a change of location or position (or its maintenance) must commit himself to one of two options. He must either ascribe the motion to an external cause expressed as an ergative argument or else represent it as spontaneous or controlled by the theme itself. In the first case the verb will be transitive, in the second case intransitive.

But, in sharp contrast to the change-of-state situation, the two alternatives are not invariably covered by the same lexical item. Although many verbs of motion exhibit the anticausative alternation, the intransitive use of a transitive verb finds itself blocked by the existence of a separate intransitive verb.

Two of the most frequent motion verbs, *ekarri* 'to bring' and *eraman* 'to carry away', fail to alternate, as their intransitive use is blocked by the existence of *etorri* 'to come' and *joan* 'to go away'.

Furthermore, certain verbs of motion are inherently transitive, as they contain semantic features involving the nature of the causing event, for example, the exertion of force in the case of verbs like *bultzatu* 'to push' or *tiratu* 'to pull'.

For similar reasons, verbs of throwing, like *bota*, *jaurti(ki)*, and *aurtiki*, are inherently transitive. Only Baztanese and a few neighboring varieties permit *bota* to be intransitive with the meaning 'to fall down'.

As to the remaining verbs of motion, the following picture emerges:

1. Verbs denoting merely the presence or absence of movement.

These are all alternating: *mugitu* or *higitu* 'to move'; *gelditu* or *geratu* 'to stop', 'to stay', 'to remain'.

2. Verbs denoting "inherently directed motion"—an apt characterization I borrow from Levin and Rappaport Hovav 1995.

These verbs tend to be alternating, with very few exceptions. Examples are all deallatives, as well as *aienatu* 'to chase', 'to flee'; *atera* 'to take out', 'to go out', 'to exit'; *bihurtu* 'to send back', 'to turn back'; *itzuli* 'to send back', 'to turn back'; *jaitsi* 'to lower', 'to go down'; and *sartu* 'to put inside', 'to insert', 'to go inside', 'to enter'.

[*N.B.* Unlike its synonym *atera*, the verb *irten* 'to go out' is strictly intransitive.]

The main exception here is the verb *jaso* 'to lift', whose intransitive use appears to be blocked by the existence of *igo* 'to go up', 'to climb'.

3. Verbs requiring the end point of the motion to be expressed.
 The verb *finkatu* 'to fix', 'to settle', as well as the verbs *ezarri*, *ipini*, *jarri*, and *kokatu*, all equivalents of the English verb *to put*, are alternating, except for *ezarri*, whose intransitive use has become obsolete. Here is an illustration:

(19) a. Patxik Karmen nire aurrean jarri zuen.
 Frank put Carmen in front of me.
 b. Karmen nire aurrean jarri zen. (Urretabizkaia, *Asp*. 50)
 Carmen put herself in front of me.

4. Verbs of putting in a spatial configuration.
 These are all alternating. The main examples are *altxatu* 'to raise up', 'to rise'; *eseri* 'to seat', 'to sit down'; *etzan* 'to lay down', 'to lie down'; and *jaiki* 'to raise up', 'to rise up', 'to rise'.

[*N.B.* The synthetic forms of *etzan* denote position rather than motion and are invariably intransitive.]

Before closing this section, a word of warning: It is by no means the case that all transitivity alternations exhibited by verbs of motion conform to the anticausative pattern. We may also have to do with a pattern in which the intransitive use of the verb is basic. In this pattern, a locative phrase selected by the verb is promoted to the status of a direct object, and the theme of the motion ends up in the ergative case:

(20) a. Zubitik igaro gara.
 We have crossed over the bridge.
 b. Zubia igaro dugu.
 We have crossed the bridge.

(21) a. Miren mendi-gainera iritsi zen.
 Mary arrived at the top of the mountain.
 b. Mirenek mendi-gaina iritsi du.
 Mary has reached the top of the mountain.

(22) a. Nire gainetik jauzi zara.
 You have jumped over me.
 b. Jauzi nauzu.
 You have skipped me.

12.5 The Middle Voice

Virtually every Basque verb possesses a middle voice, in form coinciding with the intransitive periphrastic conjugation. The semantic range of this middle voice is rather broad. Even with the same verb, its value can vary between that of an agentless passive, a reflexive, or a reciprocal. On this basis I will speak of medio-passives, medio-reflexives, and medio-reciprocals, without attempting to establish a structural foundation for this diversity in interpretation.

12.5.1 Medio-passives

In marked contrast to the case of the intransitives studied in section 12.4, involvement of an external agent in the process denoted by the verb is not ruled out. What defines the middle voice is simply that the agent—*or experiencer*—is not syntactically realized as an argument of the verb. Some examples will illustrate this point:

(23) a. Gurasoen etxean ez zen sua egunero pizten. (Urretabizkaia, *Asp.* 85)
In the house of the parents fire was not lighted every day.
b. Gure etxea atzo saldu zen.
Our house was sold yesterday.
c. Ez ote dira bi txori sos batean saltzen? (Mt 10:29)
Are not two birds sold for a penny?
d. Zuhaitza fruitutik ezagutzen da. (Mt 12:33)
The tree is known by its fruit.
e. Eta nire leihotik ez da ezer ikusten. (Mendiguren, *Hamalau* 95)
And from my window one sees nothing.

[*N.B.* Note that the Basque medio-passive can often be called upon to translate English sentences with indefinite *one* or *you* as subject: *Jendea pozik ikusten zen* (Lasarte, *Gordean* 325), 'You saw the people happy'.]

As *EGLU* (II, 54–56) observes, nowadays medio-passives are restricted to third-person subjects. Thus, while *elizan sartzen da* is ambiguous between the meanings 'he enters the church' and 'he is put inside the church', *elizan sartzen naiz* can mean only 'I enter the church', not 'I am put inside the church'. Accordingly, examples like (24), still current at the end of the 19th century, are at present no longer understood:

(24) Hurrengo laurogei urtean ni ez naiz ahaztuko Kantabriako partean. (*EGL* 17: from Txirrita)
In the next eighty years I won't be forgotten in the Cantabrian region.

In order to express an indefinite animate subject, an unspecified third-person plural can always be resorted to:

(25) a. Hurrengo laurogei urtean ni ez naute ahaztuko Kantabriako partean.
In the next eighty years they won't forget me in the Cantabrian region.
b. Etxeko lanak ez egiteagatik zigortuko dute mutil hau.
They will punish this boy for not doing his homework.

Many speakers reject animate subjects in medio-passives altogether, a restriction endorsed by *EGLU* (II, 55). Other speakers, however, will still accept examples like (26a,b):

(26) a. Etxeko lanak ez egiteagatik zigortuko da mutil hau.
This boy will be punished for not doing his homework.
b. Bata harturen da eta bestea utziren. (Lk 17:34, 35, & 36; Lz)
The one will be taken and the other left.

It is interesting to observe that Leizarraga's turn of phrase, given as (26b), has not been retained by any of the later translators. They all alter the construction, using either an adjectival participle: *bata hartua izango da, eta bestea utzia* (*IB*, similarly in *JKBO*, *Lau Eb.*, Dv, Olab.) or a third-person plural subject: *bata eraman eta bestea utzi egingo dute* (*EAB*, similarly Ker.).

The constraint against first- and second-person medio-passives can also be detected in the behavior of the change-of-state verb *isildu* 'to keep quiet', 'to silence', which takes either inanimate objects as in (27a) with its corresponding medio-passive (27b), or human ones, as in (27c) with the anticausative alternant (27d):

(27) a. Zure izena isildu du.
He has kept your name quiet.
b. Zure izena isildu da.
Your name has been kept quiet.
c. Berehala isildu zaitu.
He has silenced you at once.
d. Berehala isildu zara.
You have fallen silent at once.

Notice that (27d) cannot bear the medio-passive reading 'you have been silenced at once' because of its second-person subject; it has the anticausative reading, always possible with a change-of-state verb.

Intransitive verbs too can be used in the middle voice, but, as *EGLU* points out, always in a habitual or generic sense:

(28) a. Hemendik joaten al da Basagorrira?—galdetu zuen Senekak. (Amuriza, *Emea* 114)
"Does one go this way to Basagorri?" asked Seneka.
b. Oso ondo egoten da hemen. (*EGLU* II, 51)
One stays here very nicely.

Interestingly, as B. Oihartzabal has noticed (personal communication, cf. 1992), the habitual or generic requirement only obtains for unaccusative intransitives, not for the medio-passive of an unergative intransitive, such as *mintzatu* 'to speak':

(28) c. Atzo asko mintzatu zen gai horretaz.
Yesterday, a lot was spoken about that matter.

[*N.B.* All these sentences also admit, of course, a personal interpretation: he/she/it . . .]

12.5.2 Medio-reflexives

While Basque also makes available an explicit reflexive anaphor based on the noun *buru* 'head' (see section 15.7), the middle voice itself can convey an unmistakable reflexive meaning, as in the following examples:

(29) Ez zen sekula erabat ematen. (Urretabizkaia, *Asp.* 30)
She never gave herself totally.

There is no constraint against first- or second-person subjects in medio-reflexives:

(30) a. Arriskuan ikusi naiz. (*EGLU* II, 55)
I have seen myself in danger.
b. Ez ginen inportanteak sentitzen. (Urretabizkaia, *Asp.* 23)
We did not feel ourselves important.
c. Ur-ertzean begiratu naiz. (Ibiñagabeitia, *Virgil.* 34)
I have looked at myself in the edge of the water.
d. Ispiluan begiratu al zara?
Have you looked at yourself in the mirror?

12.5.3 Medio-reciprocals

Reciprocals are generally expressed in Basque by means of the locution *batak* . . . *bestea* 'the one . . . the other', or else by the anaphor *elkar* 'each other', to be studied in chapter 15. A small set of verbs, however, allow a reciprocal interpretation of their middle-voice form. These are mainly verbs of perception that allow animate direct objects, but also a few others. Examples are attested for at least the following verbs: *aditu* 'to understand', *agurtu* 'to greet', *ezagutu* 'to (get to) know', *ikusi* 'to see', *maitatu* (or *maite*) 'to love', *ulertu* 'to understand'. Some examples follow:

(31) a. Non ikusiko gara bihar? (Agirre, *A.L.* 72)
Where shall we see each other tomorrow?
b. Ez dira egunero ikusten. (Urretabizkaia, *Sat.* 74)
They don't see each other every day.
c. Anaiak bezala maite ziren. (Alzaga, *B.L.* 44)
They loved each other like brothers.

d. Pabiloiaren atean agurtu ginen. (Atxaga, *Obab*. 129)
   We said goodbye to each other at the door of the pavillion.
e. Irribarre gozoz agurtu ziren. (Cf. *G.* 41)
   They greeted each other with a pleasant smile.

[*N.B.* Some purist grammarians frown upon medio-reciprocals, ascribing them to Spanish influence. For example, the editor of the "improved" third edition of *Garoa* expurgated the original middle construction *parra-irri gozoz agurtu ziran*, changing it to *par-irri gogoz agurtu zuten alkar* ($G.^3$ 38).]

12.6 Actor Nouns: The Suffix *-(tzai)le*

Attached to a verb radical, the nominalizer *-(tzai)le* yields a noun denoting the performer or experiencer of the action indicated by the verb. In Batua, as in all southern dialects, this process is fully productive but restricted to transitive and unergative verbs. In the northern dialects a few unaccusative verbs also claim actor nouns: *egoile* 'stayer', 'resident', *erorle* 'faller', *jile* 'comer', *joaile* 'goer'.

Nouns formed with this suffix are typically animate and indiscriminate as to gender. Some of them are also used as adjectives, in which case they may form part of an inanimate noun phrase.

The suffix comes in two shapes: a simple form *-le* and a complex form *-tzaile*. The choice between them is phonologically determined in the following fashion: the complex form is required unless the perfect participle ends in *-ri*, *-rri*, or *-n*, or the radical ends in a sibilant or an affricate.

12.6.1 The Allomorph *-le*

Before the *l* of this allomorph, two natural sandhi rules apply. The first is that an affricate simplifies to a sibilant, and the second that a nasal elides.

The verbs *eman* and *eraman* are slightly irregular in that a vowel *i* is inserted after the elision of the nasal. The main examples are

antzeztu	to perform, to act	antzezle	performer, actor
aurkeztu	to present	aurkezle	presenter
babestu	to protect	babesle	protector, patron
bereizi	to separate, to distinguish	bereizle	separator, divider
ebatsi	to steal	ebasle	stealer, thief
edan	to drink	edale	drinker
egin	to make, to do	egile	maker, author
ehortzi	to bury	ehorzle	burier, gravedigger
ekarri	to bring	ekarle	bringer, carrier
ekoitzi	to produce	ekoizle	producer
eman	to give	emaile	giver

entzun	to hear	entzule	hearer
eragin	to cause, to promote	eragile	promoter, moving spirit
erakutsi	to show	erakusle	demonstrator, demonstrative
eraman	to bear	eramaile	carrier, bearer, sufferer
erantzun	to answer	erantzule	answerer, respondent
erausi	to chatter	erausle	chatterer, chatterbox
erein	to sow	ereile	sower
eroan	to conduct	eroale	carrier, conductor
erosi	to buy	erosle	buyer, redeemer
esan	to say	esale	sayer
hautsi	to break	hausle	breaker
idatzi	to write	idazle	writer
igarri	to guess, to divine	igarle	diviner, prophet
igorri	to send	igorle	sender
ikasi	to learn	ikasle	learner, student
ikusi	to see	ikusle	seer, viewer, spectator
irabazi	to win	irabazle	winner
irakatsi	to teach	irakasle	teacher, instructor
irakurri	to read	irakurle	reader
irun	to spin	irule	spinner
jakin	to know	jakile	knower, witness
jan	to eat	jale	eater
josi	to sew	josle	sewer, seamstress, tailor
moztu	to cut, to clip	mozle	shearer, clipper
sinetsi	to believe	sinesle	believer
urgatzi	to assist	urgazle	assistant

[*N.B.* A few doublets still remain in Batua usage—for example, *aurkeztaile* for *aurkezle* and, more often, *motzaile* for *mozle*.]

After nominalization has taken place, a direct object of the verb turns into a genitive phrase: *ur honen edalea* 'the drinker of this water', *liburu honen egilea* 'the author of this book', *behi zaharren eroslea* 'the buyer of the old cows'.

If the object is indefinite or generic, compounds can be formed: *diru-ebasle* 'money stealer', *ardo-edale* 'wine drinker', *berri-ekarle* 'messenger', *berri-emaile* 'informant', *gaitze-sale* 'slanderer', *lege-hausle* 'lawbreaker', *gizajale* 'cannibal', and so on.

12.6.2 The Allomorph *-tzaile*

As the vast majority of verbs, those ending in *-tu*, almost all form their actor nouns by means of this allomorph, examples with *-tzaile* greatly outnumber those with *-le*. Strictly speaking, there is an unlimited number of them, since there is no limit to the number of verbs that can be derived by means of the magic suffix *-tu* of section 12.3. The following examples are listed for the sake of their frequency or interest:

aditu	to listen, to understand	aditzaile	listener, understander
antolatu	to organize	antolatzaile	organizer
askatu	to free, to liberate	askatzaile	liberator
atera	to take out	ateratzaile	remover, server
aztertu	to examine, to analyze	aztertzaile	examiner, investigator
bilatu	to seek, to search	bilatzaile	seeker, searcher
bildu	to gather, to collect	biltzaile	gatherer, collector
bota	to throw, to cast, to launch	botatzaile	thrower, caster, launcher
bultzatu	to push, to shove	bultzatzaile	pusher, promoter
eho	to grind	ehotzaile	grinder, miller
engainatu	to deceive, to cheat	engainatzaile	deceiver, cheat
erabaki	to decide	erabakitzaile	arbiter, jury member
erabili	to use	erabiltzaile	user
eraiki	to raise, to found, to build	eraikitzaile	founder, builder
eraso	to attack	erasotzaile	attacker
erre	to burn, to smoke	erretzaile	burner, smoker
eskaini	to offer	eskaintzaile	offerer, tenderer
esnatu	to wake up	esnatzaile	awakener
ezagutu	to know	ezagutzaile	connoisseur
galdu	to lose, to corrupt	galtzaile	loser, corrupter
garaitu	to win, to triumph	garaitzaile	winner, victor
garbitu	to clean, to wash	garbitzaile	cleaner
gonbidatu	to invite	gonbidatzaile	inviter, host
gorrotatu	to hate	gorrotatzaile	hater
harrapatu	to catch, to grab	harrapatzaile	catcher, capturer, kidnapper
hartu	to take, to receive	hartzaile	taker, receiver, creditor
hil	to kill	hiltzaile	killer, murderer
hondatu	to ruin, to waste	hondatzaile	waster, spendthrift
ikertu	to research, to explore	ikertzaile	researcher, explorer
iraindu	to insult, to offend	iraintzaile	insulter, offender
ito	to choke, to suffocate	itotzaile	strangler
jarraitu	to follow	jarraitzaile	follower, continuator, disciple
jo	to hit, to strike	jotzaile	hitter, striker, player of a musical instrument
kantatu	to sing	kantatzaile	singer
kontatu	to count, to narrate	kontatzaile	counter, teller, narrator
lagundu	to accompany, to help	laguntzaile	helper, assistant
maitatu	to love	maitatzaile	lover

menderatu	to dominate	menderatzaile	dominator, conqueror
mintzatu	to speak	mintzatzaile	speaker
neurtu	to measure	neurtzaile	measurer, assessor
osatu	to heal	osatzaile	healer
pagatu	to pay	pagatzaile	payer
partitu	to divide, to distribute	partitzaile	divider, distributor
pertsegitu	to persecute	pertsegitzaile	persecutor
salatu	to denounce	salatzaile	denouncer, accuser
salbatu	to rescue, to save	salbatzaile	rescuer, saver, savior
saldu	to sell, to betray	saltzaile	seller, salesman, traitor
segitu	to follow	segitzaile	follower, disciple
sendatu	to cure	sendatzaile	healer
sortu	to conceive, to generate	sortzaile	creator, generator, generative
tiratu	to pull, to throw, to shoot	tiratzaile	puller, thrower, shooter, shot
ukatu	to negate, to deny	ukatzaile	negator, denier
ulertu	to understand	ulertzaile	understander
urkatu	to hang	urkatzaile	hangman
zabaldu	to widen, to spread, to open	zabaltzaile	widener, opener, spreader
zaindu	to guard, to protect	zaintzaile	guard, custodian
zanpatu	to oppress	zanpatzaile	oppressor
zapaldu	to flatten, to repress	zapaltzaile	crusher, repressor
zirikatu	to prod, to provoke	zirikatzaile	provoker, tempter, stimulator
zuritu	to whiten, to flatter	zuritzaile	whitewasher, flatterer
zuzendu	to correct, to direct	zuzentzaile	corrector, rectifier

[*N.B.* Present Batua usage recognizes *garaile* along with *garaitzaile*, and *ezagule* as a literary variant of *ezagutzaile*.]

As noted in section 12.6.1, a direct object of the original verb turns into a genitive: *haren lanaren jarraitzailea* 'the continuator of his work', *berri horren zabaltzailea* 'the spreader of that news', while indefinite or generic objects can give rise to compound nouns: *hagin-ateratzaile* 'tooth puller', *urre-biltzaile* 'gold seeker', *kale-garbitzaile* 'street cleaner', *liburu-saltzaile* 'bookseller'.

12.7 Vocabulary

adierazi	to express	aurkitu	to find
afaldu	to have supper	baratza	garden
ahaztu	to forget	baserri	farm, farmhouse

batera	together
bazkaldu	to have lunch
bihurtu	to turn into, to return
bilatu	to look for, to seek
edan	to drink
egile	maker, author
ezagun	acquaintance
gehiago	more, some more, any more
gosaldu	to have breakfast
hartu	to take, to receive, to get
hitz	word
hizkuntza	language
idazle	writer
ikasle	student
irribarre	smile
jo	to hit, to strike, to beat
kezka	worry
kezkatu	to worry
morroi	servant, farmhand
neskame	housemaid, woman servant
neurri	measure, size
ogibide	livelihood, occupation, trade
pena	sorrow
sekula . . . ez	never
sorbalda	shoulder
txokolate	chocolate
utzi	to leave

12.8 Exercises

12.8.1 Translate into English

1. Zer neurritako prakak eramaten ditu irakasleak egun hauetan?
2. Txokolate hau erosi al duzu zure andregaiarekin batera baratzan jateko?
3. Ibai guztiak itsasora doaz eta itsasoa ez da inoiz ere betetzen.
4. Nolako ogibidea hartuko ote du orain zure semeak?
5. Kezka guztien artean, ez naiz ahazten zure irribarre gozoaz.
6. Noren etxeratuko dituzu umetxo horiek?
7. Sorgin zahar batek nire arreba jo eta sorgindu egin du.
8. Mundu honetan ez gara apika gehiago ikusiko.
9. Idazle honen hitzak gaizki ulertu bide dira.
10. Baratza eder batean aurkitu nintzen eta hor aurkitu zintudan.
11. Ez dut lan hau morroien sorbaldetaratuko.
12. Zuen kezkak berehala geuretu ditugu.

12.8.2 Translate into Basque

1. The housemaids always eat breakfast together with us.
2. Why have you left all your books at home?
3. What is being read in our farmhouses?

4. How does one go from our house to yours?
5. In Bilbao one eats a lot of fish.
6. How does one learn languages?
7. We will never forget our mother's language.
8. Among my acquaintances, nobody worries about our language.
9. Today I won't drink anything more in this pub.
10. This author does not use a lot of words to express her sorrows.
11. The housemaid will turn into the lady of the house, and she will then turn the servant into the master.
12. In all these farmhouses, lunch is eaten at a quarter to two.

13 The Partitive; the Verb *egin* and Its Complements; *gabe*

13.1 The Partitive

13.1.1 The Partitive Case

Originally named *negativus* by Oihenart in his 1638 work *Notitia utriusque Vasconiae* (1992), the case ending *-(r)ik* (i.e., *-rik* after a vowel or diphthong, *-ik* after a consonant) was recognized as a partitive by Lécluse in 1826: "Ce nominatif négatif peut être considéré comme un partitif" (*Manuel de la langue basque*, p. 83). [This negative nominative can be regarded as a partitive.] This designation, however, did not gain currency until after the publication of Ithurry's *Grammaire basque* (1920).

This partitive case appears to have originated as an ablative or an elative. A history of this type would account for the presence of *-rik* as an allomorph of *-tik* in the elative paradigm given in chapter 3: original *-tarik* and *-etarik* were retained in the easternmost dialects, while replaced by *-tatik* and *-etatik* elsewhere.

In the modern dialects, including Batua, its independent role as an inherent case marker is rather limited, inasmuch as it is restricted to indefinite noun phrases and appears in very few contexts. The contexts involved are divisible into two groups: 1 and 2.

1. The partitive is contained in a productive adverbial pattern of the form *N-ik N*, where *N* is a countable noun. Such adverbials specify the nature of the action as involving at least two separate instances of *N*, which are affected by the action either reciprocally or in temporal sequence. Examples are

ahorik aho	from mouth to mouth (of news going round)
alderik alde	from one side to the other, right through
aterik ate	from door to door
bazterrik bazter	from one corner to the other, here and there
besorik beso	arm in arm
biderik bide	to and fro, up and down, along the road
eskurik esku	hand in hand

etxerik etxe	from house to house
herririk herri	from village to village, from town to town
hiririk hiri	from city to city
kalerik kale	from street to street
mendirik mendi	from mountain to mountain
oherik ohe	from bed to bed
zokorik zoko	from nook to nook

With *N* denoting a period of time, the phrase *N-ik N* also exists and admits three different interpretations. Thus, for *egunik egun*, the *DGV* (VI, 476–477) provides the following meanings:

a. day by day, from day to day (serially)
b. by the day (in comparatives)
c. day after day (every day)

Similarly, for *aste* 'week', *ordu* 'hour', *urte* 'year': *asterik aste*, *ordurik ordu*, *urterik urte*.

2. The partitive may be used to mark a noun phrase indicating the range of quantification. There are three types of quantification that are pertinent:

a. *Superlative constructions*. The partitive is one of the means to indicate the range of a superlative. Taking *ederren* 'most beautiful', superlative of *eder* 'beautiful' as an example, we get: *Donostiako emakumerik ederrena* 'the most beautiful woman of San Sebastian'. Alternatives are the plural elative: *Donostiako emakumeetatik ederrena*, the plural inessive: *Donostiako emakumeetan ederrena*, or even no case ending at all: *Donostiako emakume ederrena*.

b. *Indefinite quantifier expresssions*. Although the usual form of the noun phrases governed by indefinite quantifiers is the indefinite absolutive (see section 2.3.2, item 8), indefinite quantifiers not containing the determiner *bat* may instead assign the partitive, as in the following example:

(1) Lehengo idazle zaharren kartarik gutxi dugu. (Etxaniz, *Nola* 41)
We have few letters of the ancient writers of the past.

This optional use, already attested in the earliest texts, has virtually disappeared from the modern language, except in the fossilized phrase *eskerrik asko* (never **esker asko*) 'many thanks'. The disappearance, however, is quite recent, since Mitxelena's writings still contain quite a few examples, all used in positive contexts: *alde ederrik aski* (*MEIG* II, 47) 'enough sunny sides', *horrelakorik aski* (*MEIG* II, 94) 'plenty of such', *punturik aski* (*MEIG* III, 147) 'enough points', *gauza jakingarririk aski* (*MEIG* VIII, 23) 'plenty of interesting things', *lanik aski* (*MEIG* VIII, 41) 'plenty of work', *euskaldunik asko* (*MEIG* I, 57) 'many Basques', *lore ederrik asko* (*MEIG* IX, 105) 'many beautiful flowers', *horrelakorik* *franko* (*MEIG* IV, 77) 'a lot of such', *liburu eta artikulurik franko* (*MEIG* VI, 62) 'a lot of books and articles', *gauza berririk gutxi* (*MEIG* I, 54) 'few new things', *horrelakorik gutxi* (*MEIG* VIII, 179) 'few such things'.

It is worth noting that in exclamatory sentences an indefinite quantifier may delete with the partitive remaining:

(2) Bada txakurrik Madrilen!
    There are an awful lot of dogs in Madrid!

c. *Existential quantifiers*. Among the existential quantifiers, only *inor* 'anybody' and *ezer* (or its northern synonym *deus*) 'anything' allow the partitive on the noun phrase indicating their scope. Alternatives to the partitive are the plural elative and the plural inessive, which are also used with the more positively asserting quantifiers *norbait* 'somebody' and *zerbait* 'something'.

The partitive noun phrase may either precede or follow the quantifier. Examples with *ezer* follow:

(3) a. Ez dago ezer txarrik. (*MEIG* II, 114 = *MIH* 344)
       There is nothing wrong.
    b. Ez zekien Liberen bihotz-barrengorik ezer. (T. Agirre, *Uztaro* 114)
       He knew nothing of what was inside Libe's heart.
    c. Beste penarik ez daukat ezer. (Basarri, in Uztapide, *Noizb.* 64)
       Of other sorrows I have nothing.
    d. Ogibiderik ez dauka ezer. (*G.* 368)
       He has nothing (in the way) of a livelihood.

[*N.B.* Observe that the quantifier *ezer* has been extraposed to the end of its clause in examples (3c) and (3d).]

Examples with *inor* follow:

(4) a. Beretzat ez zegoen beste gizonik inor. (Agirre, *Kres.* 190)
       For her there was no other man.
    b. Toki horretan ez zeukan inor ezagunik. (Agirre, *Kres.* 184)
       In that place she had nobody (in the way) of acquaintances.
    c. Izkotarren etxean ez du senitartekorik inor bizi. (Mokoroa, 20)
       In the house of the Izko clan he has nobody living of his family.

With the partitive present, the indefinite pronouns *ezer* and *inor* will normally be omitted—for many speakers even obligatorily—provided they occur in the absolutive form, that is, bear no case endings. This deletion will account quite neatly for the existence and behavior of the partitive determiner analyzed in the next subsection, at least historically, and perhaps synchronically as well.

13.1.2 The Partitive Determiner

In nonaffirmative contexts, that is, precisely in those where the indefinite pronouns *ezer* and *inor* are favored over *zerbait* and *norbait*, absolutive noun phrases admit the partitive determiner *-(r)ik*, which operates like an article on a par with *-a*, *-ak*, *bat*, and *batzu*. In particular, absolutive noun phrases occurring within the scope of a negative, interrogative, or conditional element will allow and quite often require the partitive, provided their referent is construed as indefinite, or rather, nonspecific.

Leaving conditionals and comparatives aside for later chapters, our discussion here will be mainly confined to the use of the partitive in negative or interrogative sentences.

In negative sentences, use of the partitive is obligatory for indefinite absolutives. Thus, while the noun phrase *txokolatea* complete with its article *-a* can mean either 'some chocolate' or 'the chocolate' in the affirmative statement (5a), the same noun phrase can only be interpreted as 'the chocolate' in the corresponding negative (5b), since for the indefinite meaning 'any chocolate' the partitive form *txokolaterik* is required, as seen in (5c):

(5) a. Gaur txokolatea erosi dut.
Today I have bought some/the chocolate.
b. Gaur ez dut txokolatea erosi.
Today I have not bought the chocolate.
c. Gaur ez dut txokolaterik erosi.
Today I have not bought any chocolate.

Since the partitive determiner is restricted to the absolutive case, subject noun phrases allow it only when the verb is intransitive. Thus we find

(6) a. Ez omen da hamabost urteko neska itsusirik. (T. Agirre, *Uzt.* 53)
The saying goes that there are no ugly maidens of fifteen.
b. Etxe honetan arratoirik ere ez da gelditzen. (Amuriza, *Hil* 165)
Not even rats are staying in this house.
c. Baina ez zen Albanian inspektorerik azaldu. (Atxaga, *Obab.* 44)
But no inspector appeared at Albania.
d. Orain ez da lapurrik etorriko. (Garate, *Esku* 128)
No thief will come now.

With transitive verbs only the direct object allows the partitive, never the subject:

(7) a. Ez dut adiskiderik. Ez da premiarik ere. (*MEIG* IX, 96)
I have no friends. There is no need either.
b. Ez dut saririk eskatzen. (*TOE* II, 266)
I am not asking for any reward.
c. Nire aurrean ez zuen inoiz drogarik hartu. (Garate, *Iz.B.* 35)
She never took (any) drugs in my presence.

As confirmed by the verb forms in all the examples presented, a partitive noun phrase invariably counts as singular. This statement is true even for noun phrases otherwise restricted to the plural, such as dvandva compounds of the type *anai-arreba* 'brother(s) and/or sister(s)':

(8) a. Baditut anai-arrebak.
I have brothers and sisters.
b. Ez dut anai-arrebarik.
I have no brothers or sisters.

Even proper nouns are liable to be turned into indefinites by the partitive:

(9) a. Moxolorik ez da agertuko. (*G.* 314)
No Moxolo will appear.
b. Ez da Maria Vöckel-ik sekula egon. (Atxaga, *Obab.* 106)
There never has been a Maria Vöckel.

More generally, an indefinite partitive may sometimes be preferred over a more straightforward designation for rhetorical purposes:

(10) a. Baina gaur nire arrebarik ez duzu ikusiko. (*G.* 308)
But today you won't see any sister of mine. (Only one sister, Malen, was wanted.)
b. Apika nire izenik ez dakizue? (Atxaga, *Obab.* 400)
Maybe yoû don't know my name?

The partitive can be freely used in yes-no questions, without any expectation of the answer being negative:

(11) a. Ba al duk izenik? (*LBB* 264)
Do yoú have a name?
b. Ba al da euskal musikarik ? (*MEIG* I, 55)
Is there Basque music?
c. Ostu al duzu oilorik? (Urruzuno, *E.Z.* 61)
Have you stolen any hens?
d. Zure neurriko soinekorik aurkitu al duzu? (*EGLU* I, 131)
Have you found any dresses in your size?

As long as they are mere requests for information, wh-questions do not admit the partitive. Those wh-questions, however, that are in fact meant as denials, or at least indicate disbelief or consternation on the part of the speaker, may very well contain the partitive.

A certain rhetorical style, such as the one pervading Axular's classical work *Guero*, is particularly conducive to questions of this type:

(12) a. Non da giristino goiztiarrik? (Ax. 172)
Where are there any prompt Christians?
b. Nork edirenen du ene baitan faltarik? (Ax. 448)
Who will find any faults in me?
c. Nork izanen du sorbaldarik sostengatzeko, indarrik jasateko, eta pairurik eta pazientziarik sofritzeko? (Ax. 599)
Who will have a shoulder to support him, strength to bear it, and stamina and patience to endure it?

Modern literature too provides plenty of examples:

(13) a. Non aurkituko du honelako etxerik? (*TOE* III, 203)
Where will he find a home like thís?
b. Non aurkitu holako emakumerik, ordea? (Garate, *NY* 115)
Where to find any such woman, however?

In negative, interrogative or conditional clauses, the intensifier *batere* 'at all' (derived from *[ez] ... bat ere* '[not] even one ...') may co-occur with a partitive noun phrase, whether preceding or following:

(14) a. Ez du batere beldurrik. (Etxaniz, *Antz*. 106)
He has no fear at all.
b. Ez dut gezurrik batere esaten. (Txill., *Let*. 115)
I am not telling any untruth at all.
c. Batere ez zuen molderik. (Xalbador, *Odol.* 41)
He had no skill at all.

Purely affirmative contexts do not normally allow the partitive, but certain factors may trigger it. Thus the partitive is a very common feature with indefinite noun phrases introduced by the determiner *beste* (section 11.5), also in affirmative clauses:

(15) a. Badu beste kezkarik. (Garate, *NY* 44)
He has other worries.
b. Hori besterik da. (*LBB* 159, 188)
That's something else.
c. Beste gizonik bihurtu zen. (Orixe, *S.Cruz* 127)
He became another man.

Some speakers allow the partitive in a clause introduced by an adverb meaning 'perhaps':

(16) Beharbada, izango dut, semerik haren bitartez. (Gn 16:2)
Maybe I will have sons through her.

Likewise, the presence of an adverb meaning 'only' accounts for the partitive in some affirmative sentences.

Exclamatory sentences readily admit the partitive. The most natural explanation for why they do so is the application of quantifier deletion, as seen in example (2) in section 13.1.1.

I have saved to the end an important observation that up to now has escaped the grammarians' attention: Some putatively eligible noun phrases unexpectedly reject the partitive, even in negative contexts. These are noun phrases containing interrogative pronouns (*zer ordu*[**rik*] 'what time', *zein ogen*[**ik*] 'what guilt', etc.) on the one hand, and the indefinite pronouns *zerbait*, *norbait*, *ezer*, and *inor* on the other. In short, just those noun phrases not modifiable by *ezer* or *inor* do not allow the partitive. An eastern synonym of *ezer*, the noun *deus*, does allow the partitive, but then, the combination *deusik deus* also happens to be attested (Mirande, *Pr.* 142), unlike the impossible **ezerik ezer*.

These facts plainly corroborate my hypothesis that the partitive determiner evolved out of the partitive case by deletion of indefinite *ezer* or *inor* (cf. the end of section 13.1.1), and may even argue for a synchronic derivation along that line. Why some speakers admit the partitive on the diminutive forms *ezertxo* and *inortxo* remains a mystery, however.

More details about the use of the partitive can be found in my articles de Rijk 1972c, 1996b.

13.2 Particularities of the Verb *egin*

The verb *egin*, easily the most frequently employed verb in Basque, covers a wide range of meanings. Besides being the regular counterpart of both *to do* and *to make* in English, in various contexts it also serves to convey the senses of the English verbs *to act*, *to pretend*, *to spend (time)*, *to live through*, *to bet*, and several more, as revealed by the various subdivisions of the entry *egin* in the *DGV* (VI, 413ff.). While a serious treatment of the semantics of this or any other verb falls far outside the scope of this work, a number of syntactic constructions headed by *egin* and countenanced by its semantic profile are of more than sufficient interest to warrant discussion, however brief, in any grammar of Basque.

13.2.1 Adjectives with *egin*

Morphologically complex adjectives can be combined with the verb *egin* in its meaning 'to make': *Eta bai, zoriontsu egin zuen egun hartan Ainhoa* (Atxaga, *Bam.* II, 55) 'And yes, he made Ainhoa happy that day'. Plain adjectives, however, prefer deadjectival *-tu* verbs: *edertu* 'to make beautiful', *laburtu* 'to make short'.

In a noncausative use, however, *egin* can combine with any adjective: transitively: 'to pass off as being Adj.' and, more frequently, intransitively: 'to seem Adj.', as in *Sararen eskaera hau Abrahami gogor egin zitzaion* (*TZ* I, 47) 'This request of Sara's seemed harsh to Abraham'.

Curiously enough, reduplicated adjectives and even reduplicated verb radicals can combine with *egin*, resulting in an intensification of the meaning of the corresponding *-tu* verb:

bero-bero egin	to make very hot, to beat up
gorri-gorri egin	to make very red
txiki-txiki egin	to make very small, to smash
zabal-zabal egin	to open very wide
zurbil-zurbil egin	to make very pale

And with verb radicals:

asper-asper egin	to exasperate
neka-neka egin	to wear out
sumin-sumin egin	to infuriate

For more examples, see *DGV* VI, 417.

13.2.2 Allatives with *egin*

When governing an allative noun phrase, transitive *egin* means 'to turn' and intransitive *egin* means 'to get used (to)': *Bulegora egin du* 'He has turned to the office', *Bulegora egin da* 'He has gotten used to the office'.

13.2.3 Genitives with *egin*

Like English *to do* in *to do a part*, transitive *egin* can mean 'to act' as in *papera egin* 'to act a part', 'to pretend'. Mitxelena wrote:

(17) Honek ez du portuko gazte ezjakinarena egiten, bera da gazte hori. (*MEIG* I, 124)
He doesn't act the part of the ignorant youngster at the harbor, he is that youngster.

Note that the concept 'part', for which only loanwords are available (*paper*, *parte*), is not overtly expressed: *gazte ez jakinarena* 'that of the ignorant youngster'. Provided that the whole nominal is governed by the verb *egin*, ellipsis of a head noun meaning 'part', 'role' following a genitival modifier is a fully productive process. Other examples are

astoarena egin	to play the ass
belearena egin	to play the raven (i.e., leave without paying)
eriarena egin	to play the patient, to pretend to be ill
gorrarena egin	to play deaf
handiarena egin	to play the adult
hilarena egin	to play possum
judasena egin	to play Judas, to turn traitor
zoroarena egin	to play the fool

The nominalized adjective occurring in this construction can be a negated perfect participle:

ez adituarena egin	to pretend not to have heard (or: understood)
ez entzunarena egin	to pretend not to have heard

ez ikusiarena egin — to pretend not to have seen
ez jakinarena egin — to pretend not to have known
ez ulertuarena egin — to pretend not to have understood

In examples of the latter type the genitive can be dispensed with:

(18) Baina nik ez aditua egin nuen. (Atxaga, *Obab*. 91)
But I pretended not to have heard.

Even the article is not essential here: *ez aditu egin* (Atxaga, *Obab*. 144).

Much less current than the construction treated so far is a superficially similar idiom where the noun phrase is also based on a genitive and governed by *egin*, but is plural instead of singular: *astoarenak egin* 'to do stupid things', *zoroarenak egin* 'to do foolish things'. Here the abstract head noun corresponds to 'action' rather than 'part', since the plural expression refers to acts typical of the base noun, not to any part being played.

13.2.4 Ergatives with *egin*

Used in a perfect tense with an ergative subject but without a direct object, the verb *egin* acquires the meaning 'to be up', 'to be over', 'to be gone':

(19) Nire indarrak egin du. (Larréguy I, 233)
My strength is up. (is gone)

With *aldi* 'turn', 'period', 'time' instead of *indar*, we have examples such as

(20) a. Zure aldiak egin du.
Your time is up.
b. Ia gure aldiak egin du.
Our time is almost up.

As will be seen in the chapter devoted to time adverbials, the noun *aldi* is usually deleted in the presence of a modifier, which then takes over the case ending originally borne by *aldi*. Applying this observation to (20a) and (20b), we get the more usual (21a) and (21b):

(21) a. Zureak egin du! (Garate, *Alaba* 60)
You're done for!
b. Ia gureak egin du. (*Xenp*. 410)
It's almost the end of us.

[*N.B.* An intransitive variant of (19) featuring the instrumental instead of the ergative also exists:

(22) Egin da nire indarraz.
My strength is gone.]

13.2.5 Weather Expressions with *egin*

Weather conditions can be expressed by the durative verb *ari* to be discussed in chapter 16, but also by the verb *egin* used with a direct object denoting an atmospheric phenomenon, but without overt subject. The object noun bears the article *-a*. Here are some examples:

elurra egin	to snow
euria egin	to rain
harria egin	to hail
izotza egin	to freeze
txingorra egin	to hail

In contrast, air temperature is expressed by combinations of *egin* with bare nouns that are also adjectives: *bero* 'heat', 'hot'; *epel* 'warmth', 'lukewarm'; *hotz* 'cool', 'cold'. Compare the Spanish forms *hacer calor* and *hacer frío*.

bero egiten du	it is hot
epel egiten du	it is mild
hotz egiten du	it is cold

13.3 Bare Noun Objects of *egin*

In section 7.1.4 mention was made of Beth C. Levin's perceptive observation that Basque intransitive verbs are overwhelmingly unaccusative. As an immediate consequence, it follows that English unergatives must correspond in the main to transitive constructions in Basque, if they are to have any equivalents at all.

Basque counterparts to the English unergative verbs do indeed exist: they take the shape of an *egin* idiom consisting of the transitive verb *egin* with a bare noun as a direct object. There is of course no implication that all *egin* idioms of this type correspond to unergative intransitives in English; instead, many of them will be translational equivalents of transitive verbs.

We will now pass in review various semantic classes of *egin* idioms, verifying, wherever applicable, their correspondence to unergative verbs in English.

In performing this task, care must be taken to distinguish *egin* idioms from superficially similar expressions, such as *hauts egin* 'to pulverize' and *huts egin* 'to miss', where the bare noun is not a direct object but a kind of object complement, a construction that does not concern us at this point.

13.3.1 Manner-of-Motion Idioms

Verbs specifying manner of motion form a standard example of unergative verbs. In Basque too, a few such verbs can be found: *dantzatu* 'to dance', *irristatu* 'to slip', *murgildu* 'to dive', the latter perhaps rather depicting "inherently directed motion." Instead of by intransitive verbs, however, manner of motion is much more frequently expressed by a transitive *egin* idiom. As seen in the examples, manner of motion is taken in a broad sense, including what would be more aptly described as the circumstances of the motion:

bidaia	journey	bidaia egin	to travel
bide	road	bide egin	to move along, to advance
dantza	dance	dantza egin	to dance
estropezu	stumbling (block)	estropezu egin	to stumble
hanka	leg	hanka egin	to run off, to escape
herren	lameness	herren egin	to limp
igeri	swimming	igeri egin	to swim
ihes	flight	ihes egin	to flee
irrist	slip	irrist egin	to slip
jauzi	leap	jauzi egin	to leap, to jump
labain	slip	labain egin	to slip
larrapast	slip	larrapast egin	to slip
laster	speed	laster egin	to run
murgil	dive, plunge	murgil egin	to dive, to duck
salto	jump	salto egin	to jump
zabu	swing	zabu egin	to swing, to rock
zirkin	stir	zirkin egin	to budge, to dodge

13.3.2 Idioms of Emission

To express the emission of light or sound, another domain of unergative verbs, Basque has a small number of morphologically transitive verbs at its disposal, such as *distiratu* 'to glitter', *burrunbatu* 'to hum', and *durundatu* 'to clang', already mentioned in section 12.3.3. Their number, however, is minimal in comparison to that of the *egin* idioms belonging to this class:

adausi	bark	adausi egin	to bark
aldarri	cry	aldarri egin	to cry
argi	light	argi egin	to give light, to shine
arrantza	braying	arrantza egin	to bray
auhen	lament	auhen egin	to lament
burrunba	buzzing	burrunba egin	to buzz
deiadar	cry, shout	deiadar egin	to cry, to shout
dir-dir	shine, gleam	dir-dir egin	to shine, to gleam
dirdira	shine, gleam	dirdira egin	to shine, to gleam
distira	shine, glory	distira egin	to shine, to glimmer
diz-diz	shine	diz-diz egin	to shine, to flash

eztanda	explosion	eztanda egin	to explode
garrasi	scream	garrasi egin	to scream
heiagora	shriek	heiagora egin	to shriek
hots	sound	hots egin	to sound, to call, to shout
irrintzi	neigh, screech	irrintzi egin	to neigh, to screech
karranka	grating	karranka egin	to grate
kirrinka	creak	kirrinka egin	to creak
kurrinka	grunt	kurrinka egin	to grunt
marmar	grumble	marmar egin	to grumble
marru	mooing, lowing	marru egin	to moo, to low, to roar
marruma	roar, howl	marruma egin	to roar, to howl
ñir-ñir	shine	ñir-ñir egin	to shine, to glimmer
oihu	scream, yell	oihu egin	to scream, to yell
orro	roar	orro egin	to roar
pio	peep, chirp	pio egin	to peep, to chirp
txilio	scream	txilio egin	to scream
txio	chirp	txio egin	to chirp
uhuri	hooting, hoot	uhuri egin	to hoot
ulu	wail, howl	ulu egin	to wail, to howl
zapart	crack, bang	zapart egin	to crack, to explode
zaunka	bark	zaunka egin	to bark
zurrunga	snore	zurrunga egin	to snore
zurrust	gulp	zurrust egin	to gulp

13.3.3 Idioms of Communication and Interaction

In the idioms listed here, the function of the bare noun is to specify either the nature or the result of an act of verbal or nonverbal communication. The English equivalents are usually transitive verbs:

agiraka	reproach	agiraka egin	to scold
agur	greeting	agur egin	to greet, to say goodbye
ahakar	reproach	ahakar egin	to scold
aitor	testimony	aitor egin	to testify
apa	kiss	apa egin	to kiss
arnegu	blasphemy, curse	arnegu egin	to blaspheme, to curse
arren	plea	arren egin	to implore
axut	provocation, defiance	axut egin	to defy, to provoke
berba	word, speech	berba egin	to speak
birao	blasphemy	birao egin	to curse, to blaspheme
burla	mockery	burla egin	to scoff

dei	call	dei egin	to call, to invite
diosal	greeting	diosal egin	to greet
erregu	prayer, request	erregu egin	to pray, to request
errieta	quarrel, reproof	errieta egin	to quarrel, to reprove
ezetz	refusal, no	ezetz egin	to shake one's head in refusal
galde	question	galde egin	to ask, to question
hitz	word	hitz egin	to speak
irain	offense, insult	irain egin	to offend, to insult
iseka	mockery	iseka egin	to ridicule
keinu	wink, gesture	keinu egin	to wink, to gesture
laido	offense, insult	laido egin	to offend, to insult
laztan	hug, kiss	laztan egin	to hug, to kiss
muin	kiss (not on face)	muin egin	to kiss (not the face)
oles	hailing, call	oles egin	to hail, to call out
otoitz	prayer	otoitz egin	to pray
pot	kiss	pot egin	to kiss
trufa	mockery	trufa egin	to ridicule
txalo	applause	txalo egin	to applaud
uko	denial	uko egin	to deny
zin	oath	zin egin	to swear, to take an oath

13.3.4 Idioms of Mental Activity

The bare noun denotes a mental activity other than communication or the result of it:

amets	dream	amets egin	to dream
duda	doubt	duda egin	to doubt
gogoeta	thought, reflexion	gogoeta egin	to reflect, to think
jaramon	attention	jaramon egin	to pay attention
kasu	attention	kasu egin	to pay attention
kontu	account	kontu egin	to take care, to imagine
zalantza	uncertainty	zalantza egin	to have doubts, to doubt

13.3.5 Idioms of Bodily Activity

The bare noun denotes either the activity itself, the result, or the instrument of it. The English equivalents are unergative verbs, unless transitive.

abaro	shelter	abaro egin	to take shelter
aharrausi	yawn	aharrausi egin	to yawn
atximur	pinch	atximur egin	to pinch
atzapar	claw, scratch	atzapar egin	to claw, to scratch

barau	fast	barau egin	to fast
barre	laugh	barre egin	to laugh
beltzuri	frown	beltzuri egin	to frown
bultza	pushing	bultza egin	to push
dominìstiku	sneeze	dominìstiku egin	to sneeze
eztul	cough	eztul egin	to cough
gernu	urine	gernu egin	to urinate
hatz	finger (obsol.)	hatz egin	to scratch
ikara	trembling	ikara egin	to tremble
imurtxi	pinch	imurtxi egin	to pinch, to steal
irri	laugh, jeer	irri egin	to laugh, to jeer
irribarre	smile	irribarre egin	to smile
jolas	play, recreation	jolas egin	to play
kaka	shit	kaka egin	to shit
kosk	bite	kosk egin	to bite
lagun	companion, mate	lagun egin	to accompany
listu	saliva, spit	listu egin	to spit
lo	sleep	lo egin	to sleep
muzin	grimace	muzin egin	to grimace, to disdain
negar	crying	negar egin	to cry, to weep
oka	vomiting, vomit	oka egin	to vomit
ostiko	kick	ostiko egin	to kick
piper	pepper, truancy	piper egin	to play hooky, to play truant
pixa	piss, urine	pixa egin	to piss
planto	halt, stop	planto egin	to make halt, to stop
putz	blow, puff	putz egin	to blow, to puff
saka	push, shove	saka egin	to shove, to push
so	look, glance	so egin	to look, to glance, to watch
tira	pull	tira egin	to pull, to draw (on)
tu	saliva, spit	tu egin	to spit
txistu	whistle, saliva	txistu egin	to whistle, to spit
txiza	piss, urine	txiza egin	to piss
ufa	blow, puff	ufa egin	to blow, to puff
usain	smell	usain egin	to smell
usin	sneeze	usin egin	to sneeze
zimiko	pinch	zimiko egin	to pinch
zintz	snot	zintz egin	to blow one's nose
zotin	hiccup, sob	zotin egin	to hiccup, to sob
zurrust	sip, gulp	zurrust egin	to gulp
zurrut	slug, gulp	zurrut egin	to tipple, to drink, to sip

13.3.6 Idioms of Human Activity

Listed under this heading are some activities restricted to human beings or human collectivities. The bare noun denotes the activity itself, its result, or its instrument.

bekatu	sin	bekatu egin	to sin
bortxa	violence	bortxa egin	to do violence, to violate
egur	firewood	egur egin	to cut firewood
gerra	war	gerra egin	to wage war
gudu	battle, war	gudu egin	to give battle, to wage war
hoben	guilt	hoben egin	to offend, to sin
jai	day off, festivity	jai egin	to take a day off, to celebrate
men	dominion	men egin	to obey
oker	wrong	oker egin	to do wrong
peto	miss	peto egin	to miss
su	fire	su egin	to fire, to shoot
uzkur	reluctance	uzkur egin	to shy away, to shrink
zotz	small rod	zotz egin	to draw lots

13.3.7 Idioms of Experiences

The idioms listed here necessarily involve an animate patient or experiencer:

dolu	sorrow, grief	dolu egin	to grieve, to cause sorrow
gogait	boredom	gogait egin	to get bored
iruzur	deception	iruzur egin	to deceive
kili	tickle	kili egin	to tickle
kili-kili	tickle	kili-kili egin	to tickle
min	pain	min egin	to hurt, to cause pain

13.3.8 Miscellaneous Idioms

The following examples are hard to classify:

buru	head	buru egin	to resist, to encounter
enbarazu	obstacle	enbarazu egin	to stand in the way
gaitz	evil, harm	gaitz egin	to do harm, to do evil
kalte	harm, damage	kalte egin	to harm, to damage
leher	bursting	leher egin	to burst
mesede	good turn, favor	mesede egin	to do good, to do a favor
molokot	bankruptcy	molokot egin	to go bankrupt
on	good, benefit	on egin	to do good, to benefit
oztopo	obstacle	oztopo egin	to stand in the way
porrot	bankruptcy, failure	porrot egin	to go bankrupt, to fail

13.3.9 Grammatical Observations on *egin* Idioms

1. Sometimes an *egin* idiom and a *-tu* verb derived from its bare noun coexist in a speaker's vocabulary—for example, *burla egin* and *burlatu* 'to mock', *dantza egin* and *dantzatu* 'to dance', *dei egin* and *deitu* 'to call'. In such a case meaning differentiation tends to set in. Thus many speakers make several of the following distinctions:

agur egin	to say goodbye	agurtu	to greet
amets egin	to dream in sleep	amestu	to daydream
jolas egin	to play	jolastu	to amuse oneself
leher egin	to wear oneself out	lehertu	to burst
min egin	to cause pain	mindu	to offend
otoitz egin	to pray	otoiztu	to beseech
saka egin	to push against (things)	sakatu	to push (people)

2. An intriguing connection between semantic definiteness and *egin* idioms has been discovered by Itziar Laka (1993). In closing section 2.3.1, it was mentioned that noun phrases often allow an indefinite interpretation even when marked by the definite article *-a*. Incidentally, noun phrases headed by a singular count noun appear to have lost this option nowadays.

Now consider the following three sentences:

(23) a. Lana bilatuko dut.
I will look for some work.
b. Txokolatea egingo dut.
I will make the/some chocolate.
c. Lana egingo dut.
I will do the (*some) work.

In short, while both the noun phrase *lana* and direct objects of the verb *egin* generally allow an indefinite interpretation, the combination *lana egin* can only be construed as definite: 'to do the work'. What this restriction means is that the indefinite interpretation of *N-a* in *N-a egin* is unavailable just in case a corresponding *N egin* idiom exists.

3. *Egin* idioms have been explained by some grammarians as an instance of incorporation of the object noun into the verb *egin*. It is unclear, however, how this proposal accounts for the syntactic separability of noun and verb. The noun, indeed, will be ousted from its canonical preverbal site as soon as the sentence contains a focus constituent other than this action noun:

(24) a. Gogotik egin dute lan. (*MEIG* VIII, 97)
They have worked gladly.
b. Orduan, egun hartan, egingo dute barau. (Lk 5:35)
Then, on that day, they will fast.

c. Gaur bertan egin dut ihes handik. (1 Sm 4:16)
   I fled from there just today.
d. Horrek leku hezeetan egiten du lo. (Jb 40:16; Dv)
   He sleeps in humid places.

4. To show that the morpheme *N*, retaining its status as an independent noun, still acts as the direct object of the verb *egin*, we can invoke its ability to accept the partitive determiner under the usual conditions. It must be noted, however, that the partitive here is merely optional even in negative clauses. Some examples follow:

(25) a. Ez dut irribarrerik egin. (Gn 18:15)
   I have not smiled.
b. Ez dut negarrik egiten. (*LBB* 137)
   I am not crying.
c. Deabruak ez du lorik egiten. (*E.H.* 528)
   The devil does not sleep.
d. Ez dugu gogaitik egingo guk. (*P.Ab.* 179)
   We won't get bored.
e. Ez al duzu ametsik egiten? (*LBB* 204)
   Don't you dream?
f. Eztulik ere ez du egin nire aurrean. (*LBB* 139)
   She hasn't even coughed in my presence.

If a particular *egin* idiom consistently rejects the partitive, that idiom has become fossilized, as has happened to the example *alde egin* 'to leave' (from *alde* 'side', but also 'distance'), more commonly spelled *aldegin*, of which *egin* is no longer a part. For many speakers, this observation also applies to *hitz egin* 'to speak', which accounts for the meaning difference that *EGLU* (II, 45) finds between (26a) and (26b):

(26) a. Ez du hitz egin.
   He has not spoken.
b. Ez du hitzik egin.
   He has not said a word.

Yet, more conservative speakers insist that (26b) is ambiguous and shares one meaning with (26a).

5. While many object nouns of *egin* are idiomatic and do not admit any modifiers, others can be expanded into full noun phrases. Then, needless to say, the article *a* or some other determiner will be required. Here are some examples:

(27) a. Lo luzea egin du.
   He has slept a long time.

b. Gerizan egiten du bere loa. (Ax. 39)
   He takes his sleep in the shade.
c. Negar handiak egin zituzten. (*TZ* II, 103)
   They wept profusely.

13.4 Bare Noun Objects of Other Verbs

Only a few of the most frequent verbs admit bare nouns as direct objects. In this respect, no verb measures up to *egin*; the verb *eman* 'to give' comes out second best, with roughly a third of the number of nouns *egin* can boast of. A list of examples will be given in section 15.6.6, as part of our analysis of the use of the verb *eman*. The third place can be claimed by the verb *hartu* 'to take', and the fourth belongs to the verb **edun* 'to have'. The idioms made up by those two verbs will be discussed in the next subsections.

13.4.1 Bare Noun Objects of *hartu*

For a proper assessment of the following idioms, the reader should be aware that the verb *hartu*, usually glossed as 'to take', also has a nonagentive use with the value of English 'to get' or 'to receive'.

Assuming the following list to be nearly exhaustive, we may count slightly over a dozen *hartu* idioms in standard Basque:

adore	vigor, courage	adore hartu	to gain vigor, to take courage
arnasa	breath	arnasa hartu	to breathe, to take a breather
atseden	rest	atseden hartu	to rest
atsegin	pleasure	atsegin hartu	to take pleasure
damu	repentance	damu hartu	to repent, to resent
gorroto	hatred, hate	gorroto hartu	to conceive a hatred
indar	strength	indar hartu	to gain strength
kalte	harm, damage	kalte hartu	to suffer damage
kargu	charge, responsibility	kargu hartu	to take charge, to call to account
kontu	account, attention	kontu hartu	to look after, to pay attention
min	pain	min hartu	to get hurt, to hurt oneself
pena	sorrow, trouble	pena hartu	to feel sorrow, to take trouble
poz	joy	poz hartu	to be glad, to rejoice
toki	place	toki hartu	to substitute

In all these expressions, the object noun may be modified by an adjective, but the presence of a determiner such as *-a* or *bat* will then be required: *min handia hartu* 'to hurt oneself badly', *pena ederra hartu* 'to be greatly sorry'.

Phrases like *katibu hartu* 'to take captive', *lagun hartu* 'to take as a companion', and *preso hartu* 'to take prisoner' do not belong here, as the bare noun fulfills the function of an object complement rather than a direct object, present elsewhere in the clause. Use of the partitive also provides a diagnostic. While incompatible with object complements, the partitive determiner is possible for true direct objects in negative contexts, although for such bare nouns it is optional rather than obligatory. Accordingly, for 'he is not hurt', we get either *ez du min hartu* or *ez du minik hartu*, with no difference in meaning (*EGLU* II, 45).

13.4.2 Bare Noun Objects of **edun*

To qualify as a genuine direct object, the bare noun must optionally admit the partitive in negative contexts and be incompatible with other absolutive objects. Only a small number of examples pass this test, among them several idioms with the meaning 'to matter':

ardura	care, worry	ardura *edun	to matter
axola	care, worry	axola *edun	to matter
inporta	import, importance	inporta *edun	to matter

Other examples are

arrazoi	reason	arrazoi *edun	to be right (cf. French *avoir raison*)
damu	regret	damu *edun	to have regrets, to regret
gorroto	hatred	gorroto *edun	to hate
min	pain	min *edun	to have pain, to ache
pena	sorrow, grief	pena *edun	to feel sorrow, to be grieved

As will be shown in the next chapter, *damu* can occur also as an object complement to **edun*, and even more often nowadays as a verb.

As for *gorroto*, it is the object noun of **edun* only when accompanied by a dative noun phrase denoting the hated person or thing. The latter can also be assigned absolutive case, in which event *gorroto* is either an object complement or a verb.

In the western dialects, that is, Biscayan and most of Guipuzcoan, the verb *eduki* tends to replace **edun* as a notional verb. Yet most of the bare nouns given in this subsection do not appear as objects of *eduki*, but *arrazoi*, *min*, and *pena* do:

(28) a. Zure andreak arrazoi du. (*TOE* III, 46)
Your wife is right.
b. Arrazoi daukak. (Arrue, *G.B.*[2] 93)
Yoú are right.

(29) a. Bihotzean min dut. (Lizardi, *BB* 66)
My heart aches. (Lit: I have pain in the heart.)
b. Non daukak min? (San Martin, 45)
Where do yoú hurt?

13.5 Constructions with *gabe*

Like many words of some antiquity in Basque (cf. *bero* 'heat', 'hot'; *gose* 'hunger', 'hungry'), the lexical item *gabe* (or its western variant *bage*, Biscayan *baga*) represents a noun as well as an adjective. As a noun it means 'lack', whence also 'poverty', as an adjective 'lacking', 'devoid'. This adjective may then again convert into a stative adverb or postposition, thus giving rise to the most frequent use of *gabe*: as an equivalent of the English preposition *without*.

The word *gabe* rarely occurs by itself; it is nearly always preceded by a complement phrase, usually overtly realized but sometimes merely understood, as in *zure baimenarekin edo gabe* 'with your permission or without (it)'. Other examples are *gabe nago* 'I am without' and *gabe aldegin zuen* 'he left without', where it is left to the context to clarify the meaning.

The range of complements taken by *gabe* is largely independent of its syntactic category. The actual form taken by the complement will depend on the nature of what is lacking.

By far the most common situation in ordinary discourse is that the lack the speaker wants to convey refers to an entire class, without distinguishing between its members. The corresponding complement will be a semantically indefinite noun phrase, syntactically realized in one of three ways: a bare noun phrase, a partitive one, or one ending with the indefinite article *bat*.

The first option may well have predated the others (*DGV* VIII, 87). Examples are *deusen beldur gabe* (Ax. 150) 'without fear of anything' and *beste gertaera aipagarri gabe* (Azkue, *Ardi* 113) 'without other mentionable events'.

Nowadays there is a strong tendency to reserve this option for single nouns and use the partitive for more complex noun phrases: *diru gabe* or *dirurik gabe* 'without money', *duda gabe* or *dudarik gabe* 'without (any) doubt', *neke gabe* or *nekerik gabe* 'without (any) effort'; but only *neke handirik gabe* 'without great effort', *gurasoen baimenik gabe* (T. Agirre, *Uztaro* 193) 'without consent of the parents', *akats haundirik gabea* (Uztapide, *Sas.* 75) 'one free of great flaws'.

In this construction, the intensifier *batere* 'at all' may accompany the partitive: *batere arrazoirik gabe*, or alternatively, *arrazoirik batere gabe* 'without any reason at all'. Likewise for adjectival *gabe*: *harrokeriarik batere gabea* (Uztapide, *Sas.* 23) 'one free of any arrogance at all'. Less often, the particle *ere* 'also', 'even' intervenes between the partitive and *gabe*: *hitzik ere gabe* (*G.* 203) 'without even speech', *aztarrenik ere gabe* (*MEIG* VIII, 184 = *MIH* 400) 'without even a trace'.

The third option, the use of the indefinite article *bat* before *gabe*, is actually quite rare, and to some speakers unacceptable. Yet it is attested here and there in the literature: *hitz bat gabe atera zen* (Barbier, *Piarres* I, 181) 'he went out without a word'; *arima bat gabe* (J. Etchepare, *Ber.* 177) 'without a soul'; *intziri bat gabe* (*Xenp.* 323) 'without a groan'; *zimurtxo bat gabea da* (Azkue, *Ardi* 31) 'she is without one little wrinkle'. Inclusion of the adjective *bakar* 'single' will render the phrase more acceptable: *haritz bakar bat gabe* (Duvoisin, *Lab.* 315) 'without a single oak tree'.

Given the need to also express something lacking that does not relate to an entire open category, but rather to one or more individuated referents, it stands to reason that any definite noun phrase (including a pronoun) can occur as a complement of *gabe*. Except for the noun, which also allows genitival complements, *gabe* governs the absolutive case: *senarra eta semeak gabe* (*TZ* I, 249) 'without (her) husband and sons', *gobernamenduaren baimena gabe* (H.U., *Zez.* 154) 'without the permission of the government', *bere lehenbiziko adiskidetxoa gabe* (*MEIG* IX, 105) 'without his first little friend', *eraskin hori gabeak* (*MEIG* VIII, 175 = *MIH* 390) 'the ones without that addition', *zu gabe* 'without you', *hori gabe* 'without that'.

Finally, the lack to be conveyed may also refer to the performance of an action. In that event, the complement of *gabe* will be an infinitival clause ending in the unmarked form of the verb: its perfect participle. The subject of this infinitival clause is left out if it is identical to that of the main clause:

(30) a. Artzain zaharra atera zen mendirantz inori ezer esan gabe. (*G.* 203)
The old shepherd went out toward the mountain without telling anybody anything.
b. Nobel saria urrutitik ere ikusi gabe, zerbait ikusi dut. (*MEIG* VIII, 184 = *MIH* 400)
Without having seen the Nobel Prize even from afar, I have seen something.

When the subject of the infinitival clause is different from that of the main clause, it can and must be expressed:

(31) Nik esan gabe badakizue. (Uztapide, *Sas.* 321)
Yoû know it without my saying it.

13.5.1 Nominal *gabe*

Unless used in its secondary meaning of 'poverty', the noun *gabe* 'lack' normally takes a preposed complement and a case ending. Since this noun serves to indicate a state of want, the definite inessive *-an* is the most common case ending used, but in the northern dialects the indefinite inessive *-tan* and the definite or indefinite instrumental *-(a)z* also occur. In the southern dialects, the instrumental in this context expresses a causal relationship only: *jan gabez* 'by not eating'.

Besides the usual complements such as absolutives, partitives, and infinitival clauses as mentioned in the previous section, *gabe*, exercising its prerogative as a noun, also allows genitival complements:

guztiaren gabean	lacking everything (lit. "in the lack of everything")
beste giltzaren gabean	lacking other clues (lit. "in the lack of other clues")
zure gabean	lacking you (lit. "in the lack of you")

Actually, nominal use of *gabe* is somewhat rare in modern Basque. Much more common is the employment of *falta* 'lack' or its northern near synonym *eskas* 'shortage' if the absence is perceived as a lack, or else the noun *ez* 'nonexistence', 'absence', a denominative of the negation *ez*, which has a more neutral connotation.

The complements of these nouns are the same as those of nominal *gabe*, except for the partitive, allowed by *ez* only. Some examples should be welcome at this point:

diru faltan	for lack of money, lacking money
argi faltaz	for lack of light, lacking light
loaren faltan	for lack of sleep, lacking sleep
guztiaren faltan	for lack of everything, lacking everything
saiatu faltan	for lack of trying
hitz eskasean	short of words, lacking words
beste zerbaiten eskasean	for lack of something else
hori jakin eskasean	for lack of knowing that, without knowing that
lan ezean	in the absence of work
maitasun ezaz	through the absence of love
batasunik ezean	in the absence of unity
nik ikusi ezean	without my seeing it, if I don't see it

Given the present scarcity of the noun *gabe* and hence of the corresponding inessives, one is inclined to wonder whether adverbial *gabe* itself counts as a postposition to which can be attached the linking morpheme *-ko* in order to form the much employed adnominals headed by *gabeko*, instead of these being derived from the little used inessives.

13.5.2 Adjectival *gabe*

Even if somewhat in danger of being overshadowed by its more versatile competitor *gabeko* (Biscayan variant *bako*, from *bagako*), adjectival *gabe* is still widely used:

(32) a. Guztiz ederra zara, ene laztana, ederra eta akatsik gabea! (Sg 4:7)
You are wholly beautiful, my beloved, beautiful and free of any flaw!

b. Urteak gorabehera zimurtxo bat gabea da mutxurdin hau. (Azkue, *Ardi* 31)
Despite her years this spinster is without one little wrinkle.

c. Hau ustekabe uste gabea! (Amuriza, *Hil* 202)
What an unexpected surprise!

d. Inori kalte egin gabeak ziren. (Garate, *Erd.* 127)
They were people who had harmed nobody.

Although a monstrosity like *guraso tonto eta Jaungoikoaren beldur gabeak* (JJMg., *Bas. Esc.* 223) 'stupid and devoid of the fear of God parents' is attested (1816), attributively used *gabe* tends to have as a complement only single nouns, either bare or with the partitive: *kale poz gabea*, 'a street without joy', *gau hodei gabea* 'a night without clouds', *bere erruki azkenik gabea* 'his compassion without end', *eskolarik gabeak* 'those without schooling'.

This fact explains why adnominal *gabeko* rather than adjectival *gabe* has been used in the following phrases: *inoren kalte gabeko gezur arin bat* (Ubillos, 152) 'a slight lie without harm to anyone'; *garrantzia gabeko galderatxo bat* (*LBB* 113) 'a little question without importance'. The alternative would have been to use adjectival *gabe* in apposition: *gezur arin bat inoren kalte gabea; galderatxo bat garrantzia gabea.*

A perception that the adnominal *gabeko* is currently being overused to the detriment of adjectival *gabe* may have prompted the author G. Garate in his work *Erdarakadak* to point to (33b) as being preferable to (33a):

(33) a. Nor da bekaturik gabekoa? (Garate, *Erd.* 127)
Who is free of sin?
b. Nor da bekaturik gabea? (Garate, *Erd.* 127)
Who is free of sin?

13.5.3 Adverbial *gabe*

Being actually a stative adverb, the postposition *gabe* optionally admits the stative suffix -*(r)ik*, a homonym of the partitive determiner, which I mentioned in section 11.1:

(34) Ez da deus lortzen saiatu gaberik. (*MEIG* IV, 120)
Nothing is achieved without trying.

While in most of the Basque Country *gaberik* is a relatively uncommon stylistic variant of adverbial *gabe*, its Biscayan counterpart *barik* (from earlier *bagarik*) is the normal—and often only—form used for 'without' in the Biscayan dialect. It has been accepted in Batua as a synonym of *gabe*.

A typical Biscayan feature now also found in (southern) Batua is the use of *barik* to mean 'instead of', a meaning usually expressed by *ordean* or *beharrean*:

(35) a. Ura barik ardoa edan du. (Garro, 358)
He has drunk wine instead of water.
b. Hemendik barik hortik joango zara. (Garate, *Erd.* 49)
Instead of along here, you will go along there.

This usage is sometimes imitated in Batua, making use of *gabe* instead of *barik*:

(35) c. Elizatik gabe tabernatik gatoz.
We are coming from the pub instead of from the church.

In other cases too, *gabe* serves to bring about constituent negation even in the standard language. With adverbial constituents, such as those of time and place, *gabe*, not *ez*, must be used for the purpose of negation: *aspaldi gabe* 'not long ago', *Lekeitiotik urruti gabe* (*MEIG* II, 99) 'not far from Lekeitio'.

In the northern dialects, the negation of a time adverbial by means of *gabe* has narrowed its sense to mean 'before': *bihar gabe* 'before tomorrow', *luzaro gabe* 'before long', *igandea gabe* 'before Sunday', *iluna gabe* 'before dark'.

The same process applies to adverbial infinitival clauses: *ilundu gabe* 'before it gets dark', *oilarrak jo gabe* 'before the cock crows', *gu jaio gabe* 'before we were born', *ni hil gabe* 'before I die'.

Between an allative phrase and *gabe*, a verb of motion can be understood without being expressed: *Bilbora gabe* 'without going to Bilbao', *elizara gabe* 'without going to church', *inora gabe* 'without going anywhere', *urrutira gabe* 'without going afar', *xehetasunetara gabe* 'without going into details', *bere lagunarengana gabe* (Garate, *Esku* 134) 'without going to his friend'.

The same deletion applies where *gabe* means 'before': *etxera gabe* 'before going home', *aurrera gabe* 'before going on', *ohera gabe* 'before going to bed', *ni mundura gabe* 'before I came into the world'.

The deletion can also apply before *ezean*, the most common example being *nora ezean* 'lacking where to go', fossilized to *noraezean* 'inevitably'.

Before closing this section I should mention the existence in the western dialects of an alternative to the construction where the perfect participle is followed by *gabe*. This is the attachment of the suffix *-ke* to the verbal noun. Thus *hori egiteke* 'without doing that', *hitzik esateke* 'without saying a word', *elizan sartzeke* 'without entering the church', and *hona etortzeke* 'without coming here' can substitute for *hori egin gabe*, *hitzik esan gabe*, *elizan sartu gabe*, and *hona etorri gabe*.

13.6 The Parasuffix *gabe*

Although *gabe* is an independent lexical item, not a suffix, there are a great many compounds with *gabe* as a final member, so that the term parasuffix is appropriate. Since *gabe* is simultaneously a noun and an adjective, as a matter of principle its compounds too should each belong to both syntactic categories. While this is indeed the case for some examples (*dohakabe* 'misfortune' and 'unfortunate'; *errugabe* 'innocence' and 'innocent'; *eskergabe* 'ingratitude' and 'ungrateful'; *logabe* 'sleeplessness' and 'sleepless'), in actual fact most compounds have specialized as either nouns or adjectives. In both cases, the first member of the compound is a noun, aside from a few, mostly recent, exceptions, where it is a verb.

13.6.1 Nominal Compounds with *gabe*

The meaning of the compound is a total lack of what is denoted by its first member, sometimes even its complete opposite. The number of nominal compounds is fairly small compared to that of the adjectival ones:

atse	pleasure	atsekabe	displeasure, sorrow
bide	(correct) way	bidegabe	injustice
doha	bliss	dohakabe	misfortune
erru	guilt	errugabe	innocence
esker	thankfulness	eskergabe	ingratitude
lo	sleep	logabe	sleeplessness
nahi	will	nahigabe	suffering, distress
uste	expectation	ustekabe	surprise

[*N.B.* In some of the oldest compounds, the form *-kabe* appears instead of *-gabe*, likewise for adjectival *antsikabe*. The reason why is unclear: perhaps an earlier laryngeal?]

13.6.2 Adjectival Compounds with *gabe*

Given the sheer abundance of such compounds, only a sample can be presented:

antsia	worry, care	antsikabe	careless
ardura	care	arduragabe	careless
axola	care, worry	axolagabe	careless
azken	end	azkengabe	endless, unending
bazter	edge	baztergabe	edgeless, unlimited
beldur	fear	beldurgabe	fearless
berdin	match	berdingabe	matchless
bihotz	heart	bihozgabe	heartless
bizar	beard	bizargabe	beardless
bizi	life	bizigabe	lifeless, inanimate
buru	head	burugabe	headless, stupid
diru	money	dirugabe	moneyless
era	manner	eragabe	immoderate, irregular
erru	guilt	errugabe	innocent
erruki	pity, compassion	errukigabe	pitiless, merciless
esker	thanks	eskergabe	ungrateful
eskola	schooling	eskolagabe	unschooled, uneducated
fede	faith	fedegabe	unbelieving, unbeliever
ganora	skill	ganoragabe	awkward, clumsy
gatz	salt	gatzgabe	saltless, insipid, pointless
gogo	desire	gogogabe	listless, indifferent
grina	passion	grinagabe	dispassionate
hezur	bone	hezurgabe	invertebrate, boneless
hoben	guilt, sin	hobengabe	innocent, sinless
hondar	ground, bottom	hondargabe	bottomless, unfathomable
indar	force, strength	indargabe	strengthless, weak, void

itxura	appearance	itxuragabe	misshapen, shapeless, absurd
kalte	harm	kaltegabe	harmless, inoffensive
lotsa	shame	lotsagabe	shameless, brazen
molde	form, skill	moldegabe	unformed, inept, clumsy
muga	limit, border	mugagabe	limitless, unlimited, indefinite
neurri	measure	neurrigabe	unlimited, immoderate
odol	blood	odolgabe	bloodless, anemic, apathetic
pare	match	paregabe	matchless, unequaled, exceptional
toles	fold, pleat	tolesgabe	artless, ingenuous, sincere
zentzu	(good) sense	zentzugabe	senseless, foolish, nonsensical
zori	(good) fate	zorigabe	unfortunate, ill-fated, unlucky
zuzen	right, correct	zuzengabe	unjust, unfair

In most cases, only intonation will distinguish these lexical compounds from the corresponding syntactic collocations: *beldurgabe* 'fearless', *lotsagabe* 'shameless', compared to *beldur gabe* 'without fear', *lotsa gabe* 'without shame'.

There also are a few compounds derived from verbs:

eten	to break (off)	etengabe	continuous, ceaseless
ezkondu	to marry	ezkongabe	unmarried (from earlier *ezkondugabe*)
heldu	to ripen	heldugabe	unripe, immature
hezi	to tame	hezigabe	untame, wild, indomitable
sinetsi	to believe	sinesgabe	unbelieving, incredulous

13.7 Vocabulary

Egin idioms:

amets egin	to dream
barau egin	to fast
barre egin	to laugh
birao egin	to curse
dei egin	to call, to invite
eztul egin	to cough
garrasi egin	to yell
ihes egin	to flee
irribarre egin	to smile
kalte egin	to do harm, to harm
lan egin	to work
lo egin	to sleep
negar egin	to cry, to weep
oihu egin	to shout
otoitz egin	to pray
zapart egin	to crack, to explode
zaunka egin	to bark
zin egin	to take an oath

Other words:

arnasa	breath
behintzat	at least
benetan	really, for real
berriketa	chatter, gossip
damu	regret
erotu	to turn crazy
erruki	pity, compassion
esne	milk
etengabe	continuous, ceaseless
gaixo	poor, unfortunate
irakurle	reader
kalte	harm, damage

luzaro	for a long time, long	trebe	skillful
maitasun	love	urruti	far
sukalde	kitchen	zor	debt

13.8 Exercises

13.8.1 Translate into English

1. Zurekin amets egiten dut egunero, ba al dakizu hori?
2. Zure berriketa etengabeak laster erotuko nau.
3. Herririk herri ibili da ama gaixoa, alabatxo maitea inon aurkitu gabe.
4. Ibaira barik elizarantz abiatu zen atzerritar lotsatia.
5. Egin al zenuten lana hona gabe?
6. Benetan damu dut ez etorriaz.
7. Arnasa luze bat hartu eta leize sakonera jaitsi nintzen.
8. Gaztelu zahar honetan ez da behin ere otoitz egin.
9. Ehun liberaren zorretan gelditzen zara gurekin.
10. Alkateari egia esateak ez du kalterik egingo.
11. Zuk nola dakizu egia, inork zuri ezer esan gabe?
12. Gure baratzatik oso urruti gabe txerri asko ikusten dira.

13.8.2 Translate into Basque

1. Our skillful reader read no books this week.
2. One never drinks milk in San Sebastian.
3. Why do the maids always laugh in our kitchen?
4. Who are they working for?
5. Some fishermen never talk without shouting.
6. For lack of love, Mary cried a long time.
7. Where are our students sleeping these days?
8. How do they live so long without money?
9. The teacher never spoke a word without coughing.
10. It was cold yesterday, but at least it did not snow.
11. My parents have no pity for anyone.
12. We have no debts at all, at least in this city.

14 Object Complements of **edun*; Modal Verbs

14.1 Object Complements of **edun*

As noted in item 11 of section 2.3.2, bare nouns may act as subject or object complements to verbs, such as *morroi* 'servant' in *morroi joan* 'to go away into service' or *katibu* 'captive' in *katibu eraman* 'to lead into captivity'.

The verb **edun* 'to have' is quite prone to such object complements:

(1) a. Pello seme dugu.
Pete is our son. (Lit. "We have Pete [as] a son.")
b. Patxi adiskide dut.
Frank is my friend. (Lit. "I have Frank [as] a friend.")

With full noun phrases instead of mere nouns used as object complements, the article *a* must occur on the complement:

(2) a. Pello seme bakarra dugu.
Pete is our only son.
b. Patxi adiskide handia dut.
Frank is my great friend.

In similar fashion, the adjective *maite* 'dear' readily assumes the role of an object complement to **edun*, and in the southern dialects even to its synonym *eduki*. Notice, incidentally, that German has an exactly parallel construction: *liebhaben* 'to love', where *lieb* 'dear' functions as a separable prefix, as *maite* seems to in Basque:

(3) a. Maite dituzu eta maite zaituzte. (*P.Ab.* 105)
You love them and they love you.
b. Nagusiek hain maite zeukaten. (Cf. *TZ* II, 219)
The rulers loved him so much.
c. Nork du maite? (Orixe, in *OrOm* 289)
Who loves him?

d. Jacob izan nuen maite eta ez Esau. (Rom 9:13)
   Jacob I loved, and not Esau.
e. Zu zara nire legea; zu bakarrik zaitut maite. (*TOE* II, 331)
   You are my law; I only love you.
f. Ho, nik zu zaitut maite . . . (Larzabal, *Hiru* 59)
   Oh, I love you . . .

When the bare adjective *maite* is expanded into a full phrase *oso maite* 'very dear', the object complement construction is still possible, but will now entail the article *-a*, similar to what we saw in examples (2a,b):

(4) a. Oso maitea zuen Salbatorek. (K. Iturria, in S. Mitxelena, *IG* I, 452)
   Salbator loved him very much.
b. Jonatanek oso maitea zuen Dabid. (1 Sm 19:1)
   Jonathan loved David very much.

Another example of an object complement to **edun* is furnished by the noun *zor* 'debt'. The resulting phrase means 'to have as a debt' and is the normal equivalent in Basque of the English verb *to owe*:

(5) a. Zuk, berriz, zenbat duzu zor? (Lk 16:7; Dv)
   You, now, how much do you owe?

Postverbal occurrence of *zor* with **edun* is still found acceptable by many speakers, especially in Biscay:

(5) b. Nork izango ditu hamar miloi libera zor?
   Who will owe ten million francs?

Similarly, in the northern dialects, the noun *iduri* 'likeness' can appear as an object complement of **edun*, yielding the meaning 'to be like', 'to resemble':

(6) Nor dute iduri? (Lk 7:31; Dv)
   Who are they like?

Some nouns denoting emotions are also commonly applied to the objects inspiring that emotion. This property makes them fitting candidates to act as object complements of **edun*. The following emotive nouns can be mentioned as examples: *atsegin* 'pleasure', *atsekabe* 'distress', *damu* 'regret' (albeit not often found in this construction), *erruki* 'pity', *gorroto* 'hatred', *gupida* 'compassion', *hastio* 'loathing', *higuin* 'disgust', *narda* 'repulsion', *opa* 'wish'.

Classical scholars will not need to be reminded of Latin parallels, such as *odio habere* 'to hate' and *ludibrio habere* 'to mock', 'to ridicule', which, however, display dative case forms, instead of the absolutive—or possibly caseless—forms found in Basque.

Generally, the object complement will be treated as focus, so that it will occur immediately in front of the verb **edun*:

(7) a. Ez beldur izan, Maria, Jainkoak atsegin zaitu. (Iraizoz, 5)
Don't be afraid, Maria, God delights in you.
b. Damu dugu bekatua. (S. Mitxelena, *IG* II, 140)
We repent of sin. (or 'regret sin')
c. Israelko semeak erruki ditut. (*TZ* I, 108)
I pity the sons of Israel.
d. Nik ez ote dut erruki izango Ninibe hiri haundia? (*Biblia K.E.* 197)
Shall I then not pity the great city Niniveh?
e. Gorroto biziz gorroto izan ditut. (Ps 139:22)
I have hated them with intense hatred.
f. Bata gorroto izango du eta bestea maite. (Mt 6:24)
He will hate the one and love the other.
g. Maite ez nauzu, higuin nauzu. (*TZ* I, 221)
You don't love me, you detest me.

Occasionally, however, some other constituent is focused on, in which event the object complement will be situated in the postverbal position, as it was in examples (3c,d,e,f). Examples with emotive nouns as complements are

(8) a. Zuk, ordea, bihotz leiala duzu atsegin. (Ps 51:8)
You, however, relish a loyal heart.
b. Fede gaiztokoak ditut gorroto. (Ps 119:113)
I hate those with bad faith. (Vulgate: *Iniquos odio habui.*)
c. Hizkuntza guztiak izango dituzte higuin. (*MEIG* VIII, 136 = *MIH* 215)
They will detest all languages.
d. Bat izanen du higuin eta bestea maite. (Mt 6:24; Dv)
He will detest one and love the other.
e. Hain dute hastio askok euskara ... (H.U., *Aurp.* 201)
So much do many people loathe Basque ...
f. Hori zuen opa noski artista trebe honek. (*MEIG* II, 65 = *MIH* 177)
That is, of course, what this skillful artist wished for.

This type of object complement construction has clearly been lexicalized to a considerable degree. On the one hand, emotive nouns do not appear as object complements to any verbs other than **edun* and its intransitive counterpart *izan*; on the other hand, some semantically quite similar nouns, such as *poz* 'joy', never take on this function. Interestingly enough, to all intents and purposes the nouns appearing in this construction present the same characteristics as the separable prefixes attached to many verbs in Dutch and German—except for their confinement to **edun* and *izan*, and their origin as nouns rather than adjectives or adverbs.

Now, in the field of diachronic syntax, there is an ample body of evidence showing that a shift from separable to inseparable prefixes is a perfectly natural process, well attested in the history of various languages. It should therefore come as no surprise that this is indeed what has been happening in many varieties of Basque over the past centuries. For a majority of speakers in Guipuzcoa and, to a somewhat lesser extent, in Biscay also, many or even all of the prefixes have become inseparable. To put it in other words, postverbal position of the emotive noun in positive clauses has ceased to be an option for those speakers, so that, for example, *nork maite du?* 'who loves him?' has replaced an earlier *nork du maite?*

Following this change, however, there remains no syntactic evidence pointing to an object complement, for now the structural relation between an object complement like *maite* and the accompanying notional verb **edun* will entirely mirror that between a verbal participle like *maitatzen* and its corresponding auxiliary **edun*: *maite dut* acting precisely like *maitatzen dut* and *ez dut ... maite*, with auxiliary attraction overruling inseparability, behaving exactly like *ez dut ... maitatzen*.

Under these circumstances, restructuring may very well set in and a new verb will be born; it will have the characteristics of a preterito-present verb, on a par with those analyzed in section 14.2.

A clear sign of the reality of this change in syntactic category is the appearance of future participle forms such as *maiteko*, *gorrotoko*, and *zorko*, inasmuch as the future suffix *-ko* is restricted to verbs and totally out of place with object complements. Thus one never encounters **Deabrua beti etsaiko dut* as an alternative to the sentence *Deabrua beti etsai izango dut* 'I will always have the devil as an enemy'. Yet, we do find

(9) a. Deabrua beti gorrotoko dut.
I will always hate the devil.
b. Nik maiteko zaitut beti. (Lasarte, *Gordean* 92)
I will love you always.
c. Nik maite zaitut eta haurra ere maiteko dut. (Izeta, *Nigarrez* 98)
I love you and I will love the child too.
d. Eta arnasa ere zorko duzu. (*P.Ab.* 74)
And you will owe even your breath.
e. Iduriko zenuen zeruko izarra. (From the traditional Navarrese song "Xarmagarria zira," *Xaramela* 292, Arratia IV, 121, etc.)
You would look like a star in the sky.

But, as our analysis predicts, active users of sentences such as *Nor duzu maite?* 'Who do you love?' or *Zenbat duzu zor?* 'How much do you owe?' never resort to forms like *maiteko* or *zorko*. Thus, contrary to what some grammarians—myself included—have claimed, there are no rules of the type *maite izango* ⇒ *maiteko*, *zor izango* ⇒ *zorko*.

The presence of an object complement can also be ruled out by the occurrence of a degree adverbial in a form restricted to verbs. An example is *txit asko*:

(10) Txit asko maite zaitut. (Bilintx, 190)
I love you very much.

While intensifiers like *oso* and *txit* appear across all syntactic categories (cf. section 11.2.1), object complements when modified require the article *-a*, as demonstrated by examples (2a,b). The absence of an article in examples (11a,b,c) shows therefore that we are no longer dealing with object complements, but with verbs:

(11) a. Txit maite zaitut. (Bilintx, 191)
I love you very much.
b. Baina Jonathas, Saulen semeak txitki maite zuen Dabid. (1 Sm 19:1; Dv)
But Saul's son Jonathan loved David very much.
c. Oso maite dut gazta zahar hori. (*EHM* 754)
I love that old cheese very much.

14.2 Preterito-present Verbs

Similar in this respect to the modal verbs of Germanic, the Basque modals are preterito-present verbs: what looks like a periphrastic perfect tense form actually indicates the present. From *behar* 'to need', *nahi* 'to want', western Biscayan *gura* 'to want', *gogo* 'to intend', *asmo* 'to intend' (literary only), we get *behar dut* 'I need', *nahi dut* 'I want', *gura dut* 'I want', *gogo dut* 'I intend', *asmo dut* 'I intend', to which we may compare *bota dut* 'I have thrown' from the ordinary verb *bota* 'to throw'. Preterito-present verbs have regular future participles (*beharko*, *nahiko*, *gurako*, *gogoko*, *asmoko*) and coincide with their radical forms, but in order to form the remaining participles the auxiliary verb **edun* has to be resorted to, that is, nowadays in most areas transitive *izan*. Thus, for *behar* we have the following forms: perfect participle *behar izan*, imperfect participle *behar izaten* with the corresponding verbal noun *behar izate*; and likewise for all other preterito-present verbs. An analogical future participle *behar izango* has also made its appearance, but it is losing out to the older form *beharko*, despite its promotion by the influential grammarian R. M. Azkue (1923–1925, II, sec. 1000), who held that *behar* was no verb and hence could not take the future suffix *-ko*.

Now that their morphological characteristics have been fully stated, we can leave these modal verbs for the time being, as their syntactic behavior will be analyzed separately in the next sections.

Instead, we will turn to the nonmodal preterito-present verbs, which also exist in Basque, the most frequent one being *uste* 'to think' or 'to believe', to be taken up in chapter 18. Some other common examples happen to be Romance loans: *balio* 'to be worth', *falta* (or northern *peitu*) 'to lack', *merezi* 'to deserve', *opa* 'to wish' (always a verb when used with an indirect object), and *kosta* 'to cost', also employed as an ordinary verb. Only *balio* and *falta* will be illustrated here; for *opa*, see section 15.1.

The verb *balio* has all the meanings of French *valoir*: 'to be worth', 'to be equivalent to', 'to be worthwhile', 'to be valid'. Here are some examples:

(12) a. Haren bihotzak urrea balio du. (T. Agirre, *Uztaro* 300)
His heart is worth gold.
b. Ikusi dugu, baina ez zuen begiratzea ere balio. (Jnn., *SBi* 4)
We have seen him, but he wasn't even worth looking at.
c. Euskarak ez du ogia irabazteko balio. (Agirre, *Kres.* 83)
Basque is no use for earning (one's) bread.
d. Horrek ez du balio.
That doesn't count.

The verb *falta* occurs transitively in the meaning 'to lack' or 'to miss', and also intransitively when it means 'to be absent'. Some examples of its use are

(13) a. Nire maitasun honek falta du ordaina. (Bilintx, 91)
This love of mine lacks reciprocity.
b. Emakumearen eskua falta izan zen handik aurrera. (*LBB* 96)
A woman's hand was missing from then on.
c. Solas luzeetan ez da faltako bekatua. (Zerbitzari, 58)
In long conversations sin won't be lacking.
d. Falta izan al zenuten ezer? (Lk 22:35)
Did yoû lack anything?

[*N.B.* The virtually synonymous *-tu* verbs *baliatu*, *faltatu*, *merezitu*, *opatu*, and *kostatu* (actually more common than *kosta*) are not preterito-present verbs. Verbs ending in *-tu*, as a matter of fact, never are.]

Relatively recent members of the set of nonmodal preterito-present verbs are those arising from the diachronic change discussed in section 14.1, such as *maite* 'to love', *gorroto* 'to hate', *erruki* 'to pity', and *zor* 'to owe'. Their future participles *maiteko*, *gorrotoko*, *errukiko*, and *zorko* are thus of recent vintage and are still rejected by many speakers, who prefer the traditional *maite izango*, *gorroto izango*, *erruki izango*, and *zor izango*. The question as to exactly how recent those controversial participles are must await further inquiry. It may be noted that *zorko* is already attested in *El doctor Peru Abarka*, a novel written by J. A. Mogel before 1802, although not published until 1881.

The other, much older, preterito-present verbs may actually have arisen in the same way as this latter group, but for such early verbs as the modals *nahi* and *behar* no evidence whatsoever seems to remain of an earlier object complement stage.

14.3 Syntax of *nahi*

14.3.1 The Verb *nahi* 'to want'

In this section, we will analyze in some detail the complement system of the preterito-present verb *nahi* 'to want'. Its Biscayan synonym *gura* does not warrant separate attention, since it displays exactly the same behavior as *nahi*.

To begin with the simplest possible option, noun phrases readily occur as direct objects of *nahi*:

(14) a. Giltza nahiko duzu? (Atxaga, *Obab.* 67)
You will want the key?
b. Zer nahi du niganik? (Larzabal, *Senp.* 116)
What does he want from me?
c. Ez dut haren dirurik nahi. (*TOE* II, 273)
I don't want any of his money.

Nominalized clauses too can function as direct objects of *nahi*:

(15) a. Ni erotzea nahi al duzu? (Garate, *Hades* 39)
Do you want me to go crazy?
b. Zerbait ekartzea nahi al duzu? (*TOE* III, 132)
Do you want (someone) to bring you something?
c. Ez zuen inork jakiterik nahi. (Mk 7:24)
He didn't want anyone to know it.
d. Nora joatea nahi duzu nire zaharrean? (*TOE* II, 206)
Where do you want me to go in my old age?
e. Zer nahi zenuen nik Gazteizen egitea? (*MEIG* IX, 73)
What did you want me to do in Vitoria?

The last three examples present some points of interest: In (15c), the nominalized clause *inork jakitea* 'anyone knowing it' counts as an absolutive noun phrase, and, as such, being in a negative context, admits the partitive determiner.

In (15d), the nominalized clause has been broken up by the main clause verb *nahi duzu*. The explanation for this fact is straightforward. Within the nominalized clause the focus *nora* must attach to its verb *joan*; this combination, realized as *nora joatea*, in turn functions as the focus of the main clause and must therefore move to the main verb *nahi*, leaving behind the temporal adjunct *nire zaharrean* 'in my old age'.

In (15e), the wh-pronoun *zer* 'what' has (optionally) been moved out of the subordinate clause to take up focus position before the main verb *nahi*. (Compare 15d.)

[*N.B.* In all these examples, an alternative construction could have been used: finite complement clauses in the subjunctive mood. This type of complement will be discussed in chapter 21.]

To explain the examples to be given shortly, we need the notion of subject for both transitive and intransitive clauses, and we need this concept to be defined as the ergative constituent of the former and the absolutive one of the latter. The need for a subject of this type is generally taken as a proof that Basque is not a syntactically ergative language, as mentioned already in section 9.2.1.

What the following examples go on to show is this: whenever the subject of the main verb *nahi* is presupposed to be the same as (i.e., is coreferential with) that of the subordinate clause, the whole sentence will collapse into a single clause. (Only optionally so for some speakers, as the grammarian P. Goenaga [1985b] has observed.)

The subordinate subject remains unexpressed, and instead of the verbal noun we find the unmarked form of the subordinate verb: its perfect participle. The resulting construction illustrates what I will call *direct infinitival complementation*, direct in the sense of not being mediated by any suffix borne by the subordinate verb.

(16) a. Zertarako nahi duzu bizi? (San Martin, 84)
What do you want to live for?
b. Zer nahi duzu hartu? (Lertxundi, *Aise* 104)
What do you want to drink? (Lit. "to take")
c. Nork nahi du, ordea, etxerik eta lurrik erosi? (H.U., *Zez*. 65)
But who wants to buy any houses or grounds?
d. Denek nahi zuten Salomon ikusi. (1 Kgs 10:24 = 2 Chr 9:23)
Everybody wanted to see Solomon.
e. Nahi izan dut oihukatu: sendatua naiz! (Aintziart, 102)
I have wanted to shout: I am cured!

The subordinate verb *bizi* in (16a) is intransitive, so that its subject, if expressed, would be in the absolutive case. But in the other examples the subordinate verb is transitive, and its subject, if overt, would show the ergative case. Yet the *nahi* construction treats all examples in exactly the same way. In short then, morphological case is irrelevant to the process.

For the main clause to be negative makes no difference:

(17) a. Ez dut nahi joan sukaldera. (*TOE* II, 88)
I don't want to go to the kitchen.
b. Ez, ez dugu nahi izan sobera lan hartu. (H.U., *Zez*. 19)
No, we have not wanted to take on too much work.

Usually, especially in the southern dialects, a different constituent order is preferred, in which the subordinate verb precedes the main verb *nahi* and forms with it a single constituent, a compound verb, as P. Goenaga aptly labeled it in his contribution "Nahi eta behar" (1985b).

Technically speaking, this kind of structure results from infinitival predicate raising, a well-known subcase of head-to-head movement, here triggered by the optional raising verb *nahi*. Some examples are

(18) a. Zer esan nahi duzu? (Lertxundi, *Aise* 105)
What do you want to say? (i.e., "What do you mean?")
b. Nork hil nahi zaituzte? (*TZ* II, 198)
Who wants to kill yoú?

c. Nork entzun nahi du elbarriaren ipuina? (*LBB* 92)
Who wants to hear the paralytic's tale?

d. Nik nire emazte egin nahi zaitut. (*TOE* II, 270)
I want to make you my wife.

e. Nire gurasoek ezagutu nahi zaituzte. (*LBB* 46)
My parents want to know you.

f. Begiz jan nahi ninduen. (Larzabal, *Hil.* 58)
He wanted to eat me with the eyes.

To explain the shape taken by the auxiliary in these examples, we must be aware that the main verb has to agree with the direct object originating from the subordinate clause, since the latter has ceased to be extant.

Examples with a negative main clause follow:

(19) a. Ez zaitut inondik galdu nahi. (*TOE* II, 115–116)
In no way do I want to lose you.

b. Ez dut ohera gabe biluzi nahi. (Ax. 235)
I don't want to undress before going to bed.

c. Nik ez dut ezer jakin nahi. (*TOE* II, 26, 75, 295)
I don't want to know anything.

d. Ez du etorri nahi izaten nire etxera. (*TOE* I, 72)
He doesn't (usually) want to come to my house.

In parts of the northern dialect region, and occasionally in some earlier Guipuzcoan writers as well, the verb *nahi* is transparent; that is, it takes the transitive auxiliary **edun* when governing a transitive verb and the intransitive auxiliary *izan* when governing an intransitive verb. Some examples of the intransitive auxiliary are

(20) a. Ama, ni ere nahi naiz ezkondu. (From the Low Navarrese song "Kaila kantuz," Riezu, 208)
Mother, I too want to get married.

b. Susana baratzeko putzuan mainatu nahi izan zen. (*TZ* II, 176)
Susanna wanted to bathe in the well in the garden.

c. Hura, berriz, ez zen sartu nahi. (Lk 15:28; Dv)
He, however, didn't want to go in.

d. Eta ez ziren nahi etorri. (Mt 22:3; Dv)
And they didn't want to come.

e. Eta ez ziren joan nahi izan. (Mt 22:3; Intx.)
And they didn't want to go.

(More examples are in *EGLU* II, 446; cf. also Goenaga 1985b.)

In the modern standard language, even in the north, *nahi* is practically always opaque; that is, it takes the auxiliary **edun*, regardless of the nature of the lower verb.

[*N.B.* Judging from the data furnished by the *DGV* (IX, 16–17), *gura* never co-occurs with the intransitive auxiliary, except of course in medio-passives.]

14.3.2 The Deverbal Noun *nahi* 'will' and Its Synonym *borondate*

This section will probe into the complement system of the deverbal noun *nahi* meaning 'will' and compare it to that of its near synonym *borondate*, unrelated to any verb.

To begin with, either noun allows an animate genitival complement, requiring a subjective reading. Thus the phrase *andre gazte baten nahia*, like *andre gazte baten borondatea*, unambiguously stands for 'a young lady's will'—in contrast to the phrase *andre gazte baten beharra*, which can mean 'the need for a young lady' as well as 'a young lady's need'.

Inanimate genitival complements are rejected by the noun *borondate* but are, in principle, possible with *nahi*. On account of their being inanimate, they only allow an objective reading. The following example is from P. Charritton:

(21) Bada beti guregan zorion handi baten nahia.
There always is in us a will for a great happiness.

An unmodified inanimate noun, while never forming a compound with *borondate*, may do so with *nahi*: *zorion-nahi* 'will for happiness'. The genitive phrase *zorionaren nahia* (Lapeyre, 73) 'the will for happiness' is equally acceptable.

Nominalized clauses do not appear as genitival complements of the noun *nahi*, perhaps because this noun, unlike the homophonous verb, imposes an equisubject constraint on its sentential complement. Where this constraint is met, the complement verb in its unmarked form will act as a connecting link between the sentential complement and the noun *nahi*. This point is shown by the following examples:

(22) a. Jainkoa ondo serbitu nahia laster agertu zuen. (*TZ* II, 159)
He soon showed the will to serve God well.
b. Honek beste handizkietan Daniel galdu nahia sortzen zuen. (*TZ* II, 205)
This created among the other aristocrats the will to ruin Daniel.
c. Dama, ni zuri hitzegin nahiak narama maitasun eztiz. (Lasarte, *Gordean* 91)
Lady, the desire (lit. "will") to speak to you agitates me with a sweet love.

This structure, a direct infinitival complement in the terms of the preceding section, is not available to *borondate*. With this word, the adnominal form of the verbal noun must be used instead, an option open to all complement-taking nouns, including *nahi*: *Jainkoa ondo serbitzeko borondatea* (*nahia*) 'the will to serve God well', *Daniel galtzeko borondatea* (*nahia*) 'the will to ruin Daniel', *zuri hitzegiteko borondatea* (*nahia*) 'the will to speak to you'.

Noun phrases denoting actions can also serve as complements to such nouns as *borondate* and *nahi*. The noun phrase then takes the allative case form followed by the adnominal suffix *-ko*: *lanerako borondatea* (*nahia*) 'the will to work'. More usual, however, is *lanerako gogoa* 'the desire to work', for which see section 14.4.1.

A final difference between *nahi* and *borondate* concerns morphology rather than syntax. There is in Basque a fair number of lexical compounds with a verb radical as the first member and *nahi* as the second and final member. There are, however, none such with *borondate* as a last member. These compounds function both as adjectives and as nouns. Some examples are

agertu	to display	agernahi	ostentatious, ostentation
aldatu	to change	aldanahi	eager(ness) to change
goratu	to rise	goranahi	ambitious, ambition
ikasi	to learn	ikasnahi	eager(ness) to learn
ikusi	to see	ikusnahi	curious, curiosity

Our analysis has now led to the following conclusion: There are two types of complement systems to nouns. The first is that of ordinary nouns, which we will call the *borondate* system, characterized by the appearance of the adnominal suffix *-ko*, at times preceded by a locative case ending such as allative *-ra* or tendential *-rantz*.

The second is that of deverbal nouns, which we will call the *nahi* system, presenting the additional options of an objective genitive and direct infinitival complements.

The divergence in syntactic behavior observed between *nahi* and *borondate* confirms my notion that *nahi* is a deverbal noun, and not, as P. Goenaga and many other grammarians seem to assume, a denominal verb.

True enough, synchronic status—which is what we are concerned with—does not necessarily reflect historical development. While I have no evidence one way or another, it is certainly conceivable that, as a matter of history, the verb *nahi* did derive from an earlier noun acting as an object complement to **edun* in the manner sketched for the verb *maite* in section 14.1.

To complete this section, we may note that verb phrases containing the noun *nahi* are occasionally resorted to in order to express volition, although for that purpose use of the verb *nahi* is much more common. Of such rarely used verb phrases, most often heard are those where the definite inessive form *nahian* is combined with a suitable intransitive verb, such as *izan* in the north, and *egon* or *ibili* in the south:

(23) a. Zuek ikusi nahian nago. (Rom 1:11)
I want to see yoû.
b. Aspalditxoan nengoen berari bertso batzuk egin nahian. (Lasarte, *Gordean* 68)
A while ago I wanted to make some verses on it.
c. Bertsolariak indartu nahian omen zabiltzate. (*MEIG* I, 117)
(It is said that) Yoû want to strengthen the bards.
d. Ongile denak eskertu nahian nabil. (Lasarte, *Gordean* 323)
I want to thank all benefactors.

Transitive clauses with the noun *nahi* as the direct object of **edun* or *eduki* are of course also possible:

(24) a. Mutilek bazuten kalte egin nahia.
The boys had the will to do harm.
b. Ez zuten ausaz kalte egin nahirik. (Orixe, *Aitork.* 68–69)
They had perhaps no will to do harm.

Many speakers actually find (24b) unacceptable, apparently because the verb *nahi*, which does not admit the partitive determiner, is expected to occur here rather than the noun *nahi*, which does. Yet, everybody accepts

(24) c. Ez zuten ausaz kalte egin nahi handirik.
They had perhaps no great will to do harm.

14.4 Syntax of *gogo* and *asmo*

As the complement systems of the nouns *gogo* and *asmo* will be seen to conform to the *borondate* type instead of to the *nahi* type, *gogo* and *asmo* must be denominal verbs rather than deverbal nouns. The noun *gogo* is therefore basic, and it will be discussed before the verb. Both uses of *asmo* will be dealt with in a final subsection.

14.4.1 The Noun *gogo* 'mind'

The meaning of the noun *gogo*, found in all Basque dialects, exactly covers that of English *mind*, although puristic authors have seized upon it to render also the concepts of 'spirit' (*izpiritu*) and 'soul' (*arima*). Like its English gloss, it naturally encompasses the notions of 'disposition', 'appetite', and 'desire'. Thus the actual content of *gogo* tends to be an object of desire, referred to either by a noun phrase or by a clause whose subject remains unexpressed, since it coincides with the person entertaining the desire. With the noun *gogo*, the genitive never appears as a connective; what is required instead is the adnominal suffix *-ko*, in the case of a noun phrase optionally preceded by the allative *-ra*: *berriketarako gogo handia* (T. Agirre, *Uztaro* 149) 'a great fancy for gossip', *berriketako gogoa* (*TOE* I, 83) 'a fancy for gossip', *emaztetako gogoa* (Ax. 377) 'a fancy for women', *bazirauen jokatzeko gogoak* (Ax. 611) 'the appetite for gambling lasted', *kalera irteteko nire gogo horretan* (Lertxundi, *Aise* 103) 'in this fancy of mine to go out into the street'.

The most common way of voicing a desire is to use *gogoa* as a direct object of the verb **edun*, or its western substitute *eduki*:

(25) a. Honek berriketarako gogoa dauka. (Azkue, *Bein B.* 53)
He has a mind for gossip.
b. Ez dut haserrerako gogorik. (Urretabizkaia, *Zerg.* 26)
I am not in the mood for a row.
c. Gure herria ikusteko gogoa banuen aspaldian. (*TOE* I, 133)
For a long time I have had the desire to see our village.

d. Nik ez dut hilengana makurtzeko gogorik. (Amuriza, *Emea* 8)
I have no desire to bow to the dead.
e. Badaukat, bai, Donostiara iristeko gogorik! (Lertxundi, *Aise* 77)
Do I ever feel like arriving in San Sebastian!

The adnominal complement can extrapose to the end of the main clause:

(26) a. Banuen gogoa Bazko afari hau zuekin egiteko! (Lk 22:15)
How I longed to eat (lit. 'do') this Passover supper with you!
b. Gogorik al dun gaur arratsaldean nirekin Izpegira etortzeko? (Garate, *E.E.* 106)
Do you feel like coming with me to Izpegi this afternoon?

14.4.2 The Denominal Verb *gogo* 'to intend'

The verb *gogo* was originally exclusive to the northern dialects, but it has now been borrowed into the southern literary standard. Consistent with its meaning 'to intend', it only takes sentential objects, the subject of which will not be expressed, as it must be identical to that of the main verb *gogo*. The subordinate verb, therefore, always assumes the unmarked form:

(27) a. Zer egin gogo duzu? (Ax. 212)
What do you intend to do?
b. Gogo zuen etxean egon. (Etxamendi, 74)
He intended to stay home.
c. Ezkila lehen bezala jo gogo du. (Lafitte, *Murtuts* 36)
He intends to sound the bell as before.

[*N.B.* When borrowing this verb from northern usage, southern dialect speakers, who have only the meaning of the homophonous noun to rely on, tend to assign to the verb the meaning 'to desire'. Still, correct Batua usage distinguishes between *joateko gogoa dut* 'I feel like going' and *joan gogo dut* 'I intend to go'.]

14.4.3 Syntax of *asmo*

The noun denoting 'intention' or 'plan' is not *gogo*, but *asmo*. Its complement system is largely identical to that of *gogo*, with adnominal complement clauses occurring most frequently:

(28) a. Non geratzen dira zoko hauek ezagutzeko asmoak? (Lertxundi, *Aise* 69)
What has become of the plans to get to know these parts? (Lit. "Where remain . . .")
b. Zarautzera joan nintzen Patxi Barberoren omenaldian kantatzeko asmotan. (Xalbador, *Odol.* 267)
I went to Zarauz with the intention to sing in the Patxi Barbero celebration.

An exclusive feature of the literary style is the use of *asmo* as a preterito-present verb, with the syntax and meaning of the verb *gogo*:

(29) Zer egin asmo duzu?
What do you intend to do?

14.5 Syntax of *behar*

14.5.1 The Verb *behar*

The complement system of the preterito-present verb *behar*, our first object of study in this section, has a great deal in common with that of the verb *nahi*.

First of all, the verb *behar* can take noun phrases as direct objects. When it does, the verb will be glossed as 'to need'; with sentential complements the gloss 'must' or 'to have to' will be more appropriate. Some examples with noun phrase objects will illustrate:

(30) a. Odol hotza behar duzu. (Atxaga, *Behi* 25)
You need cold blood.
b. Nork zer behar du? (*Larzabal* I, 23)
Who needs what?
c. Hi behar haut. (Garate, *Alaba* 103)
I need yoú.
d. Baina ez nau inork behar hemen. (*MEIG* IX, 110)
But nobody needs me here.
e. Sermoirik ez dugu behar. (*TOE* I, 371)
We don't need sermons.
f. Liburuak behar dira. (*EGLU* II, 449)
Books are needed. (A medio-passive, see section 12.5.1.)

Being noun phrases, nominalized clauses are also expected to occur as direct objects of *behar*, and indeed, the *EGLU* grammar provides some instances:

(31) a. Polizia etortzea behar zenuen. (*EGLU* II, 448)
You needed the police to come.
b. Zuk esatea behar genuen. (*EGLU* II, 449)
We needed you to say it.

In fact, however, such sentences are categorically rejected by northern speakers, and no examples of this type are recorded in the *DGV*, even from southern sources. Observing furthermore that no finite complement clauses ever occur with *behar*, we arrive at the following inference: for the majority of speakers, the verb *behar* imposes an equisubject constraint, which will lead to direct infinitival complementation, characterized by the suppression of the subordinate subject and the perfect participle form assumed by the subordinate verb:

(32) a. Irakurlea behar dugu errespetatu. (H.U., *Aurp*. 31)
We must respect the reader.

b. Guztiek behar zuten jakin haren berri. (H.U., *Zez.* 54)
   They all had to know about it.
c. Orduan behar nuen nik mintzatu. (Aintziart, 82)
   I should have spoken then.
d. Ez dira behar sinetsi. (H.U., *Zez.* 62)
   They are not to be believed. (Medio-passive)
e. Gaurko lokatzetan beharko du zikindu. (*MEIG* II, 136 = *MIH* 334)
   He must dirty himself in today's quagmires.

With the sole exception of (32e), all the examples given stem from the northern dialect area. In the southern area, unless the language is intended to be poetic, predicate raising (cf. section 14.3.1) is obligatory. Examples of this are

(33) a. Nik zer esan behar dut? (*TOE* II, 183)
   What am I to say?
b. Jan egin behar zaituztet. (*LBB* 188)
   I must eat yoû.
c. Horrela bizi behar al dun, alaba? (*LBB* 49)
   Do yoù have to live that way, daughter?
d. Nirekin dantzatu beharko duzu rumba hau. (*LBB* 203)
   You will have to dance this rumba with me.
e. Hori ez du inork jakin behar. (*TOE* II, 52)
   Nobody must know that.
f. Ez al nauzue urkatu behar? (*LBB* 117)
   Don't yoû have to hang me?
g. Adorerik ez da galdu behar. (*TOE* II, 226)
   One mustn't lose courage. (Medio-passive)

Behar is the only verb in common use for expressing deontic modality. Accordingly, its meaning encompasses that of English *need, must, should, have to, be to*, and so on. It has nondeontic uses as well, for example, for indicating impendency:

(34) a. Euria egin behar du. (Lafitte 1962, sec. 655)
   It is going to rain.
b. Igandean gurekin bazkaldu behar omen duzu. (*LBB* 46)
   It seems that on Sunday you are going to have lunch with us.

This particular use is especially frequent in wh-questions:

(35) a. Zer esan behar du herriak? (*LBB* 173)
   What are the people going to say?
b. Zer egin behar dut nik zu gabe? (*LBB* 157)
   What am I going to do without you?

c. Eta beste zure andrearekin zer egin behar duzu? (*TOE* III, 137)
And what are you going to do with your other wife?
d. Noiz zentzatu behar duzu? (*TOE* III, 93)
When are you going to come to your senses?
e. Nork esan behar zuen? (*LBB* 171)
Who would have said so?

Like the verb *nahi*, but perhaps more widely so (cf. *DGV* IV, 303–304, for geographical distribution and historical testimonies), the verb *behar* is transparent for some speakers; that is, it can take the intransitive auxiliary *izan* when governing an intransitive verb:

(36) a. Ez nintzen ezkondu behar. (Lafitte, *Murtuts* 36)
I shouldn't have got married.
b. Zure haurrak nola behar dira han bizi? (H.U., *Zez.* 72)
How are your children going to live there?
c. Gaur abiatu behar gara ... (Gerriko I, 17)
We must start out today ...

Still, the majority usage in the modern standard language is for the verb *behar* to be opaque, that is, to take the transitive auxiliary **edun* in all cases.

Needless to say, transparent use of this verb should not be confused with its mediopassive, which is possible for all speakers, regardless of the verb governed:

(37) Hotz-hotzean erabakiak hartu behar dira. (*TOE* III, 106)
Decisions must be taken in utter coolness.

14.5.2 The Deverbal Noun *behar*

The noun *behar*, which has the central meaning of 'necessity' or 'need', takes various types of complements to convey the specific content of what is needed:

1. Noun phrases in the genitive: *hire sos zikinen beharra* 'the need for yoúr dirty pennies', *zure beharra* 'the need for you' (objective genitive; the subjective genitive 'your need' is also possible).

While this is the only option open to pronouns, unmodified nouns can also enter into compounds with *behar*: *zorion behar* 'need for happiness', *emakume behar* 'need for a woman'.

2. Nominalized clauses are accepted either in the genitive or in the adnominal form: *apaizek euskara ikastearen beharra* or *apaizek euskara ikasteko beharra* 'the need for the priests to learn Basque'.

[*N.B.* Since *apaizek euskara ikastearen nahia* 'the will for the priests to learn Basque' does not occur, the complement system of *behar* is even richer than that of *nahi*.]

3. When the complement clause lacks an explicit subject, the unmarked form of the verb is preferred: *euskara ikasi beharra* 'the need to learn Basque', *hori esan beharra* (*MEIG* IX, 80) 'the need to say that'.

[*N.B.* In the meaning 'necessity' rather than 'need', the noun *behar* forms lexical compounds with—mostly intransitive—verb radicals as a first member. The verb then loses its verbal properties and can no longer take complements. Examples are

aldatu	to change	alda-behar	inconstancy, inconstant
beheratu	to go downhill	behera-behar	necessity of decay
bukatu	to end	buka-behar	finitude, finite
mintzatu	to speak	mintza-behar	need to speak]

Verb phrases containing the noun *behar* and its complement are often resorted to in order to express the meaning of the English verb *to need.* Most common among these is *beharra *edun*, or, alternatively, *beharra eduki* in Biscay and western Guipuzcoa:

(38) a. Zergatik du hil beharra? (1 Sm 20:32)
Why does he need to die?
b. Herriko etxeraino joan beharra dut. (*TOE* II, 138)
I need to go as far as the city hall.
c. Hori al zenuen esan beharra? (*TOE* II, 133)
Did you need to say that?

The noun *behar*, like most other nouns, must take the partitive in negative contexts:

(39) a. Mitxelena jaunak ez du nire aurkezpen beharrik. (M. Ugalde, in *MEIG* IX, 52)
Mr. Mitxelena does not need my introduction.
b. Ez duzu gutaz arduratu beharrik. (*MEIG* IX, 98)
You don't need to worry about us.
c. Ez dut nik joan beharrik izango. (*TOE* II, 236)
I won't need to go.
d. Ez daukat nik zurekin hitz egin beharrik. (Garate, *Alaba* 54)
I have no need to talk to you.
e. Esan beharrik ez daukazu. (Atxaga, *Z.H.* 44)
You don't need to say it.

When the need is not to be ascribed to any entity in particular, existential *izan* or *egon* can be employed as a main verb:

(40) a. Bazen zure beharra gure etxe honetan. (*LBB* 157)
There was a need for you in this house of ours.
b. Hainbeste gauza antolatu beharra dago. (*TOE* II, 123)
So many things need to be taken care of.
c. Lau Ebanjelioen itzulpen berri baten beharrik ba ote zegoen? (*MEIG* III, 100)
Was there any need for a new translation of the four Gospels?

As an equivalent of the English phrase *in need of*, the definite inessive *beharrean*—in the northern dialects also the indefinite inessive *beharretan*—often enters into predications with the help of a suitable verb. This is usually *izan* 'to be' or *egon* 'to stand', 'to be', but it can also be *aurkitu* 'to find' or *eduki* 'to have', 'to keep':

(41) a. Nire laguna laguntza beharrean da. (Duvoisin, *Lab.* 9)
My fellow-man is in need of help.
b. Denaren beharrean izango zarete. (*TOE* II, 109)
Yoû will be in need of everything.
c. Burua makurtu beharrean gaude. (Zaitegi, *Plat.* 54)
We are in need to bend our heads.
d. Gu bizi izateko, oraintxe nago bozkario beharrean. (*TOE* III, 153)
For us to live, I am in need of joy precisely now.
e. Zure beharrean aurkitzen naiz. (Oñatibia, 235)
I find myself in need of you.
f. Saul bere hitza jan beharrean aurkitu zen. (*TZ* I, 262)
Saul found himself in need to break his word. (Lit. 'eat his word')

By a slight shift of meaning, *beharrean* also occurs as a postposition with the value 'instead of': *z beharrean s* 's instead of z'. Further examples follow:

(42) a. Konpondu beharrean, hondatu egin du. (*EHM* 157)
Instead of repairing it, he has ruined it.
b. Berak egin beharrean, amak egiten zuen negar. (Oskillaso, *Kurl.* 38)
Instead of him doing so, the mother was crying.

14.6 Expressing Habit: Constructions with *ohi*

In southern Batua, *ohi* is a preterito-present verb with the meaning 'to be in the habit', 'to use to'. It combines with a subordinate verb in the same way as *nahi* (section 14.3.1) making up with it a compound verb as a result of infinitival predicate raising. The compound verb is transparent; that is, it always agrees with the subordinate verb in transitivity. This fact is shown by the following examples:

(43) a. Ez naiz ibaira erori ohi.
I am not in the habit of falling into the river.
b. Jendea ezkondu egin ohi da. (Saizarbitoria, 122)
People are wont to get married.

(44) a. Ez dugu jan ohi. (*EGLU* II, 505)
We don't usually eat it.
b. Bazko-Jaiero preso bat askatu ohi zuen Pilatok. (Mk 15:6)
Each Passover, Pilate used to release a prisoner.

c. Egin izan ohi ditu horrelako gauzak. (Saizarbitoria, 132)
He has been in the habit of doing such things.

In northern Basque, *ohi* is not a verb but merely a proclitic particle denoting habitualness. Given its meaning, it requires an imperfective verb form:

(45) a. Ez ohi naiz ibaira erortzen.
I am not in the habit of falling into the river.
b. Jendea ezkontzen ohi da.
People are wont to get married.

(46) a. Ez ohi dugu jaten.
We don't usually eat it.
b. Presuna haserrekorrak ez ohi du begi-orde anitz higatzen. (Ax. 280)
An irascible person doesn't usually wear out many pairs of glasses.

In northern usage, *ohi* can be used as the final member of a nominal compound, where it has the meaning of the English prefix *ex-*: *lehendakari ohia* 'the ex-president'.

[*N.B.* There also is a verb *ohitu* 'to get used to' and when transitive 'to accustom to', employed in the north as well as in the south. Its syntax will be discussed in section 16.5.5.3.]

14.7 The Incentive Suffix *-garri*

The suffix *-garri*, etymologically related to the verb *ekarri* 'to bring', can be added to nouns denoting a state and, even more massively, to transitive verb radicals. In either case, the meaning of the resulting form is 'incentive (in a broad sense) to the state, process, or action described by the base'.

Although forms with this suffix can in principle be nouns as well as adjectives, a particular form may very well favor one category over the other in actual language use, sometimes to the point of virtual exclusiveness.

14.7.1 Denominal Incentives

Most nouns denoting a state admit the suffix *-garri*. The resulting form is an adjective meaning 'conducive to the state mentioned', which is also utilizable as a name for an object having this property.

In the examples commonly encountered, it is the physiological or psychological state of a human being that we are concerned with:

ahalke	shame	ahalkegarri	shameful
beldur	fear	beldurgarri	fearsome, frightful
damu	regret, repentance	damugarri	regrettable, deplorable

egarri	thirst	egargarri	causing thirst
erruki	pity	errukarri	pitiable
gogait	boredom, annoyance	gogaikarri	boring, tedious, annoying
goragale	queasiness, nausea	goragalegarri	nauseating
gose	hunger	gosegarri	causing hunger
gupida	compassion	gupidagarri	piteous, pathetic
gutizia	desire, longing	gutiziagarri	desirable, attractive
higuin	disgust	higuingarri	disgusting
ikara	shiver, trembling	ikaragarri	terrible, terrifying
interes	interest	interesgarri	interesting
izu	fright	izugarri	frightful, horrible
kezka	worry	kezkagarri	worrisome, disquieting
laido	dishonor	laidogarri	insulting, offensive
lilura	fascination	liluragarri	fascinating, enchanting
lotsa	shame	lotsagarri	shameful
maita-	love	maitagarri	lovable, fairy
mira	wonder	miragarri	wonderful, marvelous
mozkor	drunkenness	mozkorgarri	intoxicating, intoxicant
narda	repulsion	nardagarri	repulsive
nazka	repulsion, disgust	nazkagarri	disgusting, repulsive
osasun	health	osasungarri	healthy, salutary
pena	sorrow	penagarri	sorrowful, painful
poz	joy	pozgarri	gratifying, consoling
urrikari	compassion	urrikalgarri	pitiful, piteous
zalantza	uncertainty	zalantzagarri	doubtful, controversial

It would seem that there are also incentive adjectives derived from nouns not referring to a state, such as *kaltegarri* 'harmful' and *mesedegarri* 'beneficial'. In fact, however, such examples are based on *egin* idioms and are therefore not truly denominal.

Thus, *kaltegarri* and *mesedegarri* derive from *kalte egingarri* and *mesede egingarri* by *egin* deletion, a process still optional for some speakers. Other examples are

atsegin egin	to please	atsegingarri	pleasing, pleasurable, delightful
atsekabe egin	to distress	atsekabegarri	distressing, distressful
barre egin	to laugh	barregarri	comic, funny, ridiculous
irri egin	to laugh, to mock	irrigarri	ridiculous, laughable, laughingstock
min egin	to hurt	mingarri	painful, hurtful
negar egin	to cry	negargarri	deplorable, dismal
oka egin	to vomit	okagarri	nauseating, vomitive
onura egin	to profit	onuragarri	beneficial, profitable
probetxu egin	to profit	probetxugarri	profitable, advantageous

14.7.2 Deverbal Incentives

Let us call a deverbal adjective "objective" if it is interpreted as a property belonging to the object of the verb. Typical examples among the incentives are *barkagarri* 'forgivable', *irakurgarri* 'worth reading', and *jakingarri* 'worth knowing'. Nonobjective incentives also exist: *argigarri* 'clarifying', *engainagarri* 'deceptive', and *nekagarri* 'tiring'. Then again, some incentives have objective as well as nonobjective uses. With *erdeinagarri*, derived from the verb *erdeinatu* 'to despise', we have an objective use in *atsegin erdeinagarria* 'a contemptible pleasure' and a nonobjective one in *irri erdeinagarria* 'a contemptuous laughter'. Similarly, *adigarri*, from the verb *aditu* 'to understand', means 'explanatory' or 'explanation' in its nonobjective use and 'clear' or 'understandable' in its objective use.

Mostly, however, the nature of the verb determines whether the corresponding incentive will be objective or not. Thus, all deadjectival verbs and pure change-of-state verbs, in general, yield nonobjective incentives:

aberastu	to enrich	aberasgarri	enriching, fertile, fruitful
altxatu	to rise, to lift up	altxagarri	uplifting, leavening
apaindu	to decorate	apaingarri	decorative, ornamental, ornament
arindu	to alleviate	aringarri	lenitive, palliative
ase	to satiate, to satisfy	asegarri	filling, satisfying
aspertu	to bore, to annoy	aspergarri	boring, bothersome, annoying
behaztopat	to stumble	behaztopagarri	stumbling block, obstacle, hindrance
beratu	to soften, to mollify	beragarri	softening, mollifying
berotu	to heat, to warm up	berogarri	warming, stimulating, blanket
bete	to fill, to fill up	betegarri	filling, satiating, stopgap
biguindu	to soften, to smoothen	biguingarri	softening, smoothing
bizi	to live, to enliven	bizigarri	revitalizing, enlivening, food
bizkortu	to brighten up, to revive	bizkorgarri	fortifying, reviving, tonic
deitu	to call	deigarri	striking, flamboyant, attractive
edertu	to embellish, to adorn	edergarri	ornamental, decorative, ornament
eragin	to stimulate, to cause	eragingarri	stimulating, incentive, stimulus
erdiratu	to cut in half	erdiragarri	heartrending, tearing
eritu	to fall ill, to sicken	erigarri	sickening, unwholesome, pathogenic
erotu	to drive crazy	erogarri	maddening, unhinging
erre	to burn	erregarri	burning, combustible, fuel
estali	to cover	estalgarri	covering, cover-up
eztitu	to sweeten	eztigarri	sweetening, edulcorative
freskatu	to refresh	freskagarri	refreshing, cooling, refreshment
galdu	to ruin, to corrupt	galgarri	ruinous, corrupting, detrimental
gehitu	to increase	gehigarri	additive, increase, supplement
gogortu	to harden, to fortify	gogorgarri	hardening, fortifying, buttress
gortu	to deafen	gorgarri	deafening

gozatu	to sweeten, to flavor	gozagarri	sweetening, comforting, seasoning
harritu	to astonish, to amaze	harrigarri	astonishing, amazing, surprising
hil	to kill, to die	hilgarri	deadly, lethal
hondatu	to destroy, to ruin	hondagarri	disastrous, destructive
horditu	to intoxicate	hordigarri	intoxicating, intoxicant
hunkitu	to touch, to affect	hunkigarri	touching, moving
igarri	to guess	igargarri	suggestive, sign, signal, mark
indartu	to strengthen	indargarri	strengthening, fortifying
iraindu	to insult	iraingarri	insulting
iraun	to last	iraungarri	lasting, durable
ito	to choke, to smother	itogarri	suffocating, smothering, asphyxiating
itsustu	to deface, to uglify	itsusgarri	defacing, uglifying
itsutu	to blind	itsugarri	blinding
kilikatu	to tickle, to excite	kilikagarri	tickling, exciting
kiskali	to scorch	kiskalgarri	scorching
kutsatu	to contaminate	kutsagarri	contaminating, contagious
lohitu	to soil, to stain	lohigarri	dirtying, soiling, staining
lotu	to tie, to connect	lokarri	tie, connection, cord, lace
luzatu	to extend, to postpone	luzagarri	prolonging, delaying, extension
ondu	to improve, to ripen	ongarri	fertilizer, manure
osatu	to heal, to complete	osagarri	healing, complementary, complement
salbatu	to save, to rescue	salbagarri	saving, salutary
samindu	to embitter	samingarri	bitter, painful
sendatu	to cure	sendagarri	curative, remedy
suspertu	to enliven, to cheer up	suspergarri	invigorating
tentatu	to tempt	tentagarri	tempting
trabatu	to hamper, to obstruct	trabagarri	hampering, obstructive
urduritu	to make nervous	urdurigarri	enervating, nerve-wracking
zoratu	to drive crazy, to charm	zoragarri	enchanting, wonderful, marvelous

In contrast, verbs denoting an action or process where the intervention of a willful agent or experiencer is essential will yield objective incentives. Included are thus all prototypical verbs, verbs of obtaining or transfer, verbs of production or consumption, verbs of ordering, requesting, and advising, and verbs of communication, thinking, cognition, or perception.

As it is a property of the verbal object that provides the stimulus to the action, the incentive adjective can be glossed as 'conducive to being V-ed' or 'worth V-ing'. The following examples will serve to illustrate this point:

aditu	to hear	adigarri	worth hearing, spectacular
agurtu	to revere, to greet	agurgarri	reverend, honorable, distinguished
aipatu	to mention	aipagarri	worth mentioning, mentionable
baliatu	to use	baliagarri	useful

baztertu	to put aside	baztergarri	objectionable, negligible
bereizi	to distinguish	bereizgarri	distinctive, characteristic
deitoratu	to lament	deitoragarri	lamentable, deplorable
dudatu	to doubt	dudagarri	doubtful
errespetatu	to respect	errespetagarri	respectable
estimatu	to appreciate	estimagarri	appreciable, estimable
etsi	to give up, to despair	etsigarri	desperate, hopeless
ezagutu	to recognize	ezaugarri	characteristic, mark, feature
eztabaidatu	to dispute	eztabaidagarri	disputable, controversial
fidatu	to trust	fidagarri	trustworthy
gogoratu	to recall	gogoragarri	memorable
gomendatu	to recommend	gomendagarri	recommendable, advisable
gomutatu	to remember	gomutagarri	memorable
hautatu	to choose, to select	hautagarri	eligible, electable
ikusi	to see, to visit	ikusgarri	worth seeing, curious
irakatsi	to teach	irakasgarri	instructive, educational
jarraitu	to follow	jarraigarri	worth following, exemplary
kondenatu	to condemn	kondenagarri	reprehensible, blameworthy
laudatu	to praise	laudagarri	praiseworthy
miretsi	to admire, to wonder	miresgarri	admirable, wonderful, marvelous
nabaritu	to notice	nabarigarri	noticeable, notable
nabarmendu	to exhibit, to show off	nabarmengarri	notable, showy
ohartu	to realize, to notice	ohargarri	remarkable, notable
ohoratu	to honor	ohoragarri	worthy of honor, honorable
oroitu	to recall	oroigarri	memorable, souvenir
ospatu	to celebrate	ospagarri	worth celebrating
sinetsi	to believe	sinesgarri	believable, credible, proof
susmatu	to suspect	susmagarri	suspicious
txalotu	to applaud	txalogarri	applaudable, praiseworthy

14.7.3 Pseudoincentives

A semantic change has been in progress for some time weakening the meaning of objective incentives from 'worth V-ing' to plain 'V-able'. It stands to reason that Romance influence, in particular the need to translate Romance adjectives ending in *-able* and *-ible* uniformly into Basque, has been a weighty contributor to this process.

While some speakers still resist the change, adjectives like the following are frequently encountered in contemporary writings and have the approval of the Basque Academy:

egin	to do	egingarri	feasible, practicable, viable
eraman	to bear	eramangarri	bearable, tolerable
gertatu	to happen	gertagarri	incidental, contingent, possible

jasan	to put up with	jasangarri	bearable, tolerable
konprenitu	to understand	konprenigarri	understandable
mugitu	to move	mugigarri	movable
pentsatu	to think	pentsagarri	thinkable, conceivable
ulertu	to understand	ulergarri	understandable
zenbatu	to count	zenbakarri	countable

The new meaning has even been conferred upon some nonobjective incentives: *zubi altxagarria* 'a drawbridge', *gaitz sendagarria* 'a curable ailment'.

14.7.4 Bibliographical Note on Incentives

The following articles can be read as a commentary to Azkue's statement "*Garri.* En su sentido obvio es sufijo adjetival y designa lo que el latino *-bilis* ..." (In its obvious sense it is an adjectival suffix and designates the same thing as Latin *-bilis* ...) (Azkue, 1923–1925, sec. 132, p. 98): Eguskitza 1930, Azkarate 1990b, Artiagoitia 1995.

14.8 Vocabulary

alargun	widow, widower	ingeles	English, Englishman
asmo	intention, plan	interesgarri	interesting
aspergarri	boring, annoying	itxi	to close
aste	week	izugarri	frightful
balio	worth, value	kondenatu	to condemn
behar	necessity, need	konpondu	to fix, to repair
beldurgarri	dreadful, frightful	liluragarri	fascinating, enchanting
erogarri	maddening	lotsagarri	shameful
erruki	pity	maitagarri	lovable, lovely, fairy
gainera	besides, moreover	mintzatu	to speak, to talk
gogaikarri	boring, annoying	miresgarri	admirable, wonderful, marvelous
gogo	mind, appetite, fancy	nahi	will
harrigarri	astonishing, amazing, surprising	sinetsi	to believe
		teilatu	roof
ikaragarri	terrible, terrifying	zoragarri	enchanting, wonderful, marvelous
ikasi	to learn	zoriontsu	happy

14.9 Exercises

14.9.1 Translate into English

1. Hotz izugarriagatik ongi itxi behar dituzue etxeko ate eta leiho guztiak.

2. Mirenek gure etxeko teilatua konpontzea nahi dut.

3. Euskara ikasteko urrutira joateko beharrik ez dugu ikusten.
4. Ingelesa ikasi beharrean euskara ikasi zuten, eta oso ondo gainera.
5. Euskara ongi jakiteko, asko ikasi beharrean gaude oraindik.
6. Gaur ez daukat liburuetarako gogorik.
7. Liburu merke honek ez du balio irakurtzerik.
8. Gaur behintzat ez da inor sinetsi behar.
9. Ez zenuen bide luzerik egin beharrik nire emaztearekin mintzatzeko.
10. Zure emazte liluragarriaren beharrean aurkitzen nintzen omenaldi hartan.
11. Gure alabarekin ezkondu gogo al duzu, bai ala ez?
12. Gure alabarekin ezkontzeko gogorik al duzu, bai ala ez?

14.9.2 Translate into Basque

1. We must condemn you, but we will not condemn this lovely widow.
2. Don't you need anything to drink?
3. I want you to build an amazing house for me.
4. Who doesn't want to be frightfully happy?
5. I don't feel at all like selling my wonderful house to you.
6. I don't want to die before seeing San Sebastian.
7. We don't want you to need us.
8. Who will ever pity you?
9. I really intend to go home without you.
10. I must read this boring book, but I don't want to.
11. Nobody wants to love me this week.
12. Who wants who to work on that maddening farm?

15 Dative Agreement; Reflexives and Reciprocals

15.1 Dative Agreement and Its Morphology

In section 5.3 the distribution of the adnominal suffix *-ko* motivated the claim that not only absolutives but also ergatives and datives are noun phrases, all other case endings giving rise instead to postpositional phrases. Now, while in English agreement in the finite verb merely involves its subject, in Basque, as noted in sections 9.1 and 10.1, it equally applies to the direct object, and, as to be seen shortly, to the indirect object as well.

As a result, a neat characterization of agreement obtains in Basque: the finite verb agrees with all the nominal constituents within its clause. In particular, a finite verb will agree in person and number with any dative clause mate. This will be illustrated by the following examples, making use of the preterito-present verb *opa* 'to wish' (cf. section 14.2):

(1) a. Mutil honek neskatxa horri egun zoriontsua opa dio.
This boy wishes that girl a happy day.
b. Mutil honek neskatxa horiei egun zoriontsua opa die.
This boy wishes those girls a happy day.

(2) a. Mutil hauek neskatxa horri egun zoriontsua opa diote.
These boys wish that girl a happy day.
b. Mutil hauek neskatxa horiei egun zoriontsua opa diete.
These boys wish those girls a happy day.

(3) a. Mutil honek neskatxa horri egun zoriontsuak opa dizkio.
This boy wishes that girl happy days.
b. Mutil honek neskatxa horiei egun zoriontsuak opa dizkie.
This boy wishes those girls happy days.

(4) a. Mutil hauek neskatxa horri egun zoriontsuak opa dizkiote.
These boys wish that girl happy days.
b. Mutil hauek neskatxa horiei egun zoriontsuak opa dizkiete.
These boys wish those girls happy days.

What these examples show is the appearance of eight different forms of the auxiliary verb **edun* in accord with the singular versus plural number of each of the noun phrases in the sentence.

The actual forms involved are never suppletive; they obey an obvious pattern. This holds true for dative agreement forms in general, a fact which greatly facilitates the learning process.

Implementation of dative agreement proceeds by suffixation of dative markers to the verbal stem. For the third person, the dative markers are *-o* in the singular, and *-e* (dialectally *-ote*) in the plural. For the first and second persons, the dative markers are identical to the ergative ones: *-da*, *-ga*, *-na*, *-gu*, *-zu*, *-zue*.

Some common verbs insert a pre-dative marker *-ki-* between the dative marker and the stem. These are *atxiki* 'to adhere', *egon* 'to be (there)', 'to stay', *ekarri* 'to bring', *erabili* 'to use', *eraman* 'to bear', *etorri* 'to come', *ibili* 'to walk', and *joan* 'to go'.

Furthermore, the verb *eman* 'to give' uses a pre-dative marker *-i-*, and the verb **ion* 'to say' a pre-dative marker *-ts-* (see section 15.4.2). All other verbs add the dative marker directly to the stem, or else lack synthetic dative forms altogether.

In a dative verb form, except for those of **ion* 'to say', the plural will be indicated by the unmarked pluralizer suffix *-z-*, linked to the subject of an intransitive verb or the object of a transitive one. In its presence, use of the pre-dative marker *-ki-* is obligatory, so that the segment *zki* is shared by all dative forms with plural objects (or subjects in the case of intransitives), regardless of the shape of the pluralizer used in the corresponding nondative forms.

Ergative subject suffixes, when present, directly follow dative markers. Given that the two sets of markers are identical except for the third person, often only linear order will tell whether a particular marker represents the ergative or the dative.

Synthetic dative forms of the verbs *egin* 'to do', *ikusi* 'to see', and *jakin* 'to know', which all lack a pre-dative marker, are exceedingly rare even in elevated or poetic style. When we do encounter them, we find the vowel *a* in the present tense marker replaced by *e*, enabling us to distinguish *dei degit* 'he is calling to me' from *dei dagit* 'I am calling', *dekus(a)t* 'he sees it on me' from *dakus(a)t* 'I see it', and *dekit* 'he knows it about me' from *dakit* 'I know it'.

Synthetic dative forms of the verb *egon* are very common, carrying meanings served by a variety of English verbs: *to fit*, *to behoove*, *to concern*, *to refer*, *to keep* (*to*):

(5) a. Ontzi horri estalki hau dagokio. (*E.H.* 204)
This lid fits that container.
b. Morroia bataiatzea nagusiari dagokio. (Atxaga, *Behi* 16)
It is up to the boss to christen the servant.
c. Ohiturari nagokio. (*MEIG* VII, 44)
I am keeping to the custom.

I will now use this verb to illustrate the full array of dative markers. Notice that even with a plural subject the stem of the verb remains *-go-*, since the pluralizer required in all dative forms is *-z-*, instead of the usual *-de* of this verb.

Here then is the complete paradigm of the verb *egon*, serving as a representative of all intransitive verbs that make use of the pre-dative marker *-ki-*:

(niri) dagokit	it fits me	(niri) dagozkit	they fit me
(hiri) dagokik	it fits yoú	(hiri) dagozkik	they fit yoú
(hiri) dagokin	it fits yoù	(hiri) dagozkin	they fit yoù
(hari) dagokio	it fits him	(hari) dagozkio	they fit him
(guri) dagokigu	it fits us	(guri) dagozkigu	they fit us
(zuri) dagokizu	it fits you	(zuri) dagozkizu	they fit you
(zuei) dagokizue	it fits yoû	(zuei) dagozkizue	they fit yoû
(haiei) dagokie	it fits them	(haiei) dagozkie	they fit them

And in the past tense:

(niri) zegokidan	it fitted me	(niri) zegozkidan	they fitted me
(hiri) zegokian	it fitted yoú	(hiri) zegozkian	they fitted yoú
(hiri) zegokinan	it fitted yoù	(hiri) zegozkinan	they fitted yoù
(hari) zegokion	it fitted him	(hari) zegozkion	they fitted him
(guri) zegokigun	it fitted us	(guri) zegozkigun	they fitted us
(zuri) zegokizun	it fitted you	(zuri) zegozkizun	they fitted you
(zuei) zegokizuen	it fitted yoû	(zuei) zegozkizuen	they fitted yoû
(haiei) zegozkien	it fitted them	(haiei) zegozkien	they fitted them

Either alone or coupled with a suitable adverb, such as *ongi* 'well' or *gaizki* 'badly', dative forms of the verbs *egon*, *etorri*, or *joan* can be used to express either the fit or the becomingness of an article of clothing:

(6) Soineko hori ondo doakio/datorkio/dagokio. (*DCV* 1051)
That dress fits her well. (or: becomes her)

Dative forms of the verb *etorri* can mean 'to suit', especially when combined with a suitable adverb:

(7) Ordu hori gaizki datorkit.
That hour does not suit me.

Dative forms of the verb *joan* can mean 'to matter':

(8) Guri zer dihoakigu? (Mt 27:4; Dv)
What does it matter to us?

[*N.B.* Since *-ihoa* is an allowed alternative to the stem *-oa* (cf. section 6.2.3), forms such as *dihoakio* or *dihoakigu* commonly occur as variants of *doakio* or *doakigu*.]

Among the transitive verbs with synthetic dative forms are *ekarri* 'to bring', *eraman* 'to carry (off)', and *eman* 'to give'. Here are some examples:

(9) a. Berri onak al dakarzkiguzu? (1 Kgs 1:42)
Are you bringing us good news?
b. Berri onak dakarzkizut. (2 Sm 18:31)
I am bringing you good news.
c. Etsai gaiztoak daramakio. (Cf. Ax. 561)
The evil enemy is leading her away from him.
d. Agindu berri bat damaizuet. (Jn 13:34; *EAB*)
I am giving yoû a new commandment.
e. Zorion betea damaiot neure maiteari. (Sg 8:10)
I am giving full happiness to my beloved.

[*N.B.* Synthetic forms of *eman* are restricted to the literary language.]

Since dative agreement ensures recoverability, it is not surprising that pro-drop applies to dative pronouns (cf. section 9.5). As a result, one single verb form may represent a sentence containing three arguments:

(10) a. Bagenekarkien.
We were bringing it to them.
b. Badaramazkigute.
They are carrying them away for us. (Or 'from us')

[*N.B.* For the prefix *ba-*, see section 8.6.1.]

15.2 Vestigial Synthetic Dative Forms

The three verbs to be introduced in this section require dative complements. Although they do admit synthetic forms, these have to be considered vestigial in that within contemporary usage they only appear in subordinate clauses or elevated discourse.

15.2.1 Synthetic Forms of *jarraiki*/*jarraitu* 'to follow'

To express the concepts 'to follow', 'to pursue', and 'to continue', northern Basque uses *jarraiki*, and southern Basque *jarraitu*, both also making use of the Romance loan *segitu*, all requiring dative complements. While all of these verbs were originally intransitive, *jarraitu* and *segitu* have now become transitive: *Mutilak neskatxari jarraitu* (*segitu*) *dio* 'The boy has followed the girl'.

Synthetic dative forms of the stem *-rrai-* exist, but are quite rare and confined nowadays to a rather elevated literary style. They have remained intransitive:

(11) a. Idoloak adoratzeari zerraizkion. (*TZ* II, 60)
They continued adoring idols.

b. Honela darraio Umandi: ... (*MEIG* IV, 41 = *MIH* 84)
Umandi continues in this way: ...
c. Eta honela darraio gaiari: ... (*MEIG* VII, 90)
And he pursues the subject in this way: ...

15.2.2 Synthetic Forms of *jario* 'to flow'

Intransitive *jario* 'to flow', 'to emanate', has the future participle *jarioko*, but lacks an imperfect participle. For this, the synonymous verb *jariatu* is resorted to. The verb *jario* requires a dative constituent indicating the source of the flow, while the flowing substance is encoded by the absolutive subject.

Synthetic forms exist; their stem is *-ri-*, and no pre-dative marker appears:

(12) a. Izerdia darit (zeridan).
I am (was) dripping with sweat.
b. Malkoak darizkizu (zerizkizun) begietatik.
Tears are (were) flowing from your eyes.

A few examples taken from the literature follow:

(13) a. Zure aurrean lotsa eta beldurra darie aingeruei. (Añibarro, *E.L.*[3] 144)
In front of you shame and fear emanate from the angels.
b. Neskatxari negar isila zerion. (*LBB* 45)
A silent weeping was emerging from the girl.
c. Zauritik odola zerion gurdiaren zoruraino. (1 Kgs 22:35)
The blood ran out of his wound all the way to the floor of the chariot.
d. Zure ezpainei eztia darie. (Sg 4:11)
Honey drops from your lips.
e. Maitasun-sagarrei usain eztia darie. (Sg 7:14)
A sweet fragrance exudes from the mandrakes (love-apples).
f. Adurra zerion ezpainetatik gaztaia jan nahiaz. (B. Mogel, 58)
The saliva was dripping from his lips from the desire to eat the cheese.
g. Ezekielen begiei sua zerien. (Lertxundi, *Urtero* 187)
Fire flew out of Ezekiel's eyes.

Outside of the literary style, only those forms with a third-person dative marker occur, and then mainly in subordinate clauses.

15.2.3 Synthetic Forms of *atxiki*

Traditionally restricted to the northern dialects, the transitive verb *atxiki* either takes an absolutive object, when it means 'to hold on to', 'to keep', or a dative object, when it means 'to take hold of', 'to grasp', and also 'to be fond of'.

Such synthetic forms as survive require a dative complement and carry the meaning 'to adhere', 'to be attached (to)', in both senses of the term. They are intransitive, and as such seem to correspond to the anticausative use of the verb. The standard paradigms of the Basque Academy show a stem *-txe-* and a pre-dative marker *-ki-*. Given the rarity of these forms, only two examples will be provided:

(14) a. Sua datxekio auzoko etxeari. (Cf. Oihenarte, *Prov.* 672)
Fire is sticking to the neighbor's house. (i.e., the house is burning)
b. Gure txabolak elizari datxezkio.
Our huts are attached to the church.

Although the academy lists a complete paradigm, only *datxekio* and *datxezkio* (or rather their dialectal variants *datxiko* and *datxizko*) occur in common parlance, and only in subordinate clauses.

15.3 Dative Forms of the Auxiliaries

Because of their overwhelming practical importance, the auxiliary paradigms, while quite regular, will be given in full for the convenience of the reader.

15.3.1 Dative Forms of Intransitive *izan* 'to be'

In the past tense dative forms of *izan* we find the regular base form *zitza-* (for which see section 6.2.2) augmented by a vowel *i*, quite possibly a fossilized pre-dative marker: *zitzai-*. This form may have given rise to the present tense base *-tzai*, whose affricate simplifies to *z* in word-initial position.

With the further stipulation that the dative verbal markers are added directly to these verbal bases, the regular formation rules as studied in section 6.2.2 will account for the whole following paradigm, in which I have used *izan* as an auxiliary for the intransitive verb *agertu* 'to appear'.

agertzen da	he appears	agertu zen	he appeared
agertzen zait	he appears to me	agertu zitzaidan	he appeared to me
agertzen zaik	he appears to yoú	agertu zitzaian	he appeared to yoú
agertzen zain	he appears to yoù	agertu zitzainan	he appeared to yoù
agertzen zaio	he appears to him	agertu zitzaion	he appeared to him
agertzen zaigu	he appears to us	agertu zitzaigun	he appeared to us
agertzen zaizu	he appears to you	agertu zitzaizun	he appeared to you
agertzen zaizue	he appears to yoû	agertu zitzaizuen	he appeared to yoû
agertzen zaie	he appears to them	agertu zitzaien	he appeared to them
agertzen dira	they appear	agertu ziren	they appeared
agertzen zaizkit	they appear to me	agertu zitzaizkidan	they appeared to me
agertzen zaizkik	they appear to yoú	agertu zitzaizkian	they appeared to yoú
agertzen zaizkin	they appear to yoù	agertu zitzaizkinan	they appeared to yoù

agertzen zaizkio	they appear to him	agertu zitzaizkion	they appeared to him
agertzen zaizkigu	they appear to us	agertu zitzaizkigun	they appeared to us
agertzen zaizkizu	they appear to you	agertu zitzaizkizun	they appeared to you
agertzen zaizkizue	they appear to yoû	agertu zitzaizkizuen	they appeared to yoû
agertzen zaizkie	they appear to them	agertu zitzaizkien	they appeared to them
agertzen naiz	I appear	agertu nintzen	I appeared
agertzen natzaik	I appear to yoú	agertu nintzaian	I appeared to yoú
agertzen natzain	I appear to yoù	agertu nintzainan	I appeared to yoù
agertzen natzaio	I appear to him	agertu nintzaion	I appeared to him
agertzen natzaizu	I appear to you	agertu nintzaizun	I appeared to you
agertzen natzaizue	I appear to yoû	agertu nintzaizuen	I appeared to yoû
agertzen natzaie	I appear to them	agertu nintzaien	I appeared to them
agertzen haiz	yoú appear	agertu hintzen	yoú appeared
agertzen hatzait	yoú appear to me	agertu hintzaidan	yoú appeared to me
agertzen hatzaio	yoú appear to him	agertu hintzaion	yoú appeared to him
agertzen hatzaigu	yoú appear to us	agertu hintzaigun	yoú appeared to us
agertzen hatzaie	yoú appear to them	agertu hintzaien	yoú appeared to them
agertzen gara	we appear	agertu ginen	we appeared
agertzen gatzaizkik	we appear to yoú	agertu gintzaizkian	we appeared to yoú
agertzen gatzaizkin	we appear to yoù	agertu gintzaizkinan	we appeared to yoù
agertzen gatzaizkio	we appear to him	agertu gintzaizkion	we appeared to him
agertzen gatzaizkizu	we appear to you	agertu gintzaizkizun	we appeared to you
agertzen gatzaizkizue	we appear to yoû	agertu gintzaizkizuen	we appeared to yoû
agertzen gatzaizkie	we appear to them	agertu gintzaizkien	we appeared to them
agertzen zara	you appear	agertu zinen	you appeared
agertzen zatzaizkit	you appear to me	agertu zintzaizkidan	you appeared to me
agertzen zatzaizkio	you appear to him	agertu zintzaizkion	you appeared to him
agertzen zatzaizkigu	you appear to us	agertu zintzaizkigun	you appeared to us
agertzen zatzaizkie	you appear to them	agertu zintzaizkien	you appeared to them
agertzen zarete	yoû appear	agertu zineten	yoû appeared
agertzen zatzaizkidate	yoû appear to me	agertu zintzaizkidaten	yoû appeared to me
agertzen zatzaizkiote	yoû appear to him	agertu zintzaizkioten	yoû appeared to him
agertzen zatzaizkigute	yoû appear to us	agertu zintzaizkiguten	yoû appeared to us
agertzen zatzaizkiete	yoû appear to them	agertu zintzaizkieten	yoû appeared to them

15.3.2 Dative Forms of **edun* 'to have'

Dative forms of **edun* are perfectly regular but for one tiny detail: the stem of the verb is *-i-* instead of *-u-*. There is no pre-dative marker.

Because of their frequent occurrence, I will list all the forms with a third-person singular object, using *eman* 'to give' as the main verb. Since synthetic forms of this verb are not used in the colloquial language, a form such as *ematen dut* means both 'I give' and 'I am giving'. This is the paradigm:

ematen dut	I give it	eman nuen	I gave it
ematen diat	I give it to yoú	eman nian	I gave it to yoú
ematen dinat	I give it to yoù	eman ninan	I gave it to yoù
ematen diot	I give it to him	eman nion	I gave it to him
ematen dizut	I give it to you	eman nizun	I gave it to you
ematen dizuet	I give it to yoû	eman nizuen	I gave it to yoû
ematen diet	I give it to them	eman nien	I gave it to them
ematen duk	yoú give it	eman huen	yoú gave it
ematen didak	yoú give it to me	eman hidan	yoú gave it to me
ematen diok	yoú give it to him	eman hion	yoú gave it to him
ematen diguk	yoú give it to us	eman higun	yoú gave it to us
ematen diek	yoú give it to them	eman hien	yoú gave it to them
ematen dun	yoù give it	eman huen	yoù gave it
ematen didan	yoù give it to me	eman hidan	yoù gave it to me
ematen dion	yoù give it to him	eman hion	yoù gave it to him
ematen digun	yoù give it to us	eman higun	yoù gave it to us
ematen dien	yoù give it to them	eman hien	yoù gave it to them
ematen du	he gives it	eman zuen	he gave it
ematen dit	he gives it to me	eman zidan	he gave it to me
ematen dik	he gives it to yoú	eman zian	he gave it to yoú
ematen din	he gives it to yoù	eman zinan	he gave it to yoù
ematen dio	he gives it to him	eman zion	he gave it to him
ematen digu	he gives it to us	eman zigun	he gave it to us
ematen dizu	he gives it to you	eman zizun	he gave it to you
ematen dizue	he gives it to yoû	eman zizuen	he gave it to yoû
ematen die	he gives it to them	eman zien	he gave it to them
ematen dugu	we give it	eman genuen	we gave it
ematen diagu	we give it to yoú	eman genian	we gave it to yoú
ematen dinagu	we give it to yoù	eman geninan	we gave it to yoù
ematen diogu	we give it to him	eman genion	we gave it to him
ematen dizugu	we give it to you	eman genizun	we gave it to you

ematen dizuegu	we give it to yoû	eman genizuen	we gave it to yoû
ematen diegu	we give it to them	eman genien	we gave it to them
ematen duzu	you give it	eman zenuen	you gave it
ematen didazu	you give it to me	eman zenidan	you gave it to me
ematen diozu	you give it to him	eman zenion	you gave it to him
ematen diguzu	you give it to us	eman zenigun	you gave it to us
ematen diezu	you give it to them	eman zenien	you gave it to them
ematen duzue	yoû give it	eman zenuten	yoû gave it
ematen didazue	yoû give it to me	eman zenidaten	yoû gave it to me
ematen diozue	yoû give it to him	eman zenioten	yoû gave it to him
ematen diguzue	yoû give it to us	eman zeniguten	yoû gave it to us
ematen diezue	yoû give it to them	eman zenieten	yoû gave it to them
ematen dute	they give it	eman zuten	they gave it
ematen didate	they give it to me	eman zidaten	they gave it to me
ematen diate	they give it to yoú	eman ziaten	they gave it to yoú
ematen dinate	they give it to yoù	eman zinaten	they gave it to yoù
ematen diote	they give it to him	eman zioten	they gave it to him
ematen digute	they give it to us	eman ziguten	they gave it to us
ematen dizute	they give it to you	eman zizuten	they gave it to you
ematen dizuete	they give it to yoû	eman zizueten	they gave it to yoû
ematen diete	they give it to them	eman zieten	they gave it to them

With a third-person plural object, the pluralizer *-zki-* will be suffixed to the stem: *ematen dizkiozu* 'you give them to him', *eman zenizkidan* 'you gave them to me', and so on. Dative forms with a first- or second-person object are easily put together: *ematen niozu* 'you give me to him', *ematen gaizkiezue* 'you give us to them', *emango zaizkiot* 'I will give you to him'; and similarly with a synthetically conjugated verb: *banaramakiozu* 'you are leading me to him', *bazaramazkiet* 'I am leading you to them'. For all their morphological transparency, dative forms of this sort, while found in older texts, are now avoided by native speakers everywhere, and therefore absent from the Basque Academy's paradigms. Yet a 1961 Guipuzcoan gospel version still has *Apaizburuek ekarri zaizkidate nigana* (Jn 18:35; *Lau Eb.*) 'The chief priests have brought you to me'.

15.4 Dative Paradigms of Two Transitive Verbs

In view of some slight irregularities in the conjugation of these verbs, full paradigms will be provided for *iritzi* 'to deem' and **ion* 'to say'.

15.4.1 Paradigm of the Verb *iritzi* 'to deem'

The transitive verb *iritzi* 'to deem', 'to consider (as)', requires a dative complement denoting the object of assessment.

(15) Zer irizten die jendeak eskribauei? (*MEIG* I, 72)
What do people think of public notaries?

Synthetic forms of this verb are fairly common. They are based on a stem *-eritz-*, a form derived from *eritzi*, which is the original shape of this verb.

While the Guipuzcoan dialect employs a pre-dative marker *-ki-*, in the standard language the dative markers are added directly to the stem. Since no epenthesis applies before these person markers, sandhi rule 3 of section 1.2.6 comes into play, turning the sequences *tz+da*, *tz+ga*, and *tz+gu* into *zta*, *zka*, and *zku*. The same rule also applies to the nasal stop *n*, so that *tz+na* turns into *zna*.

The theoretical sequence *zka* thus obtained will surface as *-zk* word-finally, and otherwise as *-za-*, according to a peculiarity of the suffix *-ga* already noted in section 9.1: its consonant will elide whenever its vowel *a* does not.

Together with the natural simplification of the sequence *tz+zu* to *tzu*, these processes account for the following paradigm:

derizat	I deem yoú	nerizan	I deemed yoú
deriznat	I deem yoù	neriznan	I deemed yoù
deritzot	I deem him	neritzon	I deemed him
deritzut	I deem you	neritzun	I deemed you
deritzuet	I deem yoû	neritzuen	I deemed yoû
deritzet	I deem them	neritzen	I deemed them
deriztak	yoú deem me	heriztan	yoú deemed me
deritzok	yoú deem him	heritzon	yoú deemed him
derizkuk	yoú deem us	herizkun	yoú deemed us
deritzek	yoú deem them	heritzen	yoú deemed them
deriztan	yoù deem me	heriztan	yoù deemed me
deritzon	yoù deem him	heritzon	yoù deemed him
derizkun	yoù deem us	herizkun	yoù deemed us
deritzen	yoù deem them	heritzen	yoù deemed them
derizt	he deems me	zeriztan	he deemed me
derizk	he deems yoú	zerizan	he deemed yoú
derizna	he deems yoù	zeriznan	he deemed yoù
deritzo	he deems him	zeritzon	he deemed him
derizku	he deems us	zerizkun	he deemed us
deritzu	he deems you	zeritzun	he deemed you

deritzue	he deems yoû	zeritzuen	he deemed yoû
deritze	he deems them	zeritzen	he deemed them
derizagu	we deem yoú	generizan	we deemed yoú
deriznagu	we deem yoù	generiznan	we deemed yoù
deritzogu	we deem him	generitzon	we deemed him
deritzugu	we deem you	generitzun	we deemed you
deritzuegu	we deem yoû	generitzuen	we deemed yoû
deritzegu	we deem them	generitzen	we deemed them
deriztazu	you deem me	zeneriztan	you deemed me
deritzozu	you deem him	zeneritzon	you deemed him
derizkuzu	you deem us	zenerizkun	you deemed us
deritzezu	you deem them	zeneritzen	you deemed them
deriztazue	yoû deem me	zeneriztaten	yoû deemed me
deritzozue	yoû deem him	zeneritzoten	yoû deemed him
derizkuzue	yoû deem us	zenerizkuten	yoû deemed us
deritzezue	yoû deem them	zeneritzeten	yoû deemed them
deriztate	they deem me	zeriztaten	they deemed me
derizate	they deem yoú	zerizaten	they deemed yoú
deriznate	they deem yoù	zeriznaten	they deemed yoù
deritzote	they deem him	zeritzoten	they deemed him
derizkute	they deem us	zerizkuten	they deemed us
deritzute	they deem you	zeritzuten	they deemed you
deritzuete	they deem yoû	zeritzueten	they deemed yoû
deritzete	they deem them	zeritzeten	they deemed them

[*N.B.* In this verb and a few others, the third-person singular dative marker *-o-* may be replaced by *-a-*. Thus, *deritzat*, *deritza*, *deritzate*, and so on may occur instead of *deritzot*, *deritzo*, *deritzote*, and so on. Furthermore, the sequence *-tze* in the third-person plural forms freely alternates with *-zte*.]

Some examples illustrating the use of this verb may be welcome here:

(16) a. Euskara experimentala deritzat Olabideren hizkerari. (*MEIG* II, 112)
I consider Olabide's language experimental Basque.

b. Eta zer deritzazu eskutitzaren mamiari? (Garate, *E.E.* 91)
And what do you think of the contents of the letter?

c. Zorakeria hauei ele-eder deritzate. (Orixe, *Aitork.* 26)
They consider these inanities literature.

d. Zer deritza Pellok ahari honi? Oso ederra deritza. (Oskillaso, *El vasco de hoy* I, 322)
What does Pete think of this ram? He finds it very beautiful.

e. Nik gaizki deritzat etxea saltzeari. (*E.H.* 427)
I think it is bad to sell the house.

When used with an impersonal third-person subject, *iritzi* takes on the meaning 'to be named':

(17) a. Tarte eder honi Urrezko Aldi deritza. (S. Mitxelena, *IG* II, 102)
This beautiful interval is called Age of Gold.
b. Nola deritzu (zuri)? Arantxa derizt (niri).
What are you called? I am called Arantxa.

Intransitive dative forms of this verb, as commonly encountered for this meaning in the Guipuzcoan dialect, are not countenanced by the Basque Academy for the literary standard:

(18) a. *Bolsa honi deritzaio kapulea. (Iturriaga, *Dial.* 6)
This sheath is called *kapule* (cocoon).
b. *Nola deritzaizu? Arantxa deritzait (niri).
What are you called? I am called Arantxa.

At present, impersonal datives of *iritzi* are confined to relative clauses. In other contexts, medio-passives of the verb *deitu* 'to call' or the verb phrase *izena *edun* 'to have the name' are resorted to for the purpose of naming:

(19) a. Nola deitzen zara? Arantxa deitzen naiz.
What (lit. *how*) are you called? I am called Arantxa.
b. Nola (or *zer*) duzu izena? Arantxa dut izena.
What is your name? My name is Arantxa.

15.4.2 Paradigm of the Verb **ion* 'to say'

While not requiring the presence of a dative complement, the verb **ion* 'to say' does have synthetic dative forms. The paradigm exhibits features that seem typical of the Biscayan dialect: an object pluralizer *-z* (actually *-za*) and a pre-dative marker *-ts-*, triggering the operation of sandhi rule 3 of section 1.2.6. By virtue of its application, the sequences *ts+da*, *ts+ga*, and *ts+gu* are simplified to *sta*, *ska*, and *sku*, and, similarly, *ts+na* yields *sna*.

Given the peculiarity of the suffix *-ga* recalled to memory in section 15.4.1, the sequence *ska* will surface as *-sk* in word-final position, and as *-sa-* elsewhere. Since the sequence *ts+zu* naturally turns into *tsu*, the following paradigm results:

diot	I say it	nioen	I said it
diosat	I say it to yoú	niosan	I said it to yoú
diosnat	I say it to yoù	niosnan	I said it to yoù
diotsot	I say it to him	niotson	I said it to him

diotsut	I say it to you	niotsun	I said it to you
diotsuet	I say it to yoû	niotsuen	I said it to yoû
diotset	I say it to them	niotsen	I said it to them
diok	yoú say it	hioen	yoú said it
diostak	yoú say it to me	hiostan	yoú said it to me
diotsok	yoú say it to him	hiotson	yoú said it to him
dioskuk	yoú say it to us	hioskun	yoú said it to us
diotsek	yoú say it to them	hiotsen	yoú said it to them
dion	yoù say it	hioen	yoù said it
diostan	yoù say it to me	hiostan	yoù said it to me
diotson	yoù say it to him	hiotson	yoù said it to him
dioskun	yoù say it to us	hioskun	yoù said it to us
diotsen	yoù say it to them	hiotsen	yoù said it to them
dio	he says it	zioen	he said it
diost	he says it to me	ziostan	he said it to me
diosk	he says it to yoú	ziosan	he said it to yoú
diosna	he says it to yoù	ziosnan	he said it to yoù
diotso	he says it to him	ziotson	he said it to him
diosku	he says it to us	zioskun	he said it to us
diotsu	he says it to you	ziotsun	he said it to you
diotsue	he says it to yoû	ziotsuen	he said it to yoû
diotse	he says it to them	ziotsen	he said it to them
diogu	we say it	genioen	we said it
diosagu	we say it to yoú	geniosan	we said it to yoú
diosnagu	we say it to yoù	geniosnan	we said it to yoù
diotsogu	we say it to him	geniotson	we said it to him
diotsugu	we say it to you	geniotsun	we said it to you
diotsuegu	we say it to yoû	geniotsuen	we said it to yoû
diotsegu	we say it to them	geniotsen	we said it to them
diozu	you say it	zenioen	you said it
diostazu	you say it to me	zeniostan	you said it to me
diotsozu	you say it to him	zeniotson	you said it to him
dioskuzu	you say it to us	zenioskun	you said it to us
diotsezu	you say it to them	zeniotsen	you said it to them
diozue	yoû say it	zenioten	yoû said it

diostazue	yoû say it to me	zeniostaten	yoû said it to me
diotsozue	yoû say it to him	zeniotsoten	yoû said it to him
dioskuzue	yoû say it to us	zenioskuten	yoû said it to us
diotsezue	yoû say it to them	zeniotseten	yoû said it to them
diote	they say it	zioten	they said it
diostate	they say it to me	ziostaten	they said it to me
diosate	they say it to yoú	ziosaten	they said it to yoú
diosnate	they say it to yoù	ziosnaten	they said it to yoù
diotsote	they say it to him	ziotsoten	they said it to him
dioskute	they say it to us	zioskuten	they said it to us
diotsute	they say it to you	ziotsuten	they said it to you
diotsuete	they say it to yoû	ziotsueten	they said it to yoû
diotsete	they say it to them	ziotseten	they said it to them

[*N.B.* In this paradigm as in that of *iritzi*, the third-person singular dative marker -*o*- may be replaced by -*a*-: *diotsot* or *diotsat*, *geniotson* or *geniotsan*, and so on.]

Dative forms of **ion* are exceptional in that the object pluralizer -*z*- follows the ergative person markers (with the exception of -*ga* and -*na*), not the stem: *diotsudaz* 'I say them to you', *niotsuzan* 'I said them to you', and so on.

Incidentally, the past tense forms show that the full form of this pluralizer is -*za*, not just -*z*, in which case the form would have been **niotsuzen*. This observation is further corroborated by the forms *diostazak* 'yoú say them to me' and *diostazan* 'yoù say them to me', where the pluralizer precedes the ergative markers, in contrast to what happens with all other ergative markers: *diostazuz* 'you say them to me', *diotsuguz* 'we say them to you', *diotsodaz* 'I say them to him', and so on.

15.5 Some Issues of Dative Syntax

15.5.1 The Possessive Dative

As noted at the end of section 15.1, dative pronouns do not need to be spelled out, since a compact agreement marker on the finite verb provides a sufficient clue to their underlying presence. It is clear that such implicit dative pronouns are a great asset to the language. One aim for which these are put to work is to avoid the use of possessive pronouns, a category which Basque, even more so than Spanish, seems to somewhat disapprove of. Thus a dative verb form can replace the possessor of an ergative subject (example 20), an absolutive subject (examples 21a,b), an absolutive object (examples 22a,b), and various more or less peripheral noun phrases (examples 23a,b). Needless to say, the strategy can be applied only when the clause in question does not already contain a dative complement.

(20) Dardar degit barruak. (Sg 5:4)
My insides tremble. (Dardar dagi nire barruak.)

(21) a. Zauria sendatu al zaio? (*LBB* 144)
Did his wound heal? (Bere zauria sendatu al da?)
b. Hizkuntza larri dabilkigu. (*MEIG* VII, 172)
Our language is in a crisis. (Gure hizkuntza larri dabil.)

(22) a. Semea hil didak. (Atxaga, *Gizona* 346)
Yoú have killed my son. (Nire semea hil duk.)
b. Gaixotu egiten dizkidazu nerbioak. (Atxaga, *Gizona* 172)
You are overstraining my nerves. (Gaixotu egiten dituzu nire nerbioak.)

(23) a. Poliziak atzetik dihoazkio. (Garate, *NY* 53)
The policemen go after him. (Poliziak haren atzetik dihoaz.)
b. Labaindu egin zitzaion gutuna eskuetatik. (Atxaga, *Obab*. 314)
The letter slipped out of his hands. (Labaindu egin zen gutuna haren eskuetatik.)

[*N.B.* Nonavoidance of possessive pronouns does not lead to ungrammaticality. The parenthesized alternatives may be less idiomatic, but they are fully grammatical.]

15.5.2 The Dative and the Middle Voice

The presence of a dative complement is no impediment to the use of the middle voice. Medio-passives including a dative are by no means uncommon:

(24) a. Ez zaizue lastorik emango. (Ex 5:18)
No straw will be given to yoû.
b. Dena kentzen zaigu.
Everything is being taken away from us.

Medio-reflexives with a dative complement also occur in literature:

(25) a. Ematen natzaizu osoki eta behin betikoz. (Jnn., *SBi* 386)
I give myself to you totally and once and for all.
b. Nire etsai higuinari eman hatzaio. (Duhalde, 146)
Yoú have given yoúrself to my detested enemy.

15.5.3 Dative Agreement and the Modal Verbs

Characteristic for the construction named direct infinitival complementation in section 14.3.1 is that it behaves as one single clause, so that agreement between its noun phrases and the modal verb complex is compulsory in the standard language:

(26) a. Eutsi egin nahi zien amets-irudi haiei. (Atxaga, *Gizona* 9)
He wanted to hold on to those dream images.

b. Zer esan behar diot orain Pili-ri? (*LBB* 125)
What am I to say now to Pili?

Here, dative auxiliary forms must be employed, although semantically those dative noun phrases do not belong to the modal main verb, but to the lower verbs *eutsi* and *esan*.

Against this background, an interesting fact was pointed out by Goenaga (1985b). As noted in sections 14.3.1 and 14.5.1, the majority usage in the standard language is for the modal verbs to be opaque, that is, to be transitive regardless of the nature of the lower verb. But, as Goenaga noticed, the appearance of a dative complement renders a modal verb transparent: an intransitive lower verb will then induce an intransitive auxiliary form:

(27) a. Usoa haurrari hurbildu nahi zaio. (Goenaga 1985b, 951)
The pigeon wants to get closer to the child.
b. Zama lurrera erori behar zaio. (Cf. *EGLU* II, 452)
His burden is going to fall onto the ground.

Without a dative complement, we would have instead

(28) a. Usoak hurbildu nahi du.
The pigeon wants to get closer.
b. Zamak lurrera erori behar du.
The burden is going to fall onto the ground.

15.5.4 Dative versus Absolutive Government

Whether a particular verb takes an absolutive or a dative object is usually obvious from its meaning and thus tends to agree with the behavior of its English counterpart, if there is one.

There are just a few commonly used verbs that need some commentary:

1. The verb *begiratu* 'to look' can occur without any complement, but when it does have one, it must be either a dative or an allative phrase:

(29) a. Luisek berriro begiratzen du. (Urretabizkaia, *Sat.* 13)
Louis looks again.
b. Luisek neskari begiratzen dio. (Urretabizkaia, *Sat.* 13)
Louis looks at the girl.
c. Lopez-Mendizabal-eren hiztegira begiratu dugu. (*TOE* I, 102)
We have looked in Lopez-Mendizabal's dictionary.

2. In the standard language, the verb *deitu* 'to call' indifferently allows a dative or an absolutive object. In the Biscayan dialect it takes dative objects, in Guipuzcoan dative or absolutive ones, and in all other dialects absolutive ones only.

(30) a. Leihotik deitu zion (zuen). (*E.H.* 182)
He called him from the window.

b. Margo deitzen du. (Larzabal, *Senp.* 132)
She calls Margo.

3. With the verb *eskertu* 'to thank', a dative refers to the person thanked, while the absolutive denotes the favor received. When the latter is omitted, the person thanked can be the absolutive object.

(31) a. Askoz eskertzen dizut liburua.
I thank you very much for the book.
b. Nola ez Jauna eskertu? (Uztapide, *Sas.* 125)
How (could we) not thank the Lord?

4. For both meanings of the verb *lagundu* 'to accompany', 'to help', Biscayan and Guipuzcoan prefer a dative complement, the other dialects an absolutive one. The standard language allows either:

(32) a. Etxera lagundu dizut/zaitut (*EGLU* II, 26)
I have accompanied you home.
b. Jaunak laguntzen die. (Ps 37:40)
The Lord helps them.
c. Jaunak lagunduko ditu. (Ps 36:40; Dv)
The Lord will help them.

5. For the use of the verb *utzi* 'to leave', see section 16.3.1.

15.6 Particularities of the Verb *eman*

The verb *eman*, with the basic meaning 'to give' (in the Labourdin and Navarrese dialects also used for 'to put'), is, after *egin* 'to do' and *izan* 'to be', the third most frequently used verb in Basque. Given this prominence, certain particulars regarding its use and meaning in various contexts should find a place in this grammar. Only those usages that are sufficiently widespread to be deemed part of the standard language will be considered. Other minor ones can be found in the *DGV* (VI, 628–631).

15.6.1 *Eman* Expressing Indulgence in a Habit

With the meaning 'to give oneself up (to)', 'to indulge (in)', *eman* occurs in phrases of the following type:

alferkeriari eman	to indulge in laziness
ardoari eman	to indulge in wine
drogari eman	to indulge in drugs
jokoari eman	to take up gambling
tabernari eman	to take to frequenting pubs
zurrutari eman	to take to excessive drinking

Such phrases are usually given an ergative subject as in example (33a), but the intransitive form (33b) also has its partisans:

(33) a. Alkateak drogari eman zion.
The mayor took to drugs.
b. Alkatea drogari eman zitzaion.
The mayor took to drugs.

These alternatives can be explained on the same assumptions that will also account for a slightly more general case in the next subsection, namely, that (33a) is based on an understood object noun phrase *bere burua* 'himself' and that (33b) is a medio-reflexive (for which see section 12.5.2).

15.6.2 Inceptive Use of *eman* and *ekin*

Since a habit can be viewed as a particular sequence of activities repeated by the same performer, use of *eman* to denote the transition to a single activity appears to be a natural extension of the preceding usage. The activity in question is encoded by a nominalized clause whose subject coincides with that of the main verb (namely, *eman*) and remains therefore unexpressed. The nominalization serves as the indirect object of *eman*, hence its dative case marker:

(34) a. Orduan ibaia igarotzeari eman zioten. (*TZ* I, 176)
Then they proceeded to cross the river.
b. Eskuak garbitzeari eman zitzaion. (*TB*, 126)
He proceeded to wash his hands.

It appears that the 19th-century author Francisco Ignacio de Lardizabal (1806–1855), from whom these examples are taken, felt free to choose in this construction either a transitive or an intransitive frame. Indeed, the intransitive (34b) is an obvious medio-reflexive, and, as for (34a), the assumption of an understood (strongly) reflexive direct object *beren burua* will account for its transitive structure—given that a plural subject may license a singular reflexive, as will be seen in section 15.7. Comparable constructions with overt reflexives, such as *alferkeriari bere burua eman* 'to give oneself up to laziness' are well attested in the older literature, albeit by now all but obsolete. Moreover, a parallel development is found in English, where *indulging oneself* and *engaging oneself in something* lose their reflexives and turn into *indulging* and *engaging in something* tout court.

When the activity involved corresponds to an *egin* idiom (section 13.3), the expected verbal noun *egite* is omitted and the dative ending *-ari* attaches directly to the activity noun. Common examples of the resulting idiom are

barreari eman	to break into laughter
bideari eman	to take to the road
eztulari eman	to start coughing

ihesari eman	to take to flight
korrikari eman	to start running
lanari eman	to set to work
lasterrari eman	to break into a sprint
negarrari eman	to break into tears

In current usage, the intransitive form of these locutions has all but disappeared, and even the transitive form is restricted to the literary style, the colloquial preferring other expressions, such as those using the verb *ekin*, to which we will now shift our attention.

The primary sense of the verb *ekin* is 'to tackle', as in *etsaiari ekin* 'to tackle the enemy'. The meaning of 'applying oneself to a task' is thereby included.

As with *eman*, the indirect object can be a nominalized clause, but also allowed are noun phrases in general, not merely nouns corresponding to *egin* idioms:

(35) a. Legeak ikasteari ekin nion Deustuko Unibertsitatean. (Garate, *Hades* 63)
I applied myself to studying law at the University of Deusto.
b. Azkenean kanpoan ere lapurretari ekingo dio. (Garate, *NY* 67)
At the end he will engage in thievery outdoors too.
c. Ekin nion, beraz, igoerari. (Atxaga, *Obab*. 330)
So I set out upon the ascent.

In contemporary Batua, the meaning of *ekin* has weakened to that of mere inception, no longer implying much application or effort on the part of the subject, which, however, must be animate, unlike that of the verb *hasi* 'to begin'. For instance,

(36) a. Beste emisora bat bilatzeari ekin zion. (Atxaga, *Gizona* 330)
He started to look for another radio station.
b. Isilaldi bati ekin zion. (Atxaga, *Behi* 59)
He commenced a moment of silence.

The Basque Academy (*Euskera* 22 [1977], 809) has listed paradigms for synthetic forms of *ekin*. They are intransitive: *nakio* 'I apply myself to it', *gakizkio* 'we apply ourselves to it', *nenkion* 'I applied myself to it', *genkizkion* 'we applied ourselves to it', and so on. As of now, modern usage has not revived these archaic forms.

In the northern dialects, intransitively used *lotu* 'to attach oneself' is employed instead of *ekin*: *lanari lotu* 'to set to work'.

15.6.3 Metaphoric *eman*

Basque usage embodies an interesting metaphor by which thoughts and projects are presented as gifts originating from certain human organs, such as *barru* 'inner self', *bihotz* 'heart', *buru* 'head', and *gogo* 'mind'. Being the subject of *eman*, the organ noun has the form of a definite ergative, while the content of the thought is expressed by an absolutive noun phrase, or perhaps more often, a finite complement clause (for which see chapter 19). Some examples are

(37) a. Hori guztia eman zidan buruak.
All that has occurred to me.
b. Ematen zidan niri barruak. (Garate, *E.E.* 139)
I was thinking that.
c. Gogoak eman zion bilatzea Ahias profeta. (*TZ* II, 60)
It occurred to him to seek out the prophet Ahias.

[*N.B. Gogoak eman* can also mean 'to feel like (doing something)'.]

15.6.4 *Eman* Indicating Appearance

When used without a dative complement, the verb *eman* can express outward appearance:

(38) a. Zeruak maindire zikin bat ematen zuen. (Atxaga, *Z.H.* 32)
The sky looked like a dirty sheet.
b. Txorimaloa ematen duzu.
You look like a scarecrow.
c. Denak ematen zuen berri. (Atxaga, *Gizona* 42)
Everything looked like new.
d. Hala ematen du.
It looks that way.
e. Ez dugu ondo emango. (Uztapide, *Sas.* 202)
We won't look good.

15.6.5 Time-related *eman*

With a direct object denoting a period of time, *eman* translates as 'to pass' or 'spend':

(39) a. Oso aldi ederra eman genuen. (Garate, *NY* 27)
We passed a very nice time.
b. Goiz osoa kanpoan eman zenuen? (Garate, *Esku* 95)
Did you spend the whole morning outside?

15.6.6 Bare Noun Objects of *eman*

Comparable to the *egin* idioms studied in section 13.3, there are also *eman* idioms, where a bare noun acts as a direct object to this verb. In many instances, use of the article is also possible, and sometimes more common. Thus one gets *aurpegi eman* or *aurpegia eman* 'to resist', *belarri eman* or *belarria eman* 'to give ear', *bizkar eman* or *bizkarra eman* 'to turn one's back', *bular eman* or *bularra eman* 'to breast-feed', *gogo eman* or *gogoa eman* 'to pay attention', and so on.

The main examples are:

abisu	advice, notice	abisu eman	to notify
adore	courage, spunk	adore eman	to encourage, to stimulate
aholku	advice	aholku eman	to advise
amore	love, yielding	amore eman	to give in, to yield
antz	likeness	antz eman	to make out, to recognize, to notice
argi	light	argi eman	to give light, to illuminate
arnasa	breath	arnasa eman	to blow, to stimulate
aterpe	shelter	aterpe eman	to give shelter, to shelter
atseden	rest	atseden eman	to give rest
atsegin	pleasure	atsegin eman	to give pleasure
atsekabe	sorrow	atsekabe eman	to cause sorrow, to distress
aurpegi	face	aurpegi eman	to face, to resist
auzi	lawsuit	auzi eman	to sue
axola	worry, importance	axola eman	to attach importance
begi	eye	begi eman	to consider, to look at
belarr	ear	belarri eman	to give ear, to listen
berri	news	berri eman	to inform, to notify
bide	way, road	bide eman	to give the opportunity, to enable
bihotz	heart	bihotz eman	to encourage, to cheer up
bizkar	back	bizkar eman	to turn one's back
branka	prow	branka eman	to face
bular	breast	bularra eman	to breast-feed
buru	head	buru eman	to finish, to resist
damu	regret, remorse	damu eman	to cause regret
esku	hand	esku eman	to give a hand, to help
fede	trust, faith	fede eman	to trust, to attest
gibel	backside, liver	gibel eman	to turn one's back, to despise
gogo	mind	gogo eman	to pay attention, to mind
haize	wind	haize eman	to blow
harrika	lapidation	harrika eman	to stone
hats	breath	hats eman	to blow
higuin	disgust	higuin eman	to cause disgust
hitz	word	hitz eman	to promise
huts	void, fault	huts eman	to fail, to let down, to disappoint
indar	strength	indar eman	to give strength
kasu	attention	kasu eman	to pay attention, to watch
kontu	account	kontu eman	to give account, to report
leku	place, site	leku eman	to give place, to welcome

lotsa	shame	lotsa eman	to put to shame, to shame
lur	earth	lur eman	to bury
min	pain	min eman	to hurt
muin	kiss (not on face)	muin eman	to kiss
musu	kiss	musu eman	to kiss
ostatu	inn, tavern	ostatu eman	to lodge, to house
pena	sorrow, grief	pena eman	to cause grief
pot	kiss	pot eman	to kiss
poz	joy	poz eman	to delight, to gladden
su	fire	su eman	to set on fire, to give a light

Examples (40a,b) show that the object noun can be postponed to the verb, and examples (40c,d) display the partitive, which is, however, never obligatory in these idioms.

(40) a. Agian, horregatik ematen zion beti musu sudurrean. (Urretabizkaia, *Sat.* 7)
Perhaps, that is why she always kissed him on the nose.
b. Eman zien su eta bota zituen azeriak filistearren garisoroetara. (Jgs 15:5)
He set them on fire and threw the foxes into the cornfields of the Philistines.
c. Ez diot amorerik eman. (*MEIG* VIII, 134 = *MIH* 212)
I have not yielded to it.
d. Besteari antzik ez zion eman. (Irazusta, *Bizia* 122)
He did not make out the other one.

[*N.B.* Notwithstanding example (40d) (dating from 1950), it is far more common to employ an inseparable verb *antzeman*, see *DGV* II, 173–174 and *E.H.* 46.]

15.7 Strongly Reflexive Nominals

A strongly reflexive nominal in Basque consists of the noun *buru*, which normally means 'head', preceded by a possessive pronoun and followed by the article *-a* (plural *-ak*) or, much more rarely, a demonstrative corresponding to the first or second person.

With an antecedent in the third person, the possessive used will be *bere* or its plural *beren*; otherwise, the personal reflexives introduced in section 6.1.3 (*neure*, *heure*, *geure*, *zeure*, *zeuen*) are preferred, though the unmarked possessives (*nire*, *hire*, *gure*, *zure*, *zuen*) also occur, especially in the northern dialects.

A strongly reflexive nominal must be case-marked in the usual way. It will trigger third-person agreement in the verb, whatever the person features of the antecedent, which, as a rule, denotes an animate being, but can also be inanimate. Some examples follow:

(41) a. Nik hala esan nion neure buruari: . . . (Atxaga, *Bi Let.* 48)
I said to myself thus: . . .

b. Ezagutzen al duzu zeure burua? (Garate, *Hades* 39)
Do you know yourself?
c. Suak jan egiten zuen bere burua. (Atxaga, *Obab.* 51)
The fire ate itself up.
d. Bere burua hil behar ote du? (Jn 8:22)
Is he going to kill himself, one wonders?
e. Zergatik bota nahi zenuen zeure burua? (Atxaga, *Behi* 172)
Why did you want to throw yourself away?

Some speakers allow an evaluative adjective to follow *buru*: *bere buru gaixoa* 'his poor self', *neure buru triste hau* 'this sad self of mine'.

In the event of a plural antecedent, a singular reflexive is nowadays preferred, although a plural one remains acceptable. The following examples illustrate this point:

(42) a. Beren burua eman dute. (2 Cor 8:5; *Biblia*)
They have given themselves.
b. Jaunari eman zizkioten beren buruak. (2 Cor 8:5)
They gave themselves to the Lord.

(43) a. Geure burua engainatzen dugu. (1 Jn 1:8)
We are deceiving ourselves.
b. Geure buruak engainatzen ditugu. (1 Jn 1:8; *IB*)
We are deceiving ourselves.

Despite a coreferential antecedent within the same clause, a nominal cannot be strongly reflexive unless it also counts as an argument of the verb. Noun phrases, thus also all dative nominals (see section 5.3), automatically qualify, but postpositional phrases may be nuclear or peripheral, depending on the argument structure of the verb. Under coreference, peripheral nominals will appear as weak reflexives only; that is to say, their form will be based on the anaphor *bera* (cf. section 6.1.5) for the third person or its personal counterparts *neu*, *heu*, *geu*, *zeu*, and *zeuek* for the other persons. Instead of these five, we may also find unmarked pronouns, especially in the northern dialects.

The following examples show weak reflexives:

(44) a. Ardo hau beretzat gorde nahi du.
He wants to keep this wine for himself.
b. Zuhaitzek erregea izendatu nahi zuten berentzat. (Jgs 9:8)
The trees wanted to appoint a king for themselves.
c. Utzi ditut neuretzat zazpi mila gizon. (Rom 11:4)
I have left for myself seven thousand men.

In the matter of choosing between weak and strong reflexives, disagreements between native speakers are not uncommon. Most likely, they stem from differences in argument structure as internalized by individual speakers. Thus, examples (45b,c), and to a lesser extent (46b), are acceptable to some, but not to others:

(45) a. Zer diozu zeure buruaz? (Jn 1:22)
What do you say about yourself?
b. Zer diozu zutaz? (Jn 1:22; Ker)
What do you say about yourself?
c. Zutaz zer diozu? (Jn 1:22; *JKBO*)
What do you say about yourself?

(46) a. Neure buruarekin haserre nago.
I am angry with myself.
b. Neurekin haserre nago. (Northern form: *Nitaz haserre naiz.*)
I am angry with myself.

In the genitive case form as well, the use of weak versus strong reflexives—*bere* versus *bere buruaren*, *neure* versus *neure buruaren*, and so on—is governed by a strict locality rule, the choice being left to the convenience of the speaker in only a few exceptional contexts.

When a strong reflexive occurs as a genitival modifier, it must find its semantic justification within the very noun phrase to which it belongs. Accordingly, we can have *bere buruaren etsai hori* 'that enemy of himself', *bere buruaren jabe* (*bat*) '(a) master of himself', *zeure buruaren hondamena* 'your self-inflicted downfall', *neure buruaren ardura* 'my care for myself', *beren buruen nazka* 'the loathing for themselves', and *bere buruaren argazkia* 'the self-taken photograph of himself'.

When this condition is not met, weak reflexives will appear. Even under coreference with the subject of the clause, it will be *bere etxea* 'his (own) house', and likewise *bere argazkia* 'his (own) photograph', which may well refer to a picture of himself, provided it was taken by someone else.

There are two contexts where strong genitival reflexives may occur contrary to the rule just given. The most general one is the genitival complement of a location noun or postposition, provided the location noun is not employed in a strict spatiotemporal sense. Thus, one gets *bere buruaren gainean* 'over (about) himself', *bere buruaren alde* 'in his own favor', and *bere buruaren kontra* 'against himself'; but only *bere gainean* 'on top of himself', *bere aldean* 'next to himself', and *bere atzean* 'behind himself'; whereas *bere buruaren atzean* can only mean 'behind his head'.

The other exceptional context is defined by idiomatic phrases of the type *norbaiten berri jakin* 'to know about somebody', *zerbaiten berri eman* 'to give information about something', *zerbaiten kontu eman* 'to give an account of something'. Choosing a strong reflexive inside these phrases allows the speaker to clarify that the intended coreference applies to the subject of the clause in question and not to some previous noun phrase, as permitted in the southern dialects if a weak reflexive like *bere* were to be used. (See section 6.1.5.)

For the antecedent of a strong reflexive to be the subject of its clause is overwhelmingly common. Yet when there is an experiencer distinct from the subject, this experiencer will often be the only possible antecedent. Hence, there can be dative antecedents:

(47) a. Euskaldun ona izateko, eskas ageri zait neure burua zenbait aldetatik. (*MEIG* II, 92)
To be a good Basque, my own self appears to me deficient in certain respects.
b. Pellori ez zaio bere burua atsegin.
Pete doesn't like himself. (Lit. "To Pete, his own self is not pleasing.")
c. Mireni bere burua erakutsi nion ispiluan.
I showed Mary herself in the mirror.

In these examples the anaphoric relation is irreversible: an absolutive noun phrase cannot serve as an antecedent to a dative experiencer.

As we saw in section 12.1.11, the absolutive object of an emotive verb represents the experiencer and the ergative subject the cause or source of the experience. Here too, only the experiencer can act as an antecedent. A striking consequence is the appearance of strong reflexives in the ergative case:

(48) a. Neure buruak kezkatu eta izutzen nau.
My own self worries and frightens me.
b. Zeuen buruek zoratzen zaituztete.
Yoûr own selves are driving yoû crazy.
c. Bere buruak liluratzen du nire anaia. (Saltarelli, 113)
His own self fascinates my brother.

Even with some nonemotive verbs ergative strong reflexives can be found:

(49) a. Zeure buruak egin zaitu esklabo, ez beste inork. (Saltarelli, 113)
Your own self has made you a slave, no one else.
b. Neure buruak ere ematen dit franko lan. (*TOE* I, 92)
My own self too is giving me plenty of work.
c. Neure buruak gidatu nau.
My own self has guided me.

With most verbs, however, ergative strong reflexives are ruled out. Examples like (50a,b) meet with near universal rejection:

(50) a. *Neure buruak gorrotatzen nau.
My own self hates me.
b. *Neure buruak ere ez dit hori barkatuko.
Even my own self won't forgive me that.

The following example, accepted by some and rejected by others, shows a modifier of the subject acting as the antecedent for a strong reflexive:

(51) Zure amets haiek zeure buruari kalte egingo diote. (Cf. Saltarelli, 110)
Those dreams of yours will harm you. (Lit. 'yourself')

For logophoric use, Basque prefers weak reflexives (*neu*, *heu*, *bera*, etc.) or emphatic pronouns (*nerau*, *herori*, etc.), although in this function strong reflexives can be occasionally encountered in the literature, including Mitxelena's writings, for example, *MEIG* VII, 37, middle of second paragraph.

A short bibliographical note will end this section: With the sole exception of Saltarelli 1988 (pp. 104–120), existing grammars (even *EGLU*) say very little about the use of *bere burua*. The fairly detailed survey of textual data in the *DGV* (V, 671–675) is all the more welcome, even though the syntactic analysis remains superficial and some examples of nonreflexive *buru* have been allowed to creep in. Readers familiar with early government and binding theory may wish to consult Salaburu 1986.

15.8 Reciprocals

In Basque, reciprocity can be expressed in two ways: analytically, using an anaphoric phrase *bata bestea*, literally 'the one the other'; or synthetically, with the help of the anaphoric noun *elkar* 'each other'. This too originated as an analytic expression: *hark-har*, according to a plausible etymology proposed by Uhlenbeck (1927).

As true anaphors, both require a higher ranking antecedent in the same clause. Therefore, in sharp contrast to what we saw for *bere burua*, a reciprocal cannot be the subject of its clause, hence the lack of an ergative case form. For the same reason, a reciprocal appearing in the absolutive case must have the subject as an antecedent—again, unlike *bere burua*. In the event of an oblique reciprocal, either the direct object (as in example 52) or again the subject will act as the antecedent. Indeed, I have found no examples in which a dative or a postpositional phrase serves as an antecedent to a reciprocal anaphor. (Cf. *E.H.* 213.)

Another difference between reciprocals and strong reflexives is that the former need not be arguments of the verb, but can be peripheral nominals:

(52) Haiek ez ditu Jainkoak bata bestearentzat (elkarrentzat) egin. (Zapirain, *M.* 90)
Those, God has not made for each other.

15.8.1 The Synthetic Reciprocal *elkar*

The reciprocal anaphor *elkar* declines like an indefinite noun phrase (*elkarri*, *elkarren*, *elkarrekin*, etc.) and triggers third-person singular agreement in the verb, regardless of the nature of its antecedent, which is normally plural, although indefinites like *inork* are also acceptable. The anaphor contrasts with pronouns in having only a short form for the instrumental: *elkarrez*, never **elkarretaz* (cf. section 6.1.3). Syntactically, the word *elkar* must be regarded as an inherently animate noun, as it requires the presence of the formative *-gan* (optionally preceded by the genitive) in the locative cases, even when the antecedent is inanimate:

(53) a. Aitonak bereizten zituen . . . elkarrengandik ahotza eta gari-alea. (T. Agirre, *Uzt.* 159)
Grandfather separated the chaff and the grain from each other.
b. Liburu horiek bakandu behar dira elkarrengandik. (*EGLU* I, 351)
Those books must be kept apart from each other.

[*N.B.* Perhaps by force of analogy, the same constraint applies when *bata bestea* is used instead of *elkar*: *bata bestea(ren)gandik*, never **bata bestetik*.]

Further examples of the use of elkar follow:

(54) a. Elkar engainatzen dute. (Jer 9:4)
They cheat each other.
b. Elkar saldu eta gorrotatuko dute. (Mt 24:10)
They will betray and hate each other.
c. Zuek elkar dirudizue. (J. A. Mogel, *Ip.* 132 [52])
Yoû resemble each other.
d. Gure bi etxeek elkar ukitzen dute. (*EHM* 1066)
Our two houses touch each other.
e. Elkarri idazten genion. (*MEIG* IX, 95)
We were writing to each other.
f. Musu eman zioten elkarri. (Atxaga, *Gizona* 344)
They kissed each other.
g. Elkarri aurkeztu genizkion adiskide ez-ezagunak. (Garate, *Musk.* 50)
We introduced the unacquainted friends to each other.
h. Miren eta Xabier elkarrenganantz bultzatu ditut.
I have pushed Mary and Xavier toward each other.
i. Elkarrekin maitemindu ziren. (Garate, *NY* 141)
They fell in love with each other.

The sociative *elkarrekin* (but not *bata bestearekin*) also functions as the normal counterpart of the English adverb *together*:

(55) a. Elkarrekin egiten al dute lo? (Atxaga, *Bi An.* 24)
Do they sleep together?
b. Gurasoek elkarrekin ikusi gaituzte. (*E.H.* 213)
The parents have seen us together.
c. Elkarrekin afaldu genuen "Artzak" jatetxean. (Garate, *Alaba* 26)
We dined together in the restaurant "Artzak."

The use of the form *elkarren* as a genitival modifier is subject to considerable variation between speakers, many of them conforming to a narrow system, while others follow a broad system, and still others, it seems, are guided by some intermediate system. Only the extremes, the narrow and the broad system, will be described here.

In the narrow system, the use of *elkarren* is roughly similar to that of *bere buruaren*. That is, outside of a few special contexts, the use of *elkarren* must be justified within the very noun phrase it is a part of. This will usually be the case when the modifier *elkarren* can be glossed in English as *mutual* or *reciprocal*. Thus, in the narrow system, *elkarren* typically modifies relational nouns: *elkarren adiskideak* 'friends with each other', *elkarren anaiak* 'brothers to each other', *elkarren antza* 'a likeness to each other', that is, 'a mutual likeness' (cf. *DGV* VI, 590).

Paramount among the exceptional contexts allowing *elkarren* to refer back to the subject or object of the minimal clause containing it is the genitival complement of a location noun or postposition, this time without any restriction whatsoever. Examples are *elkarren alde* 'in favor of each other', *elkarren aldean* 'next to each other', *elkarren artean* 'between each other', *elkarren atzean* 'behind each other', *elkarren gainean* 'about each other' or 'on top of each other', and *elkarren kontra* 'against each other'. The other context to be adduced is that provided by certain idiomatic verb phrases, as exemplified by *elkarren berri jakin* 'to know about each other', *elkarren kontu eman* 'to give an account of each other', and so on.

Whenever this system fails to license the use of *elkarren*, its followers will avail themselves of the synonymous phrase *bata bestearen*.

For the adherents of the broad system, *elkarren* and *bata bestearen* are interchangeable in all contexts. For them, *elkarren* is similar to *elkar* itself, in that its antecedent can be the subject or object of the minimal clause containing the noun phrase modified by *elkarren*. From the many examples cited in the *DGV* (VI, 590) violating the narrow system, I only quote two:

(56) a. Ezagutzen ditugu elkarren ahotsak. (Uztapide, *Sas*. 262)
We know each other's voices.

b. ... elkarren begietatik amodioa edanaz. (Bilintx, 78 [*Juramentuba* III])
... drinking love from each other's eyes.

15.8.2 Analytic Reciprocals

Reciprocal *bata bestea* 'each other' must be carefully distinguished from its etymological source *bata ... bestea* 'the one ... the other', which contains two syntactically independent noun phrases, each to be declined separately. In the reciprocal form, however, *bata* is inseparable from *bestea*, which carries the case ending of the whole unit, declined like a definite singular noun phrase. Thus, contrast the nonreciprocal example (57a) with the reciprocal (57b):

(57) a. Batak bestea maite du.
The one loves the other.
b. Gurasoek bata bestea maite dute.
The parents love each other.

When the antecedent is ergative, as in (57b), then there exists also a hybrid form (57c) containing two noun phrases: *batak*, displaying the antecedent's ergative case, and *bestea*, with the absolutive case marking proper to the object of the verb:

(57) c. Gurasoek batak bestea maite dute.
The parents love each other.

This construction with its plural verb form will be called a quasi reciprocal. Another instance of it is (58b), as opposed to the true reciprocal in (58a):

(58) a. Bata bestea maite dugu.
We love each other.
b. Batak bestea maite dugu.
We love each other.

[*N.B.* Another quasi-reciprocal construction, *bakoitzak bestea* 'each the other', current in certain areas of Biscay, is not part of the standard language.]

Except perhaps for the genitival form, reciprocal *bata bestea* occurs much less frequently than its synonym *elkar*. Still, examples from both contemporary and older literature are not hard to find:

(59) a. ... bata bestea galtzeko beldurra. (Urretabizkaia, *Asp*. 36)
... the fear of losing each other.
b. Egipto guztian inork ere, bata bestea ez zuen ikusten. (*TZ* I, 114)
In the whole of Egypt, nobody could see each other.
c. Atal guztiak bata besteaz arduratzen dira. (1 Cor 12:25)
All parts care for each other.
d. Bata bestearekin ez haserretzeko, ... (Ax. 314)
In order not to get angry at each other, ...
e. Mila kilometrotara geunden bata bestearengandik. (Mintegi, 106)
We were a thousand kilometers from each other.
f. Gertakariak agudo bata bestearen gainera datoz. (*TOE* III, 151)
The events are coming fast on top of each other.

As is clear from examples such as (59c), the antecedent of *bata bestea* may denote any number of referents, and not just two, as the singular form of *bata bestea* might suggest. There exists, however, an optional plural form *batzuk besteak*:

(60) a. Hark batzuk besteengandik bereizi egingo ditu. (Mt 25:32)
He will divide them from each other.

b. Hala ez ziren batzuek besteengana hurbildu. (Ex 14:20)
That way, they didn't come near to each other.

Another version of this Exodus text, that of *Biblia*, employs the singular form *bat bestearengana*, *bat bestea* being an alternative for *bata bestea* in the eastern dialects.

15.9 Compounds with *buru* and *elkar*

15.9.1 Compounds with *buru* 'self'

Among the many compounds with *buru* as a first member, there are only very few where *buru* means 'self' rather than 'head'. These are mostly adjectives:

iritzi	opinion	buruiritzi	conceited
jabe	owner, master	burujabe	autonomous, independent
zale	devotee, lover	buruzale	egoistic, selfish

15.9.2 Compounds with *elkar*

Nominal compounds with *elkar* as the first member have been created, mostly in the 20th century, to express some useful concepts:

bide	road, way	elkarbide	connection
bizitza	life	elkarbizitza	life together, symbiosis
ekintza	action, deed	elkarrekintza	interaction
gune	stretch, spot	elkargune	junction, intersection
hizketa	speech	elkarrizketa	dialogue, conversation, interview
kide	member, counterpart	elkarkide	copartner, associate
lan	work	elkarlan	teamwork, joint venture
leku	place, site	elkarleku	juncture
lotura	tie	elkarlotura	correlation
meza	Catholic mass	elkarmeza	concelebrated mass
min	pain, craving	elkarmin	craving for each other
truke	exchange	elkartruke	mutual exchange
zale	devotee, fan	elkarzale	devotees of each other

15.10 Vocabulary

argazki	photograph
aurkeztu	to present, to introduce
barre	laughter, laugh
batera	simultaneously, jointly, together
batez ere	especially, particularly

besarkatu	to embrace, to hug
bidali	to send
ekin	to tackle, to apply oneself, to begin
elkartu	to join, to unite, to gather together
ezti	honey, sweet
garbitu	to clean, to wash
gogoz	willingly, gladly, with pleasure
lurralde	land, territory
musu	to kiss
su eman	to set fire (to)

15.11 Exercises

15.11.1 Translate into English

1. Hamar bat gizonek loreak bidaltzen zizkidaten egunero. (Atxaga, *Obab.* 287)
2. Gezur handi horiek zergatik diostazuz?
3. Bihar arratsaldean etorriko natzaizu etxera.
4. Modu horretan hitz egiteari barregarri deritzot. (*EGLU* II, 101)
5. Laster barreari eman genion, oso gogoz gainera. (Garate, *Hades* 27)
6. Nire aitaren hizkuntza ondo ikasteari ekin nion. (Atxaga, *Obab.* 99)
7. Ni neure buruarentzat ere aspergarria naiz.
8. Zuek ere elkarri oinak garbitu behar dizkiozue. (Jn 13:14; *IB*)
9. Besarkatu zuten elkar, eta negar egin zuten elkarrekin. (1 Sm 20:41)
10. Miren eta Itziar bata besteari aurkeztu diot.
11. Elkarrenak izateko hitza bata besteari eman zioten.
12. Ez dira biak etsaiak, baina gutxik elkartzen ditu biak. (Beobide, 201)

15.11.2 Translate into Basque

1. You mustn't sell the house to your brothers.
2. A child has been born to us, God has given us a son.
3. Many young witches have kissed me this week.
4. This land is said to be dripping with milk and honey.
5. I (for one) consider that woman very beautiful.
6. All the children in this house broke into tears together.

7. Why are you setting fire to the table?
8. We don't want to kill ourselves.
9. He spoke to me also about himself, particularly about himself.
10. Have you ever seen a photograph of yourself?
11. What, I wonder, have yoû done to each other?
12. My brother and I don't want to go into each other's house.

16 Causatives and Gerundives

16.1 Archaic Causatives

Under the traditional assumption that derivation does not include number agreement and other conjugational mechanisms, there is only one derivational process applying to verbal stems in Basque: prefixation of a causativoid formative shaped *ra-*. Combining with stems of some canonical verbs exclusively, this prefix never shows up in word-initial position. In the nonfinite forms, it will be preceded by the verbal prefix *e-* or *i-*, and in the finite paradigm, the stem as a whole is invariably preceded by a person or tense marker.

Despite the assimilation into the standard language of two or three neologisms dating from the last decade of the 19th century, the prefix *ra-* has been nonproductive for centuries. As an inevitable consequence, semantic change has affected the initially causative relationship, greatly obscuring it in many instances. It is for this reason that I chose to refer to these as "archaic" causatives, in contrast to the productive causatives formed with the suffix *-arazi* to be discussed in section 16.2.

In the following examples, at least the remnants of a causative relationship can still be detected. The first item on our list, *atxiki*, looks like a noncanonical verb; the basis of the causative *eratxiki*, however, is *etxiki*, an older canonical form, now deemed nonstandard.

atxiki	to adhere, to attach (intr.)	eratxiki	to adhere, to attach (trans.)
ebaki	to cut	erabaki	to decide
edoski	to suck	eradoski	to suckle
egin	to do, to make	eragin	to activate, to influence, to promote
egotzi	to throw out, to throw off	eragotzi	to bar, to prohibit, to prevent
ekarri	to bring	erakarri	to cause to bring, to produce, to attract
entzun	to hear	erantzun	to answer
esan	to say	erasan	to cause to say
etorri	to come	eratorri	to derive, to bring forth (neologism)
etzan	to lie, to lie down	eratzan	to cause to lie, to lay down

ezagutu	to know, to acknowledge	erazagutu	to make known, to reveal
ibili	to walk, to function	erabili	to handle, to treat, to use
igan	to ascend	iragan	to pass (by), to pass away, to go through
igarri	to guess	iragarri	to announce, to predict
igo	to climb	igaro	to pass through, to pass away, to pass
ikasi	to learn	irakatsi	to teach
ikusi	to see	erakutsi	to show
ito	to choke	irato	to strangle
itzarri	to wake up (intr.)	iratzarri	to wake up (trans.)
izan	to be	irazan	to create (neologism)
izeki	to burn	irazeki	to kindle
jaiki	to rise, to get up	eraiki	to raise, to found, to build, to provoke
jaitsi	to go down, to descend	eraitsi	to bring down, to fell, to milk
jalgi	to come out, to go out	eralgi	to sift, to spend
jasan	to bear, to suffer	erasan	to affect
jauzi	to leap, to bounce, to explode	erauzi	to pull out, to pull away, to blast
joan	to go, to go away	eroan	to carry, to bear, to conduct, to drive

[*N.B.* According to the *DGV* (VI, 766), also *eraman*, a most common synonym of *eroan*, is a causative of *joan*: **eraoan* > **eraban* > *eraman*.]

An older meaning of *erantzun* still surviving in 19th-century Souletin—'to make heard' (with further development into 'to reproach')—shows that *erantzun*, although now the normal term for 'to answer', was originally a causative of *entzun* 'to hear'. The form *igaro* arose by metathesis from *irago*, a nonstandard form still in use around Oiartzun.

The initial *i* of the verbs *ibili* and *ikusi* stems from an assimilatory process that altered the original forms *ebili* and *ekusi*, still underlying the causative verbs *erabili* and *erakutsi*.

Incidentally, no adequate explanation has been found so far as to why stem-final sibilants undergo sharpening to affricates in the causative form, as seen in *erakutsi* 'to show', *irakatsi* 'to teach', and *erautzi* 'to pull out', a widespread variant of the standard form *erauzi*.

The verbs *edan* 'to drink' and *egon* 'to stay', 'to be' also used to have archaic causatives: *edaran* 'to water', 'to give to drink' (metathesis of *eradan*) and *eragon* 'to make stay'. The latter is now obsolete and the former nearly so.

For curiosity's sake, I venture to end this section with a pairing of verbs, in which there is little or no indication from the meaning that a causative relationship might once have obtained, even though the shape of the second verb coincides exactly with that of a *ra*-derivation of the first:

itxi	to close, to shut	iritsi	to reach, to obtain
jakin	to know	irakin	to boil
jantzi	to put on, to dress	erantzi	to take off, to undress

jo	to hit, to strike	ero	to kill (obs.), now adjective 'insane'
josi	to fasten, to pin, to sew	erosi	to buy

16.2 Productive Causatives

16.2.1 Formation of Causative Verbs

A causative counterpart to virtually any Basque verb can be uniformly derived by suffixing to its radical the causative auxiliary *arazi* (radical *araz*, imperfect participle *arazten*, future participle *araziko*). The resulting causative verb is written as a single word:

bete	to fill, to fulfill	betearazi	to cause to fill, to make fulfilled
ezagutu	to know, to recognize	ezagutarazi	to make known, to cause to recognize
gelditu	to stop, to stay	geldiarazi	to make stop, to make stay
heldu	to arrive, to come	helarazi	to cause to arrive, to make come
hil	to die	hilarazi	to put to death, to cause to kill
jo	to hit, to strike	joarazi	to make hit, to cause to strike
joan	to go (away)	joanarazi	to make go (away)

[*N.B.* A decree of the Basque Academy stipulates one exception to the general rule: the causative of *aditu* 'to hear', 'to understand' is *adierazi*, not **adiarazi*.]

A radical-final *a* elides before the initial *a* of *arazi*, as in the following examples:

aipatu	to mention	aiparazi	to cause to mention
aldatu	to change	aldarazi	to cause to change
gertatu	to happen	gertarazi	to cause to happen

When a verb radical ends in a strong *r*, it must be remembered (see section 1.2.2.3) that this strong *r* is spelled *rr* in front of a vowel:

etorri	to come	etorrarazi	to cause to come
hartu	to take, to receive	harrarazi	to cause to take (or receive)
lehertu	to burst	leherrarazi	to cause to burst
sartu	to enter	sarrarazi	to cause to enter
sortu	to arise	sorrarazi	to cause to arise, to provoke

While the regular causative of the verb *egin* 'to do' is *eginarazi*, with the *egin* idioms (see section 13.3) the archaic causative *eragin* is preferred, as in these examples:

barre egin	to laugh	barre eragin	to make laugh
ihes egin	to flee	ihes eragin	to put to flight
lo egin	to sleep	lo eragin	to put to sleep
negar egin	to cry, to weep	negar eragin	to make cry
ok(a) egin	to throw up	ok(a) eragin	to make throw up
usin egin	to sneeze	usin eragin	to make sneeze

16.2.2 Syntax of Causative Verbs

Needless to say, all causative verbs require ergative subjects, since they are perforce transitive.

What now happens to the causee, that is, the original subject of the basic verb underlying the causative? Its fate depends on the nature of the basic verb. If this is intransitive, its subject is absolutive and will remain so in the causative construction, acting then as a direct object to the causative verb. If, however, the basic verb is transitive, its originally ergative subject will turn into a dative noun phrase serving as an indirect object to the causative verb.

Here are examples with a basic intransitive:

(1) a. Semeak geldiarazi du zaldia. (H.U., *Aurp.* 74)
The son has made the horse stop.
b. Etzanarazi nuen Ines. (Haranburu, *Its.* 128)
I made Ines lie down.
c. Barkatu zien bere anaiei, eta etorrarazi zituen Egiptora. (Ubillos, 21)
He forgave his brothers, and made them come to Egypt.

The following examples with a basic transitive:

(2) a. Edurnek Galarretari haur bati bezala edanarazi zion. (Garate, *E.E.* 131)
Edurne made Galarreta drink it like a child.
b. Janarazi diozu zuk Adani sagar debekatua? (J. B. Aguirre, *Erak.* II, 90)
Have you made Adam eat the forbidden apple?
c. Biziak jakinarazi dit gauza bat: ... (Aintziart, 94)
Life has made me aware of one thing: ...
d. Bideko lagun bat bederen nahi zioten harrarazi. (Lapitze, 50)
They wanted to make him take at least a traveling companion.

Notice that (2d) provides a counterexample to Saltarelli's claim that *-arazi* is incompatible with verbs taking animate direct objects. Examples (3a,b), denounced by him as ungrammatical, are considered somewhat "heavy" by my consultants, yet in no way unacceptable, let alone ungrammatical. Hence, his claim must be rejected.

(3) a. Jonek Xabierri Mikel hilarazi dio. (Saltarelli, 221)
John made Xavier kill Michael.
b. Jonek Xabierri Mikel ikusarazi dio. (Saltarelli, 221)
John made Xavier see Michael.

As *EGLU* (II, 63–64) has noticed, only causatives derived from a transitive verb allow medio-passives. Thus, corresponding to (4a), one can get a medio-passive (4b), but there is no medio-passive (5b) to match (5a), derived from an intransitive verb.

(4) a. Irakasleak hamar liburu irakurrarazi dizkigu.
The teacher has made us read ten books.

b. Hamar liburu irakurrarazi zaizkigu.
We have been made to read ten books.

(5) a. Irakasleak beti geldiarazten gaitu.
The teacher always makes us stay.
b. *Beti geldiarazten gara.
We are always made to stay.

Impersonal (i.e., unspecified) third-person plural forms, however, are possible for all causative verbs:

(6) a. Hamar liburu irakurrarazi dizkigute.
They have made us read ten books.
b. Beti geldiarazten gaituzte.
They always make us stay.

With causatives based on a transitive verb, the causee can be left unspecified. If so, the verb form will show no dative marking, unless the base verb itself provides for a dative complement:

(7) a. Aita ekarrarazi zuten. (Garate, *NY* 62)
They had the father brought in.
b. Nahi dut harrarazi. (Larréguy I, 374)
I want to have him taken.
c. Abimelekek Sara bere jauregira eramanarazi zuen. (Cf. *TZ* I, 43)
Abimelek had Sara carried off to his palace.
d. Lan anitzez bere burua ezagutarazi du azkenean. (H.U., *Aurp*. 78)
Through a lot of work he has finally made himself known.

Given a causative based on a transitive verb fitted with a dative complement, introducing a causee leads to a clause with two datives. On this account, there are two dialects: an eastern one, and a western one covering Biscay and most of Guipuzcoa. Eastern speakers have no problem, as long as it is the causee that is marked inside the verb:

(8) Gure aitak amari gona gorria erosarazi dit.
My father made me buy a red skirt for mother. (Not: made mother buy . . . for me)

Unable to tolerate two datives in one clause, western speakers will change the dative to the benefactive, using *amarentzat*, or forgo the causative construction altogether.

What about the causatives of the so-called deponent verbs, that is, the logically intransitive verbs of section 12.2.1? What case to assign to the causee of such causatives as *distirarazi* 'to cause to glitter (shine)'; *durundarazi* 'to cause to clang', 'to sound'; *irakinarazi* 'to boil (trans.)'; *iraunarazi* 'to cause to last', 'to preserve'; and *izarniarazi* 'to cause to twinkle (shine)'?

Given the rule stated at the head of this section, we should expect the dative. This is, in fact, by and large what happens in the south, more precisely, in the Guipuzcoan dialect.

(The Biscayan dialect has nothing to contribute to the discussion, since its speakers use other causative auxiliaries, such as *eragin* and *erazo*, which impose the dative case on all causees.) In the northern dialects, the modern trend is to use the absolutive case. In the older literature, while Souletin texts consistently employed the absolutive, 19th-century Labourdin authors still vacillated between the dative (attested in Leizarraga, both Etxeberris, and Axular) and the more recent absolutive.

In this complex state of affairs, the Basque Academy came up with a compromise solution: a decree dated September 29, 1995, prescribes the dative when the causee is animate and the absolutive otherwise. Conforming examples from the literature are not hard to come by:

(9) a. Jendeari bere lo nagian iraunarazteko ez dugu kritikaren beharrik. (*MEIG* I, 140)
To make the people persist in their lazy sleep, we have no need of the critique.
b. Gerritik gora ez zuen ezer, eta horrek iraunarazi zion bizirik. (Zavala, in Goñi, 15)
Above the waist he had nothing (wrong), and that kept him alive.

[*N.B. Bizirik* 'alive' here is a stative adverb, not a partitive. See section 11.2.]

(10) a. Tabako hostoak irakinarazten zituzten ur garbian. (J. Etchepare, *Bur.* 26)
They would boil the tobacco leaves in clean water.
b. Irakinarazi berehala orratza eta zizta-ontziak. (Etxaniz, *Antz.* 97)
Boil at once the needle and the ampules.

An unfortunate aspect of the academy's decision is that it introduces an artificial split, unattested in any spoken variety of the language. It also runs counter to the majoritarian usage in the Guipuzcoan dialect, to which Mitxelena, among others, bears witness:

(11) Norbaitek eta zerbaitek iraunarazi dio hizkuntzari. (*MEIG* IX, 62)
Someone and something has caused the language to last.

16.3 Permissive Causatives

Causatives formed with *-arazi* are not used to express mere permission. For this purpose, Basque grammar makes use of a construction based on the verb *utzi* 'to leave'. A brief discussion of this verb is therefore in order.

16.3.1 The Verb *utzi* and Its Government

The verb *utzi* possesses all the meanings of French *laisser* or Spanish *dejar*, thus: 'to abandon', 'to leave', 'to leave behind', 'to leave out', 'to cease', and so on. Its grammatical object, when it is an ordinary noun phrase or pronoun, regularly takes the absolutive case in all dialects:

(12) a. Ene Jainkoa, ene Jainkoa, zergatik utzi nauzu? (*TB* 136; Ps 22:2; Mt 27:46)
My God, my God, why have you left me?

b. Ikasketak utzi ditu. (*EHM* 1078)
He has left his studies.

In the northern dialects, the same rule obtains also for grammatical objects consisting of a nominalized clause: *erretzea utzi du* 'he has quit smoking'. In the southern dialects, however, this type of object requires the dative case:

(13) a. Erretzeari utzi dio. (*EGL* 214)
He has quit smoking.
b. Danutak segituan utzi zion igeri egiteari. (Atxaga, *Gizona* 217)
Danuta soon ceased to swim.
c. Orduan, amak negar egiteari utzi zion. (Tb 5:23)
Then, the mother stopped crying.

When the nominalized clause contains an activity noun as the object of the verb *egin*, the same phenomenon described for *eman* in section 15.6.2 arises here too: the verbal noun *egite* will often be omitted so that the dative ending *-ari* ends up directly attached to the activity noun itself:

(14) a. Amak negarrari utzi zion.
Mother stopped crying.
b. Lanari utzi dio. (*EHM* 1078)
He has stopped working.
c. Bekatuari utzi behar diogu.
We must stop sinning.

16.3.2 Syntax of Permissive Causatives

A permissive causative clause employs *utzi* (or its synonym *laga*, see section 16.3.3) as its main verb, which then takes the causee as an object: direct (i.e., absolutive) in the northern dialects, and indirect (i.e., dative) in the southern ones. The permitted action is encoded by a nonfinite complement clause, ending in the imperfect participle (gerund) in the western dialects and in the allative form of the verbal noun in the eastern ones. Thus, compare (15a) and (15b):

(15) a. Joaten utziko dizuet, ez zaituztet gehiago geldiaraziko. (Ex 9:28)
I will let yoû go, I won't make yoû stay anymore.
b. Utziko zaituztet joatera, eta ez zaituztet geldiaraziko gehiago. (Ex 9:28; Urt.)
I will let yoû go, and I won't make yoû stay anymore.

As *EGLU* (II, 105) points out, the northern dialects distinguish permissive *kantatzera utzi* 'to let him sing' from circumstantial *kantatzen utzi* 'to leave him singing'. While the southern dialects make use of the form *kantatzen* in both cases, the same distinction will reveal itself in the case marking, since the object of *utzi* will be in the absolutive just as long as it does not represent a causee.

In this connection, reference should be made to a highly perceptive discussion of *utzi* by Goenaga (1984, sec. IV, 5). To summarize one of his main insights: Basque grammar takes the notion of permission operating in permissive causatives very seriously, insisting that there can be no permissive causative, unless the causee in some way or other actively participates in the process at hand. Thus, according to Goenaga, instead of (16a), we will get (16b), which is not a permissive causative, but has a structure similar to that of (16c):

(16) a. *Andonik liburuari erortzen utzi dio.
Anthony has let the book fall.
b. Andonik liburua erortzen utzi du. (Goenaga 1984, 223)
Anthony has let the book fall.
c. Andonik liburua mahai gainean utzi du. (Ibid.)
Anthony has left the book on the table.

That the verb *utzi* requires absolutive instead of dative objects when there is no active participation in the process on the part of this object, is abundantly confirmed by examples from the literature:

(17) a. Noragabe joaten utzi genuen ontzia. (Acts 27:15)
We let the ship go without direction.
b. Utzi biak batera hazten. (Mt 13:30)
Let the two grow up together.
c. Zergatik ez nauzue hiltzen utzi. (Etxaniz, *Antz*. 98)
Why have yoû not let me die?

A borderline case is that of a boiling liquid, where we find both the permissive causative (18a) and the circumstantial (18b):

(18) a. Urari irakiten utzi diot.
I have let the water boil.
b. Ura irakiten utzi dut.
I have left the water boiling.

16.3.3 Permissive Causatives with the Verb *laga*

In southern Batua, the preterito-present verb *laga* (or its regular synonym *lagatu*) can occur as a synonym of *utzi* in all its uses, including the permissive causative:

(19) a. Ez dut bakarrik laga. (*LBB* 22)
I have not left her alone.
b. Lanari laga beharrean aurkitu ziren. (*TZ* I, 27)
They found themselves in the necessity to stop working.
c. Laga umeei niregana etortzen. (Manzisidor, 347)
Let the children come to me.

d. Lagatzen al didazue hitz egiten? (Etxaniz, *Antz.* 49)
   Are you letting me speak?
e. Istil-otsak ez du ordurik kontatzen laga. (*LBB* 106)
   The sound of falling rain does not let one count the hours.

16.4 Introducing the Gerundive

A gerundive in Basque is a complement headed by an imperfect participle unaccompanied by a finite verb form. The participle heading a gerundive usually occurs at its very end, and will be called a gerund.

Basque also employs another type of gerundive, which will be labeled a "kinetic" gerundive. The only difference from ordinary gerundives is that, instead of an imperfect participle, the kinetic gerundive uses the allative form of the verbal noun, which, in this construction, will be termed the "kinetic" gerund.

As we will see in the course of this chapter, there is good evidence that the ordinary gerund is actually an inessive form of the verbal noun, albeit distinct from the definite inessive ending in *-an*. Accordingly, the two types of gerundives are isomorphic: both are locative nominalizations, one inessive, the other allative.

16.4.1 General Properties of the Gerundive

Unable to stand by itself, a gerundive must be embedded as a verbal complement to a main predicate. The subject of a gerund cannot be overtly realized; it must be either unspecified or coreferential with a nuclear noun phrase (i.e., an argument) inside the main clause. Thus we will speak of noncontrolled, subject-controlled, and direct or indirect object–controlled gerunds or gerundives.

A gerundive has no room for a time adverbial of its own. What this fact implies for the interpretation of the sentence is that there can be no time interval between the action denoted by the gerund and that expressed by the main verb. In other words, the two actions are inseparable and hence simultaneous. Indeed, in the Biscayan dialect, simultaneity is all that is required for a gerundive to appear, as evidenced by the following example from the Azcoitian author N. Etxaniz:

(20) Zure izena bedeinkatzen hilko naiz. (Etxaniz, *Antz.* 91–92)
     I will die blessing your name.

Rejecting such indiscriminate use, the other dialects reserve the gerundive for a limited set of constructions defined by the meaning class of the main verb or predicate. These various uses will be surveyed in the rest of this chapter.

The first study of Basque gerundives I am aware of is that by Goenaga (1984). A convenient Spanish summary of this work can be found in Goenaga 1985a, hereafter referred to as Goenaga, *Comp.*

16.4.2 Noncontrolled Gerundives Occurring with *Tough*-like Adjectives

The only instance I know of a noncontrolled gerundive is the one found with *tough*-like adjectives, that is, adjectives such as *erraz* 'easy' and *zail*, *gaitz*, *neke*, and *nekez*, all roughly meaning 'difficult'. More often than not, when appearing as predicates, they take a nominalized clause as subject:

(21) a. Zahar eta berrien artean hautatzea ez da erraz. (*MEIG* VII, 150 = *MIH* 113)
Choosing between the old and the new ones is not easy.
b. Zail da harekin bat ez etortzea. (*E.H.* 766)
It is difficult not to agree with him.
c. Zaila da benetan Jainkoaren erreinuan sartzea. (Mk 10:24)
It is really hard to enter into the kingdom of God.

As long as the embedded clause contains neither a specified subject nor a time adverbial, nothing prevents it from being turned into a gerundive complement comparable to the second supine in Latin, such as *facile dictu* 'easy to say'. Examples are

(22) a. Ez da gaitz erantzuten. (*MEIG* VIII, 72)
It is not hard to answer.
b. Zail izango da hori jakiten. (Garate, *Iz.B.* 42)
It will be difficult to get to know that.
c. Ez da erraz egia jakiten. (*LBB* 79)
It is not easy to get to know the truth.
d. Herrietan gaitza da gauzak isilik eukitzen. (San Martin, 87)
In the villages it is hard to keep things quiet.

The grammatical process known as "*tough*-movement" in certain circles operates also in Basque, where it is, however, restricted to direct objects. As a result, a direct object originating inside a gerundive may end up as the subject of the main predicate, provided this belongs to the *tough* class. The following examples illustrate this process:

(23) a. Liburu hauek errazak dira irakurtzen. (Goenaga, *Comp.* 512)
These books are easy to read.
b. Etxe hau erraz da garbitzen. (Cf. Ax. 540)
This house is easy to clean.
c. Idazlearen eginkizuna erraz da adierazten, gaitz betetzen. (*MEIG* VII, 153 = *MIH* 116)
The duty of a writer is easy to explain, (but) hard to fulfill.

[*N.B.* Notice that the examples given here and subsequently conform to our earlier observation that use of the article *-a* is optional with predicates taking impersonal or sentential subjects (see section 2.3.1, item 7, and also 18.2.2). Despite the lexical subject, this optionality also applies to instances of *tough*-movement.]

16.4.3 Modal Use of *Tough*-like Adjectives

The adjectives discussed in the preceding subsection can be employed in a modal sense: *erraz* may correspond to English *likely*, the others to English *unlikely*. Used in that meaning, their syntactic behavior is quite different from that analyzed in 16.4.2. First and foremost, far from being ruled out, overt subjects are virtually required within the nominalized subject clause. The following examples are typical:

(24) a. Ez da erraza aberats bat han sartzea. (S. Mitxelena, *IG* II, 70)
It isn't likely that a rich person enters there.
b. Gaitz da itsuak koloreen berri jakitea. (Ax. 504)
It is unlikely that a blind person knows about colors.

It follows that gerundives, which disallow overt subjects, are unable to appear with these adjectives when used in their modal sense. Furthermore, *tough*-movement, as in (23a,b,c), is not available here either. What we do find is a raising rule, fully analogous to the raising rule triggered by *likely* and *unlikely* in English. Since this process removes the subject from the embedded clause, a gerundive complement is no longer ruled out and will in fact appear:

(25) a. Itsasgizonak errazak dira moskortzen. (Cf. Urruzuno, *Urz* 63)
Sailors are likely to get drunk.
b. Mozkortuagatik(an) gaitza da erortzen, lagun gabe etxera badaki etortzen. (*Xenp.* 252)
Despite having got drunk he is unlikely to fall, (and) knows how to get home without an escort.

Contemporary Basque, however, has lost this raising rule. Examples (25a,b), which date from the 19th century, are no longer acceptable to native speakers.

16.5 Subject-Controlled Gerundives

Plain (i.e., nonkinetic) gerundives are governed by four semantic classes of main verbs: aspectual verbs, verbs of cognition, "psychological" verbs, and conative verbs.

16.5.1 Gerundives with Aspectual Verbs

In Basque, aspectual notions are expressed as a rule by lexical verbs taking gerundive complements. In this subsection, we will discuss the duratives *ari*, *egon*, *ibili*, and *jardun*, continuative *jarraitu*, inceptive *hasi*, and terminative *amaitu*. We will also include predicates measuring the duration of the action considered.

16.5.1.1 Durative *ari*

By far the most common way to express durative aspect involves the preterito-present verb *ari*, which conveys the meaning of 'being engaged in some activity or process'. In line with section 14.2, its perfect participle is *ari izan*, its imperfect participle *ari izaten*, its verbal noun *ari izate*, and its future participle *ariko* or *ari izango*. This verb is always intransitive, except where used in reference to weather conditions, when it takes an absolutive object, but no subject. Here are some examples:

(26) a. Euria ari du. (*LBB* 102; Urretabizkaia, *Sat*. 84)
It is raining.
b. Haizea ari du. (*E.H.* 56)
It is windy.
c. Bero ari zuen itsuski. (Barbier, *Lég*. 62)
It was horribly warm.

While it is possible for the verb *ari* to appear without a complement, as in *alferrik ari zara* (Urretabizkaia, *Asp.* 88) 'you are acting in vain', it mostly co-occurs with an inessive noun phrase that serves to specify the activity engaged in.

Common examples are *borrokan ari* 'to be fighting', *eztabaidan ari* 'to be arguing', *hizketan ari* 'to be conversing', *jolasean ari* 'to be playing', *lanean ari* 'to be working', *lapurretan ari* 'to be stealing', *otoitzean ari* 'to be praying', and *txantxetan ari* 'to be joking'. More elaborate noun phrases are also possible: *lan zikin hartan ari nintzen* 'I was engaged in that dirty work'.

Characteristic activities of the human body are not expressed this way, but make use of indefinite instrumental nouns combined with *ari*: *barrez ari* 'to be laughing', *eztulez ari* 'to be coughing', *irriz ari* 'to be mocking', *irribarrez ari* 'to be smiling', *negarrez ari* 'to be weeping', *oihuz ari* 'to be screaming'.

Furthermore, activities consisting of repetitions of the same action are readily conveyed by adverbs formed with the suffix *-ka* (see section 33.1.11) used together with *ari*: *barreka ari* 'to keep laughing', *deika ari natzaio* (Sg 5:6) 'I keep calling out to him'.

Finally, to return to our main concern, the verb *ari* also takes gerundive complements, presenting the activity they denote as being an ongoing one, that is, as a durative action or process.

Whatever the nature of the gerundive complement, the verb *ari* remains intransitive—the sole exception being a gerundive describing meteorological phenomena, as in

(27) a. Argitzen ari du. (Atxaga, *Sara* 146)
It is getting light.
b. Elurra urtzen ari du. (*EGLU* II, 438)
The snow is melting.

Mostly, the gerundive complement acts as the focus of the main verb and thus occupies the focus site directly in front of *ari*:

(28) a. Hiltzen ari zara. (Atxaga, *Obab*. 403)
You are dying.

b. Fermin liburu bat irakurtzen ari zen. (Lertxundi, *Aise* 56)
Fermin was reading a book.
c. Orain sendagilearen etxea garbitzen ariko da ama. (Lertxundi, *Aise* 14)
Mother will now be cleaning the doctor's house.
d. Zer kantatzen ari haiz? (Amuriza, *Emea* 122)
What are you singing?

Occasionally, some other constituent will be focused on, in which event the gerundive—or what remains of it—will be relegated to a position after the verb:

(29) a. Zertan ari zara pentsatzen? (Atxaga, *Gizona* 32)
What are you thinking of?
b. Ari al zarete telebista ikusten? (Atxaga, *Gizona* 14)
Are you watching television?
c. Ume bat bezala ari haiz portatzen! (Atxaga, *Obab*. 104)
You are behaving like a child!

We may note that *ari* does not require its subject to be animate:

(30) a. Igotzen ari da liburuen prezioa. (*EGLU* II, 437)
The price of books is rising.
b. Ilea urdintzen ari zaio. (Goenaga)
His hair is turning gray. (Possessive dative, see section 15.5.1)
c. Zorrak pilatzen ari zitzaizkion. (Garate, *Esku* 189)
His debts were piling up.

As *EGLU* points out, the gerund *egiten* can be omitted when its object is an interrogative or indefinite pronoun:

(31) a. Zer ari zara? (Garate, *Esku* 180)
What are you doing?
b. Ezer ez dira ari. (*EGLU* II, 438)
They are not doing anything.
c. Hura ere zerbait ari da. (*EGLU* II, 438)
He too is doing something.

[*N.B.* In earlier Basque, *egiten* could also be omitted when part of an *egin* idiom: *bekatu ari* 'to be sinning', *otoitz ari* 'to be praying'.]

While a few speakers have generalized the use of *ari* along the lines of the English progressive, for the great majority *ari* still represents a genuine durative. It cannot be used to convey instantaneous action, so that, while example (32a) is possible, (32b) is not:

(32) a. Bonbak oraintxe lehertzen ari dira.
The bombs are exploding right now.

b. *Bonba oraintxe lehertzen ari da.
The bomb is exploding right now.

By virtue of its dynamic meaning, *ari* is incompatible with stative verbs:

(33) Andre horretaz ongi gogoratzen (*ari) naiz.
I remember that lady very well.

16.5.1.2 Durative *egon*

As noted in section 6.2.2, the verb *egon*, originally meaning 'to stay', has evolved in southern Basque into a perfect analogue of the Spanish verb *estar*, to be glossed in English by various verbs of position, including 'to sit', 'to stand', 'to lie'—depending on the situation at hand.

Gerundive complements may occur to describe concomitant action:

(34) a. Hantxe egoten ginen etxean, gaztainak jaten eta suari begira. (Atxaga, *Bi Let.* 33)
We would be sitting there at home, eating chestnuts and looking at the fire.
b. Pedro ere haiekin zegoen berotzen. (Jn 18:18)
Peter too was standing with them, warming himself.

When combined with a gerundive, the verb *egon* has a strong tendency to blur its lexical meaning and to fade into a grammatical tool conveying duration of a state, or even, purists' protests notwithstanding, an activity:

(35) a. Miliari esateko irrikatzen nago. (Etxaniz, *Antz.* 39)
I am yearning to tell it to Emily.
b. Orain zeruan gozatzen dago bere eternidadea. (*Xenp.* 335)
He is now in heaven enjoying his eternity.
c. Hogei lagunen lanak egiten dago makina bakarra. (Basarri, 132)
A single machine is doing the jobs of twenty persons.

16.5.1.3 Durative *ibili*

To express durative aspect in the case of an activity spread out over a relatively long period of time, the verb *ibili* 'to walk' is preferred to *ari*:

(36) a. Hiru urte ibili ziren elkarri eskutitzak idazten. (Garate, *NY* 144)
They were writing letters to each other for three years.
b. Etxea lorez apaintzen ibili naiz egunero. (Arrese, *O.B.* 67)
I have been decorating the house with flowers every day.
c. Gu elkar hiltzen ibili ginen. (Uztapide, *Sas.* 124)
We had been killing each other.

As with *ari*, the gerund *egiten* can be omitted when its object is an interrogative or indefinite pronoun:

(37) Zer zabiltza, Garazi? (*TOE* I, 112)
What are you doing (these days), Grace?

[*N.B.* Unlike that of *ari*, the subject of *ibili* must be animate.]

16.5.1.4 Durative *jardun*

Lacking the verb *ari*, the Biscayan dialect forms its duratives with the verb *egon* or, provided the activity is described by a transitive verb, with *jardun* 'to be busy doing (or talking)', a verb also occurring in Batua (see sections 9.1 and 9.3.1). As was stated in section 12.2.1, this verb takes instrumental objects when it means 'to discuss', otherwise inessive ones: *berriketan jardun* 'to engage in gossip', *bertsotan jardun* 'to be improvising verses'.

Although many Guipuzcoan authors, who employ the verb as a stylistic variant of *ari*, tend to make it intransitive, *jardun* differs from *ari* in being transitive and also requiring animate subjects.

Gerundive complements are permitted, but only if they are based on a transitive gerund:

(38) a. Hemen ere baziharduen eriak sendatzen. (*TB* 85)
Here too he was occupied in healing the sick.
b. Jendeari erakusten (better: *irakasten*) luzaro jardun zuen. (*TB* 43)
He had been teaching the people for a long time.

As A. Elordieta, a Biscayan linguist, has observed to me (oral communication), *jardun* typically corresponds to the type of durative expressed by the English verb 'to keep':

(39) a. Goizeko lau eta erdiak arte edaten jardun zuten. (Garate, *NY* 45)
They kept drinking until half past four in the morning.
b. Noiz arte jardun behar digu gizon horrek zorigaitza sortzen? (Ex 10:7)
Until when is that man going to keep wreaking havoc on us?

16.5.1.5 Continuative *jarraitu*

The verb *jarraitu*, introduced in section 15.2.1, can mean both 'to follow' and 'to continue'. In the latter meaning it admits gerundive complements, as does also its colloquial synonym *segitu*:

(40) a. Guk otoitz egiten jarraituko dugu. (*TOE* I, 292)
We will continue to pray.
b. Lurrean idazten jarraitu zuen. (Jn 8:8)
He continued to write on the ground.
c. Lehen bezala etortzen jarraitzen zuen. (Haranburu, *Itsas.* 79)
He went on coming as before.
d. Bihar segituko dugu hitz egiten. (Atxaga, *Obab.* 147)
We will talk again tomorrow.

16.5.1.6 Inceptive *hasi*

Equivalent to the English verb *to begin*, *hasi*, when used intransitively, has exactly the same complement system as *ari*: inessive noun phrases denoting activities, instrumental nouns denoting characteristic activities of the human body, and *-ka* adverbs for iterative actions:

(41) a. Argia gabe hasiko ziren lanean. (Barbier, *Lég*. 60)
They would begin working before daylight.
b. Negarrez hasi zen haurra ozenki. (Gn 21:16)
The child began to weep loudly.
c. Piarres hasten da oihuka. (*P.Ad.* 50)
Peter starts to shout and shout.

Unlike *ari*, however, *hasi* can take direct objects outside the meteorological domain:

(42) a. Egun berean hasi zuen arloa. (*G.* 315)
He began the task the same day.
b. Hasi zuten etxerako bidea. (Agirre, *Kres.* 43)
They began the way home.
c. Laminek gau hartan bertan hasi zuten beren lana. (Barbier, *Lég*. 25)
That same night the elves began their work.

But, when taking gerundive complements, *hasi* again conforms to *ari* in being intransitive as long as the complement does not refer to meteorological phenomena:

(43) a. Iluntzen hasi du. (Lekuona, *Eun dukat* 33)
It has started to get dark.
b. Hamaikak aldean hasi zuen lainoa kentzen. (Salaberria, 114)
Around eleven o'clock the fog began to clear.

It is usual for the gerundive to act as focus and thus to appear directly in front of the main verb *hasi*:

(44) a. Zerbait jaten hasten da. (Etxaniz, *Antz*. 88)
She begins to eat something.
b. Haren gerria, bernak, bularrak eta gorputz osoa laztantzen hasi zen. (Lertxundi, *Aise* 64)
He began to fondle her waist, legs, breasts, and whole body.
c. Nire loreak zimeltzen hasi dira. (Goenaga, *Comp*. 519)
My flowers have begun to fade.

It is quite possible, however, for there to be a different focus, or no focus at all:

(45) a. Noiz hasi zinen euskaraz ikasten? (*MEIG* I, 105 = *MIH* 145)
When did you begin to learn Basque?

b. Garai ederrean hasten haiz pentsatzen. (Atxaga, *Gizona* 30)
   At a fine time yoú begin to think.
c. Hasi ziren zotz egiten. (*TZ* I, 187)
   They began to draw lots.

Another inceptive to be mentioned is the verb *abiatu* 'to set out', 'to start', which also takes gerundive complements:

(46) Gogoz abiatu naiz euskal hiztegi honen atalaurrean hitz batzu moldatzen. (*MEIG* VII, 25)
     With pleasure I have set out to formulate a few words in the introduction to this Basque dictionary.

16.5.1.7 Terminative *amaitu*

The grammarian P. Goenaga reflects the usage of most non-Biscayan speakers when he remarks that the verbs meaning 'to end', *amaitu* and *bukatu*, are averse to admitting gerundive complements. Traditionally, the indefinite instrumental form of the verbal noun appears here: *garbitzez bukatu* 'to finish cleaning', *agur egitez amaitu* 'to end saying farewell'. Goenaga accordingly marks the grammatical status of his example (47a) as doubtful, but adds that speakers hesitate and that some of them make free use of this construction. According to the *DGV* (I, 870; V, 603), the earliest example dates from 1927.

(47) a. Gizonak autoa garbitzen amaitu du. (Goenaga, *Comp.* 518)
        The man has finished washing the car.
     b. Jaunaren bide zuzenak okertzen ez duzu amaituko? (Acts 13:10; Ker.)
        Will you not cease to pervert the straight ways of the Lord?
     c. Nexkatxa janzten amaitzen ari zen. (Garate, *Leh.* 22)
        The girl was finishing with dressing.
     d. Badakizue zein liburu amaitu nuen irakurtzen atzo? (*Durangoko . . . lehiaketa* 26)
        Do yoû know which book I finished reading yesterday?

16.5.1.8 Gerundives with Predicates Measuring Duration

The activity or process whose duration is described by the main predicate of the sentence is expressed by a gerundive complement:

(48) a. Noek kutxa hau egiten urte asko igaro zituen. (*TZ* I, 23)
        Noah spent many years making this ark.
     b. Minutu luzeak ematen ditu azal zuri leuna lehortzen. (Urretabizkaia, *Sat.* 19)
        He is taking many (lit. 'long') minutes to dry the smooth white surface.
     c. Urteak daramatzazu esnea banatzen. (*LBB* 62)
        You have been distributing milk for years.

d. Gau eta egun zuri (south: *zugan*) pentsatzen daramat ene bizia. (Xalbador, *Odol.* 114)
I spend my life thinking of you day and night.

16.5.2 Gerundives with Verbs of Cognition

All verbs of cognition admit gerundive complements, provided the object of cognition is how to perform a certain action, to be encoded by the gerundive. Since the subject of cognition is the intended performer of that action, we are dealing with a case of subject control, except for causative cognition verbs such as *irakatsi* 'to teach' and *erakutsi* 'to show', for which see section 16.7.1.

The verb *jakin* 'to know' furnishes the most common examples of this construction:

(49) a. Ba al dakik bizikleta gainean ibiltzen? (Atxaga, *Obab.* 261)
Do yoú know how to ride on a bicycle?
b. Ez nuen garaiz ezetz esaten jakin. (*TOE* II, 89)
I didn't know how to say no in time.
c. Nork daki gauzen zergatia argitzen? (Eccl 8:1)
Who knows how to explain the reason of things?

In the presence of a gerundive complement, the verb *jakin* may indicate nothing more than a habit, in which case its subject is allowed to be inanimate:

(50) a. Sendagileek gezur asko esaten dakite. (Etxaniz, *Antz.* 121)
Doctors are wont to tell a lot of lies.
b. Nahigabeak ez daki orduak neurtzen. (Etxaniz, *Antz.* 130)
Sorrow is in no habit of measuring hours.

Regarding the verb *ahaztu* 'to forget', note the following contrast:

(51) a. Amonak pianoa jotzen ahaztu egin du.
Grandmother has forgotten how to play the piano.
b. Amonak pianoa jotzea ahaztu egin du.
Grandmother has forgotten to play the piano.

The same applies to intransitive use of *ahaztu* (for which see section 12.1.9):

(52) a. Euskaraz hitz egiten ahaztu zaio. (*E.H.* 17)
He has forgotten how to speak Basque.
b. Euskaraz hitz egitea ahaztu zaio. (*E.H.* 17)
He has forgotten to speak Basque.

The following are some examples of gerundives with other cognition verbs:

(53) a. Ez dut ikasi emakumezkoen gorabehera eta matrikulak konprenitzen. (*TOE* III, 205)
I haven't learned to understand the whims and wiles of females.

b. Poliziari inor ez salatzen ikasi behar duzu. (Garate, *NY* 35)
You have to learn not to betray anyone to the police.
c. Nik ez dut hitzik egiten asmatzen. (*TOE* III, 205)
I am not managing to speak a word. (i.e., I cannot find anything to say.)

16.5.3 Gerundives with "Psychological" Predicates

Predicates denoting a psychological state may take gerundive complements referring to the action presented as the cause of this state. Examples are manifold:

(54) a. Nekatu naiz ederki honaino etortzen. (*TOE* I, 143)
I have gotten pretty tired coming all the way here.
b. Lotsatu egiten nintzen ama laztantzen. (Garate, *Hades* 66)
I was getting ashamed to hug my mother.
c. Beatriz maitagarria ez zen aspertzen pianoa jotzen. (Oñatibia, 210)
The lovely Beatrice never tired of playing the piano.
d. Aspertu egin al dira poloniarrak hire ogia jaten? (Atxaga, *Gizona* 166)
Have the Poles had enough of eating yoúr bread?
e. Orain arte bakarrik bizitzen etsi dugu. (*TOE* II, 35)
Up to now we have been resigned to living alone.
f. Beldur al haiz bakarrik etortzen? (Amuriza, *Emea* 99)
Are yoú afraid to come alone?
g. Zergatik ez zarete ikaratzen Moisesen kontra hitz egiten? (*TZ* 1, 142)
Why aren't you scared to talk against Moses?

Predicates denoting the expenditure of effort to reach a certain goal form a transition between the psychological predicates of this section and the conative ones of the next. If the goal involves an action to be carried out by the subject of the main predicate, it can be encoded by a gerundive complement:

(55) a. Zergatik burua nekarazi . . . gaizkilea bilatzen? (Garate, *Esku* 52)
Why wear out his head searching for the criminal?
b. Lanak izango ditugu horretaz libratzen. (*MEIG* VII, 42)
We will have trouble getting free of that.
c. Lan haundiak hartu dituzu nire fitxa ikasten. (Atxaga, *Z.H.* 89)
You have taken great pains to learn my file.
d. Kazetariak haizatzen nahiko lan izango zuten. (Garate, *Esku* 134)
They would have plenty of work to chase away the journalists.

16.5.4 Gerundives with Conative Predicates

A nonfinite sentential complement of a conative predicate (for which see section 12.1.6) takes the form of a subject-controlled gerundive:

(56) a. Saiatu naiz gerlariekin hitz egiten. (Atxaga, *Obab.* 246)
I have tried to speak with the soldiers.
b. Zertarako saiatu geure buruak dotoretzen? (Amuriza, *Hil* 111)
Why try to make ourselves pretty?
c. Munduak . . . , goiz edo berandu, saiatu beharko zuen makurrak zuzentzen. (*MEIG* IX, 96)
Sooner or later, the world would have to try to rectify its wrongs.
d. Haren uste ona irabazten ahalegindu nintzen. (Garate, *Alaba* 47)
I did my best to gain her confidence.
e. Itxurak gordetzen ahalegindu nintzen, ordea. (Garate, *Musk.* 70)
I did my best to keep up appearances, however.
f. Apaizak ahaleginak egin zituen haren arima lokalizatzen. (Amuriza, *Hil* 66)
The priest did all he could to locate her soul.

The eastern dialects make use of the kinetic gerundive after conative predicates. Using examples with the mainly northern verbs *entseatu* 'to try', *bermatu* 'to try hard', and *lehiatu* 'to strive', we find *zutitzera entseatu* 'to try to get up'; *ate hertsitik sartzera bermatu* 'to try hard to enter by the narrow gate' (cf. Lk 13:24; Dv); and *hari atsegin egitera lehiatu* 'to strive to please him' (cf. 2 Cor 5:9; *Biblia*).

Other subject-controlled kinetic gerundives, not restricted to the eastern dialects, will be treated in the next section.

16.5.5 Subject-Controlled Kinetic Gerundives

In section 8.6.1 focus was defined as a constituent embodying the answer to a tacit wh-question. With an ordinary gerundive as focus, the interrogative will take the form *zertan* 'in what', but with a kinetic gerundive the corresponding interrogative will be *zertara* 'to what'. In other words, while ordinary gerundives are inessives, kinetic gerundives are allatives; hence their affinity to verbs of motion.

16.5.5.1 Kinetic Gerundives with Verbs of Motion

A kinetic gerundive may appear as an allative complement to a verb of motion. It serves as an essential part of the sentence in that, if left out, the utterance would be pointless, although the sentence might still be grammatical. Examples are

(57) a. Autoa hartzera nindoan. (Atxaga, *Gizona* 107)
I went to get the car.
b. Zu joango al zara kazetari horrekin hitz egitera? (Atxaga, *Gizona* 107)
Will you go to speak to that journalist?
c. Ni itotzera zatozte. (*TOE* II, 220)
You're coming to strangle me.

d. Baina lurra emakumeari laguntzera etorri zen. (Rv 12:16)
But the earth came to help the woman.

Quite often, however, a clause purporting to be a kinetic gerundive does not, in fact, substitute for an allative complement; rather, it appears in addition to such a complement. In that case, what we are faced with could well be a purpose clause disguised as a gerundive.

As an illustration, take the following pair of nearly identical utterances:

(58) a. Zertara hator herri honetara? Guri neskak kentzera? (Atxaga, *Bi Let.* 42)
What are yoú coming to this town for? To take our girls away from us?
b. Zertarako hator herri honetara? Guri neskak kentzeko?
What are yoú coming to this town for? So as to take our girls away from us?

In this context, the putative gerundive *guri neskak kentzera* in (58a) has exactly the same semantic import as the purpose clause *guri neskak kentzeko* 'in order to take our girls away from us' in (58b).

In a similar vein, comparing various renditions of the New Testament phrase 'Have you come to destroy us?', we find *JKBO* employing *galtzeko etorri* in Lk 4:34, but *galtzera etorri* in Mk 1:24. The *IB* version has *galtzeko* in both texts, yet uses *galtzera* in Lk 9:55.

It was shown in section 7.2.3 that a nonfinite purpose clause needs an underlying allative justifying the occurrence of the adnominal form of the verbal noun. Therefore, all we require to account for our data is an optional process of *-ko* deletion (thus bleeding allative deletion) to apply in just those purpose clauses that depend on a verb of motion (or refraining from motion: *gurekin bazkaltzera gelditu* [*TOE* I, 211] 'to stay to have lunch with us'). Such a mechanism would explain the following examples:

(59) a. Kanpora atera naiz zigarro bat erretzera. (Atxaga, *Gizona* 25)
I have stepped out to smoke a cigarette.
b. Palmondora igoko naiz haren fruituak hartzera. (Sg 7:9)
I will climb up into the palm tree to grasp its fruits.
c. Gora al zoaz afaltzera? (Atxaga, *Gizona* 247)
Are you going upstairs to have supper?
d. Baina haiek ez ziren zu hiltzera etorri. (Amuriza, *Emea* 45)
But they didn't come to kill you.
e. Oraindik ez al dira poloniarrak gosaltzera azaldu? (Atxaga, *Gizona* 202)
Haven't the Poles appeared yet to have breakfast?

16.5.5.2 Kinetic Gerundives with Verbs of Change

Inasmuch as a change can be viewed as a metaphoric extension of the concept of motion, it is not surprising that verbs of change also admit kinetic gerundives:

(60) a. Otso hau aldatu da bildots izatera? (Mogel, *C.C.* 39)
Has this wolf changed into being a lamb?
b. Otso hau bihurtu da bildots izatera? (Mogel, *C.O.* 50)
Has this wolf turned into being a lamb?

Several verbs of motion can serve to indicate change. Thus the verb *etorri* 'to come' can come to mean 'to end up (as)'—for example,

(61) a. Berdintsuak izatera etorri gara. (Irazusta, *Bizia* 125)
We have come to be somewhat similar.
b. Besteren limosnaz bizitzera etorri ziren. (Gerriko I, 424)
They ended up living by the alms of others.

Simple forms of the verb *joan* 'to go' may combine with a kinetic gerundive to announce impending actions or events. For examples, see section 16.5.6.

The verb *heldu* 'to arrive' or 'to come' can be used to describe a change for the better:

(62) Gudalburu izatera heldu ziren. (2 Chr 12:22)
They came to be army captains.

The verb *iritsi*, likewise meaning 'to arrive', assumes the meaning 'to manage' when it occurs with a kinetic gerundive:

(63) a. Nola iritsi naiz gaizkilea aurkitzera? (Garate, *Esku* 174)
How have I managed to find the criminal?
b. Hori ulertzen iristen naiz. (Lertxundi, *Aise* 71)
I (can) manage to understand that.

The verb *makurtu* 'to bend' combined with a kinetic gerundive means 'to stoop':

(64) Ez dira euskararik ikastera makurtuko. (Cf. *MEIG* VII, 159)
They won't stoop to learn any Basque.

With a main verb denoting motion, the terminal form of the verbal noun may be utilized instead of the allative in order to characterize the goal as either excessive or particularly hard to reach:

(65) Deboziozko lan guztiak debekatzeraino iritsi ziren. (Arrue, *May.* 201)
They went as far as to prohibit all works of devotion.

16.5.5.3 Kinetic Gerundives with Verbs of Accustoming

To express 'falling into a habit' or 'getting accustomed to something', use of the verb *ohitu* is most common, although its Biscayan synonym *ekandu* and the northern verb *usatu* also are permitted in the standard language. Since both allative and inessive complements are possible (*gauza berrietara* 'to the new things', *lanean* 'to work'), kinetic gerundives as well as ordinary ones may occur:

(66) a. Lapurreta txikiak egitera ohitu zen. (Gerriko II, 15)
He got used to committing small thefts.
b. Bakarrik bizi izaten ohitu zen. (Garate, *Leh.* 102)
He got used to living alone.
c. Zure ahoa ez dadila ohitu zin egiten. (Ecclus. 23:9)
May your mouth not get used to oath taking. (For the third-person singular present tense subjunctive *dadila*, see chapter 21.)

Note the (object-controlled) kinetic gerundive a few lines down in the same text:

(66) d. Ez ohitu zeure ahoa itsuskeriak esatera. (Ecclus. 23:13)
Do not accustom your mouth to speak obscenities.

16.5.5.4 Kinetic Gerundives with Verbs of Daring

Verbs of daring (*ausartu* 'to dare', its colloquial synonym *atrebitu*, Biscayan *azartu*, and northern *menturatu*) admit allative complements and hence kinetic gerundives:

(67) a. Ez da inor ezertara ausartzen, ez jatera, ez mintzatzera. (*MEIG* IX, 110)
Nobody dares anything, neither eat nor speak.
b. Luis ez zen galderarik egitera ausartu. (Urretabizkaia, *Sat.* 66)
Luis didn't dare ask any questions.
c. Nola menturatu zarete etortzera? (Amuriza, *Hil* 214)
How did yoû dare to come?
d. Ez gara atrebitzen ikustera gizon haren aurpegia. (Gn 44:26; Ur.)
We don't dare see that man's face.

In the western dialects and also in southern Batua, inessive complements (*zertan ausartu*), and hence ordinary gerundives, are also allowed:

(68) a. Nolatan ausartzen zara hemen sartzen nire baimenik gabe? (Labayen, *Su Em.* 168)
How do you dare to come in here without my permission?
b. Inor ez zen ausartu ezer esaten. (Garate, *Esku* 173)
No one dared to say anything.

16.5.6 The Proximate Future Tense

When combined with a kinetic gerundive, a synthetic form of the verb *joan* 'to go' is prone to assume the status of an auxiliary, taking part in the creation of a proximate future tense. It will directly follow the gerund in a positive clause and precede it in a negative one, thus copying the behavior of an auxiliary in regard to its participle. As the examples show, there are no constraints on the subject of this construction:

(69) a. Galtzera goaz! (Mt 8:25)
We're going to perish!

b. Soinua bukatzera dihoa. (*LBB* 198)
The music is going to end.
c. Hogeita hamazazpi urte betetzera noa. (Atxaga, *Z.H.* 89)
I am going to be thirty-seven years old. (Lit. 'to complete 37 years')
d. Neskamearekin ezkontzera omen zoaz. (*TOE* I, 192)
They say that you're going to marry the maid.
e. Horma zahar hori erortzera doa. (*EGLU* II, 35, 467)
That old wall is going to fall down.

In negative clauses the meaning element of proximity in time tends to fade, so that we are left merely with a more peremptory alternative to the ordinary future tense:

(70) a. Baina ez noa inori esatera. (Atxaga, *Gizona* 107)
But I'm not going to tell anyone.
b. Etxea ez zihoan uztera. (*LBB* 98)
He wasn't going to leave the house.

16.6 Raising Out of Gerundives

An aspectual verb or a verb of motion governing a gerundive complement may allow the direct object of the gerund to be raised into the main clause. A slightly wider class of verbs allows an indirect object of the gerund to be similarly raised.

16.6.1 Indirect Object Raising

A dative complement which the meaning of the sentence clearly assigns to the gerund and which therefore belongs inside the gerundive, may appear instead within the main clause, as evidenced by dative agreement on its verb. Not all main verbs allow this construction. It occurs predominantly with verbs of motion and aspectual verbs, although for some speakers verbs of daring and conatives are also included. A rather natural way to account for this phenomenon is to assume that such verbs optionally trigger a movement rule raising indirect objects, usually in the shape of pronouns, out of the gerundive complement into the main clause.

Examples involving the proximate future tense are not uncommon:

(71) a. Azken nahia irakurtzera noakizue. (Garate, *Esku* 18)
I am going to read the last will to yoû.
b. Ez noakizu liburu honen egilea aurkeztera. (K. Mitxelena, in Etxaide, *16 Seme* 7)
I'm not going to present the author of this book to you.

Verbs of motion generally allow dative raising:

(72) a. Horregatik joan nintzaion agur esatera. (Atxaga, *Obab.* 254)
That's why I went to say goodbye to him.

b. Ni joango natzaizu laguntzera. (2 Sm 10:11)
I will go to help you.
c. Hire ama etorriko zaik laguntzera. (Lertxundi, *Aise* 28)
Yoúr mother will come to help yoú.

Here are some examples with aspectual verbs:

(73) a. Hori esaten ari nintzaion atezainari. (*TOE* I, 295)
I was (just) saying that to the doorkeeper.
b. Zorrak pilatzen ari zitzaizkion. (Garate, *Esku* 189)
The debts were piling up on him.
c. Orduan, anaiak hitz egiten hasi zitzaizkion. (Gn 45:15)
Then, the brothers began to speak to him.
d. Bisitak ugaritzen hasi nintzaion. (Atxaga, *Obab*. 133)
I began to increase my visits to him.
e. Gizon pottoloari irriñoz begiratzen geratu nintzaion. (Garate, *Ald.* 18)
I had been looking at the chubby man with a little smile.
f. Eskutitzak idazten jarraitu zion Pellok Mireni.
Pete went on writing letters to Mary.

And these examples have conative verbs:

(74) a. Ni saiatu nintzaion ateak zabaltzen.
I tried to open doors for him.
b. Dirua bidaltzen ahalegindu natzaio.
I have done my best to send him money.

These have verbs of daring:

(75) a. Eta geroztik ez zitzaion inor galdetzera ausartzen. (Mk 12:34; *Lau Eb.*)
And thereafter nobody dared to ask him.
b. Atrebituko natzaio berriz ere mintzatzera ene Jainkoari. (Chourio III, 10.1)
I will dare once more to speak to my God.

Raising can apply in a sentence more than once:

(76) Iritzia eskatzera hurbiltzera ere ez natzaio atrebitzen.
I don't dare to even approach him to ask him his opinion.

16.6.2 Direct Object Raising

An animate direct object can be raised out of gerundive complement governed by a verb of motion or an aspectual verb. In the process, the object is demoted to a dative. Examples usually involve the verbs *joan* 'to go' or *etorri* 'to come':

(77) a. Aitari ikustera noakio. (Lafitte 1962, sec. 482, p. 223)
I am going to see Father.

b. Banoakio iratzartzera. (Jn 11:11; *EAB*)
I am going to wake him up.
c. Jendetza handiak urrutietatik zihoazkion adoratzera. (*TB* 205–206)
From distant areas masses of people were going to adore her.
d. Asko joaten zitzaizkion ikustera. (*TB* 223)
Many people were going to see him.
e. Don Jorje Nabera ardura joaten zitzaion ikustera. (Lapitze, 88)
Don Jorje Nabera often went to see him.
f. Bisitatzera etorri zaigu Andoni. (Goenaga, *Comp.* 521)
Anthony has come to visit us.
g. Eta ikustera etorri zintzaizkidaten. (*TB* 102–103)
And yoû came to see me.

But there also are examples with the aspectual verb *hasi* 'to begin':

(78) a. Idumearrak eta siriarrak hasi zitzaizkion zirikatzen. (*TZ* II, 50)
The Idumeans and the Syrians began to challenge him.
b. Andoni jotzen hasi zaizu zuri. (Goenaga, *Comp.* 521)
Anthony has begun to hit you.

It is noteworthy that Goenaga finds (79), the unraised version of (78b), hardly acceptable, on account of its absolutive personal pronoun:

(79) ?Andoni zu jotzen hasi da.
Anthony has begun to hit you.

Raising of inanimate direct objects is attested solely in the proximate future tense construction. Here no demotion to dative takes place, so that the verb *joan* can be saddled with a plural object marker not otherwise part of its paradigm:

(80) a. Liburu horiek irakurtzera doatza. (Lafitte 1962, sec. 482, p. 223)
He is going to read those books.
b. Etsaiari armak hartzera nindoazkion. (Lafitte 1962, sec. 482, p. 223)
I was going to take the weapons from the enemy.
c. Bi hitz esatera noazkizu. (Cf. Gerriko I, 437)
I am going to say a couple of words to you.

Examples of this type, however, are exceedingly rare. It seems that the overwhelming majority of speakers adhere to a structure-preserving constraint on morphology, in virtue of which they reject "impossible" verb forms.

16.7 Object-Controlled Gerundives

This section will deal with gerundives whose subject is controlled by the direct or indirect object of the main verb.

16.7.1 Gerundives in Causativoid Contexts

Permissive causatives (discussed in sections 16.3.2 and 16.3.3) are typical instances of object-controlled gerundives. As we saw in section 16.3.2, the western dialects (Biscayan and Guipuzcoan) employ an ordinary gerundive, the others a kinetic one:

(81) a. Ez dit ezer edaten uzten. (*TOE* II, 12)
He doesn't let me drink anything.
b. Asetasunak ez du aberatsa lo egitera uzten. (Eccl 5.11; Dv)
Repleteness doesn't let the rich man sleep.

Incidentally, verbs denoting the opposite concept, as are *debekatu* and *eragotzi*, both meaning 'to forbid' as well as 'to prevent', usually take absolutive nominalizations as complements: *sartzea eragotzi* 'to forbid to enter', 'to prevent entering'. Occasionally one also meets *sartzez eragotzi*, *sartzetik eragotzi*, *sartzera eragotzi*, or *sartzen eragotzi* (Garate, *NY* 24).

Western usage preserves a few instances of a gerundive governed by the verb *eman* 'to give' in a construction we might call the periphrastic causative: *aditzen eman* 'to give to understand'. The Guipuzcoan dialect has lost this option, except for two examples: *edaten eman* 'to give to drink' and *jaten eman* 'to give to eat'. Syntactically, the construction is highly interesting for its twofold control: both the subject and the object of the gerund are controlled, the former by the indirect object and the latter by the direct object of the main verb *eman*:

(82) a. Zeruko ogia eman zien jaten. (Jn 6:31)
He gave them bread from heaven to eat.
b. Semeari edaten eman zion. (*TZ* I, 48)
She gave it to her son to drink.

Causative cognition verbs (see section 16.5.2) provide yet another instance of indirect object control, as the subject of their gerund is controlled by the dative noun phrase representing the causee. Most commonly involved are the archaic causatives *irakatsi* 'to teach' and *erakutsi* 'to show' (often used for 'to teach'):

(83) a. Idazten irakatsi zigun.
He taught us how to write.
b. Zuk erakusten didazu zerura begiratzen. (Urretabizkaia, *Sat.* 76)
You are showing me how to look at the sky.
c. Erakutsiko dinat nik hire haizeak gordetzen. (*LBB* 158)
I'll teach yoù to keep yoùr airs to yourself.

Intuitively, helping someone to do something and teaching someone to do something seem to be performances belonging to the same category. Thus one would expect the verb *lagundu* 'to help' to take the same type of complement as *irakatsi* 'to teach'. This prediction is borne out:

(84) a. Lagunduko dizut bidoia sartzen? (Atxaga, *Gizona* 36)
Shall I help you bring in the drum?
b. Jainkoak lagundu zion filistearrak garaitzen. (2 Chr 26:7)
God helped him defeat the Philistines.

While the other meaning of *lagundu*, that is, 'to accompany', does not admit sentential complements at all in the northern dialects, in the south a kinetic gerundive is possible:

(84) c. Ez al didak brotxea aukeratzera lagundu behar? (Atxaga, *Gizona* 314)
Aren't yoú going to accompany me to choose the brooch?

16.7.2 Gerundives with Verbs of Perception

Provided the object of perception is expressed in the absolutive or dative case, that is, as an NP, not a PP, all perception verbs allow gerundive complements whose subject is controlled by the noun phrase denoting that object. Starting with the prototypical perception verb *ikusi* 'to see', we can find the following:

(85) a. Ez dugu atea zabaltzen ikusi. (*MEIG* I, 199)
We have not seen the door open(ing).
b. Nork ikusi du inor hiltzen? (Garate, *E.E.* 122)
Who has seen him kill(ing) anyone?
c. Jai bakoitzean nexka berria ikusten zaitut maitatzen. (*LBB* 319)
At each festival I see you loving a new girl.

A gerundive complement can have a medio-passive structure (see section 12.5.1):

(86) a. Ardoa nik behin ikusi nuen egiten.
I once saw wine being made.
b. Etxe hori ikusi dugu jasotzen.
We have seen that house being built.
c. ?*Etxe hori ikusi dugu zuek jasotzen.
We have seen that house being built by yoû.

Since gerunds reject overt subjects and medio-passives are unable to mark agents, example (86c) should be ungrammatical, which it is for most, though not all, speakers.

Action nouns in the inessive case may substitute for a gerundive, for instance, *dantzan* 'at dance' instead of *dantzatzen* 'dancing':

(87) a. Ez zaitut inoiz dantzan ikusi. (Oñatibia, 286)
I have never seen you dancing. (Lit. "at dance")

It is therefore plausible that the final *n* of the gerund represents the inessive case, a conclusion buttressed by the further observation that, here as before, gerundives can be questioned using inessive *zertan* 'in what':

(87) b. Zertan ikusi dituzu ehiztariak? Azeriak hiltzen.
(Engaged) in what did you see the hunters? Killing foxes.

I will now present some examples of gerundives with perception verbs other than *ikusi*. Regarding the verbs meaning 'to hear', *entzun* and *aditu*, I recall that their objects, when animate, occur in the dative case form, at least in the south. In the north, animate objects are usually in the absolutive, although the dative can be found also.

(88) a. Mintzo bat entzun nuen niri esaten: . . . (Acts 11:7)
I heard a voice saying to me: . . .
b. Zure aitari entzun diot Esauri esaten: . . . (Gn 27:6)
I have heard your father say to Esau: . . .
c. Sartzen entzun dut. (*EGLU* II, 103)
I have heard him come in.

(89) a. Guk bere ahotik esaten aditu diogu. (*TB* 120)
We have heard him say it from his own mouth.
b. Aditu dut zure aita mintzatzen zure anaia Esaurekin. (Gn 27:6; Dv)
I have heard your father speak with your brother Esau.

(90) a. Goizeko orduetan etortzen sumatu zuen. (Garate, *Alaba* 22)
She had noticed her coming in the morning hours.
b. Sentitzen zaitut sala berrian jaikitzen. (Satrustegi, 25)
I notice you getting up in the new parlor.
c. Asaben odola bere zainetan irakiten nabaritzen zuen. (Garate, *E.E.* 7)
He felt the blood of his ancestors boiling in his veins.
d. Ene laguna hautematen dut ahultzen. (J. Etchepare, *Ber.* 99)
I notice my companion getting weaker.

Also *aurkitu* 'to find' and *harrapatu* 'to catch' can occur as verbs of perception:

(91) a. Emakume hau ezkontz-nahasten aurkitu dugu. (Jn 8:4; *IB*)
We have found this woman committing adultery.
b. Gure nazioa nahaspilatzen harrapatu dugu gizon hau. (Lk 23:2)
We have caught this man subverting our nation.

16.7.3 Object-Controlled Kinetic Gerundives

First of all, warning should be sounded that not all allative nominalizations lacking an overt subject qualify as kinetic gerundives. Quite a few verbs will take allative complements that allow internal time adverbials, and for that reason fail our test of what constitutes a gerundive:

(92) a. Larunbatean afaltzera gonbidatzen haut. (Garate, *Ald.* 72)
I invite yoú to (have) dinner on Saturday.

b. Bihar hiltzera kondenatu zuten atzo.
   They condemned him yesterday to die tomorrow.

Crucial evidence for the aberrant status of such examples is the fact that they also occur in the westernmost variety of Biscayan, since this subdialect totally lacks kinetic gerundives and employs ordinary ones instead: *Loreak erosten noa* 'I'm going to buy flowers'.

As we will see, genuine object-controlled kinetic gerundives all occur in causativoid contexts. Two of these have already been discussed: permissive causatives in the eastern dialects (examples 15b and 81b) and transitive *ohitu* 'to accustom' (example 66d). The remaining contexts will fall into three groups: periphrastic causatives with *eman*, verbs of displacement, and verbs of forcing.

16.7.3.1 Periphrastic Causatives with *eman*

In the eastern dialects, kinetic gerunds of verbs of ingestion, cognition, or perception can combine with the verb *eman* 'to give' to form a quasi-causative structure: X gives Y to Z with the intention for Z to Verb Y, where "Verb" represents the action denoted by the gerund. This gerund has no overt arguments or adjuncts: its subject is controlled by the indirect object of *eman*, and its object by the direct object of that verb.

The Guipuzcoan dialect has borrowed *aditzera eman* 'to give to understand', and a few additional ones are apt to occur in the southern literary standard, such as *ezagutzera eman* or *jakitera eman* 'to make known'.

In the northern dialects, several more are in use, among which are *ikustera eman* or *erakustera eman* 'to show' and, especially, *edatera eman* 'to give to drink' and *jatera eman* 'to give to eat', for which the southern dialects use the ordinary gerund: *edaten eman* and *jaten eman* (see section 16.7.1).

16.7.3.2 Kinetic Gerundives with Verbs of Displacement

Semantically, verbs of displacement, such as *ekarri* 'to bring' and *bidali* 'to send', are causatives of verbs of motion. As a consequence, it is natural for them to take kinetic gerundives with object control, since the object of the verb acts as the causee, and thus corresponds to the subject of the motion verbs studied in section 16.5.5.1. The following examples are typical:

(93) a. Horiek gosaltzera daramatzagu. (*TOE* I, 346)
   Those we are taking away to have breakfast.
 b. Nork eraman du Katalin, jostatzera izarrakin? (*LBB* 266)
   Who has taken away Katalin to play with the stars?
 c. Ardoa erostera bidali naute. (Goenaga, *Comp.* 529)
   They have sent me to buy wine.

Here, as in section 16.5.5.1, we meet with purpose clauses disguised as gerundives:

(94) a. Amak mataza hauek garbitzera bidali nau ibai honetara. (*LBB* 161)
Mother has sent me to this river to wash these skeins.
b. Iruñeatik ekarri dute hiltzera. (Garate, *Leh.* 134)
They have brought her from Pamplona to die.

16.7.3.3 Kinetic Gerundives with Verbs of Forcing

Forcing someone to some action can be viewed as a metaphoric extension of displacement; hence the appearance of the kinetic gerundive:

(95) a. Berari kalte egitera bultzatu ninduan. (Jb 2:3)
Yoú pushed me to do him harm.
b. Pauso txar bat ematera bultzatu ninduten. (Atxaga, *Gizona* 278)
They incited me to make a false step.
c. Nagusiak berarekin ezkontzera behartu omen zuen. (Garate, *NY* 51)
The boss allegedly forced her to marry him.
d. Egunero jan beharrak lana hartzera behartzen ninduen. (Garate, *Alaba* 9)
The need to eat every day was forcing me to take the job.

16.8 The Nature of Gerundives

16.8.1 Gerundives as Indefinite Inessives

The consistent distributional similarity we have observed between gerundives and inessive action nouns (e.g., *lanean* 'at work') strongly suggests that gerundives are in fact inessive nominalizations. Yet our case would even be stronger if we could show that the form *-n* is independently required as an inessive ending for the verbal noun. Happily, we can do so—by availing ourselves of nominal compounds with a verbal noun as their final member: *sagar-biltze* 'apple-gathering', *liburu-saltze* 'book-selling', *bizar-mozte* 'beard-cutting'.

As the grammarian Goenaga has aptly demonstrated, such compounds do not represent nominalizations, since they are unable to function as sentential complements. Thus, alongside example (96a), we do not get (96b):

(96) a. Bizarra moztea erabaki dut. (Goenaga, *Comp.* 562)
I've decided to cut (my) beard.
b. *Bizar-moztea erabaki dut. (Ibid.)
*I've decided to beard-cut.

Indeed, while it is true that a few juxtapositions of a direct object and its verb have resulted in the creation of new transitive verbs (*Jauna hartu* 'to take the Lord' > *jaunartu* 'to take communion', *itxura aldatu* 'to change the appearance' > *itxuraldatu* 'to transform'), a Basque verb essentially lacks the ability to incorporate its direct object, whether definite or indefinite. Accordingly, there are no verbs of the type **sagar-bildu* 'to apple-gather', **liburu-saldu* 'to book-sell', **bizar-moztu* 'to beard-cut'.

To return to our nominal compounds, they are action nominals and occur in the same contexts as other action nouns. When the context requires an inessive, however, we find the ending *-n*, not *-an* as in *lanean*:

(97) a. Bizar-mozten ari da.
He is busy beard-cutting.
b. Bizar-mozten ikusi dugu.
We have seen him beard-cutting.
c. Bizar mozten ez du oraindik ikasi. (Goenaga, *Comp.* 562)
He hasn't yet learned how to beard-cut.

Similar examples may be found in the literature:

(98) a. Bartel patata zuritzen ari zen sukaldean. (Amuriza, *Hil* 9)
Bartel was busy potato-peeling in the kitchen.
b. Lepo mozten ari dira. (Esd. III [= 1 Esd.], 4.5; Dv)
They are busy throat-cutting.

Since the responsibility for the unusual inessive has to lie with the final member of the compound, the conclusion must be that the verbal noun has indeed the property of requiring inessive *-n* in certain contexts. This form cannot belong to the definite paradigm, this being already preempted by the form *-an* found in *etortzean* 'in coming'. It has to be part of the indefinite paradigm, thereby explaining the absence of an indefnite form with the ending *-tan*. In fact, indefinite forms of verbal nouns never take *-ta-*; these apparently conform to the place-name declension of section 3.5: *etortzen*, *etortzetik*, *etortzera*, *etortzeraino* follow the pattern of *Bilbon*, *Bilbotik*, *Bilbora*, *Bilboraino*.

Gerundives, we thus conclude, are indefinite inessives of nominalized clauses. Given that gerundives were characterized as tenseless complements (see section 16.4.1), it seems natural to infer that it is precisely the lack of tense that makes them indefinite. If this assumption is correct, then definite inessive complements should also exist and should admit tense. This prediction is borne out:

(99) Jokoa, azken finean, ezagunaren eta ezezagunaren arteko orekagunea aurkitzean datza. (*MEIG* VI, 146)
The game consists, after all, in finding the balance between the known and the unknown.

Here, a time adverbial can be inserted into the complement: *lehenbailehen aurkitzean* 'in finding as soon as possible'.

For reasons not altogether clear to me, subjects of definite nominalizations are much less narrowly controlled than those of indefinite ones. Thus, in Basque as in English, in the definite (100a), either I or Itziar is going home, whereas in the indefinite (100b), it has to be Itziar:

(100) a. Itziar ikusi dut etxeratzean.
I've seen Itziar going home.
b. Itziar ikusi dut etxeratzen.
I've seen Itziar go home.

16.8.2 Kinetic Gerundives as Indefinite Allatives

The same reasoning as in section 16.8.1 leads to the conclusion that kinetic gerundives are indefinite allatives of nominalized clauses. But allative *-ra*, unlike inessive *-n*, also occurs in the definite paradigm. Assuming again that definiteness is correlated with the presence of tense, we now have an explanation for the nongerundive allative complements in section 16.7.3: these are simply definite allatives of nominalized clauses.

The insights now at hand allow us to redefine sections 16.4 to 16.8 as an attempt to account for the distribution of indefinite nominalizations. In section 29.2 attention will be paid to definite nominalizations in their function as sentential complements.

16.9 Denominal Agentives: The Suffixes *-gile* and *-gin*

Attached to a noun *N*, either one of the suffixes *-gile* and *-gin* yields a nominal denoting a being who, professionally or at least regularly, produces, processes, or cultivates N. Despite the obvious connection of the suffix *-gile* to the agentive noun *egile* 'maker' of section 12.6.1, and that of the suffix *-gin* to the active sense 'he who has made' of the perfect participle *egin*, no aspectual difference between the two suffixes can be detected in historical Basque. Although recent fashion seems to favor *-gile* over *-gin* in the literary standard, for most of the eligible nouns either suffix will do:

ardo	wine	ardogile	winemaker (ardogin)
arma	weapon	armagile	arms manufacturer (armagin)
bizar	beard	bizargile	barber (bizargin)
diru	money	dirugile	minter, coiner, moneymaker (dirugin)
egur	firewood	egurgile	woodcutter (egurgin)
eltze	pot	eltzegile	potter (eltzegin)
etxe	house	etxegile	builder, architect (etxegin)
ezkontza	marriage	ezkontzagile	marriage broker, matchmaker (ezkontzagin)
ezti	honey	eztigile	honey maker, beekeeper (eztigin)
gaitz	evil	gaizkile	evildoer, malefactor, criminal (gaizkin)
gazta	cheese	gaztagile	cheese maker (gazta(n)gin)
gozo	sweet	gozogile	confectioner (gozogin)
horma	wall	hormagile	mason (hormagin)

irudi	picture, image	irudigile	illustrator (irudigin)
kanpai	church bell	kanpaigile	bell founder (kanpaigin)
kanta	song	kantagile	songwriter (kantagin)
lege	law	legegile	legislator, legislative (legegin)
oihal	fabric	oihalgile	textile manufacturer (oihalgin)
ontzi	vessel	ontzigile	shipbuilder, potter (ontzigin)
sare	net	saregile	net maker (saregin)
saski	basket	saskigile	basket maker (saskigin)
soka	rope	sokagile	rope maker (sokagin)
ume	offspring, child	umegile	offspring maker, fertile (umegin)
upel	cask, barrel	upelgile	cooper, barrel maker (upelgin)
urre	gold	urregile	goldsmith (urregin)
uztar	yoke	uztargile	yoke maker (uztargin)
zapata	shoe	zapatagile	shoe manufacturer, shoemaker, cobbler (zapatagin)
zilar	silver	zilargile	silversmith (zilargin)

With nouns entering in *egin* idiom (see section 13.3) and a few others, *-gin* derivatives are avoided in actual practice. Yet their virtual existence must be assumed in order to account for the corresponding derivatives formed with the suffix *-tza* (discussed later in this section). For the following examples, then, only *-gile* is used:

bake	peace	bakegile	peacemaker
birao	blasphemy, swearword	biraogile	blasphemer, curser
galde	question	galdegile	questioner, inquirer, petitioner
ipuin	story	ipuingile	story writer, storyteller, fibber
iruzur	deception	iruzurgile	deceiver, swindler, fraud
kalte	harm, damage	kaltegile	harmer, damager, offender
kondaira	chronicle, history	kondairagile	chronicler, historian
lan	work, job	langile	worker
liburu	book	liburugile	author, printer, bookbinder
liskar	quarrel	liskargile	quarreler
mesede	favor	mesedegile	benefactor, patron
oihu	scream, cry	oihugile	town crier
on	good	ongile	benefactor
oski	shoe	oskigile	shoe manufacturer, shoemaker, cobbler
oso	whole	osagile	healer, doctor
sendo	healthy	sendagile	doctor, physician

[*N.B.* The derivatives *osagile* and *sendagile* are exceptional in showing Minor Apocope (section 3.8.1) and also in being based on adjectives (or verbs) rather than nouns.]

To refer to some of the oldest professions, only *-gin* derivatives are in use:

eme	female	emagin	midwife
haragi	meat	harakin	butcher (attested since 1301)
harri	stone	hargin	quarrier (attested since 1360)
ikatz	coal	ikazkin	charcoal burner
ile	hair, wool	ilagin	woolman, fuller
lur	earth	lugin	farmer (Biscayan only)
ogi	bread	okin	baker
zur	wood	zurgin	joiner, carpenter

While the suffix *-tza* will be discussed in section 25.8.2, it may be mentioned at this point that it can attach to agentives with *-gin* in order to designate productive activities and professions:

harakin	butcher	harakintza	butchery (also: massacre)
langin	worker	langintza	industry, craft
legegin	legislator	legegintza	legislation
okin	baker	okintza	baking trade
sendagin	physician	sendagintza	medical profession, medical art

As was mentioned earlier, the forms *langin* and *sendagin* have a peculiar status: they are discarded in favor of *langile* and *sendagil*e whenever the suffix *-tza* is not present.

In theory, the suffix *-tza* can be added also to agentives with *-gile*; in practice, however, this option is hardly ever taken.

Derivatives with *-gintza* occur in the literature also in a concrete meaning, that is, referring to the premises in which a professional activity is concentrated: *bizargintza* 'barbershop', *ezkontzagintza* 'matrimonial agency', *okintza* 'bakery'. Today's literary standard rejects this usage, adopting instead the suffix *-tegi* of section 3.8.2: *bizartegi* 'barbershop', *gozotegi* 'candy shop', *harategi* 'butcher shop', *lantegi* 'workshop'. But for 'bakery', *okindegi*, based on *okin* 'baker', is nowadays preferred to the older term *ogitegi*, presumably for reasons of euphony.

16.10 Vocabulary

16.10.1 Verbs

ahalegindu	to do one's best
amaitu	to end
aspertu	to get bored, to get fed up
ausartu	to dare
behartu	to force
erakutsi	to show, to teach

erre	to smoke, to burn, to roast
eskatu	to ask (for), to request
ferekatu	to caress
galdu	to lose (all senses)
harrapatu	to catch
hautsi	to break
idatzi	to write
irakatsi	to teach
iritsi	to reach, to arrive
jo	to beat, to hit
lagundu	to help, to accompany
maitatu	to love
saiatu	to try
salatu	to betray, to denounce
ulertu	to understand
zabaldu	to widen, to open
zaindu	to guard, to protect

16.10.2 Other Items

baimen	permission
eskutitz	letter
ez . . . inoiz	never
gaitz	evil, ailment, calamity
gaizkile	criminal, evildoer
garesti	expensive
gaztaina	chestnut
gizen	fat (adj.)
harakin	butcher
harakintza	butchery, massacre
harategi	butcher shop
hezur	bone
isil	silent, quiet
jauregi	palace
langile	worker, workman
mihi	tongue (also: *mingain*)
nagi	lazy
okin	baker
okindegi	bakery
sendagile	doctor, physician

txahal	calf
zail	difficult
zoro	crazy, silly

16.11 Exercises

16.11.1 Translate into English

1. Mihiak ez du hezurrik hausten, baina bai hautsarazten. (Landerretche, 67)
2. Mirenek Joni bere burua garbiarazi dio. (A. Eguzkitza)
3. Noren eskutitzak errearazi ote dizkiozu gaur goizean neskameari?
4. Txahal gizen bat hilaraziko al didazu?
5. Sendagile honek ez dit bere alabei musu ematen utzi nahi.
6. Gauzak isilean edukitzen ongi zekien. (Garate, *Esku* 116)
7. Galtzen ere jakin egin behar da. (*TOE* II, 85)
8. Pello zakurrak eta katuak jotzen ari omen zen bere andregai berriaren etxe aurrean.
9. Nola ez zara aspertzen egunero liburu bera irakurtzen?
10. Ez naiz hona etorri inori erakustera euskara maitatzen. (*MEIG* VII, 131)
11. Nola iritsiko naiz andre maitagarri haren gerri polita ferekatzera?
12. Alkatea ez da behin ere gure langileei baimena eskatzeraino jaitsi.

16.11.2 Translate into Basque

1. What made the doctor write us that silly letter?
2. Yesterday the doctor came to tell me the truth.
3. We didn't see you come out of the bakery.
4. The criminal didn't dare open the door to the palace.
5. I've tried to be a good teacher, but the students haven't let me.
6. What is forcing you to be so lazy?
7. Those expensive books are hard to find.
8. The baker didn't let the butcher help him guard the calves.
9. Few people know how to roast chestnuts.
10. Won't you ever begin to understand these things?
11. The criminals weren't going to betray themselves so easily.
12. Why don't you help the black cat catch all those mice?

17 Conditionals; the Prolative

17.1 Conditional Sentences

A full conditional sentence consists of two clauses: a protasis embodying a condition and an apodosis stating a consequence. Usually, the protasis precedes the apodosis, but the reverse order is also found. If the protasis is a finite clause, its main verb must carry the prefix *ba-*: *bada* 'if he is', *badu* 'if he has', *badator* 'if he is coming', *ikusten badu* 'if he sees', and so on.

With periphrastic verb forms there is no danger of mistaking this prefix for the homophonous affirmative particle of sections 8.3 and 8.6.1, as this particle—extremely rare with periphrastic verb forms anyway—always causes preposing of the auxiliary: *badu ikusten* 'he does see it'. For any verb form, synthetic and periphrastic alike, ambiguity can be forestalled by making use of the optional conjunction *baldin*, to be discussed in section 17.1.2. While conspicuously frequent with synthetic verb forms, its use is never obligatory. Furthermore, in most varieties of Basque, conditional *ba-* and affirmative *ba-* induce dissimilar intonation contours on the phonological phrase they are heading and can therefore, in principle, be told apart. Particulars will not be detailed here, since they differ substantially according to region.

In the next section, the scope of our discussion will be confined to conditional sentences in the indicative mood. Subsequent sections (17.2 and 17.3) will then deal with the conditional mood, a special set of verb forms employed when a speaker wants to convey his expectation that the condition involved will not in fact be realized.

17.1.1 The Indicative Mood: Constituent Order within the Protasis

There is a noticeable tendency for the protasis to be verb-final, particularly when the clause is positive:

(1) a. Inork behi bat hiltzen badu, urkatu egiten dute segituan. (Atxaga, *Behi* 165)
If anyone kills a cow, they hang him at once.

b. Norbaitek Gizonaren Semearen kontra zerbait esaten badu, barkatuko dio Jainkoak. (Mt 12:32)
If someone says something against the Son of man, God will forgive him.
c. Nork egingo dizue kalte, zuek beti on egiten saiatzen bazarete? (1 Pt 3:13)
Who will do yoû harm, if yoû always try to do good?

Postverbal constituents are not altogether ruled out, however:

(2) a. Bakarrik gelditu bada munduan, horretan ez du hobenik. (Satrustegi, 96)
If he has been left alone in the world, it is not his fault. (Lit.: "If he has stayed alone in the world, in that he has no guilt.")
b. Bestela, itsua badabil itsu-mutil, ongi jaioak gaude. (*MEIG* I, 140)
Otherwise, if a blind person acts as a guide to the blind, we will be in a fine state. (Literally: well born.)
c. Itsu bat jartzen bada beste baten itsu-aurreko, biak zulora eroriko dira. (Mt 15:14; *IB*)
If a blind person puts himself up as a guide to the blind, both will fall into a pit.

What happens when the protasis is a negative clause depends on the dialect. In a large eastern area, the auxiliary precedes its participle just as in other negative clauses, while in the Biscayan dialect the order remains the same as in a positive clause, with the negated auxiliary directly following the participle. The standard language takes its cue from the central zone, where both orders are equally common.

The following are examples with preposed auxiliary:

(3) a. Nik ez zaitut utziko, zuk ez banauzu uzten. (Larzabal, *Hiru* 13)
I won't leave you, if you don't leave me.
b. Ez baduzu jaten, ez zara haundituko. (Satrustegi, 192)
If you don't eat, you won't grow up.
c. Gaixoa ez bada sendatzen, medikuak du errua. (*TOE* I, 375)
If the patient doesn't recover, it is the doctor's fault.
d. Berehala ez baduzue alde egiten, zakurrak puskatu egingo zaituzte. (Garate, *Iz.B.* 74)
If yoû don't leave at once, the dog will tear yoû to pieces.

These are examples with unmoved auxiliary:

(4) a. Erabiltzen ez bada, hil egiten da euskara. (Gandiaga, 95)
If it is not being used, Basque dies.
b. Gehiago ardorik edaten ez badun, aberastuko gaitun. (*Goldaraz* 22)
If yoù drink no more wine, yoù will make us rich.
c. Itzultzen ez badiozu, zinez hilko zarete. (Gn 20:7)
If yoû do not restore her to him, yoû will surely die.

d. Etxea Jaunak eraikitzen ez badu, alferrik ari dira etxegileak (Ps 127:1)
If the Lord does not build the house, the builders are working in vain.

17.1.2 The Conjunction *baldin*

A protasis may include an optional conjunction, *baldin*, whose function, according to Azkue, is merely to highlight the condition: "no tiene traducción directa, su oficio es dar más fuerza á la condición" (it has no straight translation, its function is to strengthen the condition). (1905–1906, I, 129) Nowadays its canonical position is directly in front of the conditional prefix *ba-*:

(5) a. Ni zerbait izan baldin banaiz, hizkuntzalaria izan naiz. (*MEIG* IX, 73)
If I have been something, I have been a linguist.
b. Gorde nahi baldin badu, gordeko du. (*MEIG* IV, 59)
If he wants to keep it, he will keep it.
c. Beste eredurik ez baldin badakar, ez du mintzatzeko eskubiderik. (*MEIG* VIII, 144)
If he isn't contributing any other model, he has no right to speak.
d. Ez baldin baduzue sinesten, eroriko zarete. (Is 7:9; Dv)
If yoû do not believe, yoû will come to fall.

An older usage, still accepted in the literary language, places *baldin* at the very head of the protasis:

(6) a. Baldin hala ez bada, euskaldunek berek dute falta eta ez euskarak. (*Ax*. 19)
If it is not that way, the Basques themselves are at fault and not the Basque language.
b. Baldin gaur arratsean gordetzen ez bazara, bihar hil beharko zara. (*TZ* I, 263)
If you don't hide this evening, you will have to die tomorrow.
c. Baldin ez badut negar egiten, harrizkoa dut bihotza. (Agirre, *Kres*. 29)
If I do not weep, I have a heart made of stone.
d. Baldin Hazparne itzaltzen bada, ez dugu Euskal Herririk. (Xalbador, *Odol*. 161)
If Hazparne disappears, we have no Basque Country.

In this clause-initial use, *baldin* may be followed by an expletory *eta* 'and':

(7) Baldin eta handik irteten banaiz, zu eta zureak nire federa konbertituko zarete. (Beobide, 167)
If I come out of there, you and your family will convert to my faith.

17.1.3 Avoidance of Future Tense Forms

Future tense forms, while very common in the apodosis, are avoided in the protasis. Present tense forms occur where future tense ones might have been expected on the ground that the action has not yet occurred:

(8) a. Pilomenak jakiten badu, larrutuko zaitu. (*LBB* 140)
If Philomene gets to know it, she will skin you.
b. Osaba zerritegira etortzen bada, ez diot sartzen utziko. (Atxaga, *Bi An*. 48)
If Uncle comes to the pigsty, I won't let him enter.
c. Ostera ikusten bagara, emango dizut eskua. (Atxaga, *Z.H.* 138)
If we see each other again, I will shake hands with you.
d. Ostiraletan etortzen bazara, plazer haundiz hitzegingo dut zurekin. (Atxaga, *Obab*. 174)
If you come on Fridays, I will talk to you with great pleasure.

As Saltarelli (1988, 47) has noticed, the southern dialects allow a peculiar type of conditional whose protasis even requires a future tense. The apodosis of these conditionals states a necessary condition for the protasis to come true:

(9) a. Batasuna premiazkoa da, hizkuntza biziko baldin bada. (Cf. *MEIG* VIII, 46)
Unification is necessary, if the language is going to live.
b. Horrela izango da aurrera ere, biziko baldin bada. (*MEIG* IV, 35)
It will be like that in the future too, if it is to live.

17.1.4 Untypical Apodoses

Given the function fulfilled by the apodosis, it may seem odd that it can take the form of a question:

(10) a. Baina egia badiot, zergatik ez didazue sinesten? (Jn 8:46)
But if I tell the truth, why do you not believe me?
b. Hik ez badakik, nork ote daki? (Garate, *Leh*. 126)
If yoú don't know it, who does, I wonder?
c. Eta nik ez badut hitzegiten, nola jakingo dute? (Atxaga, *Gizona* 328)
And if I don't talk, how will they know?
d. Zer esan behar du herriak, hori jakiten badu? (*LBB* 173)
What is the village going to say, if it comes to know it?

To help interpret these conditionals, we may supply a missing statement such as "then the question arises. . . ." A similar expedient may explain imperative apodoses as well:

(11) a. Gaizki hitzegin badut, esan zertan. (Jn 18:23)
If I have spoken wrongly, say why.
b. Autoraino lagundu nahi badidak, etorri nirekin. (Atxaga, *Gizona* 326)
If yoú want to keep me company as far as to the car, come with me.
c. Barkatu, itxaronarazi badizuet. (*TOE* II, 212)
Forgive (me), if I have kept yoû waiting. (Lit. 'made yoû wait')

(For the perfect participle as a short form of the imperative, see chapter 22.)

17.2 Morphology of the Conditional Mood

The conditional mood covers three paradigms: first, a paradigm confined to the protasis, which we will refer to as "protasis forms," and then two paradigms, the "conditional forms," used in the apodosis: the "present conditional" and the "past conditional."

17.2.1 A Truncation Process

The morphology of all three paradigms is based on that of the past indicative, discussed in section 10.1. To simplify our exposition, it will be convenient to introduce the concept of a truncated verb form. Truncation as defined here can apply to any finite verb, and it consists in the removal, if applicable, of the past tense suffix *-n* together with the epenthetic vowel possibly inserted before it, followed by the restoration of any person or number suffix to its pristine shape: *-t* to *-da*, *-k* or *-a* to *-ga*, *-n* to *-na* (cf. section 9.1).

With respect to the verb *izan* 'to be', there is a special provision stipulating that the final *a* of its stem *-iza-* be retained in all its truncated forms. Hence, truncation will produce *naiza* from *naiz*, *nintza* from *nintzen*, *gina* from *ginen*, and so on.

Finally, instead of applying to the actual third-person singular past tense form *zen*, truncation is stipulated to operate on the analogical construct **zitzen*, producing the form *zitza*. Accordingly, the truncated past tense paradigm of *izan* 'to be' runs *nintza*, *hintza*, *zitza*, *gina*, *zina*, *zinete*, *zira*.

No special provision needs to be stated for the verb **edun* 'to have'. Thus from *ninduan* 'yoú had me', we get *ninduga*; from *nindunan* 'yoù had me', *ninduna*; from *ninduen* he had me', *nindu*; from *ninduzun* 'you had me', *ninduzu*; and so on. The forms with a third-person direct object are likewise regular: *nu*, *hu*, *zu*, *genu*, *zenu*, *zenute*, *zute*; and with a plural object: *nitu*, *hitu*, *zitu*, *genitu*, *zenitu*, *zenituzte*, *zituzte*.

17.2.2 Morphology of Protasis Forms

Protasis forms always occur in combination with the conditional prefix *ba-*. They can be obtained from truncated past tense forms by substituting an eventuality prefix shaped *l(e)-* for the past tense marker *z(e)-* if it is there, and then applying the usual word-final adjustments described in section 9.1.

A single irregularity needs to be mentioned, again applying to the verb *izan* 'to be'. Here the expected final *a* is missing just in case it would follow an affricate: *banintz* 'if I were', but *bagina* 'if we were'.

In view of the close relationship between protasis forms and the already familiar past tense forms, it would be rather otiose to provide exhaustive paradigms. However, the reader may find it helpful to commit to memory a few sample paradigms, such as the following:

From *egon*:

banengo	if I stood (or: were)
bahengo	if yoú stood
balego	if he stood
bageunde	if we stood
bazeunde	if you stood
bazeundete	if yoû stood
baleude	if they stood

From *izan*:

banintz	if I were
bahintz	if yoú were
balitz	if he were
bagina	if we were
bazina	if you were
basinet	if yoû were
balira	if they were

balitzait	if he were to me
balitzaik	if he were to yoú
balitzain	if he were to yoù
balitzaio	if he were to him
balitzaigu	if he were to us
balitzaizu	if he were to you
balitzaizue	if he were to yoû
balitzaie	if he were to them

From **edun*:

banu	if I had it	banitu	if I had them
bahu	if yoú had it	bahitu	if yoú had them
balu	if he had it	balitu	if he had them
bagenu	if we had it	bagenitu	if we had them
bazenu	if you had it	bazenitu	if you had them
bazenute	if yoû had it	bazenituzte	if yoû had them
balute	if they had it	balituzte	if they had them

baninduk	if yoú had me	bagintuk	if yoú had us
banindun	if yoù had me	bagintun	if yoù had us
banindu	if he had me	bagintu	if he had us
baninduzu	if you had me	bagintuzu	if you had us
. . .		. . .	

balit	if he had it for me	balizkit	if he had them for me
balik	if he had it for yoú	balizkik	if he had them for yoú
balin	if he had it for yoù	balizkin	if he had them for yoù
balio	if he had it for him	balizkio	if he had them for him
baligu	if he had it for us	balizkigu	if he had them for us
balizu	if he had it for you	balizkizu	if he had them for you
balizue	if he had it for yoû	balizkizue	if he had them for yoû
balie	if he had it for them	balizkie	if he had them for them

17.2.3 Morphology of the Present Conditional

To derive the present conditional forms from the truncated past tense forms, we again substitute the eventuality prefix *l(e)-* for the past tense marker *z(e)-* and add an irreality suffix *-ke* to the end of the form, unless an ergative person marker or a pluralizer *-te* is present, in which event *-ke* will directly precede these. We then apply the usual word-final adjustment rules of section 9.1.

A small number of verbs display minor irregularities, also found in the past conditional forms. The verb *izan* 'to be' inserts a formative *-te-* in just those forms where the irreality suffix *-ke* would otherwise touch the stem. Thus we have *litzateke* 'he would be', but *litzaidake* 'he would be for me'. (The Guipuzcoan dialect forgoes the use of this formative.) Moreover, the second-person plural is irregular: *zinatekete*.

Plural object forms of the verb **edun* 'to have' acquire a pluralizer *-z* suffixed to the stem, while the plural prefix *it-* is also retained: *lituzke* 'he would have them'. Furthermore, the pluralizer *-tza* of the verbs *ibili* 'to walk' and its archaic causative *erabili* 'to use' changes to *-z* before the irreality suffix *-ke*: *lebilzke* 'they would walk', *lerabilzke* 'he would use them'.

For the sake of completeness, I will end with some particulars whose import remains purely academic, given that synthetic conditionals of the verbs in question occur only at the loftiest levels of poetic style. We thus note that the verbs *entzun* 'to hear', *ikusi* 'to see', and its archaic causative *erakutsi* 'to show' change their pluralizer *-zki* to *-z*: *lentzuzke* 'he would hear them', *lekusazke* 'he would see them', *lerakutsazke* 'he would show them'. Under the 1977 normalization decree of the Basque Academy, conditional forms of *ikusi* with a plural direct object require the augmented stem *-kusa-*, whereas the conditional forms of *erakutsi* with a singular object utilize the apocopated stem *-rakuts-*, as follows: *lekusazke* 'he would see them', *lerakuske* 'he would show it', *lerakutsazke* 'he would show them'.

For the convenience of the learner, some useful paradigms follow:

egon:

nengoke	I would stand (or: be)
hengoke	yoú would stand

legoke	he would stand
geundeke	we would stand
zeundeke	you would stand
zeundekete	yoû would stand
leudeke	they would stand

izan:

nintzateke	I would be
hintzateke	yoú would be
litzateke	he would be
ginateke	we would be
zinateke	you would be
zinatekete	yoû would be
lirateke	they would be
litzaidake	he would be to me
litzaiake	he would be to yoú
litzainake	he would be to yoù
litzaiokehe	he would be to him
litzaiguke	he would be to us
litzaizueke	he would be to yoû
litzaieke	he would be to them

**edun*:

nuke	I would have it	nituzke	I would have them
huke	yoú would have it	hituzke	yoú would have them
luke	he would have it	lituzke	he would have them
genuke	we would have it	genituzke	we would have them
zenuke	you would have it	zenituzke	you would have them
zenukete	yoû would have it	zenituzkete	yoû would have them
lukete	they would have it	lituzkete	they would have them
nindukek	yoú would have me	gintuzkek	yoú would have us
ninduken	yoù would have me	gintuzken	yoù would have us
ninduke	he would have me	gintuzke	he would have us
nindukezu	you would have me	gintuzkezu	you would have us
nindukezue	yoû would have me	gintuzkezue	yoû would have us
nindukete	they would have me	gintuzkete	they would have us
lidake	he would have it for me	lizkidake	he would have them for me
liake	he would have it for yoú	lizkiake	he would have them for yoú
linake	he would have it for yoù	lizkinake	he would have them for yoù
lioke	he would have it for him	lizkioke	he would have them for him

liguke	he would have it for us	lizkiguke	he would have them for us
lizuke	he would have it for you	lizkizuke	he would have them for you
lizueke	he would have it for yoû	lizkizueke	he would have them for yoû
lieke	he would have it for them	lizkieke	he would have them for them

[*Note*: Whenever there is an ergative person marker, the suffix *-ke* will immediately precede it; whenever there is a dative person marker, the suffix *-ke* will immediately follow it. Hence we have *zintuzket* 'I would have you', *nizuke* 'I would have it for you'.]

17.2.4 Morphology of the Past Conditional

All we need to do to derive the past conditional forms from the truncated past tense forms is to add the irreality suffix *-ke* in the same way as before and convert the result into a past tense form by completing it with the characteristic past tense ending: *-en* if the form ends in *-ke*, *-n* otherwise.

Since it now occurs in a nonfinal position, the *g* of the second-person marker *-ga* is elided as usual.

Over and above the irregularities also found in the present conditional, there is one additional stipulation: the third-person singular form of *izan* 'to be' suffers the loss of its initial syllable: *zatekeen* 'he would have been' instead of **zitzatekeen* (cf. Guipuzcoan *zitzakeen*).

Notice that past conditionals do not employ the eventuality prefix *l(e)-*. Here again, some paradigms may be welcome:

egon:

nengokeen	I would have stood (or: been)
hengokeen	yoú would have stood
zegokeen	he would have stood
geundekeen	we would have stood
zeundekeen	you would have stood
zeundeketen	yoû would have stood

izan:

nintzatekeen	I would have been
hintzatekeen	yoú would have been
zatekeen	he would have been
ginatekeen	we would have been
zinatekeen	you would have been
zinateketen	yoû would have been
ziratekeen	they would have been
zitzaidakeen	he would have been to me
zitzaiakeen	he would have been to yoú

zitzainakeen	he would have been to yoù
zitzaiokeen	he would have been to him
zitzaigukeen	he would have been to us
zitzaizukeen	he would have been to you
zitzaizuekeen	he would have been to yoû
zitzaiekeen	he would have been to them

***edun:*

nukeen	I would have had it	nituzkeen	I would have had them
hukeen	yoú would have had it	hituzkeen	yoú would have had them
zukeen	he would have had it	zituzkeen	he would have had them
genukeen	we would have had it	genituzkeen	we would have had them
zenukeen	you would have had it	zenituzkeen	you would have had them
zenuketen	yoû would have had it	zenituzketen	yoû would have had them
zuketen	they would have had it	zituzketen	they would have had them
nindukean	yoú would have had me	gintuzkean	yoú would have had us
nindukenan	yoù would have had me	gintuzkenan	yoù would have had us
nindukeen	he would have had me	gintuzkeen	he would have had us
nindukezun	you would have had me	gintuzkezun	you would have had us
nindukezuen	yoû would have had me	gintuzkezuen	yoû would have had us
ninduketen	they would have had me	gintuzteketen	they would have had us
zidakeen	he would have had it for me	zizkidakeen	he would have had them for me
ziakeen	he would have had it for yoú	zizkiakeen	he would have had them for yoú
zinakeen	he would have had it for yoù	zizkinakeen	he would have had them for yoù
ziokeen	he would have had it for him	zizkiokeen	he would have had them for him
zigukeen	he would have had it for us	zizkigukeen	he would have had them for us
zizukeen	he would have had it for you	zizkizukeen	he would have had them for you
zizuekeen	he would have had it for yoû	zizkizuekeen	he would have had them for yoû
ziekeen	he would have had it for them	zizkiekeen	he would have had them for them

17.3 Syntax of Conditional Forms

17.3.1 Use of Synthetic Conditionals

Just those verbs with synthetic past indicative forms in common use also exhibit synthetic forms in the conditional mood. This fact, by the way, may count as evidence for the psychological reality of the morphological connection between the conditional mood and the ordinary past tense. In contrast to a periphrastic protasis verb, where the time reference is rather vague in that the hypothetical fulfillment of the condition expressed may be projected into a more or less distant future, a synthetic protasis always concerns the very present, as shown in the following examples:

(12) a. Ni errege baldin banintz, erregina zinateke. (*LVP* VIII-2)
If I were king, you would be queen.
b. Hemen bazina edo hor banengo, zure begi tristeak alaitzen saiatuko nintzateke. (Urretabizkaia, *Sat.* 94)
If you were here or I were there, I would try to cheer up your sad eyes.
c. Jainkoa balitz zuen aita, maite nindukezue. (Jn 8:42; *JKBO*)
If God were yoûr father, yoû would love me.
d. Nik ere hala pentsatuko nuke, zaharra banintz. (Zapirain, *M.* 20)
I also would think that way, if I were old.
e. Zure larruan banengo, ez nuke ezetzik esango (*TOE* II, 35)
If I were in your skin, I wouldn't say no.
f. Ezetz banio, gezurra esango nuke. (Zapirain, *M.* 82, 197)
If I were to say no, I would be telling a lie.
g. Negar egingo luke nire amak, baleki. (Iparragirre, from the song "Nire amak baleki," Arratia IV, 159, *Xaramela* 306)
My mother would cry if she knew it.

[*N.B.* The apodosis may concern the past even if the protasis refers to the present, and vice versa:

(13) a. Gaizkilea ez balitz, ez genizukeen ekarriko. (Jn 18:30)
If he weren't a criminal, we wouldn't have brought him to you.
b. Labana eskuan ikusi balute, ez lukete hori esango. (Zapirain, *M.* 159)
If they had seen the knife in his hand, they wouldn't say that.]

17.3.2 Periphrastic Conditionals

We will first discuss the verbal structure of the protasis, then that of the apodosis. When the hypothetical fulfillment of the condition expressed by the protasis is envisioned as happening in the past, the protasis form of the auxiliary will combine with the perfect participle of the main verb: *etorri balitz* 'if he had come', *egin balu* 'if he had done it'.

In all other cases, the protasis form of the auxiliary combines with the future participle in the southern dialects or with the imperfect participle in the northern ones: *etorriko balitz* (*etortzen balitz*) 'if he were to come', *egingo balu* (*egiten balu*) 'if he were to do it'.

As for the apodosis, the southern dialects employ the future participle of the main verb combined with the present or past conditional of the auxiliary as required by the action's location in time: *etorriko litzateke* 'he would come', *egingo luke* 'he would do it', *etorriko zatekeen* 'he would have come', *egingo zukeen* 'he would have done it'. The northern dialects, however, make use of conditional forms belonging to the potential mood, for which see chapter 24. The examples in this section, therefore, are all taken from southern sources, thus reflecting the southern variety of standard Basque.

First, the following are examples of present conditionals:

(14) a. Oraintxe bazterren batean atzemango banu, itoko nuke. (*TOE* I, 350)
If I were to catch him right now in some corner or other, I would strangle him.
b. Aitak jakingo balu, haserretuko litzateke. (*TOE* III, 83)
If Father got to know it, he would get angry.
c. Ni ezagutuko baninduzue, nire Aita ere ezagutuko zenukete. (Jn 8:19)
If yoû knew me, yoû would know my Father too.
d. Gau bat pasatu nahi banu hemen, bi hilabeteko irabaziak beharko nituzke. (Atxaga, *Grl.* 21)
If I wanted to spend one night here, I would need the earnings of two months.

Attention may be drawn to the existence of a hybrid type of conditional, where a conditional protasis combines with an indicative apodosis. In this type, it seems that the apodosis is asserted regardless of the fulfillment of the condition expressed by the protasis:

(15) a. Nik ere jantzi nahi baldin banitu, badauzkat horiek aukeran. (Uztapide, in *B.Tx.* 60, 32)
If I too wanted to wear them, I've got them in abundance.
b. Norbaitek kontrako arrazoirik baldin balu, ni gertu nago arrazoi horiek entzuteko. (*MEIG* IV, 52)
If someone should have opposing arguments, I am prepared to hear those arguments.

Following are examples of past conditionals:

(16) a. Hil ez banu, salatu egingo nindukeen. (Garate, *NY* 97)
If I hadn't killed her, she would have denounced me.
b. Amak esan ez balit, ni ez nintzatekeen hura ikustera joango. (Garate, *Hades* 59)
If Mother hadn't told me, I wouldn't have gone to see her.
c. Zer esango ote zukeen Etxepare zaharrak horrelakorik entzun balu? (*MEIG* VI, 182)
What would the old Etxepare have said, one wonders, if he had heard anything like that?

Addition of *izan* to a perfect participle in the protasis is quite common, in transitive as well as in intransitive clauses:

(17) a. Gauza bera esango zukeen zerua oskarbi egon izan balitz. (Urretabizkaia, *Sat.* 102)
He would have said the same thing if the sky had been clear.
b. Horrelakorik egin izan balu, abisatu egingo zukeen. (Garate, *Alaba* 19)
If she had done anything like that, she would have warned (us).

We may note at this point that a protasis, whether in the indicative or conditional mood, constitutes a negative polarity context; that is, it allows partitive noun phrases:

(18) a. Elkarri egiazko maitasunik baldin badiote, argitasuna etorriko da. (*TOE* III, 187)
If they have (any) true love for each other, clarity will come.
b. Hilko al zenuke gaur, aukerarik bazenu? (Amuriza, *Emea* 40)
Would you kill him today, if you had any chance?

Colloquially, and quite often in literary usage as well, the past future indicative substitutes for the past conditional:

(19) a. Hori jakin banu, ez nintzen joango. (Zapirain, *M.* 157)
If I had known that, I wouldn't have gone.
b. Zu hemen izan bazina, gure anaia ez zen hilko. (*TB* 90; cf. Jn 11:21)
If you had been here, our brother would not have died.
c. Zaldia saldu banu, asto bat beharko nuen. (*EGLU* II, 415)
If I had sold the horse, I would have needed a donkey.

17.4 Nonfinite Protases

17.4.1 Allative Protases

Instead of a finite protasis clause, a nonfinite one may occur taking the shape of a nominalized clause in the allative case. Since this clause, based on the "verbal noun," is incapable of showing tense, its exact translation will depend on the tense and mood of the apodosis.

Given an indicative apodosis (excepting the past future tense, since this is the colloquial equivalent of a past conditional), the protasis will also be interpreted in the indicative mood:

(20) a. Zuk hala ez esatera, galdua naiz. (Mogel, *Cat. Basc.* 87 [32])
If you don't say so, I am lost.
b. Honela jarraitzera, hezurretan gelditutko zarete. (Atxaga, *Grl.* 55)
If yoû continue this way, yoû will end up all bones.

When the apodosis displays a conditional form, the protasis too must be interpreted in that mood, perfect or imperfect depending on the apodosis being past or present:

(21) a. Zu izatera, jertse bat hartuko nuke. (Atxaga, *Z.H.* 55)
If I were you, I would take a sweater.
b. Baita zu ere erreko zintuzkete, erejerik zugan aurkitzera. (S. Mitxelena, *IG* I, 419)
And they would burn you too, if they found a heretic in you.
c. Jakitera, han gelditutko nintzatekeen. (*EGLU* II, 105)
If I had known, I would have stayed there.

With a past future tense in the apodosis, a conditional mood reading of an allative protasis is likewise in order, but its aspectual value remains ambiguous. Taken out of context, example (22a) could have been rendered as 'If anything had happened, the organization would have asked her to account', and (22b) as 'If he had not arrived on time, Michael would have got nervous':

(22) a. Ezer gertatzera, organizazioak berari eskatuko zizkion kontuak. (Atxaga, *Gizona* 29)
If anything were to happen, the organization would ask her to account.
b. Garaiz ez iristera, Mikel urduri jarriko zen. (Atxaga, *Gizona* 183)
If he didn't arrive on time, Michael would get nervous.

17.4.2 Negative Protases with *ezik* or *ezean*

With a negative clause to serve as a protasis, another nonfinite pattern can be employed, this time based on the perfect participle. This pattern consists of an adverbialized clause, where the adverbializer attaches to the negation *ez*, which has been shifted to final position, directly behind the perfect participle. The adverbializer comes in two shapes without a clear difference in meaning: it can be either the stative suffix *-ik* of section 11.1 or the inessive ending *-ean*.

While a clause of this kind is properly speaking a circumstantial complement, as in *nora joan jakin ezik* (Labayen, *Su Em.* 215) 'not knowing where to go', it regularly serves as a protasis in a conditional sentence:

(23) a. Mirariak ikusi ezik, ez duzue zuek sinesten. (Jn 4:48; *Lau Eb.*)
If yoû do not see miracles, yoû do not believe.
b. Hain burugabe jokatuko al lirateke, arraunlarien gorabeherak jakin ezik? (T. Agirre, *Uzt.* 220)
Would they behave so foolishly, if they didn't know the condition of the rowers?

(24) a. Izerditzea ona da, gero hoztu ezean. (Garate, *Erd.* 116)
Sweating is good, provided one doesn't get chilled afterward.
b. Zer egin zizukeen ..., zuk borrokarik nahi ezean? (Orixe, *Aitork.* 155)
What would it have done to you ..., if you had wanted no fight?

17.4.3 Protasis Absorption

The condition embodied in a conditional sentence, while normally expressed in a separate protasis, can at times be conveyed by a constituent of the apodosis itself, in which case no protasis will be in evidence.

Specifically, comparing (25a) to (25b) and (26a) to (26b), it appears as if an original protasis clause can have its auxiliary or copula deleted, provided the remains can be absorbed somehow into the main clause:

(25) a. Zer egingo luke hire amatxok, hi gabe balitz?
What would yoúr mommy do, if she were without yoú?
b. Zer egingo luke hire amatxok hi gabe? (Garate, *Hades* 53)
What would yoúr mommy do without yoú?

(26) a. Guztiak aipatuko balira, luze litzateke.
If one were to mention them all, it would be (too) long.
b. Guztiak aipatzea luze litzateke.
Mentioning them all would be (too) long.

17.5 Free Conditionals

Often enough, sentences formulated in the conditional mood are encountered without the support of a protasis of any sort, not even one that has been absorbed into the main clause, as seen in section 17.4.3. We will call such sentences free conditionals.

In trying to describe their semantic value, we observe that, despite the absence of a protasis clause, free conditionals convey an indirectness or lack of total commitment characteristic of hypothetical statements in general. On the basis of this observation, we will assume that there is an unspoken condition present in the mind of the speaker that accounts for the conditional form. In other words, a free conditional is explained as being an apodosis to an implicit protasis.

Obviously, the speaker is not free to choose this protasis at his caprice; otherwise, communication would be impossible. Rather, usage has sanctioned a small set of options, each giving rise to a particular interpretation of the conditional. In Basque, according to my data, there are three main categories: politeness conditionals, opportunity conditionals, and deontic conditionals.

17.5.1 Politeness Conditionals

An implicit protasis meaning 'if not too presumptuous on my part' or 'if not too inconvenient to you' gives rise to a condtional utterance indicating politeness:

(27) a. Mesede bat eskatu nahi nizuke. (Garate, *G.E.* 9)
I would like to ask you a favor.
b. Gure gaixo batek zurekin hitz egin nahi luke. (Garate, *Alaba* 69)
A patient of ours would like to talk to you.
c. Bidaliko al zenituzke, Marcel? (Atxaga, *Obab.* 303)
Would you send them, Marcel?

An even greater degree of politeness is achieved by phrasing the request as a negative question, again formulated in the conditional mood:

(27) d. Ez zenieke zerbait esango *Egan*-en irakurleei? (*MEIG* I, 101)
Wouldn't you say something to the readers of *Egan*?

As in English, another common way of phrasing a request is to express a desire:

(28) a. Gustora hartuko nuke kafe beroa. (Urretabizkaia, *Sat.* 84)
I would gladly take some warm coffee.
b. Gaua igarotzeko lehorra nahi nuke, Jauna. (Garate, *NY* 113)
I would like a dry spot to spend the night, sir.

17.5.2 Opportunity Conditionals

An implicit protasis meaning 'if asked', 'if given the opportunity', or 'if need be' leads to a type of conditional to be named opportunity conditional:

(29) a. Lan hau hartuko al zenuke? (Garate, *Alaba* 21)
Would you take on this job?
b. Egia osoa jakin nahi al zenuke? (Garate, *Alaba* 66)
Would you like to know the whole truth?
c. Zein beste arrazoi aipatuko zenuke? (*MEIG* IX, 77)
Which other reason would you mention?
d. Alabak bizia ere emango luke aitaren alde. (Zapirain, *M.* 144)
The daughter would give even her life for her father.

17.5.3 Deontic Conditionals

An implicit protasis meaning 'if one wanted to do the right thing' or 'if things were as they ought to be' generates conditionals we can name deontic. The verb *behar* is usually part of the utterance:

(30) a. Amagatik andre oro behar luke goratu. (*LVP*, III-18)
Because of his mother he should praise all women.
b. Jendaila horrek ez luke hemen egon behar. (Atxaga, *Grl.* 19)
That riffraff should not stay here.
c. Euskarari iraunarazteko saiatu behar ote litzateke? (*MEIG* I, 71)
Should one perhaps endeavor to make Basque survive?
d. Zer egin behar litzateke, bada? (*MEIG* I, 49)
What would one then have to do?
e. Euskaltzaleek komeni lukete astiro irakurtzea. (*MEIG* III, 70)
Bascophiles would do well to read it attentively.

17.6 Concessive *ere*

The particle *ere*, introduced in section 1.3.3 in the sense 'also', has in fact a much wider meaning: it also serves as the regular equivalent of English *even*: *Ez dute ogirik ere jateko* 'They don't even have bread to eat'. This, then, may explain why adding *ere* to a protasis constitutes one of the ways of forming concessive clauses in Basque. The particle *ere* must directly follow the finite verb, as in the following examples:

(31) a. Arrazoia badut ere, ez diot erantzungo. (Jb 9:15)
Though I am right, I won't answer him.
b. Zurekin hil behar badut ere, ez zaitut inola ere ukatuko. (Mt 26:35)
Even if I have to die with you, I will surely not deny you.
c. Baina nahi ez baditugu ere, behar ditugu. (*MEIG* V, 145)
But even if we don't want them, we need them.
d. Baina ez baldin bazen ere bera mediku, argitzen zituen medikuak. (H.U., *Aurp.* 78)
But although he was not a doctor himself, he educated the doctors.

A concessive clause based on a protasis in the conditional mood will normally be interpreted as a counterfactual:

(32) a. Eta epaituko banu ere, nire epaia baliozkoa litzateke. (Jn 8:16)
And even if I were to judge, my judgment would be valid.
b. Profetak gauza zailen bat agindu izan balizu ere, ez al zenukeen egingo? (2 Kgs 5:13)
Even if the prophet had commanded you some hard thing, wouldn't you have done it?

17.7 The Adnominal Inessive *-kotan*

The suffix *-kotan*, consisting of adnominal *-ko* followed by the indefinite inessive *-tan* (cf. Azkue, 1905–1906, I, 502), combines exclusively with verbal nouns and can assume three meaning values: intention, condition, and point of time.

17.7.1 Intentional *-kotan*

In the following examples the suffix *-kotan* expresses intention:

(33) a. Eleberri bat egitekotan omen zebilen. (*MEIG* V, 137)
It was rumored that he planned to do a novel.
b. Egon naiz etxea erretzekotan ere, baina . . . (Atxaga, *Obab.* 40)
I have even had the intention to burn the house, but . . .
c. Semea ezkontzekotan dabilkizu aspaldi. (*TOE* III, 186)
Your son has been planning to marry for a long time.

As the grammarian P. Goenaga proposed in 1978, this use of the suffix *-kotan* can be explained by positing ellipsis of the noun *asmo* 'intention':

(34) a. Zerbait irabazteko asmotan saldu zuen autoa. (Goenaga, *G.B.* 333; *G.B.*^{2} 372)
He sold the car intending to earn something.

b. Zerbait irabaztekotan saldu zuen autoa. (Goenaga, *G.B.* 333; *G.B.*^{2} 372)
He sold the car intending to earn something.

17.7.2 Conditional *-kotan*

The suffix *-kotan* combined with a verbal noun often serves to express a condition:

(35) a. Semea izango duzue, baina haren arima gero niretzat izatekotan. (*LBB* 179)
You will have a son, but on condition that afterward his soul will be for me.
b. Argia sortaldetik etortzekotan, ez ote zaigu Txinatik agertuko? (*MEIG* II, 140)
If the light comes from the east, won't it appear unto us from China, I wonder?
c. Inori ezer egitekotan, niri izango da. (S. Mitxelena, *IG* I, 228)
If they do anything to anybody, it will be to me.

This use of *-kotan* can be explained by ellipsis of the noun *kontu* 'event', 'matter', as suggested by K. Mitxelena in 1976 (see Villasante 1976, 187). Compare these examples:

(36) a. Ezkontzeko kontutan, gaztea nahi du.
In the event of marrying, he wants a young person.
b. Ezkontzekotan, gaztea nahi du. (*TOE* II, 61)
If he marries (at all), he wants a young person.

[*N.B.* For this meaning, the northern dialects also use the adnominal instrumental *-koz*, dialectally *-kotz*.]

17.7.3 Temporal *-kotan*

Temporal use of the suffix *-kotan* is easily accounted for by ellipsis of the noun *puntu* 'point':

(37) a. Abiatzeko puntutan ginen, . . .
We were on the point of departing, . . .
b. Abiatzekotan ginen, . . . (*EGLU* II, 107)
We were about to depart, . . .

17.8 The Prolative *-tzat* 'as (a) . . .', 'for (a) . . .'

Originally, "prolatif" was Ithurry's name for the case marked by the ending *-tzat*, that is, our benefactive case (1920, 12). The name was adopted by Lafitte, who distinguished the "prolatif du possessif," that is, the ordinary benefactive based on the genitive, from the "prolatif ordinaire," that is, the ending *-tzat* without a preceding genitive morpheme (1962, secs. 857–858). More recently, Basque grammarians reserve the term "prolative" for the latter use, preferring the designation "destinative" to Lafitte's "prolatif du possessif."

As noted in *EGLU* (I, 446–447), the prolative is restricted to object complements; it is because of this restriction that we never find it on pronouns or determined noun phrases. Needless to say, object complements should be carefully distinguished from translative objects, for which verbs such as *bihurtu* and *bilakatu* (both meaning 'to turn into') are subcategorized. It is therefore no surprise that these two verbs are incompatible with the prolative, as pointed out in *EGLU* (I, 448). *EGLU*'s third example, *izendatu* 'to appoint', does take object complements for some speakers, and hence it can co-occur with a prolative.

Since object complements are never determined noun phrases, the prolative does not display the threefold number distinction characteristic of Basque case endings. It also differs from these in its failure to induce epenthesis after a consonantal stem: *hutstzat* 'as empty' (commonly pronounced [*h*]*utzat*). Therefore, instead of treating it as a case, I will consider prolative *-tzat* a semantically empty postposition subcategorized for bare noun phrases and adjectives. As an example of its use, consider example (38):

(38) Erregetzat hartu ninduten gizon haiek. (*EGLU* I, 449)

As *EGLU* points out, example (38) has two different readings (38a) and (38b), which, for want of better terms, I will call "resultative" versus "evaluative":

(38) a. These men took me as (their) king. (resultative)
b. These men took me for a king. (evaluative)

These two types of prolative will be discussed in separate subsections.

17.8.1 The Resultative Prolative

An object complement describing the outcome of a change of state or status undergone by the direct object as a result of the action of the verb must be governed by the prolative, at least in colloquial usage. In the literary language, use of the prolative is often optional, as will be seen in some of the examples that follow. In contemporary practice, however, its omission by and large evokes an archaic flavor, proper to church hymns and other poetry: *zeru-lurren jabe ezagut dezagun* (G. Lerchundi, *Kantikak* 252) 'let us recognize Him as master of heaven and earth' (Guipuzcoan: *aitortu dezagun*; for the subjunctive *dezagun*, see chapter 21). Prototypical instances of this prolative concern adoption and marriage:

(39) a. Aita izango nau hark ni, eta seme izango dut nik hura. (2 Sm 7:14)
He will have me for a father, and I will have him for a son.
b. Aitatzat izango nau hark ni, eta semetzat izango dut nik hura.
He will have me for a father, and I will have him for a son.

(40) a. ?Seme hartu dute Iñaki. (Rejected by *EGLU* I, 448)
They have taken Iñaki as a son.
b. Semetzat hartu dute Iñaki. (*EGLU* I, 448)
They have adopted Iñaki as a son.

(41) a. Labanek Rahel bere alaba eman zion emazte (Gn 29:28; *Biblia*)
Laban gave him his daughter Rachel as wife.
b. Labanek bere alaba Rakel eman zion emaztetzat. (Gn 29:28)
Laban gave him his daughter Rachel as wife.

(42) a. Bere alaba Jenobeba emazte eman zion. (Arrue, *G.B.* 36)
He gave him his daughter Genevieve as wife.
b. Bere alaba emaztetzat eman zion. (Arrue, *G.B.*[2] 9)
He gave him his daughter as wife.

Venturing outside the realm of family relations, we may note the following phrases where the prolative is normal, albeit optional:

oparitzat eman	to give as a gift
ordaintzat eman	to give in exchange
saritzat eman	to give in reward
zergatzat eman	to pay in tribute, as taxes
aitzakiatzat hartu	to use as a pretext
gaitzat hartu	to take as a theme
oinarritzat hartu	to use as a base
joputzat saldu	to sell as a slave

Finally, the prolative can occur with such verbs as *aitortu* 'to confess', 'to acknowledge'; *ezagutu* 'to know', 'to recognize'; and *aukeratu* and *hautatu*, both meaning 'to choose', 'to elect':

(43) a. Semea baldin baduzu ere, guk ez dugu aitortzen anaiatzat. (*TOE* III, 181)
Even though he is your son, we do not acknowledge him as (our) brother.
b. Hau neure alabatzat ezagutuko dut. (Iztueta, 241)
I will recognize her as my daughter.
c. Nola aukeratu zenuen gaitzat Lizardiren poema hori? (*MEIG* I, 48 = *MIH* 154)
How come you chose that poem by Lizardi as a theme?

Mostly, the resultative prolative governs a single noun, yet a prenominal modifier is allowed: *bere populuaren aitzindaritzat hautatu* (Larréguy I, 207) 'to choose as a leader of his people'; *betiereko jabegotzat eman* (Gn 17:8) 'to give as an everlasting holding'.

While adjective-based evaluative prolatives are extremely common, I have found no clear examples of resultative ones of this type.

17.8.2 The Evaluative Prolative

In combination with certain verbs, the prolative can serve as a tool to formulate an appraisal of a referent X with regard to a quality Y, provided the latter can be encoded as an object complement. A small number of transitive verbs, of which a nominal referring to

X is to be the direct object, is available for this purpose, to wit, **edun, eduki, eman, etsi, hartu*, and *jo*.

As it is not the core meaning of these verbs to express an appraisal, it must be assumed that the prolative activates a meaning component of the verb that is either secondary (as for *etsi* and *jo*) or even merely latent. The prolative therefore is an essential part of the construction and cannot be omitted, except with the verbs *etsi* and *jo* in some southern dialect areas. We will treat the relevant verbs one by one:

1. *jo* 'to hit'. In southern Batua, and particularly in the dialect of southern Guipuzcoa, this verb can assume the meaning 'to consider':

(44) a. Oso haundi jotzen dugu. (*LBB* 169)
We consider him very great.
b. Arabatik ardoa kontrabando ekartzea bekatu handi jotzen zuen. (Anduaga, 80)
Smuggling wine from Alava he deemed a great sin.
c. Egiazko erruduna bera joko zuten. (Zapirain, *M.* 182)
They would consider himself the true culprit.

Most speakers, however, prefer to make use of the prolative:

(45) a. Kaxkartzat jo gaituzte. (*MEIG* VIII, 159 = *MIH* 373)
They have deemed us insignificant.
b. Erotzat joko haute, seme. (Etxaniz, *Antz.* 52)
They will think yoú crazy, son.
c. Zu, beti etsai, eta etsai amorratutzat joko zaitut. (*TOE* I, 348)
As for you, I will always deem you an enemy, and a rabid enemy.

2. *eman* 'to give'. An accompanying prolative activates the meaning 'to consider', a meaning otherwise foreign to the verb, except perhaps where age is concerned:

(46) a. Ez lioke inork hirurogei urte emango. (Zabala, 26)
Nobody would think him sixty years old.
b. (Ni) tximu hutstzat eman? (B. Mogel, *Ip.* 112)
Deeming me a mere monkey?
c. San Pablo berehala hiltzat eman zuten. (*TB* 195)
They instantly gave St. Paul up for dead.

[*N.B.* ontzat eman: to approve
txartzat eman: to disapprove]

3. *hartu* 'to take'. The compound verb *onartu* 'to approve' (from *on* 'good' and *hartu*) suggests a virtual meaning 'to regard'. In the current state of the language a prolative is needed to bring out this latent meaning:

(47) a. Gure agindua huskeriatzat hartzen dute. (Zapirain, *M.* 114)
They regard our command as a trifle.

b. Judak emagaldutzat hartu zuen. (Gn 38:15)
Judah took her for a prostitute.

c. Zergatik hartzen gaituzu animaliatzat? Zergatik jotzen inozotzat? (Jb 18:3)
Why do you regard us as brutes? Why consider us foolish?

[*N.B.* ontzat hartu: to take well, to approve, to accept
txartzat hartu: to take ill, to disapprove, to reject
The following distinction is not always observed:
haintzat hartu: to take as such (from *hain* 'so', see section 11.2.2)
aintzat hartu: to take seriously]

4. *eduki* 'to hold'. Like its English equivalent, this verb can express belief or opinion. While finite complement clauses are restricted to the northern dialects (*DGV* VI, 385), use of the prolative is common to north and south alike:

(48) a. Andoni irakasle zintzotzat daukagu. (*EGLU* I, 448)
We consider Tony a reliable teacher.

b. Daniel eta bere lagunak ere asmatzailetzat zeuzkaten. (*TZ* II, 180)
They also considered Daniel and his companions as soothsayers.

c. Napoleon ontzat daukate batzuek, gaiztotzat besteek. (*MEIG* VIII, 72 = *MIH* 267)
Some people regard Napoleon as good, the others (regard him) as evil.

5. *edun* 'to have'. Used by certain speakers just like *eduki*:

(49) a. Osasungarritzat dut nik lana neurriz egitea. (*EGL* 491)
I consider it healthy to do work in moderation.

b. Hiltzat ninduzuen. (Etxaniz, *Antz*. 98)
You thought me dead.

6. *etsi* 'to desist'. This verb readily occurs with the prolative in phrases such as *galdutzat etsi* 'to give up as lost'. More importantly, however, as a back-formation from its compounds (*gaitzetzi* 'to reject', *gutxietsi* 'to despise', *onetsi* 'to approve', etc.), *etsi* also acquired the meaning 'to consider'. In this meaning, it can take the prolative, but examples are few, and, on the whole, fairly recent:

(50) Edertzat etsi zuen Jaungoikoak Ebe atsegintokian. (T. Agirre, *Uzt*. 53)
God regarded Eve as beautiful in the Garden of Eden.

17.8.3 The Prolative Adnominal -*tzako*

In accord with its postpositional status, we expect the prolative to be free to turn into an adnominal modifier with the assistance of the adnominal suffix *-ko* (chapter 5). But to the best of my knowledge, phrases of the type *lapurtzako sorgina* 'the witch presumed to be a thief' are nowhere attested. What we do find, however, are examples of the substantive use of the adnominals in question, witness K. Mitxelena's phrase *teologo eta teologotzakoei* (*MEIG* VII, 27) 'to the theologians and the presumed theologians'. Other examples are

aita	father	aitatzako	adoptive father, presumed father
alaba	daughter	alabatzako	adoptive daughter, presumed daughter
ama	mother	amatzako	adoptive mother, presumed mother
bekatu	sin	bekatutzako	presumed sin
ero	lunatic	erotzako	presumed lunatic
gezurti	liar	gezurtitzako	presumed liar
lapur	thief	lapurtzako	presumed thief
seme	son	semetzako	adoptive son, presumed son
senargai	fiancé	senargaitzako	presumed fiancé
sorgin	witch	sorgintzako	presumed witch
zintzo	honest (man)	zintzotzako	a supposedly honest man

Notice that *aitatzako*, *alabatzako*, and the like carry two quite different meanings, as a reflex of the double function of the prolative: resultative or evaluative.

Incidentally, the most common instance of the suffix *-kotzat* is found in the phrase *aintzakotzat hartu* 'to take into account', a pleonastic variant of *aintzat hartu*.

17.9 The Parasuffix *tasun* '-ness'

Occurring in technical language only, the noun *tasun* denotes the concept of a property or quality. As a productive parasuffix, it combines with adjectives, adnominals, nouns, and even some pronouns and adverbs, from which it forms names of properties or states. Alongside this abstract meaning, the resulting noun may also denote a typical instantiation of the quality in question.

Since this type of compounding is fully productive, at least for adjectives and nouns (e.g., *mahaitasun* 'the quality of being a table'), only a small number of illustrations will be given for each stem category.

With adjectives as stem:

argi	light, clear	argitasun	luminosity, clearness, clarification
aske	loose, free	askatasun	freedom
baker	alone, single	bakartasun	solitude (also *bakardade*)
erraz	easy	erraztasun	easiness, facility, convenience
estu	tight, strict	estutasun	tightness, distress, difficulty
gora	high	goratasun	height, highness, elevation
maite	beloved	maitasun	love (haplology from *maitetasun*)
on	good	ontasun	goodness (cf. *ondasunak*, 'goods')
oso	whole, complete	osotasun	completeness (cf. *osasun* 'health')

urri	scarce	urritasun	scarcity, dearth
xehe	minute	xehetasun	detail
zehatz	precise	zehaztasun	precision, detail

With adnominals as stem:

betiko	eternal	betikotasun	eternity
elkarrekiko	reciprocal, mutual	elkarrekikotasun	reciprocity, mutuality
gaurko	present-day	gaurkotasun	actuality, topicality
nolako	what kind of	nolakotasun	quality
oraingo	current, modern	oraingotasun	currentness, actuality, topicality

With nouns as stem:

adiskide	friend	adiskidetasun	friendship (also *adiskidantza*)
aita	father	aitatasun	fatherhood, paternity
ama	mother	atasun	motherhood, maternity
anaia	brother	anaitasun	brotherhood, fraternity
etsai	enemy	etsaitasun	enmity
herri	people	herritasun	peoplehood
herritar	citizen	herritartasun	citizenship, nationality
jabe	owner	jabetasun	ownership, independence
lur	earth	lurtasun	earthliness
muga	limit, border	mugatasun	limitation
zorion	happiness	zoriontasun	happiness

[*N.B.* Either *gizatasun* or *gizontasun* can be used for 'human nature', although the latter form more often denotes 'manliness'.]

With pronouns and the like:

anitz	many	aniztasun	plurality
bat	one	batasun	unity
elkar	each other	elkartasun	solidarity, cooperation, covenant
ni	I	nitasun	ego
nor	who	nortasun	identity, personality
zer	what	zertasun	essence

With adverbs as stem:

atzera	backward	atzeratasun	backwardness, reticence
maiz	often	maiztasun	frequency

17.10 Vocabulary

aintzakotzat hartu	to pay attention to, to take seriously
aintzat hartu	to pay attention to, to take seriously

apustu	bet
aukera	choice, opportunity
aukeratu	to choose, to elect
bidaia	journey, voyage
ezkertiar	leftist (see section 6.7)
gizarte	society
haserretu	to get angry, to make angry
hilondoko	(last) will, testament
izeba	aunt
ontzat hartu	to take well, to approve, to accept
osaba	uncle
ostera	again
sufritu	(always transitive) to suffer
xentimo	penny
zor *edun	to owe

17.11 Exercises

17.11.1 Translate into English

1. Asko baduk, asko beharko duk. (Proverb, *R.S.* 124)
2. Deabruarekin itsasoratzen bahaiz, berarekin egin beharko duk bidaia. (Proverb)
3. Sorgin harekin ezkondu banintz, neure burua hil nukeen.
4. Ezkertiartzat jo izan balituzte, haien biziak ez zuen xentimorik balioko. (*LBB* 66)
5. Eta orain, hilondokoa erakutsiko bazenit, esker beroak emango nizkizuke. (Garate, *G.E.* 46)
6. Nora gindoazke, sinetsiko ez bagenio elkarri? (Labayen, *Su Em.* 171)
7. Neure etxean banengo, banekike zer egin.
8. Nik ikusi ezean, ez nuke sinetsiko. (Garate, *Erd.* 116)
9. Zure arreba etxean izatekotan, berehala etorriko natzaio.
10. Egia esatekotan, egia osoa zor dugu. (*MEIG* VIII, 155 = *MIH* 369)
11. Gizarteak oraindik ere ez ditu ontzat hartzen. (Garate, *NY* 157)
12. Nirekin haserretu zen, ez nau aintzakotzat hartzen. (*TOE* I, 67)

17.11.2 Translate into Basque

1. If you suffer, I also suffer.
2. If yoû live in that manner, yoû will die.

3. My wife would laugh if she heard that.
4. If the gypsy wants to buy the house, he will have to have the money.
5. What would you do if it had happened to you?
6. If I win this bet, I will invite you to supper.
7. Even if he had read a lot of books, he would have remained a big ass.
8. My aunt will want to read those books, provided they are interesting.
9. I will take yoû as my people.
10. Some ladies would take you as a husband.
11. My uncle considers himself a woman and will pay no attention to our words.
12. The young widow has chosen Mary and me as companions.

18 Direct and Indirect Questions; Finite Complement Clauses

18.1 Constituent Questions

18.1.1 Direct Questions

Yes-or-no questions have been sufficiently discussed in section 8.1.5; only constituent questions remain to be examined. As pointed out in section 8.6.1, the interrogative they contain must occur in focus position, that is, directly in front of the verb, at least in finite clauses. Interrogatives can be interrogative pronouns or interrogative adverbials. When pronouns, they admit the basic case endings of section 2.2.1. There are four of them: *nor* 'who', *zer* 'what', *zein* 'which', and *zenbat* 'how much' or 'how many'. The latter is properly speaking an interrogative quantifier, which takes case endings in its substantival use only: *Zenbatek egin dute?* 'How many (people) have done it?' For the declension of these pronouns, see section 2.3.2, item 6. Except for *nor*, they can all occur adjectivally, in which case *zer* may be reduced to *ze*:

(1) a. Ze(r) ordu da? (*E.H.* 624)
What time is it?
b. Ze gai erabiltzen da eta zein hizkuntzatan? (*MEIG* I, 100)
What subject is treated and in which language?

Interrogative adverbials are precisely those interrogatives that admit the adnominal suffix *-ko*. There are three groups:

1. Locational: *non* 'where', together with its other locative case forms: *nondik* 'from where', *nora* 'to where', *norantz* 'in what direction', *noraino* 'up to where', 'how far'.
2. Temporal: *noiz* 'when', and its elative *noiztik* (or its bookish variant *noizdanik*) 'since when'. Instead of the allative *noizera*, only found in the noninterrogative *noizetik noizera* 'from time to time', the adnominal *noizko* 'for when' appears. A terminative *noizdaino* 'until when' exists, but *noiz arte* or *noiz artean* is preferred.
3. Referring to manner: *nola* (or its synonyms *nolaz, nolatan*) 'how' and its adnominal *nolako* 'what kind of': *nolako apaiza* 'what kind of a priest' (note the presence of the article *-a*).

Interrogatives can be reinforced by the addition of an expletive giving vent to the speaker's astonishment or irritation. The most common expletive is *arraio* 'thunderbolt' (also 'ray'), but several other ones also occur. Examples are

(2) a. Nola arraio ezagutu ote du aitak horrelako neska bat? (Haranburu, *Ausk.* 35)
How in the world did Father get to know such a girl, I wonder?

b. Zer arraioren bila dabil gure Peru? (*MEIG* II, 140 = *MIH* 338)
What the hell is our Peter searching for?

c. Nor arraiorekin ote dabil Xu? (Haranburu, *Ausk.* 76)
Who the hell is Xu going around with, I wonder?

d. Eta non arraiotik deitzen didak? (Haranburu, *Ausk.* 54)
And where the hell are yoú calling me from?

e. Zer arraiopola gertatu da hemen? (Garate, *G.E.* 21–22)
What the hell has happened here?

f. Nola demontre biziko naiz? (from the traditional song "Pipa hartuta," *Xaramela* 266)
How the deuce shall I live?

g. Zer mila demonio pasatzen da hemen? (*LBB* 180)
What the devil is happening here?

h. Zer mila sorgin pentsatu dute zure haurrek? (J. B. Etcheberry, 217)
What on earth did your children think?

[*N.B.* With a case ending, there are usually two options, for example, *norekin arraio* 'with who the hell' or *nor arraiorekin* as in (2c), *nondik arraio* 'where the hell from' or *non arraiotik* as in (2d).]

Basque allows more than one constituent of a clause to be questioned, but the details differ according to dialect or speaker. While some speakers—especially those from (western) Biscay—disallow more than one interrogative in front of the verb, admitting at most questions of the form *Nork jan behar du nor?* (Amuriza, *Emea* 28) 'Who is to eat whom?' others find no fault with the fronting of two or more interrogatives, provided these have NP status, that is, are ergative, absolutive, or dative. What they allow can be characterized as a multiply-filled focus site: the interrogatives must occur in a fixed order (to wit, ergative-dative-absolutive), and nothing can be inserted between these. Textual examples are not very numerous:

(3) a. Nork nori eman ote dio?—galdetuko du norbaitek. Erdarak euskarari, ala euskarak erdarari? (A. Zavala, *E.Z.B.B.* I, 20)
"Who has given it to whom?" someone will ask. "Spanish to Basque, or Basque to Spanish?"

b. Nork nori zer eman dio? (Saltarelli, 21)
Who has given what to whom?

[*N.B.* Note the expression *noiz nola* 'it depends'.]

In the northern dialects, a multiple question often functions as a rhetorical device to express a strong denial:

(4) a. Nork zer eginen du? (Tartas, *Onsa* 40)
   Who will do what? (i.e., nobody will do anything)
   b. Nork zer behar du? (*Larzabal* I, 23)
   Who needs what? (i.e., nobody needs anything)
   c. Mintzorik eta hizkuntzarik izan ez balitz, nork zer irakatsiko zuen? (Etcheberri Sarakoa, 262)
   If there had been no speech or language, who would have taught what?

To conclude this section, we recall the existence of nonfinite constituent questions. As mentioned in section 7.2.2, in Guipuzcoan and Biscayan the perfect participle is employed instead of the radical. Examples are

(5) a. Nor ezar haren orde? (J. B. Etcheberry, 73)
   Who to put in his place?
   b. Zergatik negar egin? (From the traditional song "Isil isilik dago," *Xaramela* 174)
   Why cry?
   c. Zer egin hori jakiteko? (Garate, *Alaba* 45)
   What to do to find that out?
   d. Nola ulertu istilu hori? (Garate, *Alaba* 37)
   How to understand that mess?

18.1.2 Indirect Questions; Wh-Complements

While all indirect questions make use of wh-complements, not all wh-complements serve to formulate questions. Therefore, limiting the scope of the discussion to questions would lead to needless duplication, and it is for this reason that I will at once address the wider topic of wh-complements in general.

We will start by briefly dealing with nonfinite wh-complements. Lacking as they do an overt complementizer, their subordinate clause ends with the radical form of the verb, or, in southern usage, also the perfect participle. Examples are

(6) a. Ez dakit klinikara joan ala hemen geldi. (*TOE* III, 152)
   I don't know whether to go to the clinic or stay here.
   b. Orain ez dakit hemen gelditu ala joan. (*TOE* III, 201)
   I don't know now whether to stay here or go.
   c. Ez nekien zer erantzun. (M. Onaindia, *Gau Ip*. 43)
   I didn't know what to answer.
   d. Jainkoak erakusten zien nondik joan. (*TZ* I, 119)
   God showed them which way to go.

A nonfinite complement clause may have more than one fronted interrogative:

(6) e. Berak agintzen du non zer lan egin. (*G.* 365)
He commands where to do which job.

Our study of finite complements should begin by reporting a fundamental fact. In Basque, all finite complements require the presence of an overt nondeletable complementizer realized as a suffix onto the finite verb of the subordinate clause. In particular, finite wh-complements call for a wh-complementizer, a verb suffix, for which I will use the symbol -*N*. This suffix consists of two allomorphs in complementary distribution: -*n* and -*en*, the selection of which is determined by the nature of the final morpheme of the verb form.

The allomorph -*n* will occur in the following three contexts:

1. After a person marker, including third-person plural -*te*, but not third-person singular ∅.
2. After a stem-final *a* not belonging to the verb *izan* 'to be'.
3. After the past tense suffix -*n*.

Elsewhere, the allomorph -*en* appears.

Ad 1. The complementizer is attached prior to the operation of the word-final adjustment rules of section 9.1. Hence, from *dut*, *dun*, *duk* we get *dudan*, *dunan*, *duan* (with intervocalic -*g*- deletion). Given that the *g* of the suffix -*ga* elides whenever *a* remains (see section 9.1), *dakark* and *darabilk* will yield *dakarran* and *darabilan*.
Ad 2. Stems ending in vowels other than *a* take -*en*: *dagoen*, *dirudien*, versus *daukan*, *daraman*. The final *a* occurring in some present tense forms of *izan* requires the allomorph -*en*, before which the *a* is elided. Thus from *da*, *gara*, *zara*, *dira* we get *den*, *garen*, *zaren*, *diren*.
Ad 3. Actually, all past tense forms remain unchanged under the addition of the complementizer -*n*, since there is no epenthesis and geminate -*nn* is simplified to -*n*.

A wh-complement need not contain an interrogative word, in which case it will correspond to an English *whether* complement:

(7) a. Ez dakit ezagutzen duzun. (Lertxundi, *Hamasei* 58)
I don't know whether you know him.
b. Ez dakit gezurra den hori. (Larzabal, *Hiru* 55)
I don't know whether that is a lie.
c. Honek galde egiten dio hartu duen esnea. (J. B. Etcheberry, 293)
He asks him whether he has taken the milk.

Guipuzcoan speakers like to insert the interrogative particle *al* (section 8.1.5) into indirect yes-or-no questions—provided these are genuine questions governed by a main verb meaning 'to ask':

(8) a. Entzuten al duzun galdetzen dizut. (Lertxundi, *Aise* 102)
I am asking you if you hear.

b. Ez al zizuten galdetu beti hemen bizi behar al zenuen? (Irazusta, *Bizia* 66)
Didn't they ask you whether you had to live here always?
c. Joango al den galdegin diote. (*EGLU* II, 512)
They have asked him if he will go.

The dubitative particle *ote* (section 8.1.6) is less picky about the contexts it appears in. Thus it may occur in wh-complements of the verb *jakin* 'to know', as long as the main clause is negative or interrogative:

(9) a. Kontuz! Ez dakizu senargairik ba ote duen. (*TOE* III, 94)
Watch out! You don't know if she happens to have a fiancé.
b. Nork daki inguru hauetakoak ez ote zareten? (Jo 9:7)
Who knows if you don't happen to be from these parts?

Unlike interrogative *al*, dubitative *ote* can occur in indirect constituent questions:

(10) a. Zer gertatu ote zen ezin pentsatuz, ... (*TB* 167)
Unable to guess what (on earth) had happened, ... (For *ezin*, see chapter 24.)
b. Ez dakit zer ekarri ote duen. (Mujika 1988, 464)
I don't know what (on earth) he has brought.
c. Zertako hots egin ote dion galdetzen dio bere buruari. (Satrustegi, 96)
He is asking himself why (on earth) he has called him.

In wh-complements of the verbs *egon* and *beldur izan*, in particular, the presence of *ote* is all but obligatory.

As it happens, on both sides of the Pyrenees a wh-complement may depend on a synthetic first-person form of the verb *egon*, then to be translated as 'to wonder'. The particle *ote* is seldom absent from such complements:

(11) a. Markos ote datorren nago. (*TOE* III, 118)
I wonder if Markos is coming.
b. Zerbait esan ote zidan nengoen. (Itziar, 79)
I wondered if he said something to me.
c. Nago kofesio ona egin ote dudan. (Larzabal, *Senp.* 38)
I wonder if I have made a valid confession.

In marked contrast to its English equivalent *to be afraid*, the Basque expression *beldur izan* (cf. section 7.5) usually governs wh-complements:

(12) a. Beldur naiz nire etxekoak haserretuko ote zaizkidan. (T. Agirre, *Uzt.* 62)
I am afraid that my family will get angry with me.
b. Beldur naiz ez den azkena izango. (Satrustegi, 171)
I am afraid that it won't be the last one.

As in French and Spanish, an expletory negation *ez* can be optionally inserted into the complement clause of *beldur izan*:

(13) a. Beldur naiz ez ote den erotuko. (Atxaga, *Obab*. 247)
I am afraid that she will go mad.
b. Beldur naiz ez ote diogun kalte ikaragarria egingo. (Zapirain, *M*. 115)
I am afraid that we will do her tremendous harm.

The reader will have noticed that the wh-complement follows the main clause in an overwhelming majority of examples. This, as a matter of fact, is the canonical position of any finite complement clause. In practice, the governing main verb mostly occupies the position directly preceding the sentential complement, but this usage is by no means compulsory, as the following examples show:

(14) a. Zer dakizu zuk zer zor diodan nik inori? (Garate, *Alaba* 75)
What do you know (about) what I owe anyone?
b. Nik erakutsiko diot horri bi eta bi zenbat diren! (*LBB* 161)
I'll show her how much two and two is!

A sentential complement can be topicalized by fronting:

(15) a. Nora zoazen ba al dakizu? (Zaitegi, *Sof*. 76)
Do you know where you are going?
b. Baina hori nongoa den ere ez dakigu. (Jn 9:29)
But even where he is from, we don't know.
c. Nahigabetzen gaituen ala ez, Jainkoak daki. (*MEIG* I, 84)
Whether it distresses us or not, God knows.

An embedded constituent question contains focus (to wit, the interrogative constituent) and therefore tends to occur in focus position:

(16) a. Nork ukitu zaituen galdetzen duzu? (Mk 5:31)
You are asking who has touched you?
b. Norantz joko dugun galdetzen dut. (Lertxundi, *Aise* 69)
I am asking what direction we will take.
c. Zer gertatu zaizun esan al diozu? (Garate, *Alaba* 72)
Have you told him what happened to you?
d. Etxe hau nork gobernatzen duen ez dakit. (*MEIG* IX, 109)
I don't know who is managing this house.

An embedded yes-or-no question too can be focus:

(17) a. Zerbait nahi ote duen galdegitera noa. (*TOE* III, 33)
I am going to ask if he wants something.
b. Barnean zegoen ala ez jakin behar zen lehenik. (Satrustegi, 124)
One first had to know whether he was inside or not.

Quasi-focus position (see section 8.6.2) is also open to a wh-complement:

(18) a. Zuetariko inork ez dit nora noan galdetzen. (Jn 16:5)
No one among yoû asks me where I am going.
b. Baina ez diat oraindik zer nahi duan ulertzen. (Urretabizkaia, *Sat.* 23)
But I still don't understand what yoú want.

Not all embedded constituent questions, however, are in focus or quasi focus. In fact, wh-complements of a factive main verb, such as *jakin* 'to know', *ulertu* 'to comprehend', and *konturatu* 'to realize', hardly ever are focus, so that with these main verbs the canonical order prevails:

(19) a. Inesi ez nion kontatu zer gertatu zen. (Haranburu, *Its.* 99)
I didn't tell Ines what had happened.
b. Ez du inork jakingo nongoa den. (Jn 7:27)
No one will know where he is from.
c. Ez dakit zer esan nahi duzun. (Haranburu, *Its.* 37)
I don't know what you mean.
d. Inork ez zuen ulertu zergatik esan zion hori. (Jn 13:28)
No one understood why he said that to him.
e. Konturatzen al zara norekin bizi zaren? (Garate, *Alaba* 55)
Do you realize who you are living with?

Given that the prefix *ba-* occurs only when there is no focus constituent other than the verb (section 8.6.1), a synthetic main verb thus prefixed will impose canonical order on its subordinate clause:

(20) a. Zuk badakizu nor naizen. (*MEIG* VIII, 138)
You know who I am.
b. Ba al dakik zer den maitasuna? (Atxaga, *Obab.* 88)
Do yoú know what love is?

Turning now to the order of constituents inside the complement clause, we find that by and large the same constraints apply as in a main clause. There is one noteworthy exception: Auxiliary Attraction (section 8.2.2) is merely optional. Thus for the single option in a main clause (*Euskara zergatik ez da hilko?* 'Why won't Basque die?'), there are two in a subordinate clause:

(21) a. Esango dizut euskara zergatik ez den hilko.
I will tell you why Basque won't die.
b. Esango dizut euskara zergatik hilko ez den.
I will tell you why Basque won't die.

Likewise:

(22) a. Mirenek galdetu digu etxea oraindik ez (al) den erori.
Mary has asked us if the house hasn't fallen down yet.
b. Mirenek galdetu digu etxea oraindik erori ez (al) den.
Mary has asked us if the house hasn't fallen down yet.

(23) a. Beldur naiz gure etxea ez ote den erori.
I am afraid that our house has fallen down.
b. Beldur naiz gure etxea erori ez ote den.
I am afraid that our house has fallen down.

As noted by Dr. A. Arejita and confirmed by other Biscayan observers, indirect questions with more than one fronted interrogative are admitted by all speakers, including those who reject direct questions of that type. Indirect multiple questions, then, are much more widely attested than direct ones:

(24) a. Badakizu gero zer non dagoen. (*P.Ab.* 52)
Then you know what lies where.
b. Nor nor den nork ezagutu? (*P.Ab.* 95)
Who is to recognize who is who?
c. Nire amaren alabari ez dio Ana-Marik zer zer den erakutsiko. (Azkue, *Ait. Bild.* 8–9)
To my mother's daughter Ana-Mari shall not show what is what.
d. Nik zer dakit ba nor non dabilen? (*G.* 199)
What do I know who is walking where?
e. Bere kezka guztia: ama nor non zuen jakitea. (Garate, *NY* 29)
All his concern (was): finding out who (and) where his mother was.

18.1.3 Presentative Sentences

The allative adverbs *hona*, *horra*, and *hara*, when used as presentatives (see section 6.3.2), can take a wh-complement containing a fronted interrogative. The interpretation of this construction is straightforward:

(25) a. Hona nola ezagutu nuen. (*MEIG* V, 137)
This is how I got to know him.
b. Jauna, horra zer hatzeman dudan. (Lapitze, 19)
Sir, this is what I have found.
c. Horra zer egin duen Jaunak enetzat. (Lk 1:25; *JKBO*)
That is what the Lord has done for me.
d. Hara zer esaten dizuedan nik, Paulok: . . . (Gal 5:2)
This is what I, Paul, say to yoû: . . .
e. Hara nondik datorkigun oraingo larrialdi hau. (Gn 42:21)
That is whence this present distress is coming upon us.

When an event or situation is to be presented, the same syntactic pattern is used with locative *non* 'where' acting as the interrogative needed. The frequent occurrence of the historical present inside the complement testifies to the vividness of the construction. Some examples are

(26) a. Eta hona non datorkigun Loidi bere lehenbiziko nobelarekin. (*MEIG* II, 60)
And lo and behold, here comes Loidi to us with his first novel.
b. Hona non sortu zaigun bat-batean . . . nobelista bat. (*MEIG* II, 60)
Lo and behold, here has been born unto us all of a sudden a novelist.
c. Arratsean, horra non datorren gizon zahar bat soroko lanetik. (Jgs 19:16)
In the evening, behold, an old man is coming from his work in the field.
d. Eta horra non ikusten duen emakumea bere oinetan etzanik. (Ru 3:8)
And lo and behold, he sees a woman lying at his feet.
e. Hara non diren mendi maiteak, hara non diren zeiaiak. (Iparragirre, from song "Nire etorrera" [= "Hara non diren"], Arratia I, 87, *Xaramela* 45)
Look, there are the beloved mountains; look, there are the plains.

18.1.4 Exclamative Wh-Clauses

Exclamative utterances headed by an interrogative (e.g., *zer* 'what', *zein* 'which', *nola* 'how', *nolako* 'what kind of', *zenbat* 'how many') take the form of a wh-complement clause without an overt main clause:

(27) a. Zer gizon handia den! (*EGLU* I, 34)
What a great man he is!
b. Zer sorgin parea eginen duzuen biek! (Barbier, *Sup.* 169)
What a pair of witches yoû two will make!
c. Zenbat aldiz bildu nahi izan ditudan zure semeak! (Mt 23:37; *IB*, and Lk 13:34; *IB*, *JKBO*)
How many times have I wanted to gather your sons together!
d. Ze onak dauden gerezi horiek! (Atxaga, *Gizona* 175)
How good those cherries are!
e. Zein zoriontsu naizen eta bat-batean bizia zein ederra kausitzen dudan! (Landart, 102)
How happy I am and how nice I find life all of a sudden!
f. Zein makalak izan garen! Lotsatu egiten naiz! (Atxaga, *Behi* 153)
How spineless we had been! I feel ashamed!

18.1.5 Partitive Wh-Complements

A minority of speakers in southern Guipuzcoa like to attach the partitive ending *-ik* to the complementizer of a wh-complement subordinate to a negative main clause. The Basque

Academy has spoken out against this localism in the standard language. Two examples follow:

(28) a. Ez dakigu nor denik. (*Lau Eb.* 246)
We don't know who he is.
b. Eskritura santak ez digu Ester noiz hil zenik esaten. (*TZ* II, 199)
Holy scripture doesn't tell us when Esther died.

18.1.6 The Conjunction *ea*

A wh-complement can be introduced by the conjunction *ea* when the sentence as a whole conveys a search for missing information, that is, amounts to a genuine question. As in these examples:

(29) a. Hazaeiek galdetu zion ea zertako negar egiten zuen. (*TZ* II, 91)
Hazael asked him why he was crying.
b. Ea non bizi zaren nahi nuke jakin. (Xalbador, *Odol.* 118)
I would like to know where you live.
c. Begiratu nuen ea zer gertatzen zen. (Atxaga, *Grl.* 57)
I looked to see what was happening.
d. Ea zer dioten elkarri entzun behar dugu. (Larzabal, *Senp.* 88)
We must hear what they are saying to each other.

Indirect yes-or-no questions too can be introduced by *ea*:

(30) a. Ea dirurik falta ote zen galdetu zion etxekoandreari detektibeak. (Garate, *Esku* 127)
The detective asked the lady of the house if any money happened to be missing.
b. Biharamonean ea elkarrekin aterako ote ginen galdetu nion. (Garate, *Alaba* 26)
The next day I asked her if we would (i.e., could) go out together.
c. Beste zenbaiti ere galdetu izan diet bat-batean ea itzuliko zidaten. (*MEIG* I, 207)
I have also asked some other people out of the blue if they would translate it for me.

The strongly inquisitive meaning of *ea* empowers it to be employed also without an overt main clause, as we see in the following examples:

(31) a. Egon, ea datorkion Elias salbatzera! (Mt 27:49)
Wait, let's see if Elias comes to save him!
b. Ea zenbat daukadan. (Amuriza, *Hil* 207)
Let me see how much I have.
c. Joño, ea gauzak pixka bat zuzentzen ditugun! (*MEIG* IX, 71)
Damn it, let's try to rectify things a bit!

d. Ea organizazioak zerbait esaten duen. (Atxaga, *Gizona* 41)
Let's hope the organization says something.
e. Amak ea jaitsiko ote zaren afaltzera! (Garate, *Hades* 19)
Mother asks if you'll come down to have supper!

Notice that in order to account for the ergative noun phrase *amak* in (31e), we must assume a syntactic process deleting a main verb of the type *galdetu* 'to ask' or *esan* 'to say'.

With an overt main clause, use of *ea* is merely optional in the standard language. But in the dialect of many speakers, especially in Biscay, its use is obligatory with certain main verbs, such as *galdetu* 'to ask'.

18.1.7 The Suffix *-etz*

The suffix *-etz* (dialectal variants *-entz*, *-ez*) represents a reinforcement of the complementizer *-N*, optionally used in order to mark the sentence as a genuine yes-or-no question. Although attested in older Biscayan—as late as Añibarro (1748–1830)—its use at present is confined to the northern dialects, from which it is occasionally borrowed into Batua texts. Examples are

(32) a. Nork daki lainoak direnetz? (J. Etchepare, *Ber*. 151)
Who knows whether these are clouds?
b. Nago ea buru gogorra duzunetz. (Duvoisin, *Lab.* 133)
I wonder if you have a thick head.
c. Nago hala ere, ez dudanetz Afrika hautatuko. (Landart, 101)
Yet, I wonder if I won't choose Africa.
d. Badakizu, jauna, ez denetz hori hitzez hitz egia. (*Artho Xur*. 7)
You know, lord, if that isn't word for word the truth.
e. Hori egia denetz laster ikusiko dugu. (Garate, *G.E.* 116)
We'll soon see if that is true.

18.1.8 The Interrogative Interjection *auskalo*

The colloquial interjection *auskalo*, translatable as 'heaven knows', originated in 19th-century Guipuzcoan, with the Spanish idiom *a buscarlo* 'go look for it' as its source. It has been adopted into southern Batua:

(33) a. Non da Anton? ... Auskalo! ... Aspaldi ez dugu haren berririk. (Etxaniz, *Antz.* 102)
Where is Tony? ... Heaven knows! ... We haven't had news of him for a long time.
b. —Egun on, Kornelio, non da nire senarra?—Eta zer galdetzen didazu niri? Auskalo! (Lertxundi, *Hamasei*. 25)
Good morning, Neil, where is my husband?—Why do you ask me? Who knows!

What is interesting about this interjection is that it can introduce indirect questions:

(34) a. Auskalo zer egingo duen bestela. (Atxaga, *Z.H.* 65)
Heaven knows what she will do otherwise.
b. Auskalo zenbat kazetari etorriko diren gaur. (Atxaga, *Gizona* 80)
Heaven knows how many journalists will come today.
c. Auskalo zer informazio daukaan hik. (Atxaga, *Gizona* 112)
Heaven knows what information yoú have.
d. Auskalo zenbat denboraz jo duen ni esnatu arte. (Haranburu, *Ausk.* 140)
Who knows how long it rang until I woke up.

18.2 Finite Complement Clauses in the Indicative Mood

In Basque, verbs of communication, cogitation, cognition, perception, opinion, certainty, and uncertainty take finite complement clauses in the indicative mood. (Subjunctive complements will be treated in chapter 21). Unlike their English counterparts, and apart from *beldur* (*izan*), emotive verbs (section 12.1.11), such as *harritu* 'to astonish' and *poztu* 'to rejoice', do not admit finite complement clauses.

18.2.1 The Complementizer -*LA*

Corresponding in function to the English complementizer *that*, Basque possesses a finite complementizer, which I will represent as -*LA*. As section 18.1.2 implied, -*LA* is a non-deletable suffix onto the finite verb of the subordinate clause. It has two allomorphs -*la* and -*ela*, whose distribution is determined by the nature of the final morpheme of the subordinate verb, in exactly the fashion described for -*n* and -*en* in section 18.1.2.

Thus, the allomorph -*la* occurs in these three contexts:

1. After a person marker, including third-person plural -*te*, but not third-person singular ∅.
2. After a stem final *a* not belonging to the verb *izan* 'to be'.
3. After the past tense suffix -*n*.

Elsewhere, the allomorph -*ela* appears.

Ad 1. The complementizer is attached prior to the operation of the word-final adjustment rules of section 9.1. Hence, from *dut*, *dun*, *duk* we get *dudala*, *dunala*, *duala* (with intervocalic -*g*- deletion). Given that the *g* of the suffix -*ga* elides whenever *a* remains (see section 9.1), *dakark* and *darabilk* will yield *dakarrala* and *darabilala*.

Ad 2. Stems ending in a vowel other than *a* take -*ela*: *dagoela*, *dirudiela* versus *daukala*, *daramala*. The final *a* occurring in some present tense forms of *izan* requires the allomorph -*ela*, before which the *a* is elided. Thus from *da*, *gara*, *zara*, *dira* we get *dela*, *garela*, *zarela*, *direla*.

Ad 3. In the absence of epenthesis, the past tense *-n* elides before *-la*, thus avoiding the inadmissible cluster *nl*.

As in the case of wh-complements, the canonical nonfocus position of a subordinate clause is to follow the main clause. Examples are

(35) a. Badakizu oso emakume ederra nintzela. (Atxaga, *Obab.* 287)
You know that I was a very beautiful woman.
b. Antzematen da euskalduna zarela. (Atxaga, *Z.H.* 22)
One notices that you are Basque.
c. Ez al duzu ikusten janzten ari naizela? (Atxaga, *Z.H.* 37)
Don't you see that I am getting dressed?
d. Ez dut esan nahi ez dakiela euskaraz mintzatzen. (*MEIG* I, 238)
I don't mean that he doesn't know how to speak Basque.

A subordinate clause can be topicalized:

(36) a. Baina Gotzonek ni hil ninduela zeharo sinetsi zuen Iñakik. (Garate, *Esku* 191)
But Iñaki really believed that Gotzon had killed me.
b. Zerurik badela sinesten al duzu? (Garate, *Hades* 39)
Do you believe that there is a heaven?

When a subordinate clause contains focus, as a rule the whole clause will occur in focus position in front of the main verb. Thus, in (37a) *ona* is focus, in (37b) *sekula*, in (37c) *laster*, and in (37d) *Booz izeneko baten soroan*:

(37) a. Eta Jainkoak ona zela ikusi zuen. (Gn 1:10, 12, 18, 21, 25)
And God saw that it was good.
b. Sekula ez zinela etorriko uste nuen. (Atxaga, *Obab.* 106)
I thought that you would never come.
c. Medikua ere laster etorriko dela uste dut. (*TOE* III, 154)
I think that the doctor too will come soon.
d. Noren soroan egin duzu lan? . . . Rutek, orduan, Booz izeneko baten soroan lan egin zuela kontatu zion Noemiri. (Ru 2:19)
In whose field did you work? . . . Ruth then told Naomi that she had worked in the field of someone named Boaz.

In particular, subordinate clauses containing an interrogative tend to be in focus position:

(38) a. Nor naizela uste duzue? (Labayen, *Su Em.* 186)
Who do yoû think I am?
b. Eta zuek, nor naizela diozue? (Mt 16:15, Lk 9:20)
And as for yoû, who do yoû say I am?

c. Bultza nork egin dizula uste duzu? (Garate, *Alaba* 71)
The push, who do you think gave it to you?

d. Zer dela uste duzu barberua? (*P.Ab.* 45)
What do you think a barber is?

Finally, a subordinate clause may occupy the quasi-focus site (cf. section 8.6.2):

(39) Ez nuke eroa dela esango.
I wouldn't say that he is crazy.

Little needs to be said about the order of constituents within the *-LA* clause. Compared with a main clause, the only difference I am aware of is that nonapplication of Auxiliary Attraction (section 8.2.2) is condemned much less harshly:

(40) a. Uste dut alkatea ez dela etorri.
I think that the mayor has not come.

b. ?Uste dut alkatea etorri ez dela.
I think that the mayor has not come.

18.2.2 Sentential Subjects

Certain intransitive verbs and predicates take *-LA* complements that can be viewed as their sentential subjects. Along with the verb *iruditu* 'to seem', we may cite as examples the adverb *argi* 'clear' and the inessives *agerian* 'in the open' and *bistan* 'in sight', which form predicates conveying 'obviousness' when combined with a suitable verb: stative *egon* (more rarely *izan*) 'to be' or dynamic *ezarri, ipini, jarri,* all meaning 'to put'. A few examples will do as illustrations:

(41) a. Ez nindutela konprenitzen iruditzen zitzaidan. (Atxaga, *Obab.* 99)
It seemed to me that they didn't understand me.

b. Dena ongi joango zela iruditu zitzaien. (Garate, *NY* 94)
It seemed to them that everything would go fine.

c. Faniri zerbait gertatzen zaiola bistan dago. (Haranburu, *Ausk.* 39)
It is obvious that something is happening to Fani.

d. Bistan dago bi alde dituela teoria honek. (*MEIG* III, 107)
It is obvious that this theory has two aspects.

e. Eta bistan da ez dakiela. (*MEIG* VI, 117)
And it is obvious that he doesn't know it.

Turning now to adjectives and their sentential complements, we need to distinguish between deverbal adjectives and all others. The nonderived adjective *bitxi* 'strange' furnishes a typical example of the behavior of the latter class. Its sentential complement is either nonfinite, being a nominalization based on the verbal noun or the perfect participle, or else a wh-complement with an interrogative, never a *-LA* clause:

(42) a. Bitxi(a) da abuztuan elurra egitea.
It is strange that it snows in August.
b. Bitxi(a) da abuztuan elurra egin (izan)a.
It is strange that it has snowed in August.
c. Bitxi(a) da abuztuan nola egiten duen elurra.
It is strange how it snows in August.

Deverbal adjectives, however, inherit from their verbal origin the capacity to admit -*LA* clauses. Consider the adjectives *interesgarri* 'interesting', *harrigarri* 'astonishing', and *ohargarri* 'remarkable'. Of these three, only the last one, *ohargarri*, can take a -*LA* clause. The first one, *interesgarri*, does not qualify at all, since it is derived from a noun (*interes*); the next one is derived from the emotive verb *harritu* 'to astonish' that rejects -*LA* clauses (section 18.2); only *ohargarri* is derived from a verb (*ohartu* 'to remark', 'to notice') that does take -*LA* complements. We thus get

(43) Ohargarria da galderak bai, baina erantzunak ez daramala *ba*-rik. (*MEIG* VI, 162)
It is remarkable that the question does, but the answer does not carry any *ba*.

Some deverbal adjectives are zero derived; that is, they are homophonous with perfect participles. The main examples are *ageri* 'apparent' from the verb *ageri* 'to appear'; *ezagun* 'obvious' from the verb *ezagun*, a more archaic variant of *ezagutu* 'to recognize', 'to know'; *jakin* 'well-known' from the verb *jakin* 'to know'; and *nabari* 'evident' from the verb *nabari(tu)* 'to perceive', 'to notice'. Since the verbs take -*LA* complements, the adjectives do too:

(44) a. Ageri da eri dela gure Maria. (H.U., *Zez.* 62)
It is apparent that my Maria is ill. (For *gure* 'my', see section 6.1.3, item 2.)
b. Ageri da engainatu dituela konfesoreak. (Mogel, *C.C.* 187)
It is apparent that he has deceived his confessors.
c. Gizon azkarra dela ezagun da. (*TOE* I, 113)
It is obvious that he is a clever person.
d. Apaiztegiko kutsua ez zaizula joan ezagun da. (*TOE* I, 79)
It is obvious that the taint of the seminary has not left you.
e. Jakina da bi klasetan banatu zituela euskalkiak. (*MEIG* VI, 66)
It is well-known that he divided the Basque dialects in two classes.
f. Nabari zaio ez dela hemengoa. (*E.H.* 581)
It is obvious (about him) that he is not from here.
g. Nabari zaio euskalduna ez dela. (Aulestia, 422)
It is obvious (about him) that he is not Basque.

While adjectives acting as predicates in combination with the copula *izan* normally require the article -*a* (see section 2.3.1, item 7), they no longer do so when equipped with a sentential complement, finite or not. Still, in southern Batua, having the article is the more colloquial option, leaving it out, the more literary one (*EGLU* I, 261). Zero-derived adjectives fitted with a sentential complement, however, always reject the article *-a*; see examples (44a–g).

Predicate nouns combined with the copula *izan* still require the article *-a* even in the presence of a sentential subject or complement. Thus with *egia* 'truth' and *gezur* 'lie', 'falsehood', we get

(45) a. Egia al da inoiz zizparekin irten eta ia garbitu zintuela? (Amuriza, *Emea* 58)
Is it true that one time she went out with a rifle and almost killed you?
b. Gezurra da Frantziako erregea urzalea dela.
It is false that the king of France is a teetotaler.

It can be maintained that these complement clauses are not licenced directly by the nominal predicates *egia* and *gezur* but depend on a covert verb of saying: *Egia* (*esatea*) *al da* . . . (*esatea*) 'Is it (telling) the truth (to say) that . . .'. As a matter of fact, *-LA* clauses depending on a verb of saying left unexpressed are by no means unusual:

(46) a. Nik, aldiz, ez nintzela joanen, ihes egin nuen goiko salara. (Arrosagaray, 17)
I, however, (saying) that I wouldn't go, fled to the room upstairs.
b. Hala uste zuela berak. (Atxaga, *Grl.* 146)
He (said) that he thought so.

18.2.3 Exclamative *-LA* Clauses

In one type of exclamatory sentence, the affirmative particle *bai* 'yes' can be followed by a *-LA* complement clause:

(47) a. Bai ederki bizi garela hemen! (*MEIG* IX, 102)
How nicely we are living here!
b. Bai ona zarela nirekin, Jauna! (Ru 2:13)
How good you are for me, sir!

A contrastive adverb or topic can be placed before *bai*:

(48) a. Orain bai mintzo zarela argi! (Jn 16:29)
How clear you are speaking now! (unlike before)
b. Hik bai egin beharko dunala negar! (Garate, *NY* 138)
How much yoù will need to weep! (unlike the persons mentioned before)

18.3 The Complementizer *-NA*

The complementizer *-NA* optionally substitutes for *-LA* (*-na* for *-la*, *-ena* for *-ela*) when the following two conditions are both met:

1. The main predicate either presupposes or asserts the truth of its complement clause.
2. The complement clause is not in focus (cf. Altube 1929, sec. 116).

Although this complementizer is native to Biscay and part of Guipuzcoa only, and even there unfamiliar to many, it has been readily accepted into the southern variety of the standard language. Use of *-NA* is most common on complements of factive verbs, especially *jakin* 'to know':

(49) a. Banekien gizon zorrotza zarena. (Mt 25:24)
I knew that you are a hard man.
b. Diruzalea ez zarena badakit. (Garate, *G.E.* 10)
I know that you are not money hungry.
c. Ikasi zuen ... gizonak gauza guztietan txit apala izan behar zukeena. (*G.*[3] 8)
He had learned that man should be very humble in all things.
d. Gazte hauek ez dira konturatzen, etxeko lan guztiak jai arratsetan guri uzten dizkiguna. (Itziar, 24)
These youngsters don't realize that on festival evenings they leave all the household jobs to us.

The complementizer *-NA* is also possible, however, after main predicates that do not presuppose but assert the truth of their complements:

(50) a. Eta seguru nago gure asmoa ontzat hartuko dutena. (*TOE* III, 42)
And I am sure that they will approve our plan.
b. Biek oso elkar maite dutena ez dut nik inongo zalantzarik egiten. (Garate, *Alaba* 28–29)
I have no doubt whatsoever that the two love each other very much.
c. Agirian dago sortaldeko ahoberokeria bat dena hori. (*Lau Eb.* 110)
It is obvious that that is a case of oriental exaggeration.
d. Haien esanetan gezurrik ez zena garbi zegoen. (Garate, *Alaba* 35)
It was clear that there was no lie in their statements.
e. Bai, badakusat oso ederra zarena. (Garate, *Alaba* 71)
Yes, I see that you are very beautiful.
f. Nik aitortzen dizuet eskasa nintzena. (Uztapide, *Noizb.* 103)
I admit to yoû that I was inadequate.

Many speakers obey the constraint that *-NA*, unlike *-LA*, must be clause-final. (But see example 50c.) For them, example (51a) is not possible with *-NA* instead of *-LA*:

(51) a. Badakigu etorri dela sorgin hori.
We know that that witch has come.
b. Badakigu sorgin hori etorri dena.
We know that that witch has come.

18.4 The Partitive Complementizer *-NIK*

The complementizer *-NIK* optionally substitutes for *-LA* (*-nik* for *-la*, *-enik* for *-ela*) when a complement not in focus occurs in a negative polarity context. As *-NIK* appears in just those contexts that allow the partitive determiner *-(r)ik* (section 13.1.2), to which it seems to be formally related, we will henceforth refer to it as the partitive complementizer. While totally unknown in the northern dialects, it is frequently seen in the southern ones—much more so than *-NA*—and hence in southern Batua. Examples of the use of *-NIK* will be presented according to context:

1. With a negated main verb of any kind

(52) a. Ez dut uste oker nagoenik. (*MEIG* V, 143)
I don't think that I am wrong.
b. Ez diot inork gaizki egin zuenik. (*MEIG* VII, 163)
I am not saying that anybody acted wrongly.
c. Ez duk esango hitzontzia naizenik. (Garate, *Esku* 116)
You won't say that I am a chatterbox.
d. Ez nekien hain berandu zenik. (Atxaga, *Z.H.* 111)
I didn't know that it was so late.
e. Ez dirudi gaixo dagoenik. (Atxaga, *Obab.* 139)
He doesn't appear to be ill.
f. Ez dut nik ukatuko auzi hori larria denik. (*MEIG* IX, 55)
I won't deny that that matter is important.

2. With an interrogative main clause

(53) a. Uste al duzu lotan egongo denik? (*TOE* III, 208)
Do you think he will be asleep?
b. Zerriek hitz egiten dutenik inoiz entzun al da? (Garate, *Ald.* 12)
Has it ever been heard that pigs talk?
c. Ba al zenekiten On Lorentzok ezkontzeko asmorik zuenik? (Garate, *G.E.* 92)
Did yoû know that Don Lorenzo had any plans to get married?

3. With a rhetorical constituent question in the main clause

(54) a. Nork esan du gizon honek nire aitari kalte egin dionik? (Garate, *Alaba* 55)
Who said that this man has done my father harm?
b. Nork esan dizu Zinkunegi italianoa denik? (*TOE* I, 94)
Who told you that Zinkunegi is an Italian?
c. Nork esan dizu zuri ni libre nagoenik? (Garate, *Musk.* 42)
Who told you that I am free?

4. With a protasis main clause

(55) Uste baduzue aditz kontuan ere berehalako batasuna behar dugunik, . . . (*MEIG* VII, 160)
If yoû think that we need immediate unification in the matter of the verb too, . . .

5. With inherently negative main predicates, such as *ukatu* 'to deny' and *ahaztu* 'to forget'

(56) a. Hala ere, Kathleen hil zuenik ukatu (zuen) orduan ere. (Garate, *NY* 85)
Still, then too he denied that he had killed Kathleen.
b. Eta Jainkoaren beharrean garenik ahaztu egiten zaigu. (Irazusta, *Joan.* 182)
And we are forgetting that we are in need of God.

18.5 Negative Raising and Hyperraising

18.5.1 Negative Raising

With verbs of opinion like *uste izan* 'to think', 'to believe', negative complement clauses are exceedingly rare. However, sentences with negated *uste* as a main verb seem to report more than a mere absence of opinion regarding the truth of the subordinate clause. Taken together, these two observations provide evidence for a syntactic process of negative raising: a negation *ez* that clearly belongs in the subordinate clause shows up instead in the main clause.

If negative raising exists, however, complementizer selection must obviously follow it and should therefore be handled within the syntactic component also:

(57) a. Uste dut ez dutela (*dutenik) bukatu.
I think that they haven't finished.
b. Ez dut uste bukatu dutenik. (*MEIG* IX, 75)
I don't think that they have finished.

18.5.2 Syntax of *irudi* 'to seem'; Hyperraising

As shown in section 9.3.1, the verb *irudi* 'to seem' appears to take nominal complements:

(58) a. Gaur etxe honek errota dirudi. (*TOE* III, 93)
Today this house is like a mill. (so many visitors)
b. Haren begiek tximistak ziruditen. (*TB* 147)
His eyes were like flashes of lightning.

The verb *irudi* readily admits finite complement clauses: wh-complements ('it seems as if . . .') but, more commonly, *-LA* clauses ('it seems that . . .'). Some examples are

(59) a. Etorkizun handiko pilotaria ote den dirudi. (Basarri, 89)
It seems as if he may perhaps be a jai alai player with a great future.

b. Lotan daudela dirudi. (*TOE* I, 162)
It seems that they are asleep.
c. Altubek arrazoi zuela dirudi horretan. (*MEIG* VIII, 101)
It seems that Altube was right in that. (For *arrazoi zuen*, see section 13.4.2.)
d. Bahitu egin dutenik ez dirudi, beraz. (Garate, *Alaba* 22)
It doesn't seem, therefore, that she was kidnapped.

Just as in English, the subject of the subordinate clause can be raised into the main clause. Unlike what happens in English, however, the remaining complement clause stays finite. Thanks to this phenomenon, known as hyperraising, an absolutive subject of an intransitive predicate can be promoted to an ergative subject of the main clause:

(60) a. Orain, badirudi euskarak ahaike dela. (Ax. 19)
Now, Basque seems to be timid.
b. Mutilak jatorra eta ona dela dirudi. (Zapirain, *M.* 144)
The boy seems to be nice and pleasant.
c. Zatitxo batek badirudi ez dagoela ongi itzulia. (*MEIG* II, 78)
A little fragment seems not to be correctly rendered.

Returning now for a moment to examples (58a,b), we notice that the verb *ziruditen* in (58b) fails to agree with the plural noun *tximistak* 'flashes'. Therefore, such nominal complements do not have the status of direct objects, but appear to be remnants of *-LA* clauses (*errota dela, tximistak zirela*) after deletion of the subordinate verb.

Another characteristic of the verb *irudi* is that it allows negative raising. It may have applied in the following examples:

(61) a. Ez dirudi gaixo dagoenik. (Atxaga, *Obab.* 139)
He doesn't seem to be ill.
b. Ez zirudien ondo ikusten zuenik. (Atxaga, *Obab.* 155)
He didn't seem to see well.

Even the deceptively simple example (61c) is an example of negative raising, if, as I have claimed, it is based on an underlying clause *mutila ez dela motela*:

(61) c. Mutilak ez dirudi motela. (*TOE* I, 136)
The boy doesn't seem sluggish.

Warning: The (morphologically) transitive verb *irudi* is not to be confused with the intransitive verb of similar meaning *iruditu*, which requires a dative experiencer and does not allow raising:

(62) a. Norbait erori ote den iruditu zait. (*TOE* II, 95)
It seemed to me as if somebody fell.
b. Urduri zegoela iruditu zitzaidan. (Garate, *Alaba* 27; Atxaga, *Obab.* 95)
It seemed to me that he was nervous.

18.6 Cross-Clause Focus Movement

As pointed out in section 18.2.1, the normal way for Basque to cope with a situation where the focus F of the sentence is contained inside a subordinate clause S, is to leave F in focus position within S and place S as a whole in the focus site of the main clause. However, when the main verb belongs to a small set of verbs—the so-called bridge verbs—there is an alternative possibility involving "long" movement. In virtue of long movement, the focus constituent slips out of the subordinate clause and surfaces again in the focus site of the main clause.

Speakers may differ as to which verbs are bridge verbs, but *uste* (*izan*) 'to believe' and *esan* 'to say' are always included, and *ukatu* 'to deny' as well as all factive verbs are excluded. Long movement mostly applies with interrogatives as focus, but is not obligatory even then. Here are some examples, all taken from written sources:

(63) a. Honela diozu eginen duzula. (Ax. 235)
Thus you say you will do.
b. Nor diote naizela jendeek? (Lk 9:18; HE)
Who do the people say I am?
c. Zer uste zuten emango ziela Jainkoak? (Ubillos, 60)
What did they think that God would give them?
d. Zer uste duzue egin zuela? (Satrustegi, 182)
What do yoû think he did?
e. Zer uste huen zela bizitzea? (Atxaga, *Behi* 15)
What did yoú think that living was?
f. Norekin uste duzu etorri zinela? (Urretabizkaia, *Sat*. 84)
With whom do you think you came?
g. Noiz eta norekin esan duzu joan zarela zinera? (Saltarelli, 21)
When and with whom have you said that you have gone to the movies?

18.7 More on Topic

18.7.1 Cross-Clause Topic Fronting

As we noticed in section 8.5, like many languages, Basque may call into play a process of topic fronting, by which a sentence topic achieves prominence by virtue of moving to a topic slot in front of the sentence. Note the absence of postposition stranding: in Basque, the fronted constituent perforce brings along any postposition or case ending belonging to it.

Long movement is allowed: a topic can be moved out of a finite subordinate clause, and it can do so even across a main verb that (like *ukatu* 'to deny') does not permit cross-clause focus movement. Some examples are

(64) a. Etorkizunekoa, ez dakigu emanen zaigunetz. (Ax. 155)
As to that of the future, we don't know if it will be given us.
b. Paperak, ez dakit nola galdu dituen. (*EGLU* I, *E* 27)
As for the papers, I don't know how he lost them.
c. Alabak, ez dakit zer egin nahiko duen. (*TOE* III, 186)
As to the daughter, I don't know what she will want to do.
d. Sendagilerik, ez dut uste inoiz beharko dudanik. (*MEIG* VI, 160)
A(ny) doctor, I don't think that I'll ever need.
e. Zure izeba horrekin, ez dut ukatu Pariseratu naizenik.
With that aunt of yours, I have not denied that I have gone to Paris.

18.7.2 Verb Topicalization

For various reasons, a speaker may want to insist on the action conveyed by the verb, quite apart from its participants. This happens in particular when there is a contrast, overtly expressed or merely implied, with a different action involving the same participants. Many languages, including northern Basque, have to rely on intonational means to achieve the effect desired. Southern Basque, however, also commands a syntactic resource: it can treat the verb as an emphatic topic. This strategy may be described as a topicalization process that keeps the affected verb in place, but puts a copy of it in front of the sentence in the shape of the unmarked verb form, the perfect participle. To illustrate, we begin with a few examples with overt contrast:

(65) a. Esan ederki, baina egin, zer egiten dugu? (Orixe, in *OrOm* 290)
As to saying (it), fine, but as to doing (it), what do we do?
b. Gustatu bai, baina harritu, ez zuten horrenbeste harritzen. (Atxaga, *Obab*. 356)
Please, yes, but amaze, they didn't amaze that much.
c. Hil, ez gara guztiok hilko, baina bai guztiok izatez aldatuko. (1 Cor 15:51; *IB*)
As to dying, we will not all die, but we will all be changed in nature.

We now continue with some examples where the contrast is merely implicit, or where the topicalization has other motives. Since English lacks a convenient way of topicalizing the verb, the translations given may appear somewhat strained:

(66) a. Entzun, ez zuen ezer entzuten. (Garate, *Esku* 120)
As to hearing, he didn't hear anything.
b. Sortu, 1948an sortu zen. (*MEIG* I, 257)
Origin-wise, it originated in 1948.
c. Ezagutu, Salamancan ezagutu nuen Altuna. (*MEIG* IV, 111)
As regards acquaintance, I became acquainted with Altuna in Salamanca.
d. Aipatu, ez du bere burua baizik aipatzen. (*MEIG* VIII, 27)
As far as citing goes, he only cites himself.

Like any sentence topic, a fronted verb may be followed by *ere* 'also' or 'even':

(67) a. Eta gosaldu ere, ez zuen sukaldean presaka gosaldu. (Atxaga, *Obab*. 292)
And as for breakfasting too, he didn't breakfast in the kitchen hurriedly.
b. Eta sinestu ere, ez dakit sinestuko zizuen. (Atxaga, *Gizona* 29)
And as far as believing goes (too), I don't know whether he believed you.

In the western dialects, the second instance of a verb may be replaced by the dummy verb *egin* 'to do':

(68) a. Eta sinestu ere, ez dakit egin zizuen.
And as far as believing goes (too), I don't know whether he believed you.
b. Saiatu, behintzat, egingo gara. (Atxaga, *Obab*. 24)
Try, at least, we will (do).

18.8 Noun Complementation

Since verbal nouns are in fact nominalized sentences (section 7.2.3), it follows that they will allow finite complements whenever the corresponding verb does:

nor nor den jakitea	knowing who is who
euskalduna dela jakitea	knowing that he is Basque

Other nouns, however, do not have this facility. True enough, nouns such as *aitzaki* 'pretext', *berri* 'news', *froga* 'proof, *itxaropen* 'hope', *poz* 'joy', *zurrumurru* 'rumor', and many others can be paired with *-LA* clauses; yet they cannot take these complements directly, but only with the help of an intervening morpheme linking the clause to the noun. As to the choice of this morpheme, there is disagreement among speakers. One option assimilates the *-LA* clause to an NP, and, accordingly, makes use of the genitive:

(69) Guda-ontzi ahul haiek arrisku denetatik askatzen zituztelaren ustetan (Oñatibia, 19)
In a belief that those weak warships freed them from all danger

18.8.1 Adnominal *-ko*

The standard language, however, seems to have taken another option. It employs the adnominal morpheme *-ko*, thus assimilating the *-LA* clause to a PP. As J. E. Emonds has convincingly argued (1985, chap. 7) that complementizers are universally adpositions, so that *-LA* must have the status of a postposition, this option claims the support of syntactic theory. It is seconded by etymology, since the complementizer *-LA*, in all likelihood, is to be identified with the allative case marker *-ra*, whose original shape was *-la*, as shown in section 11.1.6. Moreover, use of the adnominal *-ko* corresponds to older usage in all dialects and is still widely resorted to today:

(70) a. Jainkoa badelako froga bat (J. B. Etcheberry, 158)
A proof that God exists
b. Adiskide garelako ezaugarritzat (*P.Ab.* 53)
As a sign that we are friends
c. Santiago zaharrena Espainiara etorri zelako berriak (*TB* 186)
Reports that James the Elder came to Spain
d. Norabait joan beharra zutelako aitzakian (T. Agirre, *Uzt.* 41)
Under the pretext that they had to go somewhere
e. Bizi garelako seinale (*MEIG* IV, 32 = *MIH* 66)
As a sign that we are living
f. Egoera mingarri batetik askatzen gintuelako pozez (Garate, *Musk.* 92)
From joy that he was freeing us from a painful situation
g. Bere partea izango duelako itxaropenez (1 Cor 9:10; *IB*, *EAB*)
In the hope that he will have his part
h. Ikasle hura hilko ez zelako zurrumurrua (Jn 21:23)
The rumor that that disciple would not die
i. Bloy pitzadura batean erori zelako albistea (Atxaga, *Obab.* 345)
The news that Bloy had fallen into a crevice
j. Ongi jarri zarelako berriak baditut. (Etxaniz, *Irul. Neg.* 86)
I have reports that you are quite recovered.
k. Menscher ero zegoelako hotsa (Atxaga, *Obab.* 280)
The rumor that Menscher was crazy

Noun complements have two characteristics: they immediately precede the noun, and they must end in the finite verb, even when the clause is negative (cf. example 70h). The noun *beldur* is somewhat exceptional in that, like the verbal idiom *beldur izan* 'to be afraid', it admits wh-complements directly:

(71) a. Sua sortuko den beldurrez (Labayen, *Su Em.* 165)
Out of fear that fire will break out
b. Besteren batek emaztea ostuko ote zion beldurrez (Etxaniz, *Antz.* 89)
Out of fear that someone or other would perhaps steal his wife

But the verbal idiom *beldur izan* also admits *-LA* complements, and the noun *beldur* therefore allows *-lako* clauses as well:

(72) a. Beldur naiz hau nuela azken itzulia. (Xalbador, *Odol.* 232)
I am afraid that this was the last return for me.
b. Biraolari gisa harrika emango ez didatelako beldurra (*MEIG* V, 110)
The fear that they will stone me as a blasphemer

[*N.B.* For nonfinite noun complements, see section 19.2.5.]

18.8.2 The Suffix *-lakoan* 'in the belief that . . .'

On page 222 of Lardizabal's work *Testamentu zarreko kondaira I* (*TZ* I), we find the meaning 'in the belief that he had left her forever' expressed in two ways. Once, in accordance with section 18.8.1, as *betiko utzi zuelako ustean*, but also as *betiko utzi zuelakoan*. What this usage shows is that the noun *uste* 'belief' can be deleted when preceded by a sentential complement and followed by the inessive ending *-an*. We thus witness the emergence of a suffix attachable to a finite verb: *-lakoan* 'in the belief that . . .'. Other examples of its use are

(73) a. Hartu zuen ostalariaren astoa, berea zuelakoan. (From "Makilakixki," *Eusk. Ip.* 33)
He took the innkeeper's donkey, thinking that he had his own.
b. Eztia nekarrelakoan behazuna ekarri dut. (*G.* 231)
Thinking that I was bringing honey, I have brought gall.
c. Mesede ederra egin zioten hari, kalte egiten ziotelakoan. (Uztapide, *LEG* I, 50)
They did him a big favor, thinking that they were doing him harm.
d. Barbero batengana eraman omen zuten, hark sendatuko zuelakoan. (Atxaga, *Bi An.* 9)
They took him to a barber, in the belief that he would cure him.

Inasmuch as the expression *ustean egon* acts as a common alternative to *uste izan* 'to believe', the verb *egon*, present or understood, can turn a *-lakoan* phrase into the main predicate of the sentence:

(74) a. Neroni ere erraza ez delakoan nago. (*MEIG* V, 121)
I myself also believe that it is not easy. (For *neroni* 'myself', see section 28.2.5.)
b. Detektibe batek lana hobeki egingo lukeelakoan gaude. (Garate, *Alaba* 20)
We believe that a private detective would do the job better.
c. Nor zarelakoan zaude? (Jn 8:53)
Who do you think you are?
d. Hutsaren truke errespetatzen zaituelakoan, ala? (Jb 1:9)
You believe he reveres you for nothing, do you? (Lit. "in exchange for nought")

When preceded by a sentential complement, the noun *uste* can likewise be deleted when it is followed by the article *-a*. Such deletion again results in a suffix attachable to a finite verb: *-lakoa* 'the belief that . . .'. Examples are

(75) a. Oso zabaldua zen herriaren artean Mesiasa ustekabean azalduko zelakoa. (*Lau Eb.* 82)
The belief that the Messiah would appear unexpectedly was very widely spread among the people.
b. Etxean daudelakoa daukat.
I have the idea that they are at home.

Note the expression . . . *-lakoa egin* 'to act as if . . .':

(76) Dena daki, eta ez baleki, dakielakoa egiten du. (Mintegi, 94)
He knows everything, and should he not know it, he acts as if he does.

18.9 A Nominal Suffix of Reprehension: *-keria*

Attached to adjectives, appropriate nouns, and a few verbs, the suffix *-keria*, possibly abstracted from Spanish *porquería* meaning 'muck' or 'filth', yields nouns naming a vice, failing, or deficiency on the part of a human being. The nouns can be used also to denote an action or activity typical of the vice in question. Only very few examples are at variance with this characterization—for example, *huskeria* 'trifle', from *huts* 'empty', 'nought'. Since the meaning of the derivation is not always fully predictable from the base, I will present an extensive catalog of examples.

1. Adjectives as a base

aberats	rich	aberaskeria	excessive show of richness
ahalkegabe	shameless	ahalkegabekeria	shamelessness
ahul	weak	ahulkeria	weakness, depression
alderdikoi	partial, biased	alderdikoikeria	partiality
alfer	idle, lazy	alferkeria	idleness
anker	cruel	ankerkeria	cruelty
antsikabe	careless	antsikabekeria	carelessness
arduragabe	negligent	arduragabekeria	negligence
argal	thin, weak	argalkeria	weakness
arin	light, frivolous	arinkeria	levity, frivolity
ase	satiated, replete	asekeria	gluttony
ausart	bold, daring	ausarkeria	audacity, impudence
axolagabe	heedless, careless	axolagabekeria	heedlessness, carelessness
barregarri	comic, ridiculous	barregarrikeria	grotesqueness, ludicrousness
beltz	black	beizkeria	black deed, villainy
berri	new	berrikeria	modernism
bigun	soft	bigunkeria	indolence, softness
bihozgabe	heartless	bihozgabekeria	heartlessness
bihurri	naughty	bihurrikeria	naughtiness, mischief
biluzi	naked	biluzkeria	nudity
bitxi	strange	bitxikeria	eccentricity
burugabe	headless	burugabekeria	headlessness
dirukoi	avaricious	dirukoikeria	greed, avarice
doilor	vile, mean	doilorkeria	meanness, villainy
epel	lukewarm, tepid	epelkeria	halfheartedness, tepidity
eragabe	unruly, disorderly	eragabekeria	unruliness, disorderly conduct
ergel	imbecilic, silly	ergelkeria	imbecility, silliness

ero	insane, crazy	erokeria	insanity, craziness
eskergabe	ungrateful	eskergabekeria	ungratefulness, thanklessness
ezti	sweet	eztikeria	adulation, flattery
gaizto	wicked, bad	gaiztakeria	wickedness, evil deed, misdeed
gangar	fatuous, conceited	gangarkeria	fatuity, conceitedness
ganoragabe	indolent, awkward	ganoragabekeria	indolence, awkwardness
gogor	hard, harsh	gogorkeria	hardness, harshness
gordin	raw, unripe	gordinkeria	coarseness, vulgarity, obscenity
gozo	delicious, sweet	gozokeria	worldly pleasure
harro	arrogant, proud	harrokeria	arrogance, conceit, pride
handi	great, big	handikeria	ostentation, conceit, vanity
inozo	naive, silly	inozokeria	foolishness, silliness
itsu	blind	itsukeria	blindness, obstinacy
itsusi	ugly	itsuskeria	villainy, obscenity
izugarri	terrible	izugarrikeria	atrocity
kaiku	idiotic, stupid	kaikukeria	idiocy, stupidity
koldar	cowardly	koldarkeria	cowardice
labain	slippery, false	labainkeria	adulation, falseness, lewdness
lasai	relaxed, calm	lasaikeria	slackness, wantonness
leun	smooth	leunkeria	adulation, smooth talk
likits	sticky, filthy, lewd	likiskeria	filth, lewdness
lizun	moldy, lascivious	lizunkeria	lasciviousness, obscenity
lotsagabe	shameless	lotsagabekeria	shamelessness, impudence
maite	dear, beloved	maitekeria	infatuation, adultery
makur	bent, crooked, wrong	makurkeria	crookedness, evil, injustice
motel	dull, insipid	motelkeria	dullness, insipidity
motz	short, blunt	mozkeria	bluntness, abruptness
mozkor	drunk	mozkorkeria	drunkenness
nabarmen	outstanding, conspicuous	nabarmenkeria	extravagance, eccentricity
nagi	lazy	nagikeria	laziness
neurrigabe	unlimited	neurrigabekeria	excess, exhorbitance
oker	crooked, wrong	okerkeria	crookedness, injustice
sabelkoi	gluttonous	sabelkoikeria	gluttony
samin	bitter	saminkeria	bitterness, resentment
tentel	foolish	tentelkeria	foolishness
txaldan	stupid, silly	txaldankeria	stupidity
txar	bad	txarkeria	evil action, wrong
txiki	small	txikikeria	small-mindedness, trifle
zabar	lax, indolent	zabarkeria	laxness, neglect
zantar	filthy, ugly	zantarkeria	filth, obscenity
zaputz	unsociable, aloof	zapuzkeria	unsociability, aloofness
zatar	dirty, ugly	zatarkeria	smut, obscenity
zeken	stingy	zekenkeria	stinginess

zentzugabe	irrational, absurd	zentzugabekeria	absurdity
zikin	dirty	zikinkeria	filth, obscenity
zikoitz	stingy	zikoizkeria	stinginess, avarice
zital	mean, vile	zitalkeria	meanness, villainy
ziztrin	insignificant, trivial	ziztrinkeria	pettiness
zoro	foolish, crazy	zorakeria	foolishness, craziness
zozo	foolish	zozokeria	foolishness
zuhur	cautious, thrifty	zuhurkeria	stinginess
zuri	white	zurikeria	adulation, cajolery

2. Nouns as a base

a. Nouns with human referents as a base

ar	male	arkeria	machismo
azti	wizard, sorcerer	aztikeria	wizardry, sorcery
etsai	enemy	etsaikeria	hostility, rivalry
haur	child	haurkeria	childishness, puerility
jauntxo	potentate, tyrant	jauntxokeria	despotism, tyranny
lapur	thief	lapurkeria	theft, robbery
maisu	schoolteacher	maisukeria	pedantry
nagusi	boss	nagusikeria	tyranny, despotism
ohoin	thief, swindler	ohoinkeria	theft, swindle, fraud
sorgin	witch	sorginkeria	witchcraft, sorcery
ume	child	umekeria	childishness, puerility

b. Nouns referring to animals as a base

abere	animal	aberekeria	beastliness, bestiality, brutality
apo	toad	apokeria	gibe, jeer, taunt
asto	donkey	astakeria	stupidity, nonsense, stupid act
azeri	fox	azerikeria	slyness, cunning, guile
katu	cat	katukeria	glibness, cajolery
mando	mule	mandakeria	stupidity
oilar	cock	oilarkeria	arrogance
oilo	chicken	oilokeria	cowardice, timidity
sator	mole	satorkeria	conspiracy, intrigue
urde	male pig	urdekeria	filth, obscenity
zakur	hound, dog	zakurkeria	treachery, dirty trick
zerri	pig	zerrikeria	immorality, obscenity

c. Miscellaneous nouns as a base

alderdiside	party	alderdikeria	partisanship, partiality
amets	dream	ameskeria	illusion

azal	surface, hide	azalkeria	superficiality, hypocrisy
azpi	underside	azpikeria	machination, treachery
baso	woods, wilderness	basakeria	savagery, brutality
bidegabe	injustice, injury	bidegabekeria	unfairness, injustice
bortxa	coercion, duress	bortxakeria	coercion, violence
ezerez	nothing	ezerezkeria	trifle, insignificance
gai	material	gaikeria	materialism
indar	strength, force	indarkeria	violence
itxura	appearance	itxurakeria	hypocrisy, pretense
kirten	handle, idiot	kirtenkeria	idiocy, stupidity, horseplay
lohi	mud	lohikeria	filth, lasciviousness
talde	group	taldekeria	herd instinct, gregariousness
uste	belief, opinion	ustekeria	prejudice, superstition

3. The perfect participle of a few verbs as base

galdu	to lose, to ruin	galdukeria	dissipation, debauchery
saldu	to sell, to betray	saldukeria	treachery, treason
sinetsi	to believe	sineskeria	superstition

18.10 Vocabulary

agindu	to command, to promise
aipatu	to mention, to cite
ala	or
amorratu	rabid
antzeman	to notice, to guess
astakeria	stupid action, stupidity, nonsense
azkar	strong, fast, quickly, clever
berehala	immediately, at once
bistan egon	to be obvious
erantzun	to answer
ezbehar	disaster, misfortune
gaiztakeria	evil action, misdeed, evil
galdegin	to ask (also *galde egin*)
galdetu	to ask
itxaropen	hope, expectation
konpondu	to repair, to manage
kontatu	to tell, to count
konturatu	to realize
kontuz	watch out!, look out!, attention!

laino	fog, mist, cloud
lehenbizi	at first, initially
makal	spineless, weak, cowardly
mesede	favor
motel	dull, tasteless, insipid
nahigabe	distress, sorrow
nahigabetu	to distress
urduri egon	to be nervous
urduri jarri	to make nervous, to become nervous
uste	opinion, belief
uste *edun	to believe, to think
zalantza	hesitation, doubt

18.11 Exercises

18.11.1 Translate into English

1. Ez dakit nola arraio konponduko ginatekeen bera gabe. (Haranburu, *Ausk.* 75)
2. Mundua zeharo erotu ote den nago.
3. Ez genekien bizi zenetz ere, eta hain aberatsa zela. (Zubiri, *Art.* 76)
4. Ezbeharretan ezagutzen omen da nork maite gaituen. (Zapirain, *M.* 216)
5. Astakeria izugarriak egin dituzula konturatu dela entzun diot Mireni esaten.
6. Ez dut nahi non nabilen inork jakiterik. (Irazusta, *Bizia* 67)
7. Sendagile horrengatik, ba al dakizu nor hil den?
8. Jonek badaki bere semeak arazoak dituena eta bere emazteak ere badaki hori.
9. Pello ez da konturatzen ero denik eta bere emaztea ere ez da konturatzen horretaz.
10. Pellok uste du ezbehar bat gertatuko zaiola eta bere emazteak ere hala uste du.
11. Joni iruditzen zaio itxaropenik ez dagoela beretzat eta bere emazteari ere hala iruditzen zaio.
12. Mirenek agindu zion senarrari ez zuela gehiago gezurrik esango eta bere ahizpak ere hala agindu zion.

18.11.2 Translate into Basque

1. I don't know what is happening to me.
2. We don't know who has taught you what.
3. I don't know whether he believed us or not.
4. Do you realize what you have done?
5. I don't think that I have ever seen you.

6. I didn't think that they would forget me so quickly.
7. Does your father know when we will come to see him?
8. They have told me that it is obvious that my dogs are rabid.
9. I don't think that anyone will believe that that man has killed his wife.
10. He promised me that he would never see that girl anymore.
11. I didn't know whether I wanted to live outside the Basque Country or not.
12. We believe that the mayor wrote you that there were two thousand witches living in this village.

19 Relative Clauses

19.1 Introduction

Since the structure of most Basque relative clauses will be seen to differ substantially from that of their English counterparts, we need a definition broad enough to cover both types. An admittedly sketchy attempt will be offered here; for a more serious endeavor the reader is advised to turn to Chr. Lehmann's 1984 monograph *Der Relativsatz*.

We will speak of a relative clause whenever a sentence displaying a nominal gap—thus technically a propositional function—serves to restrict the extensional meaning of a noun phrase (restrictive relative) or to provide additional information about it (nonrestrictive relative). In the interpretive process, the noun phrase in question assumes the semantic role of the nominal gap, which must be in a position to count as the topic of the relative clause. This noun phrase will be named the head of the relative, regardless of its actual location, external or internal to this clause. Let us consider some examples from English:

(a) Books you like tend to be expensive.

(b) The book I read yesterday is an absolute masterpiece.

(c) Mary Whitehouse, who isn't exactly a bachelor's dream, is getting married shortly.

The relative clause *you like* in example (a) with its gap in object position semantically filled by the head nominal *books* limits this concept to a more restricted one: 'books you like'. In example (b), the relative clause *I read Ø yesterday* uniquely identifies the reference of the head noun *book*, as evidenced by the use of the definite article *the*. In example (c), the relative merely provides additional information about its head, which, being a proper name, has unique reference in any case. This example also features a relative pronoun (*who*), which apparently serves as the subject of the relative clause. With an inanimate head, the relative pronoun *which* would have occurred, a form that could have been inserted in examples (a) and (b) as well.

Although it is true that in most languages that have them such pronouns are case-marked according to their function inside the relative clause, we will nonetheless consider these as mere syntactic tools whose presence does not invalidate our definition of a relative as involving a structural gap. The same stipulation will also apply to resumptive pronouns, personal, demonstrative, or interrogative, occurring in certain types of relatives in anaphoric relation with the head nominal. Assuming a definition along these lines, Basque has an amazing array of relativization strategies, which I will discuss in the order of their importance in contemporary usage:

1. Prenominal finite relatives and their derivates
2. Nonfinite relatives (participial and infinitival)
3. Adjoined finite relatives
4. Corelatives
5. Relatives based on fronted interrogatives (Romance strategy)

19.1.1 General Structure of Prenominal Finite Relatives

There is no question that a prenominally embedded finite clause illustrates the main relativization strategy in all known varieties of Basque. Two traits characterize this kind of relative: (1) the head is external to the relative; and (2) head and relative together form a constituent of the main clause.

As a subordinate clause, a finite relative in Basque requires an overt subordinator. For this purpose, Basque grammar, at least in the main strategy, avails itself of the wh-complementizer *-N* (for which see section 18.1.2), possibly because relatives and indirect questions can both be viewed as containing a semantic gap, which makes them propositional functions rather than assertions. When the complementizer *-N* helps to make up a relative clause, it will be christened "relativizer."

Except when the head is reduced to the pronoun alias article *-a*, all relatives of this type must be verb-final. Hence, the relativizer *-N* effectively signals the end of the relative clause and links it to the head nominal that follows it. We are now ready for some examples:

(1) a. Nor ote da nire emaztearen ohean dagoen emakume itsusi hori? (*LBB* 162)
Whoever is that ugly woman who is lying in my wife's bed?
b. Zaintzen nauen frantsesa alboko gelan dago. (Atxaga, *Sara* 75)
The Frenchman who is guarding me is in the neighboring room.
c. Hor daramazun agendatxoa behar dugu. (Garate, *Iz.B.* 74)
We need that little notebook you are carrying there.
d. Laguntzat eman didazun emakumeak fruitua eskaini dit. (Gn 3:12)
The woman you gave me for a companion offered me the fruit.
e. Nik lepoa moztu nion Joan huraxe piztu da. (Mk 6:16)
That (very) John whose neck I cut off has revived. (Possessive dative, section 15.5.1)

On account of multi-pro-drop (section 9.5), the presence of a syntactic gap inside these relatives is not immediately obvious. It can be demonstrated only by the impossibility of inserting a pronoun coreferential to the head. Thus in the relative clause of example (1d), an ergative subject pronoun (*zuk*) and an indirect object pronoun (*niri*) can be readily inserted; not, however, a direct object pronoun *hura* or *bera*. Proceeding this way, we find an absolutive subject gap in (1a), an ergative subject gap in (1b), absolutive object gaps in both (1c) and (1d), and an indirect object gap in (1e). These examples, I may add, do not exhaust the possibilities: still other types of gaps will make their appearance in section 19.1.2.

Notice that in the event of a negative relative, the verb-final requirement imposes a constituent order not allowed in an independent negative:

(2) a. Ez dago hutsik egiten ez duen gaizkilerik. (Garate, *Esku* 73)
There is no criminal who makes no mistakes.
b. Bizia salbatu ez zidan laguna (Atxaga, *Grl.* 18)
The mate who didn't save my life
c. Bidartek ikusten ez zituen malkoak txukatu zituen. (Garate, *Esku* 86)
She dried tears that Bidart didn't see.

When the noun phrase immediately following the relative starts with a genitival or adnominal constituent, either the former or the latter may serve as the head of the relative. Compare the following:

(3) a. Hauek ziren, behinik behin, gogoan dudan gaitzaren ezaugarriak.
These, at any rate, were the symptoms of the disease I remember.
b. Hauek ziren, behinik behin, gogoan ditudan gaitzaren ezaugarriak. (*MEIG* IX, 97)
These, at any rate, were the symptoms of the disease I remember.

Only the singular object verb form *dudan* versus plural *ditudan* shows that in (3a) it is the disease that is remembered, whereas in (3b) it is the disease's symptoms. As a matter of fact, lacking such a number distinction, we are left with an ambiguity even intonation is unable to resolve.

Somewhat more troublesome in practice is the ambiguity that results from the impossibility of case-marking the gap involved in relativization. Here again, multi-pro-drop is a complicating factor. In examples (4a–c) there is no problem:

(4) a. Gizonari haurra eman dion emakumea hil da.
The woman who has given the child to the man has died.
b. Apaizak gizonari eman dion emakumea hil da.
The woman whom the priest has given to the man has died.
c. Apaizak haurra eman dion emakumea hil da.
The woman to whom the priest has given the child has died.

But now consider example (4):

(4) Eman dion emakumea hil da.

In this example only the context or situation can tell whether the gap is ergative as in (4a), absolutive as in (4b), or dative as in (4c). Three different readings of (4) are therefore possible: (a) 'The woman who has given it to him has died'; (b) 'The woman whom he has given to him has died'; (c) 'The woman to whom he has given it has died'.

19.1.2 Acceptability and the Syntactic Function of the Gap

It is a natural question to ask whether there are constraints on relativization that have to do with the syntactic function of the gap inside the relative clause. Various researchers, including myself, have tried to answer this question with the help of native speakers, but their reactions to test sentences tend to be hesitating and inconsistent over time, and thus fail to yield a clear-cut answer.

In my article (1972a) "Relative Clauses in Basque: A Guided Tour," I distinguished two dialects: a restricted one, where only relatives with morphologically represented gaps are consistently accepted—that is, those relatives where the verb shows agreement with the gap, as in the examples of section 19.1.1—and a more lenient one where the gap can be also instrumental, inessive, elative, or allative. But, as I have since come to realize, speaking of dialect here merely obscures the issue. As I noted at the time, this usage of that term denotes nothing more than a set of idiolects, given the fact that the two putative dialects completely interpenetrate, that is, no geographical or sociolectal distribution can be specified in any way. Moreover, speakers are anything but consistent. A sentence rejected one day may be accepted without question a few weeks later. Furthermore, it can be observed time and again that syntactically identical structures give rise to widely diverging judgments. Thus, *EGLU* adduces the following contrast:

(5) a. Izena ahaztu dudan norbaitek esan dit. (*EGLU* V, 187)
Somebody whose name I have forgotten has told me.
b. *Etxeraino joan naizen norbaitek esan dit. (*EGLU* V, 187)
Somebody (up) to whose house I have gone has told me.

As far as relativization is concerned, the two sentences have identical structures: they both display a genitival gap. Yet, while example (5a) is accepted by virtually everyone, (5b) is universally rejected as utter gibberish.

Last but not least, the findings by Oihartzabal (1985b) deserve to be mentioned. Using 20 native speakers of the northern dialects, Oihartzabal has demonstrated that relative clauses quite beyond the range of even the tolerant "dialect" and qualified by him as "très choquants, voire incompréhensibles" (very shocking, really incomprehensible) in isolation, are accepted without comment when embedded in a suitable context.

These facts may be explained as follows: Inasmuch as the gap involved in relativization is not marked for case, any Basque relative presents a decoding problem, and it is the difficulty of solving it which determines the native hearer's reaction to the sentence. Now, some language users have little patience to spend on the task of decoding, whereas others are prepared to go to much greater lengths. Hence the two "dialects" distinguished earlier. This, however, is clearly not a matter of linguistic competence. Obviously, this decoding process often crucially involves information present in the preceding discourse or current situation and thus cannot be dealt with in the realm of sentence grammar. We therefore reach a rather paradoxical conclusion: We must maintain that the output of the Basque relativization strategy is in principle grammatical, even in cases where it is vehemently rejected by all native speakers.

In the remainder of this section, I will review the various types of gaps not covered in section 19.1.1 and present some of the instances I have encountered in texts. There is no implication that these examples are necessarily acceptable to all native speakers, even though they all originate from native speakers.

The following are examples of genitival gaps:

(6) a. Txutxo, gaur arte izenik ere ez nekien txakurra, . . . (Satrustegi, 61)
Txutxo, the dog whose name I didn't even know until today, . . .
b. Kodigoa ezagutzen ez nuen sistema baten barruan aurkitzen nintzen. (Garate, *Hades* 12)
I found myself inside a system whose code I didn't know.
c. Zer esango dute aldegiten badut lehen hain zalea izan naizen festetatik? (Mogel, *C.C.* 144)
What will they say if I stay away from the festivities that I was so fond of earlier?
d. Ea deretxorik pagatu behar den gauzarik bilatzen dugun. (Iraola, 40)
See if we find any thing that one must pay duties on.
e. Nafarroako erregeek gainean zin egiten zuten liburu handia (J. Etchepare, *Ber*. 49)
The big book that the kings of Navarra swore upon
f. Piarresek puskak gainean ezartzen dituen armairua (Oihartzabal, *R.B.* 84)
The chest that Peter puts his things on
g. Gibelean jarri naizen gizona (Oihartzabal, *Pro-drop* 77)
The man behind whom I've sat down

[*N.B.* Relatives with genitival gaps governed by location nouns are not acceptable to speakers of the southern dialects. In examples (6e–g), they must insert the genitive resumptive pronoun *bere*, for which see section 19.1.4.]

The following are examples of instrumental gaps:

(7) a. Aurkitu ote dute akusatu ninduten krimenaren egilea? (*EGLU* V, 186)
Have they found the author of the crime they accused me of?
b. Zuek ez zenuten gu konturatu ginen arriskua ikusten. (Goenaga, *G.B.*[2] 289)
Yoû didn't see the danger we realized.
c. Mintzaldia egin duzun idazlea ez nuen ezagutzen. (Oihartzabal, *Pro-drop* 67)
I didn't know the author about whom you have given the lecture.

The following are examples of inessive gaps:

(8) a. Bizi zareten baserria berekin eramango luke. (Zapirain, *M.* 55)
She would take with her the farm yoû live on.
b. Geunden gela haren erretaulez betea zegoen. (Landart, 69)
The room we sat in was full of her paintings.
c. Gaua egin behar zuen etxeraino jarraitu zitzaizkion. (*TB*, 48)
They followed him as far as the house in which he was to spend the night.
d. Laster joango haiz, Arantxa, beste maitasun batzuk izango ditunan etxera. (Itziar, 23)
Yoù will soon go, Arantxa, to a house in which yoù will have some other love relationships.
e. Berandu agertu nintzen, gainera, leku hutsik gelditzen ez zen mundura. (*MEIG* IX, 94)
Moreover, I appeared too late in a world in which no empty place remained.
f. Lo zatzan lurra emango dizuet zuri eta zure ondorengoei. (Gn 28:13; Ur.)
The land on which you are lying asleep I will give to you and your descendants.

With a head nominal denoting time an inessive gap is quite common and seems to raise no decoding problems:

(9) a. Abenduaren hamaika; ni amarenganik atera nintzen eguna. (Landart, 11)
December eleven; the day I came out of my mother.
b. Lanik egiten ez dudan egunetan pattarrarekin bukatzen dut. (Garate, *Alaba* 65)
On the days I am not working I finish with brandy.
c. Zoragarria izango da zu ezkontzen zaren eguna. (Lasarte, *Gordean* 91)
The day you are getting married will be wonderful.
d. Etorriko da senar berria kenduko dieten eguna. (Mk 2:20; *IB*)
The day will come in which they'll take the groom away from them.

The following are examples of elative gaps:

(10) a. Zoaz etorri zinen lekura! (*TOE* III, 158)
Go to the place you came from!
b. Itzuliko naiz atera naizen nire etxera. (Mt 12:44; *JKBO*)
I will return to my house, out of which I have gone.
c. Dabilen bideak harrapatuko du. (Azkue, *E. Y.* III, 187)
The road along which he goes will catch up with him.
d. Zihoan bide guztietara ateratzen zitzaion Simon. (1 Mc 13:20)
Simon confronted him on all the roads he went along.

The following are examples of allative gaps:

(11) a. Kendu dugu igo behar ez zuen tokitik. (J. A. Mogel, in Mahn, 50)
We have removed him from the place he should not have ascended to.

b. Harria bota didan begitik ez dut ezer ikusten. (Peillen, 77)
I see nothing with the eye she threw (me) a stone at.

c. Eta Hura joaten zen herriska, herri eta auzoetan, gaixoak larrainetan ipintzen zizkioten. (Mk 6:56; *IB*)
And in the villages, towns, and hamlets He went to, they put the sick out for Him on the threshing floors.

The gaps that now remain to be considered involve the case markers based on the genitive (*-(r)ekin* 'with', *-(r)entzat* 'for', *-(r)engatik* 'because of', as well as the animate locatives *-(r)engan* etc.) or on the allative (*-raino* 'up to', *-rantz* 'toward'). Discounting some special cases to be described later, I have been able to find no instances of such gaps in Basque texts, nor were the examples I constructed acceptable to the native speakers I consulted. In my 1972 publications on the subject, these case functions were therefore labeled "non-relativizable," a qualification which was subsequently adopted by the Basque linguists P. Goenaga and X. Artiagoitia (cf. section 19.6).

For reasons set out at the beginning of this section, Goenaga and I now have come to embrace Oihartzabal's position that relative clauses formed with non-relativizable case endings are unacceptable because of decoding difficulties, instead of being ungrammatical. Some additional support for this view is provided by the nature of the two criteria handling the special cases that I have alluded to: the Parallel Case criterion and the Functional Predestination criterion.

The Parallel Case criterion, first stated by I. M. Echaide (1912, 54), can be phrased as follows: Relative clauses where the case marking of the head coincides with that of the gap are always acceptable. Thus the following examples are acceptable even though they involve the non-relativizable endings *-(r)ekin* 'with' or *-(r)engatik* 'because of':

(12) a. Joan naizen gizonekin eraman dut. (Alzo, 81)
I have carried it together with the men I have gone with.

b. Zergatik hautsi behar duk behin oheratzen haizen neska guztiekin? (Saizarbitoria, 77–78)
Why do yoú have to break off with all the girls with whom yoú go to bed once?

c. Pellok bere burua hil zuen emakumearengatik Andresek ere bere burua hil nahi du. (Oihartzabal, *R.B.* 75)
Andrew too wants to kill himself because of the woman because of whom Pete killed himself.

The Functional Predestination criterion was discovered by this author in 1972 and can be stated thus: Relative clauses where the head is a noun predisposed to a certain syntactic function are acceptable whenever the gap fills that function.

Thus one may consider the noun *arrazoi* 'reason' to be predisposed to the function expressed by the ending *-(r)engatik* 'because of', which is why example (13) is acceptable despite this ending's non-relativizable status:

(13) Neure burua hil nahi nuen arrazoiaz ez naiz gogoratzen. (Oihartzabal, *R.B.* 75)
I don't remember the reason why I wanted to kill myself.

Clearly, satisfaction of either of these criteria trivializes decoding, a fact from which acceptability naturally follows. If, however, ungrammaticality were at stake, it is hard to see how fulfillment of these criteria would manage to turn ungrammatical clauses into grammatical ones.

19.1.3 Adnominally Linked Relatives

Inasmuch as the adjectival nature of the relative clause is undeniable, there would seem to be no need to saddle the relativizer -*N* with an additional linking morpheme (-*ko*) to help connect the relative to the head that follows it. Nevertheless, use of the adnominal form is possible as long as the gap in the relative does not have the function of an absolutive. Thus one finds

(14) a. Ni bizi naizeneko balera honetan, elizatxo bat da. (Orixe, in *OrOm* 290)
In this valley where I live, there is a little church.
b. Ume nintzeneko egunak joan ziren. (E. Azkue, 193)
The days when I was a child have gone.
c. Eta aitarentzat ur bila nihoaneko iturriaren hotsa (Azurmendi, 74)
And the sound of the fountain where I went for water for my father
d. Iritsiko zaizue Gizonaren Semea etorriko deneko egun bat bederen ikusi nahi izango duzueneko garaia. (Lk 17:22)
The time will arrive (for yoû) when yoû will want to see at least one day on which the Son of Man will come.
e. Noan berriro atera nintzeneko neure etxera. (Mt 12:44, Lk 11:24)
Let me go again to my own house from which I went out. (For the subjunctive form *noan*, see section 21.6)

The examples cited so far all contain locative gaps: inessive, allative, or elative ones. While these are undoubtedly the most common, other types of gaps also occur: instrumental, as in (15a); dative, as in (15b); and ergative, as in (15c). Only absolutive gaps do not seem to allow the adnominal form of the relative.

(15) a. Ezta ere atzo hots egin zidaneko bere ahotsaren doinua. (Haranburu, *Ausk.* 10)
Nor the tone of the voice with which she called me yesterday.
b. Antipasek berak lepoa motzarazi zioneko Joan huraxe bera dela uste du. (*Lau Eb.* 82)
Antipas believes that he is that same John whose neck he himself had cut off.
c. Zera dioeneko (pasarte) hura aurkitu zuen: ... (Lk 4:17; *Lau Eb.*)
He found that (passage) that says the following: ...

The adnominal form is never obligatory. Even with inessive gaps, the plain form still predominates.

19.1.4 Resumptive Pronouns

In Basque, a gap cannot signal its syntactic function; an overt pronoun can. For this reason, in many cases where the regular relativization strategy leads to unacceptable results, insertion of a pronoun referring to the head of the relative makes the sentence clear and therefore acceptable. Such resumptive pronouns are normally in the third person: *bera* (plural *berak*) in the south, *hura* (plural *haiek*) in the north. The following examples are all from the south:

(16) a. Beretzat lan egiten dudan ugazaba (Altube, *Erd.* 137)
The boss I am working for
b. Ez da beragatik bizia emango nukeen gizonik. (*EGLU* V, 189)
There is no man for whom I would give my life.
c. Hau da neure atsegin guztiak Beregan ditudan nire seme kutuna. (Manzisidor, 120)
This is my beloved son in whom I have all my contentments.
d. Bere alaba ezagutzen dudan gizona (Altube, *Erd.* 137)
The man I know his daughter

Where the regular strategy works, the resumptive strategy is blocked. Hence, no resumptive pronouns appear in the absolutive, ergative, or dative cases. In this connection, it is worth noting that location nouns can be combined with resumptive pronouns in the southern dialects only; in the north the regular strategy applies, witness examples (6e–g). The following examples illustrate this point:

(17) a. Bere azpian ezkutatu nintzen mahaia txiki samarra zen.
The table I hid under was rather small.
b. Bere atzetik zabiltzan neskatxak ez zaitu maite.
The girl you are chasing after does not love you.

[*N.B.* To date, resumptive pronouns have featured in grammatical treatises rather more than in actual speech or writing. A typical (southern) informant response to the examples in this section is "They are acceptable, but, personally, I wouldn't use them."]

19.1.5 Complex Relatives

A relative clause can be a complex sentence with its gap situated inside a subordinate clause. The latter may be finite or nonfinite.

First, we present some examples of relativization out of a nonfinite subordinate clause:

(18) a. Bart ikustera joan ginen filma (*EGLU* V, 183)
The movie we went to see last night
b. Hark nahi du berak esaten atrebitzen ez den gauzak bestek esatea. (Lasarte, *Gordean* 269)
He wants somebody else to say the things he doesn't dare to say himself.

c. Zoaz ibaira eta hartu han gordetzeko agindu nizun gerrikoa. (Jer 13:6)
Go to the river and take the belt that I commanded you to hide there.

Some examples of relativization out of a clause with a wh-complementizer follow:

(19) a. Etorriko ote den ez dakizun gizona (Oihartzabal, *R.B.* 47)
The man you don't know whether he will come
b. Salatuko ote zaituen beldur zaren gizona (*EGLU* V, 181)
The man you are afraid will denounce you

Some examples of relativization out of regular finite complements follow:

(20) a. Hara non duzuen gaur etorriko ez zela zenioten gizona! (López Mendizabal, 353)
There yoû have the man who yoû said would not come today!
b. Eta neskatxa hilaren ondoan agertu zen Peru Okotzena zela esan duzuen aiztoa ere. (Albisu, 64)
And also the knife you have said belonged to Peru Okotz appeared near the dead girl.
c. ... berriro ez zenutela ikusiko esan zizuen lurraldera (Dt 28:68)
... to a land that He had told yoû that yoû would not see again
d. Hau al da itsu jaio zela diozuen zuen semea? (Jn 9:19; *IB*)
Is this yoûr son who yoû said was born blind?
e. Laguntza emanen dizula uste duzun gizona (*EGLU* V, 181)
The man you believe will give you assistance

The examples listed so far show one embedding only. However, there is no principled limit to the depth of the embedding. Example (21), taken from my dissertation (1972b), was acceptable to all my informants:

(21) Zoroa dela guztiek dakitela esan zizutela idatzi zenidala uste dudan ijitoak musu eman zidan. (*DLV* 130)
The gypsy I believe you wrote me they told you everybody knows is crazy kissed me.

19.1.6 Structural Constraints on Relativization

There is no sentential subject constraint in Basque:

(22) Amorratuak direla bistan dagoen zakur horiekin ez dut ibili nahi. (*DLV* 136)
I don't want to walk with those hounds that it is obvious are rabid.

The coordinate structure constraint is valid for Basque, except, of course, for "across the board" cases like example (23):

(23) Bi urteren buruan itzularazi egingo ditut toki honetara erregeak bertatik hartu eta Babiloniara eraman zituen tenpluko tresnak. (Jer 28:3)

In two years time I will return to this place the temple vessels which the king took from here and carried off to Babylon.

The complex noun phrase constraint also holds. No constituent inside a noun phrase complement or relative clause can be relativized:

(24) a. *Eroa zelako seinaleak ikusi nituen taxi gidariak itsuski jo ninduen.
*The taxi driver who I saw signs that he was crazy beat me up badly.
b. *Eraiki duen etxea desegin duten etxegilea gaixotu egin da.
*The architect who they tore down the house that he built has fallen ill.
c. *Idatzi duen emakumea ezagutzen dudan liburua gogoz irakurri dut.
*I have read with pleasure the book that I know the woman who wrote.

Questioning of constituents inside relative clauses, however, is permitted, since no movement is involved:

(25) a. Nondik datorren ere ez dakidan jendeari eman behar al dizkiot? (1 Sm 25:11)
Must I give them to people I don't know even from where they come?
b. Nork kantatzen dituen abestiak gustatzen zaizkizu? (Oihartzabal, *Pro-drop* 73)
The songs that who sings do you like?
c. Nork eman zizun liburua galdu duzu? (*EGLU* V, 199)
You lost the book who gave you?
d. Nor bizi den etxean sartu da polizia? (*EGLU* V, 199)
In the house where who lives did the police enter?
e. Noiz ikusi duzun filmaz mintzo zara? (*EGLU* V, 199)
You are talking about a movie you saw when?

19.1.7 Stacked Relatives

More than one relative clause may modify the same head:

(26) a. Guztiok maite dugun mesede handiak egin dizkigun lagun batek esan du. (*EGLU* V, 203)
A friend who has done us great favors whom we all love has said it.
b. Eta orain datorkit gogora gaztetan ikasi nuen asko esan gura duen ipuin hau. (*P.Ab.* 88)
And this tale, that means a lot, which I learned in my youth, now comes to mind.
c. Irakurri ditugun idatzi zituen liburu batzuk oso interesgarriak dira. (*DLV* 136)
Some books that he wrote that we have read are very interesting.

19.1.8 Relatives with Pronominal Heads

In the type of relative we have been studying, personal pronouns cannot be heads, but demonstratives can be:

(27) a. Ez esan inori ikusi duzuen hau. (Mt 17:9; *IB*)
Don't tell anyone this which yoû have seen.
b. Armairu gainean daukazun hori zer da? (Iraola, 31)
What is that which you keep on top of the cupboard?
c. Zer da basamortuan gora datorren hori? (Sg 3:6)
What is that coming up from the wilderness?
d. Datorren horrekin seigarren txanda izango dut. (Garmendia, 45)
With that one that is coming, it will be my sixth time.

Demonstrative pronouns with human referents can also be heads of relatives, even though these are the functional equivalents of third-person pronouns of other languages:

(28) a. Nor ote dugu bekatuak barkatu ere egiten dituen hau? (Lk 7:49)
Who is this who even forgives sins?
b. Nortzuk dira eta nondik datoz zuriz jantzirik dauden hauek? (Rv 7:13; *IB*)
Who are these that are robed in white and from where do they come?
c. Ez al duzu ikusten bizikletan datorren hori? (Urruzuno, *E.Z.* 137)
Don't you see that one who is coming on a bicycle?
d. Nor dira hor datozen horiek? (Cf. Iraola, 71)
Who are those who are coming there?
e. Zu zara Israel nahastu duzun hura? (1 Kgs 18.17; Dv)
Are you that one who has troubled Israel?

Actually, even the meaning of a first- or second-person singular can be accommodated by a demonstrative head: *hau* will substitute for *ni*, *hori* for *hi* or *zu*. For purposes of verb agreement, these demonstratives count as first- or second-person forms:

(29) a. Hainbeste maite zaitudan honek esaten dizut. (Oihartzabal, *R.B.* 65)
I, who love you so much, say it to you.
b. Guztiak betetzen dituzun horrek, Zutaz osoz betetzen al dituzu? (Orixe, *Aitork.* 11)
Do You, who fill all things, fill them with Yourself completely?
c. Bikain zaren Horri higuin zaizu haien maketsa. (Orixe, *Aitork.* 380)
Their imperfection is loathsome to You, who are perfect.

For the first- or second-person plural, the inclusive enclitic pronoun *-ok*, to be discussed in section 19.7, may occur as a head:

(30) a. Batasuna sortu nahiz hasi ginenok "bitasuna" sortu dugu. (*MEIG* VII, 164)
We who started with the aim to create unity have created "two-ness."
b. Jules Verneren liburuak . . . gogoz irakurri ditugunontzat, badu film honek beste atsegin iturririk. (*MEIG* I, 181)
For us who have read Jules Verne's books with pleasure, this film has another source of delight.

c. Ai, zuek lege-maisuok, jakituriaren giltza kendu duzuenok! (Lk 11:52; *Lau Eb.*)
Alas for yoû, lawyers, who have taken away the key of wisdom!

Like English *one*, the numeral *bat* can have pronominal status; therefore, it may occur as the head of a relative:

(31) a. Nirekin plater beretik jaten ari den batek salduko nau. (Mt 26:23)
One who is eating from the same plate with me will betray me.

b. Nongoa den ez dakidan bati emango dizkiot moztaileentzat prestatu ditudan ogi eta ardikiak? (*TZ* I, 272)
Shall I give the bread and sheep cutlets I have prepared for the shearers to one who I don't know where he is from?

19.1.9 Preclitic Relatives

At this point we need to take a closer look at the article *-a* and see that what we have somewhat irresponsibly been calling a definite article is actually a pronoun recruited as a determiner. As a matter of fact, in the Biscayan dialect *a* still serves as a demonstrative: *gizon a* 'that man' (superseded in certain regions by the innovation *a gizona*). In all other dialects, the form *a* has turned into an enclitic, having been replaced by *hura* in its demonstrative use. Nonetheless, it has retained its pronominal status, as shown by constructions such as *ederra* 'the beautiful one' (see section 1.3.2) and *Patxirena* 'that of Frank' (see section 2.4).

Therefore, it should be no surprise that the "article" *-a* can act as the head of a relative. Thus the Greek phrase *to agathon* in Rom 7:13, best translated as plain *ona*, was rendered both in *EAB* and in the standard version as *ona zen hura* (with tendentious past tense), but as *ona dena*, using *-a*, in four other versions (Dv, Olab., Ker., and *Biblia*).

This type of relative, of course, is the equivalent of what is known as a free relative in English grammar. Yet I prefer to introduce the term "preclitic" relative, to remind us of the fact that this relative too has a head, namely, the clitic pronoun *-a*.

As *EGLU* points out, in comparison to the standard ones, preclitic relatives are more limited in the types of gaps they can accommodate: only absolutive, ergative, or dative gaps occur. Thus there are no examples like **Hango etxea da ni bizi naizena* (*EGLU* V, 212) 'The house over there is where I live'.

As we may remember from section 1.3.2, there is a twofold interpretation for a nounless noun phrase such as *ederra*: specific, that is, 'the beautiful one I am referring to', or generic, that is, 'whatever is beautiful'. Considered out of context, preclitic relatives are similarly ambiguous. In actual speech, however, one or the other reading tends to be more salient. Thus, examples (32a–d) involve specific reference:

(32) a. Konprenitzen duzu orain esan nahi dudana? (Saizarbitoria, 100)
Do you understand now what I mean?

b. Ez dago ondo egiten ari zaretena. (Neh 5:9)
It is not good what yoû are doing.
c. Begiek gezurtatzen zuten ahoek ziotena. (*LBB* 149)
The eyes were belying what the mouths were saying.
d. Eskandalu bat da hemen gertatzen dena. (Larzabal, *Hiru* 121)
It's a scandal what is happening here.

Generic reference obtains in the following examples:

(33) a. Ari denak egiten ditu hutsak. (Xalbador, *Odol.* 39)
Who works makes mistakes.
b. Bik dakitena laster jakingo dute hamaikak. (Garate, *Esku* 135)
What two (people) know, a lot (of people) will soon know.
c. Askoren ustez, beste ezertarako balio ez dutenek legeak ikasten dituzte. (Garate, *Esku* 62)
In the opinion of many, those that are no good for anything else study law.
d. Izan ere, duenari eman egingo zaio; ez duenari, ordea, daukan apurra ere kendu egingo. (Mk 4:25)
Indeed, to him who has shall be given; from him who doesn't have, however, even the little he has shall be taken away.

Basque proverbs quite often contain generic relatives:

(34) a. Senarra duenak jauna badu. (López Mendizabal, 255)
Who has a husband has a lord.
b. Urak dakarrena, urak darama. (López Mendizabal, 256)
What the water brings, the water carries away.
c. Nahi duena esaten duenak, nahi ez duena entzungo du. (López Mendizabal, 252)
Who says what(ever) he likes (to say), will hear what he doesn't like (to hear).
d. Behia jezten ez dakienarentzat, behi guztiak dira antzuak. (Urruzuno, *E.Z.* 121)
All cows are barren for him who doesn't know how to milk.

As demonstrated by these examples, the preclitic relative bears whatever case marker is required to signal its function in the main clause. The partitive too may occur:

(35) a. Katalinek eta amonak nahi dutenik ez da gertatuko. (*G.* 270)
None of what Kathleen and Grandmother want will happen.
b. Donostian ez da hau ez dakienik. (Garate, *Esku* 46)
There is no one in San Sebastian who doesn't know this.
c. Bada oraindik haren ateraldi eta erantzunik gogoan dituenik Errenterian. (*MEIG* VIII, 153)
In Rentería, there still are quite a few people who remember her witticisms and repartees.

As I argued in section 13.1.1, the partitive determiner owes its existence to the deletion of an indefinite pronoun: *ezer* in (35a), *inor* in (35b), and *franko* in (35c). These pronouns can also be retained in the context we are dealing with:

(36) a. Ez dut beregan barkapena merezi duenik ezer aurkitzen. (Berrondo, 79)
I don't find anything in him that deserves forgiving.
b. Ez dut frantses "angoisse" hitzak daukan bortiztasuna duenik ezer aurkitzen. (Aintziart, 61–62)
I have found nothing that has the forcefulness the French word "angoisse" has.
c. Bai al da Gipuzkoa osoan nik ezagutuko ez nukeenik inor? (T. Agirre, *Uzt.* 241)
Is there anybody in all of Guipuzcoa whom I wouldn't know?
d. Ez dakizue gauza isilak asmatzen niri eramaten didanik inor ez dela? (*TZ* I, 96)
Don't yoû know that there is nobody who outdoes me in discovering hidden matters?
e. Jendeak esaten du hala ez denik franko.
People say a lot of things that are not so.

An alternative strategy is deleting the partitive marker rather than the indefinite pronoun. As a result of this, the latter turns into a pseudohead: it is linked to the relative like a head but lacks a semantic role within it. Examples are

(37) a. Purgatorioko suan pagatu beharko duzun ezer ez daukazu? (Arrue, *May.* 96)
Do you have nothing you will have to pay for in the fire of purgatory?
b. Arrebari ez zaio Luisek egiten duen ezer gustatzen. (Urretabizkaia, *Sat.* 76)
His sister likes nothing that Luis does. (Spanish: *nada de lo que hace Luís*)
c. Munduan ba al da logikarekin jokatzen duen inor? (Saizarbitoria, 67)
Is there anyone in the world who acts logically? (Lit. 'with logic')
d. Atzo bizi zen franko bada hilik egun. (*Ast. Las.* 74)
Plenty who were living yesterday are dead today.

Another pseudohead is the universal quantifier *guzti.* In examples (38a,b) *guzti* is a modifier of the head *-a*; it is not itself the head.

(38) a. Egin dudan guztia esan dit. (Jn 4:39)
He has told me all I have done.
b. Hori da naizen guztia. (Xalbador, *Odol.* 345)
That's all I am.

A diminutive suffix *-txo* (in the eastern dialects *-tto*) corresponding to the head of a relative is tacked onto the relative itself if and only if the head is pronominal:

(39) a. "Naiz" esaten dut naizentxo honek. (Orixe, in *Olerti* [1961] 93)
I, who am so little, keep saying "I am."

b. Hala ere, goretsi nahi zaitu duzuntto honek. (Orixe, *Aitork.* 2)
Yet, this little one whom you have wants to praise you.
c. Gabe zarentxo bat baduzu oraindik. (Lk 18:22; Olab.)
There is (lit. 'you have') still one little thing that you are without.

The criterion just stated confirms that the suffix *-a* of preclitic relatives is indeed a pronominal head:

(40) a. Ikasi duguntxoa ... besteren hizkuntzan ikasi dugu. (*MEIG* VII, 188)
What little we have learned, we have learned in someone else's language.
b. Hemen dihoakizu dakiguntxoa. (*MEIG* I, 219)
Here goes (to you) what little we know.
c. Ahal dentxoa egiten dut behintzat (*TOE* III, 63)
At least, I am doing what little one can.
d. Zordun gara zenbait kultura sailetan, duguntxo pixkaren zordun. (*MEIG* IV, 43)
We are indebted in certain areas of culture, indebted for the little bit we have.

Whether a head pronoun is a clitic or not, however, does have syntactic repercussions. For one thing, preclitic relatives are special in that a nonfocused constituent can hop across the verb, yielding a word order unavailable with any other type of head. Some examples are

(41) a. Egiten digunari gaizki, zergatik egin behar diogu ongi? (Ax. 322)
Toward him who acts badly toward us, why should we act nicely?
b. Ahoan duenari min, eztia zaio samin. (Garate, *Esku* 51)
Honey is bitter to him who has a sore in the mouth.
c. Dakienak beldur eukitzen, badaki gizon izaten. (López Mendizabal, 244)
Who knows how to be afraid knows how to be a man.

19.1.10 Instrumental Comment Clauses

One of the meanings of the instrumental case is 'according to', as in *itxuraz* 'according to appearance', *izenez* 'in name', *legez* 'according to law', *nire iritziz* 'in my opinion', *ohituraz* 'according to custom'. With this same meaning, the instrumental ending may attach to a preclitic relative:

(42) a. Ameriketan bai, nire senarrak esaten duenez. (*TOE* III, 88)
In America it is, according to what my husband says.
b. Neronek egun hauetan ikusi dudanez, jende gutxi dabil hemen. (Garate, *G.E.* 128)
According to what I've seen these days myself, few people are walking here.

Instrumental relatives, in fact, correspond to comment clauses introduced by *as* in English:

(43) a. Baina, ikusten dudanez, ez nau inork behar hemen. (*MEIG* IX, 110)
But, as I see, nobody needs me here. (i.e., according to what I see, . . .)
b. Dirudienez, beraz, edo nik deritzadanez behintzat, *etxe-jupua* ez zen . . . habea. (*MEIG* I, 225)
As it seems therefore, or at least as it seems to me, *etxe-jupua* was no beam.

When its main verb means 'to know', the instrumental relative can be translated using *as far as*:

(44) a. Dakidanez, Madrilen bizi zen (*MEIG* IX, 90)
As far as I know, he lived in Madrid.
b. Eta orain arte, nik dakidanez, ez du inork ezer aurkitu. (*MEIG* IX, 81)
And up to now, as far as I know, nobody has found anything.

Like the English conjunction *as*, the instrumental clause may assume a causal force:

(45) a. Hitzaurreaz bi hitz esango nituzke, Tolstoizalea naizenez. (*MEIG* II, 85)
I would (like to) say a couple of words about the preface, as I am a Tolstoi fan.
b. Neu bakarrik izango nauzu gainetik, errege naizenez. (Gn 41:40)
Only me shall you have above you, as I am the king.

19.1.11 Appositive Relatives

Appositions exist in Basque as they do in many other languages. So far we have not given them much consideration; yet in connection with relative clauses they take on such an importance that we must now give them our full attention.

In Basque, as in most languages with overt case marking, an apposition to a noun phrase agrees with it in case:

(46) a. Neska batek, oso politak, maite zaitu.
A girl, a very pretty one, loves you.
b. Neska bati, oso politari, emango dizkiot loreak.
I will give the flowers to a girl, a very pretty one.
c. Behi bati, ederrari, luzaro begiratu dio.
He has looked for a long time at a cow, a beautiful one.

The above examples are typical in that the apposition must be adjacent to the coreferential noun phrase, unless both are used in the absolutive case, as in examples (47a,b):

(47) a. Neska bat etorri zitzaigun, oso polita. (*EGLU* I, 298)
A girl came up to us, a very pretty one.
b. Behi bat erosi dut, ederra.
I have bought a cow, a beauty.

In the same way, relative clauses headed by a demonstrative pronoun can be put in apposition to a coreferential antecedent:

(48) a. Baldin nik, zuen Jaun eta Maisu naizen honek, oinak garbitu badizkizuet, zuek ere elkarri garbitu behar dizkiozue. (*TB* 108)
If I, who am yoûr Lord and Teacher, have washed yoûr feet, yoû also should wash one another's feet.
b. Zuk, ezagutzen nauzun horrek, badakizu ezetz. (Atxaga, *Grl.* 153)
You, who know me, know that it is not so.
c. Campionek, hainbeste aldiz gogoratzen dugun hark, . . . (*EGLU* I, 312)
Campion, whom we so often bring to mind, . . .

Similarly, we often find a preclitic relative serving as an apposition:

(49) a. Banuen astakume polit bat, oso maite nuena. (Urruzuno, *Urz* 48)
I had a nice young donkey, which I loved very much.
b. Eta hau zer da? Katu bat, joan den neguan hil zitzaiguna. (Iraola, 113)
And what is this? A cat, which died on us last winter.
c. Ni naiz zuen anaia, zuek saldu ninduzuena. (*TZ* I, 98)
I am yoûr brother, whom yoû sold.
d. Beti gogoan zauzkadan dama, izarra dirudizuna, eguzkiaren beharrik gabe argi egiten duzuna, . . . (Bilintx, 95)
O lady, whom I always keep in mind, you who look like a star, who shine without need for the sun, . . .
e. Berriz agertu zen aingerua haren emazteari, landan jarria zegoenari (Jgs 13:9; Dv)
The angel again appeared to his wife, who was sitting in the field.

Note the obligatory case agreement between the antecedent and the head of the relative. Like other appositions, an appositive relative can be syntactically separated from its antecedent, provided its case is absolutive. Examples of separation are

(50) a. Eta ohar bat, bidenabar, inork txartzat hartzea nahi ez nukeena. (*MEIG* IV, 135)
And one remark, which, by the way, I wouldn't want anyone to take amiss.
b. Astakume bat aurkituko duzue, gainean inor jarri ez zaiona. (Lk 19:30)
Yoû will find a young donkey, on which no one has sat.
c. Herritar guztiak hartaz mintzatzen ziren puta bat izan balitz bezala, ifernuko suak beretuko zuena. (Landart, 18)
All the townspeople spoke about her as if she was a whore, whom hellfire was going to get.

Appositive relatives in Basque do not need to be nonrestrictive, although, in fact, most of them are. The restrictive ones either involve indefinite antecedents, as in (51a–c), or antecedents denoting time, as in (52a–c).

(51) a. Zuk ez al duzu lehengusu bat filarmonika jotzen duena? (Iraola, 54)
Don't you have a cousin who plays the accordion?

b. Harginik ez da edaten ez duenik. (Zavala, *Txirr.* 46)
There is no stonecutter who doesn't drink.

c. Jende asko ezagutu dut goizean aldarte txarretan esnatzen zirenak. (Garate, *Leh.* 15)
I have known a lot of people who woke up in the morning in a bad mood.

(52) a. Etorriko da denbora deabruak laguntzarik eginen ez dizuna. (Ax. 518)
A time will come that the devil will give you no help.

b. Noiz iritsiko da eguna nirea izango zaitudana? (Bilintx, 192)
When will the day arrive that you will be mine?

c. Baina gero izango zirela egunak bi ere egingo zituztenak. (Urruzuno, *E.Z.* 28)
But that later there would be days that it would even lay two (eggs).

What we have seen just now amounts to an alternative strategy for relativization: the appositive strategy, in which a preclitic relative follows an antecedent noun phrase that agrees with it in case. This strategy works for all nonrestrictive clauses and for some restrictive ones (examples 51a–c and 52a–c). Not all restrictive relatives, however, permit appositive variants. There are none for *datorren astean* 'in the coming week', or *joan den urtean* 'in the past year'. Since our main strategy works for restrictive and nonrestrictive clauses alike, the language often allows a choice between the two options. Thus all the examples given under (49) and (50) have prenominal alternatives; for example, (49c) corresponds to (53a); and (50b), to (53b). It follows from section 19.1.7 that even (53c), a stylistically monstrous variant of (49d), is grammatical.

(53) a. Ni naiz Egiptorako saldu zenuten Jose zuen anaia. (Gn 45:4; Ur.)
I am Joseph yoûr brother, whom yoû sold into Egypt.

b. Oraindik inor eseri ez zaion astakume bat aurkituko duzue. (Lk 19:30; *Lau Eb.*)
Yoû will find a young donkey on which no one yet has sat.

c. Eguzkiaren beharrik gabe argi egiten duzun izarra dirudizun beti gogoan zauzkadan dama . . .
O lady, whom I always keep in mind, you who look like a star, who shine without need for the sun, . . .

19.1.12 Postnominal Relatives

Older usage in all dialects allowed a postnominal variant of the standard relative in which the determiner and case marker of the head follow the relative. Thus alongside the normal *eri den gizonaren ohea* 'the bed of the man who is sick', we also find, but with much less frequency, *gizon eri denaren ohea* (Gèze, 64). Postnominal relatives must be carefully distinguished from appositive ones where the determiner of the antecedent comes before the relative. Thus examples (54a,b) are appositives, while (55a,b) are postnominal relatives:

(54) a. Horrako zure seme hori, zure ondasunak emagalduekin jan dituen hori, . . . (Lk 15:30)
That son there of yours, who has consumed your goods with prostitutes, . . .
b. Jainko biziaren Semea, mundu honetara etorri zarena. (Jn 11:27; Dv)
(that You are) the Son of the living God, who have come into this world.

(55) a. Seme gaizto andre galduekin bere gauza guztiak hondatu dituen hori, . . . (*TB* 81)
That wicked son who has squandered all his things with loose women, . . .
b. Zu zarela, Jesus Kristo, Jainko biziaren Seme mundura etorri zarena, . . . (*TB* 91)
That You are Jesus Christ, the Son of the living God, who have come into the world, . . .

Some further examples are

(56) a. Etxe erosi nuena ederra zen. (Archu, 151)
The house I bought was beautiful.
b. Hura zen . . . jainkozko gizon, asko neke erabili zuen bat. (Duvoisin, *L.Ed.* 35)
He was . . . a pious man who went through a lot of trouble.
c. Gizon aspaldi ikusi ez nituenak aurkitu nituen han. (*EGLU* V, 179)
I found people there that I had not seen for a long time.
d. Euskaldun zahar zerbait dakitenak alde dituzte. (J. Etchepare, *Bur.* 145)
They have on their side the elderly Basques who know something.
e. Gure lagun min hartu zuen hori egun berean joan omen zen sendagilearengana. (Lasarte, *Gordean* 35)
That friend or ours who had been hurt went to the doctor that same day.

Postnominal relatives mainly survive among the older speakers of the northern dialects.

19.2 Nonfinite Relatives

Discounting for the moment corelatives (for which see section 19.4), there are two types of nonfinite relative clauses in Basque: participial ones based on the perfect participle on the one hand, and infinitival ones based on the adnominal form of the verbal noun on the other. Both types normally precede their heads, although short participial relatives can be postponed for stylistic reasons.

The array of syntactic functions available to the gap is in principle the same as for finite relatives. Many speakers, however, have ended up assimilating these relatives to the participial constructions of Spanish or French; their usage, in consequence, licenses absolutive gaps only.

The way in which the participle is linked to the head of the relative is a matter of dialect geography. To describe the situation very roughly, the bare participle is used in the north; adnominal stative *-(r)iko* in the west; its synonym *-tako* in the center; and the older form of the adnominal stative *-(r)ikako* in the east. In the present literary standard, all four forms may occur.

19.2.1 Bare Participial Relatives

Only speakers of the northern dialects allow preposed participial relatives without an adnominal ending. We will list some examples, involving various types of gaps. We begin with some examples presenting an absolutive gap, corresponding to the subject in examples (57a,b) and to the direct object in (58a,b).

(57) a. Iragan denbora ez da gehiago gurea. (Larzabal, *Senp.* 116)
The time that has passed is no more ours.
b. Uztazaleari itzuri buruxkak bilduko ditut. (Ru 2:2; Dv)
I will gather the ears that have escaped from the reaper.

(58) a. Horiei egin kaltea nola behar dut erreparatu? (Larzabal, *Senp.* 36)
How am I to compensate the harm I caused them?
b. Osaba misionestak utzi liburuak, denak leituak nituen. (Aintziart, 72)
The books my uncle the missionary had left, I had read them all.

The following examples are more interesting. In (59a) we have an inessive gap, in (59b) an inessive gap referring to time, and in (59c) an elative gap.

(59) a. Abraham Jaunaren aitzinean egon tokira joan zen. (Gn 19:27; *Biblia*)
Abraham went to the place where he has stood before the Lord.
b. Mundu hau utzi eguna hurbil zuen. (Orixe, *Aitork.* 231)
The day when she was to leave this world was near (for her).
c. Etorri bideaz bihurtu zen. (Nm 24:25; Dv)
He returned by the road he came.

Postponed participial relatives occur in all dialects:

(60) a. ... ene beribileko lagun sakelorenaz gabetua ... (J. Etchepare, *Ber.* 69)
... my friend in the automobile who had been relieved of his pocket watch ...
b. Mahaizainak ur ardo bihurtua dastatu zuen. (Jn 2:9; *EAB*)
The table steward tasted the water that had turned into wine.
c. ... emakume itsusi baztangak zulatu batekin (Iraola, 53)
... with an ugly woman pitted by the pox

Perfect participle phrases also serve as appositions, again in all dialects:

(61) a. Agertu zen gizon bat Jainkoak bidalia. (Jn 1:6)
There appeared a man, sent by God.
b. Farisauek ekarri zioten orduan emazteki bat, ezkontza hausten atzemana. (Jn 8:3; *JKBO*)
The Pharisees then brought to him a woman caught committing adultery.

19.2.2 Participial Relatives with *-(r)ikako*

The stative suffix *-(r)ik* can be combined with any perfect participle. The result will be named a "stative" participle. Its use will be detailed in section 25.5.4. For the moment, all we are concerned with is the corresponding adnominal. This adnominal ends in *-(r)ikako* or *-(r)iko*, depending on whether the older form of the stative *-(r)ika* or its modern form *-(r)ik* is taken as a base.

Participial relatives with the ending *-(r)ikako* survive in the dialects of Labourd and Navarra, including also several varieties of High Navarrese. Some examples follow:

(62) a. Orantzarik gabe eginikako ogia (Mendiburu, *Ot.Gai.* II, 336)
Bread made without yeast
b. Kalifornian sos parrasta eginikako amerikano bat (Zubiri, *Art.* 228)
An "American" who has made a heap of money in California
c. Ezkontza, Jainkoak eginikako legea (Larzabal, *Hil.* 38)
Marriage, an institution God made
d. ... emanikako hitza ongi beterik. (Izeta, *Nigarrez* 23)
... having fulfilled neatly the word that he had given.

19.2.3 Participial Relatives with *-(r)iko*

Participial relatives based on the (modern) adnominal form of the stative participle are fairly common in literary Biscayan, and hence also occur in Batua. Here are some examples with an absolutive subject gap:

(63) a. Itsasoetan luzaro ibiliriko ontzi-agintari azkor zintzoa (Agirre, *Kres.* 79)
An intelligent, respectable shipmaster who had ranged the seas for a long time
b. Gure herrian berriki sorturiko fauna bat da. (Haranburu, *Ausk.* 112)
It is a fauna newly arisen in our country.
c. Liburu honetarako zergatik ez dituk hartu gertaturiko gauzak eta mintzaturiko hizkuntza? (Sarrionandia, 42)
For this book, why didn't yoú take things that have happened and language that has been spoken?

With an absolutive object gap we have

(64) a. Bizitza, idiota batek kondaturiko ipuina da. (Sarrionandia, 47)
Life is a tale told by an idiot.
b. Egia da semeen gainean Jaungoikoak eta Izadiak emaniko aginpidea daukatela gurasoek. (Agirre, *Kres.* 95)
It is true that over their sons the parents have the authority given by God and Nature.

Examples with an ergative subject gap also exist:

(65) Baina predikua entzuniko askok sinetsi egin zuten. (Acts 4:4)
But many who had heard the sermon believed.

Stylistic inversion of this construction is possible, although rare—for example, *meza aginduriko batzuk* (Mogel, *D.C.* 174) 'some masses promised'; *lur eskainirikoan* (Arrese Beitia, *Olerk.* 261) 'into the land promised'.

19.2.4 Participial Relatives with *-tako*

Rather than *-(r)ik*, the Guipuzcoan dialect employs the suffix *-ta*, a shortened form of the conjuction *eta*, to create an equivalent of stative participles: *hilda* 'having died', *ikusita* 'having seen', and *emanda* 'having given' instead of *hilik*, *ikusirik*, and *emanik*. They too allow adnominal forms and hence give rise to participial relatives. In fact, such *-tako* adnominals constitute the most common nonfinite relative, not only in the Guipuzcoan dialect, but also in the southern variety of the standard language.

Artiagoitia's (1991) claim that participial relatives allow the same kinds of gaps as finite relatives do is easily verified by means of examples gathered from modern texts. There is an absolutive subject gap in examples (66a–c) and an absolutive object gap in (67a,b):

(66) a. Hiru ziren kanpotik etorritako jaunak. (Satrustegi, 28)
The gentlemen who had come from outside were three (in number).
b. Beitzez jantzitako emakume batek loreak jartzen ditu hilobi batean. (Saizarbitoria, 169)
A woman dressed in black is putting flowers on a grave.
c. Mahaizainak ardo bihurtutako ura dastatu zuen. (Jn 2:9)
The table steward tasted the water that had turned into wine.

(67) a. Ez zituen nik hautatutako bi adiskideak onartu. (Lertxundi, *Aise* 21)
He did not accept the two friends I had chosen.
b. Arestian neskatxari egindako argazkia erakutsi nion. (Garate, *Iz.B.* 36)
I showed her the picture I had just taken of the girl.

There is an ergative subject gap in (68a,b) and a dative gap in (69):

(68) a. Erailearen aita erretiroa hartutako polizia zen. (Garate, *NY* 124)
The father of the killer was a policeman who had taken his retirement.
b. Parisen sinesmena galdutako gazte bat (Intza, *Azalp.* 35)
A youngster who had lost his faith in Paris

(69) Bertso hauek jarri nizkion autopistak etxea harrapatutako aitona horri. (Lasarte, *Gordean* 175)
I put together these verses for that grandfather, whom the highway grabbed the house from.

An inessive gap occurs in (70a–c) and an elative one in (71a–c):

(70) a. Ni jaiotako harana ikusi nuen. (Atxaga, *Behi* 45)
I saw the valley in which I was born.
b. Nagusi horrek berea omen zuen jaiotako baserria. (M. Elicegui and A. Zavala, *P.E.* 145)
That landlord reputedly owned the farm on which he was born.
c. Abrahan Jaunarekin egondako lekura joan zen. (Gn 19:27)
He went to the place where Abraham had stood with the Lord.

(71) a. Berriro sartzen gara irtendako etxera. (Arrese Beitia, *Olerk.* 116)
We again enter the house we came out of.
b. Bidart etorritako bidean gora itzuli zen. (Garate, *Esku* 120)
Bidart returned along the road by which he had come.
c. Saiatu zen, halere, ibilitako bidean atzera egiten. (Atxaga, *Obab.* 322)
He tried, nevertheless, to go back on the road by which he had traveled.

Examples with genitival, instrumental, or allative gaps do not happen to occur in the texts I have perused, but can easily be constructed and seem quite acceptable:

(72) a. Ni hain zalea izandako inauteriak galarazi dituzte.
They have forbidden the carnivals I was so fond of.
b. Zuek ez zenuten gu konturatutako arriskua ikusten.
Yoû didn't see the danger we realized.
c. Gu igotako tokia arriskutsua zen.
The spot we had climbed to was dangerous.

An example of stylistic inversion with the head preceding the participial relative is occasionally encountered:

(73) Orta zeritzan herri inguruan gelditu ziren elizatxo utzitako batean. (Beobide, 63)
They stopped in the vicinity of a village named Orta in a little abandoned church.

19.2.5 Noun Complementation and Infinitival Relatives

Finite complements to nouns were described in section 18.8.1. Nonfinite ones also occur and make use of the adnominal form of the verbal noun:

(74) a. Sagardo pixka bat edateko aitzakia (*TOE* I, 62)
A pretext for drinking a bit of cider
b. Zuei laguntzeko baimena eskatzera noa. (Agirre, *Kres.* 177)
I am going to ask permission to accompany yoû.
c. Banekien ez zuela inoiz argia ikusteko itxaropen handirik. (Mirande, *Pr.* 197)
I knew that it had not much hope to ever see the light.

d. Paulo Ameriketara joateko paperak ari da egiten. (Izeta, *Nigarrez* 104)
Paul is busy getting the documents for going to America.

Now consider the following sentences:

(75) a. Oihenartena ez da inor harritzeko gauza. (*MEIG* V, 27)
Oihenarte's attitude is not a matter to surprise anyone.
b. Hauek ez dira ume batek esateko hitzak. (Arejita)
These are no words for a child to say.
c. Horiek dira andreari kontatzeko gezurrak. (Arejita)
Those are lies to tell the wife.
d. Beti izan haiz andreari gezurrak kontatzeko gizona.
Yoú have always been a man to tell lies to the wife.

These examples, to which could be added such common phrases as *edateko ura* 'drinking water' and *etxeratzeko ordua* 'time to go home', differ from the earlier ones in several respects, despite some superficial similarity. To begin with, the adnominalized clauses in these examples have an unmistakable modal flavor, in clear contrast with the plainer sense of their counterparts in (74a–d). Even more to the point, the adnominalized clauses in (75a–d), again unlike those in (74a–d), display gaps anaphorically related to a noun in the main clause. As this is precisely the definition of a relative clause proposed in the introduction to this chapter, I will follow Artiagoitia in designating them as infinitival relatives.

Infinitival relatives behave like other relatives in accepting pronominal heads, including, of course, the clitic pronoun *-a*. Some examples are

(76) a. Nor dira joatekoak? (Ex 10.8; Dv)
Who are the ones that are supposed to go?
b. Zu al zara etortzekoa? (Mt 11:3)
Are you the one that is supposed to come?
c. Fani noiz da etortzekoa? (Haranburu, *Ausk.* 135)
When is Fani supposed to come?
d. Kafkaren zenbait fruitu ez bide dira denbora-pasa irakurtzekoak. (*MEIG* IV, 135)
Certain productions of Kafka's are presumably not meant to be read as a pastime.

Some of these preclitic relatives have been lexicalized:

edateko (what is meant to be drunk)	beverage
egiteko (what has to be done)	task, occupation, work
esateko (what has to be said)	reproach, complaint
jateko (what is meant to be eaten)	food

19.3 Adjoined Relatives

An adjoined clause can be defined as a clause that has no syntactic role within the main clause, yet is subordinate to it, being neither coordinate nor independent. Incidentally, in Basque, it is easy to verify subordination for finite clauses, as it is signaled by an affix on the verb.

In some languages, adjoined clauses constitute the main—and sometimes only—strategy for relativization. In Basque, adjoined relative clauses do occur but are somewhat peripheral compared with the prenominal ones using the relativizer *-N*.

19.3.1 The Subordinator *bait-*

In Basque, all finite nonmain clauses must carry a mark of subordination on their finite verbs. Thus conditionals display the prefix *ba-*; and finite clauses governed by a verb receive a complementizer suffix: *-LA*, *-NA*, *-NIK*, or *-N*, the latter also attaching to adnominal relatives, as described in section 19.1.1. All finite clauses not carrying a suffix based on one of these complementizers require the subordinating prefix *bait-* in the eastern dialects or the complementizer *-N* in the others, that is, Guipuzcoan and Biscayan. In the eastern part of Guipuzcoa, the prefix *bait-* has survived, but solely in a causal use, for which see section 23.3.2.

The final *t* of the prefix has virtual existence only. It causes the following consonant to sharpen and then drops. That is, following plosives (*d* or *g*) become unvoiced by application of sandhi rule 1 of section 1.2.6, and sibilants (here *z*) turn into affricates (*tz*). Thus, with the present tense of the verb *izan* 'to be' we get *bainaiz*, *baihaiz*, *baita*, *baikara*, *baitzara*, *baitzarete*, *baitira*.

The nonfocus particle *ba* is incompatible with this prefix, but the negative *ez* can precede it: *ez baitu egin*. Notice that the prefix does not block Auxiliary Attraction, which is still obligatory.

19.3.2 Relativization with *bait-*

Clauses where the verb bears the prefix *bait-* form a classic example of adjoined clauses. These admit a great variety of uses, one of which represents a relative clause. In observing the structure of this kind of relative, we find that there is an anaphoric relation between a pronoun—possibly zero—in the adjoined clause and a noun phrase in the main clause, to which the adjoined clause acts as a comment. Note, however, that this noun phrase, which we will call the head, does not combine with the relative into a single constituent, as it does in adnominal relatives.

The canonical position for an adjoined relative is after the main clause. Examples are

(77) a. Lili bat ikusi dut baratze batean, desiratzen bainuke nire sahetsean. (From the song "Lili bat ikusi dut," *Ene H.* 26; *Xaramela* 199.)
In a garden I have seen a flower that I would wish (to have) at my side.

b. Badira "ranchero" nagusi eder batzu, oroz gainetik, euskaldun alabak nahi baitituzte emaztetzat. (Larzabal, *Hiru* 16)
There are some handsome ranch owners who, above all, want Basque daughters for a wife.

c. Hor heldu zaio Basajauna, neska hartu eta eramaten baitu berekin. (Barbier, *Lég*. 129)
There comes at her the Ogre, who takes the girl and carries her off with him.

d. ... dozena bat antzara, Piarresek ez baitzituen ikusi ere (*P.Ad*. 53)
... a dozen geese, which Peter didn't even see

e. Pellok neskatxa bat aurkitu du, guztiz maite baitu.
Pete has found a girl whom he loves very much.

As we noticed for adnominal relatives in section 19.1.1, the occurrence of zero pronouns produced by multi-pro-drop can give rise to ambiguity. Thus example (77e) could be used as well to mean 'Pete has found a girl who loves him very much'. Beyond this, however, there are no decoding problems to cope with, since an overt pronoun will indicate its function within the relative by its case marker. Accordingly, there are plenty of adjoined relatives whose prenominal version would be unacceptable to many speakers:

(78) a. Zer da gure adimena, hartaz baikaude guztiz hantuak? (J. Etchepare, *Bur*. 156–157)
What is our intelligence, about which we are bragging (so) much?

b. Astakume bat aurkituko duzue, haren gainean ez baita egundaino inor jarri. (Lk 19:30; *EAB*)
Yoû will find a young donkey, upon which nobody has ever sat. (For *egundaino* 'until today', see section 20.1.1.)

c. Egiptoera zaharrean hitzegin zuen, hots, hizkera batean inork haren fonetika orduan ez baitzekien. (Mirande, *Pr*. 345)
She spoke in ancient Egyptian, that is to say, in a speech form whose phonetics nobody at the time knew.

Another favored position of the adjoined relative is right after the topic of the main clause. This is illustrated in the following examples:

(79) a. Etxe hori, motozikleta atarian baitago, apaizarena da. (Heard by Mitxelena in Echalar)
That house, where there is a motorcycle at the entrance, belongs to the priest.

b. Mattin ene adiskideari, ez baita hura ere nornahi, gertatu zaizkio horrelakoak. (*EGLU* V, 245)
To my friend Mattin, who isn't just anybody either, such things have happened.

c. Lehen Saulen armak, ttipiak eta arinak baitziren, handiz eta pisuz utzi zituen, eta orain jigante handi batenak iruditzen zaizkio ttipi eta arin? (Ax. 90)
Earlier he had left off as too big and heavy Saul's weapons, which were small and light, and now those of a big giant seem to him small and light?

Incidentally, these examples, especially (79c), belie a claim made by Chr. Lehmann, who posited: "Since an adjoined relative clause is not a constituent of the main clause, it never appears within it, but always at its margin, being either preposed or postposed" (1986, 666).

Preposed adjoined relatives are quite rare and will not be discussed here. For two plausible examples, see Lafitte's *Grammaire basque* (1962, sec. 772, p. 406).

19.3.3 Sentential Relatives

Relative clauses with a sentence as a head are ruled out as far as the main relativization strategy is concerned. Adjoined relatives with a sentence as the antecedent, however, are quite common. Examples are

(80) a. Garatik hirirako bi zubiak ere behar dituzte zabaldu, ez baita goizegi izanen. (H.U., *Gontzetarik* 30)
They also have to widen the two bridges from the station into the town, which will not be (any) too soon.

b. Taularen gainean etzan naiz zenbait egunez, ez baita batere goxo. (J. Etchepare, *Bur*. 114)
I have lain on a wooden board for a few days, which was not at all pleasant.

c. Federiko enperadoreak ez zuen bere mendean ardorik edan, anitz baitzen aleman batentzat. (Ax. 406)
Emperor Frederick did not drink wine in his lifetime, which was quite something for a German.

19.4 Corelatives

A correlative relative, in short, a corelative, is an adjoined clause containing an interrogative phrase, usually a pronoun, anaphorically related to a noun phrase (or pronoun) in the main clause. In Basque, a corelative precedes the main clause, to which it may optionally be linked by the conjunction *eta*, especially when the particle *ere* 'also' is present. If finite, its verb is marked by the complementizer -*N* in western usage and by the subordinator *bait-* in eastern usage (cf. section 19.3.1).

(81) a. Nire aitak norentzat prestatua duen, hari emango zaio. (Mt 20:23)
It will be given to him for whom my father has prepared it.

b. Nora gidatzen gaituzun, hara joango gara. (Jo 1:16)
We will go where you direct us.

(82) a. Nork sobera besarkatzen baitu, gutxi hersten du. (Voltoire, 194)
Who takes in too much, grasps little.

b. Nor hark igorri baitu, hura zuek ez duzue sinesten. (Jn 5:38)
You do not believe him whom he has sent.

When following an interrogative, the particle *ere* 'also' has the force of English *-ever*:

(83) a. Gizonak zer ere ereiten baitu, hura biltzen ere du. (Ax. 216)
Man will reap whatever he sows.
b. Non ere izaten baita gorputza, han bilduko dira arranoak (Mt 24:28; Etx.)
The vultures will gather wherever the corpse is.
c. Zer ere baitzuen eskas eta hura ematen zion. (J. Etchepare, *Bur.* 72)
She gave him whatever he was lacking.

The verb in the corelative may be reduced to its unmarked form, the perfect participle:

(84) a. Bakoitzak zer erein, huraxe bilduko du. (Gal 6:7)
Everyone will gather just what he sows.
b. Zu non jarri bizitzen, hantxe jarriko naiz ni ere. (Ru 1:16)
Where you settle to live, I will settle too.

In proverbial sayings of this type, the verb may be lacking altogether:

(85) a. Zure aberastasuna non, zure bihotza han. (Mt 6:21)
Where your wealth (is), there (is) your heart.
b. Eguzkia nora, zapiak hara. (*P.Ab.* 122)
(Put) the linen where the sun (is).

As *EGLU* (V, 256) points out, the corelative may be intercalated into the main clause as long as the anaphor follows it:

(86) Gero badaramatzate zein tokitara iduritzen ere baitzaie, eta hara. (J. Etchepare, *Bur.* 161)
Afterward they lead them to whichever spot they deem fit.

19.5 Relatives Based on Fronted Interrogatives

The borrowed strategy of relatives based on fronted interrogatives yields a mostly nonrestrictive relative following the head and characterized by the presence of a case-marked fronted interrogative, usually *zein* 'which', behaving like a relative pronoun in the Romance languages.

This strategy is mentioned here for historical reasons only, since it plays no role in the contemporary standard. This point is confirmed by *EGLU* (V, 218), which prefaces its 22-page analysis with the remark that the construction has been used in all dialects and centuries up to the 20th century. Also Villasante, while advocating its use for reasons of convenience, has to admit that it is never used in the spoken language (1976, 88). It reeks of outdated homilies and is spurned by a vast majority of present-day speakers.

As for its presence in classical Basque literature, considering that this consisted largely of translations and adaptations of Romance originals, it is hardly surprising that the Romance relativization strategy was resorted to for rendering the involved relative structures encountered in the originals. What is surprising is that such moderate use was made of this convenient strategy.

As a detailed study of the strategy's application is available in *EGLU*, my remarks will be confined to a few basic points. Some classical authors, among whom the most ancient, such as Leizarraga, Axular, Tartas, and Beriain, use the same indefinite declension of *zein* as found in other functions (cf. section 2.3.2, item 6), whereas others use a definite form *zeina*, influenced, no doubt, by French *lequel* or Spanish *el cual*. Since the relative is a finite subordinate clause, its verb must carry a subordinator: the prefix *bait-* in the eastern dialects or the complementizer *-N* in the western ones.

(87) a. Halatan ez da gelditzen lau besanga baizik zeinetarik ateratzen baitira gando berriak. (Duvoisin, *Lab*. 374)
That way only four branches remain, out of which emerge new shoots.
b. ... eskerrak eman Jaungoikoari, zeinen eskuetatik datozkigun on guztiak. (*P.Ab.* 56)
... giving thanks to God, from whose hands all good things come to us.

Some Guipuzcoan authors, however, omit this subordinator—for example, Larramendi (sometimes only) and Lardizabal (always). On page 273 of Larramendi's grammar, there are two instances of *zeina*-based relatives, the first of which clearly lacks a complementizer:

(88) a. Etxe hau, zeinaren zu bide zara jabe (Larramendi, 273)
This house, of which you are reputed to be the owner
b. Eliza hau, zeinari eman zioten gure gurasoek hainbeste urre (Larramendi, 273)
This church, to which our parents gave so much gold

19.6 Historical and Bibliographical Note on Relativization

The first grammarian to take up the study of Basque relatives was Larramendi, author of a grammar titled *El imposible vencido*, published in 1729. Chapter 2 of part II is entirely devoted to relativization; in its ten pages the main relativization strategy is applied to ergative and absolutive gaps only, while the remaining cases are accommodated by the Romance strategy (see examples 88a,b in section 19.5).

Larramendi's text is reproduced almost verbatim in Lardizabal's *Gramática vascongada* of 1856, which, on the whole, follows Larramendi's work rather closely. The next treatment of Basque relativization I am aware of is by the hand of I. M. Echaide, an electrical engineer, who despite his handicap of not being a native speaker of the language was elected president of the Basque Academy in 1951, a post he held until his demise in 1962. In his 1912 study *Sintaxis del idioma éuskaro*, Echaide discusses the main relativization strategy at great length, extending it to dative gaps also. To him we are indebted moreover for the Parallel Case criterion cited in section 19.1.2.

Fieldwork among mainly Guipuzcoan speakers enabled me to make my own contribution. My MIT dissertation (1972b) entitled *Studies in Basque Syntax: Relative Clauses*, a comprehensive summary of which appeared under the title "Relative Clauses in Basque: A Guided Tour," in *The Chicago Which Hunt* (1972a), was followed by a later article "Erlatiboak idazle zaharrengan" (1980). (All three are included in *DLV*.) My position at the time was that there are two "dialects" to be distinguished: a restrictive one as described by Echaide and another one, which I labeled "the main system," where instrumental, inessive, elative, and allative gaps also yield acceptable relatives.

Resting on roughly the same premises are the more formal treatments of P. Goenaga in his work *Gramatika bideetan* (1978, considerably enlarged second edition in 1980) and X. Artiagoitia, who applied the Null Operator Hypothesis of Government and Binding theory to the issue in his 1992 article "Why Basque Doesn't Relativize Everything."

A dissenting voice came from B. Oihartzabal, who not only took exception, quite correctly, to some incidental claims in my dissertation, but, more crucially, objected to the putative dialect distinction and propounded, in effect, that (almost) everything can be relativized, provided a suitable context is shared by the speaker and his listeners. I may mention, incidentally, that my current views on the matter, outlined here in section 19.1.2, are not altogether different from Oihartzabal's. Among his publications, the most relevant are *Les relatives en basque* (1985b) abbreviated here as *R.B.*, and his 1989 "Pro-drop and the Resumptive Pronoun Strategy in Basque," abbreviated here as *Pro-drop*.

For nonfinite relatives, the reader may be referred to Artiagoitia's 1991 essay "Aspects of Tenseless Relative Clauses in Basque," to be studied in conjunction with Oihartzabal's 1998 investigation "Analyse des infinitives adnominales en basque."

More information on the use of adjoined clauses, including relatives, can be found in the relevant sections (767–778) of P. Lafitte's *Grammaire basque* (1962). Also worth reading is the instructive 1966 essay by Lafon "La particule *bait* en basque; ses emplois morphologiques et syntaxiques," and finally, the *DGV*, in which ten dense pages are allotted to the prefix *bait-* in its various uses (III, 702–712).

Last, but not least, for all the topics treated in this chapter, those who can should take advantage of *EGLU*, authored by the grammar committee of the Royal Basque Academy. In this collective work, the perceptive section on relative clauses (*EGLU* V, 173–270) dating from 1999 unmistakably betrays the hand of the linguist-grammarian B. Oihartzabal.

19.7 The Inclusive Article *-ok*

The inclusive article *-ok* optionally replaces the plural article *-ak* on a noun phrase when its referent is directly implicated in the speech act of the utterance containing it. Like the article *-a(k)* itself, it is actually a clitic pronoun and partly covers the meaning of both *hauek* and *horiek*.

Its declension is regular, with *o* replacing the *e* of the ordinary plural forms: *gizonok* (both absolutive and ergative), *gizonoi*, *gizonon*, *gizonokin*, *gizonoz*, *gizonontzat*, *gizonongatik*, and so on. A stem-final *a*, elides: *alabok*, *elizok*.

There also are locative forms, such as *urteotan* 'in the years we are talking about'—for example, *hirurogeita hamar urteotan* (Zec 7:5) 'in these seventy years'.

In accordance with the preceding definition, three uses of *-ok* can be distinguished:

1. Marking matters already mentioned in the same discourse

(89) a. Aipatu ditudan xehetasunok garbiro azaltzen digute . . . (*MEIG* II, 117)
The details that I have mentioned clearly demonstrate to us that . . .
b. Eta guztiok gramatikaz baliatzen dira beti. (*MEIG* III, 63)
And all of these always make use of grammar.
c. Egiak dira horiok guztiok. (Ax. 562)
All of these are truths.

2. Marking the addressee, if plural

(90) a. Galdu didazue aita-semeok afaritako gogo guztia. (*P.Ab.* 103)
Yoû, father and son, have spoiled my whole appetite for dinner.
b. Zuei diotsuet, orain, ene adiskideoi: . . . (Lk 12:4; *IB*)
To yoû, my friends, I now say: . . .

When beginning to address an audience, use of *-ok* is quite common, although optional—for example, *anaia maiteok* (Garate, *Ald.* 78) 'dear brothers'; *egun on, jaun-andreok* (*LBB* 194) 'good morning, ladies and gentlemen'; *arratsalde on, guztioi* (*MEIG* VII, 161) 'good afternoon to yoû all'.

3. Marking a group to which the speaker belongs

(91) a. Zor berria dugu euskaldunok Orixerekin. (*MEIG* II, 75)
We Basques have a new debt to Orixe.
b. . . . arrotzak eta euskaldunak, etsaiak eta geuk, denak eta denok. (*G.* 194)
. . . the foreigners and the Basques, the enemies and ourselves, they all and we all.
c. Hala bada guk ere, gerotik gerora gabiltzanok, kontsolatzen ditugu geure buruok. (Ax. 73)
So then we, who procrastinate endlessly, also console ourselves.
d. Berretura hartaz, bere burua eta guztiok ere galdu gintuen. (Ax. 72)
By this addition, she ruined herself and all of us too.

For *-ok* as the head of a relative, see examples (30a–c) in section 19.1.8.

19.8 The Property Suffix *-dun*

The productive suffix *-dun* (with lowered pitch), etymologically related to the verb **edun* 'to have', functions as the positive counterpart to the parasuffix *gabe* 'without', analyzed in section 13.6. It operates on noun phrases X lacking a determiner; the result, which may serve both as a noun and as an adjective, expresses the meaning 'having X'. Altube's stricture (1929, 262–269) that only alienable possession qualifies hardly seems to fit contemporary usage.

In its adjectival use, the derivative is free to either precede or follow the noun phrase it modifies: *zentzudun emaztea* or *emazte zentzuduna* 'the sensible wife'. In accordance with sandhi rule 3 of section 1.2.6, stems ending in an affricate yield derivatives ending in a sibilant followed by *-tun*, cf. *akastun*, *bihoztun*, *hiztun*, *ugaztun*. An exception is *kirats* 'stench', which yields *kirasdun* 'stinking'. Given that the suffix *-garri* derives from the verb *ekarri* (section 14.7) and the suffix *-gin* from the verb *egin* (section 16.9), it seems obvious that the suffix *-dun* derives from the verb **edun*. This is not to claim, however, that this suffix originated as a phonetic contraction of the relative third-person singular present tense form *duen*, a peculiar view held by many grammarians (e.g., Uhlenbeck, Azkue, Villasante, Irigoyen) for which there is little or no justification.

Some derivatives in common use are the following:

adar	branch, horn	adardun	branchy, horned
ahal	power, ability	ahaldun	powerful
akats	nick, defect, fault	akastun	nicked, defective, faulty
ardura	care	arduradun	caretaker, administrator
arima	soul	arimadun	animated being, animated
arma	weapon	armadun	armed person, armed
asto	donkey	astodun	ass driver, peddler
azken	end	azkendun	finite being, finite
betaurrekoak	glasses	betaurrekodun	(person) wearing glasses
bihotz	heart	bihoztun	one with a heart, kindhearted, brave
bizar	beard	bizardun	(person) with a beard, bearded
bizi	life	bizidun	living creature, living
buru	head	burudun	having a head, cautious, clever
damu	regret, remorse	damudun	penitent, repentant, remorseful
deabru	devil	deabrudun	possessed of the devil, devilish
ele	speech	eledun	spokesperson (*elebidun* 'bilingual')
erdara	foreign language	erdaldun	non-Basque speaker
erru	guilt	errudun	culprit, guilty
esker	thanks	eskerdun	thankful
esne	milk	esnedun	milch, milkman
euskara	Basque language	euskaldun	Basque-speaker, Basque-speaking
fede	faith, trust	fededun	believer, faithful
galtzak	trousers	galtzadun	adult male, layperson, secular
gona	skirt	gonadun	adult female, priest, monk
hartzeko	assets, credit	hartzekodun	creditor

haur	child	haurdun	pregnant (woman), having children
hitz	word	hiztun	lecturer, speaker, chatterbox
hoben	blame, guilt	hobendun	culprit, guilty
indar	strength, force	indardun	strong (person)
izate	being	izatedun	(a) being, existent
jabe	owner	jabedun	owned property, copyrighted
kargu	charge, post	kargudun	officeholder, official
konkor	hump, bump, lump	konkordun	hunchback, humped
min	pain, grief	mindun	sufferer, aggrieved (person)
prakak	pants	prakadun	adult male, layperson, secular
sineste	belief	sinestedun	believer
txapel	beret, hat	txapeldun	wearing a hat, champion
ugatz	breast, teat	ugaztun	mammal, mammiferous
zaldi	horse	zaldun	horseman, nobleman, knight
zentzu	sense	zentzudun	sensible (person)
zor	debt	zordun	debtor, indebted

Verbal nouns based on a transitive verb can also take this suffix provided they end in *-te* rather than *-tze*. These derivatives, as a rule, are not used adjectivally but denote a habitual or even professional performer of the action concerned. The final vowel *e* of the verbal noun is elided by virtue of Major Apocope (section 3.8.1, here applying to disyllables also), after which sandhi rule 1 of section 1.2.6 turns the resulting cluster *td* into *t*.

The following examples have occurred in the literature:

edate	drinking	edatun	big drinker, drunkard (cf. *edale*, 'drinker')
erakuste	showing	erakustun	teacher (more common: *irakasle*)
eroste	buying	erostun	professional buyer (*erosle*, 'buyer')
ikaste	learning	ikastun	student, apprentice (*ikasle*, 'pupil')
irabazte	earning, winning	irabaztun	earner, winner
irakaste	teaching	irakastun	teacher, doctor
jakite	knowing	jakitun	scholar, erudite (*jakile*, 'witness')
jate	eating	jatun	big eater, glutton
joste	sewing	jostun	seamstress (also *josle*)
saleroste	trading	salerostun	trader, merchant (also *salerosle*)
sineste	believing	sinestun	believer (also *sinestedun*)

An exceptional form is *izandun*, based as it is on the perfect participle rather than on the verbal noun. It has two meanings: 'being', derived from intransitive *izan* 'to be', and 'wealthy', derived from transitive *izan* 'to have'.

To end this section, I will list some examples taken from Basque literature, in which the suffix *-dun* is attached to a whole phrase instead of a single noun.

1. With an adjective present: *oin luze arinduna* (J. A. Mogel, *Ip*. 153 [61]) 'one with agile long legs'; *gizon buru gogordunak* (*TB* 170) 'men with hard heads'; *aita xahar ile xuridunak* (Oxobi, 178) 'elderly fathers with white hair'; *mutil txapel gorriduna* (Azkue, *E.Y.* IV, 67) 'boy with the red beret'; *andre gona gorriduna* (Azkue, *E.Y.* IV, 67) 'lady with the red skirt'; *zuhaitz enbor lodidunak* (Kirikiño, *Ab*. 19) 'trees with thick trunks'.
2. With an indefinite quantifier: *Jaungoiko askodunak* (*DGV* X, 170: F. Bart., *Ikas*. I, IV) 'those with many gods'; *barru gutxidunak* (Kirikiño, *Ab*. 19) 'those with little content'.
3. With a numeral present: *zazpi burudun sugea* (Cardaberaz, *Eg*. II, 173) 'a serpent with seven heads'; *ehun begiduna* (J. A. Mogel, *Ip*. 153 [61]) 'one with a hundred eyes'; *zulo bidun eskopeta bat* (Kirikiño, *Ab*. [II], 94) 'a two-barreled shotgun'; *hogei etxedun* (Orixe, *Eusk*. 39) 'one having twenty houses'; *bi begidun oro* (Orixe, *Poem*. 523) 'all those having two eyes'.
4. With a preceding adnominal: *harrizko bihoztuna* (Agirre, *Kres*. 187) 'having a heart of stone'; *zu bezalako amonadun gazteok* (Amuriza, *Hil* 58) 'we youngsters with a grandmother such as you'.

19.9 Vocabulary

adiskide	friend
ahaztarazi	to cause to forget (see section 16.2.1)
aingeru	angel
aski	enough
aspaldi	long ago
azaldu	to appear, to show up
bakar	alone, unique
bakarrik	alone
berehala	at once, immediately, forthwith
bidali	to send
bihurtu	to return, to become
bizirik	alive
gaizki	evil, badly
gustatu	to please, to like
itzuli	to return
jabe	owner
Jainko(a)	God
kalte	harm, damage
kendu	to take away
kolko	bosom, chest
konponketa	repair

lapur	thief
lapurtu	to steal
lehen	earlier, before, formerly, first, at first
leku	spot, place
lodi	thick
maitagarri	lovable, lovely
ordaindu	to compensate, to pay
pagatu	to pay
sutsuki	ardently, passionately
ustel	rotten, putrid, perverse
zaharo	old age
zigarro	cigarette

19.10 Exercises

19.10.1 Translate into English

1. Liburuak gustatzen zaizkion ikaslea da Pello. (*EGLU* V, 185)
2. Bakarrik etorri den haurrari eman zaion sagarra ustela da.
3. Kolkoan dakarzun hori ekarri ez bazenu, ez zinatekeen hemendik bizirik aterako. (Garate, *Ald.* 8)
4. Umea nintzeneko egunak aspaldi joan ziren.
5. Jon kalean dabilen neskarekin ezkondu nahi luke Patxik. (*EGLU* V, 189)
6. Zekarkionak zekarkionari zekarkiona zekarkion.
7. Ogia orain jan didaten honi ardoa kendu didazu. (Echaide 1912, 49)
8. Dakidanez, ez dizut behin ere kalterik egin.
9. Dakidana zuk ere badakizu; dakizuna nik ez dakit dakidan.
10. Lehen ikasitako gauza asko zaharoak ahaztarazten dizkigu.
11. Zuen alaba sutsuki maite dut, guztiz maitagarria baita.
12. Nor ere bizi baita etxe hartan, hark pagatu beharko du haren konponketa. (*EGLU* V, 247)

19.10.2 Translate into Basque

1. I do the evil that I do not want.
2. Have you seen that thick book that no one will ever read?
3. Do I have to read the book that you have written?
4. Yes, you must read this book, which is very interesting.
5. The lady to whom I promised the horse doesn't want it.

6. I will go to the place where yoû are sending me.
7. A good friend is an angel that God sends us.
8. Where is the gypsy that you told me would show up?
9. What you do, you must do well.
10. You have to know what you are doing.
11. All stolen books must be returned forthwith.
12. What is enough is enough.

20 Time Adverbials

20.1 Time Adverbs

20.1.1 Declension of Time Adverbs

Given their meaning and function, the declension of time adverbs in Basque is limited to the locative system and naturally excludes the directional *-rantz*. In practice, we only need to be concerned with the elative and terminal cases, since the allative, as we will see, appears mainly with the adnominal *-ko* combined into destinative *-rako*, and the inessive, as a rule, is not morphologically realized on adverbs. Syntactically, however, we will assume the inessive case to be present on most of these adverbs, not so much on the strength of the analogy with comparable adverbials, such as *igandean* 'on Sunday', *egun hartan* 'on that day', and *orduan* 'at that time', but because they allow the adnominal form: *oraingo* 'of now', *gaurko* 'of today', *geroko* 'of later'.

With regard to inessive adverbs, it is interesting to observe that indefinite inessive noun phrases denoting a period in life can be treated as adverbs, as shown by their ability to be followed by the elative marker *-tik*, not otherwise added to inessive forms: *gaztetandik* 'since one's youth'; *haurretandik* 'since childhood'; *mutikotandik* 'since boyhood'; *txikitandik* and *umetandik*, both meaning 'since early childhood'. By the same token, adnominals like *gaztetango* will occur, as well as the regular *gaztetako*.

Note that when case endings are attached to adverbs no epenthesis takes place. Thus, with the adverb *egun* 'today', we get *egundik* 'from today on', to be distinguished carefully from *egunetik* 'from the day on', where *egun* is used as a noun. An exception is made for adverbs ending in the morpheme *bait*, which do require epenthesis: *noizbaitetik* 'from a certain time on'.

As regards the elative, the northern dialects feature a special form when referring to time: *-danik*, originally an independent word governing the inessive: *bere amaren sabelean danik* (Lk 1:15; Lz, HE) 'from his mother's womb'. In present-day Low Navarrese, where it is thriving, *danik* governs the absolutive: *bere amaren sabela danik* (Lk 1:15; *JKBO*) 'from his mother's womb', *iragan urtea danik* (Lh. 196) 'since the past year'. The literary language has borrowed it as a suffix, treating it as a prestigious variant of temporal *-tik*, while limiting its occurrence to adverbs. Thus we find *oraindanik* 'from now on', *ordudanik* 'from then on', and *aspaldidanik* 'since long'; also *gaztedanik* 'since one's youth' and *haurdanik* 'since childhood'; and even two spatial adverbs: *hurbildanik* 'from nearby' and *urrundanik* 'from afar'.

With the exception of a few set phrases where it follows an elative form and shows epenthesis—for example, *gaurtik biharrera* 'overnight' (in the north: *egunetik biharrera* 'from one day to the next')—the allative ending does not appear on time adverbs unless accompanied by the adnominal ending *-ko*.

In contexts where the allative might be expected to occur, the location noun *arte* (section 4.1.3.6) or its terminal *arteraino* will appear instead: *gaurtik bihar arte* 'from today until tomorrow'.

The locative destinative *-rako* 'for' has taken on a temporal meaning, like Spanish *para*, corresponding to English *by*: *datorren iganderako* 'by next Sunday'. With adverbs ending in a consonant, allative deletion (section 5.2.3) is obligatory. Hence we have

(1) Noizko behar dituzu oinetako hauek? Biharko ala etzirako?
By when do you need these shoes? By tomorrow or by the day after tomorrow?

The terminal case has the form *-raino* after a vowel and *-daino* after a consonant, barring epenthesis as in *noizbaiteraino* 'up to a certain time'—for example,

(2) Oraindaino ez da gauza handia. (Irazusta, *Joan.* 194)
Up to now it is no big thing.

Actually, the terminal case is little used in time specifications. Much more common is the location noun or postposition *arte*: *orain arte* 'up to now', *bihar arte* 'until tomorrow', *gero arte* 'until later'.

The declension of the interrogative *noiz* 'when' neatly summarizes what we have seen so far: inessive *noiz*; (destinative) adnominal *noizko*; elative *noiztik* or *noizdanik*; terminal *noizdaino*, usually replaced by *noiz arte*.

When *noiz* appears as part of a noninterrogative set phrase, it seems to have nominal status, as it is then declined according to the definite singular paradigm of section 3.2 with its usual epenthesis. The following expressions, all meaning 'from time to time', illustrate this point: *noizean noiz*, *noizean behin*, *noizik noizera*, *noizetik noizera*.

20.1.2 Inventory of Time Adverbs

Time adverbs can be divided into adverbs denoting location in time, adverbs of frequency, and adverbs of duration.

20.1.2.1 Adverbs of Location in Time

Adverbs indicating location in time are again subdivisible into three groups: a general group with *orain* 'now' as a prototype; a group concerned with days, having *gaur* 'today' as a prototype; and a group involving years, with *aurten* 'this year' as a prototype.

1. The main members of the *orain* group are

antzina	long ago
behiala	long ago
behinola	long ago (only used in the south)
aspalditxo	a long while ago (also *aspaldixko*)
aspaldi	quite a while ago (cf. *aspaldiko* 'old chum')
lehen	in the past, before, formerly
artemein	lately
berriki	recently (also *berritan*)
oraintsu	a short time ago, recently
orain	now (recall that *oraindik* and *oraino* only mean 'still')
gero	later on, afterward (cf. *gero ere* 'in the end')

Some of these adverbs can also be used as nouns: *aspaldi* 'period extending from quite a while back up to now' (whence, *aspaldian* 'for a long time', *aspaldi guztian* 'all this time', *aspaldi honetan* 'for a long time already'); *lehen* 'past' (e.g., *haren lehena* 'his past'); *orain* 'present' (thus, *orainean* 'in the present'); *gero* 'future' (thus, *geroan* 'in the future', *gero-aren beldur* 'fear of the future').

Actually, for the concepts 'past', 'present', and 'future', including their use as grammatical notions, compounds with *aldi* 'time' (sections 20.3 and 20.9) are more common: *lehe-naldi, orainaldi, geroaldi.*

Parallel to *aspaldi* is the noun *aresti* meaning 'period extending from a short while back on the same day up to now', whence *arestian* (or *aresti batean*) 'a while ago'.

Regarding the adverb *gero*, attention must be drawn to its use as a postposition in the meaning 'since' or 'after'. Its instrumental *geroz* and its irregular elative *geroztik* also share this function. All three postpositions normally govern the instrumental case. Examples are *atzoz gero(z)* 'since yesterday', *orduz gero(z)* 'since then', and *zortziez gero(z)* 'since eight o'clock'; *aurreko igandeaz gero* (T. Agirre, *Uzt.* 235) 'since the previous Sunday'; *aurreko astelehenaz geroztik* (T. Agirre, *Uzt.* 162) 'since the previous Monday'; *egun hartaz geroz* (Atxaga, *Obab.* 325) 'since that day'; *Arakistainez gero* (*MEIG* III, 44) 'since Arakistain'; and *Etxeparez geroz* (*MEIG* IV, 93) 'since Etxepare'.

Nonfinite clauses too can be accommodated by the postposition *gero*, provided they are based on the perfect participle, which then takes the instrumental form. Examples are *izena aipatuz gero* (*MEIG* II, 125) 'after mentioning the name' and *gartzelatik ateraz gero* (Atxaga, *Z.H.* 78) 'after coming out of prison'. It is worth noting that this construction also allows a conditional reading: 'if one mentions the name', 'if one comes out of prison'.

In the southern dialects, the sequence *-ez gero* has amalgamated, forming a new postposition *ezkero*, governing the absolutive case. A recommendation issued by the Royal Basque Academy in January 1995 advises against the use of *ezkero* after a perfect participle or any other verb form, but allows it elsewhere. Thus, in Batua, we may find written *atzo ezkero* 'since yesterday', *ordu ezkero* 'since then', *noiz ezkero* 'since when', *zortziak ezkero* 'from eight o'dock on', *osteguna ezkero* (*TOE* I, 89) 'since Thursday', *egun hau ezkero* (*TB* 191) 'from this day on', and *San Paul ezkero* (Orixe, *Q.A.* 77) 'from Saint Paul on'. Also accepted in Batua are the typically southern adverbs *honezkero* 'from now on' and *harrezkero* (and its relatively recent synonym *horrezkero*) 'from then on', forms based on the oblique stems of the demonstrative pronouns (cf. section 9.6.1), with dialectal *harr-* (derived from ergative *hark*, commonly pronounced *harrek*) instead of standard *har-*.

Aside from their use as time indicators, the adverbs *lehen* 'first' and *gero* 'later' can also be employed to situate an event with respect to another event. Other forms serving this purpose are the elative *lehendik* 'first', the archaic ablative *ondoren* 'afterward', and the inessive noun *jarraian* 'in continuation', that is, 'next'.

2. The *gaur* group contains the following members:

laurdenegun	on the second day before yesterday
herenegun	on the day before yesterday
atzo	yesterday
bart	last night
gaur	today (northern meaning: 'this evening', 'this night')
egun	today (cf. *egungo egunean* 'nowadays')
bihar	tomorrow
etzi	on the day after tomorrow
etzidamu	on the second day after tomorrow
etzikaramu	on the third day after tomorrow

Any adverb in this group can occur as the initial member of a nominal compound whose final part consists of a noun denoting a part of the day: *goiz* 'morning', *arratsalde* 'afternoon', *arrats* 'evening', *gau* 'night'. Since these compounds are nouns, they must be overtly case-marked: *bihar goizean* 'tomorrow morning', *gaur gauean* 'tonight', *atzo arratsaldean* 'yesterday afternoon', *bart arratsean* 'last evening', a common alternative to plain *bart*.

Although the regular adnominal of *bart* is *bartko*, declined forms of *bart* are usually avoided by compounding it with either *arrats* 'evening' or *gau* 'night'. Thus we get *bart arratseko* or *bart gaueko* instead of *bartko*, and *bart arratsetik* or *bart gauetik* instead of *bartik* or *bartdanik*.

3. The *aurten* group has only three members:

iaz	last year
aurten	this year
geurtz	next year (rare, much more common is *datorren urtean*)

These forms do not enter into compounds. Instead, adnominal constructions appear: *iazko udan* 'in last year's summer', *aurtengo neguan* 'in this year's winter'.

20.1.2.2 Adverbs of Frequency

Adverbs denoting frequency are

behin	once (*urtean behin* 'once a year', *beste behin* 'once more')
bakan	seldom
maiz	often (*maiztxo* 'quite often')
ardura	often (northern oniy)
usu	often (easternmost dialects, especially Souletin: *üsü*)
sarri	often (also *sarriro*, *sarritxo* 'quite often')
etengabe	incessantly
beti	always (*betidanik* 'since always', *betiko* 'eternal')
inoiz	ever (with *ez*: never)
sekula	ever (with *ez*: never)

[*N.B.* The original meaning of *sarri* 'dense' has produced two divergent sense developments: adjectival 'frequent' and adverbial 'often' in the western areas, and 'closely following', whence 'soon', in the eastern ones, where *sarri arte* 'until soon' is a common parting phrase on a par with 'see you soon' in English.]

Frequency adverbs can be created ad libitum with the help of the suffix *-bider*, etymologically a dative plural of the noun *bide* 'way'. It can be applied to numerals above 1, and also to certain quantifiers, for example, *zenbat*, *hainbat*, *hainbeste*, *asko*, *aski*, *gutxi*, and so on. Always written separately, the suffix may well be evolving toward the status of a noun. Examples are *bi bider* 'two times' (not, of course, **bider bi*), *hiru bider zazpi* 'three times seven', *mila bider* 'a thousand times', *zenbat bider* 'how many times', and *asko bider* 'many times' (again, not **bider asko*).

20.1.2.3 Adverbs of Duration

Adverbs of duration are

luzaro	for a long time, at great length
laburki	briefly

These adverbs, in fact, fall under the broad category of manner adverbs, for which see chapter 11.

20.1.3 Noun-Based Time Adverbials

Usually, an adverbial of time or duration has as its nucleus a noun denoting a time interval. The main instances of such nouns are *mende* 'century', *gizaldi* 'generation' (also 'century'), *urte* 'year', *hil* 'month' (also *hilabete*), *aste* 'week', *egun* 'day', *gau* 'night', *ordu* 'hour' (in the northern dialects *oren*), *minutu* 'minute', *segundu* 'second', *une* 'moment', and *memento* 'moment'.

Some nouns express relative time: *bezpera* 'eve', 'the previous day' (also *aurreko egun*); *biharamun* 'the following day' (also *hurrengo egun*); *biharamunago* 'the second following day'. These can be combined with a genitive phrase, or, in the case of a verbal noun, the adnominal: *igandearen bezpera* (*MEIG* VII, 97) 'the day before Sunday'; *ezkoneguna, ondo izanaren biharamuna* (cf. Oihenarte, *Prov.* 155) 'the wedding day (is) the first day after being all right'; *hiltzeko bezpera* 'the day before dying'. Unsurprisingly, the noun *biharamun* also means 'hangover'.

It may be useful at this point to recall that, unlike adverbs, adverbials denoting location in time must be overtly marked for the inessive case, or, in the northern dialects, the instrumental, as follows: *gau batean* (or *gau batez*) '(on) one night', *egun bero-bero batean* (. . . *batez*) 'on a very warm day', *Eguberri bezpera gauean* 'on the night of Christmas Eve', *biharamunean* '(on) the next day', *biharamun goizean* '(on) the next morning'.

In section 4.1.3.4 it was observed that the notion of posteriority can be expressed by the forms *ondoan* or *ondotik*, to which may be added *ondoren*: *batzarraren ondoan* 'after the meeting', *euri ondoko eguzkia* 'the sun after the rain', *bata bestearen ondotik* 'one after the other', *Mitxelenaren ondoren* 'after Mitxelena'.

But, when *after* is replaceable in English by *after a lapse of* or *at the end of* it is aptly rendered instead by *buruan* 'at the head' governing the genitive: *laurehun urteren buruan* (*MEIG* V, 25) 'after four hundred years', *bederatzi urte hauen buruan* (Etxaniz, *Antz.* 74) 'after these nine years', *egun batzuen buruan* (Jgs 14:8) 'after a few days', *azterketa nekagarrien buruan* (*MEIG* VIII, 157 = *MIH* 371) 'at the end of tiring investigations'.

Another location noun applicable to time is *barru* 'interior'. Preceded by a phrase measuring length of time, its inessive *barruan*, or more commonly the bare form *barru*, expresses 'within': *hiru hilabete barruan* (B. Enbeita, 136) 'within three months', *beste bi hilabete barruan* (Etxaide, *J.J.* 54, changed to *barru* in subsequent editions) 'within two more months', *berrehun urte barru* (*MEIG* I, 56 = *MIH* 132) 'within two hundred years', *egun gutxi barru* (*MEIG* IX, 99) 'within not many days'. The time phrase in this construction is often put into the genitive: *egun gutxiren barruan* (*TB* 232; Bilintx, 130) 'within not many days', *zazpi egunen barruan* (Jgs 14:12) 'within seven days', *ordu gutxiren barru* (Uztapide, in *B.Tx. 62*, 88) 'within not many hours'.

20.1.4 Noun-Based Adverbials of Duration

(For noun-based adverbials of frequency, see section 20.3.3.)

Adverbials of duration take one of three forms: the definite inessive, the indefinite instrumental, or, in combination with a stative main verb, the absolutive form. This function of the inessive appears to be an exclusive feature of the southern dialects. Some examples follow:

(3) a. Hemen lan egiten dut egunero zortzi edo hamar orduan. (*LBB* 80)
Here I work every day for eight or ten hours.
b. Mamia behar da zuritu . . . eta ur berotan eduki hogeita lau orduan. (Iturriaga, *Dial.* 107)
The flesh must be peeled and kept in hot water for twenty-four hours.
c. Eskritura Santak ez digu esaten orduko gizonak zergatik hainbeste urtean bizi izaten ziren. (*TZ* I, 19)
Holy Scripture does not tell us why the people at that time lived for so many years. (Compare *hainbeste urtetan* 'in so many years'.)

The northern dialects make use of the indefinite instrumental, common also in the literary usage of the south:

(4) a. Zenbait minutuz ez du inork txintik ateratzen. (*MEIG* IX, 110)
For a few minutes no one utters a sound.
b. Ehun eta hogeita hamazazpi urtez bizi izan zen Ismael. (Gn 25:17)
Ismael lived for a hundred and thirty-seven years.
c. Hantxe egon zen berrogei egunez eta berrogei gauez. (Ex 24:18; Ker.)
He stayed there for forty days and forty nights.

With a stative main verb, the plain absolutive is possible:

(5) a. Ordu laurden bat eduki nauzu hor kanpoan. (Atxaga, *Obab.* 64)
You have kept me out there for a quarter of an hour.
b. Zu gabe orain ez nuke nahi minutu bat ere bizi. (Xalbador, *Ezin B.* 58)
Without you I wouldn't want to live now even for one minute.

When the nouns *aste* 'week', *ordu* 'hour', and *urte* 'year' appear inside adverbials of duration, instead of the numeral *bat*, speakers of the southern dialects prefer to use a suffix *-bete*, derived from the adjective *bete* 'full':

(6) a. Astebetean besterik ez nuen lanik egin Operan. (Labayen, *Su Em.* 208)
I worked in the Opera for not more than one week.
b. Handik astebetera Ameriketarako bidea prestatu zioten. (*LBB* 30)
One week from then they arranged her trip to America.
c. Handik ordubete ingurura, beste batek berriro esan zuen: . . . (Lk 22:59)
About one hour from then, someone else said again: . . .
d. Nik Parisen urtebetez erakutsi dut soziolinguistika. (*MEIG* IX, 81)
I have taught sociolinguistics in Paris for one year.

Accordingly, we get the following paradigm with *epe*, 'term', 'period':

ordubeteko epean	within a term of one hour
egun bateko epean	within a term of one day

astebeteko epean	within a term of one week
hilabeteko epean	within a term of one month
urtebeteko epean	within a term of one year
mende bateko epean	within a term of one century

Although in *hilabete* 'month' the suffix *bete* is frozen (*zenbat hilabete?* 'how many months?'), it nevertheless also retains the meaning 'one month': *hilabete iraun zuen* 'it lasted one month'. Therefore both *hilabeteko epea* and *hilabete bateko epea* occur.

Duration adverbials consisting of an inessive time phrase followed by the adverb *zehar* were mentioned in section 4.1.3.2. Examples are *urtean zehar* 'throughout the year', *urte luzeetan zehar* 'all through long years', and *hiru hilabetetan zehar* 'all through three months'. This use of *zehar* is unknown in the northern dialects.

The duration of a state still lasting at the time of speaking can be focalized by placing the duration adverbial in an existential frame, using intransitive *izan* 'to be' in the southern dialects and impersonally construed transitive **edun* 'to have' in the northern dialects. The state concerned is commonly expressed by a finite subordinate clause with the complementizer *-LA*. First, here are some examples from the southern dialects:

(7) a. Noiztik ezagutzen dut? Urteak dira. (*LBB* 90)
Since when do I know her? It has been years.
b. Zenbat denbora da erotuta zabiltzala? (Iraola, 96)
How long is it that you have been walking around crazy?
c. Badira hiru egun nirekin dabiitzala. (Mt 15:32; *Lau Eb.*)
It is three days that they have been walking with me.
d. Aspaldiko Austin! Urteak dira elkar ikusi ez dugula. (*G.* 191)
Austin old chum! It has been years that we haven't seen each other.

Now, here are some examples with **edun*, mainly from the northern dialects:

(8) a. Zenbat denbora du ifernuko pena horietan zaudela? (Ax. 602)
How long is it that you have been in those pains of hell?
b. Hamabost egun badu hemen garela. (Larzabal, *Hiru* 30)
It is fifteen days that we have been here.
c. Hamazazpi urte badu ez dudala ikusi. (Lapitze, 195)
It is seventeen years that I haven't seen him.
d. Ni hemen nagoela zazpi urte badu. (Garate, *E.E.* 136)
It is seven years that I have been here.
e. Hamazazpi urte ditu bidetan eskale dabilela. (Etxaniz, *Antz.* 89)
It is seventeen years that she has been walking on the roads as a beggar.

Notice that the main verb in such examples is usually singular (*du*), except in (8e), which stems from a southern author.

20.1.5 Telling How Long Ago

For specifying the time depth of an event, that is, telling how long ago something happened, Basque makes use of the same existential frame employed to express the duration of a state still present (section 20.1.4), using intransitive *izan* in the southern dialects and impersonal **edun* in the northern ones, as illustrated by the following examples:

(9) a. Aitona hil zela bi urte badira. (*G.* 364)
  It is two years ago that Grandfather died.
 b. Bada ordubete esan diodala. (Labayen, *Su Em.* 167)
  It is an hour ago that I told him so.
 c. Hamasei bat urte dira liburua argitaratu nuela. (*LBB* 285)
  It is about sixteen years ago that I published the book.

(10) a. Laurogeita lau urte badu zendu zela. (Oxobi, 21)
  It is eighty-four years ago that he passed away.
 b. Gu biak esposatu ginela baditu hamabost urte. (Mattin, 99)
  It is fifteen years ago that we two got married.

When the time specification does not figure as the main predicate of the sentence but functions adverbially, subordinate clauses with *-la*, as discussed in section 20.8.1, will appear with the verb *dela* or its plural *direla* for the users of *izan*, and the verb *duela* or its plural *dituela* for the users of **edun*:

(11) a. Orain dela 30 urte elkarrekin jan genuen harako zoko hartan. (*G.* 191)
  We ate together thirty years ago in such and such a spot.
 b. Oraindik egun asko ez dela, gizon bat gelditu dute bi guardak. (Iraola, 39)
  Not yet many days ago, two guards stopped a man.
 c. Orain direla hogeita hamar bat urte hasi ginen euskaldunok batasunaren bila. (Oskillaso, *Kurl.* 9)
  About thirty years ago we Basques set out on the search for unity.

(12) a. Duela aste bat amak esan dit: ... (Aintziart, 94)
  A week ago my mother said to me: ...
 b. Duela gutxi bilera bat izan zen. (*MEIG* VII, 130)
  A short time ago there was a meeting.
 c. Gauzek, ... dituela berrogeita hamar mende bezala diraute. (J. Etchepare, *Bur.* 164)
  The things ... remain like fifty centuries ago.

In the presence of a time expression specifying the departure point from which to count, such as *orain* 'now' in (11a), the subordinate verb form in *-la* can be omitted. The resulting ambiguity is clarified by the tense of the main verb—for example,

orain ehun urte	a hundred years ago/a hundred years from now
orain urteak	years ago/years from now
gaur zortzi	a week ago/a week from today
gaur hamabost	two weeks ago/two weeks from today

20.2 Time Clauses Based on the Noun *ordu*

As Mitxelena was well aware of by 1976 (see Villasante 1976, 102), several types of time clauses, finite and nonfinite, are produced by *ordu* ellipsis: the noun *ordu* 'time' is deletable when followed by a locative case ending, provided there is a directly preceding constituent for this ending to attach to: a relative clause or an adnominal modifier. Thus *ordu* ellipsis readily accounts for forms like *lehenbizikoan* 'at first'.

20.2.1 The Noun *ordu* and Its Paradigm

In its noncountable use the noun *ordu* 'time' is common to all dialects, although the northern ones in some contexts prefer the word *tenore*. The countable sense of *ordu* 'hour' (*zenbat ordu?* 'how many hours?', cf. section 4.2) will play no part in this chapter. Incidentally, length of time is conveyed by *ordu* in its countable sense only; otherwise, the term *denbora* is used, as in *zenbat denbora?* 'how long?' (see examples 7b and 8a in section 20.1.4).

The noun *ordu* possesses a peculiarity not shared with any of its near synonyms (*denbora*, *tenore*, *garai*, *une*, etc.). On a par with the English noun *time*, its definite locative forms retain deictic force: for example, *orduan* 'at the time', that is, 'at that time'.

The last phrase, to all intents and purposes, serves as the functional equivalent of the English temporal adverb *then* (or, for that matter, French *alors*). Moreover, nontemporal uses of *orduan*, where it means 'in that case', 'therefore', are run-of-the-mill according to G. Garate, who at the same time condemns these as barbarisms (Garate, *Erd.* 245). Instances of this are easily found in 20th-century texts representing the Guipuzcoan colloquial:

(13) a. Edariak galdua dago.—Orduan oker dabil? (Soroa Lasa, *Bar.* 53)
He has been ruined by drink.—Then he walks crookedly?
b. Egunak hemen pasatzen, orduan? (*LBB* 37)
Spending some days here then?
c. Zer behar du orduan? (Labayen, *Su Em.* 167)
What does he need then?

Other locative case forms of *ordu* are *ordutik* (or *ordudanik*) 'since then'; *ordura* 'to then' (always combined with a preceding elative, unless followed by *arte*: *ordura arte*, 'until then'); and *orduraino* 'until then' (more commonly *ordu arte*).

Finally, there is the adnominal allative *ordurako* as well as the plain adnominal *orduko* (in the northern dialects also *ordukotz*, an archaic instrumental), which, while allowing the meaning 'for then' (i.e., 'for that time'), usually mean 'by then'.

20.2.2 Finite Time Clauses: Conjunctions *-nean*, *-neko*, and So On

Finite time clauses are characterized by the occurrence of certain conjunctions suffixed onto the subordinate verb. These are: *-nean* 'when'; *-netik* 'from the moment that', 'since'; *-neko* or *-nerako* 'by the time that' or 'as soon as'; *-neraino* or *-n arte* 'until'. Morphophonemically, the initial *-n* of these suffixes behaves like the relativizer *-N*, that is, *da* + *-nean* > *denean*, *du* + *-nean* > *duenean*, *duk* + *-nean* > *duanean*, *zen* + *-nean* > *zenean*. Examples of such clauses are

(14) a. Kalera ateratzen denean ez du euririk ari. (Urretabizkaia, *Sat.* 21)
When he goes out into the street it is not raining. (For *ari du*, see section 16.5.1.1.)
b. Euria ari duenean ez naiz sekula ateratzen. (Urretabizkaia, *Asp.* 80)
When it is raining I never go out.
c. Krispin harrapatu zutela ikasi zuenean, poztu zen epailea. (Zapirain, *M.* 195)
The judge was happy when he learned that they had caught Crispin.

(15) a. Nirekin mintzatu zinenetik, zure ugazaita hiltzeko asmoa hartu zenuen. (Garate, *Alaba* 97)
From the moment you spoke with me, you had in mind to kill your stepfather.
b. Gure ama hil zenetik ez nuen nik negarrik egin. (Garate, *Iz.B.* 85)
I hadn't cried since my mother died. (For *gure ama* 'my mother', see section 6.1.3.)

(16) a. Apaiza etorri zeneko, ez zen gauza ezertarako. (*LBB* 56)
By the time the priest came, he wasn't fit for anything.
b. Sendatu nintzeneko, herriko elizara eraman ninduten. (Landart, 12)
As soon as I was cured, they carried me to the village church.

[*N.B.* Note the common expression *dagoeneko* 'by the time it is', that is, 'by now'.]

(17) a. Baina hurrengo aldiz ikusi nuenerako, Karmen ezkontzeko bezperatan zegoen. (Urretabizkaia, *Asp.* 53)
But by the time I saw her next, Carmen was on the eve of getting married.
b. Amaitu dutenerako beren barrenek atseden handi bat hartu dute. (Eizagirre, 222)
As soon as they had finished, their minds experienced a great relief.

(18) a. Umeak beren hegalez ibiltzeko on direneraino ... (*P.Ad.* 42)
Until the young are fit to travel by their own wings ...
b. Zulatu lurra, ... zeruaren ametsik ez deneraino, infernu-kiratsa deneraino ... (Azurmendi, 64)
Dig the earth, ... until there is no dream of heaven, until there is the stench of hell ...
c. Utzi lo egiten nahi duen arte. (Sg 2:7, 3:5, 8:4)
Let her sleep as long as she wants to.

d. Aita galdu genuen arte, artzaintza izan zen ene lan nagusia. (Xalbador, *Odol.* 29)
Until the time we lost our father, shepherding had been my main job.

(For the apparently double meaning of *arte* 'until' and 'as long as', see section 20.4.5.)

There also is a suffix *-nera* 'to when', always used with a preceding elative; see section 20.2.1. Examples are

(19) a. Gaurtik datorrenera. (Azkue, *DVEF* II, 79)
From today to when he comes.
b. Zenbat denbora izan zen ihes egin zenienetik hil zenituenera? (Amuriza, *Emea* 44)
How long was it from when you fled them to when you killed them?

As the preceding examples suggest, the canonical position of a time clause is preceding the main clause. It is, however, also possible for it to follow, or even to occur in focus position inside the main clause, as in (20d):

(20) a. Diru asko al zeraman bart etxetik irten zenean? (Garate, *Esku* 158)
Was she carrying a lot of money when she went out of the house last night?
b. Ibilaldi hori zinez gustatzen zitzaidan, bereziki denbora ederra zenean. (Landart, 79)
I really liked that walk, especially when the weather was nice.
c. Ez zuen lorik egiten janzki hura bere etxeko eskaileretan aurkitu zuenetik. (Lertxundi, *Urtero* 55)
He did not sleep since he found that suit on the stairs of his house.
d. Egia garratz horiek gibeleko mina duzunean bakarrik esaten dituzu. (*MEIG* IX, 108)
You say those bitter truths only when you have a bilious attack.

Although clauses of this kind tend to be verb-final, postverbal constituents are not totally excluded:

(21) a. Pasatzen naizenean zure leihopetik . . . (From the fisherman's song "Isil isilik dago," *Xaramela* 174)
When I pass underneath your window . . .
b. Geure asaba zaharren odola daukagun arte zainetan, . . . (K. Enbeita, 44)
As long as we have the blood of our ancient forefathers in our veins, . . .

There is convincing evidence that time clauses of the type shown in this section are derived from relative clauses by means of *ordu* ellipsis. First, let us look at the *Dialogues basques*, an 1857 work in which the same Spanish text is translated into Guipuzcoan by Iturriaga and into Biscayan by Uriarte. Iturriaga uses *-nean* clauses quite often, but on three occasions he employs a relative clause construction with the head *ordu*: *Berotzen asten dan orduan* (p. 57) "cuando empieza a calentarse" (when it begins to heat up); *Gatzatu dan orduan* (p. 87) "cuando se ha cuajado" (when it is curdled); *Gatz au chit urtu dan orduan* (p. 88) "cuando esta sal se haya derretido enteramente" (when this salt is completely dissolved). Uriarte, however, employs *danian*, Biscayan for *denean*, throughout. Iturriaga's *orduan* constructions, converted into Batua morphology, are still quite acceptable today.

Furthermore, a century later, N. Etxaniz's work *Lur berri billa* shows the following two clauses on the same page:

(22) a. Apaizak elkarrenganako baimena eman zien ordutik... (*LBB* 121)
From the time that the priest had given them permission to unite ...
b. Baina orain, apaizak baimena eman zienetik... (*LBB* 121)
But now, since the priest had given them permission ...

Finally, we may observe that, no matter how frequent *-neko* clauses are, their synonyms containing a relative clause followed by *orduko* also keep appearing:

(23) a. Kotxetik atera nintzen orduko, alkatea etorri zen. (Lasarte, *Gordean* 303)
By the time I had gotten out of the car, the mayor had come.
b. Neskak, ikusten duen orduko, hala esango dit: ... (Zapirain, *M.* 90)
The girl, as soon as she sees him, will say this to me: ...
c. Arretaz ekin dio lanari, etxeratu zen orduko. (T. Agirre, *Uzt.* 29)
He set to work with care, as soon as he got home.

20.2.3 The Participle Suffixes *-takoan* and *-(r)ikoan* 'after'

Example (24a) shows that (22a) admits a participial counterpart (24b), from which (24c) can be derived by *ordu* ellipsis:

(24) a. Txerria hildako astea eta ezkondutako urtea, onenak. (Garmendia, 60)
The year the pig has been slaughtered and the year one has married are the best.
b. Gatz hau urtutako orduan, gazitzen da orobat beste aldetik. (Cf. Iturriaga, *Dial.* 88)
At the time when the salt is dissolved, one salts it likewise on the other side.
c. Gatz hau urtutakoan, gazitzen da orobat beste aldetik.
Once this salt is dissolved, one salts it likewise on the other side.

Since this construction is based on the stative form (with *-ta* equivalent to *-(r)ik* used outside Guipuzcoa) of the perfect participle, the time reference of the head *orduan* is to the state resulting from the completion of the action of the verb in the subordinate clause, and is therefore posterior to the action itself. This fact explains how the suffixes *-takoan* and *-(r)ikoan* function as equivalents of the English conjunction *after*, as seen in the following examples:

(25) a. Etxera etorritakoan ez haserretu behintzat. (*TOE* II, 54)
At least, do not get angry after coming home.
b. Zu eseritakoan nire txanda izango da. (*TOE* II, 246)
After you have sat down it will be my turn.

c. Hori gero etorriko da etsaiak oinperatu eta zanpatutakoan. (Eizagirre,16)
   That will come later after the enemies have been trampled and crushed.

d. Iraultza bukatutakoan, zin egiten dinat antolatuko dugula hori ere. (Amuriza, *Hil* 210)
   After the revolution has ended, I swear to yoù that we will arrange that too.

Use of the suffix -*(r)ikoan* appears to be restricted to the southern part of Biscay:

(26) Aitaren bihotz honek bihotza galdurikoan, . . . (Arrese Beitia, *Olerk*. 162)
After this father-heart has lost its heart, . . .

[*N.B.* A suffix -*(r)ikakoan*, although theoretically possible, does not seem to be attested.]

20.2.4 Verbal Nouns with the Suffix -*koan* 'when'

As observed in section 19.2.5, the noun *ordu* can be the head of an infinitival relative:

(27) Ez da hau lo egiteko ordua. (Duvoisin, *L.Ed.* 74)
This is not the time to sleep.

When the head *ordu* is case-marked with the definite singular inessive, as in *ordaintzeko orduan* (*LBB* 40) 'at the time to pay', the Guipuzcoan dialect allows *ordu* ellipsis, giving rise to a suffix -*koan* with the meaning 'when', admissible also in the standard language. Examples are

(28) a. Zortzi lagun ginen mahaian eguerditan, eta afaitzekoan bi besterik ez ginen agertu. (Orixe, *Q.A.* 48)
   We were eight fellows at the table at noon, and at the time to eat dinner no more than two of us appeared.

b. Mogel hartuko dut abiatzekoan. (*MEIG* IV, 130)
   When starting out, I will take Mogel.

c. Hitz-elkartze berrietan hautatzekoan, bi indar ari zaizkigu beti lanean. (*MEIG* VIII, 148)
   When choosing among new compounds, we always have two forces at work.

20.2.5 The Suffix -*rakoan* 'when going to'

According to section 5.1, mere addition of the adnominal suffix -*ko* will turn an allative adverbial into an adjectival modifier of a following noun phrase. In consequence, to express the concept 'it is time for us to go to the church', Basque has no need for a verb like *joan* 'to go', as *Elizarako ordua dugu* (Etxaniz, *Antz*., 46) will do. Now, phrases like *elizarako ordua* when put into the inessive allow *ordu* ellipsis in all dialects, whence *elizarakoan* 'when going to church'. Similarly, we have

etxerakoan	when going home, on the way home
harakoan	when going there, on the way there

honakoan	when coming here, on the way back
lotarakoan	when going to sleep
mahairakoan	when going to table
oherakoan	when going to bed
zureganakoan	when going to you

Since verbal nouns can also take the allative, as in *hiltzera doa* 'he is going to die' (section 16.5.6), we likewise get *hiltzerako orduan* (Argaiñaratz, 228), and then by *ordu* ellipsis *hiltzerakoan*, glossed by S. Pouvreau as 'allant mourir', that is, 'when going to die'. Examples can be found from Axular up to the present day:

(29) a. Hiltzerakoan zure galde egin zuen. (Ax. 329)
When about to die, he asked for you.
b. Hiltzerakoan bakarrik aitortu zuen hori bere semeari. (Barbier, *Sup*. 231)
Only when about to die did he confess that to his son.
c. Azienda erosterakoan ... (Duvoisin, *Dial*. 94)
When going to buy cattle ... (French original: "Quand on va acheter le bétail")
d. Liburu bat erosterakoan, hautatzen jakin behar duzu. (Lertxundi, *Urtero* 124)
When about to buy a book, you have to know how to choose.
e. Gizonak utzi egin zuen, Marthak seme bat edukitzerakoan. (Garate, *NY* 51)
The man left her when Martha was going to have a son.

In modern usage, the original meaning of *-rakoan* 'when going to' tends to get blurred into plain 'when', especially among speakers who lack the suffix *-koan* in their active vocabularies. Thus one finds

(30) a. Malkoak zerizkion hori esaterakoan. (Garate, *Hades* 53)
Tears streamed from her when she said that.
b. Bizkor ibili zen motelera itzultzerakoan. (Atxaga, *Z.H.* 78)
She walked quickly when going back to the motel.
c. Setatsuaz hitzegiterakoan, zakar aritzeko joera daukat. (Atxaga, *Behi* 152)
When talking about Setatsua, I have a tendency to be harsh.

20.2.6 Instrumental Clauses Governed by the Postposition *gero*

In section 20.1.2.1, nonfinite instrumental clauses governed by the postposition *gero*, its instrumental *geroz* (preferred in the north), or its elative *geroztik* were already discussed in sufficient detail. Their finite counterparts, also expressing posteriority, will be presented in this section. In these, the instrumental ending is tagged onto a final relativized verb form, as seen in the following examples:

(31) a. Alargundu zenez gero, elizatik aldegin gabe bizi zen. (*TB* 21)
After she became a widow, she lived inseparable from the church.

b. Ez digu inork ezer ostu ni hemen naizenez gero. (*TOE* I, 290)
Nobody has stolen anything from us since I have been here.

c. Jesuiten ikastetxera eraman nuenez gero asko aldatu da. (*TOE* III, 169)
After I took him to the school of the Jesuits, he (has) changed a lot.

The following examples have *geroztik*:

(32) a. Hartueman handia izan zuen aitaginarrebarekin Mikelek ezkondu zenez geroztik. (T. Agirre, *Uzt.* 17)
Michael had a lot of contact with his father-in-law after he got married.

b. Itzulpen ugari izan dugu euskal literatura hasi zenez geroztik. (*MEIG* IV, 40)
We have had plenty of translations since Basque literature began.

Just like English *since*, the postposition *gero* also has a causal sense:

(33) a. Hitzegiten hasi naizenez gero, guztia esan behar dizuet. (*TOE* III, 181)
Since I have begun to speak, I must tell yoû everything.

b. Lur beraren umeak direnez geroz, zuzen berak dituzte. (J. Etxepare, *Bur.* 59)
Since they are children of the same earth, they have the same rights.

Except for these two, the preceding examples can all be derived by means of *ordu* ellipsis, as example (34) makes clear. Relatives using *orduz*, however, although perfectly grammatical, are much rarer in practice than those featuring *orduan*, *ordutik*, or *orduko*. Perhaps for that reason, speakers may have lost awareness of the connection between *-nez gero* and *orduz gero*, which would also explain, in part, the emergence of the causal use shown in examples (33a,b). At any rate, the special status of *-nez gero* clauses warrants treating these separately instead of relegating them to section 20.2.2, where they belong by right of origin.

(34) Davitek zeraman bizia, Saül etsaitzat agertzen zitzaion orduz geroz, osoki zen urrikalgarria. (Larréguy I, 286)
The life David led was very pitiable since the time that Saul appeared to him as an enemy.

20.2.7 Nonfinite Time Clauses with *orduko* and *ordurako*

Among the various case forms of *ordu*, only the adnominals *orduko* and, albeit to a lesser extent, *ordurako*, govern nonfinite clauses. As usual, these clauses must be based on the perfect participle, as the unmarked form of the verb. The meaning of the *orduko* and *ordurako* constructions equals that of *-neko* clauses, that is, ‘by the time that . . .’ or ‘as soon as . . .’.

The nonfinite clause may contain its own explicit subject, as in (35a,b):

(35) a. Hi jaio orduko, banekizkian nik gauza hauek. (Urruzuno, *E.Z.* 111)
By the time yoú were born, I already knew these things.

b. Nire arrebatxoa jaio orduko konturatu nintzen ni nintzela amaren kuttuna. (Garate, *Hades* 58)
As soon as my little sister was born, I realized that I was Mother's favorite.

When the subject of the subordinate clause is not overtly expressed, it is usually the same as that of the main clause, as happens in examples (36a,b,c). Otherwise, the subject may be impersonal, as in (37a), or identical to the discourse topic, as in (37b).

(36) a. Atea zabaldu orduko, ama lurrean dakuste. (Etxaniz, *Antz.* 96)
As soon as they open the door, they see (their) mother (lying) on the ground.
b. Haurrak elkarrekin euskaraz mintzo hauteman orduko, gaztigatzen gintuen. (Xalbador, *Odol.* 26)
As soon as he caught us children speaking Basque with each other, he punished us.
c. Laurak oihu egin zuen ni sartzen ikusi orduko. (Atxaga, *Obab.* 246)
Laura shouted as soon as she saw me come in.

(37) a. Zopa ekarri orduko hasten da. (*MEIG* IX, 108)
As soon as the soup is brought in, he begins.
b. Eskuaz hunkitu orduko gaitzak uzten du. (Lapitze, 156)
As soon as he touches him with the hand, the ailment leaves him.

Nonfinite clauses with *ordurako* are unknown in the north, and no longer current in the south either. The following examples date from the 19th century:

(38) a. Mutilak esan zion hartu ordurako: . . . (Bilintx, 176)
As soon as he had taken it, the boy said to him: . . .
b. Zuhaitzen orriak ihartzen hasi ordurako, andre Luzia ihartu zen. (Agirre, *A.L.* 119)
As soon as the leaves of the trees began to wither, Lady Lucia withered.
c. Ezagutu ordurako maitatu ziren biak. (Agirre, *A.L.* 134)
The two loved each other as soon as they knew each other.

20.3 Time Expressions Based on the Noun *aldi*

The noun *aldi* occasionally adopted by purists as a substitute for the loanword *denbora* 'time', properly means 'interval of time', 'period'. It is a term of common occurrence, also serving where English makes use of more specific designations, as in the following examples:

sinfoniaren aldiak	the parts of the symphony
ilargiaren aldiak	the phases of the moon
partidaren bigarren aldia	the second half of the match

lau aldiko motorra	a four-stroke engine
noren aldia da?	whose turn is it?

There is a synchronic process of *aldi* ellipsis: Given the presence of a suitable premodifier, a head noun *aldi* can be optionally deleted when followed only by a determiner or quantifier, preferably in the inessive case. There are also some examples in the instrumental case, and with *hurren* or *hurrengo* 'next' as premodifiers the location noun *arte* may appear, yielding the meaning 'until next time'. Apart from *hurren*, suitable premodifiers are *beste* 'other', adnominals, and relative clauses.

Interestingly, Old Castilian too had a rule of *vez* ellipsis: *cada que el golpe oye* 'every time when he hears the blow', *cada que quisieres* 'any time you would want' (Metzeltin 1979, 95).

20.3.1 Time Specifications Based on *aldi*

Inessive phrases with *aldi* as the head can serve to specify location in time, in which event the length of the period denoted by *aldi* becomes irrelevant, so that it can be glossed as 'time' or 'occasion'. Time specifications of this type have a crucial property: it is that the head noun *aldi* itself is dispensable when preceded by suitable modifier. Some typical examples are as follows:

behingo batean = behingo aldi batean	once upon a time, in one moment
beste batean = beste aldi batean	at another time
beste batzuetan = beste aldi batzuetan	at some other times
besteetan = beste aldietan	at the other times
gaurkoan = gaurko aldian	on today's occasion, today
gaurko honetan = gaurko aldi honetan	on this occasion of today
geroko batean = geroko aldi batean	on a later occasion
halako batean = halako aldi batean	on a certain occasion
honelakoetan = honelako aldietan	on occasions such as these
horrelakoetan = horrelako aldietan	on occasions such as those
halakoetan = halako aldietan	on such occasions
hurrengoan = hurrengo aldian	on the next occasion, the next time
lehengoan = lehengo aldian	the other day, lately
lehengo batean = lehengo aldi batean	on a recent occasion
oraingoan = oraingo aldian	at the present occasion, at present
oraingo honetan = oraingo aldi honetan	at this present time

With instrumental phrases (English *for*) *aldi* ellipsis is virtually obligatory:

behingoz = behingo aldiz	for once
gaurkoz = gaurko aldiz	for today
lehen(da)bizikoz = lehen(da)biziko aldiz	for the first time
oraingoz = oraingo aldiz	for the time being, for the present

The parting phrase *hurren arte* (or *hurrengo arte*) 'until next time' also results from *aldi* ellipsis.

20.3.2 Duration Adverbials Based on *aldi*

Consistent with its meaning 'interval of time', *aldi* can head adverbials of duration. There are four case forms to choose from: inessive, instrumental, allative adnominal, or plain adnominal. Thus *aldi batean*, *aldi batez*, *aldi baterako*, and *aldi bateko* all mean 'for a while'. The latter form is also used to modify noun phrases: *aldi bateko lana* 'work for a while'; *aldi luzeko lana* 'work for a long while'.

20.3.3 Frequency Adverbials Based on *aldi*

As was mentioned in section 20.1.2.2, frequency adverbials based on numerals can be formed with the suffix *-bider*, as in *bi bider* 'twice'. At least as common, if not more so, are phrases involving the noun *aldi*, the case marking used being the indefinite inessive or instrumental. For 'once', however, only *behin* appears, not **aldi batetan* or **aldi batez*.

Inessive frequency adverbials, unlike instrumental ones, allow *aldi* ellipsis, as long as there remains a formative for the inessive ending to attach to. Thus, we have

bi aldiz	bi alditan	bitan	twice
hiru aldiz	hiru alditan	hirutan	three times
lau aldiz	lau alditan	lautan	four times
bost aldiz	bost alditan	bostetan	five times

[*N.B.* The forms *bostetan* 'five times' and *hamaiketan* 'eleven times' are often used in the meaning 'quite often'.]

Inessive frequency adverbials not based on numerals can also undergo *aldi* ellipsis:

anitzetan = anitz alditan	many times, often
askotan = aldi askotan	many times, often
bakanetan = aldi bakanetan	few times, seldom
batzuetan = aldi batzuetan	some times, sometimes
frankotan = aldi frankotan	plenty of times, quite often
gehienetan = aldi gehienetan	most times, mostly
gutxitan = aldi gutxitan	few times, seldom
guztietan = aldi guztietan	on all the occasions
sarritan = aldi sarritan	frequent times, frequently
zenbaitetan = zenbait alditan	some times, sometimes
zenbatetan = zenbat alditan	how many times

As many of the examples show, even in the absence of a premodifier, modification by a quantifier is a sufficient condition for the noun *aldi* to be expendable.

20.3.4 Finite Clauses Identifying Occasions: Conjunctions Based on *aldi*

Finite subordinate clauses serving to specify the occasion or time frame of an action all end in the relativizer -*N* followed by an appropriate conjunction or suffix. These are *bat* 'once when'; -*etan* 'the times that', 'on the occasions when'; *bakoitzean* 'each time that'; *gehienetan* 'on most occasions that'; *guztietan* 'on all occasions that'; *bakanetan* 'on the rare occasions that'; and -*ero* 'on every occasion that'. One or more examples of each will be given as an illustration:

(39) a. Begiak luzatu zituen batean hiru gizon bere ondoan zutik ikusi zituen. (*TZ* I, 39)
Once when he lifted his eyes, he saw three men standing near him. (*zutik* 'erect')

b. Anginarekin ohean zegoen batean, anaiaren gelara sartu nintzen. (Urretabizkaia, *Asp*. 41)
Once when he lay in bed with tonsillitis, I went into my brother's room.

c. Erantzun diot nik ere, nire Jaungoikoak deitu didanetan? (Mendiburu, *Ot. Gai* II, 18)
Have I also answered Him, the times my God has called me?

d. Halaxe aurkitzen nuen, behintzat, nik, baserri hartan sartzen nintzenetan. (Jautarkol, *Ip*. 71)
That, at least, is how I found her, the times that I came into the farmhouse.

e. Badut orain, etxeratzen naizenetan, nora jo neure egarria berdintzeko. (*MEIG* VIII, 183)
I now have, the times I come home, a place to go in order to quench my thirst.

f. Guria egiten den bakoitzean, garbitu behar da azpia urarekin. (Iturriaga, *Dial*. 83)
Each time one makes butter, the ground must be cleaned with water.

g. Eztula egiten duen bakoitzean, badirudi kristal guztiak hautsi behar dituela. (Iraola, 23)
Each time he produces a cough, it seems he must break all the windowpanes.

h. Nire ametsetara etortzen zaren bakoitzean, beti zu gaixo. (Urretabizkaia, *Mait*. 47)
Each time you come into my dreams, you (are) always sick.

i. Umeei goxoak ematen zizkien zetorren gehienetan. (cf. Jautarkol, *Ip*. 45)
He gave sweets to the children most of the times he came.

j. Nik behintzat horrelakorik aski topatu dut liburua zabaldu dudan guztietan. (*MEIG* II, 94)
I, at least, have encountered plenty of such, all the times I have opened the book.

k. Esnatzen nintzen bakanetan, euriaren hotsa aditzen nuen.
The rare times I woke up, I heard the sound of the rain.

l. Lekunberrira joaten nintzenero, beti lelo bera zuen zapatariak. (Orixe, *Q.A.* 40)
Every time I went to Lecumberri, the cobbler always had the same babble.

m. Garrasi hirukoitz batez erantzun ohi zuen norbaitek proposamenen bat egiten zionero. (Atxaga, *Grl.* 92)
She was in the habit of answering with a triple shout every time that some one made her some kind of proposal.

Given that in all these examples insertion of the noun *aldi* in front of the conjunction leads to an acceptable relative without changing the meaning of the sentence, it is obvious that these constructions result from the process of *aldi* ellipsis. Moreover, examples with relatives where *aldi* is retained also occur in the literature:

(40) a. Sermoiak eta gauza onak aditzera joaten dira diren aldietan. (Mendiburu, *I.Arg.* I, 297)
They go to listen to sermons and good things on the occasions that they are there.

b. Burra egiten den aldi bakoitzean, behereak garbitu behar du urarekin. (Duvoisin, *Dial.* 83; compare example 39f)
Each time that one makes butter, the floor needs to be cleaned with water.

c. Ni iratzarri naizen aldi bakoitzean ametsetan aurkitu zaitut urduri samar. (Garate, *Leh.* 15)
Each time I woke up I found you quite restless, dreaming.

d. Esnatzen nintzen aldi bakanetan, euriaren hotsa aditzen nuen sabaian. (Atxaga, *Obab.* 245)
The rare times I woke up, I heard the sound of the rain on the ceiling.

e. Ikusten zaitudan aldiero, ahazten zaizkit beste gauza guztiak. (Bilintx, 193)
Every time that I see you, I forget all other things.

In principle, all conjunctions of this section can also occur together with participial relatives, as in

(41) Ni ikusitako bakoitzean, umea nola genuen galdetuko zidan. (Amuriza, in Lazkaotxiki II, 535)
Each time he saw me, he would ask me how our child was.

20.4 Temporal Use of Location Nouns

The location nouns *aurre* and *aitzin* both meaning 'frontside', can be used to express anteriority; *ondo* 'succession' and *oste* 'backside' posteriority; *arte* and *bitarte*, both meaning 'interval', delimitation in time. Appearing mainly in the inessive and sometimes in the elative case, they allow clausal complements. In some respects, they are similar to English conjunctions such as *before* and *after*, except for occurring at the end rather than the beginning of the clause.

By far the most common clausal complement takes the form of a nonfinite clause terminating in a perfect participle. Occasionally, nonfinite clauses ending in the adnominal form of the verbal noun, or even finite relatives, also appear as complements. Nominal complements also occur. In outline, their structure conforms to the pattern described for spatial use in chapter 4: absolutive complements for *arte* and *bitarte*, genitival complements for the others. The compound construction, however, is much more restricted here than in its spatial use, as many speakers only allow it with nonmodified nouns.

These location nouns and their properties will be discussed in the following sections one by one.

20.4.1 Anteriority Expressed with *aurrean* or *aurretik*

The location noun *aurre* belongs only to the western dialects: Guipuzcoan and Biscayan. For the purpose of expressing anteriority, some speakers prefer the inessive, others the elative. The literary language allows either form: *aurrean* or *aurretik*. The term *aurretik*, however, also means 'in advance': *egun batzuez* (or *batzuek*) *aurretik* 'a few days in advance'.

Examples with nominal complements are *lo aurrean* 'before sleep', *bazkari aurretik* 'before dinner', *Freuden aurretik* 'before Freud', and *gure gerrate aurretik* (Alzola, 113) 'before our war' (here many speakers require the genitive: *gure gerratearen aurretik*). Among the clausal complements, perfect participle clauses are the most common:

(42) a. Zer ari zen Jainkoa zeru-lurrak egin aurrean? (Orixe, *Aitork.* 315)
What was God doing before making heaven and earth?
b. Ez dut jango esateko dudana esan aurretik. (Gn 24:33)
I won't eat before saying what I have to say.

Examples constructed with a relative clause occur rather infrequently:

(43) a. Etzatera zihoazen aurrean, hiriko zahar-gazteek ... etxea inguratu zuten. (*TZ* I, 41)
Before they went to lie down, the men of the city, young and old, surrounded the house.
b. Gure arrebari hala esan omen zion, hil behar zuen aurrean: ... (Uztapide, *LEG* I, 31)
Before she was going to die, she (reportedly) spoke thus to my sister: ...

The construction with an adnominal verbal noun may by now well be obsolete:

(44) a. Zerura igotzeko aurrean, esku hau utzi zien. (Ubillos, 151)
Before ascending to heaven, he left them this power.
b. Ezkontzeko aurrean galdetu zuen Mikallak: ... (*G.* 260)
Before getting married, Mikalla asked: ...

Note finally the interesting diminutives *aurretxoan* and *aurretxotik*, which mean 'a little before', 'shortly before'.

20.4.2 Anteriority Expressed with *aitzin, aitzinean,* or *aitzinetik*

Geographically, *aitzin* is complementary to *aurre*; that is, its use is restricted to the eastern dialects. Three morphological options are available in denoting anteriority: the bare form *aitzin* (etymologically an inessive of *aitzi*, cf. *aitzitik* 'on the contrary'), the inessive *aitzinean*, or the elative *aitzinetik*. The last form, however, is foreign to the Labourdin dialect, except in the meaning 'in advance': *egun batzuez aitzinetik* 'a few days in advance'.

A noteworthy feature of the eastern dialects is that they lack syntactic compounding (see section 4.1.2). Therefore, only lexical compounds form an alternative to the genitival construction. By way of illustration, where the western dialects have two forrns: *bazkari aurrean* (syntactic) and *bazkalaurrean* (lexical), the eastern dialects must do with one: *bazkalaitzin(ean)* 'after lunch'.

Further examples with nominal complements are *gauerdi aitzin* 'before midnight', *negu aitzin* 'before the winter', and *ezteien aitzinetik* 'before the wedding'.

As to clausal complements, those based on the perfect participle are most common:

(45) a. Ehiza hil aitzin, jalerik ez gonbida! (Mattin, 109)
Do not invite eaters before killing the game!
b. Urrunetik ikusi zuteneko, hura hurbildu aitzin, hilen zutela hitzartu ziren. (Gn 37:18; *Biblia*)
As soon as they saw him from afar, before he came close, they agreed that they would kill him.
c. Ahariak ez du ardirik jokatu behar hiru urte bete aitzinean. (Duvoisin, *Lab.* 272)
A ram must cover no sheep before he is three years old.
d. Eritu aitzinetik ongi ezagutzen zuen bere senarra. (Cf. Irigaray, 185)
Before he fell ill, she knew her husband quite well.

The two other types of clausal complements are attested as well:

(46) a. Zahartzeko aitzinean entseatu naiz ongi bizitzera. (Ax. 186)
Before growing old, I have tried to lead a good life.
b. Ebaki behar da loratu den aitzinean. (Duvoisin, *Lab.* 95)
It must be cut before it has bloomed.

There also is a diminutive form: *aitzinttoan* 'a little before':

(47) Erromara heldu zen 1538 aitzinttoan. (Arradoy, *S.Fran.* 136)
He came to Rome a little before 1538.

20.4.3 Posteriority Expressed with *ondoren, ondoan,* or *ondotik*

With 'contiguity' as its basic meaning, the location noun *ondo* also serves to express succession in time, as already noted in section 4.1.3.4. Geographically speaking, there is a dichotomy: a western area comprising Biscay and most of Guipuzcoa employs the form *ondoren* (ostensibly a genitive, but historically a contraction of the archaic ablative *ondorean*, still surviving as a relic in Biscayan usage), while the remaining area makes use of the inessive *ondoan*. The elative *ondotik*, occurring mainly in the eastern regions, seems to be restricted to noun phrase complements: *gertakari horien ondotik* 'after those events', *zuzi luze baten ondotik* 'after a long trial', *egin duenaren ondotik* 'after what he has done'.

Of course, *ondoren* and *ondoan* likewise allow nominal complements: *iraultza ondoren* 'after the revolution', *Freuden ondoren* 'after Freud', *gure afariaren ondoan* 'after our supper', *Oiñatiko batzar ondoan* (*MEIG* VIII, 142) 'after the meeting in Oiñate', which many speakers would prefer to amend to *Oiñatiko batzarraren ondoan*.

As a rule, clausal complements make use of the perfect participle:

(48) a. Zerbait edan ondoren erraz berotzen dira gizonezkoak. (*TOE* II, 144)
After drinking something men get easily heated up.
b. Gure berri jakin ondoren, euskararen berri onak zabalduko ditu Europan. (*MEIG* VI, 48)
After learning about us, he will spread the good news about Basque in Europe.
c. Azkenean, egin ondoan, guztiak erretzen zituen. (Ax. 23)
At the end, after making them, he burned them all.
d. Batxilera egin ondoan, fabrikan hasi nintzen lanean. (*MEIG* VIII, 154)
After getting my high school diploma, I began to work in the factory.

Only two instances of relative clause complements have come to my notice:

(49) a. . . . neure superbiozko bestimendaz biluzi naizen ondoan . . . (Argaiñaratz, 91)
. . . after I have stripped myself of my garment of arrogance . . .
b. Piztu naizen ondoan, ordea, joango naiz Galileara. (Mt 26:32; Ur.)
After I have risen, however, I will go to Galilee.

Here too there is a diminutive form: *ondotxoan* 'a little after', 'shortly after'.

20.4.4 Posteriority Expressed with *ostean*

While the location nouns *atze* and *gibel* 'backside' have no temporal connotation, the inessive *ostean* of their Biscayan equivalent *oste* is actually one of the most common terms for 'after' in the Biscayan dialect and can be used in the literary standard as well. With nominal complements: *eguerdi ostean* 'after midday', *lo gozoaren ostean* 'after a nice sleep', *bazkariaren ostean* 'after the lunch', *bazkari ostean* or *bazkalostean* 'after lunch'.

Clausal complements require the perfect participle:

(50) a. Latinezko otoitz batzuek esan ostean, galdetu zion: . . . (Jautarkol, *Ip.* 60)
After saying a few Latin prayers, he asked him: . . .
b. Une luze batean itxaron ostean, brankako partetik kanpoko argia sartzen hasi zen. (Oskillaso, *Gab.At.* 164)
After they had waited a long time, outside light started to come in from the prow area.

20.4.5 Delimitation Expressed with *arte*

Time has come to complete and partially amend my earlier treatment of the temporal uses of the location noun *arte* 'interval' presented in section 4.1.3.6.

Besides the uninflected form *arte*, unemployed until well into the 18th century but now predominant, there also are inflected forms to be reckoned with: terminal *arteraino*; *arteino* (see section 20.5) with its phonetic variants *arteo*, *artino*, and *artio*; and inessive *artean*, the only form attested in *Refranes y Sentencias* of 1596 (= *R.S.*).

Up to the middle of the 20th century, according to the data in the *DGV*, all these forms could be used indiscriminately in the manner described in section 4.1.3.6: expressing the meaning 'as long as' or 'while' in a stative context (including continuous or habitual action) and the meaning 'until' in others. But during the latter half of the 20th century a new system arose in the western dialects and has imposed itself on southern Batua. In it, uninflected *arte*, and its by now rare alternatives *arteraino* and *arteino*, are used only to convey the meaning 'until', while inessive *artean* is reserved for the senses 'as long as' and 'while'. Our discussion of this system will start with *arte* and its various types of complements and then proceed to the syntax of *artean*.

As noted in section 4.1.3.6, there are two options for nominal complements of *arte*: syntactic compounding, as in *afari arte* 'until supper' and *afaltzeko ordu arte* 'until supper time', or else absolutive complements requiring a determiner: *ikusi zintudan eguna arte* 'until the day I saw you', *arratsaldeko bostak arte* 'until five P.M.'.

Clausal complements of *arte* can be finite, taking the shape of relative clauses, or nonfinite and based on the perfect participle:

(51) a. Ez zuten ezkontza-harremanik izan, Mariak semea izan zuen arte. (Mt 1:25)
They had no marital relations, until Mary had gotten her son.
b. Ni etortzen naizen arte hori hemen gelditzea nahi badut, zuri zer? (Jn 21:23; *IB*)
If I want him to stay here until I come, what is it to you?

(52) a. Ni etorri arte hori gelditzea nahi baldin badut, zuri zer? (Jn 21:23; *EAB*)
If I want him to stay until I come, what is it to you?
b. Nire semetzat ez haut hartuko ama erakutsi arte. (Lazkao-txiki II, 28)
I won't take yoú as my son until yoú show me yoúr mother.

In both types of clausal complements, an initial conjunction *harik*, partitive of *hura*, may be inserted for emphatic purposes. It is invariably followed by *eta*:

(53) a. Eta ez nituen sinesten harik eta nik neronek ikusi ditudan arteraino. (*TZ* II, 48)
And I did not believe them until I saw them myself.
b. Ez dizut baketan utziko, harik eta nahi dudana lortu arte. (Erkiaga, *Arran.* 123)
I won't leave you in peace until I obtain what I want.

In the southern system, inessive *artean* takes no nominal complements. Clausal complements are usually finite, assuming the form of relative clauses, although nonfinite clauses based on the perfect participle are also possible:

(54) a. Ez, Axari naizen artean! (Arrinda, 111)
No, (not) as long as I am Axari!
b. Eta hori gertatzen zen artean, bestea han egoten omen zen, oholen bestaldean. (San Martin, 87)
And while that was happening, the other was standing there, behind the boards.

(55) a. Euskal odola nire zainetan bizi artean, ekingo dizut kantari. (Jautarkol, *B.* 58)
As long as Basque blood is alive in my veins, for you I'll make an effort to sing.
b. Oturuntzak iraun artean bi anaiek ez zioten elkarri hitzik egin. (Etxaide, *J.J.* 28)
As long as the meal lasted, the two brothers did not speak to each other.

In the northern dialects the traditional system survives unaltered. There, *arte* and *artean* remain synonymous, so that *arte* encompasses the meaning 'as long as' and *artean* the meaning 'until':

(56) a. Bizi naizen arte eta bai heriotzean, argi egingo duzu ene bihotzean. (Xalbador, *Odol.* 318)
As long as I live and also in death, you will make light in my heart.
b. Nik, eskolan abiatu artean, ez nuen behin ere frantses hitz bat entzun. (Xalbador, *Odol.* 25)
As for me, until I started school, I had never heard a French word.

20.4.6 Delimitation Expressed with *bitarte*

The location noun *bitarte*, originally a back formation from *bitartean*—that is, *bi eta artean* 'two and between'—has the meaning 'interval', both spatial and temporal. Its inessive *bitartean* and, since the middle of the 19th century, also uninflected *bitarte*, can serve as the head of a delimitation clause. Noun phrase complements are uncommon, except for single nouns: *lan bitartean* 'during work', *lo bitartean* 'during sleep'. Used independently, *bitartean* has the sense 'meanwhile'. When combined with a relative clause, its most common complement, *bitarte(an)* accommodates three English meanings: 'until', as in *gaixotu nintzen bitarte* (Uztapide, *Sas.* 137) 'until I fell ill'; 'while', as in *hitzegiten duen bitartean* (Saizarbitoria, 73) 'while he is speaking'; and 'as long as', as in *ni bizi naizen bitartean* (*TOE* I, 53) 'as long as I live', sometimes used in a nontemporal sense ('provided'): *politika ez den bitartean* (Irazusta, *Bizia* 50) 'as long as it is not politics'. One more example of each use may be welcome:

(57) a. Eseri nire eskuinean, zeure etsaiak oinazpian jartzen dizkizudan bitartean. (Mt 22:44)
Sit at my right hand until I put your enemies under your feet.
b. Orain apaiza hor dagoen bitartean hitzegin nahi nizueke. (*TOE* III, 180)
Now, while the priest is there, I would like to speak to yoû.

c. Ez dugula eta ez dakigula ez dakigun bitartean ez gara izateko eta jakiteko bidean sartuko. (*MEIG* IV, 44)
As long as we don't know that we don't have and don't know, we won't get onto the path to having and knowing.

Except for the meaning 'as long as', a perfect participle construction is also possible:

(58) a. Beste zerbait utzi beharko didazu, antxumea bidali bitartean. (Gn 38:17)
You'll have to leave me something else, until you send the kid.
b. Egunkari hau irakurri bitartean, Jainkoak daki zein gogoeta ilun hits egin nuen. (Garate, *Iz.B.* 103)
While I read this diary, God knows what sad, dark thoughts I had.
c. Gizonak gaztak egin bitarte, andreak babak egosi. (Uztapide, *Sas.* 64)
While the man is making cheese, the lady is cooking beans.

[*N.B.* Once common to the whole speech area, use of *bitarte(an)* is now confined to the western dialects.]

20.5 The Delimitative Suffix *-ino*, as in *deino*

An obsolete case ending *-no*, originally meaning both 'until' and 'as long as', and still recognizable in the pleonasm *arteno* 'until', has survived in the eastern dialects as a suffix on relativized verb forms, but solely in the meaning 'as long as'. Degemination, of course, applies: *den* + *-no* > *deno*. Examples are

(59) a. Munduan naizeno, munduaren argia naiz. (Jn 9:5; Lz, Dv, *JKBO*)
As long as I am in the world, I am the light of the world.
b. On zeno ez da lanetik gelditu. (H.U., *Aurp.* 97)
He didn't cease working as long as he was well.
c. Ene bihotza, bizi naizeno, izanen zaizu fidela. (Xalbador, *Odol.* 115)
My heart will be faithful to you as long as I live.

In certain regions, *-no* was replaced by *-ño*, originally an expressive variant (see section 1.2.5). On account of its exclusive use by the prestigious Axular and, in his wake, by Mitxelena, it is this form that—de facto—became part of the literary standard. To take an example, a relativized verb *den* gives rise to a sequence *den* + *ño*, which Axular and his contemporaries, noticing the anticipatory effect of the palatal on the preceding vowel, represented in writing as *deiño*. Since such forms have long lost their expressive character, standard orthographic conventions omit this tilde, as palatalization is automatic after a diphthong ending in *i*. Hence the present spelling *deino*, and similarly, *naizeino*, *dudaino*, *duguino*, and so on. Some examples from the literature:

(60) a. Zamaria gazte deino hezten da. (Ax. 87)
One trains a mule while it is young.

b. Aldamenean behar ninduen, eritegia zabalik zegoeino. (*MEIG* IX, 97)
He needed me at his side, as long as the infirmary was open.

c. Euskal literaturaren oroitzapenak lurrean diraueino, ez da noski itzaliko haren izena eta omena. (*MEIG* V, 117)
As long as the memory of Basque literature lasts on earth, his name and fame will not fade away.

[*N.B.* Sarasola's *E.H.* lists *arteino* but not *arteno* as part of the standard vocabulary.]

20.6 Constructions with *eta* Denoting Posteriority

A convenient way of specifying the extent to which the action described by the main clause is posterior to that expressed by a nonfinite subordinate clause terminating in a perfect participle is the use of a suitable time adverbial connected to the latter by means of the conjunction *eta* 'and'. Suitable adverbials are allatives like *egun gutxitara* 'not many days hence' and *handik gutxira* 'a little afterward'; inessives such as *biharamunean* 'on the next day' and *berehalakoan* 'immediately'; and plain adverbs of the type *laster* 'soon', *berehala* 'at once'. Examples of this construction are

(61) a. Lehen etsipenak, ezkondu eta bi urtera jo zuen. (Garate, *NY* 100)
The first depression hit her two years after she got married.

b. Azkenean jaio egin nintzen 1936ko gerra bukatu eta handik gutxira. (Atxaga, *Behi* 31)
At long last I was born a little after the 1936 war ended.

c. Joan eta berehalakoan itzuli zen. (Echebarria, *Eib.* 154)
Immediately after he went, he came back.

d. Medikua harrapatu eta berehala hemen naiz. (*TOE* I, 66)
Immediately after fetching the doctor, I'll be here.

With the uninformative adverb *gero* 'later' occurring in this context, nothing but sheer posteriority is conveyed. As a matter of fact, this seems to be a much-favored means for expressing posteriority in Biscay and western Guipuzcoa:

(62) a. Etxe osoa erakutsi eta gero, saloi zabalera zuzendu ditu. (Onaindia, *Lam.* 135)
After showing them the whole house, she directed them to the spacious hall.

b. Agindu zaizuen guztia egin eta gero, esan ... (Lk 17:10)
After doing all that is commanded yoû, say ...

c. Hemen, hil eta gero ere, amandrearen eskua ageri da. (*LBB* 75)
Here, Grandmother's hand is conspicuous, even after she died.

The adverb *gero* may be omitted. In this event, intonation ensures that the construction is not mistaken for an ordinary instance of coordination. In particular, *eta*, usually atonic, will bear an appreciable degree of stress and will have a clear intonation break behind it. Examples are

(63) a. Orobat, afaldu eta, kaliza hartu zuen ... (1 Cor 11:25; Dv)
Likewise, after he has supped, he took the cup ...
b. New Yorktik etorri eta azken orrazketak eman nizkion. (Garate, *Iz.B.* 13)
After I came back from New York, I gave it the finishing touches.

20.7 Impendency Predicates

Mostly, postpositional phrases such as *zorian* 'on the verge' are called upon to furnish impendency predicates, yet southern Batua also has a special suffix available for the purpose.

20.7.1 The Impendency Suffix *-r*

The suffix *-r*, a truncated allative according to Lafitte (1962, sec. 466, p. 218), attaches only to (definite) verbal nouns, turning these into predicates denoting a state near to accomplishment of the action conveyed by the verb.

When a copula is required, that is, in case of primary predication, it will be *egon* if the base verb is intransitive and *eduki* if it is transitive—in accordance with the usual practice in the southern dialects for predicates denoting a state:

(64) a. Eguzkia erortzear zegoen mendi ostera. (Amuriza, *Hil* 51)
The sun was about to sink behind the mountain.
b. Gaixo hori hiltzear dago. (*EGLU* II, 481)
That patient is on the point of dying.

(65) a. Baimen-aldia amaitzear neukan. (Etxaide, *Xanti* I, 207)
I had nearly finished my furlough.
b. Zuk emandako liburua irakurtzear daukat. (*EGLU* II, 481)
I have almost read the book you gave me.

Note the subject complement in example (66a) and the object complement in (66b):

(66) a. Beste mutil bat zegoen zutik, kantuz hastear. (Amuriza, *Hil* 200)
Another boy was standing upright, about to start singing.
b. Galtzear aurkitu ninduen. (Orixe, *Aitork.* 125)
She found me almost lost.

The same suffix appears in the northern dialects even in conversational style, but there it attaches to the indefinite form of the verbal noun and, in contrast to southern usage, implies the nonoccurrence of the final accomplishment. The copulas used are *izan* and **edun*:

(67) a. Zabal-zabala erortzer zen Jon Doni Petri. (Barbier, *Lég.* 65)
Saint Peter nearly fell flat on the ground.

b. Hori entzutean, bihotza gelditzer zitzaidan. (Landart, 136)
When I heard that, my heart nearly stopped beating.

(68) a. Nola egiter nuen hamaiketakoa Azkainen. (*P.Ad.* 49)
How I almost had elevenses in Azcain.
b. Xahutzer naute lurrean. (Ps 118:87; Dv)
They have almost annihilated me on earth.

20.7.2 The Impendency Postposition *zorian*

Being the inessive of the noun *zori* 'destiny', the postposition *zorian* can be glossed as 'just about to ...' or 'on the verge of ...'. It follows the adnominal form of the verbal noun:

(69) a. Ateak puskatzeko zorian zeuden. (Gn 19:9; Ur.)
The doors were just about to break.
b. Nire etsaien eskuetan erortzeko zorian nago. (*TZ* I, 224)
I am on the verge of falling into the hands of my enemies.
c. Erretoreak, algaraz lehertzeko zorian, dio: ... (Muxika, *P.Am.* 36)
The parish priest, nearly bursting with laughter, says: ...

Compounds are also used: *galzorian* 'on the verge of ruin', *hilzorian* 'at death's door'. As nouns, *galzori* has been employed for 'danger' and *hilzori* for 'agony'.

20.7.3 The Impendency Postposition *aginean*

Borrowed from literary Biscayan, the postposition *aginean*, inessive of *(h)agin* 'molar', combines with a perfect participle to convey an impending threat (cf. the English phrase *in the teeth of* [*danger*]). Examples include *hil aginean* 'about to die', *hondatu aginean* 'about to sink', and *ito aginean* 'about to drown'.

20.7.4 The Impendency Adjective *hurran*

Originally, a northern adjective meaning 'nearby', *hurran* occurs in Batua as a postmodifier of a perfect participle *V*, weakening its meaning to 'almost V'. Examples are *hil hurran da* 'he almost died', *saldu hurran ditu* 'he almost sold them', *gosez hil hurranak* 'the starving', and *higatu hurranak dira* (Jo 9:13; Dv) 'they are almost threadbare'. A variant *hurren* occurs with the same meaning; see section 11.3.

20.8 Circumstantial Clauses

20.8.1 Finite Circumstantials in *-LA*

Not all clauses whose verb bears the suffix *-la* actually are complements of a verb, expressed or understood. They can be circumstantials, setting the background against which the action or event of the main clause takes place. For these, an English gloss using *while* is often appropriate.

While the complementizer *-LA* and the circumstantial suffix *-la* share the same segmental morphophonemics, there is a clear contrast with respect to intonation, inasmuch as the latter, but not the former, induces the anormal toneme (see section 1.2.3) on the verb form, as pointed out by Mitxelena in 1976 (see Villasante 1976, 201).

By definition, a circumstantial predicate must be durative. Perfective verb forms, therefore, are excluded; yet periphrastic imperfectives are rare also, because they tend to be iterative or habitual rather than durative, especially in the past tense. With rare exceptions, what we find are synthetic verb forms, or else durative constuctions with *ari*, *egon*, *ibili*, and *jardun*, as were discussed in section 16.5.1.

Normally, the subordinate clause precedes the main clause, but it is possible for it to follow, or to be intercalated into the main clause as its focus. Some typical examples should clarify matters:

(70) a. Oraintxe txipiroi batzuek jaten ari nintzela, Donostiatik datorren beste papera hartu dugu. (*TOE* I, 77)
Just now, while I was eating some squid, we received the other paper that comes from San Sebastian.
b. Lo nengoela agertu zitzaidan aingeru oso eder bat. (Urruzuno, *E.Z.* 15)
While I was asleep, a very beautiful angel appeared to me.
c. Esna dagoela ez du inork ametsik egiten. (Urruzuno, *E.Z.* 15)
Nobody dreams while he is awake.
d. Gerra bukatzear zegoela bere senarra eta beste bi soldadu afusilatu zituzten. (Atxaga, *Behi* 60)
While the war was about to end, they shot her husband and two other soldiers.
e. Zer egin ez nekiela etxetik irten nintzen. (Garate, *Leh.* 33)
I went out of the house not knowing what to do.

Final *-la* clauses often serve as an expedient to recall the obvious:

(71) a. Jokoan ari ziren, aurrean edariak zituztela. (Garate, *Alaba* 52)
They were playing (cards) with their drinks in front of them.
b. Hona non azaldu den Rebeka, pegarra sorbaldan duela. (Gn 24:45)
Behold, Rebecca came out with her jar on her shoulder.

When being focus, the *-la* clause takes focus position inside the main clause:

(72) Hargin guztiek ezpata gerrian zeramatela egiten zuten lan. (Neh 4:12)
All the bricklayers worked while wearing their swords at their waists.

20.8.2 Finite Circumstantials in *-larik*

In southern usage, the suffix *-larik* is a mere stylistic alternative to *-la*, meaning 'while' (cf. Mitxelena in Villasante 1976, 201). Examples are

(73) a. Oraindik zuen artean nagoelarik esan dizuet hau. (Jn 14:25; *IB*)
I have told yoû this while I am still among yoû.
b. Apaizgoan urte askotxo daramazkidalarik, ez dut ikasi emakumezkoen gorabehera eta matrikulak konprenitzen. (*TOE* III, 205)
While I have been spending a great many years in the priesthood, I haven't learned to understand the whims and wiles of females.

In northern usage, the suffix *-larik* has widened its meaning so as to include also location in time, so much so that in many regions it has all but replaced *-nean*:

(74) Poxi bat gosea eztitu delarik, solasak haste. (Arradoy, *K.G.* 28)
When hunger has been somewhat alleviated, talk starts.

20.8.3 Nonfinite Circumstantials

As was intimated in section 7.2.3, an important type of nonfinite clause is based on a case-marked verbal noun. And in fact, the definite inessive of the verbal noun is the basic ingredient of a nonfinite circumstantial. Inessive clauses, however, need not be circumstantials, but can also specify location in time. Whether or not they do seems to depend on the aspect of the main clause. If this is imperfective, the inessive clause is likely to be a circumstantial, and if not, a *when*-clause. Contrast examples (75a) and (75b):

(75) a. Zatiño hori entzutean, beldurrak hartzen ninduen. (Landart, 96)
While I heard that little fragment, fear was overtaking me.
b. Hitzen soinua entzutean, ikaratu egin zen. (Urretabizkaia, *Asp.* 78)
When hearing the sound of the words, he got frightened.

20.9 Compounds with *aldi*

The broad meaning of the noun *aldi*, encompassing 'period' as well as 'occasion' (French *fois*, Spanish *vez*, cf. section 20.3.1), renders it eminently fitting for use as a parasuffix; and, indeed, compounds having *aldi* as a final member are numerous as well as ubiquitous. The base of this parasuffix, that is, the initial member of the compound, can be an adjective describing a state, a verb radical, or a noun that can be readily associated with a state, activity, or process.

With an adjective describing a state as base, the compound denotes the period or moment during which this state lasts. With a verb radical as base, the compound expresses the period of duration if the verb is stative, and it merely individuates the activity if the verb is nonstative. With a noun as base, a similar situation obtains. If the noun refers to a state or time, the compound denotes the corresponding period. If the noun is associated with a particular activity, then again the compound individuates that activity. The association of an activity with a particular noun is mostly obvious, although, at times, somewhat idiosyncratic. Thus the activity associated with *egun* 'day' is atmospheric, whence *eguraldi* 'weather'; and the activity euphemistically associated with *belaun* 'knee' is procreation, whence *belaunaldi* 'generation'.

With regard to phonology, note that a base-final *a* is elided before the *a* of *aldi* (as in *dantzaldi, kezkaldi*), even when this *a* is the result of Minor Apocope (section 3.8.1), as in *bidaldi, gogaldi*, and *nekaldi*.

The following are examples with adjectives as base:

behere	low	beheraldi	slump, ebb tide, decline
beltz	black	beltzaldi	affliction, time of sorrow
bero	hot	beroaldi	hot spell, moment of fervor
eri	sick	erialdi	bout of illness, period of illness
ero	insane, crazy	eroaldi	fit of craziness, period of insanity
estu	narrow, tight	estualdi	scrape, tight spot
gaixo	ill, sick	gaixoaldi	bout of illness, period of illness
goibel	cloudy, sad	goibelaldi	period of sadness, moment of sadness
gora	high, up	goraldi	boom, flood tide, rise
hordi	drunk	hordialdi	drunken fit, period of intoxication
hotz	cold	hotzaldi	cold spell, chill, coolness
ilun	dark	ilunaldi	dark period, eclipse
larri	urgent, grave	larrialdi	predicament, crisis
makal	weak	makalaldi	period of weakness, depression
mozkor	drunk	mozkorraldi	drunken fit, period of intoxication
samur	tender	samurraldi	burst of tenderness
zoro	crazy, silly	zoraldi	fit of craziness, period of madness

These are examples with verbs as base:

agertu	to appear	agerraldi	apparition, visit, scene
begiratu	to look	begiraldi	glance, look
beheratu	to decrease	beheraldi	decline, drop, decrease
burutatu	to come to mind	burutaldi	whim
busti	to wet, to soak	bustialdi	soaking, bath
dantzatu	to dance	dantzaldi	dancing session
egon	to stay	egonaldi	stay, period of residence
entzun	to hear	entzunaldi	hearing, audience, audition
eraso	to attack	erasoaldi	attack
erori	to fall	eroraldi	fall, decline, drop
erre	to burn, to bake	errealdi	blaze, firing, batch
ferekatu	to caress	ferekaldi	caress, stroking, petting bout
garbitu	to clean, to wash	garibaldi	cleaning, washing, purification
gelditu	to stop, to remain	geldialdi	pause, stagnation
geratu	to stop, to remain	geraldi	pause, stagnation

gertatu	to happen	gertaldi	event
gorritu	to blush	gorrialdi	fit of blushing, blush
gozatu	to enjoy	gozaldi	time of enjoyment, recreation
hartu	to take	harraldi	dose, portion
hasi	to begin	hasialdi	beginning
hegatu	to fly	hegaldi	flight
ibili	to walk	ibilaldi	walk, trip
igaro	to pass	igaroaldi	past time, past tense
igo	to climb	igoaldi	climb, ascent, ascension
ikertu	to investigate	ikerraldi	investigation, inspection
iragan	to pass	iraganaldi	past time, past tense
iraun	to last	iraunaldi	duration, period of validity
ireki	to open	irekialdi	opening
jaiki	to rise	jaikialdi	uprising
jaitsi	to go down	jaitsaldi	descent, drop
jan	to eat	janaldi	feeding, meal
jo	to hit, to beat	joaldi	blow, beating, strike
jokatu	to gamble, to play	jokaldi	move, game
jolastu	to play	jolasaldi	playing time, recreation time
jorratu	to weed	jorraldi	weeding
kantatu	to sing	kantaldi	singing session, song recital
mintzatu	to speak	mintzaldi	lecture
moztu	to cut off	motzaldi	shearing period, shearing
omendu	to pay homage	omenaldi	homage, celebration
saiatu	to try	saialdi	attempt, try
sartu	to enter	sarraldi	entrance, entry
tentatu	to tempt	tentaldi	temptation

A few common verbs make use of the verbal noun instead of the radical:

ekin	to undertake	ekitaldi	activity, exercise, act (in play)
erakutsi	to show	erakustaldi	lesson, show
ikasi	to learn	ikastaldi	course, lesson, study
ikusi	to see	ikustaldi	visit, meeting, inspection
irakatsi	to teach	irakastaldi	course, lesson

The following examples have a noun as base:

atseden	rest, relaxation	atsedenaldi	rest period, rest
atsegin	pleasure, delight	atseginaldi	time of pleasure
barau	fast, fasting	baraualdi	fasting period, fast
barre	laughter	barrealdi	fit of laughter

behar	need	beharraldi	time of need
bide	road, way	bidaldi	journey, trip
bihotz	heart	bihotzaldi	impulse, feeling
ehiza	hunting	ehizaldi	hunt
esku	hand	eskualdi	touch, stroke, help
estreina	first use, inauguration	estreinaldi	opening, performance, premiere
ez	nought, lack	ezaldi	penury, period of scarcity
ezti	honey	eztialdi	honeymoon
eztul	cough	eztulaldi	coughing fit, cough
gaitz	evil, ailment	gaitzaldi	crisis, attack of illness
gero	future	geroaldi	future time, future tense
gibel	backside, liver	gibelaldi	retrogression, decline
gizon	man	gizaldi	generation, century
gogo	mind	gogaldi	state of mind, mood
goiz	morning	goizaldi	morning time, morning weather
gorputz	body	gorputzaldi	state of the body, condition
guda	war, battle	gudaldi	time of war
haize	wind	haizaldi	gust of wind
haserre	anger	haserrealdi	angry mood, spurt of anger, quarrel
hitz	word	hitzaldi	lecture, speech
hizketa	speech	hizketaldi	conversation, talk
ihes	escape, flight	ihesaldi	escape, flight
itxaso	sea	itsasaldi	sea voyage, sea trip
izotz	frost, ice	izotzaldi	frost, freeze
izu	fright	izualdi	scare, moment of fright
jai	feast, public holiday	jaialdi	festival, feast
kezka	worry	kezkaldi	time of worry, spell of worry
lan	work	lanaldi	working time
lehen	past	lehenaldi	past time, past
lo	sleep	loaldi	period of sleep, nap
lore	flower	loraldi	flowering season, bloom, heyday
muga	border, opportunity	mugaldi	opportunity, occasion
negar	weeping, crying	negarraldi	period of sorrow, crying fit
negu	winter	negualdi	winter season
neke	fatigue, effort	nekaldi	time of hardship, time of suffering
oinaze	torment, pain	oinazealdi	time of torment, time of pain
opor	vacation	oporraldi	vacation period, vacation
orain	present	orainaldi	present time, present tense
poz	joy	pozaldi	time of joy
sabel	belly	sabelaldi	eating binge, litter

solas	talk	solasaldi	conversation
uda	summer	udaldi	summer season
ume	young, child	umealdi	litter
ur	water	uraldi	flood, inundation

20.10 Vocabulary

bihurtu	to become
edozein	any . . . whatsoever
eguraldi	weather
erdara	non-Basque language
esan nahi	to mean
eskaini	to offer
feria	fair, market
handitu	to get big, to grow up
haurkeria	puerility, childish way
hobeto	better
igaro	to pass, to cross
jaso	to lift, to receive, to get
modu	manner
muga	border
prestu	noble, honest
ze(r) moduz	how, in what condition

20.11 Exercises

20.11.1 Translate into English

1. Besterik egiten ez dakizuenean nireganatzen zarete.
2. Gu irten ginenean elurra hastear zegoen. (*EGLU* II, 481)
3. Dakarrenean dakar dakarrenak dakarrena.
4. Gizondu orduko haurkeriak utzi ditut. (*MEIG* IV, 25)
5. Iluntzerakoan abiatu ginen etxerantz eta iluntzean etxeratu.
6. Edozein gauza egiterakoan, norentzako eta zertarako ari garen galdetzen diogu geure buruari. (*MEIG* VII, 75)
7. Gernikako ferian Pernando ikusi zuen batean, zer moduz zegoen galdetu zion adiskide batek.
8. Aita gelan sartzen den guztietan haurrak negarrez hasten dira.
9. Gernikatik igarotzen naizen bakoitzean goibelaldi bat izaten dut.
10. Hobeto sentitzen al zara zure zigarroak erre eta gero? (Atxaga, *Z.H.* 79)

11. Gure baserrietan jende prestuek dirauten artean, Euskarak iraungo du. (Cardaberaz, *E.B.O.* 65)
12. Donostian biziko gara dirua duguino.

20.11.2 Translate into Basque

1. We will talk when I return.
2. When the weather is nice, we don't want to stay home.
3. When I am growing up, will I speak Spanish?
4. What do you think he means when he says that?
5. Six months have passed since you were here.
6. My father died while I was in America.
7. As soon as he opened his eyes, he saw it.
8. Each time we come to see the priest, he offers us wine.
9. It is a year ago that Grandmother died.
10. He doesn't want to say a word until he receives the money.
11. While everybody else knew it, I didn't know it.
12. After crossing the border, she became another woman.

21 The Subjunctive

21.1 Introduction

The Basque verbal system provides a set of forms generally referred to as the subjunctive mood because its function corresponds by and large to that of the subjunctive in the surrounding Romance languages.

The evidence of Leizarraga's 1571 New Testament version, where the forms in question function solely as perfectives, shows that older Basque did not have a subjunctive mood, and even now colloquial usage largely avoids it, using the indicative in many adverbial contexts where Spanish has the subjunctive and preferring nonfinite constructions to subjunctive complements. In colloquial style, the subjunctive mainly occurs in hortatives (section 21.6) and optatives (section 21.7), uses in which it has no competitor.

In both these uses, the subjunctive occurs in what appears to be an independent main clause. Yet the nonexistence of allocutive subjunctives (see chapter 29) suggests a subordinate status for such clauses, possibly to be analyzed as complements of a covert performative requiring the subjunctive. Moreover, the fact that subjunctive verb forms invariably end in a complementizer lends further support to such an analysis. This complementizer is either -*LA*, which, as Goenaga (1997) has shown, chiefly occurs in contexts involving communication, or -*N*, traditionally considered part and parcel of the subjunctive form itself.

Clauses built on a subjunctive main verb will be named subjunctive clauses, unless the complementizer -*LA* is present, in which case we will use the term conjunctive clause. Similarly, we will speak of subjunctive and conjunctive complements. There are three subjunctive tense forms: present, past, and the rarely used hypothetical, identical to the past except for the third-person subject forms. In these, the eventuality prefix *l*- of section 17.2.2 replaces initial *z*-.

21.2 Subjunctive Morphology

Generally speaking, all subjunctives are periphrastic forms and consist of the verb radical—in the southern colloquial the perfect participle—combined with a subjunctive auxiliary. As to synthetic forms, there are but two contexts where a synthetic indicative together with a complementizer can act the part of a subjunctive: hortatives (with *-N* as complementizer) and optatives (with *-LA* as complementizer).

21.2.1 Subjunctive Forms of the Intransitive Auxiliary

Morphologically, subjunctive forms of intransitive *izan* belong to the otherwise unattested verb **edin* with the hypothesized meaning 'to become'. Its stem *-di-* reduces to zero when preceding the pre-dative marker *-ki-* (section 15.1) and takes *-tez* as a pluralizing suffix.

As was stated in the introduction, subjunctive forms are customarily cited together with the complementizer *-N*. Note, however, that the vowel *e*, normally intercalated between the *n* of this complementizer and a stem ending in *i* (cf. *dirudien* in section 18.1.2) or between such a stem and the past tense ending *-n* (section 6.2.2), while still retained in the eastern dialects, has been dropped in the standard forms.

For the reader's convenience, the intransitive subjunctive paradigm will now be presented in full detail, leaving out only the forms of the hypothetical, predictable as they are from the past tense forms. To save space, no glosses are provided; instead, the corresponding indicatives appear within parentheses.

nadin	(naiz)	nendin	(nintzen)
hadin	(haiz)	hendin	(hintzen)
dadin	(da)	zedin	(zen)
gaitezen	(gara)	gintezen	(ginen)
zaitezen	(zara)	zintezen	(zinen)
zaitezten	(zarete)	zintezten	(zineten)
daitezen	(dira)	zitezen	(ziren)

While seemingly irregular, the plural forms result from regular sound change. Thus present tense *gaitezen* results from **gaditezen* by the loss of intervocalic *d*, a process possibly facilitated by the following dental. Somewhat less transparently, past tense *gintezen* derives from **genditezen* by the loss of an intervocalic nasal followed by its restoration: **genditezen* > **geñitezen* > **gẽĩtezen* > **gĩtezen* > *gintezen*.

The dative forms conform to the usual pattern if we posit a zero stem followed by the pre-dative marker *-ki-* of section 15.1:

dakidan	(zait)	zekidan	(zitzaidan)
dakian	(zaik)	zekian	(zitzaian)
dakinan	(zain)	zekinan	(zitzainan)
dakion	(zaio)	zekion	(zitzaion)
dakigun	(zaigu)	zekigun	(zitzaigun)
dakizun	(zaizu)	zekizun	(zitzaizun)
dakizuen	(zaizue)	zekizuen	(zitzaizuen)
dakien	(zaie)	zekien	(zitzaien)

dakizkidan	(zaizkit)	zekizkidan	(zitzaizkidan)
dakizkian	(zaizkik)	zekizkian	(zitzaizkian)
dakizkinan	(zaizkin)	zekizkinan	(zitzaizkinan)
dakizkion	(zaizkio)	zekizkion	(zitzaizkion)
dakizkigun	(zaizkigu)	zekizkigun	(zitzaizkigun)
dakizkizun	(zaizkizu)	zekizkizun	(zitzaizkizun)
dakizkizuen	(zaizkizue)	zekizkizuen	(zitzaizkizuen)
dakizkien	(zaizkie)	zekizkien	(zitzaizkien)
nakian	(natzaik)	nenkian	(nintzaian)
nakinan	(natzain)	nenkinan	(nintzainan)
nakion	(natzaio)	nenkion	(nintzaion)
nakizun	(natzaizu)	nenkizun	(nintzaizun)
nakizuen	(natzaizue)	nenkizuen	(nintzaizuen)
nakien	(natzaie)	nenkien	(nintzaien)
hakidan	(hatzait)	henkidan	(hintzaidan)
hakion	(hatzaio)	henkion	(hintzaion)
hakigun	(hatzaigu)	henkigun	(hintzaigun)
hekien	(hatzaie)	henkien	(hintzaien)
gakizkian	(gatzaizkik)	genkizkian	(gintzaizkian)
gakizkinan	(gatzaizkin)	genkizkinan	(gintzaizkinan)
gakizkion	(gatzaizkio)	genkizkion	(gintzaizkion)
gakizkizun	(gatzaizkizu)	genkizkizun	(gintzaizkizun)
gakizkizuen	(gatzaizkizue)	genkizkizuen	(gintzaizkizuen)
gakizkien	(gatzaizkie)	genkizkien	(gintzaizkien)
zakizkidan	(zatzaizkit)	zenkizkidan	(zintzaizkidan)
zakizkion	(zatzaizkio)	zenkizkion	(zintzaizkion)
zakizkigun	(zatzaizkigu)	zenkizkigun	(zintzaizkigun)
zakizkien	(zatzaizkie)	zenkizkien	(zintzaizkien)
zakizkidaten	(zatzaizkidate)	zenkizkidaten	(zintzaizkidaten)
zakizkioten	(zatzaizkiote)	zenkizkioten	(zintzaizkioten)
zakizkiguten	(zatzaizkigute)	zenkizkiguten	(zintzaizkiguten)
zakizkieten	(zatzaizkiete)	zenkizkieten	(zintzaizkieten)

21.2.2 Subjunctive Forms of the Transitive Auxiliary

Morphologically, subjunctive forms of **edun* belong to the otherwise unattested verb **ezan*, stem *-za-*, with the hypothesized meaning 'to make'. Its pluralizer is identical to that of **edun*: a prefix *it-*. Its present tense marker has the shape *de-* instead of *da-* just in case the direct object is third person; its *e* elides before the *i* of the pluralizer, while the *a* in the other forms remains. Thus we get the contrasts *dezazun* versus *nazazun* and *ditzan* versus *gaitzan*. The following paradigm is now fully accounted for:

dezadan	(dut)	nezan	(nuen)
dezaan	(duk)	hezan	(huen)
dezanan	(dun)	hezan	(huen)
dezan	(du)	zezan	(zuen)
dezagun	(dugu)	genezan	(genuen)
dezazun	(duzu)	zenezan	(zenuen)
dezazuen	(duzue)	zenezaten	(zenuten)
dezaten	(dute)	zezaten	(zuten)
ditzadan	(ditut)	nitzan	(nituen)
ditzaan	(dituk)	hitzan	(hituen)
ditzanan	(ditun)	hitzan	(hituen)
ditzan	(ditu)	zitzan	(zituen)
ditzagun	(ditugu)	genitzan	(genituen)
ditzazun	(dituzu)	zenitzan	(zenituen)
ditzazuen	(dituzue)	zenitzaten	(zenituzten)
ditzaten	(dituzte)	zitzaten	(zituzten)
nazaan	(nauk)	nintzaan	(ninduan)
nazanan	(naun)	nintzanan	(nindunan)
nazan	(nau)	nintzan	(ninduen)
nazazun	(nauzu)	nintzazun	(ninduzun)
nazazuen	(nauzue)	nintzazuen	(ninduzuen)
nazaten	(naute)	nintzaten	(ninduten)
hazadan	(haut)	hintzadan	(hindudan)
hazan	(hau)	hintzan	(hinduen)
hazagun	(haugu)	hintzagun	(hindugun)
hazaten	(haute)	hintzaten	(hinduten)
gaitzaan	(gaituk)	gintzaan	(gintuan)
gaitzanan	(gaitun)	gintzanan	(gintunan)
gaitzan	(gaitu)	gintzan	(gintuen)
gaitzazun	(gaituzu)	gintzazun	(gintuzun)
gaitzazuen	(gaituzue)	gintzazuen	(gintuzuen)
gaitzaten	(gaituzte)	gintzaten	(gintuzten)
zaitzadan	(zaitut)	zintzadan	(zintudan)
zaitzan	(zaitu)	zintzan	(zintuen)
zaitzagun	(zaitugu)	zintzagun	(zintugun)
zaitzaten	(zaituzte)	zintzaten	(zintuzten)

zaitzatedan	(zaituztet)	zintzatedan	(zintuztedan)
zaitzaten	(zaituzte)	zintzaten	(zintuzten)
zaitzategun	(zaituztegu)	zintzategun	(zintuztegun)
zaitzateten	(zaituztete)	zintzateten	(zintuzteten)

[*N.B.* In accordance with sandhi rule 5 of section 1.2.6 the sequence *-n* + *z-* is realized as *-ntz-*.]

We now proceed to the subjunctive dative forms of **edun*:

diezadaan	(didak)	hiezadan	(hidan)
diezadanan	(didan)	hiezadan	(hidan)
diezadan	(dit)	ziezadan	(zidan)
diezadazun	(didazu)	zeniezadan	(zenidan)
diezadazuen	(didazue)	zeniezadaten	(zenidaten)
diezadaten	(didate)	ziezadaten	(zidaten)
diezaadan	(diat)	niezaan	(nian)
diezaan	(dik)	ziezaan	(zian)
diezaagun	(diagu)	geniezaan	(genian)
diezaaten	(diate)	ziezaaten	(ziaten)
diezanadan	(dinat)	niezanan	(ninan)
diezanan	(din)	ziezanan	(zinan)
diezanagun	(dinagu)	geniezanan	(geninan)
diezanaten	(dinate)	ziezanaten	(zinaten)
diezaiodan	(diot)	niezaion	(nion)
diezaioan	(diok)	hiezaion	(hion)
diezaionan	(dion)	hiezaion	(hion)
diezaion	(dio)	ziezaion	(zion)
diezaiogun	(diogu)	geniezaion	(genion)
diezaiozun	(diozu)	zeniezaion	(zenion)
diezaiozuen	(diozue)	zeniezaioten	(zenioten)
diezaioten	(diote)	ziezaioten	(zioten)
diezaguan	(diguk)	hiezagun	(higun)
diezagunan	(digun)	hiezagun	(higun)
diezagun	(digu)	ziezagun	(zigun)
diezaguzun	(diguzu)	zeniezagun	(zenigun)
diezaguzuen	(diguzue)	zeniezaguten	(zeniguten)
diezaguten	(digute)	ziezaguten	(ziguten)
diezazudan	(dizut)	niezazun	(nizun)
diezazun	(dizu)	ziezazun	(zizun)

diezazugun	(dizugu)	geniezazun	(genizun)
diezazuten	(dizute)	ziezazuten	(zizuten)
diezazuedan	(dizuet)	niezazuen	(nizuen)
diezazuen	(dizue)	ziezazuen	(zizuen)
diezazuegun	(dizuegu)	geniezazuen	(genizuen)
diezazueten	(dizuete)	ziezazueten	(zizueten)
diezaiedan	(diet)	niezaien	(nien)
diezaiean	(diek)	hiezaien	(hien)
diezaienan	(dien)	hiezaien	(hien)
diezaien	(die)	ziezaien	(zien)
diezaiegun	(diegu)	geniezaien	(genien)
diezaiezun	(diezu)	zeniezaien	(zenien)
diezaiezuen	(diezue)	zeniezaieten	(zenieten)
diezaieten	(diete)	ziezaieten	(zieten)

Characteristic of these transitive dative forms is the unexplained segment *-ie-* invariably preceding the stem *-za-*. Note also the insertion of an *i* glide between the stem and a vocalic dative marker, thus preserving the *a* of the stem, which would otherwise elide. Here as in all other dative forms, a plural object is marked by a suffix *-zki* directly after the stem: *diezazkiogun* (dizkiogu), *geniezazkien* (genizkien), and so on.

21.3 Subjunctive Complement Clauses

The following categories of predicates allow subjunctive complements:

1. Volitive and desiderative predicates
2. Predicates of ordering and requesting (*verba petendi*)
3. Conative predicates
4. Predicates expressing necessity or suitability
5. Predicates granting permission
6. Emotive predicates (in accordance with section 18.2, only *beldur* qualifies)

21.3.1 Complements of Volitive or Desiderative Predicates

With *nahi* 'to want' and other volitive predicates, colloquial usage prefers nonfinite complements in the form of nominalizations:

(1) a. Nor etortzea nahi zenuen? (Labayen, *S.G.* 161)
Who did you want to come?

b. Zer nahi zenuen nik Gasteizen egitea? (*MEIG* IX, 73)
What did you want me to do in Vitoria?

In a more formal style, however, subjunctive complements are also possible:

(2) a. Dirurik gabe, nora nahi duzu joan nadin? (*TOE* III, 57)
Without money, where did you want me to go?
b. Zer nahi duzu nik egin dezadan? (Larzabal, *Hil.* 16)
What do you want me to do?
c. Eta zer nahi zenuen egin nezan? (*TOE* III, 128)
And what did you want me to have done?
d. Hil nazan nahi al duzu? (1 Kgs 18:9)
Do you want him to kill me?
e. Ez zuen ustel bat zela pentsa zezaten nahi. (Atxaga, *Gizona* 303)
He didn't want them to think that he was a wimp.
f. Belle eta Gretak ez zuten inork lotu zitzan nahi. (Atxaga, *Gizona* 68)
Belle and Greta didn't want anyone to tie them up.
g. Guiomar isil zedin desio zuen. (Atxaga, *Gizona* 317)
He wished Guiomar would be quiet.

The preterito-present verb *opa* 'to wish someone something' and its synonym *opatu* can take conjunctive complements:

(3) a. Opa diogu zeruan goza dadila. (Txirrita, *B.* I, 44)
We wish (him) that he may have a good time in heaven.
b. Nik opa diet zeruan gerta daitezela. (Uztapide, *Sas.* 341)
I wish (them) that they may find themselves in heaven.

21.3.2 Complements of Predicates of Ordering and Requesting

In a fairly formal style, *verba petendi* can take finite complements, which are either subjunctive or conjunctive:

(4) a. Alferrik aginduko diezu isil daitezen. (S. Mitxelena, *IG* I, 396)
You will (i.e., would) command them in vain to keep silent.
b. Paseoarekin segi genezan eskatu nion. (Atxaga, *Obab.* 177)
I begged him that we continue with our walk.
c. Otoitz egiten nuen dena ondo atera zedin. (Atxaga, *Grl.* 98)
I kept praying that all would turn out well.

(5) a. Jesusek zorrotz agindu zien inork ere ez zezala jakin. (Mk 5:43)
Jesus sternly charged them that no one should know it.
b. Berak eskatu du etor zaitezela. (*TOE* III, 179)
She herself has asked for you to come.
c. Otoizten zaitut jarrai dezazula. (Iturriaga, *Dial.* 59)
I beg you to continue.

Nonfinite complements based on the adnominal form of the verbal noun are more common in colloquial style. Some examples are

(6) a. Jesusek inori ez esateko agindu zien zorrotz. (Lk 9:21)
Jesus sternly ordered them to tell no one.
b. Amak musu emateko agindu zidan. (Garate, *Hades* 59)
Mother ordered me to kiss her.
c. Berarengana joateko eskatzen dizu. (Garate, *Alaba* 12)
He is asking you to go to him.
d. Bilbotik irteteko aholkatu zidaten medikuek. (Garate, *Hades* 57)
The doctors advised me to leave Bilbao.

Occasionally, the verbal noun itself may occur instead of the adnominal:

(7) a. Eriberibilean neu ere joatea eskatzen nion. (Garate, *Alaba* 81)
I asked him to let me go too in the ambulance. (For *neu* 'myself', see section 28.2.5.1.)
b. Nire lanak liburu asko irakurtzea eskatzen du.
My job requires reading a lot of books.

As verbs of communication can be used to convey orders and recommendations, they too can take adnominal complements and, in a more formal style, conjunctive ones:

(8) a. Nire anaia horrek lasai egoteko dio. (*G.* 257)
That brother of mine says to be at ease.
b. Etortzeko esan nion. (Irazusta, *Bizia* 95)
I told him to come.
c. . . . gaztigatzen diozu tabernariari eduki dezala zenbait egunez bahi hura. (Ax. 80)
. . . you notify the bartender that he should keep that pledge for a few days.
d. Esan zion ez zedila inoiz ere bereiz bere anaietatik. (Beobide, 282)
He told him that he should never separate himself from his brothers.

A main verb meaning 'to say' can be left out in this type of construction provided its ergative subject remains. This possibility gives rise to phrases such as *amak etortzeko* (Alzo, 65), also mentioned by Azkue in his *Morfología Vasca* (1923–1925, II, sec. 917, p. 673), where it is said to be equivalent to *amak etor zaitezela dio* 'Mother says that you should come'.

21.3.3 Complements of Conative Predicates

As observed in section 16.5.4, conative predicates typically take gerundive complements. These, however, are subject controlled; yet the equisubject constraint imposed on the English verb *to try* fails to apply to Basque conatives. These are similar in this respect to their Romance counterparts—witness the French example *Je vais tâcher qu'il me voie* (Proust), literally 'I am going to try that he see me'. In Basque, subjunctive complements of conative verbs are fairly common and may occur even when the two subjects are identical. Some typical examples are

(9) a. Arantxa ere saiatzen zen bere senar Inaxiok Ander zerbait zirika zezan. (Itziar, 103)
Arantxa too was trying to get her husband Inaxio to prod Andrew a bit.
b. Etxeko gauzak ondo joan daitezen ahaleginduko naiz. (*TOE* II, 194)
I will do my best to ensure that the firm's affairs go well.
c. Zergatik ez zara ahalegindu lebitarrek Judan . . . zerga bil zezaten? (2 Chr 24:6)
Why didn't you do your best to make sure that the Levites collected the tax in Judah?
d. Ahaleginak egiten zituzten Bordalaisek kanta berriak ikas zitzan. (Atxaga, *Sara* 117)
They were doing all they could to get Bordalais to learn new songs.
e. Guztiok ataka honetatik atera zaitezen ahaleginak egingo ditugu. (*TOE* II, 222)
All of us will do all we can (to see) that you get out of this fix.
f. Zeruko erreinuan sar gaitezen egin ditzagun ahaleginak. (*Xenp.* 320)
Let us do all we can (to ensure) that we enter into the kingdom of heaven.

Although they may not be typical conatives, the verb *lortu* with its synonym *eskuratu* should also be mentioned at this point. These verbs mean 'to be successful in one's efforts' and can be variously glossed as 'to obtain', 'to achieve', 'to succeed', or 'to manage'. They allow nominalizations as well as subjunctive complements:

(10) a. Era honetara lortuko dugu irakurleak ulertzea. (Etxaide, *Alos* 12)
In this way we will succeed in (getting) the reader to understand.
b. Babeslekutik atera zedin lortu zuen. (2 Mc 4:34)
He succeeded in (getting) him to come out of the sanctuary.

21.3.4 Complements of Predicates Expressing Necessity or Suitability

A nominalization constitutes the most common type of complement for a predicate indicating either necessity or suitability:

(11) a. Beharrezkoa al da hori egitea? (*LBB* 57)
Is it necessary to do that?
b. Ez da on gizona bakarrik egotea. (Gn 2:18)
It is not good for man to be alone.

Yet subjunctive complements are not all that uncommon either:

(12) a. Ikusten duzunean ez zaituztela sinetsi nahi, eta premia dela sinets zaitzaten, dagizun orduan juramentu. (Ax. 250–251)
When you see that they do not want to believe you and that it is necessary that they believe you, then swear.

b. Ez da ongi gizona bakarrik izan dadin. (Lapeyre, 115)
It is not good that man should be alone.
c. Ez da komeni nire seme-alabek zurekin ikus nazaten. (*TOE* III, 193)
It is not fitting that my children should see me with you.
d. Ordu zen noizbait lagunak egin gintezen.
It was time that we should finally get to be friends. (Xalbador, *Odol.* 215)

21.3.5 Complements of Predicates Granting Permission

While predicates granting permission normally take gerundive complements (see section 16.3.2), subjunctive complements occasionally occur in the southern literary style:

(13) a. Nagusiak ez zion uzten eskolara arratsaldez ere etor zedin. (Atxaga, *Obab.* 48)
The boss did not let him come to school also in the afternoons.
b. Ez dizut utziko nire aita eta Agarrengatik gaizki esaka art zaitezen. (*TOE* III, 199)
I won't have you go around speaking badly about my father and Agar.
c. Etxeko seme-alabak konformatuko dira ni berriz ezkon nadin. (*TOE* III, 187)
The sons and daughters of the household will accept that I marry again.

[*N.B.* The verb *konformatu* can also mean 'to settle', in which meaning it takes indicative complements, as in example (14):

(14) Konformatu ziraden (= *ziren*) elkarren artean ezkonduko zirela hurrengo urtean. (*Balad.* 230)
They settled between themselves that they would get married the following year.]

Verbs of prohibition, such as *debekatu* and *galarazi* do not seem to take subjunctive complements. With the verb *eragotzi* 'to prevent', I have found one Guipuzcoan example:

(15) Egundaino ez digute eragotzi elkar ikusi eta mintza gaitezen. (*TOE* II, 331)
They have never prevented us from seeing each other and talking to each other.

21.3.6 Complements of Emotive Verbs

As noted in section 18.2, of all the emotive verbs (section 12.1.11) only *beldur* (and *beldurtu*) 'to be afraid', 'to fear' takes finite complements. These complements will be indicative as long as the event feared is in the past or present:

(16) a. Beldur naiz zerbaitetan huts egin dudan eta lehendanik gaiztotu naizen. (Ax. 446)
I am afraid that I have failed in something and have become worse than before.
b. Beldur naiz giristinoetarik ere, gehienek bide hura bera hartzen duten. (Ax. 141)
I am afraid that of the Christians too, the majority is taking that same road.
c. Beldur naiz ... bekaturen bat estali dizula. (Mogel, *C.C.* 128)
I am afraid that she has concealed from you some kind of sin.

When the event feared is still to come, classical usage seems to require the subjunctive. Axular's usage illustrates this point:

(17) a. Beldur naiz utz ez dezan. (Ax. 92–93)
I am afraid that he may not abandon it.
b. Beldur zen entzun zezan berehala Jainkoak. (Ax. 53)
He was afraid that God might hear him immediately.

Later, use of the subjunctive became optional in such contexts. With a future event, Duvoisin mostly uses the subjunctive, but also sometimes the indicative, a usage which is very common nowadays:

(18) a. Eta beldurtu zen ez zuela izanen dirurik gerlako gastuentzat. (1 Mc 3:30; Dv)
And he got afraid that he might not have money for the war's expenses.
b. Beldur naiz nire etxekoak haserretuko ote zaizkidan. (T. Agirre, *Uzt.* 62)
I am afraid that the members of my household may get mad at me.
c. Beldur naiz ondore txarra ekarriko duen. (Satrustegi, 145)
I am afraid that it may bring a bad consequence.
d. Beldur naiz ez ote den erotuko. (Atxaga, *Obab.* 247)
I am afraid that she may go mad.

Yet, the subjunctive remains possible:

(19) a. Frantsesak beldur ziren lagunak etor zekizkion libratzera. (LF, *Murtuts* 47)
The French were afraid that his fellows might come to free him.
b. Zerbait gerta dakion beldur izan dira. (Satrustegi, 164)
They have been afraid that something may happen to him.

[*N.B.* Note that the particle *ote* never appears in subjunctive complements.]

21.4 Use of the Subjunctive in Adverbial Clauses

Purpose clauses constitute the most typical adverbial context for the subjunctive. In addition, the expression of prospective action in delimitatives and other time clauses needs to be considered. There, use of the subjunctive, while optional, is quite fashionable in formal style.

21.4.1 Purpose Clauses: Finite and Nonfinite

In older Basque, purpose clauses were characterized by a suffix *-tzat* attached to a subjunctive verb form—as in *jasan ditzadantzat* (Duvoisin, *L.Ed.* 41) 'so that I suffer them'. Nowadays the suffix is omitted, so that purpose clauses have come to be identical with subjunctive adverbials.

A purpose clause normally follows the main clause:

(20) a. Dirua parrastaka ematen dut egunero jan dezagun. (*MEIG* IX, 109)
I give money galore for us to eat every day.
b. Esango dizuet zer den film hori, ikusi gabe lasai geldi zaitezten. (*MEIG* I, 131)
I will tell yoû what that movie is (like), so that yoû can rest easy without seeing it.
c. Ezer egin behar ote genuke, gal ez dadin? (*MEIG* I, 56)
Should we perhaps do something, so that it won't get lost?

But when the purpose clause functions as topic or focus, it will precede the main clause:

(21) a. Jainkoak heriotzatik gorde gaitzan, kandela bedeinkatua piztuko dugu. (Etxaniz, *Antz*. 12)
For God to preserve us from death, we will light a blessed candle.
b. Bekaturik egin ez dezazuen idazten dizuet hau. (1 Jn 2:1)
I am writing this to yoû so that yoû will not sin.

Negative purpose clauses also exist and require no special morphology. Note, however, that in purpose clauses, in contrast to other subjunctive clauses, the negated auxiliary must follow the participle. This fact can be taken as evidence that *-tzat* deletion is still a synchronic process. Examples are

(22) a. Bidera irten beharko natzaio, ama haserre ez dadin. (*TOE* I, 225)
I must go out to meet him on the way, so that Mother won't get mad.
b. Ez diezagula Jainkoak hitzegin, hil ez gaitezen. (Ex 20:19)
Let not God speak to us, lest we die.
c. Besoetan eramango zaituzte, harriekin estropezu egin ez dezazun. (Ps 91:12, Mt 4:6, Lk 4:11)
They will carry you in their arms, lest you trip over stones.

Nonfinite purpose clauses are also very common and make use of the adnominal form of the verbal noun:

(23) a. Teexak berehala jantzarazi zion Joanixiok ikusteko. (Irazusta, *Joan.* 171)
Theresa at once made her put it on for Joanixio to see.
b. Ez dizut eskutitz hau nire burua zuritzeko idazten. (Garate, *Musk*. 128)
I am not writing you this letter in order to excuse myself.

21.4.2 Delimitatives and the Subjunctive

In a delimitative context involving prospective action, use of the subjunctive is optional. Constructions with *arte*, taken from the standard Bible version, will serve as illustrations:

(24) a. Ez dizut utziko, bedeinka nazazun arte. (Gn 32:27)
I will not leave you, until you bless me.

b. Jeseren seme hori lurrean bizi dadin arte, ez haiz seguru izango. (1 Sm 20:31)
   As long as that son of Jesse lives upon the earth, yoú will not be safe.
c. Hilabete osoan jango duzue, sudurretatik atera dakizuen arte.
   Yoû shall eat it for a whole month, until it comes out of yoûr nostrils. (Nm 11:20)

In all such examples, the indicative is equally possible and, in fact, more common: *bedeinkatzen nauzun arte, bizi den arte, ateratzen zaizkizuen arte*. In colloquial style, however, use of the perfect participle prevails: *bedeinkatu arte, bizi arte, atera arte.*

21.4.3 Prospective Action and the Subjunctive

When a *-nean* or *-neko* clause (see section 20.2.2) relates to prospective action, many southern writers like to make use of the subjunctive:

(25) a. Haz nadinean, Alemania osoa pasatuko dut hura bilatzen. (Garate, *NY* 29)
   When I'll have grown up, I will cross the whole of Germany looking for her.
b. Zahar zaitezenean ere, izango duzu hiltzeko astirik. (Garate, *Leh.* 20)
   When you'll have grown old too, you will have time to die.
c. Itzul nadinean esango didazu. (*TOE* I, 207)
   You will tell me when I return.
d. Berak erantzun zezanean egingo zion gutun berri bat. (Atxaga, *Obab.* 43)
   When he replied, she would write him a new letter.
e. Ongi daki Jainkoak, hartatik jan dezazuenean, begiak zabalduko zaizkizuela. (Gn 3:5)
   God knows very well that, when yoû eat from it, yoûr eyes will be opened.

This use of the subjunctive is likely to be imputable to Spanish influence. It is quite unknown in the northern dialects, and not a genuine part of colloquial usage in the south either. The following examples, all from southern sources, show the indicative form employed with prospective action:

(26) a. Patxi etortzen denean hasiko dugu bilera. (*EGLU* II, 420)
   When Frank comes, we will start the meeting.
b. Haunditzen naizenean, erdaraz mintzatuko al naiz? (Satrustegi, 192)
   When I grow up, will I speak Spanish?
c. Hitzegingo dugu itzultzen naizenean. (Atxaga, *Grl.* 127)
   We will talk when I return.
d. Berarekin hitzegiten duzunean, ederki ulertuko duzu. (Zapirain, *M.* 90)
   When you speak with her, you will understand it perfectly.
e. Gatz hau guztiz urtu denean, gazitzen da berdin beste aldetik. (Uriarte, *Dial.* 88)
   When this salt is completely dissolved, one salts it likewise on the other side.

In (26e) we have the indicative, despite the presence of the subjunctive in the Spanish original: *cuando esta sal se haya derretido enteramente. . . .*

21.5 Subjunctive Relatives

Use of the subjunctive in relative clauses is not a feature of colloquial Basque. Yet in situations where a more elegant style is called for, referential indefiniteness may sanction the use of the subjunctive inside a relative. According to the Basque grammarian B. Oihartzabal, this practice, while present in older northern texts, is nowadays confined to southern literary usage. Examples are not at all easy to find:

(27) a. Ez dio bat ere gerta dakion egitekok kalterik eginen, bat ere bekaturik ez duenari. (Ax. 442)
To one who has no sin at all, any trouble that might happen to him will do no harm at all.
b. Hasi zen emakume hari pozgarri izan zekizkion hitzak esaten. (Cf. *EGLU* V, 199)
He started to say words that might be comforting to that woman.
c. Ez diet egin diezazkidaten galderei erantzunik emango.
I will give no answer to the questions they may ask me.
d. Egin dezazuen guztia egin maitasunez. (1 Cor 16:14)
All that yoû do, do it in love.

Example (28), a kind of corelative, is dismissed by B. Oihartzabal as an obvious loan translation from French *quoi que vous fassiez* . . . , quite untypical of normal usage.

(28) Edozer egin dezazuen, guztia Jesus Jaunaren izenean izan dadila. (Col 3:17; *Biblia*)
Whatever yoû do, may it be in the name of the Lord Jesus.

21.6 Hortatives

I will use the term hortative for all subjunctive main clauses because they all serve to exhort a group of persons of which the speaker forms part to carry out the action denoted by the verb, or in a negative context, to refrain from doing so. Thus hortatives only occur in the present tense, and must have a first-person subject, usually plural, but occasionally singular.

The term main clause here is used in a superficial sense; I argued in section 21.1 that a hortative should be analyzed as a subjunctive complement of a covert performative main clause. As shown by the following examples, there is a strong tendency for hortatives to be verb-initial:

(29) a. Edan dezagun oparo ardo gozo hori. (*LBB* 335)
Let us drink that sweet wine abundantly.
b. Salba ditzagun geure buruak! (Atxaga, *Obab*. 328)
Let us save ourselves!
c. Saia gaitezen oraingo gauzak oraingo begiz ikusten. (*MEIG* VIII, 151)
Let us try to see today's things with today's eyes.

d. Hurbil nadin gauza harrigarri hori ikustera. (Ex 3:3)
Let me get close to see that amazing thing.

e. Eman dezagun, bada, horrela dela. (*MEIG* VII, 172)
Let us grant, then, that it is so.

[*N.B.* Note the special meaning of *eman* in this context: 'to grant', 'to assume'.]

The following are examples of negative hortatives:

(30) a. Mateorekin ez gaitezen haserre. (Etxaniz, *Antz.* 141)
Let us not quarrel with Mateo.

b. Baina ez dezagun gurdia idien aurrean jar(ri). (Atxaga, *Grl.* 148)
But let us not set the cart before the oxen.

c. Baina ez nadin gehiago luza, azal dezadan dokumentua. (Atxaga, *Obab.* 26)
But let me delay no more, let me present the document.

[*N.B.* Compare this with the purpose clause: Baina gehiago luza ez nadin . . . 'But, so as not to delay anymore, . . .'.]

There also are synthetic hortatives, usually consisting of a present indicative synthetic verb form with the complementizer -*N* added:

(31) a. Goazen azkar. (Atxaga, *Gizona* 338)
Let's go quickly.

b. Noan beregana. (Jautarkol, *Ip.* 21)
Let me go to her.

c. Gatozen bigarren puntura. (*MEIG* VIII, 173)
Let's come to the second point.

d. Natorren berriz harira. (*MEIG* VII, 163)
Let me come once again to the topic. (Lit. 'to the thread')

In contrast to periphrastic ones, synthetic hortatives always relate to an immediate course of action. Thus *joan gaitezen Bilbora* means 'let us go to Bilbao' (that is, at the proper time, perhaps still to be agreed on), whereas *goazen Bilbora* means 'let's go to Bilbao (right now)'.

Perhaps for that reason, synthetic hortatives are incompatible with negation. A few transitive verbs have hortative forms not based on the indicative. The main examples are *demagun* (*MEIG* VII, 169) 'let us assume', from the verb *eman* 'to give' whose indicative, if used, would be *damagu*, and *desadan* 'let me say' (northern form *derradan*), from the verb *esan* 'to say', whose indicative, if used, would be *dasat*.

21.7 Optatives

Conjunctive main clauses are used to express an order, request, or wish on the part of the speaker. I will therefore refer to them by the term optative. Like hortatives, and for the same reason, optatives are main clauses only in appearance. It is clear from their definition that optatives, unlike hortatives, need impose no constraint on the nature of their subjects, and that they are confined to the present tense. Examples are

(32) a. Hau ez dadila sekulan berriro gerta. (Mendiguren, *Hamalau* 110)
Let this never happen again.
b. Egin dezala nahi duena. (*TOE* III, 60)
Let him do what he wants.
c. Luzaro bizi daitezela! (*MEIG* I, 195)
May they live long!
d. Zeruak gorde gaitzala! (*LBB* 28)
May heaven protect us!
e. Ikus dezadala zure irudia, entzun dezadala zure ahotsa. (Sg 2:14)
Let me see your figure, let me hear your voice.

Synthetic optatives also exist and consist of a present indicative synthetic verb form to which the complementizer -*LA* has been added:

(33) a. Bere herrira dihoala! (*G.* 352)
Let him go to his own village!
b. Datorrela Jose. (*G.* 287)
Let Joseph come.
c. Dagoela jan gabe. (*MEIG* IX, 109)
Let him stay without dinner.
d. Ez zoazela. (Bilintx, 138)
May you not go away.

As (33d) shows, synthetic optatives may co-occur with negation, unlike synthetic hortatives.

Of the obsolete verb *jin* 'to give' (see de Rijk 1985) only imperative and optative forms remain:

(34) a. Egun on dizula Jainkoak! (Etxaniz, *Irul. Neg.* 82)
May God give you a good day!
b. Jainkoak gabon dizuela. (*LBB* 156) (*gabon* = *gau on*)
May God give yoû a good night.

[*N.B.* The intransitive version of *jin* survives as a periphrastically conjugated verb in the eastern dialects, in which it has largely replaced *etorri* 'to come'.]

In the southern speech area, congratulations are conveyed by another optative relic: *bejondeizula, Ana!* (Etxaniz, *Antz.* 19) 'Congratulations to you, Ana!'; *Bejondeigula!* (*G.* 353) 'Congratulations to us!'. As *DGV* (IV, 525) explains, the person markers in these forms were originally ergative (**Biaje on dagizula* 'May you make a pleasant trip'), but have been reinterpreted as datives—whence *Bejondeiola* (*MEIG* IV, 42 = *MIH* 85) 'Good for him', 'Congratulations to him'.

21.8 Use of the Hypothetical Tense

Whereas a subjunctive complement to a conditional verb normally occurs in the present tense, in formal writing the hypothetical tense may be resorted to for the sake of elegance. Mitxelena's writings provide some examples:

(35) a. Ez luke nahi gerta lekion berarí gertatua. (*MEIG* I, 163)
She would not like what happened to herself to happen to her.
b. Ez nuke nahi inork hau txartzat har lezan. (*MEIG* VII, 185)
I wouldn't like anyone to take this amiss.
c. Esplikatu dudana besteren gogoeten ispilu zuzen izan ledin nahi nuke. (*MEIG* VIII, 136)
I would like what I have just explained to be a correct reflection of other people's thoughts.

Purpose clauses belonging to a conditional sentence form another optional context for the hypothetical tense:

(36) Baldin aita batek bere alabari dirua emango balio etxe bat eros lezan, zorotzat joko lukete denek.
If a father were to give money to his daughter in order for her to buy a house, everybody would consider him crazy.

21.9 Action Nominals with the Suffix -*keta*

The suffix -*keta* combines with most nonstative verb radicals and some nouns to form action nouns. Axular's usage seems to show that -*keta* used to be a nominalizing suffix operating on clauses (see Villasante 1974, 95). This is still the case in the southeastern varieties of the Biscayan dialect. There, for almost all verbs ending in the suffix -*tu*, derivatives with -*keta* have replaced the verbal noun, with inessive forms in -*ketan* serving as imperfect participles (see Zuazo 1999, 68).

Generally, the derived nouns indicate activities and processes. But for some verbs, the result of the activity may be much more salient than the activity itself, in which case the derived noun takes on a result sense. Clear examples are *erosketa* 'purchase', *irakurketa* 'interpretation', and *salaketa* 'denunciation', 'accusation'.

In its morphological aspects, the derivational process is quite regular. Verbs whose perfect participle ends in -*n* lose this consonant: *eragiketa* 'operation' from *eragin* 'to activate'. Slightly irregular is the form *heziketa* 'taming', 'education', where *hezketa* is the form expected. As a matter of fact, a more usual designation for 'education' is *hezkuntza*.

On account of their practical importance, a great many instances of deverbal action nouns with *-keta* are listed here:

agurtu	to greet	agurketa	greeting
aldatu	to change	aldaketa	change
antolatu	to organize, to set up	antolaketa	organization, adaptation
ari(tu)	to act, to work	ariketa	activity, exercise
asmatu	to figure out, to invent	asmaketa	invention, riddle
astindu	to shake	astinketa	shaking, shake, beating
aurkitu	to find, to discover	aurkiketa	find, finding, discovery
aztertu	to investigate, to examine	azterketa	examination, investigation
banatu	to distribute	banaketa	distribution
bereizi	to distinguish, to separate	bereizketa	distinction, separation
bidali	to send	bidalketa	sending, dispatch
bihurtu	to return	bihurketa	return, restitution
bilatu	to look for, to search	bilaketa	search
bildu	to gather, to collect	bilketa	gathering, collection
biluzi	to strip, to bare	biluzketa	stripping, baring
dastatu	to taste	dastaketa	tasting
egosi	to boil to digest	egosketa	boiling, digestion
ehortzi	to bury	ehorzketa	burial
ekarri	to bring	ekarketa	bringing, supply
erabili	to use, to handle	erabilketa	use, handling
eragin	to activate, to stimulate	eragiketa	operation
erakutsi	to show	erakusketa	showing, exposition, exhibition
eratu	to form, to organize	eraketa	formation, organization
erori	to fall	erorketa	fall
erosi	to buy	erosketa	purchase
erre	to burn, to smoke	erreketa	burning, smoking
eskolatu	to instruct, to train	eskolaketa	instruction, training
estali	to cover, to conceal	estalketa	covering, concealment
ezabatu	to wipe off	ezabaketa	deletion
frogatu	to prove	frogaketa	demonstration, proof
galdetu	to ask, to question	galdeketa	questioning, interrogation
garbitu	to clean, to wash	garbiketa	cleaning, washing, liquidation
grabatu	to record	grabaketa	recording
harrapatu	to catch, to capture	harrapaketa	capture
hausnartu	to ruminate, to muse	hausnarketa	rumination, meditation
hautatu	to select	hautaketa	selection
hautsi	to break	hausketa	breaking, rupture
hedatu	to extend, to spread	hedaketa	extension, spreading

hezi	to tame, to educate	heziketa	taming, education
hil	to kill	hilketa	killing
ibili	to walk	ibilketa	walking
idatzi	to write	idazketa	writing
ikasi	to learn	ikasketa	studying, study
ikertu	to investigate	ikerketa	investigation, research
ikusi	to see	ikusketa	vision, sight
inausi	to prune	inausketa	pruning
irabiatu	to churn, to disturb	irabiaketa	turning, disturbance
irakurri	to read	irakurketa	reading, interpretation
irarri	to engrave, to print	irarketa	engraving, printing
irauli	to turn over	iraulketa	overturning, turning, swing
isuri	to pour, to shed	isurketa	pouring, shedding
itaundu	to ask	itaunketa	questioning, interrogation
itzuli	to return, to translate	itzulketa	overturning, return, translating
jaso	to lift, to raise	jasoketa	lifting, raising, building
jolastu	to play	jolasketa	play, amusement
jorratu	to weed, to treat	jorraketa	weeding out, cultivation
josi	to sew	josketa	sewing
jostatu	to have fun	jostaketa	entertainment, pastime (*josteta*)
kendu	to take away	kenketa	removal, subtraction
konpondu	to settle, to repair	konponketa	settlement, repairing
kontatu	to tell, to count	kontaketa	narration, counting
labaindu	to slip, to slide	labainketa	slipping, sliding
lehertu	to burst, to explode	leherketa	bursting, explosion
lehiatu	to challenge, to compete	lehiaketa	challenging, competition
leundu	to soften, to polish	leunketa	softening, polishing, caress
miatu	to search, to inspect	miaketa	search, inspection
moldatu	to form, to adapt	moldaketa	adaptation, formation
moztu	to cut, to shear	mozketa	cutting, shearing
mugatu	to limit	mugaketa	delimitation, restriction
nahasi	to mix, to mix up	nahasketa	mixture, confusion
negoziatu	to negotiate	negoziaketa	negotiation
neurtu	to measure	neurketa	measuring
ordaindu	to compensate, to pay	ordainketa	paying, payment, payoff
orraztu	to comb	orrazketa	combing, revision
osatu	to complete, to heal	osaketa	completion, healing, cure
pentsatu	to think	pentsaketa	thought
prestatu	to prepare	prestaketa	preparation
probatu	to try out, to taste	probaketa	experiment, trial, tasting
saiatu	to try, to attempt	saiaketa	attempt, trial, experiment

salatu	to denounce, to accuse	salaketa	denunciation, accusation
salerosi	to trade	salerosketa	trade
sendatu	to cure	sendaketa	cure
soildu	to raze, to crop	soilketa	razing, devastation
sortu	to generate, to create	sorketa	generating, creating
telefonatu	to phone	telefonaketa	phoning
txertatu	to graft, to inject	txertaketa	grafting, insertion
txukundu	to tidy	txukunketa	tidying, cleaning up
urratu	to tear, to rend	urraketa	tearing, tear, rift
zapaldu	to trample, to oppress	zapalketa	trampling, oppression
zatitu	to divide	zatiketa	dividing, division
zenbatu	to count	zenbaketa	counting
zigortu	to whip, to punish	zigorketa	whipping, punishment
zorroztu	to sharpen	zorrozketa	sharpening
zulatu	to pierce, to drill	zulaketa	piercing, drilling, boring
zuritu	to whitewash, to flatter	zuriketa	whitewashing, flattery
zuzendu	to straighten, to correct	zuzenketa	correction

The suffix *-keta* can be added also to some nouns, the result likewise denoting an action related to the base noun. With names of tools the derivation is fully productive (e.g., *mailuketa* 'hammering' from *mailu* 'hammer'); otherwise its scope is fairly limited. Sometimes an apparently unpredictable allomorph *-eta* appears, which is held by some scholars to be the original form of this suffix. The main examples are

arnas	breath	arnasketa	breathing
arrain	fish	arrainketa	fishing
berri	report, news	berriketa	gossip, twaddle, talk
ele	word	eleketa	conversation
gogo	mind	gogoeta	thought, meditation, idea
hil	death, dead	hileta	funeral, wailing, lamentation
hitz	word	hizketa	speech, talk
indar	strength	indarketa	exertion, effort
lapur	thief	lapurreta	theft
sari	reward, prize	sariketa	contest, competition
sexu	sex	sexuketa	sexual relations
solas	talk	solasketa	conversation
tiro	shot	tiroketa	shooting
txapel	beret, hat	txapelketa	championship
ume	young, child	umeketa	procreation
zezen	bull	zezenketa	bullfight
zotz	tiny stick, toothpick	zozketa	drawing lots

Forms of address are also expressed with the suffix *-keta*: *hiketa* 'familiar address using *hi*'; *zuketa* 'polite address using *zu*'; *beroriketa* 'superpolite address using *berori*'. *Hiketa* to a male is called *toketa*, to a female *noketa*.

A few of these denominal action nouns may have originated as compounds with the noun *keta* 'quest, search', a loanword surviving only in the northern dialects. It is responsible for compounds such as *egurketa* 'search for firewood', *lanketa* 'search for work', *urketa* 'search for water', and *zorriketa* 'search for lice'.

21.10 The Nominal Suffix *-keta* Denoting Abundance

A suffix *-keta* surviving only in the eastern dialects can be added to some concrete nouns *N*, with the resulting noun indicating a considerable quantity of *N* present in one place. Examples are

ardi	sheep	ardiketa	herd of sheep
behi	cow	behiketa	herd of cows
behor	mare	behorketa	herd of mares
diru	money	diruketa	pile of money, fortune
egur	firewood	egurketa	heap of firewood
elur	snow	elurketa	abundance of snow
euri	rain	euriketa	abundance of rain
jende	people	jendeketa	crowd of people
lur	earth	lurketa	heap of earth
mendi	mountain	mendiketa	range of mountains

Place names still indicate that this suffix used to be employed with names of plants and trees all over the Basque-speaking area: *Amezketa*, that is, a place with many white oaks (*ametz*); *Harizketa*, that is, a place with many oak trees (*haritz*); *Sarasketa*, that is, a place with many willows (*sarats*).

21.11 Vocabulary

agindu	to command, to order, to promise
arrazoi *edun	to be right
berriketa	gossip, twaddle, talk
bukatu	to finish
eskatu	to ask for, to urge
eskuargi	flashlight, pocket torch
hizketa	speech, talk, conversation
ikasketa	studying, study
ikastola	Basque school

komeni	fitting, suitable
larru	hide, skin
lehenbailehen	as soon as possible

21.12 Exercises

21.12.1 Translate into English

1. Euskaraz ez dakienak ikas dezala lehenbailehen.
2. Goazen etxera, afaria hotz ez dakigun.
3. Ez da komeni elkarrekin hizketan ikus gaitzaten. (*TOE* II, 366)
4. Ez nuke nahi gure berriketak entzun ditzaten. (*TOE* III, 89)
5. Nork ez luke nahi bakea etor ledin?
6. Ordu da erretzeari utz diezaiozun.
7. Nola nahi duzue zuen haurrek ezer ikas dezaten, ikastolara joaten uzten ez badiezue?
8. Buka dezagun sorginek lehenbailehen buka dezagun nahi duten lana.
9. Nahi duenak nahi duena egin dezala; ni etxera noa.
10. Nahi ez duenak del dezaten otso, ez dezala jantz otso-larrurik. (Ax. 403)
11. Gure arrebak lagun diezazun ahaleginduko naizela agintzen dizut.
12. Zure arreba nirekin ezkon dadin ahalegin zaitezela agintzen dizut.

21.12.2 Translate into Basque Using the Subjunctive Whenever Possible

1. I have brought this book for Frank to see.
2. Have I ever told you to write a book?
3. We did not want you to do this work.
4. I am urging you now not to burn my book.
5. It is fitting that witches should live with witches.
6. May the devil take you!
7. I do not want anyone to know your name.
8. Let me see what has happened.
9. I carried a flashlight so as not to lose the way.
10. Let us now grant that Mr. Gorostiaga is right.
11. Paul urged everybody to eat something.
12. I will pay you when I finish my studies.

22 Imperatives and Jussives

22.1 Introduction

The Basque verbal system makes available a set of forms we may call imperative forms, as they fulfill the same function as the imperative mood in the surrounding Romance languages. Morphologically, these are second-person subject forms, and sentences constructed with them have indeed second-person subjects, as evidenced by the optional occurrence of the corresponding subject pronouns and also by the existence of reflexive imperatives with phrases like *heure burua*, *zeure burua*, and *zeuen buruak* discussed in section 15.7.

A felicitous uttering of an imperative sentence performs an imperative speech act directed at the addressee of the utterance. The term "imperative speech act" is meant to cover three pragmatic categories: commanding, requesting, and advising. Which of these three we are dealing with in a particular utterance can be determined by the presence of certain adverbials or particles and, above all, by the various modalities of sentence intonation.

Furthermore, Basque distinguishes itself from the Romance languages and, for that matter, from the Germanic and Slavic languages as well, by maintaining a special mood, the jussive, used when the intended agent of a command, request, or advice on the part of the speaker is not identical with the addressee of the utterance. Thus jussive forms are third-person subject forms.

To cope with the situation where Basque employs jussives, the Romance languages must resort to the subjunctive mood, thus adding to the functions of the latter.

22.2 Imperative Morphology

The imperative is no exception to the overall pattern of Basque verbal morphology: intransitive verbs are treated differently from transitive ones. Another fact to be noted is that the imperatives of the verbs *izan* 'to be' and **edun* 'to have', also serving as auxiliaries, do not follow the regular paradigm but are based instead on the corresponding subjunctive forms.

22.2.1 Synthetic Imperatives of Intransitives Other Than *izan*

Whereas most verbs have no synthetic conjugations (section 6.2.1), the following intransitives do possess synthetic imperatives: *egon* 'to stay', 'to be'; *ekin* 'to take up', 'to persist'; *etorri* 'to come'; *etzan* 'to lie down'; *ibili* 'to walk'; *izan* 'to be'; *jarraitu* 'to follow'; *joan* 'to go'.

Only the verb *izan* 'to be' has special forms for the imperative, for which see section 22.2.3. The imperatives of all other intransitives are segmentally identical to the second-person present tense forms, from which, however, they are readily distinguished by their characteristic falling intonation pattern. Examples are

hator	come (yoú)	hago	stay (yoú)
zatoz	come (you)	zaude	stay (you)
zatozte	come (yoû)	zaudete	stay (yoû)

hoa	go (yoú)
zoaz	go (you)
zoazte	go (yoû)

habil	walk (yoú)
zabiltza	walk (you)
zabiltzate	walk (yoû)

[*N.B.* Imperatives of *egon* also convey the meaning of the English idiom *wait a moment*.]

The verbs *ekin* and *jarraitu* require a dative complement. As intransitive use of *ekin* is virtually obsolete, only the imperative of *jarraitu* will be exemplified:

harrait	follow me (yoú)	harraio	follow him (yoú)
zarraizkit	follow me (you)	zarraizkio	follow him (you)
zarraizkidate	follow me (yoû)	zarraizkiote	follow him (yoû)

Dative imperatives of *etorri* and *joan* seldom occur in speech but are found in texts:

(1) a. Zatozkit, etzan nirekin, ene arreba. (2 Sm 13:11)
Come to me, lie with me, my sister. (For *etzan*, see section 22.3.3.)
b. Zatozkidate bihar ordu honetan Izreelera. (2 Kgs 10:6)
Come to me in Jezreel tomorrow at this time.

[*N.B.* Instead of *zatoz*, *zatozte*, the Guipuzcoan dialect has devised a special imperative form *atoz*, *atozte*, and the Labourdin dialect has *zato* instead of *zatoz*. These forms are not acceptable in Batua.]

22.2.2 Synthetic Imperatives of Transitives Other Than **edun*

The following transitive verbs allow synthetic imperatives: all verbs listed in section 9.1 except for **ion* 'to say'; in addition, *eman* 'to give' and *iritzi* 'to consider (as)' introduced in chapter 15, as well as a number of verbs that allow a synthetic imperative while lacking a synthetic indicative: *erosi* 'to buy'; *esan* 'to say'; *eutsi* 'to grip'; *igorri* 'to send'; *ihardetsi* 'to answer'; *irakatsi* 'to teach'; *jin* 'to give'; *utzi* 'to leave', 'to lend', 'to let'. Note, however, that synthetic imperatives are limited to forms with third-person direct objects.

For a transitive verb with a singular third-person direct object, synthetic imperatives consist of the verb radical—in some cases slightly modified at the end—completed by a second-person ergative marker: *-ga* (yielding *-k* by the word-final adjustment rules of section 9.1), *-na* (yielding *-n* after a vowel), *-zu*, or *-zue*. With a dative complement present or understood, there will also be a dative person marker in prefinal position—just as in the indicative.

The modifications undergone by the radical are minor in nature: elision of final *-n* or *-t* and, except in the presence of a dative marker, addition of the vowel *a* to a final sibilant or affricate. Thus with *eman* 'to give', *ezagutu* 'to recognize', and *erakutsi* 'to show', we get

emak	give (yoú)
eman	give (yoù)
emazu	give (you)
emazue	give (yoû)
ezaguk	recognize (yoú)
ezagun	recognize (yoù)
ezaguzu	recognize (you)
ezaguzue	recognize (yoû)
erakutsak	show (yoú)
erakutsan	show (yoù)
erakutsazu	show (you)
erakutsazue	show (yoû)

Not counting **edun*, there are three irregular verbs using the stem instead of the radical: *eduki* 'to hold', *jardun* 'to be busy (with)', *jin* 'to give'.

Thus the imperative forms of *eduki* are based on its stem *-uka-* prefixed by *e-*: *eukak, eukan, eukazu, eukazue*.

The verb *jardun* makes use of its stem *-ihardu-*: *iharduk, ihardun, iharduzu, iharduzue.*

Transitive *jin* 'to give' is restricted to optatives (section 21.7) and imperatives. It has no periphrastic conjugation. In its imperative use, it requires a first-person indirect object. When this is singular, the stem is *-in-*: *indak, indan, indazu, indazue* 'give it to me'. When this is plural, the stem reduces to *-i-*: *iguk, igun, iguzu, iguzue* 'give it to us'. None of these forms occur colloquially.

As regards the morphology of dative forms, we recall from section 15.1 that some verbs require a pre-dative marker: *dakarkidazu* 'you are bringing it to me', *dakarkiozu* 'you are bringing it to him'. No such markers are found in imperatives: *ekardazu* 'bring it to me'. However, between the radical and a third-person dative marker, a vowel *i* intervenes (as in *ekarriozu* 'bring it to him'), which is merely optional for a radical ending in a sibilant or affricate: *utziozu* or *utzozu* 'lend it to him'. (Compare *uztazu* 'lend it to me', *uzkuzu* 'lend it to us'.)

In all dative forms, plurality of the direct object is indicated by a pluralizer *-zki-* preceding the dative person marker. Radicals ending in a sibilant or affricate insert the vowel *a* before *-zki-*: *utzazkidazu* 'lend them to me'.

As to plural direct objects in nondative forms, synthetic imperatives, as a rule, give way to periphrastic forms. Yet verbs with past participles ending in a nasal—always *-n*—do allow synthetic imperatives with plural direct objects. These are constructed with the pluralizer *-itza-* —apparently borrowed from the imperative of **edun*—suffixed to the modified radical: *eramaitzazu* 'carry them off'.

The only remaining exceptions are *ezagutu*, whose imperative also employs the pluralizer *-itza-*, and, finally, *eduki* with its pluralizing infix *z* also appearing in the imperative forms: *euzkazu* 'hold them'.

To end this section, we may conclude that transitive verbs, unlike intransitives, evince a clear contrast between indicative and imperative morphology, the main difference residing in the absence from the latter of the present tense marker *d(a)-*.

22.2.3 Imperative Forms of Intransitive *izan* 'to be'

In forming its imperative, intransitive *izan* resorts to its subjunctive stem *-di-*, which, as seen in section 21.2.1, reduces to zero when preceding the pre-dative marker *-ki*. As a matter of fact, the imperative forms can be obtained from the corresponding second-person subject forms of the subjunctive present by removing the final complementizer and applying the usual word-final adjustment rules of section 9.1 to the outcome. This procedure results in the following paradigm:

hadi	be (yoú) (cf. subj. *hadin*)	zaitez	be (you) (cf. subj. *zaitezen*)
hakit	be to me (cf. subj. *hakidan*)	zakizkit	be to me (cf. subj. *zakizkidan*)
hakio	be to him (cf. subj. *hakion*)	zakizkio	be to him (cf. subj. *zakizkion*)
hakigu	be to us (cf. subj. *hakigun*)	zakizkigu	be to us (cf. subj. *zakizkigun*)
hakie	be to them (cf. subj. *hakien*)	zakizkie	be to them (cf. subj. *zakizkien*)

[*N.B.* The standard form *zaitez* has been borrowed from the Biscayan dialect. The remaining dialects prefer a form without a final sibilant: *zaite* or *zite*.]

zaitezte	be (yoû) (cf. subj. *zaitezten*)
zakizkidate	be to me (cf. subj. *zakizkidaten*)
zakizkiote	be to him (cf. subj. *zakizkioten*)

zakizkigute	be to us (cf. subj. *zakizkiguten*)
zakizkiete	be to them (cf. subj. *zakizkieten*)

In contemporary usage, these forms appear as auxiliaries only:

(2) a. Izan zaitezte errukitsuak. (Lk 6:36)
Be compassionate.
b. Ez zaitez sinplea izan. (Atxaga, *Grl.* 82)
Don't be silly.

22.2.4 Imperative Forms of Transitive **edun* 'to have'

Like intransitive *izan*, transitive **edun* relies on its subjunctive stem *-za-* to coin its imperatives. These too can be obtained from the corresponding second-person subject forms of the subjunctive present by removing the final complementizer and applying the word-final adjustment rules described in section 9.1, provided one important difference be taken into account. I am referring, of course, to the present tense marker, which is lacking in all transitive imperatives, as noted in section 22.2.2. Hence the omission of the otherwise expected *d-* in the forms with a third-person direct object. In this way, the following paradigm is fully accounted for:

ezak	have (yoú) it	(cf. subj. *dezaan*)
ezan	have (yoù) it	(cf. subj. *dezanan*)
ezazu	have (you) it	(cf. subj. *dezazun*)
ezazue	have (yoû) it	(cf. subj. *dezazuen*)
itzak	have (yoú) them	(cf. subj. *ditzaan*)
itzan	have (yoù) them	(cf. subj. *ditzanan*)
itzazu	have (you) them	(cf. subj. *ditzazun*)
itzazue	have (yoû) them	(cf. subj. *ditzazuen*)
nazak	have (yoú) me	(cf. subj. *nazaan*)
nazan	have (yoù) me	(cf. subj. *nazanan*)
nazazu	have (you) me	(cf. subj. *nazazun*)
nazazue	have (yoû) me	(cf. subj. *nazazuen*)
gaitzak	have (yoú) us	(cf. subj. *gaitzaan*)
gaitzan	have (yoù) us	(cf. subj. *gaitzanan*)
gaitzazu	have (you) us	(cf. subj. *gaitzazun*)
gaitzazue	have (yoû) us	(cf. subj. *gaitzazuen*)
iezadak	have (yoú) it to me	(cf. subj. *diezadaan*)
iezadan	have (yoù) it to me	(cf. subj. *diezadanan*)
iezadazu	have (you) it to me	(cf. subj. *diezadazun*)
iezadazue	have (yoû) it to me	(cf. subj. *diezadazuen*)

iezaiok	have (yoú) it to him	(cf. subj. *diezaioan*)
iezaion	have (yoù) it to him	(cf. subj. *diezaionan*)
iezaiozu	have (you) it to him	(cf. subj. *diezaiozun*)
iezaiozue	have (yoû) it to him	(cf. subj. *diezaiozuen*)
iezaguk	have (yoú) it to us	(cf. subj. *diezaguan*)
iezagun	have (yoù) it to us	(cf. subj. *diezagunan*)
iezaguzu	have (you) it to us	(cf. subj. *diezaguzun*)
iezaguzue	have (yoû) it to us	(cf. subj. *diezaguzuen*)
iezaiek	have (yoú) it to them	(cf. subj. *diezaiean*)
iezaien	have (yoù) it to them	(cf. subj. *diezaienan*)
iezaiezu	have (you) it to them	(cf. subj. *diezaiezun*)
iezaiezue	have (yoû) it to them	(cf. subj. *diezaiezuen*)

As usual in dative forms, a plural direct object is marked by a suffix *-zki* directly after the stem: *iezazkidazu* 'have (you) them to me'.

Nowadays, imperative forms of **edun*, like those of *izan*, only occur as auxiliaries:

(3) a. Zure haur batez bezala nitaz arta izan ezazu otoi. (Duvoisin, *L.Ed.* 186)
Please take care of me like one of your children.
b. Horretan kontua izan ezazue, neskatxak eta mutilak. (Uztapide, *Noizb.* 101)
Have caution in that matter, girls and boys.

Use of the participle *izan* is obligatory in these and similar examples.

22.3 Syntax of Imperatives

22.3.1 Synthetic Imperatives

There are two important points to be made about the syntactic behavior of synthetic imperatives. First of all, they form a noteworthy exception to the statement in section 8.6.1, which claimed that any synthetic verb form is incomplete and requires the prefix *ba-* unless completed by a preceding focus constituent. As we will see shortly, imperatives often occur clause-initially and admit no prefix whatsoever. The second point has typological interest. Unlike periphrastic ones, synthetic imperatives are incompatible with negation in all dialects: *ez zoaz* can only be indicative 'you are not going' and **ez ekarzu* does not exist at all.

The following are typical examples of imperative sentences:

(4) a. Zatoz ohera, hoztu egingo zara. (Urretabizkaia, *Sat.* 89)
Come to bed, you will get cold.
b. Hoa laster sugea hiltzera. (Atxaga, *Bi An.* 106)
Go quickly to kill the snake.

c. Esadazu orain egia. (Atxaga, *Obab.* 381)
Tell me now the truth.
d. Egizu nahi duzuna. (*TOE* I, 180)
Do what you want.
e. Egizkidazu argiekin hiru piztualdi. (Garate, *G.E.* 10)
Give me (lit. make me) three flashes with the lights.
f. Uztazu zure ahotsa entzuten. (Sg 8:13)
Let me hear your voice.

Initial position for the imperative verb is typical but by no means obligatory. Various constituents of the sentence may precede:

(5) a. Zu isilik zaude, Lierni! (*TOE* III, 49)
You be quiet, Lierni!
b. Gainerako guztiok zoazte bakean zeuen aitarengana. (Gn 44:17)
All the rest of yoû, go in peace to yoûr father.
c. Seme hori indazu, Eliasek esan zion. (*TZ* II, 64)
"Give me that son," Elijah said to her. (Cf. *emadazu semea* in 1 Kgs 17:19)
d. Nik diodana egizu! (Labayen, *Su Em.* 193)
Do what I say!
e. Mutil honi kinina emaiozue. (Zapirain, *M.* 65)
Give this boy quinine.

To call someone's attention or to address someone, western Basque makes use of the paradigm *aizak*, *aizan*, *aizu*, *aizue*—most likely representing contractions of the imperative of *aditu* 'to hear', 'to listen'. Some examples are

(6) a. Aizu laguna, lagun on-ona, ez al da iritsi ordua? (Atxaga, *Behi* 13)
Hey buddy, excellent buddy, hasn't the time arrived?
b. Aizu, baina hori beste kontu bat da. (*MEIG* IX, 84)
But listen, that is another matter.
c. Aizak, emango diat alaba. (Zavala, *Txirr.* 150)
Listen, I will give yoú a daughter.
d. Aizan Andoni, ba al dakin zer egin behar genukeen? (*LBB* 72)
Listen Andoni, do yoù know what we should do?

An unexplained paradigm *to* (familiar, to a male), *no* (familiar, to a female), *tori* or *tori-zu* (polite, unmarked), *torizue* (to several people) is used for urging someone to accept a gift that is being offered, or else a punishment on the verge of being wrought:

(7) a. Tori nire pastela. (Atxaga, *Bi An.* 40)
Take my cake.
b. Hark esan zidan: "Tori eta irentsi . . ." (Rv 10:9)
He said to me: "Take it and swallow it . . ."

c. Torizu orain bostekoa eta izan ongi etorria. (Uztapide, *Noizb*. 17)
Take my handshake and be welcome.
d. Torizu nire erantzuna! (Zapirain, *Etork*. 84)
Take my answer! (She spits at him)
e. To, to, hau ere, eta urririk, kontuaren gaineko! (Barbier, *Sup*. 149)
Take, take this too, and free of charge, on top of the bill!
f. No, Xaneta! Hori hiretako! (Barbier, *Sup*. 149)
Take, Jeannette! That's for yoù!

In the eastern dialects, the forms *to* and *no* can also be used for calling someone's attention or addressing someone, in the same fashion as *aizak* and *aizan* in the western dialects:

(8) a. To, Pello, horra Olhetako bidea. (*P.Ad*. 52)
Look, Pete, there's the road to Olheta.
b. No, Maria, ez otoi, kexa! (Barbier, *Sup*. 122)
Listen, Maria, please don't get angry!

Finally, in the northern dialects, *to* can be employed as an interjection of surprise to either sex:

(9) a. To, hi ere atxoaren beldur haiz? (*Larzabal* I, 36)
(To the maid): Hey, are you also afraid of the little old lady?
b. To, zu hemen Jana-Mari! (*Larzabal* I, 213)
Hey, you here, Jeanne-Marie!
c. To, kanperoaren alaba, Benita, heldu da! (Larzabal, *Hiru* 32)
Hey, the field guard's daughter, Benita, is coming!

22.3.2 Periphrastic Imperatives

Periphrastic imperatives consist of a combination of an imperative auxiliary with the radical or perfect participle of the main verb. The latter option is preferred in the Guipuzcoan and Biscayan colloquial, but the former is the recommended practice for Batua, in accord with older usage.

As in the indicative, the auxiliary immediately follows the main verb in an affirmative clause. Examples are

(10) a. Joan zaitez Euskal Herrira bolada baterako. (Atxaga, *Gizona* 206)
Go to the Basque Country for a while.
b. Jon, Jon, irakur ezazu hau! (Garate, *Leh*. 37)
John, John, read this!
c. Utz itzazu bakean. (Atxaga, *Gizona* 312)
Leave them in peace.
d. Utz iezaiozu behintzat jaten. (*MEIG* IX, 109)
Let him at least eat.

e. Har iezadazu neskatxa hori emaztetzat. (Gn 34:4)
   Get me that girl as a wife.
f. Emazte—esan zion Giuseppari—utzi ezazu zakua, eta zatozkit laguntzera. (Etxaniz, *Antz.* 145)
   "Wife," he said to Giuseppa, "put the bag down and come help me."

In the western dialects, but not in the eastern ones, negative periphrastic imperatives also occur and display auxiliary attraction; that is to say, just as in indicatives, the negated auxiliary precedes the radical (or perfect participle) and need not be contiguous to it:

(11) a. Ama, ez ezazu horrelakorik esan! (T. Agirre, *Uzt.* 120)
   Mother, don't say such things!
b. Mesedez! Ez nazazue hil! (Amuriza, *Hil* 217)
   Please! Don't kill me!
c. Ez ezak erokeriarik esan. (Atxaga, *Gizona* 94)
   Don't talk rubbish.
d. Lagun hori ez iezadak gehiago etxera ekarri. (Garate, *Hades* 27)
   Don't bring that fellow to my house anymore.
e. Ez zaitez hain suminkorra izan. (Atxaga, *Sara* 93)
   Don't be so irritable.
f. Tira, alaba, ez hadi horrela atsekabe! (Garate, *NY* 138)
   Come on, Daughter, don't get so distressed!

To express such meanings the eastern dialects resort to nonfinite imperatives: *ez horrelakorik erran* (section 22.3.3), or else optatives: *ez dezazula horrelakorik erran* (section 21.7). (*Erran* is the eastern equivalent of *esan*.)

We may note that K. Mitxelena, who was born in Rentería, conforms to eastern usage in rejecting negative imperatives and using optatives where such would be expected:

(12) a. Ez zaitezela ordea engaina, irakurle. (*MEIG* I, 123)
   Don't, however, delude yourself, reader.
b. Ez gaitzazula lotsaraz kanpotarren aurrean. (*MEIG* IX, 110)
   Don't make us ashamed in front of strangers.

22.3.3 Nonfinite Imperatives

Imperative speech acts do not require an imperative verb form. Either the perfect participle, in accord with a practice predominating in the western dialects, or the radical, widely used in the remaining dialects, can be employed wihout auxiliary to convey commands, requests, or advice, as long as the nature of the speech act is clear from the sentence intonation.

Following are some examples with the perfect participle:

(13) a. Jaso eskuak! (Garate, *Leh.* 101)
   Hands up!

b. Mikel, entzun orain ondo. (Atxaga, *Gizona* 337)
Now listen carefully, Michael.
c. Hartu furgoneta eta etorri nire atzetik. (Atxaga, *Gizona* 334)
Take the truck and come after me.
d. Utzi hori nire gain. (*TOE* II, 250)
Leave that to me.
e. Ondo lo egin! (Atxaga, *Gizona* 164, *Sara* 141)
Sleep well!
f. Igo mendira niregana eta zaude han. (Ex 24:12)
Climb up to me on the mountain and wait there.

The following examples involve negation:

(14) a. Ez jaitsi besoak! (Atxaga, *Gizona* 298)
Don't lower your arms!
b. Ez berandu etorri! (*TOE* III, 78)
Don't come late!
c. Ez niri begiratu. (Atxaga, *Gizona* 41)
Don't look at me.
d. Baina ez deitu niri. (Atxaga, *Gizona* 196)
But don't call me.
e. Ez uste izan hori, Agustine! (*TOE* III, 36)
Don't think that, Agustine!

Some examples from western authors using the radical follow:

(15) a. Ikus *FLV* I (1969), 113–132. (*MEIG* VII, 94)
See *FLV* I (1969), 113–132.
b. Barka, mesedez, aipamenaren luzea. (*MEIG* V, 96)
Please forgive the length of the quotation.
c. Hik segi nahi duana egiten. (Atxaga, *Gizona* 35)
Yoú, go on doing what yoú want.
d. Hala, sar ohean! (Garate, *Leh.* 20)
So, get into bed!
e. Utz baketan sendagileak. (Garate, *Alaba* 62)
Leave the doctors in peace.

Like the perfect participle, the radical can co-occur with negation:

(16) a. Ez tira! (Atxaga, *Sara* 14)
Don't shoot!
b. Ez niri uki! (Garate, *Leh.* 20)
Don't touch me!

c. Baina ez pentsa arazoa hain erraz konpondu denik. (Atxaga, *Gizona* 236)
   But don't think that the problem has been resolved that easily.
d. Ez nire hitzak gaizki har. (Garate, *E.E.* 71)
   Don't take my words wrong.
e. Hura berriz eni ez aipa. (Larzabal, *Senp.* 38)
   Don't mention that to me again. (*eni*: northern form for *niri*, cf. *ene*)

22.3.4 Command Softeners

As we observed in section 22.1, imperative utterances are instrumental in performing at least three different types of speech acts: commanding, requesting, and advising. Since the act of commanding requires rather special pragmatic conditions to be socially acceptable, speakers often feel the need to make clear that the intended speech act is not one of commanding but rather the more acceptable one of requesting. This can be effected by intonational means, but also by the use of certain adverbs, to be termed "command softeners," of which *please* is a typical example in English. While in general command softeners increase politeness, at times they are seen to have an opposite effect. The reason for this seems to be their implication that the speaker has a considerable stake in the addressee's complying with what thereby turns out to be a request, whereas the same utterance without the softener could be taken as proffering disinterested advice.

In standard Basque, four command softeners are in common use. In the south we find the instrumental adverb *mesedez* or much more rarely *faborez*, both meaning 'as a favor' (cf. Spanish *por favor*). They can be combined for greater effect: *mesedez eta faborez*. Somewhat stronger than *mesedez* and known in all dialects is *arren*, also occurring as a noun meaning 'plea', cf. *arren egin* 'to implore'. Finally, the obsolete as noun *otoi* 'prayer' (nowadays *otoitz*), still found in the idiom *otoi egin* 'to beseech', regularly appears as a command softener in the northern dialects, in which it has replaced an earlier loan translation *plazer baduzu* 'if you please'.

All command softeners can appear in finite as well as nonfinite imperatives and, given their status as sentence adverbs, may occur within the sentence in any position open to those (cf. section 11.4).

First, here are some examples of clause-initial command softeners:

(17) a. Mesedez, Guiomar, esna hadi pixka bat. (Atxaga, *Gizona* 157)
   Please, Guiomar, wake up a bit.
b. Mesedez, niri sermoirik ez bota. (Atxaga, *Gizona* 29)
   Please, don't launch a sermon at me.
c. Mesedez, utzi ene aitamei zuen artean bizitzen. (1 Sm 22:3)
   Please, let my father and mother live among yoû.
d. Arren, atera nazazu lehenbailehen hemendik. (Garate, *NY* 39)
   For goodness' sake, get me out of here as soon as possible.

e. Arren, Ezkira, utz iezadazu kontatzen. (Garate, *Leh.* 116)
For goodness' sake, Ezkira, let me tell it to you.

f. Otoi, Jana-Mari, zaude isilik. (Larzabal, *Senp.* 128, 132)
Please, Jeanne-Marie, be quiet.

g. Otoi, otoi, geldiaraz ezazu makila! (Barbier, *Lég.* 65)
Please, please, make the stick stop!

h. Otoi, ez negarrik egin! (Haranburu, *Job* 72)
Please, don't cry!

Examples of clause-final command softeners are

(18) a. Sar zaitez, sar, mesedez. (Garate, *Esku* 66)
Come in, come in, please.

b. Mesedez! Utz nazan mesedez! (Amuriza, *Hil* 100)
Please! Let me off, please!

c. Hemendik aurrera hola jokatu, mesedez. (Atxaga, *Gizona* 246)
Act that way from now on, please.

d. Ekarri giltza, faborez. (Atxaga, *Obab.* 48)
Bring the key, please.

e. Maita nazazu arren! (Bilintx, 91)
Love me for heaven's sake!

f. Sarraraz ezazu, sarraraz, otoi! (Larzabal, *Hil.* 22)
Have him come in, have him come in, please!

g. Kafe bat, mesedez. (Atxaga, *Z.H.* 42)
One coffee, please.

Here are some examples of clause-internal command softeners:

(19) a. Emadazu, arren, ur pixka bat zeure pegarretik. (Gn 24:17)
Give me, I beg you, a little water from your jar.

b. Bidal ezazu, arren, Lazaro gure aitaren etxera. (Lk 16:27)
Send, I beg you, Lazarus to my father's house.

c. Uztazu, otoi, herriari hitzegiten. (Acts 21:39)
Let me, please, speak to the people.

d. Erantzun, mesedez, gutun honi. (1 Mc 12:18)
Answer, please, this letter.

e. Ez gorde, arren, deus ere. (1 Sm 3:17)
Please, don't hide anything whatsoever.

f. Ez, arren, biraorik inori egotzi. (*P.Ab.* 70)
Please, don't throw curses at anyone.

Command softeners are not confined to imperative sentences. They may occur whenever a request is made or implied and serve to strengthen its force:

(20) a. Bere anaiari mesedez irakurtzen jarraitzeko esan zion. (Irazusta, *Bizia* 123)
She told her brother to please go on reading.
b. Mesedez eskatu nion harekin hausteko. (Garate, *NY* 16)
I asked him to please break off with her.
c. Mesedez, zaldi hau edukiko didazu apur batean? (Kirikiño, *Ab.* 22)
Please, will you hold this horse for a moment?
d. Mesedez, Villoslada jaunarekin hitz egin nahi nuke. (Garate, *E.E.* 43)
I would like to speak with Mr. Villoslada, please.

22.3.5 Monitive *gero*

The temporal adverb *gero* 'afterward' (section 20.1.2.1) can occur as a monitive particle in imperative, jussive, and optative sentences. It then conveys a warning that something dire is to happen, should the advice in question be ignored. As a rule this particle occurs in a nonfinite clause, usually one expressing a prohibition. Its favorite position is right after the negation *ez*:

(21) a. Ez gero niri gezurrik esan. (Iraola, 62)
Be sure not to tell me lies.
b. Ez gero inori ezer esan. (Agirre, *Kres.* 15)
Be sure not to tell anybody anything.
c. Ez gero poliziari gaztiga! (Garate, *NY* 35)
Be sure not to notify the police!

Actually, however, any position open to sentence adverbs also accommodates *gero*:

(22) a. Ez niri gero Donostia ukitu! (*TOE* I, 83)
Mind you do not run down San Sebastian to me!
b. Ez ahaztu gero Jauna zuen Jainkoa. (Dt 8:11)
Be careful not to forget the Lord yoûr God.
c. Nor denik ez esan gero! (*TOE* I, 182)
Be careful not to say who it is!

The particle *gero* can be used in positive commands as well:

(23) a. Horra hiru izen polit. Kontuan hartu, gero! (*LBB* 93)
Look, three pretty names. Be sure to pay attention to them!
b. Begira gero! (Mt 16:6, Mk 8:15)
Be sure to watch out!

Finite imperatives containing *gero* are fine with some speakers but rejected by others:

(24) a. Kontuz ibil zaitez, gero!
Be sure to walk carefully!

b. Egin ezazu, gero, lan hori!
   Be sure to do that work!

22.4 Jussive Morphology

Jussives in Basque are third-person-subject verb forms with a modal force very much like that of the imperative. Basque grammatical tradition therefore has referred to them as third-person imperatives.

The main morphological characteristic of the Basque jussive is an initial prefix *be-* present in most forms. As to the syntactic category of this prefix, B. Oihartzabal (2000) in his "Note à propos des formes jussives préfixées en *b-* du basque" made the attractive proposal that it is a complementizer, so that jussive clauses, on a par with optative ones, are main clauses only in appearance.

This complementizer *be-*, whose *e* elides before *i*, replaces the present tense marker *da-*, understandably absent in jussives. The remaining part of a jussive form is identical to the corresponding form of the indicative or, in the case of the auxiliaries, the truncated subjunctive—that is, the subjunctive after removal of the final complementizer *-N* and application of the word-final adjustment rules of section 9.1.

22.4.1 Synthetic Jussives of Intransitives Other Than *izan*

Precisely those intransitives that allow synthetic imperatives also allow synthetic jussives. There is one trivial exception: the verb *jario* 'to flow' (see section 15.2.2) does possess synthetic jussives, although, for obvious semantic reasons, it lacks an imperative. The morphology of these intransitive jussives fully conforms to the description given in the preceding section:

egon	etorri	etzan	ibili	joan
bego	betor	betza	bebil	bihoa
beude	betoz	beutza	bebiltza	bihoaz

Note that the jussive of *joan* is based on the long stem *-ihoa-* found in *dihoa* and *dihoaz*, and not on the short stem *-oa-* of *doa* and *doaz*.

Except for *etzan*, dative forms also exist: *begokit*, *betorkit*, *bebilkit*, *bihoakit*, and so on. The verbs *jarraitu* 'to follow' and *jario* 'to flow' only have dative forms:

berrait	berraizkit	berit	berizkit
berraik	berraizkik	berik	berizkik
berrain	berraizkin	berin	berizkin
berraio	berraizkio	berio	berizkio
berraigu	berraizkigu	berigu	berizkigu
berraizu	berraizkizu	berizu	berizkizu

berraizue	berraizkizue	berizue	berizkizue
berraie	berraizkie	berie	berizkie

22.4.2 Synthetic Jussives of Transitives Other Than **edun*

With the single exception of **ion* 'to say', only those transitive verbs that allow synthetic imperatives can have synthetic jussives. But not even all of these possess such forms. In contemporary usage as mandated by the Basque Academy, there are no synthetic jussives for the verbs *erosi* 'to buy', *esan* 'to say', *igorri* 'to send', *ihardetsi* 'to answer', *irakatsi* 'to teach', *jin* 'to give', and *utzi* 'to leave', all of which have synthetic imperatives.

Morphology here is completely regular. Inasmuch as synthetic jussives, like synthetic imperatives, are limited to third-person direct objects, all forms result from the corresponding indicatives by replacing initial *da-* or *de-* with *be-* and initial *di-* with *bi-*.

By way of illustration, five paradigms will be presented: those of *eduki* 'to hold', *egin* 'to make', *entzun* 'to hear', **ion* 'to say', and *jakin* 'to know'. They consist of four forms each, since both subject and direct object can be either singular or plural.

eduki	egin	entzun	*ion	jakin
beuka	begi	bentzu	bio	beki
beukate	begite	bentzute	biote	bekite
beuzka	begitza	bentzuzki	bioz	bekizki
beuzkate	begitzate	bentzuzkite	biotez	bekizkite

In contrast to the more erratic behavior of imperatives (see section 22.2.2), jussives always require the same pluralizer for their direct objects as in the indicative. A similar remark applies to the presence or absence of a pre-dative marker in the dative paradigms: *bekarkit, bekarkio* like *dakarkit, dakarkio*; but imperative *ekardazu, ekarriozu*.

22.4.3 Jussive Forms of Intransitive *izan* 'to be'

Just like its imperative, the jussive of *izan* is morphologically akin to its subjunctive present. This time, however, the third-person subject forms are to be taken as starting points. From these, the final complementizer has to be stripped off, after which the word-final adjustment rules of section 9.1 must apply. Last, the initial tense marker *da-* will be replaced by the complementizer prefix *be-*. This process yields the following paradigm:

bedi	(cf. subj. *dadin*)	bitez	(cf. subj *ditezen*)
bekit	(cf. subj. *dakidan*)	bekizkit	(cf. subj. *dakizkidan*)
bekik	(cf. subj. *dakian*)	bekizkik	(cf. subj. *dakizkian*)
bekin	(cf. subj. *dakinan*)	bekizkin	(cf. subj *dakizkinan*)
bekio	(cf. subj. *dakion*)	bekizkio	(cf. subj. *dakizkion*)
bekigu	(cf. subj. *dakigun*)	bekizkigu	(cf. subj. *dakizkigun*)

bekizu	(cf. subj. *dakizun*)	bekizkizu	(cf. subj. *dakizkizun*)
bekizue	(cf. subj. *dakizuen*)	bekizkizue	(cf. subj. *dakizkizuen*)
bekie	(cf. subj. *dakien*)	bekizkie	(cf. subj. *dakizkien*)

These forms are used in periphrastic constructions only—for example,

(25) a. Eta Jainkoak esan zuen: "Izan bedi argia." (Gn 1:3)
And God said: "Let there be light."
b. Zure dirua zure galmen izan bedi. (*TB* 173)
Let your money be your undoing. (For *galmen*, variant of *galpen*, see section 22.8.)
c. Aski izan bekit forma mintzatzea. (*MEIG* VII, 99)
Let it be sufficient for me to talk about the form.

In a few set expressions where *izan* functions as a substantive verb, the antiquated jussives *biz* and *bira* appear instead of *izan bedi* and *izan bitez*. The main example is *hala biz* occasionally used for *amen*, and often written as one word:

(26) a. Beraz, hala biz; denean hizpidean zaude. (Zaitegi, *Sof.* 72)
Thus, let it be so; you are right in everything.

Also, the following expression has the same archaic flavor as its English equivalent:

(26) b. Bira iraganak iragan. (Ax. 126)
Let bygones be bygones.

22.4.4 Jussive Forms of Transitive **edun* 'to have'

Just like the intransitive auxiliary, transitive **edun* resorts to its subjunctive stem to construct jussive forms. In the main, the procedure matches that for *izan*: third-person present subjunctives as starting points, removal of the final complementizer, and subsequent application of the word-final adjustment rules of section 9.1.

Also, initial *d-*, remnant of the tense marker *da-*, is replaced by *b-*, as part of the complementizer *be-*, whose vowel elides before *e* and *i*. But note that in the first- and second-person object forms, where the tense marker has given way to personal prefixes, no complementizer prefix is added in Batua.

This procedure, then, accounts for the following paradigm:

beza	let him have it	(cf. subj. *dezan*)
bezate	let them have it	(cf. subj. *dezaten*)
bitza	let him have them	(cf. subj. *ditzan*)
bitzate	let them have them	(cf. subj. *ditzaten*)
naza	let him have me	(cf. subj. *nazan*)
nazate	let them have me	(cf. subj. *nazaten*)

gaitza	let him have us	(cf. subj. *gaitzan*)
gaitzate	let them have us	(cf. subj. *gaitzaten*)
haza	let him have yoú	(cf. subj. *hazan*)
hazate	let them have yoú	(cf. subj. *hazaten*)
zaitza	let him have you	(cf. subj. *zaitzan*)
zaitzate	let them have you	(cf. subj. *zaitzaten*)
zaitzate	let him have yoû	(cf. subj. *zaitzaten*)
zaitzatete	let them have yoû	(cf. subj. *zaitzateten*)

As these forms are invariably part of a periphrastic construction anyway, I will add the verb *eman* 'to give' in order to facilitate the translation of the dative forms:

(eman) biezat	let him (give) it to me	(cf. subj. *diezadan*)
(eman) biezadate	let them (give) it to me	(cf. subj. *diezadaten*)
(eman) biezak	let him (give) it to yoú	(cf. subj. *diezaan*)
(eman) biezaate	let them (give) it to yoú	(cf. subj. *diezaaten*)
(eman) biezan	let him (give) it to yoù	(cf. subj. *diezanan*)
(eman) biezanate	let them (give) it to yoù	(cf. subj. *diezanaten*)
(eman) biezaio	let him (give) it to him	(cf. subj. *diezaion*)
(eman) biezaiote	let them (give) it to him	(cf. subj. *diezaioten*)
(eman) biezagu	let him (give) it to us	(cf. subj. *diezagun*)
(eman) biezagute	let them (give) it to us	(cf. subj. *diezaguten*)
(eman) biezazu	let him (give) it to you	(cf. subj. *diezazun*)
(eman) biezazute	let them (give) it to you	(cf. subj. *diezazuten*)
(eman) biezazue	let him (give) it to yoû	(cf. subj. *diezazuen*)
(eman) biezazuete	let them (give) it to yoû	(cf. subj. *diezazueten*)
(eman) biezaie	let him (give) it to them	(cf. subj. *diezaien*)
(eman) biezaiete	let them (give) it to them	(cf. subj. *diezaieten*)

As always, a plural direct object is marked by a suffix *-zki* directly after the stem: (*eman*) *biezazkit* 'let him (give) them to me'.

All jussives of **edun* are limited nowadays to periphrastic constructions; that is, they only occur as auxiliaries. Two examples will illustrate:

(27) a. Gizon bakoitzak izan beza bere emaztea. (1 Cor 7:2)
Let each man have his own wife.
b. Izan bezate behar dena. (Hiribarren, *Esk*. 69)
Let them have what is needed.

22.5 The Syntax of Jussives

The syntactic behavior of jussives is largely identical to that of imperatives.

22.5.1 Synthetic Jussives

Like synthetic imperatives, synthetic jussives are incompatible with negation and, while often sentence-initial, never take the prefix *ba-* of section 8.6.1. A few examples will suffice:

(28) a. Bihoa sukaldera. (*TOE* II, 197)
Let her go to the kitchen.
b. Bego oraindik neskatxa gurekin hamar bat egun. (Gn 24:55)
Let the girl still stay with us for ten days or so.
c. Beude zabalik zure begiak. (Neh 1:6)
Let your eyes be open.
d. Betorkigu zure erreinua. (Mt 6:10; *Lau Eb.*)
Let your kingdom come to us.

22.5.2 Periphrastic Jussives

Like imperatives, periphrastic jussives make use of the radical form of the verb or, in western colloquial style, the perfect participle. In an affirmative clause the auxiliary immediately follows the radical or participle; in a negative clause, it precedes:

(29) a. Egin bedi Jaungoikoaren borondatea! (Etxaniz, *Ito* 200)
Let God's will be done!
b. Barka biezat Aita Barandiaranek. (*MEIG* I, 239)
Let Father Barandiaran forgive it me.
c. Ez beza inork pentsa gaurko zenbaiten asmoak erabat baztertzekoak direla deritzodanik. (*MEIG* V, 36)
Let no one think that I feel that the proposals of certain contemporaries are to be totally discarded. (For *deritzodanik*, see sections 15.4.1 and 18.4.)
d. Ez beza inork bere burua engaina! (1 Cor 3:18)
Let no one delude himself!

22.6 Use and Function of the Jussive

22.6.1 Jussive Forms as Deferential Imperatives

As seen in section 6.1.6, the deferential mode of address using *berori* or its plural *beroriek* requires the use of third-person verb forms. The corresponding imperatives, therefore, also have to be third-person forms—that is, jussives. Examples of such jussives are

(30) a. Hitzegin beza, don Markox. (Etxaniz, *Ito* 173)
Speak, Mr. Markox.

b. Bai jauna! Sar bedi aurrera! (*TOE* III, 135)
Yes, sir! Come on in!
c. Goiz dabil, eskribau jauna, eseri bedi! (*TOE* II, 231)
You are out early, Mr. Notary, sit down!
d. Ez beza horrelakorik esan, aita. (*G*. 117)
Don't say such things, Father.
e. Hitzegin biezaio mutilari—agindu zuen emakumeak. (Atxaga, *Bi An*. 14)
"Speak to the boy," commanded the woman.

To all intents and purposes, these jussives behave as ordinary imperatives. The grammatical subject of the sentence denotes the addressee of the utterance, who is also the intended agent of the imperative speech act. Let us therefore agree to distinguish between these deferential jussives and those in which the conditions we just mentioned do not hold. Only the latter will be termed genuine jussives.

22.6.2 Genuine Jussives and Their Use

Genuine jussives involve commands, requests, or advice directed at some intended agent—just as imperatives do. But in the latter the intended agent coincides with the addressee of the utterance and at the same time serves as the referent of its grammatical subject. Now, whenever either of these two conditions is not satisfied, we will meet a jussive sentence with a jussive verb form. Thus there are two kinds of genuine jussives: one in which the intended agent coincides with the addressee of the utterance but is not its grammatical subject, and one in which the intended agent is distinct from the addressee.

The first kind is illustrated by examples (31a,b) and requires no further discussion:

(31) a. Zure beso-kakoek estutu nazate. (*LBB* 329)
Let the curves (lit. "hooks") of your arms clench me.
b. Zure hitza ere betor bat haienarekin. (2 Chr 18:12)
Let your word too agree with theirs.

The second kind can be seen in examples (32a–d), in which the addressee of the utterance is clearly not the intended agent:

(32) a. Berak betozkigu, eta berek atera gaitzate. (*TB* 200)
Let them come themselves, and themselves take us out.
b. Eman biezat musu! (Sg 1:2)
Let him kiss me!
c. Bestek bio arrazoizkoa den ala ez iritzi hori. (*MEIG* VIII, 29)
Let someone else say whether this opinion is reasonable or not.
d. Naaman nigana betor eta jakin beza Israelen profeta badela. (*TZ* II, 86)
Let Naaman come to me and let him know that there is a prophet in Israel.

When the only difference between the reference of the intended agent and that of the addressee is that the former is a quantified version of the latter—for example, as in 'each of yoû' versus 'yoû'—either the jussive or the imperative may occur:

(33) a. Sar bedi bakoitza bere etxean. (Amuriza, *Hil* 130)
Let everyone go into his own house.
b. Sar zaitezte bakoitza zeuen etxean.
Each of yoû go into your own house.

(34) a. Azter beza, bada, nork bere burua. (1 Cor 11:28)
Let everyone, then, examine himself.
b. Azter ezazue, bada, nork bere burua.
Each of yoû, then, examine himself.

22.6.3 Jussives versus Optatives

As observed in section 21.7, optatives are ambiguous in contemporary usage as they may express either an order (or request) or a wish on the part of the speaker. No such ambiguity obtains for jussives; these clearly have imperative force. Uttering a jussive is nothing less than an attempt to control the world. Consider the following:

(35) a. Baina Jainkoa ez bekigu mintza, hil ez gaitezen. (Ex 20:19; *Biblia*)
But let not God speak to us, lest we die.
b. Baina ez diezagula Jainkoak hitzegin, hil ez gaitezen. (Ex 20:19)
But let (or: may) not God speak to us, lest we die.

While example (35a) is unmistakably a request to God, (35b) may be taken as either that or a simple wish.

In many pronouncements occurring in the New Testament it is unessential to distinguish between wishes and orders, inasmuch as a wish on the part of a person of authority comes close to an order at any rate. Accordingly, several New Testament passages can, and have been, rendered either way:

(36) a. Bi soineko dituenak, eman biezaio bat, ez duenari. (Lk 3:11; *IB*)
Who has two garments, let him give one to him who does not have it.
b. Bi soineko dituenak eman diezaiola bat ez duenari. (Lk 3:11; *EAB*)
Let (or: may) he who has two garments give one to him who does not have it.

(37) a. Norbait egarri bada, etor bekit eta edan beza. (Jn 7:38; *JKBO*)
If someone is thirsty, let him come to me and let him drink.
b. Inor egarri bada, nigana etorri eta edan dezala. (Jn 7:37; *Lau Eb.*)
If anyone is thirsty, let him come to me and drink.

(38) a. Ez beza jakin zure ezkerrak zer egiten duen eskuinak. (Mt 6:3)
Let your left hand not know what your right hand does.

b. Ez dezala jakin ezkerrak zure eskubiak zer egiten duen. (Mt 6:3; *Lau Eb.*)
May your left hand not know what your right hand does.

(39) a. Gizon bakoitzak izan beza bere emaztea. (1 Cor 7:2)
Let every man have his own wife.
b. Gizon bakoitzak bere emaztea eduki dezala. (1 Cor 7:2; *IB*)
May every man have his own wife.

While jussives and optatives seem interchangeable in examples of this sort, it would be a mistake to assume that they always are. For one thing, the strong imperative force of example (25a) *Izan bedi argia!* 'Let there be light!' cannot be conveyed by the optative *Izan dadila argia*, which would generally be interpreted as 'May there be light'. Furthermore, a playwright in giving stage directions uses the jussive, or else the indicative, but never the optative mood. The following examples are all stage directions:

(40) a. Bihoaz barrura hirurok. (*TOE* II, 378)
Let these three go inside.
b. Bi aldiz irakur beza. (*TOE* II, 388)
Let him read it out two times.
c. Besotik eutsi bekio. (*TOE* I, 335)
Let him grip him by the arm.
d. Edan bezate zutik daudela. (Labayen, *Su Em.* 213)
Let them drink while standing up.
e. Zaldi irrintziak entzun bitez. (*TOE* II, 326)
Let neighs be heard.
f. Oihala eror bedi geldiro. (*TOE* III, 184)
Let the curtain fall slowly.

Likewise, the jussive, not the optative, is used in an errata sheet:

(41) 9. orrialdea, 5. lerroa: Dio: *ihardun*; bio: *jardun*.
Page 9, line 5: It says: *ihardun*; let it say: *jardun*.

22.7 Deverbal *-men* Indicating Capability

The suffix *-men* originated most probably as a shortened version of *-mendu*, still in use in the eastern dialects, which itself is a borrowing from Latin *-mentum*. The suffix combines with verb radicals (including the preterito-present verbs *ahal* and *nahi*) and yields nouns denoting either a state of mind or a capability.

The morphology is transparent. Note, however, the elision of a final nasal: *entzumen* from *entzun*, *usaimen* from *usaindu*. Cluster simplification operates in the usual way: for example, *apalesmen* from *apalets* + *men*.

The following listing may well be comprehensive:

aditu	to understand	adimen	understanding, intellect
ahal	to be able	ahalmen	capability, faculty, power
ahaztu	to forget	ahazmen	forgetfulness, forgetting
apaletsi	to disparage	apalesmen	humility
asmatu	to invent	asmamen	ingenuity, resourcefulness, imagination
aukeratu	to choose	aukeramen	free will
aztoratu	to dismay, to alarm	aztoramen	dismay, consternation, alarm
begiratu	to look, to guard	begiramen	caution, respect, reverence
bereizi	to separate, to distinguish	bereizmen	resolving power
dastatu	to taste	dastamen	sense of taste
ederretsi	to admire	ederresmen	admiration
entzun	to hear	entzumen	sense of hearing, hearing
eragin	to activate	eragimen	impulse, impetus, incentive, influence
erotu	to go mad	eromen	madness, insanity
etsi	to desist, to despair	etsimen	resignation, desperation, despair
ezagutu	to know, to recognize	ezagumen	cognition
gogoratu	to recall	gogoramen	memory, faculty of recall
goretsi	to extol	goresmen	praise, eulogy
gozatu	to enjoy	gozamen	enjoyment, delight, comfort
harritu	to be astonished	harrimen	astonishment, amazement
hartu	to take	harmen	reach, range
hautatu	to select	hautamen	free will
hedatu	to extend	hedamen	extension
heldu	to reach, to grip	helmen	reach, range, scope
higitu	to move	higimen	power of motion
iguriki	to wait, to expect	igurikimen	expectation, hope
ikasi	to learn	ikasmen	learning capacity
ikusi	to see	ikusmen	eyesight, range of vision
iragarri	to announce, to predict	iragarmen	gift of prophecy
irakurri	to read	irakurmen	reading skill
iruditu	to imagine	irudimen	imagination, fantasy
itsutu	to blind	itsumen	blinding, blindness
itxaron	to wait, to expect	itxaromen	expectation, hope
mintzatu	to speak	mintzamen	faculty of speech
nahasi	to mix, to confuse	nahasmen	confusion
nahi	to want	nahimen	will
ohartu	to notice, to note	oharmen	consciousness, perception
oroitu	to remember	oroimen	memory
pairatu	to suffer	pairamen	suffering, endurance
pentsatu	to think	pentsamen	faculty of thought
sentitu	to feel	sentimen	emotion
sinetsi	to believe	sinesmen	faith

sortu	to generate	sormen	creativity, generative power
ugaldu	to reproduce	ugalmen	reproductivity
ukitu	to touch	ukimen	sense of touch
ulertu	to understand	ulermen	understanding, intellect
urrikaldu	to pity	urrikalmen	compassion, pity
usaindu	to smell	usaimen	sense of smell
zoratu	to go wild	zoramen	rapture, thrill, ecstasy

A few of these nouns can be turned into adjectives by adding the suffix *-tsu* discussed in section 8.7: *adimentsu* 'intelligent', *ahalmentsu* 'powerful' (more commonly *ahaltsu*), *begiramentsu* 'respectful', *sentimentsu* 'sensitive', 'intense'.

There also is a denominal suffix *-men*, which may represent a shortened version of the noun *mende* 'control'. It operates on a few nouns only:

aho	mouth	ahamen	mouthful, morsel
beso	arm	besamen	armful
esku	hand	eskumen	handful, reach (also *eskumende*)

22.8 Deverbal *-pen* Indicating Result

Combining with mainly transitive verb radicals, the suffix *-pen* yields abstract nouns denoting the outcome of the action, or perhaps put more accurately, perfective action nominals. The form *-pen*, most likely, originated as a syncopated variant of *-tamen*, where the suffix *-men* (from *-mendu*, see section 22.7) was added to the verbal noun instead of to the radical. Once the form *-pen* was established, it was applied also to verbs whose verbal nouns ended in *-tze* instead of *-te*.

As to the shape of this suffix, it is important to note that its initial *p* turns into *m* after certain verb radicals, which then renders the suffix identical in form to the suffix *-men* of quite different meaning studied in section 22.7. Some of these cases are accounted for by a dissimilatory process applying to a *p* not protected by an adjacent consonant, when it follows a radical with a labial plosive in either of its last two syllables.

The remaining cases have to be explained on an individual basis. We get *aldamen* instead of *aldapen* under the influence of its homonym *aldamen* 'vicinity', *galmen* alongside *galpen* on account of its synonym *galmende*, *hertsamen* alongside *hertsapen* because of its synonym *hertsamendu*, *hitzarmen* instead of *hitzarpen* under the influence of *harmen* 'reach', *hondamen* instead of *hondapen* on account of its synonym *hondamendi*, *laudamen* instead of *laudapen* as a loan from Bearnese, *luzamen* alongside *luzapen* on account of its synonym *luzamendu*, *salmen* alongside *salpen* because of its synonym *salmenta*, and *ukamen* alongside *ukapen* on account of its synonym *ukamendu*.

Most of the examples in the following list are confined to the written style of the language:

abiatu	to set out, to depart	abiamen	beginning, preparation
adierazi	to declare, to explain	adierazpen	declaration, explanation
agertu	to manifest, to express	agerpen	manifestation, expression, apparition
ahantzi	to forget	ahanzpen	oblivion
ahaztu	to forget	ahazpen	oblivion
aipatu	to mention, to cite	aipamen	mention, citation, quote
aitortu	to confess	aitorpen	confession
aitzinatu	to advance	aitzinapen	advancement, progress
aldatu	to change	aldamen	change
apaldu	to humiliate	apalmen	humiliation
apaletsi	to disparage	apalespen	disparagement
aplikatu	to apply	aplikapen	application
argitaratu	to publish	argitalpen	publication
askatu	to free, to liberate	askapen	deliverance, liberation
aukeratu	to choose	aukerapen	choice
aurkitu	to find, to discover	aurkipen	find, finding, discovery
aurreratu	to progress, to advance	aurrerapen	advancement, progress
baietsi	to approve	baiespen	approval
baieztatu	to affirm, to confirm	baieztapen	affirmation, confirmation, assertion
baitu	to consent	baimen	consent, permission
barkatu	to forgive	barkamen	forgiveness, pardon
bedeinkatu	to bless	bedeinkapen	blessing
beheratu	to lower	beherapen	drop, decline, reduction, discount
bereizi	to separate, to distinguish	bereizpen	separation, distinction
berrerosi	to ransom, to redeem	berrerospen	ransom, redemption
bihurtu	to return, to render	bihurpen	conversion, rendering
bildu	to gather, to collect	bildumen	collection, summary
dastatu	to taste	dastapen	tasting, taste
ederretsi	to admire	ederrespen	marvel
egiaztatu	to verify, to confirm	egiaztapen	verification, confirmation
egin	to do	egipen	deed, action
ekarri	to bring	ekarpen	contribution
ekoiztu	to produce, to yield	ekoizpen	product, production, yield
eragotzi	to impede, to hinder	eragozpen	impediment, obstacle
erakutsi	to show	erakuspen	sample, model, paragon
erantzun	to answer	erantzupen	answer, reaction
erdietsi	to achieve, to obtain	erdiespen	achievement, attainment
erosi	to buy	erospen	redemption (*erosketa* 'purchase')
eskolatu	to school, to train	eskolapen	schooling, training
etsi	to resign oneself	etsipen	resignation, despair
ezeztatu	to deny, to contradict	ezeztapen	negation, denial
ezkutatu	to hide	ezkutapen	secret, mystery
frogatu	to prove, to test	frogapen	proof, trial, ordeal
gaitzetsi	to condemn	gaitzespen	condemnation

galdu	to lose, to ruin	galpen	loss, undoing, ruin
garaitu	to overcome, to win	garaipen	victory, win
gezurtatu	to refute, to belie	gezurtapen	refutation, falsification
gogoratu	to recall, to occur	gogorapen	recollection, idea, thought
goratu	to raise, to increase	gorapen	rise, raise, increase, praise
goretsi	to esteem, to praise	gorespen	(high) esteem, praise
gutxietsi	to disdain	gutxiespen	disdain
hautetsi	to select, to elect	hautespen	election, selection
hautsi	to break	hauspen	break, rupture, infraction
hertsatu	to harass, to implore	hertsamen	harassment, imploration
hitzartu	to agree	hitzarmen	agreement, treaty, pact
hobetsi	to prefer	hobespen	preference
hondatu	to destroy, to ruin	hondamen	destruction, ruin
igorri	to send	igorpen	sending, shipping
ihardetsi	to answer	ihardespen	reply, answer
ikasi	to learn	ikaspen	lesson
ikusi	to see	ikuspen	sight, view, vision
irabazi	to earn, to gain, to win	irabazpen	earnings, gains, profit
iragarri	to announce, to predict	iragarpen	announcement, prediction
irakatsi	to teach	irakaspen	teaching, lesson
iraun	to last	iraupen	duration, constancy
iritzi	to deem, to consider	irizpen	opinion, report
irudi	to seem	irudipen	impression, illusion
isuri	to spill, to shed	isurpen	spillage, effusion
ito	to choke	itomen	choking, suffocation, drowning
itsatsi	to stick, to adhere	itsaspen	attachment
itxaron	to wait, to expect	itxaropen	expectation, hope
itxuratu	to shape, to simulate	itxurapen	appearance, illusion, pretense
itzuli	to return, to render	itzulpen	return, rendering, translation
izendatu	to nominate	izendapen	nomination
jarraitu	to follow, to continue	jarraipen	continuation
jazarri	to persecute	jazarpen	persecution
kutsatu	to infect, to contaminate	kutsapen	infection, contagion, taint
laburtu	to shorten, to abridge	laburpen	abridgement, abbreviation
laudatu	to praise	laudamen	praise
luzatu	to lengthen, to delay	luzapen	prolongation, deferment, delay
ohartu	to notice, to note	oharpen	observation, note, warning
onartu	to approve, to accept	onarpen	approval, acceptance
onetsi	to approve, to bless	onespen	approval, blessing
oroitu	to remember	oroipen	recollection, memory, souvenir
pentsatu	to think	pentsamen	thought
prestatu	to prepare	prestamen	preparation
proposatu	to propose	proposamen	proposal
sailkatu	to classify	sailkapen	classification

salatu	to denounce	salapen	denouncement, accusation
salbatu	to rescue, to save	salbamen	rescue, salvation
salbuetsi	to exempt, to except	salbuespen	exception, exemption
saldu	to sell	salpen	sale (also *salmen*, *saltzapen*)
salerosi	to trade	salerospen	trading, business
sariztatu	to reward	sariztapen	reward
sentitu	to feel	sentipen	feeling
sinetsi	to believe	sinespen	belief
sorotsi	to assist	sorospen	assistance
txertatu	to graft, to vaccinate	txertapen	grafting, embedding, vaccination
ukatu	to deny, to refuse	ukamen	denial, refusal, disavowal
ukitu	to touch	ukipen	contact, touch
xahutu	to cleanse, to liquidate	xahupen	cleansing, liquidation, expense
zuzendu	to correct, to rectify	zuzenpen	rectification, correction

A comparison with the suffix *-men* of section 22.7 shows that the literary language has the potential to make the following distinctions:

apalesmen	humility	apalespen	humiliation
aukeramen	free will	aukerapen	choice
dastamen	sense of taste	dastapen	tasting
ederresmen	admiration	ederrespen	marvel
gogoramen	memory	gogorapen	recollection, idea
ikasmen	learning capacity	ikaspen	lesson
ikusmen	eyesight	ikuspen	view
iragarmen	gift of prophecy	iragarpen	announcement, prediction
irudimen	power of imagination	irudipen	impression, illusion
oharmen	consciousness, perception	oharpen	observation, warning, note
sentimen	emotion	sentipen	feeling
sinesmen	faith	sinespen	belief

22.9 Deverbal *-tzapen* Indicating Result

The nonproductive suffix *-tzapen* merely represents an augmented version of the suffix *-pen*, the meaning of which it shares. Thus the derived noun denotes the outcome of the activity expressed by the verb. Compared with *-pen*, instances of *-tzapen* are sparse. It occurs with *erori* 'to fall', *hasi* 'to begin', and a handful of verbs ending in *-tu* or *-du*. After a radical ending in a sibilant or affricate, the initial affricate turns into a *t*: *-tapen*.

Sarasola's *Euskal Hiztegia* (1996) contains the following examples:

argitu	to clarify	argitzapen	explanation, clarification
beheratu	to lower	beheratzapen	decline, drop, low spirits
berritu	to renew	berritzapen	renewal, renovation

erori	to fall	erortzapen	fall, decay, decline
galdu	to lose, to ruin	galtzapen	loss, undoing, ruin
garbitu	to clean, to wash	garbitzapen	purification, ablution
goratu	to raise, to increase	goratzapen	rise, raise, increase, praise
hasi	to begin	hastapen	beginning
oroitu	to remember	oroitzapen	recollection, souvenir, keepsake
saldu	to sell	saltzapen	sale
zehaztu	to specify	zehaztapen	specification

To these could be added

bihurtu	to return	bihurtzapen	restitution
edertu	to adorn, to embellish	edertzapen	adornment, embellishment
egokitu	to adapt	egokitzapen	adaptation
erditu	to give birth	erditzapen	childbirth
erre	to burn	erretzapen	combustion
handitu	to enlarge	handitzapen	enlargement
hurbildu	to approach	hurbiltzapen	rapprochement, approach
sortu	to generate	sortzapen	conception, origin, birth

22.10 Vocabulary

arima	soul
arren	for goodness' sake, please
arrotz	stranger
asto	donkey, ass
baimen	permission, consent
bake	peace
barkatu	to forgive
barru	inside (see section 4.1.3.2)
baso	(drinking) glass
begi	eye
begiratu	to look (used with dative)
bilatu	to look for
eragozpen	obstacle
esklabu/o	slave (also *jopu*)
faborez	please
gora	up, upstairs (see section 3.2)
gorroto (izan)	to hate (see sections 14.1 and 14.2)
hitz	word

hondamen	ruin, destruction
ireki	to open
kendu	to take away, to avert
kezka	worry
lozale	sleepyhead (see section 10.7.1)
luzapen	delay, deferment
mesedez	please
morroi	servant
musu	kiss
mutiko	boy, lad (from *mutil* 'boy' + diminutive *-ko*)
nonbait	somewhere
ordez	instead
oroipen	recollection, souvenir
oroitzapen	recollection, souvenir
saiatu	to try
sentimen	emotion
sentipen	feeling
urre	gold
utzi	to leave, to abandon, to let
zoratu	to drive wild, to enthrall

22.11 Exercises

22.11.1 Translate into English

1. Begira iezadak, begira, begiz-begi! (*MEIG* IX, 109)
2. Barka iezadazu, arren. (*MEIG* IX, 110)
3. Kezka horiek utz itzak eta goazen. (Zapirain, *Etork.* 158)
4. Esazu, arren, arreba zaitudala. (Gn 12:13)
5. Esadak norekin habilen, esango diat nor haizen. (López Mendizabal, 245)
6. Utz ezazu urrea eta bila ezazu arima. (Amuriza, *Orom.* 196)
7. Zoaz gora eta esaiozu Mireni, arren, datorrela guregana. (Garate, *G.E.* 31)
8. Har nazazu esklabutzat mutikoaren ordez, eta doala hau anaiekin. (Gn 44:33)
9. Amnon nire anaia gurekin betor. (*TZ* II, 22)
10. Hemen baserrian etxe barrura arrotzik ez har! (Garate, *E.E.* 87)
11. Ken niregandik begi horiek, zoratu egiten naute. (Sg 6:5)
12. Emazu ni ijitoa naizela eta zu sorgina, zer gertatuko litzaiguke?

22.11.2 Translate into Basque

1. Anna! Bring another glass.
2. Leave the girl in peace!
3. Tell me whether it is true.
4. Try to forget that.
5. Open the back door, please.
6. Leave us here somewhere.
7. Don't be a sleepyhead.
8. Send me, please, a servant and a donkey.
9. Come, little one, give father a kiss.
10. Do what you want.
11. Don't forget that we hate each other.
12. Don't say a word when nothing is being asked of you.

23 Causal, Explanatory, and Concessive Clauses

23.1 Indicating Cause

While this grammar's main concern remains the western variant of Euskara Batua, in the present chapter considerable attention will be paid to eastern usage also, as the literary practices of western writers owe a great deal to their northeastern neighbors, particularly in the realm of explanatory clauses.

The oldest means for indicating cause or reason is the instrumental case. It still occurs in this function where a state of mind or physical condition is involved: *beldurrez* 'out of fear', *gosez* 'out of hunger', *lotsaz* 'out of shame', *minez* 'out of pain', *pozez* 'out of joy'; see section 27.2 for more examples.

23.1.1 Causal Postpositional Phrases

Well before the 15th century the form *gatik* (originally *gaitik*, elative of *gai* 'matter') evolved into a case ending and superseded the instrumental as a means for forming causal adverbials:

(1) a. Jagoitikoz ukanen dut nik zugatik dolore. (*LVP* VI–30)
    Henceforth I will have anguish because of you.
  b. Amagatik andre oro behar luke goratu. (*LVP* III–18)
    Because of his mother he should praise all women.
  c. Eskerrik asko afariagatik. (Atxaga, *Gizona* 41)
    Many thanks for the supper.

This case ending also occurs with verbal nouns, that is, with nominalized clauses: *euskaraz mintzatzeagatik zigortu* 'to punish for speaking Basque'.

In combination with verbal nouns, western Basque may also employ the suffix *-arren*: *euskaraz mintzatzearren zigortu* 'to punish for speaking Basque'. Either *-arren* or *-gatik* can substitute for the adnominal *-ko* in nominalized purpose clauses (cf. section 21.4.1). Some examples with *-arren* follow:

(2) a. Nik seme bat edukitzearren zer emango nukeen ez dakit. (Garate, *Leh.* 17)
I don't know what I would give in order to have a son.
b. Zerbait egitearren, legeak ikasteari ekin nion Deustoko Unibertsitatean. (Garate, *Hades* 63)
In order to do something, I took up studying law at the University of Deusto.
c. Ilunpera egokitzearren geldiune bat egin zuen. (Atxaga, *Gizona* 24)
He made a pause in order to adapt himself to the darkness.

This construction, borrowed from Biscayan, is confined to western Basque. Use of *arren* with nonsentential noun phrases is obsolete, except for a few relics such as *beldurrarren* 'out of fear', *lotsarren* 'out of shame', and *pozarren* 'out of joy' (also stative: 'happily'). For the role of *-arren* in concessives, see section 23.7.4.

23.1.2 Causal Clauses Using *-lako(tz)*

Causal clauses are encountered more often than causal phrases, perhaps because reason or cause tends to be linked up with a complex state of affairs best conveyed by a finite clause. The main grammatical tool for constructing causal clauses is a suffix *-lako* applied to the finite verb, at least in western usage. In eastern usage, the suffix is shaped *-lakotz*, where *-tz* shows an archaic form of the instrumental case ending. This construction has to compete with an alternative absent from the western speech area: use of the prefix *bait-* attached to the finite verb, accompanied or not by a clause-initial conjunction *zeren*.

As to origin, causal *-lako* can be identified with the suffix used to link sentential complements to nouns (sec. 18.8.1), provided one allows a non-overt instrumental noun to account for the meaning 'cause or reason'. Barring the use of an interrogative like *zergatik* as a causal conjunction—a controversial construct shunned by many speakers and most writers—a *-lako* clause constitutes the only possible reply to a *why*-question in western practice:

(3) a. Zergatik joan hintzen?—Berak deitu ninduelako. (Garate, *G.E.* 59)
"Why did yoú go?" "Because he invited me (himself)."
b. Zergatik baztertzen dute euskara mojek?—Apaizek eta fraileek ere zapuzten dutelako. (Garate, *Esku* 103)
"Why do nuns reject Basque?" "Because priests and friars also repudiate it."
c. Zergatik hil zenituen?—Behartu nindutelako. (Amuriza, *Emea* 44)
"Why did you kill them?" "Because they forced me to."
d. Zergatik ez ninduen hil?—Zizpak bi tiro bakarrik zituelako. (Amuriza, *Emea* 44)
"Why did she not kill me?" "Because the gun only had two shots."
e. Zergatik jokatu dut horrela? Maite ez zaituztedalako ote? (2 Cor 11:11)
Why have I acted like that? Because I do not love yoû perhaps?

Whereas notionally one may wish to distinguish between objective causes, logical grounds, and subjective reasons, Basque grammar provides no formal means for doing so.

For all of these, the *-lako* clause serves equally well. Thus, objective causes are called up in these examples:

(4) a. Nik, behar den lekuan bilatu ez dudalako agian, ez dut *Guero*-n aurkitzen. (*MEIG* VII, 57)
As for me, I do not find it in *Guero*, perhaps because I haven't looked for it in the proper place.
b. Ez daki ze ordu den, bainatu ondoren ordularia nonbait ahaztu zaiolako. (Urretabizkaia, *Sat.* 126)
He doesn't know what time it is, because he has forgotten (i.e., left) his watch somewhere after taking a bath.

Logical grounds are expressed in

(5) a. Mudakorrak dira gizonen irakaspenak, gizonak berak hala direlakotz. (Lapeyre, 233)
Men's teachings are changeable because men themselves are so.
b. Etxekoandrea naizelako baditut nire eginbeharrak. (*TOE* II, 68)
I have my chores because I am the lady of the house.

Subjective reasons are communicated in

(6) a. Nahi duzulako zaude hemen. (López Mendizabal, 201)
You are here because you want to (be).
b. Zauritu ninduelako, gizona hil dut. (Gn 4:23)
I have killed a man, because he wounded me.

The neutral site for causal clauses not in focus or quasi focus is after the main clause:

(7) a. Eragotzi diogu, gu bezala, ez darraikizulako. (*TB* 71)
We have forbidden it him, because he is not, like us, following you.
b. Ez zara agertu, beldur zinelako. (*TOE* I, 337)
You did not appear, because you were afraid.
c. Eta berehala noa, luzapena eguerdian bukatzen delako. (*TOE* II, 272)
And I am going at once, because the respite ends at noon.
d. Ez nizuen hori hasieratik esan, ni zuekin nengoelako. (Jn 16:4)
I didn't tell yoû that from the beginning, because I was with yoû.

Deviations from this neutral order, however, are possible and result in enhanced vividness. In particular, a causal clause may be preposed, that is, occur between the sentence topic and the main clause, as in example (4a). Other examples of preposed clauses are

(8) a. Piztia txarren eskuetan gaudelako, heriotzari aurrez-aurre begiratu behar diogu. (*TOE* I, 350)
Because we are in the hands of vicious beasts, we have to look at death face to face.

b. Hiru urte lehenago lapur bat aurkitzen lagundu ziolako, oso adiskide zuen. (Garate, *Esku* 154)
Because he had helped him find a thief three years earlier, he was his good friend.
c. Ilea erdi bustirik dagoelako, hotza sentitzen du. (Urretabizkaia, *Sat*. 124)
Because his hair is half wet, he feels cold.

When answering a *why*-question constitutes the chief purpose of uttering a sentence, its causal clause is in focus (see section 8.6.1) and will normally occupy the focus site directly preceding the main verb. Examples follow:

(9) a. Nahi dudalako bizi naiz hemen. (Atxaga, *Obab*. 170)
I live here because I want to.
b. Eta bihotzez maite nauzulako egin dituzu gauza handi hauek. (1 Chr 17:19)
And you have done these great things because you wholeheartedly love me.
c. Ikusi nauzulako sinetsi al duzu? (Jn 20:29)
Have you believed because you have seen me?
d. Irtenbiderik ez zeukatelako gelditu dira, gogoz bestera, ez daukatenari baliorik ematen diotelako. (Atxaga, *Obab*. 139)
They have stayed because they had no escape—against their wishes—not because they attach any value to what they have.
e. Niri, berriz, egia diodalako ez didazue sinesten. (Jn 8:45)
Me, on the other hand, yoû do not believe because I tell the truth.

Use of anticipatory *horregatik* 'because of that' enables the speaker to shift the focus clause to the end of the main clause:

(10) a. Horregatik saldu zidan bada etxe hau, bera Dublinera zihoalako. (Atxaga, *Obab*. 357)
That is then why he sold me this house, because he was going to Dublin.
b. Horregatik maite nau Aitak, neure bizia ematen dudalako. (Jn 10:17)
That is why the Father loves me, because I give my own life.

With a negative main clause, a causal clause may be focus, as in example (9e); yet more often it is quasi focus, that is, focus of the positive statement that is being denied (see section 8.6.2). Examples are

(11) a. Gaztearen iritziek ez dute, gazte baten ahotik jaulki direlako, amen-amenik merezi. (*MEIG* IX, 64)
A young person's opinions do not deserve acclaim (just) because they have emerged from a young person's mouth.
b. Zaharra ez da, zahar delako eta kito, errespetagarri. (*MEIG* IX, 64)
An old person isn't venerable just because he is old.
c. Ni ere ez naiz nahi dudalako txikia, e? (Lazkao-Txiki I, 39)
Me too, I'm not small because I want to be, am I?

d. Mutil hau ez dago hemen nahi duelako. (Satrustegi, 59)
This boy isn't here because he wants to (be).

As mentioned in section 18.2, emotive verbs do not allow finite complement clauses. They do, however, take *-lako* clauses, which are, in many instances, translational equivalents of English *that*-clauses. Some examples are

(12) a. Ingelesez daudelako, ez dut uste inork harritu behar lukeenik. (*MEIG* VIII, 110)
That they are in English, I don't think anyone should be surprised.
b. Damu dut hainbeste diru nire alde jokatu dutelako. (*TOE* II, 86)
I am sorry that they have gambled away so much money on me.
c. Arras pozik nago nire senarrari eman diotelako. (Garate, *Esku* 82)
I am very glad that they have given it to my husband.
d. Poztu egiten zara aurreko emakumea beltza delako. (Oñederra, 114)
You are glad that the woman in front is black.

While the causal clauses we have seen so far were all verb-final, this word order, though preferred, is not compulsory, as illustrated by the following examples:

(13) a. Beraz zor dizkiogu eskerrak Jaungoikoari gure bizitzari iraun arazteko ematen digulako zer jan. (*P.Ab.* 68)
Therefore, we owe thanks to God because he gives us food to eat to sustain our lives.
b. Ez diot ezer aipatu, berak badakielako gorabehera guztia. (Arejita, *Eusk. Josk.* 190)
I haven't mentioned anything to him, because he already knows the whole problem himself.
c. Gauerako denak joaten ziren, orduan agertzen zelakotz hil haren arima. (Ariztia, 48)
By nightfall they all went away, because it was then that the soul of that dead man used to appear.

Similarly, in negative causal clauses, the preferred verb-final order seen in examples (3e), (4a), and (9d) can be modified by applying the well-known rule of Auxiliary Attraction (although not all speakers allow it here):

(14) a. Patxik, ez zuelako Maite ikusi, galdetu zidan haren berri. (Cf. Tamura 1985, 77.)
Because Frank didn't see Maite, he asked me about her.
b. ... unibertsitateetan ez zuelako euskarak lekurik. (Zuazo, *Sendabel.* 20)
... because in the universities Basque had no place.
c. Eliza ez zen oraino jendez betea, meza ez zelakotz hasia. (*P.Ad.* 47)
The church was not yet full of people, because the mass had not started.
d. Hori gertatu izan da Protestanteen artean, ez dutelakotz buruzagi bat Jesu-Kristok emana. (Lapeyre, 243)

That has happened among the Protestants because they do not have a leader given by Jesus Christ.

To conclude this section, I will present some instances of questioning a constituent inside a causal clause. While not all speakers accept these, many do, and not merely as echo-questions, as in English. The interrogative element, of course, remains in situ.

(15) a. Zer egin duelako zigortu dute?
They have punished him because he has done what?
b. Nor datorrelako zoaz etxera?
You are going home because who is coming?
c. Nork kantatzen duelako joango zara antzokira?
You will go to the theater because who is singing?
d. Nora zoazelako saldu duzu etxea?
You have sold the house because you are going where?

23.2 Explanatory *eta* Clauses

23.2.1 The Enclitic Use of the Conjunction *eta*

Consider these two sentences:

(16) a. Aita, barkatu iezaiezu, ez dakite zertan ari diren eta. (Lk 23:34; *Lau Eb.*)
Father, forgive them, for they do not know what they are doing.
b. Aita, barka iezaiezu, ez dakite eta zer ari diren. (Lk 23:34; *IB*)
Father, forgive them, for they do not know what they are doing.

The final clauses in both examples are instances of what we will refer to as "explanatory *eta* clauses." These are characterized by the enclitic use of the conjunction *eta*, occurring either at the end of the clause or shifted onto the finite verb, as in (16b). It is to be noted that enclitic *eta* is pronounced *ta* after a vowel and *da* after *n* or *l*, otherwise *eta*.

Some further examples of this predominantly western construction are

(17) a. Utzi nazazu, egunsentia da eta. (*TZ* I, 74 = Gn 32:26; Ur.)
Leave me, for it is daybreak.
b. Zatozte pixka bat barrura, oraindik badugu astia eta. (Etxaniz, *Antz.* 44)
Come inside a bit, for we still have time.
c. Hi egon hadi isilik, ez dakik ezer eta! (Atxaga, *Obab.* 149)
Yoú be quiet, for yoú don't know anything!
d. Gauden isilik. Martina eta Andresa barrura datoz eta. (Etxaniz, *Antz.* 42)
Let us be quiet, for Martina and Andresa are coming inside.
e. Lenbailehen dihoala, ez digu mutil horrek nahigabea besterik ematen eta. (*TOE* I, 233)
Let him go as soon as possible, for that boy is giving us nothing but sorrow.

As these examples show, it is quite common for the principal clause to be imperative, hortative, or jussive; yet declarative clauses too can be followed by an explanatory *eta* clause:

(18) a. Ez dizuet esango guztia, luze litzateke eta. (*TOE* I, 245)
I won't tell you everything, for it would be lengthy.
b. Neuk jarraituko dut, aspaldi ez dut hitzegin eta. (Atxaga, *Grl.* 104)
I will continue, for I haven't spoken for a long time.
c. Agudo amaitzen dut. Hitzaldi luzeak ez ditudala maite badakizue eta. (*TOE* I, 302)
I am finishing quickly, for yoû know I don't like lengthy speeches.
d. Horiek zuentzat. On Permin gozozalea ez dela badakit eta. (*TOE* I, 211)
Those (are) for yoû, for I know that Don Fermín is not fond of sweets.

It happens, albeit rarely, that the explanatory clause precedes the principal clause:

(19) a. Azkeneko eguna da eta, goazen guztiok dantzara! (From the song "Kat(t)alin," Fernandez, 68; *Euskal Kantak* 160)
Since it is the last day, let us all go (to) dance!
b. Etxean ez dugu hartzen paper hori eta, eman behar didazu. (*TOE* I, 75)
Since we do not get that paper at home, you must give it to me.

We may even find the explanatory clause intercalated within the principal clause:

(20) Bere lagunak, agure zen eta, zeukan lepoa makurra. (E. Azkue, 244)
His friend, since he was an old man, had a bent neck.

As to the syntactic analysis of these examples, let us note, first of all, that an explanatory *eta* clause S_2 is in no way subordinate, as it lacks a complementizer and allows allocutive verb forms (see chapter 29). Also, unlike a genuine causal clause, it can be neither focus nor quasi focus; in fact, it is not a constituent of the principal clause S_1 at all.

Since the presence of the conjunction *eta* hints at sentence coordination as the origin of the construction, the Basque grammarian P. Goenaga proposes (oral communication) that sentences (17a) and (18a), for example, are transforms of (21a) and (21b), respectively:

(21) a. Egunsentia da eta utzi nazazu.
It is daybreak and leave me.
b. Luze litzateke eta ez dizuet esango guztia.
It would be lengthy and I won't tell yoû everything.

Schematically: S_2 *eta* $S_1 \rightarrow S_1$, S_2 *eta*

As a root transformation in the sense of Emonds (1970, 1976), this operation only applies in main clauses; this fact explains why sentences with explanatory *eta* can never be embedded.

I think, however, that this proposal must be rejected on several grounds. Indeed, the alleged transformation is structurally unprecedented, fails to explain the meaning of the construction, does not account for the speaker's intuition that S_2 is an autonomous sentence—as evidenced by the punctuation of some of our examples—and, finally, is unable to accommodate the fact that S_1 and S_2 can be uttered by different locutors, as in the following examples taken from Labayen's play *Irunxeme*:

(22) a. Salome: Hura begietatik sartu zaizula dirudi.
Peli: Itsua ez naiz eta. (*TOE* I, 227)
Salome: She has gotten into you through the eyes, it seems.
Peli: After all, I'm not blind.
b. Agustine: Jeikiak dira aspaldi.
Itziar: Elizara joan-etorria egin dute eta. (*TOE* I, 236)
Agustine: They have been up for a long time.
Itziar: Indeed, they have made a trip to church.
c. Eneko: Beltzen artean biziko naizela ba al deritzozu?
Orreaga: On Kristobal eta han bizi dira eta. (*TOE* I, 209)
Eneko: Do you approve of me living among blacks?
Orreaga: Don Cristóbal and his family live there, after all.

Such examples cease to be a problem if we abandon Goenaga's proposal and simply assume that *eta* stands for *eta horregatik* 'and that's why it is so'. This assumption neatly accords with the meaning of the construction. For, as A. Arejita (1985, 194) correctly points out, explanatory *eta* clauses provide no cause or reason, but rather a justification for uttering the principal clause. This interpretation explains why such clauses cannot be in focus, and also why they are appropriate with all sorts of speech acts, unlike *-lako* clauses.

With a declarative principal, an explanatory *eta* clause may present a justification on the level of content, as in examples (18a–d), or else on the epistemic level. In the latter case, the argument presented in S_2 does not address the validity of the state of affairs expressed by S_1, but merely purports to show why the speaker believes S_1 to be true. The following examples illustrate such epistemic justification, where *eta* may be interpreted as *eta horregatik diot* 'and that's why I say so':

(23) a. Miren ez da etorriko, bere amak hala esan dit eta.
Mary won't come, for her mother has told me so.
b. Honezkero bide erdian datoz, garaia da eta. (*TOE* I, 226)
By now they are halfway in coming, for it is (the) time.
c. Baietz, lapurra! Nik ikusi dut sartzen eta. (*TOE* I, 190)
Yet, (it is) a thief! For I have seen him go in.

23.2.2 A Subject-Bound Justification Using *-LA ... eta*

As shown in section 18.2.2, *-LA* clauses depending on an implicit verb of saying are quite common—for example,

(24) a. Gazteenak bera jaitsiko zela. (Barandiaran, *Mundo* I, 84)
The youngest one (said) that he would go down himself.
b. Hala uste zuela berak. (Atxaga, *Grl.* 146)
He (said) that he thought so.

When such a *-LA* clause acts as a basis for an explanatory *eta* clause, the justification offered is to be ascribed to the subject of the implicit verb of saying, usually identical to the subject of the principal clause—hence the term "subject-bound justification." English translations of this construction can take various forms:

(25) a. Ezetz besteek, hark ez zuela horretarako balio eta. (Barandiaran, *Mundo* I, 83)
The others (said) no, adducing that he was not up to that.
b. Juanak bere ama ikusi behar zuela eta Basaburuko bidea hartu zuen. (*LBB* 49)
Juana took the road to Basaburu on the plea that she had to see her mother.
c. Sendagile bat sartu da gaixoren bat dagoela eta. (Garate, *Iz.B.* 63)
A doctor has come in on the plea that there was some sick man.
d. Etxean gatza ugari dagoela eta ez dezazula bazkaria gehiegi gazitu. (López Mendizabal, 246)
Do not salt the food too much on the principle that there is plenty of salt in the house.

Sometimes the subject of the verb of saying differs from that of the principal clause:

(26) a. Migeli txiki gelditu zitzaizkiola eta, nik jantzi beharko nituen oheko jantzi haiek, urtebete barru. (Lertxundi, *G.K.* 77)
On the pretext that they had become too small for Miguel, I would have to wear those nightclothes within one year.
b. Hor Lizarretako barrutian izan gara. Semeak ikusi behar zuela eta. (*TOE* I, 160)
We've been in the area of Lizarreta. On the pretext that his son had to see it.

Where existential *izan* or its synonym *egon* is the main verb of the explanatory clause, something's existence provides a subjective justification for the action stated in the principal clause. This action may then be said to be *on account of* the subject of the explanatory clause, or even *because* of it. Examples are

(27) a. Eguraldi txarra zegoela eta, hurrengo egunerako ezkontza atzeratu omen zuten. (Barandiaran, *Mundo* I, 86)
On account of the bad weather they postponed the wedding to the next day.
b. Goizeko zalaparta izan dela eta senarra ihesi joan zait. (*TOE* II, 362)
On account of this morning's disturbance my husband has fled.
c. Ez dut berriro mundua madarikatuko gizakia dela eta. (Gn 8:21)
I will not curse the world again because of man.
d. Zer dela eta, orduan, hasieran azaldu ditudan kezkak? (*MEIG* II, 68)
Why, then, the reservations I expressed at the beginning?

Note that *zer dela eta* can be appropriately rendered as 'why'. Similar translations are *hau/hori dela eta* 'because of this/that' and *hauek/horiek direla eta* 'because of these/those'. This very phrase *dela eta*, or, with a plural referent, *direla eta*, is often resorted to for indicating the topic of a discourse or reflection, possibly because the speaker considers the topic as providing itself sufficient justification for its discussion:

(28) a. Arraina dela eta, horrenbeste auzi. (Uztapide, *Sas.* 221)
So much dispute about fish.
b. Plajioa dela eta, ideiak oso garbi dauzkate. (Atxaga, *Grl.* 157)
On plagiarism, their ideas are very clear.

In essay headings and other headlines the principal clause remains implicit: *Allende dela eta* (*MEIG* VIII, 36) 'On Allende'; *Euskararen izter-lehengusuak direla eta* (*MEIG* VI, 121) 'On the distant relatives of Basque'.

23.3 Causal and Explanatory Uses of the Prefix *bait-*

23.3.1 Causal and Explanatory *bait-* Clauses in Eastern Usage

It is time now to return to the subordinating prefix *bait-*, the morphophonemics of which were described in section 19.3.1. Indeed, among the various semantic functions that a clause whose verb bears this prefix can fulfill with respect to a main clause, two are tied to the concerns of this chapter. First of all, in eastern usage, such a clause can provide a reason or cause, therefore being interchangeable with a *-lakotz* construction. Alternatively, it may contain a justification, either for the validity of the statement in the main clause or for uttering it. In this use it is an exact synonym of an explanatory *eta* clause.

We find a reason expressed in the following examples:

(29) a. Nola ez naizen beldur? Ez baitut deusetan ere faltarik. Kontzientzia baitut ona eta garbia. (Ax. 449)
Why I am not afraid? Because I have no failings in anything whatsoever. Because my conscience is good and pure.
b. Zertako? Ziztatzen bainínduten. (Barbier, *Lég.* 64)
Why? Because they were stinging me.
c. Ez omen baita ere denborarik galtzeko, hona zertako etorri naizen. (*P.Ad.* 72)
Because supposedly there is no time at all to lose, this is why I have come.

Causal *bait-* clauses may occur in coordination with causal *-lakotz* clauses, either as the first or as the second conjunct:

(30) a. Epela baitzara eta ez zarelakotz ez hotza ez beroa, hasiko natzaizu ene ahotik aurtikitzen. (Rv 3:16; Dv)
Because you are lukewarm and because you are neither cold nor warm, I will start ejecting you from my mouth. (For *hasiko natzaizu*, see section 16.6.2.)

b. Hori erran zuen, ez behardunez axola zuelakotz, baina ohoina baitzen. (Jn 12:6; *JKBO*)
He said that, not because he cared about the poor, but because he was a thief.

Combined with an imperative main clause, a *bait-* clause will be explanatory rather than causal. Thus, example (31a) is synonymous with (16b), and (31b) with (17a), both of these explanatory *eta* clauses:

(31) a. Aita, barka iezaiezu, ez baitakite zer ari diren. (Lk 23:34; *EAB*)
Father, forgive them, for they do not know what they are doing.
b. Utz nazazu joatera, argi-hastea baita. (Gn 32:27; *Biblia*)
Let me go, for it is daybreak.

I may add here that all western examples given in the next section are also acceptable to northern speakers.

23.3.2 Explanatory *bait-* Clauses in Western Usage

The grammatical device of an adjoined *bait-* clause has been borrowed into western Basque, but only in its function as an explanatory clause. In the easternmost part of Guipuzcoa the construction has been adopted into the spoken language; in the rest of the area it is also known but looked upon as highly literary, quite unlike the synonymous *eta* clauses.

The justifying function of *bait-* clauses, like that of other explanatory clauses, extends to all sorts of speech acts: assertions, imperatives, and even questions.

The following examples contain assertions:

(32) a. Zure bila ote datozen beldur naiz. Atean soldadu pila bat baitago. (*TOE* I, 335)
I am afraid they are coming for you, for there is a bunch of soldiers at the door.
b. Ondo dagoen ala ez esan behar didazu. Guk ez baitugu euskara liburuetan ikasi. (*TOE* I, 102)
You must tell me if it is correct or not, for we haven't learned Basque in books.
c. Entzun, ez zuen ezer entzuten, bikotea urrun samar baitzegoen. (Garate, *Esku* 120)
As to hearing, he heard nothing, for the couple was rather far away.
d. Bizitza osoan ez baitzen inoiz mozkortu, gaizki sentitzen hasi zen. (Arana, 26)
As he had never got drunk in his whole life, he began to feel bad.

These have imperatives:

(33) a. Jan ezazue gogoz, zuek ez baituzue errurik. (Amuriza, *Hil* 45)
Eat heartily, for yoû are not guilty. (Lit. 'have no guilt')
b. Igo hadi gainera, gaur azken afaria baitugu. (Amuriza, *Hil* 141)
Climb up on it, for tonight we have a last supper.

These have questions:

(34) a. Zergatik esan behar nizun? zuk ez baitidazu galdetu. (*TOE* I, 365)
Why did I have to tell you? After all, you have not asked me.
b. Nola gertatuko da, ba, hori, nik ez baitut gizonik ezagutzen? (Lk 1:34; *Lau Eb.*)
How will that, then, happen? After all, I know no man.

In spoken usage, a *bait-* clause regularly follows the main clause, as in most examples cited so far. In literary style, however, it is possible for a *bait-* clause to precede, as in (32d), or even to be inserted into the main clause, as shown by Mitxelena:

(35) a. Eta hemen, teatroan baikaude, hitzak ez dira eranskin huts. (*MEIG* I, 127)
And here, as we are in the theater, words are no empty additions.
b. Ez nuke honekin, lekua ez baita batere egokia, aurrera jo nahi. (*MEIG* VI, 175)
I should not like, as the place is not at all suitable, to proceed further with this.

With respect to word order within *bait-* clauses, we must note that *bait-* is actually a proclitic, on a par with the modal particles of section 8.1.1 with which it is incompatible. It follows that *bait-* does not alter regular word order. In particular, it does not block Auxiliary Attraction in negative clauses: *ez baitu egin*, and not **egin ez baitu*. Compare this with *egin ez duelako* 'because he has not done it', which is more current then *ez duelako egin*.

23.4 Explanatory Instrumental Clauses

23.4.1 Explanatory Instrumental Clauses Governed by *gero(z)*

It was mentioned in section 20.2.6 that finite instrumental clauses governed by the postposition *gero(z)*, originally expressing the temporal sense of English *since*, have also developed the causal sense of English *since*. However, inasmuch as neither Basque *-ez gero* clauses nor English *since* clauses can be used in reply to a 'why' question, the term "causal" here is hardly appropriate. What a Basque *-ez gero* or an English *since* clause in fact does is justify the main clause on the basis of information the speaker assumes the hearer is already aware of. Therefore, *-ez gero* clauses are comparable to explanatory *eta* clauses in view of their justifying character, but only the latter can contain new information. Thus, examples (36a) and (36b) are both possible but have different implications:

(36) a. Zaudete pixka batean, lagunduko dizuet eta. (Atxaga, *Gizona* 103)
Wait a moment, for I will accompany yoû.
b. Lagunduko dizuedanez gero, zaudete pixka batean.
Since I will accompany yoû, wait a moment.

In the context of (36a), the intention of accompanying represents new information, whereas for (36b) to be appropriate, this action must have been previously agreed upon.

From what has been explained so far, it would seem that all *-ez gero* clauses could be replaced by explanatory *eta* ones. This, however, is not the case, because of a divergence in the level of justification. With a declarative principal clause, an explanatory *eta* clause, as observed at the end of section 23.2.1, provides a justification either on the content level or on the epistemic level, but only an *-ez gero* clause can serve to provide a justification on the speech act level, a possibility illustrated by the following examples:

(37) a. Gauza horietaz ari garenez gero, gure seme horrek beste nahigabe bat emango digu. (*TOE* I, 235)
Since we are talking about those things, that son of ours will be giving us another pain.
b. Amerika aipatu duzunez gero, Santo Domingoko zenbait berri galde egin behar dizkizut. (*TOE* I, 220)
Since you have mentioned America, I have to ask you (for) some information about Santo Domingo.
c. 1700ean, urte hori ezarri digutenez gero abiapuntutzat, zenbait gauzaren jabe da oraindik Euskal Herria. (*MEIG* VI, 49)
In 1700, since they have set us that year as a starting point, the Basque Country still has disposition over certain things.

Here, obviously, the explanatory clause does not justify the main clause in any way as to its validity. Rather, it justifies the act of uttering it and, in particular in (37c), the act of uttering a sentence with the year 1700 as its topic. No equivalent *eta* clause is possible for these examples.

Most instances of the *-ez gero* construction, however, convey a justification on the content level, for which purpose explanatory *eta* clauses would serve equally well, provided the linear order of the clauses is inverted. Indeed, as the *-ez gero* clause makes use of old information to prepare the ground for the main clause, it nearly always precedes, whereas the *eta* clause normally follows the principal clause. Typical examples are

(38) a. Ni apaiza naizenez gero, aholkularitzat hartu nau. (Garate, *Esku* 173)
Since I am a priest, he has taken me as adviser.
b. Gerezi sasoian gaudenez gero, ona litzateke gereziren bat ikustea. (Atxaga, *Grl.* 40)
Since we are in the cherry season, it would be nice to see some cherry or so.
c. Galtzak zikindu dizkizudanez gero, beste kafe bat hartzera gonbidatzen zaitut. (Garate, *Iz.B.* 29)
Since I have stained your pants, I invite you to have another cup of coffee.

The *-ez gero* clause can be preceded by a sentence topic fronted out of the main clause:

(39) a. Aho literatura, paperik erabiltzen ez duenez gero, berez da suntsikorra. (*MEIG* IV, 62)
Oral literature, since it doesn't use paper, is ephemeral by nature.

b. Txemak, oporretan dagoenez gero, oso pozik lagunduko lizuke. (Garate, *Iz.B.* 38)
Txema, since he is on vacation, would help you very gladly.

As we say in the case of explanatory *eta* clauses (examples 17a–e), the main clause need not be declarative, but it can be imperative, jussive, hortative, or optative. Some examples are

(40) a. Gertatua gertatu denez gero, egizu nahi duzuna. (*MEIG* IX, 111)
Since what has happened has happened, do what you want.
b. Zilegi izan bekit, gai ez naizenez gero bestetarako, zenbait gauza esatea azentuaz. (*MEIG* VI, 98)
Let it be allowed to me, since I am not qualified for anything else, to say a few things about the accent.
c. Gatozen Etxeparegana, Etxeparegandik gehiegi saihestu garenez gero. (*MEIG* V, 27)
Let us come to Etxepare, since we have strayed too far from Etxepare.
d. Amerikanoarekin ezkondu nahi ez zuenez gero, egin dezala gogoak ematen diona. (*TOE* II, 27)
Since she didn't want to marry the American, let her do what she feels like.

Questions too, rhetorical or genuine, are eligible as main clauses:

(41) a. Gauzak eskura datozkigunez gero, zergatik ez jaso aukeran duguna? (*LBB* 84)
Since things are coming into our hands, why not pick up what opportunity offers?
b. Su emailetzat hartzen gaituzunez gero, zergatik ez hitzegin argi eta garbi? (Labayen, *Su Em.* 212)
Since you take us for arsonists, why not speak up plainly?
c. Horien irizkide ez haizenez gero, lotsak ez al hau gorritzen? (Zaitegi, *Sof.* 175)
As yoù are not like-minded with them, are yoù not red with shame?
d. Lanbide berriak agertu direnez gero, nola ez dira norgehiagoka berriak sortzen? (*MEIG* I, 111)
Since new professions have appeared, how come there are no new contests arising?

23.4.2 Explanatory Use of Ungoverned Instrumental Clauses

Although the option is seldom taken on account of the resulting ambiguity, the postposition *gero* can be dispensed with in western usage, since instrumental clauses by themselves can have "causal" force, as noted in section 19.1.10. To examples (45a,b) of that section, I may add

(42) a. Alargun hau gogaikarri zaidanez, degiodan justizia. (Lk 18:5)
As this widow is a bother to me, let me do justice to her.

b. Ezer gertatu ez zenez, bertan utzi zuten. (Atxaga, *Gizona* 100)
As nothing happened, they left it right there.

[*N.B.* This meaning of the instrumental clause is not found in the northern dialects.]

23.4.3 A Northern Alternative: *-az gainean*

In the northern dialects a less common alternative to the *-ez geroz* construction exists consisting of the definite inessive of the location noun *gain* 'upper side' preceded by the definite instrumental form of a finite relative. Examples are

(43) a. Utziko zaitut joatera hala desiratzen duzunaz gainean. (Cerquand, 75)
I will let you go since you so desire.
b. Bai, bai, erosiko diat saldu nahi duanaz gainean. (Cerquand, 49)
Yes, yes, I will buy it from yoú since yoú want to sell it.
c. Jakin nahi duzunaz gainean, hona beti zer gertatzen zaigun: . . . (Barbier, *Lég*. 24)
Since you want to know, here is what always happens to us: . . .
d. Hirira bazoazenaz gainean, nahi duzu eraman ene xamarra? (*DRA* 1669)
Since you are going to town, do you want to wear my jacket?

23.5 Causal Clauses Based on Fronted Interrogatives

As the scope of this grammar is largely limited to standard Basque in its written form, constructions confined to colloquial use in a particular dialect are usually left aside. Exceptionally, however, a Guipuzcoan colloquial use of *zergatik* will be briefly touched upon because it constitutes the most straightforward illustration of an interrogative used as a causal conjunction.

More space has been devoted in another subsection to the use of *zeren* as a conjunction in the eastern dialects, where it occurs in writing as well as in speech. A final subsection examines the use of *zeren* in the southern literary language, into which it has been borrowed from northern usage.

23.5.1 Causal Conjunctions in the Guipuzcoan Vernacular

In the Guipuzcoan vernacular the interrogative adverbs *zergatik* 'why' and *nola* 'how' occur as causal conjunctions. Used together with the complementizer *-N*, a *zergatik* clause expresses a cause or reason, and a *nola* clause a justification, as does also a postponed coordinate *zergatik* clause, that is, a final *zergatik* clause without a complementizer.

It is no accident that the examples which follow all date from the 19th century. Indeed, from the early 20th century on, constructions of this type, while current in conversation, have been shunned in writing as unworthy calques from Spanish *porque* and *como*, inconsistent with Basque idiom. Thus the following examples are hardly acceptable in Batua:

(44) a. Badakizu zergatik egiten dudan, zu zarela medio, hainbeste negar? Zergatik ni zuretzako argizaria naizen, eta zu niretzako eguzkia zaren, eta eguzkiak argizaria nola ez du urtuko? (Bilintx, 191)
Do you know why in connection with you I weep so much? Because for you I am wax, and for me you are the sun, and how will the sun not melt the wax?
b. Nola eztizalea naizen txit, ez nintzen argizariaz oroitzen. (Iturriaga, *Dial.* 10)
As I am very fond of honey, I did not remember the wax.
c. Agudo plater pare bat, zergatik gosearekin ez dugu ikusten. (Soroa Lasa, *A.O.* 71)
Quick a couple of dishes, for we are blind with hunger.

[*N.B.* The Biscayn vernacular uses *ze* for a causal conjunction instead of *zergatik*.]

23.5.2 Interrogative-Based Conjunctions in Eastern Usage

In eastern usage, the only interrogative widely used as a causal conjunction is *zeren*, the genitive form of *zer* 'what'. This form used to be common in the meaning 'why' and is still found as such in certain contexts, for example, *Ez dut zeren ukatu* (Lhande, 1083) 'I have no reason to deny it'.

When used in combination with the complementizer *-N*, the conjunction *zeren* has a strictly causal sense and thus is interchangeable with the suffix *-lakotz* (cf. example 45d). The conjunction *zeren* also occurs combined with the subordinating prefix *bait-*, in which case the ambiguity characteristic of the latter is retained: the clause can be either causal or explanatory (cf. section 23.3.1).

Finally, we find coordinate *zeren* clauses, in which the verb carries no subordinating affix. Such clauses are invariably explanatory.

The following examples of causal *zeren* combined with the complementizer *-N* are taken from Labourdin authors:

(45) a. Emaztekia, zergatik egiten duzu negar? Magdalenak ihardetsi zuen: Negar egiten dut zeren eraman duten ene Jainkoa, eta zeren ez dakidan non ezarri duten. (Larréguy, II, 286)
Woman, why are you weeping? Magdalena replied: I am weeping because they have taken away my God, and because I do not know where they have put Him.
b. Zergatik? Zeren ez zaituztedan maite? (2 Cor 11:11; Dv)
Why? Because I do not love yoû? (Cf. example 3e.)
c. Zeren zaren hain ona, urriki dut zuri egin irainez. (Duvoisin, *L.Ed.* 100)
Because you are so good, I am sorry for the insults done to you.
d. Ez diozu zuk ene izenari altxaturen etxerik, zeren zaren gerla-gizona, eta odola isuri duzulakotz. (1 Chr 28:3; Dv)
You shall build no house for my name, because you are a man of war, and because you have shed blood.

Clear instances of a causal *bait-* clause introduced by *zeren* are

(46) a. Zergatik behar diogun geure etsaiari barkatu. Lehenbiziko arrazoia: Zeren Jainkoak manatzen baitu. (Ax. 321)
Why we must forgive our enemy. First reason: Because God commands it.
b. Gelditzen dira jokotik, zeren akabatzen baitzaie kandela. (Ax. 611)
They stop playing, because their candle is burning out.
c. Emaztekia, zergatik egiten duzu negar? Ihardesten du: Zeren eraman baitute ene Jauna, eta ez dakit non ezarri duten. (Jn 20:13; Dv)
Woman, why are you weeping? She replies: Because they have taken my Lord away, and I do not know where they have put him.

Duvoisin's Bible translation also provides clear instances of explanatory *bait-* clauses introduced by *zeren*:

(47) a. Izan zituen hirurogeita hamar seme, zeren baitzituen asko emazte. (Jgs 8:30; Dv)
He had seventy sons, for he had many wives.
b. Senda ezazu ene arima, zeren bekatu egin baitut. (Ps 40:5; Dv)
Heal my soul, for I have sinned.
c. Erne zaudete beraz zuek ere, zeren uste ez duzuen orduan etorriko baita gizonaren Semea. (Lk 12:40; Dv)
Be alert, therefore, yoû also, for the Son of man will come at a time yoû do not expect.

Coordinate *zeren* clauses abound in Axular and occur more sparingly in later authors:

(48) a. Ez dut ebatsi nahi, zeren menturaz justiziak atzeman nintzake, urka edo azota. (Ax. 68)
I don't want to steal, for the law could possibly catch me, hang or flog me. (For the potential *nintzake*, see section 24.1.3.)
b. Ez dut jokatu nahi, zeren jokoa ez da errenta, menturaz gal nezake. (Ax. 68)
I do not want to gamble, for gambling is no stipend, I could possibly lose. (For the potential *nezake*, see section 24.2.3.)
c. Zuk ere ikasi behar duzu eraiten, zeren zahartzen ari naiz. (Duvoisin, *Lab.* 66)
You too must learn how to sow, for I am getting old.
d. Aldi bakoitz, ene libertatetik zati bat erortzen zait, zeren ez dakit nora banoan. (Aintziart, 99)
Each time, a part of my freedom falls away from me, for I don't know where I am going.

Just like explanatory *eta* clauses, explanatory *zeren* clauses may be treated as an independent sentence:

(49) a. Ez dut eskuetan dudanaz gabetu nahi. Zeren menturaz gero, nahi dudanean, ez nuke. (Ax. 68)
I don't want to give up what I have in my hands. For maybe later, when I want it, I might not have it.

b. Anitzetan ere Eskritura Sainduan konparatzen da bekatorea ardi errebelatuarekin. Eta arrazoiekin. Zeren anitz gauzatan baitirudite elkar. (Ax. 77–78)
Often in Holy Scripture the sinner is compared to a stray sheep. And with reason. For in many things they resemble each other.

Like *baldin* (section 17.1.2), *zeren* may be followed by an expletory *eta*, already found in Leizarraga's New Testament translation (Heb 5:12). Other examples are

(50) a. Bai pena hau merezi du gizon eskergabeak zeren eta hautsi (di)tuen Jainkoaren legeak. (Etxeberri Ziburukoa, *Man.* I, 42)
Ungrateful man indeed deserves this punishment because he has broken God's laws.

b. Hori ez zait gogoratu ere, zeren eta baitakit emazte anitz . . . ez direla nik hemen mintzatu nahi ditudanetarik. (Zubiri, 242)
That didn't even occur to me, for I know that many women are not among those I want to talk about here.

We observe a pleonastic combination with *-lakotz* in (50c):

(50) c. Arras gogotik mintzatzen naiz gizon honetaz, zeren eta abantzu ene herritarra delakotz. (Zubiri, 104)
I speak about this man quite gladly, because he is more or less my fellow villager.

A less used alternative to *zeren* in the northern dialects is *ezen*. Examples are

(51) a. Laboraria Jainkoaren obretan ari da; ezen Jainkoak egin ditu gizon guztiak, eta laborariaren eskutik hazten ditu. (Duvoisin, *Lab.* 8)
The farmer is busy with God's work; for God has made all men, and feeds them out of the farmer's hand.

b. Segur naiz plazer eginen diodala, ezen bera ere kantari polita da. (Xalbador, *Odol.* 293)
I am sure that I will do him a favor, for he too is a fine singer himself.

23.5.3 Use of *zeren* in Western Batua

Although interrogative as well as "causal" use of *zeren* was once common to the whole Basque-speaking area, its employment nowadays by western authors represents a cultural borrowing from northern usage. As with *bait-* clauses, only the explanatory use has been adopted. Nor is this practice uncontroversial. Many literati in Guipuzcoa and Biscay have been holding to the opinion that clause-initial causal conjunctions are superfluous and inconsistent with Basque idiom. None are found in the works of Txomin and Toma Agirre, A. Labayen, S. Mitxelena, N. Etxaniz, J. Etxaide, G. Garate, and many others. As for K. Mitxelena, disregarding his publication *Zenbait hitzaldi*, a student's translation of his linguistics lectures originally delivered in Spanish, only one instance of *zeren* can be found in his extensive writings (*MEIG* VI, 26). The novelist B. Atxaga, in contrast, makes free use of *zeren*:

(52) a. Ez daude inon, zeren ihes egin baitute. (Atxaga, *Behi* 20)
They are nowhere, for they have fled.
b. Baina ailegatu eta ezuste bat izan nuen, zeren gailurra eta haren inguru guztiak leku mortuak baitziren. (Atxaga, *Obab*. 330)
But once arrived I got a surprise, for the summit and all its surroundings were deserted places.
c. Bertako objetu guztiak ... arrotz egiten zitzaizkidan, zeren eta errealitatea ez baitzen aski indartsu ametsa ezeztatzeko. (Atxaga, *Obab*. 336)
All the objects there looked strange to me, for reality was not potent enough to undo the dream.
d. Ez dute sekulan harrapatuko. Zeren klasikoak ... izenez eta estanpetan bakarrik baitira ezagunak. (Atxaga, *Obab*. 338)
They will never catch him. For the classics are known only by name and by picture.

Many western authors, however, tend to restrict the use of *zeren* to cases where the explanatory clause is fairly complex. Of this, St. John's gospel provides some examples:

(53) a. Ez dut nik zuen alde Aitari erregutu beharrik izango, zeren Aitak berak maite baitzaituzte, ni maite izan nauzuelako. (Jn 16:26–27)
I will have no need to pray to the Father for yoû, for the Father himself loves yoû, because yoû have loved me.
b. Horregatik esan dizuet, zeuen bekatuan hilko zaretela, zeren ni naizena naizela sinesten ez baduzue, zeuen bekatuetan hilko baitzarete. (Jn 8:24)
That is why I have told yoû that yoû would die in yoûr own sin, for, if yoû do not believe that I am what I am, yoû will die in yoûr own sins.

As pointed out in *EGLU* (III, 178), sometimes a coordinate *zeren* clause is the only option. From our discussion in this and prior sections it is obvious that all alternatives require a finite verb available for affixation, which is precisely what is lacking in what we may refer to as cases of indirect justification. Here the justification for the main clause is couched in terms of a proverb or quotation or conveyed by a question or exclamation. Since the verb in such phrases, if at all present, is immune to modification, the conjuction *zeren* alone will mark the phrase as explanatory. The following examples illustrate this point:

(54) a. Ez deus egiteaz beraz ikasten da gaizki egiten, zeren, *otiositas est mater nugarum, noverca virtutum.* (Etxeberri Sarakoa, 187; cf. Ax. 39)
Merely by doing nothing one learns to do evil, for *otiositas est mater nugarum, noverca virtutum.* (Idleness is the mother of frivolities, [and] the stepmother of virtues.)

b. Jende hau ... bat-batean aurkitzen da ... mintzabiderik gabe; zeren, zer dela eta hasiko ziren jaun haiek Afrika erdiko hizkuntza basatiak ikasten? (K. Mitxelena, *Z.H.* 43)
These people suddenly find themselves without the power of speech, for, why would those gentlemen start learning the uncouth languages of central Africa?

c. Munduaren gain garaipena ematen diguna gure sinesmena da. Zeren, nork garaitzen du mundua, Jesus Jainkoaren Seme dela sinesten duenak baizik? (1 Jn 5:4–5)
What gives us victory over the world is faith. For, who overcomes the world but he who believes that Jesus is the Son of God?

d. Kanpoa desiratzen du, zeren, libertatea zeinen eder den! (Cf. Sallaberry, 48)
He longs for the outside, for, how nice is freedom!

Note, however, that in all these examples *zeren* can be replaced by the sentence adverb *izan ere* 'indeed'. Thus the text of 1 Jn 5:5 in the *IB* version is virtually identical to example (54c), except for this replacement: *Izan ere, nor da mundua garaitzen duena ...*

23.6 Inferential Adverbs

For use as signposts in the development of a complex argument, Basque possesses a considerable number of adverbs with meanings such as 'then', 'therefore', 'in that case': *bada* 'well then', *beraz* 'thus', *hartara* 'in that way', *horregatik* 'therefore', *hortaz* 'consequently', *orduan* 'then', and so on. Among these, *beraz* and *bada* will be singled out here for separate treatment: *beraz* as a typical representative of this group and *bada* on account of its various idiosyncrasies.

23.6.1 Inferential *beraz*

Etymologically, the form *beraz*, instrumental of *bera* 'the same' (section 6.1.5), matches the English phrase *by the same token*. Except in Souletin, where *arren* holds sway, it is the most common illative adverb, corresponding in use to English *therefore*, *thus*, or causal *so*:

(55) a. Bere diruak han zituen oso-osorik. Ez dute beraz ebasteko hil. (Larzabal, *Senp.* 58)
His valuables were there, intact. So they've not killed him in order to steal.

b. Senitartekoak gara biok. Beraz, ez dugu bion artean liskarrik izan behar. (Gn 13:8)
We two are kinsmen. Therefore, we must have no quarreling between us two.

As a sentence adverb, its position within the sentence is rather free. The most favored location, however, is directly after the finite verb, as in example (55a); thereafter, initial position; and also, but less frequently, the second position in the sentence. All three options can be illustrated from K. Mitxelena's writings:

(56) a. Hortik dator, beraz, gure harridura honen gutuna irakurtzean. (*MEIG* VI, 70)
Thence comes, therefore, our astonishment upon reading his letter.
b. Ongi etorria zor diegu beraz. (*MEIG* VIII, 111)
We owe them, therefore, a welcome.
c. Ez nioke, beraz, deus kendu nahi. (*MEIG* VI, 121)
I would not want, therefore, to take anything away from him.
d. Saia gaitezen, beraz, kultura baten alde onez lehenbailehen jabetzen. (*MEIG* IV, 45)
Let us try, therefore, to appropriate the good sides of a culture as soon as possible.

The following examples have initial *beraz*:

(57) a. Beraz, *rey* ez da euskal hitza. (*MEIG* VII, 128)
Therefore, *rey* is not a Basque word.
b. Beraz, nik ez nuke esango inork oraingo hizkuntza baztertzen duenik. (*MEIG* IX, 76)
Therefore, I wouldn't say that anyone rejects the present-day language.

These have *beraz* in second position:

(58) a. Batzuetan, beraz, ez da erraz izango euskal ordaina asmatzea. (*MEIG* VI, 90)
Sometimes, therefore, it won't be easy to invent a Basque equivalent.
b. Lehen bokalaren iturburua jakiteko, beraz, lagungarri dugu forma trinkoak edukitzea. (*MEIG* VI, 192)
In order to discover the source of the first vowel, therefore, it is helpful for us to have synthetic forms.

23.6.2 The Particle *bada*

The particle *bada*, which in conversational style is pronounced and written as *ba*, may count as an inferential particle, as evidenced by the scores of examples in *EGLU* where *bada* and *beraz* are interchangeable (*EGLU* III, 136–140).

EGLU, however, goes on to show that in many other contexts *bada* and *beraz* are far from interchangeable. This is in part because *bada* has a weaker illative force, as was pointed out by P. Lafitte: "*Bada* a un sens assez imprécis: en syllogisme on l'utilise pour traduire *or*, et c'est *beraz* qui traduit *donc*." (*Bada* has a rather imprecise meaning: in a syllogism it is used to translate *or* [now, but now], and it is *beraz*, which translates *donc* [therefore, thus].) (Lafitte 1962, sec. 400, p. 178)

More significantly, however, *bada* differs from *beraz* in that over and above its illative use it serves to provide phonic support for the sentence intonation, so as to enable it to better convey all sorts of emotional states, such as surprise, doubt, distrust, disapproval, and so on.

Its English translation, therefore, may vary from context to context, but in use it generally corresponds to Spanish *pues* and, somewhat less closely, to French *alors* or English *then* in their nontemporal sense.

It is most commonly located directly after the finite verb, but initial, second, or final positions are also possible.

To illustrate the various uses of *bada*, I will start with assertions and then proceed to other speech acts:

(59) a. *Inguru* da euskaldun guztiok darabilgun hitza, baita zuberotarrek ere. Hori da, bada, euskal hitza. (*MEIG* VII, 131)
Inguru is a word we Basques all use, the Souletins also. That, therefore, is a Basque word.
b. Hori da ba nik esan nuena. (Muxika, *P.Am.* 29)
So that's what I said.
c. Lana! Lana! Lan egitea ere nahikoa astakeria da ba. (*G.* 199)
Work! Work! Working, too, is plenty of bullshit, you know.

Bada appears in exclamations:

(60) a. Ni ez naute ba berriz harrapatuko! (*TOE* II, 79)
I say, they won't catch me again!
b. Banengoen, ba! (*LBB* 162)
I rather thought as much!

Bada is freely used in imperatives, jussives, and hortatives:

(61) a. Dena bustia etorriko zara, nire Txomin; alda zaitez, bada. (Zabala, *Gabon* 31)
You must have come all wet, my Txomin, go change, then.
b. Baina zurekin nahi nuke hitzegin.—Esan bada, entzuten zaitut. (Haranburu, *Ausk.* 97)
But I would like to talk to you.—Say it then, I hear you.
c. Azter beza, bada, nork bere burua, ogitik jan aurretik. (1 Cor 11:28)
Let everyone, then, examine himself before eating from the bread.
d. Eman dezagun, bada, horrela dela. (*MEIG* VII, 172)
Let us grant, then, that it is so.

As *EGLU* observes, use of *bada* with an imperative can convey a challenge or mark irritation:

(61) e. Bakarrik egingo dut.—Egizu bada! (*EGLU* III, 155)
I will do it alone.—Then do it!

In questions too, use of *bada* is accompanied quite often by a nonneutral sentence intonation betraying emotional involvement on the part of the questioner:

(62) a. Judua ote naiz, bada, ni? (Jn 18:35)
Am I then a Jew?
b. Zer gertatu zen, bada? (Garate, *NY* 15)
What, then, happened?
c. Nor da bada jende hori? (Atxaga, *Obab*. 332)
Who are those people then?
d. Zenbat eskatzen duzu, ba, txahalagatik? (*G.* 87)
How much, then, do you ask for the calf?
e. A! Hor zaude.—Non nahi duzu ba egotea? (Haranburu, *Ausk*. 137)
Ah! There you are.—Where then do you want me to be?
f. Nik ez diot esan.—Nola daki bada? (*EGLU* III, 157)
I haven't told him.—How does he know it then?
g. Ez du hori esan.—Zer bada? (*EGLU* III, 156)
He hasn't said that.—What then?

[*N.B.* With a slightly sarcastic intonation, *zer ba* can mean 'what else did you expect?' or 'come now!'.]

Placed at the head of the sentence, *bada* fulfills the same function as English *well* or *well then*:

(63) a. Ba, egia esan, gaur ez dut asko bazkaldu. (Atxaga, *Gizona* 216)
Well, to tell the truth, I haven't had much for lunch today.
b. Txabola honetan gertatzen dena jakin nahi duk, ez da? Bada, gau osoa edukiko duk jakiteko! (Atxaga, *Obab*. 393)
Yoú want to know what happens in this hut, don't yoú? Well then, yoú will have the whole night to find out.
c. Bada, ikasi nahi ez duanez gero, Ameriketara joango haiz. (*TOE* I, 208)
Well then, since yoú don't want to study, yoú'll go to America.
d. Dena daki.—Bada, ez digu ezer esan. (*EGLU* III, 158)
He knows everything.—Well, he hasn't said anything to us.
e. Nik ez diot esan.—Bada, norbaitek esan dio. (*EGLU* III, 158)
I haven't told him.—Well, somebody told him.

Use of *ba* in conversation is not always justified by the preceding context, as it was in most of the examples presented so far. It may also function as a hesitation particle or a stopgap:

(64) a. Nora eraman duzue autoa konpontzera?—Badago ba Igeldo bidean garaje bat, ba haraxe. (*EGLU* III, 160)
Where did yoû take the car to be fixed?—There is, you know, a garage on the Igeldo road; well, there (is where we took it).
b. Esango diot ba, Jauna, argiro. (Urruzuno, *E.Z.* 124)
Now, I will tell you, sir, clearly.
c. Berrehun ... ez dakit ba berorrek nahiko ote dituen. (Urruzuno, *E.Z.* 124)
Two hundred ... I don't know, now, whether you will want them.

As a reaction to a positive statement, *bai ba* means 'no wonder' and *ez ba* or *ba ez* 'on the contrary'. As a reaction to a negative statement, however, *bai ba* or *ba bai* means 'on the contrary' and *ez ba* 'no wonder'. (For particulars on intonation, see *EGLU* III, 153–154.)

An exclamation featuring an expletory negative *ez* combined with postverbal *ba* expresses amazement or even indignation at the state of affairs conveyed by the sentence:

(65) a. Izan ere, harritzekoa zen! Orratz hura ... Pagodirena ez zen ba! (Loidi, 85)
It was indeed amazing! That pin ... it was actually Pagodi's!
b. Leihoa hesten ari nintzela, erori ez zitzaidan, ba, eskutik! (*LBB* 144)
While I was closing the window, it actually went and fell out of my hand!
c. Dirua ez zioten ba eskatu! (*G.* 371)
They actually asked him for money!
d. Kotxea ez didate ba eskatu! (Haranburu, *Ausk.* 39)
They have actually asked me for my car!
e. Sinetsi ere! Bidart detektibea bera ez zen, bada! (Garate, *Esku* 168)
Unbelievable! It actually was detective Bidart himself!

This construction also serves as an emphatic positive answer to a yes-no question, implying indignation at the question even being asked:

(66) a. Gogoratzen al zara nitaz?—Gogoratuko ez naiz ba! (Oñederra, 100)
Do you remember me?—Sure enough I remember!
b. Ezagutzen al duzu hor atzean zutik dagoen emakume hori?—Ezagutuko ez dut, ba? (Amuriza, *Emea* 50)
Do you know that woman who is standing there in the back?—(How) would I not know her?

Note that Auxiliary Attraction (section 8.2.2) is optional here: *ez naiz ba gogoratuko!* and *ez dut ba ezagutuko?* are equally possible.

As intimated at the beginning of this section, *bada* in most of its uses matches Spanish *pues*. As a result of the extensive bilingualism among southern Basques, there has been a tendency to perfect this match by allowing *bada* to also act as a causal conjunction. Yet, after Azkue (1923–1925, sec. 725, p. 491) and Altube (1929, 210) inveighed against this practice, use of *bada* as a conjunction became stigmatized and is now shunned by most speakers. Nevertheless, *EGLU*, adducing its time-honored presence in the southern literary tradition, seems to condone it:

(67) a. Aspertu egin naiz, bada bakarrik utzi naute. (*EGLU* III, 187)
I got bored, for they have left me alone.
b. Eraman ezazu, bada on egingo dizu. (*EGLU* III, 189)
Take it with you, for it will do you good.

23.7 Concessive Constructions

A concessive construction voices an objection to the validity of the main clause (content concessive), to the speaker's ability to realize its validity (epistemic concessive), or to the propriety of the speaker uttering the main clause (illocutionary concessive). Concessive clauses might therefore be construed as explanatory clauses for the negation of the main clause, though the objection presented is invariably made light of by the speaker, since it fails to keep him from asserting the main clause in spite of it. Small wonder, then, that concessive clauses and explanatory ones share some properties, among which is the inability to take focus or quasi focus.

The location of a concessive with respect to the main clause is, on the whole, rather free. It may precede or follow, or be intercalated in it.

Standard Basque has several ways of forming concessives, to be discussed in the following separate subsections. About the different types or levels of concessives distinguished in this section no more will be said, as inquiry has shown that they are distributed equally among the various constructions.

Textual concessives—that is, concessives objecting to a preceding discourse unit rather than a single proposition—are a different matter. Not being bound to a particular clause, they cannot be accommodated by a verbal affix, but only by a conjunction, in this case *nahiz* (*eta*). (See section 23.7.5.)

23.7.1 Concessive Postpositional Phrases

The motivational case ending *-gatik* has a concessive sense as well:

(68) a. Hiru tatxa horiengatik, neskatxek maite naute ni. (From the song "Gizon gazteak ezkontzeko," *Xaramela* 131)
Despite those three faults the girls love me.
b. Amengatik, semeek nahi dutena egiten dute. (*DRA* 1749)
In spite of their mothers, the sons do what they want.

Then there is the noun *gorabehera*, literally 'up and down', which also acts as a postposition governing the absolutive case. It expresses two meanings: 'in spite of' and 'aside from'. Mitxelena's essays brim with examples: *Arakistainen lekukotasuna gorabehera* (*MEIG* VII, 40) 'despite Arakistain's testimony'; *gramatikak gorabehera* (*MEIG* VI, 167) 'in spite of the grammar books'; *zenbait aldaera gorabehera* (*MEIG* VI, 73) 'apart from a few variants'; *euskalkia gorabehera* (*MEIG* VII, 72) 'aside from the Basque dialect'. The meaning 'aside from', that is, 'discounting', also explains the expression *gutxi gorabehera* 'approximately'.

A similar, but less employed, postposition is *goiti-beheiti*: *zuen esamesak goiti-beheiti* (*TOE* II, 25) 'in spite of yoûr taunts'.

An idiomatic construction based on the deletion of *direlarik* 'while they are' (see section 20.8.2) can be resorted to when the concession concerns an unmodified plural noun. Some examples will make this point clear:

(69) a. Hutsak huts, badu liburu honek alde ederrik aski. (*MEIG* II, 47)
Despite the mistakes, this book has plenty of nice features.
b. Ez da bera, itxurak itxura, nire artaldekoetarik. (*MEIG* VI, 108)
Despite appearances, he is not among those of my flock.
c. Eragozpenak eragozpen, plazara ginen Etxeparez geroz. (*MEIG* IX, 33)
Despite the impediments, we have made ourselves known from Etxepare on.
d. Huskeriak huskeria ados naizela esango nuke guztira, puntu guztietan ez bada ere. (*MEIG* VII, 160)
Some trifles aside, I would say that on the whole I agree, if not on all points.
e. Bazekien gertatuko zela, tartekoak tarteko beregana etorriko zinela. (Oñederra, 63)
He knew it would happen, that you would come to him despite all that was in the way.

23.7.2 Concessive Clauses Using *-gatik*

One way of forming nonfinite concessives, albeit not the most common one, is to use the motivational case ending *-gatik* in combination with the definite form of the perfect participle:

(70) a. Zahartuagatik dago oso dezentea. (Txirrita, in Zavala, *Txirr.* 178)
Despite having grown old, he is quite all right.
b. Pixka batean ez naiz ahaztuko sartuagatik lurpean. (Txirrita, in Zavala, *Txirr.* 242)
I won't be forgotten for a while, although put under ground.
c. Elizaren laguntza hori izanagatik ere, aski harrigarria izan da eta da euskararen iraupena. (*MEIG* VI, 33)
Even despite there having been that help from the Church, the survival of Basque has been and is quite amazing.

Finite concessives with *-gatik* are possible but rare: *zahar naizenagatik* (Ax. 193) 'although I am old'.

23.7.3 Conditional Concessives with *ere*

As shown in section 17.6, adding *ere* 'even' to the protasis of a conditional produces a concessive. To the examples given there I may add

(71) a. Gezurra badirudi ere, bidaiak on egin dio. (Atxaga, *Sara* 149)
Incredible though it may seem, the journey has done him good.
b. Baina Itziarrek, jan bazuen ere, ez zuen janari onaz gozatu. (Arana, 18)
But Itziar, even though she ate it, did not enjoy the good food.
c. Bizitza ez da gelditu, beldurrak hala eskatzen badio ere. (Oñederra, 152)
Life has not stopped, even though fear is begging it to do so.

Not just finite conditionals, but any clause susceptible to a conditional interpretation can turn into a concessive by the addition of *ere*:

(72) Zer esango duen jakin gabe ere, ontzat hartuko nituzke orain bertan bere iritziak. (*MEIG* VII, 165)
Even without knowing what he will say, I would endorse his opinions right now.

23.7.4 Concessive Clauses Using the Suffix *-arren*

In southern Basque, the most favored device for forming concessive clauses is the suffix *-arren*, the causal use of which was illustrated in section 23.1.1. It can form finite as well as nonfinite concessives, in both of which it is commonly written as a separate word.

In a finite clause *-arren* follows the relativized form of the verb:

(73) a. Bai hala da, askotan ez dirudien arren. (*TOE* II, 212)
Yes, that is so, although often it does not seem so.
b. "Gure hotela" deitu izan diote, han bi egun besterik egin ez zituzten arren. (Iturbe, 102)
They have been calling it "our hotel," although they only spent two days there.
c. Hara, hauts eta errauts besterik ez naizen arren, ene jaun horri mintzatzera ausartzen naiz. (Gn 18:27)
Behold, though I am nothing but dust and ashes, I venture to speak to my Lord.
d. Senda nazazu, zure aurka bekatu egin dudan arren. (Ps 41:5)
Heal me, though I have sinned against you.

In the nonfinite construction *-arren* follows the perfect participle or, in negative clauses, sometimes the negative *ez*:

(74) a. Filosofoak ezagutzen du gauza batzuek jakin arren, badirela beste anitz hark ez dakizkienak. (Etxeberri Sarakoa, 203)

The philosopher recognizes that although he knows some things, there are many other things that he doesn't know.

b. Ezkontzak, egoera ederra izan arren, baditu bere atsekabe eta alde txarrak. (*MEIG* I, 128)
Marriage, though it is a nice state, has its griefs and bad points.

c. Bospasei beribil igaro arren, bat ere gelditu ez. (Garate, *Alaba* 61)
Although five or six cars came by, none stopped.

d. Zuk inor maite ez arren ere, badira zu maite zaituztenak. (Amuriza, *Hil* 148)
Even though you love no one, there are those who love you.

23.7.5 Concessive Clauses Using the Conjunction *nahiz*

The indefinite instrumental of the noun *nahi* 'will' (section 14.3.2) may be employed as a clause-initial conjunction for concessive clauses. Nowadays, a finite verb in a concessive clause requires the complementizer *-N*; in older usage *-LA* was also an option.

(75) a. Ez zuten haurrik nahiz aspaldi esposatuak ziren. (*P.Ad.* 71)
They had no children although they had been married a long time.

b. Nahiz ez den gaztelua, maite dut nik sorlekua. (Elzb. *Po.* 195)
Even though it is no castle, I love my birthplace.

While the factuality of a concessive is normally presupposed, as in Spanish, a speaker may cancel this presupposition by resorting to a subjunctive verb form:

(75) c. Eta hori da uste duguna nahiz aitor ez dezagun. (*MEIG* VIII, 142 = *MIH* 222)
And that is what we believe even though we may not admit it.

Nonfinite concessives are constructed with the perfect participle:

(76) a. Hiru egun pozik pasa genituen nahiz diru gutxi ekarri. (Uztapide, *Sas.* 174)
We happily spent three days although we had brought little money.

b. Baietz ba ihardetsi nion, nahiz horietaz gauza gutxi jakin. (Landart, 26)
I then answered him positively, although I knew little about those matters.

In southern usage and no earlier than the end of the 19th century, concessive *nahiz* is optionally followed by expletory *eta*, no doubt on analogy with *baldin* and *zeren*:

(77) a. Nahiz eta leihotik Obabako mendi zaharrak ikusten nituen, kosta egiten zitzaida nire gelan nengoenaz jabetzea. (Atxaga, *Obab.* 336)
Although I could see the old mountains of Obaba through the window, I had trouble realizing the fact that I was in my room.

b. Egia esan, nahiz eta harrokeria dirudien, uste dut Euskaltzaindiak fidantza apur bat merezi duela. (*MEIG* VII, 172)
To tell the truth, arrogance though it may seem, I think that the Basque Academy deserves a little trust.

c. Ez du irakurgai honek inoren ilerik laztuko, nahiz eta loak hartzerakoan irakurri. (*MEIG* III, 85)
This reading will make nobody's hair curl, even when read right before falling asleep.

While an affix (*-gatik*, *ba-*, *-arren*) requires a suitable clause to attach to, a conjunction can afford to be less fussy about its syntactic requirements. Thus the following example shows a textual concessive expressed in the shape of a question preceded by the conjunction *nahiz eta*.

(77) d. (After a discourse composed of three sentences in which he voices his suspicion of being followed, the speaker continues, saying:)
Nahiz eta, pentsatzen jarrita, zergatik zaindu behar naute ni? (Atxaga, *Sara* 114)
Although, come to think of it, why should they be watching me?

23.7.6 Concessive Adverbials

In K. Mitxelena's writings, a notable paradigm of essayistic style, the following concessive adverbials occur: *alabaina*, *guztiarekin ere*, *guztiaz ere*, *haatik*, *hala(z) ere*, *halarik ere*, *hala eta guzti(z) ere*, *hala(z) guztiz (ere)*, *halere*, *horregatik*, and *horratik*, all meaning 'nevertheless'.

With the exception of the long forms *hala eta guzti(z) ere* and *hala(z) guztiz (ere)*, which prefer clause-initial position (*EGLU* III, 123), the distribution of these sentence adverbials is like that of *beraz* (section 23.6.1), that is, rather free. Among these concessive adverbials the one most frequently used in speech as well as in writing is *hala ere* 'even so', a form, often contracted to *halere*, common to the entire Basque-speaking area (*EGLU* III, 121).

While the motivational demonstratives *hargatik* and *horregatik* show ambiguity between a causal and a concessive use, meaning either 'because of that' or 'in spite of that', their contractions *haatik* and *horratik* are concessive only.

Although not strictly concessives, the following expressions are worth noting: *dena den* or *dena dela*, both meaning 'however it may be', 'anyhow'.

23.8 Deverbal *-kor* Marking Inclination

Attaching to verb radicals, the suffix *-kor* (with lowered pitch) yields adjectives with the meaning 'prone to the state or activity denoted by the verb'. In the case of an adjective based on a transitive verb a question then arises. Does it describe a propensity to act or to be acted upon? Inquiry has shown that the deverbal adjective indicates a propensity to act, except with verbs taking direct objects demonstrably affected by the action, such as *erabili* 'to use', *kilikatu* 'to tickle', *manatu* 'to command', and *moldatu* 'to form', where the derived adjectives have a passive sense: *erabilkor* 'easy to use', 'manageable', 'handy';

kilikor (haplology from *kilikakor*) 'ticklish'; *manakor* 'submissive', 'obedient'; and *moldakor* 'flexible', 'supple', 'accommodating'.

As to typical change-of-state verbs (section 12.4.2), the derivational process seems to operate on the intransitive sense only, given the fact that *errekor* means 'readily burning' and not 'readily burned', *hauskor* 'easily breaking' and not 'easily broken', and *hilkor* 'liable to death' and not 'liable to murder'. In the listing that follows the transitive sense of such verbs will therefore be ignored.

In contrast to adjectives derived with the suffix *-ti* (section 9.7) or *-koi* (section 10.6), adjectives with this suffix apply to animate as well as inanimate referents: *sendagai eraginkorra* 'an effective medicine', *poz iragankorra* 'a transitory joy'.

A variant form *-or* exists in the Biscayan dialect. Only *errukior* 'compassionate' and *erabakior* 'resolute' have penetrated into the standard language, replacing the less euphonious *errukikor* and *erabakikor*.

The four adjectives with passive meaning cited previously have not been included in the following list of current *-kor* derivatives, which turns out to contain no further examples of passive adjectives.

adierazi	to express	adierazkor	expressive
aditu	to listen, to understand	adikor	affable, understanding, attentive
ahantzi	to forget	ahanzkor	forgetful
ahaztu	to forget	ahazkor	forgetful
aldatu	to change	aldakor	changeable, variable, versatile
amaitu	to end	amaikor	finite
anaitu	to become brothers	anaikor	brotherly
atsekabetu	to distress	atsekabekor	sorrowful, morose
barkatu	to forgive	barkakor	forgiving, merciful, lenient
bekaiztu	to envy	bekaizkor	envious
berandu	to be late	berankor	tardy, slow in coming
bizi (izan)	to live	bizkor	lively, energetic, quick, clever
bukatu	to end	bukakor	finite
damutu	to be sorry	damukor	remorseful, penitent
dudatu	to doubt	dudakor	irresolute, hesitating, sceptical
egin	to do	eginkor	active, effective
egon	to stand, to be	egonkor	stable
ekarri	to bring	ekarkor	productive, fertile
eman	to give	emankor	productive, fertile, generous
engainatu	to err, to deceive	engainakor	error prone, deceptive
eragin	to activate	eraginkor	effective, stimulating
erakarri	to attract	erakarkor	attractive, appealing
eraman	to carry, to bear	eramankor	uncomplaining, patient
erantsi	to adhere, to stick	eranskor	adhesive, sticky, contagious
eritu	to fall ill	erikor	sickly

erori	to fall	erorkor	unstable, wobbly, precarious
erre	to burn	errekor	inflammable, combustible
etorri	to come	etorkor	compliant, yielding, docile
gaixotu	to fall ill	gaixokor	sickly
galdu	to perish, to ruin, to lose	galkor	perishable, pernicious
gertatu	to happen	gertakor	impending, probable
gizendu	to get fat	gizenkor	prone to fatness
haserretu	to get angry	haserrekor	short-tempered, irascible
hautsi	to break	hauskor	breakable, fragile, brittle
hedatu	to spread	hedakor	rapidly spreading, expansive
higitu	to move	higikor	mobile, restless, shifting
hil	to die	hilkor	mortal (cf. *hilezkor* 'immortal')
ibili	to walk	ibilkor	fond of walking or traveling
igaro	to pass	igarokor	transitory, ephemeral, passing
igo	to ascend	igokor	upwardly mobile, aiming high
ikaratu	to tremble	ikarakor	jumpy, shy, easily frightened
iragan	to pass	iragankor	transitory, transient, transitive
iraun	to last	iraunkor	lasting, eternal
irentsi	to swallow, to devour	irenskor	devouring
iruditu	to imagine, to seem	irudikor	suspicious, imaginary, figurative
isildu	to keep silent	isilkor	taciturn, silent
itsatsi	to adhere, to stick	itsaskor	adhesive, sticky, contagious
izutu	to get frightened	izukor	easily alarmed, shy
jarraitu	to continue	jarraikor	continuous, assiduous, persistent
jasan	to suffer	jasankor	long-suffering, tolerant, patient
jelostu	to get jealous	jeloskor	jealous, prone to jealousy
jostatu	to play	jostakor	playful, frolicsome
kutsatu	to contaminate, to infect	kutsakor	contagious, contaminating
labaindu	to slide, to slip	labainkor	prone to slip
laztandu	to caress	laztankor	caressing, tender
lehertu	to burst, to explode	leherkor	tending to burst, explosive
lotsatu	to become ashamed	lotsakor	bashful, timid, shy
luzatu	to procrastinate	luzakor	procrastinating, slow acting
maite (izan)	to love	maitekor	amorous, affectionate
mugitu	to move	mugikor	mobile, restless, shifting
pasatu	to pass	pasakor	passing, ephemeral
pentsatu	to think	pentsakor	pensive, thoughtful, meditative
poztu	to be glad	pozkor	jovial, jolly, cheerful
sartu	to enter	sarkor	penetrating, incisive
sentitu	to feel	sentikor	sensitive, feeling, emotional
sinestu	to believe	sineskor	credulous
sumindu	to get furious	suminkor	short-tempered, irascible
suntsitu	to disappear	suntsikor	ephemeral

ugaldu	to reproduce	ugalkor	prolific, fertile
ukatu	to deny, to refuse	ukakor	negative, pessimistic
usteldu	to rot	ustelkor	perishable, corrupt
zabaldu	to widen	zabalkor	expansive, diffusive
zikindu	to soil	zikinkor	easily soiled

In addition to their expected meaning 'prone to slip', the adjectives *irristakor* and *lerrakor*, derived from the intransitives *irristatu* and *lerratu* both meaning 'to slide' as well as 'to slip', also express the meaning 'slippery', thus substituting for **irristarazkor* and **lerrarazkor* corresponding to the causatives *irristarazi* and *lerrarazi*: *lintzura irristakor hori* (*MEIG* VI, 146) 'that slippery marsh', *bide lerrakor hau* 'this slippery road'.

A few adjectives, seemingly derived from nouns, are based on *egin* idioms (section 13.3):

barre egin	to laugh	barrekor	quick to laugh, smiling
ihes egin	to flee	iheskor	evasive, elusive, fleeting
irri egin	to laugh, to jeer	irrikor	quick to laugh, smiling
kalte egin	to harm	kaltekor	harmful
kili(kili) egin	to tickle	kilikor	exciting, titillating
manu egin	to command	manukor	submissive, docile
zalantza egin	to have doubts	zalantzakor	doubting, irresolute

[*N.B.* The passive sense of *manukor* must be explained by analogy, cf. *manakor*.]

A small number of non-deverbal neologisms dating from the first half of the 20th century have become current: *bihozkor* 'cordial', 'warmhearted', 'heartfelt', from *bihotz* 'heart'; *baikor* 'optimistic', from *bai* 'yes'; *ezkor* 'pessimistic' from *ez* 'no'; *orokor* 'universal', 'general', from *oro* 'all'.

23.9 The Adjectival Suffix *-bera* Marking an Inordinate Proclivity

Originally an adjective meaning 'soft' (now replaced by *bigun* or *beratz*), the suffix *-bera* produces adjectives describing a somewhat inordinate proclivity to the state or process indicated by the base. The suffix is not productive, attaching to about a dozen nouns and twice as many verbs, most of which require an animate subject. Where the direct object is demonstrably affected by the action of the verb, a passive meaning results for the derived adjective, as in the following examples:

egosi	to cook, to digest	egosbera	easy to cook, easy to digest
kilikatu	to tickle	kilikabera	ticklish
moldatu	to form	moldabera	ductile, malleable, supple

Otherwise the meaning is active:

aldatu	to change	aldabera	changeable, fickle
barkatu	to forgive	barkabera	forgiving, merciful, lenient

eritu	to fall ill	eribera	sickly
erori	to fall	erorbera	unstable, wobbly
gaixotu	to fall ill	gaixobera	sickly
hautsi	to break	hausbera	fragile, brittle
hunkitu	to be touched	hunkibera	easily touched, touchy
ikusi	to see	ikusbera	curious
irristatu	to slide, to slip	irristabera	prone to slip, slippery
maitatu	to love	maitabera	amorous
samurtu	to become tender	samurbera	easily mollified
sentitu	to feel	sentibera	(over)sensitive, sentimental
sinetsi	to believe	sinesbera	credulous

[*N.B.* Remember that change-of-state verbs behave as intransitives (*hautsi*, *aldatu*).]

While the nouns serving as a base for *bera* are not easily classified, the adjectives derived invariably describe a property of animate beings:

eder	beauty	ederbera	sensitive to beauty
egarri	thirst	egarbera	overly prone to thirst, thirsty
erruki	compassion	errukibera	compassionate
gaitz	ailment, evil	gaizbera	sickly, inclined to evil
gose	hunger	gosebera	ever hungry
hotz	cold	hozbera	very sensitive to cold
irri	laughter	irribera	quick to laugh, cheerful
izerdi	sweat	izerbera	easily sweating, sweaty
izu	fright	izubera	easily alarmed, shy
ke	smoke	kebera	very sensitive to smoke
min	pain	minbera	overly sensitive, touchy
sumin	rage, irritation	suminbera	short-tempered, easily enraged

From *bihotz* 'heart' there is *bihozbera* 'softhearted', and from *gogo* 'mind' *gogabera* 'sensitive', 'lenient'. These, however, are not instances of the suffix *-bera*, but rather exocentric compounds with the adjective *bera* 'soft'. Also a compound is the adjective *onbera* 'kind', from *on* 'good' and *bera* 'soft'.

23.10 Vocabulary

afalondo	time after dinner (cf. section 4.1.3.4)
amore eman	to give in, to yield (cf. section 15.6.6)
arriskutsu	dangerous (cf. section 8.7)
baizik	but (i.e., Spanish *sino*, German *sondern*)
berandu	late

elur	snow
erantsi	to add, to stick on
eri	ill, sick
gaixo	ill, sick
gezurti	mendacious, liar (cf. section 9.7)
gogo *edun	to be eager, to feel like
igande	Sunday
Iparralde	Northern Region of the Basque Country
irakin	to boil
jakintsu	learned, knowledgeable
maisu	teacher, expert
mami	substance, curds
nekarazi	to tire out, to disturb
ohe	bed
sinesmen	faith (cf. section 22.7)
txartel	ticket
zehatz	exactly, in detail
zine	movie theater
zorionak eman	to congratulate

23.11 Exercises

23.11.1 Translate into English

1. Ez dizuet idatzi egia ez dakizuelako, badakizuelako baizik. (1 Jn 2:21; *EAB*)
2. Ez dakiguna ez dakigulako dakigu dakiguna.
3. Goazen azkar zinera. Txartelik hartzeke gaude oraindik eta. (Itziar, 41) (Cf. section 13.5.3.)
4. Don Frantziskok ez zion ezer erantsi nahi izan telefonoz horrelako gauzak aipatzea arriskutsua zela eta. (Garate, *Esku* 172)
5. Zer dela eta zatozte horren berandu?
6. Eliza Ama Santuak bere maisuak dituenez gero, ez dagokigu guri liburu honen mamiaz mintzatzea. (*MEIG* II, 47)
7. Horren jakintsua zarenez gero, ni noiz hilko ote naizen ere ba al dakizu? (*LBB* 183)
8. Arrazoi dudan arren, gezurtitzat nauka. (Jb 34:6)
9. Lan berrian hasteko gogoa du, zehatz nolakoa den ez dakien arren. (Oñederra, 31)
10. Denak irakurtzearren erosi ditut liburu zahar hauek.
11. Nahiz Iparraldekoa den, ulertzen du hemengo euskara. (Arejita, *Eusk. Josk.* 181)
12. Amore eman behar izan dugu, nahiz odolak irakin.

23.11.2 Translate into Basque

1. We have come home because we were hungry.
2. Mary does not want to buy wine because she doesn't drink it herself.
3. I love you because you are who you are.
4. On the plea that it is cold outside, Pete does not want to get up out of bed.
5. I must congratulate you that you have such a brother.
6. Adducing that he has lost the Faith, he is not going to church.
7. Since you know everything, you do not need to learn anything.
8. Since it was Sunday, he had no fear of disturbing anyone.
9. I don't know whether I will come, for it is snowing.
10. Stay at home, for you are ill.
11. You should not have said that, even though it is true.
12. Even though I am asking rather late, what plans do you have for the time after dinner?

24 Expressing Potentiality

24.1 Morphology of the Potential Mood

In Basque the concept of potentiality can be expressed morphologically, lexically, or syntactically: morphologically, by the use of a special verbal paradigm known as the potential mood; lexically, with the help of the nouns *ahal* 'possibility' or *ezin* 'impossibility' combined with ordinary verb forms; syntactically, by means of the verbal noun used with a verb indicating possession or existence.

This first section will be concerned exclusively with the auxiliary verbs *izan* 'to be' and **edun* 'to have', the reason being that Batua has only four other verbs having synthetic potential forms, and these will be more conveniently discussed in section 24.4.3. Discounting this minor exception, all potential verb forms are periphrastic and consist of the radical (section 7.2.2) of the verb combined with the potential form of an auxiliary.

Although the radical has all but disappeared from western colloquial practice, academic Batua norm insists on its use, allowing only one exception: with denominal or deadjectival verbs the perfect participle may be employed instead—for example, *ur* or *urtu*, *gizon* or *gizondu*, *gaurko* or *gaurkotu*, *bere* or *beretu*, *lodi* or *loditu*, *hobe* or *hobetu*, *hizka* or *hizkatu*, *garai* or *garaitu* (recommendation of the Basque Academy, February 1995).

The potential mood allows for three tense forms: present potential, conditional potential, and past potential. In addition, there are two seldom used protasis paradigms: present potential protasis forms (section 24.5.1) and remote potential protasis forms (section 24.5.2).

24.1.1 Truncation Applied to the Subjunctive

As the truncation process applicable to a finite verb form, introduced in section 17.2.1, will be somewhat helpful here too, it may be convenient to repeat the relevant instructions: Remove any suffix not denoting person or number together with any epenthetic vowel inserted before it, and restore any person or number suffix to its pristine shape: *-t* to *-da*, *-k* or *-a* to *-ga*, *-n* to *-na*. While in section 17.2 the process was applied to the past tense indicative, it will now be applied to the subjunctive, past as well as present.

24.1.2 Morphology of the Present Potential

The present potential forms are obtained by adding the irreality suffix *-ke* to the end of the truncated forms of the subjunctive present; but if there is an ergative marker or a pluralizer *-te*, *-ke* will directly precede these. Last, the usual word-final adjustment rules of section 9.1 will apply.

The verb *izan* displays a slight irregularity in that the *d* of its subjunctive stem *-di-* always elides. Furthermore, as we may recall from section 17.2.3, contact between this stem and the irreality suffix *-ke* is avoided by the insertion of a buffer morpheme *-te-*. For the learner's convenience, the chief paradigms of the auxiliaries will be listed here, perfectly regular though they are.

The present potential of intransitive *izan* follows:

izan naiteke	I can be
izan haiteke	yoú can be
izan daiteke	he can be
izan gaitezke	we can be
izan zaitezke	you can be
izan zaitezkete	yoû can be
izan daitezke	they can be

gerta dakidake	it can happen to me
gerta dakiake	it can happen to yoú
gerta dakinake	it can happen to yoù
gerta dakioke	it can happen to him
gerta dakiguke	it can happen to us
gerta dakizuke	it can happen to you
gerta dakizueke	it can happen to yoû
gerta dakieke	it can happen to them

As is usual in the presence of a dative marker, a plural subject will require the pluralizer *-zki*: *etor dakizkidake* 'they can come to me'.

When the verb takes a first-person subject, we have

etor nakiake	I can come to yoú	etor gakizkiake	we can come to yoú
etor nakinake	I can come to yoù	etor gakizkinake	we can come to yoù
etor nakioke	I can come to him	etor gakizkioke	we can come to him
etor nakizuke	I can come to you	etor gakizkizuke	we can come to you
etor nakizueke	I can come to yoû	etor gakizkizueke	we can come to yoû
etor nakieke	I can come to them	etor gakizkieke	we can come to them

With a first-person singular indirect object, we have

etor hakidake	yoú can come to me
etor dakidake	he can come to me

etor zakizkidake	you can come to me
etor zakizkidakete	yoû can come to me
etor dakizkidake	they can come to me

The present potential of the transitive auxiliary **edun* is as follows:

ikus dezaket	I can see it	ikus ditzaket	I can see them
ikus dezakek	yoú can see it	ikus ditzakek	yoú can see them
ikus dezaken	yoù can see it	ikus ditzaken	yoù can see them
ikus dezake	he can see it	ikus ditzake	he can see them
ikus dezakegu	we can see it	ikus ditzakegu	we can see them
ikus dezakezu	you can see it	ikus ditzakezu	you can see them
ikus dezakezue	yoû can see it	ikus ditzakezue	yoû can see them
ikus dezakete	they can see it	ikus ditzakete	they can see them

ikus nazakek	yoú can see me	ikus gaitzakek	yoú can see us
ikus nazaken	yoù can see me	ikus gaitzaken	yoù can see us
ikus nazake	he can see me	ikus gaitzake	he can see us
ikus nazakezu	you can see me	ikus gaitzakezu	you can see us
ikus nazakezue	yoû can see me	ikus gaitzakezue	yoû can see us
ikus nazakete	they can see me	ikus gaitzakete	they can see us

ikus hazaket	I can see yoú	ikus zaitzaket	I can see you
ikus hazake	he can see yoú	ikus zaitzake	he can see you
ikus hazakegu	we can see yoú	ikus zaitzakegu	we can see you
ikus hazakete	they can see yoú	ikus zaitzakete	they can see you

ikus zaitzaketet	I can see yoû
ikus zaitzakete	he can see yoû
ikus zaitzaketegu	we can see yoû
ikus zaitzaketete	they can see yoû

Also regular are the forms with an indirect object:

eman diezaaket	I can give it to yoú
eman diezanaket	I can give it to yoù
eman diezaioket	I can give it to him
eman diezazuket	I can give it to you
eman diezazueket	I can give it to yoû
eman diezaieket	I can give it to them

Those with a plural direct object are regular too:

eman diezazkiaket	I can give them to yoú
eman diezazkinaket	I can give them to yoù

eman diezazkioket	I can give them to him
eman diezazkizuket	I can give them to you
eman diezazkizueket	I can give them to yoû
eman diezazkieket	I can give them to them

Similarly, forms with other persons as subject are regular.

24.1.3 Morphology of the Conditional Potential

The conditional potential paradigm can be obtained from the truncated past subjunctive paradigm by substituting the eventuality prefix *l(e)-* for the past tense marker *z(e)-* (as in section 17.2) and adding the irreality suffix *-ke* to the resulting form in the same way as in section 24.1.2, that is, to the end of the form, except in the presence of an ergative marker or pluralizer *-te*, which will follow *-ke*. The usual word-final adjustment rules, where needed, also apply.

Nothing more needs to be said about the forms of the transitive auxiliary **edun*, but the nondative singular subject forms of the intransitive auxiliary *izan* require some further adjustments. To begin with, these undergo the same processes as in the present potential: reduction of the stem *-di-* to *-i-* and insertion of the buffer morpheme *-te-* before *-ke*. Then a further development takes place: elision of the intervocalic nasal, monophthongization of the resulting *ei* into *i*, followed by restoration of the elided nasal in postvocalic position. Schematically: **neniteke* > **nẽĩteke* > **nĩteke* > *ninteke*.

All this results in the following paradigm:

izan ninteke	I could be
izan hinteke	yoú could be
izan liteke	he could be
izan gintezke	we could be
izan zintezke	you could be
izan zintezkete	yoû could be
izan litezke	they could be

The remaining forms of *izan* need no comment:

gerta lekidake	it could happen to me
gerta lekiake	it could happen to yoú
gerta lekinake	it could happen to yoù
gerta lekioke	it could happen to him
gerta lekiguke	it could happen to us
gerta lekizuke	it could happen to you
gerta lekizueke	it could happen to yoû
gerta lekieke	it could happen to them

With a plural subject we get

etor lekizkidake	they could come to me
etor lekizkiake	they could come to yoú
etor lezkizkinake	they could come to yoù
etor lekizkioke	they could come to him
and so on	

Taking a first-person subject, we have

etor nenkiake	I could come to yoú	etor genkizkiake	we could come to yoú
etor nenkinake	I could come to yoù	etor genkizkinake	we could come to yoù
etor nenkioke	I could come to him	etor genkizkioke	we could come to him
etor nenkizuke	I could come to you	etor genkizkizuke	we could come to you
etor nenkizueke	I could come to yoû	etor genkizkizueke	we could come to yoû
etor nenkieke	I could come to them	etor genkizkieke	we could come to them

With a first-person singular indirect object, we have

etor henkidake	yoú could come to me
etor lekidake	he could come to me
etor zenkizkidake	you could come to me
etor zenkizkidakete	yoû could come to me
etor lekizkidake	they could come to me

Although perfectly regular, the paradigms of the transitive auxiliary **edun* are listed for the convenience of the learner as follows:

ikus nezake	I could see it	ikus nitzake	I could see them
ikus hezake	yoú could see it	ikus hitzake	yoú could see them
ikus lezake	he could see it	ikus litzake	he could see them
ikus genezake	we could see it	ikus genitzake	we could see them
ikus zenezake	you could see it	ikus zenitzake	you could see them
ikus zenezakete	yoû could see it	ikus zenitzakete	yoû could see them
ikus lezakete	they could see it	ikus litzakete	they could see them
ikus nintzakek	yoú could see me	ikus gintzakek	yoú could see us
ikus nintzaken	yoù could see me	ikus gintzaken	yoù could see us
ikus nintzake	he could see me	ikus gintzake	he could see us
ikus nintzakezu	you could see me	ikus gintzakezu	you could see us
ikus nintzakezue	yoû could see me	ikus gintzakezue	yoû could see us
ikus nintzakete	they could see me	ikus gintzakete	they could see us
ikus hintzaket	I could see yoú	ikus zintzaket	I could see you
ikus hintzake	he could see yoú	ikus zintzake	he could see you
ikus hintzakegu	we could see yoú	ikus zintzakegu	we could see you
ikus hintzakete	they could see yoú	ikus zintzakete	they could see you

And with a second-person plural object, we have *ikus zintzaketet* 'I could see yoû', *ikus zintzakete* 'he could see yoû', *ikus zintzaketegu* 'we could see yoû', and *ikus zintzaketete* 'they could see yoû'.

Also regular are the forms showing an indirect object in addition to their third-person direct object, singular or plural:

eman niezaake — I could give it to yoú
eman niezanake — I could give it to yoù
eman niezaioke — I could give it to him
eman niezazuke — I could give it to you
eman niezazueke — I could give it to yoû
eman niezaieke — I could give it to them

eman niezazkiake — I could give them to yoú
eman niezazkinake — I could give them to yoù
eman niezazkioke — I could give them to him
eman niezazkizuke — I could give them to you
eman niezazkizueke — I could give them to yoû
eman niezazkieke — I could give them to them

The forms with other persons as subject are also regular:

eman hiezadake — yoú could give it to me
eman liezadake — he could give it to me
eman zeniezadake — you could give it to me
eman zeniezadakete — yoû could give it to me
eman liezadakete — they could give it to me

24.1.4 Morphology of the Past Potential

The past potential paradigm can be obtained from the truncated past subjunctive paradigm by adding the irreality suffix *-ke* in the same way as in section 24.1.3 and completing the resulting form with the past tense suffix *-n*, or *-en* when immediately following *-ke*. The nondative singular subject forms of the intransitive auxiliary *izan* present the same developments as in section 24.1.3, so that the following paradigm results:

izan nintekeen — I could have been
izan hintekeen — yoú could have been
izan zitekeen — he could have been
izan gintezkeen — we could have been
izan zintezkeen — you could have been
izan zintezketen — yoû could have been
izan zitezkeen — they could have been

With a dative marker we get

gerta zekidakeen	it could have happened to me
gerta zekiakeen	it could have happened to yoú
gerta zekinakeen	it could have happened to yoù
gerta zekiokeen	it could have happened to him
gerta zekigukeen	it could have happened to us
gerta zekizukeen	it could have happened to you
gerta zekizuekeen	it could have happened to yoû
gerta zekiekeen	it could have happened to them

With a plural subject, we will have *etor zekizkidakeen* 'they could have come to me', *etor zekizkiakeen* 'they could have come to yoú', and so on.

Taking a first-person subject produces

etor nenkiakeen	I could have come to yoú
etor nenkinakeen	I could have come to yoù
etor nenkiokeen	I could have come to him
etor nenkizukeen	I could have come to you
etor nenkizuekeen	I could have come to yoû
etor nenkiekeen	I could have come to them

etor genkizkiakeen	we could have come to yoú
etor genkizkinakeen	we could have come to yoù
etor genkizkiokeen	we could have come to him
etor genkizkizukeen	we could have come to you
etor genkizkizuekeen	we could have come to yoû
etor genkizkiekeen	we could have come to them

These are the forms with a first-person singular dative marker:

etor henkidakeen	yoú could have come to me
etor zekidakeen	he could have come to me
etor zenkizkidakeen	you could have come to me
etor zenkizkidaketen	yoû could have come to me
etor zekizkidakeen	they could have come to me

The paradigms of the transitive auxiliary **edun* need no comment:

izan nezakeen	I could have had it
izan hezakeen	yoú could have had it
izan zezakeen	he could have had it
izan genezakeen	we could have had it
izan zenezakeen	you could have had it

izan zenezaketen	yoû could have had it
izan zezaketen	they could have had it
izan nitzakeen	I could have had them
izan hitzakeen	yoú could have had them
izan zitzakeen	he could have had them
izan genitzakeen	we could have had them
izan zenitzakeen	you could have had them
izan zenitzaketen	yoû could have had them
izan zitzaketen	they could have had them
ikus nintzakean	yoú could have seen me
ikus nintzakenan	yoù could have seen me
ikus nintzakeen	he could have seen me
ikus nintzakezun	you could have seen me
ikus nintzakezuen	yoû could have seen me
ikus nintzaketen	they could have seen me
ikus gintzakean	yoú could have seen us
ikus gintzakenan	yoù could have seen us
ikus gintzakeen	he could have seen us
ikus gintzakezun	you could have seen us
ikus gintzakezuen	yoû could have seen us
ikus gintzaketen	they could have seen us
ikus hintzakedan	I could have seen yoú
ikus hintzakeen	he could have seen yoú
ikus hintzakegun	we could have seen yoú
ikus hintzaketen	they could have seen yoú
ikus zintzakedan	I could have seen you
ikus zintzakeen	he could have seen you
ikus zintzakegun	we could have seen you
ikus zintzaketen	they could have seen you
ikus zintzaketedan	I could have seen yoû
ikus zintzaketen	he could have seen yoû
ikus zintzaketegun	we could have seen yoû
ikus zintzaketeten	they could have seen yoû

The indirect object forms are also regular. A few examples will therefore suffice:

eman hiezadakeen	yoú could have given it to me
eman ziezadakeen	he could have given it to me
eman zeniezadakeen	you could have given it to me

eman zeniezadaketen yoû could have given it to me
eman ziezadaketen they could have given it to me

24.2 Use of the Potential Mood and Its Tenses

24.2.1 Semantic Coverage of the Potential Mood

The potential in Basque covers most of the meanings of the English modals *can*, *could*, *may*, and *might*. In particular, the concepts of ability, possibility, opportunity, and permissibility can all be expressed by this mood. Any of the three tense paradigms could be chosen to verify this statement; for simplicity's sake I will use the present potential.

We find ability expressed in

(1) a. Nahi baduzu, garbi nazakezu. (Mt 8:2)
If you want, you can cleanse me.
b. Sinesten al duzue hori egin dezakedana? (Mt 9:28)
Do yoû believe that I can do that? (For *-na*, see section 18.3.)
c. Bakarrik tarta jan dezaket. (Atxaga, *Gizona* 291)
I can only eat pastry.

Possibility is involved in

(2) a. Oker egon naiteke. (*MEIG* VIII, 177 = *MIH* 393)
I may be wrong.
b. Non eros ditzakegu patatak? (Atxaga, *Bam.* III, 36)
Where can we buy potatoes?
c. Atentatu bat egitera gentozela pentsa dezakete. (Atxaga, *Gizona* 30)
They may think that we came to carry out a terrorist attack.
d. Esan al daiteke egiaren zati bat osoa esan gabe? (Oñederra, 174)
Can one tell a part of the truth without telling the whole?

Opportunity is conveyed in

(3) a. Hortxe aurki ditzakezu haren bizitzari buruzko zenbait xehetasun ere. (*MEIG* V, 46)
There you can also find some details about his life.
b. Hori ikusi nahi duenak Aita Villasantek iaz argitara zuen liburuxkan ikus dezake. (*MEIG* VIII, 162 = *MIH* 376)
He who wants to see that can see it in the booklet that Father Villasante published last year.
c. Ezkondu berria naiz eta ez naiteke joan. (Lk 14:20)
I am newly married and (so) I cannot go.

Permissibility is meant in

(4) a. Eser al naiteke zure ondoan? (Garate, *Hades* 31)
May I sit next to you?
b. Nahi duzunean has zaitezke zeure ipuina kontatzen. (Arana, 22)
You may start telling your tale whenever you want. (For *zeure*, see section 6.1.4.)
c. Jakin al daiteke isileko hori? (Etxaniz, *Antz.* 153)
May one know that secret?
d. Niregatik nahi duena egin dezake honek. (Atxaga, *Gizona* 127)
As far as I am concerned, he can do what he wants.

24.2.2 Use of the Present Potential

The present potential can be used not only for the present and future, as in (5a–d), but also in cases where time is irrelevant, as in (6a–c).

(5) a. Orain aurkez ikus dezakezu. (Zaitegi, *Sof.* 13)
Now you can see it in front of you.
b. Zer egin daiteke orain? (*LBB* 26)
What can be done now?
c. Beste film bat egiten ari omen da Chaplin. Zer esan diezaguke, azken hitza esan ondoan? (*MEIG* I, 137 = *MIH* 319)
Rumor has it that Chaplin is making another film. What can he tell us after having said the last word?
d. Datorren urtean ikus dezakegu.
We can see it next year.

(6) a. Itxura, ordea, engainagarria izan daiteke. (*MEIG* V, 52 = *MIH* 250)
Appearance, however, can be deceptive.
b. Nor salba daiteke, orduan? (Mk 10:26)
Then, who can be saved?
c. Ez gaitezke zu gabe salba. (Lapeyre, 136)
We cannot be saved without you.

24.2.3 Use of the Conditional Potential

The conditional potential properly belongs to the conditional mood, as it appears in just those contexts where the present conditional (section 17.2.3) would have occurred but for the need to express potentiality. Accordingly, we may find it associated with a protasis in the conditional mood:

(7) a. Ilargitik hona balitz, zerbait esan nezake. (Muxika, *P.Am.* 38)
If it were from the moon to here, I could say something. (Pernando's reply after having been challenged to tell the distance from here to the moon.)

b. Zuk nahi bazenu, berehala Ameriketara joan gintezke. (Alzaga, *Ram.* 51)
If you wanted to, we could go at once to America.

c. Onar nezake oinazea, baneki nondik datorren. (Aintziart, 83)
I could accept the suffering, if I knew where it is coming from.

As with ordinary conditionals (section 17.4.3), the condition need not be stated in a separate clause:

(8) a. Abiada honetan Cordoban izan gintezke eguerdi aldera. (Haranburu, *Ausk.* 63)
At this speed we could be in Cordoba by noon.

b. Ehun urtean ere ezin ikasi nezake. (*P.Ab.* 159)
I could not learn it even in a hundred years.

Free conditionals, as described in section 17.5, also occur with potential forms:

(9) a. Horrelakorik gerta al liteke? (Atxaga, *Obab.* 95)
Could anything like that happen?

b. Edozeini gerta lekioke horrelakorik. (*MEIG* VI, 182)
Something like that could happen to anyone.

[*N.B.* Note that a potential clause licenses the partitive.]

In particular, there are politeness conditionals, as in section 17.5.1:

(10) a. Jan al nezake zerbait, mesedez? (Arana, 43)
Might I eat something, please?

b. Barruko jatetxean bazkal genezake, ez? (Oñederra, 161)
We could eat in the restaurant inside, couldn't we?

There also are opportunity conditionals, as in section 17.5.2:

(11) a. Garbitasun horretaz mintza gintezke luzaroan. (*MEIG* VIII, 135 = *MIH* 214)
About that purity we could speak a long time.

b. Lekukorik aski aurki genezake nekerik gabe. (*MEIG* VI, 102)
We could find plenty of witnesses without any effort.

Deontic conditionals, as in section 17.5.3, also occur:

(12) a. Nola esan zenezakete gauza onik? (Mt 12:34)
How could yoû say anything good?

b. Zer egin nezake nire alabaren bizia zuzentzeko? (*LBB* 47)
What could I do to put right my daughter's life?

As *EGLU* (II, 433–434) notes, there is a tendency among western language users to blur the distinction between the present potential and the conditional potential, so much so that many speakers dispense with the former altogether in favor of the latter, considered more refined. The increasing influence of Batua norms, especially in Guipuzcoa, counteracts this tendency.

Also noted by *EGLU* (II, 415, 433) is that in most of the northern dialect area the conditional potential is interpreted as an ordinary conditional; that is, *eros nezake* matches southern *erosiko nuke* 'I would buy', while the potentiality sense requires the use of *ahal*: *eros ahal nezake*, or more commonly, *erosten ahal nuke* 'I could buy'.

24.2.4 Use of the Past Potential

The past potential has a double function in Basque. It can be the past tense counterpart of the present potential, as in (13a–d) where it translates as *could* or *might*, but it also can be the perfect aspect counterpart of the conditional potential, as in (14a–d) where it translates as *could have* or *might have*.

(13) a. Margariren etxeko atea zabalik ikus zitekeen. (Arana, 106)
The door of Margari's house could be seen wide open.
b. Ez nuen uste gogoz egiten ari naizen egiteko hori gogoz egin zitekeenik. (*MEIG* V, 137 = *MIH* 296)
I didn't think that the task I am doing with pleasure could be done with pleasure.
c. Agian, oraindik, eman zezakeen buelta bat plazaraino. (Urretabizkaia, *Asp*. 80)
Perhaps she could still take a walk as far as the town square.
d. Inork ere ez zezakeen kantu hura ikas. (Rv 14:3)
Nobody could learn that song.

(14) a. Huts horiek erraz osa zitezkeen, euskaldunok nahi izan bagenu. (*MEIG* II, 111 = *MIH* 341)
Those gaps could have been filled easily, if we Basques had wanted to.
b. Indiarrek sor zezaketen gaurko fisika, bide horretatik abiatu izan balira. (*MEIG* II, 141 = *MIH* 339)
The Indians could have created today's physics, if they had set out on those trails.
c. Gizon hau aska zitekeen, enperadoreagana jo izan ez balu. (Acts 26:32)
This man could have been freed, if he had not appealed to the emperor.
d. Garesti asko sal zitekeen eta dirua behartsuei eman. (Mt 26:9)
It might have been sold very expensively and the money given to the poor.

In contrast to the conditional paradigm of section 24.2.3, the past potential needs no intervening *ahal* to express potentiality in the northern dialects:

(15) a. Ederki sal zitekeen hori eta saria pobreei eman. (Mt 26:9; *JKBO*)
That might have been sold very nicely and the proceeds given to the poor.
b. Erregeren alaba eri zen, eta inork ez zezakeen senda. (Barbier, *Lég*. 136)
The king's daughter was ill, and nobody could cure her.
c. Eta irri egitetik ez zitekeen geldi gehiago. (Barbier, *Lég*. 137)
And she couldn't stop laughing anymore.

24.3 Syntax of *ezin* in Negative Potential Clauses

Any potential verb form can be negated using the regular negation particle *ez*, in which event Auxiliary Attraction (section 8.2.2) obligatorily applies:

(16) a. Barreneko hutsa ez dezake kanpoko ezerk bete. (*MEIG* I, 152 = *MIH* 326)
Nothing outside can fill the emptiness inside.
b. Ez dakioke horrelakorik gerta euskaldun irakurleari. (*MEIG* V, 139 = *MIH* 298)
Such a thing cannot happen to a Basque reader.
c. Ez dezake beste inorekin egin. (Haranburu, *Its*. 92)
She cannot do it with anybody else.

Yet, more often than not, in a potential clause *ez* is replaced by a negative particle *ezin* conveying impossibility:

(17) a. Ezin dezakegu gehiago esan. (*MEIG* II, 60 = *MIH* 359)
We cannot say more.
b. Barojak Euskal Herria maite zuenik ezin daiteke uka. (*MEIG* VIII, 74 = *MIH* 269)
It cannot be denied that Baroja loved the Basque Country.
c. Algeriako gerla hau ezin dezaket onar. (Aintziart, 43)
I cannot accept this Algerian war.
d. Zu eta ene burua ezin ditzaket engaina. (Xalbador, *Odol*. 265)
I cannot deceive you and myself.

Syntactically, however, *ezin* differs from *ez* in having the option of leaving the auxiliary where it belongs: right after the main verb, as illustrated by these examples:

(18) a. Inork ezin bi nagusi zerbitza ditzake. (*TB* 39)
Nobody can serve two bosses.
b. Arbola onak ezin fruitu gaiztorik eman dezake. (*TB* 41)
A good tree cannot give bad fruit.
c. Eta ezin inork handik atera dezake. (Gerriko I, 347)
And no one can take him out of there.

While some speakers allow *ezin* to head the whole verb phrase as in (18a–c), others require it to head the verb itself, assuming it has not been combined with the auxiliary as in examples (17a–d). Thus, unlike (18a–c), (19a–c) are accepted by all speakers:

(19) a. Eta ezin alda daiteke jabearen baimenik gabe. (*MEIG* II, 79 = *MIH* 171)
And it may not be altered without consent of the owner.
b. Ezin uka daiteke osasungarriak direnik. (*MEIG* V, 29 = *MIH* 288)
It cannot be denied that they are healthy. (For *-nik*, see section 18.4.)

c. Ezin sinets dezakegu akabatuko garela. (Ax. 64)
We cannot believe that we will come to an end.

24.4 Synthetic Potential Forms

24.4.1 Use of Synthetic Potential Forms of *izan* 'to be'

When the verb *izan* occurs as a copula, periphrastic potential forms are obligatory:

(20) a. Benetan, oso arriskutsua izan daiteke. (Atxaga, *Gizona* 26)
Really, it may be very dangerous.
b. Ikastoletan erabiltzen den euskara ez daiteke izan, eta ez da, inoren amaren hizkuntza. (*MEIG* VIII, 139 = *MIH* 218)
The Basque that is used in Basque schools cannot be, and is not, the language of anybody's mother.
c. Bizikleta izan zitekeen nire amona, bi gurpil izan balitu. (*MEIG* II, 141 = *MIH* 339)
My grandmother could have been a bicycle, if she had had two wheels.

But synthetic potential forms of *izan* do occur when it is used as a verb of existence or location. In fact, the form *badaiteke*, a third-person singular present potential with the affirmative prefix *ba-* (section 8.6.1), serves as an idiomatic equivalent of the English phrase (*it*) *is possible*, while its negation *ezin daiteke* matches (*it*) *is impossible*. The corresponding affirmative form of the conditional potential *baliteke* conveys much less assurance and comes down to a rather unconvinced *maybe* in English:

(21) a. Badaiteke hori ere. (*LBB* 86)
That too is possible.
b. Hori ezin daiteke. (Etxaniz, *Ito* 201)
That is impossible.
c. Nik uste dut nonbait ikusi zaitudala zu.—Ni? Baliteke. (Iraola, 53)
I think I have seen you somewhere.—Me? Maybe.

In formal parlance, finite complement clauses may occur and must be subjunctive, as shown by example (22a). Normal practice, however, makes use of nonfinite subject clauses based on the verbal noun. The embedded subject may remain unexpressed and is then interpreted as coinciding with the discourse topic, as happens in examples (22b,f,g).

(22) a. Badaiteke zuekin geldi nadin. (1 Cor 16:6; *Biblia*)
It is possible that I will stay with yoû.
b. Badaiteke zuekin gelditzea. (1 Cor 16:6)
It is possible that I will stay with yoû.
c. Badaiteke nik gauzak ilun ikustea. (*TOE* II, 56)
It is possible that I am taking a gloomy view of things.

d. Badaiteke inoiz oker ibiltzea Axular. (*MEIG* II, 121 = *MIH* 352)
It is possible that Axular goes wrong sometimes.
e. Nola daiteke, bada, guretako bakoitzak bere jatorrizko hizkuntzan horiei entzutea? (Acts 2:8)
How is it possible, then, that each of us hears them in his own native language?
f. Baliteke zu bizirik uztea. (1 Kgs 20:31)
Maybe he will leave you alive.
g. Baliteke hurrengoan zuri ere horrelako bitxiren bat ekartzea. (Garate, *Iz.B.* 50)
Maybe next time I will also bring you some jewel like that.

24.4.2 Use of Synthetic Potential Forms of **edun* 'to have'

Synthetic potential forms of **edun* readily occur, but their meaning is 'can do', never 'can have'. This fact, I may point out, provides the main evidence for R. Lafon's claim that the subjunctive stem *-za-* of **edun* properly belongs to an otherwise unattested verb **ezan* signifying 'to do'. Examples of these synthetic potentials are:

(23) a. Apaizak ere ez dezake deus askorik. (*MEIG* I, 134 = *MIH* 311)
The priest too can do nothing much.
b. Badakit dena dezakezula zuk. (Jb 42:2)
I know that you can do everything.
c. Nezakeen guztia egin dut. (*TOE* II, 100)
I have done all I could do.
d. Jende honekin nik bakarrik ezin dezaket. (*TZ* I, 141)
I cannot cope with these people alone.

24.4.3 Synthetic Potential Forms of Other Verbs

In the paradigms comprising the 1977 normalization decree of the Basque Academy, only four verbs (besides *izan* and **edun*) are shown as having synthetic potential forms: *egon* 'to stand', 'to stay', *etorri* 'to come', *ibili* 'to walk', and *joan* 'to go'. The morphology of these forms is completely regular as it follows the rules given in section 24.1; however, the indicative is to be taken as a base, since these verbs lack a separate subjunctive. Inasmuch as the instructions in sections 17.2.3 and 17.2.4 differ from those in sections 24.1.3 and 24.1.4 merely in operating on the indicative past instead of the subjunctive past, it follows that for these verbs the conditional potential is identical to the present conditional, and the past potential to the past conditional. The remaining paradigm, the present potential, follows the rules given in section 24.1.2, again taking the indicative as a base. If there is a dative marker, truncation as defined in section 24.1.1 will restore it to its pristine shape: *-t* to *-da*, *-k* to *-ga* (reducing to *-a* after the pre-dative marker *ki-*), *-n* to *-na*. Since these verbs do not carry a pluralizer *-te* nor an ergative marker, the irreality morpheme *-ke* always appears at the end of the form.

With the verb *ibili*, the irregularity noted in section 17.2.3 applies here too: its pluralizer *-tza* reduces to *-z* before the irreality suffix *-ke*. Applying the rules, we get *dagoke* from *dago*, *daudeke* from *daude*, *dabilzke* from *dabiltza*, and *doake* from *doa*. With a dative marker we get *dagokidake* from *dagokit*, *dagokiake* from *dagokik*, *dagokioke* from *dagokio*, *doakiguke* from *doakigu*, *datorkizuke* from *datorkizu*, and so on. In western Batua, all such forms are rather uncommon and have a decidedly bookish flavor when they do occur. Examples are

(24) a. Gure gogoa ezin dagoke gogoeta gabe. (Ax. 369)
Our mind cannot stay without thought.
b. Bere larruan ez dagoke. (*DGV* XI, 310)
He cannot stay in his skin. (That is, he is beside himself.)
c. Inor nigana ezin datorke, ni bidali ninduen nire aitak ez badakar. (*TB* 61)
Nobody can come to me, if my father who sent me does not lead him.
d. Ezin zetorkeen bat, beraz, Larramendirekin. (*MEIG* V, 104)
He could not agree, therefore, with Larramendi.
e. Bazoazke zeure etxera, hantxe aurkituko duzu senarra. (*TOE* II, 407)
You may go home, it is there that you will find your husband.
f. Badoazke lasai Josetxu eta Txantxo Miamira. (*MEIG* I, 134)
Josetxu and Txantxo can go unperturbed to Miami.

24.5 Morphology and Use of Potential Protasis Forms

As *EGLU* shows, ordinary potential forms may occur in a conditional clause:

(25) a. Etor badaiteke, datorrela berehala! (*EGLU* II, 377)
If he can come, let him come at once!
b. Ordain badezakezu, ordain ezazu. (*EGLU* II, 377)
If you can pay, pay.
c. Etor bazitekeen, zergatik ez zen etorri? (*EGLU* II, 378)
If he could come, why didn't he come?

Yet in elevated style special potential protasis forms may be encountered, which are similar to the protasis forms in section 17.2.2 in lacking the irreality suffix *-ke*. There are two tense paradigms: present potential protasis forms and remote potential protasis forms. These will be treated in separate subsections.

24.5.1 Present Potential Protasis Forms

Morphologically, present potential protasis forms are obtained from the truncated forms of the subjunctive present merely by applying the word-final adjustment rules of section 9.1. No other modifications take place. Without the irreality suffix *-ke* there is no buffer morpheme *-te-* and no elision of the *d* of the intransitive subjunctive stem *-di* in the singular forms.

Given the rarity of these forms as well as their perfect regularity, only two paradigms need to be shown by way of illustration:

etor banadi	if I can come	ikus badezat	if I can see
etor bahadi	if yoú can come	ikus badezak	if yoú can see
etor bahadi	if yoù can come	ikus badezan	if yoù can see
etor badadi	if he can come	ikus badeza	if he can see
etor bagaitez	if we can come	ikus badezagu	if we can see
etor bazaitez	if you can come	ikus badezazu	if you can see
etor bazaitezte	if yoû can come	ikus badezazue	if yoû can see
etor badaitez	if they can come	ikus badezate	if they can see

Examples are

(26) a. Aitak esan du joan badadi agurtuko duela. (*EGLU* II, 376)
Father has said that he will greet him if he can come.

b. Predikariak bidaliagatik, zer probetxu izanen dute, baldin elkar adi ez badezate? (Etxeberri Sarakoa, 281)
Even though preachers are sent, what use will they have, if they cannot understand each other?

c. Norbaitek ikus ez badeza, argibide hau eskainiko diot. (*MEIG* II, 117)
If someone cannot see it, I will offer him this example.

d. Nire eskea ontzat har badezazue, eskerrak aurrez. (Etxaniz, *Nola* 15)
Thanks in advance, if yoû can grant my request.

As was observed in section 24.2.1, the potential mood in Basque can be used to express the concept of possibility. Practice shows that the vague notion of possibility inherent in any hypothetical clause may suffice to justify the use of the potential. As a consequence, potential protasis forms sometimes have to be glossed in English by the modal *should* or even a simple indicative instead of by the full-fledged potentiality modals *could* or *might*.

(27) a. Egun edo bihar *eizan* idazten has banadi, aldez aurretik ematen diot edozeini esku ero-etxe batean sar nazan. (*MEIG* IV, 39 = *MIH* 82)
If today or tomorrow I should start writing *eizan*, in advance I give everybody the right to put me in a madhouse.

b. Ez du behin ere Jainkoak uzten gizona, baldin gizonak lehenik utz ez badeza Jainkoa. (Ax. 103)
God never abandons a man, if the man does not first abandon God.
(Axular's translation of St. Augustine's dictum *Nunquam prius Deus deserit hominem nisi prius ab homine deseratur*.)

24.5.2 Remote Potential Protasis Forms

Morphologically, remote potential protasis forms can be obtained from the truncated forms of the subjunctive past by applying the word-final adjustment rules of section 9.1. Only one other alteration is needed: substitution of the eventuality prefix *l(e)-* for the past tense marker *z(e)-*, exactly as in sections 24.1.3 and 17.2. As in section 24.5.1, only two paradigms will be shown:

etor banendi	if I should come	ikus baneza	if I should see
etor bahendi	if yoú should come	ikus baheza	if yoú should see
etor baledi	if he should come	ikus baleza	if he should see
etor bagintez	if we should come	ikus bageneza	if we should see
etor bazintez	if you should come	ikus bazeneza	if you should see
etor bazintezte	if yoû should come	ikus bazenezate	if yoû should see
etor balitez	if they should come	ikus balezate	if they should see

While these forms, as some 19th-century grammarians seem to suggest, once may have borne the sense of a past, or otherwise remote, potentiality, for the last several centuries their meaning has been that of a mere hypothetical, to wit, a lofty variant of the protasis forms of section 17.2.2 in southern literary style as well as their replacement in the greater part of the northern area (cf. Ithurry 1920, 76). Accordingly, they have to be glossed with the modal *should* or the indicative, rather than with *could*, as the following examples illustrate:

(28) a. Barre egingo luke lasai jendeak horrelakorik ikus baleza. (*MEIG* II, 80 = *MIH* 171)
People would laugh heartily if they saw anything like that.
b. Zer edo zer gerta baledi, badakin nire etxeko telefono zenbakia. (Garate, *E.E.* 79)
If something should happen, yoù know my home phone number.
c. Zutaz ahaz(tu) banendi, Jerusalen, geldi bekit eskua elbarri. (Ps 137:5)
If I should forget you, O Jerusalem, may my hand be crippled.

Genuine potentiality is conveyed by putting the particle *ahal* (or its negation *ezin*) in front of the auxiliary:

(29) a. Nahi ez dugula bekaturik egin ahal bageneza, hamaikek, . . . , galduko genuke zerua. (Zapirain, *Odol.* 154)
If we could sin while we don't want to, a lot of us, . . . , would lose paradise.
b. Zenbait herritarren kezkak arindu nahi nituzke orain, arin ahal banitza. (*MEIG* VIII, 153 = *MIH* 367)
I would now like to alleviate the worries of certain citizens, if I could alleviate them.

24.6 The Lexical Potential

As the potential mood has no more than three tense forms to chose from, it should come as no surprise that it cannot convey certain states of affairs. For one thing, the present potential lacks a perfect aspect form, since the past potential can be a perfect aspect counterpart of the conditional potential only. Furthermore, although the present potential may apply to the future, it is unable to contrast the future with the present. Last, the potential mood has no subjunctive; neither has it nonfinite forms to serve as alternatives.

Fortunately, there exists an alternative to the potential mood, able to accommodate all tenses. It is a construction where the lexical item *ahal* 'possibility' or its antonym *ezin* 'impossibility' combines with a regular form of the main verb, hence its designation "lexical potential."

The Biscayan grammarian S. Altube has claimed that the lexical potential always indicates actualized possibility or impossibility, as seen in his examples *ahal dudalako bizi naiz honela* 'I live this way because I am able to' and *ezin ibili naiz* 'I am unable to walk', allegedly allowable only when one has been walking and cannot go on. As a consequence of this view, Altube denounces the use of the lexical potential to convey permission or prohibition. (Altube 1929, sec. 199)

Other grammarians, notably Azkue and Mitxelena, have disputed this claim (Azkue 1923–1925, II, sec. 998; Mitxelena's footnote on page 103 of Villasante 1980). Incidentally, I should point out that Altube's phrase *ahal dudalako* is actually not a lexical potential at all, but an instance of *ahal* **edun* 'to have the possibility'. According to the evidence I have collected, eastern practice must be distinguished from western practice. In the former, there are no restrictions on the use of the lexical potential; in fact, it has all but replaced the potential mood. In the latter, however, the lexical potential can serve to indicate ability, opportunity, and permissibility, but not sheer possibility. Thus, we can get example (30a) but not (30b):

(30) a. Ez da egia bi eta bi bost izan daitezkeela.
It is not true that two and two can be five.
b. *Ez da egia bi eta bi bost izan ahal direla.
*It is not true that two and two are able to be five.

Most often then, the English glosses *able* and *unable* are quite appropriate for *ahal* and *ezin* and will be used here as much as possible.

Eastern usage will be separately dealt with in section 24.6.3 for *ahal* and in section 24.6.4 for *ezin*. One characteristic of the lexical potential, however, is constant throughout the whole area: it does not affect the transitivity or intransitivity of the clause it appears in. In particular, an intransitive auxiliary will remain intransitive.

24.6.1 The Lexical Potential Using *ahal* in Western Usage

In western practice, the lexical potential is based on a verb phrase ending in a perfect participle. Its canonical position is right in front of *ahal*, which itself is immediately followed by an indicative (or, if need be, subjunctive) auxiliary. This particular order results from the application of infinitival predicate raising (see section 14.3.1), obligatory with *ahal* in western usage unless an emphatic focus blocks its operation, as seen in example (31b).

(31) a. . . . eta gero lapurtu ahal izango dio etxea. (Mk 3:27; *Lau Eb.*)
. . . and after that he will be able to rob his house. (Possessive dative, section 15.5.1)
b. Eta orduan ahal izango dio etxea ostu. (Mt 12:29; *Lau Eb.*)
And it is then that he will be able to rob his house.

As potential *ahal* and interrogative *al* (section 8.1.5) are homonyms in western Basque, the simple tenses (past or present) of the lexical potential give way to the potential mood, except in subordinate clauses, which exclude the interrogative. Examples are

(32) a. Ea beste bat noiz bidali ahal didazun. (Cf. Bilbao, 135)
Let's see when you can send me another one.
b. Ezer egin ahal baduzu, erruki zaitez gutaz eta lagun iezaguzu. (Mk 9:22)
If you are able to do anything, take pity on us and help us.
c. Baldin gizonen batek kontatu ahal badu lurreko hautsa, zure jatorria ere konta dezake. (Gn 13:16; Ur.)
If some person is able to count the dust of the earth, he can also count your progeny. (Notice: No lexical potential in the main clause!)

With the perfect participle *izan* heading the auxiliary, the lexical potential conveys perfect aspect:

(33) a. Aski goiz etorri ahal izan da. (*EGLU* II, 458)
He has been able to come quite early.
b. Horregatik idatzi ahal izan ditut. (Atxaga, *Bam.* I, 18)
That's why I have been able to write them.

A past tense auxiliary headed by *izan* yields a past perfect:

(34) a. Lehen maitasun horren aztarnak antzeman ahal izan zituen bere baitan. (Atxaga, *Obab.* 92)
He had been able to notice within himself the relics of that first love.
b. Bakar batean sartu ahal izan nituen gauza guztiak. (Rozas, 134)
I had been able to put all the things in a single one (i.e., a single suitcase).

Future tense is expressed by the use of the future participle *izango* heading the auxiliary, as in examples (31a,b). Other examples are

(35) a. Hemen ez ditugun esertokiak eskaini ahal izango dizkizuet. (*TOE* I, 331)
I will be able to offer yoû the seats that we haven't got here.
b. Noiz entzun ahal izango dugu "Illeta" Donostian? (*MEIG* I, 47 = *MIH* 153)
When will we be able to hear "Illeta" in San Sebastian?

Nonfinite constructions with *ahal* also occur: *ulertu ahal izatea* 'being able to understand'.

The lexical potential with *ahal* can be negated only when the auxiliary is complex; otherwise the lexical potential with *ezin* has to be used:

(36) a. Egun horietan ez nuen ikusi ahal izan. (Garate, *Alaba* 27)
I was not able to see her in those days.
b. Nik ez nukeen aurkitu ahal izango. (Atxaga, *Obab*. 23)
I wouldn't have been able to find it.

[*N.B.* Some speakers find such examples bookish and prefer to substitute *ezin* forms in all negative clauses.]

24.6.2 The Lexical Potential Using *ezin* in Western Usage

To convey inability, lack of opportunity, or unlawfulness, *ezin* can be employed together with a perfect participle and an ordinary auxiliary, transitive or intransitive according to the nature of the participle, in the same way as *ahal*. But *ezin*, unlike *ahal*, freely occurs in main clauses even in the simple present:

(37) a. Ni noan tokira zuek ezin zarete joan. (Jn 8:21)
Where I am going you are unable to go.
b. Ezin al du berak nahi duena egin bere etxean, ezin al da nahi duenean sartu? (Oñederra, 100)
Can't he do what he wants in his own house, can't he come in when he wants to?

There are two options with regard to word order: *ezin* may attract the auxiliary as *ez* does, or it may leave the auxiliary in situ, that is, right after the perfect participle. Nowadays, the former option is the more common one. Examples are

(38) a. Ezin dut eraman futbola. (Atxaga, *Gizona* 26)
I cannot stand soccer.
b. Ezin nuen nire maitalea baztertu. (Atxaga, *Obab*. 288)
I was unable to turn my lover away.
c. Ezin al ditugu hemen utzi? (Atxaga, *Sara* 122)
Can't we leave them here?
d. Itziarrek ezin izan zuen aukera pasatzen utzi. (Arana, 18)
Itziar had been unable to let the opportunity pass.

In this word order, future tense can be expressed with the help of a future auxiliary containing *izango*, or else by using *ezingo* instead of *ezin*. Examples are

(39) a. Ezin izango diote gertatzen zaizunari izenik jarri. (Oñederra, 155)
They will be unable to put any name to what is happening to you.
b. Ezin izango nituzke denak kontatu. (Atxaga, *Bam*. II, 93)
I would be unable to tell them all.

(40) a. Ezingo naiz mutilzahar gelditu. (*G*. 33)
I will be unable to remain a bachelor.
b. Ezingo zaitut infernura bota. (Etxaniz, *Nola* 29)
I will be unable to throw you into hell.

When the second option is chosen of keeping the auxiliary in situ, it is customary for *ezin* to immediately precede the main verb, thus yielding the compact order *ezin* + participle + auxiliary, as in the following examples:

(41) a. Ezin asmatu dut haserretu gabe hitz bat esaten. (*TOE* II, 121)
I cannot manage to say one word without getting angry.
b. Baina ezin sendatu izan didate. (Mt 17:16; *Lau Eb*.)
But they have been unable to cure him for me.
c. Gu ezin joan izaten gara oso maiz. (Uztapide, *LEG* I, 34)
We are unable to go very often.

In this word order, future tense will be expressed by the future participle of the main verb, as seen in the following examples:

(42) a. Ni nagoen tokira zuek ezin etorriko zarete. (Jn 7:34; *Lau Eb*.)
You will be unable to come to the place where I am.
b. Izeba ikusi gabe ezin aterako naiz etxe honetatik. (*TOE* II, 202)
I will be unable to leave this house without seeing the aunt.
c. Ezin kenduko diozu legezko duena. (*TOE* II, 174)
You will not be allowed to take her legal portion away from her.

Although somewhat unusual, it is possible to intercalate a constituent between *ezin* and the main verb:

(43) a. Ezin lorik egingo dut. (*P.Ab*. 164)
I will be unable to sleep.
b. Ezin txartelik emango dizut. (Linazasora, 53)
I won't be able to give you a certificate.
c. Ezin burutik kendu dut Eneko Ameriketara dihoana. (*TOE* I, 242)
I am unable to put Eneko who is going to America out of my head.

24.6.3 The Lexical Potential Using *ahal* in Eastern Usage

Present or past potentiality is expressed by the imperfect participle followed by *ahal* and not the perfect participle encountered here in western usage:

(44) a. Egia ezagutzen ahal du. (Lapeyre, 112)
He is able to know the truth.
b. Hilabeteak egoten ahal da nahirik gabe. (Aintziart, 96)
One can stay without volition for months.

Here, in contrast to western practice, *ahal* constructions can be freely negated by means of *ez* even in the present tense:

(45) a. Ez du . . . garaitzen ahal. (Barbier, *Lég*. 131)
He cannot overcome him.
b. Ezagutzen ez dena ez da maitatzen ahal. (Zubiri, 218)
One cannot love what one doesn't know.

Of course, the auxiliary can be in the past tense, but also in the perfect tense:

(46) a. Zer ihardesten ere ahal nuen? (Barbier, *Sup*. 180)
What indeed could I answer?
b. Horri esker ikasten ahal izan dut munduko zenbait berri. (Xalbador, *Odol*. 27)
Thanks to him I have been able to learn some news about the world.

Yet, in general, for the perfect aspect, the perfect participle is used, nearly always reinforced by *izan*:

(47) a. Ez du kordokatu ahal. (Lk 6:48; Dv)
It (i.e., the torrent) has not been able to shake it (i.e., the house).
b. Ez du kordokatu ahal izan. (Lk 6:48; *JKBO*)
It (i.e., the torrent) has not been able to shake it (i.e., the house).
c. Nola honen laster atzeman ahal izan duzu? (Gn 27:20; Dv)
How have you been able to capture it this quickly?
d. Ez dut idatzi ahal izan fisikoki. (Aintziart, 100)
I have not been physically able to write.

[*N.B.* The examples with *izan* coincide with western practice, where its presence is obligatory.]

The traditional system for future potentiality, which makes use of the future participle of the main verb, survived into the first half of the 20th century but is now obsolete:

(48) a. Nor da igurikiren ahal duena? (Rv 6:17; Lz)
Who will be able to stand it?
b. Nork iraunen ahal du? (Ps 129:3; Dv)
Who will be able to last?
c. Dirutan ere ez da eskuratuko ahal. (J. Etchepare, *Eusk. G*. 138–139)
Even for money one won't be able to obtain it.

d. Ez du bere azken hatsa botako ahal. (Barbier, Lég. 22)
He won't be able to exhale his last breath.

With a future participle ending in *-en*, it is possible to use *ahalko*, future form of *ahal* (Lafitte 1962, sec. 656.d):

(48) e. Ez dakit lo handirik eginen ahalko dudan. (Barbier, *Sup*. 126)
I don't know whether I will be able to do a lot of sleeping.

The modern way to convey future potentiality in eastern usage also makes use of the form *ahalko*, but combines it with the imperfect participle of the main verb:

(49) a. Egun batez, ez ditut baztertzen ahalko egiazko galde eta erantzunak. (Aintziart, 49)
One day, I won't be able to put aside the real questions and answers.
b. Deusek ... ez gaitu bereizten ahalko ... Jainkoaren maitasunaganik. (Rom 8:39; *Biblia*)
Nothing will be able to separate us from God's love.
c. Zer egiten ahalko zuen hainbeste haurren aitzinean? (Landart, 62)
What would she be able to do in front of so many children?

Occasionally, one finds the perfect participle put to service, similar to western practice:

(49) d. Ezdeusek ez du aldaratu ahalko bere sailetik. (J. Etchepare, *Bur*. 110–111)
Nothing will be able to keep him from his enterprise.

24.6.4 The Lexical Potential Using *ezin* in Eastern Usage

Traditionally, the eastern regions had but two uses for the lexical potential with *ezin*. The first of these employs the perfect participle of the main verb and conveys verified impossibility:

(50) a. Ezin egundaino garaitu zuten bere etsaiek. (Ax. 381)
His enemies had never been able to overcome him.
b. Egundaino ezin jasan dut haren ahalkesunaren handia. (Jb 31:23; Dv)
I have never been able to bear the greatness of his majesty.
c. Medikuek deus ezin egin dute. (Barbier, Lég. 135)
The doctors have been unable to do anything.

Sometimes the perfect participle *izan* is added, as in western practice:

(50) d. Ezin egin izan zuten. (Ex 8:18; Dv)
They had been unable to do it.

Second, *ezin* combined with the future participle of the main verb indicates future impossibility. Note therefore that *ezin* does not occur in the simple tenses, so that present impossibility cannot be expressed by it. Negative *ahal* clauses appear instead.

(51) a. Ezin mintzaturen haiz. (Lk 1:20; Lz)
Yoú will be unable to speak.
b. Ezin mintzatuko zara. (Lk 1:20; Dv)
You will be unable to speak.

This traditional system was abandoned by the middle of the 20th century in favor of negative *ahal* clauses. However, since the last decade of that century, the younger generation, influenced by southern Batua, has begun to adopt the western use of *ezin*.

24.6.5 Nonfinite Relatives with *ezin*

Basque grammar allows for a postponed nonfinite relative based on a perfect participle preceded by *ezin*. The construction refers to the present, as would be expected in western usage where *ezin* combines with a perfect participle to convey present impotentiality. What is remarkable is that this construction is also widely used in the eastern dialects, in which present impotentiality cannot be expressed by means of a lexical potential with *ezin*, as noted in section 24.6.4.

(52) a. Eri bat da hospitalean, inork ezin hurbildua, inork ezin ikusia. (Lapitze, 167)
There is a patient in the hospital, whom no one can approach, whom no one can visit.
b. Ez duzu eginen, inork ezin egina da eta! (Barbier, *Lég.* 70)
You won't do it, for it is something no one can do!
c. Oi, ene maite ezin ukana, zein zaren xarmagarria! (Xalbador, *Odol.* 114)
O, my dear love, impossible to have, how charming you are!
d. Hau ezin eramana zait. (Labayen, *Su Em.* 165)
This is something impossible for me to bear.

Attributive use, as in (52c), is quite common: *etsai ezin ikusia* (Goyhetche, 300) 'the invisible enemy'; *gau ezin jasan hura* (Orixe, *Q.A.* 58) 'that insufferable night'.

24.6.6 Adnominal Instrumentals with *ezin*

Although the construct *ezin* followed by a perfect participle can be employed adjectivally as shown in section 24.6.5, a more common procedure nowadays is to adverbialize this construct using the instrumental ending *-z* and then turn it into an adnominal by adding the morpheme *-ko* discussed in section 5.1. Widely used in the north from the 17th century on, these forms in *-zko* have recently become part and parcel of southern literary usage as well, quite possibly on account of their use by Mitxelena. From the dozens of examples occurring in his works, I cite *ezin asezko gosez* (*MEIG* VII, 33), 'with an insatiable hunger'; *ezin barkatuzko hutsuneak* (*MEIG* VI, 43), 'unforgivable gaps'; *ezin ukatuzko ezberdintasuna* (*MEIG* VI, 174), 'an undeniable difference'; and *ezin zurituzko bidegabekeria* (*MEIG* VI, 169), 'an inexcusable unfairness'.

24.7 Some Other Uses of *ahal*

24.7.1 The Modal Quantifier *ahala*

Nominals headed by verb radicals, such as *nahi ahal guztia* 'all one might want', *edan ahal guztia* 'all one can drink', *pentsa ahal guztiak* 'all things conceivable', and *egin ahal guztiak* 'all things one can do', represent relics of the adjectival use of *ahal* in the meaning 'possible', now obsolete (cf. *DGV* I, 18). After this use was lost, these phrases became opaque, with the result that the quantifier *guzti*, felt to be redundant, could be left out. I will refer to the ensuing noun phrases as *ahala* quantifiers: singular ones, such as *nahi ahala* and *edan ahala*, and plural ones, such as *pentsa ahalak* and *egin ahalak*. Here are some sentences as illustrations:

(53) a. Pentsa ahalak aurtiki arteino ez da isiltzen. (Ax. 292)
He doesn't fall silent until he has blurted out everything conceivable.
b. Izurdeak ... sartzen dira arrain piloaren erdian, jan ahalak jaten eta irents ahalak irensten. (Agirre, *Kres*. 24)
The dolphins get into the middle of the school of fish, eating all they can and swallowing up all they can.
c. Hemen segitu egin beharko duzu, jarraitu, kosta ahala kosta. (Oñederra, 152)
You will have to go on here, continue, at all costs.
d. Artalea jan ahala botatzen badizuete, ez dago problemarik. (Amuriza, *Hil* 107)
If they throw grains of corn to yoû, all yoû can eat, there is no problem.

Given examples such as (53d), it was but one more step for singular *ahala* quantifiers to be used prenominally:

(54) a. Hik jan behar duk nik egin ahala talo! (Uztapide, *LEG* II, 110)
Yoú must eat as many corncakes as I can make!
b. Eska ahala mesede egiten dizkigu. (S. Mitxelena, *IG* II, 234)
She does us as many favors as we can ask for.

Such *ahala* quantifiers can also modify adverbs: *ikus ahala urrun* (Hiriart-Urruty, *Zez*. 159) 'as far as one can see'; *begiek ikus ahala urrun* (Barbier, *Sup*. 196) 'as far as the eyes can see'.

A few Labourdin authors use *ahal* instead of *ahala*: *irabaz ahal sosak* (Hiribarren, *Esk*. 183) 'as many pennies as one can earn'; *begiz ikus ahal urrun* (J. Etchepare, *Bur*. 26) 'as far as one can see with the eye'.

In the southern dialects, the perfect participle often occurs instead of the radical: *irentsi ala* instead of *irents ahala*.

[*N.B.* The plural noun *eginahalak* 'efforts' owes its existence to the plural quantifier *egin ahalak*. The distinction between *egin ahalak egin* 'to do all one can' and the verb phrase *eginahalak egin* 'to make efforts', however, is merely academic.]

To express the meaning 'as much as is impossible to V', one makes use of the phrase *ezin V ahala*, where *V* represents the radical or, in the south, the perfect participle of the verb, as follows: *ezin konta ahala* or *ezin zenbatu ahala* 'countless'; *ezin esan ahala* 'indescribably many'; *ezin sinets ahala* 'unbelievably many'; *ezin jasan ahala* 'insufferably many'. These too can occur prenominally, in which case either *ahal* or *ahala* may be used: *ezin konta ahala paper* (*MEIG* VI, 59) 'countless papers'. The adnominal construction—for example, *ezin konta ahaleko multzoan* (*MEIG* VI, 116) 'in a countless quantity'—can serve as an alternative.

24.7.2 The Conjunction *ahala*

Immediately following a perfect participle, the form *ahala* can function as a conjunction corresponding to English *as*, being understood as 'gradually as' when the preceding verb is durative, and conveying 'as soon as' otherwise.

Durative examples are

(55) a. Zorrak gehitu ahala, dirutza urritzen zihoakigun. (*MEIG* VIII, 43)
As debts increased more and more, our capital went dwindling.
b. Neba, droga hartu ahala, petralduz joan zen. (Garate, *NY* 139)
The brother was getting meaner the more he was taking drugs.
c. Urteek, joan ahala, irakatsi digute gauza ederrak aberatsentzat sortu zituela Jainkoak. (*MEIG* III, 87)
As they went by, the years have taught us that the beautiful things were made by God for the rich.

Nondurative examples are

(56) a. Andresek, sartu ahala, lehen begiraldiaren lehen segundoan, ikusten du zahartu egin zarela. (Oñederra, 118)
As he is coming in, in the first second of his first glance, Andrew sees that you have aged.
b. Beste gaixo bat sendatu ahala, neke madarikatu hura nagusitzen zitzaion. (Arana, 121)
As he cured another patient, that cursed fatigue overpowered him.

24.8 The Syntactic Potential

I use the term "syntactic potential" to refer to a construction consisting of the verbal noun combined with a verb of possession: *eduki* in southern parlance and **edun* in the north, as well as in literary usage in the south. There also is an impersonal form, which has *egon* or *izan* as the main verb.

The syntactic potential always conveys a potentiality outside of the subject's control; that is, it never indicates ability or the lack of it. What it does indicate is possibility, opportunity, or permissibility. Some examples involving possibility follow:

(57) a. Alferrik duzu, on Lander. Ez daukazu ihes egiterik. (Garate, *G.E.* 131)
It's no use, Don Lander. You can't escape. (For *alferrik*, see section 25.5.2.)
b. Leize handi bat dago zuen eta gure artean; nahita ere, ez dauka inork hemendik zuengana igarotzerik. (Lk 16:26)
There is a great chasm between yoû and us; even if he wanted to, no one can cross from here to yoû. (For *nahita*, see section 25.7.)
c. Oso gazia dago, ez dago jaterik. (Haranburu, *Ausk.* 49)
It is very salty, one cannot eat it.
d. Zurekin ez dago eztabaidan aritzerik. (*TOE* I, 93)
There is no way of arguing with you.

In the following examples, opportunity is at issue:

(58) a. Ez dut mendira joaterik, lana egin behar dut. (Garate, *Erd.* 117)
I am not free to go to the mountains, I have to do some work.
b. Ez dakit ezer egiterik edukiko dudan. (Atxaga, *Grl.* 110)
I don't know whether I will have an opportunity to do anything.
c. Berriz erosterik ez da izanen geroan. (Lv 27:20; *Biblia*)
There will be no opportunity afterward to buy it again.

In the following examples, permissibility is at stake:

(59) a. Zure pentsu pixka bat jaterik ba al daukat? (Atxaga, *Behi* 99)
May I eat a bit of your feed?
b. Gaur ez daukazue hemendik inora joaterik afaldu arte. Hau Joanitoren enkargua da. (Lasarte, *L.G.* 102)
Today yoû aren't allowed to go anywhere from here until supper. This is Joanito's order.
c. Nobela horren zatiren bat irakurtzerik ba al dago? (Etxeberria, *Egun* 226)
May one read some part or other of that novel?
d. Ez dago gizonaz etsitzerik. (*MEIG* I, 195)
One shouldn't despair of man.

In all examples given so far, the verbal noun occurred in a context requiring the partitive. This choice is typical for this construction and constitutes the only option for most speakers. Some speakers, however, do use the construction in affirmative statements. Then, of course, the verbal noun will have the article *-a*:

(60) a. Ikustea daukak. (Bilbao, 162)
Yoú can see it.

b. Hik ikustea badaukak, baina nik? (Atxaga, *Obab*. 93)
   Yoú can see her, but what about me?
c. Etortzea du. (Alzo, 60)
   He is free to come.
d. Orduan, nola daude gauzak? Jakitea daukadan neurrian, noski. (Atxaga, *Gizona* 325)
   How, then, do things stand? Insofar as I'm permitted to know, of course.

When a syntactic potential occurs affirmatively in the past tense, the communicative intent of the speaker is seen to go well beyond the literal meaning. His intention is not so much to express a past possibility per se, but rather to voice dispproval or regret in regard to an opportunity forever passed up. Illustrations are

(61) a. Joatea zenuen. (*TOE* I, 113)
   You should have gone.
b. Autoen prezioak gora egin du: lehenago erostea zuen. (*EGLU* II, 471)
   The price of cars has gone up: he should have bought it sooner.
c. Lehentxeago etortzea zuten, ez zen sarraskia gertatu izango. (*TOE* II, 357)
   They should have come a little sooner, the massacre would not have happened.

[*N.B.* For the comparatives *-ago* and *-txeago*, see sections 26.4.1–2.]

24.9 The Nouns *gauza* and *gai* as Predicates of Ability

24.9.1 The Predicate *gauza*

With an adnominal verb phrase *V* preceding it, the noun *gauza*, denoting 'matter' as well as 'thing', can function as a predicate meaning 'able to cause activity V':

(62) a. Harritzeko gauza da. (*P.Ab*. 180)
   It is an amazing matter. (Lit. 'matter for getting amazed')
b. Ez da barre egiteko gauza. (Labayen, *Su Em*. 211)
   It is no laughing matter. (Lit. 'matter for laughing')

In the western dialect area, the sense of this predicate has been extended to also include the meaning 'able to perform activity V', as seen in

(63) a. Ez naiz ibiltzeko gauza. (Etxaniz, *Antz*. 144)
   I am not able to walk.
b. Bai, hori ikusteko gauza banaiz ni ere. (Iturbe, 64)
   Yes, I too am able to see that.
c. Ez da sekula arrautza bat frijitzeko gauza izan. (Urretabizkaia, *Zerg*. 23)
   He has never been able to fry one egg.

The verbal complement of *gauza* may be fronted by topicalization:

(64) a. Liburuxka bat besterik agerrarazteko ez zen gauza izan. (*MEIG* VI, 55)
Nothing but one booklet had he been able to publish.
b. Laguntza eskatzeko ere ez zara gauza. (Oñederra, 104)
Ask for help, you are not able to either.

Extraposition of the verbal complement to the end of the clause is another option:

(65) a. Gauza dela euskara horrelako gaiak adierazteko? (*MEIG* VIII, 128 = *MIH* 205)
That Basque is able to express such topics?
b. Gauza al zarete nik edan behar dudan edari saminetik edateko? (Mt 20:22)
Are you able to drink the bitter potion that I am to drink?

The activity in question may be denoted by a noun phrase, which then takes the form of an adnominal allative:

(66) a. Ez naiz dantzarako gauza. (*TOE* I, 99)
I am not fit for dancing.
b. Lanerako gauza ez. (Irazusta, *Bizia* 85)
Not fit for work.
c. Egun osoan ez nintzen ezertarako gauza izan. (Iturbe, 23)
The whole day I wasn't fit for anything.

24.9.2 The Predicate *gai*

The noun *gai*, an archaic term for 'thing' now restricted to mostly abstract senses ('material', 'matter', 'topic'), can serve as a predicate denoting ability, much as *gauza* does. It differs from the latter, however, in occurring over the whole Basque-speaking area and, more importantly, in having a somewhat wider meaning, as it also encompasses 'suitability' and 'worthiness'.

Thus, in the examples under (67) *gauza* would serve just as well, but not in the examples under (68), with the possible exception of (68a), where some speakers do seem to allow *gauza* to substitute for *gai.*

(67) a. Ez da gai izaten beste euskalkiz mintzatzeko. (*MEIG* VII, 135)
He is not (as a rule) able to speak in another Basque dialect.
b. Asmatuko du zerbait. Askotan izan da gai. (Oñederra, 105)
He will think up something. He has often been able to.
c. Berak haiei erakutsi nahi zien euskara gai zela edozer gauza esateko. (*MEIG* VII, 125)
He wanted to show to them that Basque was suited for saying anything whatsoever.

(68) a. Elizatxoa ez zen gai jende hura kabitzeko. (Zabala, *Gabon* 105)
The little church was not suited for holding that mass of people.
b. Aipatzeko gai litekeen jauregirik ez dugu ikusten. (J. Etchepare, *Ber*. 96)
We see no palace that would be worth mentioning.
c. Izen eder horren gai ez gara sendi. (Batua: *sentitzen*) (Xalbador, *Odol*. 237)
We don't feel ourselves worthy of that beautiful name.
d. Ez naiz gai sar zaitezen nire aterpean. (Duvoisin, *L.Ed*. 48)
I am not worthy that you should enter into my shelter.

[*N.B.* The loanwords *dina* and *duin* are more usual terms for 'worthy'.]

24.10 Compounds with *ezin* and Its Near Synonym *gaitz*

24.10.1 Adjectival Compounds with *ezin* 'impossible'

Taking transitive verb radicals *V* as the first member, *ezin* forms adjectival compounds with the meaning 'impossible to V'. The process is fully productive.

Two points of morphophonemics are to be noted. After a verb radical ending in *-r*, a *t* is intercalated: *agortezin*, *elkartezin*, *irakurtezin*, *neurtezin*, *ulertezin*. Instead of a monosyllabic radical, the corresponding perfect participle will appear, unless the monosyllable contains a diphthong: *galduezin*, *heziezin*, *salduezin*, *utziezin*, but *hautsezin*.

Some useful examples are

adierazi	to express	adieraezin	inexpressible
aditu	to listen, to understand	adiezin	unintelligible
agortu	to exhaust	agortezin	inexhaustible
aldatu	to change	aldaezin	unchangeable
ase	to satiate	aseezin	insatiable
barkatu	to forgive	barkaezin	unforgivable
bukatu	to end	bukaezin	endless
elkartu	to combine, to join	elkartezin	incompatible
entzun	to hear	entzunezin	inaudible
esan	to say	esanezin	unsayable, unutterable
eskuratu	to obtain	eskuraezin	unobtainable
eten	to snap, to break	etenezin	unbreakable, irrevocable
ezagutu	to recognize	ezagutezin	unrecognizable
frogatu	to prove	frogaezin	unprovable
galdu	to lose	galduezin	inadmissible
hautsi	to break	hautsezin	unbreakable
hezi	to tame, to train	heziezin	untameable, untrainable
ikusi	to see	ikusezin	invisible
irakurri	to read	irakurtezin	unreadable, illegible

itzali	to put out	itzalezin	inextinguishable, quenchless
itzuli	to turn back	itzulezin	irreversible, untranslatable
jan	to eat	janezin	uneatable, inedible
jasan	to suffer	jasanezin	insufferable, unbearable
kontatu	to tell, to count	kontaezin	countless, uncountable
lortu	to attain	lortuezin	unattainable
luzatu	to extend, to postpone	luzaezin	unextendable, undelayable
mugatu	to limit, to restrict	mugaezin	unlimitable, limitless
mugitu	to move	mugiezin	unmovable
nekatu	to tire out	nekaezin	tireless, indefatigable
neurtu	to measure	neurtezin	immeasurable
onartu	to accept, to approve	onartezin	unacceptable
pentsatu	to think	pentsaezin	unthinkable, inconceivable
saldu	to sell	salduezin	unsalable, unmarketable
sendatu	to heal, to cure	sendaezin	unhealable, incurable
sinetsi	to believe	sinetsezin	unbelievable, incredible
sumatu	to perceive	sumaezin	imperceptible, unnoticeable
ukatu	to deny	ukaezin	undeniable
ukitu	to touch	ukiezin	untouchable, inviolable
ulertu	to understand	ulertezin	incomprehensible, unintelligible
usteldu	to spoil, to corrupt	ustelezin	unspoilable, incorruptible
utzi	to leave	utziezin	indispensable, unrenounceable
zehaztu	to specify	zehatzez	indeterminable, unspecifiable

24.10.2 Nominal Compounds Headed by *ezin*

Compound nouns with the meaning 'inability to V' can be formed from perfect participles *V* with the help of the noun *ezin* 'impossibility' as a first member. Of the following list, only *ezinegon*, *ezinetorri*, and *ezinikusi* appear in Sarasola's *Euskal Hiztegia*.

ahaztu	to forget	ezinahaztu	memorability, inability to forget
ase	to be satiated	ezinase	insatiability
egin	to do	ezinegin	incapacity, impossibility
egon	to stay	ezinegon	restlessness, nervousness
eraman	to bear	ezineraman	unbearableness, intolerance, envy
esan	to say	ezinesan	inability to say, stutter
etorri	to come	ezinetorri	inability to come, discord
etsi	to give up	ezinetsi	inability to give up, desperation
gorde	to hide	ezingorde	inability to hide
ibili	to walk	ezinibili	inability to walk
ikusi	to see	ezinikusi	envy, animosity, ill will
jasan	to suffer	ezinjasan	aversion

Notice that section 24.6.5 implies the following distinction for transitive verbs: *ezin asea* 'the insatiable one', *ezinasea* 'the insatiability'; *ezin eramana* 'the unbearable one (or thing)', *ezineramana* 'the unbearableness'; *ezin ikusia* 'the invisible one (or thing)', *ezinikusia* 'the envy'.

24.10.3 Adjectival Compounds Using the Parasuffix *gaitz* 'difficult'

With transitive verb radicals *V* as a first member, the adjective *gaitz* forms adjectival compounds with the meaning 'hard to V'. In theory, this is a weaker meaning than that of the *ezin* compounds of section 24.10.1, but in actual practice the difference tends to be merely academic.

As to phonology, recall that according to sandhi rule 3 of section 1.2.6 an affricate will turn into the corresponding sibilant before the plosive *g* of *gaitz*. Under the same rule, this plosive will then be devoiced. The latter change, however, is not reflected in the spelling, except for *hauskaitz* from *hautsi* 'to break'. The voiceless allomorph *-kaitz* occurs in certain other items as well. Sometimes this is attributable to voicing dissimilation, as in *gozakaitz*, *menderakaitz*, and *moldakaitz* (but *sendagaitz*); other cases remain unexplained: *izukaitz*, *zentzakaitz*. The form *zenbakaitz* is based on the radical *zenbat*. With the monosyllabic radical *hez*, the perfect participle appears instead: *hezigaitz*.

Common examples are

adit	to listen, to understand	adigaitz	hard to understand
aldatu	to change	aldagaitz	hard to change
ase	to be satiated	asegaitz	hard to satisfy
barkatu	to forgive	barkagaitz	hard to forgive
egosi	to boil, to digest	egosgaitz	hard to digest, hard to take
elkartu	to combine, to join	elkargaitz	hard to combine, incompatible
erabili	to handle, to use	erabilgaitz	hard to use
eraman	to bear	eramangaitz	hard to bear
entzun	to hear	entzungaitz	hard to hear
erre	to burn	erregaitz	hard to burn
esan	to say	esangaitz	hard to say
eskuratu	to get hold of	eskuragaitz	hard to get hold of
ezabatu	to wipe off	ezabagaitz	hard to wipe off
fidatu	to trust	fidagaitz	hard to trust, distrustful
frogatu	to prove	frogagaitz	hard to prove
gozatu	to savor, to enjoy	gozakaitz	disagreeable, surly, tasteless
hautsi	to break	hauskaitz	hard to break
hezi	to tame	hezigaitz	hard to tame, fierce, wild
ikasi	to learn	ikasgaitz	hard to learn
ikertu	to investigate	ikergaitz	hard to investigate, inscrutable

irakurri	to read	irakurgaitz	hard to read
itzali	to put out	itzalgaitz	hard to put out
izutu	to frighten	izukaitz	hard to frighten, fearless
jan	to eat	jangaitz	hard to eat
jasan	to suffer	jasangaitz	hard to suffer
konprenitu	to understand	konprenigaitz	hard to understand
kontatu	to tell, to count	kontagaitz	hard to tell, hard to count
kontentatu	to satisfy	kontentagaitz	hard to satisfy, hard to please
menderatu	to dominate	menderakaitz	hard to subdue, indomitable
moldatu	to shape	moldakaitz	hard to shape, awkward, clumsy
mugatu	to limit, to determine	mugagaitz	hard to determine
neurtu	to measure	neurgaitz	hard to measure
onartu	to accept, to approve	onargaitz	hard to accept
sendatu	to heal, to cure	sendagaitz	hard to heal, hard to cure
sinetsi	to believe	sinesgaitz	hard to believe
sumatu	to perceive	sumagaitz	hard to perceive
ulertu	to understand	ulergaitz	hard to understand
zentzatu	to straighten up	zentzakaitz	hard to straighten up

24.10.4 Adjectival Compounds with *erraz* 'easy'

The adjective *erraz* 'easy', antonym of *gaitz*, enters into compounds with transitive verb radicals in the same way as *gaitz* does. The resulting adjective means 'easy to V'. As with *ezin*, a *t* is intercalated after a radical ending in *r*. Only a few items are in common use:

aditu	to listen, to understand	adierraz	easy to understand
ezagutu	to recognize	ezaguterraz	easy to recognize
ikasi	to learn	ikaserraz	easy to learn
itzuli	to render	itzulerraz	easy to translate
sendatu	to heal, to cure	sendaerraz	easy to heal, easy to cure
sinetsi	to believe	sinetserraz	easy to believe
ulertu	to understand	ulerterraz	easy to understand

24.11 Vocabulary

alfer	idle
apo	toad
asmatu	to invent, to imagine
bart	last night
bildu	to collect

eskaini	to offer
ezkondu	to marry (off)
hondatu	to squander
irabazi	to earn, to win
irentsi	to swallow
iritzi	opinion
jakina	of course
lekuko	witness
luzaro	for a long time
sentitu	to feel
suge	snake
tuntun	silly, stupid
uzta	harvest

24.12 Exercises

24.12.1 Translate into English

1. Nola adieraz ote daitezke gauzak hitzik gabe? (*MEIG* I, 161)
2. Uzta ederra bil genezake luzaro gabe. (*MEIG* I, 81 = *MIH* 135)
3. Ezin duzu irentsi ezer gertatu ez denik. (Oñederra, 112)
4. Hori irents dezakeenak apoak eta suge biziak ere irentsiko luke. (*MEIG* VIII, 175)
5. Nik, jakina, ezin nezakeen horrelakorik sinets. (*MEIG* IX, 97)
6. Eskola ikusi gabe ez daukat ezer egiterik. (Atxaga, *Obab.* 44)
7. Gerta zitekeenaz eta ez zitekeenaz mintzatzea ez da berriketa alferra besterik izaten. (*MEIG* II, 141 = *MIH* 339)
8. Ezin asmatu dut nola aukeratu nuen emazte tuntun hau. (Lertxundi, *Aise* 94)
9. Nik ezin al dut nire iritzia esan, edo zer? (*TOE* II, 281)
10. Ezkon ezazu semea nahi duzunean eta alaba ahal duzunean. (López-Mendizabal, 247)
11. Dena ahal du sinesten duenak. (Mk 9:23)
12. Gizonek ez dezaketena Jainkoak badezake. (Lk 18:27; *EAB*)

24.12.2 Translate into Basque

1. I cannot take anything from you.
2. I don't know how you can do that.
3. Even an ass can understand these things.

4. What you are carrying I can carry too.
5. I could have died last night.
6. What could I have done otherwise?
7. I was unable to understand what was happening.
8. May I know what has happened to you?
9. Then nobody would be able to say anything.
10. Do yoú feel yoúrself able to love me?
11. They will offer you all the wine you can drink.
12. Mary squanders her money as she earns it.

25 Complex Predicates; Transitive Predication and Predicatives

25.1 Complex Predicates

Just like the verbal noun (section 7.2.3), the perfect participle (section 7.2.1) has a dual nature. As a participle, it manifests verbal properties in that it allows case-marked arguments and adverbial adjuncts. At the same time, it has adjectival status, since it can act as the head of an adjectival clause predicating a state resulting from the action of the verb—whence its characterization as a perfect aspect form.

The internal structure of such complex predicates is severely constrained. On the one hand, no arguments of the verb, but only heavy constituents such as postpositional phrases, can follow the participle. On the other hand, whatever precedes it must be focus in the adjectival clause.

Consequently, only speakers allowing a multiply filled focus site (section 18.1.1) will admit the combination of a manner adverb with an explicit object, as these would count as two separate foci. Thus the sentence *Gutun hau zuk gaizki idatzia da* 'this letter has been badly written by you' is rejected by most speakers, unlike *Gutun hau zuk eskuz idatzia da* 'this letter has been handwritten by you', in which *zuk eskuz* 'by you by hand' may be considered a single concept.

25.1.1 Participial Predication with *izan*

Used with *izan* 'to be' as a copula, a perfect participle clause functions as a predicate relating the subject noun phrase to a state of affairs resulting from the action denoted by the participle. The subject of the predicate will henceforth be named the "theme." Some examples follow:

(1) a. Noemi Moab lurraldetik etorria da. (Ru 4:3)
Naomi has come (lit. "is come") from the Moab region.
b. Hemendik urrutira joana da. (T. Agirre, *Uzt.* 194)
She has gone far away from here.
c. Fortunato, aita agertu zenean, etxera sartua zen. (Etxaniz, *Antz.* 147)
When his father appeared, Fortunato had gone into the house.

d. Hiru gerra haunditan eta lau txikitan ibilia naiz. (Amuriza, *Orom.* 273)
I have been engaged (lit. "walked") in three big and four small wars.

e. Makina bat lehenago joanak badira gure adinekoak. (Uztapide, *Sas.* 21)
Quite a few of our peers have gone earlier already.

f. Itsasgizonen andre asko da alargun gelditua. (Lasarte, *Gordean* 265)
Many seamen's wives have ended up as widows.

Notice that the affirmative prefix *ba-*, incompatible with auxiliaries, can attach to the copula (example 1e) and that the biclausal nature of these examples is brought out by the word order found in example (1f), inasmuch as the order *da alargun gelditu* is excluded in an affirmative clause, at least in southern usage.

As compared to the corresponding monoclausal sentences with bare participles, the meaning of which is often ambiguous between a perfect or a mere past, the biclausal ones indicate a state rather than an action and are thus unambiguously perfects. When we are dealing with an intransitive participle as in the examples given so far, its understood subject will be linked by coreference to the theme. But with a transitive participle the speaker has a choice, as either its subject or its direct object may provide the required linking. We have subject linking in the following examples:

(2) a. Ni ere zerbait sufritua naiz. (Amuriza, *Orom.* 223)
I too have suffered some.

b. Asko ikusia naiz, geroztik, nire bizitza luzean. (*G.* 209)
I have seen a lot, since then, in my long life.

c. Zerbait ikasia naiz Xerapi kuranderarekin. (*TOE* I, 91)
I have learned something from the healing lady, Xerapi.

d. Hau ere ibilaldi luzeak egina zen. (*MEIG* II, 52)
He too had made long journeys.

Alternatively, the direct object of the participle clause may be coreferential to the theme. In that event, the participle clause allows an explicit subject:

(3) a. Hau ez da nik asmatua. (*MEIG* VIII, 150 = *MIH* 230)
This has not been invented by me.

b. Kortatxoko basoa Urruzulak erosia zen. (Uztapide, *LEG* I, 155)
The Kortatxo woods had been bought by Urruzula.

c. Badakit nork emanak diren. (Izeta, *Dirua* 71)
I know by whom they have been given.

d. Gizonezkoren batek eskuz idatzia zen. (Garate, *Alaba* 101)
It had been written by hand by some male.

Similar examples also exist without an ergative subject. In most of these the participle clause has been detransitivized by one of the processes discussed in section 12.5, usually the medio-passive:

(4) a. Bertso hauek Asteasun kantatuak omen dira. (Uztapide, *LEG* II, 30)
These verses are reputed to have been sung in Asteasu.
b. Noiz egina da argazki hau? (Garate, *G.E.* 94)
When has this photograph been made?
c. Denak dira deituak, baina gutxi aukeratuak. (Mt 22:14; *EAB*)
All have been called, but few chosen.
d. Lan guztiak eginak dira. (*LBB* 86)
All jobs have been done.

25.1.2 Resultative Passives

The reader will have noticed that sentences such as (3a–d) serve as translational equivalents of English passives inasmuch as their ergative noun phrase must be rendered in English by a *by*-phrase. Whether or not the Basque sentences themselves count as passives is a matter of definition. They do, if coreferentiality between the subject of the copula and the implicit direct object of the participle is taken as the sole criterion. They do not, if the definition stipulates a change in case marking, since the case assigned by the participle differs in no way from that found in any transitive clause. As a matter of fact, such a change, usually from ergative to instrumental, is occasionally attested in the literature, chiefly in northern texts:

(5) a. Hi, Etxahun, nongo zori madarikatuaz joa bizi haiz ba munduan? (*Larzabal* I, 241)
Yoú, Etxahun, struck by what sort of cursed fatality are yoú living in the world?
b. Satanez tentatua zen. (Mk 1:13; Dv)
He was tempted by Satan. (*tentabatur a satana*; other translations use *Satanek*)

This use of the instrumental, virtually unknown in the south, is generally held to be a calque from French. *EGLU*'s remark that the ergative is to be preferred (*EGLU* I, 433) fully agrees with contemporary practice.

It is important to point out that with the agent expressed, whether by an ergative or otherwise, putative passive clauses in Basque are invariably perfective in character; in other words, we are dealing with resultative passives. Imperfective passives are accommodated by the medio-passive construction, in which, however, no syntactic realization of the agent is possible (section 12.5.1).

Exceptionally, Leizarraga's New Testament translation of 1571 does combine medio-passives with instrumental agents:

(6) a. Ezagutzen ditut neure ardiak, eta ezagutzen naiz neure ardiez. (Jn 10:14; Lz)
I know my own sheep and am known by my own sheep. (*ginōskomai hupo tōn emōn*)
b. ... ekartzen zutela laurez eramaten zen paralitiko bat. (Mk 2:3; Lz)
... while they were bringing a paralytic who was being carried by four (men). (*paralutikon airomenon hupo tessarōn*)

c. . . . zeren egun ihardetsi behar baitut Juduez akusatzen naizen gauza guziez. (Acts 26:2; Lz)
. . . as I am to answer today concerning all the things I am being accused of by the Jews. (*peri pantōn hōn egkaloumai hupo Ioudaiōn*)

This usage, however, is to be ascribed to a short-lived innovation prompted by an understandable yet misguided craving for a fully literal translation of the sacred Greek original. Constructions of this type have remained totally unacceptable to the Basque community.

25.1.3 Bibliographical Note on the Basque Passive

A lot of half-truths and sometimes sheer nonsense have been perpetrated by various ill-informed authors on the subject of the alleged Basque passive. Two reliable discussions in English are those of Trask (1985a) and Ortiz de Urbina & Uribe-Etxebarria (1991).

25.1.4 Participial Predicates with *egon*

In southern Basque the verb *egon* often serves as a copula with predicates denoting a state rather than a property (section 7.5). In Batua this use of *egon* is optional; *izan* may always replace it, unlike the corresponding use of *estar* in Spanish, which is obligatory. Since participial predicates—that is, adjectival clauses headed by a perfect participle—describe states, use of *egon* as a copula is widespread in southern Batua. We start with some intransitive examples:

(7) a. Bietako bat ezkondua dago. (Atxaga, *Obab*. 115)
One of the two is married.
b. Ia denek hila zegoela zioten. (Mk 9:26)
Nearly everybody said that he was dead.
c. Ibai bazterretan eseriak geunden negarrez. (Ps 137:1)
In tears we were seated by the sides of the river.
d. Herri honetaz aspertua ere banago. (*TOE* I, 74)
I am fed up with this village even.

Medio-passive constructions can be considered derived intransitives:

(8) a. Zer dago idatzia Moisesen legean? (Lk 10:26)
What is written in the law of Moses?
b. Zertaz dago egina burua? (Atxaga, *Obab*. 251)
What is the head made of?
c. Bazkaria egina dago. (Irazusta, *Bizia* 98)
Lunch is ready. (Lit. "has been made")
d. Aukerak eskainiak daude. (*MEIG* VIII, 47)
The choices have been offered.
e. Barkatua dago. (Etxaniz, *Ito* 141)
It has been forgiven.

The subject of a transitive participle remains implicit when identical to that of the main clause:

(9) a. Aspaldidanik hitza emana nago. (*TOE* I, 150)
I have given my word long ago.
b. Maiz elkarrekin lan egina geunden. (Garate, *Alaba* 38)
We had often worked together.
c. Hemen ostatuan arrautza frijitu pare bat hartua nago. (*TOE* I, 87)
Here in the inn I have taken a couple of fried eggs.
d. Mudantza askotxo gaude geure begiz ikusiak. (Basarri, 140)
We have seen quite a lot of changes with our own eyes.

When the participial clause contains an ergative agent, the tendency is to use *izan* rather than *egon* as a copula. But, on occasion, speakers from eastern Guipuzcoa still resort to *egon*, especially in contexts where the emphasis is entirely on the resulting state, rather than on the action that brought it about. More than elsewhere, acceptability judgments here differ greatly from speaker to speaker:

(10) a. Sukaldeko mahaia pipiak joa dago. (P. Goenaga)
The kitchen table is infested by woodworms.
b. Gure hizkuntza diglosiak joa dago. (cf. *MEIG* VI, 49)
Our language is affected by diglossia.
c. Nire gona gorria zerrenak zulatua dago. (P. Goenaga)
My red skirt has moth holes in it. (Lit. "has been holed")
d. Sagar hauek zure txerriek marruskatuak daude. (P. Goenaga)
These apples have been rubbed by your pigs.
e. Honelaxe baitago Profetak idatzia: ... (Mt 2:5; *Lau Eb.*)
For thus it is written by the Prophet: ...
f. Medikuek esana zegoen ez zuela haurrik izango. (Garate, *NY* 63)
She'd been told by doctors that she would have no children.

25.2 Transitive Predication

25.2.1 Simple Transitive Predication

An interesting feature of Basque conversational style is the occurrence of transitive clauses with **edun* as a copula expressing predication. Instead of the regular theme + predicate structure with the intransitive copula *izan*, we find a transitive structure ergative + theme + predicate requiring a transitive copula: **edun*.

In this way, the language makes available an additional argument, to be interpreted as connected in some way with the predication: a connection sometimes factual, sometimes purely emotional. Since English frequently lacks this option, the translations given in this section must be mere approximations, as they do not reflect the full import of the Basque originals.

In conversational practice, it is mostly the speaker or a group he forms part of that we find associated with the predication, so that the ergative argument tends to be first person, singular or plural:

(11) a. Nor dut neure aldeko? (2 Kgs 9:32)
Who is on my side?
b. Nirea haut! (*LBB* 188)
Yoú are mine.
c. Nire irakaspena ez dut neurea. (Jn 7:16)
My teaching is not my own.

(12) a. Nor zaitugu, ba? (*LBB* 178)
Who are you, then?
b. Zer dugu, gazte? (*MEIG* IX, 111)
What is the matter, young man?
c. Eta noiz dugu, ba, egun hori? (Etxaniz, *Antz.* 19)
And when is then that day?

A speaker may choose to involve the addressee in his predication:

(13) a. Tori, ama.—Zer duzu hau? (*LBB* 74)
Take it, Mother.—What is this?
b. Horretan Don Abraham ez duzu batere zeken. (*TOE* III, 169)
In this Don Abraham is not at all stingy.

Not infrequently the use of structures of this type may be motivated by the tendency to avoid possessive pronouns (cf. section 15.5.1), as these are normally omitted when they correspond to the subject of the clause:

(14) a. Salome alaba dut. (*TOE* I, 245)
Salome is my daughter.
b. Gabriel nuen izena. (Atxaga, *Grl.* 115)
Gabriel was my name.
c. Orain datozenak adiskideak ditugu. (*TOE* II, 335)
Those coming now are our friends.
d. Baina, Pernando, non duzu semea? (Muxika, *P.Am.* 41)
But, Pernando, where is your son?
e. Andrea leitzarra du. (Uztapide, *LEG* II, 15)
His wife is from Leitza. (For *-arra*, see section 6.6.)
f. Izpiritua goibel du eta bihotza eri. (Hiribarren, *Egia* 101)
His spirit is glum and his heart aching.

Example (14f) stems from the Labourdin dialect. In southern usage the verb *egon* is the preferred copula for predicates indicating a state (section 7.5):

(15) a. Publioren aita aspaldian gaixo zegoen.
Publius's father had been sick for a long time.
b. Bi gizon zeuden behean bere zain.
Two men were waiting for her downstairs. (For *zain*, see section 25.5.1.)

Accordingly, *egon*'s transitive counterpart *eduki* can be marshaled to serve as a transitive copula:

(16) a. Publiok aita aspaldian ... gaixo zeukan. (*TB* 220)
Publius's father had been sick for a long time.
b. Bi gizon zeuzkan behean zain. (Arana, 73)
She had two men waiting for her downstairs.

As shown by the preceding examples, the ergative slot in this construction can be filled by a third-person argument.

As to the use of these structures, Azkue has remarked: "Ces locutions, presque intraduisibles et difficiles à concevoir dans une autre langue, sont très usuelles parmi les auteurs qui, en écrivant, pensent en basque." (These locutions, almost untranslatable and difficult to imagine in another language, are very common among authors who, while writing, think in Basque.) (Azkue, *DVEF* I, 447)

25.2.2 Participial Transitive Predication

Transitive predication structures as studied in the previous section also occur with participial clauses used as predicates, indicating a state resulting from the action of the verb underlying the participle. The theme of the predication, the only overt absolutive in the sentence, must be coreferential to the understood subject of an intransitive or medio-passive participle and with the understood object of a transitive one. To illustrate, I will give two examples with an intransitive participle, followed by several examples of medio-passive participles:

(17) a. Mende erdia joana dugu. (*MEIG* VIII, 98)
Half a century has passed (to our detriment).
b. Ama hila al duzu? (Etxaniz, *Antz*. 86)
Is your mother dead?
c. Begiak nahigabez lausotuak ditut. (Ps 6:8)
My eyes are dimmed because of grief.
d. Gizona, barkatuak dituzu bekatuak. (Lk 5:20)
Man, your sins are forgiven.
e. Buru osoa zauritua duzue, bihotza erabat eroria. (Is 1:5)
Your whole head is wounded, your heart utterly faint.

f. Denbora guztia hartua izaten dut. (Garate, *Alaba* 46)
I tend to have all my time taken up.

g. Aspaldi eskatua nuen artikuluren bat *Jakin*-erako, gai honetaz. (*MEIG* IX, 23)
Long ago, I had some article requested from me for *Jakin*, on this subject.

With a transitive participle clause not detransitivized by the medio-passive, there is a subject and a direct object to consider. As to the latter, it invariably coincides with the theme of the predication and hence remains unexpressed. As for the subject of the participle, it normally coincides with the ergative argument of the transitive copula, in which case it also remains unexpressed. Some southern speakers, however, allow the subject of the participle to be different from that of the copula. Then, of course, it needs to be overtly expressed in pre-participle position, as in

(18) Hau zure aitak emana dut. (Arrue, *G.B.* 93)
I have this given by your father.

When the participle lacks an explicit subject, a systematic ambiguity arises between an identical subject reading and a medio-passive reading:

(19) a. Autoa konpondua dut. (P. Goenaga)
I have fixed the car *or* My car is fixed.

b. Garbituak ditut oinak. (Sg 5:3)
I have washed my feet *or* My feet are washed.

c. Txartela eskatua dut. (*TOE* II, 155)
I have requested a ticket *or* My ticket has been requested.

Since the finite verb in such examples has the status of a copula, it sometimes takes the affirmative prefix *ba-*, incompatible with auxiliaries (section 8.6.1). Furthermore, at least in southern usage, affirmative auxiliaries always follow their participle (section 8.4), but copulas may precede a participial predicate provided the latter is not in focus. The following examples, therefore, support a biclausal analysis:

(20) a. Nik eraspen haundia diot Santiagori. Lehen ere bi txango eginak baditut. (Zapirain, *Odol.* 86)
I have a great devotion to James. I have also made two trips before.

b. Lehenago ere une ederrak baditu guri emanak. (Basarri, in Uztapide, *Noizb.* 49)
Earlier too he already has given us nice moments.

c. Josek ere baditu sos batzuk bilduak. (Izeta, *Nigarrez* 92)
Joseph too has raised some funds (a few pennies).

d. Historia franko badituzu zuk mundu honetan ikusiak. (Uztapide, *Sas.* 138)
Quite a few happenings you have seen in this world.

e. Zuen lurra eta zuen etxea penaz zenuten utzia. (Basarri, 182)
In sorrow yoû have left yoûr land and yoûr home.

f. Zer duzu ikusia? (**ikusi*) (F. Yurramendi)
What have you seen?

Given that there are participial predicates with *egon* (section 25.1.4), we also find transitive predication structures with *eduki*, the transitive counterpart of *egon*. Examples are

(21) a. Horregatik nahigabetua daukagu bihotza. (Lam 5:17)
That is why our hearts are saddened.
b. Gauza hauek lehen seguru asko dauzkazu irakurriak. (Uztapide, *Sas*. 283)
These things you have certainly read before.
c. Eta zuri zer erantzun ere pentsatua daukat azkar. (Uztapide, *Noizb*. 26)
And I have quickly thought up what to answer you, too.

(22) a. Eskuak izoztuak zeuzkan. (Urretabizkaia, *Asp*. 90)
Her hands were frozen. (Lit. "She had the hands frozen.")
b. Elizabetek berak Plentziako etxea ere ikusia zeukan. (Garate, *Alaba* 42)
Elisabeth herself had seen the house in Plencia also.
c. Andonik hilabete buruan lurra erosia zeukan eta makinak eskatuak ere bai. (Irazusta, *Bizia* 63)
After one month Anthony had bought the land and ordered the machines as well.
d. Ernio menditik kablea jarria zeukaten. (Lasarte, *Gordean* 29)
They had put up a cable from mount Ernio.

According to P. Goenaga (personal communication), the participle here can have no expressed ergative subject: there is no counterpart to example (18) with *daukat* instead of *dut*.

25.2.3 Perfect Participles and Number Agreement

Biclausal structures as studied in the previous section fail to account for all instances of definite participles in transitive clauses. This failure is particularly obvious when the finite verb carries a dative marker. Since an indirect object within the participle clause is prevented from agreeing with the copula of the main clause (cf. example 20b), it is hard to see how this copula could ever acquire a dative marker. Yet examples with dative marking do occur—although perhaps not before 1940:

(23) a. Lehenago ere mila duro askotxo aurreratuak dizkizu. (*TOE* II, 221)
Earlier too, it (our bank) has lent you quite a few thousand duros.
b. Hebron inguruko herrixkak emanak zizkioten jabetzan Kalebi. (Jo 21:12)
They had already given the villages around Hebron to Caleb in possession.

These examples along with many others will be neatly accounted for by postulating the existence of an optional rule of number agreement of the perfect participle with the direct object in any syntactically transitive clause functioning as a true perfect. The agreement is implemented by the occurrence of the definite article on the participle: singular *-a*, plural *-ak*.

It now appears that definite participles created by number agreement automatically assume the resultative meaning characteristic of perfect participles when acting as predicates (cf. section 25.1). It follows, in dealing with a present perfect, that applying number agreement to the participle will have the effect of emphasizing the relevance of the action to the present moment.

The reader should recall at this point that, in Basque, the present perfect, as set forth in section 7.3.2, merely situates the action within a time interval characterizable as an extended present, without requiring any current relevance. But as soon as a definite participle conveys the action, current relevance must be assumed. Some examples will illustrate:

(24) a. Kemen guztia galdua dut. (*TOE* II, 209)
I have lost all energy.
b. Ahaztua dut zer esan zidan Franziskok. (Haranburu, *Its.* 25)
I have forgotten what Francisco told me.
c. Zure eskutitza gogoz irakurria dut. (Etxaniz, *Nola* 33)
I have read your letter with pleasure.
d. Behin eta berriro irakurria dut. (*MEIG* I, 71 = *MIH* 149)
I have read it time and again.
e. Gure bankoak agindu hori emana dit. (*TOE* II, 218)
Our bank has given me that order.

As to the past perfect, matters are even simpler. Following section 7.3.2, this tense form is employed for the regular past as well as the pluperfect (see examples 15a–c in chapter 7). Using the definite form of the participle, however, forces the pluperfect reading, in accord with its resultative nature:

(25) a. Danielek bere indar guztiaz joa zuen. (Atxaga, *Bi An.* 54)
Daniel had struck him with all his strength.
b. Jaunari eskainia nion zilar hau. (Jgs 17:3)
I had dedicated this silver to the Lord.
c. Saltzaileak seinale hau jarria zien: ... (Mk 14:44)
The betrayer had arranged with them this signal: ...
d. Nik sermoi guztia perretxikoez egina nuen. (Garate, *Ald.* 78)
I had made the whole sermon about mushrooms.
e. Josuek agindu hau emana zion herriari: ... (Jo 6:10)
Joshua had given the people this command: ...

In contrast to northern usage, where the definite singular form of the participle can be employed to signal current relevance even if no direct object is present or implied, southern usage requires a syntactic direct object: *jana dut* can mean 'I have eaten' in the north, but only ‘I have eaten it’ in the south. Furthermore, for many southern speakers, the direct object has to be definite, or, at least, subdefinite. The term “subdefinite,” coined by E. Wayles Browne (personal communication), is needed to describe facts like the following: The English sentence *Five books are on my desk* is acceptable only if those five form part of a larger set of books whose whereabout are subject to inquiry. Otherwise, the sentence *There are five books on my desk* must be used. Similarly, for many southern speakers of Basque, the sentence *Bost liburu irakurriak ditut* is acceptable only if there is a prearranged larger set of books that the speaker was supposed to read.

25.3 Attributive Use of Perfect Participle Clauses

Our discussion so far has been limited to the predicative use of perfect participle clauses. Yet attributive use of a perfect participle clause also occurs, although, at least in southern usage, participial relatives with *-tako* (section 19.2.4) are considerably more common.

As a rule, in an attributive participle clause no argument or even adjunct follows the participle and only focus may precede it, just as in predicative use (section 25.1). Thus examples tend to be short: *sorgin berandu etorria* ‘the belated witch’, *liburu trenean galdua* ‘the book lost in the train’, *emakume senarrak utzia* ‘the woman left by her husband’, *irakasle edan samarra* ‘the fairly tipsy teacher’. (Notice the active meaning of *edan* ‘to drink’ here.) Additional examples have been given in section 19.2.1, where they were listed under the heading “postponed participial relatives.” To the appositional examples cited there, I may add *Zaldibarren neskatoa, zazpi urtez gaitzak joa*, ‘the girl of Zaldibar, struck by illness for seven years’ and *gona gorri-gorria, zazpi jostunek josia*, a bright red skirt, sewn by seven seamstresses’.

25.4 Adjectives Modifying Perfect Participles: *berri* and *zahar*

Since adjectives allow modification by other adjectives, as in *urdin argi* ‘light blue’ and *gorri ilun* ‘dark red’, perfect participles, adjectival as they are, can be expected also to be modifiable by adjectives. For semantic reasons, the only adjectives that qualify are *berri* ‘new’ and, although much less common, *zahar* ‘old’. When combined with the participle, these adjectives act as adverbs, to wit, ‘recently’ or ‘just’ and ‘quite a while ago’, meanings they assume in no other context.

First, we present some instances of attributive use: *Lazaro piztu berria* (*TB* 93) ‘the recently resurrected Lazarus’; *Juduen errege jaio berria* (Mt 2:2) ‘the newborn king of the Jews’; *esne jetzi berria* (Iturriaga, *Dial.* 86) ‘recently drawn milk’; *makina sortu berri bat* (Irazusta, *Bizia* 112) ‘a newly developed machine’.

And here are some examples of predicative use:

(26) a. Lantegitik etorri berri da. (*TOE* III, 26)
He has just come from the factory.

b. Inazio ikusi berri dut. (Lapitze, 143)
 I have just seen Ignatius.
c. Ikusi berri dugunez, . . . (*MEIG* VII, 118)
 As we have just seen, . . .
d. Erregeri egin berri diodan bisitak ez zuen beste asmorik. (*TOE* II, 368)
 The visit I have just made to the king had no other purpose.

[*N.B.* Combinations with *zahar*, as in *jan zahar* 'not having eaten for quite some time', describe a state and, as such, tend to occur with *egon* rather than *izan*. Note the expression *jan zaharrean* 'many hours after the last meal'.]

A participle clause combining with *berri* or *zahar* always represents a true perfect, not a recent past. Accordingly, as discussed in sections 25.2.2 and 25.2.3, the participle may assume the definite form under certain conditions. The definite article will then be attached to the adjective, since this will be the final constituent of the participle phrase. Examples are

(27) a. Nik ama hil berria nuen orduan. (Uztapide, *LEG* II, 13)
 My mother had just died then.
b. Frantzia gudan sartu berria zen. (Oñatibia,14)
 France had just entered the war.
c. Ikusi berria nuen "Psychosis". (*MEIG* I, 199)
 I had just seen "Psycho."
d. Liburutegiak erosi berria du eskuizkribu bat. (*MEIG* I, 231)
 The library has just bought a manuscript.
e. Ez nintzen edan zaharra. (Garate, *Iz.B.* 33)
 I had drunk not long before.

This predicative participle construction can occur also as a nonfinite adverbial clause. The adjective then takes the inessive ending, either indefinite in *-tan* or, much more commonly, definite in *-an*:

(28) a. Albistea hartu berrian enparantzara irteteko asmoa zeukan. (Agirre, *A.L.* 97)
 Just after receiving the news, he had the intention to go out to the village square.
b. Hasi berrian nolanahiko paperak sorrarazi zituen Iraultzak. (*MEIG* VI, 53)
 When it had just started, the Revolution produced all kinds of papers.

25.5 Predicatives

25.5.1 Definition of Predicatives

There is a lexical category in Basque that hitherto was only mentioned in passing in section 11.1 under the rather questionable designation "'stative' adverbs." It will now claim our full attention. Its members, invariable in form, function as predicates mostly indicating a state. They occur as subject or object complements and can also serve as the main predicate of the clause, in which case they take *egon* or *ibili* or another colorless verb as a copula, rarely *izan*. They do not occur attributively. Asunción Martínez (1996) refers to them as "predicative adjectives." Given their morphological invariability, I hesitate to include them in the adjectival category, and therefore prefer the shorter term "predicatives." Saltarelli (1988, 251), not altogether implausibly, considers them postpositions. Typical examples are

adi	attentive
ados	in agreement
artega	anxious, restless
ateri	cleared up, dry (of weather only)
(with preceding dative or allative) begira	looking (at)
(with preceding genitive) begira	waiting for, expecting, watching
(with preceding genitive) bila	looking for, in search (of)
esna	awake
gaixo	sick, ill
gertu	close by, near
igeri	floating, swimming
(governing the genitive, dative, or elative) ihesi	fleeing (from)
(with preceding dative or elative) itzuri	evading, shirking
lo	asleep
oskarbi	unclouded
prest	prepared, ready, willing
(governing the genitive) truk	in exchange (for) (northern)
(governing the genitive) truke	in exchange (for) (southern)
(governing the genitive) zain	waiting (for)

Some of these predicatives are derived from semantically related nouns: *adi* 'attention', *ateri* 'dry weather', *ihesi* 'flight', *lo* 'sleep', *oskarbi* 'clear sky', *zain* 'guard'.

Quite a few adjectives denoting states are able to function as predicatives. That is, their bare form can occur as subject or object complements, and they can take *egon* or *ibili* as a copula. Examples of these are

alai	merry, cheerful, in high spirits
apain	elegant, well dressed, dressed up
aske	loose, free, independent
bare	calm, imperturbable
dotore	elegant, smartly dressed
ernai	alert, awake

erne	alert, awake
estu	narrow, in a tight spot, anxious
gabe	without
geldi	still, motionless, calm
goibel	cloudy, gloomy, somber
haserre	angry
ilun	dark, obscure, somber
irmo	firm, resolute, determined
itun	sad, sorrowful, glum
larri	anxious, worried, distressed
lasai	unworried, carefree, calm
libre	free
sendo	resolute, firm
tente	upright, standing, firm
triste	sad, mournful, dreary
txukun	neat, tidy
urduri	nervous, jittery

Another set of adjectives, many of them describing a state, do not occur as predicatives, unless provided with the stative suffix *-(r)ik*, for which see the next subsection.

25.5.2 The Stative Suffix *-(r)ik*

The suffix we now need to discuss, referred to as "the stative suffix" in section 11.1, has the shape *-rik* after a vowel and *-ik* after a consonant, and is therefore a homonym of the partitive suffix. Its function is to create predicatives.

The suffix is, at most, semiproductive. It mainly attaches to adjectives; their eligibility, however, if not arbitrary, seems to depend on a poorly understood semantic condition. Furthermore, the suffix can be applied to any ordinal: *hirugarrenik* 'in the third place'. It can also be attached to some nouns indicating a bodily or mental state. Moreover, there are some fossilized forms in which it occurs with a noun-adjective combination. Finally, the stative suffix can occur with any perfect participle. Discussion of this topic, however, will be postponed to section 25.5.4.

First, I will list the examples with adjectival stem I have been able to find:

ahul	weak	ahulik	in weak condition
alfer	idle	alferrik	in vain, to no avail
bakar	sole, unique	bakarrik	alone, only
bero	warm	berorik	warm, in a warm state
bete	full	beterik	full, satiated
biluz	nude	biluzik	naked

bizi	alive	bizirik	alive
ero	crazy	erorik	crazy
gazte	young	gazterik	when young, as a youngster
gordin	raw, unripe, uncooked	gordinik	in a raw state, in unripe condition
hil	dead	hilik	dead
hordi	drunk	hordirik	drunk
hotz	cold	hotzik	cold, in a cold state
huts	empty	hutsik	empty
isil	silent, quiet	isilik	silent, silently
itsu	blind	itsurik	blind, blindly
on	good	onik	in good health, on good terms
oso	whole, complete	osorik	in its entirety, in one piece
soil	bare, barren, bald	soilik	only, merely
urri	scanty, scarce	urririk	free of charge
zabal	wide, broad, open	zabalik	wide, open
zahar	old	zaharrik	when old, as an old person
zintzil	hanging down	zintzilik	hanging down
zoro	foolish, crazy	zororik	crazy, in a crazy fit
zut	straight up, vertical	zutik	standing, erect

In addition, some predicatives (*esna*, *gaixo*) and some adjectives able to act as such (*gabe*, *geldi*, *ilun*, *itun*, *triste*) also allow the stative suffix.

As we can see, there often is little or no difference in meaning between the adjective and the corresponding predicative. There is, however, a difference in syntactic behavior: *betea da* and *beterik dago* both mean 'it is full' and *zoroa zen* and *zororik zegoen* (Bilbao, 121) 'he was crazy'. Yet, in principle, use of *izan* reflects a property, thus suggesting a lasting trait, whereas use of *egon* evokes a state, which may or may not be temporary. With some adjectives the distinction is quite clear: *isila da* 'he has a silent disposition' versus *isilik dago* 'he is keeping silent'; *itsua da* 'he is blind' versus *itsurik dago*, which may also mean 'he is blinded'.

Since the stative suffix is rather picky in what it attaches to, many adjectives lack a predicative form. The corresponding manner adverb will then be resorted to instead. Thus, instead of the nonexisting **ederrik* and **txarrik*, we find *ederki* and *gaizki*: *ederki dago hori* (*MEIG* IV, 44) 'that is a beautiful state of affairs'; *gaizki dago* (*G.* 345) 'he is in a bad state' (i.e., 'seriously ill'). This use of *gaizki* may well have provided the impulse for its antonym *ongi* (or *ondo*) to virtually replace the predicative *onik*: *ondo nago* or *ongi nago* being much more common than *onik nago* to express 'I am in good health'. Moreover, to express the meaning 'only', either the predicative *soilik* or the manner adverb *soilki* will do. Yet *soilik*'s synonym *bakarrik* has no corresponding manner adverb.

We now leave adjectives and go on to other supports for the stative suffix. First, let us look at ordinals.

The stative suffix can be added to any ordinal (section 2.1.2), although the resulting form refers to a position rather than a state:

lehen	first	lehenik	as the first, firstly, in the first place
bigarren	second	bigarrenik	as the second, secondly, in the second place
...	...		
azken	last	azkenik	as the last, lastly, in the last place

Furthermore, the stative suffix can be used with some nouns indicating a bodily or mental state, turning these into predicatives:

ase	satiety	aserik	satiated, satisfied
barau	fasting, fast	baraurik	on an empty stomach
beldur	fear	beldurrik	afraid
damu	regret	damurik	unfortunate, unfortunately
egarri	thirst	egarririk	thirsty
gose	hunger	goserik	hungry
ondoez	indisposition, malaise	ondoezik	unwell, indisposed
poz	joy	pozik	joyful, happy

From *dohain* 'gift' is derived *dohainik* 'free of charge', and from *behar* 'need', *beharrik* 'luckily', 'fortunately'.

Finally, there are a few fossilized phrases in which the stative suffix has been added to a noun-adjective combination: *aho zabalik* 'with open mouth', 'astonished', *beso zabalik* 'open-armed', *buru hutsik* 'with the head uncovered', *esku hutsik* 'empty-handed'. These are to be analyzed [N + A] + *ik*, and not N + [A + *ik*].

In general, predicatives do not take the adnominal suffix *-ko*. Yet there are a few exceptions, all showing the stative suffix: *alferrikako lana* 'useless work', *dohainikako sarrera* 'free entrance', *amodioz beterikako bihotza* (*DRA* 936) 'a heart full of love'. Since *bete* is also a verb meaning 'to fill', this example can also be viewed as a participial relative (cf. section 19.2.2).

25.5.3 The Syntax of Predicatives

Predicatives may act as subject complements, object complements, or main predicates. Examples of subject complements are

(29) a. Nikanor, ordea, gazterik hilko da. (*MEIG* III, 92)
Nicanor, however, will die young.

b. Ez naiz ni lehenik hasi. (*MEIG* VIII, 142 = *MIH* 222)
I have not started as the first.

c. Denek beso zabalik, hartuko haute. (Zapirain, *Etork.* 159)
Everyone will receive you open-armed.

d. Biluzik irten nintzen amaren sabeletik, biluzik itzuliko naiz lurraren sabelera. (Jb 1:21)
Naked I came out of my mother's womb, naked I will return to the womb of the earth.

The following are examples of object complements:

(30) a. Nik gazterik gordetzen dut bihotza. (*TOE* II, 34)
I am keeping my heart young.

b. Zuk gordinik ere kilo pare bat jango zenituzke. (*TOE* I, 77)
You would eat a couple of kilos even raw.

c. Gure maizterrek mandioak hutsik dauzkate. (*TOE* II, 394)
Our tenants have their barns empty.

d. Ezin harrapatu dut bakarrik. (*TOE* I 220)
I am unable to catch her alone.

e. Aita Uriartek ere osorik itzuli zuen. (*MEIG* II, 111)
Father Uriarte too translated it in its entirety.

These examples have predicatives as main predicates:

(31) a. Bakarrik egongo zara. (Oñederra, 153)
You will be alone.

b. Pozik al zaude *Egan*-ekin? (*MEIG* I, 82)
Are you happy with *Egan*?

c. Emakumea urduri samar zegoen. (Garate, *NY* 62)
The woman was rather nervous.

d. Ni onik nago, ama. (Etxaniz, *Irul.Neg.* 96)
I am fine, Mother.

e. Gaixorik egon nintzen ia hilabetean. (Agirre, *Kres.* 78)
I was sick for almost a month.

f. Egunero daude zuretzako ateak zabalik. (*TOE* I, 176)
The doors are open for you every day.

Finally, here are some examples where the predicative contains a complement:

(32) a. Igel bat zegoen behin idi bati begira. (Goyhetche, 6)
Once a frog was looking at an ox.

b. Ez nabil erantzunbeharrari itzuri. (*MEIG* IV, 73)
I am not shirking the responsibility.

c. Jende guztia zure bila dabil. (Mk 1:37)
Everyone is searching for you.

d. Bihotz-bihotzez nabilkizu bila. (Ps 119:10)
With my whole heart I am searching for you.
e. Zeren zain zaudete? (2 Mc 7:30)
What are yoû waiting for?

25.5.4 Participial Predicatives with *-(r)ik*

In accordance with their adjectival character, all perfect participle phrases allow the stative suffix, thus turning into predicative phrases:

(33) a. Bixenta asperturik zegoen. (Irazusta, *Bizia* 97)
Bixenta was fed up.
b. Gaur nekaturik nago. (*TOE* II, 345)
I am tired today.

The phrase *nekaturik nago* is to be analyzed as 'I am in a state of having become tired', which, of course, is semantically indistinguishable from 'I am tired'.

With a transitive participle, we may have subject or object linking, just as in section 25.1.1. In the first case, the subject of the participle coincides with that of the copula (i.e., the theme), as in

(34) a. Ni sinetsirik nago kartzelatik laster aterako garela. (Garate, *Iz.B.* 107)
I am convinced that we will soon come out of prison.

Here *sinetsirik*, literally 'in a state of having believed' is aptly glossed as 'convinced'.

(34) b. Salome andregaitzat harturik dabilela jakin dut. (*TOE* I, 233)
I have found out that he has taken Salome as his fiancée.
c. Jesus zein zen ikusi nahirik zebilen. (Lk 19:3)
He wanted to see who Jesus was.

Note that the stative suffix attaches directly to the preterito-present verb *nahi*, instead of being added to the perfect participle *nahi izan*.

In the second case, the theme coincides with the direct object of the participle, in which case the latter can be preceded by an explicit ergative subject:

(35) a. Barkaturik zaude. (*TOE* I 372)
You are forgiven.
b. Goseak hilik dago. (J. Altuna, *Ip.* 19)
He is dead-hungry. (Lit. 'in a state of having been "killed" by hunger')
c. Txakur bat ibili ohi zen goseak hilik. (Uriarte, *Dial.* 21)
A dog used to be dead-hungry.
d. Gure bihotzak daude pozak zabaldurik. (J. Etxagaray, *Festara* 202)
Our hearts are expanded with joy.

Phrases ending in a perfect participle followed by *ezinik* (from *ezin* 'unable', 'impossible') will also be considered participial predicatives:

(36) a. Erantzun ezinik gelditu ziren. (Lk 14:6)
They were unable to answer. (Lit. "they remained ...")
b. Lo egin ezinik al hago? (Atxaga, *Grl.* 109)
Are yoú unable to sleep?
c. Loak hartu ezinik dago. (Etxeberria, *Egun* 11)
He is unable to fall asleep.

Note that example (36c) is an instance of object linking: 'he is in a state that sleep is unable to catch him'.

Like the ordinary participial clauses discussed in section 25.2.2, participial predicatives can be embedded in transitive predication structures. The transitive counterpart of *egon*, *eduki*, will then serve as a copula. Here too, an overt absolutive represents the theme of the predication, while the direct object of the predicative, coreferential with the theme, remains unexpressed.

(37) a. Ez daukat ... Oñatibia ahazturik. (*MEIG* III, 154)
I have not forgotten Oñatibia.
b. Rutek bere erabakia harturik zeukan. (Ru 1:18)
Ruth had taken her decision. (Lit. "... had her decision taken")
c. Joan den urtean erositakoa ezin saldurik daukagu. (*TOE* II, 197)
We are unable to sell what we have bought last year.
d. Heten alabek bizitzez asperturik naukate. (*TZ* I, 64)
The daughters of Heth make me fed up with living.

Example (37d) has *ni* 'I' as the theme and may be compared with the intransitive predication (37e):

(37) e. Bizitzez asperturik nago Heten alabengatik.
I am fed up with living because of the daughters of Heth.

Participial predicatives may occur as subject or object complements:

(38) a. Landare hau ez da zuk zaindurik hazi. (Jon 4:10)
This plant did not grow up tended by you.
b. Haiek bertan utzirik, txalupara igo zen. (Mk 8:13)
Having left them right there, he went up into the boat.

(39) a. Oso gaizki zauriturik atera dute. (*TOE* III, 142)
They pulled him out very badly wounded.
b. Nik haurrak zila ebakirik uzten ditut munduan. (Amuriza, *Hil* 193)
As for me, I am leaving the children in the world with their navel strings cut.

Here the participial predicative phrase *zila ebakirik* 'the navel string having been cut' is seen to act as a complement to the direct object *haurrak* 'children' of the main verb *utzi* 'to leave'. Quite often, however, this verb, when construed with a participial object complement, sheds its lexical meaning and fades into a mere transitive copula. Thus examples (40a) and (40b) formally contain participial object complements, yet are to be glossed as instances of transitive predication:

(40) a. Harriturik utzi zituen ikasleak esaldi honek. (Mk 10:24)
The disciples were amazed at this saying.
b. Harriturik utzi nau bere aberastasunak. (*MEIG* III, 116)
I am amazed at its richness.

In contrast with ordinary participial predicates (section 25.1 et seq.), participial predicatives also occur as circumstantials, a type of clause covering a wide range of meanings—temporal: 'after'; causal: 'because' or 'since'; conditional: 'if'; and (with *ere*) concessive: 'even if', 'although'. Examples are

(41) a. Etxeraturik emakumeak umearekin, Porrot gelditu zen oraindik atzera. (Urruzuno, *Ip*. 181)
After the women had gone home with the child, Porrot still remained behind.
b. Herriko gizonetarik zenbaitek hala nahirik, eskola berria egin zuten. (Barbier, *Sup*. 142)
Because some of the village people wanted it, they made a new school.
c. Zenbat zor dizugu, horrela zuk gu lagundurik? (Barbier, *Sup*. 142)
How much do we owe you for helping us in that way?
d. Zuetako norbaitek, semeak ogia eskaturik, harria emango ote dio? (Mt 7:9)
If his son asks for bread, will anyone among yoû give him a stone?
e. Hala izanik ere, ez duzu horrela mintzatu behar. (*TOE* II, 346)
Even if it is so, you mustn't talk that way.
f. Zenbait aldiz, berak ez nahirik ere, negarra nagusitzen zitzaion. (Lapitze, 191)
At times, although he didn't want it, tears overwhelmed him.

Notice that no shared subject constraint obtains here. In fact, as can be seen in examples (41a) and (41e), the circumstantial and the main clause do not need to share any constituent at all.

25.6 Ergative Predicates

A small number of nouns denoting bodily or mental states have two curious properties: They function as adjectival predicates in combination with certain intransitive verbs acting as a copula, such as, *egon* 'to be', *ibili* 'to walk', and *gelditu* 'to remain'. Moreover, they can take the ergative case when doing so. These nouns are *beldur* 'fear', *bero* 'warmth', *egarri* 'thirst', 'longing', *gose* 'hunger', *hotz* 'cold', *logale* 'sleepiness', and *logura* 'sleepiness'. Examples are

(42) a. Horrelako liburu lodixkoa irakurtzen hasteko beldurrak dago. (*MEIG* III, 93)
He is afraid to start reading such a rather thick book.
b. Emadazu edaten ur pittin bat, egarriak nago eta. (Jgs 4:19)
Give me a little water to drink, for I am thirsty.
c. Horrelako zerbaiten egarriak geunden aspaldian. (*MEIG* III, 134)
We were longing for something like that for a long time.
d. Beste batzuetan goseak, egoten naiz. (Anduaga, 62)
Some other times I am hungry.
e. Hotzak badago edo badago goseak,... (Xalbador, *Odol.* 299)
Whether he is cold or whether he is hungry,...

These ergative predicates also occur as subject or object complements:

(43) a. Hotzak esnatu zen. (*LBB* 17)
She woke up cold.
b. Noiz aurkitu zintugun goseak? (Mt 25:37)
When did we find you hungry?
c. Ez da beldurrak ibili beharrik. (Uztapide, *LEG* I, 72)
One does not have to walk (there) terrified.
d. Gau guztian hantxen egon ginen, euritan, hotzak, logaleak eta batere lorik egin gabe, estalpe bat ere ez zegoelako, eta goseak, zer janik ez genuelako. (Salaberria, 110)
We stayed there the whole night, in the rain, cold, sleepy without getting any sleep at all, because there was no shelter at all, and hungry, because we had nothing to eat.

As pointed out by Mitxelena (1972c, 115), the anomalies observed in these examples—that is, the unmotivated ergative case of certain nouns coupled with their predicative use—can be readily explained by assuming ellipsis of a predicative participle semantically similar to *hilik*. Indeed, all we have to assume is that, to take an example, sentence (35b) *Goseak hilik dago* came to be shortened to *Goseak dago*. Such an assumption neatly accounts for the absence of **pozak dago*, since there is no **pozak hilik dago* 'he is dying from joy'.

A similar, albeit less likely, explanation starts from gerundives exceptionally (cf. section 16.4.1) allowing ergative subjects:

(44) a. Beroak erretzen zaude. (Arrue, *G.B.*[2] 81)
You are burning from heat. (Lit. "in a state where heat is burning you")
b. Ni goseak akabatzen nago. (Haranburu, *Ausk.* 43)
I am perishing from hunger. (Lit. "in a state where hunger is killing me")

25.7 Participial Predicatives with *-ta*

In most of Guipuzcoa and many parts of Biscay, the stative suffix *-(r)ik* seldom combines with perfect participles. There, participial predicatives are commonly formed with a suffix *-ta*, originating from the conjunction *eta* (cf. examples 63a,b in section 20.6). Participial predicates with *-ta* are considered fully acceptable in the literary standard, although quite unknown in the northern dialects. After a stem-final *n* or *l*, *-ta* changes into *-da*: *eginda*, *hilda*.

Apart from *nahita*, replacing *nahi izanda*, and *ezinda* (*G.* 195), *-ta* attaches to perfect participles only.

In meaning or use, participial predicatives with *-ta* differ in no way from those with *-(r)ik*: all examples listed in section 25.5.4 could be repeated with *-ta*.

Some examples of this construction as a main predicate follow:

(45) a. Oso kezkatuta nago. (Atxaga, *Obab.* 56)
I am very worried.
b. Zeharo maiteminduta zegoen. (Iturbe, 113)
He was totally in love.
c. Gabirian ere izanda nago. (Uztapide, *LEG* II, 135)
I have been in Gabiria too.
d. Ikasleak zeharo harrituta zeuden esan honekin. (Mk 10:24; *Lau Eb.*)
The disciples were greatly amazed at this saying.
e. Neskatxa ez dago hilda; lo dago. (Mt 9:24)
The girl is not dead; she is asleep.

The following are examples of transitive predication:

(46) a. Ez daukat ahaztuta. (*TOE* II, 123)
I have not forgotten it.
b. Hiretzat ere aukeratuta neukan norbait. (*G.* 145)
For yoú too I had chosen someone.

These are examples of subject complements:

(47) a. Harrek janda hil zen. (Acts 12:23; Ker.)
He died consumed by worms.
b. Besotik hartuta beregana ekarri ninduen. (Garate, *Hades* 71)
Taking me by the arm, she drew me to herself.

These are examples of object complements:

(48) a. Errota haundiko zubipean auto bat amilduta ikusten dugu. (*TOE* III, 144)
Under the bridge by the great mill we see a car fallen off the road.

b. Aurrena, etzanda ohean jar dezagun. (*TOE* III, 149)
First, let us put her lying down on the bed.

Finally, here are some examples of circumstantial participial predicatives not sharing a constituent:

(49) a. Katalin hilda, nola biziko naiz, ba? (Etxaniz, *Irul.Neg*. 110)
Now that Katalin is dead, how shall I then live?
b. Aitaren izena entzunda, begiak lausotu egin zitzaizkion Ikerri. (Garate, *Esku* 46)
After he had heard his father's name, Iker's eyes clouded over.
c. Eserita, gauzak lasaiago esaten dira. (*TOE* II, 213)
Things are more comfortably said sitting down.
d. Zuetako norbaitek, semeak ogia eskatuta, harria emango ote dio? (Mt 7:9; *IB*)
If his son asks for bread, will anyone among yoû give him a stone?

25.8 Miscellaneous Suffixes

25.8.1 The Nominal Suffix *-(kun)tza*

The suffix *-(kun)tza* attaches to verb radicals and creates perfective action nouns. I use the term "perfective" because, in contrast with the *-keta* derivatives of section 21.9, most of which present the action as being in progress, the *-(kun)tza* derivatives denote the action in its totality—more like a fact instead of a process.

The suffix consists of two allomorphs in complementary distribution, *-tza* and *-kuntza*, where only the latter is semiproductive. The allomorphy here has a purely lexical character, no semantic or formal criteria being apparent. No more than 20 verbs take *-tza*. The antiquity of this suffix is brought out by the irregular forms *egoitza*, *emaitza*, *etzauntza*, and *igaraitza*, to be explained historically by intervocalic nasal elision in the older forms of the participles: **egoni*, **emani*, **etzanu*, **igarani*. The following list may well be exhaustive:

agindu	to command	agintza	commandment, order, authority
agindu	to promise	agintza	promise (eastern usage)
berdindu	to equate, to compare	berdintza	equality, comparison
egin	to do	egintza	action, deed
egon	to stay, to be	egoitza	residence
eman	to give	emaitza	gift
eragin	to activate, to influence	eragintza	activity, impulse, influence
erein	to sow	ereintza	sowing, seeding
eskaini	to offer, to dedicate	eskaintza	offer, offering, dedication
etzan	to lie down	etzauntza	resting place, couch
ezagutu	to get to know, to recognize	ezagutza	acquaintance, recognition

ezkondu	to marry	ezkontza	marriage
garaitu	to overcome	garaitza	victory
higuindu	to loathe	higuintza	loathing
iguriki	to wait, to expect	igurikitza	waiting, patience, hope
iragan	to pass, to cross	iragaitza	passing, passage, transit
irauli	to turn over	iraultza	turning, revolution
jaio	to be born	jaiotza	birth
jakin	to know	jakintza	knowledge, erudition, science
lagundu	to accompany, to help	laguntza	help, assistance, aid

[*N.B.* The conjunction *baldin* 'if' has given rise to the neologism *baldintza* 'condition'.]

All other verbs take the allomorph *-kuntza*. Some examples are

aditu	to listen, to understand	adikuntza	understanding
aitortu	to confess	aitorkuntza	confession
aldatu	to change	aldakuntza	change
asmatu	to invent	asmakuntza	invention
atzeratu	to go back, to regress	atzerakuntza	reticence, retreat, retrogression
aurkitu	to find	aurkikuntza	discovery
aurreratu	to advance, to progress	aurrerakuntza	progress, advancement
ausartu	to dare	ausarkuntza	daring
bahitu	to pawn, to kidnap, to confiscate	bahikuntza	confiscation
banatu	to distribute, to separate	banakuntza	distribution, separation
bereizi	to distinguish, to separate	bereizkuntza	distinction, separation
berritu	to renew, to renovate	berrikuntza	renovation, innovation
bihurtu	to return	bihurkuntza	restitution
bilatu	to look for, to search	bilakuntza	search, scrutiny, investigation
eraiki	to raise, to found, to build	eraikuntza	construction, building
erratu	to stray, to err	errakuntza	error, mistake
erre	to burn	errekuntza	burning, combustion
esan	to say	esakuntza	saying, expression, maxim
garbitu	to clean, to wash	garbikuntza	cleaning, purification
gertatu	to happen	gertakuntza	happening, event, case
haserretu	to anger, to get angry	haserrekuntza	anger, fury
hazi	to grow, to grow up	hazkuntza	upbringing, breeding
hedatu	to spread, to expand	hedakuntza	spreading, expansion
hezi	to train, to tame	hezkuntza	training, education
hobetu	to improve, to better	hobekuntza	improvement
ibili	to walk	ibilkuntza	walking, walk
idatzi	to write	idazkuntza	writing
ikasi	to learn	ikaskuntza	learning, study
ikertu	to investigate	ikerkuntza	research, investigation
jaso	to lift, to build	jasokuntza	lifting, building

manatu	to command	manakuntza	command, commandment
ohitu	to get used to	ohikuntza	custom, tradition
pairatu	to suffer	pairakuntza	suffering
saiatu	to try	saiakuntza	experiment, test
salatu	to denounce, to accuse	saiakuntza	denouncement, accusation
sendatu	to cure, to heal	sendakuntza	healing, recovery
zapaldu	to crush, to oppress	zapalkuntza	repression, oppression

[*N.B.* The form *hizkuntza* 'language' appears to be based on the noun *hitz* 'word', influenced perhaps by the idiom *hitz egin* 'to speak'.]

25.8.2 The Profession Suffix *-tza*

The suffix *-tza* forms nouns indicating a profession or status and attaches to nouns denoting a practicioner of the profession or an individual having that status. Examples are

alargun	widow(er)	alarguntza	widow(er)hood
alkate	mayor	alkatetza	mayorship
argazkilari	photographer	argazkilaritza	photography
artzain	shepherd	artzaintza	shepherding
buruzagi	leader	buruzagitza	leadership
errege	king	erregetza	kingship
eskribau	notary	eskribautza	notaryship
gidari	guide	gidaritza	guidance
hizkuntzalari	linguist	hizkuntzalaritza	linguistics
irakasle	teacher	irakasletza	teachership, teaching
jabe	owner	jabetza	ownership
morroi	servant	morrontza	servitude
mugazain	border guard	mugazaintz	profession of border guard
nagusi	boss, master	nagusitza	superiority, predominance
nekazari	farmer	nekazaritza	agriculture
neskame	maidservant	neskametza	job of being a maidservant
ohoin	thief	ohointza	thievery
seme	son	semetza	sonship
soldadu	soldier	soldadutza	military service
sorgin	witch	sorgintza	witch power, witchcraft
sukaldari	cook, chef	sukaldaritza	cooking, cuisine
zaindari	caretaker, protector	zaindaritza	guardianship, protection
zuzendari	director, principal	zuzendaritza	directorship, management

From *arrantzari* 'fisherman' we do not get **arrantzaritza*, but *arrantza* 'fishing'. The derivational stem *morron-* of the noun *morroi* 'servant' is explained by its evolution from an older form **morroni*.

As stated in section 16.9, all agentives with the suffix *-gin* allow *-tza*: *emagintza* 'midwifery', *ikazkintza* 'charcoal burning', *okintza* 'bread-baking profession'.

25.8.3 The Collective Suffix *-tza*

The collective suffix *-tza* added to a concrete noun denoting some item or substance indicates an accumulation of that item or substance. It is no longer productive. Examples are

arto	maize	artotza	field of maize
basa	mud	basatza	muddy place, mudhole
belar	grass	belartza	grassy area, haystack
diru	money	dirutza	pile of money, capital
elorri	thistle	elortza	site full of thistles
elur	snow	elurtza	heavy snowfall
euri	rain	euritza	heavy rainfall, downpour
gari	wheat	garitza	field of wheat
harea	sand	hareatza	sandy area
hondar	sand	hondartza	beach
jende	people	jendetza	big crowd
landare	plant	landaretza	vegetation

25.8.4 The Nominal Suffix *-kunde*

Of northern origin, the deverbal suffix *-kunde*, linked by P. Lhande to the Latin suffix *-cundia*, seems to act by and large as a more stylish synonym of *-(kun)tza*. Relatively few of its derivatives are in common use:

aiher (izan)	to resent	aiherkunde	resentment, animosity
aurkitu	to find	aurkikunde	discovery
bahitu	to confiscate, to kidnap	bahikunde	confiscation, guarantee
egin	to do	egikunde	action, act, deed
eratu	to organize	erakunde	organization
garaitu	to overcome	garaikunde	victory
hautetsi	to elect	hauteskunde	election
hazi	to grow	hazkunde	growth
ohitu	to get used (to)	ohikunde	custom
zabaldu	to spread	zabalkunde	diffusion, advertising

The nouns *desirkunde* 'sort of wish' and *nahikunde* 'sort of will', 'whim' must be excluded from this list on account of their divergent meaning. They have originated as compounds with the noun *kunde* (cf. *DGV* XI, 114) 'kind', 'sort'.

Given their somewhat solemn flavor, it comes as no surprise that *-kunde* derivatives have been resorted to for the purpose of creating neologisms for Christian holidays and key concepts. The main examples are as follows:

agertu	to appear, to show	Agerkunde	Epiphany, apparition
erosi	to buy	eroskunde	redemption
gizatu	to become human	gizakunde	incarnation
igo	to ascend	Igokunde	Ascension
jaso	to lift up	Jasokunde	Assumption
piztu	to revive	pizkunde	resurrection, revival

25.9 Vocabulary

aipatu	to mention
amets	dream
behin eta berriro	once and again, repeatedly
bidali	to send
bidesari	road toll
eskale	beggar
jokaera	conduct, behavior
lasai	peacefully, comfortably
latz	harsh
lehor	dry
maitemindu	to fall in love
ontzi	vessel, ship, container
sahats	willow
salbatu	to save
sarritan	often
senar	husband
senide	relative, sibling
urduritasun	nervousness, nervosity
urruti	far
zain egon	to be waiting
zintzilik	hanging
zitara	lyre

25.10 Exercises

25.10.1 Translate into English

1. Herri askotan kantatuak gara elkarrekin. (Lasarte, *Gordean* 29)
2. Sarritan lo egina nago zure arrebarekin.
3. Gogora datorkit irakurri berria dudan zerbait. (*MEIG* VII, 26)

4. Senarraren senideen jokaera latza ezin eramanik aurkitzen naiz. (Oñatibia, 168)
5. Bidesaria ordaindurik, ontziratu egin zen. (Jon 1:3)
6. Urte guztian zebilen etxe bat erosi nahirik.
7. Adiskide batek bidalirik, ikusiak ditut zuk aipatutako paper zaharrak.
8. Barojak ikusiak, entzunak, eginak, pentsatuak irakurtzen ditugu. (*MEIG* VIII, 76 = *MIH* 272)
9. Ur ondoko sahatsetan utziak genituen zitarak zintzilik. (Ps 137:2)
10. Neure aspaldiko ametsak ahazturik bizi naiz mundutik urruti.
11. Egun hauetan neure emaztea ulertu ezinik nabil.
12. Noiztik egon zara nitaz maiteminduta?

25.10.2 Translate into Basque

1. Everything has been caused by your nervousness.
2. It seems that you were saved by a cat.
3. Our sins have been forgiven.
4. Many teachers in this city have ended up as beggars.
5. We have lost all we had.
6. Some other times I am hungry.
7. Having read these good books, I can die peacefully.
8. My daughter has just died.
9. What is written in the law?
10. The house we are living in has been sold repeatedly.
11. My mouth is dry.
12. Are you waiting for me?

26 Comparatives

26.1 Comparatives of Similarity: *bezala* and *legez*

In standard Basque, comparatives denoting similarity are commonly expressed by means of the postposition *bezala* 'as', 'like', directly following the basis of comparison. Less frequently employed is the indefinite instrumental of *lege* 'law', *legez*, in this function originally restricted to the Biscayan dialect. Finally, a genitival construction with the noun *pare* 'peer', 'counterpart' used as a postposition may also serve to voice a comparison.

Morphologically, *bezala* belongs to the group of deictic manner adverbs ending in *-la* (section 11.1.6), which points to a possible origin by dissimilatory rhotacism from **berala*, meaning 'in the same way'. Four main uses of *bezala* (as well as *legez*) can be distinguished, to be discussed in separate subsections.

26.1.1 Comparative *bezala*

In trying to elucidate the meaning and syntax of comparatives, it is expedient to start from a full clause premodifying *bezala* as the basis of comparison. Such a clause, if finite, will end in a finite verb carrying the relativizer suffix *-N*; if nonfinite, it will end in a perfect participle:

(1) a. Hitz egiten duen bezala idazten du. (*E.H.* 141)
He writes like he speaks.

b. Barka iezazkigu gure zorrak, guk gure zordunei barkatzen dizkiegun bezala. (Mt 6:12; Ur.)
Forgive us our debts, as we forgive them our debtors.

c. Ez zituen Bonapartek Elizak agindu bezala argitaratzen. (*MEIG* II, 111)
Bonaparte did not publish them as prescribed by the Church.

To account for the many instances in which the basis of comparison does not consist of a full clause, grammarians have postulated a process of "comparative stripping" (see, e.g., McCawley 1988, 305, 687ff). Under this process, constituents inside the basis of comparison can be dispensed with as long as they also appear in the main clause. As a consequence, the remaining basis need not consist of a single constituent (see examples 2a and 2b), although it often does (examples 2c, 2d, and 2e).

(2) a. Orain bihotza urtua daukat gatza urean bezala. (From song "Amodioa zoin den zoroa," Arratia I, 81)
Now my heart has melted like salt in water.
b. Oinaze bizitan aurkituko zara, emakumea erdiminetan bezala. (Jer 13:21)
You will find yourself in sharp pain, like a woman in childbirth.
c. Egin bedi zure nahia, zeruan bezala lurrean ere. (Mt 6:10; *IB*)
Your will be done, also on earth as in heaven.
d. Katuak bezala zazpi bizi ote dauzkak? (Zapirain, *Odol.* 141)
Do yoú have seven lives like a cat, I wonder?
e. Erabaki bezala egin zuten. (*LBB* 72)
They did as (they had) decided.

Bezala can follow a sentence in the conditional mood, yielding an 'as if' meaning:

(3) a. Ezer aditu ez balu bezala, Luisek ez du inongo seinalerik ematen. (Urretabizkaia, *Sat.* 33)
As if he had heard nothing, Luis is giving no signal whatsoever.
b. Buruan mailu haundi batekin jo banindute bezala geratu naiz. (Itziar, 144)
It was to me as if they had hit me on the head with a big hammer.
c. Hasieratik, aspaldiko lagunak bagina bezala, mintzatu gintzaizkion elkarri. (Garate, *Alaba* 26)
From the beginning we spoke to each other as if we were old friends.

Note the following commonly used expressions in which the verb *den* or *zen* is optional:

ahal (den) bezala	as well as one can
behar (den) bezala	as it should be, properly
nahi (den) bezala	to one's heart's content
ohi (den) bezala	as usual
uste (den) bezala	as expected

The phrase *ez bezala* is used for 'unlike':

(4) a. Ni, Orixe ez bezala, Galileo ondokoa naiz. (*MEIG* VIII, 161)
As for me, unlike Orixe, I am heir to Galileo.
b. Etxepare osorik har daiteke, Leizarraga ez bezala. (*MEIG* VII, 80)
Etxepare can be taken in its totality, unlike Leizarraga.

The postpositional status of *bezala* is confirmed by the existence of the adnominal form *bezalako*:

(5) a. Beste asko bezalako egun bat. (Irazusta, *Joan.* 181)
A day like many others.

b. Ohi ez bezalako zerbait badu horratik film honek. (*MEIG* I, 124)
This film does have something unusual nevertheless.
c. Zuek bezalako seme bat izango banu, . . . (Atxaga, *Gizona* 127)
If I had a son like yoû (have), . . .

26.1.2 Annotative *bezala*

Comment clauses, usually introduced by *as* in English, are expressed in Basque in two ways: by means of instrumental relatives (section 19.1.10) and relatives followed by *bezala*. There is no meaning difference between the two types: -*Nez* clauses and -*N bezala* clauses are interchangeable. Examples are

(6) a. Denek dakigun bezala, Azkue iritzi horren etsaia izan zen. (*MEIG* VII, 126)
As we all know, Azkue was an opponent of that view.
b. Batzar honetan esan den bezala, batasuna ez du Euskaltzaindiak egingo. (*MEIG* IX, 50)
As has been said at this meeting, it is not the Basque Academy that will bring about unity.

A perfect tense comment clause may take the shape of a reduced relative, in which *bezala* directly follows a perfect participle:

(7) a. Esan bezala gure saioa arratsaldean izaten zen. (Uztapide, *LEG* II, 190)
As said, our session normally was in the afternoon.
b. Jesusek aitzinetik ikusi bezala, hasi lana utzi behartu zitzaion Jon Doni Petriri. (Barbier, *Lég*. 61)
As Jesus had seen in advance, Saint Peter was forced to abandon the work he had begun.

Note that comparative stripping does not apply to comment clauses.

26.1.3 Qualifying *bezala*

Qualifying *bezala* signifies 'as (a)', meaning 'in the capacity of', and must therefore follow a noun phrase rather than a clause. This noun phrase may be bare, or it may carry the article -*a*, without any difference in meaning:

(8) a. Horra etorri zen lanera, ehule bezala, gure aitona. (*MEIG* IX, 41)
That is where my grandfather came to work as a weaver.
b. Funtsezko zimentarri bezala, honako puntu hauek azpimarratuko nituzke nik. (*MEIG* VIII, 113)
As a basic foundation, I would underline the following points.
c. Ordu berean adiskide bezala hartu zuten. (Arradoy, *S.Fran*. 163)
At that same moment, they accepted him as a friend.
d. Legezko semea bezala jarri zuten bataioko liburuan. (*LBB* 30)
They put him in the baptismal register as a legitimate son.

G. Garate (*Erd.* 58–61) censures this use of *bezala* as an unwarranted romanism, accepting it only where it means 'as if he were', as in example (8d). Otherwise, *bezala* should be omitted altogether (e.g., in 8a) or replaced by the prolative *-tzat* (section 17.8) in (8b) and (8c).

26.1.4 Approximative *bezala*

Following a measure phrase or some other numerical specification, *bezala* indicates lack of precision; it is thus to be glossed in English by adverbs such as *approximately* or *about.*

(9) a. Haren alde ateratu dira laurehun gizon bezala. (Acts 5:36; Dv)
About four hundred men came out in his defense.
b. Zerua isiltasunean gelditu zen oren erdi bat bezala. (Rv 8:1; Dv)
Heaven remained in silence for about half an hour.
c. Zenbat urte bezala? (Orixe, *Q.A.* 39)
About how many years?
d. Herritik kilometro bat bezala dago *La Fanderia* izeneko pentsu-fabrika, eta hemendik kilometro eta erdi bezala dago Sagasti baserria. (Salaberria, 14)
About one kilometer from the village is a feed plant called La Fanderia, and about a kilometer and a half from here is the Sagasti farmhouse.

[*N.B.* More common equivalents of *approximately* are *inguru* and *gutxi gorabehera*.]

26.1.5 Comparative *legez*

In a large part of the Biscayan speech area, *legez* (often pronounced *lez*) is much more common than *bezala*, of which it is an exact synonym, including its four main uses. Southern Batua too makes occasional use of it for the sake of stylistic variety.

First, here are some examples of comparative *legez*:

(10) a. Ez dago gaur Mundakan ni legez neskarik. (E. Azkue, 177)
There is today in Mundaca no girl like me. (better: *ni legezko*)
b. Katua saguaren zain legez daude. (*P.Ab.* 107)
They are like a cat waiting for a mouse.
c. Emakume ero batek le(ge)z egiten duzu hitz. (Jb 2:10; Ker.)
You are speaking like a crazy woman.

Given its low frequency in Batua, I will present one example each of annotative *legez*, qualifying *legez*, and approximative *legez*:

(11) a. Hitzen kontuari lotu beharko natzaio, zor dudan legez. (*MEIG* VII, 37)
I will have to stick to the topic of words, as I am committed to do.
b. Ikusten duena kontatzen du, jakile legez. (*MEIG* III, 126)
He tells what he sees, as a witness.

c. Urtarrilean zenbat legez ikasle geratu zirela uste duzu? (Kirikiño, *Ab.* (II) 134)
About how many students do you think were left in January?

26.1.6 Comparative *pare*

The noun *pare* 'pair', 'peer', 'counterpart' also acts as a postposition introducing comparisons. It only takes genitival complements:

(12) a. Gaur medikuen pare gara. (*P.Ab.* 45)
Today we are like doctors.
b. Badirudi ur garbiaren pare behar duela izan behar bezalako prosak. (*MEIG* VII, 153)
It seems that proper prose must be like clean water.

The adnominal form *pareko* serves for adjectival uses:

(13) a. Urre gorriaren pareko dira utzi zizkigun orrialdeak. (*MEIG* VII, 69)
The pages he left us are like pure gold.
b. Ez dago deus ere horren parekorik. (*MEIG* III, 104)
There is nothing at all like that.

26.2 Comparatives Denoting Equality in Quality

In standard Basque, comparatives denoting equality in quality, also known as equatives, are expressed by means of the postposition *bezain* immediately following the basis of comparison. Directly following *bezain*, there will be a standard of comparison, usually consisting of an adjective (including, of course, perfect participles) possibly acting as the modifier of a noun, a predicative or a manner adverb. As a simple example illustrating this kind of comparative, we may take

(14) a. Anttoni Edurne bezain polita da. (*E.H.* 141)
Tony is as pretty as Edurne.

Just as we did for *bezala* clauses, we will start from a hypothetical full clause as the basis of comparison. That is, example (14a) is derived from the nonexistent (14b) by the process of comparative stripping (section 26.1.1).

(14) b. *Anttoni Edurne polita den bezain polita da.
*Tony is as pretty as Edurne is pretty.

Structure (14b) fails to occur because comparative stripping is obligatory for the embedded constituent matching the standard of comparison—in this case, *polita* 'pretty'. Stripping of the embedded copula, however, is optional:

(14) c. Anttoni Edurne den bezain polita da.
Tony is as pretty as Edurne is.

Other examples where the embedded clause is still detectable thanks to the finite verb are

(15) a. Lastima da egon ohi den bezain garesti egotea gatza. (Iturriaga, *Dial.* 69)
It is a pity that salt is as expensive as it normally is.
b. Ederki dago hori; ez, ordea, uste dugun bezain ederki. (*MEIG* IV, 44)
That is a beautiful state of affairs; not, however, as beautiful a state as we believe.
c. Mugak ez dira behar genituzkeen bezain zabalak. (*MEIG* VI, 86)
The limits are not as broad as we would need them to be.
d. Dioten bezain gauza argia ote da hori? (*MEIG* I, 143)
Is that as clear a matter as they say, I wonder?

At this point, a highly interesting peculiarity of comparative stripping should be noted: it overlooks the difference between an adjective and an adverb as long as the two are formally identical:

(16) a. Zen bezain sutsu jokatu zen. (T. Agirre, *Uzt.* 187)
She acted as full of verve as she was.
b. Den bezain argi azaldu du guztia. (P. Goenaga)
Literally: He has explained everything as lucid as he is.

Here the adjectives *sutsu* and *argi* have been removed from the basis of comparison on the strength of the homonymous adverbs in the main clause.

In examples (17a,b) and (18a,b) comparative stripping has wiped out the embedded verb. In (17a,b) the remaining basis of comparison consists of two separate constituents, whereas in (18a,b) only one constituent of the basis has survived:

(17) a. Baina zaharrak erosoak bezain nekagarriak gertatzen dira bide berriak. (*MEIG* I, 197)
But the new ways turn out to be as fatiguing as the old ones (are) smooth.
b. Erdaraz ugari bezain euskaraz urri idatzi zuen Larramendik. (*MEIG* VI, 60)
Larramendi wrote as sparsely in Basque as (he did) plentifully in Spanish.

(18) a. Hori badakizue honezkero, nik bezain ongi. (*MEIG* I, 141)
Yoû know that by now, as well as I (do).
b. Non-nahi bezain ondo biziko litzateke Malentxo gure etxean. (T. Agirre, *Uzt.* 195)
In our house Malentxo would live as well as anywhere.

Perfect synonyms of the *-neko* temporal clauses studied in section 20.2.2 arise when instead of the adverb *ondo* 'well', as in example (18b), the adverb *laster* 'soon' (or one of its synonyms) is chosen as the standard of comparison:

(19) a. Bestela busti bezain laster lehortzen da. (Iturriaga, *Dial.* 44)
Otherwise, it dries up as soon as one moistens it.

b. Elizatik etxeratu bezain laster, sukaldean sartu zen Libe. (T. Agirre, *Uzt.* 111)
As soon as she came home from church, Libe went into the kitchen.
c. Zuk alde egin bezain laster idazten dut. (Urretabizkaia, *Sat.* 99)
I am writing as soon as you had left.

The examples given so far provide ample confirmation for my initial claim that the standard of comparison, as a rule, consists of an adjective, predicative, or adverb. Exceptions, nonetheless, occur. Indeed, on occasion, a predicate noun or even a certain type of verb will act as a standard of comparison:

(20) a. . . . ez ote dira edozein Mikel Agirre edo Pedro Perez bezain gizon? (*MEIG* VIII, 76 = *MIH* 272)
. . . aren't they as much of a human being as any Miguel Aguirre or Pedro Perez?
b. Hor burdin gorri bezain berotuko eta beraturen naiz. (Duvoisin, *L.Ed.* 87)
There I will get as hot and soft as red iron.

The mechanism described in this section readily enables us to compare two qualities as to intensity. Thus, taking *luze den* 'is long' as the basis of comparison and *zabala* 'wide' as the standard, we can get *oihal hau luze bezain zabala da* 'this piece of cloth is as wide as (it is) long'. Mostly, however, a speaker making use of such a structure has no comparison in mind at all. The construction is resorted to for quite a different purpose: it conjoins the two predicates, at the same time ascribing a high intensity to each of them. The structure may occur predicatively, as in example (21a), or attributively, as in (21b,c):

(21) a. Ugari bezain zorrotz zen hizketan, aberats bezain zehatz eta doi. (*MEIG* VIII, 81 = *MIH* 47)
In conversation he was as acute as copious, as exact and precise as (he was) rich.
b. Bi edo hiru lagunen boz ozen bezain bakarra gorabehera. (*MEIG* IV, 30)
Despite the as solitary as resounding voice of two or three persons.
c. Euskararen bide luze bezain malkarrak. (*MEIG* VI, 25)
The as long as bumpy ways of the Basque language.

26.3 Comparatives Denoting Equality in Quantity

While equality in quality is expressed in Batua by the sole postposition *bezain*, equality in quantity or degree can be signified by a variety of comparative postpositons directly following the basis of comparison: *adina*, *hainbat*, *bezainbat*, *beste*, *bezainbeste*, *adinbat*—all of them to be glossed as 'as much as', 'as many as'. The last two, however, may be safely ignored here on account of their extreme scarcity in standard Basque.

If need be, to spell out what the quantity compared consists of, a noun phrase in its bare form (cf. section 2.3.2) may be included in the sentence—usually, but not necessarily, directly following the comparative postposition.

26.3.1 The Comparative Postposition *adina*

Confined to comparatives, the postposition *adina*, far more frequent than any of its synonyms in Batua, must follow a basis of comparison. Just as in the previous sections, this basis will be assumed to be a full clause, subsequently subject to comparative stripping. No such stripping has occurred in the following examples:

(22) a. Aitak ezagutzen du bere burua ezagut daitekeen adina. (Ubillos, 126)
The Father knows himself as much as He can be known.
b. Ez nau, berorrek uste duen adina, aberats izateak harrotzen. (Agirre, *Kres*. 147)
Being rich does not gratify me as much as you think.

Although it is impossible with *bezala* and *bezain*, a nonfinite clause ending in an adnominal verbal noun occurs as a basis of comparison for *adina* and its synonyms:

(23) a. Oinaze eta minak eramateko adina indar eta bihotz izango duzue? (*TB* 89)
Will yoû have as much strength and courage as to bear the torments and pains?
b. Erregalotan ere, bazuen tren bat kargatzeko adina. (Uztapide, *Sas*. 271)
In presents too, he had as much as to load a train with.
c. Bizitzeko adina badu gorputzak. (*MEIG* IX, 95)
The body does have enough to live on.

In the following examples comparative stripping has reduced the basis of comparison to one single nominal, except for (24a), whose two nominals *hire idiak* 'your ox' and *uretan* 'in water' lack counterparts in the main clause and are therefore immune to comparative stripping:

(24) a. Ardotan hire idiak uretan adina edaten duk eta. (*TOE* I, 101)
For yoú drink as much of wine as yoúr ox of water.
b. Zuek adina edozein astok daki. (Kirikiño, *Ab*. 27)
Any ass knows as much as yoû do.
c. Gizonaren biziak ez zuen arkakuso batenak adina balio. (*LBB* 40)
A man's life was not worth as much as that of a flea.
d. Ez da libururik hiztegi batek adina huts bil dezakeenik. (*MEIG* VII, 72)
There is no book that can collect as many mistakes as a dictionary.

Copula stripping has resulted in the following expressions:

ahal adina	as much as possible
behar adina	as much as needed, enough
lehen adina	as much as before
nahi adina	as much as wanted
uste adina	as much as expected

Adina and its synonyms have undergone a natural meaning extension leading from 'as much as' to 'as good as':

(25) a. Bere irakaslea adina izango da. (Lk 6:40; *IB*)
He will be as good as his teacher.
b. Oraindik ez haiz hire nagusia adina. (Muxika, *P.Am.* 50)
Yoú are still not as good as yoúr master.

Given that *adina* is a postposition, clauses based on it can be made attributive by means of the adnominal suffix *-ko*:

(26) a. Mostaza-hazia adinako fedea izango bazenute,... (Mt 17:20, cf. Lk 17:6; *IB*)
If yoû had faith (of) the size of a mustard seed,...
b. Sartzen dira itsas-barrura etxeak adinako baga zuri sendoen artetik. (Agirre, *Kres.* 18)
They enter into the open sea in between strong white waves as big as houses.

We can have attributes to a null pronoun:

(27) a. Patrixirentzat ere, ez zen bere Xegundu adinakorik. (*LBB* 122)
For Patricia too, there was no one as good as her Segundo.
b. Zama jasotzen gu adinakorik bada, betor bide-erdira! (*LBB* 166)
If there is anyone as good as we in lifting loads, let him come to the middle of the road!

26.3.2 The Comparative Postposition *hainbat*

Comparative *hainbat*, together with its seldom used homologues *honenbat* and *horrenbat*, needs no external basis of comparison and is therefore able to function as a quantifier synonymous with *hainbeste* 'so much/many': *hainbat aldiz* (*G.* 331) 'for so many times'; *hainbat urteren buruan* (*MEIG* VI, 31) 'after so many years'; *hainbat eta hainbat eremutan* (*MEIG* VII, 187) 'in such a great many domains'. (Note the use of the bare form of the noun following, in accordance with section 2.3.2.)

The same structures observed with *adina* are found when *hainbat* does occur with a (preceding) basis of comparison. Thus in examples (28a,b) this basis is a full clause:

(28) a. Hartzen duen hainbat ematen du. (Iturriaga, *Dial.* 61)
It gives as much as it takes.
b. Zuk maite zenuen hainbat berak maite zintuen. (Irazusta, *Bizia* 125)
He loved you as much as you loved him.

After stripping of the embedded verb, three nominal fragments remain in example (29a), but only a single noun phrase in (29b) and (29c):

(29) a. Nik bihotzean atsegin hainbat ur ez dago itsasoan. (Xalbador, *Ezin B.* 62)
There is not as much water in the sea as I (have) pleasure in my heart.
b. Nik honi zuri hainbat eman nahi diot. (*TB* 88)
I want to give to him as much as to you.

c. Inoiz, inork ez zaitu nik hainbat maitatuko (Haranburu, *Ausk.* 29)
Nobody will ever love you as much as I.

Like *adina*, *hainbat* can have the meaning 'as good as':

(30) Aski du ikasleak irakaslea hainbat izatea, eta morroiak nagusia hainbat. (Mt 10:25; *EAB*)
It is enough for the pupil to be as good as the teacher, and for the servant to be as good as the master.

26.3.3 The Comparative Postposition *bezainbat*

The postposition *bezainbat* belongs to the eastern dialect area and is rarely encountered in southern Batua. A few examples will therefore suffice:

(31) a. Hartzen duen bezainbat ematen du. (Duvoisin, *Dial.* 61)
It gives as much as it takes.
b. Edan ezazu nahi bezainbat. (Etxaniz, *Antz.* 153)
Drink as much as you want.
c. Edaten du ahal bezainbat. (Orixe, *Aitork.* 216)
He drinks as much as possible.
d. Giputz hauek, gainera, ez ziren lapurtar haiek bezainbat euskararen alde ahalegindu. (*MEIG* IV, 118)
Moreover, these Guipuzcoans did not exert themselves in favor of Basque as much as those Labourdins.

On a par with its synonyms, *bezainbat* can express the meaning 'as good as'. For examples, see *DGV* V, 184. Just like *bezain*, *bezainbat* can conjoin two predicates while ascribing a high degree to each of them:

(32) a. Behin bazen apaiz bat ona bezainbat bitxia. (Barbier, *Sup.* 188)
Once there was a priest as eccentric as he was good.
b. Logikazale bezainbat musikazalea baitzen. (Mirande, *Pr.* 168)
For he was as fond of music as he was of logic.

The locative form *bezainbatean* expresses the meaning 'as to'. The governed noun phrase takes the form of an instrumental, often followed by the relativized copula *den* or its definite instrumental *denaz*: *nitaz denaz bezainbatean* (Ax. 53) 'as for me'; *hizkuntzaren historiaz den bezainbatean* (*MEIG* VII, 94) 'as regards the history of the language'; *jendeez bezainbatean* (J. Etchepare, *Bur.* 27) 'as to the people'.

26.3.4 The Comparative Postposition *beste*

For the purpose of denoting equality in quantity or degree, the Biscayan dialect makes use of the postposition *beste*, etymologically connected to the determiner *beste* 'other' discussed in section 11.5. Although its use is allowed in the standard language, in practice, only Biscayan speakers will employ it. To illustrate, a few examples will do:

(33) a. Mariñok ez du inoiz eduki orain daukan beste diru. (Oskillaso, *Gab.At.* 27).
Marino has never had as much money as he has now.
b. Esango zenuke abade izateko beste badakiela. (*P.Ab.* 154)
You would say that he knows as much as to be a priest.
c. Non etxean beste babes? (*G.* 374)
Where (is there) as much support as at home?
d. Ai! Jakin izan banu gaur beste! (San Martin, 25)
Ah! If I had known as much as today!

The meaning extension to 'as good as' has taken place here too:

(34) a. Ez zen inor beren aita izan zen beste. (*G.* 18)
Nobody was as good as their father had been.
b. Hamar emakume ere ez ziren gizon bat beste. (Bilbao, 165)
Even ten women were not as good as one man.

When preceded by an adnominal purpose clause (section 7.2.3), *beste* may acquire the potential sense 'able':

(35) Zahar eta andreak ez omen ziren haraino igotzeko beste. (S. Mitxelena, *IG* II, 57)
The elderly and the ladies were (allegedly) not able to climb up there.

26.4 Comparatives Denoting Superiority

Comparatives denoting superiority, in other words, those plainly designated as "comparatives" in traditional parlance, are characterized by the postposition *baino* directly following the basis of comparison, provided there is one, as well as by a special comparative form of the predicate acting as the standard of comparison.

26.4.1 Morphology of Comparatives

Except for a few cases of suppletion, the comparative degree of a predicate is formed by attachment of the comparative suffix *-ago*. In standard Basque, there is but one morphophonemic rule to apply: elision of stem-final *a*. As illustrations, I here present some examples involving adjectives, adverbs, and nouns:

gora	high, loud	gorago	higher, louder
maite	dear, beloved	maiteago	dearer, more beloved
txar	bad	txarrago	worse
zoro	crazy, silly	zoroago	crazier, sillier
gaizki	badly	gaizkiago	worse
gutxi	few	gutxiago	fewer

maiz	often	maizago	more often
ugari	abundantly	ugariago	more abundantly
abere	beast	abereago	more of a beast
gaitz	evil, harm	gaitzago	greater evil, greater harm
gau	night	gauago	more night
gizon	man	gizonago	more of a man

The suppletive forms are *gehiago* (colloquially often pronounced *geio*) 'more', comparative of *asko* 'much', and *hobe* 'better', comparative of *on* 'good', as well as the corresponding adverbs *hobeto*, comparative of *ondo* 'well', and *hobeki*, comparative of *ongi* 'well'.

Case endings follow *-ago* where adjectives are concerned, but precede it in the case of nouns. Thus we have *hiri handiagora* 'to the larger city' and *etxe txikiagoan* 'in the smaller house', but *aurrerago* 'more to the front', *gusturago* 'more comfortable', *gogoanago* 'more in mind', *gogozago* 'more willingly', *kontuzago* 'more carefully', and *osagarritanago* 'in better health'.

26.4.2 Comparatives and Adverbs of Degree

Adverbs of degree are divisible into those able to characterize the extent of superiority expressed by a comparative and those that are unable to co-occur with comparatives. In turning first to intensifiers (section 11.2.1), we must discuss western and eastern usage separately.

In western usage, the possibilities are rather limited, as the main intensifier *oso* and most of its synonyms are unable to modify comparatives. Apart from the virtually obsolete *txit* (*txit ahaltsuago* [Gn 26:16; Ur.] 'much more powerful'), the rather colloquial *dexente* 'sufficiently', 'considerably' (*EGLU* I, 284), and an occasional *izugarri* (*izugarri haundiagoa* [Villasante, *Jainkoa* 43] 'terribly bigger'), only the instrumental form of *asko*, *askoz*, or *askotaz* (section 6.1.3), acts as an intensifier with comparatives:

(36) a. Guk baino askoz gutxiago daki Ximonek. (*LBB* 122)
Simon knows a lot less than we.
b. Aldizkariak askoz hobeak dira egungo egunean. (*MEIG* VI, 43)
The magazines are much better nowadays.
c. Hori baino ere txiroago zen gure Migel Permin. Askotaz txiroago. (Bilbao, 115)
Our Miguel Fermin was poorer even than that. A lot poorer.
d. Herri hizkera askotaz ere askatuagoa izaten da. (*MEIG* VII, 129)
Popular speech tends to be much more liberated.

Eastern usage is a lot freer in allowing intensifiers to modify comparatives. Thus one of the most common intensifiers, *biziki*, freely occurs with comparatives: *biziki ederrago* (J. Etchepare, *Bur.* 93) 'much more beautiful'. Likewise, *izigarri* 'terribly', *itsuski* 'horribly', and *gogorki* 'strongly', whose meaning in colloquial style fades into a mere intensifier to be glossed 'tremendously', are used with comparative as well as noncomparative predicates.

The adverb *aise* 'easily' also serves as an intensifier, but only with comparatives: *aise hobeki* (Mattin, 118; *MEIG* VI, 115) 'much better'; *aise usuago* (*MEIG* VI, 59, 170) 'much more often'.

Not all intensifiers, however, co-occur with comparatives, even in eastern usage: *arras*, *arrunt*, and *guztiz*, for example, do not.

As to *anitz* and *hagitz*, eastern counterparts of *asko* 'much', they readily modify comparatives, either with or without an instrumental ending: *anitzez gehiago eta hobeki* (Duvoisin, *L.Ed.* 84) 'much more and better'; *harria baino anitz urrunago* (Barbier, *Lég.* 127) 'much farther than the stone'; *hagitzez dohatsuago* (Chourio, I, 25.9) 'much happier'.

To indicate but a slight degree of superiority, all dialects make use of the suffix *-xe*, intercalated between *-ago* and the stem:

haundixeago	a little bigger
beranduxeago	a little later
urrutixeago	a little farther
geroxeago	a little later
gehixeago	a little more
gutxixeago	a little less
honaxeago	a little more in this direction
horraxeago	a little more in that direction
haraxeago	a little farther from here

With the suppletive *hobe*, *hobeki*, *hobeto* a pleonastic *-ago* is added:

hobexeago	a little better
hobekixeago	a little better (adv.)
hobetoxeago	a little better (adv.)

To these forms an optional phrase of the type *pixka bat* 'a bit' can be proposed:

pixka bat goraxeago (*MEIG* VI, 54)	a little bit higher
apur bat gehixeago (*MEIG* VII, 55)	a little bit more

Also without *-xe* is the phrase *apur bat geroago* (Atxaga, *Obab.* 139) 'a little afterward'.

As seen in section 11.2.3, this suffix *-xe* is also used with perfect participles ending in *-tu* when they function adjectivally: *ahaztuxe(a)* 'somewhat forgotten', *zahartuxe(a)* 'somewhat aged'.

26.4.3 Syntax of Comparatives

To begin with, comparatives form an exception to the rule stated in section 1.3.3 according to which nominal or adjectival predicates construed with the copula *izan* must take the article *-a*. With comparative nouns and adjectives, not used as an attribute, use of the article is merely optional (*EGLU* I, 283):

(37) a. Zu orain zarena baino gazteago zen emakume hura. (Oñederra, 141)
That woman was younger than what you are now.
b. Nik uste nuen baino luzeago, mardulago eta ederrago da. (Garate, *Iz.B.* 94)
He is handsomer, more robust, and taller than I thought.

As we did for clauses with *bezala* and *bezain*, here too we will assume the basis of comparison to start out as a full clause, to which subsequent comparative stripping may apply. So as not to lose ourselves needlessly in a theoretical quagmire, I will take two rather simple examples to illustrate this approach:

(38) a. Gure bihotza baino haundiagoa da Jainkoa. (1 Jn 3:20; *IB*)
God is greater than our heart.
b. Gu baino azkarrago ibili zen Okerra. (Atxaga, *Obab.* 359)
Okerra walked faster than we.

We will view examples (38a,b) as the result of comparative stripping applied to the hypothetical (39a,b):

(39) a. *Gure bihotza haundia den baino haundiagoa da Jainkoa.
*God is greater than our heart is great.
b. *Gu ibili ginen moduan baino azkarrago ibili zen Okerra.
*Okerra walked faster than the way we walked.

This approach explains how *baino* can have two separate constituents to govern:

(40) a. Badihoaz honelako edo halako herrira ... umeak gozotegira baino pozago. (*G.* 81)
They go to such or such a village happier than children to the candy store.
b. Joseba lanean baino erneago ibili zen musean Andoni. (*EGLU* V, 280)
Anthony acted more alert playing "mus," than Joseph working.

In many languages, nouns do not have comparative forms. In Basque, they do:

(41) a. Hori gaitzaren ordez gaitzagoa sartzea da. (*MEIG* VIII, 146 = *MIH* 226)
That means introducing in place of the ailment a worse one.
b. Ni baino gizonago portatu haiz. (Amuriza, *Hil* 197)
Yoú have behaved more manly than I.
c. Azeriak berak baino azeriagoak dira. (*P.Ab.* 165)
They are more foxy than the foxes themselves.
d. Abereak baino abereago egin naiz! (Duvoisin, *L.Ed.* 65)
I have become more beastly than the beasts!
e. Handia dugu, ba, gaua nola ez den bihurtu gauago. (Azurmendi, 37)
It is strange for us, then, how the night has not become more night.

The comparatives *nahiago* and *beharrago* of the nouns *nahi* 'will' and *behar* 'need', just like the comparative *maiteago* of the adjective *maite* 'dear', can function as object complements (section 14.1) of the verb **edun*, that is, transitive *izan*. This usage gives rise to sentences such as

(42) a. Isaakek maiteago zuen Esau; Rebekak, aldiz, Jakob zuen maiteago. (Gn 25:28)
Isaac was fonder of Esau; Rebecca, on the contrary, was fonder of Jacob.
b. Nik zu zaitut maiteago arraintxoek ura baino. (From song "Itsasoa lano," *Xaramela* 169)
I love you more than the little fish the water.

(43) a. Garai batean pilota genuen ogia baino nahiago.
For a period we preferred the pilota game to bread.
b. Hark, egia esan, nahiago zuen Leizarraga Axular baino. (*MEIG* IX, 62)
He, to tell the truth, preferred Leizarraga to Axular.

(44) a. Itsasaldekoa baino beharrago zain osasunarentzat lehorraldeko haizea. (T. Agirre, *Uzt*. 123)
The inland wind is more necessary for yoùr health than the sea wind.
b. Arnasa baino beharrago zaitun NN. (Etxaniz, *Nola* 12)
NN who needs you more than breathing.

The predicate *nahiago* also admits a conditional clause as complement:

(45) a. Nahiago nuen hemen egon balitz! (Satrustegi, 112)
I had preferred it if he had stayed here.
b. Iturritik baino zure suiletik emango bazenit, nahiago nuke. (Etxaniz, *Antz*. 153)
I would prefer it if you gave me from your pail rather than from the fountain.
c. Nahiago nuke, egia esan, bestela izan balitz. (*MEIG* VIII, 155 = *MIH* 369)
I would prefer it, to tell the truth, if it had been otherwise.

As to the order of constituents in a comparative clause, the canonical order is for the basis of comparison to precede and for the standard of comparison to immediately follow the postposition *baino*. Yet deviations from this order are not unusual. *EGLU* presents some examples in which a constituent from the main clause intervenes between the basis of comparison and the standard, thus occupying the focus site of the main clause:

(46) Lana baino alferkeria maiteago dugu. (*EGLU* V, 406)
We prefer laziness to work.

Furthermore, in examples (42b) and (43b) the standard precedes the basis of comparison.

I will close this subsection with the important observation that Basque possesses no comparatives denoting inferiority in quality. In particular, there is no straightforward way of rendering the English sentence *Mary is less pretty than Eve*. Since *Miren Eba baino itsusiagoa da* 'Mary is uglier than Eve' won't do, the only possibility is to resort to a negated equative: *Miren ez da Eba bezain polita* 'Mary is not as pretty as Eve'.

26.4.4 Comparatives Expressing Anteriority and Posteriority

Comparatives expressing temporal relations, such as anteriority and posteriority, could not be treated in chapter 20 because the reader was assumed to be still unacquainted with the structure of the Basque comparative. This omission will now be rectified.

As to anteriority, either with respect to a given time or to a given event, it is quite often indicated by a comparative clause with *lehen* 'formerly' or its comparative form *lehenago* 'earlier' taken as a standard of comparison. When a given time is at issue, this time specification itself serves as a basis of comparison: *bostak baino lehen* (*G.* 294) 'before five o'clock'; *1700 baino lehenago* (*MEIG* VI, 52) 'before 1700'; *luzaro baino lehen* (Zaitegi, *Sof.* 24) 'before long'; *orain baino lehen* (Uztapide, *Sas.* 244) or *orain baino lehenago* (Uztapide, *Sas.* 279) 'before now'.

Where anteriority with respect to a given event is concerned, the basis of comparison will be a perfect participle clause describing the event:

(47) a. Oilarrak jo baino lehen, hiru aldiz ukatuko nauzu. (Mt 26:34)
Before the cock crows, you will deny me three times.
b. Nik ez nuen ezagutu eritegira etorri baino lehen. (Garate, *NY* 30)
I didn't know her before she came to the hospital.
c. Zuek eskatu baino lehenago ere badaki zuen Aitak zer behar duzuen. (Mt 6:8; *Lau Eb.*)
Yoûr Father knows what yoû need even before yoû ask for it.
d. Pentsa ezazu une batez lasai, erantzun baino lehenago. (Garate, *Esku* 96)
Think calmly for a moment, before you answer.

Comparative stripping, of course, may sometimes reduce this clause to a single constituent:

(48) a. Bera ni baino lehen iritsi zen. (Haranburu, *Ausk.* 77)
She arrived before I (did).
b. Gipuzkoan hemezortzigarren mendean ez dira hainbeste Larramendi baino lehenago idatzi zuten lekukoak. (*MEIG* IV, 59)
In Guipuzcoa in the eighteenth century there are not so many witnesses who wrote before Larramendi.

Like English *sooner*, the comparative form *lehenago* can be employed in a nontemporal sense: 'rather':

(49) a. Horrela uste banu, lehenago egingo nioke uko euskaltzaletasunari zentzuari baino. (*MEIG* VIII, 128 = *MIH* 204)
If I thought so, I would renounce bascophily rather than common sense.

b. Emakume egarria nuela esan? Lehenago lurpean sartu! (*LBB* 87)
   To say that I had a longing for women? (I would) rather have buried myself underground.

Posteriority, usually expressed by means of *ondoren* or *ondoan* (section 20.4.3), can also be indicated using the comparative form of *gero* 'afterward', namely, *geroago* 'later'. In this case, however, the time or event acting as the point of reference is normally left unstated. In the rare instances when it is expressed, it will be by an elative noun phrase—for example, *gauerditik geroago* 'after midnight' or *handik geroago* 'after that'—or by a perfect participle clause followed by *eta* 'and' (cf. section 20.6), hardly ever by a basis of comparison followed by *baino*.

What we do find preceding *geroago* are measure phrases specifying the length of the relevant time interval. In older usage such measure phrases take the instrumental case; nowadays they tend to be absolutive: *Bi mila urtez geroago* (*TZ* I, 42) 'two thousand years later'; *Ordu erdi batez geroago* (T. Agirre, *Uzt*. 79) 'half an hour later'; *zortzi urtez geroago* (*MEIG* VIII, 154 = *MIH* 368) 'eight years later'; but *ordubete geroago* (Agirre, *A.L.* 76) 'one hour later'; *ordu erdi geroago* (Bilbao, 102) 'half an hour later'; *hiru hilabete geroago* (Arana, 99) 'three months later'.

26.4.5 Comparatives Denoting Superiority or Inferiority in Quantity

Comparatives denoting superiority in quantity are formed in the same way as those denoting superiority in quality, using *gehiago* 'more', comparative of *asko* 'much', as a standard of comparison. The nature of the quantity will remain unexpressed when inferrable from the sentence or its context:

(50) a. Alargun behartsu honek beste guztiek baino gehiago bota du kutxara. (Mk 12:43)
   This poor widow has cast more into the box than all the others.
b. Emakumeek beti dakigu gizonek uste baino gehiago. (Urruzuno, *E.Z.* 141)
   We women always know more than the men think.
c. Inoiz baino gehiago jan arazi zidan. (Haranburu, *Its*. 118)
   She made me eat more than ever.

When needed, the nature of the quantity involved can be indicated by a bare noun phrase governed by *gehiago*:

(51) a. Zuk baino diru gehiago dut. (*E.H.* 94)
   I have more money than you.
b. Haiek baino neke gehiago jasan dut. (2 Cor 11:23)
   I have suffered more fatigue than they.
c. Jende gehiago hil zuen kazkabar-harriak israeldarren ezpatak baino. (Jo 10:11)
   The hailstone(s) killed more people than the sword of the Israelites.

[*N.B.* Note that *gehiago* phrases are always construed as singulars.]

Sometimes the two quantities compared have different natures:

(52) a. Laudorio eta goramen baino kritika zorrotz gehiago egin omen diot Azkueren obra nagusiari. (*MEIG* VII, 72)
I am said to have made on Azkue's main work more sharp criticism than eulogy and praise.
b. Diru baino amets gehiago zuen agureak. (*EGLU* V, 277)
The old man had more dreams than money.
c. Buruan ile duzun baino bekatu gehiago egin duzu. (cf. Ax. 125)
You have committed more sins than you have hair on the head.

Not all uses of *gehiago* involve quantity, even when it appears as the standard of comparison. Thus *gehiago* can have the sense 'more important', 'more valuable':

(53) Ez ote da bizia janaria baino gehiago? (Mt 6:25)
Is not life more than food?

Moreover, *gehiago* occurs as an adverbial standard of comparison, since, like *asko*, it may function as an adverb of degree accompanying a verbal predicate (cf. section 11.2.1). Examples are

(54) a. Txori guztiek baino gehiago balio duzue. (Lk 12:7)
Yoû are worth more than all birds.
b. Odolkia baino gehiago estimatzen da odolki emailea. (Garate, *Atsot.* 10247)
The giver of a blood sausage is more appreciated than the blood sausage.
c. Jone ez zitzaion bera baino gehiago gustatzen. (Atxaga, *Gizona* 290)
He did not like Jone more than her.

In noncomparative contexts, *gehiago* may appear as a negative polarity item with the meaning 'any more':

(55) a. Nirekin ez duzue gehiago lanik izango. (*LBB* 27)
Yoû will have trouble with me no more.
b. Mutila ez zen sekula gehiago ohetik jaiki. (Garate, *Leh.* 71)
The boy didn't ever get up from his bed anymore.

Inferiority in quantity is expressed by the same structure as superiority, but with *gutxiago* 'less' instead of *gehiago* 'more'. A few examples will therefore suffice:

(56) a. Lehen baino pisu gutxiago zeramala laster antzeman zion astoak. (Muxika, *P.Am.* 50)
The donkey noticed quickly that he was carrying less weight than before.
b. Ez da guztia gure irispidera heldu, gutunak eta antzekoak besterik baino gutxiago. (*MEIG* VI, 59)
Not everything has come into our reach, letters and the like less than anything else.

c. Gutxi idatzi zuen euskaraz, besteri eragin baino gutxiago. (*MEIG* VII, 69)
He wrote little in Basque, less than he made others do.

d. Uste dut ez naizela superapostolu horiek baino gutxiago. (2 Cor 11:5)
I believe that I am not less than those superapostles.

26.4.6 The Topping Particle *are*

In present-day usage—for the past, see *DGV* II, 386—the particle *are*, to be glossed in English as *still*, *yet*, or *even*, must co-occur with a comparative immediately following it. Its function is to indicate an even higher degree of a quality already mentioned or implied, unless the comparative is *gutxiago*, where the degree will be lower than another quality already known to be low. Some examples will make this function clear:

(57) a. Itziar zaharra da. Mikel, berriz, are zaharragoa. (*EGLU* I, 290)
Itziar is old. Michael, however, is even older.

b. Mikel Itziar baino zaharragoa da, Andoni are zaharragoa. (*EGLU* I, 290)
Michael is older than Itziar, Tony even older (than Michael).

c. Lur eder bat, Holanda, herri xarmangarriak eta hiri are xarmangarriagoak dituena. (Atxaga, *Grl.* 46)
A beautiful land, Holland, one that has charming villages and even more charming cities.

d. Eta hor geldituko naiz are istilu gorriagoetan ez murgiltzearren. (*MEIG* VI, 143)
And I will stop here so as not to plunge into even knottier problems.

The phrase *are gehiago* may be shortened to *areago*:

(58) a. Zu gaiztoa zara eta hura areago. (Garate, *Erd.* 243)
You are bad and he even more so.

b. Zuhur jokatu beharrean gaude, areago ugal ez daitezen. (Ex 1:10)
We have to act shrewdly, lest they increase even more.

Although in a somewhat different context, the same meaning ‘even’ can be expressed by the use of *ere* in construction with *baino*:

(59) a. Profeta baino ere handiagoa. (Mt 11:9 = Lk 7:26)
Someone even greater than a prophet.

b. Zure azken egintzak lehenengoak baino ere bikainagoak dira. (Rv 2:19)
Your latest deeds are even more excellent than the first ones.

26.4.7 Comparatives as Intensifiers

To take an adjective or an adverb both as the standard and as the basis of comparison is a favored device for expressing a high degree of the element in question. Examples of this structure are

(60) a. Ilun baino ilunago dago beroien zentzua zer den. (*MEIG* VI, 95)
It is extremely obscure what their sense is.
b. Txukun baino txukunago agertzen dira beti. (*MEIG* III, 81)
They always appear extremely neat and tidy.
c. Nik ondo baino hobeto gogoratzen ditut Caulfielden gorabeherak. (Atxaga, *Grl.* 126)
I remember Caulfield's adventures extremely well.
d. Musarrok, noski, ederki baino ederkiago zekien hau. (*MEIG* VI, 162)
Musarro, of course, knew this perfectly.
e. Maiz baino maizago entzuna dute horren izena. (*MEIG* III, 146)
They have heard its name extremely often.

Occasionally, the basis of comparison is a synonym of the standard:

(60) f. Argi baino garbiroago erakusten digu aurkitzea ez dela aski. (*MEIG* V, 101)
He shows us most clearly that it is not enough to find it.

An easier way to create high-degree predicates out of comparatives is to prepose *ezin* 'impossible' to them: *ezin ederrago* 'extremely beautiful', *ezin gutxiago* 'preciously little', *ezin hobe* 'extremely good', *ezin hobeki* 'extremely well', and so on. The Souletin dialect, oddly enough, uses the comparative of *ezin* rather than that of the adjective or adverb: *ezinago eder* 'very beautiful'.

26.4.8 Time Correlations

Basque has rather a neat way of describing qualities increasing with time. It consists in the use of a comparative preceded by *gero eta, geroago eta*, or, in northern usage, *beti (eta)*. Here are some examples with *gero*:

(61) a. Aurrera zihoala, gero eta urduriago zegoen. (Arana, 12)
As she went on, she got more and more nervous.
b. Gero eta azkarrago ibiltzen zara. (Oñederra, 145)
You walk faster and faster.
c. Gero eta abilago haiz lagunak engainatzen. (Atxaga, *Gizona* 21)
You are getting better and better at deceiving your companions.

The following are examples with *geroago*:

(62) a. Jendea geroago eta ederkiago janzten da. (Iraola, 73)
People are dressing more and more smartly.
b. Geroago eta gorroto gehiago zion. (*TZ* I 64)
He hated him more and more.
c. Geroago eta okerrago zihoan haren osasuna. (*LBB* 73)
His health went from bad to worse.

These examples use *beti:*

(63) a. Euskaldun egon beti, beti eta gehiago euskaldun. (Barbier, *Sup*. 38)
Always stay Basque, more and more Basque.

b. Baina, orroa beti eta handiago, beti eta hurbilago entzuten nuen. (Barbier, *Lég*. 149)
But, I was hearing the roar increasingly louder, increasingly nearer.

c. Ikusten dut beti eta hobe zoazela. (Xalbador, *Odol*. 342)
I see that you are becoming better and better.

26.4.9 Proportional Sentences

A proportional sentence presents two actions, processes, or circumstances as correlating in degree of intensity. In Basque, sentences of this type involve a sequence of two clauses: the first one nonfinite, consisting of an initial *zenbat eta* followed by a comparative phrase; the second one, finite or verbless, headed by either *hainbat eta* or *orduan eta* followed by another comparative phrase. First, I will cite some examples using *hainbat eta:*

(64) a. Zenbat eta gehiago saiatu egintza horien arrazoi bila, hainbat eta nekezago aurkituko dute. (Eccl 8:17)
The more they try to search for the reason of those works, the harder they will find it.

b. Badirudi, hala ere, zenbat eta gehiago nik zuek maite izan, hainbat eta gutxiago maite nauzuela zuek ni. (2 Cor 12:15)
Yet, it seems that the more I love yoû, the less yoû love me.

c. Zenbat eta urte gutxiago, hainbat eta txikiagoa prezioa. (Lv 25:16)
The fewer the years, the lower the price.

In northern usage, *zenbat* and *hainbat* require the instrumental ending, optionally preceded by the genitive: *zenbatez ... hainbatez*, or *zenbatenaz ... hainbatenaz*, already used by Leizarraga (see *DGV* I, 360).

The following examples have *orduan eta:*

(65) a. Zenbat eta gehiago agindu, orduan eta areago zabaltzen zuten. (Mk 7:36)
The more he ordered them (not to), the more widely they continued to proclaim it.

b. Baina zenbat eta zanpatuago, orduan eta ugariago eta hedatuago egin ziren. (Ex 1:12)
But the more they were oppressed, the more they increased and spread out.

c. Aspaldixko ikasi genuen jende horiek zenbat eta bakezaleago, orduan eta beldurgarriago izaten direla. (*E.H.* 778)
We have learned long ago that the more peace-loving those people are, the more terrifying they tend to be.

26.4.10 Comparatives Preceded by *hainbat*

The quantifier *hainbat* preposed to a comparative has the same meaning as the English phrases 'so much the ...', 'all the ...'—for example, *hainbat gogaikarriago* 'all the more annoying', *hainbat errazago* 'so much the easier', *hainbat gehiago* 'all the more'. As this kind of phrase is not attested until the middle of the 18th century, with *hainbat hobe* 'so much the better' and *hainbat gaizto(ago)* 'so much the worse' being the only examples up to the beginning of the 20th century, one may well suspect those phrases to be calques from neighboring Romance languages (cf. Bearnese *tan miélhou* and *tan pire* in the north, and Castilian *tanto major* and *tanto peor* in the south). A few examples as illustrations will suffice:

(66) a. Hainbat gaiztoago egiten ez dutenentzat. (Duvoisin, *Lab.* 219)
So much the worse for those who don't do it.
b. Hainbat hobeto niretzat, horrela balitz. (Agirre, *A.L.* 137)
So much the better for me, if it were like that.
c. Izan zituzten nahigabe gogorrek hainbat beroago jartzen zituzten beren bihotz zintzoak. (Cf. Echeita, *Jos.* 353)
The harsh sorrows they had had were making their honest hearts all the warmer.

26.4.11 Comparatives Preceded by *zein baino zein*

A construction consisting of the comparative form of an adjective preceded by the phrase *zein baino zein*, in which *zein* is an interrogative pronoun meaning 'which one', serves to indicate that a high degree of the property denoted by the adjective obtains uniformly within a certain group. Examples are

(67) a. Denak zein baino zein ederragoak! (Oñatibia, 197)
All of them equally beautiful.
b. Denak zaunkaka zetozen, zein baino zein amorratuago. (Arana, 12)
They were all coming barking, all equally furious.
c. Bederatzi mahaiko, eta zeinek baino zeinek jateko gogo ederragoa. (Etxaniz, *Nola* 22)
Nine people at the table, all of them with the same great appetite.
d. Hiru opari eskaini zizkioten, zein baino zein galgarriagoak. (*LBB* 161)
They offered her three presents, all equally pernicious.

26.5 Superlatives

26.5.1 Morphology of Superlatives

Except for one or two cases of suppletion, the superlative degree of a predicate is formed by attachment of the superlative suffix *-en*, a homonym of the genitive plural ending, which may well be its ultimate source. In standard Basque, there is but one morphophonemic rule to apply: elision of stem-final *a*. I will illustrate this with some examples involving adjectives, adverbs, and nouns:

gora	high, loud	goren	highest, loudest
maite	dear, beloved	maiteen	dearest, most beloved
txar	bad	txarren	worst
zoro	crazy, silly	zoroen	craziest, silliest
gaizki	badly	gaizkien	worst
gutxi	few	gutxien	fewest
maiz	often	maizen	most often
ugari	abundantly	ugarien	most abundantly
abere	beast	abereen	most of a beast
gaitz	evil, harm	gaitzen	greatest evil, greatest harm
gau	night	gauen	most night
gizon	man	gizonen	most of a man

The suppletive forms are *gehien* 'most', superlative of *asko* 'much', and, in northern usage or elevated style, *hoberen* 'best', superlative of *on* 'good', and *hobekien* 'best', superlative of *ongi* 'well'. In southern usage, the superlatives of *on*, *ondo*, and *ongi* are regular: *onen*, *ondoen*, *ongien*.

Case endings follow *-en* where adjectives are concerned but precede it in the case of nouns. Thus we have *hiri handienera* 'to the largest city' and *etxe txikienean* 'in the smallest house', but *gogoanen* 'most in mind', *gogozen* 'the most willingly', *gusturen* 'the most comfortable', and *kontuzen* 'the most carefully'.

26.5.2 Syntax of Superlatives

As *EGLU* points out (I, 281), it is possible for a superlative adjective to directly modify a noun phrase: *udako gau beroena* (Atxaga, *Gizona* 345) 'the warmest night of the summer'. This, in fact, is the preferred option for ranking adjectives such as *gazteen* 'youngest' or *zaharren* or *nagusien* 'eldest' when applied to relatives: *alaba gazteena* 'youngest daughter', *alaba nagusiena* (Gn 29:26) 'eldest daughter'. Also the adjective *gehien* 'most' fairly often modifies its noun phrase directly.

In general, however, direct modification is somewhat rare. The reason is not far to seek. A noun phrase construed with a superlative is naturally interpreted as providing the domain over which the superlative ranges, so that use of the partitive case ending seems called for (section 13.1.1). Hence we have phrases such as the following: *munduko ipuinik onena* (Arana, 21, 128) 'the best tale in the world'; *munduan den emakumerik ederrena* (*MEIG* I, 157) 'the most beautiful woman existing in the world'; *guk dugun eragozpenik larriena* (*MEIG* IX, 83) 'the greatest difficulty that we have'; *nire lagunik onena* (Garate, *Hades* 23) 'my best friend'; *jantzirik garestienak* (Garate, *NY* 161) 'the most expensive clothes'.

As seen in section 13.1.1, the partitive cannot be attached to a definite noun phrase. Instead, an inessive or elative ending is then used: *zuetan txikiena* (Lk 9:48) 'the least of yoû'; *apostoluetan txikiena* (1 Cor 15:9) 'the least of the apostles'; *liburuetatik politena* (*EGLU* I, 281) 'the prettiest of the books'.

Not only superlative adjectives, but also superlative nouns enter in construction with a directly preceding partitive noun phrase. This is aptly illustrated by a peculiar type of locution in which a superlative noun modifies its stem noun equipped with the partitive ending:

agurerik agureena (*MEIG* IX, 63)	the most senior of seniors
gizonik gizonena (Agirre, *A.L.* 115)	the manliest of men
bere lagunik lagunena (Atxaga, *Obab.* 42)	her very best friend

These examples have a final inessive:

bizitzarik bizitzarenean	in the midst of life
borrokarik borrokarenean	in the thick of the struggle
hondarrik hondarrenean (*MEIG* II, 99; V, 21; VII, 188; VIII, 163)	at bottom, basically
zokorik zokorenean (*MEIG* VIII, 100)	in the most hidden corner

Just like the corresponding comparatives, the superlatives *nahien* and *beharren* of the nouns *nahi* 'will' and *behar* 'need', as well as the superlative *maiteen* of the adjective *maite* 'dear', can function as object complements (section 14.1) of the verb **edun*, that is, transitive *izan*. Examples are

(68) a. Kendu beharko da maiteen duguna ere. (Cf. *MEIG* VIII, 149 = *MIH* 229)
Even what we most love will have to be removed.
b. Bietako zeinek izango ote du maiteen? (Lk 7:42)
Which of the two will love him most?

(69) a. Ez alegia, berak amestu eta nahien izan zuen neskatila. (Erkiaga, *Arran.* 176)
Not, indeed, the girl that he had dreamed of and that he had most wanted.
b. Horixe dut nahien. (Azkue, 1923–1925, I, sec. 339, p. 219)
That is what I most want.

(70) a. Zer da nik egin beharren nukeena? (Duvoisin, *L.Ed.* 75)
What is it that I would most need to do?
b. Ikus dezala berak zer den beharren duguna. (Azkue, *Ardi* 41)
Let him see himself what it is that we most need.

Without the meaning being affected, a superlative predicative or adverb may appear bare or take one of two endings: either *-a*, most likely the singular article (cf. French: *le mieux*, *le plus souvent*), or *-ik*, possibly identical with the partitive suffix. These possibilities are illustrated by the following examples taken from *EGLU*:

(71) a. Etxe hura dago hurbilen/hurbilena/hurbilenik. (*EGLU* V, 315)
That house is the nearest.
b. Zeu bizi zara ondoen/ondoena/ondoenik. (*EGLU* V, 310)
It is you who are living the most comfortably.
c. Peru bizi da hobekien/hobekiena/hobekienik. (*EGLU* V, 315)
It is Pete who is living most comfortably.

In potentiality contexts—that is, when the superlative is preceded by *ahalik* (*eta*), *albait*, or *hainbat* (see section 26.5.3)—no partitive ending appears.

An interesting construction Batua has borrowed from the Biscayan dialect consists of a superlative preceded by the adnominal form of *inoiz* 'ever': *inoizko* 'of ever'. It must be glossed in English by a superlative followed by *of all* or by a comparative: *more than ever*.

(72) a. Inoizko soinurik gozoenak jotzen hasi zen. (Bilbao, 157)
She started to play the sweetest melodies of all.
b. Inoizko ipuinik politena entzun dugu gaur. (Bilbao, 71)
Today we have heard the prettiest tale of all.
c. Senar hori laster izango duzu inoizko zoriontsuen. (Bilbao, 95)
That husband will soon be happier than ever.

The partitive form *inoizkorik* can also be used in this construction: *inoizkorik zoriontsuen* (Bilbao, 166) 'happier than ever'. A rarely found alternative for *inoizko* is *guztizko*: *guztizko ondoen* (Bilbao, 203) 'as well as possible'.

26.5.3 Superlatives and Potentiality

To express the meaning 'as *X* as possible', where *X* is an adjective, predicate, or adverb, Basque makes use of a superlative preceded by one of the following phrases: *ahalik* (*eta*), *albait*, or *hainbat*.

The most common of these is *ahalik* optionally followed by *eta*. A superlative adjective constructed with *ahalik* (*eta*) always takes the article *-a*, both in its predicative and in its attributive use: *ahalik* (*eta*) *handiena* 'as big as possible'. When the adjective is used attributively, *ahalik* (*eta*) may precede the whole noun phrase, as in *ahalik deiadar handiena* (Arrue, *G.B.* 80) 'as loud a shout as possible' or *ahalik eta etxe ederrena* (*E.H.* 16) 'as beautiful a house as possible', or it may precede just the adjective, as in *luma ahalik onenak eta ederrenak* (*P.Ab.* 177) 'feathers as good and beautiful as possible'.

With predicatives or adjectives in this construction, the general practice had been to employ the article *-a*, until southern authors at the end of the 19th century began to leave it out, a practice that continued in southern usage for most of the 20th century—for example, *ahalik urrutien* (*MEIG* I, 142) 'as far as possible', *ahalik argien* (*MEIG* I, 85) 'as clear as possible', *ahalik ongien* (*MEIG* II, 41) 'as comfortably as possible', *ahalik ondoen eta azkarren* (Oñatibia, 251) 'as well and as fast as possible'.

At least since 1995, the Basque Academy has been advocating a return to the traditional system still preserved in northern usage. Southern authors now tend to use the definite form:

(73) a. Igaro ezak denbora ahalik goxoena. (Garate, *Iz.B.* 49)
Spend the time as pleasantly as possible.
b. Ahalik eta ondoena itzultzen saiatu naiz. (Atxaga, *Obab.* 369)
I have tried to translate it as well as possible.
c. Ahalik eta lasterrena abiatzea komeni zaigu. (Atxaga, *Gizona* 340)
We do well to start out as quickly as possible.

[*N.B.* Instead of *ahalik*, a relative clause may appear: *ahal den gutxiena* (*TOE* II, 63) 'as little as is possible'.]

Similar structures exist with *albait* or *hainbat* instead of *ahalik*. These constructions are limited to the southern area, and mainly used in Biscay. Here too, adjectives require the definite form, and, when they are used attributively, *albait* (and likewise *hainbat*) may either precede the whole noun phrase, as in *albait medikurik onena* (JJMg, *Bas.Esc.* 78) 'the best possible doctor', or just the adjective, as in *kantari albait onena* (Arrese Beitia, *Ama E.* 464) 'the best possible singer'. Predicatives and adverbs, however, do not take the article: *albait ondoen* (*E.H.* 28) and *hainbat ondoen* (*E.H.* 343) 'as well as possible'.

26.6 Excessives

26.6.1 Morphology of Excessives

Except for one case of suppletion, the excessive form of a predicate is formed by attachment of the excessive suffix *-egi*. In standard Basque, there is but one morphophonemic rule to apply: elision of stem-final *a*. Some examples involving adjectives, adverbs, and nouns will serve to illustrate:

gora	high, loud	goregi	too high, too loud
maite	dear, beloved	maiteegi	too dear
txar	bad	txarregi	too bad
on	good	onegi	too good
gaizki	badly	gaizkiegi	too badly
gutxi	few	gutxiegi	too few
maiz	often	maizegi	too often
ongi	well	ongiegi	too well
abere	beast	abereegi	too much of a beast
asto	ass	astoegi	too much of an ass
gizon	man	gizonegi	too much of a man
haur	child	haurregi	too much of a child

The only instance of suppletion is *gehiegi* 'too many', 'too much', excessive of *asko* 'many', 'much'. It has two synonyms in southern Batua: *sobera* of eastern provenance and *larregi* (or its stem *lar*) of Biscayan origin.

Case endings follow *-egi* where adjectives are concerned but precede it in the case of nouns: *hiri handiegira* 'to the too big city', but *gogoanegi* (*MEIG* IX, 28) 'too much in mind'.

The suffix *-egi*, while holding sway over a large central region within the Basque-speaking territory, does not extend to the easternmost or westernmost areas. The eastern Basques (Azkue, 1923–1925, I, sec. 337, p. 218) make use of preposed *sobera*: *sobera handi* rather than *handiegi*; and in western Biscay, preposed *lar* is employed: *lar handia* instead of *handiegia*.

26.6.2 Excessives and Adverbs of Degree

In southern parlance, excessives are utterly incompatible with adverbs of degree. In northern usage, on the contrary, the same adverbs occurring with comparatives also appear with excessives, as does the suffix *-xe*: *handixeegi* 'a little too big', *gehixeegi* 'a little too much'. The Baztanese dialect, from which *EGL* has borrowed its example sentence *New York aise handiegia da* (*EGL* 461) 'New York is much too big' enjoys a middle position in that it admits *aise* as the sole adverb of degree modifying excessives.

As a matter of fact, southern usage reflects the situation in Spanish, where *demasiado* 'too' cannot be modified in any way, whereas the north matches the French state of affairs, where phrases such as *beaucoup trop grand* and *un peu trop grand* are commonplace.

26.6.3 Syntax of Excessives

Just like comparatives, excessives form an exception to the rule stated in section 1.3.3 according to which nominal or adjectival predicates in construction with the copula *izan* must take the article *-a*. With excessive nouns and adjectives, not used as an attribute, use of the article is optional (*EGL* 128):

(74) a. Etxe hori handiegi da zuretzat. (*EGL* 128)
That house is too big for you.
b. Berritsuegi da langile ona izateko. (*EGLU* I, 294)
He is too garrulous to be a good worker.

Excessives can appear attributively:

(75) a. Jantzi ederregia da hau zuretzat. (*EGLU* I, 293)
This is too beautiful a dress for you.
b. Ikusmin gehiegiak galtzen gaitu. (Orixe, *Q.A.* 161)
Excessive curiosity ruins us.

Just like the quantifiers *gutxi* 'few' and *asko* 'much' themselves, their excessives *gutxiegi* and *gehiegi* require the bare form of the preceding noun phrase they are in construction with: *ardo gutxiegi* 'too little wine', *jende gehiegi* 'too many people'. The situation is similar for *gehiegi*'s synonym *larregi*: *eskale larregi* 'too many beggars' (also: *eskalerik lar*). The eastern quantifier *sobera*, usually preposed, optionally follows a noun phrase in the absolutive case: *ezti sobera jatea* (Ax. 137) 'eating too much honey' but only *sobera liburuz mintzo zen* 'he spoke about too many books'.

Quite frequently, excessive predicates co-occur with nonfinite purpose clauses ending in *-tzeko* (section 7.2.3):

(76) a. Gazteegi zara hiltzeko. (Oñederra, 142)
You are too young to die.
b. Narrasegi nago honelako etxe txukunean sartzeko. (Etxaniz, *Antz*. 86)
I am too shabby to enter such a neat house.
c. Goizegi da ... igaro berria dugun mende erdia aztertzeko eta epaitzeko. (*MEIG* IV, 31)
It is too early to examine and judge the half century we have just passed through.

As happens in English and many other languages, the use of excessives in a negative context is normally interpreted as an understatement rather than expressing real excessiveness:

(77) a. Ez gaitu gehiegi maite euskaldunok. (*MEIG* VIII, 75 = *MIH* 270)
He doesn't love us Basques too much.
b. Elizgizonek ez dute maiteegi izan Euskara. (*MEIG* IV, 116)
Clerics have not loved the Basque language too much.

26.7 The Suffix of Approximation: *-tsu*

A homonym of the suffix of abundance discussed in section 8.7, the suffix *-tsu* of approximation can be employed with various types of words and sometimes phrases to express the meaning 'approximately'. We find *-tsu* used with the following:

1. Numerals and numeral phrases, as long as the notion of approximateness makes pragmatic sense: *hogeitsu* 'around twenty', *berrehuntsu* 'around two hundred', *milatsu* 'around one thousand', *bost urtetsu* 'about five years'.
2. Interrogatives: *nortsu* 'roughly who', *zertsu* 'roughly what', *nontsu* 'whereabouts', *noratsu* 'to about where', *noiztsu* 'around when', *noizkotsu* 'by about when', *nolatsu* 'roughly how', *zenbatsu* 'about how many'. Some examples are

(78) a. Oxalde: nortsu zen eta zertsu bizitza eraman zuen. (Oxobi, 189)
Oxalde: (roughly) who he was and (roughly) what kind of life he led.
b. Hona zertsu zioen. (*DRA* 9, 3970)
Here is roughly what he said.

c. Lehendik ba omen zekien nontsu egoten ziren karabineroak. (Salaberria, 17)
He was said to know from before whereabouts the border guards used to be.
d. Laborariak aski du jakitea noiztsu egiten diren lanak. (Duvoisin, *Lab.* 202–203)
It is enough for the farmer to know roughly when the jobs are done.
e. Zenbatsu urte dituzu? (Azkue, *DVEF* II, 430)
Roughly how old are you?

3. Deictic manner adverbs: *honelatsu, horrelatsu, halatsu* 'roughly this' (cf. section 11.1.6).
4. Some comparative postpositions: *bezalatsu* 'roughly similar', *hainbatsu, bezainbatsu,* both meaning 'roughly as much as'.
5. Some comparative adverbs: *berdintsu, orobatsu, paretsu,* all meaning 'roughly the same'.
6. Certain time adverbs and phrases: *oraintsu* 'recently', *bateratsu* 'almost simultaneously', *urte honen hastapentsuan* 'around the beginning of this year', *urte honen azkentsuan* 'around the end of this year', *ordutsu hartan* 'around that time', *zer ordutsutan?* 'around what time?'.
7. The location nouns *inguru* and *erdi*: *ingurutsuan* 'more or less in the neighborhood', *erditsuan* 'in about the middle', *erditsu* 'about half'—for example, *ordu erditsuko isilaldia* (Rv 8:1) 'a silence of about half an hour'.
8. Forms based on the superlative *gehien* 'most'. Although *gehientsuak* might be expected to be a mitigation of *gehienak* 'most (of them)', in practice the two forms are largely synonymous. Nor is there a difference in meaning with the pleonastic form *gehientsuenak*, quite common in southern usage. The same is true for the locative forms *gehienetan*, *gehientsuetan*, and *gehientsuenetan*, all meaning 'in most cases', 'mostly'.

26.8 The Suffix of Precision: *-xe*

Deictics optionally take the suffix *-xe* to indicate precision, especially when they are focus or, much more rarely, topic of their clause, or are contained within a phrase with one of those functions.

Forms bearing this suffix will be called emphatics. The term "deictics" is meant to cover demonstrative adverbs, demonstrative pronouns, deictic manner adverbs including *bezala* (section 26.1), and deictic time adverbs such as *orain* and *orduan*, as well as punctual time clauses.

26.8.1 Morphology of Emphatics

First of all, let us note that two of the sandhi rules of section 1.2.6 are relevant here. According to sandhi rule 5, *-xe* turns into *-txe* when following *-n* or *-r*. Sandhi rule 2 applies in part only. A plosive (*k*) will indeed drop before *-xe*, which, however, does not turn into *-txe*. The main emphatic forms of the demonstrative adverb paradigm will illustrate:

hementxe	hortxe	hantxe
hemendixe	hortixe	handixe
honaxe	horraxe	haraxe

The elided *k* in the elative forms may be reestablished at the end of the form: *hemendixek*, *hortixek*, *handixek*. Alternatively, *hementxetik*, *hortxetik*, *hantxetik* can be used.

In the oblique cases of the demonstrative pronouns, the suffix *-xe*, as a rule, precedes the case ending, as seen in the following paradigms:

Basic Cases: Singular

Absolutive	hauxe	horixe	huraxe
Ergative	honexek	horrexek	harexek
Dative	honexeri	horrexeri	harexeri
Genitive	honexen	horrexen	harexen
Sociative	honexekin	horrexekin	harexekin
Instrumental	honexetaz	horrexetaz	harexetaz

In the dative and the sociative, *-xe* may also follow the case ending: *honixe*, *horrixe*, *harixe*; *honekintxe*, *horrekintxe*, *harekintxe*.

The emphatic benefactive is based on the emphatic genitive: *honexentzat*, *horrexentzat*, *harexentzat*.

The emphatic motivational can be formed in two ways: either by adding *-xe* to the plain motivational: *honegatixe*, *horregatixe*, *hargatixe*; or by starting from the emphatic genitive with or without its final *-n*: *honexe(n)gatik*, *horrexe(n)gatik*, *harexe(n)gatik*.

Basic Cases: Plural

Absolutive	hauexek	horiexek	haiexek
Ergative	hauexek	horiexek	haiexek
Dative	hauexei	horiexei	haiexei
Genitive	hauexen	horiexen	haiexen
Sociative	hauexekin	horiexekin	haiexekin
Instrumental	hauexetaz	horiexetaz	haiexetaz

The same remarks apply as in the singular paradigm. Thus the suffix *-xe* may follow the case ending in the dative and sociative: *haueixe*, *horieixe*, *haieixe*; *hauekintxe*, *horiekintxe*, *haiekintxe*.

The emphatic benefactive is based on the emphatic genitive here too: *hauexentzat*, *horiexentzat*, *haiexentzat*.

Again, the emphatic motivational can be formed in two ways: either by adding *-xe* to the plain motivational: *hauegatixe*, *horiegatixe*, *haiegatixe*; or by starting from the emphatic genitive with or without its final *-n*: *hauexe(n)gatik*, *horiexe(n)gatik*, *haiexe(n)gatik*.

Locative Cases: Singular

Inessive	honetantxe	horretantxe	hartantxe
	honexetan	horrexetan	harexetan
Elative	honetatixe	horretatixe	hartatixe
	honexetatik	horrexetatik	harexetatik
Allative	honetaraxe	horretaraxe	hartaraxe
	honexetara	horrexetara	harexetara
Terminal	honetarainoxe	horretarainoxe	hartarainoxe
	honexetaraino	horrexetaraino	harexetaraino

Locative Cases: Plural

Inessive	hauetantxe	horietantxe	haietantxe
	hauexetan	horiexetan	haiexetan
Elative	hauetatixe	horietatixe	haietatixe
	hauexetatik	horiexetatik	haiexetatik
Allative	hauetaraxe	horietaraxe	haietaraxe
	hauexetara	horiexetara	haiexetara
Terminal	hauetarainoxe	horietarainoxe	haietarainoxe
	hauexetaraino	horiexetaraino	haiexetaraino

As these paradigms show, in the locative emphatics the suffix *-xe* may either follow or precede the case ending.

The animate forms involving *-gan* (*-gandik*, *-gana*, *-ganaino*) are based on the emphatic genitive, with or without its *n*: *honexe(n)gan*, and so on. In the inessive, there is also *hone-gantxe*, *horregantxe*, and so on.

The synonymous construction with *baitan* can be constructed either with the emphatic genitive or with the emphatic absolutive: *honexen baitan* or *hauxe baitan*, and so on. The situation is similar for *baitarik*, *baitara*, *baitaraino*.

The emphatic deictic manner adverbs present no problems: *honelaxe*, *horrelaxe*, *halaxei*, *bezalaxe*.

Among time adverbs, the following have emphatic forms:

berehala	at once	berehalaxe	instantly
orain	now	oraintxe	right now
orduan	then	orduantxe	right then
ordutik	since then	ordutixe	exactly since then

Furthermore, all adnominal forms allow the suffix *-xe*: *hemengoxe*, *horkoxe*, *hangoxe*, *honetakoxe* (or *honexatako*), *horretakoxe* (or *horrexetako*), *honelakoxe*, *berehalakoxe*, *oraingoxe*, *ordukoxe*, *ordurakoxe*, and so on.

26.8.2 Use of Emphatics

While emphatics are known in the entire Basque-speaking area, their frequency decreases markedly from west to east. Thus in the Biscayan dialect their use is very common, less so in Guipuzcoan, and even less in High Navarrese and the northern dialects. With respect to the latter, it is telltale that the suffix *-xe* is nowhere mentioned in Lafitte's *Grammaire basque* (1962), although Haize Garbia's more recent *Grammaire basque pour tous* (1978) does cite *holaxe* 'ainsi même' (just so) and *oraintxe* 'maintenant même' (right now) (p. 44), and also mentions exclamations such as *Hauxe da komedia!* 'quelle comédie!' (what a comedy!) (p. 52). As to the factors, if any, constraining the use of emphatics in the eastern area, nothing much can be averred on account of their rareness of occurrence.

Shifting our attention to the western area, where emphatics are far from rare, we find that pragmatic concepts involving topic and focus appear to be a paramount factor governing their distribution. According to the Biscayan grammarian A. Arejita, emphatics are restricted to focus phrases (1985, 32, 33), a statement corroborated by an overwhelming majority of examples:

(79) a. Halaxe jokatuko nuela esan nion neure buruari. (Atxaga, *Behi* 138)
I said to myself that I would act just so.
b. Hauxe agintzen dizuet: maita dezazuela elkar. (Jn 15:17)
This is what I command yoû: that yoû love one another.
c. Eta Mitxelenak berak ere horixe egingo du. (*MEIG* VI, 182)
And that is what Mitxelena himself will do also.
d. Horretxek ez du beharbada gehiegi poztuko. (*TOE* II, 55)
Just that is perhaps what won't make her too happy.
e. Urte horiexetan argitara zen Bilbon *Eguna* egunkaria. (*MEIG* VI, 26)
It was just in those years that the daily *Eguna* was published in Bilbao.
f. Gure amak holakoxe aldarteak izaten zituen. (Garate, *Esku* 45)
My mother tended to have just such changes in feelings.
g. Afaldu ordukoxe oheratu ziren gau hartan guztiak. (T. Agirre, *Uzt.* 73)
That night everyone went to bed right after eating supper.

Another Biscayan grammarian, E. Osa (1990, 45), amended Arejita's statement, quite correctly claiming that emphatics can also occur as topics, either preposed or extraposed:

(80) a. Bada horretxek hiri, seaskakoa hintzela, hainbeste on egin zian. (Arrue, *G.B.* 127)
Well now, that very person did yoú so much good while yoú were a baby in the cradle.
b. Merezi luke, ba, horretxek bertso bat. (Urruzuno, *E.Z.* 30)
That very person would deserve a verse.

It may be noted that emphatic topics cannot co-occur with a marked focus: **Liburu hauxe nork irakurriko du?* 'Who will read this very book?'; **Liburu hauxe apaiz horretxek* *irakurriko du* 'Precisely that priest will read this very book.' But why these sentences are greatly improved when *ere* 'also' is added to the topic remains a mystery.

26.9 Manner Expressions

26.9.1 Use of the Noun *era* 'manner' and Its Synonyms

The Basque terms for 'manner' are *era* and *modu* in southern usage and *gisa* and *molde*, also meaning 'form', in the north. When used adverbially, they take indifferently the locative *-an* or the allative *-ra*; in the north they also take the instrumental *-z*, while *gisa* can also dispense with case endings: *era horretan* 'in that way'; *era guztietara* 'in every way'; *komediante moduan* 'in the manner of a comedian'; *frantzes modura* 'in the French way'; *gisa honetan* 'in this way'; *nahi zuten gisara* 'in the way they wanted'; *zenbat gisaz?* 'in how many ways?'; *Euskal herriko seme gisa* 'in the manner of a son of the Basque Country'; *neure molde apurrean* 'in my own little way'.

To specify the action that the manner in question applies to, either a relative clause or a nonfinite noun complement in *-tzeko* can be used: *indiarrek ogia egiten duten modua* 'the manner in which the Indians make bread', *mintzatzeko modu hutsa* 'a mere manner of speaking'.

Adnominals, genitives, and bare absolutives can also occur as premodifiers: *baserriko modura* 'in the manner of the farm'; *kristau fidelen moduan* (S. Mitxelena, *IG* II, 122), *kristau fidel moduan* (S. Mitxelena, *IG* II, 118) 'in the manner of loyal Christians'.

An important southern locution is *ze(r) modu(z)*, roughly synonymous with *nola* 'how'. There is no counterpart with *era, gisa*, or *molde*.

(81) a. Zer modu dago alaba? (*TOE* I, 66)
How is your daughter?
b. Zer moduz dihoa gerra hori? (Salaberria, 65)
How is that war going?

Unlike *nola*, it can be used in elliptic utterances, without a verb:

(82) a. Abaltzisketan zer modu? (Muxika, *P.Am.* 47)
How is it in Abaltzisketa?
b. Zer moduz, Angel? (*LBB* 144)
How are you, Angel?

26.9.2 Deverbal Compounds with *era*

The noun *era* meaning 'manner' acts as a parasuffix in southern Basque, combining with verb radicals. The resulting noun denotes the manner in which the action is carried out, but it may also come to indicate the action itself. Except for *jantzi*, bisyllabic verbs ending in *-i* make use of the perfect participle instead of the radical: *hasiera*, *haziera*, *heziera*. After radicals ending in a sibilant or affricate, a *k* will be intercalated and the affricate simplified to the corresponding sibilant: *ikuskera*, *idazkera*, *sineskera*. After radicals ending in a nasal, *k* is likewise intercalated, except when the radical is identical to the perfect participle, in which case the *n* is simply dropped: *egoera*, *esaera*, *izaera*, but exceptionally *egikera*.

Two lists of examples will be presented. In the first, the manner sense is still discernible, in the second, the derivation merely denotes the action or state itself.

aditu	to hear, to understand	adiera	understanding, meaning, attention
aldatu	to change	aldaera	variation, variant
amaitu	to end	amaiera	ending, end
bizi (izan)	to live	biziera	lifestyle, way of life
bukatu	to end	bukaera	ending, end
ebaki	to cut	ebakera	way of cutting, pronunciation
egin	to do	egikera	way of acting, style, act
egokitu	to adapt, to adjust	egokiera	adaptation, opportunity
egon	to stay	egoera	situation, state
erabili	to use	erabilera	manner of use, utilization
erantzun	to answer	erantzuera	way of answering, answer
esan	to say	esaera	expression, saying
hartu	to receive	harrera	reception
hasi	to begin	hasiera	beginning
hazi	to grow, to raise	haziera	cultivation, education
hezi	to tame, to train	heziera	taming, training, education
hitz egin	to speak	hizkera	way of speaking, speech
ibili	to walk	ibilera	walk, gait
idatzi	to write	idazkera	style of writing, spelling
ikusi	to see	ikuskera	outlook, view, vision
irten	to go out	irteera	way out, exit, solution, departure
izan	to be	izaera	way of being, personality, character
jantzi	to clothe, to dress	janzkera	way of dressing, dress style, fashion
jarri	to place, to put	jarrera	stance, attitude
jokatu	to play, to act	jokaera	manner of playing, behavior, conduct
orraztu	to comb, to groom	orrazkera	hairdo, hairstyle
pentsatu	to think	pentsaera	way of thinking, mentality, thought
portatu	to behave	portaera	behavior, conduct
prestatu	to prepare	prestaera	manner of preparation, preparation
sartu	to enter	sarrera	way in, entrance, ticket, introduction
sortu	to generate, to conceive	sorrera	origin, generation, conception

bildu	to gather, to collect	bilera	gathering, meeting
entzun	to hear	entzuera	fame, reputation
etorri	to come	etorrera	coming, arrival
eskatu	to ask for	eskaera	request, petition
ezagutu	to be acquainted	ezaguera	knowledge, acquaintance, consciousness
galdetu	to ask	galdera	question

galdu	to lose	galera	loss, ruin, defeat, perdition
gelditu	to stop	geldiera	stop, halt
gertatu	to happen	gertaera	happening, event
gertutu	to prepare	gertuera	preparation
igo	to go up, to climb	igoera	ascension, climb
ilundu	to darken	ilunkera	dusk, nightfall
itxi	to close	itxiera	closing, shutdown
jo	to hit, to head (for)	joera	tendency, inclination, leaning
laburtu	to shorten	laburrera	abbreviation
sinetsi	to believe	sineskera	belief
utzi	to abandon	utziera	abandonment

[*N.B.* From the noun *gorputz* 'body' has been derived *gorpuzkera* 'build', 'physical constitution'.]

26.9.3 Deadjectival Nouns with *-era*

Some adjectives can be turned into names for the corresponding property by adding a suffix *-era*, related or not to *era* 'manner'. These adjectives include all those measuring the dimensions of an object, but some others as well:

altu	high	altuera	height
garai	high	garaiera	height
geldi	quiet, slow	geldiera	quiet, slowness
goi	high	goiera	height
gor	deaf	gorrera	deafness
handi	big	handiera	bigness, size
isil	still, silent	isilera	stillness, silence
itsu	blind	itsuera	blindness
labur	short, brief	laburrera	shortness, brevity
lodi	thick	lodiera	thickness
luze	long	luzera	length
sakon	deep	sakonera	depth
sor	numb	sorrera	numbness
zabal	wide, broad	zabalera	width, breadth

26.10 Vocabulary

aberats	rich
alferkeria	laziness
aztal	calf, heel
bakan	rare
bakartasun	solitude

basamortu	desert
berriz	again, on the contrary
edari	drink
egiazki	really, truly
gaixo	poor, miserable, sick
goiz	early
inguratu	to surround
iragan	to pass
izter	thigh
izugarrizko	terribly
jatetxe	restaurant
jolas egin	to play
lagunarte	society, company
larri	big, grave, serious, urgent
lirain	graceful, svelte
lodi	thick, fat
merezi	to deserve
min	dear, intimate
pozoi(n)	poison
sakondu	to deepen, to delve into
tristura	sadness

26.11 Exercises

26.11.1 Translate into English

1. Ba ote da geure burua adiskide minez inguraturik ikustea bezain gauza ederrik? (*MEIG* I, 82)
2. Maita nazazu bada, nik zaitudan hainbat. (Bilintx, 93)
3. Mirenek izugarrizko aztal lodiak ditu eta izterrak areagoak.
4. Gauza horiek ahazteko, edari pixka bat adinakorik ez da. (*LBB* 87)
5. Zu zara munduan maiteena zaitudana; zu zara maiteena izatea merezi duzuna. (Bilintx, 194)
6. Pozarik handienetatik tristurarik larrieneraino iragan nintzen. (Haranburu, *Its*. 94)
7. Nahi adina jolas egin dun nirekin: hi nire katu, ni hire xagu. (*LBB* 238)
8. Malentxo zen bezain lirain eta eder gutxi izaten dira. (T. Agirre, *Uzt*. 53)
9. Neskatxa gaixoa inoizko lodiena egin zen.
10. Beharren dudana berehalaxe erostea nahiagoko nuke.
11. Euskara zenbat eta gehiago sakondu, hainbat eta ederrago aurkitzen dugu.
12. Ez da izurririk, ez eta ere pozoinik, alferkeriak bezainbat kalte egiten duenik. (Etxeberri Sarakoa, 182)

26.11.2 Translate into Basque

1. My husband is richer than I thought.
2. Most women know a lot more than their husbands.
3. We love company more than the solitude of the desert.
4. Who is the prettiest lady that you have ever known?
5. Is Carmen really as pretty as her father says?
6. This word is extremely rare.
7. Basque always used to be spoken there, much more than today.
8. You order the most expensive dish in the cheapest restaurant, I, on the contrary, the cheapest one in the most expensive one.
9. We must buy as little as possible.
10. It was too early to go to see anybody.
11. Whereabouts have yoû left yoûr witches?
12. Where could I find better students than yoû?

27 Use of the Instrumental Case

27.1 Introduction; Instrumentals Expressing Means

The case ending -*z*, introduced in section 2.2.1, was termed "médiatif" by Inchauspe in 1858 (*Le verbe basque*, 8). While this term is still used by P. Lafitte in his *Grammaire basque* (1962, 55), it has been replaced among modern Basque grammarians by the designation "instrumental," already in vogue well before 1920 according to H. Gavel: ". . . le *z* est simplement la désinence caractéristique du cas de la déclinaison basque que certains appellent *instrumental* et qui a divers emplois, dont quelques-uns sont analogues à ceux de l'ablatif latin" (. . . the *z* is simply the ending of the case in the Basque declension that some call "instrumental" and which has various uses, some of which are analogous to the Latin ablative) (1920, 153).

Because of its multifarious uses, the instrumental is the hardest of all Basque cases to deal with in semantic terms. As a result of my investigations, it seems to me that its core meaning is that of "means" and "cause," but that, in addition, it serves (or has served) as a default case to be employed when no other case is appropriate. Hence the astonishing variety of its uses, which the reader will find reflected in the organization of this chapter:

27.1 Instrumentals Expressing Means
27.2 Instrumentals Expressing Cause or Motive
27.3 Instrumental Predicatives
27.4 Instrumentals Expressing Manner
27.5 Instrumentals Expressing Criteria
27.6 Instrumentals Measuring Differences
27.7 Instrumentals Relating to Time
27.8 Instrumentals Governed by Postpositions
27.9.3 Instrumentals Expressing Aboutness
27.10 Instrumental Complements
27.11 Nonfinite Instrumental Clauses

For several of these uses the instrumental is not the only option available. In many areas of the country, especially the southern ones, the instrumental has become somewhat archaic and tends to be replaced by other cases. The sociative, in particular, may substitute for the instrumental in many of its uses. Paradoxically, it is in the rendering of the concept of means that the sociative's competition is most noticeable. In the spoken language of the south, the sociative is absolutely predominant, and the instrumental, if used at all in this function, assumes the character of a derivational suffix shaped *-z*, turning some nouns into adverbs.

In the northern colloquial, the instrumental occurs more freely. Expressions of moderate complexity, such as *harri batez hil* 'to kill with one stone' or *ganibet zorrotzez ebaki* 'to cut with a sharp knife' are common even in ordinary conversation. Yet, more complex indications of means will normally be expressed using the sociative.

Written practice, however, can often be seen to diverge considerably from spoken usage in this respect, especially in the south. An explanation can be found in a near-general consensus among linguistically sophisticated persons to the effect that the current preference for the sociative represents an unfortunate development brought on by the eclecticism of the Spanish preposition *con* or its French counterpart *avec*. In other words, use of the sociative as a substitute for the instrumental constitutes a romanism to be avoided in polished style. Accordingly, Mitxelena, one of the founding fathers of Euskara Batua, recommended in 1968: "The so-called instrumental, I think, we should try to keep. With regard to that ... one should point out that *ezpataz jo* 'to hit with the sword' is more proper (lit. "more pure," *garbiago*) than *ezpatarekin jo*" ("Euskararen batasun bideak," *MEIG* VII, 150; translation mine). Therefore, writers influenced by this point of view will tend to encode the notion of means by an instrumental phrase, regardless of complexity. Since our example sentences are taken from actual texts, the reader should be aware of this point.

As the category of means encompasses a wide variety of semantic functions, I have found it convenient to divide the subject matter into several subcategories to be discussed under separate headings. Exhaustiveness being rather hard to achieve in this case, some arbitrariness may be condoned in my choice of the following seven headings: Instrumentals Denoting Implements (27.1.1), Instrumentals Denoting the Material for Performing the Action (27.1.2), Body Parts Acting as Means (27.1.3), Instrumentals Denoting Mediative Action (27.1.4), Instrumentals Denoting Means of Expression (27.1.5), Instrumentals Denoting Means of Conveyance (27.1.6), and Instrumentals Denoting Medium of Transportation (27.1.7). To these, two more subsections have been added: one to deal with the pattern *N-z N* (27.1.8), which links up with section 27.1.7 in describing motion through intermediate points, and a final section on instrumental postpositions expressing means (27.1.9).

Finally, lest it remain buried among the details of the coming investigations, I wish here to highlight an interesting result: *The distinction between alienable and inalienable posses-*

sion is seen to play a role in Basque grammar, inasmuch as indefinite instrumentals allow a genitival modifier only if the latter expresses inalienable possession.

27.1.1 Instrumentals Denoting Implements

It seems fitting to start our explorations into the use of the instrumental case by examining prototypical instrumentality, that is, a situation where a concrete object serves as a means to carry out the action of the verb. The examples will be listed without comment, in increasing order of phrasal complexity. As set forth in section 27.1, the more complex examples do not reflect spoken practice.

(1) a. Guraize zorrotzez, trist, trast, moztu zizkion goi-ezpaineko bizarrak. (*G.* 118)
With sharp scissors, snip, snap, she cut off the hairs of the mustache on his upper lip.
b. Burdinazko makilaz hautsiko dituzu. (Ps 2:9)
You will break them with an iron rod.
c. Txakurrak eginiko zauria osatzen da txakurraren ileaz. (*P.Ab.* 119)
The wound made by a dog is healed with the hair of the dog.
d. Perlaz eta diamantaren itxurako harri batzuez apaindu. (J. Etchepare, *Bur.* 136)
To decorate with pearls and some stones with the appearance of diamonds.
e. Lehortu gabeko zazpi soka berriz lotuko banindute, ahuldua geldituko nintzateke. (Jgs 16:7)
I would turn weak if they were to bind me with seven new ropes not yet dried.
f. Ezertarako erabili ez den sokaz ondo lotzen banaute, galdu egingo dut indarra. (Jgs 16:11; Ker.)
I will lose my strength if they bind me tightly with a rope that has not been used for anything.

27.1.2 Instrumentals Denoting the Material for Performing the Action

The material used as the basis for performing the action of the verb is generally expressed by an instrumental phrase. In fact, use of the instrumental here seems to be considerably more common than it is concerning implements. Our discussion will consist of two parts: the first dealing with verbs of production and the second with other verbs allowing this kind of instrumental.

Among the verbs of production listed in section 12.1.4, only the following are apt to state their starting material and thus permit the instrumental: *egin* 'to make', *eratu* 'to fashion', *moldatu* 'to form', *osatu* 'to put together'. The most general of these verbs, *egin*, allows even human material, as in example (2b) and also (2c), which literally means 'she made something else of herself'.

(2) a. Zazpi kriseilu egin zituen urre garbiz. (Ex 37:23)
He made seven lamps of pure gold.

b. Ez dakit zer egin neure haur gaixoez. (*TOE* II, 235)
I don't know what to do with my poor children.

c. Barbituriko pastila piloa irentsirik, bere buruaz beste egin du. (Garate, *Leh.* 88)
She has committed suicide, having swallowed a heap of barbiturate tablets.

d. Jainkoak gizonari kendu zion zatiaz emakume bat eratu zuen. (*E.H.* 226; cf. Gn 2:22; Ker.)
God fashioned a woman out of the piece He had taken from the man.

e. Jainko Jaunak lur-hautsez gizona moldatu zuen. (Gn 2:7)
The Lord God formed man from the dust of the earth.

f. Inguruko erdarek bestetandik harturiko gaiez osatzen dituzte beren hitz eskolatuak. (*MEIG* IV, 43 = *MIH* 86)
The surrounding tongues put together their learned words from material taken elsewhere.

While the instrumental here may be predominant, at least in written usage, the elative or sociative is also possible:

(3) a. Eta Jainko Jaunak Adami kendu zion saihets-hezurretik egin zuen emaztekia. (Gn 2:22; Dv)
And the Lord God made a woman from the rib bone He had taken from Adam.

b. Gizonari hartu saihets-hezurretik Jainko Jaunak emaztea eraiki zuen. (Gn 2:22; *Biblia*)
From the rib taken from the man the Lord God built a woman.

c. Hezur honekin lehenengo emakumea egin zuen. (*TZ* I, 13)
With this bone, He made the first woman.

Also many verbs not dealing with production are able to specify the material used in their performance, and preferably do so by means of an instrumental phrase. Examples (4a–h) are based on the following verbs: *apaindu* 'to decorate', *ase* 'to be satiated', *bete* 'to fill', *elikatu* 'to feed', *estali* 'to cover', *inguratu* 'to surround', *jantzi* 'to clothe', *kargatu* 'to load'.

(4) a. Hementxe aseko zara nire maitasunez; bertan apainduko zaitut zeruko dohainez. (*G.* 286)
Right here you will be sated with my love; this is where I will adorn you with gifts from heaven.

b. Bete itzazue ontziak urez. (Jn 2:7; *IB*)
Fill the vessels with water.

c. Irin garbiz, eztiz eta olioz elikatzen zinen. (Ez 16:13)
You were nourished with pure flour, honey, and oil.

d. Egipto guztia igelez estali zen. (*TZ* I, 111)
All Egypt became covered with frogs.

e. Lanbroak bere ganduz estaltzen zituen bazterrak. (*MEIG* IX, 94)
   The mist covered the surroundings with its haze.
f. Honetarako ingura daiteke hautserre beroz. (Iturriaga, *Dial.* 87)
   For that purpose, one can border it with hot ashes.
g. Izotzak arbolak zilarrez jantzi zituen. (*MEIG* IX, 103)
   The frost had clothed the trees with silver.
h. Abrahamek egurraz kargatu zuen Isaak. (Zerbitzari, 20)
   Abraham had loaded Isaac with the firewood.

A particularly common example of this construction is furnished by the verb *josi*, whose usual meaning is 'to sew', but if combined with an instrumental, it can take on the meaning 'to overwhelm', 'to shower':

(4) i. Ukabilkadaz josi zuten. (*E.H.* 463)
   They overwhelmed him with punches.

In particular, combined with a suitable instrumental, the definite form of the perfect participle *josia*, as well as the corresponding predicatives *josirik* and *josita*, occur as predicates expressing abundance: *arantzez josia* 'crammed with thorns', *balaz josia* 'riddled with bullets', *diruz josia* 'rolling in money', *izarrez josia* 'packed with stars', *zauriz josia* 'covered with wounds', *zorrez josia* 'burdened with debts'.

As we may recall from section 2.3.2, the indefinite form of a noun phrase or postpositional phrase (e.g., *etxe*, *etxeri*, *etxerekin*) has a highly restricted distribution because of syntactic constraints. In particular, mere semantic indefiniteness does not provide sufficient justification for its use.

Indefinite instrumentals, however, are exempt from the syntactic constraints other indefinites are subject to. Thus, whenever number distinction is inapplicable, as with mass nouns, or simply irrelevant, the indefinite instrumental will appear; witness *urre garbiz* 'of pure gold' in example (2a), *lur-hautsez* 'from the dust of the earth' in example (2e), or *urez* 'with water' in example (4b). Interestingly, in the following example from Genesis, in which the singular is made explicit in the preceding sentence (*saihets-hezur bat kendu zion* [Gn 2:21] 'He took from him one rib'), we find the indefinite form (optionally) used nonetheless:

(5) Jainko Jaunak gizonari kenduriko saihets-hezurrez emakumea moldatu eta gizonari eraman zion. (Gn 2:22)
   The Lord God fashioned a woman with the rib He had taken from the man and led her to the man.

As soon as a sociative or an elative is substituted for the instrumental, the definite form will be employed: *urre garbiarekin* 'with pure gold', *lur-hautsetik* 'from the dust of the earth', *saihets-hezurretik* (not *hezurretatik*) 'from the rib'. No alternative exists for the instrumental complement of the verb *bete* 'to fill': only *urez*, not *urarekin* is possible in (4b).

Except in cases of inalienable possession (cf. section 27.1.3), as exemplified by *nire maitasunez* 'with my love' in (4a), or *bere ganduz* 'with its haze' in (4e), where *bere* 'its' must refer to *lanbro* 'mist', an instrumental denoting material cannot be preceded by a possessive phrase. A sociative or an elative must appear instead: *nire urre garbiarekin egina* or *nire urre garbitik egina* 'made from (or *with*) my pure gold', not **nire urre garbi(a)z egina.*

27.1.3 Body Parts Acting as Means

Instrumental noun phrases whose head denotes a part of the body can assume several semantic functions, all relating to the notion of means. Three main functions may be distinguished. The body part may serve as a tool for carrying out a concrete action, a means of perception, or a means of expression. As means of expression will be discussed separately in section 27.1.5, the present section only needs to deal with body parts as tools or perceptive organs. As to these, we are dealing, of course, with the seats of the senses: *begi* 'eye', *belarri* 'ear', *sudur* 'nose', *mihi* 'tongue'. For our syntactic investigation, we may confine our attention to *begi* 'eye' as being the most common representative of this set. Similarly, *esku* 'hand' will serve as a typical example of a body part used as a tool. In the following discussion, *esku* 'hand' and *begi* 'eye' will be treated together, as their syntactic properties when used as part of instrumental phrases appear to be largely the same. Without any difference in meaning, either a definite or an indefinite instrumental can be used, both for *esku* 'hand' and *begi* 'eye':

(6) a. ... eskuaz lepoa igurzten ziolarik. (Bilbao, 64)
... while he was patting his neck with the hand.
b. Eskuaz har ditzakezue galburuak. (Dt 23:26)
Yoû may take ears by hand.

(7) a. Horma zulatu nuen eskuz. (Ez 12:7)
I made a hole through the wall by hand.
b. Begi, oin eta eskuz keinuak egiten ditu engainatzeko. (Prv 6:13)
With eyes, feet, and hands he makes gestures in order to deceive.

(8) a. ... begiez nola zenekusan zure jabe handia. (*LVP* I-126)
... how with the eyes you saw your great master.
b. ... begiez ez ikusteko, belarriez ez entzuteko, buruaz ez konprenitzeko. (Mt 13:15; *EAB*)
... so as not to see with the eyes, not to hear with the ears, not to understand with the head.

(9) a. Ez ditut begiz ikusi nahi. (*TOE* II, 79)
I don't want to see them with the eyes.

b. ... begiz ez ikusteko, eta belarriz ez entzuteko; ... (Mt 13:15; *IB*)
... so as not to see with the eyes, and not to hear with the ears; ...

Both these options are still available when the instrumental has a possessive modifier:

(10) a. ... bere eskuez egin dituen ontzien pean. (Lapeyre, 51)
... under the ships that he has made with his own hands.
b. ... bere eskuz desegin. (Prv 14:1)
... destroy with her own hands.

(11) a. Bere eskuz eramango du. (Lv 7:30)
He shall carry it with his own hands.
b. Neure eskuz idazten dizuet. (Gal 6:11)
I am writing to yoû with my own hand.

(12) a. Zeure begiez ikusi baduzu ere, ... (Prv 25:7)
Even if you have seen it with your own eyes, ...
b. Ez bezate beren begiez ikus, ... (Mt 13:15)
Let them not see with their eyes, ...

(13) a. Bakoitzak bere begiz ikusten ditu gauzak. (E. Larre in Xalbador, *Odol.* 15)
Each person sees things with his own eyes.
b. Gauza harrigarri haiek egiak ziren ala ez, bere begiz egiaztatzeko gogoa sortu zitzaion. (T. Agirre, *Uzt.* 174)
A desire arose in him to verify with his own eyes whether those amazing things were true or not.

The free occurrence of the indefinite instrumental in these examples is interesting and requires comment. As explained in section 27.1.2, a general propensity of the instrumental to the indefinite where semantic indefiniteness or irrelevance is involved will account for examples such as (7a,b) and (9a,b). Examples (11a,b) and (13a,b), however, present a problem. In general, a possessive modifier induces the definite form of the phrase modified. This statement is true even for the instrumental:

(14) Heure mailuaz jo ezak etsai oro. (Mirande, *Po.* 69)
Hit all enemies with yoúr hammer. (For *heure*, see section 6.1.3.)

Here, according to my informants, the indefinite *heure mailuz* is impossible.

What then accounts for examples (11a,b) and (13a,b)? To all appearances, Basque grammar at this point distinguishes between alienable and inalienable possession. Only in case of the latter is an indefinite instrumental admissible—although not obligatory, as shown by examples (10a,b) and (12a,b). Obviously, body parts are a paradigm example of inalienably possessed items; examples of a different type will be seen in section 27.1.4. Although complex instrumental phrases tend to be avoided, instrumentals involving adjectives, numerals, or demonstratives can be found and are acceptable to many speakers:

(15) a. Gauza hilkorrak bakarrik egin ditzake bere esku gaiztoez. (Ws 15:17)
He can make only mortal things with his evil hands.
b. Bere esku kutsatuz hartu zituen ontzi sakratuak. (2 Mc 5:16)
He took the sacred vessels with his impure hands.
c. Beraiek ez dituzte behatz batez ere mugitu nahi. (Mt 23:4; *EAB*)
They themselves don't want to move them even with one finger.
d. Ene begi hauetaz berriz ikusiko zaitut. (Lapeyre, 262)
With these mine eyes I will see you again.

To conclude this section, a few noteworthy idioms involving *begiz* will be listed:

begiz jo	to take a look at, to glance at, to choose
begiz galdu	to lose sight of
ezin begiz ikusi	to hate the sight of, to loathe
begi onez ikusi	to approve
begi gaiztoz ikusi	to disapprove
begi txarrez ikusi	to disapprove

27.1.4 Instrumentals Denoting Mediative Action

So far, we have considered means embodied in concrete objects: tools, materials, body parts. This is an unwarranted limitation. Instead of a concrete object, an instrumental phrase may denote an action represented as a means helping to perform the action encoded by the main verb. Examples of such mediative action are

(16) a. Musu batez saltzen al duzu Gizonaren Semea? (Lk 22:48)
Is it with a kiss that you betray the Son of man?
b. Judasenak nagusitu ziren Jainkoaren laguntzaz. (2 Mc 12:11)
Judas's men prevailed with God's help.
c. Inork bere iritziz eta burubidez lagundu nahi badigu, mila esker. (*MEIG* I, 87 = *MIH* 141)
Many thanks if anyone wants to help us with his opinions and advice.

In examples (16b,c) the instrumental has a possessive modifier in which the possessor represents the agent of the mediative action. The identity of this agent, however, is to be considered a defining part of the action; if changed, the mediative action will change with it. Here too, therefore, we may speak of inalienable possession, so that the indefinite instrumental in these examples is explained in the same way as in section 27.1.3.

27.1.5 Instrumentals Denoting Means of Expression

Instrumentals denoting means of expression most often consist of single words. In many cases, they are hard to distinguish from manner adverbs. The following instrumentals are to be considered means of expression:

egitez	in deed, in fact
hitzez	in word, verbally (*hitz batez* 'in one word')
izkribuz	in writing
keinuz	by gestures, winking
seinalez	by signs

Some bodily organs may serve as means of expression:

ahoz	by mouth, orally (*aho batez* 'unanimously')
ezpainez	with the lips
mihiz	with the tongue

And, as opposed to the preceding: *bihotzez* 'with the heart', 'sincerely'.

Languages constitute a means of expression par excellence:

alemanez	in German (also *alemanieraz*)
arabieraz	in Arabic
errusieraz	in Russian
espainieraz	in Spanish
euskaraz	in Basque (*euskara batuaz* 'in Unified Basque')
frantsesez	in French
gaztelaniaz	in Castilian
ingelesez	in English

The term *erdaraz* also deserves to be listed. *Erdara* originally denoted any language other than Basque, but nowadays it is taken to refer more specifically to the language in competition with Basque: French in the north and Spanish in the south.

[*N.B.* Adjectival use of language names requires the use of the adnominal suffix *-ko*: *ingelesezko liburuak* 'English books'. Yet *euskara* and *erdara* also allow an alternative construction: use of a nominal compound: *euskal liburuak* 'Basque books', *erdal liburuak* 'non-Basque books'.]

Let us end with some sentences that illustrate the use of the instrumental as a means of expression:

(17) a. Poe-ren hitzez azal dezakegu. (*MEIG* V, 138 = *MIH* 297)
We can explain it with the words of Poe.

b. Herri honek ezpainez ohoratzen nau. (Mt 15:8 = Mk 7:6)
This people honors me with the lips.

c. Hizkuntza arrotzez hitzegingo diot herri honi. (1 Cor 14:21)
I will speak to this people in a foreign language.

d. Setazko ahotsez oso lasai mintzatu zitzaidan. (Garate, *Alaba* 58)
He spoke to me very calmly in a persistent voice.

e. Ez da gai izaten beste euskalkiz mintzatzeko, ahoz nahiz izkribuz. (*MEIG* VII, 135 = *MIH* 95)
As a rule, he isn't able to speak in another Basque dialect, either orally or in writing.

27.1.6 Instrumentals Denoting Means of Conveyance

Nouns denoting a vehicle or some other means of transport allow the indefinite instrumental to indicate that this vehicle is used in transportation:

autobusez	by bus
automobilez	by car
autoz	by car
beribilez	by car
hegazkinez	by airplane
kamioiz	by truck
mandoz	by mule
motorrez	by motorbike
oinez	on foot
ontziz	by ship
taxiz	by taxi
zaldiz	on horseback

Examples follow:

(18) a. Autobusez joatea duzu hoberena. (Atxaga, *Z.H.* 11)
It is best for you to go by bus.
b. Handik hamabi orduan igoko ziren Bogotara, nahiz trenez nahiz beribilez. (Irazusta, *Bizia* 49)
From there they would go up to Bogota in twelve hours, by train or by car.
c. Bide hura ez nuen ontziz, zaldiz edo oinez egin beharrik. (Orixe, *Aitork.* 200)
I didn't have to travel that way by ship, on horseback, or on foot.

If the vehicle is individualized and accordingly expressed by a noun phrase instead of a single noun, the locative or the sociative will appear instead of the instrumental:

(19) a. Ama-alabak azkenengo trenean beren herrira joan ziren. (Irazusta, *Bizia* 119)
Mother and daughter went to their village by the last train.
b. Azkeneko trenean badator, garai hori behar du etxeratzeko. (Zabala, *Gabon* 35)
If he is coming by the last train, he will need that time to get home.

27.1.7 Instrumentals Denoting Medium of Transportation

An indefinite instrumental can be used to indicate the medium through which transportation takes place. Examples are

airez	by air
autopistaz	by superhighway
bidez	by road
itsasoz	by sea
lehorrez	by land
lurrez	by land
mendiz	through the mountains
urez	by water

Only this generic sense can be expressed by the instrumental. As soon as the medium is individualized, other constructions must be used, such as a locative phrase followed by *barrena* or *zehar*, as seen in section 4.1.3.2: *Gazaranzko bidean barrena* (*TB* 173) 'along the road toward Gaza', *bide batean barrena* (Muxika, *P.Am.* 27) 'along a road', *Arantzazuko bidean zehar* (*E.H.* 775) 'all along the road to Aranzazu'.

27.1.8 The Adverbial Pattern *N-z N* of Reiteration

A productive pattern consisting of an indefinite instrumental noun immediately followed by the same noun in its bare form accommodates more than one meaning, depending on the type of noun. With mass nouns *N*, it means 'through N'; with nouns designating a body part, it usually expresses a situation of reciprocity; and with other countable nouns *N*, it indicates a reiterative process or action of going from one *N* to the next.

It should be noted here that the partitive pattern *N-ik N* of section 13.1.1, restricted however to countable nouns, presents a synonymous alternative to the instrumental pattern: *ahoz aho* or *ahorik aho* 'from mouth to mouth', *eskuz esku* or *eskurik esku* 'hand in hand', *kalez kale* or *kalerik kale* 'from street to street', and so on.

Some fairly representative examples will now be listed, distributed over five meaning categories:

1. With appropriate mass nouns: 'through'

airez aire	through the air
elurrez elur	through the snow

2. With appropriate body parts: reciprocity

aurpegiz aurpegi	face to face
aurrez aurre	face to face, directly opposite
begitartez begitarte	face to face
begiz begi	eye to eye, eyeball to eyeball
bekoz beko	face to face
besoz beso	arm in arm
bihotzez bihotz	heart to heart, intimately
buruz buru	face to face, from beginning to end

eskuz esku	hand in hand
oinez oin	on someone's footsteps, closely behind
orpoz orpo	on someone's heels, closely behind

3. With nouns denoting a place: from N to N

adarrez adar	from branch to branch, rambling
alboz albo	from side to side
aldez alde	from side to side, right through
atez ate	from door to door
bazterrez bazter	from one side to the other, along the edge
bidez bide	up hill and down dale, along the road
etxez etxe	from house to house
herriz herri	from village to village
hiriz hiri	from city to city
kalez kale	from street to street
mendiz mendi	from mountain to mountain, through the mountains
munduz mundu	all over the world
ohez ohe	from bed to bed
orrialdez orrialde	from page to page
zokoz zoko	from corner to corner, in all corners

4. With nouns denoting time: from N to N

egunez egun	from day to day, day in day out, exactly on this day
mendez mende	from century to century, through the ages
orduz ordu	from hour to hour, every hour, precisely at this hour
orenez oren	from hour to hour, every hour, precisely at this hour
unez une	from moment to moment, every moment
urtez urte	from year to year, every year

5. Miscellanous: from N to N

ahoz aho	from mouth to mouth
arriskuz arrisku	from danger to danger
galdeketaz galdeketa	from interrogation to interrogation
gizaldiz gizaldi	from generation to generation
medikuz mediku	from doctor to doctor
nahikundez nahikunde	from fancy to fancy, from whim to whim
urratsez urrats	step by step, foot by foot

27.1.9 Use of the Instrumental Postpositions *bidez, bitartez,* and *medioz*

When an animate being is represented as a means for the action denoted by the verb, a genitival phrase followed by one of three instrumental postpositions will occur instead of an animate instrumental. These postpositions, also usable with an inanimate genitive, are *bidez* 'by way of', *bitartez* 'by intervention of', and *medioz* 'by means of'. Some examples will illustrate their use:

(20) a. Lagun zahar baten bidez ikasi zuen. (Irazusta, *Bizia* 63)
He learned it through an old friend.
b. Honen bidez bidaltzen dizuet eskutitz hau. (*LBB* 79)
I am sending yoû this letter through him.
c. Jaunak mirari baten bidez gorde zuen. (*TZ* I, 264)
The Lord protected him by means of a miracle.

(21) a. Egin dut nire eskabidea Antonio Donearen bitartez. (*G.* 185)
I have made my petition through Saint Anthony.
b. Erantzunak musikalarien bitartez etorriko zaizkigu. (*MEIG* IV, 93)
The answers will come to us through the musicians.
c. Euskara batuak, izkribuzko batasunaren bitartez, juduentzat adina jentilentzat egina behar du izan. (*MEIG* VII, 160)
Unified Basque, through unity in writing, has to be made for Gentiles as much as for Jews.

The postposition *medioz* is used mainly in the north:

(22) a. Bekatua munduan sartu da gizon bakar baten medioz. (Lapeyre, 124)
Sin has come into the world through one single man.
b. Arimaren medioz gizonak egia ezagut dezake. (Lapeyre, 112)
Man can know the truth through the soul.
c. Gure hitz-altxorra ugaritu beharrean aurkitzen gara, dela hitz sortuen medioz, dela bestetariko hitz arrotzen bitartez. (*MEIG* VII, 187)
We are finding ourselves in need of increasing our stock of words, whether through invented words or by foreign words from elsewhere.

27.2 Instrumentals Expressing Cause or Motive

Cause or motive is generally expressed by means of the motivational ending *-gatik*, derived from *gai* 'matter' followed by the elative *-tik*. The motivational is attested as early as the 16th century, for example, in Etxepare's *Linguae Vasconum Primitiae* published in 1545:

(23) a. Amagatik andre oro behar luke goratu. (*LVP* III-18)
Because of his mother, he ought to praise all women.
b. Haiek biak galdu ditut, amorea, nik zugatik. (*LVP* IX-22)
These two I have lost, my love, because of you.

Whereas these examples involve animate nouns, there are a great many inanimate nouns whose indefinite instrumental can be used with causal force. Among these are all nouns denoting a bodily or mental state, such as

ahalkez	out of shame
beldurrez	out of fear
damuz	out of remorse
egarriz	from thirst
erdeinuz	out of disdain
gorrotoz	out of hatred
gosez	from hunger
grinaz	out of passion
harrokeriaz	out of arrogance
haserrez	out of anger
lotsaz	out of shame
minez	from pain
nagikeriaz	out of laziness
oinazez	from great pain
penaz	from sorrow
pozez	out of joy

Examples of a different sort can be cited too:

beharrez	out of necessity
bortxaz	by force
denboraz	with time
erruz	out of guilt
ezinbestez	perforce
faltaz	through lack
ohituraz	out of habit
zaharrez	out of old age
zorionez	by good luck, fortunately
zoritxarrez	by bad luck, unfortunately

[*N.B. Bere buruz* or *bere kabuz*: 'by his own initiative'.]

A few example sentences will serve as illustrations:

(24) a. Ez da gosez hilko. (*TOE* III, 177)
She won't die from hunger.
b. Begiak erreta ditut saminez. (Jb 17:7)
My eyes are burnt from bitterness.

c. Gaur egunean ezin daiteke zigarrorik piztu sua sortuko den beldurrez. (Labayen, *Su Em.* 165)
   Nowadays one cannot light a cigar out of fear that fire will break out.
d. Mendiak mugi omen daitezke fedeaz. (Oñederra, 104)
   It is said that one can move mountains by faith.
e. Geure erruz galdu genuen. (*MEIG* VII, 37)
   We lost it because of our own fault.
f. Neure indarrez libratu nintzen. (*TZ* I, 203)
   I freed myself by my own strength.
g. Hil nadila maitasunez. (*LBB* 275)
   May I die from love.
h. Horien erreguz biguntzen dira Jaungoikoaren haserreak. (Anduaga, 153)
   God's indignations are softened through their prayers.

The causal instrumental can be strengthened by the use of an idiomatic construction consisting of a (usually indefinite) instrumental noun preceded by the definite genitive of the same noun:

ahularen ahulez	out of sheer weakness
barrearen barrez	from laughing so much
beharraren beharrez	out of sheer necessity
beldurraren beldurrez	out of sheer terror
damuaren damuz	out of utter remorse
denboraren denboraz	(merely) by the passage of time
diruaren diruz	through a lot of money
egarriaren egarriz	from sheer thirst
errukiaren errukiz	from great pity
gogoetaren gogoetaz	by a lot of thinking
gosearen gosez	from sheer hunger
gozoaren gozoz	through a lot of gentleness
harroaren harroz	out of utter conceit
haserrearen haserrez	out of great fury
hitzaren hitzez	through many words
indarraren indarrez	by sheer force
indarkeriaren indarkeriaz	by sheer brutal force
izuaren izuz	out of sheer fright
kezkaren kezkaz	by a lot of worry
lanaren lanez	through a lot of work
lotsaren lotsaz	out of pure shame
maitearen maitez	out of great love

minaren minez	out of sheer pain
nagiaren nagiz	out of sheer laziness
nekearen nekez	through a lot of effort
oinazearen oinazez	from utter pain
penaren penaz	through great sorrow
pisuaren pisuz	by sheer weight
pozaren pozez	out of utter joy
urduritasunaren urduritasunez	from sheer nervousness
zaharraren zaharrez	from sheer old age
zorionaren zorionez	from sheer happiness

Some example sentences will serve as illustrations:

(25) a. Beldurraren beldurrez ez zekien zer egin ere. (Bilbao, 263)
Out of sheer terror he did not even know what to do.

b. Anaiek, izuaren izuz, ez zuten erantzuten asmatzen. (Gn 45:3)
The brothers, from sheer fright, did not manage to answer.

c. Ez zitzaion eman hizkuntza, egia, nekearen nekez bereganatu zuen. (*MEIG* II, 121 = *MIH* 351)
The language was not given to him, it is true, he appropriated it through a lot of effort.

d. Lorik egiterik ez zuen izango, noski, urduritasunaren urduritasunez. (Arana, 107)
Of course, she would have no chance to sleep, out of sheer nervousness.

e. Gogoetaren gogoetaz gertatua desagertarazteko modurik balego bezala. (*MEIG* IX, 93)
As if there was a possibility by a lot of thinking to make unhappened what had happened.

f. Hauek ez dute fitsik ere galdu nahi indarkeriaren indarkeriaz sakeleratu dutenetik. (*MEIG* IX, 24)
They don't want to lose the least little bit of what they have pocketed by sheer brutal force.

The same strengthening process can be applied also to instrumental perfect participles, provided no complements are involved. With nonstative verbs, the construction indicates repetition or duration:

edanaren edanez	from constantly drinking
emanaren emanez	by constantly giving
esanaren esanez	by repeatedly saying
eskatuaren eskatuz	by repeatedly asking
ibiliaren ibiliz	by continually walking
irakurriaren irakurriz	by constantly reading

janaren janez	from constantly eating
saiatuaren saiatuz	by continually trying

Two example sentences will serve as illustrations:

(26) a. Edanaren edanez, zabuka eta oinak lokatuta dihoaz etxera. (Mogel, *Cat. Basc.* 71 [8])
From drinking again and again, they go home reeling and tottering with their feet.
b. Maiz gertatu ohi da ... idazlea esanaren esanez asperturik bezala mintzatzen zaigula. (*MEIG* III, 88)
It frequently happens ... that an author speaks to us as if bored by his saying it so often.

With stative verbs, the construction indicates intensity:

asearen asez	from complete satiation
harrituaren harrituz	from utter astonishment
haserretuaren haserretuz	from deadly anger
ikusiaren ikusiz	from seeing (it) so much
jakinaren jakinez	from knowing it so well
nekatuaren nekatuz	from utter exhaustion

A few example sentences might be helpful:

(27) a. Kontu zaharra! Jakinaren jakinez ahazturik daukaguna. (*TOE* III, 189)
An old story! One we have forgotten already from knowing it too well.
b. Zaldiak ez zion bidetik behingoan alde egin, ezin zuelako nekatuaren nekatuz. (J. A. Mogel, *Ip.* 93 [27])
The horse did not immediately overtake him along the road, because he was unable to from utter exhaustion.
c. Nekatuaren nekatuz ezin jarraik zitezkeen ihestiarren ondotik. (Jgs 8:4; Dv)
Due to utter exhaustion they could not chase after the fugitives.

27.3 Instrumental Predicatives

During the discussion of predicatives in section 25.5, a great deal of attention was paid to the role of the stative suffix *-(r)ik* in the formation of many of these. This suffix, however, mainly attaches to adjectives, much less to nouns, except to some denoting a bodily or mental state (section 25.5.2).

The present section will show the existence of predicatives formed from certain nouns with the help of the indefinite instrumental ending. Such nouns belong to one of two categories, which will be treated in separate subsections: those denoting a bodily or mental state, on the one hand, and those denoting vocal activity, on the other. Both types admit preposed complements: genitival, adnominal, or relativized complement clauses. Adjectival modifiers have not been encountered.

Like all predicatives, they can serve as a main predicate together with a suitable copula, usually *egon*, but sometimes *ari* (*izan*), *ibili*, or, the inchoative *jarri*, and, in the event of transitive predication (section 25.2), *eduki* or *utzi*. They can also be used as secondary predicates, in which case they tend to be indistinguishable from instrumental manner adverbs, for which see section 27.4.

27.3.1 Instrumental Predicatives Expressing Bodily or Mental State

Among the instrumentals fit to act as predicatives one finds all those cited in section 27.2 as indicating a bodily or mental state. Additional examples belonging to the same category are

ametsez	dreaming
beltzuriz	frowning
dardaraz	shivering, shaking
dolorez	in sorrow
ikaraz	trembling, in terror
irribarrez	smiling
irrikaz	longing (for)
negarrez	weeping, crying
presaz	in a hurry
soz	looking, watching

First, here are some example sentences without complement:

(28) a. Ni negarrez nago. (Sarrionandia, 53)
I am crying.
b. Herriminez nago Kalifornian. (From song "Herriminez," *Xaramela* 145)
I am homesick in California.
c. Erdainkuntzagatik minez zeudela, ... (Gn 34:25)
While they were in pain because of the circumcision, ...
d. Hark ez du ezer erantzun, baina lotsaz egongo da. (Agirre, *Kres.* 166)
She hasn't replied anything, but she will be ashamed.
e. Bihotza dut saminez, begiak negarrez. (*LBB* 350)
My heart is bitter, my eyes in tears.

Now here are some examples of predicatives with complements:

(29) a. Sekulako ikaraz eta dardaraz zebilkion gorputza. (Erkiaga, *Arran.* 158)
His body was shaking and trembling terribly.

b. Zurekin hitz egiteko beldurrez ibiliko naiz hemendik aurrera. (Garate, *Musk*. 38)
   I will be afraid to speak to you from now on.
c. Kalera ateratzeko lotsaz nengoen. (Irazusta, *Bizia* 111)
   I was ashamed to go out on the street.
d. Dohatsu zuzenbidearen gosez eta egarriz daudenak. (Mt 5:6; Dv)
   Blessed are those who are hungry and thirsty for justice.
e. Ez egon haren jaki gozoen irrikaz. (Prv 23:3)
   Do not crave his tasty dishes.

27.3.2 Instrumental Predicatives Expressing Vocal Activity

Another category of instrumentals able to function as predicatives are those denoting vocal activity. I have collected the following examples:

algaraz	roaring with laughter
arneguz	blaspheming, cursing
arrenez	beseeching, imploring
auhenez	lamenting
barrez	laughing
biraoz	cursing
burlaz	mocking
deiadarrez	shouting
deiez	calling
erreguz	requesting, praying
estulez	coughing
galdez	asking
garrasiz	screaming
heiagoraz	shrieking
hotsez	clamoring
irrintziz	neighing
irriz	laughing
isekaz	scoffing
kantuz	singing
karrankaz	croaking, honking
kirrinkaz	squeaking, chirping
marmarrez	whispering, grumbling
marraskaz	bellowing, groaning
marruz	mooing, howling
oihuz	shouting
orroaz	roaring
otoitzez	praying

pioz	peeping, chirping
trufaz	taunting
txilioz	screaming
uhuriz	howling, hooting
zaunkaz	barking

Some example sentences by way of illustration follow:

(30) a. S. Franses Xavier oihuz zegoen Jainkoari: "Aski, Jauna, aski!" (Lapeyre, 278)
St. Francis Xavier kept crying out to God: "Enough, Lord, enough!"
b. Ez bakarrik deiez gaude, baizik deiadarrez. (Gerriko I, 469)
Not only are we calling, but clamoring.
c. Senartzat nahi al nauzun egon naiz galdez. (Bilintx, 129)
I have been asking whether you want me as a husband.
d. Zure anaiaren odola lurretik oihuz dagokit. (cf. Gn 4:10; Dv)
Your brother's blood is crying out to me from the ground.

With a few of these instrumental predicatives, genitival complements are possible:

(31) a. Gizarteari oihuz ari naiz zuzentasunaren galdez. (Xalbador, *Odol.* 265)
I am shouting out to society asking for justice.
b. Zure deiez gaude Ebaren ume herbestetuok. (*Kristau Ik.* 35)
We, exiled children of Eve, are calling out to you.

27.4 Instrumentals Expressing Manner

Except for idiomatic constructions of the type *beldurraren beldurrez*, which are always causal, all instrumentals cited in sections 27.2 and 27.3 can readily serve as manner adverbs. In addition, the following are worth mentioning:

arduraz	carefully
arrazoiz	with reason, justifiably
arretaz	carefully
atseginez	with pleasure
azpiz	slyly, cunningly
garaiz	on time
gertakariz	by accident, by chance
gogoz	gladly, willingly
grinaz	with passion, passionately
kontuz	carefully
nekez	with difficulty, hardly
neurriz	with moderation
zentzuz	sensibly, wisely

Following are a few simple example sentences to begin with:

(32) a. Irribarrez hartu zituen Don Pedrok. (Bilbao, 146)
Don Pedro received them smilingly.

[*N.B. Irribarrez* here may well be considered a subject complement.]

(32) b. Nekez egin nuen nire bidea. (*MEIG* IX, 137)
I made my way with difficulty.
c. Beti ausardiaz jokatu dut. (Atxaga, *Sara* 100)
I have always acted with intrepidity.
d. Guztiek begiratzen zidaten lotsaz eta beldurrez. (B. Mogel, *Ip*. 60)
They were all looking at me with respect and fear.

Instrumentals expressing manner are not restricted to single noun constructions. Adjectival modifiers are quite common:

(33) a. Plazer haundiz hitzegingo dut zurekin. (Atxaga, *Obab*. 174)
I will speak with you with great pleasure.
b. Arreta haundiz entzuten genion. (Garate, *Leh*. 67)
We were listening to him with close attention.
c. Abots finez eta astiro irakurri du bere papertxoa. (Sarrionandia, 82)
He has read his little paper slowly and with a cultured voice.
d. Andre Mariak begi gozoz eta hitz gozoagoz erantzun zidan. (Etxaniz, *Antz*. 51)
Lady Mary answered me with sweet eyes and sweeter words.
e. Benetakoa zirudien irribarre batez agurtu ditut denak. (Etxeberria, *Egun* 56)
I have greeted everybody with a smile that seemed genuine.

27.5 Instrumentals Expressing Criteria

An indefinite instrumental phrase may indicate a criterion according to which the remainder of the clause is to be understood. This value of the Basque instrumental is rendered in English by such prepositions as *as to*, *according to*, and sometimes *by*. Some example sentences will be helpful:

(34) a. Osasunez ongi nago. (Irazusta, *Bizia* 121)
As to health, I am fine.
b. Martin Saldias ez zen lanbidez zelatari. (Atxaga, *Sara* 15)
Martin Saldias was not a spy by profession.
c. Arrainez ere gaizki gabiltza. (*TOE* I, 216)
As to fish too, we are badly off.
d. Eskuz bezainbat buruz ere azkarra zara. (*TOE* III, 41)
You are quick with the head as much as with the hands.

e. Nire anaia zenak ondasunez oso poliki utzi zuen. (*TOE* II, 211)
   My late brother left her very nicely as to capital.
f. Garaiz eta aldartez, zeharo ezberdinak dira. (*MEIG* IV, 132)
   As to period and temperament, they are totally different.

The meaning of certain nouns renders them eminently suitable for indicating a criterion by means of their instrumental form. Examples of such instrumentals include

adinez	according to age, as to age (*adinez nagusi*: of age)
aldez	in one respect, in part, partly
arauz	according to the rule, by rule
egiaz	according to the truth, in truth
etorkiz	according to origin, by origin
irudiz	as it seems, by all appearances
itxuraz	in appearance, ostensibly
izatez	as to nature, by nature
izenez	as to name, in name
jaiotzez	according to birth, by birth
jatorriz	by descent, by origin
legez	according to the law, by law
ohituraz	according to custom, by custom
prezioz	as to price (*prezioz igo*: to increase in price)
ustez	as was believed, apparently, allegedly
zuzenez	according to right, by right

[*N.B.* The form *aldez* 'in part' may occur in both members of a coordinate sentence, in which case there is an alternative gloss: 'on the one hand . . . , on the other . . .'—for example,

(35) Eta aldez damu dut, eta aldez atsegin. (Ax. 11)
     And on the one hand, I am sorry, and on the other, pleased.]

Nouns signifying 'opinion' admit the indefinite instrumental expressing the meaning 'according to'. Such nouns are usually preceded by a genitival modifier. To take an example, *nire aburuz*, *nire iritziz*, *nire irudiz*, and *nire ustez* are all to be glossed as 'in my opinion'. Only *irudiz* and *ustez* also occur as adverbs, with meanings shown in the preceding list of instrumental nouns. When the noun meaning 'opinion' is qualified by an adjective, the inessive is preferred: *nire uste apalean* (*E.H.* 48) 'in my humble opinion'. Yet Mitxelena writes: *ene uste apalez* (*MEIG* VIII, 182 = *MIH* 397).

The meaning 'according to' also accounts for instrumental comment clauses (section 19.1.10), as in *Mitxelenak dioenez* 'as Mitxelena says', literally 'according to what Mitxelena says'. Note, however, that animate noun phrases do not allow this meaning of the instrumental. For 'according to Mitxelena', one has to say *Mitxelenaren arabera*, never **Mitxelenaz*.

27.6 Instrumentals Measuring Differences

Differences of the type accommodated by the use of the instrumental case arise in three contexts: with verbs indicating a change in size or quantity, comparatives, and excessives. The examples presented in this section will provide further clarification.

These examples illustrate the first context:

(36) a. Beste hamabost urtez luzatuko dizut bizia. (2 Kgs 20:6 = Is 38:5)
I will lengthen your life by another fifteen years.
b. Ez dezake inork bere bizia luzatu, ezta minutu batez ere. (Iraizoz, 133n)
Nobody can lengthen his life, not even by one minute.

Passing now to comparatives, note that we already met the instrumental adverbs *askoz* and *askotaz* 'by much' in section 26.4.2. Similar examples exist with interrogative or exclamative *zenbatez* 'by how much':

(37) a. Eta zenbatez ez da gehiago gizakia ardia baino? (Mt 12:12)
And by how much isn't a human being more valuable than a sheep?
b. Eta zenbatez zarete zuek gehiago, txoriak baino! (Lk 12:24; *IB*)
And by how much yoû are more valuable than the birds!

Phrases also occur in this function:

(38) a. Eta egun hura hamar orduz luzeago izan zen. (*TZ* II, 133)
And that day was ten hours longer.
b. Gure euskara, hura baino bi mila urte baino gehiagoz gazteagoa da. (*MEIG* II, 68)
Our Basque is younger than him by more than two thousand years.
c. Homero Detxepare baino bi mila urtez lehenago jaio zen. (*MEIG* II, 68)
Homer was born two thousand years earlier than Detxepare.
d. Buruaz handiago zen Edurne senarra baino. (*EGL* 144)
Edurne was (by) a head taller than her husband.
e. Ezkondu zen bera baino lau urtez gazteagoko Marie Peydouvan batekin. (Oxobi, 191)
He married with a certain Marie Peydouvan, four years younger than himself.

With excessives, measure phrases appear only in northern usage (cf. section 26.6.2). An example is found in Lafitte's grammar: *bi zehez luzeegi* (Lafitte, 1962, sec. 341, p. 149) 'too long by two inches'.

[*N.B.* In all these examples, the instrumental is only optional. In fact, the present-day colloquial prefers the absolutive form.]

27.7 Instrumentals Relating to Time

Time-related instrumentals divide into four semantic categories, namely, those indicating (1) duration, (2) time limit, (3) frequency, and (4) location in time.

1. Duration
As already noted in section 20.1.4, use of the indefinite instrumental is one option for expressing duration, alternatives being the definite inessive and, in certain contexts, the absolutive. Example sentences are shown in section 20.1.4, to which may be added:

(39) a. Hiru egunez atseden hartu nuen. (Neh 2:11)
I rested for three days.
b. Berrogei egunez iraun zuen uholdeak. (Gn 7:17)
The flood lasted forty days.
c. Une batez gurutzatu dira bien begiak. (Sarrionandia, 113)
For a moment, the eyes of the two met.

2. Time Limit
The instrumental can be used to indicate the time within which something happens or is to happen: *denbora laburrez* 'within a short time', *bi urtez* 'within two years', as in the following example:

(40) Harri horrek bost segundoz lurra jo du. (P. Goenaga)
That stone has hit the ground in five seconds.

[*N.B.* A common alternative is the use of *barru*: *bost segundo barru* 'within five seconds'.]

3. Frequency
Frequency adverbials based on *aldi* (section 20.3.3) require either the indefinite instrumental or the indefinite inessive: *bost aldiz* or *bost alditan* 'five times'.

4. Location in Time
To specify location in time, the inessive case is commonly used in the whole Basque-speaking area; yet the northern dialects also have available an alternative: use of the instrumental. In the south, the literary language has also started to make use of it:

(41) a. Ostegunez Itziarko Ama Birjina ikustera igo ginen. (Etxaniz, *Nola* 26)
On Thursday we went up to see Our Lady of Itziar.
b. Jerusalena abiatuko da biharamun goizez. (S. Mitxelena, *IG* II, 159)
He will start out to Jerusalem on the morning of the next day.
c. Beste egunez ere etor gintezkeen, jakin izan bagenu. (*TOE* II, 220)
We could have come on another day also, if we had known.
d. Neguko egun goibel batez heldu nintzen Villamedianara. (Atxaga, *Obab*. 131)
On a gloomy day in winter I arrived in Villamediana.

27.8 Instrumentals Governed by Postpositions

As a start, let us recall from section 3.2 that the allatives *behera* 'down' and *gora* 'up' govern the instrumental case when contributing to the description of a spatial arrangement. Examples are

buruz behera	with the head down, upside down, reverse
buruz gora	with the head raised, upside up, sloping up
ahoz behera	face down, on one's belly, forward
ahoz gora	face up, on one's back, backward

For upward or downward movement along a surface, one finds the inessive, absolutive or, less commonly, the instrumental: *aldapa(n) gora, aldapaz gora* 'up the slope', 'uphill'; *aldapa(n) behera, aldapaz behera* 'down the slope', 'downhill'.

With the meanings 'above' and 'below', that is, location without contact, or position on a scale, one employs the elative or, less commonly, the instrumental: *hodeietatik gora* or *hodeiez gora* 'above the clouds', *hogei urtetik gora* or *hogei urtez gora* 'above twenty years of age', *hamabi urtez beherakoak* 'those below twelve years of age'.

The notion 'above' can also be expressed by the location noun *gain* (section 4.1.3.1). With that meaning, *gain* and its locative forms are usually combined with the genitive. Yet the instrumental also occurs: *sorbaldaz gain* (Etxaniz, *Antz.* 143) 'above the shoulder', *neurriz gain* (*LBB* 319) 'beyond measure', *oroz gain(etik)* 'above all', *beste guztiaz gainetik* (*MEIG* III, 91) 'above everything else'. The form *gain* and its allative *gainera* are also used with the sense 'in addition to', in which event the instrumental is obligatory: *horretaz gain(era)* 'besides that', *jakintsua izateaz gain* (*MEIG* VI, 57) 'in addition to being learned', *hemen aipatuez gainera* (*MEIG* VII, 121) 'in addition to those mentioned here'.

As we observed in section 4.1.3.2, the location noun *kanpo* and its locative forms (*kanpoan, kanpora, kanpotik*) govern either the elative or the instrumental when the meaning is 'outside', but only the instrumental when the meaning is 'in addition to', 'besides'. A few examples from Mitxelena's writings: *Nafarroatik kanpora* (*MEIG* VI, 34) 'outside Navarra'; *sistemaz kanpora* (*MEIG* VII, 136) 'outside the system'; *euskaldunez kanpora* (*MEIG* VI, 49) 'besides Basques'; *hizkuntzaz kanpo* (*MEIG* VI, 50) 'besides the language'; *erlijio-gaiez kanpo* (*MEIG* VII, 32) 'besides religious topics'.

With *kanpo*'s synonym *landa*, there is a clear bipartition: it governs the elative in the meaning 'outside' and the instrumental in the meaning 'besides': *Euskal herritik landa* (*MEIG* VI, 169) 'outside the Basque Country'; *geure hizkuntzaz landa* (*MEIG* VII, 185) 'besides our language'.

The postposition *kontra* 'against' (section 4.1.3.11) does not govern the instrumental case, except in a couple of set expressions: *borondatez kontra* (*LBB* 28) 'against someone's will', *gogoz kontra* 'unwillingly', but *arauen kontra* 'against the rules'.

An instrumental phrase governed by *beste* 'other' answers the question 'other than what?'—for example, *Orixez beste usatzailerik* (*MEIG* VII, 35) 'other users than Orixe', *zenbait ohitura kaxkarrez beste* (*MEIG* VII, 35) 'other than some coarse customs'. When used as postpositions, *beste* and its allative *bestera* often strengthen their meaning from 'other' to 'against' or 'in contrast to': *gogoz beste* (Orixe, *Q.A.* 140) 'against (his) liking', *oituraz beste* (T. Agirre, *Uzt.* 28) 'against his habit', *gogoz bestera* (Orixe, *Aitork.* 138) 'against (his) liking', *bere borondateaz bestera* (Arrue, *May.* 169) 'against his will'.

Since the phrase *beste aldera* 'on (*or* to) the other side' regularly governs the instrumental, as in *Bidasoaz beste aldera* (*MEIG* VII, 127) 'on the other side of the Bidasoa river', the compound noun *bestalde* with the same meaning governs the same case: *mugaz bestaldean* (*E.H.* 137) 'on the other side of the border', *haizeaz bestaldetik* (*E.H.* 137) 'on the opposite side of the wind'.

The postposition *bestalde* (or its Labourdin form *bertzalde*) can occur as a synonym of *bestaldean*, as in *oheaz bestalde* (Mendiguren, *Hamalau* 110) 'on the other side of the bed', but also covers the meaning 'apart from', and then governs either the instrumental or the absolutive: *haietaz bestalde* (Xalbador, *Odol.* 186) 'apart from those', *izpiritu erneaz bestalde* (Xalbador, *Odol.* 61) 'apart from an alert spirit', *haur eta emaztekiak bertzalde* (Mt 14:21; Dv) 'apart from the women and children'. Used by itself as an adverb, *bestalde* means 'moreover'.

Finally, the postposition *gero* 'after' and the related forms *geroz* and *geroztik* also govern the instrumental case. For details and examples, see section 20.1.2.

27.9 How to Express Aboutness

To express the notion indicated in English by the preposition *about* when governed by a suitable verb, including all those of communication, Basque has three devices available.

27.9.1 Aboutness Expressed by *gainean* 'over'

To begin with, we can have the inessive location noun *gainean* of section 4.1.3.1 preceded by the genitive form of the noun phrase concerned. Yet the observation that *gainean* here possibly represents an imitation of Spanish *sobre* or French *sur* 'over' made in Azkue's 1905 *DVEF* (I, 314) motivated purists to shun this construction, a practice for which they were chided by Mitxelena in a 1960 essay (*MEIG* IV, 34 = *MIH* 73). Examples are

(42) a. Gauza horien gainean mintzatu zaigu. (*EGLU* I, 441)
He has talked to us about those things.
b. Aspaldian jendea isilik dago kontrabandoaren gainean. (Iraola, 38)
For a while people have been silent about smuggling.
c. Nahiko nuke zerbait jakin txindurrien gainean. (Iturriaga, *Dial.* 29)
I would like to know something about ants.

d. Ongi deritzat Baionan izenaren gainean erabaki zutenari. (*MEIG* VII, 150 = *MIH* 112)
I agree with what they decided in Bayonne concerning the noun.

According to data furnished by the *DGV* (VIII, 138), a *gainean* construction can be employed also with verbs such as *negar egin* 'to cry' and *irri egin* 'to laugh'. In this case, however, the construction seems to indicate motive rather than mere aboutness, as is evidenced by its current substitution by the motivational case, especially in the south. Indeed, once common to the whole Basque-speaking area, this construction is now virtually obsolete, having been replaced in the north by the instrumental and in the south by the motivational case:

(43) a. Ene gainean negarrik ez egin. (Lk 23:28; Dv)
Do not cry over me.
b. Ez nitaz negar egin. (Lk 23:28; *JKBO*)
Do not cry about me.
c. Ez egin negarrik niregatik. (Lk 23:28)
Do not cry because of me.

[*N.B.* In connection with these verbs, the *-(r)i buruz* idiom (see next subsection) seems to be rejected by most southern speakers, although Azkue's supplement to his dictionary (*DVEF* II, 520) presents an example from the Marquina region corresponding to Batua: *gaitzari buruz ere barre egin dut* 'I have laughed even about the illness'.]

27.9.2 Aboutness Expressed by the Idiom *-(r)i buruz*

As the *DGV* (V, 752–756) shows, the instrumental *buruz* of *buru* 'head' has quite a few different meaning values. To explain its use in signifying aboutness, the meaning 'facing' is to be taken as a starting point: *eguzkira buruz* 'facing the sun'. When the allative here is replaced by the dative, the meaning turns more abstract: 'with regard to', 'regarding'. Examples are

(44) a. Fedeak ... erakusten digu ... zer eginbide dugun gure kreatzaileari buruz.... (Lapeyre, 72)
Faith shows us what duty we have with regard to our creator.
b. Benvenistek ... ikertu ... zuen hiztunak nola jokatzen duen denborari buruz. (*MEIG* VII, 101)
Benveniste investigated how a speaker behaves with regard to time.
c. Arana Goiri eta Azkue ez ziren talde berekoak euskarari buruz. (*MEIG* V, 100)
Arana Goiri and Azkue were not part of the same group regarding Basque.

In the literary style of southern authors during the first half of the 20th century, a need was felt for a novel way of signifying 'about', since the traditional construction involving *gainean* 'over' was decried as a barbarism and the revival of this value of the instrumental had not yet taken place. For this purpose, the construction came to be chosen, given that a meaning extension from 'regarding' to also include 'about' is but a small one. Examples are

(45) a. Hona zer dioen hitz berriei buruz. (*MEIG* VII, 129)
Here is what he says about new words.
b. Engainatu nahi zaituztenei buruz idatzi dizuet hau. (1 Jn 2:26)
I have written this to yoû about those who want to deceive yoû.
c. Benetako baldarkeria oraingo garaiotan Kanti buruz hitzegitea. (Atxaga, *Grl.* 80)
Real stupidity, talking about Kant in these modern times.

27.9.3 Instrumentals Expressing Aboutness

An instrumental phrase governed by certain categories of verbs can be equivalent to an English *about* phrase. We will take this to be the case when its use can be replaced by that of the devices analyzed in sections 27.9.1 and 27.9.2 with no change in meaning. The relevant categories are verbs of communication including verbs of saying, verbs of asking, and verbs of hearing, on the one hand, and verbs of knowing, on the other.

No more reference will be made to verbs of the type *negar egin*, as it is far from obvious that the instrumental *nitaz* of example (43b) expresses aboutness.

Let us note finally that for the purpose of expressing aboutness with verbs of saying, instrumentals as well as *gainean* constructions have been resorted to from the very oldest texts on—for example, *LVP* from 1545 and the works of Leizarraga from 1571. Examples with verbs of saying follow:

(46) a. Zuen baimenarekin neure buruaz zerbait esan nahi nuke. (*MEIG* VIII, 152 = *MIH* 366)
With yoûr permission I would like to say something about myself.
b. Aitaz mintzatzen al zen? (Garate, *Alaba* 28)
Did she talk about her father?
c. Bioz mintzatuko natzaizue orain, eta batez ere bigarrenaz. (*MEIG* VII, 48)
I will now talk to yoû about these two, and especially about the second.
d. Eguneroko bizitzaz hitzegin genuen gosaldu bitartean. (Atxaga, *Obab.* 277)
While breakfasting we spoke about daily life.
e. Hartaz dago idatzia Liburu Santuan: . . . (Mt 11:10)
About him has been written in the Holy Book: . . .

The following examples have verbs of asking:

(47) a. Mundu zabalari galdegin nion ene Jainkoaz. (Orixe, *Aitork.* 250–251)
I asked the wide world about my God.
b. Norbaitek nitaz galdegiten badu, . . . (Labayen, *Su Em.* 188)
If someone asks about me, . . .

c. Hor-hemen bilan zebilela, anaiez galdetu zion gizon bati. (*TZ* I, 84)
While he was searching here and there, he asked a man about his brothers.

These have verbs of hearing:

(48) a. Beste batean entzungo dizugu horretaz. (Acts 17:32)
We will hear you about that another time.
b. Zer da zutaz entzun dudan hori? (Lk 16:2)
What is that I hear about you?
c. Aditu al duzu zerbait gerraz? (Atxaga, *Behi* 58)
Have you heard something about the war?

These have verbs of knowing:

(49) a. Ea zer dakizun hamabost eta hamaseigarren mendeaz. (Zerbitzari, 113)
Let's see what you know about the fifteenth and sixteenth centuries.
b. Nitaz ez dakidan zerbait Zutaz badakit. (Orixe, *Aitork.* 248)
I do know something about you I don't know about myself.

27.9.4 Aboutness with Respect to a Noun Phrase

To express aboutness linked to a noun phrase instead of a verb, as in 'a book about agriculture', adnominal constructions (see chapter 5) are compulsory. All three devices studied so far allow adnominal forms, as they must, since they are all based on postpositions. Thus illustrations are

(50) a. Bere egitekoen gaineko galde asko egin zizkion. (*TB* 30)
She posed him many questions about her obligations.
b. Arranondoko gauzen gaineko jardun luze batean hasi ziren. (Agirre, *Kres.* 103)
They began a long conversation about Arranondo matters.

(51) a. Humboldt etorri zitzaigun gurera, gure gauzei buruzko zenbait berri atzerrian jaso ondoan. (*MEIG* VI, 65)
Humboldt came to our territory, after he had received abroad some information about our affairs.
b. Sintaxiari buruzko saioak inoiz baino ugariago ditugu. (*MEIG* VI, 126)
Essays about our syntax are more plentiful than ever.

In contrast to the adnominals presented so far, use of the adnominal instrumental to indicate aboutness is severely constrained. In fact, the traditional system, still largely observed in the north, requires the adnominal noun phrase to be generic: *filosofiazko liburua* 'a book about philosophy', but *Kanten filosofiazko liburua* 'Kant's book about philosophy', and not 'a book about Kant's philosophy' (data provided by the northern academician P. Charritton).

Preadnominal instrumental deletion is often applicable: *nekazaritza(z)ko liburua* 'a book about agriculture'. In the northern dialects, applying it seems to have been the preferred option: *laborantzako liburua* (Duvoisin) 'a book about agriculture', *itsasoko nabigazioneko liburua* (cf. *I Nav.* 1) 'a book about maritime navigation'. (Other examples of preadnominal instrumental deletion are to be found in section 5.2.5.)

The demands of bilingual education and government are putting pressure on southern Batua to lessen the existing constraints on Basque syntax not found in Spanish. Therefore, innovations such as *Eusko Jaurlaritzazko liburua* 'a book about the Basque government' are starting to appear here and there. Yet adnominal instrumentals remain excluded for proper names (**Mitxelenazko*, **Bilbozko*), for animate noun phrases (**alkateazko* 'about the mayor'), and all plural noun phrases (**euskal liburuez* 'about the Basque books').

27.10 Instrumental Complements

27.10.1 The Antipassive Alternation

Following my interpretation of Benveniste's summary exposé (1966, 172), I will define middle verbs as those denoting an action or process that can be viewed as taking place mostly within its grammatical subject. Hence, forgetting, remembering, enjoying, mocking, having pity, giving birth, perceiving, and speaking are all cases in point. Observe, by the way, that all these verbs require animate subjects.

Basque middle verbs quite often occur in two syntactic frames: a transitive one with an ergative subject and a direct object, and an intransitive one with an absolutive subject corresponding to the ergative in the transitive frame and an instrumental complement corresponding to the direct object of the transitive construction. Schematically,

NP_1 + erg. . . . NP_2 + abs. . . . V trans.

⇓ ⇓ ⇓

NP_1 + abs. . . . NP_2 + instr. . . . V intrans.

This is known as the "antipassive alternation"—the term "antipassive," coined by the American linguist Michael Silverstein, being specifically used to refer to the intransitive version of the clause.

The transitive member of an antipassive alternation may have fallen out of use in certain areas, in which case the intransitive member no longer qualifies as an antipassive in those areas. In the southern dialects, this process has occurred with the verb *baliatu* 'to utilize', whose transitive frame only survives in the north. Present-day Batua, however, has readopted the transitive construction, so that we do have an antipassive alternation with *baliatu* in the literary language:

(52) a. Ez dugu hitz hori baliatzen. (Garate, *Erd.* 38)
We don't use this word.

b. Ez gara hitz horretaz baliatzen. (Most common form)
We don't use this word.

Here, example (52b) represents the antipassive of (52a). But in the examples that follow the antipassive (b) sentences have not been based on the transitive (a) sentences. Had they been, we would not have been able to use textually attested sentences for both frames. We now list the principal examples found in Batua:

The following examples have *ahaztu* 'to forget':

(53) a. Ahaztuko gaituzte. (*MEIG* IX, 107)
They will forget us.
b. Ez dira gutaz erabat ahaztu. (*MEIG* II, 104)
They have not completely forgotten us.

These have *gogoratu* 'to remember':

(54) a. Gogora Loten emaztea. (Lk 17:32; *EAB*)
Remember Lot's wife.
b. Gogoratzen al zara Andoniz? (Oñederra, 44)
Do you remember Anthony?

These have *oroitu* 'to remember':

(55) a. Orain ere urrun zarelarik oroituko zaitut. (*E.H.* 627)
I will remember you even now while you are far away.
b. Gure amaz oroitu nintzen. (Garate, *Alaba* 16)
I remembered my mother.

These have *gozatu* 'to enjoy':

(56) a. Iliada ... zahar-gazteek ... goza dezaketela badakit. (*MEIG* II, 67)
I know that young and old can enjoy the Iliad.
b. Maitasun horren berotasunaz luzaz dezatela goza. (Xalbador, *Odol.* 289)
May they enjoy the warmth of that love for a long time.

These have *burlatu* 'to make fun of':

(57) a. Buruzagiek burlatzen zuten Jesus. (Lk 23:35; Dv)
The rulers were making fun of Jesus.
b. Ez naiz zutaz burlatzen. (Lapeyre, 83)
I am not making fun of you.

These have *trufatu* 'to make fun of':

(58) a. Nork trufatu zaitu berriz ere? (Lafitte, *Murtuts* 41)
Who has made fun of you again?

b. Ez da Jainkoaz trufatzen. (Gal 6:7; *Biblia*)
One does not make fun of God.

These have *errukitu* 'to have pity':

(59) a. Zeuon buruak erruki(tu) itzazue. (Gerriko I, 438)
Have pity on yourselves.
b. Erruki zaitez gutaz. (Mk 9:22)
Have pity on us.

These have *erdi(tu)* 'to give birth':

(60) a. Erdituko du semea. (Mt 1:21; Ur.)
She will give birth to a son.
b. Erdiko da seme batez. (Mt 1:21; Dv)
She will give birth to a son.

These have *nabaritu* 'to sense', 'to perceive':

(61) a. Maiz nabaritzen dugu premia hori. (*MEIG* VII, 148)
We often sense that need.
b. Ongi nabaritu zen Azkue horretaz. (*MEIG* VII, 35)
Azkue sensed that very well.

With *mintzatu* 'to speak', the instrumental phrase can be explained either as a manner adverbial or as the result of an antipassive transformation:

(62) a. Hiruek, bai amak, bai alabek, mintzatzen dute euskara. (J. Etchepare, *Ber*. 86)
The three, the mother as well as the daughters, speak Basque.
b. Hiruak mintzatzen dira euskaraz.
The three speak Basque.

27.10.2 Antipassive Argument Structures

Quite a few Basque verbs require an argument structure identical to that of an antipassive; that is, they are intransitive, and they have an absolutive subject as well as an instrumental complement that can be viewed as an object. Most of these structures originated as antipassives derived from a transitive frame no longer in use. Since this grammar is not concerned with diachrony, for the sake of illustration I will merely display a few examples current in Batua, without regard to their origins.

The verb *jabetu*, denominative of *jabe* 'owner', has two main senses, one being 'to take possession of', 'to master', the other being 'to get to know', 'to grasp', 'to realize'. Either sense requires an antipassive frame in Batua:

(63) a. Une batetik bestera etxe eta ondasunez jabetuko da. (*TOE* II, 262)
From one moment to the next he will take over the house and the assets.

b. Egiaz jabetuko zara. (Atxaga, *Obab*. 107)
You will get to know the truth.
c. Ez naiz jabetzen diozunaz. (*TOE* II, 293)
I am not grasping what you are saying.

The verb *nagusitu*, denominative of *nagusi* 'boss', means 'to conquer', 'to dominate'. Its transitive use, as in example (64a), is obsolete, so that only the antipassive form survives:

(64) a. Zer pasionek gure bihotza nagusitzen dute? (Cf. Pouvreau, *Philotea* 521)
What passions dominate our heart?
b. Ez ziren beren armei esker nagusitu lurraldeaz. (Ps 44:4)
They did not conquer the land thanks to their weapons.

Although the *DGV* (XIII, 9) cites transitive uses of *ohartu* 'to notice', these are rare and unacceptable in Batua according to Sarasola (*E.H.* 606). Intransitive uses, however, are common. Furthermore, whatever is noticed is normally denoted by a finite clause or an instrumental phrase, at least in southern Batua:

(65) a. Beste zerbaitetaz ohartu nintzen. (*MEIG* VI, 140)
I noticed something else.
b. Ohartzen al nintzen gertatzen ari zenaz? (Atxaga, *Obab*. 357)
Was I aware of what was happening?

The verb *konturatu*, meaning 'to realize', also demands an antipassive frame:

(66) Kalte haundiak egin ondoan konturatu ziren horretaz. (Satrustegi, 46)
They realized that after he had done a lot of damage.

Another verb requiring an antipassive frame is *arduratu* 'to care for', 'to be interested in':

(67) Haurrez ez zen deus ere arduratzen. (Garate, *NY* 14)
He wasn't at all interested in the children.

Other examples are *maitemindu* 'to fall in love' and *zaletu* 'to grow fond (of)'.

27.10.3 Bibliographical Note on Antipassives

The first scholar to apply the term antipassive correctly within Basque syntax was Jon Ortiz de Urbina (1989, 203, note 15). A fuller treatment of the matter can be found in de Rijk 2002 and 2003.

27.10.4 Instrumentals with Emotive Verbs

A subset of emotive verbs, including *aspertu* 'to be fed up (with)', 'to be bored', *harritu* 'to surprise', 'to astonish', *kezkatu* 'to worry', *lotsatu* 'to shame', *nahigabetu* 'to distress', and *poztu* 'to rejoice', requires an instrumental phrase to denote the source of the emotion in literary Batua, provided these verbs are used intransitively. In transitive use, the source of the emotion is indicated by the ergative subject; see section 12.1.11. Examples of this use of the instrumental are

(68) a. Ez luke inork erantzun honetaz harritu behar. (*MEIG* IV, 22)
Nobody should be surprised at this answer.
b. Txirrita ... sagardoaren prezioaz kezkatzen zen. (*MEIG* VI, 70)
Txirrita was worried about the price of cider.
c. Ez zen aitaz lotsatzen? (Garate, *Alaba* 28)
Wasn't she ashamed of her father?
d. Ez naiz etsaiaren hondamendiaz poztu. (Jb 31:29)
I have not rejoiced over my enemy's disaster.
e. Mutilarekin gertatu zaizuenaz, ni ere nahigabetzen naiz. (*TOE* I, 200)
I also am grieved at what happened to yoû with the boy.

Note that these are not antipassives, since the instrumental does not correspond to the direct object of the matching transitive structure, but to its ergative subject. Nor are we dealing with the instrumental of aboutness, because there are no alternatives with *-(r)i buruz* or *-(r)en gainean*.

27.10.5 Other Instrumental Complements

It would be wrong to assume that instrumentals of aboutness, antipassive instrumentals, and complements of emotive verbs together exhaust the range of instrumental complements governed by the verb. A counterexample would be the verb *gabetu* 'to deprive', whose instrumental complement does not fall under any of those categories.

(69) a. Gabetu nahi nauzue biziaz. (Larréguy II, 200)
Yoû want to deprive me of my life.
b. Ez dut eskuetan dudanaz gabetu nahi. (Ax. 68)
I don't want to deprive myself of what I have in the hands.

A similar counterexample is the verb *hustu* 'to empty (of)'.

27.11 Nonfinite Instrumental Clauses

Finite instrumental clauses of the type *dakigunez* 'as far as we know' have been discussed in sections 19.1.10 and 27.5. Nonfinite instrumental clauses can be based on the verbal noun, but much more commonly on the perfect participle.

27.11.1 Instrumental Clauses Based on the Verbal Noun

An instrumental clause based on a verbal noun serves a causal function with respect to the main clause. The verbal noun has the form of a definite instrumental and thus ends in *-az*:

(70) a. Ez-deus egiteaz beraz ikasten da gaizki egiten. (Etxeberri Sarakoa, 187)
Just by doing nothing, one learns to do evil.
b. Astakeria handi bat egin zuten haitzetara egun guztirako joateaz. (Agirre, *Kres.* 128)
They had done something very foolish by going to the rocks for the whole day.
c. Nire seme-alabek eta nik hutsune galanta izango dugu etxean haren joateaz. (Etxaniz, *Antz.* 59)
My sons and daughters and I will experience a great emptiness at home with her going away.
d. Etxean geldi egoteaz, bat aspertzen da. (*TOE* II, 227)
One gets bored by staying idly at home.

Example (70d) allows an alternative analysis along the lines of section 27.10.4, in which the phrase *etxean geldi egoteaz* is viewed as a preposed complement of *aspertu* indicating the source of the emotion.

27.11.2 Instrumental Clauses Based on the Perfect Participle

The meaning of an instrumental clause based on the perfect participle can be either causal or merely circumstantial. In either case, there is simultaneity between the action of the subordinate clause and that of the main clause, unlike what happens with participial predicatives with *-(r)ik* or *-ta* (see sections 25.5.4 and 25.7). The instrumental may be either definite or indefinite. First we present some examples with causal meaning:

(71) a. Arrain gordina janez iraun nuen. (Atxaga, *Bam.* III, 54)
I survived by eating raw fish.
b. Droga erosteko dirua, gorputza salduz irabazten dute. (Garate, *Iz.B.* 25)
The money for buying drugs, they earn by selling their bodies.
c. Neronek galaraziko dut agintariengana joanez eta salatuaz. (*TOE* II, 149)
I will prevent it myself by going to the authorities and denouncing it.
d. Zeuen herriari su emanaz agertzen duzue zuen bilaukeria. (Etxaniz, *Antz.* 27)
You are showing your villainy by setting fire to yoûr own village.
e. Gero lo-kuluxka bat eginez, buruko mina joango zait. (*TOE* II, 229)
By taking a siesta later, my headache will go away.

Observe that in example (71e) the subject of the subordinate clause is different from that of the main clause, unlike in the previous examples.

The following examples merely express simultaneity:

(72) a. Bazter batean gelditzen da malkoak xukatuaz. (*TOE* II, 361)
She is remaining in a corner drying her tears.
b. —Antz emana nengoen—musu bat emanaz esan zion. (Irazusta, *Bizia* 119)
"I had already guessed so," she told her, giving her a kiss.

c. Honek, haurrei agur eginaz, hartu du bere etxerako bidea. (*LBB* 99)
As for him, saying goodbye to the children, he took the road home.

d. Ingurura begirada azkar bat boteaz presaka alde egin dut handik. (Etxeberria, *Egun* 216)
Casting a quick glance around, I got out of there in a hurry.

e. Hotzikara bat sentitu du goitik behera zeharkatuz. (Etxeberria, *Egun* 195)
He felt a cold shiver passing through from top to bottom.

Note that in example (72e) the subject of the subordinate clause is coreferential to the object of the main clause.

There also are instrumental clauses based on the preterito-present verbs *nahi* and *behar*: *nahi(a)z* 'wanting to . . .', *beharrez* 'needing to'. Some examples are

(73) a. Adurra zerion ezpainetatik gaztaia jan nahiaz. (B. Mogel, *Ip*. 58)
Saliva dripped from his lips from his wanting to eat the cheese.

b. Aspaldidanik dabil hemen lantegi berri bat eraiki nahiz. (*TOE* III, 44)
He has been around here for a long time wanting to build a new factory.

c. Eeeeep . . . !—oihu zegien haien gogoa sutu nahiz. (T. Agirre, *Uzt*. 232)
"Eeeeep . . . !" he shouted to them, wanting to fire up their spirits.

In southern usage, *beharrez* amounts to 'in order to', as in examples (74b,c):

(74) a. Lan ederra jarri diguzue horrenbeste galtza txuri josi beharrez. (*TOE* I, 98)
You have imposed a huge job on us, having to sew so many white pants.

b. Atera zen jan beharrez. (From song "Mehetegiko txakurra," *Xaramela* 219)
He went out in order to eat.

c. Egun batez abiatzen da Haxko, basajauna nora joaten den ikusi beharrez. (Barbier, *Lég*. 129)
One day, Haxko sets off in order to see where the sylvan man goes.

27.11.3 Instrumental Participles Combined with *joan* to Denote a Gradual Process

The verb *joan* can be combined with the indefinite instrumental form of a perfect participle to denote a gradual process. Although originally a northern construction, it is now also used in southern Batua.

(75) a. Jaunaren hitza aitzinatuz eta hedatuz zihoan. (Acts 12:24; Dv)
The word of the Lord continued to advance and to spread.

b. Egunetik egunera, ilunduz eta flakatuz doa. (Lapeyre, 45)
From day to day, it is getting obscurer and weaker.

c. Orain behinolako giro hura aldatuz doa. (Villasante, in *MEIG* III, 88)
Now that old-time atmosphere is gradually changing.

d. Etena da antzinako lokarria eta oroitzapena bera ere ezabatuz doa. (*MEIG* IX, 96)
The old bond is broken and its very memory is gradually disappearing.

e. Ordea, horren partez, areago esnatuz joan nintzen. (Atxaga, *Obab*. 336)
   However, instead of that, I was gradually waking up even more.

A southern alternative is to use the indefinite inessive of the verbal noun instead of the instrumental perfect participle:

(76) Eta neurria ez doa urritzen, hazten eta ugaritzen baizik. (*MEIG* VI, 94 = *MIH* 196)
   And the quantity is not gradually diminishing, but rather growing and increasing.

27.11.4 Negative Circumstantials: Privative *-ke*

Instead of nonfinite negative instrumental clauses, the construction using a perfect participle followed by *gabe* 'without', as shown in section 13.5, will be resorted to:

(77) a. *Hitzik ez esanez joan zen.
   He went away not saying a word.
b. Hitzik esan gabe joan zen.
   He went away without saying a word.

This construction, however, is ambiguous with respect to the tense of the subordinate clause, as it can also mean 'He went away without having said a word'. The central part of the southern area has at its disposal an alternative construction consisting of the verbal noun together with the privative suffix *-ke*. In this construction the action of the subordinate clause must be simultaneous with that of the main clause:

(78) a. Besterik esateke uzten al gaituzu? (*TOE* III, 42)
   Are you leaving us without saying anything further?
b. Hamar minutu inguru joan ziren Mateok ahorik zabaltzeke. (Etxaniz, *Antz*. 147–148)
   About ten minutes went by without Mateo opening his mouth.
c. Nora zihoan ohartzeke, aurrera eta aurrera jo zuen. (Jautarkol, *Ip*. 20)
   Without noticing where he went, he kept pushing on forward.
d. Lehen, egun bat elkar ikusteke ezin pasa; eta orain, egun oso bat ezin pasa elkarrekin. (*LBB* 121)
   Before, they could not pass one day without seeing each other, and now they cannot pass a whole day together.

27.12 The Noun *kide* and the Suffix *-kizun*

27.12.1 Compounds with *kide* 'companion', 'counterpart'

The noun *kide* 'companion' or 'counterpart' enters into nominal compounds denoting a participant in something indicated by the first member of the compound. Some first members undergo apocope (*erkide*, *irizkide*) (section 3.8.1); most others do not (*herrikide*, *zorikide*). Ancient formations show the form *-ide* instead of *kide*: *bidaide*, *gogaide*, *mintzaide*, *ohaide*, *partaide*.

Common examples of these nominal compounds are

aberri	fatherland	aberkide	compatriot
apaiz	priest	apaizkide	fellow priest
auzi	lawsuit	auzikide	opponent, adversary
auzo	neighborhood	auzokide	neighbor
batza	association	bazkide	member
batzar	congress	batzarkide	congress member, delegate
bazkari	midday meal	bazkalkide	fellow diner
bide	road	bidaide	traveling companion
biltzar	conference	biltzarkide	assembly delegate
erdi	half	erkide	partner, associate
erru	guilt	errukide	accomplice
esanahi	meaning	esanahikide	synonym
fede	faith	fedekide	fellow believer
gaitz	evil	gaizkide	accessory, accomplice
garai	period	garaikide	contemporary
gogo	mind	gogaide	kindred spirit, sympathizer
herri	village	herrikide	fellow villager
iritzi	opinion	irizkide	like-minded person
izen	named	izenkide	namesake
jabe	owner	jabekide	co-owner
lan	work	lankide	colleague, fellow worker
lehia	contest, competition	lehiakide	competitor, rival
mahai	table	mahaikide	table companion, commensal
mintzo	voice, speech	mintzaide	interlocutor
muga	border	mugakide	country sharing a border
odol	blood	odolkide	blood relation
ohe	bed	ohaide	concubine
parte	part, participation	partaide	participant
solas	talk, conversation	solaskide	interlocutor
urte	year	urtekide	classmate, contemporary
zori	destiny	zorikide	companion in misfortune

There also are a few examples where the first member is a verb radical:

bizi (izan)	to live, to reside	bizikide	spouse, contemporary, roommate
erdi	to give birth	erkide	twin brother, twin sister
ezkondu	to marry	ezkontide	spouse (*-tide* by dissimilation)
ikasi	to learn	ikaskide	fellow student

To form abstract nouns from these compounds, the suffix *-tza* of section 25.8.1 is used: *odolkidetza* 'consanguinity', *lankidetza* 'collaboration'.

27.12.2 The Deverbal Suffix *-kizun*

The deverbal suffix *-kizun* produces nouns with the primary meaning 'something intended or apt to undergo the action denoted by the verb'. With an intransitive verb radical the derived noun will be subject oriented: *etorkizun* 'what is to come', that is, 'the future'; *gertakizun* 'what is to happen', that is, 'future event'. With a transitive verb radical the noun will be object oriented: *emankizun* 'something to give'; *kontakizun* 'something to tell'.

In the western dialects, many of these derivatives can also be used for present rather than future actions, thus turning into abstract nominals: *aitorkizun* 'confession', *ikaskizun* 'lesson', *ikuskizun* 'spectacle'.

In the same dialects, a much preferred alternative for the *-kizun* derivatives is a compound with *zer* as its first member and the perfect participle as the second: *zeresan* = *esankizun*, *zerikasi* = *ikaskizun*, *zerikusi* = *ikuskizun*. These compounds also occur in Batua: *Hark ez du zerikusirik* (or *ikuskizunik*) *honekin* 'That has nothing to do with this'. (Note: *zerikusirik*, like Spanish *nada que ver*.)

Finally, some derivatives can be used adjectivally: *hilkizun* 'mortal', *ibilkizun* 'walkable', *laudakizun* 'praiseworthy', *sendakizun* 'curable'.

The morphophonemics is quite regular. Only three particularities need to be mentioned: the loss of *-ki-* by haplology in *erabakizun* (instead of expected *erabakikizun*) from *erabaki* 'to decide'; the dissimilatory elision of *k* in *ahalkeizun* 'disgrace'; and the elision of *k* in *lotsaizun* 'disgrace', most probably under the influence of its synonym *ahalkeizun*.

Examples of *-kizun* derivatives are

ahalketu	to get ashamed	alhalkeizun	something to be ashamed of, disgrace
aitortu	to confess	aitorkizun	something to confess, confession
aldatu	to change	aldakizun	something to change, variable
alderatu	to bring near, to compare	alderakizun	something to compare, comparison
asmatu	to find out, to invent	asmakizun	something to find out, riddle, puzzle
barkatu	to forgive	barkakizun	something forgivable, veniality
bete	to fill, to fulfill	betekizun	something to fulfill, assignment, duty
eman	to give	emankizun	something to give, performance, broadcast
erabaki	to decide	erabakizun	something to decide, question, decision
eraman	to bear	eramankizun	something to bear, suffering, distress
erantzun	to answer	erantzukizun	responsibility
esan	to say	esankizun	something to say, complaint, recrimination
eskatu	to ask for	eskakizun	something to ask for, claim, demand
etorri	to come	etorkizun	something to come, future
galdetu	to ask	galdekizun	something to ask, question

gertatu	to happen	gertakizun	something to happen, (future) event
hautatu	to choose	hautakizun	something to choose, alternative
hil	to die	hilkizun	something that is to die, mortal
ibili	to walk	ibilkizun	itinerary, walkable
igarri	to guess	igarkizun	riddle, prediction
ikasi	to learn	ikaskizun	something to learn, lesson
ikusi	to see	ikuskizun	something to see, spectacle, sight
irabazi	to gain	irabazkizun	(future) gain
irakatsi	to teach	irakaskizun	something to teach, lesson
irakurri	to read	irakurkizun	something to read, text
jakin	to know	jakinkizun	something to know, knowledge
kendu	to subtract	kenkizun	minuend
kexatu	to complain	kexakizun	complaint
kezkatu	to worry	kezkakizun	something to worry about, concern
kontatu	to tell	kontakizun	something to tell, tale, story
laudatu	to praise	laudakizun	something to praise, praiseworthy
lotsatu	to get ashamed	lotsaizun	something to be ashamed of, disgrace
ospatu	to celebrate	ospakizun	something to celebrate, celebration
sendatu	to cure	sendakizun	something to cure, curable
sinetsi	to believe	sineskizun	something to believe
ulertu	to understand	ulerkizun	something to understand
urrikaldu	to take pity on	urrikalkizun	someone deserving of pity

[*N.B.* From *ezin* ‘impossible’ has been derived *ezinkizun* ‘impossibility’.]

The originally future meaning of these derivations is brought out by constructions with the main verb *egon*, as are

Hori eginkizun dago. That is still to be done.
Hori etorkizun dago. That is still to come.
Hori ikuskizun dago. That remains to be seen.

27.13 Vocabulary

ahuldu	to weaken
aizkora	axe
beribil	car, automobile
beso	arm
bete	to fill, to fulfill
biharamun	the next day
borobil	round
eguerdi	noon
erabili	to use

eroso	comfortable
estali	to cover
falta	lack, fault, mistake
giltza	key
hitzeman	to promise
idazlan	article, essay
ikuskizun	sight, spectacle
ireki	to open
iritsi	to arrive
jokatu	to play, to gamble
kolpatu	to beat, to hit
luzaroan	for a long time
maila	degree
ohartu	to notice
onartu	to approve, to agree
ostu	to steal
sabel	belly
senar-emazteak	the couple
urrats	step, footstep
zorrotz	sharp

27.14 Exercises

27.14.1 Translate into English

1. Zeure ahoz hitzemana zeure eskuz bete duzu, gaur ikus dezakegunez. (1 Kgs 8:24)
2. Zure idazlana begi hobez ikusten dut zure ahizparena baino.
3. Goizeko lehenengo trenean badator, eguerdirako iritsiko da hona.
4. Senar-emazteak besoz beso etxerantz doaz. (*E.H.* 137)
5. Jende horrekin kontuz ibili beharra dago. (Atxaga, *Obab.* 136)
6. Urratsez urrats eta mailaz maila behar dugu ibili. (*MEIG* IV, 75)
7. Nola zabiltzate diruz urtez urte?
8. Irakurriaren irakurriz asko ikas daiteke gaurko munduan.
9. Besteren batek emaztea ostuko ote zion beldurrez bizi zen beti senarra.
10. Giltzak luzaroan erabiliz ireki da atea. (Sarrionandia, 75)
11. —Ba, ezta ni ere—onartu du Anartzek, esku batez bere sabel borobildua kolpatuz. (Etxeberria, *Egun* 59)
12. Bide ibiliak erosoak izan ohi dira, ezagunaren ezagunez aspertzen bagaituzte ere. (*MEIG* I, 197)

27.14.2 Translate into Basque

1. He tried to hit me with a sharp axe.
2. Are you going by train or by car? I am going by the last train of the day.
3. How often haven't I told you to come on time.
4. Through lack of bread they became weak from hunger.
5. I am getting bored by writing books about your sister.
6. By gambling constantly you are losing all you have.
7. You will cover it with pure gold.
8. Through a young witch he has gotten rich.
9. You shouldn't ask me about sights I have not seen.
10. Without living in the Basque Country, we can learn Basque.
11. Nobody noticed Tasio.
12. We didn't think much about the next day.

The Unfinished Chapters

My husband Rudolf de Rijk completed 27 of his planned 35 chapters. He had finished the preliminaries and had just begun to write chapter 28 when it was suddenly too late. Shortly before his death in 2003 he told me the chapter on allocutives (chapter 29) only needed to be translated from the Dutch as he had not much more to say about it beyond adding more examples. Though I was sad that his life's work to produce a really comprehensive grammar would not be realized, the original plan after his death was to publish what he had completed and add only a translation of the chapter on allocutives.

I knew that he developed the English version from a Dutch precursor. The new version differed considerably from the original Dutch manuscript in that he greatly expanded each chapter, adding new materials and insights gained in the years since its completion in 1986. The English version was begun in 1987. I think he mentioned that the first 16 chapters had been completed by 1994. In a sense, one could say the whole grammar as given so far is incomplete. Knowing his perfectionist tendencies, I am sure, if death had not intervened, that he would have revised all the chapters before publishing—the earlier ones in particular.

It was only in 2005 that I discovered among his papers that he had made special copies of some of the yet-to-be-treated chapters in the Dutch version. To these he had been adding notes in the margins and within the text. Seeing that some of the references were to material published quite recently, it occurred to me that it might be feasible to translate these chapters and incorporate into them the many notes and new examples he had written in.

This possibility occurred to me because his former student Fleur Veraart contacted me in late 2004, when she had just learned of his death, and offered to be of help. Because she is a native Dutch speaker and an MIT-trained linguist who is acquainted with Basque, I did not hesitate to take up her offer. She agreed then to translate the chapter on allocutives. This she did, and has also added to it her translation of the section on nonfinite sentential complements taken from another previously untranslated chapter. She has also edited and translated the Dutch manuscript that is the basis for chapter 30, incorporating a section on conjunction reduction which he had written in English, and as much of his added notes and examples for the English version as she could, sometimes only making reference to material he planned to include but had not yet written.

Not being a linguist, I confined my own efforts to the sections demanding less knowledge of linguistic terminology—those dealing mostly with morphology: chapters 28, 31, 32, and 33.

There is more material that we did not deal with. Much of it is of a pedagogical nature and was intended specifically for his Dutch readers. We did not feel capable of dealing with his chapter on idioms. We did pull out sections from these chapters and incorporate them into the chapters we treated, following a scheme for the remaining English chapters that he had written down.

Rudolf's good friends and colleagues, Professors E. Wayles Browne of Cornell University and Pello Salaburu of the University of the Basque Country, were kind enough to look at our efforts and make valuable suggestions. We remain responsible for any errors of translation and interpretation or omissions and hope the reader will understand the circumstances in which these chapters came to be added here.

Virginia de Rijk–Chan

28 Indefinite Pronouns and Related Matters; the Synthetic Future Tense

28.1 Indefinite Pronouns

We will start with a synopsis of the indefinite pronouns, to be followed up in subsequent subsections by an account of their use and properties.

I	II	III	IV	V	VI
nor	inor	norbait	nor edo nor	nornahi	edonor
zein	ezein	zenbait	zein edo zein	zein-nahi	edozein
zer	ezer	zerbait	zer edo zer	zernahi	edozer
zergatik	ezergatik	zerbaitengatik	zer edo zergatik	zernahigatik	edozergatik
non	inon	nonbait(en)	non edo non	non-nahi	edonon
nondik	inondik	nonbaitetik	non edo nondik	non-nahitik	edonondik
nora	inora	norabait	non edo nora	noranahi	edonora
noiz	inoiz	noizbait(en)	noiz edo noiz	noiznahi	edonoiz
nola	inola	nolabait	nola edo nola	nolanahi	edonola
nolako	inolako	nolabaiteko	nola edo nolako	nolanahiko	edonolako
zenbat	—	—	—	zenbat-nahi	edozenbat

[*N.B.* Most of these forms have come up in earlier chapters. See especially chapters 3, 13, and 18.]

The form of the indefinite pronouns derives from that of the interrogative ones, displayed in column I. The forms in column II, characterized by a prefix *e-* before *z-* or *i-* before *n-*, occur in the same context as the partitive determiner *-(r)ik*, that is, mainly in negative, interrogative, or conditional clauses (see sections 13.1.2 and 17.3.2).

In other contexts, such as a purely positive clause, a suffix *-bait* (earlier *-baita* from *-bait* + *da*) is added to the interrogative, thus giving the forms of column III. The forms in column IV, based on *edo* 'or', are synonymous with those in column III. They mainly occur in the Biscayan dialect but are also allowed in Batua.

Column V displays compounds with an interrogative as the first member, and the word *nahi* 'will' as the second. For example, *nornahi* signifies 'an arbitrary person', that is, 'whosoever', and can in many contexts be glossed as 'everybody'. Likewise, we have *zernahi* 'whatever', 'everything'; *zein-nahi* (also spelled *zeinahi*) 'whichever'; *non-nahi* (also spelled *nonahi*) 'wherever', 'everywhere'; *noiznahi* 'whenever', 'always'; *nolanahi* 'however', 'in every way'; and *zenbat-nahi* (also spelled *zenbanahi*) 'however many/much'.

The forms with the prefix *edo-* in column VI are synonymous with those in column V. They are used chiefly in Biscay and are also known in Guipuzcoa, but they are not found in the northern dialects, with the sole exception of *edozein* 'whichever', used everywhere.

28.1.1 Properties of *nor*

The pronoun *nor* 'who' can be employed for singular as well as for plural referents.

(1) a. Nor dira horiek? (Gn 48:8; Ur.)
    Who are those?
  b. Nor dira hauek? (Gn 48:8; *Biblia*)
    Who are these?

The southwestern dialect area, including all of Biscay, has evolved a special plural form *nortzuk* on the analogy of *batzuk* 'some' from *bat* 'one'. This form also occurs in southern Batua, although the Basque Academy prefers plain *nor* (see "Hiztegi Batua," *Euskera* 45 [2000], 674).

(1) c. Nortzuk dira hauek? (Gn 48:8)
    Who are these?
  d. Elizan nortzuk bilduko gara? (*G.* 315)
    Who (of us) will get together in church?

Mainly in negative and conditional clauses, *nor* can occur as a predicate (with *izan* 'to be') in the meaning 'brave enough', 'qualified', 'worthy':

(2) a. Ez naiz ni nor auzi hori erabakitzeko. (*MEIG* III, 118)
    I am not qualified to decide that dispute.
  b. Gu ez gara nor galdera hau erantzuteko. (*MEIG* I, 205)
    We are not qualified to answer this question.
  c. Jauna, ni ez naiz nor zu neure aterpean sar zaitezen. (Mt 8:8; Ker.)
    Lord, I am not worthy for you to enter under my roof.

28.1.2 The Word *zein*

The word *zein* means 'which' and involves a choice out of a limited number of possibilities. It is used for persons, things, and other matters, and it can appear independently or adjectivally, as well as in exclamations (see section 11.2.2):

(3) a. Haietarik bietarik, zeinek iragan ote zuen mundu honetan pena eta trabailu gehiago? (Ax. 474)
Which of those two has perhaps undergone more pain and tribulation in this world?
b. Bietako zein nahi duzue askatzea? (Mt 27:21)
Which of the two do yoû want released?
c. Zein da gure helburua? Geure buruaren atsegina ala euskararen ona eta bizia? (*MEIG* IV, 35)
Which is our goal? Our own pleasure or the welfare and existence of the Basque language?
d. Zein ur, geldia ala lasterra? (Ax. 38)
Which water, the stagnant or the running?
e. Ez al dakizue gaur zein egun dugun? (Etxaniz, *Antz.* 118)
Don't yoû know which day today is?
f. Zein leku ikaragarria hau! (*TZ* I, 65)
What an awesome place this is!

[*N.B.* Notice the use of the bare form *ur*, without an article, in example (3d). This is always the case by adjectival use of the interrogative or indefinite pronouns (see section 2.3.2).]

Batua makes a sharp distinction between *nor* and *zein*. This is in contrast to the situation in spoken Guipuzcoan where we find that *zein* = *nor*, *zenbait* = *norbait*, *zeinnahi* = *nornahi*, and *edozein* = *edonor*. For example, *Zein da hor?* (Etxaniz, *Antz.* 113) 'Who is there?'

In combination with a following reflexive form (*bera*, *bere* . . . , *berari*, etc.) or a plural reflexive form (*geure*, *zeuen*) later in the same clause, *nor* and *zein* can mean, respectively, 'everyone' ('anyone') and 'each of them' (or 'each of us', 'each of yoû'). Examples of this typical construction follow:

(4) a. Gero joan ziren nor bere etxera. (*TZ* I, 247)
Later everyone went to his own house.
b. Nori berea da zuzenbidea. (Oihenarte, *Prov.* 341)
Justice is: everyone his due.
c. Nork bere bidea hautatu behar du. (*MEIG* IX, 73)
Everyone must choose his own way.
d. Jendeak, oinazearen oinazez, nork bere mihiari hozka egiten zion. (Rv 16:10)
The people: in great pain, everyone bit his tongue.

(5) a. Gure semealabek badaukate zeinek bere etxea.
Each of our sons and daughters has his own house.
b. Beste nazione guztiek, zeinek bere lengoajean bezala, . . . (Lz, *Abc*)
Like all other nations, each in his own language, . . .

c. Eta bazihoazen oro, zein bere hirira, bere izena ematera. (Lk 2:3; Dv)
And they all went, each to his village, to give his name.

d. Soinulari hauei zeini bere tresnaren balioa ordaindu beharko zaie.
Each of these musicians shall be compensated for the value of his instrument.

[*N.B.* The compound *norbera*, meaning 'each one', 'oneself', and its possessive *norbere* 'one's own' have developed out of this construction. Some sayings are presented here as examples:

(6) a. Nork ez du maite norbere sorlekua? (Erkiaga, *Arran.* 9)
Who does not love his own birthplace?

b. Norberak ez du bere makarrik ikusten. (Azkue, *E. Y.* III, 218)
No one sees the speck in his own eye.

c. Norberak geure hutsegiteak ditugu. (*TOE* I, 244)
We each have our faults.]

28.1.3 Some Uses of *zer*

The interrogative pronoun *zer* 'what' may occur in the ergative:

(7) a. Zerk dirudi gezurra? (*LBB* 137)
What seems a lie?

b. Zerk ez zaitu harritzen? (*LBB* 133)
What doesn't surprise you?

c. Zerk erakartzen gaitu? Maite ditugun gauzekin zerk adiskidetzen gaitu? (Orixe, *Aitork.* 92)
What draws us? What enables us to conciliate with the things we love?

Adjectivally, *zer* has the meaning 'what (kind of)':

(8) a. Etxean zer lan egiten duzu? (*MIH* 148)
What (kind of) work do you do at home?

b. Zer berri dakarkiguzu? (T. Agirre, *Uzt.* 203)
What news do you bring us?

c. Zer oker egin du, bada, honek? (Lk 23:22)
What evil, then, has this man done?

d. Zer gogok eman zion zerbait egitea, lehen inoiz ezer egin gabe? (Orixe, *Aitork.* 336)
What (kind of) desire drove him to do something, without ever having done anything before?

In adjectival use, optionally *zer* > *ze* (see section 18.1.1):

(8) e. Ze berri? (*G.* 375)
What news?

f. Badakizue ze ordu den: *later than you think.* (*MEIG* VI, 136)
Yoû know what time it is: "later than you think."

g. Ze gai erabiltzen da eta zein hizkuntzatan? (*MEIG* I, 100)
What material is he using and in which language?

Besides *zer*, also *ezer*, *zerbait*, *zernahi*, and *edozer*, just like *inor* and *norbait*, can be used adjectivally. *Zer* and *zernahi* can be connected to adjectives or nouns, *inor*, *ezer*, and *zerbait* only to adjectives. Whereas *zer*, as we have shown, can lose its final *-r* in adjectival use, *ezer* does not:

(9) a. Ezer onik atera ote daiteke Nazaretetik? (Jn 1:46)
Can anything good come out of Nazareth?
b. Zerbait beroa ere jan beharko dugu. (Haranburu, *Ausk*. 29)
We will also need to eat something warm.
c. Zernahi gauza ikasten du. (Iraola, 67)
He studies everything.
d. Inor egokirik aurkitu al duzu lan hartarako?
Have you already found someone suitable for that work?
e. Norbait jakintsua behar dugu. (*EGLU* I, 92)
We need someone wise.

[*N.B. Norbait* 'someone' is not usually used adjectivally. This lacuna is partly compensated for by the independent use of the adjective concerned (see *EGLU* I, 91–92).]

Zer + *V* (perfect participle) has the meaning 'something to V, things to V': *zer jan apur bat* (Agirre, *Kres*. 154) 'a little bit to eat'; *zer esan handiak* (*G*. 38) 'a lot to say'; *beste zer esan handirik* (*TZ* I, 214) 'much else to say'; *nahikoa zer ikusi* (*G*. 86) 'plenty to see'; *zer ikusi asko* (*G*. 33) 'many things to see'; *zer egin handirik* (Etxaide, *J.J*., 116) 'much to do'; and so on. The often used *zer ikusi* is analogous to Spanish *algo que ver*.

(10) a. Ez daukazu zer esanik? (*G*. 282)
Have you nothing to say?
b. Handik begiratuta, bazegoen zer ikusia. (Uztapide, *Sas*. 351)
Looking from there, there was something to see.
c. Biak, elkarrekin zer ikusi pixka bat badute. (*LBB* 105)
The two, together they have a little bit to see.

Zer + perfect participle can also have the meaning 'motive to V, reason to V':

(11) a. Moisesek erantzun zien ez zutela zer ikaratu. (*TZ* I, 126)
Moses answered them that they had no reason to be afraid.
b. Jainkoari beldur dionak ezergatik ez du zer beldurtu. (Arrue, *G.B*. 41)
Who is afraid of God has nothing to fear.
c. Zuk horrela pentsatzea ez da zer harritu. (Bilintx, 154)
It is not surprising that you think that way.

[*N.B.* Cf. section 27.12.2 for the lexicalization of *zer* + present participle. Other examples: *zeregin* 'task', 'occupation'; *zeresan* 'gossip'; *zerikusi* 'connection'.]

28.1.4 The Phrase *nondik nora*

The meaning of *nondik nora*, literally 'from where to where' (see section 3.4), has weakened in use to 'how' or 'why':

(12) a. Nondik nora ekin zenion euskarari? (*MEIG* I, 69)
Why did you take up Basque?
b. Ez nekien nondik nora hasi. (Etxezarreta, 80)
I didn't know how to begin.
c. Nondik nora habil hi egun guztian? (Echebarria, *Eib.* 487)
Where are yoú walking to the whole day?
d. Nondik nora dakark? (Zaitegi, *Sof.* 172)
Why have yoú brought her?

The negative form *inondik inora ez* can also have an idiomatic meaning: 'in no way', 'absolutely not', 'by no means', and so on.

(13) a. Inondik inora izan ezin litekeen gauza, ez batera eta ez bester. (Echebarria, *Eib.* 342)
Something that is in no way possible, neither this way nor that.
b. Ez dut egingo inondik inora. (Aulestia, 305)
I will absolutely not do it.

Also *inondik ez* alone can have this meaning and is thus synonymous with *inola ez*:

(14) a. Ez da inondik ere aditza euskalkien arteko bereizkuntzarik larriena. (*MIH* 377)
The difference between the verbs in the Basque dialects is in no way the greatest.
b. Bestea, eria, ez da asmatua inondik ere. (*MEIG* IX, 90)
The other, the illness, is absolutely not imagined.

[*N.B.* Expressions of a higher intensity such as *absolutely*, *completely*, and *entirely* are rendered in affirmative Basque sentences by words such as *zeharo*, *erabat*, *erabateko*, *oso*, *osoki*, *guztiz*, and so on—for example,

(15) Gaur egun gauzak zeharo aldatu dira. (Aulestia, 538)
Things today have changed completely.]

28.1.5 Some Observations on the Forms in Column II

For *inor* and *ezer/deus*, see chapter 13 and de Rijk 1996b.

28.1.5.1 The Words *ezer* and *deus*

In Batua, the word *deus*, qua form traceable to Latin *genus*, has the same meaning as *ezer* 'anything' and can stand alone or in combination with an adjective.

(16) a. Ez dakigu horietaz deus. (*MIH* 250)
We do not know anything about those.

b. Hil ondoan ez da deus gehiago gutarik gelditzen. (Lapeyre, 53)
After death nothing more of us remains.
c. Ez dago deus ere horren parekorik. (*MEIG* III, 104)
There is also nothing comparable to that.

28.1.5.2 Idiomatic Expressions with *gutxi*

All the forms in Column II can form idiomatic expressions with *gutxi* 'few', 'little'. These, in contrast to the independent use of *ezer* and *deus*, occur mainly in affirmative sentences. Thus we have *ezer gutxi* and *deus gutxi* 'little' or 'hardly anything', 'almost nothing'; *inor gutxi* 'almost no one'; *inon gutxitan* 'almost nowhere'; and *inoiz gutxitan* 'seldom' or 'hardly ever'. These expressions are declined as a whole: *inor gutxik*, *inor gutxiri*, *inor gutxiren*, and so on. Here are some examples:

(17) a. Inor gutxik dakizki gaur bere eskalkiaren legeak. (*MIH* 79)
Almost no one today knows the rules of his own Basque dialect.
b. Orain, Hollywood-etik ere deus gutxi etortzen zaigu. (*MIH* 327)
Now, even from Hollywood there is hardly anything coming to us.
c. Inoiz gutxitan etortzen da hona.
He seldom comes here.
d. Bi gauza, inon gutxitan idoro daitezkeenak. (*MIH* 146)
Two things, they could be found almost nowhere.
e. Inork ezer gutxi daki emakume honetaz. (Garate, *Leh.* 36)
One knows next to nothing about this woman.

28.1.5.3 With the Diminutive Suffix *-txo*

The words *inor*, *ezer*, and *zerbait* allow the diminutive suffix *-txo* (section 1.2.5): *inortxo ez* 'nobody at all'; *ezertxo ez* 'nothing at all', 'not the slightest'; *zertxobait* or *zerbaitxo* 'a little something', 'a little bit'. These forms often occur with *ere*; see section 28.1.5.5 for more.

(18) a. Ez da inortxo ere plazan. (S. Mitxelena, *IG* I, 251)
There is nobody at all in the square.
b. Ezertxo ez nekien.
I knew nothing at all.
c. Argitaratzailea ere, egia esan behar badugu, miresten da zertxobait. (*MEIG* VI, 71)
Even the publisher, to tell the truth, is a little bit surprised.

28.1.5.4 With the Negation Marker *ez*

Negative pronouns result from combining Column II forms with the negation marker *ez*: *inor ez* 'no one', 'nobody'; *ezer ez* or *deus ez* 'nothing'; *inon ez* 'nowhere'; *inondik ez* 'from nowhere'; *inora ez* 'to nowhere'; *inoiz ez* 'never' (synonyms: *behin [ere] ez*, *sekula[n] ez*, *egundaino ez*); *inola(z) ez* 'in no way', 'by no means'. *Ez* does not have to immediately follow the pronoun:

(19) a. Aho isiletik ez da ezer jakiten. (Garate, *Atsot.* 300)
From a silent mouth there is nothing to learn.
b. Ez al zintuen atzo goizean inork hemen ikusi?
Did no one see you here yesterday morning?

[*N.B.* With *inor*, the plural verb form is sometimes used:

(19) c. Inork non zen ez zekiten. (Basarri, in Uztapide, *LEG* I, 300)
Nobody knew where he was.
d. Ez zioten inork sinetsi nahi. (Ariztia, 96)
None (of them) wanted to believe him.]

Unlike in the Romance languages, the negation marker *ez* remains even in the absence of the verb:

(20) a. Inork ikusi al zaitu?—Inork ez.
"Has anyone seen you?" "No one."
b. Ezer gertatu al zaizu?—Ezer ez.
"Has something happened to you?" "Nothing."

28.1.5.5 With the Adverb *ere*

The pronouns in Column II (and also those in Column V, but less often), particularly in negative sentences, are often immediately followed by the adverb *ere* 'also', 'even', 'either' (cf. sections 17.6 and 23.7.3). This addition of *ere* intensifies the negation but otherwise changes little in the meaning of the sentence. Some examples follow:

(21) a. Inortxok ere ez dizue poz hori kentzerik izango. (Jn 16:22; *Lau Eb.*)
No one will be able to take that joy from yoû.
b. Inortxo ere ez zen aurkitzen bertan. (Urruzuno, *Ip.* 45)
There was (absolutely) no one to be found right there.
c. Ez du haren aztarrenik inon ere aurkitzen. (*MIH* 25)
He doesn't find a trace of him anywhere.
d. Ez zaio inoiz ere damutuko. (*MEIG* III, 57)
He will never regret it.
e. Neska hori ez zaik inola ere komeni. (*LBB* 123)
In no way does that girl suit yoú.

[*N.B.* The expression *inola ere* in affirmative sentences can have the same meaning as *nolanahi ere* 'anyway', 'by any means', 'however' and is synonymous with *nolanahi den* (see *EGLU* I, 485).]

The expressions *inola(z) ere* and *inondik ere*, which in negative sentences mean 'in no way', 'by no means', can also occur in affirmative sentences but then with the meaning 'without any doubt':

(22) a. Etxekoren bat hilzorian dugu, inolaz ere. (*LBB* 74)
One of our household is close to death, no doubt about it.
b. Inondik ere, lapurra Txomin da.
Without any doubt, Txomin is the thief.
c. Deabrua dabil, inolaz ere, gure elizan. (*LBB* 171)
The devil is undoubtedly at large in our church.

28.1.5.6 The Pronoun *inor* as 'someone else'

Particularly in affirmative sentences, the pronoun *inor* 'someone', 'anyone', can also have the idiomatic meaning 'someone else' in some dialects. The reverse of *inor* is then *norbera* 'oneself' (see section 28.1.2).

(23) a. Inork du beti errua. (*DCV* 1306)
Someone else is always at fault.
b. Inoren lepotik ondo edaten dute. (*P.Ab.* 53)
While they drink lavishly at someone else's expense.

28.1.5.7 The Form *ezein*

The form *ezein* 'any' is archaic and is found practically only in old texts such as Etxepare's *Linguae Vasconum Primitiae* of 1545, as in these examples:

(24) a. Ezein jaunek ez du nahi mutil gaixtoa eduki. (*LVP* I–5)
Not a single master wants to keep a bad servant.
b. O andere excelente, ezein pare gabea . . . (*LVP* I–419)
O exalted lady, without any equal . . .

But here an instance from Mitxelena:

(24) c. Hizkuntza integrakuntza beste ezein bezain beharrezkoa dugu. (*MEIG* VI, 45)
We need language integration like anything else.

Nowadays, instead of *ezein*, one uses adjectival constructions consisting of *inola* or *inon* followed by the linking morpheme *-ko*, thus literally rendering 'of (not) any kind', 'from (not) anywhere' as in these examples:

(25) a. Ez du euskarak egundaino kalterik ekarri inongo fedeari. (Xalbador, *Odol.* 240)
Basque has never brought harm to any faith.
b. Ez naiz inolako ezkutapenekin ibili. (*MEIG* IX, 85)
I haven't been going around hiding anything.

Also the partitive can serve to render 'not any', but only if the noun in question functions in the absolutive. Moreover, this partitive can be strengthened by *inolako* or *inongo* (cf. section 13.1.2):

(26) a. Atzerrira ihes egiteko inongo arrazoirik ez daukagu.
We haven't got any reason at all to flee to a foreign country.
b. Baina guk ez dugu inongo zalantzarik horretan. (*LBB* 121)
But in that we don't have any doubt.

28.1.5.8 The Form *inoizko*

We refer the reader back to section 26.5.2 for the use of *inoizko*, the adnominal form of *inoiz* 'ever', in superlative constructions. There, it was glossed in English by 'of all' following a superlative or by 'more than ever' after a comparative. However, in other constructions the adjectival modifier *inoizko* usually has the meaning 'from earlier', 'from then': *inoizko andregaia* (*MEIG* I, 132) 'the former fiancée'; *Arnoldo ez zen inoizko Arnoldo* (Agirre, *A.L.* 95) 'Arnold was not the Arnold of old'.

28.1.6 Column III Forms

28.1.6.1 About *zenbait*

The word *zenbait* means 'some', 'few', 'one or another', 'certain', and it can be used alone or adjectivally and can refer to persons or things:

(27) a. Zenbait ohoinek ebatsi duke zure zaldia. (Duvoisin, in *DRA* 3951)
Some thief will have stolen your horse.
b. Gutarik zenbait hilen gara aurten. (Azkue, *DVEF* I, 429)
Some of us will die this year.
c. Zenbait aipatuko ditut. (*MIH* 103)
I will mention some.
d. Zenbait kritikok, berriz, harrera uzkurra egin diote. (*MIH* 317)
A critical few, on the other hand, have given him a stubborn reception.

28.1.6.2 The Expression *zerbaitengatik*

The expressions *zerbaitengatik* or *zer edo zergatik* can be translated 'not for nothing':

(28) a. Gure aita ez da elizara joaten, zerbaitengatik da sozialista. (*TOE* III, 58)
Our father doesn't go to church, it is not for nothing he is a socialist.
b. Zer edo zergatik izango da. (Atxaga, *Obab.* 98)
It will not be for nothing.

28.1.6.3 The Word *nonbait*

The word *nonbait* 'somewhere' has also the idiomatic meaning 'probably', 'apparently'. To prevent misunderstandings, one often uses the locative form *nonbaiten* for the literal meaning:

(29) a. Pello mozkorturik zegoen, nonbait.
Pello was drunk, apparently.
b. Nonbaiten sortu zen euskara. (Echebarria, *Eib.* 487)
The Basque language originated somewhere.

[*N.B.* The expressions *hor nonbait*, *han nonbait*, and *nonbait han* mean 'more or less', 'about':

(30) a. Lehendakariak hirurogeita hamar urte ditu, hor nonbait (*or* nonbait han).
The president is about seventy years old.
b. Jainkoak mendiari ematen dion belarra ardiak nonbait han aski du. (Duvoisin, *Lab.* 268)
The sheep have more or less enough in the grass which God grants the mountainous area.]

28.1.6.4 The Adverb *noizbait*

The word *noizbait* 'ever', 'at some time', 'at a certain moment' (past or future, cf. *noizbaiko* 'from earlier times') has also the idiomatic meaning 'finally', especially in combination with *ere*. In the literal meaning, one sometimes uses the locative form *noizbaiten*, although also this form here and there can have the same idiomatic meaning. First we present a number of examples with the literal meaning, and then one (31d) with the idiomatic meaning:

(31) a. Kofesatzeko manamendu hau konplitu behar da, noiz izanen baita ere, noizbait. (Ax. 532)
One must fulfill this command to confess, at some time, whenever that may be.
b. Noizbait agertuko naiz herrira. (Echebarria, *Eib.* 484)
One day I'll show up in the village.
c. Noizbaiten, ez dakit zein urtetan, izanda nago haren etxean. (Ibid.)
Once, I don't remember in which year, I was in his house.
d. Noizbait etorri zen.
He finally came.

28.1.6.5 The Word *nolabait*

The word *nolabait* 'somehow', 'in some way or other' (as in example 32a) has also the idiomatic meaning 'in a careless way' and is synonymous with *hala-hola* and *hala-hala* 'so-so'. The adnominal form *nolabaiteko* therefore means 'indifferent', 'mediocre', synonymous with *hala-holako* and *hala-halako*.

(32) a. Nolabait konpondu zen inor nekatu gabe. (Echebarria, *Eib.* 485)
In some way or other it was arranged without bothering anyone.

b. Aitor dezagun, luzatu gabe, nolabaitekotzat etsi dituela honek. (*MEIG* V, 40)
Let us admit, without further ado, that this one considers them only so-so.

[*N.B.* For the construction *etsi* ('to consider') + ... *-tzat*, see section 17.8.2.]

28.1.7 Column IV: Expressions with *edo*

An expression with *edo* is treated as a whole; thus *nor edo nork*, *nor edo nori*, *zer edo zerk*, *zer edo zeri*, and so on are no longer considered coordinating constructions. This treatment is also reflected in the pronunciation: *zer edo zer* sounds like *zeozer*, and *nor edo nor* like *nuonor* or even *nonor*.

Synonymous with *nor edo nor* are *bat edo bat* and *baten bat*, also to be translated as 'the one or other'. Besides *non edo non* 'somewhere', *non edo han* is also much used, and further, *nondik edo handik* is used for *non edo nondik*, and *nora edo hara* for *non edo nora*.

As for the corresponding expressions for *nola*: *nola edo hala* is even considerably more used than *nola edo nola*. Synonymous with *noiz edo noiz* is *behin edo behin* 'sometimes'; also frequently found is *noizean behin* or *noizik behin* 'from time to time', 'now and then'—not to be confused with *behinik behin*, which means 'at least', 'at any rate' (the same as *behintzat* and *bederen*).

28.1.8 Column V: Forms with *nahi*

28.1.8.1 The Word *zenbat-nahi*

The word *zenbat-nahi* or *zenbanahi* 'however much', 'as much as you want', 'unlimited', does occur, but it is not very usual. Normally one uses one of the following expressions: *nahi adina*, *nahi haina*, *nahi hainbat*, *nahi bezainbat* (see section 26.3), or *nahi ahala* (see section 24.7.1).

(33) a. Zenbat-nahi arrain ekarriko dut. (Echeita, *Au* 73)
I will bring as much fish as you want.

b. Bainan behar dugu, zenbat-nahi dorpe zaigun. (Lapeyre, 271)
But we must, however demanding it is of us.

c. Nahi haina diru irabaz dezakezue.
Yoû can earn as much money as yoû want.

d. Nahi ahala eduki genuen jan eta edana egun hartan (Echebarria, *Eib*. 475)
That day we got as much to eat and drink as we wanted.

28.1.8.2 The Declension of *nahi* Forms

In the declension of the *nahi* forms from Column V, one can see a wavering between two coexisting systems: an older system with *norknahi* (Ubillos, 68), *norinahi* (see Arejita 1994, 240), and so on; *zerknahi* and *zerinahi*; *nondik-nahi*, *noranahi*, and so on; and a younger system with, correspondingly, *nornahik*, *nornahiri*, and so on; *zernahik* and *zernahiri*; *non-nahitik* (or *nonahitik*), *non-nahira*, and so on.

In present-day practice in Batua, the younger system seems by far preferred. The main exception is the continued use of the locative *noranahi* instead of *non-nahira* (but see Oñatibia, 160: *nunaira*), while *nondik-nahi* (also locative) is synonymous with *non-nahitik* and *nonahitik* in the Euskaltzaindia's "Hiztegi Batua" (*Euskera* 45, 2 [2000], 673).

28.2 The Adjective *ber*

The adjective *ber* means 'same' (cf. section 6.1.5). Because of its meaning it almost always takes the definite form: *bera* 'the same'. Yet the indefinite form is not in principle excluded:

(34) Ganibet ber batek debaka ogia eta eria. (Oihenarte, *Prov.* 179)
A same knife cuts the bread and the finger. (*debaka* = *ebakitzen du*)

28.2.1 Constructions Based on *ber*

In the Souletin dialect, *ber* also means 'alone', and we find here a contrast between *ber gizon* 'the same man' and *gizon bera* 'the man alone'. In most of the other dialects, however, *ber* appears in the usual place for adjectives, that is, after the noun: *gizon bera* 'the same man'. This is true in Batua also. Some examples follow:

(35) a. Sorgin ber hori dator hona.
That same witch is coming here.
b. Sorgin berak esan du.
The same witch said it.
c. Sorgin beraren erratzaz baliatuko naiz.
I will make use of the broom belonging to the same witch.
d. Euskaldun berek dute falta.
The same Basques are to blame.

The adjective *ber* takes on the function of a restrictive clause in these sentences: it identifies the referent of the noun phrase in question. With a noun phrase that is already definite, *ber* can also appear in apposition, thus functioning like an explanatory clause. The referent of the noun phrase is in this case also evident to the hearer without *ber*; the use of *ber* serves only to focus attention on the matter to which it refers.

This explanatory constuction with *ber* has all the properties that Basque allows an apposition: *ber* stands immediately after the noun phrase in question and has the same declensional endings as the noun phrase—in this case, always in the definite form.

The English translation of this construction makes use of such terms as 'the very (one/thing we are talking about)', the word 'self', or, to make it clearer, 'in person', 'personally' for people and 'as such' for things, as in these examples:

(36) a. Sorgin hori bera dator hona.
That very witch is coming here (in person).
b. Sorginak berak esan du.
The witch has said it herself.
c. Sorginaren beraren erratzaz baliatuko naiz.
I will make use of the broom belonging to the witch herself.
d. Euskaldunek berek dute falta. (Ax. 19)
The Basques themselves are to blame.

28.2.2 With Locative Endings

In combination with locative endings (see chapter 3), appositive *ber*, just like the demonstrative pronouns, takes the suffix *-ta* (see section 9.6.2). Examples are *herri berean* 'in the same village', *zubi beretik* 'via the same bridge'; but *herrian bertan* 'in the village itself', *zubitik bertatik* 'via the bridge itself', and *herri hartan bertan* 'in that village itself', *aste hartan bertan* 'in that very week'.

28.2.3 Reduplicated *ber*

Reduplication can strengthen *ber* in both its uses: *bertsolari berbera* 'exactly the same verse singer', *bertsolaria berbera* 'the verse singer himself, personally'. Here are a couple of examples:

(37) a. Eta beti historia berbera. (Labayen, *Su Em.* 167)
And always exactly the same story.
b. Neure aberritik egotzi naute neure seme berberak. (Zaitegi, *Sof.* 123)
My very own sons expelled me from my homeland.

The forms *bera* and *berbera* can also take the precision suffix *-xe* (section 26.8):

(38) a. Irakurtzen ari zaren liburu beraxe irakurri dut nik ere.
The very same book you are reading I have also read.
b. Hona hemen bilatzen zenuen mutila berberaxe.
Here is now the very boy in person that you were looking for.

28.2.4 The Forms *bera* and *berak*

The adjective *ber* can also be in apposition to a null pronoun of the third person, thereby creating the semblance even of being a personal pronoun: *bera* 'he himself', *berak* 'they themselves'. One sees

(39) a. Bera han zegoen. (Múgica Berrondo, *DVC* 417)
He was there himself.
b. Berak dakike ongien zer egin.
He will know best himself what to do.

c. Zeregin hori egin dezala berak. (Echebarria, *Eib.* 149)
Let him do that chore himself.

d. Berek sinesten ez dutena, guri sinetsarazi nahi digute.
What they themselves don't believe, they want us to believe.

As already mentioned in section 6.1.5, *bera* used in apposition with a personal pronoun has the genitive form *bere* instead of the expected *beraren*. Thus we find *irakasle beraren liburua* 'the book of the same teacher', *irakaslearen beraren liburua* 'the book of the teacher himself', but *bere liburua* 'his own book'.

In reference to the null pronoun of the third person, it is interesting to note that the use of the null form is only possible if the pronoun in question is neither in focus nor a new "topic" and has no other case endings than one that goes with a conjugated verb form—absolutive, ergative, or dative. If this condition is not met, then the demonstrative pronouns are called for: *hau, hori, hura.*

In section 9.6.3 demonstrative pronouns as independent nominals were discussed, and it was mentioned that they serve as equivalents of the third-person pronouns, competing with *bera* (*berak* or *eurak*) in the southern variety of Batua, which employs *bera* whenever the speaker expects the hearer to be aware of a previous mention of the referent intended.

The form *bera* is used in Batua only if the nuance "self" is applicable, as in examples (39a–d). In colloquial Guipuzcoan, however, one sees a tendency to equate *bera* with the Spanish pronouns *él* and *ella.*

28.2.5 First- and Second-Person Pronouns

The form *bera* is not used in apposition with the personal pronouns of the first and second person. The reason is probably that a third-person semantic element has crept in as a result of the frequent use of the previously discussed construction $\emptyset +$ *bera* $=$ *bera* 'he himself', 'she herself'.

The meaning that a combination of these personal pronouns with *bera* would have had is expressed in another way whereby the construction of the singular forms differs somewhat from that of the plural ones.

With the first- and second-person singular we find a combined sequence of the reflexive form of the corresponding possessive pronoun and the appropriate demonstrative pronoun. The reflexive forms *neure*, *heure*, and *zeure* thereby lose their final *-e* and reduce *eu* > *e*, while the demonstrative pronouns shed their initial consonant *h-*.

There is a comparable process with the first- and second-person plural, but with the difference that the inclusive article *-ok* (section 19.7) appears in place of the demonstrative pronouns. With the second-person plural, instead of the reflexive form *zeuen*, *zeure* is used, a form that was once a plural form (see section 6.1.1).

Here is the basic paradigm for the five forms:

	Absolutive	Ergative	Dative	Genitive	Sociative
I myself	nerau	neronek	neroni	neronen	neronekin
yoú yoúrself	herori	herorrek	herorri	herorren	herorrekin
you yourself	zerori	zerorrek	zerorri	zerorren	zerorrekin
we ourselves	gerok	gerok	geroi	geron	gerokin
yoû yoûrselves	zerok	zerok	zeroi	zeron	zerokin

[*N.B.* There are variants, and the Basque Academy has not decided on standard forms as yet.]

Some examples will illustrate:

(40) a. Neure mutila bidali gabe, nerau etorri naiz.
Instead of sending my boy, I came myself.
b. ... baldin zerori nor bazara ... (Ax. 306)
... if you yourself are man enough ...
c. Neroni, egia esan, bat nentorren Txillardegirekin. (*MIH* 296)
I myself, to tell the truth, agreed with Txillardegi.
d. Eta zerok dakizue neure indar guztiarekin serbitu dudala zuen aita. (Gn 31:6; Ur.)
And yoû yoûrselves know that I have served yoûr father with all my strength.
e. Herorrek esaten dituk denak. (*LBB* 147, 150)
Yoú yoúrself are telling all.
f. Baina oraindik gerok bakarrik dakigu gertatua. (*LBB* 25)
But still only we ourselves know what happened.
g. Behartsuak zerokin beti izango dituzue, ez ordea Ni. (*TB* 94)
Yoû will always have the poor with yoû, but me (yoû will) not.

28.2.5.1 Emphatic Personal Pronouns

The precision suffix *-xe* of section 26.8, like *bera*, cannot be joined with first- and second-person pronouns. The syntactic function that these combinations would have had are filled by a system of emphatic pronouns based on the diphthong *eu*: *neu* 'Í', *heu* 'yóú ("familiar" singular)', *zeu* 'yóu (singular)', *geu* 'wé', *zeuek* 'yóû (plural)', as illustrated in the following paradigm:

	Absolutive	Ergative	Dative	Genitive	Sociative
Í	neu	neuk	neuri	neure	neurekin
yóú	heu	heuk	heuri	heure	heurekin
yóu	zeu	zeuk	zeuri	zeure	zeurekin
wé	geu	geuk	geuri	geure	geurekin
yóû	zeuek	zeuek	zeuei	zeuen	zeuekin

Just like the noun phrases with the suffix *-xe*, these emphatic pronouns are used especially when they participate in a sentence part that stands before the verb as focus or when they themselves are focus. Or they may appear as topic (cf. section 26.8.2):

(41) a. Neuk ere ongi dakit hori. (Osa 1990, 44)
Í also know that well.
b. Neuk behintzat ez dut horrelakorik esan. (Ibid.)
Í, at least, have not said anything like that.
c. Noiz jaiki zinen bada zeu? (*P.Ab.* 116)
When did yóu get up?

Their use is not compulsory:

(42) Ekarri giltza, mesedez. Nik daukat, ala?—Bai, zuk daukazu. (Arejita 1994, 223)
"(Give me) the key, please. Or do Í have it?" "Yes, yóu have it."

Moreover, the emphatic pronouns can take on a reflexive function—namely, where for syntactic-semantic reasons a reflexive construction with *buru* (see section 15.7) is not possible. This is the case particularly for the intensive genitive, already named the reflexive in section 6.1.4, but sometimes also for the endings based on it (see examples 43h,i).

[*N.B.* These possessive forms can also be focus—for example, nonreflexive *zeuria izango da errua* (*P.Ab.* 47) 'The blame will be yóurs'.]

Some examples will illustrate the use of these pronouns:

(43) a. Baina orduan ni ez nintzen neu. (Garate, *Musk.* 42)
But then I was not myself (Í).
b. Neure onak neuk nahi ditut gozatu eta maneiatu. (Ax. 235)
Í want to enjoy and manage my own goods.
c. Neu naiz denotatik zaharrena. (Echebarria, *Eib.* 483)
Í am the oldest of us all.
d. Ujentu! Heu al haiz? (Etxaniz, *Ito* 208)
Ujentu! Is it yóú?
e. Ba, heuk ere horixe egin duk.
Well, yóú also did just that.
f. Paga ezazu zerorrek, zeuk zor duzunaz geroztik. (Ax. 242)
Pay it yourself, since yóu owe it.
g. Gorputz eta arima naiz zeurea. (Agirre, *A.L.* 71)
Body and soul I am yóurs.
h. Zeren berdin ezin eraman zenitzakeen zeurekin. (Ax. 210)
Because in the end you would not have been able to take them with you.
i. Igor dezagun aitzinetik, eta daramagun geurekin ere. (Ax. 241)
Let us send ahead, and also take with us.

j. Gu gara geu, ez hobeak eta ez txarragoak, baina geu. (Echebarria, *Eib.* 307)
We are ourselves (wé), neither better nor worse, but ourselves (wé).

k. Geuk jaso dugu etxe hau eta ez izerdi gutxirekin. (Ibid.)
Wé have built this house, and with not a little sweat.

l. Zeuek zenbat emango diozue mutilari? (*G.* 37)
How much will yóû give to the boy?

m. Ez nauzue zuek aukeratu, neuk aukeratu zaituztet zuek. (Etxaniz, *Nola* 37; cf. Jn 15:16)
Yoû did not choose me, Í chose yoû.

[*N.B.* The sequences *ni neu*, *hi heu*, *zu zeu*, *gu geu*, and *zuek zeuek* appear not infrequently in the same meaning as *nerau*, *herori*, *zerori*, *gerok*, and *zerok*:

(44) a. Nik neuk ez nituen ezagutu. (Bilbao, 198)
I myself didn't know them.

b. Guk geuk daukagu inork baino gehiago. (Altube, *Erd.* 106)
We ourselves have more than anyone.]

28.2.6 With Demonstratives

The demonstrative pronouns, whether used adjectivally or independently, can in the usual way be followed by appositive *bera*, but allow also a construction analogous to the paradigm *nerau*, *zerori*, and so on:

hau bera = berau hauek berak = berauek
hori bera = berori horiek berak = beroriek
hura bera = bera haiek berak = berak (*or* beraiek)

A still more emphatic form is *hau berau*, *hori berori*, *hauek berauek*, and so on. The precision suffix -*xe* may be joined to all these forms: *hauxe bera*, *hauxe beraxe*, *berauxe*, *hauxe berau*, *hauxe berauxe*, and so on.

Some examples follow:

(45) a. Beronek asmatzen ditu galdera eta erantzunak. (Etxaniz, *Antz.* 394)
He himself thinks up the questions and answers.

b. Bitxiok eder, berori ez. (Garibay, *Refranes*, 67 [no. A55])
The jewels are beautiful, she herself not.

c. Berau da interesik haundiena eduki behar lukeena. (Echebarria, *Eib.* 150)
He himself is the one who should take the greatest interest.

d. Bada arrazoi horren beronengatik ez dut ikusi nahi. (Ax. 394)
So precisely for that reason I don't want to see her.

e. Maisu, hori itsu jaiotzeko, zeinek bekatu egin zuen? Berorrek ala horren gurasoek? (Manzisidor, 287; cf. Jn 9:2)
Master, who has sinned that he was born blind? He himself or his parents?

[*N.B.* The word *berori*, but not *hori bera*, has the idiomatic meaning 'you (deferential)', 'your "noble" . . .'.]

Also the locative adverbs *hemen* 'here', *hor* 'there', and *han* 'over there' allow appositive *bera*, which is then naturally also in the locative: *hemen bertan* (or *hemen berton*), *hor bertan* (or *hor berton*), and *han bertan*. In these combinations it is usual, though not obligatory, to leave out the first part, that is, the original adverb itself, thus giving rise to the anaphoric adverbs *bertan* 'there', 'right there' and *berton* 'here', 'right here'. *Bertatik* 'from right there' can also have a temporal meaning: 'from that moment on'.

Here are some examples:

(46) a. Patxi Zabaleta, Donostian jaioa, eta bertan bizi dena.
Patxi Zabaleta, born in San Sebastian and residing there.
b. Miren Igartea, hemen jaioa, eta berton bizi dena.
Miren Igartea, born here and residing right here.
c. Gaur, bakarrik bizi naiz ni neure herrian bertan arrotz! (Agirre, *A.L.* 46)
Today, I live alone, a stranger there in my own land!
d. Ez zara hemen etxeon berton bizi ala?—Ez. Goizuetan berton baina neure etxean. (Garate, *G.E.* 28)
"Or aren't you living right here?" "No. Here in Goizueta, but in my own house."

[*N.B.* The intensifying *berton* and *bertan* can also accompany a time expression:

(47) a. Oraintxe berton bidaldu behar dut norbait Bizkarrondonera. (Erkiaga, *Arran.* 90)
Just right now I need to send someone to Bizkarrondo.
b. Oraintxe bertontxe hil behar banu ere, berdin esango nuke. (Altube, *Erd.* 95)
Even if I had to die at this very moment, I would still say it.
c. Oraintxe berton noakio atzetik. (Bilbao, 95)
I am going after him right now.
d. Eta gaur bertan al zoaz? (Irazusta, *Bizia* 96)
And are you going (right away) today?
e. Bihar bertantxe behar dut zure erantzuna. (T. Agirre, *Uzt.* 62)
Tomorrow (for sure) I must have your answer.]

28.3 The Universal Quantifier *oro*

The Basque word *oro* has the function of a universal quantifier in the field of logic. Depending on the number of the person form and sometimes also the nature of the relevant noun phrase, *oro* has the meaning of 'each' or 'any', 'every' or 'all'. In the spoken language, *oro* is used only in the northeastern dialects, that is, Low Navarrese and especially Souletin. As for Euskara Batua, turns of phrase with *oro* are a stylistic means of giving a text a somewhat formal, or at any rate, an uncommonplace character.

In ordinary speech people make use of the adjectival quantifier *guzti* (see section 10.5) for the meaning 'every', and also the substantival quantifier *dena* 'all', 'everything' and *denak* 'everybody', 'all (of them)' (section 10.4). And *edozein* is used for the meaning 'any (at all)', while *bakoitz* does duty for the meaning nuance 'each one separately'.

28.3.1 Constructions with *oro*

The word *oro* occurs in two kinds of constructions: a normal or an appositional one. In the normal construction *oro* appears like an ordinary adjective. The form of the syntagma is then analogous to that of a noun phrase with *guzti*, with one important difference: whereas *guzti* is always definite (with the definite article), a noun phrase with *oro* is always indefinite (no article). Thus we have *esne guztia* or *esne oro* 'all milk', *andre guztiak* or *andre oro* 'all ladies'. Compare also the idiomatic expression for 'everybody': *mundu guztia* or, more stately, *mundu oro*. The fact that a noun phrase with *oro* is indefinite has the consequence that the normal construction is not possible whenever the noun phrase includes a demonstrative pronoun.

Now, as illustrations of the normal construction, we first present some examples from Etxepare's *Linguae Vasconum Primitiae* of 1545, and then some more recent ones:

(48) a. Artzain orok biltzen ditu ardiak arratsaldean. (*LVP* I–172)
Every shepherd gathers his sheep in the evening.
b. Beste nazione orok uste dute ezin deus ere skriba daite(ke)ela lengoaje hartan. (*LVP*, foreword)
All other nations think that one cannot write anything in that language.
c. Justu oro iganen da bertan goiti(k) airean. (*LVP* I–325)
The just will immediately (on the spot) rise up into the air.
d. . . . egun oro meza entzutea . . . (Ax. 497–498)
. . . the hearing mass every day . . .
e. Lur orok badu buztin eta harea. (Inchauspe, *Dial.* 10)
All soil contains clay and sand.
f. . . . bai eta ere neska gazte orori etsenplu ema(i)ten. (Azkue, *E. Y.* IV, 41)
. . . and also to give an example to all young girls.

We noticed already that this construction is not always possible. We then come to the appositional variant. Whenever we encounter a demonstrative pronoun or a noun phrase with a definite article, *oro* can then only appear in apposition. Probably the deeper reason for this limitation is that such a noun phrase does not allow a restrictive clause.

As we saw with the *bera* syntagmas, the noun phrase and the apposition are separately declined (see examples 49c–e):

(49) a. Gauza haiek oro ebatsi gauzak dira, eta haien jabeak oro hilak. (Barbier, *Lég.* 139)
Those things are all stolen things, and their owners all dead.

b. Bere bekatuak oro baditu ere konfesatu, . . . (*LVP* I–198)
Even though he has confessed his sins totally, . . .
c. Berri horien ororen jakitez . . . (Etxahun-Iruri, 140)
Learning from all those reports . . .
d. Horiengatik orogatik zer da zuen pagua? (*LVP* I–350)
What is yoûr payment (in return) for all that?
e. Neure bekatuez oroz dudan barkamendua. (*LVP* I–67)
So that I receive forgiveness for all my sins. (archaic *dudan* = *izan dezadan*)

It can happen in a sentence that the noun phrase to which *oro* stands in apposition is fronted through a process of topicalization or something similar. The *oro* apposition does not need to be fronted along with it. Thus appositive *oro*, unlike in the case of *bera*, for example, can become separated from the noun phrase it modifies. We see this possibility in the following examples:

(50) a. Ene ongi-eginak ere orai(n) oro gaitz dira. (*LVP* XIII–20)
Even my good deeds are now all bad.
b. Sainduak ere ordu hartan oro egonen isilik. (*LVP* I–287)
Even the saints will all be silent at that moment.
c. Etxeko berriak kanpoan oro salatzen dizkizu. (From the Souletin song "Ixkerraren zamaria," Sallaberry, 237)
All the news in your house she discloses outside.
d. Alaba dutenei esanen diet orori . . . (Cf. the song "Maitia, nun zira," Sallaberry, 15)
To those with a daughter, I shall say to all . . .

28.3.2 The Word *oro* as an Indefinite Pronoun

The word *oro* can also occur independently as an indefinite pronoun. As was mentioned in section 6.1.3, there is an amplified, or lengthened, form of the instrumental typical of pronouns. When *oro* functions as a pronoun, it can also take this long form: *oroz* or *orotaz* 'by all'. (According to Lafitte 1962, sec. 251f, *orotaz* should also be used when *oro* functions appositively with a noun phrase: *herriaz orotaz jabetu ziren* 'they have dominated the whole country'. It would appear from example 49e that Etxepare did not follow this rule.)

Used independently, *oro* can mean 'everything' or 'everyone'. Also important are the declined forms: *orotan* 'everywhere'; *orotarik* 'from everywhere', 'from everything'; *orotara* 'to everywhere'; *ororekin ere* 'notwithstanding everything', literally 'with all (that)'.

Expressions with *oro* that are regularly used in Batua include *oro har* 'in general', 'taking everything into consideration' and *orobat* 'the same', 'likewise', 'so also'. *Oroz gain*, *oroz gainetik*, *ororen gain*, and *ororen gainetik* all mean 'above all', 'especially'. The usual expression for this is *batez ere* or *batik bat* (*batipat*). (Translator's note: From the marginal notes on the draft manuscript one can see that de Rijk had planned to address the logical distinction between universal and existential quantifiers, and consider the analogy with Q-float.)

28.4 The Synthetic Future Tense

In addition to the periphrastic future tense already treated in chapter 7, there is a synthetic future tense, also referred to as the "archaic future tense." This tense is formed with the addition of the irreality suffix *-ke* to the present indicative forms. This suffix stands immediately before the ergative person marker, if present: *dut* 'I have', *duket* 'I will have', and *nauzu* 'you have me', *naukezu* 'you will have me'.

Also, the *-ke* precedes the suffix *-te* of the second-person plural: *zaudete* 'yoû are standing', *zaudekete* 'yoû will stand'. In the absence of the aforementioned suffixes, *-ke* comes at the very end of the verb form: *zaigu* 'he is for us', *zaiguke* 'he will be for us'. Thus it follows that *-ke* will always immediately follow an eventual dative person marker: *eman dizugu* 'we have given it to you', *eman dizukegu* 'we shall have given it to you'.

Besides the verbs *izan* and **edun*, *ibili* 'to walk' also shows an irregularity: its pluralizer *-tza* reduces to the form *-z before -ke* (cf. sections 17.2.3 and 24.4.3). Thus we have *dabiltza* 'they walk', *dabilzke* 'they will walk'.

With the verb *izan*, when there is no dative marker and the irreality suffix *-ke* would directly follow the stem, there is again the formative morpheme *-te-* acting as a buffer, to avoid contact between the stem and *-ke* (see sections 17.2.3 and 24.1.2). Last, we find in the singular forms *naiz* and *haiz* the unshortened stem *-iza-*: *naizateke* 'I will be', *haizateke* 'yoú will be' (see section 17.2.1).

With **edun*, in the presence of the object pluralizer *it-*, the stem *-u-* also takes a suffix pluralizer *-z*, immediately preceding the irreality suffix *-ke* (cf. the present conditional forms, section 17.2.3): *ditut* 'I have them', *dituzket* 'I will have them'; *gaituzu* 'you have us', *gaituzkezu* 'you will have us'.

Reminder: The present tense forms of the potential are obtained through the addition of the irreality suffix *-ke* to the truncated forms of the subjunctive present. Except for *izan* and **edun*, the synthetic forms of the subjunctive mood are really the same as those of the indicative mood—followed by the suffix *-en*. Since this suffix disappears again in the truncation process, it follows that, except for *izan* and **edun*, the synthetic future tense has the same form as the synthetic present tense of the potential:

zaudeke	you can stand, you will stand
nabilke	I can walk, I will walk
dakarkegu	we can bring, we will bring

Although the synthetic future tense forms of *izan* and **edun* can easily be derived from the present tense forms, we give here nonetheless (for convenience) the full paradigms:

naizateke	I will be
haizateke	yoú will be
dateke	he will be
garateke	we will be
zarateke	you will be
zaratekete	yoû will be
dirateke	they will be

zaidake	it will be for me	zaizkidake	they will be for me
zaiake	it will be for yoú	zaizkiake	they will be for yoú
zainake	it will be for yoù	zaizkinake	they will be for yoù
zaioke	it will be for him	zaizkioke	they will be for him
zaiguke	it will be for us	zaizkiguke	they will be for us
zaizuke	it will be for you	zaizkizuke	they will be for you
zaizueke	it will be for yoû	zaizkizueke	they will be for yoû
zaieke	it will be for them	zaizkieke	they will be for them

natzaiake	I will be for yoú	gatzaizkiake	we will be for yoú
natzainake	I will be for yoù	gatzaizkinake	we will be for yoù
natzaioke	I will be for him	gatzaizkioke	we will be for him
natzaizuke	I will be for you	gatzaizkizuke	we will be for you
natzaizueke	I will be for yoû	gatzaizkizueke	we will be for yoû
natzaieke	I will be for them	gatzaizkieke	we will be for them

hatzaidake	yoú will be for me
hatzaioke	yoú will be for him
hatzaiguke	yoú will be for us
hatzaieke	yoú will be for them

zatzaizkidake	you will be for me	zatzaizkidakete	yoû will be for me
zatzaizkioke	you will be for him	zatzaizkiokete	yoû will be for him
zatzaizkiguke	you will be for us	zatzaizkigukete	yoû will be for us
zatzaizkieke	you will be for them	zatzaizkiekete	yoû will be for them

duket	I will have it	dituzket	I will have them
dukek	yoú will have it	dituzkek	yoú will have them
duken	yoù will have it	dituzken	yoù will have them
duke	he will have it	dituzke	he will have them
dukegu	we will have it	dituzkegu	we will have them
dukezu	you will have it	dituzkezu	you will have them
dukezue	yoû will have it	dituzkezue	yoû will have them
dukete	they will have it	dituzket	they will have them

naukek	yoú will have me	gaituzkek	yoú will have us
nauken	yoù will have me	gaituzken	yoù will have us
nauke	he will have me	gaituzke	he will have us
naukezu	you will have me	gaituzkezu	you will have us
naukezue	yoû will have me	gaituzkezue	yoû will have us
naukete	they will have me	gaituzkete	they will have us
hauket	I will have yoú	zaituzket	I will have you
hauke	he will have yoú	zaituzke	he will have you
haukegu	we will have yoú	zaituzkegu	we will have you
haukete	they will have yoú	zaituzkete	they will have you

zaituzketet	I will have yoû
zaituzkete	he will have yoû
zaituzketegu	we will have yoû
zaituzketete	they will have yoû

Following are the transitive dative forms:

diaket	I will have it for yoú	dizkiaket	I will have them for yoú
dinaket	I will have it for yoù	dizkinaket	I will have them for yoù
dioket	I will have it for him	dizkioket	I will have them for him
dizuket	I will have it for you	dizkizuket	I will have them for you
dizueket	I will have it for yoû	dizkizueket	I will have them for yoû
dieket	I will have it for them	dizkieket	I will have them for them
didakek	yoú will have it for me	dizkidakek	yoú will have them for me
diokek	yoú will have it for him	dizkiokek	yoú will have them for him
digukek	yoú will have it for us	dizkigukek	yoú will have them for us
diekek	yoú will have it for them	dizkiekek	yoú will have them for them
didaken	yoù will have it for me	dizkidaken	yoù will have them for me
dioken	yoù will have it for him	dizkioken	yoù will have them for him
diguken	yoù will have it for us	dizkiguken	yoù will have them for us
dieken	yoù will have it for them	dizkieken	yoù will have them for them
didake	he will have it for me	dizkidake	he will have them for me
diake	he will have it for yoú	dizkiake	he will have them for yoú
dinake	he will have it for yoù	dizkinake	he will have them for yoù
dioke	he will have it for him	dizkioke	he will have them for him
diguke	he will have it for us	dizkiguke	he will have them for us
dizuke	he will have it for you	dizkizuke	he will have them for you
dizueke	he will have it for yoû	dizkizueke	he will have them for yoû
dieke	he will have it for them	dizkieke	he will have them for them

diakegu	we will have it for yoú	dizkiakegu	we will have them for yoú
dinakegu	we will have it for yoù	dizkinakegu	we will have them for yoù
diokegu	we will have it for him	dizkiokegu	we will have them for him
dizukegu	we will have it for you	dizkizukegu	we will have them for you
dizuekegu	we will have it for yoû	dizkizuekegu	we will have them for yoû
diekegu	we will have it for them	dizkiekegu	we will have them for them
didakezu	you will have it for me	dizkidakezu	you will have them for me
diokezu	you will have it for him	dizkiokezu	you will have them for him
digukezu	you will have it for us	dizkigukezu	you will have them for us
diekezu	you will have it for them	dizkiekezu	you will have them for them
didakezue	yoû will have it for me	dizkidakezue	yoû will have them for me
diokezue	yoû will have it for him	dizkiokezue	yoû will have them for him
digukezue	yoû will have it for us	dizkigukezue	yoû will have them for us
diekezue	yoû will have it for them	dizkiekezue	yoû will have them for them

28.4.1 Periphrastic Forms

The synthetic future tense forms of *izan* and **edun* can serve as auxiliaries to the imperfect form of the main verb to form a "synthetic" future tense for verbs that do not have synthetic forms, such as *ikasi* 'to learn', and verbs whose synthetic forms, though existent, are not often used, such as *ikusi* 'to see': *ikasten duke* 'he will (surely) learn it', *ikusten duke* (or: *dakuske*) 'he will see it (for sure)'.

Together with the perfect, the synthetic future tense forms of the auxiliary provide the "synthetic" perfect future tense: *ikasi duke* 'he will (doubtlessly) have learned it', *ikusi duke* 'he will have seen it (without a doubt)'. Cf. *EGLU* II, 412: *Gure anaia ezagutuko duzu* (= *ezagutzen dukezu* in the north); *Gure anaia ezagutuko zenuen* (= *ezagutu dukezu*). ('You will surely know our brother.')

28.4.2 Meaning and Use of the Forms

These verbal forms have undergone a semantic development. In the 1571 New Testament of Leizarraga it was still noticeable that the significance of *-ke* in combination with a verbal form of the present tense was purely aspectual: it served to clearly mark the imperfection of the process, its unfinished aspect.

This aspectual meaning has long since narrowed to a tense-mood meaning: a future tense, which is also very often used to refer to a probability in the present: *Badakikezu nor naizen.* 'You will (surely) know who I am'. Also the ordinary periphrastic future tense can, as we know, express probability in the present: *Jakingo duzu, noski, nor naizen.* 'You will surely know who I am'.

Nowadays the synthetic future tense survives in the spoken language only in the northeastern dialects, that is, in Souletin, and in some areas of Low Navarra. In present-day

Batua it is not wholely unknown, but very rare—used in literary and lofty style. (See *EGLU* II, 413–417, 429–434.)

[*N.B.* In Low Navarrese and Souletin, especially in older texts, we find for the verb *izan* the form *-te* used—but not always—instead of *-teke*: *naizate*, *haizate*, *date*, *garate*, *zarate*, *dirate* instead of *naizateke*, *haizateke*, *dateke*, *garateke*, *zarateke*, *dirateke*. These short forms are not used in Batua.]

Some examples will illustrate the use of synthetic future forms:

(51) a. Ni baitan dukezu adiskide bat. (*LVP* X–73)
In me you will have a friend.
b. Hartu duten plazer oro orduan iragan date. (*LVP* II–17)
All pleasure they have enjoyed will then be over.
c. Eta orduan denbora onaren seinalea dateke. (*G.* 37)
And then it will be a sign of good weather.
d. Nondik dukezu ur bizi hura? (Larréguy II, 136)
From where will you fetch that living water?
e. Gauza bera ezagutu dukezu zerorrek ere. (Duhalde, 539)
You yourself also will have (doubtlessly) experienced the same.
f. Zer emanen diozu, edo zer on duke zureganik? (Jb 35.7; Dv)
What will you give him, or what good will he receive from you?
g. Lan horiek beren sari ona dakarkete. (Duvoisin, *Lab.* 28)
Those works will (surely) bring their own good reward.
h. Hark badakike zer egin. (Lapitze, 89)
He will certainly know what to do.
i. Ez duke hori nahi izan Jesu-Kristok. (Lapeyre, 257)
Jesus Christ will surely not have wanted that.
j. Nire emazteak amets egin duke. (H.U., *Zez.* 61)
My wife will have dreamed it.
k. Ikusi duke bi aldiz bizkitartean! (J. Etchepare, *Bur.* 178)
Meanwhile he will (doubtlessly) have seen it twice!
l. Berehala hemen dukezue extek'andrea. (Barbier, *Sup.* 135)
Yoû will have the lady of the house here right away.
m. Bai, bai, berea duke segurki. (Barbier, *Sup.* 124).
Yes, yes, she will have hers surely.
n. Zer dukegu jateko edo edateko? (*Usk. gut.* 135)
What shall we have to eat or to drink?

[*N.B.* Leizarraga translated this text from Matthew 6:31 with the future: *Zer janen dugu edo zer edanen dugu*? 'What will we eat or what will we drink? (Duvoisin: *Zer janen dugu edo zer edanen*?)]

(51) o. Zer buruhauste berri duket? (Zaitegi, *Sof.* 111)
What new problem will I have?

p. Satanek ifernutik egin duke burla. (Xalbador, *Odol.* 111)
Satan out of hell will (doubtlessly) have laughed at it.

q. Han dirateke errotik herritarrak harriturik. (Casenave, 154)
Over there the villagers will be profoundly astonished.

r. Oraikoan zure aldi(a) zen, noiz dateke gurea? (Etxahun-Iruri, 120)
This time it was your turn, when will it be ours?

s. Jakin dukezu orain duela hamar egun Hernandorena, Elizondoko alkatea, Izpegin hil zutela. (Garate, *E.E.* 41)
You will surely have found out that they killed Hernandorena, the mayor of Elizondo, ten days ago on Izpegi.

[*N.B.* We should remember here the use of *bide* to express likelihood (section 8.1.3): *Jakin bide duzu alkatea hil dutela.* 'You must surely have found out that they have killed the mayor.']

29 Allocutive Verb Forms and Their Use; Nonfinite Sentential Complements

29.1 Allocutive Verb Forms and Their Use

29.1.1 Definition and Use of Allocutive Forms

In Basque, when one is speaking to someone whom one would address with the "familiar" pronoun *hi* (encoding "solidarity," see section 6.1.2), a special finite verb form is required in the main clause. Not only verb forms with a second-person subject are affected, but also those with a first- or third-person subject, as illustrated by the following examples. In the (a) sentences, the speaker uses the unmarked pronoun *zu*, while in the (b) and (c) sentences, the speaker uses the pronoun *hi* to address a man and a woman, respectively. The gender of the speaker is irrelevant.

(1) a. Badator zure ama eta oso haserre da zurekin.
Your mother is coming and she is very mad at you.
b. Bazatorrek/bazetorrek hire ama eta oso haserre duk hirekin.
Yoúr mother is coming and she is very mad at yoú.
c. Bazatorren/bazetorren hire ama eta oso haserre dun hirekin.
Yoùr mother is coming and she is very mad at yoù.

(2) a. Zure amak irabazi du dirua, baina zure aitak ez daki.
Your mother has earned the money, but your father doesn't know it.
b. Hire amak irabazi dik dirua, baina hire aitak ez zakik/zekik.
Yoúr mother has earned the money, but yoúr father doesn't know it.
c. Hire amak irabazi din dirua, baina hire aitak ez zakin/zekin.
Yoùr mother has earned the money, but yoùr father doesn't know it.

(3) a. Zure beldur naiz eta inork ez dit beldur hori kenduko.
I'm afraid of you, and no one will take that fear away from me.
b. Hire beldur nauk eta inork ez zidak beldur hori kenduko.
I'm afraid of yoú, and no one will take that fear away from me.
c. Hire beldur naun eta inork ez zidan beldur hori kenduko.
I'm afraid of yoù, and no one will take that fear away from me.

(4) a. Aitak gona gorria erosi dio zure amari, baina ez dakit zergatik.
Father has bought a red skirt for your mother, but I don't know why.
b. Aitak gona gorria erosi ziok hire amari, baina ez zakiat/zekiat zergatik.
Father has bought a red skirt for yoúr mother, but I don't know why.
c. Aitak gona gorria erosi zion hire amari, baina ez zakinat/zekinat zergatik.
Father has bought a red skirt for yoùr mother, but I don't know why.

The verb forms in the (b) and (c) sentences, which implicitly refer to a person who is addressed but not otherwise involved, are called allocutive forms. They can in some respects be compared to the so-called ethical dative in Romance and Germanic languages. Consider for example sentences such as "Qu'on me l'égorge tout à l'heure" (Have his throat cut at once [for me]) (Molière, *L'Avare*, V, 2, as quoted in Grevisse 1980, sec. 1063), "Regardez-moi cette misère" (Would you look at this woeful situation) (A. Thérive, *Sans âme*, 31, as quoted in Grevisse 1980, sec. 1063), and "Daß du mir nicht zu spät kommst!" (Don't show up late [on me]!) (*Duden Grammatik der deutschen Gegenwartssprache*, 634).

The ethical dative, however, differs considerably from Basque allocutive forms:

1. The ethical dative can be first or second person, while allocutive forms always relate to the (second-person) addressee.
2. The ethical dative is expressed nominally, using a personal pronoun. Basque allocutive verb forms can never be linked to an explicit personal pronoun denoting the addressee.
3. The ethical dative is an optional stylistic device. Allocutive forms in Basque are compulsory whenever they are possible.

There is a syntactic restriction on the use of allocutive forms: they should occur only in main clauses, not in subordinate clauses. They are therefore not to be combined with relative or conjunctive suffixes (*-n*, *-la*, *-nean*, *-lako*, *-larik*, etc.), with the conditional prefix *ba-*, or, in those dialects that have it, with the prefix *bait-*. This restriction is, however, not always reflected in everyday usage, and exceptions can be found, particularly in Guipuzcoan. Allocutive forms do occur with the affirmative prefix *ba-* and with the negation particle *ez*. Clauses in the subjunctive (suffix *-n* or *-la*) or imperative mood cannot contain allocutive forms. In interrogative sentences, the Guipuzcoan and Biscayan dialects allow allocutive forms, but the other dialects usually do not. Mitxelena follows western usage:

(5) Nor ausartu duk hi zauritzera? (MEIG IX, 106) (allocutive *duk* instead of *da*)
Who dared to injure yoú?

In rhetorical questions, however, allocutive forms are always allowed (cf. *EGLU* III, 157).

29.1.2 Morphology of Allocutive Forms: Intransitive Verbs

Because of the exceptional degree of variation in the allocutive verb forms from place to place, the Basque Academy did not decide on standard forms until November 1994, more than 17 years after it standardized the other verb forms.

According to the academy's rules, allocutive forms are generally derived from the corresponding nonallocutive form. The usual second-person "familiar" suffix *-ga* or *-na* is added, preceding any ergative marker—with the exception of *-te* for the third-person plural—but following all other person markers.

When the allocutive suffix follows a consonant, *e*-epenthesis always occurs: *natorrek*, *natorren* (cf., e.g., nonallocutive *dakark*, *dakarna*, formed with the homonymous ergative suffixes *-ga* and *-na*). The same rule explains the *e* in *nentorrean* (from **nentorregan*) and *nentorrenan*. The intransitive plural suffix *-z* turns out to be a reduction of *-za*: hence *gatozak*, *gatozan*.

Last, in all forms of the third person, initial *da-*, marking present tense, becomes *ze-* (or *za-*, in the northern variant of Batua).

Let us now have a look at the paradigms. We will begin with the present and past tense of the indicative mood. The forms in the conditional and the potential mood will be discussed separately, as well as the forms of the synthetic future tense. For each paradigm, the English translations will be given in the first column, followed by the nonallocutive forms, the masculine allocutive forms, and the feminine allocutive forms. We will start with intransitive verbs without a dative marker (section 29.1.2.1), followed by intransitive verbs with a dative marker (section 29.1.2.2), then transitive verbs without a dative marker (section 29.1.3.1), and finally transitive verbs with a dative marker (section 29.1.3.2).

29.1.2.1 Intransitive Verb Forms

joan 'to go'

I am going	noa	noak	noan
he is going	doa	zoak	zoan
we are going	goaz	goazak	goazan
they are going	doaz	zoazak	zoazan
I was going	nindoan	nindoaan	nindoanan
he was going	zihoan	zihoaan	zihoanan
we were going	gindoazen	gindoazaan	gindoazanan
they were going	zihoazen	zihoazaan	zihoazanan

etorri 'to come'

I am coming	nator	natorrek	natorren
he is coming	dator	za/zetorrek	za/zetorren
we are coming	gatoz	gatozak	gatozan
they are coming	datoz	za/zetozak	za/zetozan
I was coming	nentorren	nentorrean	nentorrenan
he was coming	zetorren	zetorrean	zetorrenan

we were coming	gentozen	gentozaan	gentozanan
they were coming	zetozen	zetozaan	zetozanan

ibili 'to walk'

I am walking	nabil	nabilek	nabilen
he is walking	dabil	za/zebilek	za/zebilen
we are walking	gabiltza	gabiltzak	gabiltzan
they are walking	dabiltza	za/zebiltzak	za/zebiltzan
I was walking	nenbilen	nenbilean	nenbilenan
he was walking	zebilen	zebilean	zebilenan
we were walking	genbiltzan	genbiltzaan	genbiltzanan
they were walking	zebiltzan	zebiltzaan	zebiltzanan

etzan 'to lie down'

I am lying down	natza	natzak	natzan
he is lying down	datza	za/zetzak	za/zetzan
we are lying down	gautza	gautzak	gautzan
they are lying down	dautza	za/zeutzak	za/zeutzan
I was lying down	nentzan	nentzaan	nentzanan
he was lying down	zetzan	zetzaan	zetzanan
we were lying down	geuntzan	geuntzaan	geuntzanan
they were lying down	zeutzan	zeutzaan	zeutzanan

egon 'to stand' (Spanish *estar*)

I am standing	nago	nagok	nagon
he is standing	dago	za/zegok	za/zegon
we are standing	gaude	gaudek	gauden
they are standing	daude	za/zeudek	za/zeuden
I was standing	nengoen	nengoan	nengonan
he was standing	zegoen	zegoan	zegonan
we were standing	geunden	geundean	geundenan
they were standing	zeuden	zeudean	zeudenan

izan 'to be'

I am	naiz	nauk	naun
he is	da	duk	dun
we are	gara	gaituk	gaitun
they are	dira	dituk	ditun
I was	nintzen	ninduan	nindunan
he was	zen	zuan	zunan

we were	ginen	gintuan	gintunan
they were	zinen	zituan	zitunan

[*N.B.* These allocutive forms of *izan* originate from transitive forms derived from **edun* 'to have'. Thus, literally, *nauk* is 'yoú have me', and *gintuan* is 'yoú had us'. Only the third-person past tense forms do not follow this pattern: *zuan* and *zunan* instead of *huen*, and *zituan* and *zitunan* instead of *hituen*.]

29.1.2.2 Intransitive Dative Forms

As there are no deviations from the general system (e.g., the allocutive forms *noakiok* and *noakion* correspond to nonallocutive *noakio*; *z(ih)oakiok* and *z(ih)oakion* to *d(ih)oakio; zeridak* and *zeridan* to *darit*; etc.), it is sufficient to give two paradigms here:

jarraitu 'to follow'

he is following me	darrait	za/zerraidak	za/zerraidan
he is following him	darraio	za/zerraiok	za/zerraion
he is following us	darraigu	za/zerraiguk	za/zerraigun
he is following them	darraie	za/zerraiek	za/zerraien
they are following me	darraizkit	za/zerraizkidak	za/zerraizkidan
they are following him	darraizkio	za/zerraizkiok	za/zerraizkion
they are following us	darraizkigu	za/zerraizkiguk	za/zerraizkigun
they are following them	darraizkie	za/zerraizkiek	za/zerraizkien
I am following him	narraio	narraiok	narraion
I am following them	narraie	narraiek	narraien
we are following him	garraizkio	garraizkiok	garraizkion
we are following them	garraizkie	garraizkiek	garraizkien
he was following me	zerraidan	zerraidaan	zerraidanan
and so on			

izan 'to be'

he is to me	zait	zaidak	zaidan
he is to him	zaio	zaiok	zaion
he is to us	zaigu	zaiguk	zaigun
he is to them	zaie	zaiek	zaien
they are to me	zaizkit	zaizkidak	zaizkidan
they are to him	zaizkio	zaizkiok	zaizkion
they are to us	zaizkigu	zaizkiguk	zaizkigun
they are to them	zaizkie	zaizkiek	zaizkien
I am to him	natzaio	natzaiok	natzaion
I am to them	natzaie	natzaiek	natzaien

we are to him	gatzaizkio	gatzaizkiok	gatzaizkion
we are to them	gatzaizkie	gatzaizkiek	gatzaizkien

The past tense is also entirely regular:

he was to me	zitzaidan	zitzaidaan	zitzaidanan
he was to him	zitzaion	zitzaioan	zitzaionan
he was to us	zitzaigun	zitzaiguan	zitzaigunan
he was to them	zitzaien	zitzaiean	zitzaienan
they were to me	zitzaizkidan	zitzaizkidaan	zitzaizkidanan
they were to him	zitzaizkion	zitzaizkioan	zitzaizkionan
they were to us	zitzaizkigun	zitzaizkiguan	zitzaizkigunan
they were to them	zitzaizkien	zitzaizkiean	zitzaizkienan
I was to him	nintzaion	nintzaioan	nintzaionan
I was to them	nintzaien	nintzaiean	nintzaienan
we were to him	gintzaizkion	gintzaizkioan	gintzaizkionan
we were to them	gintzaizkien	gintzaizkiean	gintzaizkienan

29.1.3 Morphology of Allocutive Forms: Transitive Verbs

With the exception of **edun* 'to have', all transitive verbs have strictly regular allocutive forms. We will therefore not print the paradigms in their entirety. Let us first look at a systematic ambiguity that occurs in most transitive allocutive verb forms with a first-person direct object. The allocutive suffix in these verb forms can usually also be interpreted as an ergative marker. This is the case in, for instance, *naramak*, *naraman*, *garamatzak*, *garamatzan*, *ninderamaan*, *ninderamanan*, *ginderamatzaan*, and *ginderamatzanan*. The only unambiguous forms are found when the verb is in the present tense, its stem ends in a consonant, and the first-person direct object is singular: *nakarrek*, *nakarren* 'he is bringing me' (alloc.), but *nakark* 'yoú are bringing me' and *nakarna* 'yoù are bringing me'.

The allocutive forms of **edun* 'to have' are irregular.

29.1.3.1 Transitive Verb Forms

ekarri 'to bring'

I am bringing it	dakart	za/zekarreat	za/zekarrenat
he is bringing it	dakar	za/zekarrek	za/zekarren
we are bringing it	dakargu	za/zekarreagu	za/zekarrenagu
they are bringing it	dakarte	za/zekartek	za/zekarten
I am bringing them	dakartzat	za/zekartzaat	za/zekartzanat
he is bringing them	dakartza	za/zekartzak	za/zekartzan
we are bringing them	dakartzagu	za/zekartzaagu	za/zekartzanagu
they are bringing them	dakartzate	za/zekartzatek	za/zekartzaten

he is bringing me	nakar	nakarrek	nakarren
he is bringing us	gakartza	gakartzak	gakartzan
I brought it	nekarren	nekarrean	nekarrenan
he brought it	zekarren	zekarrean	zekarrenan
we brought it	genekarren	genekarrean	genekarrenan
they brought it	zekarten	zekartean	zekartenan
I brought them	nekartzan	nekartzaan	nekartzanan
he brought me	nindekarren	nindekarrean	nindekarrenan
he brought us	gindekartzan	gindekartzaan	gindekartzanan
and so on			

eraman 'to carry'

I am carrying it	daramat	za/zeramaat	za/zeramanat
he is carrying it	darama	za/zeramak	za/zeraman
we are carrying it	daramagu	za/zeramaagu	za/zeramanagu
they are carrying it	daramate	za/zeramatek	za/zeramaten
I carried it	neraman	neramaan	neramanan
he carried it	zeraman	zeramaan	zeramanan
we carried it	generaman	generamaan	generamanan
they carried it	zeramaten	zeramatean	zeramatenan

erabili 'to use'

I am using it	darabilt	za/zerabileat	za/zerabilenat
he is using it	darabil	za/zerabilek	za/zerabilen
we are using it	darabilgu	za/zerabileagu	za/zerabilenagu
they are using it	darabilte	za/zerabiltek	za/zerabilten
I used it	nerabilen	nerabilean	nerabilenan
he used it	zerabilen	zerabilean	zerabilenan
we used it	generabilen	generabilean	generabilenan
they used it	zerabilten	zerabiltean	zerabiltenan

jakin 'to know'

I know it	dakit	za/zekiat	za/zekinat
he knows it	daki	za/zekik	za/zekin
we know it	dakigu	za/zekiagu	za/zekinagu
they know it	dakite	za/zekitek	za/zekiten
I knew it	nekien	nekian	nekinan
he knew it	zekien	zekian	zekinan
we knew it	genekien	genekian	genekinan
they knew it	zekiten	zekitean	zekitenan

**ion* 'to say'

I am saying it	diot	zioat	zionat
he is saying it	dio	ziok	ziona
we are saying it	diogu	zioagu	zionagu
they are saying it	diote	ziotek	zioten
I am saying them	diodaz	ziodazak	ziodazan
he is saying them	dioz	ziozak	ziozan
we are saying them	dioguz	zioguzak	zioguzan
they are saying them	diotez	ziotezak	ziotezan
I said it	nioen	nioan	nionan
he said it	zioen	zioan	zionan
we said it	genioen	genioan	genionan
they said it	zioten	ziotean	ziotenan
I said them	niozen	niozaan	niozanan
and so on			

eroan 'to drive', 'to conduct'

I am driving it	daroat	za/zeroaat	za/zeroanat
he is driving it	daroa	za/zeroak	za/zeroan
we are driving it	daroagu	za/zeroaagu	za/zeroanagu
they are driving it	daroate	za/zeroatek	za/zeroaten
I drove it	neroan	neroaan	neroanan
he drove it	zeroan	zeroaan	zeroanan
we drove it	generoan	generoaan	generoanan
they drove it	zeroaten	zeroatean	zeroatenan

jardun 'to be occupied', 'to engage in'

I am occupied	dihardut	ziharduat	zihardunat
he is occupied	dihardu	ziharduk	zihardun
we are occupied	dihardugu	ziharduagu	zihardunagu
they are occupied	dihardute	zihardutek	ziharduten
I was occupied	niharduen	niharduan	nihardunan
he was occupied	ziharduen	ziharduan	zihardunan
we were occupied	geniharduen	geniharduan	genihardunan
they were occupied	ziharduten	zihardutean	zihardutenan

The full allocutive paradigm of *eduki* 'to hold', 'to have' is as follows:

I hold it	daukat	za/zeukaat	za/zeukanat
he holds it	dauka	za/zeukak	za/zeukan

we hold it	daukagu	za/zeukaagu	za/zeukanagu
they hold it	daukate	za/zeukatek	za/zeukaten
I hold them	dauzkat	za/zeuzkaat	za/zeuzkanat
he holds them	dauzka	za/zeuzkak	za/zeuzkan
we hold them	dauzkagu	za/zeuzkaagu	za/zeuzkanagu
they hold them	dauzkate	za/zeuzkatek	za/zeuzkaten
he holds me	nauka	naukak	naukan
they hold me	naukate	naukatek	naukaten
he holds us	gauzka	gauzkak	gauzkan
they hold us	gauzkate	gauzkatek	gauzkaten
I held it	neukan	neukaan	neukanan
he held it	zeukan	zeukaan	zeukanan
we held it	geneukan	geneukaan	geneukanan
they held it	zeukaten	zeukatean	zeukatenan
I held them	neuzkan	neuzkaan	neuzkanan
he held them	zeuzkan	zeuzkaan	zeuzkanan
we held them	geneuzkan	geneuzkaan	geneuzkanan
they held them	zeuzkaten	zeuzkatean	zeuzkatenan
he held me	nindukan	nindukaan	nindukanan
they held me	nindukaten	nindukatean	nindukatenan
he held us	ginduzkan	ginduzkaan	ginduzkanan
they held us	ginduzkaten	ginduzkatean	ginduzkatenan

[*N.B.* As pointed out earlier, allocutive forms with a singular subject and *ni* or *gu* as their direct object are homonyms of nonallocutive forms that have the second person *hi* as their ergative subject: *hik nindukaan/nindukanan* 'yoú/yoù held me', *hik gauzkak/gauzkan* 'yoú/yoù hold us', and so on.]

For the verb **edun* 'to have', the allocutive paradigm is given in full as well:

I have it	dut	diat	dinat
he has it	du	dik	din
we have it	dugu	diagu	dinagu
they have it	dute	ditek	diten
I have them	ditut	ditiat	ditinat
he has them	ditu	ditik	ditin
we have them	ditugu	ditiagu	ditinagu
they have them	dituzte	ditiztek	ditizten

he has me	nau	naik	nain
they have me	naute	naitek	naiten
he has us	gaitu	gaitik	gaitin
they have us	gaituzte	gaitiztek	gaitizten
I had it	nuen	nian	ninan
he had it	zuen	zian	zinan
we had it	genuen	genian	geninan
they had it	zuten	zitean	zitenan
I had them	nituen	nitian	nitinan
he had them	zituen	zitian	zitinan
we had them	genituen	genitian	genitinan
they had them	zituzten	zitiztean	zitiztenan
he had me	ninduen	nindian	nindinan
they had me	ninduten	ninditean	ninditenan
he had us	gintuen	gintian	gintinan
they had us	gintuzten	gintiztean	gintiztenan

[*N.B.* Instead of *-u-*, the normal stem of **edun* 'to have', we consistently find *-i-* here, as with the nonallocutive dative forms of this verb. As a result, most forms with a third-person singular direct object are ambiguous: *diat*, *dik*, *diagu*, *nian*, *zian*, *genian* can also be interpreted as the nonallocutive forms associated with the dative *hiri* 'to yoú'. With a third-person plural subject, this ambiguity does not occur: the allocutive forms *ditek*, *diten*, *zitean*, *zitenan* are distinct from the nonallocutive dative forms *diate*, *dinate*, *ziaten*, *zinaten*.]

29.1.3.2 Transitive Dative Forms

The general system outlined in the introduction to section 29.1.2 applies without exceptions. For instance, the allocutive forms derived from *dakarkit* are *zekarkidak* or *zakarkidak* and *zekarkidan* or *zakarkidan; daramazkio* yields *zeramazkiok* or *zaramazkiok* and *zeramazkion* or *zaramazkion; diosku* yields *zioskuk* and *zioskun*; and *zekarkidaten* yields *zekarkidatean* and *zekarkidatenan*. For the sake of convenience, we will provide the full allocutive dative paradigm for **edun* (with a third-person singular direct object):

he has for me	dit	zidak	zidan
he has for him	dio	ziok	zion
he has for us	digu	ziguk	zigun
he has for them	die	ziek	zien
they have for me	didate	zidatek	zidaten
they have for him	diote	ziotek	zioten

they have for us	digute	zigutek	ziguten
they have for them	diete	zietek	zieten
I have for him	diot	zioat	zionat
I have for them	diet	zieat	zienat
we have for him	diogu	zioagu	zionagu
we have for them	diegu	zieagu	zienagu
he had for me	zidan	zidaan	zidanan
he had for him	zion	zioan	zionan
he had for us	zigun	ziguan	zigunan
he had for them	zien	ziean	zienan
they had for me	zidaten	zidatean	zidatenan
they had for him	zioten	ziotean	ziotenan
they had for us	ziguten	zigutean	zigutenan
they had for them	zieten	zietean	zietenan
I had for him	nion	nioan	nionan
I had for them	nien	niean	nienan
we had for him	genion	genioan	genionan
we had for them	genien	geniean	genienan

In all dative verb forms, including allocutive forms, a plural direct object is marked with the suffix -*zki*, immediately following the verb stem:

I have them for him	dizkiot	zizkioat	zizkionat
he has them for me	dizkit	zizkidak	zizkidan
I had them for him	nizkion	nizkioan	nizkionan
he had them for me	zizkidan	zizkidaan	zizkidanan

29.1.4 Allocutive Forms in the Conditional Mood

Since allocutive forms occur in main clauses only, there are no allocutive protasis forms. In apodoses, however, we do find allocutive conditional forms, in both the present and past tense (see also section 17.2).

With the exception of *izan* 'to be' and **edun* 'to have', all verbs have perfectly regular forms, which are obtained by simply adding the allocutive person marker immediately following the irreality suffix -*ke* or, in the third-person plural forms, following -*te* (of -*ke-te*):

I would come	nentorke	nentorkek	nentorken
they would stand	leudeke	leudekek	leudeken

it would fit us	legokiguke	legokigukek	legokiguken
they would bring them to me	lekarzkidakete	lekarzkidaketek	lekarzkidaketen
I would have come	nentorkeen	nentorkean	nentorkenan
he would have stood	zeudekeen	zeudekean	zeudekenan
it would have fitted us	zegokigukeen	zegokigukean	zegokigukenan
they would have brought them to me	zekarzkidaketen	zekarzkidaketean	zekarzkidaketenan

As in the indicative mood, the nondative allocutive forms of *izan* 'to be' originate from the transitive, nonallocutive forms of the verb **edun* 'to have':

I would be	nintzateke	nindukek	ninduken
he would be	litzateke	lukek	luken
we would be	ginateke	gintuzkek	gintuzken
they would be	lirateke	lituzkek	lituzken
I would have been	nintzatekeen	nindukean	nindukenan
he would have been	zatekeen	zukean	zukenan
we would have been	ginatekeen	gintuzkean	gintuzkenan
they would have been	ziratekeen	zituzkean	zituzkenan

Here too, the allocutive dative forms of *izan* are completely regular; for example,

he would be to me	litzaidake	litzaidakek	litzaidaken
they would be to us	litzaizkiguke	litzaizkigukek	litzaizkiguken
he would have been to me	zitzaidakeen	zitzaidakean	zitzaidakenan
they would have been to us	zitzaizkigukeen	zitzaizkigukean	zitzaizkigukenan

The stem of the allocutive forms of **edun* 'to have' again changes from *-u-* to *-i-*:

I would have it	nuke	nikek	niken
he would have it	luke	likek	liken
we would have it	genuke	genikek	geniken
they would have it	lukete	liketek	liketen
I would have them	nituzke	nitizkek	nitizken
he would have them	lituzke	litizkek	litizken
we would have them	genituzke	genitizkek	genitizken
they would have them	lituzkete	litizketek	litizketen
I would have had it	nukeen	nikean	nikenan
he would have had it	zukeen	zikean	zikenan
we would have had it	genukean	genikean	genikenan
they would have had it	zuketen	ziketean	ziketenan

I would have had them	nituzkeen	nitizkean	nitizkenan
he would have had them	zituzkeen	zitizkean	zitizkenan
we would have had them	genituzkeen	genitizkean	genitizkenan
they would have had them	zituzketen	zitizketean	zitizketenan
he would have me	ninduke	nindikek	nindiken
they would have me	nindukete	nindiketek	nindiketen
he would have us	gintuzke	gintizkek	gintizken
they would have us	gintuzkete	gintizketek	gintizketen
he would have had me	nindukeen	nindikean	nindikenan
they would have had me	ninduketen	nindiketean	nindiketenan
he would have had us	gintuzkeen	gintizkean	gintizkenan
they would have had us	gintuzketen	gintizketean	gintiztenenan

The allocutive dative forms of **edun* are perfectly regular. Some examples follow:

he would have it for me	lidake	lidakek	lidaken
they would have it for him	liokete	lioketek	lioketen
he would have had it for me	zidakeen	zidakean	zidakenan
they would have had it for him	zioketen	zioketean	zioketenan

29.1.5 Allocutive Forms in the Potential Mood

In all three tenses of the potential mood, the allocutive forms are completely regular. It is noteworthy that this statement is also true of the verb *izan* 'to be' which, exceptionally, does not make use here of the transitive forms of **edun* 'to have'. We will limit ourselves to just a few paradigms:

I can be	naiteke	naitekek	naiteken
he can be	daiteke	daitekek	daiteken
we can be	gaitezke	gaitezkek	gaitezken
they can be	daitezke	daitezkek	daitezken
I could be	ninteke	nintekek	ninteken
he could be	liteke	litekek	liteken
we could be	gintezke	gintezkek	gintezken
they could be	litezke	litezkek	litezken
I could have been	nintekeen	nintekean	nintekenan
he could have been	zitekeen	zitekean	zitekenan
we could have been	gintezkeen	gintezkean	gintezkenan
they could have been	zitezkeen	zitezkean	zitezkenan

I can have/do it	dezaket	zezakeat	zezakenat
he can have/do it	dezake	zezakek	zezaken
we can have/do it	dezakegu	zezakeagu	zezakenagu
they can have/do it	dezakete	zezaketek	zezaketen
I could do it	nezake	nezakek	nezaken
he could do it	lezake	lezakek	lezaken
we could do it	genezake	genezakek	genezaken
they could do it	lezakete	lezaketek	lezaketen
I could have done it	nezakeen	nezakean	nezakenan
he could have done it	zezakeen	zezakean	zezakenan
we could have done it	genezakeen	genezakean	genezakenan
they could have done it	zezaketen	zezaketean	zezaketenan

29.1.6 Allocutive Forms in the Synthetic Future Tense

Since only the verbs *izan* 'to be' and **edun* 'to have' have synthetic future tense forms that are distinct from their present tense forms in the potential mood (given in section 24.1.2), we can confine ourselves to these two verbs here. Again, the nondative allocutive forms of the verb *izan* are based on transitive forms of **edun*, and those of **edun* are characterized by a stem change from *-u-* to *-i-*. The dative forms of both verbs are perfectly regular. Therefore, we have

I will be	naizateke	naukek	nauken
he will be	dateke	dukek	duken
we will be	garateke	gaituzkek	gaituzken
they will be	dirateke	dituzkek	dituzken
he will be to me	zaidake	zaidakek	zaidaken
I will be to him	natzaioke	natzaiokek	natzaioken
and so on			
I will have it	duket	dikeat	dikenat
he will have it	duke	dikek	diken
we will have it	dukegu	dikeagu	dikenagu
they will have it	dukete	diketek	diketen
I will have them	dituzket	ditizkeat	ditizkenat
he will have them	dituzke	ditizkek	ditizken
we will have them	dituzkegu	ditizkeagu	ditizkenagu
they will have them	dituzkete	ditizketek	ditizketen
he will have me	nauke	naikek	naiken
they will have me	naukete	naiketek	naiketen

he will have us	gaituzke	gaitizkek	gaitizken
they will have us	gaituzkete	gaitizketek	gaitizketen
he will have it for me	didake	zidakek	zidaken
I will have it for him	dioket	ziokeat	ziokenat
and so on			

[*N.B.* Note that *d-* changes to *z-* only in the dative forms of **edun*: *ziokeat*, but *dikeat*.]

As mentioned at the beginning of this chapter, neither the subjunctive nor the imperative mood allows allocutive forms. We have thus dealt with the "familiar" allocutive conjugation in its entirety.

29.1.7 Allocutive Forms in Non-"Familiar" Language

When speaking to someone whom one does not address with the pronoun *hi*, one can also use allocutive verb forms. The allocutive person marker is then *-zu*, rather than *-ga* or *-na*. The use of these allocutive forms is subject to the same syntactic restriction as the use of the "familiar" allocutive forms. In other words, we do not find these forms in subordinate clauses or in interrogative, imperative, or exclamatory clauses. Unlike the "familiar" forms, however, these allocutive forms are not obligatory, except in the Low Navarrese and Souletin (and Roncalese) dialects. The forms have not yet been standardized by the Basque Academy, but the most straightforward approach would be to adopt the system used for the "familiar" forms and simply replace all allocutive person markers *-ga* or *-na* with *-zu*. This approach would yield, for example, the following principal forms of the verbs *izan* 'to be' and **edun* 'to have':

I am	naiz	nauzu
he is	da	duzu
we are	gara	gaituzu
they are	dira	dituzu
I was	nintzen	ninduzun
he was	zen	zuzun
we were	ginen	gintuzun
they were	ziren	zituzun
he is to me	zait	zaidazu
he was to me	zitzaidan	zitzaidazun
I have it	dut	dizut
he has it	du	dizu
we have it	dugu	dizugu
they have it	dute	ditezu

I had it	nuen	nizun
he had it	zuen	zizun
we had it	genuen	genizun
they had it	zuten	zitezun
I have them	ditut	ditizut
he has them	ditu	ditizu
we have them	ditugu	ditizugu
they have them	dituzte	ditiztezu
I had them	nituen	nitizun
he had them	zituen	zitizun
we had them	genituen	genitizun
they had them	zituzten	zitiztezun
he has me	nau	naizu
they have me	naute	naitezu
he had me	ninduen	nindizun
they had me	ninduten	ninditezun
he has us	gaitu	gaitizu
they have us	gaituzte	gaitiztezu
he had us	gintuen	gintizun
they had us	gintuzten	gintiztezun
I would have	nuke	nikezu
he would have	luke	likezu
I would have had	nukeen	nikezun
he would have had	zukeen	zikezun
I have to him	diot	ziozut
he has to me	dit	zidazu
they have to me	didate	zidatezu
I had to him	nion	niozun
he had to me	zidan	zidazun
they had to me	zidaten	zidatezun

29.2 Overview of Nonfinite Sentential Complements

In Basque, we find a variety of nonfinite sentential complements:

1. Direct infinitival complements, using the perfect participle (see section 14.3). This construction occurs only in complements of the verbs *nahi* 'to want', *behar* 'to have to', 'must',

asmo 'to intend', and *gogo* 'to intend' (all discussed in chapter 14), as well as *uste* 'to believe' (see chapter 18) and *hobe*, 'to be preferable' (cf. Arejita 1994, 849, and *DGV* XIII, 19–20):

(6) a. Zer egin gogo duzu? (Ax. 212)
What do you intend to do?
b. Zer uste zenuen hemen aurkitu? (cf. *P.Ab.* 124)
What did you expect to find here?
c. Hobeko duzu jan. (*P.Ab.* 64)
You'd better eat.

The understood subject of a direct infinitival complement has to be identical to the subject of the main clause. Complements with a different subject will take the form of a finite subordinate clause with *-la* when the main verb is *uste*, and of a nominalized clause with the other verbs mentioned here:

(7) a. Nori eman nahi diozu?
Who do you want to give it to?
b. Nik nori ematea nahi duzu?
Who do you want me to give it to?

2. Gerundive complements, using the imperfect participle (see section 16.4). The subject of the gerund (the imperfect participle) has to be coreferential with an argument in the main clause. The following example sentences may serve as a reminder:

(8) a. Ezin asmatu dut haserretu gabe hitz bat esaten. (*TOE* II, 121)
I cannot manage to say one word without getting angry.
b. ... eman nahi diotena eskatzen ohitu dutela jendea. (*MEIG* I, 139 = *MIH* 322)
... that they have accustomed people to ask for that which they want to give.
c. Ez al zarete hasi euskaraz idazten?
Haven't yoû started writing Basque?

3. The kinetic gerundive, using the allative form of the verbal noun (see section 16.5.5):

(9) a. Banoa zerbait erostera.
I'm going to buy something.
b. Permiti iezaguk urdalde hartara joatera. (Mt 8:31; Lz)
Allow us to go to that herd of swine.
c. Atzenean ausartu naiz bertsoak papelean jartzera ere. (Uztapide, *Sas.* 20)
I finally dared to put the verses down on paper also.

4. Complements using the adnominal (*-ko*) form of the verbal noun. This construction occurs after verbs of ordering, requesting, and advising (*verba petendi*) (see also section 21.3.2). Here is one example:

(10) Berehala etxeratzeko agintzen dizue aitak.
Father orders yoû to come home immediately.

5. Nominalized clauses, using the definite, usually absolutive, form of the verbal noun. This is the most common, unmarked nonfinite sentential complement. Unlike the first three types of complements discussed here, nominalized clauses have their own subject, which is syntactically independent of the main clause. Consider the following example:

(11) Etxean egotea erabaki dugu. (Goenaga 1985b, 949)

The interpretation of this sentence is "We decided to stay at home," unless it is clear from the context that the subject of *egotea* is different: "We decided that I/you/he/they would stay at home." It is also possible to make the subject of the nominalized clause explicit:

(12) Atzo erabaki genuen zu etortzea. (P. Goenaga)
We decided yesterday that you should come.

Note that the previous construction (number 4) is in fact a special case of 5.

[*N.B.* In negative sentences, *ez* precedes the verbal noun, but it may be separated from it.]

Factive clauses—that is, clauses that can be rephrased using a sentence starting with "the fact that"—can, as a rule, have their own subject. One therefore finds either a nominalized clause or a finite subordinate clause with *-la* following factive verbs. The use of the verbal noun is, however, certainly not limited to factive constructions.

A variety of examples follow:

(13) a. ... eta kosta egiten zitzaidan agerpen hura aintzat hartzea. (Atxaga, *Obab.* 94)
... and it was hard for me to take that appearance seriously.
b. Ez zen halakoa nik aurkitzea pentsatzen nuen eguraldia. (Atxaga, *Obab.* 131)
The weather was not such as I thought I would find it.
c. Zuk eta nik jakitea aski da. (*TOE* II, 249)
It is sufficient that you and I know it.
d. Ez da on gizona bakarrik egotea. (Gn 2:18)
It is not good for man to be alone.
e. Zerk eragozten du ni bataiatzea? (*TB* 174)
What is hindering me from being baptized?
f. Nahi-eta-nahiezkoa da zu hona etortzea. (Garate, *E.E.* 108)
It is definitely necessary that you come here.
g. Jateak ez zion hizketan egitea galerazten. (Garate, *E.E.* 12)
Eating did not keep him from talking.
h. Bazitekeen dena "happy end" batez bukatzea. (Garate, *E.E.* 51)
It could be that everything will finish with a happy ending.

i. Kosta zait nire laguntza hark onartzea. (*LBB* 91)
It is hard for me to get her to accept my help.

The verbal noun presents an aspectual ambiguity: its use doesn't indicate whether the subordinate action has been completed or not. The definite form of the perfect participle can be used to explicitly convey the perfect aspect (see also Goenaga 1984, 402, and Arejita 1994, 848, 994):

(14) a. Hamaika bider damutu zitzaion etxetik irtena. (*G.* 255)
Many times he regretted having left home.
b. . . . damu dut ez hemen gelditua. (*TOE* II, 369)
. . . I regret not having stayed here.
c. Gezurra dirudi Xabier hain azkar bere onetara etorria. (Eizagirre, 159)
It seems unbelievable that Xabier has recovered so quickly.
(Literally: It seems a lie that . . . , cf. Spanish *Parece mentira* . . .)
d. Seme onek dazau bere dongaro egina. (Mogel, *C.O.* 54)
This son acknowledges that he has done wrong.
e. Asko sentitzen dut eguraldi tzar honetan zu honaino ekarri izana. (Oñatibia, 153)
I very much regret having brought you here in such bad weather.

When the syntactic construction of the main clause requires it, the verbal noun or perfect participle can have a case ending, in particular the ergative or the instrumental:

(15) a. Asko pozten naiz zuri atsegin ematea.
I am very happy to please you.
b. Asko pozten naiz zuri atsegin emateaz.
I am very happy about pleasing you.
c. Asko pozten nau zuri atsegin emateak.
It makes me very happy to please you.

(16) a. Asko pozten naiz zuri atsegin emana.
I am very happy to have pleased you.
b. Asko pozten naiz zuri atsegin emanaz.
I am very happy about having pleased you.
c. Asko pozten nau zuri atsegin emanak. (López Mendizabal, 159)
It makes me very happy to have pleased you.

Note that the grammaticality of (15a) and (16a) alongside the (b) and (c) sentences provides evidence for a case-ending deletion rule (cf. Arejita 1994, 843). This optional rule seems to apply particularly to nonfinite complements of emotive verbs.

[*Translator's Note*: A section on nonfinite wh-complements was to have been added to this chapter. These are discussed to some extent in section 18.1.2. The author's preparatory notes for this section indicate that it would have included references to

Arejita (1994, 753, 857), *EGLU* (II, 73–74), and Ortiz de Urbina (1989, 16). Some examples, taken from the same notes, are given here:

(17) a. Ez nekien ohera joan edo bertan gera. (Lertxundi, *Aise* 11)
I didn't know whether to go to bed or to stay right there.
b. Ez dakigu nola joka. (Michelena, in Villasante 1976, 63, fn. 2)
We don't know how to play.
c. Ez dakit aldizkariak nori eman. (Ortiz de Urbina 1989, 16)
I don't know who to give the magazines to.]

30 Coordination

30.1 Conjunctions

30.1.1 Coordinating Conjunctions

The principal coordinating conjunctions are

eta 'and'
baina 'but'
edo (under certain circumstances *ala*) 'or'

As mentioned before, the *e-* in *eta* is not pronounced when immediately following a word that ends in a sonorant (i.e., a vowel, nasal, *l*, or *r*). Following a vowel, *eta* is pronounced *ta*. After any other sonorant, it is pronounced *da*. Nonetheless, in Batua, one always writes the full word *eta*. Note that *baina* can occur at the end or in the middle of the conjunct. It is then translated as 'however':

(1) a. Esnea noiz dakark baina? (Amuriza, *Hil* 19)
When are yoú bringing the milk, however?
b. Ez naiz baina eztabaidetan hasiko. (Garate, *NY* 49)
I will not, however, start an argument.

The conjunction *edo* and its substitute *ala* require a lengthier discussion, because the use of these words is the topic of some controversy among Basque grammarians. *Edo* indisputably has the meaning of inclusive 'or', like *vel* in Latin. It can also be used in cases where the speaker explicitly states that the alternatives exclude each other, when one would find *aut* in Latin. These uses of *edo* will be illustrated with an example of exclusive disjunction with *edo* from Axular, followed by two examples (one of inclusive, the other of exclusive disjunction) from the 19th-century Labourdin author Etienne Lapeyre:

(2) . . . erdi behar, edo hil. (Ax. 79)
. . . she must give birth, or die.

(3) a. Mixterioak, edo guk ezin konprenituzko gauzak, ez ote dira, bada, Erlijionean baizik aurkitzen? (Lapeyre, 67)

Mysteries, or other things that we cannot understand, are they perhaps only found in Religion?

b. Bat edo bestea: edo gezurra zioten Apostoluek, edo Juduak hobendunak ziren. (Lapeyre, 215)
It's one or the other: either the Apostles told lies, or the Jews were guilty.

In addition to the normal, semantically unmarked expression of disjunction using *edo*, a marked disjunctive form exists: *ala*. Both semantic and syntactic factors play a role in the use of *ala*. Semantically, *ala* evokes a mandatory choice between two or more possibilities presented by the speaker as mutually exclusive alternatives. Compare the following questions:

(4) a. Bihar edo etzi etorriko (al) zarete?
Will yoû be coming, tomorrow or the day after?
b. Bihar ala etzi etorriko zarete?
Will yoû be coming tomorrow or the day after?
c. Bihar edo etzi etorriko zarete?
Will yoû be coming tomorrow or the day after?

Question (4a) can be answered with *bai* or *ez*, 'yes' or 'no', while question (4b) cannot. It is possible to insert the interrogative particle *al* or the dubitative particle *ote* in (4a), but not in (4b). There are also clear intonation differences between (4a) and (4b). When pronounced with the same intonation as (4b), (4c), using unmarked *edo*, has the same meaning as (4b). (Note that this use of *edo* is frowned upon by some grammarians, e.g., José Basterrechea.)

In summary,

edo: one or another, it doesn't always matter which one
ala: either one or the other, the question is which one

In syntactic terms, the use of *ala* is limited to interrogative clauses in the broadest sense. According to grammarian Patxi Goenaga, this means all clauses containing a wh-complementizer, including direct questions, all complement clauses with the complementizer *-N* (see section 18.1.2), and nonfinite clauses using the radical form of the verb. Here are some examples of each kind:

(5) a. Hilak ala biziak dira? (Duvoisin, *Dial.* 7)
Are they dead or alive?
b. Zein parte estimatzen duzu hobe, Jainkoarena ala Deabruarena? (Ax. 505)
Which share do you consider better, God's or the devil's?
c. Zeinek bekatu egin du, honek ala honen aitamek . . . ? (Jn 9:2; Lz)
Who has sinned, he or his parents . . . ?
d. Mendira joango zara ala etxean geldituko zara? (P. Goenaga)
Will you go to the mountains, or will you stay at home?

e. Ama emazte zuen ala ez, nahi nuke galdetu. (*LVP* III–17)
I would like to ask whether his mother was a woman or not.

f. Ez digu axola Cayatte zuzen ala oker dagoen jakiteak. (*MIH* 321)
Knowing whether Cayatte is right or wrong isn't important to us.

g. Ez nekien Euskal Herritik kanpo bizi nahi nuen ala ez. (Urretabizkaia, *Asp*. 52)
I didn't know whether I wanted to live outside the Basque Country or not.

h. Joxek ez zidan esan etorriko zen ala ez. (P. Goenaga)
Joseph didn't tell me whether he would come or not.

i. Bihar erabakiko dugu joango garen ala geratu egingo garen. (P. Goenaga)
Tomorrow we will decide whether we will leave or whether we will stay.

j. Bihar erabakiko dugu joan ala gera. (P. Goenaga)
Tomorrow we will decide to leave or stay.

In the absence of a wh-complementizer, *edo* is used, even in the case of a choice between mutually exclusive alternatives:

(6) a. Andrea eder eta aberatsa, edo ero edo farata. (*R.S.* 134)
A beautiful and rich woman is either crazy or conceited.

b. Edo dantzaria haiz, edo ez haiz dantzaria. Beste aukerarik ez dago. (Atxaga, *Bi Let*. 25)
Either yoú are a dancer, or yoú are not a dancer. There is no other possibility.

c. Bietatik bat: gurekin etorri behar duk, edo etxean bakarrik gelditu.
It's one or the other: yoú have to come with us or stay home alone.

d. ... hil edo biziko auzia dugula ... (*MEIG* IX, 49)
... that we have a matter of life or death ...

As we already saw in example (4c), even when both conditions are met, the use of *ala* is not compulsory, though it is very common. Lapeyre, who is familiar with the use of *ala*, sometimes chooses *edo* where other authors use *ala*:

(7) a. Zein nahi duzue larga diezazuedan? Barabbas, ala Iesus, deitzen dena Christ? (Mt 27:17; Lz)
Who do yoû want me to release? Barabbas, or Jesus, who is called Christ?

b. Zein nahi duzue libro igor dezadan, Barrabas edo Jesus, Kristo deitua dena? (Lapeyre, 183)
Who do yoû want me to set free, Barabbas or Jesus, who has been called Christ?

30.1.2 Correlative Conjunctions

Besides the coordinating conjunctions that we have discussed, Basque also has correlatively used adverbs. These occur in each member of the coordination, with the same function and in the same position. If they are to be considered conjunctions, note that they are distinct from the conjunctions discussed in the previous section in four respects:

1. They are homonymous with a word or expression that is not a conjunction.
2. They tend to be repeated before each member of the coordination, more so than *eta*, *baina*, and *edo*/*ala*.
3. They can be preceded by *eta*, especially in the final member of the coordination.
4. They connect two or more constituents, but unlike the coordinating conjunctions discussed previously, they cannot be used to connect full sentences.

The correlative conjunctions can be grouped into three semantic classes:

Copulative

bai ... bai ...	both ... and ...
ez ... ez ...	neither ... nor ...

Disjunctive

nahiz ... nahiz ...	either ... or ... (in Biscayan also *nahi*)
zein ... zein ...	either ... or ...
dela ... dela ...	either ... or ... (in Guipuzcoan also *dala*)
biz ... biz ...	either ... or ... (now obsolete)

Distributive

nor ... nor ...	one ... the other ...
zein ... zein ...	one ... the other ...
non ... non ...	here ... there ...
noiz ... noiz ...	now ... then ...
behin ... behin ...	now ... then ...

We will now look at examples illustrating these constructions. *Bai* occurs in three types of constructions: *bai ... bai ...*; *bai ... eta bai ...*; and *bai ... bai eta ...*:

(8) a. Bai bata bai bestea etorri dira. (Rarely also *etorri da*)
Both the one and the other have come.
b. Bai bata eta bai bestea etorri dira. (Also *etorri da*)
Both the one and the other have come.
c. Bai bata, bai eta bestea etorri dira. (Also *etorri da*)
The one, as well as the other, has come.

Here are some examples from literature:

(9) a. Bai zeruan bai lurrean ... (Lz, *Adv* **1r)
In heaven as on earth ...
b. Bai Testamendu Zaharra, bai Berria Jainkoaren izenaz beteak dira. (Lapeyre, 85)
Both the Old Testament and the New are full of God's name.
c. Hau (da) teatrogizon osoa, bai antzezlari bai komeri-sortzaile legez. (*TOE* III, 280)
He is very much a man of the theater, both as an actor and as a playwright.

d. Eta desegin zituen lurraren gainean bizi ziren guztiak, gizonagandik abereraino, bai arrastakariak eta bai zeruko hegaztiak. (Gn 7:23; Ur.)
And he destroyed all that lived on the earth, from human beings to animals, both the creeping animals and the birds in the sky.

e. ... bai lehen, bai eta orai(n) ... (Lapeyre, 56)
... both in the past and in the present ...

f. ... besoak zabalik hartu dute kritikoek, bai beratxek eta bai xorrotzek. (*MEIG* II, 55)
... the critics received it with open arms, the stern ones as well as the mild ones.

Ez occurs in three constructions, analogous to those with *bai*, when used in an otherwise affirmative sentence: *ez ... ez ...*; *ez ... eta ez ...*; and *ez ... ez eta ...*:

(10) a. Ez apaizik ez mojarik etorri da.
Neither priests nor nuns have come.

b. Ez apaizik eta ez mojarik etorri da.
Neither priests nor nuns have come.

c. Ez apaizik ez eta mojarik etorri da.
Neither priests nor nuns have come.

[*N.B.* Obviously, *eta ez* can often be translated simply as 'and no' or 'and not': *Apaizak ikusi ditut eta ez mojarik* 'I have seen priests, and no nuns'.]

It is common to negate the verb in sentences with correlative conjuctions based on *ez*. Doing so requires another *ez* immediately preceding the finite verb, while *ez* preceding the first negated constituent may be dropped, yielding *ez ... ez ...* or *... ez ...* in a sentence with *ez* + V:

(10) d. Ez apaizik ez mojarik ez da etorri.
Neither priests nor nuns have come.

e. Apaizik ez mojarik ez da etorri.
Neither priests nor nuns have come.

Some textual examples follow:

(11) a. Ez berak lanik egiten du, ez besteri egiten utzi. (Altuna 1979, 305)
He doesn't work himself, nor does he allow others to.

b. Ez haragiak, ez odolak hori erakutsi dizu ... (*TB* 66)
Neither the flesh, nor the blood, has revealed that to you ...

c. Ez haragik ez odolek, ez baitizu adierazi hori zuri ... (Mt 16:17; *IB*)
(It is) neither the flesh nor the blood that has made that clear to you.

d. Haragiak ez odolak ez dik hori revelatu ... (Mt 16:17; Lz)
Neither the flesh nor the blood has revealed that ...

e. Ez dute jakitaterik ez aberastasunik. (Lapeyre, 224)
They have neither wisdom nor wealth.

f. Ez nintzen oroit, ez zenbat, ez nolako bertsoak izan ziren. (Xalbador, *Odol.* 87)
I remembered neither how many nor what kind of verses they had been.

g. Ez zituen ez hitzak leundu, ez gorrotoak estali. (*MIH* 268)
He didn't soften his words, nor did he hide his feelings of hatred.

h. Emazterik ez den lekuan ez dakusat plazerik, ez gizona ez etxea behin ere xahurik. (*LVP* III–28)
In a place where there is no woman, I don't see any pleasure, nor (do I see) the man, or the house, ever clean.

i. Inoren zilarrik, ez urrerik, ez soinekorik ez dut nahi izan. (Acts 20:33; Ker.)
I have coveted no one's silver, nor gold nor apparel.

j. Gaurko "sasi-teatroan" ez gai ez hitz eta ez ipuinik behar ez dela esaten dutenak badira. (*TOE* III, 281)
There are those who say that in contemporary "pseudo-theater" neither themes, nor words, nor stories are needed.

The disjunctive constructions *nahiz* ... *nahiz* ..., *zein* ... *zein* ..., and *dela* ... *dela* ... express the equivalence of the alternatives:

(12) a. Gure euskaldun teatrogileak, nahiz egile eta nahiz itzultzaile, lanean jarraituko dutela ez dugu batere zalantzarik. (*TOE* III, 281)
We don't have any doubt that our Basque playwrights will continue to work, whether as writers or as translators.

b. Orain, nahiz baterako eta nahiz besterako berandu da. (*TOE* II, 369)
Whether for the one or the other, it is now too late.

c. Han beti zegoen ontziren bat bete nahiz hustu beharra. (*LBB* 34)
There was always a need to load or unload some ship or other there.

d. Nahiz sinistu, nahiz ez, esan behar dut, gaztetxoa nintzela, irakurri eta azaldu ohi nituela Fedroren latinezko ipuinak. (B. Mogel, *Ip.* 37)
Believe it or not, I have to say that when I was very young, I used to read and interpret the Latin fables of Phaedrus.

e. Nahiz dela zamaria nahiz gizona, ez da biziko. (Ex 19:13; Ur.)
Whether it is a beast of burden or a man, it shall not live.

f. Nahiz dela Italia, orobat Frantzia, bietan bilatu dut anitz malizia. (From Iparragirre's song "Gitarra zahartxo bat/Gitarra joilea," cf. *Xaramela* 130; Arratia, II, 92)
Whether Italy or France, I have encountered lots of malice in both.

Either or both occurrences of *nahiz* can be replaced with *edo*:

(13) a. Edo egiaz nahiz gezurraz elikatuko naiz. (Proverb, *R.S.* 57)
Whether through the truth or through a lie, I will provide for myself.
b. Nahiz doan Frantziara edo Espainiara . . . (Etxeberri Sarakoa, 289)
Whether he goes to France or to Spain . . .
c. . . . edo lehen edo gero . . . (*R.S.* 510)
. . . whether sooner or later . . .

The author of the following example assigns different scopes to *nahiz* and *edo*: *nahiz* marks the main disjunction, while *edo* marks the subordinate disjunction:

(13) d. Zeren, nahiz gizona, nahiz emaztekia, nahiz noblea, enperadorea, edo erregeren umea, edo haren leinukoa; nahiz etorkirik apalenetik, edo txikienetik heldu dena; nahiz aberatsa, nahiz probea, nahiz gaztea, nahiz zaharra; baldin ugatzean ditiarekin edan zuen hizkuntzaz besterik ez badaki, gauza segura da, hogei egunen bidean beste herrietako hizkuntzak behartu gabe, ezin doakela. (Etxeberri Sarakoa, 275–276)
For, whether man, or woman, or nobleman, emperor, or the child or descendant of a king; or originating from the humblest or most minor lineage; or rich, or poor, or young, or old; if he doesn't know anything other than the language he drank from his mother's breast along with her milk, it is certain that he cannot travel for twenty days without needing languages of other regions.

(14) a. Zein organoa, zein biolina, zein kitarra, zein danbolina, zein tronpa, zein zartagin zahar bat, guztiekin jotzen da soinua. (Bartolomé, 32)
Whether an organ, a violin, a guitar, a drum, a Jew's harp, or an old frying pan, music is made with all of them.
b. Hil zein bizi, senarra ahalik arinen ikusi nahi izan dudalako. (Echeita, *Jay M.* 197)
Because I wanted to see my husband as soon as possible, whether dead or alive.
c. Idatzi zein idatzi ez, ordea, ez dut inoiz ahaztuko. (Mintegi, 56)
However, whether we write (each other) or not, I will never forget him.
d. Berritan olio hau da onena, bai gordinik jateko zein lapikorako. (Uriarte, *Dial.* 104)
This oil is best when fresh, whether for consuming uncooked or for the cooking pot.

(15) a. Dela koinaka, dela bermut, dela chartreuse, zernahi izenetako edari guztietarik urrats guztiez edateko. (H. U., *Zez.* 27)
To drink, at every step, all kinds of drinks regardless of their names, whether cognac, vermouth, or chartreuse.
b. . . . dela irakurtzean, dela mintzatzean . . . (J. Etchepare, *Eusk. G.* 206)
. . . whether while reading, or while speaking . . .

Most interrogatives can be used correlatively, resulting in coordination constructions with distributive meaning—for example,

(16) a. Jendea, nor zaldiz, nor oinez, etorri zen. (*EGLU* I, 89)
The people came, some by horse, others on foot.
b. Alde guztietan, non gehiago non gutxiago ... (*MIH* 107)
In all regions—more in some, less in others ...
c. Bi jokabide ikusten ditut nagusi, noiz bata, noiz bestea. (*MEIG* VII, 107)
I saw two main modes of conduct, one moment the one, the next the other.

In example (16d), *behin* 'once' is synonymous with *noiz*, and is also used correlatively:

(16) d. Behin Donostiara joaten gara, behin Bilbora.
Sometimes we go to San Sebastian, sometimes to Bilbao.

Following are some more examples:

(17) a. Bainan lur onean ereina izan dena, hura da hitza entzuten eta aditzen duena, eta fruitu dakarrena; zeinek batentzat ehun, zeinek hirurogei, zeinek hogeitamar. (Mt 13:23; Dv.)
But the one that was sown in good soil, that is the one that hears and understands the word, and bears fruit: one a hundredfold, another sixty, and another thirty.
b. Eta eman zuten fruitu, non batarik ehun, non hirurogei eta non hogeitamar. (Mt 13:8; Hualde Mayo)
And they bore fruit: in one place a hundred out of one, in another sixty, and in yet another thirty.
c. Noiz batentzat ehun, noiz hirurogei, noiz hogeitamar. (Azkue, *DVEF* II, 83)
One time a hundred to one, another sixty, and yet another thirty.
d. Honela behin batek eta behin besteak garaitzen zuen. (*TZ* I, 123)
So one moment the one triumphed, and the next the other.
e. Hemen behin iparrak eta behin hegoak jotzen du. (Amuriza, *Hil* 71)
Sometimes the northern wind blows here, other times the southern wind.

In the remainder of this chapter we will restrict ourselves to a study of coordination in its simplest form, involving the principal conjunctions *eta*, *edo*, and *ala*.

30.2 Syntactic Features of Coordination in Basque

30.2.1 Emphatic Repetition

As is the case in English, Basque conjunctions usually only occur immediately preceding the final member of the coordination:

Miren, Nekane, eta Ana	Mary, Dolores, and Anna
Patxi, Pello, Koldo, edo Andres	Frank, Pete, Louis, or Andrew

When using the conjunctions *edo* and *ala*, one has the option of expressing greater emphasis by repeating the conjunction before each member of the coordination, including the first one, as in the following examples:

(18) a. Bada, edo jaten baduzue, edo edaten baduzue, edo zerbait besterik egiten baduzue, guztia Jainkoaren gloriatan egizue. (1 Cor 10:31; Lz)
So, whether yoû eat, or whether yoû drink, or whether yoû do something else, do it all for the glory of God.
b. Beraz, edo enganatu gaitu Jainkoak, edo zorion hori nonbait aurki daiteke. (Lapeyre, 268)
Therefore either God has betrayed us, or one can find that happiness somewhere.
c. Izan dadin edo aberea edo gizona, ez da biziko. (Ex 19:13; Dv)
Whether it be beast or man, it shall not live.
d. Edo oraintxe, edo inoiz ez.
It's now or never.

(19) a. Ez da antsia, ala probeari ala Jesu Kristo berari eman . . . (Ax. 227)
It doesn't matter whether one gives to a poor man or to Jesus Christ himself . . .
b. Ala etxean gelditu, ala ahizparekin joan, beste aukerarik ez daukazu.
Either stay at home or go with your sister, you don't have any other choice.

This pattern of repetition is not used with *eta*. In order to create a similarly emphatic effect, one has the option of using copulative *bai*, as in examples (9a–f).

30.2.2 Conjunction Reduction

30.2.2.1 Constituent Level Reduction

Given a coordination where all members begin or end with the same constituent or sequence of constituents, the common part can be factored out of the whole structure, so that it will occur only once at the very end. This operation, which is not deletion but rather the analogue of bracketing in arithmetic, is known as conjunction reduction. For brevity's sake, I will call it simply reduction. Reduction is an optional process, but nonapplication often leads to stylistic awkwardness, especially when more than two conjuncts are involved. For example, the reduced form (20b) is preferred to the unreduced version (20a):

(20) a. Nik higuin dut baratxuria arrainzopan eta Mirenek maite du baratxuria arrainzopan.
I hate garlic in fish soup and Mary loves garlic in fish soup.
b. Nik higuin dut eta Mirenek maite du baratxuria arrainzopan.
I hate, and Mary loves, garlic in fish soup.

Actually, there is a third way to convey the same message: retention of the shared part in the first conjunct followed by its pronominalization in the other conjuncts. I will call this the pronominal option:

(20) c. Nik higuin dut baratxuria arrainzopan eta Mirenek maite du (bertan).
I hate garlic in fish soup and Mary loves it (in it).

For those instances of reduction involving a sequence of shared constituents starting with the main verb of the sentence, the term "backward gapping" has been used (cf. section 30.2.4 on gapping). For example, (21a) can be reduced to (21b):

(21) a. Egunak gaua dakar gurpil eroan eta goizak arratsaldea dakar gurpil eroan.
The day brings the night on the crazy wheel (of time) and the morning brings the afternoon on the crazy wheel.
b. Egunak gaua eta goizak arratsaldea dakar gurpil eroan. (Cf. Etxaniz, *Antz*. 107)
The day brings the night and the morning the afternoon on the crazy wheel.

Other examples are

(22) a. Mirenek sagar bat eta Karmenek udare bat jango du.
Mary will eat an apple and Carmen a pear.
b. Jonek bost sagar eta Patxik lau udare jango ditu.
John will eat five apples and Frank four pears.

These examples where the verbal morphology agrees with the subject and object of the final conjunct exclusively are accepted by many Basque speakers. Others, however, do not accept this type of agreement and require the verbal morphology to reflect the meaning of the whole sentence, thus indicating plurality for both subject and object:

(23) a. Mirenek sagar bat eta Karmenek udare bat jango dituzte. (Also *dute*)
Mary will eat an apple and Carmen a pear.
b. Jonek bost sagar eta Patxik lau udare jango dituzte.
John will eat five apples and Frank four pears.

The simplest possible example of this semantic agreement was provided by Lardizabal when he wrote:

(24) Abel artzaina eta Kain nekazaria ziran. (*TZ* I, 17)
Abel was a shepherd and Cain a farmer. (Plural copula in Basque)

30.2.2.2 Word-Level Reduction

In the event of a coordinate arrangement where all members present a similar structure and end in the same word, reduction is possible even when the shared word does not amount to a full constituent. The following example illustrates this possibility; the shared word *liburuak* 'the books' is part of a larger noun phrase, different in each conjunct:

(25) a. Zure liburuak, nire liburuak eta nire emaztearen liburuak hor daude lurrean.
Your books, my books, and my wife's books are lying there on the floor.
b. Zure, nire eta nire emaztearen liburuak hor daude lurrean.
Your, my, and my wife's books are lying there on the floor.

The pronominal option, of course, is also viable:

(25) c. Zure liburuak, nireak eta nire emaztearenak hor daude lurrean.
Your books, mine, and those of my wife are lying there on the floor.

Instead of a noun, the shared word may be an adjectival demonstrative or a post-position:

(26) Etxe edo herri hartatik. (Mt 10:14)
Out of that house or city. (Similarly in Lz: *etxe edo hiri hartarik.*)

(27) a. ... bihotz eta arima gabe ... (Etxepare, *LVP* XII–35)
... without heart and soul ...
b. ... Jainkoaren Lege eta amorio gabe ... (Cardaberaz, *Eg.* III, 320)
... without God's law and love ...

Examples can also be found in which *gabe* is repeated:

(28) Beraz, aita ez da nihoiz izatu semea gabe eta Espiritu Saiñdua gabe? (Argaiñaratz, *Dev.B.* 237)
Therefore, the father was never without the son and without the Holy Spirit?

Likewise, *kontra* 'against' and its synonym *aurka* can be either repeated or reduced. Some examples follow:

(29) a. Etorkiaren aurka ta oituren aurka ... (Orixe, *Aitork.* 66)
Against nature and against custom ...
b. Jaunaren aurka eta hark aukeraturiko erregearen aurka ... (Ps 2:2)
Against the Lord and against the king chosen by him ...

(30) a. ... Jaunaren eta Onek Igurtzitakuaren kontra ... (Ps 2:2; Ker.)
... against the Lord and the one anointed by him ...
b. ... Jaunaren kontra eta haren Kristoren kontra. (Ps 2:2; Dv.)
... against the Lord and his Christ.
c. ... haren eta harenen kontra ... (Ax. 70)
... against him and his people ...

Reduction is also possible with compounds ending in the same word. Thus instead of *leku izenetan eta pertsona izenetan* we have *leku eta pertsona izenetan* (*MEIG* VII, 81) 'in place and person names' (cf. also *toki eta pertson izenak* [*MEIG* III, 153]). Similarly, we have *euskal eta erdal hitzak* (*MEIG* VII, 28) 'Basque and foreign words'.

30.2.2.3 Morpheme-Level Reduction

Here we need to distinguish derivational morphology from inflectional morphology. In modern Basque, reduction applied to derivational suffixes is so rare as to be practically nonexistent. Few speakers accept *ikus eta ikaskizunak* 'spectacles and lessons' (personal communication, P. Goenaga: possible, but unusual) and none **ikas eta irakasle asko* 'many students and teachers'.

Nominal inflection, however, is quite another matter. A coordinate noun phrase in which each conjunct ends in the same inflectional morpheme or sequence of morphemes will usually allow reduction to take place. As Arejita noticed in his impressive study of J. A. Mogel's usage, reduction is excluded if one or more of the conjuncts is a personal pronoun (1994, 229). Indeed, example (31b) is rejected by all speakers I have consulted. (Cf. *EGLU* IV, 33ff.; however, in Hualde Mayo's Roncalese version of Matthew 17:26 we find *ar zazu, eta emon dazazu ni eta zoregatik* 'take it and give it for me and for yourself'.)

(31) a. Adiskide on bat daukagu zuk eta nik.
You and I have one good friend.
b. *Adiskide on bat daukagu zu eta nik.
You and I have one good friend.

Proper names, however, do not block reduction:

(32) a. Patxik eta Pellok atseginez irakurri dute liburu hori.
Frank and Pete read that book with pleasure.
b. Patxi eta Pellok atseginez irakurri dute liburu hori.
Frank and Pete read that book with pleasure.

Here is a textual example of reduction of the ergative ending:

(33) Bertako langilleek—Agirreren seme, alaba, sui ta ilobek—danak zekiten euskaraz. (Oñatibia, 117)
The workers there—Agirre's sons, daughters, sons-in-law and nephews—they all knew Basque.

The following sentence, involving the partitive ending, clearly shows reduction to be optional:

(34) Ez-da ordean ez bihirik, ez aziendarik, ez arbolarik, ez-bada lan, artha eta bururik. (Duvoisin, *Lab.* 15)
There is, however, no grain, nor cattle, nor trees, if there is no work, care or intelligence.

With the dative case, the Latin phrase *patri et fratribus* (Gn 47:11) is translated reduced by Duvoisin: *bere aita eta anayei*, and unreduced by Uriarte: *bere aitari eta anayai*, as well as by d'Urte: *bere aitari eta bere anajey*. Other examples with reduction of the dative ending are

(35) a. Neure morroi eta mirabeei ere . . . (Acts 2:18)
Unto my servants and handmaidens too . . .
b. . . . haren maxima galdu ta moda ergelei jarraiki hatzaie . . . (Duhalde, 149)
. . . yoú have followed its perverted maxims and its silly fashions . . .
c. . . . inguratzen zituen onthasun, ohore ta atseginei . . . behaturik, . . . (Duhalde, 182)
. . . looking to the wealth, honors and pleasures that surrounded them . . .

The sociative ending *-rekin* undergoes reduction in some versions of Acts 1:14 and is repeated in other ones:

(36) a. . . . Jesusen ama Maria eta anai-arrebekin . . . (Acts 1:14)
. . . with Mary the mother of Jesus and his brothers and sisters . . .
b. . . . Maria Jesusen amarekin, eta haren anayekin. (Acts 1:14; Dv)
. . . with Mary the mother of Jesus and with his brothers.

Further examples of reduction with this ending are

(37) a. Gainerakoek beheragoko eta arruntagorekin kontent ziren. (*MEIG* VII, 32)
The rest were satisfied with something lower and more ordinary.
b. Noe atzenean, bere hiru seme Sem, Kam eta Jafet eta lauren emazteakin kutxan sartu zen. (*TZ* I, 24)
Finally, Noah went into the ark with his three sons Shem, Ham and Japheth and the four men's wives.
(Cf. Gn 7:13: Egun hartan bertan sartu zen Noe untzian bere seme Sem, Kam eta Jafetekin, bere emazte eta errainekin.)
c. . . . bere emazte, hiru seme eta hiru errañakin irten zen. (*TZ* I, 24)
. . . he came out with his wife, three sons and three daughters-in-law.
(Cf. Gn 8:18: Atera zen Noe bere emazte, seme eta errainekin.)

[*Translator's Note*: Handwritten notes in the margin of the original Dutch text mention several observations on reduction in Basque made by Amundarain (1997). Amundarain points out that reduction never occurs with demonstrative pronouns (**gizon hau eta emakume hark* 'this man and that woman') or nominalized clauses (**Lanera berandu iristea eta zuzendaria iraintzeagatik bota dute Pello lanetik* 'Because of his arriving late at work and insulting the manager, they have fired Pete from the job'). He also notes that when a coordination involves more than two constituents with the same inflectional morphology, reduction almost always occurs (1997, 214, 220, 235).]

30.2.3 Leaving Out the Auxiliary

In a coordination of two or more clauses, it is possible for the auxiliary to occur only once, assuming that the tense and aspect of all clauses is the same. The northern dialects tend to retain the auxiliary in the first clause. In the southern dialects, the auxiliary generally occurs in the final clause, and the main verb in the preceding clauses will be in the unmarked form, that is, the perfect participle. In Batua both these options exist, and we find sentences like both the (a) and (b) examples that follow:

(38) a. Etxe bat erosi dugu, eta berehala saldu.
We bought, and immediately sold, a house.
b. Etxe bat erosi, eta berehala saldu dugu.
We bought, and immediately sold, a house.

(39) a. Etxe bat erosten dugu, eta berehala saltzen.
We are buying a house and selling it immediately.
b. Etxe bat erosi, eta berehala saltzen dugu.
We are buying a house and selling it immediately.

(40) a. Etxe bat erosiko dugu, eta berehala salduko.
We will buy a house and sell it immediately.
b. Etxe bat erosi, eta berehala salduko dugu.
We will buy a house and sell it immediately.

(41) a. Etxe bat eros dezagun, eta berehala sal.
Let's buy a house and sell it immediately.
b. Etxe bat erosi, eta berehala sal dezagun.
Let's buy a house and sell it immediately.

In the (b) sentences, a slight pause occurs after the first clause. Without this pause, *eta* could be interpreted as denoting posteriority of the action described in the first clause (see section 20.6):

(42) Etxe bat erosi eta, berehala saldu dugu.
After buying a house, we immediately sold it.

Synthetic verb forms behave the same way as auxiliaries:

(43) a. Tresna hauek dakartzagu, eta berehala erabiltzen.
We are bringing these tools and using them immediately.
b. Tresna hauek ekarri, eta berehala badarabiltzagu.
We are bringing these tools and using them immediately.

The auxiliary can also be left out when the clauses do not have the same subject:

(44) a. Guk etxe bat erosten dugu, eta zuek berehala saltzen.
We are buying a house, and yoû are immediately selling it.
b. Guk etxe bat erosi, eta zuek berehala saltzen duzue.
We are buying a house, and yoû are immediately selling it.

For a discussion of negated sentences of this kind, see *EGLU* IV, 70, and for examples of this construction in imperative clauses, see *EGLU* II, 72. Note that Amundarain (1997,

175) gives examples of the auxiliary being left out in sentences in which the verb in one clause is transitive (taking a form of **edun* as its auxiliary) while the verb in the other clause is intransitive (taking a form of *izan*), in both the northern and southern constructions (e.g., *Joxek jai hartu zuen eta mendira abiatu* 'Joseph took a day off and set out for the mountains').

We will now give some textual examples, starting with the northern pattern:

(45) a. Penak oro jiten dira Jainkoaren nahitik,
eta berak permititzen oro hobenagatik. (*LVP* XIII–48)
All suffering comes from God's will,
and he allows it all because of sin.

b. Nik han dakusadan zure begitartea,
eta sainduekin lauda zure majestatea. (*LVP* I–77)
So I can see your countenance there,
and praise your majesty with the saints.

c. Zeren hainbat bekatutan daramagu bizia,
eta gerok gure faltaz galtzen gure burua? (*LVP* I–171)
Why do we lead our lives in so much sin,
and lose ourselves through our own fault?

d. Zeren orduan zeure etsaia, zeure burua, eta deabrua ere garaitzen baitituzu, eta arima, eta gorputza ere bakean, soseguan eta segurean ipintzen. (Ax. 320)
For then you defeat your enemy, yourself and the devil too, and you render your soul as well as your body peaceful, calm and safe.

e. Eriak sendatzen zituen, hilak pizten, haizeak jabaltzen, itsasoa ematzen. (Lapitze, 214)
He cured the sick, revived the dead, pacified the wind, calmed the sea.

f. Laster egiten du hilerrira, irikitzen du hobia eta bere alaba bizi eta azkar hatzematen. (Lapitze, 214)
She runs to the cemetery, opens the grave, and finds her daughter alive and well.

g. Noizbaitean ere, bi zakurrak iritsi omen ziren palazioko ateetara, baita bertan txikitu deabrua, hautsi hamahiru ateak, eta beren nagusia libratu ere. (Barandiaran, *Mundo* III, 28)
Finally the two dogs reached the gates of the palace, tore the devil to pieces right then and there, broke down the thirteen doors, and liberated their master.

h. Bera ez dut ikusten, bai botsa entzuten. (From the song "Xori Errusiñula," Arratia IV, 125; *Xaramela* 297)
I do not see him himself, but I do hear his voice.

Here are some examples that follow the southern pattern:

(46) a. Eta nik gizona galdu eta alaba aurkitu nuen. (Etxaniz, *Antz*. 33)
And I lost a man and found a daughter.

b. Biok batera bazkaldu eta afaltzen zuten. (Garate, *Esku* 114)
The two of them had lunch and dinner together.

c. Hau aditu zuenean neska hori beldurtu, eta atezulotik luzatu egin omen zion behatza. (Barandiaran, *Mundo* III, 26)
When she heard this, the girl got scared, and extended her finger to him through the doorway.

d. Eta hala, ustegabe, erabat aberastu, eta herri batera jaitsi, eta han anaiarrebak eta zakurrak ondo bizi izan omen ziren. (Barandiaran, *Mundo* III, 28)
And thus, unexpectedly, they became very wealthy, and went down to a village, and there the brother and sister and the dogs lived happily.

e. Juan Martin aintzindari haundiengana joan eta Jose Larrekoaren hauzia konpondu zuen. (Izeta, *Nigarrez* 77)
Juan Martin went to the high authorities and settled the case of Jose Larrekoa.

f. Etxera joan eta ohera sartu nintzen. (Atxaga, *Bi Let*. 86)
I went home and got into bed.

g. Ni menditik etorri eta Joxek etxetik aldegin zuen. (Amundarain 1997, 178)
I came from the mountains and Joseph came from home.

30.2.4 Gapping

When coordinated clauses contain the same main verb and have identical tense and aspect (but not necessarily the same person and number), the verb phrase need only be given in the first clause and can be omitted in the subsequent clauses. The order of the constituents within the various clauses does not play a role. The following examples serve to illustrate this point:

(47) a. Orduan libraturen du anaiak anaia heriotara, eta aitak haurra. (Mk 13:12; Lz)
Then the brother will let his brother go to his death, and the father his child.

b. Oinak zerbitzatzen du eskua, eta eskuak oina. (Ax. 315)
The foot serves the hand, and the hand the foot.

c. Hilak piztuko direnean, ez dute hartuko ez gizonek emazterik, ez eta emaztekiek senarrik. (Mt 22:30; Dv)
When the dead rise, men will take no women, nor will women take men.

d. Zuk emango diozu zukua, eta nik babarrunak. (Etxaniz, *Antz*. 128)
You will give him soup, and I (will give him) beans.

e. Hamalau urte zituen orduan mutilak, eta zuk hamahiru. (Etxaniz, *Antz*. 33)
The boy was fourteen years old then, and you were thirteen.

Leaving out the verb in these cases is an example of a more general process known in linguistics as gapping. It is important to distinguish this process from reduction applied to the verb, which retains the verb in the final rather than the first clause. Moreover, reduction can only occur when the verb is placed at the end of the clause or is followed by identical material in each clause. For examples of reduction involving verbs, see examples (21)–(24) in section 30.2.2.1.

30.2.5 Coordination in Questions

In Basque, interrogative phrases immediately precede the verbal phrase but, unlike in English, need not be clause-initial (see section 8.6.1):

(48) Zuek gure alabarekin gero zer egingo duzue?
What will yoû do with our daughter later on?

Since wh-items need not be moved to sentence-initial position, certain questions in Basque have a word order that in English can only be found in echo questions. Similarly, it is possible in Basque to question only the latter of two (or more) coordinated constituents, yielding the following remarkable examples:

(49) a. Alkateak eta nork lapurtu zuten artaldea?
Who did the mayor steal the flock of sheep with?
b. Ohean bere emaztea eta nor ikusi zituen?
Who did he see in the bed with his wife?
c. Bere izena eta zer ahaztu zaizkio?
What did he forget besides his name?
d. Madrilera eta nora zihoazen?
Where did they go besides Madrid?
e. Larogei eta zenbat urte ditu?
How much older than eighty is he?

The English translations inevitably have a very different structure from the Basque sentences. Thus the literal translation of example (49a) is 'The mayor and who stole the flock of sheep?' In English, however, such a question can only be asked by someone who didn't fully hear an immediately preceding utterance like "The mayor and the midwife stole the flock of sheep." By contrast, in Basque, sentences like those in (49) are very well possible without a preceding utterance of this kind.

Questions in which the first, rather than the final, of two or more coordinated constituents is questioned are not an option in Basque. The reason for this restriction may well be that such sentences would not meet the requirement that the wh-item immediately precede the verb. In exclamatory sentences with special intonation, however, we do find this type of construction:

(50) a. Nork eta alkateak lapurtu zuen artaldea!
The mayor, of all people, stole the flock of sheep!
b. Ohean nor eta bere emaztea ikusi zuen!
In the bed he saw his own wife, of all people!

c. Zer eta bere izena ahaztu zaio!
He forgot even his own name!
d. Nora eta Madrilera zihoazen!
They went to Madrid, of all cities!
e. Zenbat eta larogei urte ditu!
He is eighty years old, eighty!

Some textual examples follow:

(51) a. Zeinek (variant of *nork*) eta Odolkik zirikatu behar bera, Moxolo! (*G.* 313)
Odolki, of all people, thought it necessary to prod him, Moxolo!
b. Nork eta Peruk esan behar! (*E.H.* 261)
Peter, of all people, should say that!
c. Nork, eta hik aukeratu duk, beraz, Txanton alkate? (Albisu, 222)
So yoú, of all people, have elected Txanton mayor?
d. Non gainera eta bere jaioterrian! (*MEIG* IV, 109)
And what's more, in his native land, of all places!
e. Halako eskeintza ... Non eta New Yorken! (Oñatibia, 179)
Such an offer ... And in New York, of all places!
f. Zahartu eta maskalduta gero ezkontzea! Norekin eta askotaz gazteago eta neskame etxean izan zenuten Agar emagaldu horrekin! (*TOE* III, 199)
To get married after growing old and weak! And with that whore Agar of all people, who is much younger and whom yoû have had in yoûr home as yoûr maid!
g. Nondik eta zerraldotik atera ziren hitz haiek. (*LBB* 185)
Those words came out of the coffin, of all places.

We should probably consider such constructions the result of a rhetorical process in which the speaker asks a question and subsequently answers it himself: *Nondik atera ziren hitz haiek*? 'Where did those words come from?' ... *Zerraldotik atera ziren hitz haiek*. 'The words came out of the coffin'. *Eta* connects the question and answer, and reduction yields example (51g). This view is supported by the following intermediate examples:

(52) a. Zer egin eta zeruko giltza puskatu zioten aingeru koskorrek San Pedrori! (F. Mendizabal, 249)
The little angels had done no less than break St. Peter's key to heaven!
b. Nor harritu eta errege harritu. (Barbier, *Lég.* 132)
The king in particular was surprised. (Literally 'Who surprised and the king surprised')
c. Eta hori noiz gertatuko eta orain gertatzen. (*MEIG* IX, 98)
And that had to happen now of all times! (Literally 'And when to happen, and happening now')

d. Zer kenduko medikuak, eta gozoa. (Atxaga, *Bi Let*. 17)
And of all things, the doctor took candy away from me.

30.2.6 Elliptic Constructions: Conjunctions as Enclitic Particles

The final constituent of a coordination is usually left out when the hearer is expected to be able to fill it in. The bare conjunction that then remains at the end of the clause forms a syntactic unit with the preceding phrase. We find this phenomenon with *eta*, *edo*, and *ala*.

Eta, when used by itself at the end of a nominal phrase, takes on the meaning of 'and the others', 'and company', if the nominal phrase refers to a living being. In other cases, it means 'and the like', 'and all that'. *Euskal hizkuntza eta literatura* (268) prescribes that unless the conjunction occurs at the very end of the sentence, a comma is required following *eta* and *edo* in these constructions. Examples from literature, however, are not all in accordance with this rule:

(53) a. Zepaik eta handik alde egin zuten. (Uztapide, *LEG* I, 95)
Zepai and the others walked away from there.
b. Amatxori eta ez beldurtzeko esan. (*TOE* I, 303)
Tell Mother and the others not to be afraid.
c. Nor bizi da etxe horretan?—Pello eta. (Azkue, *DVEF* II, 261)
Who lives in that house?—Pete and company.
d. Joxepak eta barre egin zuten. (Zapirain, *M*. 60)
Joseph and the others laughed.

(54) a. Sukaldeko ontziak, platerak eta, hautsi zituen. (*E.H*. 261)
He broke the kitchenware, the plates, and such.
b. Taberna eta izan behar dute. (Uztapide, *LEG* I, 96)
They must have had a tavern and all that.

Note that 'et cetera' in Basque is generally expressed using *eta abar* (*abar* meaning 'branch'), and 'et cetera, et cetera' using *eta, eta*.

Constructions of this kind are also possible with *edo*, which then takes on the meaning 'or something like that', 'or so':

(55) a. Hamar urte edo nituen. (Lertxundi, *G.K*. 89)
I was ten years old or so.
b. ... alaba berriz haurtzai(n) edo zeukan nonbait ... (*MEIG* IX, 98)
... his daughter however was a babysitter somewhere or something like that ...
c. Hogei edo etorri dira. (*DCV* 577)
Twenty or so have come.
d. Adimen kamutsa dudalako edo nik ez diot igartzen. (*MIH* 338)
Because I have a dull mind or something like that, I don't notice that in him.

e. Badakizu nondik datorren?—Indietatik edo. (Uriarte, *Dial.* 4)
Do you know where that one comes from?—From South America or thereabouts.
f. Losintxakerian al zatoz edo? (*TOE* III, 136)
Are you trying flattery or something? (Literally 'Are you coming in flattery or something?')
g. Dirurik edo al zegoen hemen? (Garate, *Esku* 125)
Was there money here, or something?
h. Eta zenbat behar nuen edo galdera egin zidan. (Uztapide, *LEG* I, 116)
And he asked me how much, approximately, I needed.

Compare *edo horrela*, 'or so':

(56) Errenteriakoa edo horrela izan behar zuen. (Uztapide, *LEG* II, 290)
He must have been from Renteria or thereabouts.

Following an indirect question with dubitative *ote* (section 8.1.6), *edo* can also be used to emphasize this particle. This use possibly results from an abbreviation of *edo ez*, 'or not':

(57) a. Zuen Anton-ek bere burua hil ote duen edo, diote. (Etxaniz, *Antz.* 113)
People wonder whether yoûr Tony might have committed suicide.
b. Itsaspekorik agiri ote zen edo beti itsasora begira. (Oñatibia, 22)
Always staring at the sea, wondering whether a submarine might reveal itself.

As *ala* can be considered a substitute for *edo* in certain types of questions (see section 30.1.1), one would expect that the preceding constructions with *edo* are also possible with *ala*. However, ellipsis with *ala* occurs only in direct yes-or-no questions. This restriction may be linked to the fact that unlike unmarked *edo*, *ala* presents two or more alternatives that have to be mutually exclusive. Here are some examples:

(58) a. Loteria eskaintzen al diozu ala? (*TOE* III, 37)
Are you offering him a lottery, or what?
b. Lanpetua ikusten haut. Eskribitzen, ala? (*LBB* 111)
I see that yoú are busy. Are yoú writing, or what?
c. Saldu orduko, ez zenuen zeurea, ala? (Acts 5:4; Ker.)
Was it not yours, then, before you sold it?
d. Gure hizkuntzaren egoera larriak ez zaituzte nahigabetzen ala? (*MIH* 138)
Doesn't the precarious status of our language make yoû sad, then?
e. Lo zaude ala? (*E.H.* 27)
Are you asleep, or what?

In connection with example (58e), Sarasola notes that *ala* should be considered short for *ala zer* 'or what' or for *ala ez*, 'or not'. Compare the following example:

(59) Ifernuan sartu naiz, ala zer? (Aintziart, 69)
Have I entered hell, or what?

30.2.7 Further Characteristics of *eta*

In section 23.2 we discussed the use of explanatory *eta*. The following example illustrates a somewhat related use of *eta*, at the end of an exclamatory sentence, creating more emphasis:

(60) Ez duzu ezagutu? Zure semea bera zen eta!
Didn't you recognize him? And it was your own son!

Coordinations with *eta* in which the final member of the coordination is a numeral in the definite form (*biak*, *hirurak*, *laurak*, etc.) present a striking peculiarity of Basque. When the coordinated conjuncts refer to animate beings carrying out an action together, the numeral in the final conjunct preferably indicates the total number of those involved. Since this construction is not found in English, a literal translation is not possible. Rather, we need to perform a subtraction, and infer from the sentence itself or from its context who the implicit person(s) might be. Here are some examples from literature:

(61) a. Beste lagun bat eta biak atzera joan ziren. (Uztapide, *LEG* I, 32)
He and another friend went back. (Literally: Another friend and the two went back.)
b. Beste bertso asko, andrea eta biak elkarrekin kantatzeko eginak dira. (Dorronsoro, 122)
Many other verses have been created for his wife and him to sing with each other.
c. Zestuara joan ginen aita eta biak. (Uztapide, *LEG* I, 88)
Father and I went to Cestona.

When the implicit component of the construction includes a first or second person, as in example (61c), we usually find the inclusive article *-ok* (see section 19.7) on the numeral: *biok*, *hirurok*, and so on.

(62) a. Zepai eta biok etorri ginen orduan. (Uztapide, *LEG* I, 236)
Then came Zepai and myself.
b. Nik, nagusiak eta biok egiten genituen lanak, bakarrik erraz egingo nituzkeen. (Uztapide, *LEG* I, 118)
It would have been easy for me to do by myself the work that the boss and I did together.
c. Aita eta biok mendira joan ginen. (Garate, *Ald.* 39)
Father and I went to the mountains.

While examples with *biak* and *biok* are the most common, higher numbers are also possible:

(63) a. Ama, Itziar eta hirurok gelditu ginen etxean. (Garate, *Esku* 107)
Mother, Itziar, and myself stayed at home.

b. Ba, goazen orduan, goazen Teresa eta laurok. (Atxaga, *Bi An.* 86)
Well, let's go then, Teresa and the three of us.
c. Eta holaxe ibili ginen azken udan ere, Toby, Frankie, Kent, aitona eta bostok ... (Atxaga, *Obab.* 120)
And the last summer, we also went walking just like that, Toby, Frankie, Kent, Grandfather, and myself ...

In conditional sentences with more than one protasis, expressing several conditions for the same consequence, Basque uses *eta* where English uses 'or':

(64) a. Nahi badu eta nahi ez badu nire Joxek ez du ile bat ere ikutzen nire baimenik gabe. (*TOE* I, 187)
Whether he likes it or not, my Joseph doesn't even touch one hair without my permission.
b. Baina, nahi bazuen eta ez bazuen, zaku madarikatuan sartu behar izan zitzaion. (Barbier, *Lég.* 67)
But, whether he wanted to or not, he had to go into that cursed sack.
c. Nahi baduzu eta ez baduzu, ezkondu beharra zara. (Etxaniz, *Ito* 144)
Whether you want to or not, you have to get married.
d. Orain sendoa naiz, on bazain eta ez bazain. (J. B. Etcheberry, 266)
I am healthy now, whether yoù like it or not.
e. Ez da, ordea, ez bihirik, ez aziendarik, ez arbolarik, ez bada lan, arta eta bururik. (Duvoisin, *Lab.* 15)
There is, however, no grain, nor cattle, nor trees, if there is no work, care or intelligence.

[*N.B.* This use of *eta* explains the adverb *nahitaez*, also *nahi eta ez*, 'like it or not', 'necessarily', 'inevitably'.]

It is noteworthy that the Basque sentences result directly from conjunction reduction applied to sentences with the logical form '$A \rightarrow C \wedge B \rightarrow C$', while the English translations are based on the equivalent logical form '$A \vee B \rightarrow C$'. However, note the following Basque example along the lines of the latter logical form, using disjunctive *zein*:

(65) Kobratuko duk, bai, Jainkoak nahi badu zein ez badu! (Amuriza, *Hil* 63)
Yoú will receive money, yes, whether it is what God wants or not!

30.3 The Distributive Suffix *-na*

The suffix *-na* attaches to cardinal numbers, including fractionals such as *erdi* 'half' and the interrogative *zenbat* 'how much', and turns them into distributives, that is, numeratives that indicate the amount involved per turn or per party.

Distributives can only occur in an indefinite noun phrase, and they occupy the same place in it as would the corresponding nondistributive numeral. By virtue of their meaning, they relate to a noun phrase denoting plurality elsewhere in the sentence.

As for the phonological form, we note the absence of any epenthesis. If the numeral ends in a plosive, for instance in *t*, then this consonant is dropped before *-na* in both spelling and pronunciation. Examples follow:

zenbat	how many/much	zenbana	how many/much each
erdi bat	one half	erdi bana	one half each
bat	one	bana	one each
bi	two	bina	two each
hiru	three	hiruna	three each
lau	four	launa	four each
bost	five	bosna	five each
. . .		. . .	
ehun	a hundred	ehuna	a hundred each
mila	a thousand	mila bana	a thousand each
huts	zero	husna	zero each, 0–0
. . .		. . .	

[*N.B.* A very few instances of *erdina* 'a half each' can be found in compound numbers: *sagar eta erdina* (Uztapide, *LEG* I, 271) 'one and a half apples each' and *bat eta erdina* (*Txirr.* 72) 'one and a half each'. Compare Uriarte (Ex 26:16): *bana eta erdi* 'one and a half each'.]

The following examples are from literature:

(66) a. Botila bana ardo edan dezagun. (From the Labourdin song "Mila zortzi ehun hemeretzian," Sallaberry, 184)
Let us each drink a bottle of wine.

b. Han baziren sei ontzi harrizko, bizpahiruna metreta zeukatenak. (Jn 2:6; Dv)
There were six stone containers there, each of which held two to three *metretas*.

c. Bina arima ditugu gehienek. (*MEIG* V, 135)
Most of us have two souls each.

d. Eman zizkiguten bina guri, launa besteei. (Echebarria, *Eib.* 170)
They gave us each two, and the others each four.

e. Guztiak edukiko dituzte hamarna beso luzeran, eta zabaleran bana eta erdi. (Ex 26:16; Ur.)
All shall be ten cubits each in length and one and a half each in breadth.

f. Gure etxean laurentzako gaur sei sardina,
baina ez dute egin partizio berdina;
guri bana eta berak jan digute bina

zergatikan ez partitu bat eta erdina? (*Txirr.* 72)
At home today there were six sardines for four people,
but they didn't divide them evenly;
for us one each, and they themselves ate two each,
why not divided in one and a half each?

g. Zenbana liburu erosi duzue? (Goenaga, *G.B.*[2] 92)
How many books did yoû each buy?

h. Hark bina liburu erosi ditu liburudenda guztietan. (Ibid., 90)
He bought two books in each of all the bookstores.

i. Oheratu gara biok ohe banatan. (Alkain & Zavala, 98)
The two of us went to sleep in separate beds.

In all these examples, with the exception of the last, the constituent that carries the suffix *-na* functions as direct object. In practice this is the most usual case by far. It is, however, also grammatical for other constituents to take the suffix *-na*, particularly if there is no explicit direct object in the Basque sentence. This possibility is illustrated in the following examples from Goenaga:

(67) a. Bosna gizonek lagundu digute. (*G.B.*[2] 89)
Each of us (dative) was helped by five men.

b. Guk hiruna ikasleri laguntzen diegu lanak egiten. (Ibid.)
We each help three students (dative) to do their work.

c. Bina neskak eman ziguten musu. (Personal communication, P. Goenaga)
Each of us was kissed by two girls.

d. Gu bizikleta banatan etorri gara. (*G.B.*[2] 89)
We each came on a bike.

e. Hiruna neskarekin ikusi nituen. (*G.B.* 67)
I saw them with three girls each.

31 Compounds

31.1 Compounds in Basque

The well-developed art in Basque of combining two or more words to form a new word has resulted in a lexicon rich in compounds, and many of the processes used remain productive. (For an overview, see Azkarate 1990a.)

31.2 Morphophonology of Compounds

A compound can consist of a simple sequence of two or more words that have lost their autonomy and are joined together through the intonation pattern into a new entity—for example, *ezpatadantzari* 'sword dancer' from *ezpata* 'sword' and *dantzari* 'dancer' or *suharri* 'flint' from *su* 'fire' and *harri* 'stone'.

But the process is far from always so simple. Not infrequently the final syllable of a word undergoes a change when this word is the first (or rather, nonfinal) element in a combination. Furthermore, the same change in form obtains, at least in part, in derivatives with certain suffixes, namely, *-tu*, *-garri*, *-keria*, (collective) *-tza*, *-gile*, *-gin*, *-pe*, and *-tegi*. In general, the form of the base does not change with other derivational suffixes.

31.2.1 Changes in Final Consonants

If the first element of the compound ends in a consonant, the form does not usually change. Form changes are the exception rather than the rule. Only when sandhi rules are applicable do we find them. We can differentiate two groups of these exceptions:

Rule 1. A few common words ending in *-r* (strong or weak) lose this *r* before a consonant, and the *r* changes to *h* before a vowel. This last rule applies only for single-syllable words ending in a weak *r*; the other words retain this final *r* when followed immediately by a vowel. The main examples are

adar 'branch' *adabegi* 'tree knot', *adarrondo* 'tree knot'
hamar 'ten' *hamabost* 'fifteen', *hamarratz* 'sea crab' (lit. *ten finger*)

lur 'ground'	*luberri* 'newly plowed land', *lurrikara* 'earthquake'
or 'dog'	*ozar* 'huge dog', *ohalano* 'great dane'
ur 'water'	*ubide* 'waterway', *uharte* 'island' (*ur* + *arte* 'between')
zur 'wood'	*zume* 'osier willow' (*mehe* 'thin'), *zuhirin* 'sawdust'

Rule 2. A few common words ending in *-n* lose this, or change *n* into a weak *r*. In Batua there are only three examples of importance.

In compounds, the word *egun* 'day' takes the form *egu-* before a consonant (*egutegi* 'calendar', *Eguberri* 'Christmas'), and the form *egur-* before an *h* or a vowel (*eguraldi* 'weather', *egurats* 'atmosphere' [lit. 'day breath']) unless the second element already contains an *r*: *eguargi* 'daylight', *eguerdi* 'noon' (preventive dissimilation).

The word *gizon* 'human' mostly takes the form *giza-* in compounds: *gizalaba* 'female person', *gizaldi* 'generation', *gizarte* 'society', *gizabide* 'courtesy', *gizaseme* 'male person', *gizaki* 'human being', but *gizondu* 'to become a man'. In the specific meaning 'man', the form *gizon* remains unchanged: *gizongai* 'fiancé', *gizonkeria* 'manly behavior'. New compounds are written with *giza* separate: *giza hizkuntza* 'human language'.

The word *jaun* 'lord' in old compounds has the form *jaur-*: *jauraldi* 'reign', *jaurbide* 'regime', *jauretxe* 'manor', 'palace' (also *jauregi*), *jaurerri* 'seignory', *jauretsi* 'to venerate', *jaurgoa* 'sway', but *jaundu* 'to dominate', *jauntasun* 'dominance'.

The following words are nowadays regular, but formerly had in compounds a variant with *r*: *belaun* 'knee', *ohoin* 'crook', *oihan* 'forest', *oin* 'foot', *orein* 'deer', *soin* 'torso' (cf. *sorbalda*, *sorburu* 'shoulder').

31.2.2 Changes in Final Vowels

Much more important are the changes in form that occur when the first element of a compound ends in a vowel. Then the following rules obtain:

Rule 3. The Major Apocope rule: words of more than two syllables ending in a vowel lose this vowel whenever the word is the first element in a compound, as in these examples:

itur- from *iturri* 'spring'	*iturburu* 'source'
egar- from *egarri* 'thirst'	*egartsu* 'great thirst'
berant- from *berandu* 'late'	*berantaro* 'late season'
abat- from *abade* 'abbot'	*abatandre* 'abbess'
itsas- from *itsaso* 'sea'	*itsaslapur* 'pirate'
eliz- from *eliza* 'church'	*elizgizon* 'cleric'
burdin- from *burdina* 'iron'	*burdinbide* 'railroad'
kopet- from *kopeta* 'forehead'	*kopetilun* 'angry'

Words whose last syllable begins with an *m* form an exception: *neskame* 'female servant'.

Newer loanwords and also some older ones remain unchanged: *aingeru* 'angel' (*aingerutalde* 'host of angels'), *ezpata* 'sword' (*ezpatabelar* 'cattail, reed mace'), *gaztelu* 'castle' (*gazteluzain* 'castle guard or keeper'), and so on. Moreover, by a ruling of the Basque

Academy of January 27, 1995, apocope is never compulsory when the final vowel is *a*, and only possible with the words *burdina*, *eliza*, *hizkuntza*, *kultura*, *literatura*, and *natura*, as well as all loanwords ending in *-ia*: *filosofi irakaslea*, *filosofia irakaslea*, or *filosofia-irakaslea*. (See *EGL* 47–48.)

Rule 4. The Minor Apocope rule: some two-syllable words that end in a vowel lose this vowel if it is an *i* or *u*, and final *e* and *o* become *a*. The final *u* in a few Romance loanwords changes into *a*, but most remain unchanged. Examples follow:

er- from *eri* 'finger' *erpuru* 'thumb'
har- from *harri* 'stone' *harresi* 'stone enclosure', 'wall'
her- from *herri* 'land' *(h)erbeste* 'foreign country'
or- from *orri* 'leaf' *orburu* 'artichoke'
bur- from *buru* 'head' *burezur* 'skull'
erla- from *erle* 'bee' *erlezain* 'beekeeper'
etxa- from *etxe* 'house' *etxaburu* 'main house', 'upper floor'
arta- from *arto* 'maize' *artaburu* 'ear of corn', 'corncob'
basa- from *baso* 'wilderness' *basakatu* 'wildcat'
otsa- from *otso* 'wolf' *otsabelar* 'hellebore'
oila- from *oilo* 'chicken' *oilagor* 'woodcock'
usa- from *uso* 'dove' *usazain* 'dove keeper'
kata- from *katu* 'cat' *katagorri* 'squirrel'

[*N.B.* The Minor Apocope rule is so named because only a small number of words are affected. Many Basque words with such a form remain unchanged—for example, *aste* 'week', *diru* 'money', *erbi* 'hare', *ero* 'crazy', *gose* 'hunger', *hiri* 'town', *txori* 'bird', and *zerri* 'swine'. With a number of words that do undergo apocope, this process is no longer productive but only occurs in a few passed-down compounds. This is the case, for instance, with *argi* 'light', *begi* 'eye', *idi* 'ox', and *ogi* 'bread'. Thus we have *burezur* 'skull', but also *buruhezur*, and only *burueri* 'hydrocephalus', *buruhauste* 'problem'.]

Rule 5. Some nouns ending in a vowel have a variant with a final *-n* that can be found in older compounds and derivatives. This phenomenon can be explained by the apocope rules. We are concerned here with words that originally had an intervocalic *n* which then later dropped away as a result of a general phonetic rule. (Cf. *koroa* 'crown', *ohore* 'honor', *harea* 'sand', *ahate* 'duck'—originating from Latin *corona*, *honorem*, *arena*, *anatem*.)

With compounds, however, the application of Major Apocope occasioned the loss of the intervocalic character of the *n*, thus bringing about the retention of this consonant. Because of the word boundary between the two members of the compound, this happened even when the following element began with a vowel. The main examples are

ardo 'wine' and *ardan-* (from *ardano*)
arrain 'fish' and *arran-* (from *arrani*)
balea 'whale' and *balen-* (from *balena*)

garau 'grain (of)' and *garan-* (from *garanu*)
gazta 'cheese' and *gaztan-* (from *gaztana*)
kanpai 'bell' and *kanpan-* (from *kanpane*)
katea 'chain' and *katan-* (from *katena*)
morroi 'servant' and *morron-* (from *morroni*)

As mentioned earlier, this rule applies only for older forms of derivations and compounds. With more recent forms, the *n* is usually missing. Thus we have *ardanetxe* 'winehouse' but *ardoetsai* 'wine hater', *arrantzale* 'fisherman' but *arraintzale* 'lover of fish', *balenbizar* 'whalebone' but *balegantza* 'whale oil', *garandu* 'to thresh' but *garautegi* 'granary', *gaztanbera* 'curd(s)' but *gaztazapi* 'cheesecloth', *kanpandorre* 'belfry' but *kanpaihots* 'bell ringing', *katenbegi* 'link' but *katesare* 'metallic mesh', and *morrontza* 'servitude' but *morroialdi* 'period of servitude'.

Rule 6. Numerous words ending in *-ra*, *-re*, or *-ri* display in compounds and older derivatives a variant ending in *-l*. An explanation analogous to that given for rule 5 is also possible here. For we know that an intervocalic *r* often originated from an older *l*: *zeru* 'sky' from Latin *caelum*, *goru* 'distaff' from Latin *colum*, *gura* 'desire' from Latin *gula*, and so on. Words that never had an *l*, like *amore*, have adapted to the other words. Some main examples are

abel- from *abere* 'livestock'	*abeletxe* 'stable'
afal- from *afari* 'supper'	*afalordu* 'suppertime'
aizkol- from *aizkora* 'ax'	*aizkolgider* 'helve'
amol- from *amore* 'love'	*amoltsu* 'affectionate'
atal- from *atari* 'doorway'	*ataltzain* 'doorman'
bazkal- from *bazkari* 'lunch'	*bazkalordu* 'lunchtime'
edal- from *edari* 'beverage'	*edalontzi* 'drinking vessel'
el- from *eri* 'sick'	*elgorri* 'measles'
erdal- from *erdara* 'non-Basque language'	*erdalitz* 'foreign word'
euskal- from *euskara* 'Basque language'	*Euskalerri* 'Basque country' (also *Euskal Herri*)
gal- from *gari* 'wheat'	*galburu* 'head of wheat'
gosal- from *gosari* 'breakfast'	*gosalordu* 'breakfast time'
zamal- from *zamari* 'beast of burdern', 'horse'	*zamaltzain* 'stable boy', 'groom'

For Batua, if there is a variant ending in *-l*, it is always employed in compounds. This practice is in contrast to the situation with rule 5 where the *n* variants only appear in a few forms handed down and are thus relatively rare in the language.

Rule 7. When after application of the apocope rules the plosives *g* or *d* become final consonants in the first element of a compound, then these change to *t*—also when the second element begins with a vowel, as in these examples:

art- from *ardi* 'sheep'	*artzain* 'sheepherder', *artile* 'sheep's wool'
art- from *argi* 'light'	*artizar* 'Venus'

bet- from *begi* 'eye'	*betile* 'eyelash', *betazal* 'eyelid'
harat- from *haragi* 'meat'	*haratuzte* 'abstinence from meat', *haratustel* 'rotten meat', 'gangrene'
it- from *idi* 'ox'	*itegun* 'one day's work by a team of oxen'
ot- from *ogi* 'bread'	*otordu* 'mealtime', *otapur* 'bread crumb'
sat- from *sagu* 'mouse'	*satitsu* 'shrew', *satarte* 'mousetrap'

[*N.B.* Formerly, this rule applied also for *h*: *bet-* from *behi* 'cow' (*betzain* 'cowhand'), *zot-* from *zohi* 'clod of earth' (*zotazal* 'sod', 'turf').]

31.2.3 Some Irregularities

1. In a few compounds where the first member ends in a vowel that is retained and the second member begins with a vowel or *h*, a *t* is inserted that may replace the *h*—for example, *sutondoan* 'by the fire', from *su* 'fire' and *ondo* 'closeness'; *eskutitz* 'letter', from *esku* 'hand' and *hitz* 'word'; *sutargi* 'firelight', from *su* 'fire' and *argi* 'light'.
2. Sometimes, a word that is the second element in a compound and begins with a vowel receives a *k* sound before it. This has been explained as a remnant of the linking morpheme *-ko*, as in *etxekandre* (also *etxekoandre*) 'lady of the house'. Another example is *sukalde* 'kitchen', from *su* 'fire' and *alde* 'side', but *hegoalde* 'south', from *hegoa* 'south wind' and *alde*.
3. The word *ume* 'young of animal or human' as the second element of a compound almost always takes the form *-kume*: *arkume* 'young lamb', *zakarkume* 'puppy', *zerrikume* 'piglet'. There is an exception: from *ahuntz* 'goat', through contraction, one finds *antxume* 'kid'.

31.2.4 Regular Sandhi Phenomena

Since in a compound the final sound of the first element links up directly with the initial sound of the second element, these sounds influence each other according to the normal phonological rules in Basque, but with one important exception: there is no epenthesis.

We can speak here of sandhi phenomena and shall try to give a short summary (expanding on section 1.2.6) of the relevant phonological rules. For more extensive treatments, see *FHV* and Hualde 1991.

Sandhi rule 1. When two plosives meet, the first drops, and the second is, or becomes, voiceless.

Thus $t + g = k$, as in *bekaitz* 'envy', from *begi* 'eye' (see rule 7) and *gaitz* 'bad intentions'; *arkazte* 'young sheep', from *art-* (from *ardi* 'sheep') and *gazte* 'young'; and *lokarri* 'bond', from the verbal root *lot* 'to bind' and the suffix *-garri* (section 14.7.2). (See also *baikara* 'because we are', from *bait-* and *gara* 'we are'.)

Likewise, $t + b = p$, as in *bepuru* 'eyebrow', from *bet-* (from *begi* 'eye') and *buru* 'head', 'top', and *errepide* 'highway', from *erret-* (from *errege* 'king') and *bide* 'way'. (Cf. also *bapatean* 'suddenly' from *bat-batean*.)

And, finally, that $t + d = t$ we have seen already from section 19.3.1 concerning the prefix *bait-*: *bait-* + *da* = *baita*, *bait-* + *dira* = *baitira*, and so on.

Sandhi rule 2. When a sibilant follows a plosive, the plosive drops, and the sibilant turns into the corresponding affricate.

Thus $t + s = ts$, as in *otsein* 'servant', from *ot-* (from *ogi* 'bread') and *sein* 'child'. And $t + z = tz$, as in *itzain* 'ox herder', from *it-* (from *idi* 'ox') and *zain* 'keeper'.

Sandhi rule 3. When a plosive follows an affricate, the affricate turns into a sibilant, and a voiced plosive becomes voiceless.

Thus $tz + b = zp$, as in *hizpide* 'subject matter', from *hitz* 'word' and *bide* 'way'. And $ts + d = st$, as in *mahasti* 'vineyard', from *mahats* 'grape' and the collective suffix *-di* from section 33.1.2. Compare also *harizti* 'oak forest' from *haritz* 'oak'.

Sandhi rule 4. When a voiced plosive follows a sibilant, it becomes voiceless, except in very slow, careful pronunciation. In Batua this change is usually not shown in the spelling: *ikusgarri* 'worth seeing', *ikasgai* 'lesson', *ihesbide* 'way out'.

Sandhi rule 5. In the central dialects, a sibilant turns into an affricate when following a liquid or a nasal.

Thus $l + z = ltz$, as in *abeltzain* 'herdsman', from *abel-* (from *abere* 'livestock') and *zain* 'keeper', and *euskaltzale* 'Bascophile', from *euskal-* (from *euskara* 'Basque') and *zale* 'enthusiast'. One sees also $l + s = lts$ (*galtsoro*, besides *galsoro* 'field of wheat'), $r + z = rtz$ (*haurtzain* 'babysitter'), and $r + s = rts$ (*zakurtsoka* 'dog leash').

Sandhi rule 6. When a plosive follows a nasal, there is a strong tendency for the plosive to become voiced. (Editor's note: This rule was given in section 1.2.6 but was not discussed further in de Rijk's notes for this chapter.)

31.2.4.1 Vowel Sequences

Sequences of vowels generally remain unchanged, but there are two important exceptions:

1. ***A*-Elision:** The vowel *a* is elided before any immediately following vowel. Here are illustrations for each of the five possible vowels:

a: *artale* 'kernel of corn', from *arta-* (from *arto* 'maize') and *ale* 'kernel'
e: *galtzerdi* 'sock', from *galtza* 'pants' and *erdi* 'half'
i: *sugilar* 'Nigella (bot.)', from *suga-* (from *suge* 'snake') and *ilar* 'pea'
o: *gizotso* 'werewolf', from *giza-* (from *gizon* 'man') and *otso* 'wolf'
u: *paguso* 'ringdove', 'wood pigeon', from *paga-* (from *pago* 'beech') and *uso* 'dove'

If the second member begins with an *h* instead of a vowel, then this *h* is almost always ignored by the rule and accordingly not shown in the spelling:

mugarri 'boundary stone', from *muga* 'boundary' and *harri* 'stone'
baserri 'farm', from *basa-* (from *baso* 'wilderness') and *herri* 'village'
mugizki 'article', from *muga* 'limit' and *hizki* 'morpheme'
karobi 'limekiln', from *kara-* (from *kare* 'limestone') and *hobi* 'pit'
hankuts 'with bare legs', from *hanka* 'leg' and *huts* 'empty', 'bare'

[*N.B.* In the word *otsail* 'February', from *otsa* (from *otso* 'wolf') and *hil* 'month', the final *-a* does not elide, but the *h* drops nevertheless.]

2. **Vowel contraction:** When the second member begins with the same vowel with which the first ended, the two identical vowels contract to one vowel. If the second member begins with an *h* instead of a vowel, then the *h* is ignored. Examples follow (first members ending in *-a* are already covered by the *a*-Elision rule):

e: *astegun* 'weekday', from *aste* 'week' and *egun* 'day'
i: *argilun* 'light and dark', from *argi* 'light' and *ilun* 'dark'
o: *jainkorde* 'idol', from *jainko* 'god' and *orde* 'substitute'
u: *eskuts* 'with empty hands', from *esku* 'hand' and *huts* 'empty'

The other 16 vowel combinations remain, as mentioned, unchanged (provided Minor Apocope is blocked):

asteazken 'Wednesday'	from *aste* 'week' and *azken* 'end'
ateisil 'secret door'	from *ate* 'door' and *isil* 'silent', 'secret'
esneontzi 'milk can'	from *esne* 'milk' and *ontzi* 'container'
ileurdin 'gray-haired'	from *ile* 'hair' and *urdin* 'blue', 'gray'
mendialdapa 'mountain slope'	from *mendi* 'mountain' and *aldapa* 'slope'
mendietxe 'mountain home'	from *mendi* 'mountain' and *etxe* 'house'
mendioilar 'hoopoe'	from *mendi* 'mountain' and *oilar* 'rooster'
mendiur 'mountain stream'	from *mendi* 'mountain' and *ur* 'water'
beroaldi 'heat wave'	from *bero* 'warm' and *aldi* 'time'
eroetxe 'madhouse'	from *ero* 'crazy' and *etxe* 'house'
gogoilun 'gloomy'	from *gogo* 'mind' and *ilun* 'dark'
olour 'oat beverage'	from *olo* 'oats' and *ur* 'water'
eskuargi 'flashlight'	from *esku* 'hand' and *argi* 'light'
diruetxe 'bank'	from *diru* 'money' and *etxe* 'house'
diruitzulpen 'refund'	from *diru* 'money' and *itzulpen* 'to return'
eskuorga 'handcart'	from *esku* 'hand' and *orga* 'cart'

31.2.5 Haplology

It can happen that in the formation of a compound, after application of the phonological rules already discussed, it seems that both members have contributed to a juxtaposition of two identical or similar sequences of sounds. In that case, one omits the first of the two consecutive sound sequences. This phenomenon is denoted by the term haplology, which, as we see, has not itself undergone such a simplification. In Basque compounds haplology is not unusual; one could even say it is a common phenomenon.

In the compounds of *sagar* 'apple' or *garagar* 'barley' with *ardo* 'wine', the sound sequence *ar* would occur twice in succession. Haplology prevents this repetition from happening: *sagardo* 'apple wine', *garagardo* 'beer'.

Mujika (1982, 148) finds in haplology the explanation for the word *larrosa*, which, like *arrosa*, means 'rose'. According to him, the original meaning of *larrosa* is 'wild rose', and we have here a compound of *larre* 'meadow' and *arrosa* 'rose', whereby the expected acoustic form *larrarrosa* becomes *larrosa* due to haplology. Other experts, such as Schuchardt, and following him, Michelena (see *FHV*, sec. 16.11), see in the form *larrosa* the influence of the Romance definite article *la*: *la rosa*.

The similarity of the two consecutive sound sequences does not have to be exact. The compound of *muga* 'limit', 'occasion' and *gaitz* 'bad' is *mugaitz* 'inopportune moment' (cf. *mugagaitz* 'unlimitable').

Conscious use of haplology is often found in the creation of neologisms. An example is the form *gaiztoki* 'hell' from *gaiztotoki* 'place of the evil', created with the aim of replacing the generally used loanword *infernu*.

We end here our discussion of the phonological aspects of compounds in Basque. To sum up the main points: Vowel loss and vowel changes are phenomena that occur at the end of the first member in a compound. Vowel loss at the end of the last element occurs here and there in some dialects (mainly in Souletin and Roncalese) but does not occur in Batua.

31.3 Types of Compounds

"Dans tout cela rien n'est exclusivement basque, l'indo-européaniste reconnaît tout de suite les types de mots composés qui lui sont si familiers." (In all of this, nothing is exclusively Basque. The Indo-Europeanist will immediately recognize the types of compounds that are so familiar to him.) (Uhlenbeck 1949, 70)

The principal types of compounds that we find in Basque are very much like the traditionally distinguished compounds, or composites, known from Sanskrit. We distinguish the following five groups to be discussed consecutively:

31.3.1 Copulative Compounds (Dvandva)
31.3.2 Determinative Compounds (Tatpuruṣa)
31.3.3 Descriptive Compounds (Karmadhāraya)
31.3.4 Possessive Compounds (Bahuvrīhi)
31.3.5 Phrasal Compounds

31.3.1 Copulative Compounds

Copulative compounds are compounds of the form X + Y and with the meaning ''X' and 'Y' together'.

In spite of the semantic equivalence of the two members, the ordering within the compound is firmly fixed. The shortest element, measured in syllables, invariably comes first. If the number of syllables in each of the members is the same, then the culturally determined more prominent member comes first—for example, *zahar* 'old' before *gazte* 'young'. Copulative compounds can be (1) nouns, (2) adjectives, (3) adverbs, or (4) verbs.

1. Nouns

We can differentiate between homogenous and heterogeneous compounds, depending on the semantic relationship of parts X and Y to the whole of the compound. In a semantically homogeneous compound, we find an indivisible entity that is both X and Y. In other words, X and Y are considered equal; neither X nor Y is subordinate to the other in the new entity.

In Basque there are relatively few examples of this type; some examples would be

aitajaun	(lord) Father, grandfather, godfather
amandre	(lady) Mother, grandmother
Ama-Birjina	Virgin Mother
Jainkogizon	God-man, man of God (cleric)
gizotso	werewolf (man-wolf)

One could also consider as belonging to this homogeneous category compounds indicating degrees on a scale that are composed of antithetical adjectives:

eder-itsusi (beautiful-ugly)	sense of honor, self-respect
gazi-geza (salty-saltless)	saltiness
goi-behe (high-low)	height (more often *goiera*)
hotz-bero (cold-hot)	temperature
lodi-mehe (thick-thin)	thickness (more often *lodiera*)
luze-labur (long-short)	length, duration (more often *luzera*)
on-gaizto (good-bad)	morality
txiki-haundi (small-big)	dimension (Lekuona, *IG* II, 537)

[*N.B.* The plural substantive *on-gaitzak* 'good and bad' can mean 'pros and cons'.]

"Les dvandvas basques sont toujours au pluriel." (Basque dvandva compounds are always in the plural.) (Uhlenbeck 1949, 70) A semantically heterogeneous compound is a plural substantive consisting of both X and Y components. Such an entity has no grammatical singular; these compounds occur only in indefinte (neutral) form or in the definite plural. In the spelling of the heterogeneous compounds one uses a hyphen between the two members except when doing so is contrary to the applied sandhi rules. We will divide the examples into two groups, animate and inanimate.

Group 1. Animate

aitama	parents (sometimes *aita-ama*)
aita-seme	father(s) and son(s)
amalaba	mother(s) and daughter(s)
ama-seme	mother(s) and son(s)
anai-arreba	brother(s) and sister(s)
andre-gizon	man and woman, men and women
idi-behi	ox and cow, oxen and cows
jaun-andre	ladies and gentlemen (*Jaun-andreak!* 'Ladies and Gentlemen!')
neska-mutil	girl(s) and boy(s), boy(s) and girl(s)
neskame-morroi	servants and maidservants (*morroi* had three syllables: *morroni*)
senar-emazte	married couple(s)
senar-emaztegai	engaged couple(s)
zahar-gazte	young and old
zakur-katu	dogs and cats, cat and dog

[*N.B.* Interesting is the expression *zakurkatu daude* 'they are like cat and dog'.]

The obligatory definite article of these compounds is always *-ak*, and for the indefinite, *batzuk*. Two examples will illustrate:

aitamak	the parents (one or more sets)
senar-emazteak	man and wife (one or more couples)
aitama batzuk	a set of parents, or: some parents
senar-emazte batzuk	a married couple, or: some married couples
bi aitama	two parents, a couple of parents
bi senar-emazte	two spouses, that is, a married couple

Group 2. Inanimate

aho-mihi	mouth and tongue
ate-leiho	door(s) and windows
begi-belarri	eyes and ears (*MEIG* II, 43: begi-belarri-sudur; cf. Azkarate 1993, 223)
buru-buztan	head and tail, complications
oin-esku, esku-oin	hands and feet (see Jacobsen 1982, 394)
gal-irabazi	profit and loss
galde-erantzun	question(s) and answer(s)
gau-egun	day and night
gazi-geza	salt and insipid, vicissitudes of life
gibel-aitzin	pros and cons (Aulestia, 238–239)
gogo-bihotz	heart and soul

goi-behe	high and low, foundation and roof, all inhabitants of the house
goiz-arrats	morning and evening
gose-egarri	hunger and thirst
hanka-beso	arms and legs
harreman	relationships, relations
hortzagin	teeth and molars
itsas-lehor	land and sea
jan-edan	to eat and drink
jan-edari	food and drink
joan-etorri	round-trip
musu-belarri	facial features
on-gaitz	good and bad, weal and woe
sale-erosi	trade
sar-atera	traffic
uda-negu	summer and winter
urre-zilar	gold and silver
zeru-lur	heaven and earth
zuri-beltz	vicissitudes

[*N.B.* The expressions *ezer gutxi* 'little or nothing', *inor gutxi* 'almost no one', and *inon gutxitan* 'almost nowhere' belong essentially to this group.]

Also place names can form copulative compounds to indicate the range of an area bounded or determined by the two places. The new entity, however, is no longer syntactically a place name but an ordinary plural noun: *Mundakan* 'in Mundaka', *Bermeon* 'in Bermeo', but *Mundaka-Bermeoetan* 'in the area of Mundaka and Bermeo' (see Azkue, 1923–1925, II, 392); and *Bilbo-Donostietako burgesak* 'the bourgeoisie of Bilbao and San Sebastian' (*MEIG* VI, 69).

We see something similar with the time adverbs *gaur* 'today', *bihar* 'tomorrow', and *etzi* 'the day after tomorrow'. The combinations *gaur-bihar*, *bihar-etzi*, and *gaur-bihar-etzi* are correct but act not like adverbs, but as plural nouns. In order to indicate time, they need a locative suffix:

(1) a. Gaur-biharretan bukatuko dugu lan hori.
We'll finish that work today or tomorrow.
b. Ez al duzue bihar-etzietarako utziko?
Won't yoû postpone it until tomorrow or the day after (tomorrow)?

2. Adjectives

As we saw earlier, a copulative compound composed of adjectives often yields a noun: *luze-labur* 'length', *zahar-gazte(ak)* 'young and old'. Only rarely does such a compound have the status of a real adjective. We can mention a few examples:

zuri-beltz	gray, black and white
zuri-gorri	rose, blond, red and white
gorri-zuri	light red, rose, blond, red and white
gorri-beltz	dark red, purple, red and black

It would seem that we can distinguish here both a homogeneous and a heterogeneous meaning.

3. Adverbs
It will suffice to mention here a few examples:

han-hemen	here and there
han-hor-hemen	here, there, and over there; around; about
hara-hona	to here and there
harantz-honantz	back and forth
hala-hola	so-so, vaguely, indifferent

[*N.B.* For *gaur-bihar*, which is no longer an adverb, see under nouns (item 1). Compare *aitzin-gibel* 'back and forth', 'backward' (*E.H.* 24); *goiz-arrats* 'morning and afternoon without ceasing' (Lapitze, 125; *E.H.* 326).]

4. Verbs
Copulative compounds of verbs frequently yield a noun: *har-eman* (also *harreman*) 'relations', *sal-erosi* 'trade', *sar-atera* 'traffic', 'short visit'. But some of these compounds can also continue to function as verbs:

erregosi	to fry, from *erre* 'to roast' and *egosi* 'to boil'
galde-irabazi	to gain or lose
hartu-eman	to convert, to be in circulation
jan-edan	to eat and drink
joan-etorri	to come and go, to visit

(2) a. Eta gainera abioitxo bana, eskolara joan-etortzeko. (Amuriza, *Hil* 74)
And furthermore a small airplane each to go back and forth to school with.
b. Isil-isilik jan-edan zuten. (Amuriza, *Hil* 142)
They ate and drank in dead silence.

31.3.1.1 Expressive Compounds

We can consider as belonging to the copulative compounds also those cases where the second element lacks its own identity and is simply repeating the first element, but replacing its initial sound with an *m*. Such a phenomenon has also been called "echo-compounding" (Kachru 1987, 479). Such words appear in many languages and always have an expressive character, that is, a strong emotional connotation.

We begin the discussion with the nouns. The meaning can generally be given as "all kinds of X of dubious quality." Aside from a few exceptions, these compounds also do not occur in the singular. We divide them into two groups depending on whether the base is a substantive, nominal or adjectival, or a verb.

Group 1. With Noun or Adjective as Base

aitzakia	excuse, pretext	aitzaki-maitzaki	all kinds of excuses
duda	doubt, uncertainty	duda-muda	all sorts of qualms
estakuru	pretext, excuse	estakuru-mestakuru	all kinds of excuses
ez	no, refusal	ez-mez	doubts, vacillations
gako	hook, catch	gako-mako	all sorts of problems, guiles
handi	big	handi-mandi	magnate, capitalist
hitz	word	hitz-mitz	hollow words, verbiage
hondar	scrap, dregs	hondar-mondar	leftovers
inguru	surroundings	inguru-minguru	close relations, circumlocution
iritzi	opinion	iritzi-miritzi	criticism, all kinds of opinions
irri	jeer(ing) laugh	irri-mirri	derision, irony
iseka	derision	iseka-miseka	all kinds of gibes (Garate, *Hades* 57)
isil	quiet	isil-misil	whispering
saltsa	sauce, mess	saltsa-maltsa	mess, jumble
tarte	interval	tarte-marte	odd moments
txiri	wood shaving, splinter	txiri-miri	knickknacks, bagatelle
zalantza	doubt, uncertainty	zalantza-malantza	all kinds of doubts
zehar	slant, across, askew	zehar-mehar	twist, zigzag
zoko	corner	zoko-moko	all sorts of nooks and crannies

Group 2. With Verbs as Base

aldatu	to change	alda-malda	fast changes
esan	to say	esamesa	gossip, chatter
hasi	to begin	hasi-masi	basics, rudiments
hautsi	to break	hautsi-mautsi	negotiations, arrangements
inguratu	to surround	ingura-mingura	circuitous way, roundabout, detour
itzuli	to turn (around)	itzuli-mitzuli	evasions, dodges, prevarications
nahasi	to mix, confuse	nahas-mahas	mixture, confusion, mess

[*N.B.* Note that the base usually, but not always, has the perfect participle form.]

A number of such compounds can also function as adverbs—for example, in combination with a verb such as *ibili* 'to walk' or *ari izan* 'to be busy with'. Examples are *aitzaki-mitzaki* 'prevaricating'; *estakuru-mestakuru* 'prevaricating'; *inguru-minguru* or *ingura-mingura* 'beating about the bush'; *itzuli-mitzuli* 'wriggling, twisting' (also *itzulka-mitzulka*); and *zehar-mehar* 'zigzagging'.

Some compounds of this form are always adverbial:

arteka	in turns, alternately	arteka-marteka	in odd moments (also *arte-marteka*)
erdi	half	erdi-merdi	halfhearted (also *erdi-merdia*)

isilik	quietly, silent	isilik-misilik	quietly, in secret
isilka	secretly	isilka-misilka	mysteriously, quietly
koloka	wobbly	koloka-moloka	wobbling, staggering
zeharka	indirect, sideways	zeharka-meharka	indirectly, on the side
zehatz	exact, precise	zehatz-mehatz	in great detail, meticulously
zirika	prodding, poking	zirika-mirika	steadily prodding
zoro	foolish	zoro-moro	in any old way, slapdash

The following compounds, which are no longer analyzable today, have the same expressive sound pattern:

aiko-maiko	uncertainty, excuse
kuxu-muxu	murmur (Jn 7:12; *EAB*)
txirkimirki	pouting, whining, sulking
txutxu-mutxu	whispering (also *txutxu-mutxuka*)
urkumurku	with bad intentions
zirimiri	drizzle (also *xirimiri*)
zirkimirki	half angry, grumbling
zizka-mizka	salt snack, tidbit, appetizer
zizki-mizki	trifle, small thing
zurrumurru	murmur, rumor (Jn 7:12; Ker.)

Copulative compounds are often traceable to an ellipsis of the conjunction *eta* 'and' or *edo* 'or': *aitamak*, instead of *aita eta ama* 'father and mother'; *janedanak*, instead of *janak eta edanak* 'food and drink'; *gaur-bihar*, instead of *gaur edo bihar* 'today or tomorrow'. Even though this approach leaves much unexplained, such as, for example, the fact that the word *gaur-bihar* requires a locative ending, in contrast to the syntagma *gaur edo bihar*, it is nonetheless interesting that even in the case of the expressive compounds, parallel coordinative phrases occur. Therefore, a form such as *malantza* exists not only in the compound *zalantza-malantza*, but also in the equally expressive coordinative sequence *zalantzak eta malantzak*.

To illustrate, here are some examples in context:

(3) a. ... Nik Aritz harrapatuz gero ez dut inongo zalantzarik.—Zer ardura zaizkigu hire zalantzak eta malantzak?—oihu egin zuen Galarretak. Hemen froga hobeak behar dizkiagu. (Garate, *E.E.* 126)
"Now that Aritz has been arrested, I don't have any doubt (as to his guilt)." "What does yoúr talk of doubt matter to us?" cried Galarreta. "We need better evidence here."

b. —Bai, baina ni oporretan nago eta ...
—Zer oporrak eta moporrak! Batzuetan ume bat baino okerrago haiz. (Garate, *E.E.* 64)

"Yes, but I'm on vacation and . . ."
"Vacation shmacation! Sometimes yoú're worse than a child."

c. Hik uste baino amona bekatariagoa daukak, Jon.
—Zer bekatu eta mekatu, astirik ere ez baituzu izan! (Amuriza, *Hil* 59)
"Yoú have a more sinful grandmother than yoú think, Jon."
"What about sin? You just never had the time for it yourself!"

d. —Gizona haserretzen zaigu.
—Haserre edo maserre . . . aditu hitzak. (*TOE* I, 127)
"The man is getting mad at us."
"Mad or whatever, listen to my words."

e. —Ez nekian hain sikologo ona hintzenik—bota zion alai detektibeak.
—Ze sikologo eta mikologo—erantzun zion Rodriguezek bero samar. (Garate, *Esku* 152)
"I didn't know yoú were such a good psychologist," shouted the detective cheerily.
"What psychologist!" answered Rodriguez heatedly.

31.3.2 Determinative Compounds

Determinative compounds are endocentric compounds of the form X + Y, where the first element X determines more specifically the main element Y. In short, the meaning of X + Y is Y "of" X.

A detailed classification of such compounds on the basis of the precise semantic relationship between X and Y would lead far beyond this discussion and would yield few linguistic insights, considering the fact that this semantic relationship, pragmatically seen, not infrequently applies to a single occurrence.

The word *hodeigari* 'cloud-wheat', one of the examples given by the grammarian Azkue (1923–1925, II, 393), is a striking example. Regarding the meaning of *hodeigari*, grammatically we cannot get further than that it has to do with wheat (*gari*) that has something to do with clouds (*hodei*). But here, the cultural background of Basque agricultural life supplies the explanation: *hodeigari* is what the farmers pay to practitioners who conjure against thunderclouds.

Owing to what is evidently an all but limitless diversity on the semantic level (cf. Selkirk 1982, 25), it would seem that a clear treatment could be best served by a simple (though rough) division into parts of speech. We divide the determinative compounds therefore into nominal and verbal compounds, according to whether the main base Y, and thus the entity X + Y, is a noun or a verb.

By the nominal compounds we differentiate further based on the part of speech of the first element X. If X is a noun, then it is a binominal compound; if X is a verbal root, then it is a mononominal compound.

31.3.2.1 Binominal Compounds

The following examples are chosen to give an impression of the diversity of possible semantic relationships between the first element X and the main element Y.

aker (goat) + larre (field)	*akelarre* 'witches' meeting place', 'witches' sabbath'
argi (light) + mutil (boy)	*argimutil* 'candleholder'
auzo (neighbor) + lan (work)	*auzolan* 'community work'
beso (arm) + buru (head)	*besaburu* 'shoulder', 'shoulder blade'
diru (money) + etxe (house)	*diruetxe* 'bank'
ehiza (hunting) + zakur (dog)	*ehizazakur* 'hunting dog'
esku (hand) + zapi (cloth)	*eskuzapi* 'hand towel'
etxe (house) + kalte (damage)	*etxekalte* 'squanderer', 'ruiner'
gau (night) + zain (watcher)	*gauzain* 'night watch'
gerra (war) + aurre (frontside)	*gerraurre* 'prewar'
giltz (key) + harri (stone)	*giltzarri* 'cornerstone', 'keystone'
herri (nation) + min (pain)	*herrimin* 'homesickness'
hitz (word) + ontzi (container)	*hitzontzi* 'chatterbox'
hortz (tooth) + ikara (trembling)	*hortzikara* 'teeth chattering'
indar (strength) + dema (contest)	*indardema* 'test of strength'
itsaso (sea) + ontzi (container)	*itsasontzi* 'sea vessel'
izu (fright) + ikara (trembling)	*izuikara* 'shudder'
kalte (damage) + sari (fee)	*kaltesari* 'compensation'
lo (sleep) + zaku (sack)	*lozaku* 'sleepyhead', 'lie-abed'
lur (ground) + sagar (apple)	*lursagar* 'potato' (also *patata*)
min (pain) + otso (wolf)	*minotso* 'swelling', 'growth'
odol (blood) + hots (noise)	*odolots* 'pulse beat'
oin (foot) + harri (stone)	*oinarri* 'foundation'
sudur (nose) + zulo (hole)	*sudurzulo* 'nostril'
txori (bird) + buru (head)	*txoriburu* 'bird head', 'nitwit', 'birdbrain'
uda (summer) + azken (end)	*udazken* 'autumn'
ur (water) + ontzi (container)	*urontzi* 'water glass', 'water container'
zilar (silver) + lan (work)	*zilarlan* 'silver work', 'piece of worked silver'

In interpreting compounds, existing metaphors in the speech community play a considerable role. Thus one notices that with words such as *hitzontzi* 'chatterbox' and *lozaku* 'sleepyhead' a definite difference exists between the literal meaning as compound and the actual meaning in use. The connection between the two meanings comes about through a metaphor, in this case the widespread and also in Basque very popular notion of man as vessel.

Not considered as compounds are words such as *erbinude* 'weasel' and *izterbegi* 'enemy', where the meanings of the supposed components (*erbi* 'hare', *inude* 'wet nurse'; *izter* 'thigh', *begi* 'eye') in no way whatsoever, neither directly nor via an accepted metaphor, contribute to the meaning of the word. The rejection of these examples as compounds stands completely apart from the knowledge that, historically speaking, we have to do here with dissimilated forms of other compounds: *erdinude* 'midwife' and *ezkerbegi* 'left eye'. This knowledge is unfamiliar to the ordinary speaker.

There exist also compounds with an adjective as first element. These do not form a separate category, since the adjective in these compounds always fulfills the function of a noun (abstract). Also, in general, any adjective can appear as an abstract: *ederra* 'the beautiful', for example, in the phrase *ederraren lilura* 'the enchantment of beauty'. We also have *ona* 'the good' and *isila* 'the quiet'. Compare *ederra bera* 'beauty itself'.

However, the substantive use of the adjective does not always yield in all cases the desired meaning: *maitea* 'the beloved' is not the same as *maite(ta)suna* 'love'. What we have seen with derivations applies also to compounds, namely, that a shorter base, here *maite*, takes the place of a grammatically more correct, but longer, form, here *maite(ta)sun*.

Some examples with an adjective as X follow:

alfer (useless, lazy) + ontzi (container)	*alferrontzi* 'idler', 'good-for-nothing'
argal (weak) + une (spot)	*argalune* 'weak spot'
eder (beautiful) + min (pain)	*edermin* 'desire for beauty'
isil (still) + une (spot)	*isilune* 'moment of silence'
handi (big) + uste (opinion)	*hantuste* 'self-conceit'
maite (beloved) + min (pain)	*maitemin* 'being in love'
on (good) + damu (remorse)	*ondamu* 'jealousy', 'envy'
zahar (old) + sari (fee)	*zahartsari* 'old-age pension'

[*N.B.* The compounds *oniritzi* 'approval' and *gaitziritzi* 'disapproval' probably do not go back to the noun *iritzi* 'opinion', but to the verb *eritzi* (out of *e* + *iritzi*), which means 'to think'.]

31.3.2.2 Mononominal Compounds

Mononominal compounds have a verbal root as the first element and a noun as head base. Also here the semantic relationship of the noun to the verb can be very diverse. Some examples follow:

abiatu (to set out) + puntu (point)	*abiapuntu* 'point of departure'
bidali (to send) + sari (fee)	*bidaltsari* 'postage', 'dispatch charges'
edan (to drink) + dei (call, invitation)	*edandei* 'round (of drinks)'
erakutsi (to show) + leiho (window)	*erakusleiho* 'show window', 'shopwindow'
etorri (to come) + buru (head, begin)	*etorburu* 'origin'
heldu (to arrive) + buru (head)	*helburu* 'aim'
idatzi (to write) + lan (work)	*idazlan* 'piece of writing', 'article'

ikasi (to learn) + liburu (book)	*ikasliburu* 'textbook'
irabazi (to win) + gose (hunger)	*irabazgose* 'profit hunger', 'craving for profit'
irakurri (to read) + gela (room)	*irakurgela* 'reading room'
jaio (to be born) + etxe (house)	*jaioetxe* 'birthplace (house)'
jan (to eat) + lege (law)	*janlege* 'dietary law', 'diet'
jarri (to sit down) + leku (place)	*jarleku* 'seat'
jo (to strike) + muga (border)	*jomuga* 'goal', 'object (butt)'
saldu (to sell) + toki (place)	*saltoki* 'store', '(sales) outlet'
sortu (to arise, to come into being) + leku (place)	*sorleku* 'birthplace'
ukitu (to touch) + puntu (point)	*ukipuntu* 'contact point', 'contact'

31.3.2.3 Verbal Compounds

In contrast to nominal compounds, which can be freely made up by any speaker as desired, verbal compounds, aside from the causative forms with *arazi* (see section 16.2), are nonproductive. They are undeniably part of the traditional Basque stock of words, and the underlying process of their development could well become reactivated under pressure of the need for new, especially technical, terms.

In all cases of this type of compound we are concerned with incorporation, that is, the incorporating into the verb of a noun or adjective in the neutral form, thus without an article, and mostly also without a case ending. The incorporated nominal can, with respect to the verb, fulfill one of the following functions: (1) direct object, (2) ergative subject, (3) instrumental modifier, (4) predicate nominal.

1. Examples with incorporated direct object

alde	side, distance	aldegin	to run away, to escape
bizkar	back	bizkarberotu	to thrash, to flog (from *berotu* 'to warm up')
buru	head	buruberotu	to drive/make someone crazy
era	manner	eraberritu	to reform, to renovate, to modernize
gain	top	gainartu	to dominate, to subjugate, to conquer
galde	question	galdegin	to ask
gari	wheat	garijo	to thresh wheat (from *jo* 'to hit')
gogo	mind, spirit, desire	gogobete	to please, to satisfy oneself
hats	breath	hatsartu	to breathe
hitz	word	hitzartu	to agree with/on
hitz	word	hitzegin	to speak
hitz	word	hitzeman	to promise
hortz	tooth	hortzestutu	to grit one's teeth
hots	noise	hotsegin	to call, to telephone
ile	hair	ileberritu	to shed hair, to molt
zahar	old	zaharberritu	to rejuvenate, to renew, to fix up

Incorporating a direct object does not affect the transitivity. The subject of all these verbs is in the ergative case:

(4) Pellok hitzegingo balu, mojek aldegingo lukete.
If Pete would speak, the nuns would walk out.

A number of these verbs (e.g., *eraberritu*, *galdegin*, *hitzartu*, *hitzeman*, *zaharberritu*) allow an explicit direct object:

(5) a. Hau dela eta, erabaki nuen biak eraberritzea. (Etxaide, *Eneko* 181)
For these reasons I decided to revise them both.
b. Ezkontzaren hautseraztea hitzartu zuten.
They agreed on divorce.
c. Gehienik irri egin araziko dionari hitzematen dio zinta zeta bat ederra. (*Artho Xur*. 24)
To the one who makes him laugh the most, he promises a beautiful silk ribbon.

2. Examples with incorporated ergative subject
So far as I know, there are only compounds with the verbs *jo* 'to hit' and *hartu* 'to take' that incorporate ergative subjects (but see *FHV* 528: *baztanga-pikatu* 'pockmarked'):

har	worm	harjo	wormy, to be worm-eaten
ilargi	moon	ilargijo	to be moonstruck, lunatic
itsaso	sea	itsasjo	seasick, to be seasick
lo	sleep	lokartu	to fall asleep, to die
su	fire	sukartu	to catch on fire, to get a fever

[*N.B.* Unless in *-kartu* we see preserved an older form of *hartu*, the *k* of *lokartu* and *sukartu* would point to the maintenance of the case ending of the incorporated noun before a vowel or *h*. Concerning *lokartu*, it is perhaps derived from *loakartu* (= *loak hartu*) as in *loakartu zuen* in *TB* 209 (see also *DGV* XI, 669–671).]

Ergative incorporation makes the verb intransitive:

(6) a. Eta hau esan zuenean lokartu zen. (Cf. Acts 7:60; Lz)
And when he had said this, he died.
b. Unatuak izanik biak, laster lokartu ziren. (Barbier, *Lég*. 69)
Both being exhausted, they fell quickly asleep.
c. Gure mutila sukartu zen, jakin zuenean soldadu zela. (Azkue, *DVEF* II, 235)
Our boy flared up when he heard that he was a soldier.

[*N.B.* The noun *sukar* 'fever' is probably from the verb *sukartu* and not vice versa (back-formation).]

The intransitivity of these compounds against the transitivity of those of group 1 underpins the assertion made in section 12.2.1 that transitivity in Basque depends solely on the possibility of an ergative subject, and not whether a verb allows a direct object.

3. Examples with incorporated instrumentals

ahogozatu to taste with enjoyment (cf. *ahoz gozatu* 'to enjoy with the mouth')
odolustu to bleed, to let blood (cf. *odolez hustu* 'to drain off blood')

4. Examples with incorporated predicate nominals
The most important examples with incorporated predicate nominals are compounds with the verb *etsi* in the meaning 'to consider', 'to find', 'to think'. Nowadays, the verb with this meaning is constructed with the suffix *-tzat* (see section 17.8.2):

(7) a. Aitor dezagun nolabaitekotzat etsi dituela honek. (*MIH* 238)
Let us acknowledge that he considered them only run-of-the-mill.
b. Zenbait adiskidek nire aldegitea koldarkeriatzat etsi dute. (Cf. S. Mitxelena, *IG* I, 115)
Some friends have considered my escape as cowardice.

In earlier times, the predicate nominal could appear with *etsi* without any suffix:

(8) a. Eta guztiz mirakulu esten zuten. (Mk 7:37; Lz)
And they considered it completely a wonder.
b. Aski esten du edo sobera esten du. (Ax. 114)
He finds it enough or he finds it too much.

The following compounds originate through incorporation via this construction:

alfer	useless, lazy	alferretsi	to find useless
apal	low, humble	apaletsi	to hold in contempt, to scorn
aski	enough	askietsi	to deem sufficient, to satisfy
bai	yes	baitetsi	to approve (also *baietsi*)
berandu	late	berantetsi	to become impatient
eder	beautiful	ederretsi	to admire, to find beautiful
egia	true	egietsi	to confirm as true (also *egitetsi*)
erraz	easy	errazetsi	to consider easy (Biguri 1986, 249)
ez	not	ezetsi	to disapprove
gaitz	bad, evil	gaitzetsi	to condemn, to disapprove
galdu	lost	galetsi	to give up, to consider as lost
gora	high	goretsi	to praise, to exalt
gupida	pity, compassion	gupidetsi	to be merciful, to spare (also *gupitetsi*)
gutxi	few	gutxietsi	to despise, to disdain
handi	big	handietsi	to glorify, to esteem highly
hil	dead	hiletsi	to give up for dead, to consider as dead
hobe	better	hobetsi	to consider better, to prefer
jaun	lord, sir	jauretsi	to adore, to give homage to
luze	long	luzetsi	to seem long (to someone), to become impatient
mira	admiration	miretsi	to admire, to wonder at
on	good	onetsi	to approve, to bless

sobera	too much	soberetsi	to find too much, to overestimate
zuzen	straight, just	zuzenetsi	to acquit, to justify (Mt 12:37)

[*N.B.* Hard or impossible to explain are *begietsi* 'to observe', *erdietsi* 'to obtain', *hautetsi* 'to elect', and *ihardetsi* 'to answer'.]

Some compounds with other verbs are *onartu* 'to accept', 'to approve' (synonymous with *ontzat hartu*) and *goraipatu* 'to extol' from *gora* 'high' and *aipatu* 'to mention'.

31.3.3 Descriptive Compounds

Descriptive, or attributive, compounds are endocentric compounds of the form X + Y, where the second member Y defines further the head component X. We distinguish two types depending on whether the head element is a noun or a verb.

1. If the head element X is a noun, then Y is an adjective and the compound as a whole is a noun. Here are some examples:

abere (animal, livestock) + gorri (red, naked)	*abelgorri* 'cattle'
ardo (wine) + berri (new)	*ardanberri* 'new wine'
begi (eye) + erdi (half)	*begierdi* 'contempt'
bide (way) + xidor (narrow)	*bidexidor* 'path', 'narrow way'
ele (word, story) + berri (new)	*elaberri* 'novel'
gazta (cheese) + bera (soft)	*gaztanbera* 'curd(s)'
muga (border, occasion) + on (good)	*mugon* 'good opportunity'
mutil (boy) + zahar (old)	*mutilzahar* 'confirmed bachelor'
neska (girl) + zahar (old)	*neskazahar* 'spinster'
uda (summer) + berri (new)	*udaberri* 'spring'
ume (child) + gorri (red, naked)	*umegorri* 'small child', 'greenhorn'
urre (precious metal) + bizi (living)	*urrebizi* 'mercury', 'quicksilver'
urre (precious metal) + gorri (red)	*urregorri* 'gold'
urre (precious metal) + zuri (white)	*urrezuri* 'silver'
zori (fate) + gaitz (bad)	*zorigaitz* 'misfortune', 'bad luck'
zori (fate) + on (good)	*zorion* 'good luck'
zori (fate) + txar (bad)	*zoritxar* 'bad luck', 'misfortune'

One notices the difference in form and meaning between descriptive compounds and the corresponding syntagmas: *abelgorri* and *abere gorri* 'red animal'; *gaztanbera* and *gazta bera* (also *gazta biguna*) 'soft cheese'; *udaberri* and *uda berri* 'new summer'.

2. If the head element X is a verb, then Y is an adjective or adverb and the compound as a whole has the character of an adjective.

Such compounds are also endocentric because in this respect we consider adjectives and verbs as belonging to the same category. This assumption seems to be justified in that the root form of the verb is basically nothing other than the apocopated form of the perfect participle, the adjectival status of which has been discussed in chapter 25.

We have already discussed an important example of this type of compound in section 24.10.3, namely, compounds with the adjective *gaitz* 'difficult': *asegaitz* 'hard to satisfy', *ulergaitz* 'hard to understand', and so on.

Also important are compounds of verbal roots with the adjective *berri* 'new'. Some common examples are

ateraberri	recently appeared, newly published
etorberri	newly arrived, recent, newcomer
helberri	just arrived, newcomer
hilberri	just died, recently dead
jaioberri	just born
janberri	having just eaten
sarberri	just come in, just entered, novice
sorberri	just appeared

Also to be mentioned are compounds with the adverb *sarri* 'manifold' and *urri* 'seldom', 'sparing':

edansarri	frequently drinking, often drunk
edanurri	seldom drinking, drinking little
jansarri	often eating
janurri	seldom eating, eating little, small eater, poorly fed creature

31.3.4 Possessive Compounds

Possessive compounds are exocentric compounds of the type X + Y, where the second element Y is an adjective modifying the head element X. We call this type exocentric because the compound as a whole is an adjective that nevertheless, like all adjectives, can also be used independently, which is often the case with these compounds. (Cf. Selkirk 1982, 25–26, for exocentric compounds in English.)

In Basque, adjectives of this shape are very common and fully productive. The use of these compounds has but one prerequisite: the attribution of the characteristic expressed by X + Y to a matter Z requires that X is considered to be a natural component of Z. If Z is a living being, then X can only be a body part (in broad sense) or a word such as *gogo* 'mind'. From this comes a limitation of the character of the noun X appearing as the head element of such a compound: X must be conceived as a natural part of an entity.

When this is not the case, then one must resort to other grammatical means of expression, either a relative clause or a derivation with the propensity suffix *-dun* (section 19.8); thus, unlike *neskatxa ilegorria* 'the girl with the red hair', we must say *gona gorria duen neskatxa* 'the girl that has the red skirt', or shorter, *gona gorridun neskatxa* 'the girl with the red skirt', and not use a compound. As inanimate examples, we can mention here *etxe* *zuri leihogorria* 'the white house with red windows', *eliza handi atetxikia* 'the big church with the small doors', and *hiri aberats kalegarbia* 'the rich city with the clean streets'.

Most interesting are the compounds with body parts as head component, since these, besides their literal meaning, often have a metaphoric meaning. What follows is a choice from a rich assortment of examples:

adar (horn) + bakar (single)	*adarbakar* 'one-horned', 'unicorn', 'rhinoceros'
aho (mouth) + bero (warm)	*ahobero* 'exaggerating', 'boasting', 'braggart'
aho (mouth) + zikin (dirty)	*ahozikin* 'foul-mouthed person'
aho (mouth) + zuri (white)	*ahazuri* 'flatterer', 'gourmet'
begi (eye) + argi (clear)	*betargi* 'cheerful', 'sharp-eyed' (also *begiargi*)
begi (eye) + luze (long)	*begiluze* 'observant', 'curious', 'inquisitive'
begi (eye) + oker (oblique)	*betoker* 'one-eyed', 'cross-eyed' (also *begioker*)
begi (eye) + zorrotz (sharp)	*begizorrotz* 'sharp-eyed', 'clear-sighted'
belarri (ear) + luze (long)	*belarriluze* 'long-eared', 'ass', 'pig', 'inquisitive'
belarri (ear) + motz (short)	*belarrimotz* 'short-eared', 'non-Basque', 'barbarian'
bihotz (heart) + bera (soft)	*bihozbera* 'kind', 'tender'
bihotz (heart) + bigun (soft)	*bihozbigun* 'softhearted' (also *bihotz-bigun*)
bihotz (heart) + handi (big)	*bihotzandi* 'generous', 'noble'
bihotz (heart) + zabal (broad)	*bihotzabal* 'noble', 'generous', 'amiable'
buru (head) + argi (clear)	*buruargi* 'smart', 'clever', 'bright'
buru (head) + arin (light)	*buruarin* 'foolish', 'light-headed', 'rash'
buru (head) + handi (big)	*buruhandi* 'with a big head', 'stubborn'
buru (head) + soil (bald)	*burusoil* 'with a bald head', 'bald-headed'
esku (hand) + zabal (broad)	*eskuzabal* 'with a generous hand', 'generous'
gibel (liver) + handi (big)	*gibelandi* 'with a big liver', 'phlegmatic', 'calm'
gogo (mind) + arin (light)	*gogoarin* 'frivolous', 'foolish', 'scatterbrained'
gogo (spirit) + bera (soft)	*gogabera* 'merciful', 'softhearted'
gogo (spirit) + bero (warm)	*gogobero* 'enthusiastic', 'vehement', 'fiery'
hanka (leg) + gorri (red)	*hankagorri* 'with red legs', 'bare-legged'
ile (hair) + soil (bald)	*ilesoil* 'bald', 'hairless'
larru (skin) + gorri (red)	*larrugorri* 'naked'
larru (skin) + huts (pure)	*larruts* 'naked'
mutur (snout) + handi (big)	*muturrandi* 'thick-snouted', 'mug', 'idiot'
mutur (snout) + zuri (white)	*muturtxuri* 'spoiled', 'epicure', 'gourmet'
odol (blood) + bero (warm)	*odolbero* 'hot-blooded', 'aggressive', 'violent'
odol (blood) + bizi (lively)	*odolbizi* 'nervous', 'jumpy'
odol (blood) + gaitz (evil)	*odolgaitz* 'violent', 'cruel'
odol (blood) + hotz (cold)	*odolotz* 'cold-blooded', 'in cold blood'
sudur (nose) + luze (long)	*sudurluze* 'busybody'

[*N.B.* The words *aho* and *gogo* are no longer subject to Minor Apocope in contemporary Basque. The forms *ahazuri* and *gogabera* come from an older language usage.]

Here are some examples of the use of compounds of this type in literature:

(9) a. Arrain buruhandi, haginzorrotz, larrumea. (Azkue 1923–1925, II, 393)
A fish with a big head, sharp teeth, and a thin skin.
b. Bi idi handi, kopetazuri, bizkarbeltz, adarrandiak. (Elzb. *Po*. 197)
The two big oxen with white forehead, black back, and big horns.
c. Gizon burusoil bizarzuri bat . . . (From the song "Mutil koxkor bat," *Xaramela* 230)
A man with a bald head and a white beard.
d. Etxepila bat teilatu-zahar-aundi, tximinia-ketsu, ormabeltz-sendoak. (Eizagirre, 9)
A couple of houses with big old roofs, smoked chimneys, and firm dark walls.
e. Nicolls jenerala begi eta izter eta beso-bakarra zen. (Azkue, *Ip*. 203)
General Nicolls had only one eye, one thighbone, and one arm.

31.3.5 Phrasal Compounds

One speaks of a merged form or phrasal compound when a syntagma, that is, a possible sequence of words within a sentence, gradually merges together in form and meaning.

From this definition it follows that this combination is more a matter of etymological analysis than of productive word formation. Some Basque words are results of such a phrasal compounding. A number of much-used examples are *bada-ezpada* 'just in case' (from *bada* [*eta*] *ez bada* 'if it is [so] and if it is not [so]'), from which are derived *bada-ezpadako* 'dubious', 'so-so' and *bada-ezpadakoan* 'in doubt'; *balizko* 'supposed', 'so-called' (from *balitz* 'if it were' and the linking morpheme *-ko*); *eztabaida* 'dispute', 'disagreement', 'polemic' (from *-ez da*, *-bai da* 'it isn't, it is'); *halabehar* 'fate', 'chance' (from *hala behar* 'necessarily so', 'so must it'), from which is derived *halabeharrez* 'fatefully', 'by chance' (also *halabeharrean*); *nahitaez* 'willy-nilly', 'perforce', 'like it or not' (from *nahi eta ez* 'wanted or not'), from which comes *nahitaezko* 'necessary', 'indispensable', of which the synonym is *derrigorrezko* from the Spanish expression *de rigor*; and *nonzerberri* 'busybody' (from *non zer berri?* 'What is there for news?', 'Where is there something to do?').

32 Reduplication; Parasuffixes, Prefixes, and Paraprefixes

32.1 Reduplication

The term reduplication refers to a grammatical phenomenon wherein a systematic repetition of a speech element takes place with a predictable meaning connection between the base form X and the reduplicated form XX.

This semantic relationship can differ from language to language. With Basque we can speak of an intensification or greater precision of what is expressed by the base form X. Further, it is interesting that in Basque we see here a process at word level. Only words, not parts of words or word phrases, undergo reduplication. This fact has lead some Basque grammarians to consider the reduplicated form as a compound, a compounding of the word X with itself.

Not all kinds of words in Basque are candidates for reduplication. Verbs are almost never reduplicated (*Detektibea alditxo batetan isilik egon zen, pentsa pentsatzen.* [Garate, *Esku* 124–125] 'The detective remained silent for a little while, thinking hard.'), and nouns only under certain conditions. Mostly we find reduplication of adjectives, adjectival modifiers or adjuncts (including relative clauses), stative words, adverbs, and numerals.

We shall begin by giving a number of examples in each word category and end with a discussion of the reduplication possibilities for nouns.

32.1.1 Adjectives

(1) a. Etxe hau zahar-zaharra da.
This house is ancient.
b. Bero-bero zegoen bitartean. (Muxika, *P.Am.* 44)
In the meantime it stayed very hot.
c. Ene lagun on ona. (Atxaga, *Behi* 162)
My very good friend.
d. ... eliza osoa zoko guztietan bete-betea. (Muxika, *P.Am.* 6)
... the whole church (was) chock-full to the very corners.

e. Eskatu eta hartuko duzue, zuen poza bete-betea izan dadin. (Jn 16:24)
Ask and yoû will receive, so that yoûr joy may be (over)full.

The reduplicated forms can also be used attributively:

(2) a. Bere ile gorri-gorri hori luzitzea gustatzen zaio. (Atxaga, *Bi Let.* 16)
She likes to show off that fiery red hair of hers.
b. Orduan emakume eder-ederra ikusi zuen bereganatzen.
Then he saw an extremely beautiful woman come at him.
c. Lo gozo-gozoan nengoen. (*P.Ab.* 115)
I had fallen into the most blissful sleep.

Also the adjective *guzti* 'whole', 'all' can be reduplicated:

(3) a. Liburu guzti-guztia irakurri dut.
I have read absolutely the whole book.
b. Liburu guzti-guztiak irakurri ditut.
I have read absolutely all the books.
c. Guzti-guztia esango diot. (Also *den-dena*)
I will tell him absolutely everything.
d. Guzti-guztiek zituzten hildakoak ugari. (Ws 18:12)
Absolutely all of them had innumerable dead.

32.1.2 Adjectival Modifiers

bihotzeko agurrak	cordial greetings
bihotz-bihotzeko agurrak	most cordial greetings
benetako damua	sincere remorse
bene-benetako damua	most sincere remorse
eguneroko gauza	an everyday matter
egunero-eguneroko gauza	a very everyday matter

[*N.B.* The linking morpheme *-(ta)ko* does not take part in the reduplication. We shall see that this is also the case with all case endings.]

Another type of adjectival adjunct is the relative clause (see chapter 19). Insofar as this clause consists of only one word, reduplication is also possible here.

(4) a. Zaren-zarena baitzara zutaz pena dizut nik. (*LVP* VIII–10)
Because you are precisely who you are, I am languishing.
b. Barkatu, lagun, baina den-dena ezin dizut esan. (Atxaga, *Behi* 21)
Sorry, friend, but absolutely everything I can't tell you.
c. Naizen-naizena zuri esker naiz.
Everything I am, I am thanks to you.

(5) a. Araudia dagoen-dagoenean utziko dugu.
We'll leave the rule exactly as it is.
b. Zeuden-zeudenean datoz berriz, hutsik ere zuzendu gabe. (*MEIG* VIII, 152 = *MIH* 365)
They (the essays) appear anew precisely as they were, without even mistakes corrected.

The conjunctive ending *-nean* was mentioned in section 20.2.2 as being derived from *-n orduan* 'when'. From the preceding examples it would seem that *-nean* could also have come from *-n moduan* (or *-n gisan*), and therefore can have the meaning 'like', 'such as': *dagoenean* = *dagoen moduan* 'such as he is'.

32.1.3 Stative Words

alferrik	in vain	alfer-alferrik	completely in vain
azkenik	finally	azken-azkenik	at the very last
bakarrik	alone	bakar-bakarrik	completely alone
bizirik	alive	bizi-bizirik	alive and kicking
isilik	still	isil-isilik	dead still
osorik	full	oso-osorik	absolutely full
pozik	glad	poz-pozik	overjoyed
prest	ready	prest-prest	all ready
soilik	simply	soil-soilik	simply and solely
tente	upright	tente-tente	bolt upright, unwaveringly erect
zutik	erect	zut-zutik	straight as an arrow

[*N.B.* The stative ending *-(r)ik*, as a case ending, does not take part in the reduplication.]

32.1.4 Adverbs

asko	much	asko-asko	a lot, very much
aspaldi	long ago	aspaldi-aspaldi	a very long time ago
astero	every week	astero-astero	every week without exception (Garate, *Alaba* 28)
benetan	really	bene-benetan	really and truly
berehala	at once	berehal-berehala	right then and there (Iztueta, 374)
beti	always	beti-beti	always without fail
egiatan	truly	egi(a)-egiatan	very truly
gutxi	few, little	gutxi-gutxi	very little
hala	so, thus	hala-hala	precisely so (Larzabal, *Hiru* 67)
ia	almost	ia-ia	just barely
segur	surely	segur-segur	absolutely sure

[*N.B.* See also *EGLU* I, 497. The locative ending *-tan* does not reduplicate, but the word-forming suffix *-ero* does: *egunero-egunero* 'every day without fail'. Compare *lehenbizi-lehenbizitik* 'from the very first beginning' (*MEIG* VII, 37).]

32.1.5 Numerals

ehun-ehun	precisely a hundred
bost-bostak dira	it is precisely five o'clock
bost-bostetan	at exactly five o'clock

32.1.6 Nouns

Nouns denoting a time, place, or situation can be reduplicated, but only when they are accompanied by an appropriate case ending (exception: *egi-egia* 'the whole truth' [*MEIG* I, 130]). These case endings can be the instrumental *-z* or a locational ending, to wit, *-an*, *-tik*, *-ra*, *-raino*, or *-rantz*.

The reduplication strengthens the meaning; thus time and space are more precisely indicated and a situation or state intensified.

Among the place indications we find especially the nouns denoting a location or spatial relationship mentioned in chapter 4 reduplicated:

etxe aurrean	in front of the house	etxe aurre-aurrean	right in front of the house
etxola atzean	behind the hut	etxola atze-atzean	just behind the hut (also: way behind the hut)
zubi aldean	next to the bridge	zubi alde-aldean	right next to the bridge
leize barruan	inside the cave	leize barru-barruan	in the inmost part of the cave
haritz ondoan	by the oak	haritz ondo-ondoan	right by the oak
eliza parean	opposite the church	eliza pare-parean	right opposite the church
hiri erdian	in the town center	hiri erdi-erdian	exactly in the middle of the town
zeru erdian	in heaven's midst	zeru erdi-erdian	in the very midst of heaven (Artola, in *OrOm* 62)

[*N.B.* For some speakers the genitive is necessary when combining reduplicated locationals with the preceding head word. Thus only *etxearen aurre-aurrean* is possible, even though for these speakers, besides *etxearen aurrean*, *etxe aurrean* is also possible. Compare *itsaso zabalaren ertz-ertzean* (Manzisidor, 13) 'at the very edge of the broad sea'; *atearen ondo-ondoan* (Barbier, *Lég*. 67) 'right beside the door'.]

The following are examples of other sorts of spatial relationships:

eskuinetik	from the right	eskuin-eskuinetik	wholly from the right
ezkerretik	from the left	ezker-ezkerretik	entirely from the left

goian	above, on top	goi-goian	completely above
behean	below	behe-behean	all the way below, at the bottom
zuzenean	straight on	zuzen-zuzenean	directly straight ahead

These are ordinary locationals (sometimes also used in a metaphorical sense):

mendian	in the mountains	mendi-mendian	in the midst of the mountains
etxeraino	as far as the house	etxe-etxeraino	just as far as to the house
eskuan	in the hand, by hand	esku-eskuan	right in the hand, close by hand
bihotzetik	from the heart	bihotz-bihotzetik	from the bottom of the heart

[*N.B.* We should recall here the instrumental form *bihotzez* 'with/from the heart', 'sincerely' and the reduplicated form *bihotz-bihotzez* 'with all my/one's heart', 'warmest regards', and so on. Compare *begi-begietara begiratu nionan* (Garate, *E.E.* 51) 'I looked him straight in the eyes'.]

These are time indications:

azkenean	at the last	azken-azkenean	at the very last (*MEIG* I, 159)
eguerdian	around noon	eguerdi-eguerdian	at precisely noon
gauean	at night	gau-gauean	in the dead of night
goizean	in the morning	goiz-goizean	early in the morning (*TB* 121)
hasieratik	from the beginning	hasiera-hasieratik	from the very beginning
orduan	then	ordu-orduan	exactly then
umetatik	from childhood	ume-umetatik	from the beginning of childhood

The following expressions indicate circumstances:

argitan	in the light	argi-argitan	in full light
berotan	in the warmth	bero-berotan	in the extreme heat
haizetan	in the wind	haize-haizetan	in the full force of the wind
hotzetan	in the cold	hotz-hotzetan	in the extreme cold
patxadan	in calmness	patxa-patxadan	in complete calm and rest
sutan	in the fire	su-sutan	in the blazing fire
uretan	in the water	ur-uretan	in the midst of the water

32.2 Distributive Duplication

Euskara Batua has another iterative phenomenon: "distributive duplication," borrowed from Biscayan. This duplication, only applied to place and time indicators with a locational ending, differs in form and meaning from the reduplication discussed previously—in form because the ending is also repeated, and in meaning because the repetition does not intensify or strengthen the base form. Instead, it gives a distributive, generalizing dimension to the word. The following will help to illustrate:

astean	in the week	astean astean	every week (anew)
egunean	on the day	egunean egunean	day in day out
goizean	in the morning	goizean goizean	every morning (again)
lekuan	at the spot	lekuan lekuan	everywhere
neguan	in the winter	neguan neguan	every winter, each winter again
tokian	at the place	tokian tokian	everywhere
udan	in the summer	udan udan	every summer, each summer again
urtean	in the year	urtean urtean	year in year out
zortzian	in eight (days)	zortzian zortzian	every eight days

(6) a. Urtean urtean igarotzen dute hementxe uda. (Azkue 1891, 329)
Year in year out they spend the summer here.
b. Udan udan alde egiten dute. (Ibid.)
Every summer again they go away.

32.3 Parasuffixes

The combining of nouns in Basque is a productive process. In principle, any noun can be joined with any other noun to form a compound. In practice, one distinguishes useful and nonuseful combinations. To illustrate, the compound *liburuesne* 'bookmilk' is grammatically sound, having the meaning 'milk that has something to do with books', but is not useful so long as there is no occasion to be found or even thinkable for its application.

Some words have the property of occurring with a relatively great number of other words to form useful compounds. As the second member of a compound, these words can be termed "quasi suffixes," or, as Luis M. Múgica (1978) has named them, "parasuffixes."

These are words with a rather general meaning, such as *ume* 'small area in space or time', or with a meaning that easily can be expanded metaphorically, such as *begi* 'eye', *bide* 'way', or *buru* 'head'. Some common parasuffixes have turned up in previous chapters: *gai* 'material' (section 11.7), *aldi* 'turn, time' (section 20.9), *gaitz* 'difficult' (section 24.10.3), *erraz* 'easy' (section 24.10.4), and *arte* 'gap, interval' (section 4.3).

Here we will treat the parasuffix *aro* 'period of time' and then the very important parasuffix *bide* 'way'. Because there are so many compounds with *bide* and their meanings are difficult to predict, an extensive treatment with many examples seems justified. And, to conclude, we will discuss the morpheme *pe* 'under' that occupies a singular position between suffix and parasuffix.

32.3.1 Compounds with *aro* 'period of time'

The basic meaning of the word *aro* is 'time interval', that is, a continuous period of some duration, minimally measured in days: *Eguberri aro* 'Christmas time'. Thus it is both similar to and different from the word *aldi* (section 20.3.1) where the period can be very short and, moreover, where the connotation 'incident out of a series of happenings' plays a role that is lacking in *aro*. The word *aro* has further, in the northern dialects, the meaning 'weather', especially 'good weather', and is then synonymous with *giro*: *aro gaitza* 'bad weather'.

The word *aro* occurs as a parasuffix with nouns, adjectives, and verbs that are first nominalized: *ikaste* 'learning', *zahartze* 'becoming older'. An exception is the word *ereiaro* 'time for sowing', instead of the expected *ereitaro*.

The main examples are

belar	grass	belarraro	hay-time
berandu	late	berantaro	late season, end of autumn
bide	way, journey	bidaro	(good) travel weather
bizi	life	biziaro	period of life
erein	to sow	ereiaro	time for sowing, sowing weather, June
gau	night	gauaro	night temperature, night time
gazte	young	gaztaro	youth, period of youth
goiz	morning	goizaro	beginning of season, morning temperature
hazi	seed	hazaro	planting time, sowing season, November
ikaste	learning	ikastaro	study or training period, academic course
itsaso	sea	itsasaro	(good) seafaring weather
jai	holiday, feast	jaiaro	feast period, holiday time
kristau	christian	Kristauaro	Christian era
lo	sleep	loaro, lotaro	good time for sleep, sleeping weather
lore	flower	lorearo	flowering time
luze	long	luzaro	for a long time, long-lasting, at length
mahats	grape	mahatsaro	vintage, grape harvest
motz	cut short	motzaro	shearing time (sheep), shaving time
on	good	onaro	prosperous period, time of well-being
poz	joy, happiness	pozaro	time of joy, happy times
uda	summer	udaro	summer season
urte	year	urtaro	season (*aro* can also mean 'trimester')
uzta	harvest	uztaro	harvest time
zahartze	aging	zahartzaro	old age

[*N.B.* The form *zahartzaro* was later interpreted as *zahar* + *zaro*. This assumption led to forms with *-zaro*: *gaztezaro* 'youth' next to *gaztaro*, *haurtzaro* or *umezaro* 'childhood', and *berrizaro* 'period when something is still new'.]

32.3.2 Compounds with the Parasuffix *bide*

The basic meaning of the word *bide* is 'way' or 'path'. Already since the oldest texts the word *bide* has known a great variety of uses that demonstrate the great abstractional possibilities inherent in the word. In present-day Batua the semantic dimensions are so great that it encompasses everything that can be expressed in English by such terms as *method*, *means*, *direction*, *manner*, *cause*, *opportunity*, *measure*, and *occasion*: *-ren bidez* 'with the help of' or 'by means of'; *hau dela bide* 'because of this', 'in reference to this'; *bide(a) eman* 'to give (the) opportunity'; *bide(a) hartu* 'to seize the opportunity'; *bideak hartu* 'to take measures'; and so on. This whole semantic field also plays a role in compounds.

As for the phonological form, we notice in particular that the *b* of *bide* is devoiced (*pide*) after a verb radical ending in a strong *r*, with the exception of those verb radicals that also do duty as adjectives. Thus we have *agerpide*, *azterpide*, *elkarpide*, *etorpide*, *harpide*, *ulerpide*, but *laburbide*, *okerbide*, *zeharbide*.

After an affricate, following sandhi rule 3 (section 31.2.1), *b* always becomes *p*: *erakuspide*, *irispide*. Sometimes *p* is written also after an ordinary sibilant: *aberaspide*, *adierazpide*.

In compounds with both nouns and verbs *bide* can appear as the second member. The following examples are divided into two groups:

These examples have nouns as the initial member:

arau	rule	araubide	discipline, regulation
arnasa	breath	arnasbide	respiratory system, relief
arrazoi	reason	arrazoibide	reasoning
auzo	neighbor(hood)	auzobide	local road
babes	support, protection	babesbide	recourse, refuge
burdina	iron	burdinbide	railroad, rail line
buru	head	burubide	judgment, advice, counsel, sense
diru	money	dirubide	business, sinecure, making money
erdi	middle, half	erdibide	midway, center, middle course
errege	king	erregebide	highway (also *errepide* < *erret* + *bide*)
esku	hand	eskubide	right to something
froga	proof, evidence	frogabide	argument, verification
gaitz	evil, difficult	gaizpide	scandal, vexation, opportunity to sin
gizon	man	gizabide	courtesy, decency, good relations
gurdi	cart	gurdibide	roadway, wagon trail
gurutze	cross	guruzpide	stations of the cross, martyrdom (also *gurutzebide*)
haserre	anger	haserrebide	reason for anger, dispute
haur	child	haurbide	pregnancy (*haurbidean egon* 'to be pregnant')
hitz	word	hizpide	subject matter, right (*hizpidean egon*)
ihes	flight	ihesbide	escape route, excuse, way out, loophole
indar	strength	indarbide	strengthening remedy
iritzi	opinion	irizpide	criterion, judgment
irri	laugh, jeer	irribide	cause for laughter, laughing stock
ke	smoke	kebide	chimney, smokestack

kezka	disquiet	kezkabide	reason for anxiety
lan	work	lanbide	profession, work, occupation
laster	speed	lasterbide	shortcut, shorter way
liskar	quarrel, fight	liskarbide	bone of contention
lotsa	shame	lotsabide	reason for shame
negar	tear, crying	negarbide	reason for crying, sorrow
odol	blood	odolbide	vascular system, blood circulation
ogi	bread	ogibide	livelihood, profession, occupation
oin	foot	oinbide	footpath, sidewalk
on	good	onbide	virtue, virtuous path
poz	joy	pozbide	consolation, reason for joy
saihets	side	saihespide	bypass, sidetrack, ring road
tren	train	trenbide	railway, railroad
ur	water	ubide	waterway, aqueduct, gully, ditch (also *urbide*)
zebra	zebra	zebrabide	zebra crossing (for pedestrians), crosswalk
zeru	heaven	zerubide	way to salvation
zubi	bridge	zubibide	viaduct
zur	wood	zurbide	gangway, gangboard

The following examples have verb radicals as the initial member:

aberastu	to enrich, to get rich	aberaspide	way to get rich
adierazi	to express	adierazpide	way of expressing, expression
aditu	to pay attention	adibide	example
agertu	to show, to appear	agerpide	sign, manifestation
agindu	to command	aginpide	authority, jurisdiction (from *aginte*)
ahal izan	to be able to	ahalbide	ability, possibility
aipatu	to mention	aipabide	way of mentioning, fame
alhatu	to feed, to graze	alhapide	forage, feed (also *alabide*)
antolatu	to organize	antolabide	arrangement, organization
argitu	to enlighten	argibide	evidence, explanation, information
arindu	to lighten, to ease	arinbide	comfort, relief, tranquilizer
askatu	to undo, to release	askabide	solution, liberation
asmatu	to imagine, to invent	asmabide	reason, sense
atera	to go out, to go away	aterabide	exit, way out
atzeratu	to go back, to retreat	atzerabide	reason for decline, hindrance
aukeratu	to choose	aukerabide	choice, option
aurkitu	to find	aurkibide	index, table of contents
aurreratu	to advance	aurrerabide	reason for progress, advance
azaldu	to explain	azalbide	explanation
aztertu	to investigate	azterpide	method of investigation, gauge
baliatu	to make use of	baliabide	resource, help
bilakatu	to become	bilakabide	process of evolution
bizi izan	to live	bizibide	way of living, job, profession

egiaztatu	to verify, to prove	egiaztabide	evidence, proof, verification
egin	to do, to make	eginbide	duty, task, obligation
ekin	to begin, to tackle	ekinbide	initiative
elikatu	to feed (oneself)	elikabide	method of feeding
elkartu	to bring together	elkarpide	relation, reciprocity, affinity, connection
entzun	to hear	entzunbide	acoustics
epait	to judge	epaibide	judicial process, evidence
erakutsi	to show	erakusbide	example, model (also *erakuspide*)
eratu	to form, to organize	erabide	formation, organization, formula
ernaldu	to impregnate	ernalbide	impregnation, sexual organ
erori	to fall	erorbide	pitfall, occasion to sin, offense
eskapatu	to escape	eskapabide	escape route, way out, means of escape
eskatu	to ask for something	eskabide	plea, request, petition, demand
etorri	to come	etorpide	origin, development, source
ezagutu	to recognize, to know	ezaupide	distinguishing mark, awareness, acquaintance
ezkondu	to marry	ezkonbide	keeping company, going steady
galdu	to corrupt, to ruin	galbide	road to ruin, danger, offence
garaitu	to defeat, to conquer	garaibide	strategy for conquering
garraiatu	to transport	garraiabide	means of transportation
gertu	to prepare	gertubide	preparation
gidatu	to lead, to guide	gidabide	management, leadership
hartu	to receive, to take	harpide	subscription
hautatu	to choose	hautabide	option, suffrage
hedatu	to extend, to expand	hedabide	method of spreading, means for expanding
heldu	to arrive, to grasp	helbide	address, grip, handle, grasp
hondatu	to destroy, to ruin	hondabide	road to ruin, downfall, danger
hurbildu	to approach	hurbilbide	approach, approximation
ibili	to walk	ibilbide	passage, route, trajectory
igaro	to pass	igarobide	crossing, pass, corridor
ikasi	to learn	ikasbide	educational material, examples, lessons
ikertu	to investigate	ikerbide	research method, experiment
ikusi	to see	ikusbide	view, perspective
inguratu	to encircle	ingurabide	ring road, circuit
irabazi	to earn, to win	irabazpide	livelihood, way to earn money, job
irakatsi	to teach	irakaspide	teaching method
iritsi	to reach	irispide	reach, within range, way of getting
irten	to go out	irtenbide	exit, solution, way out
isuri	to spill, to pour	isurbide	sewer, gutter, drain
itxaro	to hope	itxarobide	reason for hope, reason for confidence
itzuri	to flee, to escape	itzurbide	escape route, way out (also *itzurpide*)
izutu	to scare	izubide	terrorism, reason for fear
jardun	to work, to act	jardunbide	practice, behavior, conduct
jarraitu	to follow	jarraibide	norm, example, way of conduct

jokatu	to play	jokabide	behavior, conduct
jolastu	to amuse oneself	jolasbide	amusement, pastime, recreation
konpondu	to remedy, to mend	konponbide	settlement, solution, arrangement
laburtu	to shorten	laburbide	shortcut (*laburbidez* 'in short')
lasaitu	to reassure	lasaibide	reason for reassurance (also *lasapide*)
lerratu	to skid, to slide	lerrabide	slide, slippery road, temptation
luzatu	to defer	luzabide	delay, prolongation, hindrance
nahasi	to mix up	nahasbide	mess, confusion, chaos
okertu	to bend, to go astray	okerbide	wrong path, danger, bad way
oroitu	to remember	oroibide	remembrance, souvenir
osatu	to heal, to cure	osabide	healing method, cure
pasatu	to pass, to cross	pasabide	passage, corridor, way
pentsatu	to think	pentsabide	way of thinking, mentality
sendatu	to cure	sendabide	medical treatment, healing
sinetsi	to believe	sinesbide	reason for belief, proof, creed (also *sinespide*)
tentatu	to entice	tentabide	enticement, lure, temptation
ulertu	to understand	ulerbide	comprehension, understanding, explanation
uste izan	to think	ustebide	way of thinking (*MEIG* VI, 76)
zehartu	to cross, to deviate	zeharbide	winding road, crossroad
zuzendu	to rectify	zuzenbide	rule, justice, right

[*N.B.* The plural form *zuzenbideak* means also 'further data', 'references', and often simply 'address'.]

The compound *norabide* 'direction' is derived from the interrogative *nora* '(to) where', as in *norabide bakar(ra)* 'one way traffic', and also *norabide debekatu(a)* 'no traffic allowed'.

32.3.3 The Suffix *-pe*

The suffix *-pe* has the meaning 'under' and is probably etymologically related to the noun *behe* 'bottom', 'lower part' (section 3.2). In combination with a directional case ending (*-an*, *-ra*, *-tik*, etc.) *-pe* can serve to express the meaning 'under', like the word *azpi* (section 4.1.3.1): *liburupean* or *liburu azpian* 'under the book', *ohapetik* or *ohe azpitik* 'from under the bed'. In contrast to *azpi*, the suffix *-pe* can only occur with inanimates: 'under the cow' can only be translated by *behiaren azpian*.

The morpheme *pe* has a peculiar status as suffix; it can also appear independently, but only if preceded by a genitive and followed by a locative case ending: *lurraren pean* 'under the ground', *Mitxelenaren promesaren pean* 'under Mitxelena's promise'.

Such constructions are rather rare; mostly the compound form is used, and where that is not possible, the word *azpi*: *ohapean* 'under the bed', but *ohe horren azpian* 'under that bed'.

Though nowadays *azpian* and *-pean*, *azpira* and *-pera*, *azpitik* and *-petik* are often used interchangeably, this is not always the case, in that with *azpi* the literal (i.e., the strictly spatial) meaning is evident, and with *-pe* the figurative meaning is. Thus for the sentence "That boy can't get out from under his mother's skirt," we get

Mutil hori amaren gonaren azpitik ezin da irten. (Literally)
Mutil hori amaren gonapetik ezin da irten. (Figuratively)

In a number of set expressions where there is no or scarcely any spatial concept understood by the meaning 'under', we find only *-pean*:

agindu	command	agindupean	under the command
aho	mouth	ahopean	in a low voice, secretly (also *ahapetik*)
arau	rule	araupean	under the rule (*araupeko* 'regularly')
ardura	care	ardurapean	under the auspices
argi	light	argipean	in the light, under the light
baldintza	condition	baldintzapean	under the condition
begi	eye	begipean	under the eye
beso	arm	besapean	under the arm
bular	breast, chest	bularpean	under the breast, under the chest
eguzki	sun	eguzkipean	under the sun
ekaitz	storm	ekaizpean	under the storm
esku	hand	eskupean	under the might
euri	rain	euripean	under the rain
galda	scorching hot	galdapean	under the scorching hot (sun)
hego	wing	hegapean	under the wing, under the protection
ilargi	moon	ilargipean	sublunary
irudi	image, symbol	irudipean	under the statue, under the symbol
jasa	heavy rain	jasapean	under the cloudburst
laino	mist, fog, haze	lainopean	under the mist, under the fog
lan	work	lanpean	under the work, under piles of work
lege	law	legepean	under the law
lur	ground	lurpean	under the ground, buried
mende	dominion	menpean	under the dominion
nahigabe	sorrow, grief	nahigabepean	under the sorrow
neke	difficulty	nekepean	under the difficulty, under the punishment
oin	foot	oinpean	under the foot, underfoot
zama	burden	zamapean	under the burden

Direct derivations from the *-pe* forms with the magic suffix *-tu* are possible:

araupetu	to regulate, to make rules for
auzipetu	to sue, to bring to court
eskupetu	to subject, to dominate
giltzapetu	to put under lock and key

hegapetu	to protect, to shelter
lanpetu	to overload with work
menpetu	to conquer, to subjugate
oinpetu	to walk over, to oppress, to trample

There are also verbal derivations with the directional form *-pera*:

eskuperatu	to dominate, to oppress, to subject
giltzaperatu	to imprison, to set behind lock and key
lurperatu	to bury (for people, rather *lurra eman*)
oinperatu	to trample, to oppress, to humiliate

In accordance with the discussion of the linking morpheme *-ko* in chapter 5, adjectival modifiers of the form X + *peko* are always possible if X + *pean* is: *eskupeko berriak* 'confidential reports', *galdapeko ibilaldia* 'the march under the scorching heat', *lurpeko ibaia* 'the subterranean river'.

Through ellipsis or pronominalization of a combining noun some of these adjectival modifiers can also be used independently:

agindu	command	agindupeko	subject, servant (also *aginpeko*)
aho	mouth	ahapeko	secret, chin, confidential information
esku	hand	eskupeko	gratuity, tip, slave
gerri	waist	gerripeko	loincloth
itsaso	sea	itsaspeko	submarine
lur	ground	lurpeko	mole, troglodyte, underground/subway/metro
mende	domination	menpeko	subordinate, subject, slave
mihi	tongue	mihipeko	frenum
sudur	nose	sudurpeko	mustache

[*N.B.* Also, the word *peko* itself exists and has the same meaning as *menpeko*, thus 'slave', 'subject', 'subordinate'.]

The forms with *-pe* treated up to this point require the use of a locative ending: *araupean*, *argipetik*, *euripera*, and so on. There exist also nouns formed with *-pe* that can be found in nonlocational contexts:

(7) a. Ilunbeak ez du konprehenditu. (Jn 1.5; Lz)
The darkness has not grasped it.
b. Urpea garbitu dute. (See *DCV*, 18: under *acantilar*.)
They have dredged out the water. (Lit. "cleaned the underwater")

atertu	to stop raining	aterbe	shelter, refuge, shed, hiding place
barru	interior, inside	barrunbe	cavity, inner self
begi	eye	begipe	under the eye

belaun	knee	belaunpe	back of the knee
beso	arm	besape	underarm, armpit
buru	head	burupe	authority
eliza	church	elizpe	portico of church, crypt
etxe	house	etxepe	roof
galtzar	bosom	galtzarbe	armpit
geriza	shade	gerizpe	shady spot
haize	wind	haizebe	lee side (contrast *haizealde* 'windward')
harri	stone	harpe	cave, cavern
hosto	leaf	hostope	shade under foliage
ilun	dark	ilunbe	darkness
itsaso	sea	itsaspe	sea depth, bottom of sea
itzal	shade	itzalpe	shadowy place, shelter
izen	name	izenpe	signature
lehor	dry	lehorpe	shelter
lur	ground	lurpe	cave, catacomb, underworld
manu	commandment	manupe	submission, subjection
muga	border	mugape	ground area, district
sabel	belly	sabelpe	pubic area
ur	water	urpe	underwater
uztarri	yoke	uztarpe	slavery, serfdom, subjugation
zeru	heaven	zerupe	firmament, vault of heaven

[*N.B.* With a few words dated to an earlier time we find after an *n* or *r* *-be* instead of *-pe*.]

Naturally, derivations with the magic suffix *-tu* are possible here also, ending in *-petu* and *-peratu*:

estalpetu	to accommodate, to protect, to mask
gerizpetu	to protect, to defend, to shelter
itzalpetu	to protect, to accommodate, to imprison
izenpetu	to sign
lurpetu	to inter, to have depth, to flood
urperatu	to submerge, to dive, to be flooded, to go under
uztarpetu	to subjugate, to oppress, to yoke
uztarperatu	to take prisoner, to subjugate

The suffix *-pe* is often seen in Basque surnames. These are originally mostly names of farms or estates, thus place names. The form of the suffix here is almost always *-be*: Altube (*altu* 'height'), Arrupe (*arru* 'abyss'), Etxabe (*etxe* 'house'), Harizpe (*haritz* 'oak'), Mendibe (*mendi* 'mountain'), Olabe (*ola* with two meanings 'shepherd's hut' and 'foundry'), Uribe (*uri* 'city'—Biscayan for *hiri*).

32.4 Prefixes

Basque is a predominantly suffixing language. Only in the formation of personal forms do prefixes play a role comparable in importance to that of suffixes (see chapters 6 and 9). Elsewhere in the grammatical system suffixes are preponderant. The number of suffixes is legion, especially in morphological derivation, whereas the number of prefixes is extremely small. Batua knows only two derivational prefixes of any importance: *birr-* and *des-*.

32.4.1 The Prefix *birr-*

The prefix *birr-* with the meaning 're-', 'again' goes back perhaps to the root *bihur* of *bihurtu* 'to return'. Nominals derived with this prefix would then have been originally determinative compounds, such as *etorburu* 'origin' (from *etorri* 'to come' + *buru* 'head', 'begin') or *bidaltsari* 'postage', 'shipping costs' (from *bidali* 'to send' + *sari* 'fee'), while verbal derivatives would originally have had a coordinating character: *birjaio*: *bihurtu eta jaio* 'to be born again'; *birpiztu*: *bihurtu eta piztu* 'to rise again', 'to relight'. (Cf. the use of *arra-* in Low Navarrese and Souletin, for which see *DGV* II, 528.)

In any event, the use of *birr-* in present-day Batua is very limited. We find it used for kinship terms (adopted from Biscayan) and with a number of botanical terms. With verbs, it has a strong competitor in the form *berr-*, perhaps best viewed as a paraprefix or quasi prefix: the apocopated form of the adjective *berri* 'new' (see section 3.8.1). Verbs beginning with an *e* allow only *berr-*, never *birr-*. Note the loss of the second *r* before consonants. There is much variation among writers and dialects in words beginning with *ber-* or *bir-*. To date (March 2006) the Basque Academy has not made any decision about a standard written form. Some examples follow:

With kinship terms

ahizpa	sister (of a woman)	birrahizpa	half sister (of a woman)
aitona	grandfather	birraitona	great-grandfather
amona	grandmother	birramona	great-grandmother
anaia	brother	birranaia	half brother
arreba	sister (of a man)	birrarreba	half sister (of a man)

With botanical terms

arto	maize	birrarto	maize from the second harvest
gari	wheat	birgari	wheat from the second harvest
hazi	seed	birrazi	second seed
lore	flower	birlore	flower from the second flowering
zahi	bran	birzahi	fine bran

With verbs

aldatu	to change	birraldatu	to transplant, to change again
ikusi	to see	birrikusi	to see again, to look back

jaio	to be born	birjaio	to be reborn
landatu	to plant	birlandatu	to replant, to transplant
loratu	to bloom	birloratu	to bloom again
lotu	to join, to connect	birlotu	to rejoin, to reconnect
piztu	to light	birpiztu	to relight, to rise again (also *berpiztu*)

Most verbs use *berr-* instead of *birr-*:

agertu	to appear	berragertu	to reappear, to appear again
argitaratu	to publish	berrargitaratu	to republish, to reprint
aurkitu	to find	berraurkitu	to rediscover, to find again
egin	to do, to make	berregin	to redo, to do again
eraiki	to build, to construct	berreraiki	to rebuild, to reconstruct
erosi	to buy	berrerosi	to redeem, to buy off
esan	to say	berresan	to say again, to reiterate
ezagutu	to know	berrezagutu	to know again, to recognize again
ezarri	to put	berrezarri	to put again
galdetu	to ask	bergaldetu	to ask again (also *birgaldetu*)
hasi	to begin	berrasi	to begin anew
idatzi	to write	berridatzi	to rewrite, to write again
jarri	to place	berjarri	to place anew (also *birjarri*)
jaso	to erect, to set up	berjaso	to reerect, to set up again

32.4.2 The Prefix *des-*

The prefix *des-*, which at first entered into Basque via Romance loanwords such as *desesperantza* 'despair', quickly became used also with words of Basque origin. It is found prefixed to both nouns and verbs. The prefix *des-* has a negative meaning implying a lack—often expressed in English by the prefixes *un-* and *dis-*. (Cf. *ez-*.) Some examples follow:

With nouns

arrazoi	reason	desarrazoi	fallacy, error
bide	way	desbide	wrong track (*desbideratu* 'to deviate')
garai	time, occasion	desgarai	inconvenient time, untimeliness
herri	people, village	deserri	exile
itxaropen	hope	desitxaropen	despair
obedientzia	obedience	desobedientzia	disobedience
ohore	honor	desohore	dishonor, shame
ordu	hour	desordu	inconvenient hour (also *ezordu*)
oreka	balance	desoreka	instability, lack of equilibrium
plazer	pleasure	desplazer	displeasure

With adjectives and adverbs

atsegin	pleasant	desatsegin	unpleasant
berdin	same, equal	desberdin	different, unequal (also *ezberdin*)
egoki	fitting, suitable	desegoki	unsuitable, inappropriate
gogara	willingly	desgogara	unwillingly, reluctantly
leial	reliable	desleial	unreliable

With verbs

agertu	to appear	desagertu	to disappear
antolatu	to arrange	desantolatu	to disorganize
batu	to unite, to join	desbatu	to separate, to part
egin	to do, to make	desegin	to undo, to destroy
errotu	to take root	deserrotu	to uproot, to root out
ezkondu	to marry	desezkondu	to divorce (more often *ezkontza hautsi*)
jabetu	to appropriate	desjabetu	to expropriate, to dispossess
kargatu	to load	deskargatu	to unload
lotu	to bind, to join	deslotu	to untie, to unbind (more often *askatu*)
obeditu	to obey	desobeditu	to disobey, to contravene
ohitu	to habituate	desohitu	to dishabituate (more often *ohitura galdu*)

[*N.B. Destokitu* 'to dislocate': from *des-* + *toki* ('place') + *-tu*, a calque from Spanish *dislocar*.]

32.5 Paraprefixes

The paucity of derivational prefixes—most noticeable when trying to translate into Basque technical words with Romance prefixes—is partly compensated for in the use of paraprefixes. Paraprefixes, or quasi prefixes, are words that combine with a relatively great number of other words to form useful compounds. In Basque, paraprefixes are fewer in number and less important than parasuffixes. Leaving aside as much as possible neologisms not yet totally at home in Basque, as well as technical jargon, we will confine ourselves here to *ez-*, *basa-*, *erdi-*, and *sasi-*.

32.5.1 The Paraprefix *ez-*

The paraprefix *ez-* forms compounds with nouns and adjectives whereby *ez-* functions like the prefix *des-*. Words with *ez-* display a lowered tone at the end of the phrase. Here are some examples:

antsia	care, concern	ezantsia	indifference, unconcern
axola	care, concern	ezaxola	indifference, unconcern
behar	necessity, need	ezbehar	misfortune, adversity, mishap

berdin	same, equal	ezberdin	unequal (adjective), different
bide	way, road	ezbide	wrong (noun), unreason, injustice
deus	something	ezdeus	nothing, bagatelle
eroso	comfortable	ezeroso	uncomfortable
ezagun	known	ezezagun	unknown
garai	time, occasion	ezgarai	inconvenient time, bad occasion
gauza	thing	ezgauza	absurdity, bagatelle
ikasi	learned	ezikasi	unlettered, unlearned
izen	name	ezizen	nickname, pseudonym
jakin	knowing	ezjakin	unknowing, ignorance
lege	law	ezlege	lawlessness, unlawfulness
leku	spot, place	ezleku	prohibited place, inhospitable region
ordu	hour	ezordu	inconvenient hour, bad timing
urte	year	ezurte	bad year, lean year
uste	expectation	ezuste	surprise, unpremeditation

[*N.B.* Notice that the words *ezikasi* and *ezjakin* do not appear as verbs.]

32.5.2 The Paraprefix *basa-*

The word *baso* has the meaning 'unsettled, uncultivated area'—thus translatable as 'wilderness' or, if need be, 'forest'. When it is the first member of a compound, it takes the form *basa-* and means literally 'living in the wild' and metaphorically 'wild', 'savage', 'desolate'. Well-known examples are

abere	animal	basabere	wild animal
ahate	duck	basahate	wild duck
ahuntz	goat	basahuntz	wild goat, mountain goat
antzara	goose	basantzara	wild goose
aran	plum	basaran	blackthorn, sloe
arto	maize, millet	basarto	sorghum-millet
behi	cow	basabehi	wild cow
gaztaina	chestnut	basagaztaina	wild chestnut
gizon	man	basagizon	wild man, savage, brute
gudari	soldier	basagudari	guerilla fighter, partisan
herri	village	baserri	farm, mountain hut
jaun	lord	basajaun	forest lord, forest giant (mythological)
katu	cat	basakatu	wildcat
mahats	grape	basamahats	wild vine
mortu	desert, mountain pass	basamortu	desert
nagusi	boss	basanagusi	tyrant, despot, blustering boss
oilar	cock	basoilar	woodcock, hoopoe
pizti	beast	basapizti	wild beast

urde	swine	basurde	wild swine, boar
uso	pigeon	basuso	wood pigeon

[*N.B.* The usual word for 'farmer' is *baserritar*; others are *nezkari* or *laborari*.]

32.5.3 The Paraprefix *erdi-*

The noun *erdi* means 'middle' as well as 'half'. Both meanings play a role in nouns formed with *erdi*, but with adjectives and most verbs, only the meaning 'half' occurs—as can be seen in the following examples:

Nouns

alde	side, zone	erdialde	centerpiece, middle, neutral zone
arte	interspace, interval	erdiarte	interspace, interim, interlude
bide	way	erdibide	halfway, middle course, intermediate form
itzal	shadow	erditzal	penumbra, semidarkness
jainko	god	erdijainko	demigod
kale	street	erdikale	street in the middle, street in between
leku	place	erdileku	focus, center
maila	step, stage	erdimaila	intermediate form, average
muin	marrow	erdimuin	nucleus, core
une	spot	erdiune	core, middle point, average

[*N.B.* From *erdi* is derived the verb *erditu* 'to give birth', but words such as *erdimin* 'labor pain' will not be discussed here.]

Adjectives

alai	merry, jolly	erdialai	tragicomic, half serious, semijolly
beltz	black	erdibeltz	semiblack, gray, mulatto, colored person
bete	full	erdibete	half full, halfhearted
bizi	alive	erdibizi	half dead, half alive, barely alive
edan	drunk	erdiedan	half drunk, tipsy
egin	done	erdiegin	half done, unfinished
epel	lukewarm	erdiepel	barely lukewarm
ernai	awake, vigilant	erdiernai	half awake, half vigilant
ero	crazy, dement	erdiero	half crazy
garden	transparent	erdigarden	semitransparent
gor	deaf	erdigor	half deaf
hil	dead	erdihil	half dead
itsu	blind	erditsu	half blind
jantzi	dressed	erdijantzi	half dressed
lo	asleep	erdilo	half asleep
mozkor	drunk	erdimozkor	half drunk

soil	bald	erdisoil	half bald
zuri	white	erdizuri	half white, gray, mulatto, colored person

Verbs

adierazi	to express	erdiadierazi	to suggest, to insinuate, to express vaguely
agertu	to appear	erdiagertu	to hazily loom up
egosi	to cook	erdiegosi	to half cook
entzun	to hear	erdientzun	to half hear, to hear vaguely
erre	to burn, to roast	erdierre	to half roast, to just brown
estali	to cover	erdiestali	to half cover, to partly cover up
frijitu	to fry	erdifrijitu	to fry partly, to half fry
garbitu	to clean	erdigarbitu	to half clean, to just rinse off
hil	to die, to kill	erdihil	to almost die, to make half dead
irakurri	to read	erdirakurri	to half read, to read cursorily
ireki	to open	erdireki	to half open
ikusi	to see	erdikusi	to see vaguely, to perceive
jaiki	to rise, to get up	erdijaiki	to partially rise
mintzatu	to speak	erdimintzatu	to stammer
sendatu	to cure	erdisendatu	to partially cure, to half cure

32.5.4 The Paraprefix *sasi-*

The meaning of the word *sasi* is ‘bramble patch’. From the adjectival form *sasiko* ‘out of the bramble patch’ it has the derived meaning of ‘illegitimate child’. Another word for a natural child, incidentally, is *mendikume* ‘mountain child’. Hence, *sasi* prefixed to words often gives the meaning ‘pseudo’ to the combination. These examples will illustrate:

amnistia	amnesty	sasiamnistia	pseudo amnesty
apaiz	priest	sasiapaiz	false priest
arrazoi	reason	sasiarrazoi	fallacy, false reasoning
arrosa	rose	sasiarrosa	dog rose, wild rose
autonomia	self-government	sasiautonomia	pseudo autonomy
emazte	wife	sasiemazte	concubine
ezkontza	marriage	sasiezkontza	illicit union, cohabitation
idazle	writer	sasidazle	hack writer, writer of trash
igarle	prophet	sasigarle	false prophet
jainko	god	sasijainko	false god, idol
jakintsu	learned person	sasijakintsu	self-proclaimed expert
maisu	teacher	sasimaisu	pedant, bad teacher
olerkari	poet	sasiolerkari	poetaster, rhymer
sagu	mouse	sasisagu	muskrat, desman
saindu	saint	sasisaindu	sanctimonious person
ume	child	sasikume	illegitimate child, bastard

33 Additional Derivational Suffixes

33.1 The Additional Derivational Suffixes

In addition to the derivational suffixes already discussed, a number had been written up in an earlier Dutch version of the grammar. It was de Rijk's intention to render them into English and add them to the remaining chapters to be written. Bear in mind that these sections had been written some years earlier, and it is highly probable he would have made any necessary corrections and added comments and examples.

33.1.1 The Suffix *-go*

This suffix *-go*, from *-goa* (see *DGV* VII, 502), has a number of functions in the northern dialects, but Batua has adopted only one of these. The suffix forms abstract nouns indicating a profession, office, position, or status. The profession suffix *-tza* (section 25.8.2) is much more commonly used for this purpose; compare also *tasun* (section 17.9). Some common examples are

adiskide	friend	adiskidego	friendship (*adiskidetasun, adiskidantza*)
ahaide	family member	ahaiko	family, kinship (*ahaidego, ahaidetasun*)
apaiz	priest	apaizgo	priesthood (*apaiztasun, abadetza*)
arotz	smith, carpenter	arozgo	smithery, blacksmithing (*errementaritza*)
artzain	(sheep)herder	artzaingo	shepherding (*artzaintza*)
bikario	vicar	bikariogo	vicarship (*bikalgo, bikaritza*)
buruzagi	leader	buruzagigo	leadership, leading (*buruzagitza*)
errege	king	erregego	kingship (*erregetza*)
etsai	enemy	etsaigo	enmity (*etsaitasun*)
hargin	stonecutter	hargingo	stonecutting (*hargintza*)
ikasle	student	ikaslego	studentship (*ikasletza*)
irakasle	teacher	irakaslego	teaching profession (*irakasletza*)
jabe	owner	jabego	ownership (*jabetza*)
jaun	lord	jaurgo	authority
lagun	companion	lagungo	companionship (*laguntza*)
merkatari	tradesman, merchant	merkatalgo	commerce, trade (*merkataritza*)

nagusi	boss, master	nagusigo	mastership, superiority (*nagusitza*)
ohaide	concubine	ohaidego	concubinage (*ohaidetasun*)
ohoin	thief	ohoingo	thievery (*ohointza*)
sorgin	witch	sorgingo	witchcraft, witchery (*sorgintza*)

33.1.2 The Suffix *-di*

The suffix *-di* (earlier form *-doi*) attached to nouns indicates a natural group or aggregation of that noun. Originally it was used only in combination with names of trees and plants. Later it came to be used also with other nouns; some of these neologisms are now in common use. (Cf. the collective suffix *-tza* in section 25.8.3.)

The following examples are names of trees and plants:

ametz	muricated oak	amezti	forest of muricated oaks
aran	plum tree	arandi	grove of plum trees
arantza	thorny bush	arantzadi	thorny area
arte	evergreen oak	artadi	forest of evergreen oak
belar	grass	belardi	meadow (cf. *belartegi* 'hay-barn')
elorri	thistle	elordi	place full of thistle
ezpel	box tree	ezpeldi	grove of box trees
gaztaina	chestnut	gaztainadi	chestnut forest
gerezi	cherry	gerezidi	cherry orchard
gorosti	holly	gorostidi	place full of holly
haritz	oak	harizti	forest of oak trees
hurritz	hazel tree	hurrizti	grove of hazel trees
ilar	pea	ilardi	field of peas
intsusa	elder tree	intsusadi	grove of elder trees
intxaur	walnut	intxaurdi	walnut grove/orchard (also *intxausti*)
izai	fir tree (also *izei*)	izaidi	fir forest
lertxun	aspen	lertxundi	aspen grove
lizar	ash tree	lizardi	forest of ash trees
mahats	grape	mahasti	vineyard
makal	poplar	makaldi	grove of poplars
mizpira	medlar	mizpiradi	medlar grove
ote	gorse, furze	otadi	place covered with gorse
pago	beech	pagadi	beech forest
pinu	pine	pinudi	pine forest (also *pinadi*)
sagar	apple	sagardi	apple orchard (also *sagasti*)
sahats	willow	sahasti	place with willows
urki	birch	urkidi	birch forest
zuhaitz	tree	zuhaizti	group of trees, forest
zumar	elm	zumardi	elm forest

[*N.B.* The *s* of the variants *intxausti* and *sagasti* is due to the suffix *-tze* inserted before *-di*. (See *FHV*, sec. 14.4 [c].)]

Examples of some commonly used neologisms follow:

eder	beautiful	ederti	the fine arts
etxe	house	etxadi	group of houses, neighborhood
Eusko-	Basque (used in compounds)	Euskadi	the Basque Country (political entity)
Euskaltzain	Basque Academician	Euskaltzaindia	the Basque Academy
gazte	young man	gaztedi	youth, young people
gizon	man, human being	gizadi	mankind, humanity
izan	to be	izadi	nature, cosmos
kristau	Christian	kristaudi	Christendom
lagun	companion, comrade	lagundi	company, society
landare	plant	landaredi	flora, vegetation
lege	law	legedi	code of laws, statutes
lur	ground, earth	ludi	earth, world
maila	step, level, grade	mailadi	steps, tiers
ontzi	vessel, ship	ontzidi	fleet

33.1.3 The Suffix *-dura*

The suffix *-dura* is a nonproductive suffix of Romance origin, possibly coming from such loanwords as *tristura* 'sadness', *pintura* 'painting', and so on. Mostly found in the northern dialects, this suffix attaches only to verb radicals, yielding nouns denoting the outcome of an action of the verb—thus almost identical in meaning to the suffix *-pen* (section 22.8).

As to the shape of the suffix, note that the *d* of *-dura* changes to *t* after the semivowel *y*, that is, after a diphthong ending in *i*, as in *deitura*. This change also explains the variants *baitura* and *oitura* (in Batua written as *bahitura* and *ohitura*) alongside the older forms *bahidura* and *ohidura*.

Of course the *d* also changes into a *t* after sibilants and affricates: *nahas* + *dura* becomes *nahastura*, and *hauts* + *dura*, *haustura*.

The main examples are

abiatu	to set out, to start	abiadura	departure, start, speed
akitu	to be tired	akidura	exhaustion
apaindu	to decorate, to embellish	apaindura	decoration, embellishment
ase	to sate, to satiate	asedura	satiety, satiation
bahitu	to seize, to stand surety	bahidura	seizure, suretyship (also *bahitura*)
bihurtu	to return	bihurdura	return, restitution
deitu	to call, to name	deitura	last name
egin	to make	egitura	structure, creation

elikatu	to feed, to nourish	elikadura	nutrition, nourishment
ernaldu	to impregnate, to breed	ernaldura	impregnation, procreation
erre	to burn	erredura	burn (also *erradura*)
eten	to break off, to interrupt	etendura	break, interruption
garbitu	to clean	garbidura	cleanness, cleanliness
gogortu	to harden	gogordura	hardening, hardness
handitu	to swell up, to inflate	handidura	swelling, conceit
harritu	to be amazed, astonished	harridura	amazement, astonishment
haserretu	to get angry	haserredura	anger
hazkatu	to scratch, to itch	hazkadura	itch, pruritus
hedatu	to spread, to extend	hedadura	spread, extension
herbaldu	to weaken	herbaldura	weakness
hertsi	to shut, to enclose	hertsidura	closeness, restraint
hezurtu	to ossify	hezurdura	skeleton, bones
higatu	to wear out, to deteriorate	higadura	erosion, deterioration
higitu	to move, to stir	higidura	movement, motion
hil	to die	hildura	decay, mortification
hornitu	to supply, to provide	hornidura	provisions, supplies
hoztu	to cool off, to chill	hoztura	coldness, coolness
ibili	to walk, to move	ibildura	motion, movement
isildu	to be silent (also *ixildu*)	isildura	silence (also *ixildura*)
itsutu	to blind, to dazzle	itsudura	blindness, dazzlement
itzali	to dim, to put out	itzaldura	diminution, extinguishment
izerditu	to sweat	izerdura	perspiration, sweat (*izerdidura*)
izutu	to scare, to be frightened	izudura	fear, fright
josi	to sew	jostura	stitch, seam (also *joskura*)
kilikatu	to tickle	kilikadura	tickling, tickle
kutsatu	to contaminate	kutsadura	contamination
laburtu	to shorten, to abbreviate	laburdura	shortening, abbreviation
laztu	to shudder, to shiver	laztura	horror, shivers
lehertu	to burst, to explode	leherdura	rupture, explosion
lehiatu	to strive, to hurry	lehiadura	fervor, haste
lerratu	to slip, to slither	lerradura	slip, slippage
liluratu	to fascinate, to dazzle	liluradura	fascination, dazzlement
lizundu	to get moldy, to mildew	lizundura	mildew, mold
lotu	to link, to connect	lotura	link, connection
luzatu	to postpone, to prolong	luzadura	postponement, prolongation
metatu	to pile up, to stack	metadura	pile, stack
mindu	to sour, to hurt	mindura	sourness, anguish
mugitu	to move	mugidura	movement

nahasi	to mix, to mix up	nahastura	mixture, confusion
nekatu	to tire	nekadura	fatigue, tiredness
notatu	to sully	notadura	stain
ohitu	to get accustomed to	ohidura	custom (also *ohitura*)
pairatu	to suffer, to bear	pairadura	suffering
pisatu	to weigh	pisadura	weight
saldu	to sell	saldura	sale
sumindu	to enrage, to get angry	sumindura	ire, anger
suntsitu	to destroy	suntsidura	destruction
txunditu	to astound, to amaze	txundidura	astonishment, amazement
urratu	to tear, to rend	urradura	tear, breach
usaindu	to smell	usaindura	bad smell, odor
usteldu	to spoil, to rot	usteldura	spoilage, rot, decay
uztartu	to join, to couple	uztardura	joining, link
xahutu	to cleanse, to purify	xahudura	cleanness, purity
zikindu	to befoul, to soil	zikindura	filth, dirtiness

33.1.4 The Suffix *-ari*

The suffix *-ari*, which perhaps has its origin in the Latin suffix *-arius*, attaches—leaving aside some neologisms—to nouns, yielding nouns denoting an animate being, mostly human, holding a position or having a status associated with the basic noun, or who more or less regularly performs the action linked to this noun. (At this point, de Rijk had made a notation to refer to Eguzkitza 1993, fn. 17.)

The difference between *-ari* and the nominalizing suffix *-(tzai)le*, already discussed in section 12.6, is twofold: the latter attaches to verb radicals instead of nouns and is also used to denote performers of incidental acts; compare *kantatzaile* 'singer, someone singing' and *kantari* 'singer, vocalist'.

The suffix *-ari* has a phonologically determined variant *-lari*, which besides being used after sibilants, affricates, *-r*, or *-n*, is also found after a noneliding vowel other than *a*, and after an *a* that is secondary, that is, originating from a final *-e* or final *-o*: *joko* 'game', *jokalari* 'player'.

We should also bear in mind the discussion of apocope in sections 3.8.1 and 31.2 regarding the loss of final vowels in words of more than two syllables and the occasional loss of this vowel in words of two syllables. Consequently, from *aginte* we get *agintari*; from *aholku*, *aholkari*; but from *atze*, *atzelari* and from *oihu*, *oihulari*.

We find the ending *-dari* instead of *-lari* in some words ending in *-n*: *aitzindari*, *zaindari*, but *arraunlari* and *ipuinlari*.

An exception is also the word *ehiztari* 'hunter' from *ehiza* 'hunt'. (The expected regular form *ehizlari* is found only in Souletin.) The form *salatari* 'accuser' from *salo* 'accusation' can be explained by preventive dissimilation of **salalari*.

Following are some examples:

aginte	command	agintari	commander, chief, authority
aholku	advice, counsel	aholkulari	adviser, counselor (also *aholkari*)
aitor	confession, testimony	aitorlari	confessor, witness
aitzin	front, vanguard	aitzindari	foreman, predecessor, chief
aitzur	hoe	aitzurlari	digger
aizkora	ax	aizkolari	woodcutter
akuilu	spur, goad	akuilari	spurrer, drover, stimulator
albiste	news	albistari	news reporter, newspaper
amets	dream	ameslari	dreamer
arnegu	blasphemy	arnegari	blasphemer, apostate
arrantza	fishing	arrantzari	fisherman
arraun	oar	arraunlari	rower (also *arraunkari*)
atze	backside, rear guard	atzelari	back player (game), homosexual
aurre	frontside, vanguard	aurrelari	front player (game), pioneer
auzi	lawsuit, plea	auzilari	litigant, pleader
barranda	observation post	barrandari	scout, spy, sentry
bekatu	sin	bekatari	sinner
bertso	verse	bertsolari	verse-maker, bard, troubadour
bidaia	trip	bidaiari	traveler
bide	way, road	bidari	traveler (also *bidelari*)
borroka	fight	borrokalari	fighter (also *borrokari*)
botika	drugstore, pharmacy	botikari	pharmacist, druggist
bulego	office	bulegari	office worker, clerk
burla	taunt, mockery	burlari	taunter, mocker
dantza	dance	dantzari	dancer
denda	store, shop	dendari	shopkeeper
ehiza	hunt	ehiztari	hunter (also *ehizari*, *ehizlari*)
epai	judgment, sentence	epailari	judge, referee
erosta	wail, lamentation	erostari	wailer
errementa	iron implements	errementari	blacksmith
errota	mill	errotari	miller
eske	plea, appeal	eskelari	beggar
ezkutu	shield	ezkutari	squire, shield bearer
ezpata	sword	ezpatari	swordsman
garai	top, victory	garailari	victor, winner
gerla	war	gerlari	warrior, soldier
gerra	war	gerrari	warrior, soldier
gezi	arrow	gezilari	bowman, archer
gida	guidance, lead	gidari	guide, leader
giltza	key	giltzari	concierge, keeper of keys
gobernu	government, management	gobernari	governor, manager
golde	plow	goldelari	plowman

gudu	war, battle	gudari	(Basque) soldier
hego	wing	hegalari	flier
herresta	dragging	herrestari	dragger, reptile, hauler
hitz	word	hizlari	speaker, orator
idazki	writing, document	idazkari	secretary
ihes	flight	iheslari	refugee, fugitive
industria	industry	industrialari	industrialist
ipuin	story, tale	ipuinlari	storyteller
iritzi	opinion	irizlari	critic
joko	game, gamble	jokalari	player, gambler (also *jokari*)
josta	amusement	jostalari	entertainer, amuser (also *jostari*)
kanta	song	kantari	singer, vocalist
kontu	story, narrative	kontari	narrator (also *kontalari*)
kopla	couplet (also *kobla*)	koplari	bard, versifier (also *koblari*)
korrika	race	korrikalari	runner, cycle racer
lausengu	flattery	lausengari	flatterer
lege	law	legelari	jurist
mailegu	loan	mailegari	borrower
maite	love	maitari	lover
mandatu	message	mandatari	messenger, sender
margo	color	margolari	painter
merkatu	market	merkatari	merchant
mezu	message	mezulari	messenger, sender
misio	mission	misiolari	missionary
mus	Basque card game	muslari	mus player
oihu	scream, shout	oihulari	screamer, shouter
olerki	poem	olerkari	poet
otoitz	prayer	otoizlari	prayer leader, prayer
pilota	ball	pilotari	handball player
prediku	sermon	predikari	preacher
salo	accusation	salatari	accuser, informer
sega	scythe	segari	cutter, reaper (also *segalari*)
soinu	music	soinulari	musician
sukalde	kitchen	sukaldari	cook
taberna	tavern, bar	tabernari	tavern keeper, bartender, barman, barmaid
tratu	commerce	tratulari	businessman
txistu	Basque flute	txistulari	txistu player
zama	load, burden	zamari	beast of burden
zapata	shoe	zapatari	shoemaker, cobbler
zaunka	bark	zaunkari	barker (also *zaunkalari*)
zelata	ambush, observation	zelatari	lookout, scout, sentinel
zerbitzu	service	zerbitzari	servant
zerga	tax, duty	zergari	tax collector (also *zergalari*)

zirika	tease, goad	zirikari	teaser, provoker (also *zirikalari*)
zurrut	swig, gulp	zurrutari	tippler, gulper

Some common neologisms based on verbs are the following:

abestu	to sing	abeslari	singer, vocalist
aldeztu	to defend	aldezlari	defender
aztertu	to investigate	azterlari	investigator
idatzi	to write	idazlari	scribe
ikasi	to learn	ikaslari	student
ikertu	to research, to investigate	ikerlari	sleuth, inspector, researcher
irakurri	to read	irakurlari	reader, lector
pentsatu	to think	pentsalari	thinker, philosopher
zuzendu	to rectify, to correct	zuzendari	corrector

Well established also is the word *lehendakari* 'president' (cf. *lehen* 'first'), as well as such neologisms as these:

fisika	physics	fisikari	physicist
politika	politics	politikari	politician
teknika	technology	teknikari	technician

Also deverbal action nouns formed with *-keta* (section 21.9) can serve as base forms for the suffix *-ari*. The resulting ending *-ketari* is often contracted to *-kari*. Here are a few examples:

arraunketa	rowing	arraunkari	rower
asmaketa	invention, riddle	asmakari	inventor, soothsayer
azterketa	investigation, examination	azterkari	investigator, examiner
berriketa	news gathering, gossip	berrikari	reporter (also *berriketari*)
eleketa	conversation, chat	eleketari	talker, chatter (also *elekari*)
garbiketa	cleaning, washing	garbikari	cleaner
ibilketa	wandering, walk	ibilkari	wanderer, walker
lasterketa	footrace	lasterkari	racer, runner
solasketa	talk, conversation	solaskari	talker
urketa	water fetching	urkari	water carrier (also *urketari*)

33.1.5 The Suffix *-kari*

The suffix *-kari*, which according to Azkue is related to the word *ari* in the verbal expression *ari izan* 'to be busy with', attaches primarily to verb radicals, yielding nouns with the meaning 'something resulting from the action denoted by the verb'. Thus the occurrence of this suffix is limited to transitive verbs, and also to those intransitive verbs where the subject undergoes the action without volition—for example, *erori* 'to fall' or *gertatu* 'to happen'.

The meaning of *-kari* is thus similar to that of *-kizun* (section 27.12.2), but it does not share that suffix's inherently future orientation.

After a verb radical ending in *-a* or *-an* (which was earlier pronounced as a nasalized *-a*), the suffix takes the form *-ari*, the *-n* of *-an* eliding, and the two *a*'s become one *a*. (We still find for *edari* the Baztanese form *edanari* and the older Biscayan form *edaari*.)

An exception to all this is the monosyllabic verb stem *jan* with the derivative *janari* (in the northern dialects *janhari*).

The suffix *-kari* is no longer productive. The main examples follow:

asmatu	to invent, to think up	asmakari	invention, riddle, idea
bazkatu	to tend, to feed	bazkari	feed, food, midday meal
edan	to drink	edari	beverage (*edari bizi* 'strong drink')
egin	to do, to make	eginkari	deed, act
egosi	to cook, to boil	egoskari	stew (of legumes, Spanish *cocido*)
erori	to fall	erorkari	unsteady person, one apt to fall
erre	to bake, to burn	errari	baked goods, (own) batch of bread
esan	to say	esari	word, saying
eskatu	to ask for, to request	eskari	plea, request, petition
gertatu	to happen	gertari	event, happening (also *gertakari*)
gura izan	to will, to want	gurari	wish, desire
hazi	to grow, to raise	hazkari	crop, product
ibili	to walk	ibilkari	fidget, wanderer, restlessness
ikasi	to learn	ikaskari	lesson, learning material
ikusi	to see	ikuskari	vision, spectacle, sight
jan	to eat	janari	food
opa	to offer	opari	offering, gift
sinetsi	to believe	sineskari	article of faith, tenet, dogma
sofritu	to suffer	sofrikari	suffering (also *sofrikario*)
sortu	to create, to beget	sorkari	creature

Influenced by derivatives of intransitive verbs such as *erorkari* and *ibilkari*, translatable respectively as 'apt to fall' and 'prone to walk', the suffix *-kari* has taken on a second meaning in the northern dialects—notably in Souletin and Low Navarrese: 'disposed, inclined, apt to'.

This new meaning created the possibility for the suffix to also combine with nouns and adjectives, therefore giving it the same function as the word *zale* (the fondness parasuffix of section 10.7.1) in compounds. The form of the suffix is unchanged in this meaning: *-kari*. Some examples follow:

abere	animal	aberekari	one who loves animals, zoophile
andre	woman	andrekari	womanizer, skirt chaser
arrain	fish	arrainkari	fish lover

besta	party	bestakari	party lover
bizi	life, living	bizikari	epicure
bizkar	back	bizkarkari	sponger
egia	truth	egikari	truth-loving person
eliza	church	elizkari	devout, churchy person
handi	big	handikari	snob, ambitious person
haur	child	haurkari	person who loves children
jende	people	jendekari	sociable person
lagun	companion	lagunkari	sociable person
mendi	mountain	mendikari	mountain lover
mutiko	boy	mutikokari	boy-crazy girl, flirt
ume	child	umekari	one who loves children
zoko	corner	zokokari	shy person, recluse

33.1.6 The Suffix *-gailu*

The northern dialects as well as High Navarrese make use of a suffix *-gailu* that attaches to verb radicals yielding nouns with the meaning 'means to V'. Of these derivatives the following are also used in Batua:

apaindu	to decorate	apaingailu	ornament
azkartu	to strengthen	azkargailu	tonic
bizi izan	to live	bizigailu	sustenance, nourishment
edertu	to adorn	edergailu	ornament, adornment
gantzutu	to anoint, to embalm	gantzugailu	ointment, unguent, balsam
gorde	to keep, to hide	gordagailu	depot, storehouse, cache (also *gordailu*)
gozatu	to sweeten, to calm	gozagailu	sweetener, sedative
jostatu	to play	jostagailu	toy (also *jostailu*)
juntatu	to attach, to join	juntagailu	conjunction, joiner
ondu	to improve	ongailu	condiment, seasoning
oroitu	to remember	oroikailu	monument, memento (from *oroit* + *gailu*)
sendatu	to heal, to cure	sendagailu	medication, medicine
tapatu	to cover	tapagailu	cork, lid, stopper

[*N.B.* The sequence *-agailu* can be contracted to *-ailu*, for example in *gozagailu* > *gozailu* and *tapagailu* > *tapailu*. The contracted forms *gordailu* and *jostailu* are much more common in written Batua than the forms *gordagailu* and *jostagailu*.]

In the recent past many neologisms were coined of the type *V-gailu* to replace Spanish loanwords linked to technological advancements. The original meaning of the suffix *-gailu* has as a consequence narrowed to the more concrete meaning 'apparatus, machinery in order to V'. A hint from the grammarian Azkue (1923–1925, I, 18) seemed to have been to the point: "Si alguien se valiera de *keriak* por vicios y *gailu* por aparato no haría otra cosa que servir de instrumento consciente a evoluciones inconscientes que se sienten venir." (Anyone who would make use of *keriak* for vices and *gailu* for apparatus would be doing nothing other than consciously serve as an instrument for the unconscious developments which one senses to be coming.)

In present-day Batua, *gailu* is indeed used as an independent noun with the meaning 'apparatus', 'machine'. The examples that follow are thus not so much derivations as compounds. A further corroboration is that the word *elektragailu* does not mean 'machinery for electrification' but denotes simply 'electric apparatus'. Here are a few examples of these new forms:

berotu	to warm up	berogailu	heater
deitu	to call	deigailu	megaphone
entzun	to hear	entzungailu	earphone, hearing aid
filmatu	to film	filmagailu	movie camera
garbitu	to clean, to wash	garbigailu	washing machine
grapatu	to staple	grapagailu	stapler
haizatu	to ventilate	haizagailu	ventilator
hoztu	to cool	hozkailu	refrigerator (from *hotz* + *gailu*)
ibili	to walk	ibilgailu	vehicle
igo	to rise	igogailu	lift, elevator
ikuzi	to wash	ikuzgailu	washer
isildu	to be still	isilgailu	silencer
kalkulatu	to calculate	kalkulagailu	calculator
neurtu	to measure	neurgailu	measuring device
ordenatu	to arrange, to order	ordenagailu	computer (also *komputagailu*)
ozendu	to resound	ozengailu	loudspeaker
sortu	to engender	sorgailu	generator
zabaldu	to spread	zabalgailu	transmitter, machine for spreading
zapaldu	to flatten	zapalgailu	steamroller
zenbatu	to count	zenbakailu	adding machine, calculator
zulatu	to drill, to bore	zulagailu	drill, boring machine, perforator

[*N.B.* For 'loudspeaker', the word *bozgorailu* is also used. It is a contraction of *boz* 'voice', *gora(tu)* 'to raise', 'to intensify', and *gailu*.]

33.1.7 The Suffix *-ki* 'a separate part of a whole'

There is a productive suffix *-ki* (with lowered tone) that operates on nouns. The result is also a noun, but with the meaning 'a separate part of the whole of the basic noun', and at the same time, used as a material name, 'the material of which the whole is composed'. It is useful to divide the examples into five parts.

1. *With a numeral X as base.* The derivation with *-ki* denotes here an arbitrary component of X number:

bi	two	biki	one of twins or of a pair (also *bizki*)
hiru	three	hiruki	one of triplets or of three
lau	four	lauki	one of quadruplets or of four

[*N.B.* Exceptionally, the words *zazpiki* and *zortziki* denote premature infants, respectively, 'seventh-month infant' and 'eighth-month infant'.]

2. *With a tree name X as base.* The derivation with *-ki* means 'a piece of X-wood', or, used as a material name, 'X wood':

asmetz	muricated oak tree	amezki	wood of the muricated oak
arte	evergreen oak	artaki	wood of the evergreen oak
ezpel	box tree	ezpelki	boxwood, piece of boxwood
haritz	oak tree	harizki	oak, piece of oak wood
intxaur	walnut tree	intxaurki	wood of the walnut tree
izai	fir tree	izaiki	wood of the fir tree
lizar	ash tree	lizarki	wood of the ash tree
pago	beech tree	pagaki	beech, piece of beech wood
pinu	pine tree	pinuki	pine, piece of pinewood
zumar	elm tree	zumarki	elm, piece of elm wood

[*N.B. harizkizko mahaia* 'an oak table'; *harizki bat* 'a piece of oak wood'.]

3. *With an animal name X as base.* The derivation in *-ki* means 'a piece of X meat', or, used as a material name 'X meat':

ahate	duck	ahateki	duck meat
ahuntz	goat	ahunzi	goat meat
aker	billy goat	akerki	meat of the billy goat
ardi	sheep	ardiki	mutton
arrain	fish	arrainki	piece of fish
asto	ass, donkey	astaki	donkey meat (also used as invective)
axuri	young lamb	axuriki	meat of young lamb
behi	cow	behiki	beef
bildots	lamb	bildoski	lamb
ehizi	game	ehiziki	piece of game
eper	partridge	eperki	partridge meat
erbi	hare	erbiki	hare meat
haragi	meat	haragiki	piece of meat
idi	ox	idiki	ox meat
oilo	chicken	oilaki	chicken meat
txahal	calf	txahalki	veal
urde	swine, male pig	urdeki	swine meat, pork; bacon (*urdaki*)

zaldi	horse	zaldiki	horse meat
zerri	pig	zerriki	pork

[*N.B.* The usual word for 'meat' is *okela*, or *haragi*. An old Basque saying: *Otsoak otsokirik ez du jaten*. 'A wolf does not eat wolf meat'. See further de Rijk 1995.]

4. *Other examples in the culinary sphere:*

baratze	vegetable garden	barazki	vegetable, vegetable soup
belar	grass, herb	belarki	herb, seasoning
bizkar	back	bizkarki	back piece, shoulder cut
esne	milk	esneki	dairy product
gibel	liver	gibelki	piece of liver, liver dish
izotz	ice, frost	izozki	ice cream
mihi	tongue	mihiki	tongue dish, piece of tongue
odol	blood	odolki	blood sausage, black pudding
saihets	side, flank	saiheski	rib piece, chop
tripa	stomach, tripe	tripaki	tripe dish

[*N.B.* From the adjective *gozo* 'sweet' is derived the word *gozoki* meaning 'candy', 'tidbit', 'sweet confection'.]

5. *Other examples:*

adar	branch, horn, antler	adarki	piece of horn, antler, or branch
beira	glass	beiraki	piece of glass
enbor	trunk of tree	enborki	piece of tree trunk
euskara	Basque language	euskalki	Basque dialect
gauza	thing	gauzaki	object
gizon	man	gizaki	person, human being
itsaso	sea	itsaski	wave, sea swell
liburu	book	liburuki	volume of a book or set
oihal	cloth, fabric	oihalki	remnant, piece of cloth
ondo	underpart, tree base	ondoki	part of tree base, stump
zilar	silver	zilarki	piece of silver, silver object

[*N.B.* From the adjective *handi* (*haundi*) 'big' is derived the noun *handiki* (*haundiki*) meaning 'magnate', 'nobleman', 'aristocrat', 'rich man'.]

33.1.8 The Deverbalizing Suffix *-ki*

The suffix *-ki*, the origin of which is probably to be identified with the pre-dative marker *-ki-* (section 15.1), attaches to verb radicals to yield nouns. This manner of nominalization is not productive; only a few dozen examples are known.

The meaning of the *-ki* noun is dependent on the nature of the verb. If the verb is of the class by whose action the direct object is produced or destroyed, then the noun derived denotes whatever resulted from the action of the verb. For instance, this is the case with *idatzi* 'to write', *jan* 'to eat', *erre* 'to burn' or 'to roast', and also, to a certain extent, with the intransitive verb *izan* 'to be', 'to exist'.

But if the verb is of the class that leaves its direct object in essence unaffected, then the *-ki* noun denotes the means by which the action of the verb took place, without, in most cases, there being any agent in the narrow sense.

As illustration, the following examples are known in Euskara Batua:

adabatu	to mend, to patch	adabaki	mending piece, patch
aldatu	to change, to alter	aldaki	copy, variant
erantsi	to adhere, to add to	eranski	supplement, appendix, addition
erantzun	to answer	erantzuki	reprimand (*erantzuki egin* 'to reproach')
erre	to burn, to roast	erreki	fuel, roast (also *erraki*)
estali	to cover	estalki	cover, envelope, covering
etorri	to come	etorki	origin, lineage
idatzi	to write	idazki	letter, written matter
igo	to go up	igoki	lift, elevator (Oñatibia, 165)
iragarri	to announce	iragarki	announcement, advertisement
iragazi	to filter, to strain	iragazki	strainer, filter
isuri	to pour, to spill	isurki	drain, slope, drainage canal
izan	to be, to exist	izaki	thing, being, creature
jan	to eat	jaki	food, dish
lotu	to bind	lotzaki	strap, bandage, rope
jantzi	to dress, to clothe	janzki	garment, clothing
osatu	to supplement	osaki	supplement
sendatu	to heal	sendaki	medication
tapatu	to cover up	tapaki	lid, blanket, cover

[*N.B.* The verb *erantzun* meant earlier also 'to reproach'—thus the meaning 'reprimand' for its nominalized form *erantzuki*. For the meaning 'answer' one uses the word *erantzun*, or else *ihardespen* and also the loanword *arrapostu*. For the form *lotzaki* derived from *lotu*, compare section 22.9.]

33.1.9 The Suffix *-kin* 'remainder', 'resulting product'

The suffix *-kin* (with lowered tone) attaches to verb radicals yielding nouns with the meaning 'substance produced by the action of the verb'. If the action produces a primary product with waste matter, then the derivation with *-kin* gives preference to denoting the latter. Some examples follow:

adabatu	to mend, to patch	adabakin	mending piece, patch
atera	to take out	aterakin	extract
bidali	to send	bidalkin	ambassador, envoy, emissary
bildu	to collect, to gather	bilkin	collection, booty
bota	to throw out, to vomit	botakin	refuse, vomit
ebaki	to cut, to cut off	ebakin	remnant, clipping
edeki	to take away	etekin	earnings, profit
egosi	to boil	egoskin	something boiled, cooking liquid
eho	to weave	ehokin	weave, fabric
erantsi	to add to	eranskin	annex, addition, supplement
erditu	to halve	erdikin	remaining half, fragment
erre	to burn	errekin	burnt-off land (also *errakin*)
etorri	to come	etorkin	newcomer, immigrant
gorde	to keep	gordekin	voucher, receipt, ticket stub
harrapatu	to catch	harrapakin	prey, booty
hondatu	to spoil	hondakin	debris, cigarette butt, garbage
irabazi	to earn	irabazkin	earnings, profit, salary
isuri	to spill, to pour	isurkin	dishwater, spilled liquid
moztu	to cut, to shave	mozkin	shavings, clippings, wood chip, savings
osatu	to make up, to fill up	osakin	ingredient, supplement
urratu	to tear	urrakin	scrap, shred
utzi	to abandon	uzkin	residue, remainder
zahartu	to age	zaharkin	old thing, antique, junk
zerratu	to saw	zerrakin	sawdust, leavings from sawing
zuritu	to peel, to shuck	zurikin	peel, rind, casing

[*N.B.* From *sobera* 'too much' is derived *soberakin* 'leftovers', 'superfluous junk'. The form *errekin* (or *errakin*) also means 'fuel'. This is derived with another suffix *-kin* not used in Batua (older form *-kidin*) with the meaning 'good for . . .', 'inclined to . . .'. Dialectally, to wit in Labourdin and Low Navarrese, this suffix is also encountered with a noun as base: *haurkin* 'fond of children', *katukin* 'fond of cats', *lagunkin* or *jendekin* 'sociable, gregarious person'.]

33.1.10 The Suffix *-kin* 'instrument or organ'

Language purists have made use in the past of a suffix *-kin* with the meaning 'instrument or organ'. Nowadays, people prefer compounds with *gailu* for this meaning (see section 33.1.6). The following derivatives with this instrumental *-kin* have acquired acceptance:

entzukin	organ for hearing, hearing aid (from *entzun* 'to hear')
haizekin	fan, bellows (from *haize* 'wind')
hegazkin	airplane (from *hegaz* 'flying')
idazkin	typewriter (from *idatzi* 'to write'; also *idazmakina*)

ikuskin	organ for sight, vision, optical instrument (from *ikusi* 'to see')
iragazkin	filter, sieve, colander, strainer (from *iragazi* 'to strain', 'to filter')
neurkin	gauge, measuring instrument (from *neurtu* 'to measure')
urrutikuskin	binoculars (from *urruti* 'far' and *ikusi* 'to see')
urrutizkin	telephone (from *urruti* and *hitz egin* 'to speak')
usainkin	organ for smell (from *usaindu* 'to smell')

[*N.B.* Although in no way uncommon, *urrutizkin* is much less used than the loanword *telefono* for 'telephone'. The neologisms for 'telegraph' and 'television', respectively *urrutidazkin* and *teleikuskin*, have found no acceptance. People use almost exclusively the words *telegrafo* and *telebista*.]

33.1.11 The Suffix *-ka*

In contrast to the stative suffix *-(r)ik* that expresses a static state (section 25.5.2), the suffix *-ka* indicates a dynamic state. The suffix *-ka* attaches to nouns and a small number of adjectives yielding words describing a state indicated by the word to which it is suffixed, giving it a dynamic dimension.

In general, *-ka* does not attach to verb radicals, but there are a few exceptions: *amilka* 'falling down' from *amildu* 'to fall down'; *iraulka* 'rolling' from *irauli* 'to turn over'; *joka* 'hitting' from *jo* 'to hit' (mostly used in *ate joka* 'knocking on the door'); and *esaka* 'saying' from *esan* 'to say' (mostly used in *gaizki esaka* 'maligning'). Compare Inchauspe 1858, 10.

Depending on the nature of the base form, we can distinguish seven groups that will be discussed in succession.

Group 1. The base form is a noun (or sometimes a directional form such as *atzera*, *aurrera*, *behera*, *gora*) that together with the verb *egin* 'to make' can form a verbal expression. Such a noun denotes an action or the result of an action. If the action is continuous, that is, occurs over a necessary period of time, then the derivation with *-ka* indicates the state of the agent: *arrastaka* 'dragging out', *lasterka* 'in a rush', *presaka* 'hurried'. But if the action is momentary, then such an action occurring once or twice is not enough to call for this application of *-ka*. The derivation with *-ka* makes reference to an iterative, frequently repeated activity indicative of the state of the agent. One illustration is *eztul eginez* 'coughing' (one cough or more coughs) but *eztulka* 'coughing' (repeated coughs, coughing again and again). For brevity's sake we shall leave out this repetitive meaning in the translations to follow. The main examples in this first group are

agur egin	to greet	agurka	greeting
aharrausi egin	to yawn	aharrausika	yawning
ahausi egin	to bark	ahausika	barking
aitaren egin	to make the sign of the cross	aitarenka	crossing oneself

aldarri egin	to announce, to shout	aldarrika	calling out, with shouts
arnas egin	to breathe	arnaska	gasping (also *arnas estuka*)
arrantza egin	to bray	arantzaka	braying
arrasto egin	to leave a track	arrastaka	dragging, dragging along
atzera egin	to go back, to retreat	atzeraka	going back, retreating
auhen egin	to lament	auhenka	lamenting, moaning
aurrera egin	to progress, to advance	aurreraka	advancing, moving forward
barre egin	to laugh	barreka	laughing
behe egin	to bleat	beheka	bleating
behera egin	to go below	beheraka	going below
bultz egin	to push	bultzaka	pushing
burla egin	to mock, to poke fun	burlaka	taunting, mocking
dei egin	to call	deiaka	calling
deiadar egin	to shout	deiadarka	shouting
dominisiku	to sneeze	dominisikuka	sneezing
eztul egin	to cough	eztulka	coughing
gainez egin	to overflow	gainezka	overflowingly, excessively
galde egin	to ask, to question	galdeka	questioning, asking (also *galdezka*)
garrasi egin	to yell, to scream	garrasika	screaming, yelling
gora egin	to go up	goraka	going up
gudu egin	to fight, to brawl	guduka	fighting, brawling, warring
hasperen egin	to sigh	hasperenka	sighing
hatz egin	to scratch	hazka	scratching
hegalda egin	to fly	hegaldaka	flapping, fluttering
heiagora egin	to scream, to shriek	heiagoraka	screaming, shrieking
hitz egin	to speak	hizka	discussing, arguing, disputing
hots egin	to make noise	hoska	making noise, calling out
ihes egin	to flee	iheska	fleeing, in flight
indar egin	to force	indarka	forcing, with violence
irri egin	to ridicule, to jeer	irrika	mocking, jeering
irribarre egin	to smile	irribarreka	smiling

irrintzi egin	to neigh, to whinny	irrintzika	neighing, giving an "irrintzi"
keinu egin	to make a gesture	keinuka	gesturing, with gestures
korrok egin	to belch, to burp	korroka	belching, burping
kosk egin	to bite	koska	biting (also *koskaka*)
laster egin	to rush, to run hard	lasterka	running hard, fast, in a rush
listu egin	to spit, to expectorate	listuka	spitting
marruma egin	to low, to bellow, to moo	marrumaka	mooing, lowing, bellowing
musu egein	to kiss	musuka	kissing
negarzotin egin	to sob	negarzotinka	sobbing
oihu egin	to scream	oihuka	screaming
oka egin	to throw up, to vomit	okaka	vomiting, nauseated
oles egin	to invoke, to call upon	oleska	invoking, calling upon
orro egin	to roar	orroka	roaring
ostiko egin	to kick	ostikoka	kicking
otoitz egin	to pray	otoizka	praying
purrust egin	to grouse, to grumble	purrustaka	grumbling, mumbling, grousing
tu egin	to spit	tuka	spitting
txio egin	to peep, to squeak, to chirp	txioka	chirping, peeping, squeaking
usain egin	to smell	usainka	smelling
usin egin	to sneeze	usinka	sneezing
zabu egin	to stagger, to teeter, to rock	zabuka	staggering, teetering, rocking
zapart egin	to explode	zapartaka	exploding
zaunka egin	to bark	zaunkaka	barking (also haplology: *zaunka*)
zin egin	to swear, to take an oath	zinka	swearing, with oaths
zintz egin	to blow one's nose	zinzaka	blowing one's nose
zirkin egin	to move, to stir, to budge	zirkinka	moving, stirring, budging
zotin egin	to hiccup	zotinka	hiccupping
zurrunga egin	to snore	zurrungaka	snoring
zurrut egin	to gulp, to slurp	zurrutaka	gulping, slurping

[*N.B.* Whenever the noun stem ends in an affricate preceded by a consonant, or in a plosive other than *k*, then an epenthetic *a* appears before the ending *-ka*: *bultzaka*, *zintzaka*, *zurrutaka*.]

Group 2. The derivation with *-ka* is with a base noun denoting a material that can function as means by which the action takes place. In most cases there is a repetitive context. The main examples are

aizkora	ax	aizkoraka	hacking, with ax blows
aizto	knife	aiztoka	stabbing, with knife stabs
arraun	oar	arraunka	rowing, with oar strokes
atzapar	claw	atzaparka	clawing, scratching, with claws
esku	hand	eskuka	handling, touching
ezker	left hand	ezkerka	left, with the left hand
ezten	sting, goad, prick	eztenka	stinging, goading, with the goad
hagin	molar, tooth	haginka	biting, with the molars
harri	stone	harrika	stoning, with stones
hortz	tooth	horzka	biting, with the teeth
makila	stick, cane	makilaka	caning, with blows of the stick
mutur	snout	muturka	rooting, with the snout
oin	foot	oinka	walking, on foot, by foot
ukabil	fist	ukabilka	boxing, with the fist, with punches
ukondo	elbow	ukondoka	elbowing
zarta	staff, stick, rod	zartaka	hitting, knocking, with a tap
zigor	rod, wand, whip	zigorka	chastising, with beating
ziri	dowel, pin, wedge	zirika	pestering, prodding, challenging

[*N.B.* From *beso* 'arm' is derived *besarka* 'embracing', either from *beso* + *arte* + *ka* or *beso* + *har* + *ka*; compare *loharkatu* 'to doze off'.

Note also that the *-ka* forms can also function pragmatically as the means, reason, or cause, as in *horzka* 'with the teeth' and *makilaka* 'with swipes from a cane'.]

Group 3. The base makes reference relative to a place. Here the *-ka* form can express a static situation. The main examples are

albo	side	alboka	staggering, weaving from side to side
aldamen	side, vicinity	aldamenka	sideling, zigzagging, indirectly
atze	posterior, back side	atzeka	backing up, backward
aurre	front	aurreka	against, in front of
gain	top, surface	gainka	at the top, on top
gibel	liver, back side	gibelka	backward, backing up
han-hemen	here and there	han-hemenka	spread here and there
inguru	circle, periphery	inguruka	circling, winding around
saihets	side	saiheska	sideways, indirect, sideling

We should remember here the directional examples given in group 1 such as *aurreraka* 'going forward', *atzeraka* 'going backward', *beheraka* 'going below', and *goraka* 'going up'.

Group 4. With any arbitrary utterance *X* as base, with *X-ka* having the meaning 'again and again saying X': *jesuska* 'saying "Jesus" repeatedly'. The following examples originated in this way and slowly have become conventional:

baiezka	repeatedly saying *baietz* (repeatedly saying yes)
ezezka	repeatedly saying *ezetz* (repeatedly saying no)
otoika	repeatedly saying *otoi* (continually pleading)
berorika	addressing with *berori*
hika	addressing with *hi*
zuka	addressing with *zu*
ongi etorrika	saying "welcome" again and again

A general remark: the *-ka* derivatives discussed so far are autonomous in the sense that the base itself determined in one way or another the action lying at the foundation of the state expressed by the *-ka* form. Employed in combination with verbs such as *ari izan*, *egon*, *ibili*, *joan*, and *etorri*, the resulting stative forms could semantically be seen as sentence predicates, just as is the case with the stative forms ending in *-(r)ik*. Examples follow:

Aharrausika hago	You keep yawning.
Musuka ari dira	They are kissing.
Aiztoka hasi zitzaion	He began to stab him.
Zure inguruka dabil	He circled around you.

With the following groups of examples that is no longer the case. From now on, what the action is whose repetition results in a state does not depend on the underlying word, but only on the context. These *-ka* forms are heteronomous; they cannot function as main predicates of a sentence.

Group 5. The base is a numeral, distributive or otherwise:

hogeita hamar	thirty	hogeita hamarka	by the thirties at a time
ehun	hundred	ehunka	by the hundreds at a time
mila	thousand	milaka	by the thousands at a time
bana	each one	banaka	separately, one by one (also *banazka*)
bina	each two	binaka	in pairs, two by two
hiruna	each three	hirunaka	in groups of three, by threes
ehuna	each hundred	ehunka	in groups of a hundred, by hundreds

[*N.B.* Instead of the numeral *bat* 'one', the adjective *bakar* 'alone' is used: *bakarka* 'one by one', 'separately', with *bakarkako* 'individual' as adjectival form.]

Group 6. The base is a noun that can function as a measure. Also here the *-ka* forms refer to a repetitive process, the nature of which comes from the context.

ahamen	bite, mouthful	ahamenka	by mouthfuls, a bite at a time
aldra	group, crowd, bunch	aldraka	in groups, by groups at a time
andana	row, group	andanaka	by groups, by rows, in groups
apur	crumb	apurka	in small amounts, by bits
bihi	grain	bihika	grain by grain
erdi	half	erdika	in halves, halfhearted (*erdizka*)
espal	bundle, bunch	espalka	by bundles at a time, in bunches
gutxi	few	gutxika	little by little (*gutxika gutxika asko egiten da*)
izpi	fiber, blade, chip	izpika	bit by bit, fiber by fiber
ontzi	ship	ontzika	with shiploads at a time
oste	crowd	osteka	by crowds at a time
pila	pile, heap	pilaka	by piles at a time, in piles
pitin	little bit	pitinka	by little bits, little by little
pixka	little bit	pixkaka	by little bits, little by little
plater	plate, dish	platerka	with plates at a time
sail	part, section, crowd	sailka	in sections, in groups, by departments
saldo	herd, crowd	saldoka	with crowds at a time
saski	basket	saskika	with baskets at a time, by basketfuls
talde	herd, group	taldeka	in groups, by groups
tanta	drop	tantaka	drop by drop, by drops
txanpon	coin	txanponka	coin by coin
zama	load, freight	zamaka	by freights, by loads
zati	part, piece	zatika	by parts

Group 7. Here the base is a noun indicating a period of time:

aldi	period, turn	aldika	periodic, by turns, now and then
arte	interval	arteka	every so often
aste	week	asteka	weekly, per week
egun	day	egunka	daily, per day
epe	term	epeka	on credit, in installments
hilabete	month	hilabeteka	monthly, per month
ordu	hour	orduka	hourly, per hour
txanda	turn	txandaka	by turns, in turn
urte	year	urteka	yearly, per year

[*N.B.* We find these forms with the suffix *-ari* (treated in section 33.1.4):

aldizkari	magazine
astekari	weekly magazine, employed by the week
egunkari	diary, daily newspaper, worker for the day
hilabetekari	monthly periodical, employed per month
urtekari	yearbook]

Group 8. Some have adjectives as base:

estu	narrow	estuka	crowding
gorde	hidden	gordeka	in hiding, secret
handi	big	handika	in bulk, in large quantities
isil	quiet	isilka	quietly, in secret
itsu	blind	itsuka	blindly
lauoin	four-footed	lauoinka	creeping, on hands and feet
oker	slanted, crooked	okerka	on all fours, galloping (e.g., horse)

33.1.12 The Iterative Suffix *-katu*

The suffix *-katu* attaches to nouns and yields verbs. Its raison d'être lies in the fact that stative forms with *-ka* can occur as radicals of causative verbs. In other words, the magic suffix *-tu* (section 7.4.1) can be applied not only to nouns and adjectives, but also to stative forms.

Since most forms with *-ka* have an iterative meaning, so also do most verbs ending in *-katu*, and the remainder a durative meaning. (Cf. section 12.3.2.)

The suffix *-katu* has, to a certain extent, acquired a life of its own separate from *-ka*, as witnessed by the fact that there exist *-katu*-derived verbs for which no stative forms with *-ka* can be found. In that case the stem need not be a noun but can also be a verb or anything else. We give some illustrations:

... bezala	like ...	... bezalakatu	to become like ..., to make like ...
berdin	equal, same	berdinkatu	to equalize, to compare
ibili	to walk	ibilkatu	to wander about, to roam
ikusi	to see	ikuskatu	to explore, to visit
irauli	to turn around	iraulikatu	to turn over, to rotate (also *iraulka*)
irudi	image, to be like	irudikatu	to imagine, to envision
ordez	in place	ordezkatu	to replace, to represent
pare	equal	parekatu	to match, to compare

However, the great majority of *-katu*-derived verbs are based on a stative with *-ka*. Following are the main examples out of each of the same groups that were distinguished for the suffix *-ka*. (For the sake of brevity, we leave out the iterative meaning in the translations.)

Group 1

agur	greeting	agurkatu	to greet, to salute
aitaren	sign of the cross	aitarenkatu	to cross oneself
aldarri	shout, cry	aldarrikatu	to cry out, to exclaim
auhen	lament	auhenkatu	to lament
deiadar	scream	deiadarkatu	to scream

erren	limp	errenkatu	to limp
galde	question	galdekatu	to interrogate
gudu	dispute, battle	gudukatu	to quarrel, to fight
hegalda	wing	hegaldakatu	to flap, to flutter, to fly
hitz	word	hizkatu	to discuss, to quarrel, to argue
irri	jeer	irrikatu	to jeer, to sneer
keinu	gesture	keinukatu	to gesture
musu	kiss	musukatu	to kiss
oihu	scream	oihukatu	to scream
presa	haste	presakatu	to hasten, to rush
usain	odor, smell	usainkatu	to nose around, to sniff
zotin	gasp, hiccup	zotinkatu	to gasp, to hiccup

Group 2

aizto	knife	aiztokatu	to stab with a knife
arraun	oar	arraunkatu	to row
atzapar	claw	atzaparkatu	to scratch, to claw
esku	hand	eskukatu	to manipulate, to handle
ezten	prick, goad	eztenkatu	to sting, to prick, to goad
hagin	molar	haginkatu	to bite
harri	stone	harrikatu	to stone
hortz	tooth	horzkatu	to bite
makila	stick, cane	makil(k)atu	to give blows with a stick, to beat
oin	foot	oinkatu	to stomp, to trample
ukondo	elbow	ukondokatu	to elbow, to lean on elbow
zigor	whip, rod	zigorkatu	to scourge, to punish
ziri	pin, wedge, jab	zirikatu	to prod, to jab, to challenge, to provoke

[*N.B.* With *beso* ‘arm’ there is *besarkatu* ‘to embrace’; compare *besarka* ‘embracing’.]

Group 3

atze	back side	atzekatu	to drive back, to retreat
aurre	front side	aurkatu	to oppose, to thwart
gain	top, surface	gainkatu	to climb up, to climb, to cover
inguru	circle, vicinity	ingurukatu	to surround, to circumscribe, to encircle
saihets	side	saiheskatu	to be next to, to list

Group 4

baietz	yes, indeed	baiezkatu	to say yes repeatedly
ezetz	no	ezezkatu	to say no repeatedly
otoi	please	otoikatu	to repeatedly say “please,” to plead

Group 5

bakar	alone	bakarkatu	to isolate, to separate
bana	one each	banakatu	to separate, to distribute, to give one to each
bina	each two	binakatu	to pair off, to divide into pairs
hiruna	each three	hirunakatu	to divide in groups of three

Group 6

apur	crumb	apurkatu	to crumble, to make small
bihi	grain	bihikatu	to winnow, to shake out grain
erdi	half	erdikatu	to reduce by half, to divide in two (also *erdizkatu*)
sail	department, group	sailkatu	to catalog, to classify
talde	group	taldekatu	to group
tanta	drop	tantakatu	to drip, to distill, to fall in drops
zama	load	zamakatu	to load up, to put in piles
zati	part, piece	zatikatu	to dismantle, to divide into pieces

Group 7

aldi	period, turn	aldikatu	to alternate
txanda	turn	txandakatu	to alternate

With group 8, of the adjectives there are no derivations with *-katu*. There are, however, the usual derivatives with *-tu*, such as *estutu* 'to press', *gordetu* 'to hide', *handitu* 'to enlarge', *isildu* 'to be silent', *itsutu* 'to blind', and *okertu* 'to turn'.

[*N.B.* With loanwords with a stem ending in *-ka*—like *benedikatu* 'to bless', *maradikatu* 'to curse', *freskatu* 'to refresh', and *trukatu* 'to exchange'—naturally, no *-katu* suffix is involved.]

The suffix *-katu* is used in place of *-tu* in order to make inchoative or causative verbs from the deictic manner adverbs with *-la* (see section 11.1.6). Besides the already mentioned *bezalakatu*, there is also *bestelakatu* 'to make or become different', *halakatu* 'to make or become like', and *nolakatu* 'to make or become how (in such a way)'.

33.1.13 The Suffix *-kada*

The suffix *-kada* attaches to nouns and yields nouns that express one moment of an activity connected to the base form. Just as the suffix *-katu* is based on the verbalization of the stative forms ending in *-ka*, so is the suffix *-kada* based on the nominalization of these forms—by means of the element *-ada* borrowed from Romance.

It is clear that the iterative character of most of these stative forms is lost in the nominalization, since, as said previously, only an instance of the action is denoted.

Although the derivatives with *-kada* generally, as to meaning, concur closely with the corresponding stative forms with *-ka*, there are a few examples found where this is not the case and thus one could speak of *-kada* as an independent suffix:

bete	fullness	betekada	overful stomach, indigestion, surfeit, glut
erdara	non-Basque language	erdarakada	barbarism
sabel	belly	sabelkada	bellyful, full belly

Just as we did with *-katu*, we will use the same distinguishing groups. One notices then that the most nominalizations are to be found in groups 2 and 6, while in groups 3, 7, and 8 they are totally or almost totally lacking.

Group 1. In general one does not expect *-kada* derivations because the base itself already denotes the action and further nominalization would seem superfluous. Derivations with *-kada* only occur here if the base is not a noun but a directional form, and if the base noun is losing its character of noun in that it seldom or never appears outside the verbal expression with *egin*. This analysis yields two series of examples:

atzera	backward	atzerakada	retreat
aurrera	forward	aurrerakada	advance
behera	down	beherakada	decline
gora	up	gorakada	rise, increase

bultz	push, thrust	bultzada	push, thrust, shove
korrok	burp, belch	korrokada	burp, belch
kosk	bite	koskada	bite
oka	vomit, nausea	okada	vomit, nausea
purrust	mumble, grumbling	purrustada	mumbling, grumbling
zurrut	swallow, swig	zurrutada	swallow, swig

Group 2. The derivation with *-kada* indicates a blow or movement with the base as instrument, sometimes also the injury occasioned thereby:

aizkora	ax	aizkorada	blow from an ax, ax wound
aizto	knife	aiztokada	cut, stab from a knife, stab wound
arraun	oar	arraunkada	oar stroke
atzapar	claw	atzaparkada	scratch
bihotz	heart	bihozkada	heartbeat, impulse
buru	head	burukada	hit with the head
ezku	hand	ezkukada	slap, hit with the hand
ezpat	sword	ezpatakada	sword blow (also *ezpatada*)
ezten	stinger, awl	eztenkada	prick, sting, malicious dig
hagin	molar	haginkada	bite
harri	stone	harrikada	blow with a stone, stone's throw

hortz	tooth	horzkada	bite
makila	stick, cane	makilada	blow from a stick
oin	foot	oinkada	kick, footstep
ukabil	fist	ukabilkada	punch, hit with the fist
ukondo	elbow	ukondokada	jab or blow with the elbow
zarta	stick, rod	zartakada	hit with a stick
zigor	rod, whip	zigorkada	whiplash, punishment, chastisement
ziri	pin, peg, wedge	zirikada	poke, jab, pestering

[*N.B. ilargikada*: 'blow with the moon' (Amuriza, *Hil* 116).]

Group 3. No examples.

Group 4

berorikada	a use of the *berori* forms
hikada	a use of the solidarity *hi* forms
zukada	a use of the *zu* form

Meaningwise, the word *erdarakada* 'use of a barbaric form' would also fit in this group.

Group 5. There are examples of the following sort:

ehun	hundred	ehunkada	a hundred
mila	thousand	milakada	a thousand (not **milada*)

Group 6. Group 6 yields measurements:

aho	mouth	ahokada	mouthful, morsel
ahur	palm (of hand)	ahurkada	handful
altzo	lap	altzokada	lapful, apronful
beso	arm	besakada	armful
esku	hand	eskukada	handful (*MEIG* VI, 95: *eskutada*, with dissimilation)
golko	bosom	golkokada	armful (bosom full)
gurdi	cart, wagon	gurdikada	cartload (also *gurkada*)
ikuilu	stable	ikuilukada	stableful (Amuriza, *Hil* 15, 164)
kamioi	truck	kamioikada	truckload
katilu	bowl, cup	katilukada	bowlful, cupful (also *gatilukada*)
labe	oven	labakada	oven full
lepo	neck	lepakada	shoulder load
oin	foot	oinkada	footstep, length of a step, pace
ontzi	container, ship	ontzikada	container full, shipload
orga	wagon	orgada	wagonful, cartload
pitxer	jar, pitcher	pitxerkada	jarful, pitcherful
plater	plate, dish	platerkada	plateful, dishful
saski	basket	saskikada	basketful
tanta	drop	tantakada	drop, trickle

Regarding the syntax of these forms: As discussed in chapter 2, a phrase linked to a numeral is indefinite: *lepakada bat egur* 'a shoulder load of firewood', *bost lepakada egur* 'five shoulder loads of firewood'. In the absence of a numeral, however, the measurement receives the definite article: *lepakada egurra* 'the shoulder load of firewood'.

Here are a few more examples:

(1) a. Pitxerkada ardoa edan zuen arnasa hartu gabe. (Cf. *E.H.* 653)
He drank the jarful of wine without drawing breath.
b. Eskukada dirua badu.
He has a handful of money.
c. Har ezazu golkokada bete intxaur. (Cf. *E.H.* 326)
Take an armful (lit. chestful, bosom full) of nuts.
d. Bi platerkada tomate jan zituen.
He ate two plates of tomatoes.

Group 7. No examples, except perhaps *aldikada* 'turn', 'period' = *aldi* (Amuriza, *Hil* 185).

Group 8. No examples.

Key to the Exercises

Chapter 1

1.5.1

1. The fire is red, and the smoke black. (Or: Fire is red, and smoke black.)
2. Same as 1.
3. The daughter is beautiful, but the mother very beautiful.
4. The night is dark, the day (is) not.
5. It is a dark day today.
6. The women are pretty, but the men ugly. (Or: Women are pretty, but men ugly.)
7. The priest and the gypsy are friends.
8. Who is the boss here?
9. Many houses are white.
10. The priests and the witches are not enemies. (Or: Priests and witches are . . .)
11. The red skirt is not ugly.
12. Old apples are cheap here, but good coffee very expensive.

1.5.2

1. Ardo beltza ona da.
2. Ardo garestia da.
3. Sorgina eta ijitoak adiskideak dira.
4. Emakumea eta apaiza ez dira etsaiak ere.
5. Oiloa txikia da, baina oso goxoa.
6. Eliza asko hotzak eta ilunak dira. (Or: hotz eta ilunak dira.)

7. Eskuak beroak dira, baina oinak hotzak.
8. Liburu berria garestia da, baina zaharra merkea.
9. Zer da lana eta nor nagusia?
10. Zenbat da dirua?
11. Sorginak adiskideak dira, eta ijitoak ere adiskideak dira.
12. Eguna laburra da eta urtea ere bai. (Or: baita urtea ere.)

Chapter 2

2.8.1

1. The two gypsies are old friends.
2. The thousand chickens of the witch's daughter are black.
3. The house of the son of Pete's friend is big and beautiful.
4. The apples are for John, the bread for Louis, and the money for Frank.
5. Father is the owner of few cows, but of a lot of pigs.
6. The mothers of many kids are witches.
7. The white house is for eleven women.
8. The house of many people is nobody's.
9. Whom do the white horses belong to?
10. Why is the work of the boss's friend not good?
11. The light of the sun by day and that of the moon by night are cheap and abundant.
12. The (little) horses of the mayor's sons are good, but those of the ones of the gypsy bad.

2.8.2

1. Hamar etxeak berriak dira.
2. Mutil txikiaren zaldi zuria garestia da.
3. Emakume gorrien beldurra handia da.
4. Lau mutil eta bost neskatxa bederatzi haur dira. (Not *haurrak*, in spite of being part of the predicate.)
5. Sorgin asko gazte eta politak dira.
6. Andre gutxi da isila. (A Basque saying)
7. Etxe berria alkatearen adiskidearen alaba handiarentzat da.
8. Norentzat da dirua eta norentzat ez?

9. Diru pixka bat ez da nahikoa. (Or: Diru apur bat ez da aski.)
10. Zein liburu da apaiz zaharrarena?
11. Inor ez da ehun mila libururen jabea.
12. Norena da zakurra eta norena zaldia?

Chapter 3

3.12.1

1. From the church to the pretty girls.
2. Today from the house (home) to the church and tomorrow again from the church to the house (home).
3. From the gypsies to the priest and again from the priest to the gypsies.
4. From the beautiful books down to the nation.
5. Why always to court?
6. Why is the witch's black cat in the priest's chicken coop?
7. There are always mice in the churches and cats in the houses.
8. There is now little money in the old factories.
9. In the beautiful new churches are not many people.
10. There are three pretty girls in the small church of the new priest.
11. The beautiful sister of the mayor is a sister of a friend of Mother's.
12. From the earth toward heaven (or: toward the sky) and from (the) men toward God.

3.12.2

1. Gaur Nafarroatik Bizkairaino eta bihar Hendaiatik Parisera. (Or: Parisa.)
2. Batikanotik elizetara eta berriz elizetatik Batikanora.
3. Hiri eta herri askotatik jende gutxirengana.
4. Norengandik norengana? Mutil itsusiarengandik neskatxa politarengana.
5. Noren etxean dira sorginak beti?
6. Norantz da orain?
7. Zenbat gaztelutan dira liburu eta loreak? (Or: liburuak eta loreak?)
8. Gizon zaharra eta neskatxa gaztea Ameriketan dira.
9. Zenbait herritan sagu asko eta katu gutxi dira.
10. Gaur ez da inor lantegian.

11. Igandeetan jende gutxi da hiri handietan.
12. Zergatik orain aitaren arrebarengandik amaren ahizparengana?

Chapter 4

4.6.1

1. Behind the big workshop are two beautiful white houses.
2. Who is under the water, and who (is) on the grass?
3. Inside the old city are many pretty houses.
4. There is nothing at all under the small tables.
5. Grandmother's ring is under the mayor's foot.
6. On top of one horse are three ugly old women.
7. Aside from the witch there is nobody outside.
8. How many blind customers are there behind the white wall?
9. Around the black castle are many huge cats and few flowers.
10. There is great danger between the old mill and the new church.
11. What are the new laws about?
12. The festivities are from half past six to a quarter to nine.

4.6.2

1. Etxe zuriaren aurrean zaharra da. (Or: errota zahar bat da.)
2. Bi hiri haundien artean bide luzea da.
3. Zein mendiren atzean da etsaia?
4. Mina hezurren barrenean da.
5. Zer da mahai gorriaren azpian?
6. Hiri handietatik kanpoan otsoak eta hartzak dira.
7. Hamar andrez kanpo, ez da inor barrenean.
8. Nor da aitaren ondoan eta nor amarenean?
9. Zapata politen gainean ispilu txiki bat da. (Or: ispilutxo bat da.)
10. Zenbat ezpata dira bezeroaren mahuka handiaren barrenean?
11. Ze(r) ordutan da gaur afaria?
12. Hamar-hamarretan.

Chapter 5

5.11.1

1. Where are the good friends of yesterday?
2. Who are the three girls on top of the bed?
3. The front door was iron and the back one wooden.
4. Mary's new pants are of little value.
5. Around the old castle nearby are terrible abysses.
6. The silver belonged to the witch from the sea, and the gold to the one from the mountain.
7. The stone bridge was strong, but the wooden one very weak.
8. The statues inside the church were pretty, and those outside ugly.
9. The ties with the neighbors were very strong here.
10. The new translations from Basque are often very beautiful.
11. Words of hatred are rarely reasonable.
12. Goodbye to the fake world and the false friends!

5.11.2

1. Baionako ipuina izugarria zen.
2. Itsasoko haizea zergatik da hotza?
3. Gaurko afariaren usaina goxoa da.
4. Bilboko zubi berriak ez dira zurezkoak.
5. Herrietako etxeak ederrak dira, mendikoak ez.
6. Pelloren jantziaren oihala merkea da, baina txarra ez.
7. Katuaren errukia zen harrigarria, ez arratoiaren beldurra.
8. Euskarazko liburuak beti garestiak dira hemen.
9. Mendi gaineko gurutzearen itzala harrigarria zen.
10. Urte osoko errenta berrehun mila libera da.
11. Leize ondoko loaren arriskua argi(a) da.
12. Ezkerreko mahaia eta eskuineko ispilua aitaren aspaldiko adiskide batenak dira.

Chapter 6

6.9.1

1. (Look), there are the beloved mountains of the Basque Country!
2. Why is your uncle from San Sebastian coming here?
3. My (our) daughter is walking in the street with a young Biscayan priest.
4. How many kilometers are there from here to the sea?
5. Look here, girl, nobody is walking around here.
6. Who among your sons was at Mary's the day before yesterday?
7. I was going to my (own) house yesterday, not to yours.
8. The big rats of the old church of yoûr village are now coming up to our houses.
9. Thus, your American friend is now in the white house.
10. The black cows of the boss here are going toward the mill with the red soldiers.
11. Last night three handsome boys were walking behind you. (Or: . . . chasing after you.)
12. Then I was in an ugly city; now, however, I am in a really pretty hamlet.

6.9.2

1. Nor naiz (ni)?
2. Non nago (ni)?
3. Nora zihoazen atzo baserritar asko?
4. Orain neure aitarenera noa.
5. Altunatarrak noiz datoz gurera?
6. Zergatik ez dator gaur inor?
7. Herenegun Gernikara genbiltzan bizkaitar adiskide batekin.
8. Noren liburuak daude horko mahai txikian? (Or: horko mahai txikiaren gainean?)
9. Zure aita eta gure (nire) ama hor daude aurreko atearen atzean.
10. Hona hemen gipuzkoar apaiz bat eta bizkaitar sorgin bat.
11. Sorgina ibaiaren gainetik dabil bere ahizparenganantz.
12. Hemengo neskatxak harrigarriak dira, hangoak, aldiz, benetan izugarriak.

Chapter 7

7.9.1

1. The devil has gone out of your daughter.
2. For a long time I have not gone out of the house, and neither have you.
3. I am surprised that you still hang out with very young girls.
4. When will you marry me?
5. Until I die, yoú shall not come into our home. (For *gurean*, see section 6.4.)
6. At which hotel in Bilbao are you staying today?
7. How many hours have passed from noon until now? (Lit. "up to here.")
8. The woman came out of the workshop in a black rage (lit. "in a red anger") and went to Bilbao at once.
9. It was really astounding that we did not fall into the abyss yesterday afternoon.
10. Until we returned to Bilbao, we were neither hungry nor thirsty.
11. At that time we were afraid of the big dogs in your pub.
12. In the end, my (cf. section 6.1.3, item 2) grandmother got to San Sebastian with her chickens very late.

7.9.2

1. Zein andre etzan da nire ohe gainean bere urrezko ilearekin?
2. Sorginak gazteluaren teilatura igo ziren berehala.
3. Gure liburuak mahaitik uretara erori dira orain. (For *uretara*, see section 3.4.2.)
4. Tren lasterrak beti berandu abiatzen dira hemendik.
5. Goizero seiak laurden gutxitan esnatzen ginen. (Cf. section 4.2.)
6. Goizeko hamar t'erdietan iritsiko (helduko) gara Donostiara.
7. Zu orduan menditik jaistea ona zen.
8. Gaur asko gertatu da gure herriko tabernan.
9. Zenbat apaiz bizi dira oraindik zure etxe txikian?
10. Gaur goizean oso haserre izan naiz zurekin. (Also: zutaz)
11. Pello gure neskatxen atzetik ibiliko zen bart.
12. Mina oraindik gose izatetik dator.

Chapter 8

8.9.1

1. The interior of the sun is said to be very hot.
2. The people near the sea must have been filled with fear.
3. I do hope the mad dog of your boss will soon die.
4. Has nothing happened anywhere up to now?
5. When will you return to your excellent wife, I wonder?
6. Why, I wonder, did nobody stay in the hotel of the young witches?
7. Who is not amazed that the snow is still white?
8. You and I will never enter the pub of the gypsies.
9. We are getting ashamed to see the whole village dancing to the tune of some Americans.
10. Have yoû finally woken up?
11. Try, at least, we will.
12. I did not go back to the sea because of what happened.

8.9.2

1. Behin ba omen zen Donostiako (or: donostiar) sorgin polit bat eta soldadu beltz batekin ezkondu zen.
2. Miren ez bide da nire etxe zahar itsusian gelditukо.
3. Ijito zaharraren adiskidea ez bide zen bostetan esnatu.
4. Ez ahal da inor gauerdi arte gelditukо!
5. Nor mintzatuko ote da igandean ostatuan?
6. Bazegoen norbait hemen, edo bestela zoratu egin naiz.
7. Zu ote zinen?
8. Bermeoko (or: bermeotar) neskatxa bat ongi mintzatu (or: mintzo) zen zutaz.
9. Zein zubitatik erori zen zure semea atzo goizean?
10. Lehenago gure herriko alkateak txarrak izaten ziren, orain ez.
11. Nire anaia gutxitan etortzen da gurera, eta nire arreba inoiz ere ez.
12. Bide luzea (not: luze bat) da, baina heldu (or: iritxi) egingo gara.

Chapter 9

9.9.1

1. This wind from the sea (sea wind) brings rain.
2. At what time are yoû bringing those new tools today?
3. Whose cart (coach) are you taking to that big castle?
4. What do you say about those things, and what do those loyal friends say?
5. These farmers have thick waists and rough hands.
6. Our bashful boys don't know (about) those young witches.
7. Evil inclinations lead to death.
8. I don't know how to stand this sharp pain in the ear.
9. These old houses of ours don't look like castles.
10. How is life treating you?
11. This year we are busy at work day and night.
12. I don't know you by your name.

9.9.2

1. Nork daki euskaraz? (Or: euskara.)
2. Zerk zakartzahona?
3. Zer dakarzu hona?
4. Zure ardiak kanpora (al) daramatzazu hotz honetan?
5. Andre bikain honek ez daramatza atzoko zapatata zaharrak.
6. Zure liburu lodi horiek egunero darabiltzat.
7. Atzerritar alargun haiengana naramazu (ni)?
8. Alargun gazte horiek bizitza latza daramate.
9. Andre polit honek bere atorra(ren) azpian krabelin gorriak dauzka. (Or: ditu.)
10. Nork ez dazagu gezurti zital hori?
11. Gazte honek ez daki Mirenen izena.
12. Haiek jende leial eta bihoztia dirudite.

Chapter 10

10.9.1

1. From long ago I have had the key to all the problems in my hand.
2. I wonder what yoû said about me and my problems.
3. Did you know it all in advance?
4. I was busy with work the whole night yesterday, and my husband too.
5. Taking everything from everybody is the work of a great thief.
6. Yesterday's noisy gathering lasted the whole afternoon.
7. To tell the truth, you were spending many hours outside the house.
8. That whole day, you seemed a carnivorous mountain bear.
9. They all knew about the problems of the widow.
10. That year, I saw you at the homes of all my friends. (For *-enean*, see section 6.4.)
11. That boy was carrying inside a fierce anger toward his parents.
12. Forgiving everybody is not easy.

10.9.2

1. Nork zindekartzan hona, senarra eta guzti?
2. Lapur batek gindekartzan bere zaldi zuriaren gainean.
3. Ametsa zirundien. (Also: Amets bat zirudien.)
4. Nork harrapatuko ditu Bilboko lapur guztiak?
5. Gure egunkariak berri gutxi zekarren atzo.
6. Zure adiskideak korbata gorri bat zeraman urte guztian.
7. Denek zerbait zekarten alargun gaztearentzat.
8. Sorginek ginderamatzaten zure etxe ederrera.
9. Egun guztian (or: osoan) besoetan nindukazun.
10. (Nik) ez nekien ezer hartaz.
11. Ez nituen inoiz (or: behin ere) ijito guztiak gorrotatzen.
12. Munduko diru guztiak ez nau (ni) erosiko.

Chapter 11

11.9.1

1. Have I not seen you somewhere else?
2. It will have (i.e., must have) been somebody other than me.
3. Perhaps you have never read such books.
4. For a long time almost nobody has been coming to our meetings.
5. From my room I see the old bridge very nicely (i.e., very well).
6. Such parents know almost nothing about their children.
7. This young priest deeply examined all those problems.
8. Your fiancé hates me intensely, and I don't know why.
9. Our teacher has explained the whole lesson clearly and distinctly, in a way easy for us to understand.
10. It is not good for a mother-to-be to walk so fast.
11. I am very happy to see your fiancée. (Lit. "Seeing your fiancée rejoices me greatly.")
12. Entering blindly into such matters almost always carries (with it) fairly great dangers.

11.9.2

1. Ongi asko (or: nahikoa ondo) ikasi dut neure ikasgaia.
2. Inork gutxik irakurtzen ditu horren liburu zozoak.
3. Bat ez beste haurrak berandu etxeratu ziren. (Or: berandu etorri ziren etxera.)
4. Zergatik portatu zinen bart hain gaizki?
5. Zure sagar horiek benetan izugarri goxoak dira.
6. Zure senargaiak zuregandik zeharo (or: guztiz) bestelakoa dirudi.
7. Honelako etxe polita (or: etxe polit bat) oso gutxitan dago salgai.
8. Agian, ezer gutxi gertatuko da hemen.
9. Gaur nire senarrak ia-ia galdu ditu gure etxeko giltzak.
10. Hain egun ederrean haurrak, agian, itsasora jaitsi dira.
11. Ia arrantzale guztiek oso ongi (or: oso ederki) ulertzen dituzte gai hauek guztiak.
12. Gaurko arrantzaleek arrain asko erraz harrapatzen dute. (Or: dituzte, cf. section 9.4.)

Chapter 12

12.8.1

1. What size pants is the teacher wearing these days?
2. Did you buy this chocolate to eat in the garden together with your fiancée?
3. All the rivers go to the sea, and the sea never gets full. (Or: fills itself.)
4. What occupation will your son now take, I wonder?
5. Among all the worries, I am not forgetting your sweet smile.
6. To whose house are you taking those little kids?
7. An old witch has struck my sister and turned her into a witch.
8. Maybe we won't see each other anymore in this world.
9. The words of this writer must have been wrongly understood. (Or: misunderstood.)
10. I found myself in a beautiful garden, and there I found you.
11. I won't put this work on the servants' shoulders.
12. We have at once made your worries ours.

12.8.2

1. Neskameek gurekin batera gosaltzen dute beti.
2. Zergatik utzi dituzue zuen liburu guztiak etxean?
3. Zer irakurtzen da gure baserrietan?
4. Nola joaten da gure etxetik zurera?
5. Arrain asko jaten da Bilbon. (Or: jaten dute Bilbon.)
6. Nola ikasten dira hizkuntzak?
7. Gure amaren hizkuntza ez dugu sekula ahaztuko. (Or: inoiz ahaztuko.)
8. Nire ezagunen artean ez da inor gure hizkuntzaz kezkatzen.
9. Gaur ez dut ezer gehiago edango taberna honetan.
10. Egile honek ez du hitz asko erabiltzen bere penak adierazteko.
11. Neskamea etxekoandre bihurtuko da, eta orduan morroia nagusi bihurtuko du.
12. Baserri hauetan guztietan, biak laurden gutxitan bazkaltzen da. (Or: Baserri guzti hauetan, ordu biak laurden gutxiagotan bazkaltzen da.)

Chapter 13

13.8.1

1. I dream about you every day, do you know that?
2. Your continuous chatter will soon turn me crazy.
3. The poor mother has walked from village to village, without finding her beloved little daughter anywhere.
4. The bashful foreigner set out toward the church instead of going to the river.
5. Did yoû do the work before coming here?
6. I am really sorry not to have come.
7. I took a long breath and went down into the deep cave.
8. In this old castle one has never prayed.
9. You remain in debt to us for a hundred francs.
10. Telling the mayor the truth will do no harm.
11. How do you know the truth without anybody telling you anything?
12. Not very far from our garden one sees a lot of pigs.

13.8.2

1. Gure irakurle trebeak ez du aste honetan liburuoften irakurri.
2. Donostian ez da behin ere (or: inoiz) esnerik edaten.
3. Neskameek zergatik egiten dute beti barre gure sukaldean?
4. Norentzat egiten dute lan?
5. Arrantzale batzuek ez dute inoiz hitz egiten oihu(rik) egin gabe. (Or: egiteke.)
   Or: Arrantzale batzuk ez dira inoiz mintzatzen oihu(rik) egin gabe. (Or: egiteke.)
6. Maitasun(aren) faltaz (or: faltan), Mirenek luzaro negar egin zuen.
7. Non egiten dute gure ikasleek lo egun haueten?
8. Nola bizi dira hain luzaro diru(rik) gabe?
9. Irakasleak ez zuen inoiz (or: behin ere) hitzik egin eztul(ik) egin gabe. (Or: egiteke.)
10. Hotz egiten zuen atzo, baina ez zuen behintzat elurrik egin.
11. Nire gurasoek ez dute (or: daukate) inorentzako errukirik. (Or: errukirik inorentzat.)
12. Ez dugu (or: daukagu) batere zorrik, hiri honetan behintzat. (Or: zorrik batere.)

Chapter 14

14.9.1

1. Because of the frightful cold, you must close all the doors and windows of the house (very) well.
2. I want Mary to fix the roof of our house.
3. We see no need to go far in order to learn Basque.
4. Instead of learning English they learned Basque, and very well besides.
5. In order to know Basque well, we are still in need of learning a lot.
6. Today I am not in the mood for books.
7. This cheap book is not worth reading.
8. Today at least, no one must be believed.
9. You had no need to go a long way to talk to my wife.
10. I found myself in need of your fascinating wife at that celebration.
11. Do you intend to marry our daughter, yes or no?
12. Do you feel like marrying our daughter, yes or no?

14.9.2

1. Zu kondenatu behar zaitugu, baina alargun maitagarri hau ez dugu kondenatuko.
2. Ez al duzu ezer behar edateko?
3. Zuk niri (or: niretzat) etxe harrigarri bat jasotzea (or: eraikitzea) nahi dut.
4. Nork ez du izugarri(ki) zoriontsua izan nahi?
5. Ez dut batere gogorik zuri nire etxe zoragarria saltzeko.
6. Donostia ikusi gabe ez dut hil nahi. (Or: ez dut nahi hil.)
7. Ez dugu nahi zuk gu behar izaterik.
8. Nork izango zaitu inoiz erruki?
9. Zu gabe etxeratu gogo (or: asmo) dut benetan.
10. Liburu gogaikarri (or: aspergarri) hau irakurri behar dut, baina ez dut nahi.
11. Inork ez nau maite izan nahi (or: maitatu nahi) aste honetan.
12. Nork nahi du nork lan egitea baserri erogarri hartan?

Chapter 15

15.11.1

1. Every day about ten men sent (or: used to send) me flowers.
2. Why are you telling me those big lies?
3. Tomorrow afternoon I will come to your home.
4. I consider it ridiculous to speak in that manner. (Or: that way.)
5. We soon broke into laughter, quite gladly, besides.
6. I applied myself to learning my father's language (quite) well.
7. I am boring even to myself.
8. Yoû too must wash each other's feet.
9. They embraced each other and wept together.
10. I have introduced Mary and Itziar to each other.
11. They promised each other to belong to each other.
12. The two are not enemies, but little unites the two.

15.11.2

1. Ez diezu (zure) anaiei etxea saldu behar.
2. Haur bat jaio zaigu, Jainkoak seme bat eman digu. (Is 9:5)
3. Sorgin gazte askok musu eman didate aste honetan.
4. Lurralde honi esnea eta eztia omen darizkio.
5. Nik oso ederra deritzat (or: deritzot) emakume horri.
6. Etxe honetako haur guztiek batera negarrari eman (or: ekin) zioten.
7. Zergatik ematen diozu su mahaiari?
8. Ez dugu geure burua hil nahi.
   Ez ditugu geure buruak hil nahi.
   Ez dugu nahi geure burua hil.
   Ez ditugu nahi geure buruak hil.
9. Bere buruaz ere hitz egin dit, batez ere bere buruaz. (Mendiguren, *Hamalau* 84)
10. Zeure argazkirik inoiz ikusi al duzu?
11. Zer egin ote diozue elkarri? (Or: bata besteari.)
12. (Nire) Anaiak eta nik ez dugu bata bestearen etxean sartu nahi. (Or: batak bestearen . . .)

Chapter 16

16.11.1

1. The tongue does not break bones, but it does make (someone) break them.
2. Mary has made John wash himself. (Not: wash her.)
3. Whose letters did you make the maid burn this morning, I wonder?
4. Will you make me kill the fat calf? (*me* represents the causee, not the beneficiary!)
5. This doctor doesn't want to let me kiss his daughters.
6. He knew (very) well how to keep things quiet.
7. One has to know how to lose too.
8. Pete was allegedly beating dogs and cats in front of his new fiancée's house.
9. How come you aren't getting bored reading the same book every day?
10. I have not come here to show anyone how to love Basque.
11. How will I get to caress the pretty waist of that lovely lady?
12. The mayor has never stooped to ask permission of our workmen.

16.11.2

1. Zerk idatzarazi zion sendagileari eskutitz zoro hori guri?
2. Atzo egia esatera etorri zitzaigun sendagilea.
3. Ez zintugun ikusi okindegitik ateratzen. (Or: irteten.)
4. Gaizkilea ez zen ausartu jauregiko atea zabaltzera. (Or: zabaltzen, idekitzen.)
5. Irakasle ona izaten saiatu naiz, baina ikasleek ez didate utzi.
6. Zerk behartzen zaitu horren nagia izatera?
7. Liburu garesti horiek zail(ak) dira aurkitzen.
8. Okinak ez zion harakinari uzten berari laguntzen txahalak zaintzen.
9. Jende gutxik daki gaztainak erretzen.
10. Ez al zara inoiz gauza hauek ulertzen hasiko? (Or: hasiko gauza hauek ulertzen?)
11. Gaizkileak ez zihoazen beren buruak hain erraz salatzera.
12. Zergatik ez diozu laguntzen katu beltzari sagu guzti horiek harrapatzen? (Or: sagu horiek guztiak.)

Chapter 17

17.11.1

1. If yoú have a lot, a lot yoú will need.
2. If yoú go to sea with the devil, with him yoú will have to make the voyage.
3. If I had married that witch, I would have killed myself.
4. If they had been taken for leftists, their lives wouldn't have been worth a penny.
5. And now, if you were to show me the will, I would give you warm thanks. (More idiomatic in English: my warmest thanks.)
6. Where would we be going if we did not believe each other?
7. If I were in my (own) house, I would know what to do.
8. If I hadn't seen it, I would not believe it.
9. Provided your sister is at home, I will go to her at once.
10. If one tells the truth at all, we owe the whole truth.
11. Society still does not accept them.
12. He got angry with me; he doesn't take me seriously (or: doesn't pay attention to me).

17.11.2

1. Zuk sufritzen baduzu, nik ere sufritzen dut. (Garate, *Leh.* 115)
2. Horrela bizitzen bazarete, hil egingo zarete. (Rom 8:13)
3. Nire emazteak barre egingo luke, hori entzungo balu.
4. Ijitoak etxea erosi nahi badu, dirua izan beharko du.
5. Zer egingo zenuke zuri gertatu (izan) balitzaizu?
6. Apustu hau irabazten badut, afaltzera gonbidatuko zaitut. (*EGLU* II, 420)
7. Liburu asko irakurri (izan) balitu ere, asto handia geldituko zatekeen. (Or: zen.)
8. Nire izebak liburu horiek irakurri nahiko ditu, interesgarriak izatekotan.
9. Neure herritzat hartuko zaituztet. (Ex 6:7)
10. Zenbait andrek senartzat hartuko zintuzkete. (*TOE* I, 68) (Or: andre batzuek . . .)
11. Nire osabak emakumetzat dauka bere burua eta ez ditu gure hitzak aintzakotzat hartuko.
12. Alargun gazteak Miren eta ni laguntzat aukeratu gaitu.

Chapter 18

18.11.1

1. I don't know how in the world we would manage without him (or: her).
2. I wonder whether the world has not gone completely mad.
3. We didn't know if he was alive even, and that he was so wealthy.
4. They say (*omen*) that it is in misfortune(s) that one gets to know who loves us.
5. I have heard Mary say that she has realized that you have done terribly stupid things.
6. I don't want anyone to know where I am. (Lit. "where I walk.")
7. Because of that doctor, do you know who died?
8. John knows that his son has problems, and his wife also knows that.
9. Pete doesn't realize that he is insane, and his wife doesn't realize that either.
10. Pete thinks that a disaster will happen to him, and his wife thinks so too.
11. It seems to John that there is no hope for him, and to his wife it seems so too.
12. Mary promised her husband that she would no longer tell lies, and her sister promised so too.

18.11.2

1. Ez dakit zer gertatzen zaidan. (Mintegi, 97)
2. Ez dakigu nork zer irakatsi dizun.
3. Ez dakit sinestu zigun ala ez. (Atxaga, *Gizona* 29)
4. Konturatzen al zara zer egin duzun?
5. Ez dut uste inoiz (sekula) ikusi zaitudanik (zaitudala). (Zapirain, *M.* 216)
6. Ez nuen uste hain azkar (laster) ahaztuko nindutenik (nindutela). (Atxaga, *Obab.* 42)
7. Ba al daki zure aitak noiz etorriko gatzaizkion ikustera? (Or: garen bera ikustera.)
8. Nire zakurrak (txakurrak) amorratuak direla bistan dagoela esan didate.
9. Ez dut uste inork sinestuko duenik bere emaztea gizon horrek hil duela.
10. Sekula gehiago ez zuela neskatxa hori ikusiko agindu zidan. (Garate, *NY* 17)
11. Ez nekien Euskal Herritik kanpo bizi nahi nuen ala ez. (Urretabizkaia, *Asp.* 52)
12. Herri honetan bi mila sorgin bizi zirela idatzi zizula alkateak uste dugu.

Chapter 19

19.10.1

1. Pete is a student who likes books.
2. The apple that has been given to the child who has come alone is rotten.
3. If you had not brought that which you are carrying in your bosom, you would not have come out of here alive.
4. The days that I was a child have long gone.
5. Frank would like to marry the girl whom John is walking in the street with.
6. The one who brought it to him brought what he brought to the one to whom he brought it.
7. You have taken the wine from me, from whom they have now eaten the bread.
8. As far as I know, I have never done you any harm.
9. What I know, you also know; what you know, I don't know whether I know.
10. Old age makes us forget many things learned earlier.
11. I passionately love yoûr daughter, who is very lovable.
12. Whoever lives in that house will have to pay (for) its repair.

19.10.2

1. Nahi ez dudan gaizkia egiten dut. (Rom 7:19)
2. Inork behin ere (or: inoiz) irakurriko ez duen liburu lodi hori ikusi al duzu?
3. Idatzi duzun liburua irakurri behar al dut nik?
4. Bai, liburu hau irakurri behar duzu, oso interesgarria baita.
5. Zaldia agindu nion andreak ez du nahi.
6. Bidaltzen nauzuen lekura joango naiz. (*TOE* I, 208)
7. Adiskide ona Jainkoak bidaltzen digun aingerua da. (Irazusta, *Bizia* 104)
8. Non da azalduko zela esan zenidan ijitoa?
9. Egiten duzuna ongi egin behar duzu.
10. Zer egiten duzun jakin behar duzu.
11. Lapurtutako liburu guztiak berehala bihurtu behar dira.
12. Aski dena aski da.

Chapter 20

20.11.1

1. Yoû come to me when yoû know nothing else to do.
2. When we went out, the snow was just about to start.
3. The one who is bringing it is bringing what he is bringing when he is bringing it.
4. As soon as I became a man, I gave up childish ways.
5. We set out toward home when it was about to get dark and got home when it was getting dark.
6. When about to do anything whatsoever, we ask ourselves for whom and for what purpose we are acting.
7. Once when he saw Fernando at the Guernica fair, a friend asked him how he was.
8. All the times when Father enters the room, the children start to cry.
9. Each time that I pass by Guernica, I have a moment of sadness.
10. Do you feel better after smoking your cigarettes?
11. As long as honest people last on our farmsteads, Basque will last.
12. We will live in San Sebastian as long as we have money.

20.11.2

1. Hitzegingo dugu itzultzen naizenean. (Atxaga, *Grl.* 127)
2. Eguraldia ederra denean ez dugu etxean gelditu nahi.
3. Handitzen naizenean erdaraz mintzatuko al naiz? (Satrustegi, 192)
4. Zer uste duzu esan nahi duela hori dioenean? (Or: hori esatean.)
5. Sei hilabete igaro dira zu hemen egon zinenetik. (Garate, *E.E.* 144)
6. Ameriketan nintzela, hil zen gure aita.
7. Begiak zabaldu (or: ireki) orduko, ikusi nuen. (Atxaga, *Gizona* 216)
8. Apaiza ikustera etortzen garen bakoitzean, ardoa eskaintzen digu.
9. Bada urtebete amona hil zela.
10. Ez du hitzik esan nahi harik eta dirua jaso arte. (Also without *harik eta*.)
11. Beste guztiek zekitelarik, nik ez nekien.
12. Muga igaro ondoren, beste emakume bat bihurtu zen.

Chapter 21

21.12.1

1. Let him who doesn't know (how to speak) Basque learn it as soon as possible.
2. Let us go home so that our dinner won't get cold.
3. It is not fitting that they see us in conversation together.
4. I would not want them to hear our gossip.
5. Who would not want peace to come?
6. It is time that you stop smoking.
7. How do you want yoûr children to learn anything if yoû don't let them go to the Basque school?
8. Let us finish the work that the witches want us to finish as soon as possible.
9. Let who wants to, do what he wants; I am going home.
10. He who does not want that they call him a wolf, let him not put on a wolf's hide.
11. I promise you that I will do my best to make sure that my sister helps you.
12. I order you to do your best to see to it that your sister marries me.

21.12.2

1. Patxik ikus dezan ekarri dut liburu hau. (*EGLU* II, 422)
2. Liburu bat idatz dezazula esan al dizut inoiz?
3. Ez genuen nahi lan hau egin zenezan.
4. Nire liburua ez dezazula erre eskatzen dizut orain.
5. Komeni da sorginak sorginekin bizi daitezen.
6. Eraman (or: har) zaitzala deabruak!
7. Ez dut nahi inork zure izena jakin dezan.
8. Ikus dezadan (or: dakusadan) zer gertatu den.
9. Eskuargia neraman bidea gal ez nezan.
10. Eman dezagun orain Gorostiaga jaunak arrazoi duela. (*MEIG* VII, 128)
11. Zerbait jan zezatela eskatu zien Paulok denei. (Acts 27:33)
12. Nire ikasketak buka ditzadanean pagatuko (or: ordainduko) dizut.

Chapter 22

22.11.1

1. Look at me, look, face to face!
2. Forgive me, please.
3. Leave those worries and let's go.
4. Say, please, that you are my sister (lit. "that I have you as a sister").
5. Tell me who yoú go about with; I will tell yoú who yoú are.
6. Leave the gold and look for the soul.
7. Go upstairs and tell Mary to please come to us.
8. Take me as a slave instead of the boy, and let (lit. "may") this one go with his brothers.
9. Let my brother Amnon come with us.
10. Do not take strangers inside the house here on the farm!
11. Avert those eyes from me, they drive me wild.
12. Assume that I am a gypsy and you a witch, what would happen to us?

22.11.2

1. Ana! Beste baso bat ekar ezazu! (Labayen, *Su Em.* 169) (Or: Ekar ezazu . . .)
2. Utz ezazu baketan neskatxa. (Garate, *NY* 35) (Or: bakean)
3. Esadazu egia den. (Atxaga, *Obab.* 255)
4. Saia hadi hori ahazten. (Atxaga, *Gizona* 325) (Or: saia(tu) zaitez . . .)
5. Ireki ezazu atzeko atea, mesedez. (Atxaga, *Gizona* 97)
6. Utz gaitzazu hemen nonbait. (Atxaga, *Gizona* 321)
7. Ez zaitez lozale izan. (Prv 20:13) (Or: lozalea.)
8. Bidal iezazkidazu, arren, morroi bat eta asto bat. (2 Kgs 4:22)
9. Hator, txikia, emaiok musu bat aitari. (*MEIG* IX, 111) (Or: eman iezaiok . . .)
10. Egin ezazu nahi duzuna. (Iraola, 113) (Or: Egizu . . .)
11. Ez ezazu ahaz elkar gorroto duguna. (Etxaniz, *Ito* 150) (Or: dugula.) (For *duguna*, see section 18.3.)
12. Ez ezazu hitzik esan ezer galdetzen ez zaizunean. (Or: hitz bat . . .) (For *galdetzen ez zaizunean*, see section 12.5.1.)

Chapter 23

23.11.1

1. I have not written to yoû because yoû do not know the truth, but because yoû do know it.
2. We know what we know because we do not know what we do not know.
3. Let us quickly go to the theater, for we have not gotten tickets yet. (Lit. "for we are still without getting tickets.")
4. Don Francisco had not wanted to add anything to it on the plea that it was dangerous to mention such things on the telephone.
5. Why are yoû coming so late?
6. Since the Holy Mother Church has her experts, it does not behoove us to talk about the substance of this book.
7. Since you are so knowledgeable, do you also know when I will (or: might) die?
8. Although I am right, he considers me a liar.
9. He is eager to start at his new job, even though he doesn't know exactly what it is like.
10. I have bought these old books in order to read them all.
11. Even though he is from the Northern Region, he understands our local Basque. (Lit. "the Basque from here.")
12. We have had to give in, even though (our) blood boils.

23.11.2

1. Gose ginelako etorri gara etxera. (Arejita, *Eusk. Josk.* 188) (Or: etxeratu gara.)
2. Mirenek ez du ardorik erosi nahi, berak edaten ez duelako.
3. Zarena zarelako maite zaitut. (Or: zarena baitzara maite zaitut.)
4. Kanpoan hotz dela eta, Pellok ez du ohetik jaiki nahi.
5. Zorionak eman behar dizkizut horrelako anaia duzulako. (Garate, *Iz.B.* 65)
6. Sinesmena galdu egin duela eta, elizara ez doa. (Erkiaga, *Sinis.* 28)
7. Dena badakizunez gero, ez duzu ezer ikasi beharrik.
8. Igandea zenez gero, ez zuen inor nekarazteko beldurrik. (Garate, *Esku* 121)
9. Ez dakit etorriko naizen, elurra da eta. (Less idiomatically: elurra egiten du eta.)
10. Geldi zaitez etxean, eri baitzara. (Or: gaixo[rik] zaude eta.)
11. Ez zenukeen hori esan behar, egia izan arren. (Or: egia den arren, or: nahiz [eta] egia izan.)
12. Nahiz (eta) berandu samar galdetu, zer asmo duzu afalondorako?

Chapter 24

24.12.1

1. How can one express things without words? (Or: How can things be expressed without words?)
2. We could collect a nice harvest before long.
3. You are unable to swallow that nothing has happpened.
4. Who can swallow that would also swallow toads and live snakes.
5. I, of course, could not believe anything like that.
6. I can do nothing before seeing the school.
7. Speaking about what could and could not have happened tends to be nothing but idle talk.
8. I cannot imagine how I chose this silly wife.
9. May I not say my opinion, or what?
10. Marry off your son when you want and your daughter when you can.
11. Who believes can do everything.
12. God can do what men cannot.

24.12.2

1. Ezin dezaket zugandik ezer har (tu). (*TOE* II, 249) (Or: Ezin har dezaket zuregandik ezer.)
2. Ez dakit nola egin dezakezun hori. (Atxaga, *Gizona* 22) (Or: ... hori egin dezakezun, or: ... hori egin ahal duzun.)
3. Asto batek ere gauza hauek (or: gauzok) uler ditzake.
4. Daramazuna eraman dezaket nik ere.
5. (Ni) bart hil nintekeen. (Añibarro, *E.L.* 6)
6. Zer egin nezakeen bestela? (Oñederra, 48)
7. Ezin nuen gertatzen ari zena ulertu. (Atxaga, *Bam.* I, 30)
8. Jakin al dezaket zer gertatu zaizun? (Or: Zer gertatu zaizun jakiterik ba al daukat? or: ba al dut?)
9. Orduan inork ezingo luke ezer esan. (Etxaniz, *Ito* 195) (Or: Orduan inork ezin esango luke, or: ... ezin izango luke ezer esan.)
10. Ni maitatzeko gauza sentitzen al haiz? (Atxaga, *Obab.* 88)
11. Edan ahala ardo eskainiko dizute.
12. Mirenek bere dirua irabazi ahala honatzen du.

Chapter 25

25.10.1

1. We have sung together in many villages.
2. I have often slept with your sister.
3. Something I have just read comes to my mind.
4. I find myself unable to bear the harsh conduct of my husband's relatives.
5. After paying the fare, he went aboard.
6. The whole year he wanted to buy a house.
7. A friend having sent them, I have seen the old papers you mentioned.
8. We are reading the things Baroja has seen, heard, done, thought.
9. Upon the willows by the water(s) we had left our lyres hanging.
10. Having forgotten my old dreams, I am living far from the world.
11. These days I am unable to understand my wife.
12. Since when have you been in love with me?

25.10.2

1. Dena zure urduritasunak eragina da. (Oñederra, 139)
2. Badirudi katu batek salbatua zinela.
3. Bekatuak barkatuak zaizkigu.
4. Hiri honetako irakasle asko da/dira eskale geldituа/-ak.
5. Geneukan guztia galdua dugu.
6. Beste batzuetan goseak egoten naiz. (Anduaga, 62)
7. Liburu on hauek irakurrita/-rik, lasai hil naiteke.
8. Hil berria dut alaba. (Mt 9:18)
9. Zer dago idatzia/-ta/-rik legean?
10. Bizi garen etxea behin eta berriro saldua izan da.
11. Ahoa lehor daukat/dut.
12. Nire zain al zaude?

Chapter 26

26.11.1

1. Is there a thing as beautiful as seeing ourselves surrounded by dear friends, I wonder?
2. Love me then, as much as I love you.
3. Mary has terribly thick calves and even thicker thighs.
4. To forget those things, there is nothing like a little drink.
5. You are the one I love most in the world; you are the one who deserves to be the most beloved.
6. I passed from the greatest joy to the gravest sadness.
7. Yoù have played with me as much as yoù wanted: yoù as my cat, I as yoùr little mouse.
8. There are few as graceful and beautiful as Maud was.
9. The poor girl got fatter (thicker) than ever before.
10. I would prefer to buy immediately what I need most.
11. The deeper we delve into Basque, the more beautiful we find it.
12. There is no pestilence, and no poison either, that does as much harm as laziness.

26.11.2

1. Nire senarra uste nuen baino aberatsagoa da.
2. Emakume gehienek badakite beren senarrek baino askoz gehiago.
3. Maiteago dugu lagunartea basamortuko bakartasuna baino. (*MEIG* I, 82)
4. Nor da inoiz ezagutu duzun andrerik politena?
5. Ba al da Karmen egiazki bere aitak esaten duen bezain polita?
6. Bakana baino bakanagoa da hitz hori. (*MEIG* VII, 50)
7. Han beti euskaraz hitz egiten zen, gaur baino askoz gehiago. (Uztapide, *Sas*. 292)
8. Zuk jatetxerik merkeenean platerik garestiena eskatzen duzu, nik, berriz, garestienean merkeena.
9. Ahalik gutxiena erosi behar dugu.
10. Goizegi zen inor ikustera joateko.
11. Nontsu utzi dituzue zuen sorginak? (Barbier, *Lég*. 148)
12. Non aurki nezake zuek baino ikasle hoberik?

Chapter 27

27.14.1

1. What was promised with your mouth, you have fulfilled with your hand, as we can see today.
2. I appreciate your article more than that of your sister.
3. If he comes by the first train in the morning, he will get here by noon.
4. The couple is going homeward arm in arm.
5. One has to be careful with those people.
6. We must proceed step by step and degree by degree.
7. How are you doing moneywise from year to year?
8. By constantly reading one can learn a lot in the world of today.
9. The husband was always living in the fear that someone else might steal his wife from him.
10. Through using the key for a long time, the door opened.
11. "Well, me neither," agreed Anartz, beating his rounded belly with one hand.
12. Trodden roads tend to be comfortable, even though they bore us because we know them so well.

27.14.2

1. Ni aizkora zorrotzaz jotzen saiatu zen.
2. Trenez ala beribilez zoaz? Eguneko azkeneko trenean noa.
3. Zenbatetan ez dizut esan garaiz etortzeko?
4. Ogi faltaz, gosez ahuldu ziren.
5. Zure arrebaz liburuak idazteaz aspertzen naiz. (Or: aspertu egiten naiz.)
6. Jokatuaren jokatuz daukazun (duzun) guztia galtzen duzu.
7. Urre garbiz estaliko duzu. (Ex 25:24; *Biblia*)
8. Sorgin gazte baten bitartez aberastu zen.
9. Ikusi ez ditudan ikuskizunez ez zenidake galdetu behar.
10. Euskal Herrian bizitzeke (or: bizi gabe), euskara ikas dezakegu.
11. Tasioz ez da (zen) inor ohartu. (Etxeberria, *Egun* 110)
12. Ez genuen pentsatzen asko biharamunaz. (Xalbador, *Odol.* 183)

Vocabulary

This vocabulary and the ones at the end of each chapter are intended for the convenience of readers doing the exercises. Throughout the chapters much vocabulary is given with reference to the subjects being treated. Some lists are extensive; your attention is called to the following sections: 3.8.2 (*-tegi*); 3.9 (*-xka*); 4.3 (*arte*); 4.4 (*-tzar*); 5.6 (*-ero*); 6.5 (*-te*); 6.6 (*-tar*); 7.4.2–5 (*-tu*); 7.7 (*-xko*); 8.7 (*-tsu*); 9.7 (*-ti*); 10.6 (*-koi*); 10.7 ([-]*zale*); 11.1 (*-ro*, *-ki*); 11.7 (*-gai*); 12.6 (-[*tzai*]*le*); 13.3 (*egin* idioms); 13.6 (*gabe*); 14.7 (*-garri*); 16.9 (*-gile*, *-gin*); 17.9 (*tasun*); 18.9 (*-keria*); 19.8 (*-dun*); 20.9 (*aldi*); 21.9 (*-keta*); 22.7 (*-men*); 22.8 (*-pen*); 22.9 (*-tzapen*); 23.8 (*-kor*); 23.9 (*-bera*); 24.10 ([-]*ezin*[-], *-gaitz*, [-]*erraz*); 25.5.2 (-[*r*]*ik*); 25.8 (-[*kun*]*tza*, *-tza*, *-kunde*); 26.9.2–3 ([-]*era*); 27.12 ([-]*kide*, *-kizun*); and especially chapters 12 (transitive verbs), 31, 32, and 33.

[*Note*: The citation form of the verb is the perfect participle; * indicates a reconstructed form. The numbers following refer to some relevant sections.]

A. Basque-English

abendu(a)	December
aberats	rich
abere	animal
aberri	fatherland, homeland
abiatu	to set out, to depart (16.5.1.6)
abuztu(a)	August
adar	branch, horn
adierazi	to express (16.2.1)
adiskide	friend
aditu	to listen, to understand (12.1.10, 12.5.3, 16.7.2, 22.3.1)
afaldu	to have dinner, supper (12.1.5)
afalondo	time after dinner
afari	evening meal, dinner, supper

agertu	to appear (12.4.2)
agian	maybe, perhaps (11.4)
agindu	to command, to promise, to order; order, commandment (12.1.6)
agur	greeting, goodbye, hello
ahal	possibility, capability; able (24.1, 24.2.3–4, 24.6, 24.6.1, 24.6.3, 24.7.1–2, 26.5.3)
ahalegindu	to do one's best (12.1.6)
ahate	duck (31.2.2)
ahaztarazi	to cause to forget (16.2.1)
ahaztu	to forget (12.1.9, 16.5.2, 27.10.1)
ahizpa	sister (of a woman; 3.10)
aho	mouth
ahuldu	to weaken
aingeru	angel (31.2.2)
aintzakotzat hartu	to pay attention to, to take seriously
aintzat hartu	to pay attention to, to take seriously
aipatu	to mention, to cite (12.1.7)
aita	father (2.3.2)
aitabitxi	godfather (2.3.2)
aitona	grandfather (2.3.2)
aitortu	to confess (17.8.1)
aitzin	before, in front of (4.1.2.1, 20.4, 20.4.2)
aizkora	axe
ala	or (chap. 30)
alaba	daughter
alargun	widow, widower
aldamen	vicinity, side, nearness (4.1.3.4)
alde	in favor of, pro, for; side, region, nearby (2.2.2, 4.1.3.3)
alderdi	side, party
aldi	period, time, turn (2.1.2, 20.3, 20.9, 27.7)
aldiz	in turn, on the contrary, however
aldizkari	magazine, journal, periodical
ale	grain
alfer	lazy, useless, idle
alferkeria	laziness
alkate	mayor
ama	mother (2.3.2)
amabitxi	godmother (2.3.2)
amagai	mother-to-be
amaitu	to end, to be completed (12.4.2, 16.5.1.7)

amerikar	American
amets	dream
amets egin	to dream
ametz	Pyrenean (muricated) oak
amodio	love
amona	grandmother (2.3.2)
amore eman	to give in, to yield
amorratu	furious, rabid, mad; to be angry
anai(a)	brother (3.10)
andre	lady
andregai	fiancée
anitz	many, much (2.1.4, 2.3.2, 9.4, 11.2.1, 26.4.2)
antz	likeness
antzeman	to notice, to guess
apaiz	priest
apika	perhaps (11.4)
apiril(a)	April
apo	toad
apur bat	a little, a bit (2.3.2, 11.2.3, 26.4.2)
ar	male
aran	plum
arau	rule, norm
arazo	problem, issue
ardi	sheep
ardo	wine (31.2.2)
ardura	care, responsibility; often (in the north, 20.1.2.2)
argal	weak
argazki	photograph
argi	light, daylight, brightness; clear, bright (18.2.2, 31.2.2)
ari izan	being engaged in some activity or process (16.5.1, 16.5.1.1, 27.3, 31.3.1.1)
arima	soul
aritu	to be occupied, to be working
arma	weapon
arnasa	breath
aro	period of time (32.3.1)
arrain	fish (31.2.2)
arrantzale	fisherman
arras	totally, very (11.2.1)
arratoi	rat

arrats	evening (20.1.2.1)
arratsalde	afternoon (20.1.2.1)
arrazoi	reason
arrazoi *edun	to be right
arre	gray, muddy color
arreba	sister (of a man; 3.10)
arren	for goodness' sake, please (22.3.4)
arrisku	danger
arriskutsu	dangerous
arrosa	rose
arrotz	stranger
arte	gap, interval, stretch (4.1.3.6, 4.2, 4.3, 20.1.1, 20.4, 20.4.5, 21.4.2)
aski	enough (2.3.2, 11.2.3)
asko	much, many (2.3.2, 7.4.2, 9.4, 11.2.1, 26.4.1–2, 26.4.5, 26.5.1, 26.6.1, 26.6.3)
askotan	many times, often
asmatu	to invent, to imagine (12.1.4, 12.1.9)
asmo	intention, plan (14.2, 14.4.3, 29.2)
aspaldi	long ago (20.1.2.1)
aspalditik	since long, for a long time
aspergarri	boring, annoying
aspertu	to get bored, to get fed up; to bore (12.1.11, 27.10.4)
astakeria	stupid action, stupidity, nonsense
aste	week (20.1.3, 31.2.2)
astearte	Tuesday
asteazken	Wednesday (31.2.4.1)
astelehen	Monday
asto	donkey, ass
ate	door, gate (4.1.3.2)
atera	to go outdoors, to go out, to come out, to result, to take out (12.4.3)
atorra	shirt, blouse
atrebitu	to dare (16.5.5.4)
atsegin	pleasure; nice (14.1)
atso	old hag
atze	rear, backside, back part (4.1.2)
atzerritar	foreigner, foreign
atzo	yesterday (20.1.2.1)
aukera	choice, opportunity
aukeratu	to choose, to elect (17.8.1)
aurka	against (30.2.2.2)

aurkeztu	to present, to introduce
aurkitu	to find (16.7.2)
aurre	front, frontside, front part (4.1.2, 20.4, 20.4.1)
aurten	this year (20.1.2.1)
ausardia	intrepidity
ausartu	to dare (16.5.5.4)
auzi	trial, lawsuit, issue
auzo	neighbor, neighborhood
auzoko	neighbor, nearby
axola	care, concern
azaldu	to explain, to appear, to show up, to come out
azaro(a)	November
azkar	strong, fast, quickly; clever, smart
azken	end (noun); last (2.1.2)
azkenean	in the end, finally
azpi	bottom, lower part (4.1.3.1)
aztal	calf (body part), heel
aztertu	to examine
azti	diviner, wizard
ba (bada)	(affirmative particle) well, well then, then (8.3–4, 8.6.1, 23.6.2)
bai	yes (18.2.3, 30.1.2)
baimen	permission, consent
baina	but (30.1.1)
baita	also
baizik	but
bakan	rare, uncommon, seldom (20.1.2.2)
bakar	alone, unique
bakarrik	alone
bakartasun	solitude
bake	peace
bakoitz	each
baliatu	to utilize, to use (27.10.1)
balio	value, worth (14.2)
baratza/e	garden
barau egin	to fast
barkatu	to forgive, to pardon
barre	laughter, laugh
barre egin	to laugh (2.3.2, 16.2.1)
barren	inside, inner part, interior (4.1.3.2)
barru	inside, inner part, interior; within (4.1.3.2, 20.1.3)

bart	last night (7.3.2, 20.1.2.1)
basamortu	desert
baserri	farm, farmhouse (31.2.4.1)
baserritar	farmer
baso	drinking glass; wilderness, forest
bat	one (1.3.1–2, 2.3.2, 19.1.8, 28.1.1)
batera	together, jointly, simultaneously
batez ere	especially, particularly
batzuk	some, a few (2.3.2, 28.1.1, 31.3.1)
bazkaldu	to have lunch
bazkari	main meal, lunch
bazter	corner, edge, margin, fringe (4.1.3.9)
bederatzi	nine
begi	eye (27.1.3, 31.2.2)
begiratu	to look (used with dative)
behar	necessity, need; to need, must (14.2, 14.5, 14.5.1, 17.5.3, 26.4.3, 26.5.2, 27.11.2, 29.2)
beharbada	perhaps (11.4)
behartu	to force
behe	bottom; (lower) floor (3.2)
behi	cow
behin	once, one time (20.1.2.2, 30.1.2)
behin ere . . . (ez)	never, not even once (28.1.5.4)
behin eta berriro	once and again, repeatedly
behintzat	at least
bekaitz	envy
bekatu	sin
belar	grass, herb
belarri	ear (27.1.3)
belaun	knee
beldur	fear (2.3.2, 18.8.1, 25.6)
beldurgarri	dreadful, frightful
beltz	black
benetan	really, for real, truly, truthfully
ber(a)	same (6.1.5, 28.2)
berandu	late, too late
beraz	thus, so, therefore, by the same token (23.6.1–2)
berde	green
bere	his/her/its (6.1.5, 15.7)
berehala	at once, immediately, forthwith (20.6)

beribil	car, automobile
bero	hot, warm; heat, warmth (25.6)
berri	new; news (25.4, 31.3.3)
berriketa	chatter, gossip, talk, twaddle
berriz	again, once more, on the contrary, on the other hand
bertsolari	troubadour, improvising poet-singer (33.1.4)
besarkatu	to embrace, to hug
beso	arm
beste	other (11.5, 20.3, 27.8)
bestela	otherwise (11.6)
bete	to fill, to fulfill; full, filled, fullness (12.4.2, 27.1.2)
beti	always (20.1.2.2, 26.4.8)
bezero	customer
bi	two
bidaia	journey, voyage
bidaldi	trip
bidali	to send (12.1.3, 16.7.3.2)
bide	way, road (8.1.3, 32.3.2)
bidesari	road toll
bihar	tomorrow (20.1.2.1)
biharamun	next day, hangover (20.1.3, 20.6)
bihi	grain
bihotz	heart
bihotzez	with the heart, sincerely, cordially (27.1.5)
bihozti	affectionate
bihurtu	to turn into, to return, to become (12.4.2–3)
bikain	excellent
bilatu	to look for, to seek
bildots	lamb
bildu	to collect
bilera	gathering, assembly, reunion, meeting
birao	curse, blasphemy
birao egin	to curse
bistan egon	to be obvious (18.2.2)
bitxi	jewel; strange, eccentric, very beautiful (18.2.2)
bizar	beard
bizi	life
bizi izan	to live (2.3.2, 7.6)
biziki	very (11.2.1, 26.4.2)
bizirik	alive

biziro	keenly, greatly, very much (11.2.1)
bizitza	life, existence; floor, story (2.1.2)
bizkaitar	Biscayan
borobil	round
bost	five
brontze	bronze
bukatu	to finish, to end (16.5.1.7)
burdina	iron (31.2.2)
buru	head (4.1.3.11, 15.7, 15.9.1)
da	(he, she, it) is
damu	regret (14.1)
dantza	dance
deabru	devil
dei	call
dei egin	to call, to invite
deitu	to call, to name, to invite
dena	all, everything (10.4, 28.3)
denak	everyone (10.4, 28.3)
desagertu	to disappear
desegin	to undo, to destroy (12.4.2)
deus	anything, something (13.1.1, 28.1.5.1)
dira	(they) are
diru	money (31.2.2)
doi	precise, sufficient (2.3.2)
donostiar	(native) of Donostia (San Sebastian)
droga	drug
duda	doubt (31.3.1.1)
edan	to drink (12.1.5)
edari	drink, beverage
eder	beautiful, fine
ederki	fine, nicely, very well (25.5.2)
edo	or, about, or so (28.1.7, 31.3.1.1, chap. 30)
edozein	ány ... whatsoever (2.3.2, 28.1.2)
eduki	to hold, to contain, to have (9.1, 9.3.1, 10.1, 17.8.2, 22.2.2, 22.4.2, 24.8, 25.2.1–2, 27.3, 29.1.3)
*edun	to have (transitive of *izan*) (2.3.2, 7.1.3, 9.1, 9.3.1, 10.1, 10.3.1–2, 13.4, 13.4.2, chap. 14, 15.3.2, 17.2.2–4, 17.8.2, 19.8, 20.1.4–5, 21.2.2, 22.2, 22.2.4, 22.4.4, 24.1, 24.1.2–4, 24.4.2, 24.8, 25.2.1, 26.4.3, 26.5.2, 28.4, 28.4.1, 29.1.3–4, 29.1.6–7, 30.2.3)

egarri	thirst (25.6)
egia	truth
egiazki	really, truly
egiaztatu	to verify
egile	maker, author (12.6.1, 16.9)
egin	to do, to make, to accomplish (2.3.2, 7.1.3, 8.6.1, 9.1, 9.3.2, 10.1, 12.1.4, 12.1.7, 12.4.2, chap. 13, 22.2.2, 22.4.2, 27.1.2)
eginbide	duty, obligation
egon	to be situated, to stay (6.2.2–3, 7.5, 15.1, 16.5.1.2, 17.2.2–4, 18.8.2, 22.2.1, 22.4.1, 24.4.3, 24.8, 25.1.4, 25.2.1–2, 25.5.1, 25.6, 27.3, 29.1.2.1)
eguerdi	noon, midday (4.2)
egun	day (7.3.2, 20.1.1–3, 31.2.1)
egunkari	newspaper, diary
egur	firewood
eguraldi	weather
eguzki	sun
ekain(a)	June
ekarri	to bring (9.1, 10.1, 16.7.3.2, 29.1.3)
ekin	to tackle, to apply oneself, to begin, to take up (15.6.2, 22.2.1)
eliza	church (31.2.2)
elkar	each other (15.8.1)
elkartu	to join, to unite, to gather together
elur	snow
emakune	woman
eman	to give (2.3.2, 12.1.3, 13.4, 15.6.1–6, 16.7.1, 16.7.3.1, 17.8.2, 22.2.2, 22.4.4)
emazte	wife
eme	female
entzun	to hear, to listen (9.1, 9.3.2, 10.1, 12.1.10, 16.1, 16.7.2, 22.2.2, 22.4.2)
epaitu	to judge
era	manner, appearance, way (26.9.1)
erabili	to use, to handle, to treat, to stir (9.1, 9.3.1, 10.1, 16.1, 29.1.3)
eragozpen	obstacle
erakarri	to cause to be brought, to attract (9.1, 9.3.1, 10.1, 16.1)
erakutsi	to show, to exhibit, to teach (9.1, 10.1, 16.1, 16.7.1, 22.2.2)
eraman	to carry (off), to lead, to bear (9.1, 9.3.1, 10.1, 16.1, 29.1.3)
erantsi	to add, to stick on
erantzun	response, reply; to answer (12.1.7, 16.1)

eraztun	ring
erbi	hare (31.2.2)
erdara	language other than Basque, Spanish, French (27.1.5)
erdi	half; middle, center (4.1.3.7, 4.2, 26.7, 31.3.1.1, 32.5.3)
ere	also, even, too, either (1.3.3, 17.6, 26.4.6, 28.1.5.5)
eri	sick, ill; sickness
erle	bee
eroan	to carry, to drive, to bear (9.1, 9.3.1, 10.1, 16.1, 29.1.3)
erogarri	maddening
erori	to fall, to fall down, to fall out
erosi	to buy (12.1.3, 16.1, 22.2.2, 22.4.2)
eroso	comfortable, smooth
erotu	to turn crazy
erraz	easy, easily (16.4.2–3, 24.10.4)
erre	to smoke, to burn, to roast (12.1.5, 12.4.2)
errege	king (2.3.2)
errenta	rent, income
errota	mill
erruki	pity, compassion (14.1–2)
ertz	edge, hem, margin, fringe (4.1.3.9)
esan	word, saying; to say, to tell (10.3.2, 12.1.7, 22.2.2, 22.4.2, 31.3.1.1)
esan nahi	to mean
esanahi	meaning
eseri	to sit, to sit down (12.4.3)
eskaini	to offer
eskale	beggar
eskas	meager, inadequate, scarce, deficient (2.3.2, 11.1.4, 13.5.1)
eskatu	to ask (for), to request, to urge (12.1.6)
esker	thanks
esklabo/u	slave (also *jopu*)
esku	hand (27.1.3)
eskuargi	flashlight (31.2.4.1)
eskuin	right side, right hand; right-handed (4.1.3.10)
eskutitz	letter (31.2.3)
esnatu	to wake up (12.4.2)
esne	milk (in certain dialects: *ezne*)
estali	to cover (12.4.2, 27.1.2)
eta	and (20.6, 26.4.8–9, 26.5.3, chap. 30, 31.3.1.1)
etengabe	continuous, ceaseless (20.1.2.2)
etorri	to come (6.2.2, 16.5.5.2, 16.6.2, 22.2.1, 22.4.1, 24.4.3, 29.1.2)

etsai	enemy
etsi	to give up, to desist, to find, to consider (17.8.2, 31.3.2.3)
etxe	house
etxeko	member of the household
etzan	to lie down (6.2.2, 12.4.3, 22.2.1, 22.4.1, 29.1.2)
euri	rain
Euskal Herria	the Basque Country
euskara	Basque language (27.1.5)
ez	no, not, lack (chap. 8, 24.3, 28.1.5.4, 30.1.2, 31.3.1.1)
ez . . . inoiz	never
ezagun	acquaintance; obvious, well-known (18.2.2)
ezagutu	to recognize, to acknowledge (9.1, 9.3.2, 10.1, 12.1.9, 12.5.3, 17.8.1, 18.2.2, 22.2.2)
ezbehar	disaster, misfortune
ezer	anything, something (2.3.2, 3.4, 13.1.1, 28.1.3, 28.1.5.1)
ezin	unable, impossible; impossibility; inability (24.1, 24.3, 24.6, 24.6.2, 24.6.4–6, 24.10.1–2, 26.4.7)
ezker	left side, left hand; left-handed (4.1.3.10)
ezkertiar	leftist
ezkondu	to get married, to marry (off)
ezpata	sword
ezti	honey, sweet
eztul	cough
eztul egin	to cough
faborez	please (22.3.4)
falta	lack, fault, mistake (13.5.1, 14.2)
fede	trust; faith, religion; confidence
ferekatu	caress
feria	fair, market
franko	quite a few, enough (2.3.2, 9.4, 11.2.3)
froga	proof
fruitu	fruit
gabe	without (13.5–6, 25.5.1, 27.11.4, 30.2.2.2)
gabon	night, evening
gai	material, matter, subject (11.7, 24.9.2, 27.2)
gain	top, upper part, surface (4.1.3.1, 27.8)
gainera	moreover, besides
gaitz	difficult, evil; illness, fault, ailment, calamity (16.4.2, 24.10.3, 31.3.3)
gaixo (gaiso)	poor, unfortunate, miserable, ill(ness), sick(ness)

gaizki	bad, evil; badly (25.5.2)
gaizkile	criminal, evildoer
gaiztakeria	evil action, misdeed, evil
galburu	ear, kernel
galdegin	to ask (also: *galde egin*)
galdetu	to ask (18.1.6)
galdu	to lose, to lose (all senses), to get lost (12.4.2)
garau	grain, seed (31.2.2)
garbi	clean, pure
garbitu	to clean, to wash, to wipe out
garesti	expensive
gari	wheat
garrasi egin	to yell
gau	night (3.2, 20.1.2–3)
gauerdi	midnight
gauero	every night
gauez	by night
gaur	today (20.1.2.1)
gauza	thing, matter (24.9.1)
gazta	cheese (31.2.2)
gaztaina	chestnut
gazte	young, youngster
gaztelu	castle
gehiago	(comparative of *asko*) more, some more, any more (2.3.2, 26.4.1, 26.4.5)
gehiegi	(excessive of *asko*) too much, too many (2.3.2, 26.6.1, 26.6.3)
gela	room
gelditu	to stay, to remain, to stop, to end up (12.4.3, 25.6)
geratu	to remain, to stop, to end up
gerla	war (also: *gerra*)
gero	later, after, afterward (20.1.2.1, 20.2.6, 20.6, 22.3.5, 26.4.4, 26.4.8)
gerri	waist
gertatu	to happen, to chance to be
gezur	lie, falsehood
gezurti	mendacious, liar
giltza	key
gipuzkoar	Guipuzcoan
gizarte	society
gizen	fat
gizon	man

gogaikarri	boring, annoying
gogo	mind, appetite, fancy, liking, desire (14.4.1)
gogo *edun	to be eager, to feel like, to intend (14.2, 14.4.2, 29.2)
gogoz	willingly, gladly, with pleasure
goi	above, top; elevated (3.2)
goiz	morning, early (20.1.2.1)
gona	skirt
gora	up, upstairs, long live! (3.2, 27.8)
gorputz	body
gorri	red
gorrotatu	to hate
gorroto	hatred, hate (13.4.2, 14.1–2)
gorroto izan	to hate
gosaldu	to have breakfast (12.1.5)
gosari	breakfast
gose	hunger (25.6, 31.2.2)
goxo	nice and sweet, tasty, delicious (1.2.5)
gozo	sweet, nice, soft (1.2.5)
grina	passion
gu	we
gudu	battle, war
guraso	parent
gurdi	coach, cart, wagon
gure	our, my
gurutze	cross
gustatu	to please, to like
gutxi	few (1.2.5, 2.3.2, 4.2, 7.4.2, 9.4, 11.3, 26.6.3, 28.1.5.2)
gutxiago	less
gutxitan	few times, rarely, seldom
guzti	all (10.5, 28.3, 32.1.1)
guztiz	wholly, intensely, very (11.2.1)
haiek	those (9.6.1, 28.2.6)
hainbeste	so many (2.3.2)
haize	wind
hala	thus, in thàt (yon) way (11.1.6)
hala ere (= halere)	even so (23.7.6)
hamar	ten
han	there (far off), over there (6.3.1, 28.2.6)
handi (haundi)	big, large, great (31.3.1.1)

handitu	to get big, to grow up
hanka	leg
har	worm
haragi	meat, flesh
harakin	butcher
harakintza	butchery, massacre
haran	valley
harategi	butcher shop
harrapatu	to catch (16.7.2)
harri	stone, rock
harrigarri	astonishing, amazing, surprising, astounding
harritu	to be surprised, to be astonished, to astonish (12.1.11, 18.2, 27.10.4)
hartu	to take, to receive, to get (2.3.2, 12.1.3, 13.4.1, 17.8.2, 31.3.2.3)
hartz	bear
haserre	anger; angry (25.5.1)
haserretu	to get angry, to make angry (12.1.11)
hasi	to begin (16.5.1.6, 16.6.2, 31.3.1.1)
hau	this (9.6, 19.1.8, 28.2.6)
hauek	these (9.6, 28.2.6)
haur	child
haurkeria	puerility, childish way
hauts	ash, ashes, dust
hautsi	to break (12.4.2, 31.3.1.1)
heldu	to arrive, to ripen (16.5.5.2)
hemen	here (6.3.1, 28.2.6)
herenegun	(on) the day before yesterday (20.1.2.1)
heriotza/e	death
herra	rancor, resentment, hate
herri	country, town, village; people, nation, population
herrixka	hamlet
hezur	bone
hi	you ("familiar" sing.) (6.1.2, 9.1, 29.1.1)
hil	to die, to kill (12.4.2)
hil	month (20.1.3)
hilabete	month (20.1.3–4)
hilondoko	(last) will, testament
hiri	city, town (31.2.2)
hiru(r)	three (2.3.2)
hitz	word (25.8.1, 31.3.1.1)
hitzeman	to promise

hizketa	speech, talk, conversation
hizkuntza	language (25.8.1, 31.2.2)
hiztun	speaker
hobe	better (comparative of *on*), to be preferable (26.4.1–2, 29.2)
hobeki	better (comparative of *ongi*) (26.4.1–2)
hobeto	better (comparative of *ondo*) (26.4.1–2)
hodei	cloud
hogei	twenty
hondamen(di)	ruin, destruction
hondatu	to squander, to ruin, to collapse (12.1.5, 12.4.2)
hor	there (nearby) (6.3.1, 28.2.6)
hori	yellow
hori	that (9.6.1, 19.1.8, 28.2.6)
horiek	those (9.6.1, 28.2.6)
horma	ice, wall
hosto	leaf
hots	sound, noise; that is, in other words
hotz	cold; coldness (25.6)
hura	that (far off) (9.6.1, 28.2.6)
huts	void, emptiness, mistake, zero; empty, pure
ia	almost, nearly (11.3)
iaz (or igaz)	last year (20.1.2.1)
ibai	river
ibar	valley
ibili	to walk, to hang out, to act, to function (6.2.2, 16.5.1, 16.5.1.3, 22.2.1, 22.4.1, 24.4.3, 25.5.1, 25.6, 27.3, 28.4, 29.1.2, 31.3.1.1)
idatzi	to write (12.1.4, 12.1.7)
idazlan	article, essay
idazle	writer
igan	to ascend
igande	Sunday
igaro	to pass, to pass by, to cross, to spend time (16.1)
igo	to go up, to rise, to climb (12.4.3)
igurtzi	to rub, to pat
ihes egin	to flee (16.2.1)
ijito	gypsy
ikara	trembling, shiver, tremor; fright, scare
ikaragarri	terrible, terrifying, horribly (11.2.1)
ikaratu	to tremble with fear

ikasgai	lesson (31.2.4)
ikasi	to learn, to study (12.1.9, 28.4.1)
ikasketa	studying, study
ikasle	student
ikastola	Basque school
ikatz	coal
ikusi	to see, to view, to visit (9.1, 9.3.2, 10.1, 12.1.10, 12.5.3, 16.7.2, 28.4.1)
ikuskizun	sight, spectacle
ilargi	moon
ile	hair
ilun	dark, obscure; darkness (25.5.1)
ilunabar	sundown, dusk
indar	power, strength, force
ingeles	English, Englishman
inguratu	to surround (27.1.2, 31.3.1.1)
inguru	periphery, vicinity, environs, about (4.1.3.5, 4.2, 26.7)
inoiz	ever (20.1.2.2, 26.5.2)
inoiz . . . ez	never (20.1.2.2)
inon	anywhere
inor	anyone, anybody, someone, somebody (2.3.2, 13.1.1, 28.1.3, 28.1.5.6)
interesgarri	interesting
intsusa	elder tree (*Sambucus nigia*)
*ion	to say (9.1, 9.3.1, 10.1, 10.3.2, 12.1.7, 15.4.2, 22.2.2, 22.4.2, 29.1.3)
Iparralde	Northern Region of the Basque Country
ipuin	tale, story
irabazi	to earn, to win; earnings
iragan	to pass, to go through, to spend time (16.1)
irail(a)	September
irakasle	teacher
irakatsi	to teach (12.1.9, 16.1, 16.7.1, 22.2.2, 22.4.2)
irakin	to boil (9.1, 10.1, 12.2.1, 16.1)
irakurle	reader
irakurri	to read (12.1.7)
iraun	to last, to endure (9.1, 9.3.2, 10.1, 12.2.1)
ireki	to open
irentsi	to swallow (12.1.5)
iritsi	to arrive, to reach (16.1, 16.5.5.2)
iritzi	opinion; to deem (15.4.1, 22.2.2)

irla	island
irri	laugh
irribarre	smile
irribarre egin	to smile
irten	to go out, to exit, to leave
irudi	image, picture, statue; to resemble, to seem (transitive) (9.1, 9.3.1, 10.1, 10.3.2, 18.5.2)
isil	silent, quiet (31.3.1.1)
ispilu	mirror, reflection
itsaso	sea
itsu	blind
itsuki	blindly
itsusi	ugly
iturri	fountain, source
itxaropen	hope, expectation
itxi	to close
itxura	appearance
itzal	shadow, shade, respect
itzuli	to return, to go back, to come back (12.4.3)
itzulpen	translation
ixo	quiet!
izan	to be, to exist, to have (1.3.3, 2.3.2, 6.2.2–3, 7.1.3, 7.5, 15.3.1, 17.2.2–4, 17.3.2, 20.1.4–5, 21.2.1, 22.2, 22.2.1, 22.4.3, 24.1, 24.1.2–4, 24.4.1, 24.6.1–2, 24.8, 25.1.1, 25.1.4, 26.6.3, 28.1.1, 28.4, 28.4.1, 29.1.2, 29.1.4–7, 30.2.3)
izar	star
izeba	aunt
izen	name
izendatu	to designate
izerdi	sweat
izpiritu	spirit
izter	thigh
izu	fright
izugarri	frightful, terrible, terribly (11.2.1, 26.4.2)
izugarrizko	terribly
izutu	to be frightened, to frighten (12.1.11)
jabe	owner (27.10.2)
jai	festivity, holiday, celebration
jaiki	to get up, to rise, to rise up (12.4.3)

Jainko(a)	God (2.3.2)
jaio	to be born
jaitsi	to go down, to come down, to descend (12.4.3)
jakin	to know (9.1, 9.3.1, 10.1, 10.3.2, 12.1.9, 16.5.2, 18.2.2, 22.2.2, 22.4.2, 29.1.3)
jakina	of course, naturally
jakintsu	learned, knowledgeable, clever, wise
jan	to eat (12.1.5)
jantzi	clothing, dress, suit; to dress, to put on clothes (12.4.2, 27.1.2)
jardun	to be busy with, to engage in (9.1, 10.1, 12.2.1, 16.5.1.4, 22.2.2, 29.1.3)
jario	to flow (15.2.2, 22.4.1)
jarraitu	to follow, to continue (12.2.1, 15.2.1, 16.5.1.5, 22.2.1, 22.4.1, 29.1.2)
jarri	to sit down, to put, to set (12.4.3, 18.2.2, 27.3)
jaso	to lift, to receive, to get (12.4.3)
jatetxe	restaurant
jaun	gentleman, sir, lord, the Lord (*Jauna*) (2.3.2, 31.2.1)
Jaungoiko(a)	God (2.3.2)
jauregi	palace
jausi	to fall
jauzi	to jump
jende	folk, people (singular noun)
jo	to hit, to strike, to beat (12.1.1, 17.8.2, 31.3.2.3)
joan	to go (6.2.2, 16.5.6, 16.6.2, 22.2.1, 22.4.1, 24.4.3, 27.11.3, 29.1.2)
joera	inclination, trend
jokaera	conduct, behavior
jokatu	to play, to gamble
joko	game, play
jolas	play, game
jolas egin	to play
josi	to sew, to overwhelm (27.1.2)
jostatu	to have fun, to play
kafe	coffee
kale	street
kalte	harm, damage
kalte egin	to do harm, to harm
kamioi	truck
kanpo	outside, exterior (4.1.3.2, 27.8)
kantatu	to sing (12.1.7)

kapitulu	chapter
katu	cat
ke	smoke
keinu	gesture
kemen	energy, vigor
kendu	to take away, to avert (12.1.3)
kezka	worry
kezkatu	to worry (12.1.11, 27.10.4)
koipe	grease
kolko	bosom, chest
kolpatu	to beat, to hit
komeni	fitting, suitable
kondenatu	to condemn
konpondu	to fix, to repair, to manage (12.1.1)
konponketa	repair
kontatu	to tell, to count (12.1.7)
kontra	against (2.2.2, 4.1.3.11, 30.2.2.2)
kontrabando	smuggling
konturatu	to realize (12.1.10, 27.10.2)
kontuz!	watch out! look out! attention!
korbata	tie
krabelin	carnation
kriseilu	oil lamp
laboratu	to work, to elaborate
labur	short
lagun	companion, mate
lagunarte	society, company
lagundu	to help, to accompany (16.7.1)
laino	fog, mist, cloud
lan	work
lan egin	to work
lanbide	profession, occupation
langile	worker, workman (16.9)
lantegi	workshop, factory
lapur	thief, robber
lapurtu	to steal (12.1.3)
larri	big, grave, serious, urgent
larru	skin, hide, leather
larunbat	Saturday

lasai	peacefully, comfortably (25.5.1)
laster	fast, quick, quickly, soon (20.6, 26.2)
lasto	straw
latz	rough, harsh
lau	plain, plane, flat
lau(r)	four (2.3.2)
lege	law
lehen	first, formerly, earlier, before, at first (20.1.2.1, 26.4.4)
lehenago	formerly, previously, before (26.4.4)
lehenbailehen	as soon as possible
lehenbizi	at first, initially
lehendakari	president
lehia	diligence, haste
lehor	dry
lehortu	to dry
leial	loyal
leiho	window
leize	abyss, chasm, gorge
leku	place, spot, location, site, post
lekuko	witness
lepo	neck
libera	franc
liburu	book
liburudenda	bookstore
liburutegi	library
lili	lily, flower
liluragarri	fascinating, enchanting
lirain	graceful, svelte
liskar	quarrel
lo	sleep, asleep (25.5.1)
lo egin	to sleep (16.2.1)
lodi	thick, bulky, fat
lohi	mud
lore	flower
lotsa	shame
lotsagarri	shameful
lotsati	bashful, shy, timid
lotsatu	to be ashamed, to embarrass (12.1.11, 27.10.4)
lotu	to bind, to connect, to attach (12.1.1)
lotura	tie, link, connection

lur	earth, ground, soil
lurralde	land, territory, region
luzapen	delay, deferment
luzaro	for a long time, long (20.1.2.3)
luzaroan	for a long time
luze	long
madarikatu	accursed; to curse
mahai	table
mahats	grape
mahuka	sleeve
maiatz(a)	May
maila	degree, level
mailu	hammer
maisu	teacher, expert
maitagarri	lovable, lovely, fairy
maitasun	love
maitatu	to love (12.5.3)
maite	dear, beloved (14.1–2, 26.4.3, 26.5.2, 31.3.2.1)
maitemindu	to fall in love (27.10.2)
maiz	often (20.1.2.2)
makal	spineless, weak, cowardly
makila	cane, stick
makina bat	a great deal of, a lot of (2.3.2)
maleta	suitcase
malko	tear (from the eye)
malmutz	sly
mami	substance, curd(s)
mando	mule
martxo(a)	March
mehe	thin
mendi	mountain, hill
merezi	to deserve (14.2)
merke	cheap
mesede	favor
mesedez	please (22.3.4)
meza	mass
mihi	tongue (also *mingain*) (27.1.3)
min	pain; dear, intimate
mintzatu	to speak, to talk (27.10.1)
minutu	minute

miresgarri	admirable, wonderful, marvelous
modu	manner
moja	nun
moldatu	to form (12.1.4, 27.1.2)
mordo	bunch, group
more	purple
morroi	servant, farmhand (25.8.2, 31.2.2, 31.3.1)
motel	dull, tasteless, insipid; motel
motz	short
muga	limit, border
muin	medula, (bone) marrow
mundu	world
musika	music
musu	kiss
mutiko	boy, lad
mutil	boy, fellow, guy
nabar	piebald, grey
nagi	lazy
nagusi	boss
nahi	will, wish; to want (14.2, 14.3, 21.3.1, 26.5.2, 27.11.2, 28.1.8.1–2, 29.2)
nahigabe	distress, sorrow, suffering
nahigabetu	to distress (12.1.11, 27.10.4)
nahikoa	enough (2.3.2, 11.2.3)
narras	shabby
nazkatu	to be disgusted
negar	crying, tears, weeping
negar egin	to cry, to weep (16.2.1, 27.9.1)
negu	winter
nekarazi	to tire out, to disturb
neke	effort, tiredness, toil (16.4.2)
neska	girl, maiden
neskame	housemaid, female servant (31.2.2)
neskatxa	young girl
neurri	measure, size
ni	I
nire	my
noiz	when (18.1.1, 20.1.1)
noizbait	ever, at some time (28.1.6.4)
nola	how (18.1.1, 18.1.4)

nolabait	somehow (28.1.6.5)
non	where (18.1.1, 18.1.3)
nonbait	somewhere, apparently (28.1.6.3)
nor	who (2.3.2, 28.1.1)
norabide	direction, address
norbait	somebody (2.3.2, 13.1.1, 28.1.3)
odol	blood
ogi	bread, loaf of bread (31.2.2)
ogibide	livelihood, occupation, trade
ohar	observation, remark
ohartu	to notice (12.1.10, 27.10.2)
ohe	bed
ohitura	custom, habit
ohoin	thief
ohol	plank, board
oihal	cloth, fabric, curtain
oihan	forest
oihu	shout, scream
oihu egin	to shout
oilategi	chicken coop
oilo	chicken
oin	foot
okin	baker
okindegi	bakery (16.9)
oldar	impulse
olerkari	poet
omen	repute, rumor (8.1.2)
on	good; goodness, goods (2.3.2, 26.4.1, 26.5.1)
onartu	to approve, to agree, to accept (31.3.2.3)
ondo	well, good (25.5.2, 26.5.1)
ondo	proximity, nearness, contiguity, adjacency, succession (4.1.3.4, 20.4.3, 31.2.3)
ongi	well, good (25.5.2, 26.5.1)
ontzat hartu	to take well, to approve, to accept
ontzi	vessel, container, ship, boat
opa	wish, to wish (14.1, 15.1, 21.3.1)
orain	now (20.1.2.1)
ordaindu	to compensate, to pay (12.1.3)
ordea	however
ordez	instead

ordu	hour, time (4.2, 20.1.3, 20.2)
ordu erdi	half hour (4.2)
ordu laurden	quarter of an hour (4.2)
orduan	then, at that time, in that case (26.4.9)
orga	cart
oro	all (28.3)
oroipen	recollection, souvenir
oroitzapen	recollection, souvenir
osaba	uncle (2.3.2)
osasun	health
oski	shoe
oso	whole, very (11.2.1, 26.4.2)
ospe	fame
ostatu	hotel, inn
ostegun	Thursday
ostera	again
ostiral	Friday
ostu	to steal (12.1.3)
otoitz	prayer (22.3.4)
otoitz egin	to pray
otordu	meal
otsail(a)	February
otso	wolf
pagatu	to pay (12.1.3)
pago	beech tree
paper	paper
pare	pair, counterpart, equal, opposite side (4.1.3.8, 26.1.6)
pena	sorrow
pentsatu	to think (12.1.8)
pila/o	pile, heap
pinu	pine
piper	pepper
pixka bat	a little, a bit (2.3.2, 11.2.3, 26.4.2)
plater	plate, dish
plazer	pleasure (22.3.4)
polit	pretty
portatu	to behave
poz	joy
pozoi(n)	poison
poztu	to be glad, to rejoice, to cheer up, to delight (12.1.11, 18.2, 27.10.4)

praka(k)	pants, trousers
premia	need
prestu	noble, honest
prezio	price
sabel	belly
sagar	apple
sagardo	cider (31.2.5)
sagu	mouse
sahats	willow
saiatu	to try, to attempt (12.1.6)
sakon	deep, profound
sakondu	to deepen, to delve into
sakristau	sexton
salatu	to betray, to denounce (12.1.7)
salbatu	to save
saldu	to sell (12.1.3)
salgai	merchandise, object for sale
saltsa	sauce (31.3.1.1)
samar	somewhat (11.2.3)
santu	holy
sarde	pitchfork
sari	reward, prize
sarri	often, soon (20.1.2.2)
sarritan	often
sartu	to come in, to go in, to enter (12.4.3)
sats	muck, filth
sei	six
sekula	ever (20.1.2.2)
sekula . . . ez	never (20.1.2.2, 28.1.5.4)
seme	son
senar	husband
senar-emazteak	the couple
senargai	fiancé
sendagile	doctor, physician (16.9)
sendatu	to heal, to cure, to get well
sendo	robust, healthy, strong (7.4.2, 25.5.1)
senide	relative, sibling
sentimen	emotion
sentipen	feeling
sentitu	to feel (12.1.10)

seta	stubbornness
simaur	manure
sinesmen	faith
sinetsi	to believe
soin	shoulder, body
soinu	sound, music
soka	rope, cord
solastatu	to converse
soldadu	soldier
sorbalda	shoulder
sorgin	witch
sortu	to arise, to conceive, to originate (12.1.4, 12.4.2)
su	fire
su eman	to set fire (to)
su hartu	to catch fire, to get angry
sudur	nose (27.1.3)
sufritu	to suffer (always transitive)
suge	snake
suil	pail, bucket
sukalde	kitchen (31.2.3)
sukar	fever (31.3.2.3)
sumin	irritation
sutsuki	ardently, passionately
taberna	pub, tavern, bar
talde	group
tanta	drop
teilatu	roof
tema	obstinacy
testigu	witness
toki	place, spot
tontor	peak
toxa	pouch
trebe	skillful
tren	train
tresna	tool
tristura	sadness
tuntun	silly, stupid
txahal	calf
txakur	dog

txar	bad
txartel	ticket
txerri	pig (1.2.5)
txiki	small, little (1.2.5)
txindurri	ant
txiro	poor
txit	very (11.2.1, 26.4.2)
txoko	nice little corner
txokolate	chocolate
txori	bird (31.2.2)
txukun	neat, tidy (25.5.1)
uda	summer
udaberri	spring (31.3.3)
udazken	autumn
ugari	abundant (2.3.2)
ulertu	to understand (12.5.3)
ume	kid, child (1.2.5, 31.2.3)
une	moment (20.1.3)
ur	water
urde	male pig
urdin	blue, gray (of hair)
urduri egon	to be nervous
urduri jarri	to make nervous, to become nervous
urduritasun	nervousness
urrats	step, footstep
urre	gold
urri	scant (2.3.2)
urri(a)	October
urruti	far
urtarril(la)	January
urte	year
usain	smell, odor
uso	dove, pigeon
uste	opinion, belief
uste izan/*edun	to believe, to think (so) (2.3.2, 14.2, 18.5.1, 18.8.2, 29.2)
ustel	rotten, putrid, perverse
utzi	to leave, to abandon, to let (12.1.3, 16.3, 22.2.2, 22.4.2, 27.3)
uzta	harvest
uztail(a)	July

xaboi	soap
xede	goal, purpose
xentimo	penny
xoro	silly, foolish (1.2.5)
xume	puny, paltry, common
zabal	wide, broad
zabaldu	to widen, to open
zahar	old (25.4)
zaharo	old age
zail	difficult (16.4.2)
zain egon	to be waiting
zaindu	to guard, to protect
zakar	rough, coarse, harsh
zakur	(big) dog
zalantza	hesitation, doubt (31.3.1.1)
zaldi	horse
zapart egin	to crack, to explode
zapata	shoe
zarata	noise
zati	piece
zaunka egin	to bark
zazpi	seven
zehar	across, through, throughout (4.1.3.2, 20.1.4, 31.3.1.1)
zeharo	exactly, totally, completely (11.2.1)
zehatz	exactly, in detail, precise
zein	which (2.3.2, 3.4, 18.1.1, 18.1.4, 19.5, 26.4.11, 28.1.2)
zen	(he, she, it) was
zenbait	some (3.4, 9.4, 28.1.2, 28.1.6.1)
zenbaki	number, numeral
zenbat	how much, how many (2.1.1, 2.3.2, 3.4, 18.1.1, 18.1.4, 26.4.9)
zer	what (2.3.2, 3.4, 18.1.1, 18.1.4, 28.1.3)
ze(r) moduz	how, in what condition
zerbait	something (2.3.2, 13.1, 28.1.3)
zeren	because (23.5.2–3)
zergatik	why
zerri	pig, swine (31.2.2)
zertako	for what
zeru	sky, heaven (31.2.2)
zezen	bull

zigarro	cigarette
zilar	silver
zin egin	to take an oath
zine	movie theater
zintzilik	hanging
zintzur	throat
ziren	(they) were
zital	vile, nasty, base, infamous
zitara	lyre
zoko	hiding corner, spot (31.3.1.1)
zor	debt (14.1)
zor *edun	to owe (14.2)
zoragarri	enchanting, wonderful, marvelous
zoratu	to turn crazy, to enthrall, to drive wild
zorion	happiness, good luck (31.3.3)
zorionak eman	to congratulate
zoriontsu	happy
zoro	crazy, insane (7.4.2, 31.3.1.1)
zorrotz	sharp
zortzi	eight
zozo	silly, stupid
zu	you (singular) (6.1.2, 9.1)
zubi	bridge
zuek	you (plural) (9.1)
zuen	your (plural)
zuhaitz	tree
zulatu	to perforate (12.1.1)
zulo	hole, den, lair
zur	wood
zure	your (singular)
zuri	white
zutik	standing, upright, erect

B. English-Basque

about that	hartaz
abundant	ugari
abyss, chasm	leize
acquaintance	ezagun
affectionate	bihotzi

afternoon	arratsalde
again, yet	berriz
all, everything	dena, guzti
almost	ia
also, even	ere
always	beti
and	eta
anger	haserre
angel	aingeru
anybody	inor
anymore	gehiago
anything	ezer
apple	sagar
arm	beso
arrive, to	iritsi, heldu
ask, to	galdetu
ask for, to	eskatu
ass, donkey	asto
at least	behintzat
at once	berehala
aunt	izeba
author, maker	egile
back	atze
bad	txar
badly	gaizki
baker	okin
bakery	okindegi
Basque language	euskara
be, to	izan
beautiful	eder
become, to	bihurtu
bed	ohe
behave, to	portatu
believe, to	sinetsi
betray, to	salatu
better	hobe, hobeto
between	arte
big	handi
black	beltz

blood	odol
bone	hezur
book	liburu
bookstore	liburudenda
border	muga
boring, annoying	gogaikarri, aspergarri
born, to be	jaio
boss, master	nagusi
bottom, under	azpi
boy	mutil
bread	ogi
breakfast, to	gosaldu
bridge	zubi
bring, to	ekarri
brother	anai(a)
build, to	jaso, eraiki
but	baina
buy, to	erosi
can't	ezin
car	beribil
carry, bear, to	eraman
castle	gaztelu
cat	katu
catch, to	harrapatu
cheap	merke
child	haur, ume
choose, to	aukeratu
church	eliza
city, town	hiri
clean, pure	garbi
clear, bright	argi
clothing	jantzi
coffee	kafe
cold	hotz
come, to	etorri
come out, go out, to	atera
companion	lagun
companionship, company	lagunarte
compassion	erruki

condemn, to	kondenatu
congratulate, to	zorionak eman
cough, to	eztul egin
cover, to	estali
cow	behi
crazy, to turn	zoratu
criminal, evildoer	gaizkile
cross	gurutze
cry, to	negar egin
danger	arrisku
dare, to	ausartu
dark	ilun
daughter	alaba
day	egun
day before yesterday	herenegun
dear, beloved	maite
debt	zor
deem, to	iritzi
depart, to	abiatu
descend, to	jaitsi
devil	deabru
die, to	hil
difficult	zail
disturb, to	nekarazi
do, make, to	egin
doctor	sendagile
dog	txakur
door	ate
dream	amets
drink, to	edan
dry	lehor
each	bakoitz
each other	elkar
early	goiz
easy, easily	erraz
eat, to	jan
enemy	etsai
enough	aski, nahikoa
enter, to	sartu

ever	inoiz
evil	gaizki
excellent	bikain
expensive	garesti
express, to	adierazi
eye	begi
fabric, cloth	oihal
faith	sinesmen, fede
fall, to	erori, jausi
farmer	baserritar
farm, farmhouse	baserri
fast	laster
father	aita
fear	beldur
feel, to	sentitu
few, little	gutxi
fiancé	senargai
fiancée	andregai
find, to	aurkitu
finish, to	bukatu
fire	su
fish	arrain
fisherman	arrantzale
fitting, suitable	komeni
flashlight, torch (pocket)	eskuargi
flow, to	jario
flower	lore
foot	oin
force, to	behartu
forget, to	ahaztu
forgive, to	barkatu
formerly	lehenago
franc	libera
friend	adiskide
frightful, terrible	izugarri
front	aurre
full	bete
gamble, to	jokatu
get, to	jasu

get up, to	jaiki
girl	neskatxa
give, to	eman
glass (for drinking)	baso
go, to	joan
go up, to	igo
God	Jainko(a), Jaungoiko(a)
gold	urre
good	on, ondo
grandfather	aitona
grandmother	amona
grow up, to	handitu
guard, to	zaindu
gypsy	ijito
hair	ile
hand	esku
happen, to	gertatu
happy	zoriontsu
hate, to	gorrotatu
have, to	eduki, *edun, izan, ukan
head	buru
healthy, robust	sendo
hear, to	entzun
heart	bihotz
help, to	lagundu
here	hemen
hit, to	jo
hold, to	eduki
honey, sweet	ezti
horse	zaldi
hot, warm	bero
hotel, inn	ostatu
hour, time	ordu
house	etxe
housemaid	neskame
how	nola
how much, many	zenbat
however, on the contrary	aldiz
hunger	gose
husband	senar

influence	eragin
inside	barren
intention, plan	asmo
interesting	interresgarri
invite, to	gonbidatu
joy	poz
key	giltza
king	errege
kill, to	hil
kiss	musu
kitchen	sukalde
know, to	jakin
lack, fault	falta
lady	andre
land, territory	lurralde
language	hizkuntza
last night	bart
late, too late	berandu
laugh, to	barre egin
law	lege
lazy	nagi
learn, to	ikasi
leave, to	utzi
left, left-handed	ezker
lesson	ikasgai
letter	eskutitz
liar	gezurti
lie down, to	etzan
life	bizitza
light, daylight	argi
a little, a bit	apur bat, pixka bat
live, to	bizi izan
long	luze
long, for a long time	luzaro
long ago	aspaldi
the Lord	Jauna
lose, to	galdu
lovable	maitagarri
love	maitasun

love, to	maite izan, maitatu
loyal	leial
lunch, to	bazkaldu
maddening	erogarri
man	gizon
many, much, a lot	asko, anitz
married, to get	ezkondu
mayor	alkate
mean, to	esan nahi, esanahi
merchandise	salgai
midnight	gauerdi
milk	esne
mill	errota
mind, fancy	gogo
mirror	ispilu
money	diru
month	hilabete, hil
moon	ilargi
more, some more, any more	gehiago
morning, early	goiz
mother	ama
mountain	mendi
mouse	sagu
mouth	aho
name	izen
nearness	ondo
need, necessity	behar
nervousness	urduritasun
never	inoiz . . . ez, behin ere . . . (ez), sekula . . . ez
new	berri
newspaper, diary	egunkari
night	gau
no, not	ez
now	orain
notice, to	ohartu
obvious, to be	bistan egon
offer, to	eskaini
old	zahar
once, one time	behin

open, to	ireki, zabaldu
or	edo
other, else	beste
otherwise	bestela
outside	kanpo
owner	jabe
pain	min
palace	jauregi
parent	guraso
particularly, especially	batez ere
pass, to	igaro
pay, to	pagatu, ordaindu
pay attention, to	aintzat hartu, aintzakotzat hartu
peace	bake
peacefully	lasai
people (sing.), nation	jende, herri
perhaps, maybe	agian, beharbada
pig	txerri
pity, compassion	erruki
place	leku, toki
plate	plater
please	mesedez, arren, faborez
pretty	polit
priest	apaiz
promise, to	agindu
pub	taberna
quickly, fast, clever	azkar, laster
rabid	amorratu
rare	bakan
rat	arratoi
rather, somewhat	samar
read, to	irakurri
reader	irakurle
realize, to	konturatu
really, truly	benetan, egiazki
reason	arrazoi
recognize, to	ezagutu
red	gorri
rent	errenta

repeatedly	behin eta berriro
repute, rumor	omen
restaurant	jatetxe
return, to	bihurtu, itzuli
reward, prize	sari
rich	aberats
right, right-handed	eskuin
river	ibai
roof	teilatu
rough	latz
save, to	salbatu
say, to	esan, *ion
sea	itsaso
see, to	ikusi
seem, to	irudi
seldom, rarely	gutxitan
self	buru
sell, to	saldu
send, to	bidali
servant	morroi
shadow	itzal
shame	lotsa
sharp	zorrotz
sheep	ardi
shirt, blouse	atorra
shoe	zapata
short	labur
shout, to	oihu egin
silent, quiet	isil
show up, to	azaldu
sick, ill	eri, gaixo
sight, spectacle	ikuskizun
silly, stupid	zozo
sin	bekatu
sir	jaun
sister	ahizpa (of a woman), arreba (of a man)
skillful	trebe
skirt	gona
sleep	lo
sleep, to	lo egin

sleepyhead	lozale
sleeve	mahuka
small, little	txiki
smell, odor	usain
smoke	ke
snow	elur
soldier	soldadu
solitude	bakartasun
some, certain	zenbait
something	zerbait
sometimes	batzuetan
somewhere	nonbait
son	seme
sorrow	pena
speak, to	mintzatu, hitz egin
squander, to	hondatu
star	izar
stay, to	egon, gelditu
steal, to	lapurtu, ostu
story	ipuin
street	kale
student	ikasle
study, studying	ikasketa
suffer, to	sufritu (trans.)
summer	uda
sun	eguzki
Sunday	igande
supper	afari
surprising, astonishing	harrigarri
sweet	gozo
sword	ezpata
table	mahai
take, to	hartu
talk, to	hitz egin, mintzatu
tasty, delicious	goxo
teach, to	irakatsi
teacher	irakasle
tear(s), weeping	negar
then, at that time	orduan
thick	lodi

thief	lapur, ohoin
think, to	pentsatu
time after dinner	afalondo
today	gaur
together, simultaneously	batera
tomorrow	bihar
top	gain
totally, exactly, completely	zeharo
train	tren
truth	egia
try, to	saiatu
ugly	itsusi
uncle	osaba
understand, to	ulertu
until	harik eta
urge, to	eskatu
use, to	erabili, baliatu
very	oso, txit
vile, infamous	zital
village	herri
wake up, to	esnatu
walk, to	ibili
water	ur
way, road	bide
weaken, to	ahuldu
weather	eguraldi
week	aste
well, good	ondo, ongi
what	zer
when	noiz
where	non
which	zein
white	zuri
who	nor
whole	oso, guzti
why	zergatik
widow, widower	alargun
wife	emazte
will, wish	nahi

win, to	irabazi
wind	haize
wine	ardo
winter	negu
witch	sorgin
without	gabe
woman	emakume
wonderful, marvelous	miresgarri, zoragarri
wood	zur
word	hitz
work	lan
work, to	lan egin
workshop, factory	lantegi
world	mundu
worry, to	kezkatu
write, to	idatzi
year	urte
yes	bai
yesterday	atzo
young, youngster	gazte

Bibliography

This bibliography contains two sections: section A is titled "References," and section B is "Sources." The references (that is, scholarly works about the Basque language) are cited in text using an author-date system. For example, S. Altube's *De sintaxis euskérica* is cited as Altube 1920. However, a few works are cited so frequently that, for convenience, they have been given an abbreviation. These are included in the list at the end of this paragraph. The sources (works written in Basque that have been drawn upon for the examples) are cited in the attributions usually by author's name alone if there is only one work from that author used, or by author and title (often abbreviated) if there are several. For example, Gotzon Garate's *Izurri berria* is cited as Garate, *Iz.B.* There are also abbreviations for much-cited works, such as *LBB* for *Lur berri billa*, with a reference to its author Nemesio Etxaniz. These (and the occasional abbreviation of an author's name) are all listed alphabetically in "Sources." Many of the examples are drawn from versions of the Bible, and these citations are described in "A Note on the Biblical Sources," which follows the list of abbreviations.

Abbreviations

ASJU: *Anuario del Seminario de Filología Vasca "Julio de Urguijo"/International Journal of Basque Linguistics and Philology*
ASJU, Supp.: *Supplement to ASJU*
BSLP: *Bulletin de la Société de Linguistique de Paris*
DGV: *Diccionario general vasco*, see Michelena 1987–
DLV: *De lingua vasconum*, see de Rijk 1998
EEE: Euskal Editoreen Elkartea
EGL: *Euskal gramatika laburra*, see Euskaltzaindia 1993
EGLU: *Euskal Grammatika. Lehen Urratsak*, see Euskaltzaindia 1985–1999
FHV: *Fonética histórica vasca*, see Michelena 1977
FLV: *Fontes Linguae Vasconum*
MIT: Massachusetts Institute of Technology, Cambridge, Massachusetts
RIEV: *Revista Internacional de los Estudios Vascos/Revue Internationale des Études Basque*
UPV/EHU: Universidad del País Vasco/Euskal Herriko Unibertsitatea (University of the Basque Country)

[*Note*: Abbreviations used specifically for the example sentences are found in the list of sources (B).]

A Note on the Biblical Sources

1. *The unmarked source*: Unless a particular Bible translation is specifically mentioned in the text as the source, the passage is taken from the *Elizen Arteko Biblia* of 1994. All English translations are de Rijk's.
2. *Other sources*: A number of Bible translations were used, and these are all mentioned in the sources section of the bibliography. Following the chapter and verse numbers, the reader will find mentioned the translation used for that particular reading—for example, Lk 1:6; Dv would mean that the passage is cited from Duvoisin's translation. If a particular reading is found in several of the sources used, all are listed.
3. *List of abbreviations used to indicate the source* (see the bibliography for more details):

a. Unmarked: The 1994 Batua edition of the ecumenical *Elizen Arteko Biblia*.
b. *Biblia*: The ongoing translation into Labourdin by Marcel Etchehandy, Robert Puchulu, et al. De Rijk used four volumes published between 1979 and 1992.

c. Dv: Duvoisin's *Bible Saindua* (1858), a Labourdin version of the Vulgate.
d. *EAB*: The ecumenical New Testament Batua version of 1983 entitled *Itun Berria. Elizen Arteko Biblia.*
e. Etx.: References are to the 2nd edition of 1980 by Pello Salaburu of Bruno Echenique's Baztanese translation of Matthew for Bonaparte (1857).
f. HE: 1990 critical edition by Patxi Altuna of Joannes Haraneder's (ca. 1740) Labourdin New Testament—from the MS copy made by J. Robin.
g. Hualde Mayo: 19th-century translation of Matthew into Roncalese. See under sources.
h. *IB*: *Itun Berria*, the Catholic version of the New Testament in Batua first published in 1980; references are to the 1984 edition.
i. Intx.: Emmanuel Inchauspe's 1856 translation into Souletin of Matthew for Bonaparte.
j. *JKBO*: *Jesu Kristoren Berri Ona*, the modern Labourdin gospel version published in 1974 by the publishing house Ezkila.
k. Ker.: Jaime Kerexeta's 1976 Biscayan translation of the Bible.
l. *Lau Eb.*: *Lau ebanjelioak*, the 1961 Guipuzcoan translation of the four gospels by P. Mendizabal.
m. Lz: The oldest translation of the New Testament is that of the Protestant Joannes Leiçarraga of 1571.
n. Olab.: The Biscayan New Testament (*Itun Berria*) translation of Father Erraimun Olabide from 1931, which was published together with his Old Testament version in 1958.
o. Ur.: Translations from the Vulgate made by José Antonio Uriarte for Bonaparte. References are to his Biscayan translation of Apocalypse (1857); the Guipuzcoan version of the same (1858), and also of Matthew (1858); and the Guipuzcoan version of three Old Testament books (Genesis, Exodus, and Leviticus) published in 1859.
p. Urt.: refers to the oldest (ca. 1700) Old Testament translation, the Labourdin version by Pierre d'Urte of Genesis and part of Exodus from the 1588 Protestant French Geneva Bible.

A. References

Alberdi Larizgoitia, Jabier (1986a). "Euskarazko tratamenduen ikuspegia: I Historia apur bat." *ASJU* 20:149–202.

——— (1986b). "Alokutibotasuna eta tratamenduak euskaraz: II Markinaldeko kasua." *ASJU* 20:419–486.

——— (1995). "The Development of the Basque System of Terms of Address and the Allocutive Conjugation." In J. I. Hualde, J. A. Lakarra, and R. L. Trask (eds.), *Towards a History of the Basque Language*, 275–293. Amsterdam: John Benjamins.

——— (1996). *Euskararen tratamenduak: erabilera. Iker* 9, Bilbao: Euskaltzaindia.

Altube, S. (1920). *De sintaxis euskérica.* San Sebastian.

——— (1929). *Erderismos* (= *Euskera* X, 1–4). Bermeo: Euskaltzaindia. Reprinted in 1975. Bilbao: Indauchu.

Altuna Bengoechea, Francisco M. (1979). *Versificación de Dechepare: Métrica y pronunciación.* Bilbao: Mensajero.

Amundarain Arana, Iñaki (1997). "Juntadura eta elipsia." Doctoral dissertation, UPV/EHU.

Arejita, Adolfo (1985). *Euskal Joskera.* Bilbao: Labayru Ikastegia and Bizkaiko Aurrezki Kutxa. First published in 1978.

——— (1994). "La obra de Juan Antonio Moguel, Vol. I. Gramatica descriptiva de la lengua." Doctoral dissertation, Universidad de Deusto, Bilbao.

Artiagoitia, Xabier (1991). "Aspects of Tenseless Relative Clauses in Basque." *ASJU* 25:697–712.

——— (1992). "Why Basque Doesn't Relativize Everything." In J. A. Lakarra and J. Ortiz de Urbina (eds.), *Syntactic Theory and Basque Syntax. ASJU, Supp.* 27:11–35.

——— (1994). *Verbal Projections in Basque and Minimal Structure. ASJU, Supp.* 36.

——— (1995). "*-Garri* atzizkiaren izaera bikoitzaz: Zergatik den maitagarria bezain mingarria." *ASJU* 29:355–405.

——— (2002). "*-(t)ar* atzizkidun hitzen jokabide sintaktikoaren inguran." *FLV* 34:443–462.

Astarloa, P. P. (1803). *Apología de la lengua bascongada.* Madrid. Reprinted, 1983. Bilbao: Amigos del Libro Vasco.

——— (1883) [ca. 1804–1806]. *Discursos filosóficos sobre la lengua primitiva ó Gramática y análisis razonada de la euskara ó bascuence*. Bilbao.

Azkarate Villar, Miren (1990a). *Hitz elkartuak euskaraz. Mundaiz* 3. San Sebastian: Universidad de Deusto–EUTG.

——— (1990b). "Euskal *-garri* vs. latinezko *-bilis*: bi balio ezberdin." In E. Pérez Gaztelu and P. Urkizu Sarasua (eds.), *Patxi Altunari Omenaldia. Mundaiz* 5:19–31, San Sebastian: Universidad de Deusto-EUTG.

——— (1993). "Basque Compound Nouns and Generative Morphology: Some Data." In J. I. Hualde and J. Ortiz de Urbina (eds.), *Generative Studies in Basque Linguistics*, 222–242. Amsterdam: John Benjamins.

Azkue, Resurreción María de (1891). *Euskal izkindea (Gramática eúskara)*. Bilbao.

——— (1905–1906). *Diccionario vasco-español-francés/Dictionnaire basque-espagnol-français*, 2 vols. Bilbao. 1969 facsimile edition with appendix. Bilbao: Ed. La Gran Enciclopedia Vasca.

——— (1923–1925). *Morfología vasca. Euskera* 4–6. Reprinted in 1969 in three volumes. References are to this edition. Bilbao: Ed. La Gran Enciclopedia Vasca.

Basterrechea, José de (1974). "Estudios sobre entonación vasca según el habla de Guernica I." *FLV* 6:353–393.

——— (1975). "Estudios sobre entonación vasca según el habla de Guernica II." *FLV* 7:289–338.

——— (1981). *El vasco de hoy* I, II. Bilbao: Ed. La Gran Enciclopedia Vasca.

——— (1989). "La declinación indefinida vasca. Caso particular." *FLV* 21:183–185.

Benveniste, Émile (1966). *Problèmes de linguistique générale* I. Paris: Gallimard.

Biguri, Koldo (1986). "Koordinazioaren zenbait alderdi Duhalderen "Meditazioneak gei premiatsenen gainean" liburuan." *ASJU* 20:249–281.

Bonaparte, Prince Louis-Lucien (1863). "Carte des sept provinces basques, montrant la délimitation actuelle de l'euscara et sa division en dialectes, sous-dialectes et variétés." London.

——— (1869). *Le verbe basque en tableaux* II. London. 1991 facsimile edition in *Opera omnia vasconice* I, 221–442. Bilbao: Euskaltzaindia.

Bossong, G. (1984). "Ergativity in Basque." *Linguistics* 22:341–392.

Brettschneider, G. (1979). "Typological Characteristics of Basque." In F. Plank (ed.), *Ergativity: Towards a Theory of Grammatical Relations*, 371–384. London and New York: Academic Press.

Brown, R., and A. Gilman (1960). "The Pronouns of Power and Solidarity." In Thomas A. Sebeok (ed.), *Style in Language*, 253–276. Cambridge, MA: MIT Press. Reprinted in 1972 in P. P. Giglioli (ed.), *Language and Social Context*, 252–282. Harmondsworth: Penguin.

Caro Baroja, Julio (1973). *Sobre la religión antigua y el calendario del pueblo vasco*. San Sebastian.

Chomsky, N. (1992). "A Minimalist Program for Linguistic Theory," *MIT Occasional Papers in Linguistics* 1 (MIT Working Papers in Linguistics). Cambridge, MA.

Comrie, Bernard (1976). Review of G. A. Klimov, *Očerk obščej teorii èrgativnosti* (Moscow: Izd-vo 'Nauka'). *Lingua* 39:252–260.

——— (1978). "Ergativity." In W. P. Lehman (ed.), *Syntactic Typology*, 329–394. Austin: University of Texas Press.

——— (1985). *Tense*. Cambridge: Cambridge University Press.

Davison, A. (1984). "Syntactic Markedness and the Definition of Sentence Topic." *Language* 60:797–846.

Dixon, R. M. W. (1994). *Ergativity*. Cambridge: Cambridge University Press.

Donzeaud, Françoise (1972). "The Expression of Focus in Basque." *ASJU* 6:35–45.

Duden Grammatik der deutschen Gegenwartssprache (1995), 5th edition. Mannheim: Dudenverlag.

Echaide, Ana María (1976). "Distribución de las variantes palatalizadas y no palatalizadas de "l" y "n" debidas al contexto fónico en los dialectos vascos." *FLV* 8:163–169.

Echaide, Ignacio M. (1912). *Sintaxis del idioma éuskaro*. San Sebastian.

Eguskitza, J. (1930). "El sufijo *-garri*." *Euskera* 11:262–266.

Eguzkitza, Andolin (1993). "Adnominals in the Grammar of Basque." In J. I. Hualde and J. Ortiz de Urbina (eds.), *Generative Studies in Basque Linguistics*, 163–187. Amsterdam: John Benjamins.

Elgoibarko Euskara Mintegia (1986). *Euskal hizkuntza eta literatura.* San Sebastian: Elkar.

Emonds, Joseph E. (1970). "Root and Structure-Preserving Transformations." Doctoral dissertation, MIT.

——— (1976). *A Transformational Approach to English Syntax: Root, Structure-Preserving and Local Transformations.* New York: Academic Press.

——— (1985). *A Unified Theory of Syntactic Categories.* Dordrecht: Foris.

Euskal hizkuntza eta literatura. See under Elgoibarko Euskara Mintegia.

Euskaltzaindia, Gramatika Batzordea (1985–1999). *Euskal Gramatika. Lehen Urratsak*, I–V. Pamplona; Bilbao: Euskaltzaindia. (= *EGLU*)

——— (1993). *Euskal gramatika laburra: perpaus bakuna.* Bilbao: Euskaltzaindia. (= *EGL*)

——— (2000). "Hiztegi Batua," *Euskera* 45:482–757.

Euskera. Official organ of Euskaltzaindia, the Royal Academy of the Basque Language. Bilbao: Euskaltzaindia.

Gavel, Henri (1920). *Éléments de phonétique basque.* Paris: Champion.

Goenaga, Patxi (1978). *Gramatika bideetan.* San Sebastian: Erein.

——— (1980). *Gramatika bideetan*, 2nd revised and enlarged editon. San Sebastian: Erein.

——— (1981). "Ohizko euskal sintaxia eta sintaxi berria." In *Euskal linguistika eta literatura: bide berriak*, 139–161. Bilbao: Deustuko Unibertsitateko Argitarazioak.

——— (1984). "Euskal sintaxia: komplementazioa eta nominalizazioa." Doctoral dissertation, UPV/EHU.

——— (1985a). "Complementación y nominalización en Euskara." *ASJU* 19:493–570.

——— (1985b). "Nahi eta behar." In J. L. Melena (ed.), *Symbolae Ludovico Mitxelena Septuagenario Oblatae* II, 943–953. Vitoria.

——— (1997). "Subjunktiboaz eta aginteraz zenbait ohar: *-en* eta *-ela* atzizkien erabilera." *Iker* 10:109–132.

Grevisse, Maurice (1980). *Le Bon Usage: grammaire française, avec des remarques sur la langue française d'aujourd'hui*, 11th edition. Gembloux: Duculot.

Haize Garbia (Équipe de) (1978). *Grammaire basque pour tous*, I. *Éléments non verbaux.* Hendaye.

Harris, James (1969). *Spanish Phonology.* Cambridge, MA: MIT Press.

Heath, Jeffrey G. (1981). "The Role of Basque in Modern Linguistic Theory." *Iker* 1:433–444.

Hualde, José I. (1986). "Tone and Stress in Basque: A Preliminary Study." *ASJU* 20:867–896.

——— (1991). *Basque Phonology.* London and New York: Routledge.

——— & J. Ortiz de Urbina, eds. (2003). *A Grammar of Basque.* (Mouton Grammar Library 26.) Berlin and New York: Mouton de Gruyter.

Inchauspe, Emmanuel (1858). *Le verbe basque.* Bayonne and Paris. 1979 facsimile edition. San Sebastian: Hordago.

Ithurry, [Jean] (1920). *Grammaire basque, dialecte labourdin.* Bayonne. 1979 facsimile edition. San Sebastian: Ediciones Vascas. First published in columns of *Eskualduna*, 1894–1907.

Jackendoff, R. (1973). *Semantic Interpretation in Generative Grammar.* Cambridge, MA: MIT Press.

Jacobsen, William H., Jr. (1982). "Basque Copulative Compounds: A Problem in Irreversible Binomials." In M. Macaulay et al. (eds.), *Proceedings of the Eighth Annual Meeting of the Berkeley Linguistics Society 13–15 February, 1982*, 384–397. Berkeley: Berkeley Linguistics Society.

Joos, Martin (1952). "The Medieval Sibilants." *Language* 28:222–231. (Reprinted in 1957 in his *Readings in Linguistics* I, 372–378. Chicago: University of Chicago Press.)

Jungemann, F. H. (1956). *La teoría del sustrato y los dialectos hispano-romances y gascones.* Madrid.

Kachru, Yamuna (1987). "Hindi-Urdu." In Bernard Comrie (ed.), *The World's Major Languages*, 470–489. London: Croom Helm.

Keyser, Samuel J. (1968). Review of Sven Jacobson, *Adverbial Positions in English* (Stockholm, 1964). *Language* 44:357–374.

Kintana, Xabier (1971). "Posesiboak idazle zaharretan." *FLV* 3:75–80.

Klimov, G. A. (1973). *Očerk obščej teorii èrgativnosti.* Moscow: Izd-vo 'Nauka'. (See Comrie 1976.)

Lafitte, Pierre (1962). *Grammaire basque, (navarro-labourdin littéraire)*. 2nd revised edition. Bayonne: Amis du Musée Basque & Ikas. First published in 1944.

Lafon, René (1943). *Le système du verbe basque au XVIe siècle*, I & II. Bordeaux: Ed. Delmas. 1980 facsimile edition in one volume. San Sebastian & Bayonne: Elkar.

——— (1964). "L'adjectif épithète et les déterminants en basque." *BSLP* 59:82–104.

——— (1965). "Les deux génitifs du basque." *BSLP* 60:131–159.

——— (1966). "La particule *bait* en basque; ses emplois morphologiques et syntaxiques." *BSLP* 61:217–248.

——— (1972). "Basque." In Thomas A. Sebeok (ed.), *Linguistics in Western Europe, Current Trends in Linguistics* 9:1744–1792. The Hague: Mouton.

Laka, Itziar (1990). "Negation in Syntax: On the Nature of Functional Categories and Projections." Doctoral dissertation, MIT. (Published in 1994 as *On the Syntax of Negation.* New York: Garland.)

——— (1991). "Sentence Negation in Basque." In J. A. Lakarra (ed.), *Memoriae L. Mitxelena Magistri Sacrum* II, *ASJU, Supp.* 14:899–923.

——— (1993). "Unergatives that Assign Ergative, Unaccusatives that Assign Accusative." In J. Bobaljik and C. Phillips (eds.), *Papers on Case and Agreement* I, *MIT Working Papers in Linguistics* 18:149–172.

Lakarra Andrinua, Joseba (1996). *Refranes y Sentencias (1596). Ikerketak eta Edizioa.* Bilbao: Euskaltzaindia.

Lardizabal, Francisco Ignacio de (1856). *Gramática vascongada.* San Sebastian: I. R. Baroja.

Larramendi, Manuel de (1729). *El imposible vencido. Arte de la lengua bascongada.* Salamanca: A. J. Villagordo Alcaráz. 1979 facsimile edition. San Sebastian: Hordago.

Lécluse, Fleury de (1826). *Grammaire basque* (= *Manuel de la langue basque*). Bayonne.

Lehmann, Christian (1984). *Der Relativsatz. Typologie seiner Strukturen, Theorie seiner Funktionen-Kompendium seiner Grammatik.* Tübingen: Narr.

——— (1986). "On the Typology of Relative Clauses." *Linguistics* 24:663–680.

Lekuona, Manuel (1918). "Métrica vasca." Vitoria. (Reprinted in 1978 in *Idaz-lan guztiak.* I. *Aozko literatura*, 131–157. Tolosa: Librería Técnica de Difusión.)

Levin, Beth C. (1983a). "On the Nature of Ergativity." Doctoral dissertation, MIT.

——— (1983b). "Unaccusative Verbs in Basque." In Peter Sells and Charles Jones (eds.), *Proceedings of ALNE 13/North Eastern Linguistic Society* 13:129–144.

——— (1989). "The Basque Verbal Inventory and Configurationality." In L. Marácz and P. Muysken (eds.), *Configurationality: The Typology of Asymmetries*, 39–62. Dordrecht: Foris.

——— and M. Rapaport Hovav (1995). *Unaccusativity: At the Syntax–Lexical Semantics Interface.* Cambridge, MA: MIT Press.

Lhande, Pierre (1926–1938). *Dictionnaire basque-français.* Paris: G. Beauchesne. (= Lh.)

Linschmann, Th., and H. Schuchardt (1900). *I. Leiçarragas Baskische Bücher von 1571* (*Neues Testament, Kalender und Abc*) *im genauen Abdruck.* Strassburg: Trübner.

Lizundia, J. L., and H. Knörr (1976). "Herri eta Herritarren Izendegia." *Euskera* 21:287–315.

Martínez Arbelaiz, Asunción (1996). "Basque Nominal Morphology and Antisymmetry within the DP." Unpublished ms. of paper presented in Vienna at the 7th International Conference on Morphology.

McCawley, James D. (1988). *The Syntactic Phenomena of English* I & II. Chicago: University of Chicago Press.

Metzeltin, M. (1979). *Altspanisches Elementarbuch, I Das Altkastilische.* Heidelberg: Carl Winter Universitäts Verlag.

Michelena, Luis = Mitxelena, Koldo. See under both names.

Michelena, Luis (1972a). "Etimología y transformación." In *Homenaje a Antonio Tovar*, 305–317. Madrid: Gredos. (Reprinted in Michelena 1985, 296–308.)

——— (1972b). "A Note on Old Labourdin Accentuation." *ASJU* 6:110–120.

——— (1976). "Acentuación alto-navarra." *FLV* 8:147–162.

——— (1977). *Fonética histórica vasca*, 2nd edition, revised and enlarged. San Sebastián: Diputación de Guipúzcoa. First published in 1961, San Sebastian. (= *FHV*)

——— (1985). *Lengua e historia.* Madrid: Paraninfo.

——— (1987a). *Palabras y textos.* Vitoria: EHU/UPV.

——— (1987b–). *Diccionario general vasco/Orotoriko euskal hiztegia* (14 volumes published 1987–2002). Bilbao: Euskaltzaindia. (= *DGV*)

Mitxelena, Koldo (1968). "Euskararen batasun bideak." *Euskera* (new series) 13:203–219 (= *MEIG* VII, 135–153).

——— (1971). "Egunak eta egun-izenak." *Munibe* 23:583–591 (= *MEIG* VII, 93–110; Michelena 1987a, 269–282).

——— (1972c). *Zenbait hitzaldi.* Bilbao: Mensajero.

——— (1978). "Udal Izendegia." *Euskera* 23:313–334.

——— (1981). "Galdegaia eta Mintzagaia Euskaraz." In *Euskal linguistika eta literatura: bide berriak*, 57–81. Bilbao: Deustuko Unibertsitateko Argitarazioak.

——— (1988). *Euskal idazlan guztiak* I–IX. San Sebastián: EEE.

Múgica, Luis M. (1978). *Origen y desarrollo de la sufijación euskérica.* San Sebastian: Ediciones Vascas.

——— (= Mujika, Luis Mari) (1982). *Hitz konposastu eta eratorrien morfo-fonetika.* San Sebastian: Ediciones Vascas. (For a summary in Spanish, see his 1982 article "Morfología de la composición lexical euskérica." *FLV* 14:233–271.)

Mujika, José A. (1988). "Partículas modales de la flexión verbal." *ASJU* 22:463–478.

Müller, F. (1888). *Grundriss der Sprachwissenschaft. Nachtrage zum Grundriss aus den Jahren 1877–1887.* Vienna: Hölder.

Navarro Tomás, T. (1925). "Pronunciación guipuzcoana: Contribución al estudio de la fonética vasca." In *Homenaje ofrecido a Menéndez Pidal III*, 593–653. Madrid. (Results summarized in Jungemann 1956.)

N'Diaye, Geneviève (1970). *Structure du dialecte basque de Maya.* The Hague: Mouton.

Oihartzabal, B., see under Oyharçabal.

Oihénart, Arnaud d' (1992) [1638]. *Notitia utriusque Vasconiae, tum Ibericae, tum Aquitanicae.* Paris. Facsimile of the 2nd edition of 1656, Paris, with Spanish translation by J. Gorosterratzu and introduction by R. Cierbide. Vitoria: The Basque Parliament.

Ortiz de Urbina, Jon (1983). "Empty Categories and Focus in Basque." *Studies in the Linguistic Sciences* 13:133–156.

——— (1989). *Parameters in the Grammar of Basque.* Dordrecht: Foris.

——— and M. Uribe-Etxebarria (1991). "Participial Predication in Basque." In J. A. Lakarra (ed.), *Memoriae L. Mitxelena Magistri Sacrum* II. *ASJU, Supp.* 14:993–1012.

Osa Unamuno, Eusebio (1990). *Euskararen hitzordena komunikazio zereginaren arauera.* Leioa: UPV/EHU.

——— (1993). "Esapidearen gramatika funtzionala (egokitasunaren teoriarako)." *ASJU* 27:395–448.

Oyharçabal, B. (1983). "Le préfixe *ba* d'assertion positive en basque." *Bulletin du Musée Basque* 102:161–190.

——— (1985a). "Behato bat ezeko esaldieri." *Euskera* 30:103–115.

——— (1985b). *Les relatives en basque.* Université Paris 7.

——— (1989). "Pro-drop and the Resumptive Pronoun Strategy in Basque." In L. Marácz & P. Muysken (eds.), *Configurationality: The Typology of Asymmetries*, 63–83. Dordrecht: Foris.

——— (1992). "Structural Case and Inherent Case Marking: Ergaccusativity in Basque." In J. A. Lakarra & J. Ortiz de Urbina (eds.), *Syntactic Theory and Basque Syntax. ASJU, Supp.* 27:309–342.

——— (1998). "Analyse des infinitives adnominales en basque." *Lapurdum* 3:37–51.

——— (2000). "Note à propos des formes jussives préfixées en *b-* du basque." *Lapurdum* 5:225–235.

Perlmutter, David M. (1978). "Impersonal Passives and the Unaccusative Hypothesis." *Proceedings of the Fourth Annual Meeting of the Berkeley Linguistics Society*, 157–189. Berkeley, CA: Berkeley Linguistics Society.

Pouvreau, Silvain (1892). *Les petites oeuvres basques* [17th century], edition of J. Vinson. Chalon-sur-Saône. 1978 facsimile edition, San Sebastian: Hordago.

Pullum, G. K. (1988). "Citation Etiquette Beyond Thunderdome." *Natural Language and Linguistic Theory* 6:579–588.

Rebuschi, Georges (1978). "Cas et fonction sujet en basque." *Verbum* 1:69–98.

——— (1983). "A Note on Focalization in Basque." *Journal of Basque Studies* 4:29–42.

——— (1985). "Théorie du liage et langues non-configurationnelles: Quelques données du basque navarro-labourdin." *Euskera* 30:389–433.

——— (1986). "Théorie du liage, diachronie et énonciation: Sur les anaphores possessives du basque." *ASJU* 20:325–341.

——— (1988a). "Defining the Three Binding Domains of Basque." *ASJU* 22:233–241.

——— (1988b). "Note sur les pronoms dits 'intensifs' du basque." *ASJU* 22:827–844.

——— (1989). "L'opposition entre les génitifs réfléchis et non-réfléchis du basque, et la variation dialectale." *FLV* 21:161–181.

——— (1990). "On the Non-configurationality of Basque and Some Related Phenomena." *ASJU* 24:351–383.

——— (1991). "Binding at LF vs. Obligatory (Counter-) Coindexation at SS: A Case Study." In J. A. Lakarra (ed.), *Memoriae L. Mitxelena Magistri Sacrum* II. *ASJU, Supp.* 14:959–984.

——— (1992). "Absolute and Relativized Locality in the Binding Theory." In J. A. Lakarra & J. Ortiz de Urbina (eds.), *Syntactic Theory and Basque Syntax. ASJU, Supp.* 27:343–363.

Rijk, Rudolf P. G. de (1969). "Is Basque an SOV Language?" *FLV* 1:319–351 (= *DLV*, 13–37).

——— (1970). "Vowel Interaction in Bizcayan Basque." *FLV* 2:144–167 (= *DLV*, 39–53).

——— (1972a). "Relative Clauses in Basque: A Guided Tour." In P. Peranteau, J. Levi, and G. Phares (eds.), *The Chicago Which Hunt*, pp. 115–135. Chicago: Chicago Linguistic Society (= *DLV*, 55–69).

——— (1972b). "Studies in Basque Syntax: Relative Clauses." MIT doctoral dissertation published in *DLV*, 71–149.

——— (1972c). "Partitive Assignment in Basque." *ASJU* 6:130–173 (= *DLV*, 151–182).

——— (1978). "Topic Fronting, Focus Positioning, and the Nature of the Verb Phrase in Basque." In Frank Jansen (ed.), *Studies on Fronting*, 81–112. Lisse (the Netherlands): Peter de Ridder Press (= *DLV*, 183–201).

——— (1980). "Erlatiboak idazle zaharrengan." *Euskera* 25:525–536 (= *DLV*, 203–210).

——— (1985). "Un verbe méconnu." In José L. Melena (ed.), *Symbolae Ludovico Mitxelena Septuagenario Oblatae* II, 921–935. Vitoria (= *DLV*, 225–241).

——— (1988). "Basque Syntax and Universal Grammar." In *Euskara biltzarra. II Euskal Mundu-Biltzarra (Proceedings of the Conference on the Basque Language, II World Basque Congress)* I, 69–88. Vitoria: Eusko Jaurlaritzaren Argitalpen Zerbitzu Nagusia (Publication of the Basque Government) (= *DLV*, 251–270).

——— (1991). "Familiarity or Solidarity: The Pronoun *hi* in Basque." *RIEV* 36:373–378 (= *DLV*, 297–300).

——— (1992). "'Nunc' Vasconice." *ASJU* 26:695–724 (= *DLV*, 347–376). (Condensed English version in José I. Hualde, J. A. Lakarra, and Robert L. Trask (eds.), *Towards a History of the Basque Language*, 295–311. Amsterdam: John Benjamins, 1995.)

——— (1993). "Basque Hospitality and the Suffix *-ko*." In José I. Hualde and Jon Ortiz de Urbina (eds.), *Generative Studies in Basque Linguistics*, 145–162. Amsterdam: John Benjamins (= *DLV*, 377–390).

——— (1995). "Basque Manner Adverbs and Their Genesis." *ASJU* 29:53–82 (= *DLV*, 391–419).

——— (1996a). "Focus and Quasifocus in Basque Negative Statements." *RIEV* 41:63–76 (= *DLV*, 421–433). Author disclaims garbled version in *RIEV*.

——— (1996b). "On the Origin of the Partitive Determiner." *ASJU* 30:145–158 (= *DLV*, 435–447).

——— (1998). *De lingua vasconum: Selected Writings. ASJU, Supp.* 43 (= *DLV*).

——— (2002). "L'antipassif basque et l'hypothèse de Levin." *Lapurdum* 7:295–312.

——— (2003). "Antipasiboak euskaran." *P. Lafitteren sortzearen mendemugako biltzarra (2001/09/20–21, Baiona), Euskal Gramatikari eta literaturari. Buruzko ikerketak XXI mendearen ataran. Iker* 14 (I): 385–393.

Saksena, A. (1980). "The Affected Agent." *Language* 56:812–826.

Salaburu, Pello (1985). *Ikaslearen esku-gramatika*, 3rd edition. Bilbao: Mensajero.

——— (1986). "La teoría del ligamiento en la lengua vasca." *ASJU* 20:359–412.

——— (1989). "El movimiento de las frases-QU y el foco en vasco." *FLV* 21:7–26.

Saltarelli, Mario, et al. (1988). *Basque*. London and New York: Croom Helm.

Sarasola, Ibon (1980). "Nire/neure, zure/zeure literatur tradizioan." *Euskera* 25:431–446.

Schuchardt, Hugo (1893). *Baskische Studien* I (Über die Entstehung der Bezugsformen des baskischen Zeitworts). *Denkschriften der Kaiserlichen Akademie der Wissenschaften, Philosophisch–Historische Classe* (*Wien*) 42:1–82.

——— (1900). "Über die Einrichtung des Neudrucks, insbesondere über die Druckfehler und Varianten bei Leiçarraga." In Th. Linschmann and H. Schuchardt (eds.), *I. Leiçarragas Baskische Bücher von 1571 (Neues Testament, Kalender und Abc) im genauen Abdruck*, pp. ix–cxvi. Strassburg: K. J. Trübner.

Selkirk, Elizabeth O. (1982). *The Syntax of Words*. Cambridge, MA: MIT Press.

Tamura, S. (1985). "Hitzen ordena erabakitzeko faktoreak." *Euskera* 30:71–101.

Trask, Robert L. (1985a). "The Basque Passive: A Correct Description." *Linguistics* 23:985–991.

——— (1985b). "*-ko* atzizkia euskaraz." *Euskera* 30:165–173.

Uhlenbeck, Christian C. (1927). "Baskisch elkar." *Mededeelingen der Koninklijke Akademie van Wetenschappen, Afdeling Letterkunde*; dl.63, nr.6; Serie A. Letteren, wijsbegeerte, godgeleerdheid, 179–182. (See résumé by Georges Lacombe, 1928, in *RIEV* 19:168.)

——— (1949). "Le langue basque et la linguistique générale." *Lingua* 1:59–76.

Villasante, Luis (1962). "Illen izenak." *Euskera*, n.s., 7:328–334. (See also the pages following for the discussion in the meeting of the Euskaltzaindia.)

——— (1974). *Palabras vascas compuestas y derivadas*. Oñate: Ed. Franciscana Aranzazu.

——— (1976). *Sintaxis de la oración compuesta*. Oñate: Ed. Franciscana Aranzazu.

——— (1980). *Sintaxis de la oración simple*. Oñate: Ed. Franciscana Aranzazu.

Wilbur, Terence H. (1979a). "The Ergative, Absolutive, and Dative in Basque." *FLV* 11:1–18.

——— (1979b). *Prolegomena to a Grammar of Basque*. Amsterdam: John Benjamins.

Zuazo, Koldo (1999). *Deba ibarreko euskeria*. Eibar: Deba Arroko Udalak.

Zytsar, Ju. V. (1977). "K tipologičeskoj charakteristike èrgativnoj struktury jazyka baskov." *Voprosy Jazykoznanija* 3:37–47. (1978 Spanish translation: "Sobre el sistema ergativo del vasco [Ensayo de una comparación tipológica]." *FLV* 10:229–243.)

B. Sources

Agirre, Domingo/Txomin (1986). *Auñemendiko lorea*. R. M. Arano's edition, Bilbao: Labayru Ikastegia & Bizkaiko Aurrezki Kutxa. First published in 1898. (= *A.L.*)

——— (1912). *Garoa*. Durango: Florentine Elosu. (= *G.*)

——— (1956). *Garoa*. 3rd "improved" edition, Aranzazu. (= $G.^3$)

——— (1954). *Kresala*. 3rd edition, Zarautz: Itxaropena. First published in 1906. (= *Kres.*)

Agirre, Toma (1950). *Uztaro*. 2nd edition, Bilbao: Vasca-Irarkolan. (= *Uzt.*)

Aguirre, Juan Bautista (1850). *Eracusaldiac* I, II, III. Tolosa. 1978 facsimile edition, Donostia: Hordago. (= *Erak.*)

Aintziart, Piarres (1992). *Biziaren bazterrean*. Baiona: Maiatz.

Albisu ta Ayerdi, Anastasio (1973). *Erreka zuloan eta ....* Vitoria: ESET.

Alkain, Iñaki, & Antonio Zavala (1981). *Gerrateko ibillerak* II. Tolosa: Auspoa.

Altube, S. (1975). *Erderismos*. 2nd edition, Bilbao: Indauchu. First published in 1929 in *Euskera* X, 1–4. (= *Erd.*)

Altuna, Joseba (1927). *Ipuñak*. (Translation of stories by Oscar Wilde.) Bilbao. (= *Ip.*)

Alzaga, Toribio (1991). *Bernaiñoren larriyak.* In *Toribio Alzaga, heriotzaren 50.urte mugan, zenbait lan*, 41–56. Donostia: Eusko Jaurlaritza, etc. (First performed in 1915, San Sebastián.) (= *B.L.*)

——— (1961). *Ramuntxo.* (Based on Pierre Loti's novel.) Tolosa: Auspoa. (First performed in 1920.) (= *Ram.*)

Alzo, (Fray) Diego J. de [Dionisio Olano Galarraga] (1961). *Estudio sobre el euskera hablado.* San Sebastián: Izarra.

Alzola Guerediaga, Nicolás "Bitaño" (1967). *Atalak.* Zarautz.

Amuriza, Xabier (1985). *Emea.* Donostia: Elkar.

——— (1983). *Hil ala bizi.* Donostia: Elkar. (= *Hil*)

——— (1984). *Oromenderrieta.* Donostia: Elkar. (= *Orom.*)

Anduaga, Graziano (1961). *Aitonaren uzta. Gezaltzako aitonaren kontakizun eta bertsoekin Aita Luis Villasantek osaturiko bilduma.* Zarautz: Itxaropena.

Añibarro, Pedro Antonio (1802). *Escu-librua.* Tolosa. 1978 facsimile edition, Donostia: Hordago. (= *E.L.*)

——— (1827). *Esculiburua.* 3rd revised edition, Tolosa. (= *E.L.*^{3})

——— (1963). *Voces bascongadas ....* L. Villasante's edition, Bilbao: La Caja de Ahorros Vizcaina. (Written ca. 1800.)

Arana, Aitor (2000). *Ipuin-entzulea.* Bilbao: Euskaltzaindia & Bilbao Bizkaia Kutxa Fundazioa.

Archu, J. B. (1868). *Grammaire bilingue, française et basque/Bi mihiren gramatika uskara eta franzesa.* 3rd edition, Bayonne. 1979 facsimile edition, Donostia: Hordago.

Arejita, Adolfo (1985). *Euskal Joskera.* Bilbao: Labayru Ikastegia & Bizkaia Aurrezki Kutxa. (First published in 1978.) (= *Eusk. Josk.*)

——— (1991). "Juan Antonio Mogelen sermoiak." In J. A. Lakarra (ed.) *Memoriae L. Mitxelena magistri sacrum* I. *ASJU, Supp.* 14:277–300. (= Mogel, *Sermoi*)

Aresti, Gabriel (1979). *Ipuinak.* Donostia: Gipuzkoako Aurrezki Kutxa Probintziala. (Stories published in *Egan* between 1957 and 1962.)

Argaiñaratz, Pierre d' (1665). *Devoten Breviarioa.* Reprinted in 1910 (Vinson edition), Chalon-sur-Saône. 1978 edition is facsimile of 1910 edition. Donostia: Hordago. (Page nos. refer to first edition.)

Ariztia, Mayi (1982). *Amattoren uzta. La moisson de Grand'mère.* Donostia & Baiona: Elkar.

Arradoy, P. [Pierre Narbaitz] (1955). *Kattalinen gogoetak.* Bayonne: LFAC. (= *K.G.*)

——— (1966). *San Frantses Jatsukoa.* San Sebastián: Izarra. (= *S.Fran.*)

Arratia, J. M. de (1968–1971). *Cancionero popular del país vasco* I–IV. San Sebastián: Ed. Auñamendi.

Arrese, Emeterio (1952). *Olerki berrizte.* Zarautz: Itxaropena. (= *O.B.*)

Arrese Beitia, Felipe (1900). *Ama Euskeriaren liburu kantaria.* Bilbao. (= *Ama E.*)

——— (1887). *Diccionario manual bascongado y castellano y elementos de gramática para uso de la juventud de Vizcaya, con ejemplos en ambos idiomas.* Tolosa. (= *Dic.*)

——— (1957). *Olerkiak* [1879–1906]. Bilbao: Euskal Idazleak (= *Olerk.*)

Arrinda Albisu, Anastasio "Anes Lazkauko" (1970). *Semeno de Lazkano (anai-arteko gorroto).* Zarautz: Itxaropena.

Arrosagaray, Juan Cruz (1983). *California-tik kantuz.* Tolosa: Auspoa.

Arrue, Gregorio (1960). *Brabante-ko Genoveva-ren bizitz arrigarri miragarria.* (Translated from K. Schmid.) 2nd edition, Zarautz: Itxaropena. First published in 1885. (= *G.B.*^{2})

——— (1888). *Mayetzeco ill edo Birgina chit santari consagratutaco Mayetzeco illa.* Tolosa. (= *May.*)

——— (1987). *Santa Jenobebaren bizitza/Santa Genovevaren vicitza antziñaco demboretaco condairen.* Lino Akesolo's edition, Donostia: EEE/Erein. First published in 1868 in Tolosa: Pedro Gurruchaga. (= *G.B.*)

Artho Xur. = *Zenbait ichtorio chahar artho churitzetako.*

Ast. Las. = *Astolasterrak*, see under Urkizu, P.

Astiz Odériz, Andrés (1960). *Goldáraz'ko bertsolaria'ren kontu eta bertsoak. El versolari de Goldáraz, cuentos y poesías.* Pamplona: Institución "Príncipe de Viana."

Atxaga, Bernardo [José Irazu Garmendia] (1992). *Behi euskaldun baten memoriak.* 3rd edition, Iruñea: Pamiela. (= *Behi*)

——— (1985). *Bi anai.* Donostia: Erein. (= *Bi An.*)

——— (1984). *Bi letter jaso nituen oso denbora gutxian.* Donostia: Erein. (= *Bi Let.*)

——— (1994). *Gizona bere bakardadean.* 4th edition, Iruñea: Pamiela. (= *Gizona*)

——— (1998). *Groenlandiako lezioa.* Donostia: Erein. (= *Grl.*)

——— (1999). *Krisia* (*Bambuloren istorio Bambulotarrak*), 2nd edition. Donostia: Erein. (= *Bam.* II)

——— (1999). *Lehen Urratsak* (*Bambuloren istorio Bambulotarrak*). 2nd edition, Donostia: Erein. (= *Bam.* I)

——— (1988). *Obabakoak.* Donostia: Erein. (= *Obab.*)

——— (1996). *Sara izeneko gizona.* Villava-Atarrabia: Pamiela. (= *Sara*)

——— (1999). *Ternuako penak* (*Bambuloren istorio Bambulotarrak*). Donostia: Erein. (= *Bam.* III)

——— (1995). *Zeru horiek.* 2nd edition, Donostia: Erein. (= *Z.H.*)

——— (1986). *Ziutateaz.* 2nd edition, Donostia: Erein. First published in 1976. (= *Ziut.*)

Aulestia, Gorka (1989). *Basque–English Dictionary.* Reno: University of Nevada Press.

Ax. = Axular, P.

Axular, Pedro de (1643). *Guero* (*bi partetan partitua eta berecia*). Bordeaux: G. Milanges. 1988 facsimile edition, Bilbao: Euskaltzaindia. (= Ax.)

Azkue, Eusebio M. (1896). *Parnasorako bidea.* Bilbo. 1979 facsimile edition, Donostia: Hordago.

Azkue, Resurrección M. de (1917). *Aitaren Bildur.* Bilbao: Garmendia. (= *Ait. Bild.*)

——— (1918). *Ardi galdua.* Bilbo: Jesusen biotzaren elaztegian. (= *Ardi*)

——— (1986). *Bein da betiko.* Edition of Ines Pagola, Donostia: EEE/Erein. First published in Bilbao, 1893. (= *Bein B.*)

——— (1905–1906). *Diccionario vasco-español-francés/Dictionaire basque-espagnol-français.* 2 vols. Bilbao. 1969 facsimile edition with appendix, Bilbao: Ed. La Gran Enciclopedia Vasca. (= *DVEF*)

——— (1935–1947). *Euskalerriaren yakintza. Literatura popular del país vasco.* 4 vols. Madrid: Espasa Calpa (= *E.Y.*)

——— (1968). *Ipuiñak.* Bilbao: Ed. La Gran Enciclopedia Vasca. (= *Ip.*)

Azurmendi, Joxe (1971). *Hitz berdeak.* Oñate: Ed. Franciscana Aranzazu.

Balad. = *Euskal Baladak*, see under Lakarra, J. A.

Barandiaran, José Miguel (1934). *Euskalerri'ko leen gizona.* Donostia. (= *ELG*)

——— et al. (1960–1962). *El mundo en la mente popular vasca.* 4 volumes. Zarautz: Itxaropena; San Sebastián: Auñamendi. (= *Mundo*)

Barbier, Jean (1983). *Légendes du pays basque d'après la tradition.* Donostia: Elkar. First published in 1931, Paris: Lib. Delagrave. (= *Lég.*)

——— (1992). *Piarres* I. Edition of R. Sanchez, Bilbao: EEE/Ibaizabal. First published in Baiona, 1926.

——— (1987). *Supazter xokoan.* Edition of E. Valencia Tirapu, Donostia: EEE/Kriselu. First published in Baiona, 1924. (= *Sup.*)

Bartolomé, see Madariaga, Bartolomé.

Basarri [Ignacio Eizmendi] (1960). *Kantari nator.* Zarautz: Itxaropena.

Basterrechea, José de, see Oskillaso.

Beobide, see Beovide.

Beovide, Krispin (1992). *Asisko loria.* Edition of Iban Eguzkitza and Kristina Korella, Donostia: EEE/Sendoa. First published in Tolosa, 1885.

Bernaolacoa, Dámaso M. (1905). *Pasiño santuaren contaera.* (Translated into Biscayan from Luis de la Palma.) Durango. 1979 facsimile edition, Donostia: Hordago (= *Pas Sant*)

Berrondo, Pedro (1977). *Don Kijote Mantxako.* (Translated from Cervantes.) Zarautz: Itxaropena.

[Bertsolariak] (1963). *Bertsolarien txapelketa (30–12–1962)*. Tolosa: Auspoa. (= *B.Tx.* 62)

——— (1961). *Euskalerriko bertsolarien txapelketa (18–12–1960)*. Zarautz: Itxaropena. (= *B.Tx.* 60)

Bibli Elkarte Batuak/Sociedades Biblicas Unidas (1983). *Itun Berria. Elizen Arteko Biblia.* Iruñea: Ed. PAX. (= *EAB*)

Biblia, see under Etchehandy, Marcel.

Biblia: Kontaera ederrenak. Biblia lehen aldiz irakurtzeko. (1985). Donostia-San Sebastián: Idatz. (= *Biblia K.E.*)

Bilbao, Félix (1959). *Ipuin-barreka.* Bilbao: Euskaltzaindia.

Bilintx [Indalezio Bizkarrondo] (1986). *Bertsoak eta beste.* Edition of A. Zabala, Donostia: EEE/Etor.

B.Tx., see under Bertsolariak.

Bustinza, E., see Kirikiño.

Cardaberaz, Agustín (1760–1761). *Aita S. Ignacio Loyolacoaren egercicioac.* Volumes I–IV. Iruñea. (= *Eg.*)

——— (1964). *Euskeraren berri onak.* 4th edition, Tolosa: Auspoa. First published in 1761, Iruñea. (= *E.B.O.*)

Casenave, Junes (1976). *Santa Grazi, pastorala.* Oiñati: Ed. Franciscana Aranzazu/Jakin.

Cerquand, Jean François (1985). *Ipar euskal herriko legenda eta ipuinak* (Anuntxi Arana's edition of stories published between 1874 and 1885). Donostia: Txertoa.

Charritton, Piarres (1984). *Jean Etchepare mirikuaren (1877–1935) idazlanak.* I. *Euskal Gaiak.* Donostia-San Sebastián: Elkar. (= Etchepare, *Eusk. G.*)

Chourio, Michel de (1788). *Jesu-Christoren Imitacionea.* Baiona. 1978 facsimile edition, Donostia: Hordago. First published in Bordeaux, 1720.

Darricarrère, Jean Baptiste (n.d.). Dictionary (ms.) See *DRA* I, xiv.

DCV = *Diccionario castellano-vasco*, see under Múgica Berrondo, P.

Dechepare, see Etxepare, Bernard.

DGV = *Diccionario general vasco*, see under Michelena, L.

Dialogues basques: guipuscoans, biscaïens; labourdins, souletins; par A. P. Iturriaga, J. A. Uriarte, J. P. Duvoisin et E. Inchauspe, accompagnés de deux traductions, espagnole et française. London: L. L. Bonaparte, 1857. Facsimile editions: Donostia: Hordago, 1978; and Bonaparte: *Opera omnia vasconice* II, 309–433, Bilbao: Euskaltzaindia, 1991. (= *Dial.*)

DLV = *De lingua vasconum*, see under de Rijk.

Donosti'ko Eliz-barutirako (1951). *Kristau–Ikasbidea, guipuzkoako euskeraz (osoa).* Gasteiz: "Secretariado Catequístico". (= *Kristau Ik.*)

Dorronsoro, Joanito (1981). *Bertsotan 1789–1936.* Bilbao: Ed. Eléxpuru.

DRA = *Diccionario Retana de autoridades de la lengua vasca*, see under Sota, Manuel de la.

Duhalde, Martin (1809). *Meditacioneac gei premiatsuenen gainean.* Baiona. 1978 facsimile edition, Donostia: Hordago.

Durangoko hiria ipuin lehiaketa. Donostia: Elkar, 1985.

Duvoisin, Jean Pierre (1858). *Bible Saindua, edo Testament Zahar eta Berria.* London. 1972 facsimile edition in 3 volumes, Bilbao: Ed. La Gran Enciclopedia Vasca. (= Dv)

——— (1857). *Dialogues basques (versión labourdins).* London: L. L. Bonaparte. Facsimile editions: Donostia: Hordago, 1978; and Bonaparte: *Opera omnia vasconice* II, 309–433, Bilbao: Euskaltzaindia, 1991. (= *Dial.*)

——— (1858). *Laborantzako liburua edo bi aita semeren solasak laborantzaren gainean.* Bayona: Lamaignère. 1978 facsimile edition, Donostia: Hordago. (= *Lab.*)

——— (1987). *Liburu ederra.* Edition of M. J. Guerra, A. Iribar, and S. Laskurain, Donostia: EEE/Erein. First published in Baiona, 1856. (= *L.Ed.*)

Dv = Duvoisin, J. P.

DVEF, see under Azkue, R. M. de.

EAB = *Itun Berria. Elizen Arteko Biblia*, see under Bibli Elkarte Batuak.

Echebarria, Toribio (1965–1966). *Lexicón del euskera dialectal de Eibar* (= *Euskera*, n.s., X–XI). Bilbao: Euskaltzaindia. (= *Eib.*)

Echeita, Joseba Imanol (1913). *Au, ori ta bestia*. Durango: F. Elosu. (= *Au*)

——— (1910). *Jayoterri Maitia.* Durango: F. Elosu. (= *Jay.M.*)

——— (1909). *Josecho.* Durango: F. Elosu. (= *Jos.*)

Echenique, Bruno (1857). *El Evangelio según S. Mateo.* London. Reference is to 2nd edition; see under Salaburu Echeverría, Pello (1980). (= Etx.)

EGL = *Euskal gramatika laburra: perpaus bakuna*, see under Euskaltzaindia.

EGLU = *Euskal Gramatika. Lehen Urratsak*, see under Euskaltzaindia.

E.H. = *Euskal Hiztegia*, see under Sarasola, Ibon.

EHM = *Euskal Hiztegi Modernoa.*

Eizagirre, Joseba (1948). *Ekaitzpean.* Buenos Aires: Ed. Vasca Ekin.

Elicegui, Mikela, and Antonio Zavala (1963). *Pello Errotak jarritako bertsoak, bere alabaren argibideakin*. Tolosa: Auspoa. (= *P.E.*)

Elissamburu, Jean Baptiste (1986). *Piarres Adame.* Edition of I. Sarasola, Donostia: EEE/Elkar. First published in Pau, 1888. (= *P.Ad.*)

Elizanburu, J. B., see Elissamburu, and under Labayen, Antonio.

Elizen Arteko Biblia Elkartea (itzulpena) (1994). *Elizen Arteko Biblia.* Donostia: Idatz. (Unless otherwise designated, biblical citations are from this volume.)

Elzb. *Po.*, see under Labayen, Antonio.

Enbeita, Balendin (1974). *Nere apurra.* Tolosa: Auspoa.

Enbeita, Kepa (1971). *Gure urretxindorra. Enbeita'tar Kepa'ren bertso lanak osorik* (Onaindia's edition). Buenos Aires: Ekin.

Ene H. = *Ene Hautia*, see under Vogel, F.

Erkiaga, Eusebio (1958). *Arranegi.* Zarautz: Itxaropena. (= *Arran.*)

——— (1952). "Sinisgogorra." *Egan* 2:27–30. (= *Sinis.*)

Etcheberry, J. B. (1974). *Orotarik.* Bayonne.

Etchehandy, Marcel, and R. Puchulu (1979). *Hasera* [Genesis]. Donostia–San Sebastián & Bayonne: Elkar. (= *Biblia*)

——— (1985). *Jalgitza eta Lebitikoa* [Exodus and Leviticus]. Donostia: Elkar. (= *Biblia*)

——— (1983). *Jondoni Pauloren gutunak* [Letters from St. Paul (Romans, 1 and 2 Corinthians, Galatians, Ephesians, Philippians, Colossians, 1 and 2 Thessalonians, 1 and 2 Timothy, Titus, and Philemon)]. Donostia: Elkar. (= *Biblia*)

Etchehandy, Marcel, et al. (1992). *Hebrearrei gutuna, Jakoberen, Petriren, Joaniren, Judaren, Gutunak, Apokalipsia* [Hebrews, James, 1 and 2 Peter, 1–3 John, Jude, Revelation/Apocalypse]. Donostia: Elkar. (= *Biblia*)

Etchemendy, Paul, & Pierre Lafitte (1984). *Kantuz.* Donostia: Elkar.

Etchepare, Jean (1987). *Beribilez.* Edition of M. J. Kerejeta, Donostia: EEE/Elkar. First published in Baiona, 1931. (= *Ber.*)

——— (1980). *Buruxkak.* Donostia: Elkar. First published in 1910. (= *Bur.*)

——— *Eusk. G.*, see under Charritton, Piarres.

Etx. = Echenique, Bruno.

Etxagaray, José Vicente de (1964). *Festara.* (*Bere bertso guzien bilduma*). A. Zavala's edition, Tolosa: Auspoa.

Etxahun-Iruri [Pierre Bordazarre] (1974). *Etxahun-Iruri khantan.* J. Larrondo's edition, Pau: I.P.A.

Etxaide, Yon (1950). *Alos-Tor̃ea.* Zarautz: Itxaropena. (= *Alos*)

——— (1958). *Amasei seme euskalerri'ko.* Zarautz: Itxaropena. (= *16 Seme*)

——— (1991). *Eneko Agerroa.* (2nd revised edition of 1989). Donostia: Erein. (= *Eneko*)

——— (1964). *Gorrotoa lege.* Zarautz: Itxaropena (= *Gor*[1])

——— (1984). *Gorrotoa lege.* Donostia: Elkar. (= *Gor*[2])

——— (1955). *Joanak-Joan.* Zarautz: Itxaropena. (= *J.J.*)

——— (1984). *Xanti Andiaren kezkak.* (Translation of Pío Baroja's *Las inquietudes de Shanti Andia.*) 2 volumes. Donostia: Hordago/Lur. (= *Xanti*)

Etxamendi, E. (1975). *Azken elurra.* Bayonne: GIA.

Etxaniz, Nemesio (1958). *Euskal antzerkiak. Kontu-kontari.* Zarautz: Itxaropena. (= *Antz.*)

——— (1952). *Irulearen negaŕa.* Gasteiz: "Montepio Diocesano"-ren Irarkolan. (= *Irul.Neg.*)

——— (1968). *Ito ... edo ezkondu.* (Translation of *Mujeres en Berrigorria* by Victor Ruiz Añibarro [in the same volume]. Buenos Aires, 1949.) San Sebastián: Ed. Auñamendi. (= *Ito*)

——— (1978). *Lur berri billa.* 2nd edition, Donostia: Gipuzkoako Aurrezki Kutxa Probintziala. First published in 1967. (= *LBB*)

——— (1968). *¿Nola idatzi euskeraz?* 2nd edition, Donostia: Edili. First published in 1950. (= *Nola*)

Etxeberri Sarakoa, see under Kintana, X.

Etxeberri Ziburukoa, Joannes (1669). *Manual devotionezcoa*, I & II. First published in 1627, Bordeaux. 1978 facsimile of 2nd edition of 1669, Donostia: Hordago. (= *Man.*)

Etxeberria, Xabier (2000). *Egun denak ez dira berdin.* Donostia: Elkarlanean. (= *Egun*)

Etxepare, Bernard (Dechepare) (1545). *Linguae vasconum primitiae.* Bordeaux. 1995 facsimile edition, Bilbao: Euskaltzaindia; see also P. Altuna's critical edition of 1980, Bilbao: Menesajero. (= *LVP*)

Etxepare, Jean, see Etchepare, Jean, and under Charritton, P.

Etxezarreta, J. M. (1985). "Amildegiak ez du amairik," pp. 77–88 in Debako Kultur Elkartea, *Tene Lehiaketa 85.* Donostia: Elkar.

Euskal Herriko Elizbarrutietako Gotzaiak (1984). *Itun Berria.* 2nd edition, Donostia-San Sebastián: Idatz. First published in 1980. (= *IB*)

Euskal hiztegi modernoa (1994). Usurbil: Elhuyar Kultur Elkartea & Donostia: Elkar. (= *EHM*)

Euskal kantak (*Cantos populares del País Vasco*) (1959). Donostia.

Euskaltzaindia (1957). *Euskalerriko ipuiñak.* Zarautz: Itxaropena. (= *Eusk. Ip.*)

Euskaltzaindia, Gramatika Batzordea (1985). *Euskal Gramatika. Lehen Urratsak*–I. 2nd edition, Iruñea: Euskaltzaindia. (= *EGLU* I)

——— (1987). *Euskal Gramatika. Lehen Urratsak*–I (*Eraskina*). Bilbo: Euskaltzaindia. (= *EGLU* I, *E*)

——— (1987). *Euskal Gramatika. Lehen Urratsak*–II. Bilbo: Euskaltzaindia. (= *EGLU* II)

——— (1990). *Euskal Gramatika. Lehen Urratsak*–III (*Lokailuak*). Bilbo: Euskaltzaindia. (= *EGLU* III)

——— (1999). *Euskal Gramatika. Lehen Urratsak*–V (*Mendeko Perpausak–1: Osagarriak, erlatiboak, konparaziozkoak, ondoriozkoak*). Bilbo: Euskaltzaindia and EHU. (= *EGLU* V)

——— (1993). *Euskal gramatika laburra: perpaus bakuna.* Bilbo: Euskaltzaindia. (= *EGL*)

Euskera. Official organ of Euskaltzaindia, the Royal Academy of the Basque Language. Bilbo: Euskaltzaindia.

Eusk. Ip. = *Euskalerriko ipuiñak*, see under Euskaltzaindia.

Ezkila (ed.) (1974). *Jesu Kristoren Berri Ona.* Belloc-Urt: Ed. Ezkila. (= *JKBO*)

F. Bart. = Fray Bartolomé de Santa Teresa, see Madariaga, Bartolomé.

Fernandez Ibañez, Jesus (1978). *Cien piezas vascas para flauta dulce.* Bilbao: Ed. La Gran Enciclopedia Vasca.

FHV = *Fonética histórica vasca*, see Michelena 1977.

G. = *Garoa*, see under Agirre, Domingo.

Gandiaga, Bitoriano (1997). *Ahotsik behartu gabe.* Donostia: Erein.

Garate, Gotzon (1984). *Alaba.* Donostia: Elkar.

——— (1982). *Aldarte oneko ipuinak.* Bilbao: Ed. Mensajero. (= *Ald.*)

——— (1998). *27,173 Atsotitzak* (proverbs). Bilbao: Bilbao Bizkaia Kutxa Fundazioa. (= *Atsot.*)

——— (1981). *Elizondoko eskutitzak.* 2nd edition, Bilbao: Ed. Mensajero. (= *E.E.*)

——— (1988). *Erdarakadak.* Bilbao: Ed. Mensajero. (= *Erd.*)

——— (1985). *Esku leuna.* Donostia: Elkar. (= *Esku*)

——— (1986). *Goizuetako ezkongaiak.* Donostia: Elkar. (= *G.E.*)

——— (1983). *Hades-en erresumarantz.* Donostia: Elkar. (= *Hades*)

——— (1984). *Izurri berria.* Donostia: Elkar. (= *Iz.B.*)

——— (1980). *Lehortean ipuinak.* Bilbao: Ed. Mensajero. (= *Leh.*)

——— (1987). *Muskilak.* 2nd edition, Bilbao: Ed. Mensajero. (= *Musk.*)

——— (1988). *New York, New York.* Donostia: Elkar. (= *NY*)

Garibay, Esteban [1591]. *Refranes de Garibay*, pp. 53–75 in (edition of) J. R. Zubiaur and J. Arzamendi (1976). "El léxico vasco de los refranes de Garibay." *ASJU* 10:47–144.

Garmendia, Txomin (1982). *Bizitzaren arian.* Tolosa: Auspoa.

Garro, B. M. (1961). "Euskerazko era batzuk: dakazan gramatika oar batzukatik. B. M. Garro-k Aita L. Villasante-ri egin zion karta." *Euskera* (n.s.) 6:358–360.

Gerriko, see Guerrico.

Gèze, Louis (1873). *Éléments de grammaire basque dialecte souletin suivis d'un vocabulaire basque-français, français-basque.* Bayonne. 1979 facsimile edition, Donostia: Hordago.

Goenaga, Patxi (1985). "Complementación y nominalización en euskera." *ASJU* 19:493–570. (= *Comp.*)

——— (1978). *Gramatika bideetan.* Donostia: Erein. (= *G.B.*)

——— (1980). *Gramatika bideetan.* 2nd revised and enlarged edition, Donostia: Erein. (= *G.B.*^{2})

Goldaraz, see under Astiz Odériz.

Goñi, Francisco (1962). *Ama Birjiñaren Agertziak eta gañerako Lurdes-ko gertaera goguangarriyak.* A. Zavala's edition, Tolosa: Auspoa. First published in Durango, 1908.

Goyhetche, Leonce (1852). *Fableac edo aleguiac Lafontenenetaric berechiz hartuac.* Baiona. 1978 facsimile edition, Donostia: Hordago.

Guerrico, José Ignacio de (1858). *Cristau doctriña guztiaren esplicacioaren sayaquera* I, II. Tolosa: Mendizabal. (*DGV*: written ca. 1805.)

Haranburu-Altuna, Luis (1995). *Auskalo, Luk.* Donostia: Elkar. (= *Ausk.*)

——— (1983). *Itsasoak ez du esperantzarik.* 6th edition, Donostia: Kriselu. (= *Its.*)

——— (1975). *Job.* Donostia: Kriselu.

Haraneder, Joannes de (1990). *Jesu Christoren Evangelio Saindua.* Patxi Altuna's edition of MS dating from ca. 1740. Bilbao: Euskaltzaindia. (= HE)

Harriet, Martin (1741). *Gramatica escuaraz eta francesez, composatua francez, hitzcunça ikhasi nahi dutenen faboretan.* Bayonne: Fauvet.

HE = Haraneder, Joannes de.

Hiriart-Urruty, Jean (1995). *Gontzetarik jalgiaraziak.* Iñaki Camino's edition, Donostia: EEE/Erein.

——— (1971). *Mintzaira, aurpegia: Gizon!* (Articles pubished between 1892 and 1912 selected and with a foreword by P. Lafitte.) Baiona: IKAS & Oñati: Ed. Franciscana Arantzazu/Jakin. (= *Aurp.*)

——— (1972). *Zezenak Errepublikan.* (Edition of Joseba Intxausti of articles published between 1892 and 1912 selected by P. Lafitte.) Baiona: IKAS & Oñati: Ed. Franciscana Arantzazu/Jakin. (= *Zez.*)

Hiribarren, Jean Martin (1853). *Eskaldunac.* Baiona. 1979 facsimile edition, Donostia: Hordago. (= *Esk.*)

——— (1858). *Eskaraz eguia.* Baiona. (= *Egia*)

[Hoyarzabal, Martin de] (1677). *Liburu han da ixasoco nabigacionecoa Martin de Hoyarzabalec egiña Francezes. Eta Piarres Detcheverry, edo Dorrec escarat emana.* Baiona. 1985 facsimile edition, San Sebastián: Ed. Txertoa. (= *I Nav.*)

H.U. = Hiriart-Urruty, Jean.

Hualde Mayo, Pedro Prudencia. (19th-century translation of Matthew into Roncalese). In Estornes Lasa, José (1982). "Jesu-Kristo gore Jeinaren Ebanjelio Saintiua. Pedro Prudenzio Hualde Mayo. Oraiko ortografiaz eta anotazione batzuk." *FLV* 14:43–103.

I Nav., see under Hoyarzabal, M.

IB = *Itun Berria*, see under Euskal Herriko Elizbarrutietako Gotzaiak.

Ibiñagabeitia, Andima (1966). *Bergiliren idazlanak osorik: unai-kantak eta alor-kantak.* Bilbao. (= *Virgil.*)

Imit. (*Imitation of Christ*), see under Pouvreau, S., and Chourio, M.

Inchauspe, Emmanuel (1856). *Le Saint Evangile de Jésus-Christ selon Saint Mathieu* (traduit en basque souletin)/ *Jesus-Kristen Ebanjelio Saintia, Sen Mathiuren arauéra.* Bayonne: Lamaignère. Reprinted in 1991 in L. L. Bonaparte, *Opera omnia vasconice* II, 161–270. Bilbao: Euskaltzaindia. (= Intx.)

——— (1857). *Dialogues basques (versión souletins).* London: L. L. Bonaparte. Facsimile editions: Donostia–San Sebastián: Hordago, 1978, and in L. L. Bonaparte, *Opera omnia vasconice* II, 309–433. Bilbao: Euskaltzaindia, 1991. (= *Dial.*)

Intx. = Intxauspe, see Inchauspe.

Intza, Dámaso [Miguel Olasagarre] (1924). *Kristau ikasbidearen azalpena.* Pamplona. (= *Azalp.*)

Iraizoz, Policarpo [Agustín Zarranz] (1934). *Yesukristo gure Yaunaren bizia lau Ebangelioetatik itzez-itz atera ta.* Iruñea.

Iraola Aristiguieta, Bitoriano (1962). *Oroitzak ta beste ipui asko.* A. Zavala's edition of articles first published in *Baserritarra*, 1906–1908. Tolosa: Auspoa.

Irazusta, Jon Andoni (1950). *Bizia garratza da ....* Buenos Aires: Ed. Vasca Ekin. (= *Bizia*)

——— (1991). *Joañixio.* Edition of Gotzon Garate. Donostia: EEE/Sendoa. First published in 1946 in Buenos Aires: Ed. Vasca Ekin. (= *Joan.*)

Irigarai, see Irigaray.

Irigaray, Angel (ed.) (1958). *Prosistas navarros contemporáneos en lengua vasca. XX-garren mendeko Nafarroako Euskal idazlariak.* (Selected writings of Enrike Zubiri and Pablo Fermín Irigarai compiled by A. Irigaray). Pamplona: Institución "Príncipe de Viana".

Irigoyen, Juan Mari (1976). *Oilarraren promesa.* Bilbao: Mensajero.

Ithurralde, P. = Lafitte, P.

Iturbe, Arantxa (1995). *Lehenago zen berandu.* 2nd edition, Irun: Alberdania.

Iturriaga, Agustín Pascual de (1842). *Diálogos basco-castellanos para las escuelas de primeras letras de Guipúzcoa.* Hernani. 1857 edition of L. L. Bonaparte, London. Facsimile editions, Donostia: Hordago, 1978; and L. L. Bonaparte, *Opera omnia vasconice* II, 309–433, Bilbao: Euskaltzaindia, 1991. (= *Dial.*)

Itziar ta Agirre, Martin (1968). *Larraundi'ko sendia.* Zarautz: Itxaropena.

Izeta, Mariano (1962). *Dirua galgarri.* Tolosa: Auspoa. (= *Dirua*)

——— (1982). *Nigarrez sortu nintzan.* Donostia: Gipuzkoako Arruezki Kutxa Probintziala. (= *Nigarrez*)

Iztueta, Juan Ignacio de (1847). *Guipuzcoaco provinciaren kondaira edo historia.* Donostia: R. Baroja.

Jautarkol [Luis Jauregi] (1929). *Biozkadak.* Iruñea. (= *B.*)

——— (1953). *Ipuiak.* Zarautz: Itxaropena. (= *Ip.*)

JJMg. = Moguel, Juan José.

JKBO = *Jesu Kristoren Berri Ona*, see under Ezkila.

JMB = Barandiaran, J. M.

Jnn. = Joannategi, B.

Joannategi, Bazilio (1890). *Sainduen bizitzea, lehen zatia.* Baiona: Lasserre Baithan Imp. (= *SBi*)

Kantuz, see under Etchemendy, Paul.

Kardaberaz, see Cardaberaz.

Ker. = Kerexeta, Jaime.

Kerexeta, Jaime (1976). *Euskal Biblia* (*Bizkaieraz*). Bilbao: Bilbo'ko Elizbarrutiko Gotzaintza. (= Ker.)

Kintana, Xabier (ed.) (1971). *Joannes Etxeberri Sarakoaren lan hautatuak*. Donostia: LUR. (= Etxeberri Sarakoa)

Kirikiño [Ebaista Bustinza] (1966). *Abarrak*. Bilbao: Gráficas Bilbao. References are to the edition of Kirikiño's work collected and introduced by Aita Onaindia. The volume contains the earlier published *Abarrak* (Abando, 1918), *Bigarren abarrak* (Zornotsa/Amorebeita, 1930), and, under the heading "Eta abar . . . ," works dating from 1902–1903. (= *Ab.*)

Kristau Ik. = *Kristau-Ikasbidea*, see under Donosti'ko Eliz-barutirako.

Labayen, Antonio M. (1978). *Elizanburu. Bere bizitza ta lanak. Su vida y obras*. Donostia-San Sebastián: Auñamendi. (= Elzb. *Po.*)

——— (1966). "Su ta gar." *Egan*, 155–164. (= *S.G.*)

——— (1966). "Su–Emailleak." *Egan*, 165–215. Translated from Max Frisch, "Biedermann und die Brandstifter." (= *Su Em.*)

——— (1977). *Teatro osoa euskeraz.* (Obras completas de teatro vasco.) 3 vols. Bilbao: Ed. La Gran Enciclopedia Vasca. (= *TOE*)

Lafitte, Pierre (1945). (under pseud. P. Ithurralde): *Murtuts eta bertze . . . Artho churitzetako zonbait ichtorio chahar*. Bayonne: Coll. "Aintzina". (= LF, *Murtuts*)

Lakarra, Joseba A. (1996). *Refranes y Sentencias (1596). Ikerketak eta Edizioa* (critical edition). Bilbao: Euskaltzaindia. (Nos. refer to proverbs.) (= *R.S.*)

——— et al. (1983). *Euskal baladak* II: *Azterketa eta antología.* Donostia. (= *Balad.*)

Landart, Daniel (1989). *Aihen ahula*, 3rd edition. Donostia: Elkar.

Landerretche, Martin (1927). "Erran zuhar eta errankizun-adituzkoak," *Euskera* 1–2:66–69.

Lapeyre, Étienne (1982). *Kredo edo sinhesten dut esplikatua.* Luis Villasante's edition, Bilbao: Euskaltzaindia. First published in Baiona, 1891.

Lapitze, F. (1867). *Bi saindu hescualdunen bizia: San Iñazio Loiolacoarena eta San Franzizco Zabierecoarena.* Baiona. 1978 facsimile edition, Donostia: Hordago.

Lardizabal, Franzisko Ignazio de (1957). *Testamentu berriko kondaira edo historia.* 2nd edition, Bilbao: Euskal Idaz-lanak. First published in Tolosa, 1855. (= *TB*)

——— (1995). *Testamentu zarreko kondaira* I, II. Edition of Blanca Urgell, Donostia: EEE/Kriselu. First published in Tolosa, 1855. (= *TZ*)

Larramendi, Manuel de (1729). *El imposible vencido. Arte de la lengua bascongada*. Salamanca. 1979 facsimile edition, Donostia: Hordago.

Larréguy, B. (1775–1777). *Testamen çaharreco eta berrico historioa* I (1775), II (1777). Baiona. 1978 facsimile edition, Donostia: Hordago.

Larzabal, Piarres (1965). *Hilla esposatu* (with M. Lekuona's Guipuzcoan version). Tolosa: Auspoa. (= *Hil.*)

——— (1962). *Hiru ziren; Herriko bozak.* (Plays from 1956–1957.) Tolosa: Auspoa separata. (= *Hiru*)

——— (1991). *Piarres Larzabalen idazlanak* I, *Etxahun eta . . .* (ed. P. Xarritton). Donostia: Elkar. (= *Larzabal* I)

——— (1964). *Senpere-n gertatua* (with Villasante's Guipuzcoan version). Tolosa: Auspoa. (= *Senp.*)

Lasarte, Manuel (1975). *Gordean neuzkanak.* Tolosa: Auspoa. (= *Gordean*)

——— (1994). *Lazkao-txiki gogoan.* Oiartzun: Sendoa. (= *L.G.*)

Lau Eb. = *Lau ebanjelioak*, see under Mendizabal, P.

Lazkao-txiki [José Migel Iztueta] (1994). *Irriz eta malkoz* I, II. Oiartzun: Sendoa.

LBB = *Lur berri billa*, see under Etxaniz, Nemesio.

L.E. *Kop.*, see under Lizarraga Elkanokoa, Joakin.

Leiçarraga, Joannes (1571). *Iesus Christ gure Iaunaren Testamentu Berria*, La Rochelle. Reference is to 1900 edition of Th. Linschmann & H. Schuchardt, *I. Leiçarragas Baskische Bücher von 1571*, Strassburg: Trübner. (= Lz)

——— (1571). "Orthoitza Ecclesiasticoen forma," pp. A1r–A8r in Linschmann & Schuchardt 1900. (= *Ins.*)

——— (1571). "Batbederac iaquiteco, eta maiz iracurtzeco duen Advertimendua . . . ," pp. *8r–***1r in Linschmann & Schuchardt 1900. (= Lz, *Adv*)

——— (1571). *Abc edo Christinoen instructionea othoitz eguiteco formarequin.* In Linschmann & Schuchardt 1900. (= Lz, *Abc*)

Leizarraga, see Leiçarraga.

Lekuona, Manuel (1933). *Eun dukat.* Tolosa.

——— (1978). *Idaz-lan guztiak.* 2. *Eusko Etnografía.* Tolosa: Kardaberaz (Bilduma 23). (= *IG* II)

Lerchundi, Gabriel (1948). *Kantikak. Cantiques basques.* Urt: Abbaye N.-D. de Belloc & Bayonne: "Le Livre."

Lertxundi, Anjel (1984). *Aise eman zenidan eskua.* 3rd edition, Donostia: Erein. (= *Aise*)

——— (2000). *Goiko kale.* Irun: Alberdania. First published in 1973. (= *G.K.*)

——— (1983). *Hamaseigarrenean, aidanez.* Donostia: Erein. (= *Hamasei.*)

——— (1984). *Urtero da aurten.* Donostia: Erein. (= *Urtero*)

LF = Lafitte, Pierre.

Lh. = Lhande, Pierre.

Lhande, Pierre (1926–1938). *Dictionnaire basque-français.* Paris: Beauchesne. (= Lh.)

Linazasora, Iñaki (1970). *H gabe-ko umoria.* Zarautz: Itxaropena.

Lizardi, Xabier [J. M. Agirre] (1956). *Biotz-begietan, olerkiak* (poesías vascas, con traducción castellana). 2nd edition, San Sebastián: Valverde. First published in Bilbao, 1932.

Lizarraga Elkanokoa, Joakin (1983). *Koplak.* Critical edition of J. Apecechea Perurena of verses mostly composed between 1793 and 1813. Bilbao: Real Academia de la Lengua Vasca–Euskaltzaindia. (= L.E. *Kop.*)

Loidi Bizkarrondo, J. A. (1968). *Amabost egun urgain'en*, 4th edition. Oñate: Arantzazu. First published in Zarautz, 1955.

López Mendizabal, Isaac (1962). *Manual de conversación castellano-euskera ....* 4th edition, Donostia: Auñamendi.

LVP = *Linguae vasconum primitiae*, see under Etxepare, Bernard.

Lz = Leiçarraga.

Madariaga, Bartolomé (Fray Bartolomé de Santa Teresa) (1816). *Euskal-errijetaco olgueeta, ta dantzeen neurrizco-gatz-ozpinduba.* Iruñea. 1978 facsimile edition, Donostia: Hordago. (= Bartolomé)

——— (1816, 1817, 1819). *Icasiquizunac*, I, II, III. Iruñea. (= *Ikas.*)

Mahn, C. A. F. (1857). *Denkmaeler der baskischen Sprache.* Berlin. 1967 facsimile edition, Oosterhout: Anthropological Publications.

Manzisidor, Inazio M. (1953). *Jesukristoren bizitza.* Bilbao: Mensajero.

Materre, E. (1623). *Doctrina Christiana. Aita Esteve Materre San Franciscoren ordenaco Fraideac eguina.* 2nd edition, Bordeaux. First published in 1617. Example cited is from *DGV* V, 93.

Mattin [Mattin Treku] (1971). *Ahal dena.* Tolosa: Auspoa.

MEIG = *Mitxelenaren euskal idazlan guztiak*, see under Mitxelena, Koldo.

Mendiburu, Sebastián (1904). *Jesusen amore-nekeei dagozten zenbait otoitz-gai* II. Tolosa. First published in 1760, Iruñea. (= *Ot. Gai.* II)

——— (1760). *Jesusen amore-nequeei dagozten cembait otoiz-gai* III. Iruñea: Iruñeco libru-guille Antonio Castillaren echean. (= *Ot. Gai.* III)

——— (1982). *Mendibururen idazlan argitaragabeak* I, II. Critical edition of P. Altuna, Bilbao: Euskaltzaindia and Mensajero. (= *I.Arg.*)

Mendiguren, Xabier (1975). "Estatu Izenak." *Euskera* 20:373–387.

——— (1992). *Hamalau.* Donostia: Elkar.

Mendizabal, Fernando (1969). *Euskaldunentzat oiñarrizko gramatika euskeraz (gipuzkoeraz nagusienik) ....* Oñate: Aránzazu.

Mendizabal, P. (1961). *Lau ebanjelioak.* Zarautz: Itxaropena. (= *Lau Eb.*)

Michelena, Luis (1987–). *Diccionario general vasco/Orotariko euskal hiztegia* (14 volumes published 1987–2002). Bilbao: Euskaltzaindia; Ed. Desclée de Brouwer and Ed. Mensajero. (= *DGV*)

——— see also Mitxelena, Koldo.

MIH = *Mitxelenaren idazlan hautatuak*, see under Mitxelena, Koldo.

Mintegi, Laura (1995). *Nerea eta biok*. 2nd edition, Tafalla: Ed. Txalaparta.

Mirande, Jon (1970). *Haur Besoetakoa. Ipuin berri bat.* (*DGV*: G. Aresti edition.) Donostia: LUR. (= *HaurB.*)

——— (1976). *Miranderen idazlan hautatuak.* Bilbao: Mensajero. (= *Pr.*)

——— (1976). *Orhoituz.* (A. Eguzkitza's edition.) Donostia: Kriselu. (= *Po.*)

Mitxelena, Koldo (1988). *Euskal idazlan guztiak* I–IX. Editors: P. Altuna (I–III), B. Urgell (IV–V), J. Lakarra (VI–VII), I. Sarasola (VIII–IX). Donostia: Euskal Editoreen Elkartea (Elkar, Erein, Etor, Kriselu, Labayru, Mensajero). (= *MEIG*)

——— (1972). *Mitxelenaren idazlan hautatuak* (P. Altuna's edition). Bilbao: Mensajero. (= *MIH*)

——— (1972). *Zenbait hitzaldi.* Bilbao: Mensajero. (= *Z.H.*)

Mitxelena, Salbatore (1977, 1984). *Idazlan Guztiak* I, II. Edited by K. Iturria and J. A. Gandarias. (I) Oñati: Ed. Franciscana Arantzazu; (II) Zarautz: Itxaropena. (= *IG*)

Mogel, Bizenta A. (1963). *Ipui onak.* 3rd edition, Tolosa: Auspoa. First published in 1804. (= *Ip.*)

Mogel/Moguel, Juan Antonio (1994). *El catequista bascongado/Cristau eracasle euscalduna.* Edition of Adolfo Arejita, Bilbao: Labayru Ikastegia & Bilbao Bizkaia Kutxa. (= *Cat. Basc.*)

——— (1803). *Confesino ona.* Vitoria. (= *C.O.*)

——— (1800). *Confesio ta comunioco sacramentuen gañean eracasteac edo* .... Iruñea. (= *C.C.*)

——— (1987). *Cristaubaren icasbidea edo doctrina cristiania.* Luis Villasante's critical edition of MS written ca. end of 18th century. Bilbao: Real Academia de la Lengua Vasca–Euskaltzaindia. (= *D.C.*)

——— (1995). *Ipuinak* (Xabier Altzibar's edition). Bilbao: Labayru et al. (= *Ip.*)

——— (1881). *El doctor Peru Abarca.* Durango. 1981 facsimile edition, Bilbao: Ed. Asociacion Gerediaga. Written ca. 1802. (= *P.Ab.*)

——— *Sermoi*, see under Arejita, A.

Moguel, Juan José (1816). *Baseerritaar nequezaleentzaco escolia edo icasbidiac, guraso justu, ta jaquitun familija ondo azi ebeeneen exemplu ta eracutsijetan.* Bilbao. (= JJMg, *Bas. Esc.*)

Mokoroa, Justomari (1958). *Erraondo-ko azken danbolinteroa. Arturo Campion-en ipuia.* 3rd edition, Bilbao: Ediciones de la Academia Vasca. First published in 1925.

Múgica Berrondo, Plácido (1965). *Diccionario castellano–vasco.* Bilbao: Mensajero. (= *DCV*)

——— (1981). *Diccionario vasco–castellano.* Bilbao: Mensajero. (= *DVC*)

Mujika, José Antonio (1988). "*Partículas modales de la flexión verbal.*" *ASJU* 22:463–478.

Munita, Inozenzio (1952). *Gure mendi ta oianak. Zuaizti berriak antolatu, ta lengoak zaintzeko zuzenbide batzuek.* Tolosa.

Muxika, G. (1925). *Pernando Amezketarra. Bere ateraldi eta gertaerak.* San Sebastián. Reference is to 4th edition, n.d. Zarautz: Itxaropena. (= *P.Am.*)

Oihartzabal, B., see Oyharçabal, B.

Oihenarte, Arnaut (1971). *Atsotitzak eta neurtitzak.* Larresoro's edition. Donostia: Ed. Herri-Gogoa. First published in 1657: *Les Proverbes basques, recuellis par le S. d' Oihenart, plus les poésies Basques du mesme Auteur.* Paris. (Reference is to nos. of proverbs.) (= *Prov.*)

Olabide, Erraimun (1958). *Itun zâř eta beřia.* Bilbao: Yesu'ren Biotzaren Deya. (= Olab.)

Onaindia, M. (1983). *Gau Ipuiak.* Donostia: Haranburu. (= *Gau Ip.*)

Onaindia, (Aita) Santiago (1974). *Eskutitzak.* Bilbao.

——— (1978). *Lamiñak.* Amorebieta-Larrea. (= *Lam.*)

Oñatibia, Yon (1983). *Neke ta poz. Erbesteratu baten oroitzapenak.* Donostia: Edili.

Oñederra, Lourdes (1999). *Eta emakumeari sugeak esan zion.* Donostia: Erein.

Orixe [Nikolas Ormaetxea] (1956). *Agustiñ Gurenaren Aitorkizunak* (Confessions of St. Augustine). Zarautz: Itxaropena. (= *Aitork.*)

——— (1950). *Euskaldunak. Poema, XV kantuetan. Santos Etxeberria'ren irudiak.* Zarautz: Itxaropena. (= *Eusk.*)

——— (1972). *"Euskaldunak" poema eta olerki guztiak.* Donostia–San Sebastián: Auñamendi. (= *Poem.*)

——— (1927). In "Euskal—Literatura'ren atze edo edesti laburra." *Euskal-Esnalea* 17:192.

——— (1961). In *Olerti* (Jorr.-Bag.), 93.

——— (1987). *Quito-n arrebarekin.* Edition of I. Segurola, Donostia: EEE/Ibaizabal. (= *Q.A.*)

——— (1929). *Santa Cruz apaiza.* Donostia: Leizaola. (= *S.Cruz*)

"Orixe" Omenaldi (1965). Donostia: Euskaltzaindia. (= *OrOm*)

Ormaetxea, Nikolas, see Orixe.

OrOm = *"Orixe" Omenaldi.*

Oskillaso [José de Basterrechea] (1988). *Gabeko atorra.* Bilbao: Ibaizabal. (= *Gab.At.*)

——— (1962). *Kurloiak. Kaletarren haur-zaroa bizkaian.* Zarautz: Itxaropena. (= *Kurl.*)

——— (1981). *El vasco de hoy* I. Bilbao: La Gran Enciclopedia Vasca.

Oxobi [Jules Moulié] (1966). *Oxobi-ren lan orhoitgarri zonbait.* Bayonne: "Gure Herria."

Oyharçabal, B. (1989). "Pro-drop and the Resumptive Pronoun Strategy in Basque." In L. Marácz and P. Muysken (eds.), *Configurationality: The Typology of Asymmetries*, 63–83. Dordrecht: Foris. (= *Pro-drop*)

——— (1985). *Les relatives en basque.* Université Paris 7. (= *R.B.*)

P.Ab. = *Peru Abarca*, see under Mogel, J. A.

P.Ad. = *Piarres Adame*, see under Elissamburu, J. B.

Pas Sant, see under Bernaolacoa.

Peillen, Txomin (1973). *Gatu beltza.* Bilbao: Mensajero.

Pouvreau, Silvain (17th century). *Grammaire de la langue basque.* In *Les petites oeuvres*, 1–9. J. Vinson edition, Chalon-sur-Saône: L. Marceau, 1892. 1978 facsimile edition, Donostia: Hordago.

——— (ca. 1660). *Iesusen Imitacionea.* Donostia: Hordago, 1979. (= *Imit.*)

——— (1664). *San Frances de Sales Genevaco ipizpicuaren Philotea ....* Paris. (= *Philotea*)

Riezu, P. Jorge de (1948). *Flor de canciones populares vascas.* Buenos Aires: Ed. Vasca Ekin.

Rijk, Rudolf P. G. de (1998). *De lingua vasconum: Selected Writings. ASJU, Supp.* 43. (= *DLV*)

Rozas, Ixiar (2000). *Edo zu edo ni.* Donostia: Erein.

R.S. = *Refranes y Sentencias*, see under Lakarra, J. A.

Saizarbitoria, Ramon (1997). *Egunero hasten delako.* 5th edition, Donostia: Erein. First published in 1969.

Salaberria, Sebastián (1994). *Neronek tirako nizkin.* Oiartzun: Sendoa. Published earlier in 1964, Tolosa: Auspoa.

Salaburu Echeverría, Pello (1980). *Baztango Euskalkiaz* (I), (*Bruno Echenique-k egindako itzulpenak Bonaparteren eskakizunez*). Bilbo: Deustuko Unibertsitateko Argitarazioak. (= Etx./Echenique)

Sallaberry, Jean D. (1930). *Chants populaires du pays basque.* Paris. First published in Bayonne, 1870.

Saltarelli, Mario, et al. (1988). *Basque.* London & New York: Croom Helm.

San Martin, Juan (1984). *Zirikadak.* 2nd edition, Donostia: Elkar. First published in 1960, Zarautz: Itxaropena.

Sarasola, Ibon (1996). *Euskal Hiztegia.* Donostia: Kutxa Fundazioa. (= *E.H.*)

——— (1984–1995). *Hauta-lanerako euskal hiztegia.* Donostia: Gipuzkoa Donostia Kutxa. (= *HLEH*)

Sarrionandia, Joseba (1984). *Narrazioak.* 3rd edition, Donostia: Elkar.

Satrustegi, J. M. (1973). *Ekaitza.* Oinati: Ed. Franciscana Arantzazu.

Soroa Lasa, Marzelino (1961). *Au ostatuba!! Jostirudia euskerara moldatuba.* A. Zavala's edition, Tolosa: Auspoa. First published in 1884. (= *A.O.*)

——— (1963). *Baratzan.* Edition of A. Zavala, Tolosa: Auspoa. *DGV*: first published in 1886 in *Euskal Erria.* (= *Bar.*)

Sota, Manuel de la, Pierre Lafitte, and Lino de Akesolo (1976–1989). *Diccionario Retana de autoridades de la lengua vasca.* 9 volumes. Bilbao: Ed. La Gran Enciclopedia Vasca. (= *DRA*)

SP = Pouvreau, Silvain.

Tamura, S. (1985). "Hitzen ordena erabakitzeko fatoreak." *Euskera* 30:71–101.

Tartas, Ivan de (1666). *Onsa hilceco bidia.* Orthez. Reference is to facsimile published in Altuna's critical edition of 1987, Bilbao: Universidad de Deusto. (= *Onsa*)

TB = *Testamentu berriko* ... see under Lardizabal, F. I.

Thomas, Llewelyn (1894). *The Earliest Translation of the Old Testament into the Basque Language (A Fragment) by Pierre d' Urte of St. Jean de Luz circa 1700.* Oxford: Clarendon Press. Reprinted by AMS Press, New York, 1989. (= Urt.)

TOE = *Teatro osoa euskeraz*, see under Labayen, A.

Txill. = Txillardegi.

Txillardegi [José Luis Alvarez Enparantza] (1988). *Exkixu.* Donostia: Elkar.

——— (1957). *Leturia-ren egunkari ezkutua.* Bilbao: Euskal Idaz-lanak (Euskaltzaindia). (= *Let.*)

Txirr. = *Txirrita*, see under Zavala, Antonio.

Txirrita [J. M. Lujambio], *B.* = *Txirritaren Bertsoak*, see under Zavala, Antonio.

TZ = *Testamentu zarreko* ..., see under Lardizabal, F. I.

Ubillos, (Fray) Juan Antonio (1785). *Christau doctriñ berri-ecarlea.* Tolosa. 1978 facsimile edition, Donostia: Hordago.

Ur. = Uriarte, José A.

Uriarte, José Antonio (1857). *El Apocalipsis del apóstol San Juan/San Juan apostolubaren aguertueria* (Biskaieraz). London: L. L. Bonaparte. Facsimile edition in L. L. Bonaparte, *Opera omnia vasconice* IV, 113–151. Bilbao: Euskaltzaindia, 1991. (= Ur.)

——— (1858). *El Apocalipsis del apóstol San Juan/San Juan apostoluaren apokalipsisa* (Guipuzcoan version). London. See pp. 153–189 in preceding entry. (= Ur.)

——— (1859). *Biblia edo Testamentu zar eta berria. Guipuzcoaco euscarara itzulia.* (Genesis, Exodus, & Leviticus). London: L. L. Bonaparte. Facsimile editions: Donostia: Hordago, 1978 and in L. L. Bonaparte, *Opera omnia vasconice* IV, 307–438. Bilbao: Euskaltzaindia, 1991. (= Ur.)

——— (1857). *Dialogues basques (versión vizcaína).* London: L. L. Bonaparte. Facsimile editions: Donostia–San Sebastián: Hordago, 1978, and in L. L. Bonaparte, *Opera omnia vasconice* II, 309–433. Bilbao: Euskaltzaindia, 1991. (= *Dial.*)

——— (1858). *El Evangelio según San Mateo traducido al vascuence, dial. Guipuzcoano.* London: L. L. Bonaparte. Facsimile edition in L. L. Bonaparte, *Opera omnia vasconice* IV, 227–305. Bilbao: Euskaltzaindia, 1991. (= Ur.)

Urkizu, Patrizio (ed.) (1984). *Astolasterrak.* (*DGV*: 18th- and 19th-century folk texts). San Sebastián. (= *Ast. Las.*)

Urretabizkaia, Arantxa (1983). *Aspaldian. Espero zaitudalako. Ez nago sekula bakarri..* Donostia: Erein. (= *Asp.*)

——— (1982). *Maitasunaren magalean.* Donostia: Guipuzkoako Aurrezki Kutxa Probintziala. (= *Mait.*)

——— (1990). *Saturno.* 3rd edition. Donostia: Erein. (= *Sat.*)

——— (1983). *Zergatik panpox.* Donostia: Hordago. (= *Zerg.*)

Urretavizcaya, see Urretabizkaia.

Urruzuno, Pedro Miguel (1961). *Euskalerritik zerura ta beste ipui batzuk.* (Compilation of works published between 1894 and 1917.) Tolosa: Auspoa. (= *E.Z.*)

——— (1988). *Ipuinak.* (Stories published between 1885 and 1920, edition of L. M. Larringan.) Donostia: EEE/Kriselu. (= *Ip.*)

——— (1965). *Ur-zale baten ipuiak.* (Compilation of work published between 1885 and 1893, edition of A. Zavala.) Tolosa: Auspoa. (= *Urz*)

Urt. = Pierre d'Urte, see under Thomas, L.

Urte, Pierre d' (1715). *Dictionarium latino cantabricum.* In Patrizio Urkizu (1989), *Pierre d' Urteren hiztegia, Londres 1715* (= *Mundaiz* 1–2). San Sebastián: Universidad de Deusto.

——— (1712). *Grammaire cantabrique basque.* Bagnères-de-Bigorre, 1900.

Usk. gut. = *Uskaldunaren guthunak.*

Uskaldunaren guthunak (1946). Edizione berria (new expanded edition). Bayonne: Firmin Seris-en Salgian. (= *Usk. gut.*)

Uztapide [Manuel Olaizola Urbieta] (1975). *Lengo egunak gogoan* I, II, 2nd edition. Tolosa: Auspoa. (= *LEG*)

——— (1964). *Noizbat.* Tolosa: Auspoa. (= *Noizb.*)

——— (1976). *Sasoia joan da gero.* Tolosa: Auspoa. (= *Sas.*)

Villasante, Luis (1962). *Kristau fedearen sustraiak I. Jainkoa.* Oñati-Arantzazu. (= *Jainkoa*)

Vogel, Florentin (n.d.). *Ene Hautia* (25 chants basques). 8th edition, Saint Palais: F. Vogel. (= *Ene H.*)

Voltoire (1620). *L' interprect ou traduction du François, Espagnol & Basque de Voltoire.* Lyon. Facsimile edition, Pau: icn, 2000.

Xalbador [Fernando Aire] (1969). *Ezin bertzean.* Tolosa: Auspoa. (= *Ezin B.*)

——— (1976). *Odolaren mintzoa.* Tolosa: Auspoa. (= *Odol.*)

Xaramela (1985). Donostia: Elkar.

Xarritton, P., see Charritton, P.

Xenp. = *Xenpelar* [Petriarena, J. F.], see under Zavala, Antonio.

Zabala, Alfonso M. de (1962). *Gabon gau bat eta beste ipui asko.* (Compiled by A. Zavala.) Tolosa: Auspoa. Published between 1880 and 1889 in *Euskal Erria.*

Zaitegi eta Plazaola, Iokin (1961). *Platon'eneko atarian.* San Sebastián. (= *Plat.*)

——— (1946). *Sopokel'en antzerkiak* I. México, D.F.: "Pizkunde." (= *Sof.*)

Zapirain, Salbador "Ataño" (1988). *Etorkizuna.* Donostia: Etor. (= *Etork.*)

——— (1988). *Maitasunaren lanak.* Donostia: Etor. (= *M.*)

——— (1986). *Odol-kutsua.* Tolosa: Auspoa. (= *Odol.*)

Zavala, Antonio (1985). *Esaera zaarren bilduma berria* I (A–G) & II (I–Z). Tolosa: Auspoa. (= *E.Z.B.B.*)

——— (1962). *Txirrita* (*Bizitza ta bat-bateko bertsoak*). Tolosa: Auspoa. (= *Txirr.*)

——— (1971). *Txirritaren bertsoak* I, II. Tolosa: Auspoa. (= Txirrita, *B.*)

——— (1981). *Xenpelar bertsolaria*, 2nd edition. Tolosa: Auspoa. (= *Xenp.*)

Zenbait ichtorio chahar artho churitzetako (1909). Bayonne: Lamaignère-Foltzer. (= *Artho Xur.*)

Zerbitzari [Jean Elissalde] (1943). *Ichtorio Saindua. Testament Zaharra. Jesu-Christo. Eliza.* Lille.

Zuazo, Koldo (2000). *Euskararen sendabelarrak.* Irun: Alberdania. (= *Sendabel.*)

Zubiri, Enrike "Manezaundi" (1990). *Artikulu bilduma.* Edition of R. M. Pagola, Bilbao: EEE/Labayru Ikastegia.

Standard Basque

A Progressive Grammar

Volume 2: The Glosses
Prepared by Armand De Coene

Rudolf P. G. de Rijk

Preface

On January 6, 1989, Rudolf de Rijk and I met for the first time. This meeting was the start of a master-pupil relationship in matters Basque and linguistic which turned into a friendship that lasted until Rudolf's untimely death on June 15, 2003.

A few days before he died, he decided that a section should be added to his Basque grammar containing glosses to all the example sentences in the book and that I should be asked to do this work. Thus it was that following his funeral his wife asked me if I would be willing to take on this responsibility. Having seen the work of my friend evolve over the years from a modest introductory course (in Dutch) into the comprehensive description of the Basque language that it now is, I was proud to be asked and consented with alacrity.

My commitment at that time and throughout the period of work was based on two personal motives. First, I felt privileged to be able to honor the memory of a man of singular intellectual integrity and exemplary modesty by making his scholarly testament about Basque linguistics more accessible to the English-reading nonspecialist in the field. Second, by taking the opportunity to fulfill his request, I might yet be able to say what Koldo Mitxelena once said: *Ni zerbait izan baldin banaiz, hizkuntzalaria edo izan naiz* (*MEIG* IX, 73, given as example sentence 5a in chapter 17).

I hope the glosses will enable learners to quickly check their own analyses, and the non-Bascologist linguists to arrive at an informed view of the unique character of the Basque language in all its diachronic, diatopic, and even sociolinguistic diversity. Where links with the synchronic morphological analysis are not too difficult to establish, I also deemed it worthwhile to offer some etymological suggestions (see, for example, the word *beraz* in examples 55a–58b in chapter 23).

There are some people without whom these glosses would never have seen the light of day. To say thank you in an appropriate way to Virginia de Rijk–Chan, I can find no adequate expressions, not even in my native Dutch. Without her moral and material support and her continuing commitment to the cause, neither my glosses nor indeed the work as a whole would ever have been completed; our collaboration has only strengthened the bonds of friendship.

At the beginning of my work, Wim van der Wurff was kind enough to discuss with me the method of glossing that I was proposing to use; at later stages he checked my work for clarity and consistency. At different stages of the process, Pello Salaburu, Bernard Oyharçabal, and Itziar Laka, all of them linguists and native speakers of Basque, took time to discuss with me some tricky questions about morpho-syntactic matters. The fact that, in the end, not every problem has been resolved was only to be expected, and the hope is that further investigation will be forthcoming, perhaps partly stimulated by my own contribution to Rudolf's grammar.

With respect to the difficult question of how to deal with the definite/indefinite opposition in *a*-stems denoting kinship, especially in the ascending line, I am greatly indebted to two native speakers of the dialect of the Haute Soule, where accentual differentiation turned out to provide a decisive answer (e.g., *ene áma* vs. *bere amá*, cf. section 1.3.1 and section 2.3.2 where no explicit differentiation is found in addressing first/second person versus third person as to the indefinite/definite distinction). I value not only their expert information but also the lasting friendship that was given me by Marie-José Capdevielle from Tardets, a natural-born linguist in all but name, and Maite Bengochea from Larrau, a born storyteller in every sense of the word.

Further, I would like to thank my wife, Irina Ushakova, who joined me in 2005 from St. Petersburg to brighten my life, for her forbearance. Last, but absolutely not least, I want to express my thankfulness and regard for my young daughter Valence, whose patience and considerateness I have surely overtaxed during the many months I was engaged in my glossing work. That is the reason why I end this preface, writing *Xiberoko mintzajiaz*, by stating:

Lan hau izkiribatü düt ene alhabatto ezinago maitiarentako, azken hiru urthe horietan bere aita sobera maite ükhen beitü deüsere handirik errezibitü gabe haren ganik.

Armand De Coene
Overslag
June 2007

Contents

Symbols Used in the Glosses

Note: Superscript numbers refer to the remarks following the list.

HAU Full capitals in Basque words mark the (quasi-)focus constituent of the example sentences in Chapter 8

Hau Italics in Basque words mark the (emphatic) sentence topic of the example sentences in Chapter 8

_ Connects two English/Basque words translating one single Basque/English word form or word group

___ Indicates that the combination of two or more words/lexemes functions as a syntactico-semantic unit (e.g., *mila___demonio/sorgin* in examples 2g,h of chapter 18)

. Used to join the English translation and the immediately following label(s) glossing the same Basque word form

- Joins the two members of an English compound; marks the boundary of a fully bound morph(eme)[1]

( ) In the glosses: indicates that two different readings are possible (e.g., *hil* in *hil nazan* is glossed as ‘kill(.RAD)’, which means that, in the context in question, the given form can be read either as the perfect participle or as the radical of the verb; in the Basque sentences: restoration of phonemes/morphemes not visible due to “inflectional” contact inside or outside the given word form[2]

> Becomes

< Comes from

* Reconstructed form

** Ungrammatical sentence

? Used to mark dubious grammaticality of a phrase/clause/sentence

= Marks the boundary of partially free morph (e.g., *baldin*=in combination with the preverbal particle *ba-* equals English conditional ‘if’; although its canonical position is directly in front of *ba-*, older usage, still accepted in the literary language, places it in front of the protasis)/connects the members of a Basque compound (e.g., *kale=garbitzaile* ‘street cleaner’)

1/2/3 With verbs, indicates first/second/third person; with demonstratives, indicates the degrees of deixis (corresponding to first, second, and third person in pronouns, see sections 6.3.1 and 9.6.1)

Remarks

1. The initial prefix of a nonfinite verb form will not be hyphenated, unless the verb has a synthetic conjugation too (e.g., *ezarr-i* vs. *e-torr-i*). The constituent morphemes of the imperfect participle (cf. section 7.2.4: nominalizing suffix *-tze* of the verbal noun followed by the original inessive case ending *-n*) will not be separated by a hyphen either in order to distinguish it from the gerund, made up from the same morphological material but presenting an explicit sort of competition with the allative form of the verbal noun as the expression of the kinetic gerundive (cf. 16.5.5); for the same reason, use has been made of different labels for these forms: IPF to label the imperfect participle versus VEN.LOC for the gerund (parallel to the label VEN.ALL used for a kinetic gerundive). Unless in intervocalic position, so-called strong /R/ will always be represented as (-)*r*(-) in the analysis.

The hyphenation in the glosses is fully in line with the analyses offered by R. de Rijk. Word forms containing several morphs will always be hyphenated as such, even if they are to some extent semantically lexicalized, provided that a morphological analysis of the form is given in the text of the *Grammar*. The only exceptions are the plural ergative suffix *-ek* (cf. section 2.2.1), the universal quantifier *den* (in order to differentiate this quantifier from its etymological base *d-en*, which is a free relative clause, cf. section 10.4), and substantivized adnominals (e.g., *etxeko* 'member of the family' < *etxe-ko*).

2. Instances of so-called Minor Apocope (e.g., *maita-ro* < **maite-ro*) will not be indicated in the Basque sentences, nor will restoration be shown of *-a* before a vowel in the present tense marker *da* and plural present tense forms of *izan* followed by the wh-complementizer.

Verbs that also have synthetic forms, and whose perfect participle/radical form ends in *-n*, never get this suffix restored in other forms; instead, the bare stem is singled out in the hyphenation (e.g., compare the pair *ja-ki-n* and *ja-ki-ten* with the pair *itxaron* and *itxaro(n)-ten*). Elision of phonemes in the onset of the stem of conjugated forms of the transitive and intransitive auxiliaries will not be indicated as such, since this phenomenon is frequently and explicitly dealt with in the appropriate places of the text of the grammar. To give one example, original *ba-g-a-di-tez* will be rendered as *ba-g-a-i-tez*; the same procedure is used for the verbal prefixes *da-/ze-/le-/be-* in the case of elision of their final vowel (e.g., *l-i-te-k* from original *le-di-te-ke*); elision of final *-a* of some present tense forms of *izan* before finite complementizers -N/-LA will not be indicated either (e.g., *g-a-r-ela* instead of *g-a-r(a)-ela*).

Abbreviations Used in the Glosses

Preliminary Remarks

Following the procedure adopted by J. I. Hualde and J. Ortiz de Urbina in *A Grammar of Basque* (Berlin and New York: Mouton de Gruyter, 2003, pp. 7–8), no abbreviation/labeling is provided, unless directly relevant, when dealing with instances to be taken as default cases of the grammatical category/categories in question. The following instances will be considered default ones ("zero morphs" are never shown in the labeling):

ABS ABSOLUTIVE (see remarks under note 1 concerning the glossing of auxiliaries)

ADV ADVERB (see note 2)

ART ARTICLE

AUX AUXILIARY

DAT DATIVE in auxiliary glosses (see note 1)

DEL DELETION/ELLIPSIS

- In the case of morphological inflections on postpositional phrases (5.2)
- In the case of the following nouns: *aldi* (13.2.4 and 20.3), *asmo* (17.7.1), *era* (11.1.6), *kontu* (17.7.2), *ordu* (4.2, 20.2), *puntu* (17.7.3), *uste* (18.8.2), an instrumental noun to account for the meaning "cause–reason" in causal clauses of the *-lako(tz)*-type (23.1.2)
- In the case of the following forms: An implicit verb of saying (18.2.2 and 23.2.2), verb of subordinate -LA clauses in sentences of the type *Haren begiek tximistak ziruditen* (18.5.2), *direlarik* in an idiomatic construction used when a concession concerns an unmodified plural noun (23.7.1)

ERG ERGATIVE in auxiliary glosses (see remarks under note 1)

IDF INDEFINITE (= the bare stem) with proper nouns (2.3.2) and nonfinal members of an indefinite word group; with indefinite (with the exception of *beste*)/ interrogative–exclamative (2.3.2)/synthetic reciprocal pronouns (15.8.1); with indefinite quantifier expressions (including *bat*) (2.3.2) and with locative/allative

(16.4)/privative (27.11.4) forms of the verbal noun; also indicating the bare stem of nominals, wherever appropriate/in nonfinite instrumental clauses governed by the postposition *gero*/*geroz*/*geroztik* (20.2.6)/in constructions with distributive numeratives (30.3)

IND INDICATIVE

MAS MASCULINE

PEF PERFECT PARTICIPLE

PER PERIPHRASTIC CONJUGATION

PRS PRESENT

PTC PARTICIPLE (This label appears in the case of perfect participle forms that do not express any shade of perfective aspect, e.g., in the combination with *ezin*, for which see 24.6.5.)

3 3RD PERSON

SIN SINGULAR DEFINITE, except for the use with perfect participle forms

-SOL -SOLIDARITY (characterizing 2nd-person singular)

izan INTRANSITIVE AUXILIARY

**edun* TRANSITIVE AUXILIARY

Remarks

1. A glossing of the type "know./PLU.SYT" in a sentence with a synthetic transitive verb indicates that there is either a singular (or indefinite, as the case may be) direct object or no such object at all and a plural subject; a gloss of the type "know.PLU/.SYT" indicates a plural direct object and a third-person singular subject; in the case of "know.PLU/PLU.SYT," both direct object and subject are plural. The same method of glossing finite verb forms is used in ditransitive constructions. The relative order will always be ABS–DAT–ERG; for example, "give.DYT" indicates that both the third-person subject and both objects (direct and indirect, if there is one) are singular, whereas "give.//PLU.DYT" indicates that the subject is plural but both the objects are singular; a gloss like "give.PLU/PLU/.DYT," however, conveys that both the objects are plural while the subject is singular.

The absence of slashes, even with a ditransitive auxiliary, indicates that the subject and the two objects are all third-person singular. For dealing with two arguments represented in the intransitive auxiliary, the following relative order is adopted: DAT–ABS.

The order of labels in finite forms of the verb is as follows:

a. Person precedes number (without any intervening dot) and number precedes (qualified) gender inside the object/subject category

b. Object/subject category precedes conjugation type 〈SYN vs. ITR equals SYT vs. TRA equals DYN vs. DIT equals DYT vs. DTR〉

c. Conjugation type precedes mood

d. Mood precedes tense

e. Tense precedes type of subordination

All this can result in heavy stacking of labels, as can be seen in the following constructed example:

Miren,	ez	da-ki-t	hori-en	etsai-(e)-en	izen-ak	ema-n
Mary	not	know./1.SYT	that_one.GEN	enemy.PLU.GEN	name.PLU	give(.RAD)

d-ie-za-z-ki-gu-na-n	ala	ez.
PLU/1PLU/2SOL.FEM.DTR.POT.[PRS*].NCZ	or	not

An English translation of this example might read as follows:

Mary, I don't know whether or not you could give us the names of their enemies.

[*The label PRS in the example sentence will normally not be shown, as it is considered the default case of the category tense—hence the use of brackets in this case.]

2. Adverbial morphemes in the Basque words are separated from the bare stem by using a hyphen (e.g., *eder-ki*); bare stems used adverbially are not labeled, provided the corresponding English gloss is morphologically transparent (e.g., 'expensively' glossing *garesti* in *Garesti asko sal zitekeen* 'It might have been sold very expensively').

The Glosses

Typographical conventions used in the abbreviations are as follows:

Lexical items: lowercase (e.g., 'house'/*etxe*)
Grammatical labels: small capitals (e.g., ERG for "ergative" and BEN for "benefactive")

ABS Absolutive case
ACP Adjoined clause prefix BAIT- (19.3.1. and 23.3)
ADN Adnominalizer (5.1)
ADV Adverb
AFF Affirmative sentence particle (8.3)
ALC Allocutive verb form (29.1)
ALL Allative (3.2)
APP Approximation suffix (26.7)
BEN Benefactive (2.2.1)
CAC Causal or explanatory conjunction (23.5)
CAU Causative (16.1–2)
CDC Conditional conjunction (17.2)
CDP Conditional prefix (17.2.2)
COC Concessive conjunction (23.7.5)
COD Conditional mood (17.2) or, in combination with POT, the potentiality variant of the present conditional (24.1.3 and 24.2.3): this label covers both protasis (truncated but always accompanied by the conditional prefix) and apodosis forms

COP Comparative (26.4)
DAT Dative (2.2.1)
DEL Deletion or nonlexicalization of a head noun (to be seen, e.g., in 11.1.6 and 16.2.3)
DES Local destinative, taking on a temporal meaning in certain cases (20.1.1)
DFR Deferential mode of address (6.1.6)
DIM Diminutive: suffix *-txo*/*-tto* corresponding to the head of a relative (19.1.9); suffix *-(t)xe* intercalated between the stem and the comparative suffix *-ago* in order to indicate a slight degree of superiority (26.4.2)
DIS Suffix turning cardinal numbers into distributives (30.3)
DIT Dative clause-mate-induced forms of intransitive auxiliary (15.1)
DTR Dative clause-mate-induced forms of transitive auxiliary (15.1)
DUB Dubitative sentence particle (8.1.6)
DYN Dative clause-mate variant of synthetic forms of an intransitive verb (15.1)
DYT Dative clause-mate variant of synthetic forms of a transitive verb (15.1)
ECS Excessive form of a predicate (26.6)
EEC Explanatory function of the conjunction *eta* used as a clausal enclitic (23.2.1) and at the end of an exclamatory sentence, creating more emphasis (30.2.7)
ELA Elative (3.2)
ELP Postposition used to mark comparatives denoting equality in quality, also known as equatives (26.2)
EMC Emphatic initial conjunction *harik* invariably followed by *eta* (20.4.5)
EMP Emphatic, e.g., in forms of deictics (26.8) and in personal pronouns (28.2.5.1)
ENC Enclital position of the conjunction *eta* after a perfect participle employed to create an equivalent of stative participles (19.2.4); the same holds in the case of a final constituent of a coordination being left out: this instance of cliticization of the conjunction is found with *eta*, *edo*, and *ala* (30.2.6)
ENP Postposition used to mark comparatives denoting equality in quantity (26.3)
ERG Ergative case (2.2.1)
EXC Exclamative sentence particle (8.1.5)
EXP Expletory use of a given word (e.g., of *eta* in sentence 7 of Chapter 17 or in sentences 77a–c of Chapter 23)
FEM Feminine (9.1 and 29.1)
FRQ Frequency suffix, e.g., following finite subordinate clauses ending in the relativizer -N (see 20.3.4)
FUT Future participle (7.2.5)
GEN Genitive (2.2.1)
GSC Conjunction (*ahala*) expressing graduality or simultaneity according to the aspectual identity of the dependent verb (24.7.2)
HAB Habitualness indicated by proclitic particle (14.6)

HYP Hypothetical tense of the subjunctive (21.1, 21.8)
IDF Indefinite (1.3.1); also used, where necessary, to indicate the bare stem of (pro)nouns
IIJ Interrogative Interjection (18.1.8)
IMP Imperative (22.2)
INC Inclusive article (19.7)
INF Inferential sentence particle (8.1.3 and 23.6.2)
INS Instrumental (2.2.1)
INT Interrogative sentence particle (8.1.5)
IPF Imperfect(ive) (7.2.4). Wherever in the text of the grammar forms ending in *-t(z)en* are treated as imperfect participles, they will be labeled as IPF; in all other cases, their label will be VEN.LOC (i.e., *har-tze-n* glossed as "take.VEN.LOC" vs. *har-tzen* glossed as "take.IPF," whether or not with explicit tense/aspect value).
ITR Intransitive auxiliary (6.2)
JUS Jussive (22.4)
LCI Finite "circumstantializer" -LA(-RIK), differentiated from LCZ by inducing the anormal toneme on the verb form of the subordinate clause in question (20.8.1–2)
LCZ Finite complementizer -LA (18.2 and 21.1, 21.7)
LOC Inessive (3.1)
MAS Masculine
MON Monitive particle *gero* (temporal adverb) used in imperative, jussive, and optative sentences (22.3.5)
MOQ Modal quantifier *ahala* (24.7.1)
MOT Motivational (2.2.1)
NAZ Finite complementizer -NA (18.3)
NCZ Wh-complementizer -N (18.1.2 and 21.1), used as relativizer (19.1, 21.4.2–3, and 21.5)
NDC Suffix *-no/-ño/-ino* added to relativized verb forms in order to build finite delimitative time clauses (20.5)
NPP Negative particle lexically conveying impossibility (24.3, 24.6); see PPP
NPS Nominalized purpose clause marked by the suffix *-arren* (23.1.1)
NRE Prenominal finite relative clause ending in the complementizer/relativizer -N (19.1)
OPT Optative sentence particle (8.1.4)
PAR Partitive (8.1.6)
PCZ Partitive complementizer (18.4)
PEC Perfect participle combined with the suffix *-ta*, a shortened form of the conjunction *eta*, used in Guipuzcoan in order to create the equivalent of the stative participle (cf. STA) (19.2.4 and 25.7)

PEF Perfect (6.2.2). Perfect participle, in case the form is simply the citation form of a given Basque verb; in all other cases, forms such as *har-tu* will get no label at all (i.e., glossed as 'take' after hyphenation vs. "take.PEF" with explicit tense/aspect value).

PLU Plural (also used as plural variant in the cases where SIN appears for the singular) (1.3.3)

POC Use of the conjunction *eta* in combination with a preceding perfect participle identifying a nonfinite subordinate time clause expressing posteriority of the action described by the main clause (20.6)

POT Potential mood (24.1–5)

PPF Pluperfect (7.3.2)

PPP Antonym of NPP (*ezin* vs. *ahal*) (24.6)

PPR Preterito-present form of various modal and nonmodal verbs (14.2)

PRE Predicative (25.5.1)

PRI Privative suffix *-ke* attached to the verbal noun used in southern dialects to construe explicitly simultaneous nonfinite negative circumstantial clauses (27.11.4)

PRO Prolative (2.2.1 and 17.8)

PST Past (6.2.2)

PTC Participle (6.2.2)

RAD Radical of the verb (6.2.2 and 7.2.2)

REF Reflexive (6.1.4)

REP Reportative sentence particle (8.1.2)

RIM Suffix *-r* denoting "impendency" if attached to the definite singular (southern dialects) or indefinite (northern dialects) form of the absolutive case of the verbal noun (20.7)

SIN Singular form of the definite article used in combination with PEF (with or without *berri/zahar*) in cases where the adjectival character of this participle form is prominent (25.1.1–2, 25.1.4, and passim)

SIP Postposition used to mark comparatives denoting similarity (26.1)

SOC Sociative (2.2.1)

SOL Solidarity: pragmatic feature characterizing second-person singular (6.1.2)

SRP Postposition by means of which are expressed comparatives denoting superiority (26.4)

STA Stative: predicatives formed with the suffix *-(r)ik* attached to some adjectives/ nouns or occurring with any ordinal (25.5.2)/perfect participle (19.2.2, 25.2.2 and 25.5.4)

SUJ Subjunctive (21.2)

SUP Superlative (26.5)

SYN Synthetic form of an intransitive verb (6.2)

SYT Synthetic form of a transitive verb (9.1)
TEN Tendential (3.2)
TER Terminal (3.2)
TOP Topping particle *are* co-occurring with a comparative (26.4.6)
TRA Transitive auxiliary (7.1.3)
VEN Verbal noun (7.2.3)
WCC Conjunction introducing a wh-complement (18.1.6)
ZEP Zero (pro)noun to be postulated as head of noun phrases, e.g., of the type of *katuarena* 'the one of the cat' (2.4); also used to indicate the substantival function of numerals, adnominals, and adjectives (in which case it stands for ZEP.SIN with the perfect participles concerned)
1/2/3 First, second, or third person

The Glosses

Chapter 1

(1) Ama sorgin-a da eta alab(a)-ak ere sorgin-ak d-ir-a.
Mother.IDF witch be.SYN and daughter.PLU too witch.PLU be.PLU.SYN

(2) Sorgin-a polit-a da eta ijito-ak ere polit-ak d-ir-a.
witch pretty be.SYN and gypsy.PLU too pretty.PLU be.PLU.SYN

(3) Ama emakume ederr-a da eta alab(a)-ak ere emakume ederr-ak
Mother.IDF woman beautiful be.SYN and daughter.PLU too woman beautiful.PLU
d-ir-a.
be.PLU.SYN

(4) Ama ez da sorgin-a eta alab(a)-ak ere ez d-ir-a sorgin-ak.
Mother.IDF not be.SYN witch and daughter.PLU too not be.PLU.SYN witch.PLU

(5) Sorgin-a ez da polit-a eta ijito-ak ere ez d-ir-a polit-ak.
witch not be.SYN pretty and gypsy.PLU too not be.PLU.SYN pretty.PLU

(6) Ama ez da emakume ederr-a eta alab(a)-ak ere ez d-ir-a
Mother.IDF not be.SYN woman beautiful and daughter.PLU too not be.PLU.SYN
emakume ederr-ak.
woman beautiful.PLU

(7) Etxe-a berri-a da baina eliz(a)-a ez da berri-a.
house new be.SYN but church not be.SYN new

Chapter 2

(1) a. Astelehen-a eta astearte-a egun txarr-ak dira.
Monday and Tuesday day bad.PLU be.PLU.SYN
b. Uztail-a eta abuztu-a bero-ak dira.
July and August warm.PLU be.PLU.SYN

c. Negu-a eta udaberri-a ez dira bero-ak.
winter and spring not be.PLU.SYN warm.PLU

(2) a. Ezti-a gozo-a da.
honey sweet be.SYN
b. Apaiz isil-ak on-ak dira.
priest silent.PLU good.PLU be.PLU.SYN

(3) a. Miren sorgin-a da.
Mary witch be.SYN
b. Miren ederr-a da.
Mary beautiful be.SYN
c. Miren sorgin ederr-a da.
Mary witch beautiful be.SYN

Chapter 5

(2) a. bezero(-e-)entza(t)-ko mahai-ak
customer.PLU.BEN.ADN table.PLU
b. etsai-a-reki(n)-ko lotur(a)-ak
enemy.SOC.ADN tie.PLU
c. zeru-tika-ko ogi-a
heaven.ELA.ADN bread
d. gizon-a-gan-dika-ko gaitz-a
man.ELA.ADN evil
e. Bilbo-tik Donostia-ra-ko bide-a
Bilbao.ELA San_Sebastian.ALL.ADN road
f. matematik(a)-e-ta-r(a)-an(t)z-ko bultzad(a)-a
mathematics.PLU.TEN.ADN impulse
g. gerl(a)-a-ren kontra-ko emakume-ak
war.GEN against.ADN women.PLU

(3) a. Ez da bihotzaldi handi-(e)-eki(n)-ko poet(a)-a.
not be.SYN emotion great.PLU.SOC.ADN poet
b. Ez da bihotzaldi handi-ko poet(a)-a.
not be.SYN emotion great.ADN poet

(4) a. Jantzi gorri-a-reki(n)-ko gazte-a
suit red.SOC.ADN young
b. Jantzi gorri-ko gazte-a
suit red.ADN young

Chapter 6

(1) a. Hon-(r)a Etxahun ber-a, present da zu-rekin.
here.ALL Etxahun the_very present be.SYN you.SOC
b. Hon-(r)a Jainko-a-ren Bildots-a.
here.ALL God.GEN Lamb
c. Horr-(r)a sei bertso kale=garbitzaile-a-ri . . .
there.ALL six verse.IDF street-cleaner.DAT
d. . . . eta ha-ra zaldi zuri bat.
. . . and over_there.ALL horse white a

(2) a. Hon-(r)a hemen lapiko galant-a eta pitxer bete ardo.
here.ALL here.LOC stew nice and pitcher.IDF full.IDF wine.IDF
b. Horr-(r)a hor ni-re mutil-a.
there.ALL there.LOC I.GEN boy
c. Ha-ra ha-n zu-re Jaun-a
over_there.ALL over_there.LOC you.GEN Lord

Chapter 7

(1) Ez da on-a gizon-a bakarr-ik e-go-te-a.
not be.SYN good man alone.STA stay.VEN

(2) a. Zu hemen i-bil-tze-a on-a da.
you here.LOC walk.VEN good be.SYN
b. Zu-re hemen-go ibiler(a)-a on-a da.
you.GEN here.ADN walking good be.SYN

(3) a. Berri txarr-a korri-ka da-bil.
news bad runningly walk.SYN
b. Gatz-a ur-e-ta-n ur-tzen da.
salt water.IDF.LOC melt.IPF ITR

(4) a. Miren atzo jaio ze-n.
Mary yesterday be_born.PEF ITR.PST
b. Aintzane aurten jaio da.
Gloria this_year be_born.PEF ITR

(5) a. Bart berandu e-torr-i z-in-e-n.
last_night late(before midnight) come.PEF 2.ITR.PST
b. Bart berandu e-torr-i z-a-r-a.
last_night late(after midnight) come.PEF 2.ITR

(6) a. Goiz-e-an berandu e-torr-i z-in-e-n.
morning.LOC late come.PEF 2.ITR.PST
b. Goiz-e-an berandu e-torr-i z-a-r-a.
morning.LOC late come.PEF 2.ITR

(7) Miren eliza-ra j-oa-n ze-n atzo.
Miren church.ALL go.PEF ITR.PST yesterday

(8) Haize-a lore-(e)-en petalo-(e)-ekin josta-tzen ze-n.
wind flower.PLU.GEN petal.PLU.SOC play.IPF ITR.PST

(9) Egunero herri-ra jai(t)s-ten ze-n.
every_day village.ALL go_down.IPF ITR.PST

(10) a. Oso gutxi-ta-n Donostia-ra j-oa-ten ze-n.
very seldom San_Sebastian.ALL go.IPF ITR.PST
b. Hi-re anai(a)-a-ren kontra mintza-tzen h-in-tz-e-n.
you.GEN brother.GEN against talk.IPF 2SOL.ITR.PST

(11) a. Atzo zubi-tik eror-i ze-n.
yesterday bridge.ELA fall.PEF ITR.PST
b. Sarri-ta-n zubi-tik eror-tzen ze-n.
often bridge.ELA fall.IPF ITR.PST

(12) a. Sei-e-ta-n e-tor-tzen da.
six.PLU.LOC come.IPF ITR
b. Sei-e-ta-n e-tor-tzen ze-n.
six.PLU.LOC come.IPF ITR.PST
c. Sei-e-ta-n da-tor.
six.PLU.LOC come.SYN
d. Sei-e-ta-n ze-torr-e-n.
six.PLU.LOC come.SYN.PST

(13) a. Liburutegi-an e-go-ten da.
library.LOC stay.IPF ITR
b. Liburutegi-an e-go-ten ze-n.
library.LOC stay.IPF ITR.PST
c. Liburutegi-an da-go.
library.LOC stay.SYN
d. Liburutegi-an ze-go-en.
library.LOC stay.SYN.PST

(14) a. Andre Madalen mozkorr-a iza-ten da.
Lady.IDF Magdalen drunk be.IPF ITR

b. Andre Madalen mozkorr-a iza-ten ze-n.
Lady.IDF Magdalen drunk be.IPF ITR.PST

c. Andre Madelen mozkorr-a da.
Lady.IDF Magdalen drunk be.SYN

d. Andre Madalen mozkorr-a ze-n.
Lady.IDF Magdalen drunk be.SYN.PST

(15) a. Manolo geldi-tu ze-n arte-an ezkongai.
Manuel remain.PEF ITR.PST at_the_time bachelor.IDF

b. Orain-dik ez ze-n Jesus herri-an sar-tu.
yet not ITR.PST Jesus village.LOC enter.PEF

c. Ilun-a ze-n, eta orain-dik Jesus ez ze-n irits-i.
dark be.SYN.PST and yet Jesus not ITR.PST arrive.PEF

(16) a. Lazaro eror-i iza-n ze-n eritasun handi bat-e-an.
Lazarus fall.PEF be.PEF ITR.PST illness big a.LOC

b. Jesus ez ze-n arte-an herri-ra hel-du iza-n.
Jesus not ITR.PST at_the_time village.ALL arrive.PEF be.PEF

(17) a. Ber-e-ha(r-en)-la n-oa zu-(e)-en-gan-(r)a.
at_once go.1.SYN you.PLU.ALL

b. Bihar da-tor Kattalin.
tomorrow come.SYN Cathy.IDF

c. Bihar ezkon-tzen da emakume polit bat-ekin.
tomorrow marry.IPF ITR woman pretty a.SOC

(18) a. Taberna bat-e-ra j-oa-n-go g-a-r-a.
pub a.ALL go.FUT 1.PLU.ITR

b. Jaits-i-ko n-a-iz zu-rekin.
go_down.FUT 1.ITR you.SOC

(19) a. Eser-i-ko z-a-r-a?
sit_down.FUT 2.ITR

b. E-torr-i-ko z-a-r-a ni-rekin?
come.FUT 2.ITR I.SOC

(20) a. Liburutegi-an e-go-n-go d-ir-a orain.
library.LOC be.FUT PLU.ITR now

b. Liburutegi-an e-go-n-go z-ir-e-n atzo.
library.LOC be.FUT PLU.ITR.PST yesterday

(21) a. Ez da orain etxe-an e-go-n-go.
not ITR now house.LOC be.FUT

b. Ez ze-n atzo etxe-an e-go-n-go.
not ITR.PST yesterday house.LOC be.FUT

(22) En-e! Jesus! Ez da egi(a)-a iza-n-go!
I.GEN Jesus not ITR truth be.FUT

(23) a. Pello beti berandu irits-i iza-n da.
Pete always late arrive be.PEF ITR
b. Gu-re etsai-ak hegoalde-tik e-torr-i iza-n z-ir-e-n.
we.GEN enemy.PLU south.ELA come be.PEF PLU.ITR.PST

(24) a. Orain-dik hemen da-go; ber-e emazte-a ez da orain-dik itzul-i.
still here.LOC be.SYNT he_himself.GEN wife not ITR yet return.PEF
b. Arte-an etxe-an ze-go-en; ber-e ama ez ze-n arte-an
still house.LOC be.SYN.PST he_himself.GEN mother.IDF not ITR.PST yet
hil.
die.PEF

(25) a. Gizon-a ez da ogi-z bakarr-ik bizi.
man not ITR bread.IDF.INS alone.STA live.PPR
b. Behin bizi g-a-r-a soil-ik.
once live.PPR 1PLU.ITR alone.STA
c. Oraino bizi h-a-iz en-e-tzat.
still live.PPR 2SOL.ITR I.BEN

(26) a. Ni Azpil-e-n bizi n-a-iz.
I Azpil.LOC live.PPR 1.ITR
b. Ni Crotona kale-a-ren ondo-an bizi iza-n n-in-tz-e-n bost urte-an.
I Crotona street.GEN near live be.PEF 1.ITR.PST five year.LOC
c. Gu Donostia-n bizi-tze-a harrigarri-a ze-n.
we San_Sebastian.LOC live.VEN astounding be.SYN.PST

Chapter 8

(1) a. Len-ago Jentilbaratz(a)-an Jentil-ak bizi iza-ten omen z-ir-e-n.
formerly.COP Jentilbaratza.LOC Heathen.PLU life.PPR be.IPF REP PLU.ITR.PST
b. Gu-re ama eta ber-e ahizp(a)-a Sara-ko leize-ra j-oa-n
we.GEN mother.IDF and she_herself.GEN sister Sara.ADN cavern.ALL go.PEF
omen z-ir-e-n ongarriketa-ra.
REP PLU.ITR.PST manure_searching.ALL
c. Etxe-ko alab(a)-a oso polit-a omen da.
house.ADN daughter very pretty REP be.SYN

(2) a. Azken-e-an Miren, seme-a-ren-ga(i)-tik omen/d-irudi-e-n-e-z, itzul-i
end.LOC Mary son.MOT REP/seem.SYT.NRE.ZEP.IDF.INS return.PEF
ze-n etxe-ra.
ITR.PST house.ALL

b. Nekane Paris-e-ra j-oa-n ze-n, eta ez bakarr-ik, omen/d-irudi-e-n-e-z.
Dolores Paris.ALL go.PEF ITR.PST and not alone.STA REP/seem.SYT.NRE.ZEP.IDF.INS

c. Nor e-torr-i da? Apezpiku-a, omen.
who come.PEF ITR bishop REP

(3) a. Aberats-a bide z-a-r-a.
rich INF be.2.SYN

b. Ijito-ak gaur Donostia-ra j-oa-n bide d-ir-a.
gypsy.PLU today San_Sebastian.ALL go.PEF INF PLU.ITR

c. Apaiz-a ez bide ze-n ber-e-ha-la e-torr-i.
priest not INF ITR.PST at_once come.PEF

d. Oinaze-a-ren beldur iza-n-en bide ze-n Theresa samurr-a.
pain.GEN fear.IDF be.FUT INF ITR.PST Theresa frail

(4) Ordu-an nonbait giro hotz-a bide ze-n.
that_time.LOC somewhere.LOC climate cold INF be.SYN.PST

(5) a. Laster etxera-tu-ko ahal d-ir-a!
soon come_home.FUT OPT PLU.ITR

b. Ez ahal da oin-e-z e-torr-i-ko!
not OPT ITR foot.IDF.INS come.FUT

c. Ito-ko ahal h-a-iz!
drown.FUT OPT 2SOL.ITR

(6) a. Garai-z e-torr-i ahal g-a-r-a!
time.IDF.INS come.PEF OPT 1PLU.ITR

b. Jaungoiko-a gu-ta-z erruki-tzen ahal da!
God we.INS have_pity.IPF OPT ITR

(7) a. Laster e-torr-i-ko al da?
soon come.FUT INT ITR

b. Maiz j-oa-ten al z-a-r-a Paris-(r)a?
often go.IPF INT 2.ITR Paris.ALL

c. Ez al da irits-i ordu-a?
not INT ITR arrive.PEF time

d. Inor geldi-tzen al da eliz(a)-an?
anybody remain.IPF INT ITR church.LOC

(8) a. Gu-re nagusi-a al h-a-iz hi?
we.GEN boss INT be.2SOL.SYN you.SOL

b. Ez al z-a-r-a ni-ta-z fida-tzen?
not INT 2.ITR I.INS trust.IPF

(9) a. E-torr-i al h-a-iz, seme!
come.PEF EXC 2SOL.ITR son.IDF

b. Hemen al z-a-u-de!
here.LOC EXC be.2.SYN

(10) a. Ni ote n-a-iz n-eu-re anai(a)-a-ren zain-a?
I DUB be.1.SYN I.REF.GEN brother.GEN keeper

b. Profet(a)-(e)-en arte-ko ote da Saul ere?
prophet.PLU.GEN among.ADN.ZEP.IDF DUB be.SYN Saul.IDF also

c. Ez ote ze-n Chomsky aspaldi jaio?
not DUB ITR.PST Chomsky.IDF a_long_time_ago be_born.PEF

d. Zer-ga(i)-tik ni-re seme-a ez ote da-tor?
what.MOT I.GEN son not DUB come.SYN

(11) a. Iza-n ote da euskal eskola-rik pintur(a)-an?
be.PEF DUB ITR Basque school.PAR painting.LOC

b. Kaltegarri ote da artist(a)-a-ren-tzat erretratugintz(a)-an ari-tze-a?
harmful.IDF DUB be.SYN artist.BEN portraiting.LOC engage.VEN

(12) a. Nor ote da gizon hau?
who DUB be.SYN man this

b. Zer ote da gazte iza-te-a?
what DUB be.SYN young.IDF be.VEN

c. No-n ote da-bil-tza gu-re Malen eta Xalbador?
where.LOC DUB walk.PLU.SYN we.GEN Maggie and Xalbador

d. No-ra j-oa-n-go ote n-a-iz?
where.ALL go.FUT DUB 1.ITR

(13) a. Purrustada latz-ak ere ez d-ir-a falta. Neurri-z
grumbling harsh.PLU too not be.PLU.SYN lack.PPR measure.IDF.INS
gain-e-ko-ak ote?
top.ADN.ZEP.PLU DUB

b. Ber-e alab(a)-a Amerik(a)-e-ta-ra j-oa-n ze-n. Zer-ga(i)-tik ote?
he_himself.GEN daughter America.PLU.ALL go.PEF ITR.PST what.MOT DUB

(14) a. Miren itsusi-a da, baina Karmen ez.
Mary ugly be.SYN but Carmen not

b. Miren ohe-ra d-oa, baina Karmen ez.
Mary bed.ALL go.SYN but Carmen not

(15) a. Miren da itsusi-a, ez Karmen.
Mary be.SYN ugly not Carmen.
b. Miren d-oa ohe-ra, ez Karmen.
Mary go.SYN bed.ALL not Carmen

(16) a. Miren ez da polit-a, eta Karmen ere ez.
Mary not be.SYN pretty and Carmen also not
b. Miren ez d-oa ohe-ra, eta Karmen ere ez.
Mary not go.SYN bed.ALL and Carmen also not

(17) a. Ezer ez da-tor. / Ez da-tor ezer.
anything not come.SYN not come.SYN anything
b. Inor ez d-oa. / Ez d-oa inor.
anybody not go.SYN not go.SYN anybody

(18) a. Miren itsusi-a da.
Mary ugly be.SYN
b. Miren ohe-ra d-oa.
Mary bed.ALL go.SYN
c. Miren bihar e-torr-i-ko da.
Mary tomorrow come.FUT ITR

(19) a. Ez da Miren itsusi-a.
not be.SYN Mary ugly
b. Ez d-oa Miren ohe-ra.
not go.SYN Mary bed.ALL
c. Ez da Miren bihar e-torr-i-ko.
not ITR Mary tomorrow come.FUT

(20) a. *Miren* ez da itsusi-a.
Mary not be.SYN ugly
b. *Miren* ez d-oa ohe-ra.
Mary not go.SYN bed.ALL
c. *Miren* ez da bihar e-torr-i-ko.
Mary not ITR tomorrow come.FUT

(21) a. Jon ba-da e-torr-i.
John AFF.ITR come.PEF
b. Jon ez da e-torr-i.
John not ITR come.PEF

(22) a. Ez z-a-r-a Aizkorrri-ra igo!
not 2.ITR (Mount) Aizkorri.ALL climb.PEF

b. Ba-n-a-iz igo!
AFF.1.ITR climb.PEF

(23) a. Gu-re alkate-a zu-re ostatu-an geldi-tu-ko omen da jai-e-ta-n.
we.GEN mayor you.GEN hotel.LOC stay.FUT REP ITR festivity.PLU.LOC
b. J-oa-n al da azken-e-an Karmen ijito-en-gan-(r)-a?
go.PEF INT ITR end.LOC Carmen gypsy.PLU.ALL
c. Zer gerta-tu ote da gaur hemen?
what happen.PEF DUB ITR today here.LOC

(24) a. Gu-re herri-ra ez al z-a-r-a i-noiz e-torr-i-ko?
we.GEN village.ALL not INT 2.ITR ever come.FUT
b. Zer-ga(i)-tik ez z-in-e-n ezkon-du gu-re Miren-ekin?
what.MOT not 2.ITR.PST marry.PEF we.GEN Mary.SOC
c. Miren ez omen da mintza-tu-ko soldadu zahar bat-ekin.
Mary not REP ITR talk.FUT soldier old a.SOC
d. Karmen bada etxe-ra-tu.
Carmen AFF.ITR come_home.PEF

(25) a. Ijito bat-ekin ez da ba ezkon-tzen Miren!
gypsy a.SOC not ITR AFF marry.IPF Mary
b. Ijito bat-ekin ezkon-tzen ez da ba Miren!
gypsy a.SOC marry.IPF not ITR AFF Mary

(26) a. Bart gu-re haurtxo-a ez ze-n ba eror-i mahai-tik!
last_night we.GEN baby not ITR.PST AFF fall.PEF table.ELA
b. Bart gu-re haurtxo-a eror-i ez zen ba mahai-tik!
last_night we.GEN baby fall.PEF not ITR.PST AFF table.ELA

(27) a. Pello ez da ba e-torr-i-ko!
Pete not ITR AFF come.FUT
b. Pello e-torr-i-ko ez da ba!
Pete come.FUT not ITR AFF

(28) a. No-la ez n-a-iz ba geldi-tu-ko Donostia-n?
how not 1.ITR AFF stay.FUT San_Sebastian.LOC
b. No-la geldi-tu-ko ez n-a-iz ba Donostia-n?
how stay.FUT not 1.ITR AFF San_Sebastian

(29) a. Zer-ga(i)-tik ez ze-n geldi-tu Karmen Donostia-n?
what.MOT not ITR.PST stay.PEF Carmen San_Sebastian.LOC
b. **Zer-ga(i)-tik geldi-tu ez ze-n Karmen Donostia-n?
what.MOT stay.PEF not ITR.PST Carmen San_Sebastian.LOC

(30) a. Ez da Patxi bihar gu-rekin mendi-ra igo-ko.
not ITR Frank tomorrow we.SOC mountain.ALL climb.FUT
b. Bai, ez n-a-iz inor-ekin ino-ra inoiz j-oa-n-go.
yes, not 1.ITR anybody.SOC anywhere.ALL ever go.FUT
c. Karmen bada asko-ta-n hon-(r)a e-tor-tzen.
Carmen AFF.ITR much.LOC here.ALL come.IPF

(31) Ni-k n-e(u)-r(e_h)on-e-k ezagu(t)-tu d-u-t gazte-ta-n gu-re arte-an
I.ERG myself.ERG recognize.PEF /1.ITR youth.IDF.LOC we.GEN among
nabari ze(-n)-n ha(r-en)-la-ko susmo txarr-a *ez ote*
manifest.IDF be.ITR.SYN.NRE in_that_way.ADN suspicion bad not DUB
z-u-te(-n)-n azken fin-e-an han-go-ek, gu-k, hain
/PLU.TRA.PST.NCZ last end.LOC over_there.ADN.ZEP.PLU.ERG we.ERG so
garbi-ak g-in-e-(n)-la-rik ere (eta batzu-ek, noski, beste-ak baino
puristic.PLU be.1.PLU.SYN.PST.LCI even and some.PLU of_course other.ZEP.PLU than
garbi-ago), ida(t)z-ten g-en-u-e(n)-n baino hobe-ki, modu jatorr-ago-an, ez
pure.COP.IDF write.IPF /1PLU.TRA.PST.NCZ than well.COP fashion pure.COP.LOC not
hain modu "dorphe-an," *ida(t)z-ten.*
such fashion heavy.LOC write.IPF

(32) a. Pello poz-ik ezkon-du-ko da Karmen-ekin/*Karmen-ekin.*
Pete glad.STA marry.FUT ITR Carmen.SOC
b. *Karmen-ekin* Pello poz-ik ezkon-du-ko da.
Carmen.SOC Pete glad.STA marry.FUT ITR

(33) a. AMONA j-oa-n-go da bihar Bilbo-ra. (Nor j-oa-n-go da
Grandmother.IDF go.FUT ITR tomorrow Bilbao.ALL who go.FUT ITR
bihar Bilbo-ra?— Amona.)
tomorrow Bilbao Grandmother.IDF
b. Amona BIHAR j-oa-n-go da Bilbo-ra. (Amona noiz
Grandmother.IDF tomorrow go.FUT ITR Bilbao.ALL Grandmother.IDF when
j-oa-n-go da Bilbo-ra?— Bihar.)
go.FUT ITR Bilbao.ALL Tomorrow
c. Amona BILBO-RA j-oa-n-go da bihar. (Amona
Grandmother.IDF Bilbao.ALL go.FUT ITR tomorrow Grandmother.IDF
no-ra j-oa-n-go da bihar?— Bilbo-ra.)
where.ALL go.FUT ITR tomorrow Bilbao.ALL

(34) a. GIPUZKOA-RA j-oa-n-go n-a-iz.
Guipuzcoa.ALL go.FUT 1.ITR
b. No-ra j-oa-n-go z-a-r-a, Gipuzkoa-ra ala Bizkai-ra?
where.ALL go.FUT 2.ITR Guipuzcoa.ALL or Biscay.ALL

c. Gipuzkoa-ra ala Bizkai-ra j-oa-n-go z-a-r-a?
Guipuzcoa.ALL or Biscay.ALL go.FUT 2.ITR

(35) a. Amona BIHAR BILBO-RA j-oa-n-go da.
Grandmother.IDF tomorrow Bilbao.ALL go.FUT ITR
b. Amona noiz no-ra j-oa-n-go da?
Grandmother.IDF when where.ALL go.FUT ITR

(36) a. Zubi-tik ibai-ra nor eror-i ze-n atzo?
bridge.ELA river.ALL who fall.PEF ITR.PST yesterday
b. Gaur zer gerta-tu da gu-re eliz(a)-an?
today what happen.PEF ITR we.GEN church.LOC
c. Zenbat sorgin igaro d-ir-a gaur zu-re aurre-tik?
how_many witch pass.PEF PLU.ITR today you.GEN front_part.ELA

(37) a. Nor ez da inoiz Madril-e-n iza-n?
who not ITR ever Madrid.LOC be.PEF
b. Zer-ga(i)-tik ez d-ir-a Pello eta Karmen ostatu-an geldi-tzen?
what.MOT not PLU.ITR Pete and Carmen inn.LOC stay.IPF
c. Zenbat alaba ez d-ir-a orain-dik ezkon-du?
how_many daughter not PLU.ITR yet marry.PEF

(38) a. No-ra, orde-a, zu-rekin j-oa-n?
where.ALL however you.SOC go
b. Zer-ga(i)-tik gaur mendi-ra igo?
what.MOT today mountain.ALL go_up

(39) a. Jainko-a ON-A da.
God good be.SYN
b. JAINKO-A da on-a.
God be.SYN good

(40) a. Zu ALKATE-A al z-a-r-a?
you mayor INT be.2.SYN
b. ZU al z-a-r-a alkate-a?
you INT be.2.SYN mayor

(41) a. Elurr-a UR-TU e-gi-n da.
snow melt do.PEF ITR
b. Nekane NEKA-TU e-gi-ten ze-n.
Dolores get_tired do.IPF ITR.PST
c. Mutil-ak LOTSA-TU e-gi-n z-ir-e-n neskatx(a)-(e)-en aurre-an.
boy.PLU be_ashamed do.PEF PLU.ITR.PST girl.PLU.GEN front_part.LOC

d. EROR-I e-gi-n al da?
fall do.PEF INT ITR

e. Ia HIL e-gi-n n-a-iz.
almost die do.PEF 1.ITR

(42) a. Elurr-a ORAIN-TXE ur-tu da.
snow now.EMP melt.PEF ITR

b. Nekane AGUDO neka-tzen ze-n.
Dolores quickly get_tired.IPF ITR.PST

c. Mutil-ak ZEHA-RO lotsa-tu z-ir-e-n neskatx(a)-(e)-en
boy.PLU totally be_ashamed.PEF PLU.ITR.PST girl.PLU.GEN
aurre-an.
front_part.LOC

d. IBAI-RA eror-i al da?
river.ALL fall.PEF INT ITR

e. Ia ZU-RE-GA(I)-TIK hil n-a-iz.
almost you.MOT die.PEF 1.ITR

(43) a. AMONA d-oa gaur Bilbo-ra.
Grandmother.IDF go.SYN today Bilbao.ALL

b. Amona GAUR d-oa Bilbo-ra.
Grandmother.IDF today go.SYN Bilbao.ALL

c. Amona BILBO-RA d-oa gaur.
Grandmother.IDF Bilbao.ALL go.SYN today

(44) a. Norbait ba-d-oa gaur Bilbo-ra.
somebody AFF.go.SYN today Bilbao.ALL

b. BA-d-oa ala EZ d-oa?
AFF.go.SYN or not go.SYN

c. BaZ-A-TO(R)-Z ala baZ-OA-Z?
AFF.come.2.SYN or AFF.go.2.SYN

(45) a. Behin ba omen ze-n errege bat.
once AFF REP be.SYN.PST king a

b. BA ote DA-TOR Karmen?
AFF DUB come.SYN Carmen

c. Etxe-ko andre-a ba al da etxe-an?
house.ADN lady AFF INT be.SYN house.LOC

(46) E-TORR-I z-a-to(r)-z ala J-OA-N z-oa-z?
come come.2.SYN or go go.2.SYN

(47) a. BA-da ardo-a.
AFF.be.SYN wine

b. ARDO-A da.
wine be.SYN

(48) a. Ni BA-N-A-IZ.
I AFF.be.1.SYN
b. NI n-a-iz.
I be.1.SYN

(49) a. Ni ZAHARR-A n-a-iz.
I old be.1.SYN
b. NI n-a-iz zaharr-a.
I be.1.SYN old
c. Ni BA-N-A-IZ zaharr-a.
I AFF.be.1.SYN old

(50) Gaur zaharr-ak / BAKARR-IK ~ ZAHARR-AK BAKARR-IK / d-oa-z
today old.ZEP.PLU alone.STA old.ZEP.PLU alone.STA go.PLU.SYN
eliza(a)-ra.
church.ALL

(51) a. Orain, behin-tzat, ba-z-a-to(r)-z.
now at_least AFF.come.2.SYN
b. Apaiz-ak, orde-a, ba-d-oa-z.
priest.PLU however AFF.go.PLU.SYN

(52) a. Sorgin-ak ere ba-da-to(r)-z.
witch.PLU too AFF.come.PLU.SYN
b. Hemen ere ba-da-bil-tza.
here.LOC too walk.PLU.SYN

(53) a. Nor da-tor ijito-a-rekin? KARMEN da-tor (ijito-a-rekin).
who come.SYN gypsy.SOC Carmen come.SYN gypsy.SOC
b. Nor-ekin da-tor Karmen? IJITO-A-REKIN da-tor (Karmen).
who.SOC come.SYN Carmen gypsy.SOC come.SYN Carmen
c. Zer gerta-tzen da? BA-DA-TOR KARMEN IJITO-A-REKIN.
what happen.IPF ITR AFF.come.SYN Carmen gypsy.SOC
d. Eta *Karmen*, zer? *Karmen* ba-da-tor ijito-a-rekin.
and Carmen what Carmen AFF.come.SYN gypsy.SOC

(54) a. Nor ez da e-torr-i?
who not ITR come.PEF
b. MIREN ez da e-torr-i.
Mary not ITR come.PEF

(55) a. Zer-ga(i)-tik ez d-oa-z gaur ahizp(a)-ak eliza-ra?
what.MOT not go.PLU.SYN today sister.PLU church.ALL
b. ELURR-A-REN-GA(I)-TIK ez d-oa-z gaur ahizp(a)-ak eliza-ra.
snow.MOT not go.PLU.SYN today sister.PLU church

(56) a. Noiz ez da Patxi lanera-tzen?
when not ITR Frank go_to_work.IPF
b. IGANDE-E-TA-N ez da Patxi lanera-tzen.
Sunday.PLU.LOC not ITR Frank go_to_work.IPF

(57) Itsaso-ra eror-i z-ir-e-n sorgin-ak, baina ITO ez ze-n e-gi-n inor.
sea.ALL fall.PEF PLU.ITR.PST witch.PLU but drown not ITR.PST do.PEF anybody

(58) a. Amona ez da gaur BILBO-RA j-oa-n-go, Gazteiz-e-ra baizik.
Grandmother.IDF not ITR today Bilbao.ALL go.FUT Vitoria.ALL but
b. **Amona ez da GAUR Bilbo-ra j-oa-n-go, bihar baizik.
Grandmother.IDF not ITR today Bilbao.ALL go.FUT tomorrow but
c. Amona ez da GAUR j-oa-n-go Bilbo-ra, bihar baizik.
Grandmother.IDF not ITR today go.FUT Bilbao.ALL tomorrow but.

(59) Ez z-a-r-e-te, ala-baina, ZU-EK mintza-tzen, baina Izpiritu saindu-a.
not 2PLU.ITR however you.PLU speak.IPF but Spirit Holy

(60) Orain-dik ez n-a-iz Balantzategi-ko ikuilu-an SARTU ere egin!
yet not 1.ITR Balantzategi.ADN cowshed.LOC enter too do.PEF

(61) Aita ez da-tor OIN-E-Z gaur etxe-ra, autobus-e-z baizik.
Father.IDF not come.SYN foot.IDF.INS today house.ALL bus.IDF.INS but

Chapter 9

(1) a. Peru da-tor.
Peter come.SYN
b. Peru da-kar.
Peter bring.SYT
c. Peru-k da-kar.
Peter.ERG bring.SYT

(2) a. Arantxa da-uka.
Arantxa have.SYT
b. Arantxa-k da-uka.
Arantxa.ERG have.SYT

(3) a. Nor da-tor? Peru.
who come.SYN Peter

b. Nor da-kar? Peru.
who bring.SYT Peter

c. Nor-k da-kar? Peru-k.
who.ERG bring.SYT Peter.ERG

(4) a. Nor da-uka? Arantxa.
who have.SYT Arantxa

b. Nor-k da-uka? Arantxa-k.
who.ERG have.SYT Arantxa.ERG

(5) a. Peru-k eta Miren-e-k ogi-a da-kar-te.
Peter.ERG and Mary.ERG bread bring./PLU.SYT

b. Mutil bat-e-k arrain bat da-kar.
boy a.ERG fish a bring.SYT

(6) a. Gizon-a da-tor.
man come.SYN

b. Gizon-ak da-to(r)-z.
man.PLU come.PLU.SYN

c. Gizon-a-k da-kar.
man.ERG bring.SYT

d. Gizon-ek da-kar-te.
man.PLU.ERG bring./PLU.SYT

(7) a. Ni-k ba-d-it-u-t mila ardi.
I.ERG AFF.have.PLU/1.SYT thousand sheep.IDF

b. Ba-d-u-t andre-a, ba-d-u-t seme-a, ba-d-u-t alab(a)-a ere ni-k.
AFF.have./1.SYT wife AFF.have./1.SYT son AFF.have./1.SYT daughter too I.ERG

c. Arrosatxo-a-k bost hosto d-it-u, krabelintxo-a-k hamabi.
little_rose.ERG five leave.IDF have.PLU/.SYT little_carnation twelve

d. Midas-e-k astabelarri-ak d-it-u.
Midas.ERG donkey's_ear.PLU have.PLU/.SYT

e. Zer d-u-zu?
what have./2.SYT

(8) a. N-eu-re andre-a-k atorra zaharr-a zazpi aste-an soin-e-an da-uka.
I.REF.GEN wife.ERG shirt old seven week.SIN.LOC body.LOC keep.SYT

b. Zu-k hor da-u-z-ka-zu bi autore: Lizardi eta Agirre Asteasu-ko-a.
you.ERG there have.PLU/2.SYT two authors.IDF Lizardi and Aguirre Asteasu.ADN

(9) a. Joera berri-e-z zer d-io-zu?
trend new.PLU.INS what say./2.SYT

b. Gezurr-ak d-io-da-z?
lie.PLU tell.PLU/1.SYT

(10) a. Ni-k ez da-ki-t zer esa-n.
I.ERG not know./1.SYT what say
b. Egi(a)-a inor-k ez da-ki.
truth anybody.ERG not know.SYT
c. Ba al da-ki-zu euskara-z?
AFF INT know./2.SYT Basque.IDF.INS
d. Nor-k ez da-ki gu-re arte-an aita Plazido Mujika-ren berri?
who.ERG not know.SYT we.GEN among father Plácido Mujica.GEN news.IDF

(11) a. Zer-k z-a-kar-tza hon-(r)a?
what.ERG bring.2/.SYT here.ALL
b. Lan-a-k lan-a da-kar.
work.ERG work bring.SYT
c. Ordu-ko geldi-a-k da-kar orain-go lehi(a)-a.
time.ADN stagnant.ERG bring.SYT now.ADN hurry

(12) a. Ikastetxe-an euskara-z-ko liburu-ak da-rabil-tza-gu.
school.LOC Basque.IDF.INS.ADN book.PLU use.PLU/1PLU.SYT
b. Ur-a-k da-rabil errot(a)-a.
water.ERG move.SYT mill
c. Zerbait ba-da-ra-bil-zu zu-k hor barru-an.
something AFF.carry./2.SYT you.ERG there.LOC inside.LOC
d. Zer da-ra-bil-zu buru horr-e-ta-n?
what stir./2.SYT head that.LOC
e. Zer da-ra-bil-zu gogo-an?
what stir./2.SYT mind.LOC

(13) a. Su-a eta egurr-a ba-da-ra-ma-tza-gu.
fire and wood AFF.carry.PLU/1PLU.SYT
b. G-eu-re-gan da-ra-ma-gu heriotz(a)-a.
we.REF.LOC carry./1PLU.SYT death
c. Miren-e-k gaur minigon(a)-a da-ra-ma.
Mary.ERG today miniskirt wear.SYT
d. Luis-e-k ber-e logela-r(a)-antz z-a-ra-ma-tza.
Luis.ERG he_himself.GEN bedroom.TEN lead.2/.SYT
e. Hamar egun da-ra-ma-tza-t hemen.
ten day.IDF spend.PLU/1.SYT here.LOC

(14) a. Bide-a-k no-ra da-r-oa?
Road.ERG where.ALL lead.SYT
b. Jon-e-k orain automobil on-a da-r-oa.
John.ERG now car good conduct.SYT

(15) a. Zer-ta-n d-ihardu-zu? Ni-re lan-e-an d-ihardu-t.
what.LOC be_busy.2.SYT I.GEN work.LOC be_busy.1.SYT
b. Zer-ta-z d-ihardu-zu-e? Eguraldi-a-z d-ihardu-gu.
what.INS talk.2PLU.SYT weather.INS talk.1PLU.SYT

(16) a. Tresna-k jabe-a d-irudi.
tool.ERG master resemble.SYT
b. Zu-re gerri-a-k palmera bat d-irudi.
you.GEN waist.ERG palm_tree a resemble.SYT
c. Buenos Aires-ko berri-ek ez d-irudi-te on-ak.
Buenos Aires.ADN report.PLU.ERG not seem./PLU.SYT good.PLU
d. H-eu-re etxe=barru-an atzerritarr-a d-irudi-k.
2SOL.REF.GEN house_inner_part.LOC foreigner seem./2SOL.SYT
e. Maite, Salomon-en gurdi-a-ren behorr-a d-irudi-zu.
dear.IDF Solomon.GEN chariot.GEN mare resemble./2.SYT

(17) a. Sarajevo-k zut-ik d-irau.
Sarajevo.ERG erect.STA remain.SYT
b. Tortok(a)-(e)-en irl(a)-an ud(a)-a-k hamabi hilabete d-irau.
turtle.PLU.GEN isle.LOC summer.ERG twelve month.IDF last.SYT
c. Har-k leial d-irau.
that_one_yonder.ERG loyal.IDF remain.SYT
d. Zu-re leialtasun-a-k belaunaldi-z=belaunaldi d-irau.
you.GEN loyalty.ERG generation.IDF.INS_generation.IDF last.SYT
e. Zu-k, orde-a, Jaun-a, ba-d-irau-zu beti.
you.ERG however Lord AFF.last.2.SYT always

(18) a. Gainerako-a on-gi da-zagu-zu.
rest well know./2.SYT
b. Ba-da-zagu-zu kafetetxe hori, ez da?
AFF.know./2.SYT coffeehouse that not be.SYN
c. Jainko-a-k ba-da-zagu-z-ki zu-en bihotz-ak.
God.ERG AFF.know.PLU/.SYT you.PLU.GEN heart.PLU
d. Non-dik n-a-zagu-k?
whence know.1/2SOL.SYT

(19) a. Zer da-ntzu-t?
what hear./1.SYT
b. Ez da-ntzu ezer.
not hear.SYT anything
c. Peru, ez da-ntzu-zu zu-k?
Pete not hear./2.SYN you.ERG

(20) a. Su-a eta egurr-a da-kus-(z)-ki-t.
fire and wood see.PLU/1.SYT
b. Jainko-a-k ba-da-kus-(z)ki gauza guzti-ak.
God.ERG AFF.see.PLU/.SYT thing all.PLU
c. Ni-re begi-a-k zer da-kus?
I.GEN eye.ERG what see.SYT
d. Gu-k gauza bat da-kusa-gu garbi.
we.ERG thing one see./1PLU.SYT clearly

(21) a. Asko-ta-n da-gi-t hau.
often do./1.SYT this
b. Galde da-gi-t, Aita; ez aitor.
question.IDF make.1.SYT Father.IDF not testimony.IDF
c. Zin da-gi-t Jaun bizi-a-ren-ga(i)-tik.
oath.IDF make./1.SYT Lord living.MOT
d. Hai-en aurre-an dar=dar da-gi lurr-a-k.
yonder_one.PLU.GEN before trembling.ADV make.SYT earth.ERG

(22) a. Andre-a-k liburu-a da-kar.
lady.ERG book bring.SYT
b. Andre-ek liburu-a da-kar-te.
lady.PLU.ERG book bring./PLU.SYT
c. Andre-a-k liburu-ak da-kar-tza.
lady.ERG book.PLU bring.PLU/.SYT
d. Andre-ek liburu-ak da-kar-tza-te.
lady.PLU.ERG book.PLU bring.PLU/PLU.SYT

(23) a. Andre asko da-tor.
lady many come.SYN
b. Andre asko da-to(r)-z.
lady many come.PLU.SYN

(24) a. Andre-a-k liburu asko da-kar.
lady.ERG book many bring.SYT
b. Andre-a-k liburu asko da-kar-tza.
lady.ERG book many bring.PLU/.SYT

(25) a. Ba-z-a-ra-ma-tza-t.
AFF.carry.2/1.SYT
b. Ni-k z-a-ra-ma-tza-t.
I.ERG carry.2/1.STN
c. Zu z-a-ra-ma-tza-t.
you carry.2/1.SYT

d. Ez z-a-ra-ma-tza-t.
not carry.2/1.SYT

(26) a. Ijito aberats hon-e-k arrosa eder hau-ek neskatxa polit horr-en-tzat
gypsy rich this.ERG rose beautiful this.PLU girl pretty that.BEN
da-kar-tza.
bring.PLU/.SYT

b. Hon-e-k hau-ek horr-en-tzat da-kar-tza.
this_one.ERG this_one.PLU that_one.BEN bring.PLU/.SYT

(27) Zer d-io Itziar hon-e-k?
what say.SYT Itziar this.ERG

(28) Gu-re seme hau-ek ezkondu-ko d-ir-a alkate-a-ren alaba hori-(e)-ekin.
we.GEN son this.PLU marry.FUT PLU.ITR mayor.GEN daughter that.PLU.SOC

(29) a. Hau bakarr-ik d-io-t: Aurre-ra!
this alone.STA say./1.SYT Forward

b. Huts hori hon-e-ta-n da-tza:...
mistake that this.LOC lie.SYN

c. Gutxi g-a-r-a. Hori da arazo-a.
few be.1PLU.SYN that be.SYN problem

(30) Alargun gaixo hau ez d-oa ino-ra.
widow poor this not go.SYN anywhere.ALL

(31) Zer da-ra-bil-k hemen lapur zital horr-e-k?
what plot./2SOL.SYT here.LOC thief nasty that.ERG

(32) a. Hon-e-k ez da-ki e-zer.
this_one.ERG not know.SYT anything

b. Hai-ek horr-en-gan fede oso-a da-uka-te.
yonder_one.PLU.ERG that_one.LOC faith full have./PLU.SYT

c. Hori-(e)-en-gan-(r)a ez da inor j-oa-n-go orain.
this_one.PLU.ALL not ITR anybody go.FUT now

Chapter 10

(1) a. Gizon bat-e-k bi seme z-it-u-en.
man.ERG a.ERG two son.IDF have.PLU/.SYT.PST

b. Bi seme z-it-u-en gizon bat-e-k.
two son.IDF have.PLU/.SYT.PST man a.ERG

c. Gizon bat-e-k ba-z-it-u-en bi seme.
man a.ERG AFF.have.PLU/.SYT.PST two son.IDF

(2) a. Alargun-a-k hogei urte-ko alab(a)-a ze-uka-n.
widow.ERG twenty year.ADN daughter have.SYT.PST

b. Ba-ze-uka-te-n han kazetalari-ek gai ederr-a.
AFF.have./PLU.SYT.PST over_there.LOC journalist.PLU.ERG topic fine

(3) a. Aide-a-k kanpo=usai gozo-a ze-karr-e-n.
air.ERG field_smell sweet bring.SYT.PST

b. Laugarren alaba hon-e-k ba-ze-karr-e-n akats-en bat.
fourth daughter this.ERG AFF.carry.SYT.PST fault.IDF.GEN a

(4) a. Mikolas eta Erromana-k etxe eta seme=alab(a)-(e)-ekin nahiko-a arazo ze-ra-bil-te-n.
Mikolas and Romana.ERG house.IDF and son-daughter.PLU.SOC plenty problem handle./PLU.SYT.PST

b. Gogoeta hau-ek ze-ra-bil-tza-n Jon Bidart detektibe-a-k.
thought this.PLU stir.PLU/.SYT.PST Jon Bidart detective.ERG

(5) a. Mutil-a-k trumoi-a ze-ra-ma-n ber-e barru-an.
boy.ERG thunder carry.SYT.PST he_himself.GEN interior.LOC

b. Gizon-a-k ereinotz=usai-a ze-ra-ma-n, andre-a-k alkanfor=usai-a.
man.ERG laurel_smell carry.SYT.PST woman.ERG camphor_smell

c. Bi deabru-k su-z-ko leize bat-e-ra n-inde-ra-ma-te-n.
two devil.IDF.ERG fire.IDF.INS.ADN cave a.ALL lead.1/PLU.SYT.PST

(6) a. Inor-k ez omen ze-ki-en ezer.
anybody.ERG not REP know.SYT.PST anything

b. Baina zu-k, Maya, ba-z-ene-ki-en ni-re berri.
but you.ERG Maya AFF.know./2.SYT.PST I.GEN news.IDF

(7) a. Eta isil-a-k baietz-a z-irudi-en.
and silence.ERG assent seem.SYT.PST

b. Sorginkeri(a)-a edo zeru-ko laguntz(a)-a z-irudi-en kontu har-k.
witchcraft or heaven.ADN help seem.SYT.PST matter yonder.ERG

(8) a. Jon-e-k etxe-a sal-tzen d-u.
John.ERG house sell.IPF TRA

b. Jon-e-k etxe-a sal-du d-u.
John.ERG house sell.PEF TRA

c. Jon-e-k etxe-a sal-du-ko d-u.
John.ERG house sell.FUT TRA

(9) a. Miren-e-k sorgin-ak gorrota-tzen d-it-u.
Mary.ERG witch.PLU hate.IPF PLU/.TRA

b. Miren-e-k sorgin-ak gorrota-tu d-it-u.
Mary.ERG witch.PLU hate.PEF PLU/.TRA
c. Miren-e-k sorgin-ak gorrota-tu-ko d-it-u.
Mary.ERG witch.PLU hate.FUT PLU/.TRA

(10) a. Miren-e-k minigona gorri-gorri-a da-ra-ma.
Mary.ERG miniskirt red_red wear.SYT
b. Miren-e-k beti minigona gorri-gorri-a e-ra-ma-ten d-u.
Mary:ERG always miniskirt red_red wear.IPF TRA

(11) a. Jon-e-k txapel beltz-a ze-ra-ma-n atzo.
John.ERG beret black wear.SYT.PST yesterday
b. Jon-e-k egun hai-e-ta-n txapel beltz-a e-ra-ma-ten z-u-en.
John.ERG day yonder.PLU.LOC beret black wear.IPF TRA.PST

(12) a. Gu-re alaba-k ez z-u-en diru asko.
we(I).GEN daughter.ERG not have.SYT.PST money much
b. Gu-re alaba-k ez z-u-en diru asko iza-ten.
we(I).GEN daughter.ERG not TRA.PST money much have.IPF

(13) a. Hori aitona-k z-io-en / esa-n z-u-en.
that Grandfather.IDF.ERG say.SYT.PST say.PEF TRA.PST
b. Hori aitona-k esa-ten d-u.
that Grandfather.IDF.ERG say.IPF TRA
c. Hori aitona-k esa-ten z-u-en.
that Grandfather.IDF.ERG say.IPF TRA.PST

(14) a. Asko da-ki-gu.
a_lot know./1PLU.SYT
b. Asko ja-ki-ten d-u-gu.
a_lot know.IPF /1PLU.TRA
c. Asko ja-ki-n d-u-gu.
a_lot know.PEF /1PLU.TRA

(15) a. Den-a irits-i da orain.
everything arrive.PEF ITR now
b. Den-ak irits-i d-ir-a orain.
everybody.PLU/all_the_things.PLU arrive.PEF PLU.ITR now

(16) a. Orain den-a i-kus-ten d-u-t.
now everything see.IPF /1.TRA
b. Orain den-ak i-kus-ten d-it-u-t.
now everybody.PLU/all_the_things.PLU see.IPF PLU/1.TRA

(17) Bordalegi-ko txakurr-ek ez d-u-te den-ek e-ntzu-n-go.
Bordalegi.ADN dog.PLU.ERG not /PLU.TRA all.PLU.ERG hear.FUT

(18) a. Zu z-a-r-a gu-re / gu den-(e)-en ama.
you be.2.SYN we.GEN we all.PLU.GEN mother.IDF
b. Egi(a)-a al ze-n hura den-a?
truth INT be.SYN.PST yonder all

(19) a. Den-ak e-torr-i z-a-r-e-te.
all.ZEP.PLU come.PEF 2PLU.ITR
b. Den-ak harrapa-tu g-a-it-u-z-te.
all.ZEP.PLU catch.PF 1PLU/PLU.TRA

(20) a. Hon-(r)a ber-a-z liburu bat, den-a euskara-z.
here.ALL thus book a all Basque.IDF.INS
b. Negarr-e-z ur-tu n-a-iz den-a.
tear.IDF.INS melt.PEF 1.ITR all

(21) a. Den-ek gorrota-tzen n-a-u-te.
everybody.ZEP.PLU.ERG hate.IPF 1/PLU.TRA
b. Guzti-ek gorrota-tzen n-a-u-te.
all.ZEP.PLU.ERG hate.IPF 1/PLU.TRA

(22) Jantzi eta guzti sar-tu ze-n ibai-an.
dress.IDF and all.IDF enter.PEF ITR.PST river.LOC

(23) Ez n-a-iz ohitura hori-(e)-en zale-a.
not be.1.SYN custom that.PLU.GEN fond

(24) a. Jon oso Mirenzale-a da.
John very Mary_fond be.SYN
b. Gu-re irakasle-a Kafka eta Atxagazale amorratu-a da.
we.GEN teacher Kafka and Atxaga_fond ardent be.SYN

(25) Andre hori-ek guzti-ak pintura berrizale-ak d-ir-a.
lady that.PLU all.PLU painting new_fond.PLU be.PLU.SYN

(26) a. Pello oso neskazale-a da.
Pete very girl_fond be.SYN
b. Pello mutilzahar neskazale-a da.
Pete old_bachelor girl_fond be.SYN

Chapter 11

(1) a. On-gi e-torr-i!
well come

b. On-do i-bil-i!
well walk
c. Gizon-a eta gizarte-a eder-ki e-zagu-tzen z-it-u-e-n.
man and society very_well know.IPF PLU/.TRA.PST
d. En-e bihotz-a azkar ze-bil-e-n.
I.GEN heart vigorously walk.SYN.PST
e. Oso zintzo porta-tu g-a-r-a.
very civilly behave.PEF 1PLU.ITR
f. Den-a garbi ze-kusa-n.
everything clearly see.SYT.PST
g. Organo-a-ren not(a)-ak ozen-ki heda-tzen z-ir-e-n katedral(-)e-an.
organ.GEN note.PLU sonorously spread.IPF PLU.ITR.PST cathedral.LOC
h. Ez n-a-iz oso on-gi oroi(t)-tzen.
not 1.ITR very well remember.IPF
i. Ez d-u-zu oso erraz barka-tzen.
not /2.TRA very easily forgive.IPF

(2) a. Zer e-gi-n d-u-t zehatz?
what do.PEF /1.TRA exactly
b. Orain i-kus-ten d-u-t garbi.
now see.IPF /1.TRA clearly
c. Beste-la, zu-re-gan-(r)a j-oa-n-go n-a-iz laster.
or_else you.ALL go.FUT 1.ITR quickly
d. Eser-i e-gi-n da haundi-ki-ro.
sit_down do.PEF ITR majestically

(3) Gero, urte-(e)-en buru-an, gauz(a)-ak lasai-tu z-ir-e-n asti-ro
later_on year.PLU.GEN at_the_end_of thing.PLU ease_down.PEF PLU.ITR.PST calmly
eta poli(t)-ki.
and nicely

(4) a. Hon-e(n)-la ez g-oa-z i-nor-a.
this_way not go.1PLU.SYN anywhere.ALL
b. Horr-e(n)-la ez z-oa-z i-nor-a.
that_way not go.2.SYN anywhere.ALL
c. Ha(r-en)-la ez d-oa i-no-ra.
yonder_way not go.SYN anywhere.ALL

(5) a. Lehen ha(r-en)-la, orain horr-e(n)-la, gero ez ja-ki-n no-la.
first yonder_way now that_way afterward not know how
b. Ha(r-en)-la d-irudi.
so seem.SYT

(6) No-la-ko liburu-a? Hon-e(n)-la-ko/ horr-e(n)-la-ko/ ha(r-en)-la-ko liburu-a.
how.ADN book this_way.ADN that_way.ADN yonder_way.ADN book

(7) a. Nabarmen-du e-gi-n h-a-iz zeha-ro.
show do.PEF 2SOL.ITR totally
b. Yolanda, zora-tu al h-a-iz zeha-ro?
Yolanda go_crazy.PEF INT 2SOL.ITR totally
c. Su-tu da bizi-ro Erko zintzo-a.
get_angry.PEF ITR very Erko decent

(8) a. Zuzen-e-z irabaz-te-a oso da bide-z-ko-a.
justly earn.VEN very be.SYN legitimate
b. On-a d-irudi. - Oso da on-a, etxekoi-a eta maratz-a.
good seem.SYT very be.SYN good home-loving and diligent
c. Paula oso ze-n emakume itxura-z-ko-a eta maitagarri-a.
Paula very be.SYN.PST woman look.IDF.INS.ADN and lovable
d. Eta hura ere anitz ze-n ederr-a.
and that_one too so_much be.SYN.PST handsome

(9) a. Inspektore-a-ren erantzun-a azkarr-a iza-n ze-n oso.
inspector.GEN answer quick be.PEF ITR.PST very
b. Baina orain beste-la da oso.
but now different be.SYN very
c. Gaur gaizto-a i-kus-ten h-a-u-t oso.
today naughty see.IPF 2SOL/1.TRA very
d. Gu-re Miren alaba on-a iza-n da beti oso.
we.GEN Mary daughter good be.PEF ITR always very
e. Joxepa goibel ze-go-en oso.
Joxepa sad.PRE be.SYN.PST very

(10) a. Gu-re Miren alaba on-a iza-n da beti, oso.
we.GEN Mary daughter good be.PEF ITR always very
b. . . . eta ezagutza mingarri-a da, oso.
. . . and acquaintance painful be.SYN very
c. Bizi-a, bai, baina mingarri-a ere bai, oso.
vivid yes but painful too yes very

(11) a. Zer-ga(i)-tik jaik-i g-a-r-a hon-en goiz?
what.MOT get_up.PEF PLU.ITR this early
b. No-ra z-oa-z horr-en apain?
where.ALL go.2.SYN that elegant.IDF
c. Ha(-)in isil-a da!
so quiet be.SYN

(12) Jose ha(-)in ze-n mutil on-a!
Josef such be.SYN.PST boy good

(13) Ni ez n-a-iz ha(-)in-beste harri-tzen.
I not 1.ITR so_much be_surprised.IPF

(14) Ja-ki-n uka-n d-u beti kasik no-n ze(-n)-n egi(a)-a.
know.PEF have.PEF TRA always almost where be.SYN.PST.NCZ truth

(15) a. Ia=ia eror-i n-in-tz-e-n.
almost_almost fall.PEF 1.ITR.PST
b. Hurbil-du z-ir-e-n eta bi ontzi-ak ia=ia hondora-tze-ra-ino
draw_near.PEF PLU.ITR.PST and two boat.PLU almost_almost sink.VEN.TER
bete z(e)-it-u-z-te-n.
fill.PEF PLU/PLU.TRA.PST

(16) a. Ez ze-n ia inor e-torr-i.
not ITR.PST almost anybody come.PEF
b. Jon-e-k ez d-u ia ezer e-gi-n.
John not TRA almost anything do.PEF
c. Ia ino-n ez d-u-t aurki-tu.
almost anywhere not /1.TRA find.PEF
d. Ia inoiz ez g-a-r-a etxe-tik atera-tzen.
almost ever not 1PLU.ITR house.ELA go_out.IPF

(17) a. Inor gutxi e-torr-i ze-n.
somebody few.IDF come.PEF ITR.PST
b. Jon-e-k ezer gutxi e-gi-n d-u.
John something few.IDF do.PEF TRA
c. Ino-n gutxi-ta-n aurki-tu d-u-t.
somewhere seldom find.PEF /1.TRA
d. Inoiz gutxi-ta-n etxe-tik atera-tzen g-a-r-a.
ever seldom house.ELA go_out.IPF 1PLU.ITR

(18) a. Ni-re lan-a buka-tu hurran d-u-t.
I.GEN work finish.PEF nearly /1.TRA
b. Etxe-a sal-du hurr-en z-u-en.
house sell.PEF nearly.SUP.IDF TRA.PST
c. Hil hurr-en da. Hil hurr-en-a da.
die.PEF nearly.SUP.IDF ITR die.PEF next.SUP be.SYN

(19) a. (Agi-an) sorgin-ak (agi-an) bihar (agi-an) Zugarramurdi-ra j-oa-n-go
perhaps witch.PLU perhaps tomorrow perhaps Zugarramurdi.ALL go.FUT

d-ir-a (agi-an).
PLU.ITR perhaps

b. (Agi-an) sorgin-ak (agi-an) Zugarramurdi-ra j-oa-n-go d-ir-a (agi-an)
perhaps witch.PLU perhaps Zugarramurdi.ALL go.FUT PLU.ITR perhaps
bihar (agi-an).
tomorrow perhaps

c. (Agi-an) sorgin-ak (agi-an) ez d-ir-a (agi-an) bihar (agi-an)
perhaps witch.PLU perhaps not PLU.ITR perhaps tomorrow perhaps
Donostia-ra e-torr-i-ko (agi-an).
San_Sebastian.ALL come.FUT perhaps

d. (Agi-an) sorgin-ak (agi-an) ez d-ir-a (agi-an) Donostia-ra e-torr-i-ko
perhaps witch.PLU perhaps not PLU.ITR perhaps San_Sebastian.ALL come.FUT
(agi-an) bihar (agi-an).
perhaps tomorrow perhaps

(20) a. Agi-an bigarren ezkontza bat-e-k arin-du-ko d-u zu(-e)-en
perhaps second marriage a.ERG alleviate.FUT TRA you.PLU.GEN
alarguntz(a)-a-ren dolu-a.
widowhood.GEN grief

b. Agi-an, ez da hori nesk(a)-a-ren izen-a.
perhaps not be.SYN that maiden.GEN name

c. Gain-e-ra, agi-an lan lasai bat topa-tu-ko d-u-zu.
top.ALL perhaps work easy a find.FUT /2.TRA

d. Eta, behar-ba-da, ni-gan-dik aldegi-te-ko z-oa-z gaur.
and perhaps I.ELA run_away.VEN.ADN go.2.SYN today

e. Mentura-z zu-re-tzat da-uka dekreto hau: . . .
perhaps you.BEN have.SYT decree this

(21) a. Ero bat-en antz-a ote d-u-t agi-an . . . ?
madman a.GEN looks DUB have./1.SYT perhaps

b. Hori, orde-a, Europa zaharr-e-ko jokabide hori-e-ta-ko bat iza-n-go
that however Europe old.ADN way_of_conduct that.PLU.ADN a be.FUT
da, behar-ba-da.
ITR perhaps

c. Istilu-ren bat z-u-te-n ha-n behe-an, apika.
trouble.IDF.GEN a /PLU.TRA.PST yonder.LOC lower_part.LOC perhaps

d. Bekatu asko g-en-it-u-en, apika, baina nor-k
sin a_lot.IDF have.PLU/1PLU.SYT perhaps but who.ERG
ber-e-ak.
he_himself.GEN.ZEP.PLU

(22) a. Hiru aste ez d-ir-a, agi-an, ezer itsaso-an.
three week.IDF not be.PLU.SYN perhaps anything sea.LOC

b. Hori ez da, behar-ba-da, gizontasun prestu-a.
that not be.SYN perhaps courtesy proper

c. Hemen-dik hamar urte-ta-ra, agi-an, gaur-ko-a egun gogoragarri bat iza-n-go da.
hence ten year.IDF.ALL perhaps today.ADN.ZEP day memorable a be.FUT ITR

d. Ordu-ko, behar-ba-da, abera(t)s-tu-ko n-a-iz loteri(a)-(e)-ekin.
time.DES perhaps get_rich.FUT 1.ITR lottery.PLU.SOC

e. Bakezale-(e)-en biler(a)-ak ere ez d-ir-a, ausa-z, aski.
pacifist.PLU.GEN meeting.PLU too not be.PLU.SYN perhaps sufficient.IDF

(23) a. Zu-ta-z beste inor-k ba al da-ki berri hau?
you.INS else anyone.ERG AFF INT know.SYT news this

b. Zu beste inor-k ba al da-ki berri hau?
you else anyone.ERG AFF INT know.SYT news this

(24) a. Gu-re Jainko-a-k da-ki hori, eta zu-k ere bai, eta ez beste-k.
we.GEN God.ERG know.SYT that and you.ERG too yes and not another_one.ERG

b. Ba al da-ki beste-k?
AFF INT know.SYT another_one.ERG

c. Izen on-a beste-ri ken-tze-a ez da on-gi.
name good another_one.DAT take_away.VEN not be.SYN well.

d. Beste-ren buru-ko zorri-a da-kusa eta ez ber-e lepo-ko xerri-a.
another_one.GEN head.ADN louse see.SYT and not he_himself.GEN neck.ADN scrofula

e. Auzi-a beste-ta-n da-tza.
Dispute (something_)else.LOC lie.SYN

f. Orain, orde-a, haize-a-k beste-ta-ra g-a-ra-ma-tza.
now however wind.ERG elsewhere.ALL bring.1PLU/.SYT

(25) a. Hon-e(n)-la, ha(r-en)-la, beste-la ote da?
this_way yonder_way another_way DUB be.SYN

b. Bihar beste-la pentsa-tu-ko d-u.
tomorrow otherwise think.FUT TRA

(26) a. Nahasmendu-ra g-oa-z beste-(ren)-la, ez batasun-e-ra.
confusion.ALL go.1PLU.SYN otherwise not unity.ALL

b. E-torr-i azkar, beste-la etxe-an utz-i-ko h-a-u-t.
come quickly otherwise house.LOC leave.FUT 2SOL/1.TRA

Chapter 12

(1) a. Gu-re alab(a)-ek kezka-tzen n-a-u-te ber-e jokabide
we.GEN daughter.PLU.ERG worry.IPF 1/PLU.TRA she_herself.PLU.GEN behavior
zoro-a-rekin.
crazy.SOC

b. Gu-re alab(a)-e-z kezka-tzen n-a-iz.
we.GEN daughter.PLU.INS worry.IPF 1.ITR

(2) a. Harri-tu e-gi-ten z-u-en ber-e adiskide-a-ren portaer(a)-a-k.
astonish do.IPF TRA.PST he_himself.GEN friend.GEN conduct.ERG

b. Harri-tu e-gi-ten ze-n ber-e adiskide-a-ren portaer(a)-a-rekin.
be_astonished do.IPF ITR.PST he_himself.GEN friend.GEN conduct.SOC

(3) a. Ber-e kargu-tik dimiti-tu z-u-en.
he_himself.GEN office.ELA resign.PEF TRA.PST

b. Zer-ta-z duda-tzen d-u-zu?
what.INS doubt.IPF /2.TRA

c. Aitzurr-e-an jardu-n al d-u-zu-e?
hoe.LOC be_busy.PEF INT /2PLU.TRA

(4) a. Euskar(a)-a-k noiz arte irau-n-go d-u?
Basque.ERG when until last.FUT TRA

b. Esne-a-k iraki-n d-u.
milk.ERG boil.PEF TRA

c. Zilarr-a-k distira-tzen d-u.
silver.ERG glitter.IPF TRA

d. Eguzki-a-k argi-tzen d-u.
sun.ERG shine.IPF TRA

(5) a. Ater-tu d-u.
stop_raining.PEF TRA

b. J-oa-n da negu-a, ater-tu d-u euri-a.
go.PEF ITR winter stop_raining.PEF TRA rain

c. Har-en negarr-a ez ze-n ater-tu.
that_one.GEN crying not ITR.PST cease.PEF

(6) a. Garbi-tzen d-u.
clean.IPF TRA

b. E-zagu-tzen d-u.
recognize.IPF TRA

(7) a. Ja-ten d-u.
eat.IPF TRA

b. Irakur-tzen d-u.
read.IPF TRA

(8) a. Gu-re ogi-tik ja-ten d-u.
we.GEN bread.ELA eat.IPF TRA
b. Biblia-tik irakur-tzen d-u.
Bible.ELA read.IPF TRA

(9) a. Ate=hots-a-k esna-tu n-a-u.
door_sound.ERG wake_up.PEF 1/.TRA
b. Zortzi-e-ta-n esna-tu n-a-iz.
eight.PLU.LOC wake_up.PEF 1.ITR

(10) a. Miren-e-k senda-tu d-u Patxi.
Mary.ERG cure.PEF TRA Frank
b. Patxi senda-tu da.
Frank recover.PEF ITR

(11) a. Norbait-e-k ate-a zabal-du z-u-en.
somebody.ERG door open.PEF TRA.PST
b. Bat=bat-e-an ate guzti-ak zabal-du z-ir-e-n eta guzti-(e)-en kate(a)-ak
one.IDF-one.LOC door all.PLU open.PEF PLU.ITR.PST and all.PLU.GEN chain.PLU
eror-i.
fall.PEF

(12) a. Jaun-a, zu-k ni-ri oin-ak garbi-tu?
Lord you.ERG I.DAT foot.PLU wash
b. Garbi-tu n-in-tz-e-n eta i-kus-i e-gi-ten d-u-t.
wash.PEF 1.ITR.PST and see do.IPF /1.TRA

(13) a. Aldare hori puska-tu-ko d-u eta ber-e gain-e-ko hauts-ak zabal-du-ko
altar that shatter.FUT TRA and it_itself.GEN top.ADN ash.PLU scatter.FUT
d-it-u.
PLU/.TRA
b. Aldare hori puska-tu-ko da eta ber-e gain-e-ko hauts-ak zabal-du-ko
altar that shatter.FUT ITR and it_itself.GEN top.ADN ash.PLU scatter.FUT
d-ir-a.
PLU.ITR

(14) a. Nor-k ez d-it-u ate-ak itx-i?
who.ERG not PLU/.TRA gate.PLU close.PEF
b. Har-en ate-ak ez d-ir-a arrats-e-an itx-i-ko.
that_one.GEN gate.PLU not PLU.ITR evening.LOC close.FUT

(15) a. Kristau bihur-tu-ko n-a-u-zu.
Christian.IDF turn_into.FUT 1/2.TRA
b. Bertsolari bihur-tu al z-a-r-e-te?
bard.IDF turn_into.PEF INT 2PLU.ITR

(16) a. Ama-k haurr-a jan(t)z-ten d-u.
Mother.ERG child dress.IPF TRA
b. Haurr-a jan(t)z-ten da.
child dress.IPF ITR

(17) a. Ardo-a-k gal-du g-a-it-u.
wine.ERG ruin.PEF 1PLU/.TRA
b. Baso-an gal-du g-a-r-a.
woods.LOC get_lost.PEF 1PLU.ITR

(18) a. Hiri oso-a suntsi-tu-ko ote d-u-zu bost hori-(e)-en-ga(i)-tik?
city whole destroy.FUT DUB /2.TRA five that_one.PLU.MOT
b. Hil-ko n-a-iz, baina ez n-a-iz oso-ro suntsi-tu-ko.
die.FUT 1.ITR but not 1.ITR totally vanish.FUT

(19) a. Patxi-k Karmen ni-re aurre-an jarr-i z-u-en.
Frank.ERG Carmen I.GEN front.LOC put.PEF TRA.PST
b. Karmen ni-re aurre-an jarr-i ze-n.
Carmen I.GEN front.LOC put.PEF ITR.PST

(20) a. Zubi-tik igaro g-a-r-a.
bridge.ELA pass.PEF 1PLU.ITR
b. Zubi-a igaro d-u-gu.
bridge cross.PEF /1PLU.TRA

(21) a. Miren mendi=gain-e-ra irits-i ze-n.
Mary mountain_top.ALL arrive_at.PEF ITR.PST
b. Miren-e-k mendi=gain-a irits-i d-u.
Mary mountain_top reach.PEF TRA

(22) a. Ni-re gain-e-tik jauz-i z-a-r-a.
I.GEN top.ELA jump.PEF 2.ITR
b. Jauz-i n-a-u-zu.
skip.PEF 1/2.TRA

(23) a. Guraso-(e)-en etxe-an ez ze-n su-a egunero piz-ten.
parent.PLU.GEN house.LOC not ITR.PST fire every_day light.IPF
b. Gu-re etxe-a atzo sal-du ze-n.
we.GEN house yesterday sell.PEF ITR.PST

c. Ez ote d-ir-a bi txori sos bat-e-an sal-tzen?
not DUB PLU.ITR two bird.IDF penny one.LOC sell.IPF

d. Zuhaitz-a fruitu-tik e-zagu-tzen da.
tree fruit.ELA know.IPF ITR

e. Eta ni-re leiho-tik ez da ezer i-kus-ten.
and I.GEN window.ELA not ITR anything see.IPF

(24) Hurren-go laurogei urte-an ni ez n-a-iz aha(t)z-tu-ko Kantabria-ko parte-an.
next.ADN eighty year.LOC I not 1.ITR forget.FUT Cantabria.ADN region.LOC

(25) a. Hurren-go laurogei urte-an ni ez n-a-u-te aha(t)z-tu-ko Kantabria-ko
next.ADN eighty year.LOC I not 1/PLU.TRA forget.FUT Cantabria.ADN
parte-an.
region.LOC

b. Etxe-ko lan-ak ez e-gi-te-a-ga(i)-tik zigor-tu-ko d-u-te mutil hau.
house.ADN work.PLU not do.VEN.MOT punish.FUT /PLU.TRA boy this

(26) a. Etxe-ko lan-ak ez e-gi-te-a-ga(i)-tik zigor-tu-ko da mutil hau.
house.ADN work.PLU not do.VEN.MOT punish.FUT ITR boy this

b. Bat-a har-tu-r-en da eta beste-a utz-i-r-en.
one.ZEP take.FUT ITR and other.ZEP leave.FUT

(27) a. Zu-re izen-a isil-du d-u.
you.GEN name keep_quiet.PEF TRA

b. Zu-re izen-a isil-du da.
you.GEN name keep_quiet.PEF ITR

c. ber-e-ha(r-en)-la isil-du z-a-it-u.
at_once silence.PEF 2/.TRA

d. ber-e-ha(r-en)-la isil-du z-a-r-a.
at_once become_silent.PEF 2.ITR

(28) a. Hemen-dik j-oa-ten al da Basagorri-ra?— galde-tu z-u-en Seneka-k.
here.ELA go.IPF INT ITR Basagorri.ALL ask.PEF TRA.PST Seneca.ERG

b. Oso ondo e-go-ten da hemen.
very well stay.IPF ITR here.LOC

c. Atzo asko mintza-tu ze-n gai horr-e-ta-z.
yesterday a_lot speak.PEF ITR.PST matter that.INS

(29) Ez ze-n sekula erabat e-ma-ten.
not ITR.PST ever totally give.IPF

(30) a. Arrisku-an i-kus-i n-a-iz.
danger.LOC see.PEF 1.ITR

b. Ez g-in-e-n inportante-ak senti-tzen.
not 1PLU.ITR.PST important.PLU feel.IPF
c. Ur=ertz-e-an begira-tu n-a-iz.
water_edge.LOC look_at.PEF 1.ITR
d. Ispilu-an begira-tu al z-a-r-a?
mirror.LOC look_at.PEF INT 2.ITR

(31) a. No-n i-kus-i-ko g-a-r-a bihar?
where.LOC see.FUT 1PLU.ITR tomorrow
b. Ez d-ir-a egunero i-kus-ten.
not PLU.ITR every_day see.IPF
c. Anai(a)-ak bezala maite z-ir-e-n.
brother.PLU SIP love.PPR PLU.ITR.PST
d. Pabiloi-a-ren ate-an agur-tu g-in-e-n.
pavillion.GEN door.LOC say_goodbye.PEF 1PLU.ITR.PST
e. Irribarre gozo-z agur-tu z-ir-e-n.
smile sweet.IDF greet.PEF PLU.ITR.PST

Chapter 13

(1) Lehen-go idazle zaharr-(e)-en karta-rik gutxi d-u-gu.
past.ADN writer ancient.PLU.GEN letter.PAR few have./1PLU.SYT

(2) Ba-da txakurr-ik Madril-en!
AFF.be.SYN dog.PAR Madrid.LOC

(3) a. Ez da-go ezer txarr-ik.
not be.SYN anything wrong.PAR
b. Ez ze-ki-en Libe-ren bihotz=barrengo-rik ezer.
not know.SYT.PST Libe.GEN heart_interior.PAR anything
c. Beste pena-rik ez da-(d)uka-t ezer.
other sorrow.PAR not have./1.SYT anything
d. Ogibide-rik ez da-(d)uka ezer.
livelihood.PAR not have.SYT anything

(4) a. Ber-e-tzat ez ze-go-en beste gizon-ik inor.
she_herself.BEN not be.SYN.PST other man.PAR anyone
b. Toki hon-e-ta-n ez ze-uka-n inor ezagun-ik.
place that.LOC not have.SYT.PST anyone acquaintance.PAR
c. Izkotarr-(e)-en etxe-an ez d-u senitarteko-rik
member_of_the_Izko_family.PLU.GEN house.LOC not have.SYT relative.PAR
inor bizi.
anybody living.IDF

(5) a. Gaur txokolate-a eros-i d-u-t.
today chocolate buy.PEF /1.TRA
b. Gaur ez d-u-t txokolate-a eros-i.
today not /1.TRA chocolate buy.PEF
c. Gaur ez d-u-t txokolate-rik eros-i.
today not /1.TRA chocolate.PAR buy.PEF

(6) a. Ez omen da hamabost urte-ko neska itsusi-rik.
not REP be.SYN fifteen year.ADN maiden ugly.PAR
b. Etxe hon-e-ta-n arratoi-rik ere ez da geldi-tzen.
house this.LOC rat.PAR too not ITR stay.IPF
c. Baina ez ze-n Albania-n inspektore-rik azal-du.
but not ITR.PST Albania.LOC inspector.PAR appear.PEF
d. Orain ez da lapurr-ik e-torr-i-ko.
now not ITR thief.PAR come.FUT

(7) a. Ez d-u-t adiskide-rik. Ez da premia-rik ere.
not have./1.SYT friend.PAR not be.SYN need.PAR too
b. Ez d-u-t sari-rik eska-tzen.
not /1.TRA reward.PAR ask.IPF
c. Ni-re aurre-an ez z-u-en inoiz droga-rik har-tu.
I.GEN front._part.LOC not TRA.PST ever drug.PAR take.PEF

(8) a. Ba-d-it-u-t anai=arreb(a)-ak.
AFF.have.PLU/1.SYT brother_sister.PLU
b. Ez d-u-t anai=arreba-rik.
not have./1.SYT brother_sister.PAR

(9) a. Moxolo-rik ez da ager-tu-ko.
Moxolo.PAR not ITR appear.FUT
b. Ez da Maria Vöckel-ik sekula e-go-n.
not ITR Maria Vöckel.PAR ever be.PEF

(10) a. Baina gaur ni-re arreba-rik ez d-u-zu i-kus-i-ko.
but today I.GEN sister.PAR not /2.TRA see.FUT
b. Apika ni-re izen-ik ez da-ki-zu-e?
maybe I.GEN name.PAR not know./2PLU.SYT

(11) a. Ba al d-u-k izen-ik?
AFF INT have./2SOL.SYT name.PAR
b. Ba al da euskal musika-rik?
AFF INT be.SYN Basque music.PAR
c. Os-tu al d-u-zu oilo-rik?
steal.PEF INT /2.TR hen.PAR

d. Zu-re neurri-ko soineko-rik aurki-tu al d-u-zu?
you.GEN size.ADN dress.PAR find.PEF INT /2.TRA

(12) a. No-n da giristino goiztiarr-ik?
where.LOC be.SYN christian prompt.PAR

b. Nor-k edire-n-en d-u en-e bait(a)-an falta-rik?
who.ERG find.FUT TRA I.GEN inside.LOC fault.PAR

c. Nor-k iza-n-en d-u sorbalda-rik sostenga-tze-ko, indarr-ik jasa-te-ko,
who.ERG have.FUT TRA shoulder.PAR support.VEN.ADN strength.PAR bear.VEN.ADN
eta pairu-rik eta pazientzia-rik sofri-tze-ko?
and endurance.PAR and patience.PAR suffer.VEN.ADN

(13) a. No-n aurki-tu-ko d-u honela-ko etxe-rik?
where.LOC find.FUT TRA this_way.ADN house.PAR

b. No-n aurki-tu ho(ne)la-ko emakume-rik, orde-a?
where.LOC find this_way.ADN woman.PAR however

(14) a. Ez d-u batere beldurr-ik.
not have.SYT at_all fear.PAR

b. Ez d-u-t gezurr-ik batere esa-ten.
not /1.TRA lie.PAR at_all tell.IPF

c. Batere ez z-u-en molde-rik.
at_all not have.SYT.PST skill.PAR

(15) a. Ba-d-u beste kezka-rik.
AFF.have.SYT other worry.PAR

b. Hori beste-rik da.
that other.PAR be.SYN

c. Beste gizon-ik bihur-tu ze-n.
other man.PAR become.PEF ITR.PST

(16) Beharbada, iza-n-go d-u-t, seme-rik har-en bi-tarte-z.
maybe have.FUT /1.TRA son.PAR yonder_one.GEN through

(17) Hon-e-k ez d-u portu-ko gazte ez-ja-ki-n-a-ren-a e-gi-ten,
this_one.ERG not TRA harbor.ADN young_one not_having_known.GEN.DEL act.IPF
ber-a da gazte hori.
he_himself be.SYN young.ZEP that

(18) Baina ni-k ez_adi-tu-a e-gi-n n-u-en.
but I.ERG not_having_heard.DEL act.PEF /1.TRA.PST

(19) Ni-re indarr-a-k e-gi-n d-u.
I.GEN strength.ERG do.PEF TRA

(20) a. Zu-re aldi-a-k e-gi-n d-u.
you.GEN turn.ERG do.PEF TRA
b. Ia gu-re aldi-a-k e-gi-n d-u.
almost we.GEN period.ERG do.PEF TRA

(21) a. Zu-re-a-k e-gi-n d-u!
you.GEN.ZEP.ERG do.PEF TRA
b. Ia gu-re-a-k e-gi-n d-u.
almost we.GEN.ZEP.ERG do.PEF TRA

(22) E-gi-n da ni-re indarr-a-z.
do.PEF ITR I.GEN strength.INS

(23) a. Lan-a bila-tu-ko d-u-t.
work look_for.FUT /1.TRA
b. Txokolate-a e-gi-n-go d-u-t.
chocolate make.FUT /1.TRA
c. Lan-a e-gi-n-go d-u-t.
work do.FUT /1.TRA

(24) a. Gogo-tik e-gi-n d-u-te lan.
gladly do.PEF /PLU.TRA work.IDF
b. Ordu-an, egun har-ta-n, e-gi-n-go d-u-te barau.
time.LOC day yonder.LOC do.FUT /PLU.TRA fast.IDF
c. Gaur ber-ta-n e-gi-n d-u-t ihes han-dik.
today it_itself.IDF.LOC do.PEF /1.TRA escape.IDF over_there.ELA
d. Horr-e-k leku heze-e-ta-n e-gi-ten d-u lo.
that_one.ERG place humid.PLU.LOC do.IPF TRA sleep.IDF

(25) a. Ez d-u-t irribarre-rik e-gi-n.
not /1.TRA smile.PAR make.PEF
b. Ez d-u-t negarr-ik e-gi-ten.
not /1.TRA crying.PAR do.IPF
c. Deabru-a-k ez d-u lo-rik e-gi-ten.
devil.ERG not TRA sleep.PAR do.IPF
d. Ez d-u-gu gogait-ik e-gi-n-go gu-k.
not /1PLU.TRA boredom.PAR do.FUT we.ERG
e. Ez al d-u-zu amets-ik e-gi-ten?
not INT /2.TRA dream.PAR do.IPF
f. Eztul-ik ere ez d-u e-gi-n ni-re aurre-an.
cough.PAR too not TRA make.PEF I.GEN front_part.LOC

(26) a. Ez d-u hitz e-gi-n.
not TRA word.IDF make.PEF

b. Ez d-u hitz-ik e-gi-n.
not TRA word.PAR make.PEF

(27) a. Lo luze-a e-gi-n d-u.
sleep long do.PEF TRA
b. Geriz(a)-an e-gi-ten d-u ber-e lo-a.
shade.LOC do.IPF TRA he_himself.GEN sleep
c. Negar handi-ak e-gi-n z-it-uz-te-n.
tear big.PLU make.PEF PLU/PLU.TRA

(28) a. Zu-re andre-a-k arrazoi d-u.
you.GEN wife.ERG reason.IDF have.SYT
b. Arrazoi da-uka-k.
reason.IDF have./2SOL.SYT

(29) a. Bihotz-e-an min d-u-t.
heart.LOC pain.IDF have./1.SYT
b. No-n da-uka-k min?
where.LOC have./2SOL.SYT pain.IDF

(30) a. Artzain zaharr-a atera ze-n mendi-r(a)-antz inor-i esan gabe.
shepherd old go_out.PEF ITR.PST mountain.TEN anybody.DAT tell without.PRE
b. Nobel sari-a urruti-tik ere i-kus-i gabe, zerbait i-kus-i d-u-t.
Nobel Prize distance.ELA too see without.PRE something see.PEF /1.TRA

(31) Ni-k esan gabe ba-da-ki-zu-e.
I.ERG say without.PRE AFF.know./2PLU.SYT

(32) a. Guzti-z ederr-a z-a-r-a, en-e laztan-a, ederr-a eta akats-ik gabe-a!
wholly beautiful be.2.SYN I.GEN beloved beautiful and flaw.PAR without
b. Urte-ak gorabehera zimurtxo bat gabe-a da mutxurdin hau.
year.PLU despite little_wrinkle one without be.SYN old_maid this
c. Hau ustekabe uste gabe-a!
this surprise expectation without
d. Inor-i kalte e-gi-n gabe-ak z-ir-e-n.
anybody.DAT harm.IDF do without.PLU be.PLU.SYN.PST

(33) a. Nor da bekatu-rik gabe-ko-a?
who be.SYN sin.PAR without.ADN.ZEP
b. Nor da bekatu-rik gabe-a?
who be.SYN sin.PAR without

(34) Ez da deus lor-tzen saia-tu gabe-rik.
not ITR anything achieve.IPF try without.STA

(35) a. Ur-a ba-rik ardo-a eda-n d-u.
water instead_of.STA wine drink.PEF TRA
b. Hemen-dik ba-rik hor-tik j-oa-n-go z-a-r-a.
here.ELA instead_of.STA there.ELA go.FUT 2.ITR
c. Eliza-tik gabe taberna-tik g-a-to(r)-z.
church.ELA instead_of pub.ELA come.1PLU.SYN

Chapter 14

(1) a. Pello seme d-u-gu.
Pete son.IDF have./1PLU.SYT
b. Patxi adiskide d-u-t.
Frank friend.IDF have./1.SYT

(2) a. Pello seme bakarr-a d-u-gu.
Pete son only have./1PLU.SYT
b. Patxi adiskide handi-a d-u-t.
Frank friend great have./1.SYT

(3) a. Maite d-it-u-zu eta maite z-a-it-u-z-te.
dear.IDF have.PLU/2.SYN and dear.IDF have.2/PLU.SYT
b. Nagusi-ek hain maite ze-uka-te-n.
ruler.PLU.ERG so dear.IDF have./PLU.SYT.PST
c. Nor-k d-u maite?
who.ERG have.SYT dear.IDF
d. Jacob iza-n n-u-en maite eta ez Esau.
Jacob have.PEF /1.TRA.PST dear.IDF and not Esau
e. Zu z-ar-a ni-re lege-a; zu bakarr-ik z-a-it-u-t maite.
you be.2.SYN I.GEN law you only.STA have.2/1.SYT dear.IDF
f. Ho, ni-k zu z-a-it-u-t maite . . .
oh I.ERG you have.2/1.SYT dear.IDF

(4) a. Oso maite-a z-u-en Salbatore-k.
very dear have.SYT.PST Salbator.ERG
b. Jonatan-e-k oso maite-a z-u-en Dabid.
Jonathan.ERG very dear have.SYT.PST David

(5) a. Zu-k, berri-z, zenbat d-u-zu zor?
you.ERG again how_much have./2.SYT debt.IDF

b. Nor-k iza-n-go d-it-u hamar miloi libera zor?
who.ERG have.FUT PLU/.TRA ten million franc.IDF debt.IDF

(6) Nor d-u-te iduri?
who have./PLU.SYT likeness.IDF

(7) a. Ez beldur iza-n, Maria, Jainko-a-k atsegin z-a-it-u.
not fear.IDF be Maria God.ERG pleasure.IDF have.2/.SYT
b. Damu d-u-gu bekatu-a.
regret.IDF have./1PLU.SYT sin
c. Israel-ko seme-ak erruki d-it-u-t.
Israel.ADN son.PLU pity.IDF have.PLU/1.SYT
d. Ni-k ez ote d-u-t erruki iza-n-go Ninibe hiri haundi-a?
I.ERG not DUB /1.TRA pity.IDF have.FUT Niniveh city great
e. Gorroto bizi-z gorroto iza-n d-it-u-t.
hatred intense.IDF.INS hatred.IDF have.PEF PLU/1.TRA
f. Bat-a gorroto iza-n-go d-u eta beste-a maite.
one.ZEP hatred.IDF have.FUT TRA and other.ZEP dear.IDF
g. Maite ez n-a-u-zu, higuin n-a-u-zu.
dear.IDF not have.1/2.SYT disgust.IDF have.1/2.SYT

(8) a. Zu-k, orde-a, bihotz leial-a d-u-zu atsegin.
you.ERG however heart loyal have./2.SYT pleasure.IDF
b. Fede gaizto-ko-ak d-it-u-t gorroto.
faith bad.ADN.ZEP.PLU have.PLU/1.SYT hatred.IDF
c. Hizkuntza guzti-ak iza-n-go d-it-u-z-te higuin.
language all.PLU have.FUT PLU/PLU.TRA disgust.IDF
d. Bat iza-n-en d-u higuin eta beste-a maite.
one have.FUT TRA disgust.IDF and other.ZEP dear.IDF
e. Hain d-u-te hastio asko-k euskar(a)-a . . .
so_much have./PLU.SYT loathing.IDF many.IDF.ERG Basque
f. Hori z-u-en opa noski artista trebe hon-e-k.
that have.SYT.PST wish.IDF of_course artist skillful this.ERG

(9) a. Deabru-a beti gorroto-ko d-u-t.
devil always hate.FUT /1.TRA
b. Ni-k maite-ko z-a-it-u-t beti.
I.ERG love.FUT 2/1.TRA always
c. Ni-k maite z-a-it-u-t eta haurr-a ere maite-ko d-u-t.
I.ERG love.PPR 2/1.TRA and child too love.FUT /1.TRA
d. Eta arnas(a)-a ere zor-ko d-u-zu.
and breath too owe.FUT /2.TRA

e. Iduri-ko zen-u-en zeru-ko izarr-a.
look_like.FUT /2.TRA.PST heaven.ADN star

(10) Txit asko maite z-a-it-u-t.
very much.IDF love.PPR 2/1.TRA

(11) a. Txit maite z-a-it-u-t.
very_much love.PPR 2/1.TRA
b. Baina Jonathas, Saul-en seme-a-k txit-ki maite z-u-en Dabid.
but Jonathan Saul.GEN son.ERG very_much.ADV love.PPR TRA.PST David
c. Oso maite d-u-t gazta zahar hori.
very_much love.PPR /1.TRA cheese old that

(12) a. Har-en bihotz-a-k urre-a balio d-u.
yonder_one.GEN heart.ERG gold be_worth.PPR TRA
b. I-kus-i d-u-gu, baina ez z-u-en begira-tze-a ere balio.
see.PEF /1PLU.TRA but not TRA.PST look_at.VEN too be_worth.PPR
c. Euskar(a)-a-k ez d-u ogi-a irabaz-te-ko balio.
Basque.ERG not TRA bread earn.VEN.ADN be_worth.PPR
d. Horr-e-k ez d-u balio.
that.ERG not TRA be_worth.PPR

(13) a. Ni-re maitasun hon-e-k falta d-u ordain-a.
I.GEN love this.ERG lack.PPR TRA reciprocity
b. Emakume-a-ren esku-a falta iza-n ze-n han-dik aurre-ra.
woman.GEN hand lack be.PEF ITR.PST over_there.ELA front_part.ALL
c. Solas luze-e-ta-n ez da falta-ko bekatu-a.
conversation long.PLU.LOC not ITR lack.FUT sin
d. Falta iza-n al z-en-u-te-n ezer?
lack have.PEF INT /2PLU.TRA.PST anything

(14) a. Giltz(a)-a nahi-ko d-u-zu?
key want.FUT /2.TRA
b. Zer nahi d-u ni-gan-(d)ik?
what want.PPR TRA I.ELA
c. Ez d-u-t har-en diru-rik nahi.
not /1.TRA yonder_one.GEN money.PAR want.PPR

(15) a. Ni ero-tze-a nahi al d-u-zu?
I go_crazy.VEN want.PPR INT /2.TRA
b. Zerbait e-kar-tze-a nahi al d-u-zu?
something bring.VEN want.PPR INT /2.TRA
c. Ez z-u-en inor-k ja-ki-te-rik nahi.
not TRA.PST anyone.ERG know.VEN.PAR want.PPR

d. No-ra j-oa-te-a nahi d-u-zu ni-re zaharr-e-an?
where.ALL go.VEN want.PPR /2.TRA I.GEN old_age.DEL.LOC

e. Zer nahi z-en-u-en ni-k Gazteiz-e-n e-gi-te-a?
what want.PPR /2.TRA.PST I.ERG Vitoria.LOC do.VEN

(16) a. Zer-ta-ra-ko nahi d-u-zu bizi?
what.DES want.PPR /2.TRA live.PPR

b. Zer nahi d-u-zu har-tu?
what want.PPR /2.TRA take

c. Nor-k nahi d-u, orde-a, etxe-rik eta lurr-ik eros-i?
who.ERG want.PPR TRA however house.PAR and ground.PAR buy

d. Den-ek nahi z-u-te-n Salomon i-kus-i.
everybody.PLU.ERG want.PPR /PLU.TRA.PST Solomon see

e. Nahi iza-n d-u-t oihuka-tu: senda-tu-a n-a-iz!
want have.PEF /1.TRA shout cure.PEF.SIN 1.ITR

(17) a. Ez d-u-t nahi j-oa-n sukalde-ra.
not /1.TRA want.PPR go kitchen.ALL

b. Ez, ez d-u-gu nahi iza-n sobera lan har-tu.
no not /1PLU.TRA want have.PEF too_much work.IDF take

(18) a. Zer esa-n nahi d-u-zu?
what say want.PPR /2.TRA

b. Nor-k hil nahi z-a-it-u-z-te?
who.ERG kill want.PPR 2PLU/.TRA

c. Nor-k e-ntzu-n nahi d-u elbarri-a-ren ipuin-a?
who.ERG hear want.PPR TRA paralytic.GEN tale

d. Ni-k ni-re emazte e-gi-n nahi z-a-it-u-t.
I.ERG I.GEN wife.IDF make want.PPR 2/1.TRA

e. Ni-re guraso-ek e-zagu(t)-tu nahi z-a-it-u-z-te.
I.GEN parent.PLU.ERG know want.PPR 2/PLU.TRA

f. Begi-z ja-n nahi n-ind-u-en.
eye.IDF.INS eat want.PPR 1/.TRA.PST

(19) a. Ez z-a-it-u-t inon-dik gal-du nahi.
not 2/1.TRA somewhere.ELA lose want.PPR

b. Ez d-u-t ohera gabe biluz-i nahi.
not /1.TRA go_to_bed.RAD before.PRE undress want.PPR

c. Ni-k ez d-u-t ezer ja-ki-n nahi.
I.ERG not /1.TRA anything know want.PPR

d. Ez d-u e-torr-i nahi iza-ten ni-re etxe-ra.
not TRA come want have.IPF I-GEN house.ALL

(20) a. Ama, ni ere nahi n-a-iz ezkon-du.
Mother.IDF I too want.PPR 1.ITR get_married
b. Susana baratze-ko putzu-an maina-tu nahi iza-n ze-n.
Susana garden.ADN well.LOC bathe want be.PEF ITR.PST
c. Hura, berri-z, ez ze-n sar-tu nahi.
yonder_one new.IDF.INS not ITR.PST go_in want.PPR
d. Eta ez z-ir-e-n nahi e-torr-i.
and not PLU.ITR.PST want.PPR come
e. Eta ez z-ir-e-n j-oa-n nahi iza-n.
and not PLU.ITR.PST go want be.PEF

(21) Ba-da beti gu-re-gan zorion handi bat-en nahi-a.
AFF.be.SYN always we.LOC happiness great a.GEN will

(22) a. Jainko-a on-do serbi-tu nahi-a laster ager-tu z-u-en.
God well serve will soon show.PEF TRA.PST
b. Hon-e-k beste handizki-e-ta-n Daniel gal-du nahi-a sor-tzen z-u-en.
this.ERG other aristocrat.PLU.LOC Daniel ruin will create.IPF TRA.PST
c. Dam(a)-a, ni zu-ri hitzegi-n nahi-a-k n-a-ra-ma maitasun ezti-z.
lady I you.DAT speak will.ERG agitate.1/.SYT love sweet.IDF.INS

(23) a. Zu-ek i-kus-i nahi-an n-a-go.
you.PLU see will.LOC be.1.SYN
b. Aspalditxo-an n-en-go-en ber-a-ri bertso batzu-k e-gi-n nahi-an.
a_while_ago be.1.SYN.PST the_very_subject.DAT verse some.PLU make will.LOC
c. Bertsolari-ak indar-tu nahi-an omen z-a-bil-tza-te.
bard.PLU strengthen will.LOC REP be_busy.2PLU.SYN
d. Ongile den-ak esker-tu nahi-an n-a-bil.
benefactor all.PLU thank will.LOC be_busy.1.SYN

(24) a. Mutil-ek ba-z-u-te-n kalte e-gi-n nahi-a.
boy.PLU.ERG AFF.have./PLU.SYT.PST harm.IDF do will
b. Ez z-u-te-n ausa-z kalte e-gi-n nahi-rik.
not have./PLU.SYT.PST perhaps harm.IDF do will.PAR
c. Ez z-u-te-n ausa-z kalte e-gi-n nahi handi-rik.
not have./PLU.SYT.PST perhaps harm.IDF do will great.PAR

(25) a. Hon-e-k berriketa-ra-ko gogo-a da-uka.
this_one.ERG gossip.ALL.ADN fancy have.SYT
b. Ez d-u-t haserre-ra-ko gogo-rik.
not have.1.SYT row.ALL.ADN desire.PAR
c. Gu-re herri-a i-kus-te-ko gogo-a ba-n-u-en aspaldi-an.
we.GEN village see.VEN.ADN desire AFF.have./1.SYT.PST long_time.LOC

d. Ni-k ez d-u-t hil-(e)-en-gan-(r)a makur-tze-ko gogo-rik.
I.ERG not have./1.SYT dead.ZEP.PLU.ALL bow.VEN.ADN desire.PAR

e. Ba-da-uka-t, bai, Donostia-ra iri(t)s-te-ko gogo-rik!
AFF.have./1.SYT yes San_Sebastian.ALL arrive.VEN.ADN desire.PAR

(26) a. Ba-n-u-en gogo-a Bazko afari hau zu-ekin e-gi-te-ko!
AFF.have./1.SYT.PST desire Passover supper this you.PLU.SOC do.VEN.ADN

b. Gogo-rik al d-u-n gaur arratsalde-an ni-rekin Izpegi-ra
desire.PAR INT have./2SOL.FEM.SYT today afternoon.LOC I.SOC Izpegi.ALL
e-tor-tze-ko?
come.VEN.ADN

(27) a. Zer e-gi-n gogo d-u-zu?
what do intend.PPR /2.TRA

b. Gogo z-u-en etxe-an e-go-n.
intend.PPR TRA.PST house.LOC stay

c. Ezkil(a)-a lehen bezala jo gogo d-u.
bell before as ring intend.PPR TRA

(28) a. No-n gera-tzen d-ir-a zoko hau-ek e-zagu(t)-tze-ko asmo-ak?
where.LOC remain.IPF PLU.ITR place this.PLU know.VEN.ADN plan.PLU

b. Zarautz-e-ra j-oa-n n-in-tz-e-n Patxi Barbero-ren omenaldi-an kanta-tze-ko
Zarauz.ALL go.PEF 1.ITR.PST Patxi Barbero.GEN celebration.LOC sing.VEN.ADN
asmo-ta-n.
intention.IDF.LOC

(29) Zer e-gi-n asmo d-u-zu?
what do intend.PPR /2.TRA

(30) a. Odol hotz-a behar d-u-zu.
blood cold need.PPR /2.TRA

b. Nor-k zer behar d-u?
who.ERG what need.PPR TRA

c. Hi behar h-a-u-t.
you.SOL need.PPR 2SOL/1.TRA

d. Baina ez n-a-u inor-k behar hemen.
but not 1/.TRA anybody.ERG need.PPR here.LOC

e. Sermoi-rik ez d-u-gu behar.
sermon.PAR not /1PLU.TRA need.PPR

f. Liburu-ak behar d-ir-a.
book.PLU need.PPR PLU.ITR

(31) a. Polizi(a)-a e-tor-tze-a behar z-en-u-en.
police come.VEN need.PPR /2.TRA.PST

b. Zu-k esa-te-a behar g-en-u-en.
you.ERG say.VEN need.PPR /1PLU.TRA.PST

(32) a. Irakurle-a behar d-u-gu errespeta-tu.
reader must.PPR /1PLU.TRA respect
b. Guzti-ek behar z-u-te-n ja-ki-n har-en berri.
all.PLU.ERG have_to.PPR /PLU.TRA.PST know yonder.GEN news.IDF
c. Ordu-an behar n-u-en ni-k mintza-tu.
that_time.LOC should.PPR /1.TRA.PST I.ERG speak
d. Ez d-ir-a behar sinets-i.
not PLU.ITR need-PPR believe
e. Gaur-ko lokatz-e-ta-n behar-ko d-u zikin-du.
today.ADN quagmire.PLU.LOC must.FUT TRA make_dirty

(33) a. Ni-k zer esa-n behar d-u-t?
I.ERG what say must.PPR /1.TRA
b. Ja-n e-gi-n behar z-a-it-u-z-te-t.
Eat do must.PPR 2PLU/1.TRA
c. Horr-e(n)-la bizi behar al d-u-n, alab(a)-a?
that_way live have_to.PPR INT /2SOL.FEM.TRA daughter
d. Ni-rekin dantza-tu behar-ko d-u-zu rumba hau.
I.SOC dance have_to.FUT /2.TRA rumba this
e. Hori ez d-u inor-k ja-ki-n behar.
that not TRA anybody.ERG know must.PPR
f. Ez al n-a-u-zu-e urka-tu behar?
not INT 1/2PLU.TRA hang have_to.PPR
g. Adore-rik ez da gal-du behar.
courage.PAR not ITR lose must.PPR

(34) a. Euri-a e-gi-n behar d-u.
rain do be_going_to.PPR TRA
b. Igande-an gu-rekin bazkal-du behar omen d-u-zu.
Sunday.LOC we.SOC lunch be_going_to.PPR REP /2.TRA

(35) a. Zer esa-n behar d-u herri-a-k?
what say be_going_to.PPR TRA people.ERG
b. Zer e-gi-n behar d-u-t ni-k zu gabe?
what do be_going_to.PPR /1.TRA I.ERG you without.PRE
c. Eta beste zu-re andre-a-rekin zer e-gi-n behar d-u-zu?
and other you.GEN wife.SOC what do be_going_to.PPR /2.TRA
d. Noiz zentza-tu behar d-u-zu?
when come_to_one's_senses be_going_to.PPR /2.TRA

e. Nor-k esa-n behar z-u-en?
who.ERG say would.PPR TRA.PST

(36) a. Ez n-in-tz-e-n ezkon-du behar.
not 1.ITR.PST get_married should.PPR
b. Zu-re haurr-ak no-la behar d-ir-a ha-n bizi?
you.GEN child.PLU how be_going_to.PPR PLU.ITR over_there.LOC live
c. Gaur abia-tu behar g-a-r-a.
today start_out must.PPR 1PLU.ITR

(37) Hotz=hotz-e-an erabaki-ak har-tu behar d-ir-a.
coolness_coolness.LOC decision.PLU take must.PPR PLU.ITR

(38) a. Zer-ga(i)-tik d-u hil beharr-a?
what.MOT have.SYT die need
b. Herri-ko etxe-ra-ino j-oa-n beharr-a d-u-t.
town.ADN house.TER go need have./1.SYT
c. Hori al z-en-u-en esa-n beharr-a?
that INT have./2.SYT.PST say need

(39) a. Mitxelena jaun-a-k ez d-u ni-re aurkezpen beharr-ik.
Mitxelena Mr.ERG not have.SYT I.GEN introduction need.PAR
b. Ez d-u-zu gu-ta-z ardura-tu beharr-ik.
not have./2.SYT we.INS worry need.PAR
c. Ez d-u-t ni-k j-oa-n beharr-ik iza-n-go.
not /1.TRA I.ERG go need.PAR have.FUT
d. Ez da-uka-t ni-k zu-rekin hitz e-gi-n beharr-ik.
not have./1.SYT I.ERG you.SOC word.IDF make need.PAR
e. Esa-n beharr-ik ez da-uka-zu.
say need.PAR not have./2.SYT

(40) a. Ba-ze-n zu-re beharr-a gu-re etxe hon-e-ta-n.
AFF.be.SYN.PST you.GEN need we.GEN house this.LOC
b. Hain-beste gauza antola-tu beharr-a da-go.
so_many thing.IDF organize need be.SYN
c. Lau Ebanjelio-en itzulpen berri bat-en beharr-ik ba ote ze-go-en?
four Gospel.PLU.GEN translation new a.GEN need.PAR AFF DUB be.SYN.PST

(41) a. Ni-re lagun-a laguntza beharr-e-an da.
I.GEN fellow-man help need.LOC be.SYN
b. Den-a-ren beharr-e-an iza-n-go z-a-r-e-te.
Everything.GEN need.LOC be.FUT 2PLU.ITR
c. Buru-a makur-tu beharr-e-an g-a-u-de.
head bend need.LOC be.1PLU.SYN

d. Gu bizi iza-te-ko, orain-txe n-a-go bozkario beharr-e-an.
we live.PPR be.VEN.ADN now.EMP be.1.SYN joy need.LOC

e. Zu-re beharr-e-an aurki-tzen n-a-iz.
you.GEN need.LOC find.IPF 1.ITR

f. Saul ber-e hitz-a ja-n beharr-e-an aurki-tu ze-n.
Saul he_himself.GEN word eat need.LOC find.PEF ITR.PST

(42) a. Konpon-du beharr-e-an, honda-tu e-gi-n d-u.
repair need.LOC ruin do.PEF TRA

b. Ber-a-k e-gi-n beharr-e-an, am(a)-a-k e-gi-ten z-u-en negar.
he_himself.ERG do need.LOC mother.ERG do.IPF TRA.PST crying.IDF

(43) a. Ez n-a-iz ibai-ra eror-i ohi.
not 1.ITR river.ALL fall be_in_habit.PPR

b. Jende-a ezkon-du e-gi-n ohi da.
people get_married do be_in_habit.PPR ITR

(44) a. Ez d-u-gu ja-n ohi.
not /1PLU.TRA eat be_in_habit.PPR

b. Bazko=Jaiero preso bat aska-tu ohi z-u-en Pilato-k.
each_Passover_feast_day prisoner a release be_in_habit.PPR TRA.PST Pilate.ERG

c. E-gi-n iza-n ohi d-it-u horr-e(n)-la-ko gauz(a)-ak.
do have.PEF be_in_habit PLU/.TRA that_way.ADN thing.PLU

(45) a. Ez ohi n-a-iz ibai-ra eror-tzen.
not HAB 1.ITR river.ALL fall.IPF

b. Jende-a ezkon-tzen ohi da.
people get_married.IPF HAB ITR

(46) a. Ez ohi d-u-gu ja(n)-ten.
not HAB /1PLU.TRA eat.IPF

b. Presuna haserrekorr-a-k ez ohi d-u begi=orde anitz higa-tzen.
person irascible.ERG not HAB TRA eye_substitute many wear_out.IPF

Chapter 15

(1) a. Mutil hon-e-k neskatxa horr-i egun zoriontsu-a opa d-i-o.
boy this.ERG girl that.DAT day happy wish.PPR DTR

b. Mutil hon-e-k neskatxa hori-e-i egun zoriontsu-a opa d-i-e.
boy this.ERG girl that.PLU.DAT day happy wish.PPR /PLU/.DTR

(2) a. Mutil hau-ek neskatxa horr-i egun zoriontsu-a opa d-i-o-te.
boy this.PLU.ERG girl that.DAT day happy wish.PPR //PLU.DTR

b. Mutil hau-ek neskatxa hori-e-i egun zoriontsu-a. opa
boy this.PLU.ERG girl that.PLU.DAT day happy wish.PPR
d-i-e-te
/PLU/PLU.DTR

(3) a. Mutil hon-e-k neskatxa horr-i egun zoriontsu-ak opa d-i-z-ki-o.
boy this.ERG girl that.DAT day happy.PLU wish.PPR PLU//.DTR
b. Mutil hon-e-k neskatxa hori-e-i egun zoriontsu-ak opa d-i-z-ki-e.
boy this.ERG girl that.PLU.DAT day happy.PLU wish.PPR PLU/PLU/.DTR

(4) a. Mutil hau-ek neskatxa horr-i egun zoriontsu-ak opa d-i-z-ki-o-te.
boy this.PLU.ERG girl that.DAT day happy.PLU wish.PPR PLU//PLU.DTR
b. Mutil hau-ek neskatxa hori-e-i egun zoriontsu-ak opa
boy this.PLU.ERG girl that.PLU.DAT day happy.PLU wish.PPR
d-i-z-ki-e-te.
PLU/PLU/PLU.DTR

(5) a. Ontzi horr-i estalki hau da-go-ki-o.
container that.DAT lid this fit.DYN
b. Morroi-a bataia-tze-a nagusi-a-ri da-go-ki-o.
servant christen.VEN boss.DAT be_up_to.DYN
c. Ohitur(a)-a-ri n-a-go-ki-o.
custom.DAT keep_to./1.DYN

(6) Soineko hori on-do d-oa-ki-o / da-tor-ki-o / da-go-ki-o.
dress that well do.DYN come.DYN be.DYN

(7) Ordu hori gai(t)z-ki da-tor-ki-t.
hour that badly come.1/.DYN

(8) Gu-ri zer di-h-oa-ki-gu?
we.DAT what matter.1PLU/.DYN

(9) a. Berri on-ak al da-kar-z-ki-gu-zu?
news good.PLU INT bring.PLU/1PLU/2.DYT
b. Berri on-ak da-kar-z-ki-zu-t.
news good.PLU bring.PLU/2/1.DYT
c. Etsai gaizto-a-k da-ra-ma-ki-o.
enemy evil.ERG lead_away.DYT
d. Agindu berri bat da-ma-i-zu-e-t.
commandment new a give./2PLU/1.DYT
e. Zorion bete-a da-ma-i-o-t n-eu-re maite-a-ri.
Happiness full give.//1.DYT I.REF.GEN love.DAT

(10) a. Ba-g-ene-kar-ki-e-n.
AFF.bring./PLU/1PLU.DYT.PST
b. Ba-da-ra-ma-z-ki-gu-te.
AFF.carry.PLU/1PLU/PLU.DYT

(11) a. Idolo-ak adora-tze-a-ri ze-rrai-z-ki-o-n.
idol.PLU adore.VEN.DAT continue./PLU.DYN
b. Hon-e(n)-la da-rrai-o Umandi: . . .
this_way continue.DYN Umandi
c. Eta hon-e(n)-la da-rrai-o gai-a-ri: . . .
and this_way continue.DYN subject.DAT

(12) a. Izerdi-a da-ri-t / ze-ri-da-n.
sweat flow.1/.DYN flow.1/.DYN.PST
b. Malko-ak da-ri-z-ki-zu / ze-ri-z-ki-zu-n begi-e-ta-tik.
tear.PLU flow.2/PLU.DYN flow.2/PLU.DYN.PST eye.PLU.ELA

(13) a. Zu-re aurre-an lots(a)-a eta beldurr-a da-ri-e aingeru-e-i.
you.GEN in_front_of shame and fear flow.PLU/.DYN angel.PLU.DAT
b. Neskatx(a)-a-ri negar isil-a ze-ri-o-n.
girl.DAT weeping silent flow.DYN.PST
c. Zauri-tik odol-a ze-ri-o-n gurdi-a-ren zoru-ra-ino.
wound.ELA blood flow.DYN.PST chariot.GEN floor.TER
d. Zu-re ezpain-e-i ezti-a da-ri-e.
you.GEN lip.PLU.DAT honey drop.PLU/.DYN
e. Maitasun=sagarr-e-i usain ezti-a da-ri-e.
love_apple.PLU.DAT fragrance sweet exude.PLU/.DYN
f. Adurr-a ze-ri-o-n ezpain-e-ta-tik gaztai-a ja-n nahi-a-z.
saliva drip.DYN.PST lip.PLU.ELA cheese eat desire.INS
g. Ezekiel-en begi-e-i su-a ze-ri-e-n.
Ezekiel.GEN eye.PLU.DAT fire flow.PLU/.DYN.PST

(14) a. Su-a da-txe-ki-o auzo-ko etxe-a-ri.
fire stick_to.DYN neighbor.ADN house.DAT
b. Gu-re txabol(a)-ak eliz(a)-a-ri da-txe-z-ki-o.
we.GEN hut.PLU church.DAT be_attached./PLU.DYN

(15) Zer iri(t)z-ten d-i-e jende-a-k eskribau-e-i?
what think_of.IPF /PLU/.DTR people.ERG notary.PLU.DAT

(16) a. Euskara experimental-a d-eritz-a-t Olabide-ren hizker(a)-a-ri.
Basque experimental consider.//1.DYT Olabide.GEN language.DAT
b. Eta zer d-eritz-a-zu eskutitz-a-ren mami-a-ri?
and what think_of.//2.DYT letter.GEN contents.DAT

c. Zorakeria hau-e-i ele=eder d-eritz-e-te.
inanity this.PLU.DAT literature.IDF consider./PLU/PLU.DYT

d. Zer d-eritz-a Pello-k ahari hon-i? Oso ederr-a d-eritz-a.
what think_of.DYT Pete.ERG ram this.DAT very beautiful find.DYT

e. Ni-k gai(t)z-ki d-eritz-a-t etxe-a sal-tze-a-ri.
I.ERG wrong.IDF consider.//1.DYT house sell.VEN.DAT

(17) a. Tarte eder hon-i Urre-z-ko Aldi d-eritz-a.
interval beautiful this.DAT gold.IDF.INS.ADN age.IDF be_called.DYT

b. No-la d-erit(z)-zu (zu-ri)? Arantxa d-eri(t)z-t (ni-ri).
how be_called./2/.DYT you.DAT Arantxa be_called./1/DYT I.DAT

(18) a. **Bolsa hon-i d-eritza-i-o kapule-a.
sheath this.DAT be_called.DYT cocoon

b. **No-la d-eritza-i-zu? Arantxa d-ertitza-i-t (ni-ri).
how be_called.2/.DYT Arantxa be_called.1/DYT I.DAT

(19) a. No-la dei-tzen z-a-r-a? Arantxa dei-tzen n-a-iz.
how call.IPF 2.ITR Arantxa call.IPF 1.ITR

b. No-la / zer d-u-zu izen-a? Arantxa d-u-t izen-a.
how what have.2.SYT name Arantxa have.1.SYT name

(20) Dardar de-gi-t barru-a-k. / Dardar da-gi ni-re barru-a-k.
trembling do./1/.DYT inside.ERG trembling do.SYT I.GEN inside.ERG

(21) a. Zauri-a senda-tu al za-i-o? / Ber-e zauri-a senda-tu al da?
wound heal.PEF INT DIT he_himself.GEN wound heal.PEF INT ITR

b. Hizkuntz(a)-a larri da-bil-ki-gu. / Gu-re hizkuntz(a)-a larri
language critically.PRE walk.1PLU/.DYN we.GEN language critically.PRE
da-bil.
walk.SYN

(22) a. Seme-a hil d-i-da-k. / Ni-re seme-a hil d-u-k.
son kill.PEF /1/2SOL.DTR I.GEN son kill.PEF /2SOL.TRA

b. Gaixo-tu e-gi-ten d-i-z-ki-da-zu nerbio-ak. / Gaixo-tu e-gi-ten d-it-u-zu ni-re
weaken do.IPF PLU/1/2.DTR nerve.PLU weaken do.IPF PLU/2.TRA I.GEN
nerbio-ak.
nerve.PLU

(23) a. Polizi(a)-ak atze-tik di-h-oa-z-ki-o. / Polizi(a)-ak har-en atze-tik
police.PLU from_behind go./PLU.DYN police.PLU yonder_one.GEN after
di-h-oa-z.
go.PLU.SYN

b. Labain-du e-gi-n zi-tza-i-o-n gutun-a esku-e-ta-tik. / Labain-du e-gi-n ze-n
slip do.PEF DIT.PST letter hand.PLU.ELA slip do.PEF ITR.PST
gutun-a har-en esku-e-ta-tik.
letter yonder_one.GEN hand.PLU.ELA

(24) a. Ez za-i-zu-e lasto-rik e-ma-n-go.
not 2PLU/.DIT straw.PAR give.FUT
b. Den-a ken-tzen za-i-gu.
everything take_away.IPF 1PLU/.DIT

(25) a. E-ma-ten n-a-tza-i-zu oso-ki eta behin beti-ko-z.
give.IPF 2/1.DIT totally and once forever
b. Ni-re etsai higuin-a-ri e-ma-n h-a-tza-i-o.
I.GEN enemy detested.DAT give.PEF /2SOL.DIT

(26) a. Euts-i e-gi-n nahi z-i-e-n amets=irudi hai-e-i.
hold_on_to do want.PPR PLU/.DTR.PST dream_image yonder.PLU.DAT
b. Zer esa-n behar d-i-o-t orain Pili-ri?
what say be_to.PPR //1.DTR now Pili.DAT

(27) a. Uso-a haurr-a-ri hurbil-du nahi za-i-o.
pigeon child.DAT get_closer want.PPR DIT
b. Zam(a)-a lurr-e-ra eror-i behar za-i-o.
burden ground.ALL fall be_going_to.PPR DIT

(28) a. Uso-a-k hurbil-du nahi d-u.
pigeon.ERG get_closer want.PPR TRA
b. Zam(a)-a-k lurr-e-ra eror-i behar d-u.
burden.ERG ground.ALL fall be_going_to.PPR TRA

(29) a. Luis-e-k berri-ro begira-tzen d-u.
Louis.ERG again look.IPF TRA
b. Luis-e-k nesk(a)-a-ri begira-tzen d-i-o.
Louis.ERG girl.DAT look.IPF DTR
c. Lopez=Mendizabal-e-ren hiztegi-ra begira-tu d-u-gu.
Lopez-Mendizabal.GEN dictionary.ALL look.PEF /1PLU.TRA

(30) a. Leiho-tik dei-tu z-i-o-n / z-u-en.
window.ELA call.PEF DTR.PST TRA.PST
b. Margo dei-tzen d-u.
Margo call.IPF TRA

(31) a. Asko-z esker-tzen d-i-zu-t liburu-a.
very_much thank.IPF /2/1.DTR book

b. No-la ez Jaun-a esker-tu?
how not Lord thank

(32) a. Etxe-ra lagun-du d-i-zu-t / z-a-it-u-t.
house.ALL accompany.PEF /2/1.DTR 2/1.TRA
b. Jaun-a-k lagun-tzen d-i-e.
Lord.ERG help.IPF /PLU/.DTR
c. Jaun-a-k lagun-du-ko d-it-u.
Lord.ERG help.FUT PLU/.TRA

(33) a. Alkate-a-k drog(a)-a-ri e-ma-n z-i-o-n.
mayor.ERG drugs.DAT take_to.PEF DTR.PST
b. Alkate-a drog(a)-a-ri e-ma-n zi-tza-i-o-n.
mayor drugs.DAT indulge_in.PEF DIT.PST

(34) a. Ordu-an ibai-a igaro-tze-a-ri e-ma-n z-i-o-te-n.
then river cross.VEN.DAT proceed_to.PEF //PLU.DTR.PST
b. Esku-ak garbi-tze-a-ri e-ma-n zi-tza-i-o-n.
hand.PLU wash.VEN.DAT proceed_to.PEF DIT.PST

(35) a. Lege-ak ikas-te-a-ri e-ki-n n-i-o-n Deustu-ko
law.PLU study.VEN.DAT apply_oneself_to.PEF //1.DTR.PST Deusto.ADN
unibersitate-an
university.LOC
b. Azken-e-an kanpo-an ere lapurret(a)-a-ri e-ki-n-go d-i-o.
at_the_end exterior.LOC too thievery.DAT engage_in.FUT DTR
c. Eki-n n-i-o-n, ber-a-z, igoer(a)-a-ri.
set_out.PEF //1.DTR.PST thus ascension.DAT

(36) a. Beste emisora bat bila-tze-a-ri e-ki-n z-i-o-n.
other radio_station a look_for.VEN.DAT start.PEF DTR.PST
b. Isilaldi bati e-ki-n z-i-o-n.
moment_of_silence a.DAT commence.PEF DTR.PST

(37) a. Hori guzti-a e-ma-n z-i-da-n buru-a-k.
that all give.PEF /1/.DTR.PST head.ERG
b. E-ma-ten z-i-da-n ni-ri barru-a-k.
give.IPF /1/.DTR.PST I.DAT inner_self.ERG
c. Gogo-a-k e-ma-n z-i-o-n bila-tze-a Ahias profet(a)-a.
mind.ERG give.PEF DTR.PST seek_out.VEN Ahias prophet

(38) a. Zeru-a-k maindire zikin bat e-ma-ten z-u-en.
sky.ERG sheet dirty a look_like.IPF TRA.PST

b. Txorimalo-a e-ma-ten d-u-zu.
scarecrow look_like.IPF /2.TRA

c. Den-a-k e-ma-ten z-u-en berri.
everything.ERG look_like.IPF TRA.PST new.IDF

d. Ha(r-en)-la e-ma-ten d-u.
yonder_way look_like.IPF TRA

e. Ez d-u-gu on-do e-ma-n-go.
not /1PLU.TRA well look_like.FUT

(39) a. Oso aldi ederr-a e-ma-n gen-u-en.
very time nice pass.PEF /1PLU.TRA.PST

b. Goiz oso-a kanpo-an e-ma-n zen-u-en?
morning whole outside.LOC spend.PEF /2.TRA.PST

(40) a. Agi-an, horr-e(n)-ga(i)-tik e-ma-ten z-i-o-n beti musu sudurr-e-an.
perhaps that.MOT give.IPF DTR.PST always kiss.IDF nose.LOC

b. E-ma-n z-i-e-n su eta bota z-it-u-en azeri-ak
give.PEF /PLU/.DTR.PST fire.IDF and throw.PEF PLU/.TRA.PST fox.PLU
filistiarr-en garisoro-e-ta-ra.
Philistine.PLU.GEN wheat_field.PLU.ALL

c. Ez d-i-o-t amore-rik e-ma-n.
not //1.DTR concession.PAR give.PEF

d. Beste-a-ri antz-ik ez z-i-o-n e-ma-n.
other.ZEP.DAT likeness.PAR not DTR.PST give.PEF

(41) a. Ni-k ha(r-en)-la esa-n n-i-o-n n-eu-re buru-a-ri: . . .
I.ERG yonder_way say.PEF //1.DTR.PST I.REF.GEN head.DAT

b. E-zagu-tzen al d-u-zu z-eu-re buru-a?
know.IPF INT /2.TRA you.REF.GEN head

c. Su-a-k ja-n e-gi-ten z-u-en ber-e buru-a.
fire.ERG eat do.IPF TRA.PST it_itself.GEN head

d. Ber-e buru-a hil behar ote d-u?
he_himself.GEN head kill go_to.PPR DUB TRA

e. Zer-ga(i)-tik bota nahi z-en-u-en z-eu-re buru-a?
what.MOT throw_away want.PPR /2.TRA.PST you.REF.GEN head

(42) a. Ber(-e)-en buru-a e-ma-n d-u-te.
he_himself.PLU.GEN head give.PEF /PLU.TRA

b. Jaun-a-ri e-ma-n z-i-z-ki-o-te-n ber(-e)-en buru-ak.
Lord.DAT give.PEF PLU//PLU.DTR.PST he_himself.PLU.GEN head.PLU

(43) a. G-eu-re buru-a engaina-tzen d-u-gu.
we.REF.GEN head deceive.IPF /1PLU.TRA

b. G-eu-re buru-ak engaina-tzen d-it-u-gu.
we.REF.GEN head.PLU deceive.IPF PLU/1PLU.TRA

(44) a. Ardo hau ber-e-tzat gorde nahi d-u.
wine this he_himself.BEN keep want.PPR TRA
b. Zuhaitz-ek errege-a izenda-tu nahi z-u-te-n ber-(e)-en-tzat.
tree.PLU.ERG king appoint want.PPR /PLU.TRA.PST he_himself.PLU.BEN
c. Utz-i d-it-u-t n-eu-re-tzat zazpi mila gizon.
leave.PEF PLU/1.TRA I.REF.BEN seven thousand man.IDF

(45) a. Zer d-io-zu z-eu-re buru-a-z?
what say./2.SYT you.REF.GEN head.INS
b. Zer d-io-zu zu-ta-z?
what say./2.SYT you.INS
c. Zu-ta-z zer d-io-zu?
you.INS what say./2.SYT

(46) a. N-eu-re buru-a-rekin haserre n-a-go.
I.REF.GEN head.DAT anger.IDF be.1.SYN
b. N-eu-rekin haserre n-a-go. / Ni-ta-z haserre n-a-iz.
I.REF.SOC anger.IDF be.1.SYN I.INS anger.IDF be.1SYN

(47) a. Euskaldun on-a iza-te-ko, eskas ageri za-i-t n-eu-re buru-a
Basque good be.VEN.ADN deficient.IDF evident.IDF be.1/.DYN I.REF.GEN head
zenbait alde-ta-tik.
certain respect.ELA
b. Pello-ri ez za-i-o ber-e buru-a atsegin.
Pete.DAT not be.DYN he_himself.GEN head pleasure.IDF
c. Miren-i ber-e buru-a e-ra-kuts-i n-i-o-n ispilu-an.
Mary.DAT she_herself.GEN head show.PEF //1.DTR.PST mirror.LOC

(48) a. N-eu-re buru-a-k kezka-tu eta izu-tzen n-a-u.
I.REF.GEN head.ERG worry and frighten.IPF 1/.TRA
b. Z-eu-(e)-en buru-ek zora-tzen z-a-it-u-z-te-te.
you.REF.PLU.GEN head.PLU.ERG drive_crazy.IPF 2PLU/PLU.TRA
c. Ber-e buru-a-k lilura-tzen d-u ni-re anai(a)-a.
he_himself.GEN head.ERG fascinate.IPF TRA I.GEN brother

(49) a. Z-eu-re buru-a-k e-gi-n z-a-it-u esklabo, ez beste inor-k.
you.REF.GEN head.ERG make.PEF 2/.TRA slave.PRE not else anyone.ERG
b. N-eu-re buru-a-k ere ema-ten d-i-t franko lan.
I.REF.GEN head.ERG too give.IPF /1/.DTR plenty work.IDF
c. N-eu-re buru-a-k gida-tu n-a-u.
I.REF.GEN head.ERG guide.PEF 1/.TRA

(50) a. **N-eu-re buru-a-k gorrota-tzen n-a-u.
I.REF.GEN head.ERG hate.IPF 1/.TRA
b. **N-eu-re buru-a-k ere ez d-i-t hori barka-tu-ko.
I.REF.GEN head.ERG too not /1/.DTR that forgive.FUT

(51) Zu-re amets hai-ek z-eu-re buru-a-ri kalte e-gi-n-go d-i-o-te.
you.GEN dream yonder.PLU.ERG you.REF.GEN head.DAT harm.IDF do.FUT //PLU.DTR

(52) Hai-ek ez d-it-u Jainko-a-k bat-a beste-a-ren-tzat / elkarr-en-tzat
yonder_one.PLU not PLU/.TRA God.ERG one.ZEP other.ZEP.BEN each_other.BEN
e-gi-n.
make.PEF

(53) a. Aitona-k bereiz-ten z-it-u-en elkarr-en-gan-dik ahotz-a eta
Grandfather.IDF.ERG separate.IPF PLU/.TRA.PST each_other.ELA chaff and
gari=ale-a.
wheat_grain
b. Liburu hori-ek bakan-du behar d-ir-a elkarr-en-gan-dik.
book that.PLU keep_apart must.PPR PLU.ITR each_other.ELA

(54) a. Elkar engaina-tzen d-u-te.
each_other cheat.IPF /PLU.TRA
b. Elkar sal-du eta gorrota-tu-ko d-u-te.
each_other betray and hate.FUT /PLU.TRA
c. Zu-ek elkar d-irudi-zu-e.
you.PLU.ERG each_other resemble./2PLU.SYT
d. Gu-re bi etxe-ek elkar uki-tzen d-u-te.
we.GEN two house.PLU.ERG each_other touch.IPF /PLU.TRA
e. Elkarr-i ida(t)z-ten gen-i-o-n.
each_other.DAT write.IPF //1PLU.DTR.PST
f. Musu ema-n z-i-o-te-n elkarr-i.
kiss.IDF give.PEF //PLU.DTR.PST each_other.DAT
g. Elkarr-i aurkez-tu g-en-i-z-ki-o-n adiskide ez=ezagun-ak
each_other.DAT introduce.PEF PLU//1PLU.DTR.PST friend unacquainted.PLU
h. Miren eta Xabier elkarr-en-gan-(ra)-antz bultza-tu d-it-u-t.
Mary and Xavier each_other.TEN push.PEF PLU/1.TRA
i. Elkarr-ekin maitemin-du z-ir-e-n.
each_other.SOC fall_in_love.PEF PLU.ITR.PST

(55) a. Elkarr-ekin e-gi-ten al d-u-te lo?
each_other.SOC do.IPF INT /PLU.TRA sleep.IDF
b. Guraso-ek elkarr-ekin i-kus-i g-a-it-u-z-te.
parent.PLU.ERG each_other.SOC see.PEF 1PLU/PLU.TRA

c. Elkarr-ekin afal-du gen-u-en "Artzak" jatetxe-an.
each_other.SOC dine.PEF /1PLU.TRA.PST "Artzak" restaurant.LOC

(56) a. E-zagu-tzen d-it-u-gu elkarr-en ahots-ak.
know.IPF PLU/1PLU.TRA each_other.GEN voice.PLU

b. ... elkarr-en begi-e-ta-tik amodio-a eda-n-a-z.
... each_other.GEN eye.PLU.ELA love drink.PTC.INS

(57) a. Bat-a-k beste-a maite d-u.
one.ZEP.ERG other.ZEP love.PPR TRA

b. Guraso-ek bat-a beste-a maite d-u-te.
parent.PLU.ERG one.DEL other.DEL love.PPR /PLU.TRA

c. Guraso-ek bat-a-k beste-a maite d-u-te.
parent.PLU.ERG one.DEL.ERG other.DEL love.PPR /PLU.TRA

(58) a. Bat-a beste-a maite d-u-gu.
one.ZEP other.ZEP love.PPR /1PLU.TRA

b. Bat-a-k beste-a maite d-u-gu.
one.ZEP.ERG other.ZEP love.PPR /1PLU.TRA

(59) a. ... bat-a beste-a gal-tze-ko beldurr-a.
... one.ZEP other.ZEP lose.VEN.ADN fear

b. Egipto guzti-an inor-k ere, bat-a beste-a ez z-u-en i-kus-ten.
Egypt all.LOC anybody.ERG too one.ZEP other.ZEP not TRA.PST see.IPF

c. Atal guzti-ak bat-a beste-a-z ardura-tzen d-ir-a.
part all.PLU one.DEL other.DEL.INS care_for.IPF PLU.ITR

d. Bat-a beste-a-rekin ez haserre-tze-ko, ...
one.ZEP other.ZEP.SOC not get_angry_at.VEN.ADN ...

e. Mila kilometro-ta-ra g-e-u-n-de-n bat-a beste-a-ren-gan-dik.
thousand kilometer.IDF.ALL be.1PLU.SYN.PST one.ZEP other.ZEP.ELA

f. Gertakari-ak agudo bat-a beste-a-ren gain-e-ra da-to(r)-z.
event.PLU fast one.DEL other.DEL.GEN on_top_of come.PLU.SYN

(60) a. Har-k batzu-k beste-(e)-en-gan-dik bereiz-i e-gi-n-go d-it-u.
yonder_one.ERG some.PLU other.ZEP.PLU.ELA divide do.FUT PLU/.TRA

b. Ha(r-en)-la ez z-ir-e-n batzu-ek beste-(e)-en-gan-(a) hurbil-du.
yonder_way not PLU.ITR.PST some.PLU other.ZEP.PLU.ALL come_near_to.PEF

Chapter 16

(1) a. Seme-a-k geldi-araz-i d-u zaldi-a.
son.ERG stop.CAU.PEF TRA horse

b. E-tza-n-araz-i n-u-en Ines.
lie_down.CAU.PEF /1.TRA.PST Ines

c. Barka-tu z-i-e-n ber-e anai-e-i, eta e-torr-araz-i
forgive.PEF /PLU/.DTR.PST he_himself.GEN brother.PLU.DAT and come.CAU.PEF
z-it-u-en Egipto-ra.
PLU/.TRA.PST Egypt.ALL

(2) a. Edurne-k Galarreta-ri haur bat-i bez-(ha)-la edan-araz-i z-i-o-n.
Edurne.ERG Galarreta.DAT child a.DAT SIP drink.CAU.PEF DTR.PST

b. Jan-araz-i d-i-o-zu zu-k Adan-i sagar debekatu-a?
eat.CAU.PEF //2.DTR you.ERG Adam.DAT apple forbidden

c. Bizi-a-k ja-ki-n-araz-i d-i-t gauza bat: . . .
life.ERG know.CAU.PEF /1/.DTR thing one.IDF

d. Bide-ko lagun bat bederen nahi z-i-o-te-n harr-araz-i.
road.ADN companion a at_least want.PPR //PLU.DTR.PST take.CAU

(3) a. Jon-e-k Xabierr-i Mikel hil-araz-i d-i-o.
John.ERG Xavier.DAT Michael kill.CAU.PEF DTR

b. Jon-e-k Xabierr-i Mikel i-kus-araz-i d-i-o.
John-ERG Xavier.DAT Michael see.CAU.PEF DTR

(4) a. Irakasle-a-k hamar liburu irakurr-araz-i d-i-z-ki-gu.
teacher.ERG ten book.IDF read.CAU.PEF PLU/1PLU/.DTR

b. Hamar liburu irakurr-arazi za-i-z-ki-gu.
ten book.IDF read.CAU.PEF 1PLU/PLU.DIT

(5) a. Irakasle-a-k beti geldi-araz-ten g-a-it-u.
teacher.ERG always stay.CAU.IPF 1PLU/.TRA

b. **Beti geldi-araz-ten g-a-r-a.
always stay.CAU.IPF 1PLU.ITR

(6) a. Hamar liburu irakurr-araz-i d-i-z-ki-gu-te.
ten book read.CAU.PEF PLU/1PLU/PLU.DTR

b. Beti geldi-araz-ten g-a-it-u-z-te.
always stay.CAU.IPF 1PLU/PLU.TRA

(7) a. Ait(a)-a e-karr-araz-i z-u-te-n.
father bring_in.CAU.PEF /PLU.TRA.PST

b. Nahi d-u-t harr-araz-i.
want.PPR /1.TRA take.CAU

c. Abimelek-e-k Sara jauregi-ra e-ra-ma-n-araz-i z-u-en.
Abimelek.ERG Sara palace.ALL carry_off.CAU.PEF TRA.PST

d. Lan anitz-e-z ber-e buru-a e-zagu-t-araz-i d-u azken-e-an.
work a_lot_of.IDF.INS he.himself.GEN head know.CAU.PEF TRA end.LOC

(8) Gu-re aita-k ama-ri gona gorri-a eros-araz-i d-i-t.
we.GEN father.IDF.ERG mother.IDF.DAT skirt red buy.CAU /1/.DTR

(9) a. Jende-a-ri ber-e lo nagi-an irau-n-araz-te-ko ez d-u-gu
people.DAT he_himself.GEN sleep lazy.LOC persist.CAU.VEN.ADN not /1PLU.TRA
kritik(a)-a-ren beharr-ik.
critique.GEN need.PAR

b. Gerri-tik go(i)-ra ez z-u-en ezer, eta horr-e-k irau-n-araz-i z-i-o-n
waist.GEN top.ALL not TRA.PST anything and that.ERG remain.CAU.PEF DTR.PST
bizi-rik.
alive.STA

(10) a. Tabako hosto-ak iraki-n-araz-ten z-it-u-z-te-n ur garbi-an.
tobacco leaf.PLU boil.CAU.IPF PLU/PLU.TRA.PST water clean.LOC

b. Iraki-n-araz-i ber-e-ha-la orratz-a eta zizta=ontzi-ak.
boil.CAU at_once needle and ampule.PLU

(11) Norbait-e-k eta zerbait-e-k irau-n-araz-i d-i-o hizkuntz(a)-a-ri.
someone.ERG and something.ERG last.CAU.PEF DTR language.DAT

(12) a. En-e Jainko-a, en-e Jainko-a, zer-ga(i)-tik utz-i n-a-u-zu?
I.GEN God I.GEN God what.MOT leave.PEF 1/2.TRA

b. Ikasket(a)-ak utz-i d-it-u.
study.PLU leave.PEF PLU/.TRA

(13) a. Erre-tze-a-ri utz-i d-i-o.
smoke.VEN.DAT quit.PEF DTR

b. Danuta-k segitu-an utz-i z-i-o-n igeri e-gi-te-a-ri.
Danuta.ERG soon cease.PEF DTR.PST swim.IDF make.VEN.DAT

c. Ordu-an, am(a)-a-k negar e-gi-te-a-ri utz-i z-i-o-n.
that_time.LOC mother.ERG crying.IDF do.VEN.DAT stop.PEF DTR.PST

(14) a. Ama-k negarr-a-ri utz-i z-i-o-n.
Mother.IDF.ERG crying.DAT stop.PEF DTR.PST

b. Lan-a-ri utz-i d-i-o.
work.DAT stop.PEF DTR

c. Bekatu-a-ri utz-i behar d-i-o-gu.
sin.DAT stop must.PPR //1PLU.DTR

(15) a. J-oa-te-n utz-i-ko d-i-zu-e-t, ez z-a-it-u-z-te-t gehi-ago geldi-araz-i-ko.
go.VEN.LOC let.FUT /2PLU/1.DTR not 2PLU/1.TRA more.COP stay.CAU.FUT

b. Utz-i-ko z-a-it-u-z-te-t j-oa-te-ra, eta ez z-a-it-u-z-te-t geldi-araz-i-ko gehi-ago.
let.FUT 2PLU/1.TRA go.VEN.ALL and not 2PLU/1.TRA stay.CAU.FUT more.COP

(16) a. **Andoni-k liburu-a-ri eror-tze-n utz-i d-i-o.
Anthony.ERG book.DAT fall.VEN.LOC let.PEF DTR
b. Andoni-k liburu-a eror-tze-n utz-i d-u.
Anthony.ERG book fall.VEN.LOC let.PEF TRA
c. Andoni-k liburu-a mahai gain-e-an utz-i d-u.
Anthony.ERG book table.IDF top.LOC leave.PEF TRA

(17) a. Noragabe j-oa-te-n utz-i g-en-u-en ontzi-a.
where.ALL_without.PRE go.VEN.LOC let.PEF /1PLU.TRA.PST ship
b. Utz-i bi-ak bat-e-ra haz-te-n.
let two.ZEP.PLU one.ALL grow_up.VEN.LOC
c. Zer-ga(i)-tik ez n-au-zu-e hil-tze-n utz-i?
what.MOT not 1/2PLU.TRA die.VEN.LOC let.PEF

(18) a. Ur-a-ri iraki-te-n utz-i d-i-o-t.
water.DAT boil.VEN.LOC let.PEF //1.DTR
b. Ur-a iraki-te-n utz-i d-u-t.
water boil.VEN-LOC let.PEF /1.TRA

(19) a. Ez d-u-t bakarr-ik laga.
not /1.TRA alone.STA leave.PPR
b. Lan-a-ri laga beharr-e-an aurki-tu z-ir-e-n.
work.DAT stop necessity.LOC find.PEF PLU.ITR.PST
c. Laga ume-e-i ni-re-gan-(r)a e-tor-tze-n.
let child.PLU.DAT I.ALL come.VEN.LOC
d. Laga-tzen al d-i-da-zu-e hitz e-gi-te-n?
let.IPF INT /1/2PLU.DTR word.IDF do.VEN.LOC
e. Istil=ots-a-k ez d-u ordu-rik konta-tze-n laga.
(rain)drop_sound.ERG not TRA hour.PAR count.VEN.LOC let.PPR

(20) Zu-re izen-a bedeinka-tze-n hil-ko n-a-i-z.
you.GEN name bless.VEN.LOC die.FUT 1.ITR

(21) a. Zahar eta berri-(e)-en arte-an hauta-tze-a ez da erraz.
old.IDF and new.PLU.GEN between choose.VEN not be.SYN easy.IDF
b. Zail da har-ekin bat ez e-tor-tze-a.
difficult.IDF be.SYN that_one.SOC one not come.VEN
c. Zail-a da ben-e-ta-n Jainko-a-ren erreinu-an sar-tze-a.
hard.IDF be.SYN really God.GEN kingdom.LOC enter.VEN

(22) a. Ez da gaitz erantzu-te-n.
not be.SYN hard.IDF answer.VEN.LOC
b. Zail iza-n-go da hori ja-ki-te-n.
difficult.IDF be.FUT ITR that know.VEN.LOC

c. Ez da erraz egi(a)-a ja-ki-te-n.
not be.SYN easy.IDF truth know.VEN.LOC

d. Herri-e-ta-n gaitz-a da gauz(a)-ak isil-ik e-uki-tze-n.
village.PLU.LOC hard be.SYN thing.PLU quiet.STA keep.VEN.LOC

(23) a. Liburu hau-ek erraz-ak d-ir-a irakur-tze-n.
book this.PLU easy.PLU be.PLU.SYN read.VEN.LOC

b. Etxe hau erraz da garbi-tze-n.
house this easy.IDF be.SYN clean.VEN.LOC

c. Idazle-a-ren eginkizun-a erraz da adi-eraz-te-n, gaitz bete-tze-n.
writer.GEN duty easy.IDF be.SYN understand.CAU.VEN.LOC hard.IDF fulfill.VEN.LOC

(24) a. Ez da erraz-a aberats bat han sar-tze-a.
not be.SYN likely rich a over_there.LOC enter.VEN

b. Gaitz da itsu-a-k kolore-(e)-en berri ja-ki-te-a.
unlikely be.SYN blind.ZEP.ERG color.PLU.GEN news.IDF know.VEN

(25) a. Itsasgizon-ak erraz-ak d-ir-a moskor-tze-n.
sailor.PLU likely.PLU be.PLU.SYN get_drunk.VEN.LOC

b. Mozkor-tu-a-ga(i)-tik⟨-an⟩ gaitz-a da eror-tze-n, lagun gabe etxe-ra ba-da-ki e-tor-tze-n.
get_drunk.PEF.DEF.MOT unlikely be.SYN fall.VEN.LOC escort.IDF without.PRE house.ALL AFF.know.SYT come.VEN.LOC

(26) a. Euri-a ari d-u.
rain be_busy.PPR TRA

b. Haize-a ari d-u.
wind be_busy.PPR TRA

c. Bero ari z-u-en itsus(i)-ki.
heat be_busy.PPR TRA.PST horribly.

(27) a. Argi-tze-n ari d-u.
get_light.VEN.LOC be_busy.PPR TRA

b. Elurr-a ur-tze-n ari d-u.
snow melt.VEN.LOC be_busy.PPR TRA

(28) a. Hil-tze-n ari z-a-r-a.
die.VEN.LOC be_busy.PPR 2.ITR

b. Fermin liburu bat irakur-tze-n ari ze-n.
Fermin book a read.VEN.LOC be_busy.PPR ITR.PST

c. Orain sendagile-a-ren etxe-a garbi-tze-n ari-ko da ama.
now doctor.GEN house clean.VEN.LOC be_busy.FUT ITR mother.IDF

d. Zer kanta-tze-n ari h-a-iz?
what sing.VEN.LOC be_busy.PPR 2SOL.ITR

(29) a. Zer-ta-n ari z-a-r-a pentsa-tze-n?
what.LOC be_busy.PPR 2.ITR think.VEN.LOC

b. Ari al z-a-r-e-te telebist(a)-a i-kus-te-n?
be_busy.PPR INT 2PLU.ITR television watch.VEN.LOC

c. Ume bat bez-(h)a-la ari h-a-iz porta-tze-n!
child a SIP be_busy.PPR 2SOL.ITR behave.VEN.LOC

(30) a. Igo-tze-n ari da liburu-(e)-en prezio-a.
rise.VEN.LOC be_busy.PPR ITR book.PLU.GEN price

b. Ile-a urdin-tze-n ari za-i-o.
hair turn_grey.VEN.LOC be_busy.PPR DIT

c. Zorr-ak pila-tze-n ari zi-tza-i-z-ki-o-n.
debt.PLU pile_up.VEN.LOC be_busy.IPF /PLU.DIT.PST

(31) a. Zer ari z-a-r-a?
what be_busy.PPR 2.ITR

b. Ezer ez d-ir-a ari.
anything not PLU.ITR be_busy.PPR

c. Hura ere zerbait ari da.
yonder_one too something be_busy.PPR ITR

(32) a. Bonb(a-)ak orain-txe leher-tze-n ari d-ir-a.
bomb.PLU now.EMP explode.VEN.LOC be_busy.PPR PLU.ITR

b. **Bonb(a)-a orain-txe leher-tze-n ari da.
bomb now.EMP explode.VEN.LOC be_busy.PPR ITR

(33) Andre horr-e-ta-z on-gi gogora-tze(*-)n (*ari) n-a-iz.
lady that.INS well remember.IPF(*VEN.LOC) be_busy.PPR 1.ITR

(34) a. Han-txe e-go-ten g-in-e-n etxe-an, gaztain(a)-ak ja-te-n
over_there.LOC.EMP sit.IPF 1PLU.ITR.PST house.LOC chestnut.PLU eat.VEN.LOC
eta su-ar-i begira.
and fire.DAT looking.PRE

b. Pedro ere hai-(e)-ekin ze-go-en bero-tze-n.
Peter too yonder_one.PLU.DAT stand.SYN.PST warm_up.VEN.LOC

(35) a. Milia-ri esa-te-ko irrika-tze-n n-a-go.
Emily.DAT tell.VEN.ADN yearn.VEN.LOC be.1.SYN

b. Orain zeru-an goza-tze-n da-go ber-e eternidade-a.
now heaven.LOC enjoy.VEN.LOC be.SYN he_himself.GEN eternity

c. Hogei lagun-en lan-ak e-gi-te-n da-go makina bakarr-a.
twenty person.IDF.GEN job.PLU do.VEN.LOC be.SYN machine single

(36) a. Hiru urte i-bil-i z-ir-e-n elkarr-i eskutitz-ak ida(t)z-te-n.
three year.IDF walk.PEF PLU.ITR.PST each_other.DAT letter.PLU write.VEN.LOC
b. Etxe-a lore-z apain-tze-n i-bil-i n-a-iz egunero.
house flower.IDF.INS decorate.VEN.LOC walk.PEF 1.ITR every_day
c. Gu elkar hil-tze-n i-bil-i g-in-e-n.
we each_other kill.VEN.LOC walk.PEF 1PLU.ITR.PST

(37) Zer z-a-bil-tza, Garazi?
what walk.2.SYN Grace

(38) a. Hemen ere ba-z-ihardu-en eri-ak senda-tze-n.
here.LOC too AFF.be_busy.SYT.PST sick.ZEP.PLU heal.VEN.LOC
b. Jende-a-ri e-raku(t)s-te-n/i-ra-kas-te-n luzaro jardu-n z-u-en.
people.DAT teach.VEN.LOC for_a_long_time be_busy.PEF TRA.PST

(39) a. Goiz-e-ko lau eta erdi-ak arte eda-te-n jardu-n z-u-te-n.
morning.ADN four and half.PLU until drink.VEN.LOC keep.PEF /PLU.TRA.PST
b. Noiz arte jardu-n behar d-i-gu gizon horr-e-k zorigaitz-a
when until keep be_going_to.PPR /1PLU/.DTR man that.ERG bad_luck
sor-tze-n?
cause.VEN.LOC

(40) a. Gu-k otoitz e-gi-te-n ja-rrai-tu-ko d-u-gu.
we.ERG prayer.IDF do.VEN.LOC continue.FUT /1PLU.TRA
b. Lurr-e-an ida(t)z-te-n ja-rrai-tu z-u-en.
ground.LOC write.VEN.LOC continue.PEF TRA.PST
c. Lehen bez-(h)a-la e-tor-tze-n ja-rrai-tzen ze-n.
before SIP come.VEN.LOC continue.IPF ITR.PST
d. Bihar segi-tu-ko d-u-gu hitz e-gi-te-n.
tomorrow continue.FUT /1PLU.TRA word.IDF do.VEN.LOC

(41) a. Argi-a gabe has-i-ko z-ir-e-n lan-e-an.
daylight without.PRE begin.FUT PLU.ITR.PST work.LOC
b. Negarr-e-z has-i ze-n haurr-a ozen-ki.
tear.IDF.INS begin.PEF ITR.PST child loudly
c. Piarres has-ten da oihu-ka.
Peter start.IPF ITR shouting_and_shouting.ADV

(42) a. Egun ber-e-an has-i z-u-en arlo-a.
day same.LOC begin.PEF TRA.PST task

b. Has-i z-u-te-n etxe-ra-ko bide-a.
begin.PEF /PLU.TRA.PST house.ALL.ADN way

c. Lamin(a)-ek gau har-ta-n ber-ta-n has-i z-u-te-n
elf.PLU.ERG night yonder.LOC it_itself.IDF.LOC begin.PEF /PLU.TRA.PST
ber-(e)-en lan-a.
he_himself.PLU.GEN work

(43) a. Ilun-tze-n has-i d-u.
get_dark.VEN.LOC start.PEF TRA

b. Hamaik(a)-ak alde-an has-i z-u-en laino-a ken-tze-n.
eleven_o'clock.PLU side.LOC begin.PEF TRA.PST fog withdraw.VEN.LOC

(44) a. Zerbait ja-te-n has-ten da.
something eat.VEN.LOC begin.IPF ITR

b. Har-en gerri-a, bern(a)-ak, bularr-ak eta gorputz oso-a laztan-tze-n
yonder_one.GEN waist leg.PLU breast.PLU and body whole fondle.VEN.LOC
has-i ze-n.
begin.PEF ITR.PST

c. Ni-re lore-ak zimel-tze-n has-i d-ir-a.
I.GEN flower.PLU fade.VEN.LOC begin.PEF PLU.ITR

(45) a. Noiz has-i z-in-e-n euskara-z ikas-te-n?
when begin.PEF 2.ITR.PST Basque.IDF.INS learn.VEN.LOC

b. Garai ederr-e-an has-ten h-a-iz pentsa-tze-n.
time fine.LOC begin.IPF 2SOL.ITR think.VEN.LOC

c. Has-i z-ir-e-n zotz e-gi-te-n.
begin.PEF PLU.ITR.PST lot.IDF do.VEN.LOC

(46) Gogo-z abia-tu n-a-iz euskal hiztegi hon-en atalaurre-an hitz
pleasure.IDF.INS set_out.PEF 1.ITR Basque dictionary this.GEN introduction.LOC word
batzu molda-tze-n.
a_few formulate.VEN.LOC

(47) a. Gizon-a-k auto-a garbi-tze-n amai-tu d-u.
man.ERG car wash.VEN.LOC finish.PEF TRA

b. Jaun-a-ren bide zuzen-ak oker-tze-n ez d-u-zu amai-tu-ko?
Lord.GEN way straight.PLU pervert.VEN.LOC not /2.TRA cease.FUT

c. Neskatx(a)-a jan(t)z-te-n amai-tze-n ari ze-n.
girl dress.VEN.LOC finish.VEN.LOC be_busy.PPR ITR.PST

d. Ba-da-ki-zu-e zein liburu amai-tu n-u-en irakur-tze-n atzo?
AFF.know./2PLU.SYT which book finish.PEF /1.TRA.PST read.VEN.LOC yesterday

(48) a. Noe-k kutxa hau e-gi-te-n urte asko igaro z-it-u-en.
Noah.ERG ark this make.VEN.LOC year many spend.PEF PLU/.TRA.PST

b. Minutu luze-ak e-ma-ten d-it-u azal zuri leun-a lehor-tze-n.
minute long.PLU give.IPF PLU/.TRA surface white smooth dry.VEN.LOC

c. Urte-ak da-ra-ma-tza-zu esne-a bana-tze-n.
year.PLU spend.PLU/2.SYT milk distribute.VEN.LOC

d. Gau eta egun zu-ri / zu-gan pentsa-tze-n da-rama-t en-e bizi-a.
night and day.IDF you.DAT you.LOC think_of.VEN.LOC spend./1.SYT I.GEN life

(49) a. Ba al da-ki-k bizikleta gain-e-an i-bil-tze-n?
AFF INT know./2SOL.SYT bicycle.IDF top.LOC move.VEN.LOC

b. Ez n-u-en garai-z ezetz esa-te-n ja-ki-n.
not /1.TRA.PST in_time no.IDF say.VEN.LOC know.PEF

c. Nor-k da-ki gauz(a)-en zergati-a argi-tze-n?
who.ERG know.SYT thing.PLU.GEN reason explain.VEN.LOC

(50) a. Sendagile-ek gezur asko esa-te-n da-ki-te.
doctor.PLU.ERG lie a_lot tell.VEN.LOC be_familiar_with./PLU.SYT

b. Nahigabe-a-k ez da-ki ordu-ak neur(ri)-tze-n.
sorrow.ERG not be_familiar_with.SYT hour.PLU measure.VEN.LOC

(51) a. Amona-k piano-a jo-tze-n aha(t)z-tu e-gi-n d-u.
Grandmother.IDF.ERG piano play.VEN.LOC forget do.PEF TRA

b. Amona-k piano-a jo-tze-a aha(t)z-tu e-gi-n d-u.
Grandmother.IDF.ERG piano play.VEN forget do.PEF TRA

(52) a. Euskara-z hitz e-gi-te-n aha(t)z-tu za-i-o.
Basque.IDF.INS word.IDF do.VEN.LOC forget.PEF DIT

b. Euskara-z hitz e-gi-te-a aha(t)z-tu za-i-o.
Basque.IDF.INS word.IDF do.VEN forget.PEF DIT

(53) a. Ez d-u-t ikas-i emakumezko-(e)-en gorabehera eta matrikul(a)-ak konpreni-tze-n.
not /1.TRA learn.PEF female.PLU.GEN ups_and_downs.IDF and shift.PLU understand.VEN.LOC

b. Polizi(a)-a-ri inor ez sala-tze-n ikas-i behar d-u-zu.
police.DAT anyone not betray.VEN.LOC learn must.PPR /2.TRA

c. Ni-k ez d-u-t hitz-ik e-gi-te-n asma-tzen.
I.ERG not /1.TRA word.PAR do.VEN.LOC manage.IPF

(54) a. Neka-tu n-a-iz eder-ki hon-(r)a-ino e-tor-tze-n.
get_tired.PEF 1.ITR pretty here.TER come.VEN.LOC

b. Lotsa-tu e-gi-ten n-in-tz-e-n ama laztan-tze-n.
get_ashamed do.IPF 1.ITR.PST mother.IDF hug.VEN.LOC

c. Beatriz maitagarri-a ez ze-n asper-tzen piano-a jo-tze-n.
Beatrice lovely not ITR.PST tire_of.IPF piano play.VEN.LOC

d. Asper-tu e-gi-n al d-ir-a poloniarr-ak hi-re ogi-a ja-te-n?
have_enough_of do.PEF INT PLU.ITR Pole.PLU you.SOL.GEN bread eat.VEN.LOC

e. Orain arte bakarr-ik bizi-tze-n etsi d-u-gu.
now until alone.STA live.VEN.LOC resign.PEF /1PLU.TRA

f. Beldur al h-a-iz bakarr-ik e-tor-tze-n?
fear.IDF INT be.2SOL.SYN alone.STA come.VEN.LOC

g. Zer-ga(i)-tik ez z-a-r-e-te ikara-tzen Moises-en kontra hitz e-gi-te-n?
what.MOT not 2PLU.ITR be_frightened.IPF Moses.GEN against word do.VEN.LOC

(55) a. Zer-ga(i)-tik buru-a nek(a)-araz-i gaizkile-a bila-tze-n?
what.MOT head tire_out.CAU criminal search_for.VEN.LOC

b. Lan-ak iza-n-go d-it-u-gu horr-e-ta-z libra-tze-n.
work.PLU have.FUT PLU/1PLU.TRA that.INS free.VEN.LOC

c. Lan haundi-ak har-tu d-it-u-zu ni-re fitx(a)-a ikas-te-n.
work great.PLU take.PEF PLU/2.TRA I.GEN file learn.VEN.LOC

d. Kazetari-ak haiza-tze-n nahiko lan iza-n-go z-u-te-n.
journalist.PLU chase_away.VEN.LOC plenty work have.FUT /PLU.TRA.PST

(56) a. Saia-tu n-a-iz gerlari-(e)-ekin hitz e-gi-te-n.
try.PERF 1.ITR soldier.PLU.SOC word.IDF do.VEN.LOC

b. Zer-ta-ra-ko saia-tu g-eu-re buru-ak dotore-tze-n?
what.DES try we.REF.GEN head.PLU make_pretty.VEN.LOC

c. Mundu-a-k, goiz edo berandu, saia-tu behar-ko z-u-en makurr-ak
world.ERG early or late try have_to.FUT TRA.PST mistake.PLU
zuzen-tze-n.
rectify.VEN.LOC

d. Har-en uste on-a irabaz-te-n ahalegin-du n-in-tz-e-n.
yonder_one.GEN belief good gain.VEN.LOC do_one's_best.PEF 1.ITR.PST

e. Itxur(a)-ak gorde-tze-n ahalegin-du n-in-tz-e-n, ordea.
appearance.PLU keep_up.VEN.LOC do_one's_best.PEF 1.ITR.PST however

f. Apaiz-a-k ahalegin-ak e-gi-n z-it-u-en har-en arim(a)-a
priest.ERG endeavor.PLU do.PEF PLU/.TRA.PST yonder_one.GEN soul
lokaliza-tze-n.
locate.VEN.LOC

(57) a. Auto-a har-tze-ra n-ind-oa-n.
car get.VEN.ALL go.1.SYN.PST

b. Zu j-oa-n-go al z-a-r-a kazetari horr-ekin hitz e-gi-te-ra?
you go.FUT INT 2.ITR journalist that.SOC word.IDF do.VEN.ALL

c. Ni ito-tze-ra z-a-to(r)-z-te.
I strangle.VEN.ALL come.2PLU.SYN

d. Baina lurr-a emakume-a-ri lagun-tze-ra e-torr-i z-e-n.
but earth woman.DAT help.VEN.ALL come.PEF ITR.PST

(58) a. Zer-ta-ra h-a-tor herri hon-e-ta-ra? Gu-ri nesk(a)-ak
what.ALL come.2SOL.SYN town this.ALL we.DAT girl.PLU
ken-tze-ra?
take_away.VEN.ALL

b. Zer-ta-ra-ko h-a-tor herri hon-e-ta-ra? Gu-ri nesk(a)-ak
what.DES come.2SOL.SYN town this.ALL we.DAT girl.PLU
ken-tze-ko?
take_away.VEN.ADN

(59) a. Kanpo-ra atera n-a-iz zigarro bat erre-tze-ra.
outside.ALL step_out.PEF 1.ITR cigarette a smoke.VEN.ALL

b. Palmondo-ra igo-ko n-a-iz har-en fruitu-ak har-tze-ra.
palm_tree.ALL climb_up.FUT 1.ITR yonder_one.GEN fruit.PLU grasp.VEN.ALL

c. Go(i)-ra al z-oa-z afal-tze-ra?
top.ALL INT go.2.SYN have_supper.VEN.ALL

d. Baina hai-ek ez z-ir-e-n zu hil-tze-ra e-torr-i.
but yonder_one.PLU not PLU.ITR.PST you kill.VEN.ALL come.PEF

e. Orain-dik ez al d-ir-a poloniarr-ak gosal-tze-ra azal-du?
yet not INT PLU.ITR Pole.PLU have_breakfast.VEN.ALL appear.PEF

(60) a. Otso hau alda-tu da bildots iza-te-ra?
wolf this change.PEF ITR lamb.IDF be.VEN.ALL

b. Otso hau bihur-tu da bildots iza-te-ra?
wolf this turn_into.PEF ITR lamb.IDF be.VEN.ALL

(61) a. Berdin-tsu-ak iza-te-ra e-torr-i g-a-r-a.
similar.APP.PLU be.VEN.ALL come.PEF 1PLU.ITR

b. Beste-ren limosn(a)-a-z bizi-tze-ra e-torr-i z-ir-e-n.
other.IDF.GEN alms.INS live.VEN.ALL end_up.PEF PLU.ITR.PST

(62) Gudalburu iza-te-ra hel-du z-ir-e-n.
army_captain.IDF be.VEN.ALL come_to.PEF PLU.ITR.PST

(63) a. No-la irits-i n-a-iz gaizkile-a aurki-tze-ra?
how manage.PEF 1.ITR criminal find.VEN.ALL

b. Hori uler-tze-ra iri(t)s-ten n-a-iz.
that understand.VEN.ALL manage.IPF 1.ITR

(64) Ez d-ir-a euskara-rik ikas-te-ra makur-tu-ko.
not PLU.ITR Basque.PAR learn.VEN.ALL stoop.FUT

(65) Debozio-z-ko lan guzti-ak debeka-tze-ra-ino irits-i z-ir-e-n.
devotion.INS.ADN work all.PLU prohibit.VEN.TER go_as_far_as_to.PEF PLU.ITR.PST

(66) a. Lapurreta txiki-ak e-gi-te-ra ohi-tu ze-n.
theft small.PLU commit.VEN.ALL get_used_to.PEF ITR.PST
b. Bakarr-ik bizi iza-te-n ohi-tu ze-n.
alone.STA live.PPR be.VEN.LOC get_used_to.PEF ITR.PST
c. Zu-re aho-a ez da-di-la ohi-tu zin e-gi-te-n.
you.GEN mouth not ITR.SUJ.LCZ get_used_to.PEF oath.IDF do.VEN.LOC
d. Ez ohi-tu z-eu-re aho-a itsuskeri(a)-ak esa-te-ra.
not accustom you.REF.GEN mouth obscenity.PLU speak.VEN.ALL

(67) a. Ez da inor ezer-ta-ra ausar(t)-tzen, ez ja-te-ra, ez mintza-tze-ra.
not ITR anyone anything.ALL dare.IPF not eat.VEN.ALL not speak.VEN.ALL
b. Luis ez ze-n galdera-rik e-gi-te-ra ausar(t)-tu.
Luis not ITR.PST question.PAR make.VEN.ALL dare.PEF
c. No-la mentura-tu z-ar-e-te e-tor-tze-ra?
how dare.PEF 2PLU.ITR come.VEN.ALL
d. Ez g-a-r-a atrebi-tzen i-kus-te-ra gizon har-en aurpegi-a.
not 1PLU.ITR dare see.VEN.ALL man yonder.GEN face

(68) a. No-la-ta-n ausar(t)-tzen z-a-r-a hemen sar-tze-n ni-re baimen-ik gabe?
how dare.IPF 2.ITR here.LOC come_in.VEN.LOC I.GEN permission.PAR without.PRE
b. Inor ez ze-n ausar(t)-tu ezer esa-te-n.
anybody not ITR.PST dare.PEF anything say.VEN.LOC

(69) a. Gal-tze-ra g-oa-z!
perish.VEN.ALL go.1PLU.SYN
b. Soinu-a buka-tze-ra di-h-oa.
music end.VEN.ALL go.SYN
c. Hogeita hamazazpi urte bete-tze-ra n-oa.
twenty seventeen year.IDF complete.VEN.ALL go.1.SYN
d. Neskame-a-rekin ezkon-tze-ra omen z-oa-z.
maid.SOC marry.VEN.ALL REP go.2.SYN
e. Horma zahar hori eror-tze-ra d-oa.
wall old that fall.VEN.ALL go.SYN

(70) a. Baina ez n-oa inor-i esa-te-ra.
but not go.1.SYN anyone.DAT tell.VEN.ALL
b. Etxe-a ez zi-h-oa-n u(t)z-te-ra.
house not go.1.SYN.PST leave.VEN.ALL

(71) a. Azken nahi-a irakur-tze-ra n-oa-ki-zu-e.
last will read.VEN.ALL go.2PLU/1.DYN
b. Ez n-oa-ki-zu liburu hon-en egile-a aurkez-te-ra.
not go.2/1.DYN book this.GEN author present.VEN.ALL

(72) a. Horr-e(n)-ga(i)-tik j-oa-n n-in-tza-i-o-n agur esa-te-ra.
that.MOT go.PEF /1.DIT.PST goodbye.IDF say.VEN.ALL
b. Ni j-oa-n-go n-a-tza-i-zu lagun-tze-ra.
I go.FUT 2/1.DIT help.VEN.ALL
c. Hi-re ama e-torr-i-ko za-i-k lagun-tze-ra.
you.SOL.GEN mother.IDF come.FUT 2SOL/.DIT help.VEN.ALL

(73) a. Hori esa-te-n ari n-in-tza-i-o-n atezain-a-ri.
that say.VEN.LOC be_busy.PPR /1.DIT.PST doorkeeper.DAT
b. Zorr-ak pila-tze-n ari zi-tza-i-z-ki-o-n.
debt.PLU pile_up.VEN.LOC be_busy.PPR /PLU.DIT.PST
c. Ordu-an, anai-ak hitz e-gi-te-n has-i zi-tza-i-z-ki-o-n.
that_time.LOC brother.PLU word.IDF do.VEN.LOC begin.PEF /PLU.DIT.PST
d. Bisit(a)-ak ugari-tze-n has-i n-in-tza-i-o-n.
visit.PLU increase.VEN.LOC begin.PEF /1.DIT.PST
e. Gizon pottolo-a-ri irriño-z begira-tze-n gera-tu n-in-tza-i-o-n.
man chubby.DAT little_smile.IDF.INS look_at.VEN.LOC keep_on.PEF /1.DIT.PST
f. Eskutitz-ak ida(t)z-te-n ja-rrai-tu z-i-o-n Pello-k Miren-i.
letter.PLU write.VEN.LOC go_on.PEF DTR.PST Pete.ERG Mary.DAT

(74) a. Ni saia-tu n-in-tza-i-o-n ate-ak zabal-tze-n.
I try.PEF /1.DIT.PST door.PLU open.VEN.LOC
b. Diru-a bidal-tze-n ahalegin-du n-a-tza-i-o.
money send.VEN.LOC do_one's_best.PEF /1.DIT

(75) a. Eta gero-z-tik ez zi-tza-i-o-n inor galde-tze-ra ausar(t)-tzen.
and thereafter not DIT.PST anyone ask.VEN.ALL dare.IPF
b. Atrebi-tu-ko n-a-tza-i-o berri-z ere mintza-tze-ra en-e Jainko-a-ri.
dare.FUT /1.DIT new.IDF.INS too speak.VEN.ALL I.GEN God.DAT

(76) Iritzi-a eska-tze-ra hurbil-tze-ra ere ez n-a-tza-i-o atrebi-tzen.
opinion ask.VEN.ALL approach.VEN.ALL too not /1.DIT dare.IPF

(77) a. Aita-ri i-kus-te-ra n-oa-ki-o.
Father.IDF.DAT see.VEN.ALL go./1.DYN
b. Ba-n-oa-ki-o i-ra-tzar-tze-ra.
AFF.go./1.DYN wake_up.VEN.ALL
c. Jendetza handi-ak urruti-e-ta-tik zi-h-oa-z-ki-o-n adora-tze-ra.
crowd large.PLU distant.ZEP.PLU.ELA go./PLU.DYN.PST adore.VEN.ALL

d. Asko j-oa-ten zi-tza-i-z-ki-o-n i-kus-te-ra.
many.ZEP go.IPF /PLU.DIT.PST see.VEN.ALL

e. Don Jorje Nabera ardura j-oa-ten zi-tza-i-o-n i-kus-te-ra.
Don Jorje Nabera often go.IPF DIT.PST see.VEN.ALL

f. Bisita-tze-ra e-torr-i za-i-gu Andoni.
visit.VEN.ALL come.PEF 1PLU/.DIT Anthony

g. Eta i-kus-te-ra e-torr-i z-in-tza-i-z-ki-da-te-n.
and see.VEN.ALL come.PEF 1/2PLU.DIT.PST

(78) a. Idumearr-ak eta siriarr-ak has-i zi-tza-i-z-ki-o-n zirika-tze-n.
Idumean.PLU and Syrian.PLU begin.PEF /PLU.DIT.PST challenge.VEN.LOC

b. Andoni jo-tze-n has-i za-i-zu zu-ri.
Anthony hit.VEN.LOC begin.PEF 2/.DIT you.DAT

(79) ?Andoni zu jo-tze-n has-i da.
Anthony you hit.VEN.LOC begin.PEF ITR

(80) a. Liburu hori-ek irakur-tze-ra d-oa-tza.
book that.PLU read.VEN.ALL go.PLU/.SYN

b. Etsai-a-ri arm(a)-ak har-tze-ra n-ind-oa-z-ki-o-n.
enemy.DAT weapon.PLU take.VEN.ALL go.PLU//1.SYN.PST

c. Bi hitz esa-te-ra n-oa-z-ki-zu.
two word.IDF say.VEN.ALL go.2/PLU/1.SYN

(81) a. Ez d-i-t ezer eda-te-n u(t)z-ten.
not /1/.DTR anything drink.VEN.LOC let.IPF

b. Asetasun-a-k ez d-u aberats-a lo e-gi-te-ra u(t)z-ten.
repleteness.ERG not TRA rich.ZEP sleep.IDF do.VEN.ALL let.IPF

(82) a. Zeru-ko ogi-a e-ma-n z-i-e-n ja-te-n.
heaven.ADN bread give.PEF /PLU/.DTR.PST eat.VEN.LOC

b. Seme-a-ri eda-te-n e-ma-n z-i-o-n.
son.DAT drink.VEN.LOC give.PEF DTR.PST

(83) a. Ida(t)z-te-n i-ra-kats-i z-i-gu-n.
write.VEN.LOC teach.PEF /1PLU/.DTR.PST

b. Zu-k e-ra-ku(t)s-ten d-i-da-zu zeru-ra begira-tze-n.
you.ERG show.IPF /1/2.DTR heaven.ALL look_at.VEN.LOC

c. E-ra-kuts-i-ko d-i-na-t ni-k hi-re haize-ak
teach.FUT /2SOL.FEM/1.DTR I.ERG you.SOL.GEN air.PLU
gorde-tze-n.
keep_to_oneself.VEN.LOC

(84) a. Lagun-du-ko d-i-zu-t bidoi-a sar-tze-n?
help.FUT /2/1.DTR drum bring_in.VEN.LOC

b. Jainko-a-k lagun-du z-i-o-n filistearr-ak garai-tze-n.
God.ERG help.PEF DTR.PST Philistine.PLU defeat.VEN.LOC

c. Ez al d-i-da-k brotxe-a aukera-tze-ra lagun-du behar?
not INT /1/2SOL.DTR brooch choose.VEN.ALL accompany be_going_to.PPR

(85) a. Ez d-u-gu ate-a zabal-tze-n i-kus-i.
not /1PLU.TRA door open.VEN.LOC see.PEF

b. Nor-k i-kus-i d-u inor hil-tze-n?
who.ERG see.PEF TRA anyone kill.VEN.LOC

c. Jai bakoitz-e-an nexka berri-a i-kus-ten z-a-it-u-t maita-tze-n.
festival each.LOC girl new see.IPF 2/1.TRA love.VEN.LOC

(86) a. Ardo-a ni-k behin i-kus-i n-u-en e-gi-te-n.
wine I.ERG once see.PEF /1.TRA.PST make.VEN.LOC

b. Etxe hori i-kus-i d-u-gu jaso-tze-n.
house that see.PEF /1PLU.TRA build.VEN.LOC

c. ?**Etxe hori i-kus-i d-u-gu zu-ek jaso-tze-n.
house that see.PEF /1PLU.TRA you.PLU.ERG build.VEN.LOC

(87) a. Ez z-a-it-u-t inoiz dantza-n i-kus-i.
not 2/1.TRA ever dance.IDF.LOC see.PEF

b. Zer-ta-n i-kus-i d-it-u-zu ehiztari-ak? Azeri-ak hil-tze-n.
what.LOC see.PEF PLU/2.TRA hunter.PLU fox.PLU kill.VEN.LOC

(88) a. Mintzo bat e-ntzu-n n-u-en ni-ri esa-te-n:...
voice a hear.PEF /1.TRA.PST I.DAT say.VEN.LOC

b. Zu-re aita-ri e-ntzu-n d-i-o-t Esau-ri esa-te-n:...
you.GEN father.IDF.DAT hear.PEF //1.DTR Esau.DAT say.VEN.LOC

c. Sar-tze-n e-ntzu-n d-u-t.
come_in.VEN.LOC hear.PEF /1.TRA

(89) a. Gu-k ber-e aho-tik esa-te-n adi-tu d-i-o-gu.
we.ERG he_himself.GEN mouth.ELA say.VEN.LOC hear.PEF //1PLU.DTR

b. Adi-tu d-u-t zu-re aita mintza-tze-n zu-re anaia Esau-rekin.
hear.PEF /1.TRA you.GEN father.IDF speak.VEN.LOC you.GEN brother Esau.SOC

(90) a. Goiz-e-ko ordu-e-ta-n e-tor-tze-n suma-tu z-u-en.
morning.ADN hour.PLU.LOC come.VEN.LOC notice.PEF TRA.PST

b. Senti-tzen z-a-it-u-t sala berri-an jaik-i-tze-n.
notice.IPF 2/1.TRA parlor new.LOC get_up.VEN.LOC

c. Asab(a)-en odol-a ber-e zain-e-ta-n iraki-te-n nabari-tzen
ancestor.PLU.GEN blood he_himself.GEN vein.PLU.LOC boil.VEN.LOC feel.IPF
z-u-en.
TRA.PST

d. En-e lagun-a hautema-ten d-u-t ahul-tze-n.
I.GEN companion notice.IPF /1.TRA get_weaker.VEN.LOC

(91) a. Emakume hau ezkontz(a)=nahas-te-n aurki-tu d-u-gu.
woman this commit_adultery.VEN.LOC find.PEF /1PLU.TRA

b. Gu-re nazio-a nahaspila-tze-n harrapa-tu d-u-gu gizon hau.
we.GEN nation subvert.VEN.LOC catch.PEF /1PLU.TRA man this

(92) a. Larunbat-e-an afal-tze-ra gonbida-tzen h-a-u-t.
Saturday.LOC have_dinner.VEN.ALL invite.IPF 2SOL/1.TRA

b. Bihar hil-tze-ra kondena-tu z-u-te-n atzo.
tomorrow die.VEN.ALL condemn.PEF /PLU.TRA.PST yesterday

(93) a. Hori-ek gosal-tze-ra da-ra-ma-tza-gu.
that.PLU have_breakfast.VEN.ALL take_away.PLU/1PLU.SYT

b. Nor-k e-rama-n d-u Katalin josta-tze-ra izarr-a(k-e)kin.
who.ERG take_away.PEF TRA Katalin play.VEN.ALL star.PLU.SOC

c. Ardo-a eros-te-ra bidal-i n-a-u-te.
wine buy.VEN.ALL send.PEF 1/PLU.TRA

(94) a. Ama-k mataza hau-ek garbi-tze-ra bidal-i n-a-u ibai hon-e-ta-ra.
Mother.IDF.ERG skein this.PLU wash.VEN.ALL send.PEF 1/.TRA river this.ALL

b. Irunea-tik e-karr-i d-u-te hil-tze-ra.
Pamplona.ELA bring.PEF /PLU.TRA die.VEN.ALL

(95) a. Ber-a-ri kalte e-gi-te-ra bultza-tu n-ind-u-a-n.
he_himself.DAT harm.IDF do.VEN.ALL push.PEF 1/2SOL.TRA.PST

b. Pauso txar bat e-ma-te-ra bultza-tu n-ind-u-te-n.
step false a give.VEN.ALL push.PEF 1/PLU.TRA.PST

c. Nagusi-a-k ber-a-rekin ezkon-tze-ra behar-tu omen z-u-en.
boss.ERG he_himself.SOC marry.VEN.ALL force.PEF REP TRA.PST

d. Egunero jan beharr-a-k lan-a har-tze-ra behar-tzen n-ind-u-en.
every_day eat need.ERG job take.VEN.ALL force.IPF 1/.TRA.PST

(96) a. Bizarr-a mo(t)z-te-a e-ra-bak-i d-u-t.
beard cut.VEN decide.PEF /1.TRA

b. **Bizar=mo(t)z-te-a e-ra-bak-i d-u-t.
**beard-cut.VEN decide.PEF /1.TRA

(97) a. Bizar=mo(t)z-te-n ari da.
beard-cutting.VEN.LOC be_busy.PPR ITR

b. Bizar=mo(t)z-te-n i-kus-i d-u-gu.
beard-cutting.VEN.LOC see.PEF /1PLU.TRA

c. Bizar=mo(t)z-te-n ez d-u orain-dik ikas-i.
beard-cutting.VEN.LOC not TRA yet learn.PEF

(98) a. Bartel patata=zuri-tze-n ari ze-n sukalde-an.
Bartel potato-peeling.VEN.LOC be_busy.PPR ITR.PST kitchen.LOC
b. Lepo=mo(t)z-te-n ari d-ir-a.
Throat-cutting.VEN.LOC be_busy.PPR PLU.ITR

(99) Joko-a, azken fin-e-an, e-zagu-n-a-ren eta ez-e-zagu-n-a-ren arte-ko
Game last end.LOC known.ZEP.GEN and unknown.ZEP.GEN between.ADN
orekagune-a aurki-tze-an da-tza.
balance find.VEN.DEF.LOC lie_down.SYN

(100) a. Itziar i-kus-i d-u-t etxera-tze-an.
Itziar see.PEF /1.TRA go_home.VEN.DEF.LOC
b. Itziar i-kus-i d-u-t etxera-tze-n.
Itziar see.PEF /1.TRA go_home.VEN.LOC

Chapter 17

(1) a. Inor-k behi bat hil-tzen ba-d-u, urka-tu e-gi-ten d-u-te segi-tu-an.
anyone.ERG cow a kill.IPF CDP.TRA hang do.IPF /PLU.TRA at_once
b. Norbait-e-k Gizon-a-ren Seme-a-ren kontra zerbait esa-ten ba-d-u,
someone.ERG Man.GEN Son.GEN against something say.IPF CDP.TRA
barka-tu-ko d-i-o Jainko-a-k.
forgive.FUT DTR God.ERG
c. Nor-k e-gi-n-go d-i-zu-e kalte, zu-ek beti on e-gi-te-n
who.ERG do.FUT /2PLU/.DTR harm.IDF you.PLU always good.IDF do.VEN.LOC
saia-tzen ba-z-a-r-e-te?
try.IPF CDP.2PLU.ITR

(2) a. Bakarr-ik geldi-tu ba-da mundu-an, horr-e-ta-n ez d-u hoben-ik.
alone.STA stay.PEF CDP.ITR world.LOC that.LOC not have.SYT guilt.PAR
b. Beste-la, itsu-a ba-da-bil itsu=mutil, on-gi jaio-ak
otherwise blind.ZEP CDP.act.SYN guide_to_the_blind.IDF well born.PLU
g-a-u-de.
be.1PLU.SYN
c. Itsu bat jar-tzen ba-da beste bat-en itsu=aurreko,
blind a put_oneself_up_as.IPF CDP.ITR other a.GEN guide_to_the_blind.IDF
bi-ak zulo-ra eror-i-ko d-ir-a.
two.ZEP.PLU pit.ALL fall.FUT PLU.ITR

(3) a. Ni-k ez z-a-it-u-t utz-i-ko, zu-k ez ba-n-a-u-zu u(t)z-ten.
I.ERG not 2/1.TRA leave.FUT you.ERG not CDP.1/2.TRA leave.IPF
b. Ez ba-d-u-zu ja-ten, ez z-a-r-a haundi-tu-ko.
not CDP./2.TRA eat.IPF not 2.ITR grow_up.FUT
c. Gaixo-a ez ba-da senda-tzen, mediku-a-k d-u erru-a.
patient not CDP.ITR recover.IPF doctor.ERG TRA fault
d. ber-e-ha(r-en)-la ez ba-d-u-zu-e alde e-gi-ten, zakurr-a-k puska-tu
at_once not CDP./2PLU.TRA place.IDF make.IPF dog.ERG tear_to_pieces
e-gin-go z-a-it-u-z-te.
do.FUT 2PLU/.TRA

(4) a. E-ra-bil-tzen ez ba-da, hil e-gi-ten da euskar(a)-a.
use.IPF not CDP.ITR die do.IPF ITR Basque
b. Gehi-ago ardo-rik eda-ten ez ba-d-u-n, abera(t)s-tu-ko
more.COP wine.PAR drink.IPF not CDP./2SOL.FEM.TRA make_rich.FUT
g-a-it-u-n.
1PLU/2SOL.FEM.TRA
c. Itzul-tzen ez ba-d-i-o-zu, zin-e-z hil-ko z-a-r-e-te.
restore.IPF not CDP.//2.DTR surely die.FUT 2PLU.ITR
d. Etxe-a Jaun-a-k e-ra-ik-i-tzen ez ba-d-u, alferr-ik ari d-ir-a
house Lord.ERG build.IPF not CDP.TRA in_vain.STA be_busy.PPR PLU.ITR
etxegile-ak.
builder.PLU

(5) a. Ni zerbait iza-n baldin ba-n-a-iz, hi(t)zkuntzalari-a iza-n n-a-iz.
I something be.PEF CDC CDP.1.ITR linguist be.PEF 1.ITR
b. Gorde nahi baldin ba-d-u, gorde-ko d-u.
keep want.PPR CDC CDP.TRA keep.FUT TRA
c. Beste eredu-rik ez baldin ba-da-kar, ez d-u mintza-tze-ko
other model.PAR not CDC CDP.bring.SYT not have.SYT speak.VEN.ADN
eskubide-rik.
right.PAR
d. Ez baldin ba-d-u-zu-e sine(t)s-ten, eror-i-ko z-a-r-e-te.
not CDC CDP.2.PLU.TRA believe.IPF fall.FUT 2PLU.ITR

(6) a. Baldin ha(r-en)-la ez ba-da, euskaldun-ek ber-ek
CDC that_way not CDP.be.SYN Basque.PLU.ERG he_himself.PLU.ERG
d-u-te falt(a)-a eta ez euskar(a)-a-k.
have./PLU.TRA blame and not Basque_language.ERG
b. Baldin gaur arrats-e-an gorde-tzen ez ba-z-a-r-a, bihar hil behar-ko
CDC today evening.LOC hide.IPF not CPC.2.ITR tomorrow die have_to.FUT

z-a-r-a.
2.ITR

c. Baldin ez ba-d-u-t negar e-gi-ten, harri-z-ko-a d-u-t bihotz-a.
CDC not CDP./1.TRA crying.IDF do.IPF made_of_stone.ZEP have./1.SYT heart

d. Baldin Hazparne itzal-tzen ba-da, ez d-u-gu Euskal Herri-rik.
CDC Hazparne disappear.IPF CDP.ITR not have./1PLU.SYT Basque Country.PAR

(7) Baldin eta han-dik irte-ten ba-n-a-iz, zu eta zu-re-ak ni-re fede-ra
CDC EXP there.ELA come_out CDP.1.ITR you and you.GEN.ZEP.PLU I.GEN faith.ALL
konberti-tu-ko z-a-r-e-te.
convert.FUT 2PLU.ITR

(8) a. Pilomena-k ja-ki-ten ba-d-u, larru-tu-ko z-a-it-u.
Philomene.ERG know.IPF CDP.TRA skin.FUT 2/.TRA

b. Osaba zerritegi-ra e-tor-tzen ba-da, ez d-i-o-t sar-tze-n utz-i-ko.
Uncle pigsty.ALL come.IPF CDP.ITR not //1.DTR enter.VEN.LOC let.FUT

c. Oste-ra i-kus-ten ba-g-a-r-a, e-ma-n-go d-i-zu-t esku-a.
back_part.ALL see.IPF CDP.1PLU.ITR give.FUT /2/1.DTR hand

d. Ostiral-e-ta-n e-tor-tzen ba-z-a-ra, plazer haundi-z hitze-gi-n-go d-u-t
Friday.PLU.LOC come.IPF CDP.2.ITR pleasure great.IDF.INS talk.FUT /1.TRA
zu-rekin.
you.SOC

(9) a. Batasun-a premia-z-ko-a da, hi(t)zkuntz(a) bizi-ko baldin ba-da.
unification necessary.ZEP be.SYN language live.FUT CDC CDP.ITR

b. Horr-e(n)-la iza-n-go da aurre-ra ere, bizi-ko baldin ba-da.
like_that be.FUT ITR front_part.ALL too live.FUT CDC CDP.ITR

(10) a. Baina egi(a)-a ba-d-io-t, zer-ga(i)-tik ez d-i-da-zu-e sine(t)s-ten?
but truth CDP.tell./1.SYT what.MOT not /1/2PLU.DTR believe.IPF

b. Hi-k ez ba-da-ki-k, nor-k ote da-ki?
you.SOL.ERG not CDP.know./2SOL.SYT who.ERG DUB know.SYT

c. Eta ni-k ez ba-d-u-t hitze-gi-ten, no-la ja-ki-n-go d-u-te?
and I.ERG not CDP./1.TRA talk.IPF how know.FUT /PLU.TRA

d. Zer esa-n behar d-u herri-a-k, hori ja-ki-ten ba-d-u?
what say be_going_to.PPR TRA village.ERG that know.IPF CDP.TRA

(11) a. Gai(t)z-ki hitzegi-n ba-d-u-t, esa-n zer-ta-n.
wrongly speak.PEF CDP./1.TRA say what.LOC

b. Auto-ra-ino lagun-du nahi ba-d-i-da-k, e-torr-i ni-rekin.
car.TER keep_company want.PPR CDP./1/2SOL.DTR come I.SOC

c. Barka-tu, itxaron-araz-i ba-d-i-zu-e-t.
forgive wait.CAU.PEF CDP./2PLU/1.DTR

(12) a. Ni errege baldin ba-n-in-tz, erregina z-in-a-te-ke.
I king.IDF CDC CDP.be.1.SYN.COD queen.IDF be.2.SYN.COD

b. Hemen ba-z-in-a edo hor ba-n-en-go, zu-re begi triste-ak
here.LOC CDP.be.2.SYN.COD or there CDP.be.1.SYN.COD you.GEN eye sad.PLU
alai-tze-n saia-tu-ko n-in-tza-te-ke.
cheer_up.VEN.LOC try.FUT 1.ITR.COD

c. Jainko-a ba-li-tz zu-en aita, maite n-ind-u-ke-zu-e.
God CDP.be.SYN.COD you.PLU.GEN father.IDF love.PPR 1/2PLU.TRA.COD

d. Ni-k ere ha(r-en)-la pentsa-tu-ko n-u-ke, zaharr-a ba-n-in-tz.
I.ERG too that_way think.FUT /1.TRA.COD old CDP.be.1.SYN.COD

e. Zu-re larru-an ba-n-en-go, ez n-u-ke ezetz-ik esa-n-go.
you.GEN skin.LOC CDP.be.1.SYN.COD not /1.TRA.COD no.PAR say.FUT

f. Ezetz ba-n-io, gezurr-a esa-n-go n-u-ke.
no.IDF CDP.say./1.SYT.COD lie tell.FUT /1.TRA.COD

g. Negar e-gi-n-go l-u-ke ni-re ama-k, ba-le-ki.
crying.IDF do.FUT TRA.COD I.GEN mother.IDF.ERG CDP.know.SYT.COD

(13) a. Gai(t)zkile-a ez ba-li-tz, ez g-en-i-zu-ke-en e-karr-i-ko.
criminal not CDP.be.SYN.COD not /2/1PLU.DTR.COD.PST bring.FUT

b. Laban-a esku-an i-kus-i ba-l-u-te, ez l-u-ke-te hori esa-n-go.
knife hand.LOC see.PEF CDP./PLU.TRA.COD not /PLU.TRA.COD that say.FUT

(14) a. Orain-txe bazterr-en bat-e-an atzema-n-go ban-u, ito-ko
now.EMP corner.IDF.GEN a.LOC catch.FUT CDP./1.TRA.COD strangle.FUT
n-u-ke.
/1.TRA.COD

b. Aita-k ja-ki-n-go ba-l-u, haserre-tu-ko li-tza-te-ke.
Father.IDF.ERG know.FUT CDP.TRA.COD get_angry.FUT ITR.COD

c. Ni e-zagu-tu-ko ba-n-ind-u-zu-e, ni-re Aita ere e-zagu-tu-ko
I know.FUT CDP.1/2PLU.TRA.COD I.GEN Father.IDF too know.FUT
z-en-u-ke-te.
/2PLU.TRA.COD

d. Gau bat pasa-tu nahi ba-n-u hemen, bi hilabete-ko irabazi-ak
night a spend want.PPR CDP./1.TRA.COD here.LOC two month.ADN earning.PLU
behar-ko n-it-u-z-ke.
need.FUT PLU/1.TRA.COD

(15) a. Ni-k ere jantz-i nahi baldin ba-n-it-u, ba-da-u-z-ka-t hori-ek
I.ERG too wear want.PPR CDC CDP.PLU/1.TRA.COD AFF.have.PLU/1.SYT that.PLU
aukera-n.
abundance.IDF.LOC

b. Norbait-e-k kontra-ko arrazoi-rik baldin ba-l-u, ni gertu
someone.ERG opposing argument.PAR CDC CDP.SYT.COD I prepared.PRE
n-a-go arrazoi hori-ek e-ntzu-te-ko.
be.1.SYN argument that.PLU hear.VEN.ADN

(16) a. Hil ez ba-n-u, sala-tu e-gi-n-go n-ind-u-ke-en.
kill.PEF not CDP./1.TRA.COD denounce do.FUT 1/.TRA.COD.PST
b. Ama-k esa-n ez ba-l-i-t, ni ez n-in-tza-te-ke-en hura
Mother.IDF.ERG tell.PEF not CDP./1/.DTR.COD I not 1.ITR.COD.PST yonder_one
i-kus-te-ra j-oa-n-go.
see.VEN.ALL go.FUT
c. Zer esa-n-go ote z-u-ke-en Etxepare zaharr-a-k, horr-e(n)-la-ko-rik
what say.FUT DUB TRA.COD.PST Etxepare old.ERG like_that.ADN.ZEP.PAR
e-ntzu-n ba-l-u?
hear.PEF CDP.TRA.COD

(17) a. Gauza ber-a esa-n-go z-u-ke-en zeru-a oskarbi e-go-n iza-n ba-li-tz.
thing same say.FUT TRA.COD.PST sky clear.PRE be.PEF be.PEF CDP.ITR.COD
b. Horr-e(n)-la-ko-rik e-gi-n iza-n ba-l-u, abisa-tu e-gi-n-go
like_that.ADN.ZEP.PAR do.PEF have.PEF CDP.TRA.COD warn do.FUT
z-u-ke-en.
TRA.COD.PST

(18) a. Elkarr-i egia-z-ko maitasun-ik baldin ba-d-i-o-te, argitasun-a
each_other.DAT true love.PAR CDC CDP.have//PLU.DYT clarity
e-torr-i-ko da.
come.FUT ITR
b. Hil-ko al z-en-u-ke gaur, aukera-rik ba-z-en-u?
kill.FUT INT /2.TRA.COD today chance.PAR CDP.have./2.SYT.COD

(19) a. Hori ja-ki-n ba-n-u, ez n-in-tz-e-n j-oa-n-go.
that know.PEF CDP./1.TRA.COD not 1.ITR.PST go.FUT
b. Zu hemen iza-n ba-z-in-a, gu-re anai-a ez ze-n hil-ko.
you here.LOC be.PEF CDP.2ITR.COD we.GEN brother not ITR.PST die.FUT
c. Zaldi-a sal-du ba-n-u, asto bat behar-ko n-u-en.
horse sell.PEF CDP.TRA.COD donkey a need.FUT /1.TRA.PST

(20) a. Zu-k ha(r-en)-la ez esa-te-ra, galdu-a n-a-iz.
you.ERG so not say.VEN.ALL lost be.1.SYN
b. Hon-e(n)-la ja-rrai-tze-ra, hezurr-e-ta-n geldi-tu-ko z-a-r-e-te.
this_way continue.VEN.ALL bone.IDF.LOC end_up:FUT 2PLU.ITR

(21) a. Zu iza-te-ra, jertse bat har-tu-ko n-u-ke.
you be.VEN.ALL sweater a take.FUT /1.TRA.COD

b. Bai-ta zu ere erre-ko z-int-u-z-ke-te, ereje-rik zu-gan aurki-tze-ra.
and you too burn.FUT 2/PLU.TRA.COD heretic.PAR you.LOC find.VEN.ALL

c. Ja-ki-te-ra, han geldi-tu-ko n-in-tza-te-ke-en.
know.VEN.ALL over_there.LOC stay.FUT 1.ITR.COD.PST

(22) a. Ezer gerta-tze-ra, organizazio-a-k ber-a-ri eska-tu-ko z-i-z-ki-o-n kontu-ak.
anything happen.VEN.ALL organization.ERG she_herself.DAT ask.FUT PLU//PLU.DTR.PST account.PLU

b. Garai-z ez iri(t)s-te-ra, Mikel urduri jarr-i-ko ze-n.
time.IDF.INS not arrive.VEN.ALL Michael nervous.PRE get.FUT ITR.PST

(23) a. Mirari-ak i-kus-i ez-ik, ez d-uzu-e zu-ek sine(t)s-ten.
miracle.PLU see not.STA not /2PLU.TRA you.PLU believe.IPF

b. Hain burugabe joka-tu-ko al l-ir-a-te-ke, arraunlari-(e)-en gorabeher(a)-ak ja-ki-n ez-ik?
so foolishly behave.FUT INT PLU.ITR.COD rower.PLU.GEN condition.PLU know not.STA

(24) a. Izerdi-tze-a on-a da, gero ho(t)z-tu ez-e-an.
sweat.VEN good be.SYN afterward get_chilled not.LOC

b. Zer e-gi-n z-i-zu-ke-en, zu-k borroka-rik nahi ez-e-an?
what do.PEF /2/.DTR.COD.PST you.ERG fight.PAR want not.LOC

(25) a. Zer e-gi-n-go l-u-ke hi-re amatxo-k, hi gabe ba-li-tz?
what do.FUT TRA.COD you.SOL.GEN mommy.IDF.ERG you.SOL without.PRE CDP.be.SYN.COD

b. Zer e-gi-n-go l-u-ke hi-re amatxo-k hi gabe?
what do.FUT TRA.COD you.SOL.GEN mommy.IDF.ERG you.SOL without.PRE

(26) a. Guzti-ak aipa-tu-ko ba-l-ir-a, luze li-tza-te-ke.
all.PLU mention.FUT CDP.PLU.ITR.COD long.IDF ITR.COD

b. Guzti-ak aipa-tze-a luze li-tza-te-ke.
all.PLU mention.VEN long.IDF ITR.COD

(27) a. Mesede bat eska-tu nahi n-i-zu-ke.
favor a ask like.PPR /2/1.DTR.COD

b. Gu-re gaixo bat-e-k zu-rekin hitz e-gi-n nahi l-u-ke.
we.GEN patient a.ERG you.SOC word.IDF do like.PPR TRA.COD

c. Bidal-i-ko al z-en-it-u-z-ke, Marcel?
send.FUT INT PLU/2.TRA.COD Marcel

d. Ez z-en-i-e-ke zerbait esa-n-go *egan*-en irakurle-e-i?
not /PLU/2.DTR.COD something say.FUT *egan*.IDF.GEN reader.PLU.DAT

(28) a. Gusto-ra har-tu-ko n-u-ke kafe bero-a.
gladly take.FUT /1.TRA.COD coffee warm
b. Gau-a igaro-tze-ko lehorr-a nahi n-u-ke, Jaun-a.
night spend.VEN.ADN dry_place like.PPR /1.TRA.COD Sir

(29) a. Lan hau har-tu-ko al z-en-u-ke?
job this take_on.FUT INT /2.TRA.COD
b. Egia oso-a ja-ki-n nahi al z-en-u-ke?
truth whole know like.PPR INT /2.TRA.COD
c. Zein beste arrazoi aipa-tu-ko z-en-u-ke?
which other reason mention.FUT /2.TRA.COD
d. Alab(a)-a-k bizi-a ere e-ma-n-go l-u-ke ait(a)-a-ren alde.
daughter.ERG life even give.FUT TRA.COD father.GEN side.IDF

(30) a. Am(a)-a-ga(i)-tik andre oro behar l-u-ke gora-tu.
mother.MOT woman all should.PPR TRA.COD praise
b. Jendaila horr-e-k ez l-u-ke hemen e-go-n behar.
riffraff that.ERG not TRA.COD here.LOC stay should.PPR
c. Euskar(a)-a-ri irau-n-araz-te-ko saia-tu behar ote li-tza-te-ke?
Basque_language.DAT survive.CAU.VEN.ADN endeavor should.PPR DUB ITR.COD
d. Zer e-gi-n behar li-tza-te-ke, bada?
what do have_to.PPR ITR.COD INF
e. Euskaltzale-ek komeni l-u-ke-te asti-ro irakur-tze-a.
Bascophile.PLU.ERG convenient.PRE /PLU.SYT.COD attentively read.VEN

(31) a. Arrazoi-a ba-d-u-t ere, ez d-i-o-t e-ra-ntzu-n-go.
reason CDP.have./1.SYT even not //1.DTR answer.FUT
b. Zu-rekin hil behar ba-d-u-t ere, ez z-a-it-u-t ino-la ere
you.SOC die have_to.PPR CDP./1.TRA even not 2/1.TRA in_some_way even
uka-tu-ko.
deny.FUT
c. Baina nahi ez ba-d-it-u-gu ere, behar d-it-u-gu.
but want.PPR not CDP.PLU/1PLU.TRA even need.PPR PLU/1PLU.TRA
d. Baina ez baldin ba-ze-n ere ber-a mediku, argi-tzen
but not CDC CDC.SYN.PST even he_himself doctor.IDF educate.IPF
z-it-u-en mediku-ak.
PLU/.TRA.PST doctor.PLU

(32) a. Eta epai-tu-ko ba-n-u ere, ni-re epai-a balio-z-ko-a
and judge.FUT CDP./1.TRA.COD even I.GEN judgment value.IDF.INS.ZEP.
li-tza-te-ke.
SYN.COD.PST

b. Profet(a)-a-k gauza zail-en bat agin-du iza-n bal-i-zu ere,
prophet.ERG thing hard.GEN a command.PEF have.PEF CDP./2/.DTR.COD even
ez al z-en-u-ke-en e-gi-n-go?
not INT /2.TRA.COD.PST do.FUT

(33) a. Eleberri bat e-gi-te-ko-ta-n omen ze-bil-e-n.
novel a do.VEN.ADN.IDF.LOC REP be_busy.SYN.PST
b. E-go-n n-a-iz etxe-a erre-tze-ko-ta-n ere, baina . . .
be.PEF 1.ITR house burn.VEN.ADN.IDF.LOC even but
c. Seme-a ezkon-tze-ko-ta-n da-bil-ki-zu aspaldi.
son marry.VEN.ADN.IDF.LOC be_busy.2/.DYN for_a_long_time

(34) a. Zerbait irabaz-te-ko asmo-ta-n sal-du z-u-en auto-a.
something earn.VEN.ADN intention.IDF.LOC sell.PEF TRA.PST car
b. Zerbait irabaz-te-ko-ta-n sal-du z-u-en auto-a.
something earn.VEN.ADN.IDF.LOC sell.PEF TRA.PST car

(35) a. Seme-a iza-n-go d-u-zu-e, baina har-en arim(a)-a gero ni-re-tzat
son have.FUT /2PLU.TRA but yonder_one.GEN soul afterward I.BEN
iza-te-ko-ta-n.
be.VEN.ADN.IDF.LOC
b. Argi-a sortalde-tik e-tor-tze-ko-ta-n, ez ote zai-gu Txina-tik
light east.ELA come.VEN.ADN.IDF.LOC not DUB 1PLU/.DIT China.ELA
ager-tu-ko?
appear.FUT
c. Inor-i ezer e-gi-te-ko-ta-n, ni-ri iza-n-go da.
anyone.DAT anything do.VEN.ADN.IDF.LOC I.DAT be.FUT ITR

(36) a. Ezkon-tze-ko kontu-ta-n, gazte-a nahi d-u.
marry.VEN.ADN event.IDF.LOC young_woman want.PPR TRA
b. Ezkon-tze-ko-ta-n, gazte-a nahi d-u.
marry.VEN.ADN.IDF.LOC young_woman want.PPR TRA

(37) a. Abia-tze-ko puntu-ta-n g-in-e-n, . . .
depart.VEN.ADN point.IDF.LOC be.1PLU.SYN.PST
b. Abia-tze-ko-ta-n g-in-e-n, . . .
depart.VEN.ADN.IDF.LOC be.1PLU.SYN.PST

(38) Errege-tzat har-tu n-ind-u-te-n gizon hai-ek.
king.PRO take.PEF 1/PLU.TRA.PST man yonder.PLU.ERG

(39) a. Aita iza-n-go n-a-u har-k ni, eta seme iza-n-go d-u-t ni-k
father.IDF have.FUT 1/.TRA yonder_one.ERG me and son.IDF have.FUT /1.TRA I.ERG

hura.
yonder_one

b. Aita-tzat iza-n-go n-a-u har-k ni, eta seme-tzat iza-n-go d-u-t
father.PRO have.FUT 1/.TRA yonder_one.ERG me and son.PRO have.FUT /1.TRA
ni-k hura.
I.ERG yonder_one

(40) a. ?Seme har-tu d-u-te Iñaki.
son.IDF take.PEF /PLU.TRA Iñaki

b. Seme-tzat har-tu d-u-te Iñaki.
son.PRO adopt.PEF /PLU.TRA Iñaki

(41) a. Laban-e-k Rahel ber-e alab(a)-a e-ma-n z-i-o-n emazte.
Laban.ERG Rachel he_himself.GEN daughter give.PEF DTR.PST wife.IDF

b. Laban-e-k ber-e alab(a)-a Rakel e-ma-n z-i-o-n emazte-tzat.
Laban.ERG he_himself daughter Rachel give.PEF DTR.PST wife.PRO

(42) a. Ber-e alab(a)-a Jenobeba emazte e-ma-n z-i-o-n.
he_himself.GEN daughter Genevieve wife.IDF give.PEF DTR.PST

b. Ber-e alab(a)-a emazte-tzat e-ma-n z-i-o-n.
he_himself.GEN daughter wife.PRO give.PEF DTR.PST

(43) a. Seme-a baldin ba-d-u-zu ere, gu-k ez d-u-gu aitor-tzen
son CDC CDP.have./2.SYT even we.ERG not /1PLU.TRA acknowledge.IPF
anaia-tzat.
brother.PRO

b. Hau n-eu-re alaba-tzat e-zagu-tu-ko d-u-t.
this_one I.REF.GEN daughter.PRO recognize.FUT /1.TRA

c. No-la aukera-tu z-en-u-en gai-tzat Lizardi-ren poema hori?
how_come choose.PEF /2.TRA.PST theme.PRO Lizardi.GEN poem that

(44) a. Oso haundi jo-tzen d-u-gu.
very great.IDF consider.IPF /1PLU.TRA

b. Araba-tik ardo-a kontrabando e-kar-tze-a bekatu handi jo-tzen z-u-en.
Alava.ELA wine contraband.IDF bring.VEN sin great.IDF consider.IPF TRA.PST

c. Egia-z-ko errudun-a ber-a jo-ko z-u-te-n.
true culprit he_himself consider.FUT /PLU.TRA.PST

(45) a. Kaxkar-tzat jo g-a-it-u-z-te.
shoddy.PRO deem.PEF 1PLU/PLU.TRA

b. Ero-tzat jo-ko h-a-u-te, seme.
crazy.PRO deem.FUT 2SOL/PLU.TRA son.IDF

c. Zu beti etsai, eta etsai amorra-tu-tzat jo-ko z-a-it-u-t.
you always enemy.IDF and enemy rabid.PRO deem.FUT 2/1.TRA

(46) a. Ez l-i-o-ke inor-k hirurogei urte e-ma-n-go.
not DTR.COD anybody.ERG sixty year.IDF give.FUT
b. (Ni) tximu huts-tzat e-ma-n?
(me) monkey mere.PRO consider
c. San Pablo ber-e-ha-la hil-tzat e-ma-n z-u-te-n
St. Paul instantly dead.PRO give_up.PEF /PLU.TRA.PST

(47) a. Gu-re agindu-a hu(t)skeria-tzat har-tzen d-u-te.
we.GEN command trifle.PRO regard_as.IPF /PLU.TRA
b. Juda-k emagaldu-tzat har-tu z-u-en.
Juda.ERG prostitute.PRO take_for.PEF TRA.PST
c. Zer-ga(i)-tik har-tzen g-a-it-u-zu animalia-tzat? Zer-ga(i)-tik jo-tzen
what.MOT take_for.IPF PLU/2.TRA brute.PRO what.MOT consider.IPF
inozo-tzat?
foolish.PRO

(48) a. Andoni irakasle zintzo-tzat da-uka-gu.
Tony teacher reliable.PRO consider./1PLU.SYT
b. Daniel eta ber-e lagun-ak ere asmatzaile-tzat
Daniel and he_himself.GEN companion.PLU too soothsayer.PRO
ze-u-z-ka-te-n.
consider.PLU/PLU.SYT.PST
c. Napoleon on-tzat da-u-ka-te batzu-ek, gaizto-tzat
Napoleon good.PRO regard_as./PLU.SYT some_people.PLU.ERG evil.PRO
beste-ek.
other.ZEP.PLU.ERG

(49) a. Osasungarri-tzat d-u-t ni-k lan-a neurri-z e-gi-te-a.
healthy.PRO consider./1.SYT I.ERG work moderation.IDF.INS do.VEN
b. Hil-tzat n-ind-u-zu-e-n.
dead.PRO consider.1/2PLU.SYT.PST

(50) Eder-tzat etsi z-u-en Jaungoiko-a-k Ebe atsegintoki-an.
beautiful.PRO regard_as.PEF TRA.PST God.ERG Eve Garden_of_Eden.LOC

Chapter 18

(1) a. Ze(r) ordu da?
what time be.SYN
b. Ze(r) gai e-ra-bil-tzen da eta zein hizkuntza-ta-n?
what subject treat.IPF ITR and which language.LOC

(2) a. No-la arraio e-zagu(t)-tu ote d-u aita-k horr-e(n)-la-ko neska bat?
how EXP get_to_know.PEF DUB TRA Father.IDF.ERG like_that.ADN girl a
b. Zer arraio-ren bila da-bil gu-re Peru?
what EXP.GEN in_search_of.PRE go_around.SYN we.GEN Peter
c. Nor arraio-rekin ote da-bil Xu?
who EXP.SOC DUB go_around.SYN Xu
d. Eta no-n arraio-tik dei-tzen d-i-da-k?
and where.LOC EXP.ELA call.IPF /1/2SOL.DTR
e. Zer arraiopola gerta-tu da hemen?
what EXP happen.PEF ITR here.LOC
f. No-la demontre bizi-ko n-a-iz?
how EXP live.FUT 1.ITR
g. Zer mila___demonio pasa-tzen da hemen?
what EXP happen.IPF ITR here.LOC
h. Zer mila___sorgin pentsa-tu d-u-te zu-re haurr-ek?
what EXP think.PEF /PLU.TRA you.GEN child.PLU.ERG

(3) a. Nor-k nor-i e-ma-n d-i-o?— galde-tu-ko d-u norbait-e-k. Erdar(a)-a-k euskar(a)-a-ri, ala euskar(a)-a-k erdar(a)-a-ri?
who.ERG who.DAT give.PEF DTR ask.FUT TRA someone.ERG Spanish.ERG Basque.DAT or Basque.ERG Spanish.DAT
b. Nor-k nor-i zer e-ma-n d-i-o?
who.ERG who.DAT what give.PEF DTR

(4) a. Nor-k zer e-gi-n-en d-u?
who.ERG what do.FUT TRA
b. Nor-k zer behar d-u?
who.ERG what need.PPR TRA
c. Mintzo-rik eta hizkuntza-rik iza-n ez ba-li-tz, nor-k zer i-ra-kats-i-ko z-u-en?
speech.PAR and language.PAR be.PEF not CDP.ITR.COD who.ERG what teach.FUT TRA.PST

(5) a. Nor ezar har-en orde?
who put.RAD yonder.GEN in_place_of.PRE
b. Zer-ga(i)-tik negar e-gi-n?
what.MOT weeping.IDF do
c. Zer e-gi-n hori ja-ki-te-ko?
what do that find_out.VEN.ADN
d. No-la uler-tu istilu hori?
how understand mess that

(6) a. Ez da-ki-t klinika-ra j-oa-n ala hemen geldi.
not know./1.SYT clinic.ALL go or here.LOC stay.RAD
b. Orain ez da-ki-t hemen geldi-tu ala j-oa-n.
now not know./1.SYT here.LOC stay or go
c. Ez ne-ki-en zer e-ra-ntzu-n.
not know./1.SYT.PST what answer
d. Jainko-a-k e-ra-ku(t)s-ten z-i-e-n no-n-dik j-oa-n.
God.ERG show.IPF /PLU/.DTR.PST where.ELA go
e. Ber-a-k agin-tzen d-u no-n zer lan e-gi-n.
he_himself.ERG command.IPF TRA where.LOC what job do

(7) a. Ez da-ki-t e-zagu(t)-tzen d-u-zu-n.
not know./1.SYT know.IPF /2.TRA.NCZ
b. Ez da-ki-t gezurr-a d-en hori.
not know./1.SYT lie be.SYN.NCZ that
c. Hon-e-k galde e-gi-ten d-i-o har-tu d-u-en esne-a.
this_one.ERG question.IDF do.IDF DTR take.PEF TRA.NCZ milk

(8) a. E-ntzu-ten al d-u-zu-n galde-tzen d-i-zu-t.
hear.IPF INT /2.TRA.NCZ ask.IPF /2/1.DTR
b. Ez al z-i-zu-te-n galde-tu beti hemen bizi behar al
not INT /2/PLU.DTR.PST ask.PEF always here.LOC live.PPR have_to.PPR INT
z-en-u-e(n)-n?
/2.TRA.PST.NCZ
c. J-oa-n-go al d-en galdegi-n d-i-o-te.
go.FUT INT ITR.NCZ ask.PEF //PLU.DTR

(9) a. Kontu-z! Ez da-ki-zu senargai-rik ba ote d-u-en.
watch_out not know./2.SYT fiancé.PAR AFF DUB have.SYT.NCZ
b. Nor-k da-ki inguru hau-e-ta-ko-ak ez ote z-a-r-e-te-n?
who.ERG know.SYT part this.PLU.ADN.ZEP.PLU not DUB be.2PLU.SYN.NCZ

(10) a. Zer gerta-tu ote ze(-n)-n ezin pentsa-tu-z, . . .
what happen.PEF DUB ITR.PST.NCZ NPP guess.PTC.IDF.INS
b. Ez da-ki-t zer e-karr-i ote d-u-en.
not know./1.SYT what bring.PEF DUB TRA.NCZ
c. Zer-ta-ko hots e-gi-n ote d-i-o-n galde-tzen d-i-o ber-e
what.DES sound.IDF make.PEF DUB DTR.NCZ ask.IPF DTR he_himself.GEN
buru-a-ri.
head.DAT

(11) a. Markos ote da-torr-en n-a-go.
Markos DUB come.SYN.NCZ wonder.1.SYN

b. Zerbait esa-n ote z-i-da(-n)-n n-en-go-en.
something say.PEF DUB /1/.DTR.PST.NCZ wonder.1.SYN.PST

c. N-a-go kofesio on-a e-gi-n ote d-u-da-n.
wonder.1.SYN confession good make.PEF DUB /1.TRA.NCZ

(12) a. Beldur n-a-iz ni-re etxeko-ak haserre-tu-ko ote za-i-z-ki-da-n.
fear.IDF 1.ITR I.GEN member_of_the_family.PLU get_angry.FUT DUB 1/PLU.DIT.NCZ

b. Beldur n-a-iz ez d-en azken-a iza-n-go.
fear.IDF 1.ITR not ITR.NCZ last be.FUT

(13) a. Beldur n-a-iz ez ote d-en ero-tu-ko.
fear.IDF 1.ITR EXP DUB ITR.NCZ go_mad.FUT

b. Beldur n-a-iz ez ote d-i-o-gu-n kalte ikaragarri-a e-gi-n-go.
fear.IDF 1.ITR EXP DUB //PLU.DTR.NCZ harm tremendous do.FUT

(14) a. Zer da-ki-zu zu-k zer zor d-i-o-da-n ni-k inor-i?
what know./2.SYT you.ERG what debt.IDF //1.DTR.NCZ I.ERG anyone.DAT

b. Ni-k e-ra-kuts-i-ko d-i-o-t horr-i bi eta bi zenbat d-ir-en!
I.ERG show.FUT //1.DTR that_one.DAT two and two how_much be.PLU.SYN.NCZ

(15) a. No-ra z-oa-z-en ba al da-ki-zu?
where.ALL go.2.SYN.NCZ AFF INT know./2.SYT

b. Baina hori no-n-go-a d-en ere ez da-ki-gu.
but that_one where_from be.SYN.NCZ even not know./1PLU.SYT

c. Nahigabe-tzen g-a-it-u-en ala ez, Jainko-a-k da-ki.
distress.IPF 1PLU/.TRA.NCZ or not God.ERG know.SYT

(16) a. Nor-k uki-tu z-a-it-u-en galde-tzen d-u-zu?
who.ERG touch.PEF 2/.TRA.NCZ ask.IPF /2.TRA

b. No-r(a)-antz jo-ko d-u-gu-n galde-tzen d-u-t.
where.TEN go_to.FUT /1PLU.TRA.NCZ ask.IPF /1.TRA

c. Zer gerta-tu za-i-zu-n esa-n al d-io-zu?
what happen.PEF 2/.DIT.NCZ tell.PEF INT //2.DTR

d. Etxe hau nor-k goberna-tzen d-u-en ez da-ki-t.
house this who.ERG manage.IPF TRA.NCZ not know./1.SYT

(17) a. Zerbait nahi ote d-u-en galdegi-te-ra n-oa.
something want.PPR DUB TRA.NCZ ask.VEN.ALL go.1.SYN

b. Barne-an ze-go-e(n)-n ala ez ja-ki-n behar ze-n lehen-ik.
inside.LOC be.ITR.PST.NCZ or not know have_to.PPR ITR.PST first.STA

(18) a. Zu-e-ta-ri(k)-ko inor-k ez d-i-t no-ra n-oa-n galde-tzen.
you.PLU.ELA.ADN anyone.ERG not /1/.DTR where.ALL go.1.SYN.NCZ ask.IPF

b. Baina ez d-i-a-t orain-dik zer nahi d-u-a-n uler-tzen.
but not /2SOL/1.DTR still what want.PPR /2SOL.TRA.NCZ understand.IPF

(19) a. Ines-i ez n-i-o-n konta-tu zer gerta-tu ze(-n)-n.
Ines.DAT not //1.DTR.PST tell.PEF what happen.PEF ITR.PST.NCZ
b. Ez d-u inor-k ja-ki-n-go no-n-go-a d-en.
not TRA anyone.ERG know.FUT where.LOC.ADN.ZEP be.SYN.NCZ
c. Ez da-ki-t zer esa-n nahi d-u-zu-n.
not know./1.SYT what say want.PPR /2.TRA.NCZ
d. Inor-k ez z-u-en uler-tu zer-ga(i)-tik esa-n z-i-o(-n)-n hori.
anyone.ERG not TRA.PST understand.PEF what.MOT say.PEF DTR.PST.NCZ that
e. Kontura-tzen al z-a-r-a nor-ekin bizi z-a-r-en?
realize.IPF INT 2.ITR who.SOC live.PPR 2.ITR.NCZ

(20) a. Zu-k ba-da-ki-zu nor n-a-iz-en.
you.ERG AFF.know./2.SYT who be.1.SYN.NCZ
b. Ba al da-ki-k zer d-en maitasun-a?
AFF INT know./2SOL.SYT what be.SYN.NCZ love

(21) a. E-sa-n-go d-i-zu-t euskar(a)-a zer-ga(i)-tik ez d-en hil-ko.
tell.FUT /2/1.DTR Basque what.MOT not ITR.NCZ die.FUT
b. E-sa-n-go d-i-zu-t euskar(a)-a zer-ga(i)-tik hil-ko ez d-en.
tell.FUT /2/1.DTR Basque what.MOT die.FUT not ITR.NCZ

(22) a. Miren-e-k galde-tu d-i-gu etxe-a orain-dik ez (al) d-en eror-i.
Mary.ERG ask.PEF /1PLU/.DTR house yet not INT ITR.NCZ fall.PEF
b. Miren-e-k galde-tu d-i-gu etxe-a orain-dik eror-i ez (al) d-en.
Mary.ERG ask.PEF /1PLU/.DTR house yet fall.PEF not INT ITR.NCZ

(23) a. Beldur n-a-iz gu-re etxe-a ez ote d-en eror-i.
fear.IDF be.1.SYN we.GEN house EXP DUB ITR.NCZ fall.PEF
b. Beldur n-a-iz gu-re etxe-a eror-i ez ote d-en.
fear.IDF be.1.SYN we.GEN house fall.PEF EXP DUB ITR.NCZ

(24) a. Ba-da-ki-zu gero zer no-n da-go-en.
AFF.know./2.TRA then what where.LOC be.SYN.NCZ
b. Nor nor d-en nor-k e-zagu(t)-tu?
who who be.SYN.NCZ who.ERG recognize
c. Ni-re ama-ren alab(a)-a-ri ez d-i-o Ana=Mari-k zer zer
I.GEN mother.IDF.GEN daughter.DAT not DTR Ana-Mari.ERG what what
d-en e-ra-kuts-i-ko.
be.SYN.NCZ show.FUT
d. Ni-k zer da-ki-t ba nor no-n da-bil-en?
I.ERG what know./1.SYT AFF who where.LOC walk.SYN.NCZ

e. Ber-e kezka guzti-a: ama nor no-n z-u-e(n)-n
he_himself.GEN concern all mother.IDF who where.LOC have.SYT.PST.NCZ
ja-ki-te-a.
know.VEN

(25) a. Hon-(r)a no-la e-zagu(t)-tu n-u-e(n)-n.
here.ALL how get_to_know.PEF /1.TRA.PST.NCZ
b. Jaun-a, horr-(r)a zer hatzema-n d-u-da-n.
sir there.ALL what find.PEF /1.TRA.NCZ
c. Horr-(r)a zer e-gi-n d-u-en Jaun-a-k en-e-tzat.
there.ALL what do.PEF TRA.NCZ Lord.ERG I.BEN
d. Ha-ra zer esa-ten d-i-zu-e-da-n ni-k, Paulo-k:...
over_there.ALL what say.IPF /2PLU/1.DTR.NCZ I.ERG Paul.ERG
e. Ha-ra non-dik da-tor-ki-gu-n orain-go larrialdi hau.
over_there.ALL where.ELA come.1PLU/.DYN.NCZ now.ADN distress this

(26) a. Eta hon-(r)a no-n da-tor-ki-gu-n Loidi ber-e lehenbizi-ko
and here.ALL where.LOC come.1PLU/.DYN.NCZ Loidi he_himself.GEN first
nobel(a)-a-rekin.
novel.SOC
b. Hon-(r)a no-n sor-tu za-i-gu-n bat=bat-e-an nobelista bat.
here.ALL where.LOC born.PEF 1PLU/.DIT.NCZ one.IDF-one.LOC novelist a
c. Arrats-e-an, hor-ra no-n da-torr-en gizon zahar bat soro-ko
evening.LOC there.ALL where.LOC come.SYN.NCZ man old a.IDF field.ADN
lan-e-tik.
work.ELA
d. Eta horr-(r)a no-n i-kus-ten d-u-en emakume-a ber-e
and there.ALL where.LOC see.IPF TRA.NCZ woman he_himself.GEN
oin-e-ta-n e-tza-n-ik.
foot.PLU.LOC lie.PEF.STA
e. Ha-ra no-n d-ir-en mendi maite-ak, ha-ra
over_there.ALL where.LOC be.PLU.SYN.NCZ mountain beloved.PLU over_there.ALL
no-n d-ir-en zelai-ak.
where.LOC be.PLU.SYN.NCZ plain.PLU

(27) a. Zer gizon handi-a d-en!
what man great.DEF be.SYN.NCZ
b. Zer sorgin pare-a e-gi-n-en d-u-zu-e-n bi-ek!
what witch.IDF pair.DEF make.FUT /2PLU.TRA.NCZ two.ZEP.PLU.ERG
c. Zenbat aldi-z bil-du nahi iza-n d-it-u-da-n zur-e seme-ak!
how_many time.INS gather want.PPR have.PEF PLU/1.TRA.NCZ you.GEN son.PLU

d. Ze(r) on-ak da-u-de-n gerezi hori-ek!
what good.PLU be.PLU.SYN.NCZ cherry this.PLU

e. Zein zoriontsu n-a-iz-en eta bat=bat-e-an bizi-a zein ederr-a kausi-tzen d-u-da-n!
which happy.IDF be.1.SYN.NCZ and one.IDF-one.LOC life which nice find.IPF /1.TRA.NCZ

f. Zein makal-ak iza-n g-a-r-en! Lotsa-tu e-gi-ten n-a-iz!
which spineless.PLU be.PEF 1PLU.ITR.NCZ feel_ashamed do.IPF 1.ITR

(28) a. Ez da-ki-gu nor d-en-ik.
not know./1PLU.TRA who be.SYN.PCZ

b. Eskritura sant(a)-ak ez d-i-gu Ester noiz hil ze-(n)-n-ik e-sa-ten.
scripture holy.ERG not /1PLU/.DTR Esther when die.PEF ITR.PST.PCZ tell.IPF

(29) a. Hazael-e-k galde-tu z-i-o-n ea zer-ta-ko negar e-gi-ten z-u-e(n)-n.
Hazael.ERG ask.PEF DTR.PST WCC what.DES crying.IDF do.IPF TRA.PST.NCZ

b. Ea no-n bizi z-a-r-en nahi n-u-ke ja-ki-n.
WCC where.LOC live.PPR be.2.SYN.NCZ want.PPR /1.TRA.COD know

c. Begira-tu n-u-en ea zer gerta-tzen ze(-n)-n.
look.PEF /1.TRA.PST WCC what happen.IPF ITR.PST.NCZ

d. Ea zer d-io-te-n elkarr-i e-ntzu-n behar du-gu.
WCC what say./PLU.SYT.NCZ each_other.DAT hear must.PPR /1PLU.TRA

(30) a. Ea diru-rik falta ote ze(-n)-n galde-tu z-i-o-n etxekoandre-a-ri detektibe-a-k.
WCC money.PAR lack.IDF DUB be.SYN.PST.NCZ ask.PEF DTR.PST lady_of_the_house.DAT detective.ERG

b. Biharamon-e-an ea elkarr-ekin atera-ko ote g-in-e(-n)-n galde-tu n-i-o-n.
next_day.LOC WCC each_other.SOC go_out.FUT DUB 1PLU.ITR.PST.NCZ ask.PEF //1.DTR.PST

c. Beste zenbait-i ere galde-tu iza-n d-i-e-t bat=bat-e-an ea itzul-i-ko z-i-da-te(-n)-n.
other some.DAT also ask.PEF have.PEF /PLU/1.DTR one.IDF-one.LOC WCC translate.FUT /1/PLU.DTR.PST.NCZ

(31) a. E-go-n, ea da-tor-ki-o-n Elias salba-tze-ra!
wait WCC come.DYN.NCZ Elias save.VEN.ALL

b. Ea zenbat da-uka-da-n.
WCC how_much have./1.DYT.NCZ

c. Joño, ea gauz(a)-ak pixka bat zuzen-tzen d-it-u-gu-n!
EXP WCC thing.PLU bit a rectify.IPF PLU/1PLU.TRA.NCZ

d. Ea organizazio-a-k zerbait esa-ten d-u-en.
WCC organization.ERG something say.IPF TRA.NCZ

e. Ama-k ea jaits-i-ko ote z-a-r-en afal-tze-ra!
Mother.ERG WCC come_down.FUT DUB 2.ITR.NCZ have_supper.VEN.ALL

(32) a. Nor-k da-ki laino-ak d-ir-en-etz?
who.ERG know.SYT cloud.PLU PLU.ITR.NCZ

b. N-a-go ea buru gogorr-a d-u-zu-n-etz.
wonder.1.SYN WCC head thick /2.TRA.NCZ

c. N-a-go ha(r-en)-la_ere, ez d-u-da-n-etz Afrika hauta-tu-ko.
wonder.1.SYN yet WCC /1.TRA.NCZ Africa choose.FUT

d. Ba-da-ki-zu, jaun-a, ez d-en-etz hori hitz-e-z hitz egi(a)-a.
AFF.know./2.SYT lord not be.SYN.NCZ that word.IDF.INS word.IDF truth

e. Hori egi(a)-a d-en-etz laster i-kus-i-ko d-u-gu.
that truth be.SYN.NCZ soon see.FUT /1PLU.TRA

(33) a. No-n da Anton?... Auskalo!... Aspaldi ez d-u-gu
where.LOC ITR Tony IIJ for_a_long_time not have./1PLU.SYT
har-en berri-rik.
yonder_one.GEN news.PAR

b. —Egun on, Kornelio, no-n da ni-re senarr-a?
day good.IDF Neil where.LOC ITR I.GEN husband
—Eta zer galde-tzen d-i-da-zu ni-ri? Auskalo!
and what ask.IPF /1/2.DTR I.DAT IIJ

(34) a. Auskalo zer e-gi-n-go d-u-en beste-(ren)-la.
IIJ what do.FUT TRA.NCZ otherwise

b. Auskalo zenbat kazetari e-torr-i-ko d-ir-en gaur.
IIJ how_many journalist come.FUT PLU.ITR.NCZ today

c. Auskalo zer informazio da-uka-a-n hi-k.
IIJ what information have./2SOL.NCZ you.SOL.ERG

d. Auskalo zenbat denbora-z jo d-u-en ni esna-tu arte.
IIJ how_many time.IDF.INS ring.PEF TRA.NCZ I wake_up until

(35) a. Ba-da-ki-zu oso emakume ederr-a n-in-tz-e(n)-la.
AFF.know./2.SYT very woman beautiful be.1.SYN.PST.LCZ

b. Antzema-ten da euskaldun-a z-a-r-ela.
notice.IPF ITR Basque be.2.SYN.LCZ

c. Ez al d-u-zu i-kus-ten jan(t)z-te-n ari n-a-iz-ela?
not INT /2.TRA see.IPF get_dressed.VEN.LOC be_busy.PPR 1.ITR.LCZ

d. Ez d-u-t esa-n nahi ez da-ki-ela euskara-z mintza-tze-n.
not /1.TRA say want.PPR not know.SYT.LCZ Basque.IDF.INS speak.VEN.LOC

(36) a. Baina Gotzon-e-k ni hil n-ind-u-e(-n)-la zeha-ro sinets-i z-u-en
but Gotzon.ERG I kill.PEF 1/.TRA.PST.LCZ really believe.PEF TRA.PST
Iñaki-k.
Iñaki.ERG

b. Zeru-rik ba-d-ela sine(t)s-ten al d-u-zu?
heaven.PAR AFF.be.SYN.LCZ believe.IPF INT /2.TRA

(37) a. Eta Jainko-a-k on-a ze(-n)-la i-kus-i z-u-en.
and God.ERG good ITR.PST.LCZ see.PEF TRA.PST

b. Sekula ez z-in-e(n)-la e-torr-i-ko uste n-u-en.
ever not 2.ITR.PST.LCZ come.FUT think.PPR /1.TRA.PST

c. Mediku-a ere laster e-torr-i-ko d-ela uste d-u-t.
doctor too soon come.FUT ITR.LCZ think.PPR /1.TRA

d. Nor-en soro-an e-gi-n d-u-zu lan? . . . Rut-e-k, ordu-an, Booz izen-e-ko
who.GEN field.LOC do.PEF /2.TRA work.IDF Ruth.ERG then Boaz name.ADN
bat-en soro-an lan e-gi-n z-u-e(n)-la konta-tu z-i-o-n Noemi-ri.
a.GEN field.LOC work.IDF do.PEF TRA.PST.LCZ tell.PEF DTR.PST Naomi.DAT

(38) a. Nor n-a-iz-ela uste d-u-zu-e?
who 1.ITR.LCZ think.PPR /2PLU.TRA

b. Eta zu-ek, nor n-a-iz-ela d-io-zu-e?
and you.PLU who 1.ITR.LCZ say./2PLU.SYT

c. Bultz(a)-a nor-k e-gi-n d-i-zu-la uste d-u-zu?
push who.ERG do.PEF /2/.DTR.LCZ think.PPR /2.TRA

d. Zer d-ela uste d-u-zu barberu-a?
what be.SYN.LCZ think.PPR /2.TRA barber

(39) Ez n-u-ke ero-a d-ela e-sa-n-go.
not /1.TRA.COD crazy ITR.LCZ say.FUT

(40) a. Uste d-u-t alkate-a ez d-ela e-torr-i.
think.PPR /1.TRA mayor not ITR.LCZ come.PEF

b. ?Uste d-u-t alkate-a e-torr-i ez d-ela.
think.PPR /1.TRA mayor come.PEF not ITR.LCZ

(41) a. Ez n-ind-u-te(-n)-la konpreni-tzen irudi-tzen zi-tza-i-da-n.
not 1/PLU.TRA.PST.LCZ understand.IPF seem.IPF 1/.DIT.PST

b. Den-a on-gi j-oa-n-go ze(-n)-la irudi-tu zi-tza-i-e-n.
everything well go.FUT ITR.PST.LCZ seem.PEF PLU/.DIT.PST

c. Fani-ri zerbait gerta-tzen za-i-o-la bist(a)-an da-go.
Fani.DAT something happen.IPF DIT.LCZ sight.LOC be.SYN

d. Bist(a)-an da-go bi alde d-it-u-ela teoria hon-e-k.
sight.LOC be.SYN two aspect.IDF PLU/.TRA.LCZ theory this.ERG

e. Eta bist(a)-an da ez da-ki-ela.
and sight.LOC be.SYN not know.SYT.LCZ

(42) a. Bitxi / bitxi-a da abuztu-an elurr-a e-gi-te-a.
strange.IDF strange be.SYN August.LOC snow do.VEN
b. Bitxi / bitxi-a da abuztu-an elurr-a e-gi-n-a / e-gi-n iza-n-a.
strange.IDF strange be.SYN August.LOC snow do.PEF.SIN do.PEF have.PEF.SIN
c. Bitxi / bitxi-a da abuztu-an no-la e-gi-ten d-u-en elurr-a.
strange.IDF strange be.SYN August.LOC how do.IPF TRA.NCZ snow

(43) Ohargarri-a da galder(a)-a-k bai, baina erantzun-a-k ez da-rama-la *ba*-rik.
remarkable be.SYN question.ERG yes but answer.ERG not carry.SYT.LCZ *ba*.PAR

(44) a. Ageri da eri d-ela gu-re Maria.
apparent.IDF be.SYN ill.IDF be.SYN.LCZ we.GEN Maria
b. Ageri da engaina-tu d-it-u-ela konfesore-ak.
apparent.IDF be.SYN deceive.PEF PLU/.TRA.LCZ confessor.PLU
c. Gizon azkarr-a d-ela ezagun da.
person clever be.SYN.LCZ obvious.IDF be.SYN
d. Apaiztegi-ko kutsu-a ez za-i-zu-la j-oa-n ezagun da.
seminary.ADN taint not 2/.DIT.LCZ go.PEF obvious be.SYN
e. Jakin-a da bi klase-ta-n bana-tu z-it-u-e(n)-la
well-known be.SYN two class.IDF.LOC divide.PEF PLU/.TRA.PST.LCZ
euskalki-ak.
Basque_dialect.PLU
f. Nabari za-i-o ez d-ela hemen-go-a.
obvious.IDF be.DIT not be.SYN.LCZ from_here
g. Nabari za-i-o euskaldun-a ez d-ela.
obvious.IDF be.DIT Basque not be.SYN.LCZ

(45) a. Egi(a)-a al da inoiz zizp(a)-a-rekin irte-n eta ia garbi-tu
truth INT be.SYN one_time rifle.SOC go_out.PEF and almost kill.PEF
z-int-u-e(n)-la?
2/.TRA.PST.LCZ
b. Gezurr-a da Frantzia-ko errege-a urzale-a d-ela.
lie be.SYN France.ADN king teetotaller be.SYN.LCZ

(46) a. Ni-k, aldi-z, ez n-in-tz-e(-n)-la j-oa-n-en, ihes e-gi-n n-u-en goi-ko
I.ERG however not 1.ITR.PST.LCZ go.FUT flight.IDF do.PEF /1.TRA.PST above
sala-ra.
room.ALL
b. Ha(r-en)-la uste z-u-e(n)-la ber-a-k.
so think.PPR TRA.PST.LCZ he_himself.ERG

(47) a. Bai eder-ki bizi g-a-r-ela hemen!
AFF nicely live.PPR 1PLU.ITR.LCZ here.LOC
b. Bai on-a z-a-r-ela ni-rekin, Jaun-a!
AFF good 2.SYN.LCZ I.SOC sir

(48) a. Orain bai mintzo z-a-r-ela argi!
now AFF speech be.2.SYN.LCZ clear
b. Hi-k bai e-gi-n behar-ko d-u-na-la negar!
you.SOL.ERG AFF do need.FUT /2.SOL.FEM.TRA.LCZ crying.IDF

(49) a. Ba-n-e-ki-en gizon zorrotz-a z-a-r-ena.
AFF.know./1.SYT.PST man hard be.2.SYN.NAZ
b. Diruzale-a ez z-a-r-ena ba-da-ki-t.
money_hungry not be.2SYN.NAZ AFF.know./1.SYT
c. Ikas-i z-u-en ... gizon-a-k gauza guzti-e-ta-n txit apal-a iza-n behar
learn.PEF TRA.PST man.ERG thing all.PLU.LOC very humble be should.PPR
z-u-ke-e(n)-na.
TRA.COD.PST.NAZ
d. Gazte hau-ek ez d-ir-a kontura-tzen, etxe-ko lan guzti-ak jai
youngster this.PLU not PLU.ITR realize.IPF house.ADN job all.PLU festival
arrats-e-ta-n gu-ri u(t)z-ten d-i-z-ki-gu-na.
evening.PLU.LOC we.DAT leave.IPF PLU/1PLU/.DTR.NAZ

(50) a. Eta seguru n-a-go gu-re asmo-a on-tzat har-tu-ko d-u-te-na.
and sure.PRE be.1.SYN we.GEN plan good.PRO take.FUT /PLU.TRA.NAZ
b. Bi-ek oso elkar maite d-u-te-na ez d-u-t ni-k
two.ZEP.PLU.ERG very each_other love.PPR /PLU.TRA.NAZ not /1.TRA I.ERG
inon-go zalantza-rik e-gi-ten.
anywhere.LOC.ADN doubt.PAR do.IPF
c. Agiri-an da-go sortalde-ko ahoberokeria bat d-ena hori.
wide-open.LOC be.SYN east.ADN exaggeration a be.SYN.NAZ that
d. Hai-(e)-en esan-e-ta-n gezurr-ik ez ze(-n)-na garbi
yonder_one.PLU.GEN statement.PLU.LOC lie.PAR not ITR.PST.NAZ clear.PRE
ze-go-en.
be.SYN.PST
e. Bai, ba-da-kusa-t oso ederr-a z-a-r-ena.
yes AFF.see./1.SYT very beautiful 2.SYN.NAZ
f. Ni-k aitor-tzen d-i-zu-e-t eskas-a n-in-tz-e-(n)-na.
I.ERG admit.IPF /2PLU/1.DTR inadequate be.1.SYN.PST.NAZ

(51) a. Ba-da-ki-gu e-torr-i d-ela sorgin hori.
AFF.know./1PLU.SYT come.PEF ITR.LCZ witch that

b. Ba-da-ki-gu sorgin hori e-torr-i d-ena.
AFF.know./1PLU.SYT witch that come.PEF ITR.NAZ

(52) a. Ez d-u-t uste oker n-a-go-en-ik.
not /1.TRA think.PPR wrong.PRE be.1.SYN.PCZ
b. Ez d-io-t inor-k gai(t)z-ki e-gi-n z-u-e(n)-n-ik.
not say./1.SYT anybody.ERG wrongly act.PEF TRA.PST.PCZ
c. Ez d-u-k esa-n-go hitzontzi-a n-a-iz-en-ik.
not /2.SOL.TRA say.FUT chatterbox be.1.SYN.PCZ
d. Ez n-e-ki-en hain berandu ze(-n)-n-ik.
not know./1.SYT.PST so late.IDF be.SYN.PST.PCZ
e. Ez d-irudi gaixo da-go-en-ik.
not appear.SYT ill.PRE be.SYN.PCZ
f. Ez d-u-t ni-k uka-tu-ko auzi hori larri-a d-en-ik.
not /1.TRA I.ERG deny.FUT matter that important be.SYN.PCZ

(53) a. Uste al d-u-zu lo-ta-n e-go-n-go d-en-ik?
think.PPR INT /2.TRA sleep.IDF.LOC be.FUT ITR.PCZ
b. Zerri-ek hitz e-gi-ten d-u-te-n-ik inoiz e-ntzu-n al da?
pig.PLU.ERG word.IDF do.IPF /PLU.TRA.PCZ ever hear.PEF INT ITR
c. Ba al z-ene-ki-te-n On Lorentzo-k ezkon-tze-ko asmo-rik
AFF INT know./2PLU.SYT.PST Don Lorenzo.ERG get_married.VEN.ADN plan.PAR
z-u-e(n)-n-ik?
TRA.PST.PCZ

(54) a. Nor-k esa-n d-u gizon hon-e-k ni-re aita-ri kalte e-gi-n
who.ERG say.PEF TRA man this.ERG I.GEN father.IDF.DAT harm.IDF do.PEF
d-i-o-n-ik?
DTR.PCZ
b. Nor-k esa-n d-i-zu Zinkunegi italiano-a d-en-ik?
who.ERG say.PEF /2/.DTR Zinkunegi Italian be.SYN.PCZ
c. Nor-k esa-n d-i-zu zu-ri ni libre n-a-go-en-ik?
who.ERG say.PEF /2/.DTR you.DAT I free.PRE be.1.SYN.PCZ

(55) Uste ba-d-u-zu-e aditz kontu-an ere ber-e-ha(r-en)-la-ko batasun-a
think.PPR CDP./2PLU.TRA verb matter.LOC too immediately.ADN unification
behar d-u-gu-n-ik, . . .
need.PPR /1PLU.TRA.PCZ

(56) a. Hala___ere, Kathleen hil z-u-e(n)-n-ik uka-tu (z-u-en) ordu-an ere.
still Kathleen kill.PEF TRA.PST.PCZ deny.PEF TRA.PST then too
b. Eta Jainko-a-ren beharr-e-an g-a-r-en-ik aha(t)z-tu e-gi-ten za-i-gu.
and God.GEN need.LOC be.1PLU.SYN.PCZ forget do.IPF 1PLU/.DIT

(57) a. Uste d-u-t ez d-u-te-la (*d-u-te-n-ik) buka-tu.
think.PPR /1.TRA not /PLU.TRA.LCZ /PLU.TRA.PCZ finish.PEF
b. Ez d-u-t uste buka-tu d-u-te-n-ik.
not /1.TRA think.PPR finish.PEF /PLU.TRA.PCZ

(58) a. Gaur etxe hon-e-k errot(a)-a d-irudi.
today house this.ERG mill seem.SYT
b. Har-en begi-ek tximist(a)-ak z-irudi-te-n.
yonder_one.GEN eye.PLU.ERG lightning.PLU seem.PLU.SYT.PST

(59) a. Etorkizun handi-ko pilotari-a ote d-en d-irudi.
future great.ADN jai_alai_player DUB be.SYN.NCZ seem.SYT
b. Lo-ta-n da-u-de-la d-irudi.
sleep.IDF.LOC be.PLU.SYN.LCZ seem.SYT
c. Altube-k arrazoi z-u-e(n)-la d-irudi horr-e-ta-n.
Altube.ERG reason.IDF TRA.PST.LCZ seem.SYT that.LOC
d. Bahi-tu e-gi-n d-u-te-n-ik ez d-irudi, ber-a-z.
Kidnap do.PEF /PLU.TRA.PCZ not seem.SYT therefore

(60) a. Orain, ba-d-irudi euskar(a)-a-k ahalke d-ela.
now AFF.seem.SYT Basque.ERG shame.IDF be.SYN.LCZ
b. Mutil-a-k jatorr-a eta on-a d-ela d-irudi.
boy.ERG nice and pleasant be.SYN.LCZ seem.SYT
c. Zatitxo bat-e-k ba-d-irudi ez da-go-ela on-gi itzul-i-a.
little_fragment a.ERG AFF.seem.SYT not be.SYN.LCZ well render.PEF.SIN

(61) a. Ez d-irudi gaixo da-go-en-ik.
not seem.SYT ill.PRE be.SYN.PCZ
b. Ez z-irudi-en on-do i-kus-ten z-u-e(n)-n-ik.
not seem.SYT.PST well see.IPF TRA.PST.PCZ
c. Mutil-a-k ez d-irudi motel-a.
boy.ERG not seem.SYT sluggish

(62) a. Norbait eror-i ote d-en irudi-tu za-i-t.
somebody fall.PEF DUB ITR.NCZ seem.PEF 1/.DIT
b. Urduri ze-go-e(n)-la irudi-tu zi-tza-i-da-n.
nervous.PRE be.SYN.PST.LCZ seem.PEF 1/.DIT.PST

(63) a. Hon-e(n)-la d-io-zu e-gi-n-en d-u-zu-la.
this_way say./2.SYT do.FUT /2.TRA.LCZ
b. Nor d-io-te n-a-iz-ela jende-ek?
who say./PLU.SYT be.1.SYN.LCZ people.PLU.ERG
c. Zer uste z-u-te-n e-ma-n-go z-i-e(-n)-la Jainko-a-k?
what think.PPR /PLU.TRA.PST give.FUT /PLU/.DTR.PST.LCZ God.ERG

d. Zer uste d-u-zu-e e-gi-n z-u-e(n)-la?
what think.PPR /2PLU.TRA do.PEF TRA.PST.LCZ
e. Zer uste h-u-en ze(-n)-la bizi-tze-a?
what think.PPR /2.SOL.TRA.PST ITR.PST.LCZ live.VEN
f. Nor-ekin uste d-uzu e-torr-i z-in-e(-n)-la?
who.SOC think.PPR /2.TRA come.PEF 2.ITR.PST.LCZ
g. Noiz eta nor-ekin esa-n d-uzu j-oa-n z-a-r-ela zine-ra?
when and who.SOC say.PEF /2.TRA go.PEF 2.ITR.LCZ movies.ALL

(64) a. Etorkizun-e-ko-a, ez da-ki-gu e-ma-n-en za-i-gu-n-etz.
future.ADN.ZEP not know./1PLU.SYT give.FUT /1PLU/.DIT.NCZ
b. Paper-ak, ez da-ki-t no-la galdu d-it-u-en.
paper.PLU not know./1.SYT how lose.PEF PLU/.TRA.NCZ
c. Alab(a)-a-k, ez da-ki-t zer e-gi-n nahi-ko d-u-en.
daughter.ERG not know./1.SYT what do want.FUT TRA.NCZ
d. Sendagile-rik, ez d-u-t uste inoiz behar-ko d-u-da-n-ik.
doctor.PAR not /1.TRA think.PPR ever need.FUT /1.TRA.PCZ
e. Zu-re izeba horr-ekin, ez d-u-t uka-tu Parisera-tu n-a-iz-en-ik.
you.GEN aunt that.SOC not /1.TRA deny.PEF go_to_Paris.PEF 1.ITR.PCZ

(65) a. Esa-n eder-ki, baina e-gi-n, zer e-gi-ten d-u-gu?
say fine but do what do.IPF /1PLU.TRA
b. Gusta-tu bai, baina harri-tu, ez z-u-te-n horr-en-beste harri-tzen.
please yes but amaze not /PLU.TRA.PST that_much amaze.IPF
c. Hil, ez g-a-r-a guzti-ok hil-ko, baina bai guzti-ok izate-z alda-tu-ko.
die not 1PLU.ITR all.INC die.FUT but AFF all.INC nature.IDF.INS change.FUT

(66) a. E-ntzu-n, ez z-u-en ezer e-ntzu-ten.
hear not TRA.PST anything hear.IPF
b. Sor-tu, 1948-an sor-tu ze-n.
originate 1948.LOC originate.PEF ITR.PST
c. E-zagu(t)-tu, Salamanca-n
become_acquainted_with Salamanca.LOC
e-zagu(t)-tu n-u-en Altuna.
become_acquainted_with.PEF /1.TRA.PST Altuna
d. Aipa-tu, ez d-u ber-e buru-a baizik aipa-tzen.
cite not TRA he_himself.GEN head but cite.IPF

(67) a. Eta gosal-du ere, ez z-u-en sukalde-an presa-ka gosal-du.
and breakfast too not TRA.PST kitchen.LOC hurriedly breakfast.PEF
b. Eta sine(t)s-tu ere, ez da-ki-t sine(t)s-tu-ko z-i-zu-e(-n)-n.
and believe too not know./1.SYT believe.FUT /2PLU/.DTR.NCZ

(68) a. Eta sine(t)s-tu ere, ez da-ki-t e-gi-n z-i-zu-e(-n)-n.
and believe too not know./1.SYT do.PEF /2PLU/.DTR.NCZ
b. Saia-tu, behin-tzat, e-gi-n-go g-a-r-a.
try at_least do.FUT 1PLU.ITR

(69) Guda=ontzi ahul hai-ek arrisku den-e-ta-tik aska-tzen
warship weak yonder.PLU.ERG danger all.PLU.ELA free.IPF
z-it-u-zte(-n)-la-r-en uste-ta-n
PLU/PLU.TRA.PST.LCZ.IDF.GEN belief.IDF.LOC

(70) a. Jainko-a ba-d-ela-ko froga bat
God AFF.exist.SYN.LCZ.ADN proof a
b. Adiskide g-a-r-ela-ko ezaugarri-tzat
friend.IDF be.1PLU.SYN.LCZ.ADN sign.PRO
c. Santiago zaharr-en-a Espainia-ra e-torr-i ze(-n)-la-ko berri-ak
James old.SUP Spain.ALL come.PEF ITR.PST.LCZ.ADN report.PLU
d. No-ra-bait j-oa-n beharr-a z-u-te(-n)-la-ko aitzaki-an
somewhere.LOC go need have./PLU.SYT.PST.LCZ.ADN pretext.LOC
e. Bizi g-a-r-ela-ko seinale
life.IDF 1PLU.SYN.LCZ.ADN sign.IDF
f. Egoera mingarri bat-e-tik aska-tzen g-int-u-e(n)-la-ko poz-e-z
situation painful a.ELA free.IPF 1PLU/.TRA.PST.LCZ.ADN joy.IDF.INS
g. Ber-e parte-a iza-n-go d-u-ela-ko itxaropen-e-z
he_himself.GEN part have.FUT TRA.LCZ.ADN hope.IDF.INS
h. Ikasle hura hil-ko ez ze(-n)-la-ko zurrumurru-a
disciple yonder die.FUT not ITR.PST.LCZ.ADN rumor
i. Bloy pitzadura bat-e-an eror-i ze(-n)-la-ko albiste-a
Bloy crevice a.LOC fall.PEF ITR.PST.LC.ADN news
j. On-gi jarr-i z-a-r-ela-ko berri-ak ba-d-it-u-t.
well recover.PEF 2.ITR.LCZ.ADN report.PLU AFF.have.PLU/1.SYT
k. Menscher ero ze-go-ela-ko hots-a
Menscher crazy.PRE be.SYN.PST.LCZ.ADN rumor

(71) a. Su-a sor-tu-ko d-en beldurr-e-z
fire break_out.FUT ITR.NCZ fear.IDF.INS
b. Beste-ren bat-e-k emazte-a ostu-ko ote z-i-o(-n)-n beldurr-e-z
other.IDF.GEN a.ERG wife steal.FUT DUB DTR.PST.NCZ fear.IDF.INS

(72) a. Beldur n-a-iz hau n-u-e(n)-la azken itzuli-a.
fear.IDF 1.SYN this have./1.SYT.PST.LCZ last return
b. Biraolari gisa harri-ka e-ma-n-go ez d-i-da-te-la-ko
blasphemer.IDF as by_throwing_stones give.FUT EXP /1/PLU.DTR.LCZ.ADN

beldurr-a
fear

(73) a. Har-tu z-u-en ostalari-a-ren asto-a, ber-e-a
take.PEF TRA.PST innkeeper.GEN donkey he_himself.GEN.ZEP
z-u-e(n)-la-ko-an.
have.SYT.PST.LCZ.ADN.ZEP.LOC

b. Ezti-a n-e-karr-e(-n)-la-ko-an behazun-a e-karr-i d-u-t.
honey bring./1.SYT.PST.LCZ.ADN.ZEP.LOC gall bring.PEF /1.TRA

c. Mesede ederr-a e-gi-n z-i-o-te-n har-i, kalte e-gi-ten
favor beautiful do.PEF //PLU.DTR.PST yonder_one.DAT harm.IDF do.IPF
z-i-o-te(-n)-la-ko-an.
//PLU.DTR.PST.LCZ.ADN.LOC

d. Barbero bat-en-gan-(r)a e-ra-ma-n omen z-u-te-n, har-k
barber a.ALL take_to.PEF REP /PLU.TRA.PST yonder_one.ERG
senda-tu-ko z-u-e(n)-la-ko-an.
cure.FUT TRA.PST.LCZ.ADN.ZEP.LOC

(74) a. Ne-r(e-h)oni ere erraz-a ez d-ela-ko-an n-a-go.
I_myself also easy not be.SYN.LCZ.ADN.ZEP.LOC be.1.SYN

b. Detektibe bat-e-k lan-a hobe-ki e-gi-n-go l-u-ke-ela-ko-an g-a-u-de.
detective a.ERG job well.COP do.FUT TRA.COD.LCZ.ADN.LOC be.1PLU.SYN

c. Nor z-a-r-ela-ko-an z-a-u-de?
who be.2.SYN.LCZ.ADN.ZEP.LOC be.2.SYN

d. Huts-a-ren truke errespeta-tzen z-a-it-u-ela-ko-an, ala?
nought.GEN in_exchange_for.PRE revere.IPF 2/.TRA.LCZ.ADN.ZEP.LOC or

(75) a. Oso zabal-du-a ze-n herri-a-ren arte-an Mesias-a ustekabe-an azal-du-ko
very spread.PPF ITR.PST people.GEN among Messiah unexpectedly appear.FUT
ze(-n)-la-ko-a.
ITR.PST.LCZ.ADN.ZEP

b. Etxe-an da-u-de-la-ko-a da-uka-t.
house.LOC be.PLU.SYN.LCZ.ADN.ZEP have./1.SYT

(76) Den-a da-ki, eta ez ba-le-ki, da-ki-ela-ko-a e-gi-ten
everything know.SYT and not CDP.know.SYT.COD know.SYT.LCZ.ADN.ZEP make.IPF
d-u.
TRA

Chapter 19

(1) a. Nor ote da ni-re emazte-a-ren ohe-an da-go-en emakume itsusi hori?
who DUB be.SYN I.GEN wife.GEN bed.LOC be.SYN.NRE woman ugly that

b. Zain-tzen n-a-u-en frantses-a albo-ko gel(a)-an da-go.
guard.IPF 1/.TRA.NRE Frenchman side.ADN room.LOC be.SYN

c. Hor da-ra-ma-zu-n agenda-txo-a behar d-u-gu.
there.LOC carry./2.SYT.NRE notebook.DIM need.PPR /1PLU.TRA

d. Lagun-tzat e-ma-n d-i-da-zu-n emakume-a-k fruitu-a eskain-i d-i-t.
companion.PRO give.PEF /1/2.DTR.NRE woman.ERG fruit offer.PEF /1/.DTR

e. Ni-k lepo-a mo(t)z-tu n-i-o-(n)-n Joan huraxe pi(t)z-tu da.
I.ERG neck cut.PEF //1.DTR.PST.NRE John yonder.EMP revive.PEF ITR

(2) a. Ez da-go huts-ik e-gi-ten ez d-u-en gai(t)zkile-rik.
not be.SYN mistake.PAR make.IPF not TRA.NRE criminal.PAR

b. Bizi-a salba-tu ez z-i-da-(n)-n lagun-a
life save.PEF not /1/.DTR.PST.NRE mate

c. Bidart-e-k i-kus-ten ez z-it-u-e(n)-n malko-ak txuka-tu z-it-u-en.
Bidart.ERG see.IPF not PLU/.TRA.PST.NRE tear.PLU dry.PEF PLU/.TRA.PST

(3) a. Hau-ek z-ir-e-n, behin-ik behin, gogo-an d-u-da-n
this_one.PLU be.PLU.SYN.PST single_occasion.PAR once mind.LOC /1.TRA.NRE
gaitz-a-ren ezaugarri-ak.
disease.GEN symptom.PLU

b. Hau-ek z-ir-e-n, behin-ik behin, gogo-an d-it-u-da-n
this_one.PLU be.PLU.SYN.PST single_occasion.PAR once mind.LOC PLU/1.TRA.NRE
gaitz-a-ren ezaugarri-ak.
disease.GEN symptom.PLU

(4) a. Gizon-a-ri haurr-a e-ma-n d-i-o-n emakume-a hil da.
man.DAT child give.PEF DTR.NRE woman die.PEF ITR

b. Apaiz-a-k gizon-a-ri e-ma-n d-i-o-n emakume-a hil da.
priest.ERG man.DAT give.PEF DTR.NRE woman die.PEF ITR

c. Apaiz-a-k haurr-a e-ma-n d-i-o-n emakume-a hil da.
priest.ERG child give.PEF DTR.NRE woman die.PEF ITR

(4) E-ma-n d-i-o-n emakume-a hil da.
give.PEF DTR.NRE woman die.PEF ITR

(5) a. Izen-a aha(t)z-tu d-u-da-n norbait-e-k esan d-i-t.
name forget.PEF /1.TRA.NRE somebody.ERG tell.PEF /1/.DTR

b. **Etxe-ra-ino j-oa-n n-a-iz-en norbait-e-k esan d-i-t.
house.TER go.PEF 1.ITR.NRE somebody.ERG tell.PEF /1/.DTR

(6) a. Txutxo, gaur arte izen-ik ere ez n-e-ki-e(n)-n txakurr-a, . . .
Txutxo today until name.PAR even not know./1.SYT.PST.NRE dog

b. Kodigo-a e-zagu(t)-tzen ez n-u-e(n)-n sistema bat-en barru-an aurki-tzen
code know.IPF not /1.TRA.PST.NRE system a.GEN inside.LOC find.IPF

n-in-tz-e-n.
1.ITR.PST

c. Zer e-sa-n-go d-u-te aldegi-ten ba-d-u-t lehen hain zale-a iza-n
what say.FUT /PLU.TRA stay_away.IPF CDP./1.TRA earlier so fond be.PEF
n-a-iz-en fest(a)-e-ta-tik?
1.ITR.NRE festivity.PLU.ELA

d. Ea deretxo-rik paga-tu behar d-en gauza-rik bila-tzen d-u-gu-n.
WCC duty.PAR pay must.PPR ITR.NRE thing.PAR find.IPF /1PLU.TRA.NCZ

e. Nafarroa-ko errege-ek gain-e-an zin e-gi-ten z-u-te-(n)-n liburu
Navarra.ADN king.PLU.ERG top.LOC oath.IDF make.IPF /PLU.TRA.PST.NRE book
handi-a
big

f. Piarres-e-k pusk(a)-ak gain-e-an ezar-tzen d-it-u-en armairu-a
Peter.ERG thing.PLU top.LOC put.IPF PLU/.TRA.NRE chest

g. Gibel-e-an jarr-i n-a-iz-en gizon-a
back.LOC sit_down.PEF 1.ITR.NRE man

(7) a. Aurki-tu ote d-u-te akusa-tu n-ind-u-te(-n)-n krimen-a-ren egile-a?
find.PEF DUB /PLU.TRA accuse.PEF 1/PLU.TRA.PST.NRE crime.GEN author

b. Zu-ek ez z-en-u-te-n gu kontura-tu g-in-e(-n)-n arrisku-a i-kus-ten.
you.PLU.ERG not /2PLU.TRA.PST we realize.PEF 1PLU.ITR.PST.NRE danger see.IPF

c. Mintzaldi-a e-gi-n d-u-zu-n ida(t)zle-a ez n-u-en e-zagu-tzen.
lecture make.PEF /2.TRA.NRE author not /1.TRA.PST know.IPF

(8) a. Bizi z-a-r-e-te-n baserri-a ber-ekin e-ra-ma-n-go l-u-ke.
live.PPR 2PLU.ITR.NRE farm she_herself.SOC carry_away.FUT TRA.COD

b. G-e-u-n-de(-n)-n gel(a)-a har-en erretaul(a)-e-z bete-a ze-go-en.
stay.1PLU.SYN.PST.NRE room yonder_one.GEN painting.PLU.INS full be.SYN.PST

c. Gau-a e-gi-n behar z-u-e(n)-n etxe-ra-ino ja-rrai-tu zi-tza-i-z-ki-o-n.
night make be_to.PPR TRA.PST.NRE house.TER follow.PEF /PLU.DIT.PST

d. Laster j-oa-n-go h-a-iz, Arantxa, beste maitasun batzu-k iza-n-go
soon go.FUT 2SOL.ITR Arantxa other love_relationship some.PLU have.FUT
d-it-u-na-n etxe-ra.
PLU/2SOL.FEM.TRA.NRE house.ALL

e. Berandu ager-tu n-in-tz-e-n, gain-e-ra, leku huts-ik geldi-tzen ez
too_late appear.PEF 1.ITR.PST top.ALL place empty.PAR remain.IPF not
ze(-n)-n mundu-ra.
ITR.PST.NRE world.ALL

f. Lo z-a-u-tza-n lurr-a e-ma-n-go d-i-zu-e-t zu-ri eta zu-re
asleep.PRE lie.2.SYN.NRE land give.FUT /2PLU/1.DTR you.DAT and you.GEN
ondorengo-e-i.
descendant.PLU.DAT

(9) a. Abendu-a-ren hamaika; ni ama-ren-gan-ik atera n-in-tz-e(-n)-n egun-a.
December.GEN eleven I mother.IDF.ELA come_out.PEF 1.ITR.PST.NRE day

b. Lan-ik e-gi-ten ez d-u-da-n egun-e-ta-n pattarr-a-rekin buka-tzen d-u-t.
work.PAR do.IPF not /1.TRA.NRE day.PLU.LOC brandy.SOC finish.IPF /1.TRA

c. Zoragarri-a iza-n-go da zu ezkon-tzen z-a-r-en egun-a.
wonderful be.FUT ITR you marry.IPF 2.ITR.NRE day

d. E-torr-i-ko da senar berri-a ken-du-ko d-i-e-te-n egun-a.
come.FUT ITR husband new take_away.FUT /PLU/PLU.DTR.NRE day

(10) a. Z-oa-z e-torr-i z-in-e(-n)-n leku-ra!
go.SYN.IMP come.PEF 2.ITR.PST.NRE place.ALL

b. Itzul-i-ko n-a-iz atera n-a-iz-en ni-re etxe-ra.
return.FUT 1.ITR go_out.PEF 1.ITR.NRE I.GEN house.ALL

c. Da-bil-en bide-a-k harrapa-tu-ko d-u.
walk.SYN.NRE road.ERG catch_up_with.FUT TRA

d. Zi-h-oa(n)-n bide guzti-e-ta-ra atera-tzen zi-tza-i-o-n Simon.
go.SYN.PST.NRE road all.PLU.ALL go_out.IPF DTR.PST Simon

(11) a. Ken-du d-u-gu igo behar ez z-u-e(n)-n toki-t-ik.
remove.PEF /1PLU.TRA ascend have_to.PPR not TRA.PST.NRE place.ELA

b. Harri-a bota d-i-da-n begi-tik ez d-u-t ezer i-kus-ten.
stone throw.PEF /1/.DTR.NRE eye.ELA not /1.TRA anything see.IPF

c. Eta Hura j-oa-ten ze(-n)-n herriska, herri eta auzo-e-ta-n,
and Yonder_one go.IPF ITR.PST.NRE village.IDF town.IDF and hamlet.PLU.LOC
gaixo-ak larrain-e-ta-n ipin-tzen z-i-z-ki-o-te-n.
sick.ZEP.PLU threshing_floor.PLU.LOC put_out.IPF PLU//PLU.DTR.PST

(12) a. J-oa-n n-a-iz-en gizon-(e)-ekin e-ra-ma-n d-u-t.
go.PEF 1.ITR.NRE man.PLU.SOC carry.PEF /1.TRA

b. Zer-ga(i)-tik hauts-i behar d-u-k behin ohera-tzen h-a-iz-en
what.MOT break_off have_to.PPR /2SOL.TRA once go_to_bed.IPF 2SOL.ITR.NRE
neska guzti-(e)-ekin?
girl all.PLU.SOC

c. Pello-k ber-e buru-a hil z-u-e(n)-n emakume-a-ren-ga(i)-tik
Pete.ERG he_himself.GEN head kill.PEF TRA.PST.NRE woman.MOT
Andres-e-k ere ber-e buru-a hil nahi d-u.
Andrew.ERG too he_himself.GEN head kill want.PPR TRA

(13) N-eu-re buru-a hil nahi n-u-e(n)-n arrazoi-a-z ez n-a-iz gogora-tzen.
I.REF.GEN head kill want.PPR /1.TRA.PST.NRE reason.INS not 1.ITR remember.IPF

(14) a. Ni bizi n-a-iz-en-e-ko balera hon-e-ta-n, elizatxo bat da.
I live.PPR 1.ITR.NRE.ADN valley this.LOC church.DIM a be.SYN

b. Ume n-in-tz-e(-n)-n-e-ko egun-ak j-oa-n z-ir-e-n.
child.IDF be.1.SYN.PST.NRE.ADN day.PLU go.PEF PLU.ITR.PST

c. Eta aita-ren-tzat ur bila n-i-h-oa(n)-n-e-ko iturri-a-ren
and father.IDF.BEN water.IDF in_search_of.PRE go.1.SYN.PST.NRE.ADN fountain.GEN
hots-a
sound

d. Irits-i-ko za-i-zu-e Gizon-a-ren Seme-a e-torr-i-ko d-en-e-ko egun bat
arrive.FUT 2PLU/.DIT Man.GEN Son come.FUT ITR.NRE.ADN day one
bederen i-kus-i nahi iza-n-go d-u-zu-e-n-e-ko garai-a.
at_least see want have.FUT /2PLU.TRA.NRE.ADN time

e. N-oa-n berri-ro atera n-in-tz-e-(n)-n-e-ko n-eu-re etxe-ra.
go.1.SYN.NCZ new.ADV go_out.PEF 1.ITR.PST.NRE.ADN I.REF.GEN house.ALL

(15) a. Ezta___ere atzo hots e-gi-n z-i-da(-n)-n-e-ko ber-e
nor yesterday sound.IDF make.PEF /1/.DTR.PST.NRE.ADN he_himself.GEN
ahots-a-ren doinu-a.
voice.GEN tone

b. Antipas-e-k ber-a-k lepo-a motz-araz-i z-i-o-(n)-e-ko Joan huraxe
Antipas.ERG he_himself.ERG neck cut.CAU.PEF DTR.PST.NRE.ADN John yonder.EMP
ber-a d-ela uste d-u.
same be.SYN.LCZ believe.PPR TRA

c. Zer-a d-io-en-e-ko (pasarte) hura aurki-tu z-u-en: . . .
what.DEF say.SYT.NRE.ADN passage yonder find.PEF TRA.PST

(16) a. Ber-e-tzat lan e-gi-ten d-uda-n ugazab(a)-a
he_himself.BEN work.IDF do.IPF /1.TRA.NRE boss

b. Ez da ber-a-ga(i)-tik bizi-a e-ma-n-go n-u-ke-e(n)-n gizon-ik.
not be.SYN he_himself.MOT life give.FUT /1.TRA.COD.PST.NRE man.PAR

c. Hau da n-eu-re atsegin guzti-ak Ber-e-gan
this_one be.SYN I.REF.GEN contentment all.PLU He_himself.LOC
d-it-u-da-n ni-re seme kutun-a.
have.PLU/1.SYT.NRE I.GEN son beloved

d. Ber-e alab(a)-a e-zagu(t)-tzen d-u-da-n gizon-a
he_himself.GEN daughter know.IPF /1.TRA.NRE man

(17) a. Ber-e azpi-an ezkuta-tu n-in-tz-e(n)-n mahai-a txiki samarr-a ze-n.
it_itself.GEN under hide.PEF 1.ITR.PST.NRE table small rather be.SYN.PST

b. Ber-e atze-tik z-a-bil-tza-n neskatx(a)-a-k ez z-a-it-u maite.
she_herself.GEN back.ELA go.2.SYN.NRE girl.ERG not 2/.TRA love.PPR

(18) a. Bart i-kus-te-ra j-oa-n g-in-e-(n)-n film-a / film(a)-a
last_night see.VEN.ALL go.PEF 1PLU.ITR.PST.NRE movie movie

b. Har-k nahi d-u ber-a-k esa-te-n atrebi-tzen ez d-en
yonder_one.ERG want.PPR TRA he_himself.ERG say.VEN.LOC dare.IPF not ITR.NRE
gauz(a)-ak beste-k esa-te-a.
thing.PLU somebody_else.ERG say.VEN
(*Note:* One would expect *bera* here.)

c. Z-oa-z ibai-ra eta har-tu han gorde-tze-ko agin-du
go.SYN.IMP river.ALL and take over_there.LOC hide.VEN.ADN command.PEF
n-i-zu(-n)-n gerriko-a.
/2/1.DTR.PST.NRE belt

(19) a. E-torr-i-ko ote d-en ez da-ki-zu-n gizon-a
come.FUT DUB ITR.NCZ not know./2.SYT.NRE man

b. Sala-tu-ko ote z-a-it-u-en beldur z-a-r-en gizon-a
denounce.FUT DUB 2/.TRA.NCZ fear.IDF 2.ITR.NRE man

(20) a. Ha-ra no-n d-u-zu-e-n gaur e-torr-i-ko ez ze(-n)-la
over_there.ALL where.LOC have./2PLU.SYT.NCZ today come.FUT not ITR.PST.LCZ
z-en-io-te(-n)-n gizon-a!
say./2PLU.SYT.NRE man

b. Eta neskatxa hil-a-ren ondo-an ager-tu ze-n Peru Okotz-en-a
and girl dead.GEN side.LOC appear.PEF ITR.PST Peru Okotz.GEN.ZEP
ze(-n)-la esan d-u-zu-e-n aizto-a ere.
be.SYN.PST.LCZ say.PEF /2PLU.TRA.NRE knife too

c. ... berri-ro ez z-en-u-te(-n)-la i-kus-i-ko esan z-i-zu-e(-n)-n
... new.ADV not /2PLU.TRA.PST.LCZ see.FUT tell.PEF /2PLU/.DTR.PST.NRE
lurralde-ra.
land.ALL

d. Hau al da itsu jaio ze(-n)-la d-io-zu-e-n zu-(e)-en
this_one INT be.SYN blind.IDF be_born.PEF ITR.PST.LCZ say./2PLU.SYT.NRE you.PLU
seme-a?
son

e. Laguntza e-ma-n-en d-i-zu-la uste duzu-n gizon-a
assistance.IDF give.FUT /2/.DTR.LCZ believe.PPR /2.TRA.NRE man

(21) Zoro-a d-e(n)-la guzti-ek da-ki-te-la esan z-i-zu-te(-n)-la
crazy be.SYN.LCZ all.PLU.ERG know./PLU.SYT.LCZ tell.PEF /2/PLU.DTR.PST.LCZ
idatz-i z-en-i-da(-n)-la uste d-u-da-n ijito-a-k musu e-ma-n
write.PEF /1/2.DTR.PST.LCZ believe.PPR /1.TRA.NRE gypsy.ERG kiss.IDF give.PEF
z-i-da-n.
/1/.DTR.PST

(22) Amorratu-ak d-ir-ela bist(a)-an da-go-en zakur hori-(e)-ekin ez d-u-t
rabid.PLU be.PLU.SYN.LCZ sight.LOC be.SYN.NRE hound that.PLU.SOC not /1.TRA
i-bil-i nahi.
walk want.PPR

(23) Bi urte-ren buru-an itzul-araz-i e-gi-n-go d-it-u-t toki hon-e-te-ra
two year.IDF.GEN end.LOC return.CAU do.FUT PLU/1.TRA place this.ALL
errege-a-k ber-ta-tik har-tu eta Babilonia-ra e-ra-ma-n z-it-u-e(n)-n
king.ERG from_right_here take.PEF and Babylon.ALL carry_off.PEF PLU/.TRA.PST.NRE
tenplu-ko tresn(a)-ak.
temple.ADN vessel.PLU

(24) a. **Ero-a ze(-n)-la-ko seinale-ak i-kus-i n-it-u-e(n)-n taxi gidari-a-k
crazy be.SYN.PST.LCZ.ADN sign.PLU see.PEF PLU/1.TRA.PST.NRE taxi driver.ERG
itsus(i)-ki jo n-ind-u-en.
badly beat.PEF 1/.TRA.PST

b. **E-ra-ik-i d-u-en etxe-a desegi-n d-u-te-n etxegile-a gaixo-tu e-gi-n
build.PEF TRA.NRE house tear_down.PEF /PLU.TRA.NRE architect fall_ill do.PEF
da.
ITR

c. **Idatz-i d-u-en emakume-a e-zagu(t)-tzen d-u-da-n liburu-a
write.PEF TRA.NRE woman know.IPF /1.TRA.NRE book
gogo-z irakurr-i d-u-t.
pleasure.IDF.INS read.PEF /1.TRA

(25) a. No-n-dik da-torr-en ere ez da-ki-da-n jende-a-ri e-ma-n behar
where.ELA come.SYN.NCZ even not know./1.SYT.NRE people.DAT give must.PPR
al d-i-z-ki-ot?
INT PLU//1.DTR

b. Nor-k kanta-tzen d-it-u-en abesti-ak gusta-tzen za-i-z-ki-zu?
who.ERG sing.IPF PLU/.TRA.NRE song.PLU please.IPF 2/PLU.DIT

c. Nor-k e-ma-n z-i-zu(-n)-n liburu-a gal-du d-u-zu?
who.ERG give.PEF /2/.DTR.PST.NRE book lose.PEF /2.TRA

d. Nor bizi d-en etxe-an sar-tu da polizi(a)-a?
who live.PPR ITR.NRE house.LOC enter.PEF ITR police

e. Noiz i-kus-i d-u-zu-n film(a)-a-z / film-a-z mintzo z-a-r-a?
when see.PEF /2.TRA.NRE movie.INS talk.PPR 2.SYN

(26) a. Guzti-ok maite d-u-gu-n mesede handi-ak e-gi-n d-i-z-ki-gu-n
all.INC.ERG love.PPR /1PLU.TRA.NRE favor great.PLU do.PEF PLU/1PLU/.DTR.NRE
lagun bat-e-k esan d-u.
friend a.ERG say.PEF TRA

b. Eta orain da-tor-ki-t gogo-ra gazte-ta-n ikas-i n-u-e(n)-n asko
and now come.1/.DYN mind.ALL youth.IDF.LOC learn.PEF /1.TRA.PST.NRE a_lot
esan gura d-u-en ipuin hau.
say want.PPR TRA.NRE tale this

c. Irakurr-i d-it-u-gu-n idatz-i z-it-u-e(n)-n liburu batzu-k oso
read.PEF PLU/1PLU.TRA.NRE write.PEF PLU/.TRA.PST.NRE book some.PLU very
interesgarri-ak d-ir-a.
interesting.PLU be.PLU.SYN

(27) a. Ez esan inor-i i-kus-i d-u-zu-e-n hau.
not tell anyone.DAT see.PEF /2PLU.TRA.NRE this

b. Armairu gain-e-an da-uka-zu-n hori zer da?
cupboard top.LOC keep./2.SYT.NRE that what be.SYN

c. Zer da basamortu-an go(i)-ra da-torr-en hori?
what be.SYN wilderness.LOC top.ALL come.SYN.NRE that

d. Da-torr-en horr-ekin seigarren txand(a)-a iza-n-go d-u-t.
come.SYN.NRE that.SOC sixth turn have.FUT /1.TRA

(28) a. Nor ote d-u-gu bekatu-ak barka-tu ere e-gi-ten d-it-u-en hau?
who DUB have./1PLU.SYT sin.PLU forgive even do.IPF PLU/.TRA.NRE this_one

b. Nortzu-k d-ir-a eta no-n-dik da-to(r)-z zuri-z jantz-i-rik
who_all.PLU be.PLU.SYN and where.ELA come.PLU.SYN white.IDF.INS robe.PEF.STA
da-u-de-n hau-ek?
be.PLU.SYN.NRE this_one.PLU

c. Ez al d-u-zu i-kus-ten biziklet(a)-an da-torr-en hori?
not INT /2.TRA see.IPF bicycle.LOC come.SYN.NRE that_one

d. Nor d-ir-a da-to(r)z-en hori-ek?
who be.PLU.SYN come.PLU.SYN.NRE that_one.PLU

e. Zu z-a-r-a Israel nahas-tu d-u-zu-n hori?
you be.2.SYN Israel trouble.PEF /2.TRA.NRE that_one

(29) a. Hainbeste maite z-a-it-u-da-n hon-e-k esa-ten d-i-zu-t.
so_much love.PPR 2/1.TRA.NRE this_one.ERG say.IPF /2/1.DTR

b. Guzti-ak bete-tzen d-it-u-zu-n horr-e-k, Zu-ta-z oso-z bete-tzen al
all.PLU fill.IPF PLU/2.TRA.NRE that_one.ERG You.INS completely fill.IPF INT
d-it-u-zu?
PLU/2.TRA

c. Bikain z-a-r-en Horr-i higuin za-i-zu
perfect.IDF be.2.SYN.NRE that_one.DAT loathsome.IDF be.2/.DYN
hai-(e)-en makets-a.
yonder_one.PLU.GEN imperfection

(30) a. Batasun-a sor-tu nahi-z has-i g-in-e(-n)-n-ok "bitasun-a"
unity create aim.IDF.INS start.PEF 1PLU.ITR.PST.NRE.ZEP.INC "two-ness"
sor-tu d-u-gu.
create.PEF /1PLU.TRA

b. Jules Verne-ren liburu-ak gogo-z irakurr-i
Jules Verne.GEN book.PLU pleasure.IDF.INS read.PEF
d-it-u-gu-n-on-tzat, ba-d-u film hon-e-k beste atsegin iturri-rik.
PLU/1PLU.TRA.NRE.ZEP.INC.BEN AFF.have.SYT film this.ERG other delight source.PAR

c. Ai, zu-e-k lege=maisu-ok, jakituri(a)-a-ren giltz(a)-a ken-du
alas you.PLU lawyer.INC wisdom.GEN key take_away.PEF
d-u-zu-e-n-ok!
/2PLU.TRA.NRE.ZEP.INC.ERG

(31) a. Ni-rekin plater ber-e-tik ja-te-n ari d-en bat-e-k sal-du-ko
I.SOC plate same.ELA eat.VEN.LOC be_busy.PPR ITR.NRE one.ERG betray.FUT
n-a-u.
1/.TRA

b. No-n-go-a d-en ez da-ki-da-n bat-i e-ma-n-go d-i-z-ki-o-t
where.ADN be.SYN.NCZ not know./1.SYT.NRE one.DAT give.FUT PLU//1.DTR
mo(t)ztaile-(e)-en-tzat presta-tu d-it-u-da-n ogi eta ardiki-ak?
shearer.PLU.BEN prepare.PEF PLU/1.TRA.NRE bread.IDF and sheep_cutlet.PLU

(32) a. Konpreni-tzen d-u-zu orain esa-n nahi d-u-da-n-a?
understand.IPF /2.TRA now say want.PPR /1.TRA.NRE.ZEP

b. Ez da-go on-do e-gi-te-n ari z-a-r-e-te-n-a.
not be.SYN well do.VEN.LOC be_busy.PPR 2PLU.ITR.NRE.ZEP

c. Begi-ek gezurta-tzen z-u-te-n aho-ek z-io-te(-n)-n-a.
eye.PLU.ERG belie.IPF /PLU.TRA.PST mouth.PLU.ERG say./PLU.SYT.PST.NRE.ZEP

d. Eskandalu bat da hemen gerta-tzen d-en-a.
scandal a be.SYN here.LOC happen.IPF ITR.NRE.ZEP

(33) a. Ari d-en-a-k e-gi-ten d-it-u huts-ak.
be_busy.PPR ITR.NRE.ZEP.ERG make.IPF PLU/.TRA mistake.PLU

b. Bi-k da-ki-te-n-a laster ja-ki-n-go d-u-te
two.IDF.ERG know./PLU.SYT.NRE.ZEP soon know.FUT /PLU.TRA
hamaika-k.
a_lot(<eleven).IDF.ERG

c. Asko-ren uste-z, beste ezer-ta-ra-ko balio ez
many.GEN opinion.IDF.INS other anything.DES be_good_for.PPR not
d-ute-n-ek lege-ak ikas-ten d-it-u-z-te.
/PLU.TRA.NRE.ZEP.PLU.ERG law.PLU study.IPF PLU/PLU.TRA

d. Iza-n___ere, d-u-en-a-ri e-ma-n e-gi-n-go za-i-o; ez
indeed have.SYT.NRE.ZEP.DAT give do.FUT DIT not
d-u-en-a-ri, orde-a, da-uka-n apurr-a ere ken-du e-gi-n-go.
have.SYT.NRE.ZEP.DAT however have.SYT.REN little even take_away do.FUT

(34) a. Senarr-a d-u-en-a-k jaun-a ba-d-u.
husband have.SYT.NRE.ZEP.ERG lord AFF.have.SYT

b. Ur-a-k da-karr-en-a, ur-a-k da-ra-ma.
water.ERG bring.SYT.NRE.ZEP water.ERG carry_away.SYT

c. Nahi d-u-en-a esa-ten d-u-en-a-k, nahi ez d-u-en-a
want.PPR TRA.NRE.ZEP say.IPF TRA.NRE.ZEP.ERG want.PPR not TRA.NRE.ZEP
e-ntzu-n-go d-u.
hear.FUT TRA

d. Behi-a je(t)z-te-n ez da-ki-en-a-ren-tzat, behi guzti-ak d-ir-a
cow milk.VEN.LOC not know.SYT.NRE.ZEP.BEN cow all.PLU be.PLU.SYN
antzu-ak.
barren.PLU

(35) a. Katalin-e-k eta amona-k nahi d-u-te-n-ik ez
Kathleen.ERG and Grandmother.IDF.ERG want.PPR /PLU.TRA.NRE.ZEP.PAR not
da gerta-tu-ko.
ITR happen.FUT

b. Donostia-n ez da hau ez da-ki-en-ik.
San_Sebastian.LOC not be.SYN this not know.SYT.NRE.ZEP.PAR

c. Ba-da orain-dik har-en ateraldi eta erantzun-ik gogo-an
AFF.be.SYN now.ELA yonder_one.GEN witticism.IDF and repartee.PAR mind.LOC
d-it-u-en-ik Errenteria-n.
have./PLU.TRA.NRE.ZEP.PAR Renteria.LOC

(36) a. Ez d-u-t ber-e-gan barkapen-a merezi d-u-en-ik ezer
not /1.TRA he_himself.LOC forgiveness deserve.PPR TRA.NRE.PAR anything
aurki-tzen.
find.IPF

b. Ez d-u-t frantses "angoisse" hitz-a-k da-uka-n borti(t)ztasun-a
not /1.TRA French "angoisse" word.ERG have.SYT.NRE forcefulness
d-u-en-ik ezer aurki-tzen.
have.SYT.NRE.PAR anything find.IPF

c. Ez al da Gipuzkoa oso-an ni-k e-zagu(t)-tu-ko ez
not INT be.SYN Guipuzcoa all.LOC I.ERG know.FUT not
n-u-ke-e(n)-n-ik inor?
/1.TRA.COD.PST.NRE.PAR anybody

d. Ez da-ki-zu-e gauza isil-ak asma-tze-n ni-ri e-ra-ma-ten
not know./2PLU.SYT matter secret.PLU discover.VEN.LOC I.DAT outdo.IPF
d-i-da-n-ik inor ez d-ela?
/1/.DTR.NRE.PAR anybody not be.SYN.LCZ

e. Jende-a-k esa-ten d-u ha(r-en)-la ez d-en-ik franko.
people.ERG say.IPF TRA so not be.SYN.NRE.PAR a_lot(_of)

(37) a. Purgatorio-ko su-an paga-tu behar-ko d-u-zu-n ezer ez da-uka-zu?
purgatory.ADN fire.LOC pay have_to.FUT /2.TRA.NRE anything not have./2.SYT

b. Arreb(a)-a-ri ez za-i-o Luis-e-k e-gi-ten d-u-en ezer gusta-tzen.
sister.DAT not DIT Luis.ERG do.IPF TRA.NRE anything please.IPF

c. Mundu-an bai al da logik(a)-a-rekin joka-tzen d-u-en inor?
world.LOC AFF INT be.SYN logic.SOC act.IPF TRA.NRE anyone

d. Atzo bizi ze(-n)-n franko bada hil-ik egun.
yesterday live.PPR ITR.PST.NRE plenty AFF.be.SYN die.PEF.STA today

(38) a. E-gi-n d-u-da-n guzti-a esan d-i-t.
do.PEF /1.TRA.NRE all tell.PEF /1/.DTR

b. Hori da n-a-iz-en guzti-a.
that be.SYN be.1.SYN.NRE all

(39) a. "N-a-iz" esa-ten d-u-t n-a-iz-en-txo hon-e-k.
"I_am" say.IPF /1.TRA be.1.SYN.NRE.DIM this_one.ERG

b. ha(r-en)-la ere, gorets-i nahi z-a-it-u d-u-zu-n-tto hon-e-k.
yonder_way even praise want.PPR 2/.TRA have./2.SYT.NRE.DIM this_one.ERG

c. Gabe z-a-r-en-txo bat ba-d-u-zu orain-dik.
without.PRE be.2.SYN.NRE.DIM one AFF.have./2.SYT now.ELA

(40) a. Ikas-i d-u-gu-n-txo-a beste-ren hizkuntz(a)-an ikas-i
learn.PEF /1PLU.TRA.NRE.DIM someone_else.IDF.GEN language.LOC learn.PEF
d-u-gu.
/1PLU.TRA

b. Hemen di-h-oa-ki-zu da-ki-gu-n-txo-a.
here.LOC go.2/.DYN know./1PLU.SYT.NRE.DIM.ZEP

c. Ahal d-en-txo-a e-gi-ten d-u-t behin-tzat.
PPP ITR.NRE.DIM.ZEP do.IPF /1.TRA at_least

d. Zordun g-a-r-a zenbait kultura sail-e-ta-n, d-u-gu-n-txo
indebted.IDF be.1PLU.SYN certain culture area.LOC have./1PLU.SYT.NRE.DIM
pixk(a)-ren zordun.
little_bit.GEN indebted.IDF

(41) a. E-gi-ten d-i-gu-n-a-ri gai(t)z-ki, zer-ga(i)-tik e-gi-n behar
act.IPF /1PLU/.DTR.NRE.ZEP.DAT badly what.MOT act should.PPR

d-i-o-gu on-gi?
//1PLU.DTR nicely

b. Aho-an d-u-en-a-ri min, ezti-a za-i-o samin.
mouth.LOC have.SYT.NRE.ZEP.DAT sore.IDF honey be.DYN bitter

c. Da-ki-en-a-k beldur e-uki-tze-n, ba-da-ki gizon iza-te-n.
know.SYT.NRE.ZEP.ERG fear.IDF have.VEN.LOC AFF.know.SYT man.IDF be.VEN.LOC

(42) a. Amerik(a)-e-ta-n bai, ni-re senarr-a-k esa-ten d-u-en-e-z.
America.PLU.LOC AFF I.GEN husband.ERG say.IPF TRA.NRE.ZEP.IDF.INS

b. n-e(u)-r(e_h)on-e-k egun hau-e-ta-n i-kus-i d-u-da-n-e-z, jende
I_myself.ERG day this.PLU.LOC see.PEF /1.TRA.NRE.ZEP.IDF.INS people
gutxi da-bil hemen.
few walk.SYN here.LOC

(43) a. Baina, i-kus-ten d-u-da-n-e-z, ez n-a-u inor-k behar hemen.
but see.IPF /1.TRA.NRE.ZEP.IDF.INS not 1/.TRA anybody.ERG need.PPR here.LOC

b. D-irudi-en-e-z, ber-a-z, edo ni-k d-eritz-a-da-n-e-z
seem.SYT.NRE.ZEP.IDF.INS same.INS or I.ERG deem/1.DYT.NRE.ZEP.IDF.INS
behin-tzat, *etxe=jupu-a* ez ze-n habe-a.
at_least *etxe-jupua* not be.SYN.PST beam

(44) a. Da-ki-da-n-e-z, Madril-e-n bizi ze-n
know./1.SYT.NRE.ZEP.IDF.INS Madrid.LOC live.PPR ITR.PST

b. Eta orain arte, ni-k da-ki-da-n-e-z, ez d-u inor-k
and now until I.ERG know./1.SYT.NRE.ZEP.IDF.INS not TRA anybody.ERG
ezer aurki-tu.
anything find.PEF

(45) a. Hitzaurre-a-z bi hitz esa-n-go n-it-u-z-ke, Tolstoizale-a
preface.INS two word.IDF say.FUT PLU/1.TRA.COD Tolstoi_fan
n-a-iz-en-e-z.
be.1.SYN.NRE.ZEP.IDF.INS

b. N-eu bakarr-ik iza-n-go n-a-u-zu gain-e-tik, errege n-a-iz-en-e-z.
I.EMP only.STA have.FUT 1/2.TRA top.ELA king.IDF be.SYN.NRE.ZEP.IDF.INS

(46) a. Neska bat-e-k, oso polit-a-k, maite z-a-it-u.
girl a.ERG very pretty.ZEP.ERG love.PPR 2/.TRA

b. Neska bat-i, oso polit-a-ri, e-ma-n-go d-i-z-ki-o-t lore-ak.
girl a.DAT very pretty.ZEP.DAT give.FUT PLU//1.DTR flower.PLU

c. Behi bat-i, ederr-a-ri, luza-ro begira-tu d-i-o.
cow a.DAT beautiful.ZEP.DAT for_a_long_time look.PEF DTR

(47) a. Neska bat e-torr-i zi-tza-i-gu-n, oso polit-a.
girl a come.PEF 1PLU/.DIT.PST very pretty.ZEP

b. Behi bat eros-i d-u-t, ederrr-a.
cow a buy.PEF /1.TRA beautiful.ZEP

(48) a. Baldin ni-k, zu-(e)-en Jaun eta Maisu n-a-iz-en hon-e-k, oin-ak
CDC I.ERG you.PLU.GEN Lord and Teacher be.1.SYN.NRE this_one.ERG foot.PLU
garbi-tu ba-d-i-z-ki-zu-e-t, zu-ek ere elkarr-i garbi-tu
wash CDP.PLU/2PLU/1.DTR you.PLU.ERG also each_other.DAT wash
behar d-i-z-ki-o-zu-e.
should.PPR PLU//2PLU.DTR

b. Zu-k, e-zagu(t)-tzen n-au-zu-n horr-e-k, ba-da-ki-zu ezetz.
you.ERG know.IPF 1/2.TRA.NRE that_one.ERG AFF.know./2.SYT no

c. Campion-e-k, hainbeste aldi-z gogora-tzen d-u-gu-n
campion.ERG so_many time.INS bring_to_mind.IPF /1PLU.TRA.NRE
har-k, . . .
yonder_one.ERG, . . .

(49) a. Ba-n-u-en astakume polit bat, oso maite
AFF.have./1.SYT.PST young_donkey nice a very_much love.PPR
n-u-e(n)-n-a.
/1.TRA.PST.NRE.ZEP

b. Eta hau zer da? Katu bat, j-oa-n d-en negu-an hil
and this what be.SYN cat a go.PEF ITR.NRE winter.LOC die.PEF
zi-tza-i-gu(-n)-n-a.
1PLU/.DIT.PST.NRE.ZEP

c. Ni n-a-iz zu-(e)-en anai-a, zu-ek sal-du n-ind-u-zu-e(n)-n-a.
I be.1.SYN you.PLU.GEN brother you.PLU.ERG sell.PEF 1/2PLU.TRA.PST.NRE.ZEP

d. Beti gogo-an z-a-u-z-ka-da-n dam(a)-a, izarr-a d-irudi-zu-n-a,
always mind.LOC have.2/1.SYT.NRE lady star look_like./2.SYT.NRE.ZEP
eguzki-a-ren beharr-ik gabe argi e-gi-ten d-u-zu-n-a, . . .
sun.GEN need.PAR without.PRE light.IDF make.IPF /2.TRA.NRE.ZEP

e. Berri-z ager-tu ze-n aingeru-a har-en emazte-a-ri, land(a)-an
new.ADV appear.PEF ITR.PST angel yonder_one.GEN wife.DAT field.LOC
jarri-a ze-go-e(n)-n-a-ri.
sit.PEF.DEF be.SYN.PST.NRE.ZEP.DAT

(50) a. Eta ohar bat, bidenabar, inor-k txar-tzat har-tze-a nahi ez
and remark a by_the_way anyone.ERG bad.PRO take.VEN want.PPR not
n-u-ke-e(n)-n-a.
/1.TRA.COD.PST.NRE.ZEP

b. Astakume bat aurki-tu-ko d-u-zu-e, gain-e-an inor jarr-i ez
young_donkey a find.FUT /2PLU.TRA top.LOC anyone sit.PEF not

za-i-o-n-a.
DIT.NRE.ZEP

c. Herritar guzti-ak har-ta-z mintza-tzen z-ir-e-n puta bat iza-n
town's_people all.PLU yonder_one.INS speak.IPF PLU.ITR.PST whore a be.PEF
ba-li-tz bezala, ifernu-ko sua-k bere-tu-ko z-u-e(n)-n-a.
CDP.ITR.COD SIP hell.ADN fire.ERG seize.FUT TRA.PST.NRE.ZEP

(51) a. Zu-k ez al d-u-zu lehengusu bat filarmonik(a)-a jo-tzen d-u-en-a?
you.ERG not INT have./2.SYT cousin a accordion play TRA.NRE.ZEP

b. Hargin-ik ez da eda-ten ez d-u-en-ik.
stonecutter.PAR not be.SYN drink.IPF not TRA.NRE.DEL.PAR

c. Jende asko e-zagu(t)-tu d-u-t goiz-e-an aldarte txarr-e-ta-n
people a_lot(_of) know.PEF /1.TRA morning.LOC mood bad.IDF.LOC
esna-tzen z-ir-e(-n)-n-ak.
wake_up.IPF PLU.ITR.PST.NRE.ZEP.PLU

(52) a. E-torr-i-ko da denbor(a)-a deabru-a-k laguntza-rik e-gi-n-en ez d-i-zu-n-a.
come.FUT ITR time devil.ERG help.PAR do.FUT not /2/.DTR.NRE.ZEP

b. Noiz irits-i-ko da egun-a ni-re-a iza-n-go z-a-it-u-da-n-a?
when arrive.FUT ITR day I.GEN.ZEP have.FUT 2/1.TRA.NRE.ZEP

c. Baina gero iza-n-go z-ir-e(-n)-la egun-ak bi ere e-gi-n-go
but later be.FUT PLU.ITR.PST.LCZ day.PLU two.IDF even make.FUT
z-it-u-z-te(-n)-n-ak.
PLU/PLU.TRA.PST.NRE.ZEP.PLU

(53) a. Ni n-a-iz Egipto-ra-ko sal-du z-en-u-te(n)-n Jose zu(-e)-en anai-a.
I be.1.SYN Egypt.DES sell.PEF /2PLU.TRA.PST.NRE Joseph you.PLU brother

b. Orain-dik inor eser-i ez za-i-o-n astakume bat aurki-tu-ko d-u-zu-e.
now.ELA anyone sit.PEF not DIT.NRE young_donkey a find.FUT /2PLU.TRA

c. Eguzki-a-ren beharr-ik gabe argi e-gi-ten d-u-zu-n izarr-a
sun.GEN need.PAR without.PRE light.IDF make.IPF /2.TRA.NRE star
d-irudi-zu-n beti gogo-an z-a-u-z-ka-da-n dam(a)-a . . .
look_like./2.SYT.NRE always mind.LOC have.2/1.SYT.NRE lady

(54) a. Horr-(r)a-ko zu-re seme hori, zu-re ondasun-ak emagaldu(-e)-ekin
there.ALL.ADN you.GEN son that you.GEN good.PLU prostitute.PLU.SOC
jan d-it-u-en hori, . . .
consume.PEF PLU/.TRA.NRE that_one . . .

b. Jainko bizi-a-ren Seme-a, mundu hon-e-ta-ra e-torr-i z-a-r-en-a.
God living.GEN Son world this.ALL come.PEF 2.ITR-NRE.ZEP

(55) a. Seme gai(t)zto andre galdu(-e)-ekin ber-e gauz(a)-a guzti-ak
son wicked woman loose.PLU.SOC he_himself.GEN thing all.PLU

honda-tu d-it-u-en hori, . . .
squander.PEF PLU/.TRA.NRE that_one, . . .

b. Zu z-a-r-ela, Jesus Kristo, Jainko bizi-a-ren Seme mundu-ra e-torr-i
you be.2.SYN.LCZ Jesus Christ God living.GEN Son world.ALL come.PEF
z-a-r-en-a, . . .
2.ITR.NRE.DEF

(56) a. Etxe eros-i n-u-e(n)-n-a ederr-a ze-n.
house buy.PEF /1.TRA.PST.NRE.DEF beautiful be.SYN.PST

b. Hura ze-n . . . jainko-z-ko gizon, asko neke e-ra-bil-i
yonder_one be.SYN.PST . . . God.INS.ADN man.IDF a_lot_of trouble go_through.PEF
z-u-e(n)-n bat.
TRA.PST.NRE a

c. Gizon aspaldi i-kus-i ez n-it-u-e(n)-n-ak aurki-tu
man for_a_long_time see.PEF not PLU/1.TRA.PST.NRE.DEF.PLU find.PEF
n-it-u-en han.
PLU/1.TRA.PST over_there.LOC

d. Euskaldun zahar zerbait da-ki-te-n-ak alde
Basque elderly something know./PLU.SYT.NRE.DEF.PLU side.IDF
d-it-u-z-te.
have.PLU/PLU.SYT

e. Gu-re lagun min har-tu z-u-e(n)-n hori egun ber-e-an j-oa-n omen
we.GEN friend pain.IDF take.PEF TRA.PST.NRE that day same.LOC go.PEF REP
ze-n sendagile-a-ren-gan-(r)a.
ITR.PST doctor.ALL

(57) a. I-ra-gan denbor(a)-a ez da gehi-ago gu-re-a.
pass.PEF time not be.SYN more.COP we.GEN.ZEP

b. Uztazale-a-ri itzur-i buruxk(a)-ak bil-du-ko d-it-u-t.
reaper.DAT escape_from.PEF ear.PLU gather.FUT PLU/1.TRA

(58) a. Hori-e-i e-gi-n kalte-a no-la behar d-u-t errepara-tu?
that_one.PLU.DAT do.PEF harm how be_to.PPR /1.TRA compensate

b. Osaba misionest-a-k utz-i liburu-ak, den-ak lei-tu-ak n-it-u-en.
uncle missionary.ERG leave.PEF book.PLU all.PLU read.PEF.DEF.PLU PLU/1.TRA.PST

(59) a. Abraham Jaun-a-ren aitzin-e-an ego-n toki-ra j-oa-n ze-n.
Abraham Lord.GEN before.LOC be.PEF place.ALL go.PEF ITR.PST

b. Mundu hau utz-i egun-a hurbil z-u-en.
world this leave.PEF day near.IDF have.SYT.PST

c. E-torr-i bide-a-z bihur-tu ze-n.
come.PEF road.INS return.PEF ITR.PST

(60) a. . . . en-e beribil-e-ko lagun sakeloren-a-z gabe-tu-a . . .
. . . I.GEN automobile.ADN friend pocket_watch.INS relieve.PEF.SIN
b. Mahaizain-a-k ur ardo bihur-tu-a dasta-tu z-u-en.
table_steward.ERG water wine.IDF turn_into.PEF.DEF taste.PEF TRA.PST
c. . . . emakume itsusi baztang(a)-a-k zula-tu bat-ekin.
. . . woman ugly pox.ERG pit.PEF a.SOC

(61) a. Ager-tu ze-n gizon bat Jainko-a-k bidal-i-a.
appear.PEF ITR.PST man a God.ERG send.PEF.ZEP
b. Farisau-ek e-karr-i z-i-o-te-n ordu-an emazteki bat,
Pharisee.PLU.ERG bring.PEF //PLU.DTR.PST that_time.LOC woman a
ezkontza hau(t)s-te-n atzeman-a.
marriage.IDF break.VEN.LOC catch.PEF.ZEP

(62) a. Orantza-rik gabe e-gi-n-ika-ko ogi-a
yeast.PAR without.PRE make.PEF.STA.ADN bread
b. Kalifornia-n sos parrast(a)-a e-gi-n-ika-ko amerikano bat
California.LOC money heap make.PEF.STA.ADN "American" a
c. Ezkontz(a)-a, Jainko-a-k e-gi-n-ika-ko lege-a
marriage God.ERG make.PEF.STA.ADN law
d. . . . e-ma-n-ika-ko hitz-a on-gi bete-rik.
. . . give.PEF.STA.ADN word neatly fulfill.PEF.STA

(63) a. Itsaso-e-ta-n luza-ro i-bil-i-ri(k)-ko ontzi=agintari azkor
sea.PLU.LOC for_a_long_time travel.PEF.STA.ADN shipmaster intelligent
zintzo-a
respectable
b. Gu-re herri-an berri-ki sor-tu-ri(k)-ko fauna bat da.
we.GEN country.LOC newly arise.PEF.STA.ADN fauna a be.SYN
c. Liburu hon-e-ta-ra-ko zer-ga(i)-tik ez d-it-u-k har-tu gerta-tu-ri(k)-ko
book this.DES what.MOT not PLU/2SOL.TRA take.PEF happen.PEF.STA.ADN
gauz(a)-ak eta mintza-tu-ri(k)-ko hi(t)zkuntz(a)-a?
thing.PLU and speak.STA.ADN language

(64) a. Bizitz(a)-a, idiota bat-e-k konda-tu-ri(k)-ko ipuin-a da.
life idiot a.ERG tell.PEF.STA.ADN tale be.SYN
b. Egi(a)-a da seme(-e)-en gain-e-an Jaungoiko-a-k eta Izadi-a-k
truth be.SYN son.PLU.GEN top.LOC God.ERG and Nature.ERG
e-ma-n-i(k)-ko aginpide-a da-uka-te-la guraso-ek.
give.PEF.STA.ADN authority have./PLU.SYT.LCZ parent.PLU.ERG

(65) Baina prediku-a e-ntzu-n-i(k)-ko asko-k sinets-i e-gi-n z-u-te-n.
but sermon hear.PEF.STA.ADN many believe do.PEF /PLU.TRA.PST

(66) a. Hiru z-ir-e-n kanpo-tik e-torr-i-ta-ko jaun-ak.
three.IDF be.PLU.SYN.PST exterior.ELA come.PEC.ADN gentleman.PLU

b. Beltz-e-z jantz-i-ta-ko emakume bat-e-k lore-ak jar-tzen d-it-u
black.IDF.INS dress.PEC.ADN woman a.ERG flower.PLU put.IPF PLU/.TRA
hilobi bat-e-an.
grave a.LOC

c. Mahazain-a-k ardo bihur-tu-ta-ko ur-a dasta-tu z-u-en.
table_steward.ERG wine.IDF turn_into.PEC.ADN water taste.PEF TRA.PST

(67) a. Ez z-it-u-en ni-k hauta-tu-ta-ko bi adiskide-ak onar-tu.
not PLU/.TRA.PAST I.ERG choose.PEC.ADN two friend.PLU accept.PEF

b. Aresti-an neskatx(a)-a-ri e-gi-n-da-ko argazki-a e-ra-kuts-i n-i-o-n.
moment.LOC girl.DAT make.PEC.ADN picture show.PEF //1.DTR.PST

(68) a. Eraile-a-ren ait(a)-a erretiro-a har-tu-ta-ko polizi(a)-a ze-n.
killer.GEN father retirement take.PEC.ADN policeman be.SYN.PST

b. Paris-e-n sinesmen-a gal-du-ta-ko gazte bat
Paris.LOC faith lose.PEC.ADN youngster a

(69) Bertso hau-ek jarr-i n-i-z-ki-o-n autopist(a)-a-k etxe-a harrapa-tu-ta-ko
verse this.PLU put_together PLU//1.DTR.PST highway.ERG house grab.PEC.ADN
aitona horr-i.
grandfather that.DAT

(70) a. Ni jaio-ta-ko haran-a i-kus-i n-u-en.
I be_born.PEC.ADN valley see.PEF /1.TRA.PST

b. Nagusi horr-e-k ber-e-a omen z-u-en jaio-ta-ko
landlord that.ERG he_himself.GEN.ZEP REP have.SYT.PST be_born.PEC.ADN
baserri-a.
farm

c. Abrahan Jaun-a-rekin e-go-n-da-ko leku-ra j-oa-n ze-n.
Abraham Lord.SOC be.PEC.ADN place.ALL go.PEF ITR.PST

(71) a. Berri-ro sar-tzen g-a-r-a irten-da-ko etxe-ra.
new.ADV enter.IPF 1PLU.ITR come_out(_of) house.ALL

b. Bidart e-torr-i-ta-ko bide-an go(i)-ra itzul-i ze-n.
Bidart come.PEC.ADN road.LOC top.ALL return.PEF ITR.PST

c. Saia-tu ze-n, ha(r-en)-l(a)-ere, i-bil-i-ta-ko bide-an atze-ra e-gi-te-n.
try.PEF ITR.PST nevertheless travel.PEC.ADN road.LOC back.ALL make.VEN.LOC

(72) a. Ni hain zale-a iza-n-da-ko inauteri-ak gal-araz-i d-it-u-z-te.
I so fond be.PEC.ADN carnival.PLU forbid.PEF PLU/PLU.TRA

b. Zu-ek ez z-en-u-te-n gu kontura-tu-ta-ko arrisku-a i-kus-ten.
you.PLU.ERG not /2PLU.TRA.PST we realize.PEC.ADN danger see.IPF

c. Gu igo-ta-ko toki-a arriskutsu-a ze-n.
we climb.PEC.ADN spot dangerous be.SYN.PST

(73) Orta z-eritz-a(-n)-n herri inguru-an geldi-tu z-ir-e-n elizatxo
Orta name.DYT.PST.REN village vicinity.LOC stop.PEF PLU.ITR.PST church.DIM
utz-i-ta-ko bat-e-an.
abandon.PEC.ADN a.LOC

(74) a. Sagardo pixka bat eda-te-ko aitzaki(a)-a
cider bit a drink.VEN.ADN pretext
b. Zu-e-i lagun-tze-ko baimen-a eska-tze-ra n-oa.
you.PLU.DAT accompany.VEN.ADN permission ask.VEN.ALL go.1.SYN
c. Ba-n-e-ki-en ez z-u-e(n)-la inoiz argi-a i-kus-te-ko itxaropen
AFF.know./1.SYT.PST not have.SYT.PST.LCZ ever light see.VEN.ADN hope
handi-rik.
great.PAR
d. Paulo Amerik(a)-e-ta-ra j-oa-te-ko paper-ak ari da
Paul America.PLU.ALL go.VEN.ADN document.PLU be_busy.PPR ITR
e-gi-te-n.
make.VEN.LOC

(75) a. Oihenart-en-a ez da inor harri-tze-ko gauz(a)-a.
Oihenart.GEN.ZEP not be.SYN anyone surprise.VEN.ADN matter
b. Hau-ek ez d-ir-a ume bat-e-k esa-te-ko hitz-ak.
this.PLU not be.PLU.SYN child a.ERG say.VEN.ADN word.PLU
c. Hori-ek d-ir-a andre-a-ri konta-tze-ko gezurr-ak.
that.PLU be.PLU.SYN wife.DAT tell.VEN.ADN lie.PLU
d. Beti iza-n h-a-iz andre-a-ri gezurr-ak konta-tze-ko gizon-a.
always be.PEF 2SOL.ITR wife.DAT lie.PLU tell.VEN.ADN man

(76) a. Nor d-ir-a j-oa-te-ko-ak?
who be.PLU.SYN go.VEN.ADN.ZEP.PLU
b. Zu al z-a-r-a e-tor-tze-ko-a?
you INT be.2.SYN come.VEN.ADN.ZEP
c. Fani noiz da e-tor-tze ko-a?
Fani when be.SYN come.VEN.ADN.ZEP
d. Kafka-ren zenbait fruitu ez bide d-ir-a denbora=pasa
Kafka.GEN certain production not INF be.PLU.SYN pastime.IDF
irakur-tze-ko-ak.
read.VEN.ADN.ZEP.PLU

(77) a. Lili bat i-kus-i d-u-t baratze bat-e-an, desira-tzen bai(t)-n-u-ke ni-re
flower a see.PEF /1.TRA garden a.LOC wish.IPF ACP./1.TRA.COD I.GEN

saihets-e-an.
side.LOC

b. Ba-d-ir-a "ranchero" nagusi eder batzu, oro-z gain-e-tik,
AFF.be.PLU.SYN ranch owner handsome some.IDF all.IDF.INS top.ELA
euskaldun alab(a)-ak nahi bai(t)-t(<*d)-it-u-z-te emazte-tzat.
Basque daughter.PLU want.PPR ACP.PLU/PLU.TRA wife.PRO
(*Note:* In the cases with *bait* the original d-/g- following the prefix before devoicing have been restored in the glosses.)

c. Hor hel-du za-i-o Basajaun-a, nesk(a)-a har-tu eta e-ra-ma-ten
there.LOC arrive.PEF DIT Ogre girl take.PEF and carry_off.IPF
bai(t)-t(<*d)-u ber-ekin.
ACP.TRA he_himself.SOC

d. . . . dozena bat antzara, Piarres-e-k ez bait-z-it-u-en i-kus-i ere.
. . . dozen a goose.IDF Peter.ERG not ACP.PLU/.TRA.PST see.PEF even

e. Pello-k neskatxa bat aurki-tu d-u, guzti-z maite bai(t)-t(<*d)-u.
Pete.ERG girl a find.PEF TRA very_much love.PPR ACP.TRA

(78) a. Zer da gu-re adimen-a, har-ta-z bai(t)-k(<*g)-a-u-de guzti-z
what be.SYN we.GEN intelligence yonder_one.INS ACP.be.1PLU.SYN all.IDF.INS
han(t)-tu-ak.
puff_up.PEF.PLU

b. Astakume bat aurki-tu-ko d-u-zu-e, har-en gain-e-an ez
young_donkey a find.FUT /2PLU.TRA yonder_one.GEN top.LOC not
bai(t)-t(<*d)a egun-da-ino inor jarr-i.
ACP.ITR today.TER anyone sit.PEF

c. Egiptoera zaharr-e-an hitzegi-n z-u-en, hots, hi(t)zkera bat-e-an
Egyptian old.LOC speak.PEF TRA.PST that_is_to_say speech_form a.LOC
inor-k har-en fonetik(a)-a ordu-an ez bait-ze-ki-en.
anyone.ERG yonder_one.GEN phonetics that_time.LOC not ACP.know.SYT.PST

(79) a. Etxe hori, motoziklet(a)-a atari-an bai(t)-t(<*d)a-go, apaiz-a-ren-a da.
house that motorcycle entrance.LOC ACP.be.SYN priest.GEN.ZEP be.SYN

b. Mattin en-e adiskide-a-ri, ez bai(t)-t(<*d)a hura ere nornahi,
Mattin I.GEN friend.DAT not ACP.be.SYN yonder_one also just_anybody
gerta-tu za-i-z-ki-o horr-e(n)-la-ko-ak.
happen.PEF /PLU.DIT such.ZEP.PLU

c. Lehen Saul-en arm(a)-ak, ttipi-ak eta arin-ak bait-z-ir-e-n,
earlier Saul.GEN weapon.PLU small.PLU and light.PLU ACP.be.PLU.SYN.PST
handi-z eta pisu-z utz-i z-it-u-en, eta orain jigante handi
big.IDF.INS and weight.IDF.INS leave_off.PEF PLU/.TRA.PST and now giant big

bat-en-ak irudi-tzen za-i-z-ki-o ttipi eta arin?
a.GEN.ZEP.PLU seem.IPF /PLU.DIT small.IDF and light.IDF

(80) a. Gara-tik hiri-ra-ko bi zubi-ak ere behar d-it-u-z-te
station.ELA town.ALL.ADN two bridges.PLU also have_to.PPR PLU/PLU.TRA
zabal-du, ez bai(t)-t(<*d)a goiz-egi iza-n-en.
widen not ACP.ITR early.ECS be.FUT

b. Taul(a)-a-ren gain-e-an e-tza-n n-a-iz zenbait egun-e-z, ez bai(t)-t(<*d)a
wooden_board.GEN top.LOC lie.PEF 1.ITR a_few day.IDF.INS not ACP.be.SYN
batere goxo.
at_all pleasant.IDF

c. Federiko enperadore-a-k ez z-u-en ber-e mende-an ardo-rik
Frederick emperor.ERG not TRA.PST he_himself.GEN lifetime.LOC wine.PAR
eda-n, anitz bait-ze-n aleman bat-en-tzat.
drink.PEF quite_something ACP.be.SYN.PST German a.BEN

(81) a. Ni-re aita-k nor-en-tzat presta-tu-a d-u-en, har-i
I.GEN father.IDF.ERG who.BEN prepare.PEF.DEF TRA.NCZ yonder_one.DAT
e-ma-n-go za-i-o.
give.FUT DIT

b. No-ra gida-tzen g-a-it-u-zu-n, ha-ra j-oa-n-go g-a-r-a.
where.ALL direct.IPF 1PLU/2.TRA.NCZ over_there.LOC go.FUT 1PLU.ITR

(82) a. Nor-k sobera besarka-tzen bai(t)-t(<*d)-u, gutxi her(t)s-ten d-u.
who.ERG too_much take_in.IPF ACP.TRA little grasp.IPF TRA

b. Nor har-k igorr-i bai(t)-t(<*d)-u, hura zu-ek ez d-u-zu-e
who yonder_one.ERG send.PEF ACP.TRA yonder_one you.PLU not /2PLU.TRA
sine(t)s-ten.
believe.IPF

(83) a. Gizon-a-k zer___ere erei-ten bai(t)-t(<*d)-u, hura bil-tzen ere d-u.
man.ERG whatever sow.IPF ACP.TRA yonder reap.IPF too TRA

b. No-n___ere iza-ten bai(t)-t(<*d)a gorputz-a, han bil-du-ko d-ir-a
wherever.LOC be.IPF ACP.ITR corpse over_there.LOC gather.FUT PLU.ITR
arrano-ak.
vulture.PLU

c. Zer___ere bait-z-u-en eskas eta hura e-ma-ten z-i-o-n.
whatever ACP.TRA.PST lack.PPR EXP yonder give.IPF DTR.PST

(84) a. Bakoitz-a-k zer erein, huraxe bil-du-ko d-u.
everyone.ERG what sow yonder.EMP gather.FUT TRA

b. Zu no-n jarr-i bizi-tze-n, hantxe jarr-i-ko n-a-iz ni ere.
you where.LOC settle live.IPF over_there.LOC.EMP settle.FUT 1.ITR I too

(85) a. Zu-re abera(t)stasun-a no-n, zu-re bihotz-a han.
you.GEN wealth where.LOC you.GEN heart over_there.LOC
b. Eguzki-a no-ra, zapi-ak ha-ra.
sun where.ALL linen.PLU over_there.ALL

(86) Gero ba-da-ra-ma-tza-te zein_ toki-ta-ra iduri-tzen _ere bait-za-i-e,
afterward AFF.lead.PLU/PLU.SYT which_ place.ALL deem(_fit).IPF _ever ACP.PLU/.DIT
eta ha-ra.
COC over_there.ALL

(87) a. Ha(r-en)-la-ta-n ez da geldi-tzen lau besanga baizik zein-e-ta-rik
that_way not ITR remain.IPF four branch.IDF but which.PLU.ELA
atera-tzen bai(t)-t(<*d)-ir-a gando berri-ak.
emerge.IPF ACP.PLU.ITR shoot new.PLU
b. . . . eskerr-ak e-ma-n Jaungoiko-a-ri, zein-en esku-e-ta-tik
. . . thank.PLU give God.DAT which.GEN hand.PLU.ELA
da-to(r)-z-ki-gu-n on guzti-ak.
come.1PLU/PLU.SYN.NCZ good_thing all.PLU

(88) a. Etxe hau, zein-a-ren zu bide z-a-r-a jabe
house this which.DEF.GEN you INF be.SYN owner.IDF
b. Eliza hau, zein-a-ri e-ma-n z-i-o-te-n / z-i-o-te(-n)-n gu-re
church this which.DEF.DAT give.PEF //PLU.DTR.PST //PLU.DTR.PST.NCZ we.GEN
guraso-ek hainbeste urre
parent.PLU.ERG so_much gold

(89) a. Aipa-tu d-it-u-da-n xehetasun-ok garbi-ro azal-tzen d-i-gu-te . . .
mention.PEF PLU/1.TRA.NRE detail.INC clearly demonstrate.IPF /1PLU/PLU.DTR
b. Eta guzti-ok gramatik(a)-a-z balia-tzen d-ir-a beti.
and all.INC grammar.INS use.IPF PLU.ITR always
c. Egi(a)-ak d-ir-a hori-ok guzti-ok.
truth.PLU be.PLU.SYN that.INC all.INC

(90) a. Gal-du d-i-da-zu-e aita=seme-ok afari-ta-ko gogo guzti-a.
spoil.PEF /1/2PLU.DTR father_and_son.INC.ERG dinner.IDF.ADN appetite whole
b. Zu-e-i d-io-ts-(z)u-e-t, orain, en-e adiskide-o-i: . . .
you.PLU.DAT say./2PLU/1.DYT now I.GEN friend.INC.DAT

(91) a. Zor berri-a d-u-gu euskaldun-ok Orixe-rekin.
debt new have./1PLU.SYT Basque.INC.ERG Orixe.SOC
b. . . . arrotz-ak eta euskaldun-ak, etsai-ak eta g-eu-k, den-ak eta den-ok.
foreigner.PLU and Basque.PLU enemy.PLU and we.REF all.PLU and all.INC
c. Ha(r-en)-la bada gu-k ere, gero-tik gero-ra
so then we also time_to_come.ELA time_to_come.ALL

g-a-bil-tza-n-ok, kontsola-tzen d-it-u-gu g-eu-re buru-ok.
walk.1PLU.SYN.NRE.ZEP.INC console.IPF PLU/1PLU.TRA we.REF.GEN head.INC

d. Berretura har-ta-z, ber-e buru-a eta guzti-ok ere galdu
addition yonder.INS she_herself.GEN head and all.INC too ruin.PEF
g-int-u-en.
1PLU/.TRA.PST

Chapter 20

(1) Noiz-ko behar d-it-u-zu oinetako hau-ek? Bihar-ko ala
when.DES need.PPR PLU/2.TRA shoe this.PLU tomorrow.DES or
etzi-ra-ko?
the_day_after_tomorrow.DES

(2) Orain-da-ino ez da gauza handi-a.
now.TER not be.SYN thing big

(3) a. Hemen lan e-gi-ten d-u-t egunero zortzi edo hamar ordu-an.
here.LOC work.IDF do.IPF /1.TRA every_day eight or ten hour.SIN.LOC

b. Mami-a behar da zuri-tu eta ur bero-ta-n e-duki hogei-ta___lau
flesh must.PPR ITR peel and water hot.IDF.LOC keep twenty_four
ordu-an.
hour.SIN.LOC

c. Eskritura Sant(a)-a-k ez d-i-gu esa(n)-ten ordu-ko gizon-ak
Scripture Holy.ERG not /1PLU/.DTR tell.IPF (that)_time.ADN people.PLU
zer-ga(i)-tik hainbeste urte-an bizi iza-ten z-ir-e(-n)-n.
what.MOT so_many year.SIN.LOC life.PPR be.IPF PLU.ITR.PST

(4) a. Zenbait minutu-z ez d-u inor-k txint-ik atera-tzen.
a_few minute.INS not TRA anyone.ERG thing/word.PAR utter.IPF

b. Ehun___eta___hogei-ta___hamazazpi urte-z bizi iza-n ze-n Ismael.
hundred_and_thirty-seven year.IDF.INS life.PPR be.PEF ITR.PST Ismael

c. Hantxe e-go-n ze-n berrogei egun-e-z eta berrogei gau-e-z.
over_there.LOC.EMP stay.PEF ITR.PST forty day.IDF.INS and forty night.IDF.INS

(5) a. Ordu laurden bat e-duki n-a-u-zu hor kanpo-an.
hour quarter a keep.PEF 1/2.TRA there.LOC outside.LOC

b. Zu gabe orain ez n-u-ke nahi minutu bat ere bizi.
you without.PRE now not /1.TRA.COD want.PPR minute one even live.PPR

(6) a. Astebete-an beste-rik ez n-u-en lan-ik e-gi-n Oper(a)-an.
week.LOC else.PAR not /1.TRA.PST work.PAR do.PEF Opera.LOC

b. Han-dik astebete-ra Amerik(a)-e-ta-ra-ko bide-a presta-tu
over_there.LOC one_week.ALL America.PLU.ALL.ADN trip arrange.PEF
z-i-o-te-n.
//PLU.DTR.PST

c. Han-dik ordubete inguru-ra, beste bat-e-k berri-ro esan z-u-en:...
over_there.LOC one_hour about.ALL else someone.ERG new.ADV say.PEF TRA.PST

d. Ni-k Paris-e-n urtebete-z e-ra-kuts-i d-u-t soziolinguistik(a)-a.
I.ERG Paris.LOC one_year.IDF.INS teach.PEF /1.TRA sociolinguistics

(7) a. Noiz-tik e-zagu(t)-tzen d-ut? Urte-ak d-ir-a.
when.ELA know.IPF /1.TRA year.PLU be.PLU.SYN

b. Zenbat denbora da ero-tu-ta z-a-bil-tza-la?
how_much time be.SYN go_crazy.PEC walk_around.2.SYN.LCZ

c. Ba-d-ir-a hiru egun ni-rekin da-bil-tza-la.
AFF.be.PLU.SYN three day.IDF I.SOC walk.PLU.SYN.LCZ

d. Aspaldi-ko Austin! Urte-ak d-ir-a elkar i-kus-i ez d-u-gu-la.
old Austin year.PLU be.PLU.SYN each_other see.PEF not /1PLU.TRA.LCZ

(8) a. Zenbat denbora d-u ifernu-ko pena hori-e-ta-n z-a-u-de-la?
how_much time have.SYT hell.ADN pain that.PLU.LOC be.2.SYN.LCZ

b. Hamabost egun ba-d-u hemen g-a-r-ela.
fifteen day.IDF AFF.have.SYT here.LOC be.1PLU.SYN.LCZ

c. Hamazazpi urte ba-d-u ez d-u-da-la i-kus-i.
seventeen year.IDF AFF.have.SYT not /1.TRA.LCZ see.PEF

d. Ni hemen n-a-go-ela zazpi urte ba-d-u.
I here.LOC be.1.SYN.LCZ seven year.IDF AFF.have.SYT

e. Hamazazpi urte d-it-u bide-ta-n eskale da-bil-ela.
seventeen year.IDF have.PLU/.SYT road.IDF.LOC beggar.PRE walk.SYN.LCZ

(9) a. Aitona hil ze(-n)-la bi urte ba-d-ir-a.
Grandfather.IDF die.PEF ITR.PST.LCZ two year.IDF AFF.be.PLU.SYN

b. Ba-da ordubete esan d-i-o-da-la.
AFF.be.SYN one_hour.IDF tell.PEF //1.DTR.LCZ

c. Hamasei bat urte d-ir-a liburu-a argitara-tu n-u-e(n)-la.
sixteen a year.IDF be.PLU.SYN book publish.PEF /1.TRA.PST.LCZ

(10) a. Laurogei-ta___lau urte ba-d-u zen-du ze(-n)-la.
eighty-four year.IDF AFF.have.SYT pass_away.PEF ITR.PST.LCZ

b. Gu bi-ak esposa-tu g-in-e(-n)-la ba-d-it-u hamabost
we two.PLU get_married.PEF 1PLU.ITR.PST.LCZ AFF.have.PLU.SYT fifteen
urte.
year.IDF

(11) a. Orain d-ela 30 urte elkarr-ekin jan g-en-u-en
now be.SYN.LCI thirty year.IDF each_other.SOC eat.PEF /1PLU.TRA.PST
ha-ra-ko zoko har-ta-n.
over_there.ALL.ADN spot yonder.LOC

b. Orain-dik egun asko ez d-ela, gizon bat geldi-tu d-u-te bi
now.ELA day many not be.SYN.LCI man a stop.PEF /PLU.TRA two
guarda-k.
guard.IDF.ERG

c. Orain d-ir-ela hogei-ta___hamar bat urte hasi g-in-e-n
now be.PLU.SYN.LCI thirty a year.IDF set_out.PEF 1PLU.ITR.PST
euskaldun-ok batasun-a-ren bila.
Basque.INC unity.GEN on_the_search.PRE

(12) a. D-u-ela aste bat ama-k esan d-i-t: . . .
have.SYT.LCI week a mother.IDF say.PEF /1/.DTR

b. D-u-ela gutxi bilera bat iza-n ze-n.
have.SYT.LCI little_(while) meeting a be.PEF ITR.PST

c. Gauz(a)-ek, . . . d-it-u-ela berrogei-ta___hamar mende bezala
thing.PLU.ERG have.PLU/.SYT.LCI fifty century.IDF SIP
d-irau-te.
remain.PLU.SYT

(13) a. Edari-a-k gal-du-a da-go.— Ordu-an oker da-bil?
drink.ERG ruin.PEF.SIN be.SYN that_time.LOC crookedly walk.SYN

b. Egun-ak hemen pasa-tzen, ordu-an?
day.PLU here.LOC spend.IPF that_time.LOC

c. Zer behar d-u ordu-an?
what need.PPR TRA that_time.LOC

(14) a. Kale-ra atera-tzen d-en-e-an ez d-u euri-rik ari.
street.ALL go_out.IPF ITR.NRE.LOC not TRA rain.PAR do.PPR

b. Euri-a ari d-u-en-e-an ez n-a-iz sekula atera-tzen.
rain do.PPR TRA.NRE.LOC not 1.ITR ever go_out.IPF

c. Krispin harrapa-tu z-u-te(-n)-la ikas-i z-u-e(n)-n-e-an, poz-tu ze-n
Crispin catch.PEF /PLU.TRA.PST.LCZ learn.PEF TRA.PST.NRE.LOC be_happy ITR.PST
epaile-a.
judge

(15) a. Ni-rekin mintza-tu z-in-e(-n)-n-e-tik, zu-re ugazaita hil-tze-ko
I.SOC speak.PEF 2.ITR.PST.NRE.ELA you.GEN stepfather.IDF kill.VEN.ADN
asmo-a har-tu z-en-u-en.
intention take.PEF /2.TRA.PST

b. Gu-re ama hil ze(-n)-n-e-tik ez n-u-en ni-k negarr-ik
we.GEN mother.IDF die.PEF ITR.PST.NRE.ELA not /1.TRA.PST I.ERG tear.PAR
e-gi-n.
make.PEF

(16) a. Apaiz-a e-torr-i ze(-n)-n-e-ko, ez ze-n gauza ezer-ta-ra-ko.
priest come.PEF ITR.PST.NRE.ADN not be.SYN.PST fit.PRE anything.DES
b. Senda-tu n-in-tz-e(-n)-n-e-ko, herri-ko eliza-ra e-ra-ma-n n-ind-u-te-n.
cure.PEF 1.ITR.PST.NRE.ADN village.ADN church.ALL carry.PEF 1/PLU.TRA.PST

(17) a. Baina hurren-go aldi-z i-kus-i n-u-e(n)-n-e-ra-ko, Karmen
but nearby.SUP.ADN time.IDF.INS see.PEF /1.TRA.PST.NRE.DES Carmen
ezkon-tze-ko bezpera-ta-n ze-go-en.
get_married.VEN.ADN eve.IDF.LOC be.SYN.PST
b. Amai-tu d-u-te-n-e-ra-ko ber-(e)-en barren-ek atseden
finish.PEF /PLU.TRA.NRE.DES he_himself.PLU.GEN inner(_self).PLU.ERG relief
handi bat har-tu d-u-te.
great a take.PEF /PLU.TRA

(18) a. Ume-ak ber-(e)-en hegal-e-z i-bil-tze-ko on
young.PLU it_itself.PLU.GEN wing.PLU.INS travel.VEN.ADN fit.IDF
d-ir-en-e-ra-ino . . .
be.PLU.SYN.NRE.TER
b. Zula-tu lurr-a, . . . zeru-a-ren amets-ik ez d-en-e-ra-ino, infernu=kirats-a
dig earth heaven.GEN dream.PAR not be.SYN.NRE.TER stench_of_hell
d-en-e-ra-ino . . .
be.SYN.NRE.TER
c. Utz-i lo e-gi-te-n nahi d-u-en arte.
let sleep.IDF do.VEN.LOC want.PPR TRA.NRE as_long_as
d. Aita gal-du g-en-u-e(n)-n arte, artzaintza iza-n ze-n
father.IDF lose.PEF /1PLU.TRA.PST.NRE until_the_time shepherding be.PEF ITR.PST
en-e lan nagusi-a.
I.GEN job main

(19) a. Gaur-tik da-torr-en-e-ra
today.ELA come.SYN.NRE.ALL
b. Zenbat denbora iza-n ze-n ihes e-gi-n z-en-i-e(-n)-n-e-tik
how_much time be.PEF ITR.PST flight.IDF do.PEF /PLU/2.DTR.PST.NRE.ELA
hil z-en-it-u-e(n)-n-e-ra?
kill.PEF PLU/2.TRA.PST.NRE.ALL

(20) a. Diru asko al ze-ra-ma-n bart etxe-tik irten ze(-n)-n-e-an?
money a_lot INT carry.SYT.PST last_night house.ELA go_out.PEF ITR.PST.NRE.LOC

b. Ibilaldi hori zin-e-z gusta-tzen zi-tza-i-da-n, berezi-ki denbor(a)-a ederr-a
walk that oath.IDF.INS please.IPF 1/.DIT.PST especially weather fine
ze(-n)-n-e-an.
be.SYN.PST.NRE.LOC

c. Ez z-u-en lo-rik e-gi-ten janzki hura ber-e etxe-ko
not TRA.PST sleep.PAR do.IPF suit yonder he_himself.GEN house.ADN
eskailer(a)-e-ta-n aurki-tu z-u-e(n)-n-e-tik.
stairs.PLU.LOC find.PEF TRA.PST.NRE.ELA

d. Egia garratz hori-ek gibel-e-ko min-a d-u-zu-n-e-an bakarr-ik esa(n)-ten
truth bitter that.PLU liver.ADN ache have./2.SYT.NRE.LOC only.STA say.IPF
d-it-u-zu.
PLU/2.TRA

(21) a. Pasa-tzen n-a-iz-en-e-an zu-re leiho-pe-tik ...
pass.IPF 1.ITR.NRE.LOC you.GEN space_under_the_window.ELA

b. G-eu-re asaba zaharr-(e)-en odol-a da-uka-gu-n arte
we.REF.GEN forefather ancient.PLU.GEN blood have./1PLU.SYT.NRE as_long_as
zain-e-ta-n.
vein.PLU.LOC

(22) a. Apaiz-a-k elkarrengana-ko baimen-a e-ma-n z-i-e(-n)-n ordu-tik ...
priest.ERG unite.(VEN).ADN permission give.PEF /PLU/.DTR.PST.NRE that_time.ELA

b. Baina orain, apaiz-a-k baimen-a e-ma-n z-i-e(-n)-n-e-tik ...
but now priest.ERG permission give.PEF /PLU/.DTR.PST.NRE.ELA

(23) a. Kotxe-tik atera n-in-tz-e(-n)-n ordu-ko, alkate-a e-torr-i ze-n.
car.ELA get_out.PEF 1.ITR.PST.NRE time.ADN mayor come.PEF ITR.PST

b. Nesk(a)-a-k, i-kus-ten d-u-en ordu-ko, ha(r-en)-la esan-go d-i-t: ...
girl.ERG see.IPF TRA.NRE time.ADN yonder_way say.FUT /1/.DTR

c. Arreta-z eki-n d-i-o lan-a-ri, etxera-tu ze(-n)-n ordu-ko.
care.IDF.INS set_to.PEF DTR work.DAT get_home.PEF ITR.PST.NRE time.ADN

(24) a. Txerri-a hil-da-ko aste-a eta ezkon-du-ta-ko urte-a, on-en-ak.
pig slaughter.PEC.ADN week and marry.PEC.ADN year good.SUP.PLU

b. Gatz hau ur-tu-ta-ko ordu-an, gazi-tzen da orobat beste alde-tik.
salt this dissolve.PEC.ADN time.LOC salt.IPF ITR likewise other side.ELA

c. Gatz hau ur-tu-ta-ko-an, gazi-tzen da orobat beste alde-tik.
salt this dissolve.PEC.ADN.LOC salt.IPF ITR likewise other side.ELA

(25) a. Etxe-ra e-torr-i-ta-ko-an ez haserre-tu behin-tzat.
house.ALL come.PEC.ADN.LOC not get_angry at_least

b. Zu eser-i-ta-ko-an ni-re txand(a) iza-n-go da.
you sit_down.PEC.ADN.LOC I.GEN turn be.FUT ITR

c. Hori gero e-torr-i-ko da etsai-ak oinpera-tu eta zanpa-tu-ta-ko-an.
that later come.FUT ITR enemy.PLU trample and crush.PEC.ADN.LOC

d. Iraultz(a)-a buka-tu-ta-ko-an, zin e-gi-ten d-i-na-t antola-tu-ko
revolution end.PEC.ADN.LOC oath.IDF make.IPF /2SOL.FEM/1.DTR arrange.FUT
d-u-gu-la hori ere.
/1PLU.TRA.LCZ that too

(26) Ait(a)-a-ren bihotz hon-e-k bihotz-a gal-du-ri(k)-ko-an, . . .
father.GEN heart this.ERG heart lose.STA.ADN.LOC

(27) Ez da hau lo e-gi-te-ko ordu-a.
not be.SYN this sleep.IDF do.VEN.ADN time

(28) a. Zortzi lagun g-in-e-n mahai-an eguerdi-ta-n, eta
eight fellow.IDF be.1PLU.SYN.PST table.LOC noon.IDF.LOC and
afal-tze-ko-an bi beste-rik ez g-in-e-n ager-tu.
eat_dinner.VEN.ADN.LOC two.IDF other.PAR not 1PLU.ITR.PST appear.PEF

b. Mogel har-tu-ko d-u-t abia-tze-ko-an.
Mogel take.FUT /1.TRA start_out.VEN.ADN.LOC

c. Hitz=elkartze berri-e-ta-n hauta-tze-ko-an, bi indar ari
compound new.PLU.LOC choose.VEN.ADN.LOC two force.IDF be_busy.PPR
za-i-z-ki-gu beti lan-e-an.
1PLU/PLU.DIT always work.LOC

(29) a. Hil-tze-ra-ko-an zu-re galde e-gi-n z-u-en.
die.VEN.ALL.ADN.LOC you.GEN request.IDF make.PEF TRA.PST

b. Hil-tze-ra-ko-an bakarr-ik aitor-tu z-u-en hori ber-e seme-a-ri.
die.VEN.ALL.ADN.LOC only.STA confess.PEF TRA.PST that he_himself.GEN son.DAT

c. Aziend(a)-a eros-te-ra-ko-an . . .
cattle buy.VEN.ALL.ADN.LOC

d. Liburu bat eros-te-ra-ko-an, hauta-tze-n ja-ki-n behar d-u-zu.
book a buy.VEN.ALL.ADN.LOC choose.VEN.LOC know have_to.PPR /2.TRA

e. Gizon-a-k utz-i e-gi-n z-u-en, Martha-k seme bat e-duk-i-tze-ra-ko-an.
man.ERG leave do.PEF TRA.PST Martha.ERG son a have.VEN.ALL.ADN.LOC

(30) a. Malko-ak ze-ri-z-ki-o-n hori esa(n)-te-ra-ko-an.
tear.PLU flow./PLU.DYN.PST that say.VEN.ALL.ADN.LOC

b. Bizkor i-bil-i ze-n motel-e-ra itzul-tze-ra-ko-an.
quickly walk.PEF ITR.PST motel.ALL go_back.VEN.ALL.ADN.LOC

c. Setatsua-z hitzegi-te-ra-ko-an, zakar ari-tze-ko joer(a)-a
Setatsua.INS talk.VEN.ALL.ADN.LOC harsh.PRE be_busy.VEN.ADN tendency
da-uka-t.
have./1.SYT

(31) a. Alargun-du ze(-n)-n-e-z gero, eliza-tik aldegin gabe
become_a_widow.PEF ITR.PST.NRE.INS after church.ELA run_away without.PRE
bizi ze-n.
live.PPR ITR.PST

b. Ez d-i-gu inor-k ezer os-tu ni hemen n-a-iz-en-e-z gero.
not /1PLU/.DTR anybody.ERG anything steal.PEF I here be.1.SYN.NRE.INS since

c. Jesuit(a)-(e)-en ikastetxe-ra e-ra-ma-n n-u-e(n)-n-e-z gero asko alda-tu
Jesuit.PLU.GEN school.ALL take_to.PEF /1.TRA.PST.NRE.INS after a_lot change.PEF
da.
ITR

(32) a. Hartueman handi-a iza-n z-u-en aitaginarreb(a)-a-rekin Mikel-e-k
contact great have.PEF TRA.PST father-in-law.SOC Michael.ERG
ezkon-du ze(-n)-n-e-z gero-z-tik.
marry.PEF ITR.PST.NRE.INS after.ELA

b. Itzulpen ugari iza-n d-u-gu euskal literatur(a)-a has-i
translation plenty_of have.PEF /1PLU.TRA Basque literature begin.PEF
ze(-n)-n-e-z gero-z-tik.
ITR.PST.NRE.INS since.ELA

(33) a. Hitzegi-te-n has-i n-a-iz-en-e-z gero, guzti-a esan behar
speak.VEN.LOC begin.PEF 1.ITR.NRE.INS since everything tell must.PPR
d-i-zu-e-t.
/2PLU/1.DTR

b. Lur ber-a-ren ume-ak d-ir-en-e-z gero-z, zuzen ber-ak
earth same.GEN child.PLU be.PLU.SYN.NRE.INS since right same.PLU
d-it-u-z-te.
have.PLU/PLU.SYT

(34) Davit-e-k ze-ra-ma(-n)-n bizi-a, Saül etsai-tzat ager-tzen zi-tza-i-o-(-n)-n
David.ERG lead.SYT.PST.NRE life Saul enemy.PRO appear.IPF DIT.PST.NRE
ordu-z gero-z, oso-ki ze-n urrikalgarri-a.
time.IDF.INS since very be.SYN.PST pitiable

(35) a. Hi jaio ordu-ko, ba-n-e-ki-z-ki-a-n ni-k gauza hau-ek.
you.SOL be_born time.ADN AFF.know.PLU/2SOL/1.DYT.PST I.ERG thing this.PLU

b. Ni-re arrebatxo-a jaio ordu-ko kontura-tu n-in-tz-e-n ni n-in-tz-e(-n)-la
I.GEN little_sister be_born time.ADN realize.PEF 1.ITR.PST I be.1.SYN.PST.LCZ
ama-ren kuttun-a.
mother.IDF.GEN favorite

(36) a. Ate-a zabal-du ordu-ko, am(a)-a lurr-e-an da-kus-te.
door open time.ADN mother ground.LOC see./PLU.SYT

b. Haurr-ak elkarr-ekin euskara-z mintzo hauteman ordu-ko,
child.PLU each_other.SOC Basque.IDF.INS talk(ing).PRE catch time.ADN
gaztiga-tzen g-in(de)-(i)t-u-en.
punish.IPF 1PLU/.TRA.PST

c. Laura-k oihu e-gi-n z-u-en ni sar-tze-n i-kus-i ordu-ko.
Laura.ERG shout.IDF make.PEF TRA.PST I come_in.VEN.LOC see time.ADN

(37) a. Zop(a)-a e-karr-i ordu-ko has-ten da.
soup bring_in time.ADN begin.IPF ITR

b. Esku-a-z hunki-tu ordu-ko gaitz-a-k u(t)z-ten d-u.
hand.INS touch time.ADN ailment.ERG leave.IPF TRA

(38) a. Mutil-a-k esan z-i-o-n har-tu ordu-ra-ko:...
boy.ERG say.PEF DTR.PST take time.DES

b. Zuhaitz-(e)-en orri-ak ihar-tze-n has-i ordu-ra-ko, andre Luzia ihar-tu
tree.PLU.GEN leaf.PLU wither.VEN.LOC begin time.DES Lady Lucia wither.PEF
ze-n.
ITR.PST

c. E-zagu(t)-tu ordu-ra-ko maita-tu z-ir-e-n bi-ak.
know time.DES love.PEF PLU.ITR.PST two.ZEP.PLU

(39) a. Begi-ak luza-tu z-it-u-e(n)-n bat-e-an hiru gizon ber-e
eye.PLU lift.PEF PLU/.TRA.PAST.NRE one.LOC three man.IDF he_himself.GEN
ondo-an zut-ik i-kus-i z-it-u-en.
side.LOC erect.STA see.PEF PLU/.TRA.PST

b. Angin(a)-a-rekin ohe-an ze-go-e(n)-n bat-e-an, anai(a)-a-ren gela-ra
tonsillitis.SOC bed.LOC be.SYN.PST.NRE one.LOC brother.GEN room.ALL
sar-tu n-in-tz-e-n.
go_into.PEF 1.ITR.PST

c. E-ra-ntzu-n d-i-o-t ni-k ere, Jaungoiko-a-k dei-tu d-i-da-n-e-ta-n?
answer.PEF //1.DTR I.ERG also God.ERG call.PEF /1/.DTR.NRE.PLU.LOC

d. Ha(r-en)-la-xe aurki-tzen n-u-en, behin-tzat, ni-k, baserri har-ta-n
that_way.EMP find.IPF /1.TRA.PST at_least I.ERG farmhouse yonder.LOC
sar-tzen n-in-tz-e(-n)-n-e-ta-n.
enter.IPF 1.ITR.PST.NRE.PLU.LOC

e. Ba-d-u-t orain, etxera-tzen n-a-iz-en-e-ta-n, no-ra jo n-eu-re
AFF.have./1.SYN now come_home.IPF 1.ITR.NRE.PLU.LOC where.ALL go I.REF.GEN
egarri-a berdin-tze-ko.
thirst quench.VEN.ADN

f. Guri-a e-gi-ten d-en bakoitz-e-an, garbi-tu behar da azpi-a ur-a-rekin.
butter make.IPF ITR.NRE each.LOC clean must.PPR ITR ground water.SOC

g. Eztul-a e-gi-ten d-u-en bakoitz-e-an, ba-d-irudi kristal guzti-ak
cough make.IPF TRA.NRE each.LOC AFF.seem.SYT windowpane all.PLU
hauts-i behar d-it-u-ela.
break must.PPR PLU/.TRA.LCZ

h. Ni-re amets-e-ta-ra e-tor-tzen z-a-r-en bakoitz-e-an, beti zu gaixo.
I.GEN dream.PLU.ALL come.IPF 2.ITR.NRE each.LOC always you sick.IDF

i. Ume-e-i goxo-ak e-ma-ten z-i-z-ki-e-n ze-torr-e(-n)-n
child.PLU.DAT sweet.PLU give.IPF PLU/PLU/.DTR.PST come.SYN.PST.NRE
gehi-en-e-ta-n.
much.SUP.PLU.LOC

j. Ni-k behin-tzat horre(n)-la-ko-rik aski topa-tu d-ut liburu-a zabal-du
I.ERG at_least like_that.ADN.PAR plenty encounter.PEF /1.TRA book open.PEF
d-u-da-n guzti-e-ta-n.
/1.TRA.NRE all.PLU.LOC

k. Esna-tzen n-in-tz-e(n)-n bakan-e-ta-n, euri-a-ren hots-a adi-tzen n-u-en.
wake_up.IPF 1.ITR.PST.NRE rare.PLU.LOC rain.GEN sound hear.IPF /1.TRA.PST

l. Lekunberri-ra j-oa-ten n-in-tz-e(n)-n-ero, beti lelo ber-a z-u-en
Lecumberri.ALL go.IPF 1.ITR.PST.NRE.FRQ always babble same have.SYT.PST
zapatari-a-k.
cobbler.ERG

m. Garrasi hirukoitz bat-e-z e-ra-ntz-u-n ohi z-u-en norbait-e-k
shout triple a.INS answer be_in_habit.PPR TRA.PST someone.ERG
proposamen-en bat e-gi-te-n z-i-o(-n)-n-ero.
proposal.IDF.GEN a make.IPF DTR.PST.NRE.FRQ

(40) a. Sermoi-ak eta gauza on-ak adi-tze-ra j-oa-ten d-ir-a
sermon.PLU and thing good.PLU listen_to.VEN.ALL go.IPF PLU.ITR
d-ir-en aldi-e-ta-n.
be.PLU.SYN.NRE occasion.PLU.LOC

b. Burr(a)-a e-gi-ten d-en aldi bakoitz-e-an, behere-a-k garbi-tu behar
butter make.IPF ITR.NRE time each.LOC floor.ERG clean need.PPR
d-u ur-a-rekin.
TRA water.SOC

c. Ni i-ra-tzarr-i n-a-iz-en aldi bakoitz-e-an amets-e-ta-n aurki-tu z-a-it-u-t
I wake_up.PEF 1.ITR.NRE time each.LOC dream.IDF.LOC find.PEF 2/1.TRA
urduri samar.
restless quite.PRE

d. Esna-tzen n-in-tz-e(-n)-n aldi bakan-e-ta-n, euri-a-ren hotsa adi-tzen
wake_up.IPF 1.ITR.PST.NRE time rare.PLU.LOC rain.GEN sound hear.IPF
n-u-en sabai-an.
/1.TRA.PST ceiling.LOC

e. I-kus-ten z-a-it-u-da-n aldiero, aha(t)z-ten za-i-z-ki-t beste gauza guzti-ak.
see.IPF 2/1.TRA.NRE time.FRQ forget.IPF 1/PLU.DIT other thing all.PLU

(41) Ni i-kus-i-ta-ko bakoitz-e-an, ume-a no-la g-en-u-e(n)-n galde-tu-ko
I see.PEC.ADN each.LOC child how have./1PLU.SYT.PST.NCZ ask.FUT
z-i-da-n.
/1/.DTR.PST

(42) a. Zer ari ze-n Jainko-a zeru=lurr-ak e-gi-n aurre-an?
what be_busy.PPR ITR.PST God heaven_and_earth.PLU make front_part.LOC
b. Ez d-u-t jan-go esa(n)-te-ko d-u-da-n-a esan aurre-tik.
not /1.TRA eat.FUT say.VEN.ADN have./1.SYN.NRE.ZEP say front_part.ELA

(43) a. E-tza-te-ra zi-h-oa-z-e(-n)-n aurre-an, hiri-ko
lie_down.VEN.ALL go.PLU.SYN.PST.NRE front_part.LOC city.ADN
zahar=gazte-ek etxe-a ingura-tu z-u-te-n.
young_and_old_man.PLU.ERG house surround.PEF /PLU.TRA.PST
b. Gu-re arreb(a)-a-ri ha(r-en)-la esan omen z-i-o-n, hil behar
we.GEN sister.DAT thus speak REP DTR.PST die be_going_to.PPR
z-u-e(n)-n aurre-an: . . .
TRA.PST.NRE front_part.LOC

(44) a. Zeru-ra igo-tze-ko aurre-an, esku hau utz-i z-i-e-n.
heaven.ALL ascend.VEN.ADN front_part.LOC power this leave.PEF /PLU/.DTR
b. Ezkon-tze-ko aurre-an galde-tu z-u-en Mikalla-k: . . .
marry.VEN.ADN front_part.LOC ask.PEF TRA.PST Mikalla.ERG

(45) a. Ehiz(a)-a hil aitzin, jale-rik ez gonbida!
game kill front_part.IDF eater.PAR not invite.RAD
b. Urrun-e-tik i-kus-i z-u-te(-n)-n-e-ko, hura
far.ELA see /PLU.TRA.PST.NRE.ADN yonder_one
hurbil-du aitzin, hil-en z-u-te(-n)-la hitzar-tu z-ir-e-n.
come_close front_part.IDF kill.FUT /PLU.TRA.PST.LCZ agree.PEF PLU.ITR.PST
c. Ahari-a-k ez d-u ardi-rik joka-tu behar hiru urte bete aitzin-e-an.
ram.ERG not TRA sheep.PAR cover must.PPR three year.IDF reach front_part.LOC
d. Eri-tu aitzin-e-tik on-gi e-zagu(t)-tzen z-u-en ber-e senarr-a.
fall_ill front_part.ELA well know.IPF TRA.PST she_herself.GEN husband

(46) a. Zahar-tze-ko aitzin-e-an entsea-tu n-a-iz on-gi bizi-tze-ra.
grow_old.VEN.ADN front_part.LOC try.PEF 1.ITR well live.VEN-ALL
b. Ebak-i behar da lora-tu d-en aitzin-e-an.
cut must.PPR ITR bloom.PEF ITR.RNE front_part.LOC

(47) Erroma-ra heldu ze-n 1538 aitzintto-an.
Rome.ALL arrive.PEF ITR.PST 1538 front_part.DIM.LOC

(48) a. Zerbait edan ondo-ren erraz bero-tzen d-ir-a gizonezko-ak.
something drink contiguity.ELA easily heat_up.IPF PLU.ITR man.PLU
In glossing *ondoren*, I use the abbreviation ELA, where R. de Rijk is talking about an "archaic ablative," since this part of the semantics of the latter (Latin) case is expressed in Basque by means of the elative case.

b. Gu-re berri ja-ki-n ondo-ren, euskar(a)-a-ren berri on-ak
we.GEN news.IDF know contiguity.ELA Basque.GEN news good.PLU
zabal-du-ko d-it-u Europa-n.
spread.FUT PLU/.TRA Europe

c. Azken-e-an, e-gi-n ondo-an, guzti-ak erre-tzen z-it-u-en.
end.LOC make contiguity.LOC all.ZEP.PLU burn.IPF PLU/.TRA.PST

d. Batxiler-a e-gi-n ondo-an, fabrik(a)-an has-i n-in-tz-e-n
high_school_diploma make contiguity.LOC factory.LOC begin.PEF 1.ITR.PST
lan-e-an.
work.LOC

(49) a. ... n-eu-re superbio-z-ko bestimend(a)-a-z biluz-i n-a-iz-en
... I.REF.GEN arrogance.IDF.INS.ADN garment.INS strip.PEF 1.ITR.NRE
ondo-an ...
contiguity.LOC

b. Pi(t)z-tu n-a-i-z-en ondo-an, orde-a, j-oa-n-go n-a-iz Galilea-ra.
rise 1.ITR.NRE contiguity.LOC however go.FUT 1.ITR Galilee.ALL

(50) a. Latin-e-z-ko otoitz batzu-ek esan oste-an, galde-tu z-i-o-n: ...
Latin.IDF.INS.ADN prayer a_few.PLU say back_part.LOC ask.PEF DTR.PST

b. Une luze bat-e-an itxaron oste-an, branka-ko parte-tik kanpo-ko
time long a.LOC wait back_part.LOC prow.ADN area.ELA outside.ADN
argi-a sar-tze-n has-i ze-n.
light come_in.VEN.LOC start.PEF ITR.PST

(51) a. Ez z-u-te-n ezkontza=harreman-ik iza-n, Maria-k seme-a iza-n
not /PLU.TRA.PST marital_relation.PAR have.PEF Mary.ERG son get.PEF
z-u-e(n)-n arte.
TRA.PST.NRE interval.IDF
In other chapters, I have glossed *arte* with 'until'; in this context, however, I opt to stick as closely as possible to the origin and analysis of this construction as proposed by R. de Rijk in the paragraph concerned.

b. Ni e-tor-tzen n-a-iz-en arte hori hemen geldi-tze-a nahi
I come.IPF 1.ITR.NRE interval.IDF that_one here.LOC stay.VEN want.PPR
ba-d-u-t, zu-ri zer?
CDP./1.TRA you.DAT what

(52) a. Ni e-torr-i arte hori geldi-tze-a nahi baldin ba-d-u-t, zu-ri
I come interval.IDF that_one stay.VEN want.PPR CDC CDP./1.TRA you.DAT
zer?
what

b. Ni-re seme-tzat ez h-a-u-t har-tu-ko ama e-ra-kuts-i arte.
I.GEN son.PRO not 2SOL/1.TRA take.FUT mother.IDF show interval.IDF

(53) a. Eta ez n-it-u-en sine(t)s-ten har-ik eta ni-k n-e(u)-r(e_h)on-e-k i-kus-i
and not PLU/1.TRA.PST believe.IPF EMC EXP I.ERG I_myself.ERG see.PEF
d-it-u-da-n arte-ra-ino.
PLU/1.TRA.NRE interval.TER

b. Ez d-i-zu-t bake-ta-n utz-i-ko, har-ik eta nahi d-u-da-n-a lor-tu
not /2/1.DTR peace.IDF.LOC leave.FUT EMC EXP want.PPR /1.TRA.NRE.ZEP obtain
arte.
interval.IDF

(54) a. Ez, Axari n-a-iz-en arte-an!
no Axari be.1.SYN.NRE interval.LOC

b. Eta hori gerta-tzen ze(-n)-n arte-an, beste-a han e-go-ten
and that happen.IPF ITR.PST.NRE interval.LOC other.ZEP over_there.LOC stand.IPF
omen ze-n, ohol-(e)-en bestalde-an.
REP ITR.PST board.PLU.GEN on_the_other_side

(55) a. Euskal odol-a ni-re zain-e-ta-n bizi arte-an, e-ki-n-go
Basque blood I.GEN vein.PLU.LOC live.PPR interval.LOC apply_oneself_to.FUT
d-i-zu-t kant(a)-a-ri.
/2/1.DTR song.DAT

b. Oturuntz(a)-a-k irau-n arte-an bi anai(a)-ek ez z-i-o-te-n
meal.ERG last interval.LOC two brother.PLU.ERG not //PLU.DTR.PST
elkarr-i hitz-ik e-gi-n.
each_other.DAT word.PAR do.PEF

(56) a. Bizi n-a-iz-en arte eta bai heriotze-an, argi e-gi-n-go d-u-zu
live.PPR 1.ITR.NRE interval.IDF and also death.LOC light.IDF make.FUT /2.TRA
en-e bihotz-e-an.
I.GEN heart.LOC

b. Ni-k, eskol(a)-an abia-tu arte-an, ez n-u-en behin ere frantses hitz bat
I.ERG school.LOC start interval.LOC not /1.TRA.PST once even French word a
e-ntzu-n.
hear.PEF

(57) a. Eser-i ni-re eskuin-e-an, z-eu-re etsai-ak oinazpi-an jar-tzen
sit I.GEN right.LOC you.REF.GEN enemy.PLU bottom_of_the_foot.LOC put.IPF

d-i-z-ki-zu-da-n bitarte-an.
PLU/2/1.DTR.NRE interval.LOC

b. Orain apaiz-a hor da-go-en bitarte-an hitzegin nahi
now priest there.LOC be.SYN.NRE interval.LOC speak like_to.PPR
n-i-zu-e-ke.
/2PLU/1.DTR.COD

c. Ez d-u-gu-la eta ez da-ki-gu-la ez da-ki-gu-n
not have./1PLU.SYT.LCZ and not know./1PLU.SYT.LCZ not know./1PLU.SYT.NRE
bitarte-an ez g-a-r-a iza-te-ko eta ja-ki-te-ko bide-an sar-tu-ko.
interval.LOC not 1PLU.ITR have.FUT and know.VEN.ADN path.LOC get_onto.FUT

(58) a. Beste zerbait utz-i behar-ko d-i-da-zu, antxume-a bidal-i bitarte-an.
else something leave have_to.FUT /1/2.DTR kid send interval.LOC

b. Egunkari hau irakurr-i bitarte-an, Jainko-a-k da-ki zein gogoeta ilun
diary this read interval.LOC God.ERG know.SYT which thought dark
hits e-gi-n n-u-e(n)-n.
sad make.PEF /1.TRA.PST.NCZ

c. Gizon-a-k gazt(a)-ak e-gi-n bitarte, andre-a-k bab(a)-ak egos-i.
man.ERG cheese.PLU make interval.IDF lady.ERG bean.PLU cook

(59) a. Mundu-an n-a-iz-e(n)-no, mundu-a-ren argi-a n-a-iz.
world.LOC be.1.SYN.NRE.NDC world.GEN light be.1.SYN

b. On ze(-n-n)-no ez da lan-e-tik geldi-tu.
well.IDF be.SYN.PST.NRE.NDC not ITR work.ELA cease.PEF

c. En-e bihotz-a, bizi n-a-iz-e(n)-no, iza-n-en za-i-zu fidel-a.
I.GEN heart live.PPR 1.ITR.NRE.NDC be.FUT 2/.DIT faithful

(60) a. Zamari-a gazte d-e(n)-ino hez-ten da.
mule young.IDF be.SYN.NRE.NDC train.IPF ITR

b. Aldamen-e-an behar n-ind-u-en, eritegi-a zabal-ik ze-go-e(n)-ino.
side.LOC need.PPR 1/.TRA.PST infirmary open.STA be.SYN.PST.NRE.NDC

c. Euskal literatur(a)-a-ren oroitzapen-a-k lurr-e-an d-irau-e(n)-ino, ez da
Basque literature.GEN memory.ERG earth.LOC last.SYT.NRE.NDC not ITR
noski itzal-i-ko har-en izen-a eta omen-a.
certainly fade_away.FUT yonder_one.GEN name and fame

(61) a. Lehen etsipen-a-k, ezkon-du eta bi urte-ra jo z-u-en.
first depression.ERG get_married POC two year.IDF.ALL hit.PEF TRA.PST

b. Azken-e-an jaio e-gi-n n-in-tz-en 1936ko gerr(a)-a buka-tu eta
end.LOC be_born do.PEF 1.ITR.PST 1936.ADN war end POC
han-dik gutxi-ra.
over_there.ELA little.ALL

c. J-oa-n eta ber-e-ha(r-en)-la-ko-an itzul-i ze-n.
go POC immediately.ADN.LOC come_back.PEF ITR.PST

d. Mediku-a harrapa-tu eta ber-e-ha(r-en)-la hemen n-a-iz.
doctor fetch POC immediately here.LOC be.1.SYN

(62) a. Etxe oso-a e-ra-kuts-i eta gero, saloi zabal-e-ra zuzen-du d-it-u.
house whole show POC later hall spacious.ALL direct.PEF PLU/.TRA

b. Agin-du za-i-zu-e-n guzti-a e-gi-n eta gero, esan ...
command.PEF 2PLU/.DIT.NRE all do POC later say

c. Hemen, hil eta gero ere, amandre-a-ren esku-a ageri da.
here.LOC die POC later even grandmother.GEN hand conspicuous.IDF be.SYN

(63) a. Orobat, afal-du eta, kaliz(a)-a har-tu z-u-en ...
likewise sup POC cup take.PEF TRA.PST

b. New York-tik e-torr-i eta azken orrazket(a)-ak e-ma-n
New York.ELA come_back POC last correction_in_a_written_work.PLU give.PEF
n-i-z-ki-o-n.
PLU//1.DTR.PST

(64) a. Eguzki-a eror-tze-a-r ze-go-en mendi oste-ra.
sun sink.VEN.RIM be.SYN.PST mountain back_part.ALL

b. Gaixo hori hil-tze-a-r da-go.
patient that die.VEN.RIM be.SYN

(65) a. Baimen=aldi-a amai-tze-a-r ne-(d)uka-n.
furlough finish.VEN.RIM have./1.SYT.PST

b. Zu-k e-ma-n-da-ko liburu-a irakur-tze-a-r da-(d)uka-t.
you.ERG give.PEC.ADN book read.VEN.RIM have./1.SYT

(66) a. Beste mutil bat ze-go-en zut-ik, kantu-z has-te-a-r.
other boy a stand.SYN.PST upright.STA singing.IDF.INS begin.VEN.RIM

b. Gal-tze-a-r aurki-tu n-ind-u-en.
lose.VEN.RIM find.PEF 1/.TRA.PST

(67) a. Zabal=zabal-a eror-tze-r ze-n Jon___Doni Petri.
flat-flat fall.VEN.IDF.RIM be.SYN.PST Saint Peter

b. Hori e-ntzu-te-an, bihotz-a geldi-tze-r zi-tza-i-da-n.
that hear.VEN.DEF.LOC heart stop.VEN.IDF.RIM 1/.DYN.PST

(68) a. No-la e-gi-te-r n-u-e(n)-n hamaketako-a Azkaine-n.
how do.VEN.IDF.RIM /1.SYT.PST elevenses Azcain.LOC

b. Xahu-tze-r n-a-u-te lurr-e-an.
annihilate.VEN.IDF.RIM 1/PLU.SYT earth.LOC

(69) a. Ate-ak puska-tze-ko zori-an ze-u-de-n.
door.PLU break.VEN.ADN destiny.LOC be.PLU.SYN.PST

b. Ni-re etsai-(e)-en esku-e-ta-n eror-tze-ko zori-an n-a-go.
I.GEN enemy.PLU.GEN hand.PLU.LOC fall.VEN.ADN destiny.LOC be.1.SYN
In this context, I gloss *zorian* in line with the origin and analysis proposed by R. de Rijk.

c. Erretore-a-k, algara-z leher-tze-ko zori-an, d-io:...
parish_priest.ERG laughter.IDF.INS burst.VEN.ADN destiny.LOC say.SYT

(70) a. Orain-txe txipiroi batzu-ek ja(n)-te-n ari n-in-tz-e(-n)-la,
now.EMP squid some.PLU eat.VEN.LOC be_busy.PPR 1.ITR.PST.LCI
Donostia-tik da-torr-en beste paper-a har-tu d-u-gu.
San_Sebastian.ELA come.SYN.NRE other paper receive.PEF /1PLU.TRA

b. Lo n-en-go-e(n)-la ager-tu zi-tza-i-da-n aingeru oso eder bat.
asleep.PRE be.1.SYN.PST.LCI appear.PEF 1/.DIT.PST angel very beautiful a

c. Esna da-go-ela ez d-u inor-k amets-ik e-gi-ten.
awake.PRE be.SYN.LCI not TRA anybody.ERG dream.PAR do.IPF

d. Gerr(a)-a buka-tze-a-r ze-go-e(n)-la ber-e senarr-a eta beste bi
war end.VEN.RIM be.SYN.PST.LCI she_herself.GEN husband and other two
soldadu afusila-tu z-it-u-z-te-n.
soldier.IDF shoot.PEF PLU/PLU.TRA.PST

e. Zer e-gi-n ez n-e-ki-e(n)-la etxe-tik irten n-in-tz-en.
what do not know./1.SYT.PST.LCI house.ELA go_out.PEF 1.ITR.PST

(71) a. Joko-an ari z-ir-e-n, aurre-an edari-ak
play.LOC be_busy.PPR PLU.ITR.PST front_part.LOC drink.PLU
z-it-u-z-te(-n)-la.
have.PLU/PLU.SYT.PST.LCI

b. Hon-(r)a no-n azal-du d-en Rebeka, pegarr-a sorbald(a)-an
here.ALL where.LOC come_out.PEF ITR.NCZ Rebecca jar shoulder.LOC
d-u-ela.
have.SYT.LCI

(72) Hargin guzti-ek ezpat(a)-a gerri-an ze-ra-ma-te(-n)-la e-gi-ten
bricklayer all.PLU.ERG sword waist.LOC wear./PLU.SYT.PST.LCI do.IPF
z-u-te-n lan.
/PLU.TRA.PST work.IDF

(73) a. Orain-dik zu-(e)-en arte-an n-a-go-ela-rik esan d-i-zu-e-t hau.
now.ELA you.PLU.GEN among be.1.SYN.LCI tell.PEF /2PLU/1.DTR this

b. Apaizgo-an urte askotxo da-ra-ma-z-ki-da-la-rik, ez d-ut ikas-i
priesthood.LOC year much.DIM spend.PLU/1.SYT.LCI not /1.TRA learn.PEF

emakumezko-(e)-en gorabehera eta matrikul(a)-ak konpreni-tze-n.
female.PLU.GEN whim and wile.PLU understand.VEN.LOC

(74) Poxi bat gose-a ezti-tu d-ela-rik, solas-ak has-te.
bit a hunger alleviate.PEF ITR.LCI talk.PLU start.VEN.IDF

(75) a. Zatiño hori e-ntzu-te-an, beldurr-a-k har-tzen n-ind-u-en.
little_fragment that hear.VEN.DEF.LOC fear.ERG overtake.IPF 1/.TRA.PST
b. Hitz-(e)-en soinu-a e-ntzu-te-an, ikara-tu e-gi-n ze-n.
word.PLU.GEN sound hear.VEN.DEF.LOC get_frightened do.PEF ITR.PST

Chapter 21

(1) a. Nor e-tor-tze-a nahi z-en-u-en?
who come.VEN want.PPR /2.TRA.PST
b. Zer nahi z-en-u-en ni-k Gazteiz-en e-gi-te-a?
what want.PPR /2.TRA.PST I.ERG Vitoria.LOC do.VEN

(2) a. Diru-rik gabe, no-ra nahi d-u-zu j-oa-n n-a-di-n?
money.PAR without.PRE where.ALL want.PPR /2.TRA go(.RAD) 1.ITR.SUJ.NCZ
b. Zer nahi d-u-zu ni-k e-gi-n de-za-da-n?
what want.PPR /2.TRA I.ERG do(.RAD) /1.TRA.SUJ.NCZ
c. Eta zer nahi z-en-u-en e-gi-n n-e-za(-n)-n?
and what want.PPR /2.TRA.PST do(.RAD) /1.TRA.SUJ.PST.NCZ
d. Hil n-a-za-n nahi al d-u-zu?
kill(.RAD) 1/.TRA.SUJ.NCZ want.PPR INT /2.TRA
e. Ez z-u-en ustel bat ze(-n)-la pentsa ze-za-te(-n)-n nahi.
not TRA.PST wimp a be.SYN.PST.LCZ think.RAD /PLU.TRA.SUJ.PST.NCZ want.PPR
f. Belle eta Greta-k ez z-u-te-n inor-k lotu z-it-za(-n)-n
Belle and Greta.ERG not /PLU.TRA.PST anyone.ERG tie_up.PEF PLU/.TRA.SUJ.PST.NCZ
nahi.
want.PPR
g. Guiomar isil ze-di-n desio z-u-en.
Guiomar quiet.IDF be.SYN.SUJ.PST.NCZ wish.PPR TRA.PST

(3) a. Opa d-i-o-gu zeru-an goza da-di-la.
wish.PPR //1PLU.DTR heaven.LOC have_a_good_time.RAD ITR.SUJ.LCZ
b. Ni-k opa d-i-e-t zeru-an gerta da-i-tez-ela.
I.ERG wish /PLU/1.DTR heaven.LOC end_up.RAD PLU.ITR.SUJ.LCZ

(4) a. alferr-ik agin-du-ko d-i-e-zu isil da-i-tez-en.
in_vain.STA command.FUT /PLU/2.DTR keep_silent.RAD be.PLU.ITR.SUJ.NCZ

b. Paseo-a-rekin segi g-ene-za(-n)-n eska-tu n-i-o-n.
walk.SOC continue.RAD /PLU.TRA.SUJ.PST.NCZ beg.PEF /1.DTR.PST

c. Otoitz e-giten n-u-en den-a on-do atera ze-di(-n)-n.
prayer.IDF make.IPF /1.TRA.PST all well turn_out(.RAD) ITR.SUJ.PST.NCZ

(5) a. Jesus-e-k zorrotz agin-du z-i-e-n inor-k ez ze-za(-n)-la ja-ki-n.
Jesus.ERG sternly charge.PEF /PLU/.DTR.PST anyone.ERG not TRA.SUJ.PST.LCZ know(.RAD)

b. Ber-a-k eska-tu d-u e-tor z-a-i-tez-ela.
she_herself.ERG ask.PEF TRA come.RAD 2.ITR.SUJ.LCZ

c. Otoi(t)z-ten z-a-it-u-t ja-rrai de-za-zu-la.
beg.IPF 2/1.TRA continue.RAD /2.TRA.SUJ.LCZ

(6) a. Jesus-e-k inor-i ez esa(n)-te-ko agin-du z-i-e-n zorrotz.
Jesus.ERG anyone.DAT not tell.VEN.ADN order.PEF /PLU/.DTR.PST sternly

b. Ama-k musu e-ma-te-ko agin-du z-i-da-n.
Mother.IDF.ERG kiss.IDF give.VEN.ADN order.PEF /1/.DTR.PST

c. Ber-a-ren-gan-(r)a j-oa-te-ko eska-tzen d-i-zu.
he_himself.ALL go.VEN.ADN ask.IPF /2/.DTR

d. Bilbo-tik irte(n)-te-ko aholka-tu z-i-da-te-n mediku-ek.
Bilbao.ELA leave.VEN.ADN advise.PEF /1/PLU.DTR.PST doctor.PLU.ERG

(7) a. Eriberibil-e-an n-eu ere j-oa-te-a eska-tzen n-i-o-n.
ambulance.LOC I.REF too go.VEN ask.IPF //1.DTR.PST

b. Ni-re lan-a-k liburu asko irakur-tze-a eska-tzen d-u.
I.GEN job.ERG book a_lot_of read.VEN require.IPF TRA

(8) a. Ni-re anaia horr-e-k lasai e-go-te-ko d-i-o.
I.GEN brother that.ERG at_ease.PRE be.VEN.ADN say.SYT

b. E-tor-tze-ko esan n-i-o-n.
come.VEN.ADN tell.PEF //1.DTR.PST

c. ... gaztiga-tzen d-i-o-zu tabernari-a-ri e-duki de-za-la zenbait egun-e-z bahi hura.
... notify.IPF //2.DTR bartender keep(.RAD) TRA.SUJ.LCZ a_few day.INS pledge yonder

d. Esan z-i-o-n ez ze-di(-n)-la inoiz ere bereiz ber-e anai(a)-e-ta-tik.
tell.PEF DTR.PST not ITR.SUJ.PST.LCZ ever too separate.RAD he_himself.GEN brother.PLU.ELA

(9) a. Arantxa ere saia-tzen ze-n ber-e senar Inaxio-k Ander zerbait
Arantxa too try.IPF ITR.PST she_herself.GEN husband Inaxio.ERG Andrew a_bit

zirika ze-za(-n)-n.
prod.RAD TRA.SUJ.PST.NCZ

b. Etxe-ko gauz(a)-ak on-do j-oa-n da-i-tez-en ahalegin-du-ko n-a-iz.
firm.ADN affair.PLU well go(.RAD) PLU.ITR.SUJ.NCZ do_one's_best.FUT 1.ITR

c. Zer-ga(i)-tik ez z-a-r-a ahalegin-du lebitarr-ek Juda-n zerg(a)-a
why not 2.ITR do_one's_best.PEF Levite.PLU.ERG Judah.LOC tax
bil ze-za-te(-n)-n?
collect.RAD /PLU.TRA.SUJ.PST.NCZ

d. Ahalegin-ak e-gi-ten z-it-u-z-te-n Bordalais-e-k kanta berri-ak
all_one's_efforts.PLU do.IPF PLU/PLU.TRA.PST Bordalais.ERG song new.PLU
ikas z-it-za(-n)-n.
learn.RAD PLU/.TRA.SUJ.PST.NCZ

e. Guzti-ok ataka hon-e-ta-tik atera z-a-i-tez-en ahalegin-ak
all.INC fix this.ELA get_out(.RAD) PLU.ITR.SUJ.NCZ all_one's_efforts.PLU
e-gi-n-go d-it-u-gu.
do.FUT PLU/1PLU.TRA

f. Zeru-ko erreinu-an sar g-a-i-tez-en e-gi-n
heaven.ADN kingdom.LOC enter.RAD 1PLU.ITR.SUJ.NCZ do(.RAD)
d-it-za-gu-n ahalegin-ak.
PLU/1PLU.TRA.SUJ.NCZ all_one's_best.PLU

(10) a. Era hon-e-ta-ra lor-tu-ko d-u-gu irakurle-a-k uler-tze-a.
manner this.ALL succeed.FUT /1PLU.TRA reader.ERG understand.VEN

b. Babesleku-tik atera ze-di(-n)-n lor-tu z-u-en.
sanctuary.ELA come_out(.RAD) ITR.SUJ.PST.NCZ succeed.PEF TRA.PST

(11) a. Beharr-e-z-ko-a al da hori e-gi-te-a?
necessary INT be.SYN that do.VEN

b. Ez da on gizon-a bakarr-ik e-go-te-a.
not be.SYN good.IDF man alone.STA be.VEN

(12) a. I-kus-ten d-u-zu-n-e-an ez z-a-it-u-z-te-la sinets-i nahi, eta premi(a)-a
see.IPF /2.TRA.NRE.LOC not 2/PLU.TRA.LCZ believe want.PPR and necessity
d-ela sinets z-a-it-za-te-n, da-gi-zu-n ordu-an juramentu.
be.SYN.LCZ believe.RAD 2/PLU.TRA.SUJ.NCZ do./2.SYT.NCZ time.LOC swearing.IDF

b. Ez da on-gi gizon-a bakarr-ik i-za-n da-di-n.
not be.SYN well man alone.STA be(.RAD) ITR.SUJ.NCZ

c. Ez da komeni ni-re seme=alab(a)-ek zu-rekin ikus
not be.SYN fitting.IDF I.GEN son_and_daughter.PLU.ERG you.SOC see.RAD
n-a-za-te-n.
1/PLU.TRA.SUJ.NCZ

d. Ordu ze-n noizbait lagun-ak e-gi-n g-in-tez-e(n)-n.
time.IDF be.SYN.PST finally friend.PLU become(.RAD) 1PLU.ITR.SUJ.PST.NCZ

(13) a. Nagusi-a-k ez z-i-o-n eskola-ra arratsalde-z ere e-tor
boss.ERG not DTR.PST school.ALL afternoon.IDF.INS also come.RAD
ze-di(-n)-n.
ITR.SUJ.PST.NCZ

b. Ez d-i-zu-t utz-i-ko ni-re aita eta Agarr-en-ga(i)-tik gai(t)z-ki esa(n)-ka
not /2/1.DTR let.FUT I.GEN father.IDF and Agar.MOT badly saying.ADV
ari z-a-i-tez-en.
be_busy.PPR 2.ITR.SUJ.NCZ

c. Etxe-ko seme=alab(a)-ak konforma-tu-ko d-ir-a ni berri-z
household.ADN son_and_daughter.PLU accept.FUT PLU.ITR I again
ezkon n-a-di-n.
marry.RAD 1.ITR.SUJ.NCZ

(14) Konforma-tu z-ir-a-de-n elkarr-en arte-an ezkon-du-ko z-ir-e(-n)-la
settle.PEF PLU.ITR.PST each_other.GEN between get_married.FUT PLU.ITR.PST.LCZ
hurren-go urte-an.
next year.LOC

(15) Egun-da-ino ez d-i-gu-te e-ra-gotz-i elkar i-kus-i eta mintza
up_to_now not /1PLU/PLU.DTR prevent.PEF each_other see POC talk.RAD
g-a-i-tez-en.
1PLU.ITR.SUJ.NCZ

(16) a. Beldur n-a-iz zerbait-e-ta-n huts e-gi-n d-u-da-n eta
fear.IDF be.1.SYN something.LOC mistake.IDF make.PEF /1.TRA.NCZ and
lehen-danik gai(t)zto-tu n-a-iz-en.
before.ELA become_worse.PEF 1.ITR.NCZ

b. Beldur n-a-iz giristino-e-ta-rik ere, gehi-en-ek bide hura ber-a
fear.IDF be.1.SYN Christian.PLU.ELA too many.SUP.PLU.ERG road yonder same
har-tzen d-u-te-n.
take.IPF /PLU.TRA-NCZ

c. Beldur n-a-iz . . . bekatu-ren bat estal-i d-i-zu-la.
fear.IDF be.1.SYN sin.IDF.GEN a conceal.PEF /2/.DTR.LCZ

(17) a. Beldur n-a-iz utz ez de-za-n.
fear.IDF be.1.SYN abandon.RAD not TRA.SUJ.NCZ

b. Beldur ze-n e-ntzu-n ze-za(-n)-n ber-e-ha(r-en)-la Jainko-a-k.
fear.IDF be.SYN.PST hear(.RAD) TRA.SUJ.PST.NCZ immediately God.ERG

(18) a. Eta beldur-tu ze-n ez z-u-e(n)-la iza-n-en diru-rik gerla-ko
and get_afraid.PEF ITR.PST not TRA.PST.LCZ have.FUT money.PAR war.ADN

gastu-(e)-en-tzat.
expense.PLU.BEN

b. Beldur n-a-iz ni-re etxeko-ak haserre-tu-ko ote
fear.IDF be.1.SYN I.GEN member_of_the_household.PLU get_mad.FUT DUB
za-i-z-ki-da-n.
1/PLU.DIT.NCZ

c. Beldur n-a-iz ondore txarr-a e-karr-i-ko d-u-en.
fear.IDF be.1.SYN consequence bad bring.FUT TRA.NCZ

d. Beldur n-a-iz ez ote d-en ero-tu-ko.
fear.IDF be.1.SYN not DUB ITR.NCZ go_mad.FUT

(19) a. Frantses-ak beldur z-ir-e-n lagun-ak e-tor ze-ki-z-ki-o(-n)-n
French.PLU fear.IDF be.PLU.SYN.PST fellow.PLU come.RAD /PLU.DIT.SUJ.PST.NCZ
libra-tze-ra.
free.VEN.ALL

b. Zerbait gerta da-ki-o-n beldur iza-n d-ir-a.
something happen.RAD DIT.SUJ.NCZ fear.IDF be.PEF PLU.ITR

(20) a. Diru-a parrasta-ka e-ma-ten d-u-t egunero jan de-za-gu-n.
money galore.ADV give.IPF /1.TRA every_day eat(.RAD) /1PLU.TRA.SUJ.NCZ

b. Esan-go d-i-zu-e-t zer d-en film hori, i-kus-i gabe lasai
tell.FUT /2/1.DTR what be.SYN.NCZ movie that see without.PRE easy.PRE
geldi z-a-i-tez-te-n.
rest.RAD 2PLU.ITR.SUJ.NCZ

c. Ezer e-gi-n behar ote g-en-u-ke, gal ez da-di-n?
something do should.PPR DUB /1PLU.TRA.COD get_lost.RAD not 1.ITR.SUJ.NCZ

(21) a. Jainko-a-k heriotza-tik gorde g-a-it-za-n, kandela bedeinka-tu-a
God.ERG death.ELA preserve(.RAD) 1PLU/.TRA.SUJ.NCZ candle bless.PEF.SIN
pi(t)z-tu-ko d-u-gu.
light.FUT /1PLU.TRA

b. Bekatu-rik e-gi-n ez de-za-zu-e-n ida(t)z-ten d-i-zu-e-t hau.
sin.PAR do(.RAD) not /2PLU.TRA.SUJ.NCZ write.IPF /2PLU/1.DTR this

(22) a. Bide-ra irten behar-ko n-a-tza-i-o, ama haserre ez da-di-n.
way.ALL go_out must.FUT /1.DIT mother.IDF anger.IDF not be.SYN.SUJ.NCZ

b. Ez d-ie-za-gu-la Jainko-a-k hitzegin, hil ez g-a-i-tez-en.
not /1PLU/.DTR.SUJ.LCZ God.ERG speak die(.RAD) not 1PLU.ITR.SUJ.NCZ

c. Beso-e-ta-n e-ra-ma-n-go z-a-it-u-z-te, harri-(e)-ekin estropezu e-gi-n ez
arm.PLU.LOC carry.FUT 2/PLU.TRA stone.PLU.SOC trip.IDF make(.RAD) not
de-za-zu-n.
/2.TRA.SUJ.NCZ

(23) a. Teexa-k ber-e-ha(r-en)-la jantz-araz-i z-i-o-n Joanixio-k i-kus-te-ko.
Theresa.ERG at_once put_on.CAU.PEF DTR.PST Joanixio.ERG see.VEN.ADN
b. Ez d-i-zu-t eskut(h)itz hau ni-re buru-a zuri-tze-ko ida(t)z-ten.
not /2/1.DTR letter this I.GEN head excuse.VEN.ADN write.IPF

(24) a. Ez d-i-zu-t utz-i-ko, bedeinka n-a-za-zu-n arte.
not /2/1.DTR leave.FUT bless.RAD 1/2.TRA.SUJ.NRE until
b. Jese-ren seme hori lurr-e-an bizi da-di-n arte, ez h-a-iz
Jesse.GEN son that earth.LOC life.PPR be.1.SYN.NRE as_long_as not 2SOL.ITR
seguru iza-n-go.
safe.IDF be.FUT
c. Hilabete oso-an jan-go d-u-zu-e, sudurr-e-ta-tik atera
month whole.LOC eat.FUT /2PLU.TRA nose.PLU.ELA come_out(.RAD)
da-ki-zu-e-n arte.
2PLU/.ITR.SUJ.NRE until

(25) a. Haz n-a-di-n-e-an, Alemania oso-a pasa-tu-ko d-u-t hura
grow_up.RAD 1.ITR.SUJ.NRE.LOC Germany whole cross.FUT /1.TRA yonder_one
bila-tze-n.
look_for.VEN.LOC
b. Zahar z-a-i-tez-en-e-an ere, iza-n-go d-u-zu hil-tze-ko asti-rik.
grow_old.RAD 2.ITR.SUJ.NRE.LOC too have.FUT /2.TRA die.VEN.ADN free_time.PAR
c. Itzul n-a-di-n-e-an esan-go d-i-da-zu.
return.RAD 1.ITR.SUJ.NRE.LOC tell.FUT /1/2.DTR
d. Ber-a-k e-ra-ntzun ze-za(-n)-n-e-an e-gi-n-go z-i-o-n gutun berri
he_himself.ERG reply(.RAD) TRA.SUJ.PST.NRE.LOC make.FUT DTR.PST letter new
bat.
a
e. On-gi da-ki Jainko-a-k, har-ta-tik jan de-za-zu-e-n-e-an,
well know.SYT God.ERG yonder_one.ELA eat(.RAD) /2PLU.TRA.SUJ.NRE.LOC
begi-ak zabal-du-ko za-i-z-ki-zu-e-la.
eye.PLU open.FUT 2PLU/PLU.DIT.LCZ

(26) a. Patxi e-tor-tzen d-en-e-an has-i-ko d-u-gu biler(a)-a.
Frank come.IPF ITR.NRE.LOC start.FUT /1PLU.TRA meeting
b. Haundi-tzen n-a-iz-en-e-an, erdara-z mintza-tu-ko al n-a-iz?
grow_up.IPF 1.ITR.NRE.LOC Spanish.IDF.INS speak.FUT INT 1.ITR
c. Hitzegin-go d-u-gu itzul-tzen n-a-iz-en-e-an.
talk.FUT /1PLU.TRA return.IPF 1.ITR.NRE.LOC
d. Ber-a-rekin hitzegi(n)-ten d-u-zu-n-e-an, eder-ki uler-tu-ko d-u-zu.
she_herself.SOC speak.IPF /2.TRA.NRE.LOC perfectly understand.FUT /2.TRA

e. Gatz hau guzti-z ur-tu d-en-e-an, gazi-tzen da berdin beste
salt this completely dissolve.PEF ITR.NRE.LOC salt.FUT ITR likewise other
alde-tik.
side.ELA

(27) a. Ez d-i-o bat___ere gerta da-ki-o-n egiteko-k kalte-rik e-gi-n-en,
not DTR at_all happen.RAD DIT.SUJ.NRE trouble.IDF.ERG harm.PAR do.FUT
bat___ere bekatu-rik ez d-u-en-a-ri.
at_all sin.PAR not have.SYT.NRE.ZEP.DAT

b. Has-i ze-n emakume har-i pozgarri i-za-n
start.PEF ITR.PST woman yonder.DAT comforting.IDF be(.RAD)
ze-ki-z-ki-o-n hitz-ak esa(n)-te-n.
/PLU.DIT.SUJ.PST.NRE word.PLU say.VEN.LOC

c. Ez d-i-e-t e-gi-n d-ie-za-z-ki-da-te-n galde-r(a)-e-i erantzun-ik
not /PLU/1.DTR do(.RAD) PLU/1/PLU.DTR.SUJ.NRE question.PLU.DAT answer.PAR
e-ma-n-go.
give.FUT

d. E-gi-n de-za-zu-e-n guzti-a e-gi-n maitasun-e-z.
do(.RAD) /2PLU.TRA.SUJ.NRE all do love.IDF.INS

(28) Edozer e-gi-n de-za-zu-e-n, guzti-a Jesus Jaun-a-ren izen-e-an iza-n
whatever do(.RAD) /2PLU.TRA.SUJ.NCZ all Jesus Lord.GEN name.LOC be(.RAD)
da-di-la.
ITR.SUJ.LCZ

(29) a. Edan de-za-gu-n oparo ardo gozo hori.
drink(.RAD) /1PLU.TRA.SUJ.NCZ abundantly wine sweet that

b. Salba d-it-za-gu-n g-eu-re buru-ak!
save.RAD PLU/1PLU.TRA.SUJ.NCZ we.REF.GEN head.PLU

c. Saia g-a-i-tez-en orain-go gauz(a)-ak oraingo begi-z i-kus-te-n.
try.RAD 1PLU.ITR.SUJ.NCZ today's thing.PLU today's eye.IDF.INS see.VEN.LOC

d. Hurbil n-a-di-n gauza harrigarri hori i-kus-te-ra.
get_close.RAD 1.ITR.SUJ.NCZ thing amazing that see.VEN.ALL

e. E-ma-n de-za-gu-n, bada, horr-e(n)-la d-ela.
grant(.RAD) /1PLU.TRA.SUJ.NCZ then so be.SYN.LCZ

(30) a. Mateo-rekin ez g-a-i-tez-en haserre.
Mateo.SOC not be.1PLU.SYN.SUJ.NCZ quarrel.IDF

b. Baina ez de-za-gu-n gurdi-a idi-(e)-en aurre-an jar / jarr-i.
but not /1PLU.SUJ.NCZ cart OX.PLU.GEN before set.RAD set

c. Baina ez n-a-di-n gehi-ago luza, azal de-za-da-n
but not 1.ITR.SUJ.NCZ more.COP delay.RAD present.RAD /1.TRA.SUJ.NCZ

dokumentu-a.
document

(31) a. G-oa-z-en azkar.
go.1PLU.SYN.NCZ quickly
b. N-oa-n ber-e-gan-(r)a.
go.1.SYN.NCZ she_herself.ALL
c. G-a-to(r)-z-en bigarren puntu-ra.
come.1PLU.SYN.NCZ second point.ALL
d. N-a-torr-en berri-z hari-ra.
come.1.SYN.NCZ again thread.ALL

(32) a. Hau ez da-di-la sekul(a)-an berri-ro gerta.
this not ITR.SUJ.LCZ ever again happen.RAD
b. E-gi-n de-za-la nahi d-u-en-a.
do(.RAD) TRA.SUJ.LCZ want.PPR TRA.NRE.ZEP
c. Luza-ro bizi da-i-tez-ela!
for_a_long_time life.PPR be.PLU.SYN.SUJ.LCZ
d. Zeru-a-k gorde g-a-it-za-la!
heaven.ERG protect(.RAD) 1PLU/.TRA.SUJ.LCZ
e. I-kus de-za-da-la zu-re irudi-a, e-ntzu-n de-za-da-la zu-re
see.RAD /1.TRA.SUJ.LCZ you.GEN figure hear(.RAD) /1.TRA.SUJ.LCZ you.GEN
ahots-a.
voice

(33) a. Ber-e herri-ra di-h-oa-la!
he_himself.GEN village.ALL go.SYN.LCZ
b. Da-torr-ela Jose.
come.SYN.LCZ Joseph
c. Da-go-ela jan gabe!
stay.SYN.LCZ eat without.PRE
d. Ez z-oa-z-ela.
not go.2.SYN.LCZ

(34) a. Egun on d-i-zu-la Jainko-a-k!
day good.IDF give./2/.DYT.LCZ God.ERG
b. Jainko-a-k gabon d-i-zu-e-la.
God.ERG good_night.IDF give./2PLU/.DYT.LCZ

(35) a. Ez l-u-ke nahi gerta l-e-ki-o-n ber-a-ri gerta-tu-a.
not TRA.COD like.PPR happen.RAD DIT.SUJ.HYP.NCZ she_herself.DAT happen.PEF.ZEP
b. Ez n-u-ke nahi inor-k hau txar-tzat har l-e-za-n.
not /1.TRA.COD like.PPR anyone.ERG this amiss.PRO take.RAD TRA.SUJ.HYP.NCZ

c. Esplika-tu d-u-da-n-a beste-ren gogoet(a)-(e)-en ispilu
explain.PEF /1.TRA.NRE.ZEP other_people.IDF.GEN thought.PLU.GEN reflection
zuzen iza-n l-e-di-n nahi n-u-ke.
correct.IDF be(.RAD) ITR.SUJ.HYP.NCZ like.PPR /1.TRA.COD

(36) Baldin aita bat-e-k ber-e alab(a)-a-ri diru-a e-ma-n-go ba-l-i-o
CDC father a.ERG he_himself.GEN daughter.DAT money give.FUT CDP.DTR.COD
etxe bat eros l-e-za-n, zoro-tzat jo-ko l-u-ke-te
house a buy.RAD TRA.SUJ.HYP.NCZ crazy.PRO consider.FUT /PLU.TRA.COD
den-ek.
everybody.PLU.ERG

Chapter 22

(1) a. Z-a-to(r)-z-ki-t, e-tza-n ni-rekin, en-e arreb(a)-a.
come.1/2.DYN.IMP lie(.RAD) I.SOC I.GEN sister
b. Z-a-to(r)-z-ki-da-te bihar ordu hon-e-ta-n Izreel-e-ra.
come.1/2PLU.DYN.IMP tomorrow time this.LOC Jezreel.ALL

(2) a. Iza-n z-a-i-tez-te errukitsu-ak.
be(.RAD) 2PLU.ITR.IMP compassionate.PLU
b. Ez z-a-i-tez sinple-a iza-n.
not 2.ITR.IMP silly be(.RAD)

(3) a. Zu-re haur bat-e-z beza-la ni-ta-z arta iza-n e-za-zu otoi.
you.GEN child a.INS like I.INS care.IDF have(.RAD) /2.TRA.IMP please
b. Horr-e-ta-n kontu-a iza-n e-za-zu-e, neskatx(a)-ak eta mutil-ak.
that.LOC caution have(.RAD) /2PLU.TRA.IMP girl.PLU and boy.PLU

(4) a. Z-a-to(r)-z ohe-ra, ho(t)z-tu e-gi-n-go z-a-r-a.
come.2.SYN.IMP bed.ALL get_cold do.FUT 2.ITR
b. H-oa laster suge-a hil-tze-ra.
go.2SOL.SYN.IMP quickly snake kill.VEN.ALL
c. Esa-da-zu orain egi(a)-a.
tell./1/2.DYT.IMP now truth
d. E-gi-zu nahi d-u-zu-n-a.
do./2.SYT.IMP want.PPR /2.TRA.NRE.ZEP
e. E-gi-z-ki-da-zu argi-(e)-ekin hiru piztualdi.
make.PLU/1/2.DYT.IMP light.PLU.SOC three flash.IDF
f. U(t)z-t(<*d)a-zu zu-re ahots-a e-ntzu-te-n.
let./1/2.DYT.IMP you.GEN voice hear.VEN.LOC

(5) a. Zu isil-ik z-a-u-de, Lierni!
you quiet.STA be.2.SYN.IMP Lierni
b. Gain-e-ra-ko guzti-ok z-oa-z-te bake-an z-eu-(e)-en aita-ren-gan-(r)a.
remaining all.INC go.2PLU.SYN.IMP peace.LOC you.REF.GEN father.ALL
c. Seme hori in-da-zu, Elias-e-k esa-n z-i-o-n.
son that give./1/2.DYT.IMP Elijah.ERG say.PEF DTR.PST
d. Ni-k d-io-da-n-a e-gi-zu!
I.ERG say./1.SYT.NRE.ZEP do./2.SYT.IMP
e. Mutil hon-i kinin(a)-a e-ma-i-o-zu-e.
boy this.DAT quinine give.//2PLU.DYT.IMP

(6) a. Ai-zu lagun-a, lagun on=on-a, ez al da irits-i ordu-a?
listen.2 buddy buddy good-good not INT ITR arrive.PEF time
b. Ai-zu, baina hori beste kontu bat da.
listen.2 but that other matter a be.SYN
c. Ai-za-k, e-ma-n-go d-i-a-t alab(a)-a.
listen.2SOL give.FUT /2SOL/1.DTR daughter
d. Ai-za-n Andoni, ba al da-ki-n zer e-gi-n behar
listen.2SOL.FEM Andoni AFF INT know./2SOL.FEM.SYT what do should.PPR
g-en-u-ke-en?
/1PLU.TRA.COD.PST

(7) a. Tori ni-re pastel-a.
take.2 I.GEN cake
b. Har-k esa-n z-i-da-n: "Tori eta irents-i"
yonder_one.ERG say.PEF /1/.DTR.PST take.2 and swallow
c. Tori-zu orain bosteko-a eta iza-n on-gi e-torr-i-a.
take.2 now handshake and be(.RAD) well come.PEF.SIN
d. Tori-zu ni-re erantzun-a!
take.2 I.GEN answer
e. To, to, hau ere, eta urri-rik, kontu-a-ren gain-e-ko!
take.2SOL take.2SOL this too and free_of_charge.STA bill.GEN top.ADN.IDF
f. No, Xaneta! Hori hi-re-tako!
take.2SOL.FEM Jeannette that you.2SOL.BEN

(8) a. To, Pello, horr-(r)a Olheta-ko bide-a.
look.2SOL Pete there.ALL Olheta.ADN road
b. No, Maria, ez otoi, kexa!
listen.2SOL.FEM Maria not please get_angry.RAD

(9) a. To, hi ere atxo-a-ren beldur h-a-iz?
hey you.2SOL.FEM also little_old_lady.GEN fear.IDF be.2SOL.SYN

b. To, zu hemen Jana=Mari!
hey you.2 here.LOC Jeanne-Marie

c. To, kanpero-a-ren alab(a)-a, Benita, hel-du da!
hey field-guard.GEN daughter Benita arrive.PEF ITR

(10) a. J-oa-n z-a-(d)i-tez Euskal Herri-ra bolada bat-e-ra-ko.
go(.RAD) 2.ITR.IMP Basque Country.ALL while a.DES

b. Jon, Jon, irakur e-za-zu hau!
John John read.RAD /2.TRA.IMP this

c. Utz it-za-zu bake-an.
leave.RAD PLU/2.TRA.IMP peace.LOC

d. Utz ie-za-i-o-zu behin-tzat ja(n)-te-n.
let.RAD //2.DTR.IMP at_least eat.VEN.LOC

e. Har ie-za-da-zu neskatxa hori emazte-tzat.
get.RAD /1/2.DTR.IMP girl that wife.PRO

f. Emazte— esa-n z-i-o-n Giuseppa-ri— utz-i e-za-zu zaku-a, eta
wife.IDF say.PEF DTR.PST Giuseppa.DAT leave /2.TRA.IMP bag and
z-a-to(r)-z-ki-t lagun-tze-ra.
come.1/2.DYN.IMP help.VEN.ALL

(11) a. Ama, ez e-za-zu horr-e(n)-la-ko-rik esa-n!
Mother.IDF not /2.TRA.IMP like_that.ADN.ZEP.PAR say(.RAD)

b. Mesede-z! Ez n-a-za-zu-e hil!
please not 1/2PLU.TRA.IMP kill(.RAD)

c. Ez e-za-k erokeria-rik esa-n.
not /2SOL.TRA.IMP rubbish.PAR talk(.RAD)

d. Lagun hori ez ie-za-da-k gehi-ago etxe-ra e-karr-i.
fellow that not /1/2SOL.DTR.IMP more.COP house.ALL bring

e. Ez z-a-i-tez hain suminkorr-a iza-n.
not 2.ITR.IMP so irritable be(.RAD)

f. Tira, alab(a)-a, ez h-a-di horr-e(n)-la atsekabe!
come_on daughter not be.2.SYN.IMP so suffering.IDF

(12) a. Ez z-a-i-tez-ela orde-a engaina, irakurle.
not 2.ITR.SUJ.LCZ however delude.RAD reader.IDF

b. Ez g-a-it-za-zu-la lotsaraz kanpotarr-(e)-en aurre-an.
not 1PLU/2.TRA.SUJ.LCZ be_ashamed.CAU.RAD stranger.PLU.GEN in_front_of

(13) a. Jaso esku-ak!
raise(.RAD) hand.PLU

b. Mikel, e-ntzu-n orain on-do.
Michael listen(.RAD) now well

c. Har-tu furgonet(a)-a eta e-torr-i ni-re atze-tik.
take truck and come I.GEN after
d. Utz-i hori ni-re gain.
leave that I.GEN on
e. On-do lo e-gi-n!
well sleep.IDF do(.RAD)
f. Igo mendi-ra ni-re-gan-(r)a eta z-a-u-de han.
climb(.RAD) mountain.ALL I.ALL and wait.2.SYN.IMP over_there.LOC

(14) a. Ez jaits-i beso-ak!
not lower arm.PLU
b. Ez berandu e-torr-i!
not late come
c. Ez ni-ri begira-tu.
not I.DAT look_at
d. Baina ez dei-tu ni-ri.
but not call I.DAT
e. Ez uste iza-n hori, Agustine!
not thought.IDF have(.RAD) that Agustine

(15) a. Ikus *flv* I (1969), 113–132
see.RAD *flv* I (1969) 113–132
b. Barka, mesede-z aipamen-a-ren luze-a.
forgive.RAD please quotation.GEN long.ZEP
c. Hi-k segi nahi d-u-a-n-a e-gi-te-n.
you.SOL.ERG go_on.RAD want.PPR /2SOL.TRA.NRE.ZEP do.VEN.LOC
d. Ha(r-en)-la, sar ohe-an!
so get_into.RAD bed.LOC
e. Utz bake-ta-n sendagile-ak.
leave.RAD peace.IDF.LOC doctor.PLU

(16) a. Ez tira!
not shoot.RAD
b. Ez ni-ri uki!
not I.DAT touch.RAD
c. Baina ez pentsa arazo-a hain erraz konpon-du d-en-ik.
but not think.RAD problem so easily resolve.PEF ITR.PCZ
d. Ez ni-re hitz-ak gai(t)z-ki har.
not I.GEN word.PLU wrongly take.RAD
e. Hura berri-z en-i ez aipa.
yonder again I.DAT not mention.RAD

(17) a. Mesede-z, Guiomar, esna h-a-di pixka bat.
please Guiomar wake_up.RAD 2SOL.ITR.IMP bit a
b. Mesede-z, ni-ri sermoi-rik ez bota.
please I.DAT sermon.PAR not launch(.RAD)
c. Mesede-z, utz-i en-e aitam-e-i zu-(e)-en arte-an
please let I.GEN father_and_mother.PLU.DAT you.PLU.GEN among
bizi-tze-n.
live.VEN.LOC
d. Arren, atera n-a-za-zu lehenbailehen hemen-dik.
for_goodness'_sake get_out(.RAD) 1/2TRA.IMP as_soon_as_possible here.ELA
e. Arren, Ezkira, utz ie-za-da-zu konta-tze-n.
for_goodness'_sake Ezkira let.RAD /1/2.DTR.IMP tell.VEN.LOC
f. Otoi, Jana=Mari, z-a-u-de isil-ik.
please Jeanne-Marie be.2.SYN.IMP quiet.STA
g. Otoi, otoi, geldi-araz e-za-zu makil(a)-a!
please please stop.CAU.RAD /2.TRA.IMP stick
h. Otoi, ez negarr-ik e-gi-n!
please not crying.PAR do(.RAD)

(18) a. Sar z-a-i-tez, sar, mesede-z.
come_in.RAD 2.ITR.IMP come_in.RAD please
b. Mesede-z! Utz n-a-za-n mesede-z!
please let_off.RAD 1/2SOL.FEM.TRA.IMP please
c. Hemen-dik aurre-ra ho(rr-en)-la joka-tu, mesede-z.
here.ELA front.ALL that_way act please
d. E-karr-i giltz(a)-a, fabore-z.
bring key please
e. Maita n-a-za-zu arren!
love.RAD 1/2.TRA.IMP for_heaven's_sake
f. Sarr-araz e-za-zu, sarr-araz, otoi!
come_in.CAU.RAD /2.TRA.IMP come_in.CAU.RAD please
g. Kafe bat, mesede-z.
coffee one please

(19) a. E-ma-da-zu, arren, ur pixka bat z-eu-re pegarr-e-tik.
give./1/2.DYT.IMP I_beg_you water.IDF bit a you.REF.GEN jar.ELA
b. Bidal e-za-zu, arren, Lazaro gu-re aita-ren etxe-ra.
send.RAD /2.TRA.IMP I_beg_you Lazarus we.GEN father.IDF.GEN house.ALL
c. U(t)z-t(<*d)a-zu, otoi, herri-a-ri hitzegi-te-n.
let./1/2.DYT please people.DAT speak.VEN.LOC

d. E-ra-ntzun, mesede-z, gutun hon-i.
answer(.RAD) please letter this.DAT

e. Ez gorde, arren, deus___ere.
not hide(.RAD) please anything_whatsoever

f. Ez, arren, birao-rik inor-i egotz-i.
not please curse.PAR anyone.DAT throw

(20) a. Ber-e anaia-ri mesede-z irakur-tze-n ja-rrai-tze-ko esa-n z-i-o-n.
she_herself.GEN brother.IDF.DAT please read.VEN.LOC go_on.VEN.ADN tell.PEF DTR.PST

b. Mesede-z eska-tu n-i-o-n har-ekin hau(t)s-te-ko.
please ask.PEF //1.DTR.PST yonder_one.SOC break_off.VEN.ADN

c. Mesede-z, zaldi hau e-duki-ko d-i-da-zu apur bat-e-an?
please horse this hold.FUT /1/2.DTR moment a.LOC

d. Mesede-z, Villoslada jaun-a-rekin hitz e-gi-n nahi n-u-ke.
please Villoslada Mr.SOC word.IDF do like.PPR /1.TRA.COD

(21) a. Ez gero ni-ri gezurr-ik esa-n.
not MON I.DAT lie.PAR tell(.RAD)

b. Ez gero inor-i ezer esa-n.
not MON anybody.DAT anything tell(.RAD)

c. Ez gero polizi(a)-a-ri gaztiga!
not MON police.DAT notify.RAD

(22) a. Ez ni-ri gero Donostia uki-tu!
not I.DAT MON San_Sebastian run_down

b. Ez aha(t)z-tu gero Jaun-a zu-(e)-en Jainko-a!
not forget MON Lord.SIN you.PLU.GEN God.SIN

c. Nor d-en-ik ez esa-n gero!
who be.SYN.PCZ not say(.RAD) MON

(23) a. Horr-(r)a hiru izen polit. Kontu-an har-tu, gero!
there.ALL three name pretty.IDF attention.LOC take MON

b. Begira gero!
watch_out.RAD MON

(24) a. Kontu-z i-bil z-a-i-tez, gero!
care.IDF.INS walk.RAD 2.ITR.IMP MON

b. E-gi-n e-za-zu, gero, lan hori!
do(.RAD) /2.TRA.IMP MON work that

(25) a. Eta Jainko-a-k esa-n z-u-en: "Iza-n be-di argi-a."
and God.ERG say.PEF TRA.PST be(.RAD) ITR.JUS light

b. Zu-re diru-a zu-re galmen iza-n be-di.
you.GEN money you.GEN undoing.IDF be(.RAD) ITR.JUS

c. Aski iza-n be-ki-t form(a)-a-z mintza-tze-a.
sufficient be(.RAD) 1/.DIT.JUS form.INS talk.VEN

(26) a. Ber-a-z, ha(r-en)-la b-iz; d-en-e-an hi(t)zpide-an z-a-u-de.
thus so be.SYN.JUS everything.LOC right.LOC be.2.SYN

b. B-ir-a iragan-ak iragan.
PLU.SYN.JUS past.PLU past.IDF

(27) a. Gizon bakoitz-a-k iza-n be-za ber-e emazte-a.
man each.ERG have(.RAD) TRA.JUS he_himself.GEN wife

b. Iza-n be-za-te behar d-en-a.
have(.RAD) /PLU.TRA.JUS need.IDF be.SYN.NRE.ZEP

(28) a. B-i-h-oa sukalde-ra.
go.SYN.JUS kitchen.ALL

b. Be-go orain-dik neskatx(a)-a gu-rekin hamar bat egun.
stay.SYN.JUS still girl we.SOC ten a day.IDF

c. Be-u-de zabal-ik zu-re begi-ak.
be.PLU.SYN.JUS open.STA you.GEN eye.PLU

d. Be-tor-ki-gu zu-re erreinu-a.
come.1PLU/.DYN you.GEN kingdom

(29) a. E-gi-n be-di Jaungoiko-a-ren borondate-a!
do(.RAD) ITR.JUS God.GEN will

b. Barka b-ie-za-t Aita Barandiaran-e-k.
forgive.RAD /1/.DTR.JUS Father Barandiaran.ERG

c. Ez be-za inor-k pentsa gaur-ko zenbait-en asmo-ak
not TRA.JUS anyone.ERG think.RAD today.ADN certain.ZEP.GEN proposal.PLU
erabat bazter-tze-ko-ak d-ir-ela d-eritz-o-da-n-ik.
totally discard.VEN.ADN.ZEP.PLU be.PLU.SYN.LCZ deem.//1.DYT.PCZ

d. Ez be-za inor-k ber-e buru-a engaina!
not TRA.JUS anyone.ERG he_himself.GEN head delude.RAD

(30) a. Hitzegin be-za, don Markox.
speak(.RAD) TRA.JUS Mr.IDF Markox

b. Bai jaun-a! Sar be-di aurre-ra!
yes sir come_in.RAD ITR.JUS forward

c. Goiz da-bil, eskribau jaun-a, eser-i be-di.
early be_out.SYN Notary Mr. sit_down ITR.JUS

d. Ez be-za horr-e(n)-la-ko-rik esa-n, aita.
not TRA.JUS like_that.ADN.ZEP.PAR say(.RAD) Father.IDF

e. Hitzegin b-ie-za-i-o mutil-a-ri— agin-du z-u-en emakume-a-k.
speak(.RAD) DTR.JUS boy.DAT command.PEF TRA.PST woman.ERG

(31) a. Zu-re beso=kako-ek estu-tu n-a-za-te.
you.GEN curve_of_one's_arm.PLU.ERG clench 1/PLU.TRA.JUS
b. Zu-re hitz-a ere be-tor bat hai-(e)-en-a-rekin.
you-GEN word too come.SYN.JUS one yonder_one.PLU.GEN.ZEP.SOC

(32) a. Ber-ak be-to(r)-z-ki-gu, eta ber-ek atera
he_himself.PLU come.1PLU/PLU.DYN.JUS and he_himself.PLU.ERG take_out(.RAD)
ga-it-za-te.
1PLU/PLU.TRA.JUS
b. Ema-n b-ie-za-t musu!
give(.RAD) /1/.DTR.JUS kiss.IDF
c. Beste-k b-io arrazoi-z-ko-a d-en ala ez iritsi hori.
other_one.IDF.ERG say.SYT.JUS reason.IDF.INS.ADN be.SYN.NCZ or not opinion that
d. Naaman ni-gan-(r)a be-tor eta ja-ki-n be-za Israel-e-n profeta
Naaman I.ALL come.SYN.JUS and know(.RAD) TRA.JUS Israel.LOC prophet
ba-d-ela.
AFF.be.SYN.LCZ

(33) a. Sar be-di bakoitz-a ber-e etxe-an.
enter.RAD ITR.JUS everyone he_himself.GEN house.LOC
b. Sar z-a-i-tez-te bakoitz-a z-eu-(e)-en etxe-an.
enter.RAD 2PLU.ITR.IMP each you.REF.PLU.GEN house.LOC

(34) a. Azter be-za, bada, nor-k ber-e buru-a.
examine.RAD TRA.JUS then each.ERG he_himself.GEN head
b. Azter e-za-zu-e, bada, nor-k ber-e buru-a.
examine.RAD /2PLU.TRA.IMP then each.ERG he_himself.GEN head

(35) a. Baina Jainko-a ez be-ki-gu mintza, hil ez ga-i-tez-en.
but God not 1PLU/.DIT.JUS speak.RAD die(.RAD) not 1PLU.ITR.SUJ.NCZ
b. Baina ez d-ie-za-gu-la Jainko-a-k hitzegin, hil ez
but not /1PLU/.TRA.SUJ.LCZ God.ERG speak(.RAD) die(.RAD) not
ga-i-tez-en.
1PLU.ITR.SUJ.NCZ

(36) a. Bi soineko d-it-u-en-a-k, e-ma-n b-ie-za-i-o bat, ez
two garment.IDF have.PLU/.SYT.NRE.ZEP.ERG give(.RAD) DTR.JUS one not
d-u-en-a-ri.
have.SYT.NRE.ZEP.DAT
b. Bi soineko d-it-u-en-a-k e-ma-n d-ie-za-i-o-la bat ez
two garment.IDF have.PLU/.SYT.NRE.ZEP.ERG give(.RAD) DTR.SUJ.LCZ one not

d-u-en-a-ri.
have.SYT.NRE.ZEP.DAT

(37) a. Nor-bait egarri ba-da, e-tor be-ki-t eta edan be-za.
someone thirst.IDF CDP.be.SYN come.RAD 1.DIT.JUS and drink(.RAD) TRA.JUS
b. Inor egarri ba-da, ni-gan-(r)a e-torr-i eta edan de-za-la.
someone thirst.IDF CDP.be.SYN I.ALL come and drink TRA.SUJ.LCZ

(38) a. Ez be-za ja-ki-n zu-re ezkerr-a-k zer e-gi-ten d-u-en
not TRA.JUS know(.RAD) you.GEN left_hand.ERG what do.IPF TRA.NCZ
eskuin-a-k.
right_hand.ERG
b. Ez de-za-la ja-ki-n ezkerr-a-k zu-re eskubi-a-k zer e-gi-ten
not TRA.SUJ.LCZ know(.RAD) left_hand.ERG you.GEN right_hand.ERG what do.IPF
d-u-en.
TRA.NCZ

(39) a. Gizon bakoitz-a-k iza-n be-za ber-e emazte-a.
man every.ERG have(.RAD) TRA.JUS he_himself.GEN wife
b. Gizon bakoitz-a-k ber-e emazte-a e-duki de-za-la.
man every.ERG he_himself.GEN wife have(.RAD) TRA.SUJ.LCZ

(40) a. B-i-h-oa-z barru-ra hirur-ok.
go.PLU.SYN.JUS INSide.ALL three.INC
b. Bi aldi-z irakur be-za.
two time.IDF.INS read.RAD TRA.JUS
c. Beso-tik euts-i be-ki-o.
arm.ELA grip DIT.JUS
d. Edan be-za-te zut-ik da-u-de-la.
drink(.RAD) /PLU.TRA.JUS standing_up.STA be.PLU.SYN.LCI
e. Zaldi irrintzi-ak e-ntzu-n b-i-tez.
horse neigh.PLU hear(.RAD) PLU.ITR.JUS
f. Oihal-a eror be-di geldi-ro.
curtain fall.RAD ITR.JUS slowly

(41) 9. orrialde-a, 5. lerro-a: D-io: *ihardu-n*; b-io: *jardu-n*.
9th page 5th line Say.SYT *ihardun* say.SYT.JUS *jardun*

Chapter 23

(1) a. Jagoi-ti(k)-ko-z ukan-en d-u-t ni-k zu-ga(i)-tik dolore.
henceforth have.FUT /1.TRA I.ERG you.MOT anguish.IDF
b. Ama-ga(i)-tik andre oro behar l-u-ke gora-tu.
mother.IDF.MOT woman all.IDF should.PPR TRA.COD praise

c. Eskerr-ik asko afari-a-ga(i)-tik.
thank.PAR many supper.MOT

(2) a. Ni-k seme bat e-duki-tze-arren zer e-ma-n-go n-u-ke-en ez da-ki-t.
I.ERG son a have.VEN.IDF.NPS what give.FUT /1.TRA.COD.NCZ not know./1.SYT

b. Zer-bait e-gi-te-arren, lege-ak ikas-te-a-ri e-ki-n n-i-o-n
something do.VEN.IDF.NPS law.PLU study.VEN.DAT take_up.PEF //1.DTR.PST
Deusto-ko unibertsitate-an.
Deusto.ADN university.LOC

c. Ilunpe-ra egoki-tze-arren geldiune bat e-gi-n z-u-en.
darkness adapt_oneself.VEN.IDF.NPS pause a make.PEF TRA.PST

(3) a. Zer-ga(i)-tik j-oa-n h-in-tz-e-n?— Ber-a-k dei-tu n-ind-u-e(n)-la-ko.
what.MOT go.PEF 2SOL.ITR.PST he_himself.ERG invite.PEF 1/.TRA.PST.LCZ.ADN

b. Zer-ga(i)-tik bazter-tzen d-u-te euskar(a)-a moj(a)-ek?— Apaiz-ek
what.MOT reject.IPF /PLU.TRA Basque_language nun.PLU.ERG priest.PLU.ERG
eta fraile-ek ere zapu(t)z-en d-u-te-la-ko.
and friar.PLU.ERG too repudiate.IPF /PLU.TRA.LCZ.ADN

c. Zer-ga(i)-tik hil z-en-it-u-en?— Behar-tu n-ind-u-te(n)-la-ko.
what.MOT kill.PEF PLU/2.TRA.PST force_to.PEF 1/PLU.TRA.PST.LCZ.ADN

d. Zer-ga(i)-tik ez n-ind-u-en hil?— Zizp(a)-a-k bi tiro bakarr-ik
what.MOT not 1/.TRA.PST kill.PEF gun.ERG two shot.IDF only.STA
z-it-u-e(n)-la-ko.
PLU/.TRA.PST.LCZ.ADN

e. Zer-ga(i)-tik joka-tu d-u-t horr-e(n)-la?— Maite ez z-a-it-u-z-te-da-la-ko ote?
what.MOT act.PEF /1.TRA like_that love.PPR not 2PLU/1.TRA.LCZ.ADN DUB

(4) a. Ni-k, behar d-en leku-an bila-tu ez d-u-da-la-ko agi-an, ez
I.ERG need.IDF be.SYN.NRE place.LOC look_for.PEF not /1.TRA.LCZ.ADN perhaps not
d-u-t *Guero*-n aurki-tzen.
/1.TRA *Guero*.LOC find.IPF

b. Ez da-ki ze(r) ordu d-en, baina-tu ondo-ren ordulari-a
not know.SYT what time be.SYN.NCZ take_a_bath contiguity.ELA watch
non-bait aha(z)-tu za-i-o-la-ko.
somewhere.LOC forget.PEF DIT.LCZ.ADN

(5) a. Mudakorr-ak d-ir-a gizon-(e)-en irakaspen-ak, gizon-ak ber-ak
changeable.PLU be.PLU.SYN man.PLU.GEN teaching.PLU man.PLU he_himself.PLU
ha(r-en)-la d-ir-ela-ko-tz.
so be.PLU.SYN.LCZ.ADN.INS

b. Etxekoandre-a n-a-iz-ela-ko ba-d-it-u-t ni-re eginbeharr-ak.
lady_of_the_house be.1.SYN.LCZ.ADN AFF.have./1.SYT I.GEN chore.PLU

(6) a. Nahi d-u-zu-la-ko z-a-u-de hemen.
want.PPR /2.TRA.LCZ.ADN be.2.SYN here.LOC

b. Zauri-tu n-ind-u-e(n)-la-ko, gizon-a hil d-u-t.
wound.PEF 1/.TRA.PST.LCZ.ADN man kill.PEF /1.TRA

(7) a. E-ra-gotz-i d-i-o-gu, gu bezala, ez da-rrai-ki-zu-la-ko.
forbid.PEF //1PLU.DTR we SIP not follow.2/.DYN.LCZ.ADN

b. Ez z-a-r-a ager-tu, beldur z-in-e(-n)-la-ko.
not 2.ITR appear.PEF fear.IDF be.2.SYN.PST.LCZ.ADN

c. Eta ber-e-ha(r-en)-la n-oa, luzapen-a eguerdi-an buka-tzen d-ela-ko.
and at_once go.1.SYN respite noon.LOC end.IPF ITR.LCZ

d. Ez n-i-zu-e-n hori hasiera-tik esa-n, ni zu-(e)-ekin
not /2PLU/1.DTR.PST that beginning.ELA tell.PEF I you.PLU.SOC
n-en-go-e(n)-la-ko.
be.1.SYN.PST.LCZ.ADN

(8) a. Piztia txarr-(e)-en esku-e-ta-n g-a-u-de-la-ko heriotz(a)-a-ri,
beast vicious.PLU.GEN hand.PLU.LOC be.1PLU.SYN.LCZ.ADN death.DAT
aurrez=aurre begira-tu behar d-i-o-gu.
face.IDF.INS-face.IDF look_at have_to.PPR //1PLU.DTR

b. Hiru urte lehen-ago lapur bat aurki-tze-n lagun-du z-i-o(-n)-la-ko, oso
three year.IDF before.COP thief a find.VEN.LOC help.PEF DTR.PST.LCZ.ADN very
adiskide z-u-en.
friend.IDF have.SYT.PST

c. Ile-a erdi busti-rik da-go-ela-ko, hotz-a senti-tzen d-u.
hair half.IDF wet.STA be.SYN.LCZ.ADN cold feel.IPF TRA

(9) a. Nahi d-u-da-la-ko bizi n-a-iz hemen.
want.PPR /1.TRA.LCZ.ADN live.PPR 1.ITR here.LOC

b. Eta bihotz-e-z maite n-a-u-zu-la-ko e-gi-n d-it-u-zu gauza handi hau-ek.
and heart.IDF.INS love.PPR 1/2.TRA.LCZ.ADN do.PEF PLU/2.TRA thing great this.PLU

c. I-kus-i n-a-u-zu-la-ko sinets-i al d-u-zu?
see.PEF 1/2.TRA.LCZ.ADN believe.PEF INT /2.TRA

d. Irtenbide-rik ez ze-uka-te(-n)-la-ko geldi-tu d-ir-a, gogo-z
escape.PAR not have./PLU.SYT.PST.LCZ.ADN stay.PEF PLU.ITR wish.IDF.INS
beste-ra, ez da-uka-te-n-a-ri balio-rik e-ma-ten
contrary_to.IDF.ALL not have./PLU.SYT.NRE.ZEP.DAT value.PAR give.IPF
d-i-o-te-la-ko.
PLU.DTR.LCZ.ADN

e. Ni-ri, berri-z, egi(a)-a d-io-da-la-ko ez d-i-da-zu-e sine(t)s-ten.
I.DAT new.IDF.INS truth tell./1.SYT.LCZ.ADN not /1/2PLU.DTR believe.IPF

(10) a. Horr-e(n)-ga(i)-tik sal-du z-i-da-n bada etxe hau, ber-a Dublin-e-ra
that.MOT sell.PEF /1/.DTR.PST INF house this he_himself Dublin.ALL
z-i-h-oa(-n)-la-ko.
go.SYN.PST.LCZ.ADN

b. Horr-e(n)-ga(i)-tik maite n-a-u Aita-k, n-eu-re bizi-a e-ma-ten
that.MOT love.PPR 1/.TRA father.IDF I.REF.GEN life give.IPF
d-u-da-la-ko.
/1.TRA.LCZ.ADN

(11) a. Gazte-a-ren iritzi-ek ez d-u-te, gazte bat-en aho-tik
young.ZEP.GEN opinion.PLU.ERG not /PLU.TRA young.ZEP a.IDF.GEN mouth.ELA
jaulki d-ir-ela-ko, amen=amen-ik merezi.
emerge.PEF PLU.ITR.LCZ.ADN amen.IDF-amen.PAR deserve.PPR

b. Zaharr-a ez da, zahar d-ela-ko eta___kito, errespetagarri.
old.ZEP not be.SYN old.IDF be.SYN.LCZ.ADN just venerable.IDF

c. Ni ere ez n-a-iz nahi d-u-da-la-ko txiki-a, e?
I too not be.1.SYN want.PPR /1.TRA.LCZ.ADN small am_I

d. Mutil hau ez da-go hemen nahi d-u-ela-ko.
boy this not be.SYN here.LOC want.PPR TRA.LCZ.ADN

(12) a. Ingeles-e-z da-u-de-la-ko, ez d-u-t uste inor-k
English_language.IDF.INS be.PLU.SYN.LCZ.ADN not /1.TRA believe.PPR anyone.ERG
harri-tu behar l-u-ke-en-ik.
be_surprised should.PPR TRA.COD.PCZ

b. Damu d-u-t hainbeste diru ni-re alde joka-tu
regret.IDF have./1.SYT so_much money I.GEN side.IDF gamble_away.PEF
d-u-te-la-ko.
/PLU.TRA.LCZ.ADN

c. Arras poz-ik n-a-go ni-re senarr-a-ri e-ma-n d-i-o-te-la-ko.
very glad.STA be.1.SYN I.GEN husband.DAT give.PEF //PLU.DTR.LCZ.ADN

d. Poz-tu e-gi-ten z-a-r-a aurre-ko emakume-a beltz-a d-ela-ko.
be_glad do.IPF 2.ITR front_part.ADN woman black be.SYN.LCZ.ADN

(13) a. Ber-a-z zor d-i-z-ki-o-gu eskerr-ak Jaungoiko-a-ri gu-re bizitz(a)-a-ri
same.INS debt.IDF PLU//1PLU.DTR thank.PLU God.DAT we.GEN life.DAT
irau-n araz-te-ko e-ma-ten d-i-gu-la-ko zer jan.
last.RAD to_cause_to.VEN.ADN give.IPF /1PLU/.DTR.LCZ.ADN what eat

b. Ez d-i-o-t ezer aipa-tu, ber-a-k ba-da-ki-ela-ko
not //1.DTR anything mention.PEF he_himself.ERG AFF.know.SYT.LCZ.ADN
gorabehera guzti-a.
problem whole

c. Gau-e-ra-ko den-ak j-oa-ten z-ir-e-n, ordu-an ager-tzen
nightfall.DES all.PLU go.IPF PLU.ITR.PST that_time.LOC appear.IPF
ze(-n)-la-ko-tz hil har-en arim(a)-a.
ITR.PST.LCZ.ADN.INS dead.ZEP yonder.GEN soul

(14) a. Patxi-k, ez z-u-e(n)-la-ko Maite i-kus-i, galde-tu z-i-da-n berri.
Frank.ERG not TRA.PST.LCZ.ADN Maite see.PEF ask.PEF /1/.DTR.PST news.IDF

b. ... unibertsitate-e-ta-n ez z-u-e(n)-la-ko euskar(a)-ak leku-rik.
... university.PLU.LOC not TRA.PST.LCZ.ADN Basque_language.ERG place.PAR

c. Eliz(a)-a ez ze-n orai(n)-no jende-z bete-a, mez(a)-a ez
church not be.SYN.PST yet people.IDF.INS full mass not
ze(-n)-la-ko-tz has-i-a.
ITR.PST.LCZ.ADN.INS start.PEF.SIN

d. Hori gerta-tu iza-n da Protestante-(e)-en arte-an, ez
that happen.PEF be.PEF ITR Protestant.PLU.GEN among not
d-u-te-la-ko-tz buruzagi bat Jesu=kristo-k e-ma-n-a.
have./PLU.SYT.LCZ.ADN.INS leader a Jesus_Christ.ERG give.PEF.ZEP

(15) a. Zer e-gi-n d-u-ela-ko zigor-tu d-u-te?
what do.PEF TRA.LCZ.ADN punish.PEF /PLU.TRA

b. Nor da-torr-ela-ko z-oa-z etxe-ra?
who come.SYN.LCZ.ADN go.2.SYN house.ALL

c. Nor-k kanta-tzen d-u-ela-ko j-oa-n-go z-a-r-a antzoki-ra?
who.ERG sing.IPF TRA.LCZ.ADN go.FUT 2.ITR theater.ALL

d. No-ra z-oa-z-ela-ko sal-du d-u-zu etxe-a?
where.ALL go.2.SYN.LCZ.ADN sell.PEF /2.TRA house

(16) a. Aita, barka-tu ie-za-i-e-zu, ez da-ki-te zer-ta-n ari
Father.IDF forgive /PLU/2.DTR.IMP not know./PLU.SYT what.LOC be_busy.PPR
d-ir-en eta.
PLU.ITR.NCZ EEC

b. Aita, barka ie-za-i-e-zu, ez da-ki-te eta zer ari
Father.IDF forgive.RAD /PLU/2.DTR.IMP not know./PLU.SYT EEC what be_busy.PPR
d-ir-en.
PLU.INT.NCZ

(17) a. Utz-i n-a-za-zu, egunsenti-a da eta.
leave 1/2.TRA.IMP daybreak be.SYN EEC

b. Z-a-to(r)-z-te pixka bat barru-ra, orain-dik ba-d-u-gu asti-a eta.
come.2PLU.SYN.IMP bit a inside.ALL now.ELA AFF.have./1PLU.SYT time EEC

c. Hi e-go-n h-a-di isil-ik, ez da-ki-k ezer eta!
you.SOL be(.RAD) 2.ITR.IMP quiet not know./2SOL.SYT anything EEC

d. G-a-u-de-n isil-ik. Martina eta Andresa barru-ra da-to(r)-z eta.
be.1PLU.SYN.NCZ quiet.STA Martina and Andresa inside.ALL come.PLU.SYN EEC

e. Lenbailehen d-i-h-oa-la, ez d-i-gu mutil horr-e-k nahigabe-a
as_soon_as_possible go.SYN.LCZ not /1PLU/.DTR boy that.ERG sorrow
beste-rik e-ma-ten eta.
else.ZEP.PAR give.IPF EEC

(18) a. Ez d-i-zu-e-t esa-n-go guzti-a, luze li-tza-te-ke eta.
not /2PLU/1.DTR tell.FUT everything lengthy.IDF be.SYN.COD EEC

b. N-eu-k ja-rrai-tu-ko d-u-t, aspaldi ez d-u-t hitzegin eta.
I.EMP.ERG continue.FUT /1.TRA for_a_long_time not /1.TRA speak.PEF EEC

c. Agudo amai-tzen d-u-t. Hitzaldi luze-ak ez d-it-u-da-la maite
quickly finish.IPF /1.TRA speech lengthy.PLU not PLU/1.TRA.LCZ love.PPR
ba-da-ki-zu-e eta.
AFF. now./2PLU.SYT EEC

d. Hori-ek zu-(e)-en-tzat. On Permin gozozale-a ez d-ela
that_one.PLU 2PLU.BEN Don Fermín fond_of_sweets not be.SYN.LCZ
ba-da-ki-t eta.
AFF.know./1.SYT EEC

(19) a. Azken-e-ko egun-a da eta, g-oa-z-en guzti-ok dantza-ra.
end.ADN day be.SYN EEC go.1PLU.SYN.NCZ all.INC dance.ALL

b. Etxe-an ez d-u-gu har-tzen paper hori eta, e-ma-n behar d-i-da-zu.
house.LOC not /1PLU.TRA get.IPF paper that EEC give must /1/2.DTR

(20) Ber-e lagun-a-k, agure ze-n eta, ze-uka-n lepo-a
he_himself.GEN friend.ERG old_man.IDF be.SYN.PST EEC have.SYT.PST neck.SIN
makurr-a.
bent.SIN

(21) a. Egunsenti-a da eta utz-i n-a-za-zu.
daybreak be.SYN and leave 1/2.TRA.IMP

b. Luze li-tza-te-ke eta ez d-i-zu-e-t esa-n-go guzti-a.
lengthy.IDF be.SYN.COD and not /2PLU/1.DTR tell.FUT everything

(22) a. Salome: Hura begi-e-ta-tik sar-tu za-i-zu-la d-irudi.
Salome: yonder_one eye.PLU.ELA get_into.PEF 2/.DIT.LCZ seem.SYT
Peli: Itsu-a ez n-a-iz eta.
Peli: blind not be.1.SYN EEC

b. Agustine: Jeiki-ak d-ir-a aspaldi.
Agustine: get_up.PEF.PLU PLU.ITR for_a_long_time
Itziar: Eliza-ra joan=etorri-a e-gi-n d-u-te eta
Itziar: church.ALL trip make.PEF /PLU.TRA EEC

In the case of *joan-etorria*, both perfect participles in their function as citation form of the verb are joined together to form a so-called dvandva compound, meaning literally "going-(and)-coming."

c. Eneko: Beltz-(e)-en arte-an bizi-ko n-a-iz-ela ba al d-eritz-o-zu?
Eneko: black.ZEP.PLU.GEN among live.FUT 1.ITR.LCZ AFF INT approve.//2.DYT
Orreaga: On Kristobal eta han bizi d-ir-a eta.
Orreaga: Don Cristobal and.DEL over_there.LOC live.PPR PLU.ITR EEC

(23) a. Miren ez da e-torr-i-ko, ber-e am(a)-a-k ha(r-en)-la esa-n d-i-t eta.
Mary not ITR come.FUT she_herself.GEN mother.ERG so tell.PEF /1/.DTR EEC

b. Hon-e-z-gero bide erdi-an da-to(r)-z, garai-a da eta.
by_now way.IDF half.LOC come.PLU.SYN time be.SYN EEC

c. Baietz, lapurr-a! Ni-k i-kus-i d-u-t sar-tze-n eta.
yet thief I.ERG see.PEF /1.TRA go_in.VEN.LOC EEC

(24) a. Gazte-en-a-k ber-a jaits-i-ko ze(-n)-la.
young.SUP.ZEP.ERG he_himself go_down.FUT ITR.PST.LCZ

b. Ha(r-en)-la uste z-u-e(n)-la ber-a-k.
so think.PPR TRA.PST.LCZ he_himself.ERG

(25) a. Ezetz beste-ek, har-k ez z-u-e(n)-la horr-e-ta-ra-ko balio eta.
no.IDF other.ZEP.PLU.ERG yonder_one.ERG not TRA.PST.LCZ that.DES be_worth.PPR EEC

b. Juana-k ber-e am(a)-a i-kus-i behar z-u-e(n)-la eta Basaburuko bide-a har-tu z-u-en.
Juana.ERG she_herself.GEN mother see have_to.PPR TRA.PST.LCZ EEC Basaburu.ADN road take.PEF TRA.PST

c. Sendagile bat sar-tu da gaixo-ren bat da-go-ela eta.
doctor a come_in.PEF ITR sick.ZEP.IDF.GEN some be.SYN.LCZ EEC

d. Etxe-an gatz-a ugari da-go-ela eta ez de-za-zu-la bazkari-a gehi-egi gazi-tu.
house.LOC salt plenty.PRE be.SYN.LCZ EEC not /2.TRA.SUJ.LCZ food much.ECS salt

(26) a. Migel-i txiki geldi-tu zi-tza-i-z-ki-o-la eta, ni-k jantz-i behar-ko n-it-u-en ohe-ko jantzi hai-ek, urtebete barru.
Miguel.DAT small.IDF become.PEF /PLU.DIT.PST.LCZ EEC I.ERG wear have_to.PPR PLU/1.TRA.PST bed.ADN cloth yonder.PLU one_year within

b. Hor Lizarreta-ko barruti-an iza-n g-a-r-a. Seme-a-k i-kus-i behar
there.LOC Lizarreta.ADN area.LOC be.PEF 1PLU.ITR son.ERG see have_to.PPR

z-u-e(n)-la eta.
TRA.PST.LCZ EEC

(27) a. Eguraldi txarr-a ze-go-e(n)-la eta, hurr-en-go egun-e-ra-ko ezkontz(a)-a
weather bad be.SYN.PST.LCZ EEC close.SUP.ADN day.DES wedding
atzera-tu omen z-u-te-n.
postpone.PEF REP /PLU.TRA.PST

b. Goiz-e-ko zalapart(a)-a iza-n d-ela eta senarr-a ihes-i j-oa-n za-i-t.
morning.ADN disturbance be.PEF ITR.LCZ EEC husband flight.PRE go.PEF 1/.DIT

c. Ez d-u-t berri-ro mundu-a madarika-tu-ko gizaki-a d-ela eta.
not /1.TRA new.ADN world curse.FUT human_race exist.SYN.LCZ EEC

d. Zer d-ela eta, ordu-an, hasier(a)-an azal-du d-it-u-da-n
what be.SYN.LCZ EEC that_time.LOC beginning.LOC express.PEF PLU/1.TRA.NRE
kezk(a)-ak?
reservation.PLU

(28) a. Arrain-a d-ela eta, horr-en-beste auzi.
fish be.SYN.LCZ EEC so_much dispute

b. Plajio-a d-ela eta, idei(a)-ak oso garbi da-u-z-ka-te.
plagiarism be.SYN.LCZ EEC idea.PLU very clear.PRE have.PLU/PLU.SYT

(29) a. No-la ez n-a-iz-en beldur? Ez bai(t)-t(<*d)-u-t
how_come not be.1.SYN.NCZ fear.IDF not ACP.have./1.SYT
deus-e-ta-n___ere falta-rik. Kontzientzia bai(t)-t(<*d)-u-t on-a
anything.LOC___whatsoever failing.PAR conscience ACP.have./1.SYT good.SIN
eta garbi-a.
and pure.SIN

b. Zer-tako? Zizta-tzen bai(t)-n-ind-u-te-n.
what.BEN sting.IPF ACP.1/PLU.TRA.PST

c. Ez omen bai(t)-t(<*d)a ere denbora-rik gal-tze-ko, hon-(r)a zer-tako
not REP ACP.be.SYN too time.PAR lose.VEN.ADN here.ALL what.BEN
e-torr-i n-a-iz-en.
come.PEF 1.ITR.NCZ

(30) a. Epel-a bait-z-a-r-a eta ez z-a-r-ela-ko-tz ez hotz-a ez bero-a,
lukewarm ACP.be.2.SYN and not be.2.SYN.LCZ.ADN.INS not cold not warm
has-i-ko n-a-tza-i-zu en-e aho-tik aurtiki-tze-n.
start.FUT 2/1.DIT I.GEN mouth.ELA eject.VEN.LOC

b. Hori erra-n z-u-en, ez behardun-e-z axola z-u-e(n)-la-ko-tz, baina
that say.PEF TRA.PST not poor.PLU.INS care.IDF have.SYT.PST.LCZ.ADN.INS but
ohoin-a bait-ze-n.
thief ACP.be.SYN.PST

(31) a. Aita, barka ie-za-i-e-zu, ez bai(t)-t(<*d)a-ki-te zer ari
Father.IDF forgive.RAD /PLU/2.DTR.IMP not ACP.know./PLU.SYT what be_busy.PPR
d-ir-en.
PLU.ITR.NCZ

b. Utz n-a-za-zu j-oa-te-ra, argi=haste-a bai(t)-t(<*d)a.
let.RAD 1/2.TRA.IMP go.VEN.ALL daybreak ACP.be.SYN

(32) a. Zu-re bila ote da-to(r)-z-en beldur n-a-iz. Ate-an
you.GEN looking_for.PRE DUB come.PLU.SYN.NCZ fear.IDF be.1.SYN door.LOC
soldadu pila bat bai(t)-t(<*d)a-go.
soldier.IDF bunch a ACP.be.SYN

b. On-do da-go-en ala ez esa-n behar d-i-da-zu. Gu-k ez
well be.SYN.NCZ or not tell must.PPR /1/2.DTR we.ERG not
bai(t)-t(<*d)-u-gu euskar(a)-a liburu-e-ta-n ikas-i.
ACP./1PLU.TRA Basque book.PLU.LOC learn.PEF

c. E-ntzu-n, ez z-u-en ezer e-ntzu-ten, bikote-a urrun samar
hear not TRA.PST anything hear.IPF couple far_away rather
bait-ze-go-en.
ACP.be.SYN.PST

d. Bizitza oso-an ez bait-ze-n inoiz mozkor-tu, gai(t)z-ki senti-tze-n
life whole.LOC not ACP.ITR.PST ever get_drunk.PEF bad.ADV feel.VEN.LOC
has-i ze-n.
begin.PEF ITR.PST

(33) a. Jan e-za-zu-e gogo-z, zu-ek ez bai(t)-t(<*d)-u-zu-e
eat(.RAD) /2PLU.TRA.IMP appetite.IDF.INS you.PLU.ERG not ACP.have./2PLU.SYT
erru-rik.
guilt.PAR

b. Igo h-a-di gain-e-ra, gaur azken afari-a bai(t)-t(<*d)-u-gu.
climb_up(.RAD) 2SOL.ITR.IMP top.ALL today last supper ACP.have./1PLU.SYT

(34) a. Zer-ga(i)-tik esa-n behar n-i-zu-n?; zu-k ez bai(t)-t(<*d)-i-da-zu
what.MOT tell have_to.PPR /2/1.DTR.PST you.ERG not ACP./1/2.DTR
galde-tu.
ask.PEF

b. No-la gerta-tu-ko da, ba, hori, ni-k ez bai(t)-t(<*d)-u-t gizon-ik
how happen.FUT ITR then that I.ERG not ACP./1.TRA man.PAR
e-zagu(t)-tzen.
know.IPF

(35) a. Eta hemen, teatro-an bai(t)-k(<*g)-a-u-de, hitz-ak ez d-ir-a
and here.LOC theater.LOC ACP.be.1PLU.SYN word.PLU not be.PLU.SYN

eran(t)skin huts.
addition empty.IDF

b. Ez n-u-ke hon-ekin, leku-a ez bai(t)-t(<*d)a batere egoki-a, aurre-ra
not /1.TRA.COD this.SOC place not ACP.be.SYN at_all suitable front_part.ALL
jo nahi.
proceed want.PPR

(36) a. Z-a-u-de-te pixka bat-e-an, lagun-du-ko d-i-zu-e-t eta.
wait.2PLU.SYN.IMP moment a.LOC accompany.FUT /2PLU/1.DTR EEC

b. Lagun-du-ko d-i-zu-e-da-n-e-z gero, z-a-u-de-te pixka bat-e-an.
accompany.FUT /2PLU/1.DTR.NRE.INS since wait.2PLU.SYN.IMP moment a.LOC

(37) a. Gauza hori-e-ta-z ari g-a-r-en-e-z gero, gu-re seme horr-e-k
thing that.PLU.INS be_busy.PPR 1PLU.ITR.NRE.INS since we.GEN son that.ERG
beste nahigabe bat e-ma-n-go d-i-gu.
other pain a give.FUT 1PLU/.DTR

b. Amerik(a)-a aipa-tu d-u-zu-n-e-z gero, Santo Domingo-ko zen-bait
America mention.PEF /2.TRA.NRE.INS since Santo Domingo.ADN some
berri galde e-gi-n behar d-i-z-ki-zu-t.
information question.IDF do have_to.PPR PLU/2/1.DTR

c. 1700-e-an, urte hori ezarr-i d-i-gu-te-n-e-z gero abiapuntu-tzat,
1700.LOC year that set.PEF /1PLU/PLU.DTR.NRE.INS since starting_point.PRO
zen-bait gauza-ren jabe da orain-dik Euskal Herri-a.
certain thing.GEN possessor.IDF be.SYN now.ELA Basque Country

(38) a. Ni apaiz-a n-a-iz-en-e-z gero, aholkulari-tzat har-tu n-a-u.
I priest be.1.SYN.NRE.INS since adviser.PRO take.PEF 1/.TRA

b. Gerezi___sasoi-an g-a-u-de-n-e-z gero, on-a li-tza-te-ke
cherry.IDF___season.LOC be.1PLU.SYN.NRE.INS since good be.SYN.COD
gerezi-ren bat i-kus-te-a.
cherry.IDF.GEN some(⟨cherry⟩or_other) see.VEN

c. Galtz(a)-ak zikin-du d-i-z-ki-zu-da-n-e-z gero, beste kafe bat har-tze-ra
pants.PLU soil.PEF PLU/2/1.DTR.NRE.INS since other coffee a take.VEN.ALL
gonbida-tzen z-a-it-u-t.
invite.IPF 2/1.TRA

(39) a. Aho literatur(a)-a, paper-ik e-ra-bil-tzen ez d-u-en-e-z gero, ber-e-z
mouth literature paper.PAR use.IPF not TRA.NRE.INS since it_itself.IDF.INS
da suntsikorr-a.
be.SYN ephemeral

b. Txema-k, oporr-e-ta-n da-go-en-e-z gero, oso poz-ik lagun-du-ko
Txema.ERG vacation.PLU.LOC be.SYN.NRE.INS since very glad.STA help.FUT

l-i-zu-ke.
/2/.DTR.COD

(40) a. Gerta-tu-a gerta-tu d-en-e-z gero, e-gi-zu nahi
happen.PEF.ZEP.SIN happen.PEF ITR.NRE.INS since do./2.SYT.IMP want.PPR
d-u-zu-n-a.
/2.TRA.NRE.ZEP

b. Zilegi iza-n be-ki-t, gai ez n-a-iz-en-e-z gero
allowed.IDF be(.RAD) 1/.DIT.JUS qualified.PRE not be.1.SYN.NRE.INS since
beste-ta-ra-ko, zen-bait gauza esa-te-a azentu-a-z.
else.ZEP.IDF.DES a_few thing say.VEN accent.INS

c. G-a-to(r)-z-en Etxepare-gan-(r)a, Etxepare-gan-dik gehi-egi
come.1PLU.SYN.NCZ Etxepare.ALL Etxepare.ELA much.ECS
saihe(t)s-tu g-a-r-en-e-z gero.
stray_far_from.PEF 1PLU.ITR.NRE.INS since

d. Amerikano-a-rekin ezkon-du nahi ez z-u-en-e-z gero, e-gi-n
American.SOC marry want.PPR not TRA.PST.NRE.INS since do(.RAD)
de-za-la gogo-a-k e-ma-ten d-i-o-n-a.
TRA.SUJ.LCZ mind.ERG give.IPF DTR.NRE.ZEP

(41) a. Gauz(a)-ak esku-ra da-to(r)-z-ki-gu-n-e-z gero, zer-ga(i)-tik ez jaso
thing.PLU hand.ALL come.1PLU/PLU.DYN.NRE.INS since what.MOT not pick_up
aukera-n d-u-gu-n-a?
opportunity.IDF.LOC have./1PLU.NRE.ZEP

b. Su emaile-tzat har-tzen g-a-it-u-zu-n-e-z gero, zer-ga(i)-tik ez hitzegin
fire.IDF giver.PRO take_for.IPF 1PLU/2.TRA.NRE.INS since what.MOT not speak
argi eta garbi?
plainly and clearly

c. Hori-(e)-en iri(t)z(i)kide ez h-a-iz-en-e-z
that_one.PLU.GEN somebody_sharing_the_opinion_of.IDF not be.2SOL.SYN.NRE.INS
gero, lots(a)-a-k ez al h-a-u gorri-tzen?
since shame.ERG not INT 2SOL/.TRA make_red.IPF

d. Lanbide berri-ak ager-tu d-ir-en-e-z gero, no-la ez d-ir-a
profession new.PLU appear.PEF PLU.ITR.NRE.INS since how not PLU.ITR
norgehiagoka berri-ak sor-tzen?
contest new.PLU arise.IPF

(42) a. Alargun hau gogai(t)karri za-i-da-n-e-z, de-gi-o-da-n justizia.
widow this bothersome.IDF be.1/.DYN.NRE.INS do.//1.DYT.NCZ justice.IDF

b. Ezer gerta-tu ez ze(-n)-n-e-z, ber-ta-n utz-i z-u-te-n.
anything happen.PEF not ITR.PST.NRE.INS it_itself.IDF.LOC leave.PEF /PLU.TRA.PST

(43) a. Utz-i-ko z-a-it-u-t j-oa-te-ra ha(r-en)-la desira-tzen d-u-zu-n-a-z gain-e-an.
let.FUT 2/1.TRA go.VEN.ALL so desire.IPF /2.TRA.NRE.ZEP.INS top.LOC
b. Bai, bai, eros-i-ko d-i-a-t sal-du nahi d-u-a-n-a-z gain-e-an.
yes yes buy.FUT /2SOL/1.DTR sell want.PPR /2SOL.TRA.NRE.ZEP.INS top.LOC
c. Ja-ki-n nahi d-u-zu-n-a-z gain-e-an, hon-(r)a beti zer gerta-tzen
know want.PPR /2.TRA.NRE.ZEP.INS top.LOC here.ALL always what happen.IPF
za-i-gu-n: . . .
1PLU/.DIT.NCZ
d. Hiri-ra ba-z-oa-z-en-a-z gain-e-an, nahi d-u-zu e-ra-ma-n en-e
town.ALL AFF.go.2SYN.NRE.ZEP.INS top.LOC want.PPR /2.TRA wear I.GEN
xamarr-a?
jacket

(44) a. Ba-da-ki-zu zer-ga(i)-tik e-gi-ten d-u-da-n, zu z-a-r-ela medio,
AFF.know./2.SYT what.MOT do.IPF /1.TRA.NCZ you be.2.SYN.LCZ because
hainbeste negar? Zer-ga(i)-tik ni zu-re-tza-ko argizari-a n-a-iz-en, eta zu
so_much tear.IDF CAC I you.BEN wax be.1.SYN.NCZ and you
ni-re-tza-ko eguzki-a z-a-r-en, eta eguzki-a-k argizari-a no-la ez d-u
I.BEN sun be.2.SYN.NCZ and sun.ERG wax how not TRA
ur-tu-ko?
melt.FUT
b. No-la eztizale-a n-a-iz-en txit, ez n-in-tz-e-n argizari-a-z oroi(t)-tzen.
CAC fond_of_honey be.1.SYN.NCZ very not 1.ITR.PST wax.INS remember.IPF
c. Agudo plater pare bat, zer-ga(i)-tik gose-a-rekin ez d-u-gu i-kus-ten.
quick.ADV dish.IDF couple a CAC hunger.SOC not /1PLU.TRA see.IPF

(45) a. Emazteki-a, zer-ga(i)-tik e-gi-ten d-u-zu negar? Magdalena-k ihardets-i
woman what.MOT do.IPF /2.TRA tear.IDF Magdalena.ERG reply.PEF
z-u-en: Negar e-gi-ten d-ut zer-en e-ra-ma-n d-u-te-n en-e
TRA.PST tear.IDF do.IPF /1.TRA CAC take_away.PEF /PLU.TRA.NCZ I.GEN
Jainko-a, eta zer-en ez da-ki-da-n no-n ezarr-i d-u-te-n.
God and CAC not know./1.SYT.NCZ where.LOC put.PEF /PLU.TRA.NCZ
b. Zer-ga(i)-tik? Zer-en ez z-a-it-u-z-te-da-n maite?
what.MOT CAC not 2PLU/1.TRA.NCZ love.PPR
c. Zer-en z-a-r-en hain on-a, urriki d-ut zu-ri e-gi-n
CAC be.2.SYN.NCZ so good sorrow.IDF have./1.SYT you.DAT do.PEF
irain-e-z.
insult.PLU.INS
d. Ez d-i-o-zu zu-k en-e izen-a-ri altxa-tu-ren etxe-rik, zer-en z-a-r-en
not //2.DTR you.ERG I.GEN name.DAT build.FUT house.PAR CAC be.2.SYN.NCZ

gerla=gizon-a, eta odol-a isur-i d-u-zu-la-ko-tz.
man_of_war and blood shed.PEF /2.TRA.LCZ.ADN.INS

(46) a. Zer-ga(i)-tik behar d-i-o-gu-n g-eu-re etsai-a-ri barka-tu.
CAC must.PPR //1PLU.DTR.NCZ we.REF.GEN enemy.DAT forgive
Lehenbizi-ko arrazoi-a: Zer-en Jainko-a-k maina-tzen bai(t)-t(<*d)-u.
first.ADN reason CAC God.ERG command.IPF ACP.TRA

b. Geldi-tzen d-ir-a joko-tik, zer-en akaba-tzen bait-za-i-e kandel(a)-a.
stop.IPF PLU.ITR game.ELA CAC end.IPF ACP.PLU/.DIT candle

c. Emazteki-a, zer-ga(i)-tik e-gi-ten d-u-zu negar? Iharde(t)s-ten d-u: Zer-en
woman what.MOT do.IPF /2.TRA tear.IDF reply.IPF TRA CAC
e-ra-ma-n bai(t)-t(<*d)-u-te en-e Jaun-a, eta ez da-ki-t no-n
take_away.PEF ACP./PLU.TRA I.GEN Lord and not know./1.SYT where.LOC
ezarr-i d-u-te-n.
put.PEF /PLU.TRA.NCZ

(47) a. Iza-n z-it-u-en hirurogeita___hamar seme, zer-en bait-z-it-u-en
have.PEF PLU/.TRA.PST seventy son.IDF CAC ACP.have.PLU/.SYT.PST
asko emazte.
many wife

b. Senda e-za-zu en-e arim(a)-a, zer-en bekatu e-gi-n bai(t)-t(<*d)-u-t.
heal.RAD /2.TRA.IMP I.GEN soul CAC sin.IDF do.PEF ACP./1.TRA

c. Erne z-a-u-de-te ber-a-z zu-ek ere, zer-en uste ez
alert.PRE be.2PLU.SYN.IMP same.INS you.PLU also CAC expect.PPR not
d-u-zu-e-n ordu-an e-torr-i-ko bai(t)-t(<*d)a gizon-a-ren Seme-a.
/2PLU.TRA.NRE time.LOC come.FUT ACP.ITR man.GEN Son

(48) a. Ez d-u-t ebats-i nahi, zer-en mentura-z justizi(a)-ak atzeman
not /1.TRA steal want.PPR CAC chance.IDF.INS law.ERG catch.RAD
n-ind-za-ke, urka edo azota.
1/.TRA.POT.COD hang.RAD or flog.RAD

b. Ez d-u-t joka-tu nahi, zer-en joko-a ez da errent(a)-a,
not /1.TRA gamble want.PPR CAC gambling not be.SYN stipend
mentura-z gal ne-za-ke.
chance.IDF.INS lose.RAD /1.TRA.POT

c. Zu-k ere ikas-i behar d-u-zu erai(n)-te-n, zer-en zahar-tze-n
you.ERG too learn must.PPR /2.TRA SOW.VEN.LOC CAC get_old.VEN.LOC
ari n-a-iz.
be_busy.PPR 1.ITR

d. Aldi bakoitz, en-e libertate-tik zati bat eror-tzen za-i-t, zer-en ez da-ki-t
time each.IDF I.GEN freedom.ELA part a fall.IPF 1/.DIT CAC not know./1.SYT

no-ra ba-n-oa-n.
where.ALL AFF.go.1.SYN.NCZ

(49) a. Ez d-u-t esku-e-ta-n d-u-da-n-a-z gabe-tu nahi. Zer-en
not /1.TRA hand.PLU.LOC have./1.SYT.NRE.ZEP.INS give_up want.PPR CAC
mentura-z gero, nahi d-u-da-n-e-an, ez n-u-ke.
chance.IDF.INS later want.PPR /1.TRA.NRE.LOC not have./1.SYT.COD

b. Anitz-e-ta-n ere Eskritura Saindu-an konpara-tzen da bekatore-a ardi
often.IDF.LOC too Scripture Holy.LOC compare.IPF ITR sinner sheep
errebelatu-a-rekin. Eta arrazoi-(e)-ekin. Zer-en anitz gauza-ta-n
go_astray.PEF.SIN.SOC and reason.PLU.SOC CAC many thing.IDF.LOC
bai(t)-t(<*d)-irudi-te elkar.
ACP.resemble./PLU.SYT each_other

(50) a. Bai pena hau merezi d-u gizon eskergabe-a-k zer-en eta
indeed punishment this deserve.PPR TRA man ungrateful.ERG CAC EXP
hauts-i d-it-u-en Jainko-a-ren lege-ak.
break.PEF PLU/.TRA.NCZ God.GEN law.PLU

b. Hori ez za-i-t gogora-tu ere, zer-en eta bai(t)-t(<*d)a-ki-t emazte anitz ez
that not 1/.DIT occur.PEF even CAC EXP ACP.know./1.SYT woman many not
d-ir-ela ni-k hemen mintza-tu nahi d-it-u-da-n-e-ta-rik.
be.PLU.SYN.LCZ I.ERG here.LOC talk want.PPR PLU/1.TRA.NRE.ZEP.PLU.ELA

c. Arras gogo-tik mintza-tzen n-a-iz gizon hon-e-ta-z, zer-en eta abantzu
quite heart.ELA speak.IPF 1.ITR man this.INS CAC EXP more_or_less
en-e herritarr-a d-ela-ko-tz.
I.GEN fellow_villager be.SYN.LCZ.ADN.INS

(51) a. Laborari-a Jainko-a-ren obr(a)-e-ta-n ari da; ezen Jainko-a-k e-gi-n
farmer God.GEN work.PLU.LOC be_busy.PPR ITR CAC God.ERG make.PEF
d-it-u gizon guzti-ak, eta laborari-a-ren esku-tik haz-ten d-it-u.
PLU/.TRA man all.PLU and farmer.GEN hand.ELA feed.IPF PLU/.TRA

b. Segur n-a-iz plazer e-gi-n-en d-i-o-da-la ezen ber-a ere kantari polit-a
sure be.1.SYN favor.IDF do.FUT //1.DTR.LCZ CAC he_himself too singer fine
da.
be.SYN

(52) a. Ez d-a-u-de ino-n, zer-en ihes e-gi-n bai(t)-t(<*d)-u-te.
not be.PLU.SYN anywhere.LOC CAC flight.IDF do.PEF ACP./PLU.TRA

b. Baina ailega-tu eta ezuste bat iza-n n-u-en, zer-en gailurr-a eta
but arrive POC surprise a have.PEF /1.TRA.PST CAC summit and
har-en inguru guzti-ak leku mortu-ak bait-z-ir-e-n.
yonder_one.GEN surrounding all.PLU place deserted.PLU ACP.be.PLU.SYN.PST

c. Ber-ta-ko objetu guzti-ak arrotz e-gi-ten zi-tza-i-z-ki-da-n, zer-en eta
right_there.ADN object all.PLU strange.IDF seem.IPF 1/PLU.DIT.PST CAC EXP
errealitate ez bait-ze-n aski indartsu amets-a ezezta-tze-ko.
reality not ACP.be.SYN.PST enough potent.IDF dream undo.VEN.ADN

d. Ez d-u-te sekula-n harrapa-tu-ko. Zer-en klasiko-ak izen-e-z eta
not /PLU.TRA ever.IDF catch.FUT CAC classic.PLU name.IDF.INS and
estanp(a)-e-ta-n bakarr-ik bai(t)-t(<*d)-ir-a ezagun-ak.
picture.PLU.LOC only.STA ACP.be.PLU.SYN known.PLU

(53) a. Ez d-u-t ni-k zu-(e)-en alde Aita-ri erregu-tu beharr-ik
not /1.TRA I.ERG you.PLU.GEN side.IDF Father.IDF.DAT pray need.PAR
iza-n-go, zer-en Aita-k ber-a-k maite bait-z-a-it-u-z-te, ni maite
have.FUT CAC Father.ERG he_himself.ERG love.PPR ACP.2PLU/.TRA I love.IDF
iza-n n-a-u-zu-e-la-ko.
have.PEF 1/2PLU.TRA.LCZ.ADN

b. Horr-e(n)-ga(i)-tik esa-n d-i-zu-e-t, z-eu-(e)-en bekatu-an hil-ko
that.MOT tell.PEF /2PLU/1.DTR you.REF.PLU.GEN sin.LOC die.FUT
z-a-r-e-te-la, zer-en ni n-a-iz-en-a n-a-iz-ela sine(t)s-ten
2PLU.SYN.LCZ CAC I be.1.SYN.NRE.ZEP be.1.SYN.LCZ believe.IPF
ez ba-d-u-zu-e, z-eu-(e)-en bekatu-e-ta-n hil-ko bait-z-a-r-e-te.
not CDP./2PLU.TRA you.REF.PLU.GEN sin.PLU.LOC die.FUT ACP.2PLU.ITR

(54) a. Ez deus e-gi-te-a-z ber-a-z ikas-ten da gai(t)zki e-gi-te-n, zer-en,
not anything do.VEN.SIN.INS it_itself.INS learn.IPF ITR evil.IDF do.VEN.LOC CAC
otiositas est mater nugarum, noverca virtutum.
otiositas est mater nugarum noverca virtutum

b. Jende hau bat=bat-e-an aurki-tzen da mintzabide-rik gabe; zer-en,
people this one.IDF_one.LOC find.IPF ITR power_of_speech without.PRE CAC
zer d-ela eta has-i-ko z-ir-e-n jaun hai-ek Afrika
what be.SYN.LCZ EEC start.FUT PLU.ITR.PST gentleman yonder.PLU Africa.IDF
erdi-ko hi(t)zkuntza basati-ak ikas-te-n?
center.ADN language uncouth.PLU learn.VEN.LOC

c. Mundu-a-ren gain garai(t)pen-a e-ma-ten d-igu-n-a gu-re
world.GEN top.IDF victory give.IPF /1PLU/.DTR.NRE.ZEP we.GEN
sinesmen-a da. Zer-en, nor-k garai(t)-tzen du mundu-a, Jesus
faith be.SYN CAC who.ERG overcome.IPF TRA world Jesus
Jainko-a-ren Seme d-ela sine(t)s-ten d-u-en-a-k baizik?
God.GEN Son.IDF be.SYN.LCZ believe.IPF TRA.NRE.ZEP.ERG except

d. Kanpo-a desira-tzen d-u, zer-en, libertate-a zein-en eder d-en!
outside long_for.IPF TRA CAC freedom how nice.IDF be.SYN.NCZ

(55) a. Ber-e diru-ak han z-it-u-en oso=oso-rik.
he_himself.GEN valuable.PLU over_there.LOC PLU/.TRA.PST whole.IDF_whole.STA
Ez d-u-te ber-a-z eba(t)s-te-ko hil.
not /PLU.TRA same.INS steal.VEN.ADN kill.PEF

b. Senitarteko-ak g-a-r-a bi-ok. Ber-a-z, ez d-u-gu bi-on
kinsman.PLU be.1PLU.SYN two.INC same.INS not /1PLU.TRA two.INC.GEN
arte-an liskarr-ik iza-n behar.
interval.LOC quarreling.PAR have must.PPR

(56) a. Hor-tik da-tor, bera-z, gu-re harridur(a)-a hon-en gutun-a
there.ELA come.SYN same.INS we.GEN astonishment this_one.GEN letter
irakur-tze-an.
read.VEN.SIN.LOC

b. On-gi___etorri-a zor d-i-e-gu ber-a-z.
welcome debt.IDF /PLU/1PLU.DTR same.INS
The syntactic group adverb + perfect participle has been substantivized just as in English; therefore, despite the hyphening of *ongi* as *on-gi*, the participle has been hyphened as *etorri-a* instead of *e-torr-i-a* (cf. *soineko* 'dress' instead of *soin-e-ko*, since the adnominal has been substantivized).

c. Ez n-i-o-ke, ber-a-z, deus ken-du nahi.
not //1.DTR.COD same.INS anything take_away want.PPR

d. Saia g-a-(d)i-tez-en, ber-a-z, kultura bat-en alde on-e-z
try.RAD 1PLU.ITR.SUJ.NCZ same.INS culture a.IDF.GEN side good.PLU.INS
lehenbailehen jabe-tze-n.
as_soon_as_possible appropriate.VEN.LOC

(57) a. Ber-a-z, *rey* ez da euskal hitz-a.
same.INS *rey* not be.SYN Basque word

b. Ber-a-z, ni-k ez n-u-ke esa-n-go inor-k orain-go hi(t)zkuntz(a)-a
same.INS I.ERG not /1.TRA.COD say.FUT anyone.ERG now.ADN language
bazter-tzen d-u-en-ik.
reject.IPF TRA.PCZ

(58) a. Batzu-e-ta-n, ber-a-z, ez da erraz iza-n-go euskal ordain-a
sometimes.PLU.LOC same.INS not ITR easy.IDF be.FUT Basque equivalent
asma-tze-a.
invent.VEN

b. Lehen bokal-a-ren iturburu-a ja-ki-te-ko, ber-a-z, lagungarri
first vowel.GEN source discover.VEN.ADN same.INS helpful.IDF
d-u-gu forma trinko-ak e-duki-tze-a.
have./1PLU.SYT form synthetic.PLU have.VEN

(59) a. *Inguru* da euskaldun guzti-ok da-ra-bil-gu-n hitz-a, baita
inguru be.SYN Basque all.INC.ERG use./1PLU.SYT.NRE word as_well_as
zuberotarr-ek ere. Hori da, bada, euskal hitz-a.
Souletin.PLU.ERG too that be.SYN INF Basque word

b. Hori da ba ni-k esa-n n-u-e(n)-n-a.
that be.SYN INF I.ERG say.PEF /1.TRA.PST.NRE.ZEP

c. Lan-a! Lan-a! Lan e-gi-te-a ere nahiko-a astakeria da ba.
work work work.IDF do.VEN too plenty_of bullshit be.SYN INF

(60) a. Ni ez n-a-u-te ba berri-z harrapa-tu-ko!
I not 1/PLU.TRA INF new.IDF.INS catch.FUT

b. Ba-n-en-go-en, ba!
AFF.believe.1.SYN.PST INF

(61) a. Den-a busti-a e-torr-i-ko z-a-r-a, ni-re Txomin; alda z-a-(d)i-tez, bada.
all wet come.FUT 2.ITR I.GEN Txomin change.RAD 2.ITR.IMP INF

b. Baina zu-rekin nahi n-u-ke hitzegin. Esa-n bada, e-ntzu-ten z-a-it-u-t.
but you.SOC want.PPR /1.TRA.COD talk say INF hear.IPF 2/1.TRA

c. Azter beza, bada, nor-k ber-e buru-a, ogi-tik jan
examine.RAD TRA.JUS INF everyone.ERG he_himself.GEN head bread.ELA eat
aurre-tik.
front_part.ELA

d. E-ma-n de-za-gu-n, bada, horr-e(n)-la d-ela.
grant(.RAD) /1PLU.SUJ.NCZ INF so be.SYN.LCZ

e. Bakarr-ik e-gi-n-go d-u-t.— E-gi-zu bada!
alone.STA do.FUT /1.TRA Do.2.SYT.IMP INF

(62) a. Judu-a ote n-a-iz, bada, ni?
Jew DUB be.1.SYN INF I

b. Zer gerta-tu ze-n, bada?
what happen.PEF ITR.PST INF

c. Nor da bada jende hori?
who be.SYN INF people that

d. Zenbat eska-tzen d-u-zu, ba, txahal-a-ga(i)-tik?
how_much ask.IPF /2.TRA INF calf.MOT

e. A! Hor z-a-u-de.— No-n nahi d-u-zu ba e-go-te-a?
ah there.LOC be.2.SYN where.LOC want.PPR /2.TRA INF be.VEN

f. Ni-k ez d-i-o-t esa-n.— No-la da-ki bada?
I.ERG not //1.DTR tell.PEF how know.SYT INF

g. Ez d-u hori esa-n.— Zer bada?
not TRA that say.PEF what INF

(63) a. Ba, egi(a)-a esa-n, gaur ez d-u-t asko bazkal-du.
INF truth tell today not /1.TRA much have(_for)_lunch.PEF

b. Txabola hon-e-ta-n gerta-tzen d-en-a ja-ki-n nahi d-u-k, ez
hut this.LOC happen.IPF ITR.NRE.ZEP know want.PPR /2SOL.TRA not
da? Bada, gau oso-a e-duki-ko d-u-k ja-ki-te-ko!
be.SYN INF night whole have.FUT /2SOL.TRA find_out.VEN.ADN

c. Bada, ikas-i nahi ez d-u-a-n-e-z gero, Amerik(a)-e-ta-ra j-oa-n-go
INF study want.PPR not /2SOL.TRA.NRE.INS since America.PLU.ALL go.FUT
h-a-iz.
2SOL.ITR

d. Den-a da-ki.— Bada, ez d-i-gu ezer esa-n.
everything know.SYT INF not /1PLU/.DTR anything say.PEF

e. Ni-k ez d-i-o-t esa-n.— Bada, norbait-e-k esa-n d-i-o.
I.ERG not //1.DTR tell.PEF INF somebody.ERG tell.PEF DTR

(64) a. No-ra e-ra-ma-n d-u-zu-e auto-a konpon-tze-ra?— Ba-da-go ba
where.ALL take.PEF /2PLU.TRA car fix.VEN.ALL AFF.be.SYN INF
Igeldo bide-an garaje bat, ba ha-ra-xe.
Igeldo.IDF road.LOC garage a INF over_there.ALL.EMP

b. Esa-n-go d-i-o-t ba, Jaun-a, argi-ro.
tell.FUT //1.DTR INF sir clearly

c. Berrehun ... ez da-ki-t ba ber-(h)orr-e-k nahi-ko ote d-it-u-en.
two_hundred.IDF not know./1.SYT INF you.DFR.ERG want.FUT DUB PLU/.TRA.NCZ

(65) a. Iza-n___ere, harri-tze-ko-a ze-n! Orratz hura ... Pagodi-ren-a ez
indeed amaze.VEN.ADN.ZEP ITR.PST Pin yonder ... Pagodi.GEN.ZEP EXP
ze-n ba!
be.SYN.PST INF

b. Leiho-a he(t)s-te-n ari n-in-tz-e(n)-la, eror-i ez zi-tza-i-da-n, ba,
window close.VEN.LOC be_busy.PPR 1.ITR.PST.LCI fall.PEF EXP 1/.DIT.PST INF
esku-tik!
hand.ELA

c. Diru-a ez z-i-o-ten ba eska-tu!
money EXP //PLU.DTR.PST INF ask.PEF

d. Kotxe-a ez d-i-da-te ba eska-tu!
car EXP /1/PLU.DTR INF ask.PEF

e. Sinets-i ere! Bidart detektibe-a ber-a ez ze-n, bada!
believe even Bidart detective.SIN he_himself.SIN EXP be.SYN.PST INF

(66) a. Gogora-tzen al z-a-r-a ni-ta-z?— Gogora-tu-ko ez n-a-iz ba!
remember.IPF INT 2.ITR I.INS remember.FUT EXP 1.ITR INF

b. E-zagu(t)-tzen al d-u-zu hor atze-an zut-ik da-go-en emakume
know.IPF INT /2.TRA there.LOC back.LOC standing.STA be.SYN.NRE woman
hori?— E-zagu-tu-ko ez d-u-t, ba?
that know.FUT EXP /1.TRA INF

(67) a. Asper-tu e-gi-n n-a-iz, bada bakarr-ik utz-i n-a-u-te.
get_bored do.PEF 1.ITR CAC alone.STA leave.PEF 1/PLU.TRA
b. E-ra-ma-n e-za-zu, bada on e-gi-n-go d-i-zu.
take_with(.RAD) /2.TRA.IMP CAC good.IDF do.FUT /2/.DTR

(68) a. Hiru tatxa hori-(e)-en-ga(i)-tik, neskatx(a)-ek maite n-a-u-te ni.
three fault that.PLU.MOT girl.PLU.ERG love.PPR 1/PLU.TRA I
b. Am(a)-(e)-en-ga(i)tik, seme-ek nahi d-u-te-n-a e-gi-ten d-u-te.
mother.PLU.MOT son.PLU.ERG want.PPR /PLU.TRA.NRE.ZEP do.IPF /PLU.TRA

(69) a. Huts-ak huts, ba-d-u liburu hon-e-k alde ederr-ik aski.
mistake.PLU mistake.IDF AFF.have.SYT book this.ERG feature nice.PAR plenty
b. Ez da ber-a, itxur(a)-ak itxura, ni-re
not be.SYN he_himself appearance.PLU appearance.IDF I.GEN
artalde-ko-e-ta-rik.
flock.ADN.ZEP.PLU.ELA
c. Erago(t)zpen-ak erago(t)zpen, plaza-ra g-in-e-n Etxepare-z
impediment.PLU impediment.IDF public_life.ALL be.1PLU.SYN.PST Etxepare.INS
gero-z.
future.IDF.INS
d. Hu(t)skeri(a)-ak hu(t)skeria ados n-a-iz-ela esa-n-go n-u-k-e
trifle.PLU trifle.IDF in_agreement.PRE 1.be.SYN.LCZ say.FUT /1.TRA.COD
guzti-ra, puntu guzti-e-ta-n ez ba-da ere.
whole.ZEP.ALL point all.PLU.LOC not AFF.be.SYN even
e. Ba-ze-ki-en gerta-tu-ko ze(-n)-la, tarte-ko-ak
AFF.know.SYT.PST happen.FUT ITR.PST.LCZ place_in_between.ADN.ZEP.PLU
tarteko ber-e-gan-(r)a e-torr-i-ko z-in-e(-n)-la.
place_in_between.ADN.IDF he_himself.ALL come.FUT 2.ITR.PST.LCZ

(70) a. Zahar-tu-a-ga(i)-tik da-go oso dezente-a.
grow_old.PEF.SIN.MOT be.SYN quite all_right
b. Pixka bat-e-an ez n-a-iz aha(t)z-tu-ko sar-tu-a-ga(i)-tik lurpe-an.
while a.LOC not 1.ITR forget.FUT put_into.PEF.SIN.MOT underground.LOC
c. Eliz(a)-a-ren laguntza hori iza-n-a-ga(i)-tik ere, aski harrigarri-a iza-n da
Church.GEN help that be.PEF.SIN.MOT even quite amazing be.PEF ITR
eta da euskar(a)-a-ren iraupen-a.
and be.SYN Basque_language.GEN survival

(71) a. Gezurr-a ba-d-irudi ere, bidai(a)-a-k on e-gi-n d-i-o.
lie CDP.seem.SYT even journey.ERG good.IDF do.PEF DTR
b. Baina Itziarr-e-k, jan ba-z-u-en ere, ez z-u-en janari on-a-z goza-tu.
but Itziar.ERG eat.PEF CDP.TRA.PST even not TRA.PST food good.INS enjoy.PEF
c. Bizitz(a)-a ez da geldi-tu, beldurr-a-k ha(r-en)-la eska-tzen ba-d-i-o ere.
life not ITR stop.PEF fear.ERG so beg.IPF AFF.DTR even

(72) Zer esa-n-go d-u-en ja-ki-n gabe ere, on-tzat har-tu-ko n-it-u-z-ke
what say.FUT TRA.NCZ know without.PRE even good.PRO take.FUT PLU/1.TRA.COD
orain ber-ta-n bere iritzi-ak.
now it_itself.LOC he_himself.GEN opinion.PLU

(73) a. Bai ha(r-en)-la da, asko-ta-n ez d-irudi-en arren.
yes so be.SYN many.IDF.LOC not seem.SYT.NRE although
b. "Gu-re hotel-a" dei-tu iza-n d-i-o-te, han bi egun
we.GEN hotel call have.PEF //PLU.DTR over_there.LOC two day.IDF
beste-rik e-gi-n ez z-it-u-z-te-n arren.
else.ZEP.PAR spend.PEF not PLU/PLU.TRA.NRE although
c. Ha-ra, hauts eta errauts beste-rik ez n-a-iz-en arren, en-e
over_there.ALL dust.IDF and ash.IDF else.ZEP.PAR not be.1.SYN.NRE although I.GEN
jaun horr-i mintza-tze-ra ausar(t)-tzen n-a-iz.
Lord that.DAT speak.VEN.ALL venture.IPF 1.ITR
d. Senda n-a-za-zu, zu-re aurka bekatu e-gi-n d-u-da-n arren.
heal.RAD 1/2TRA.IMP you.GEN against sin.IDF do.PEF /1.TRA.NRE although

(74) a. Filosofo-a-k e-zagu(t)-tzen d-u gauza batzu-ek ja-ki-n arren,
philosopher.ERG recognize.IPF TRA thing some.PLU know although
ba-d-ir-ela beste anitz har-k ez da-ki-en-ak.
AFF.be.PLU.SYN.LCZ other.ZEP many yonder_one.ERG not know.SYT.NRE.ZEP.PLU
b. Ezkontz(a)-a-k, egoera ederr-a iza-n arren, ba-d-it-u ber-e
marriage.ERG state nice be although AFF.have.PLU/.SYT it_itself.GEN
atsekabe eta alde txarr-ak.
grief.IDF and point bad.PLU
c. Bos(t)pasei beribil igaro arren, bat ere geldi-tu ez.
five_or_six car.IDF come_by although one even stop.PEF not
d. Zu-k inor maite ez arren ere, ba-d-ir-a zu maite
you.ERG anyone love.PPR not although even be.PLU.SYN you love.PPR
z-a-it-u-z-te-n-ak.
2/PLU.TRA.NRE.ZEP.PLU

(75) a. Ez z-u-te-n haurr-ik nahi-z aspaldi esposa-tu-ak
not have./PLU.SYT.PST child.PAR COC a_long_time marry.PEF.PLU

z-ir-e(-n)-n.
be.PLU.SYN.PST.NCZ

b. Nahi-z ez d-en gaztelu-a, maite d-u-t ni-k sorleku-a.
COC not be.SYN.NCZ castle love.PPR /1.TRA I.ERG birthplace

c. Eta hori da uste d-u-gu-n-a nahi-z aitor ez
and that be.SYN believe.PPR /1PLU.TRA.NRE.ZEP COC admit.RAD not
de-za-gu-n.
/1PLU.TRA.SUJ.NCZ

(76) a. Hiru egun poz-ik pasa g-en-it-u-en nahi-z diru gutxi
three day.IDF happily.STA spend.PEF PLU/1PLU.TRA.PST COC money little
e-karr-i.
bring

b. Baietz ba ihardets-i n-i-o-n, nahi-z hori-e-ta-z gauza gutxi
positively.ADV INF answer.PEF //1.DTR.PST COC that(_matter).PLU.INS thing little
ja-ki-n.
know

(77) a. Nahi-z eta leiho-tik Obaba-ko mendi zaharr-ak i-kus-ten
COC EXP window.ELA Obaba.ADN mountain old.PLU see.IPF
n-it-u-e(n)-n, kosta e-gi-ten zi-tza-i-da-n ni-r-e gel(a)-an
PLU/1.TRA.PST.NCZ cost.PPR do.IPF 1/.DIT.PST I.GEN room.LOC
n-en-go-e(n)-n-a-z jabe-tze-a.
be.1.SYN.PST.NRE.ZEP.INS realize.VEN

b. Egi(a)-a esa-n, nahi-z eta harrokeri(a)-a d-irudi-en, uste d-u-t
truth tell COC EXP arrogance seem.SYT.NCZ believe.PPR /1.TRA
Euskaltzaindi-a-k fidantza apur bat merezi d-u-ela.
Basque_Academy.ERG trust.IDF little a deserve.PPR TRA.LCZ

c. Ez d-u irakurgai hon-e-k inor-en ile-rik la(t)z-tu-ko, nahi-z eta lo-a-k
not TRA reading this.ERG anyone.GEN hair.PAR curl.FUT COC EXP sleep.ERG
har-tze-ra-ko-an irakurr-i.
get.VEN.ALL.ADN.LOC read

d. Nahi-z eta, pentsa-tze-n jarr-i-ta, zer-ga(i)-tik zain-du behar
COC EXP think.VEN.LOC sit_down.PEC what.MOT watch should.PPR
n-a-u-te ni?
1/PLU.TRA I

Chapter 24

(1) a. Nahi ba-d-u-zu, garbi n-a-za-ke-zu.
want.PPR CDP./2.TRA cleanse.RAD 1/2.TRA.POT

b. Sine(t)s-ten al d-u-zu-e hori e-gi-n de-za-ke-da-na?
believe.IPF INT /2PLU.TRA that do.RAD /1.TRA.POT.NAZ

c. Bakarr-ik tart(a)-a jan de-za-ke-t.
only.STA pastry eat.RAD /1.TRA.POT

(2) a. Oker e-go-n n-a-i-te-ke.
wrong.IDF be.RAD 1.ITR.POT

b. No-n eros d-it-za-ke-gu patat(a)-ak?
where.LOC buy.RAD PLU/1PLU.TRA.POT potato.PLU

c. Atentatu bat e-gi-te-ra g-en-to(r)-z-ela pentsa de-za-ke-te.
terrorist_attack a do.VEN.ALL come.1PLU.SYN.PST.LCZ think.RAD /PLU.TRA.POT

d. Esa-n al da-i-te-ke egi(a)-a-ren zati bat oso-a esa-n gabe?
tell.RAD INT ITR.POT truth.GEN part a whole.ZEP tell without.PRE

(3) a. Hor-txe aurki d-it-za-ke-zu har-en bizitz(a)-a-ri
there.LOC.EMP find.RAD PLU/2.TRA.POT yonder_one.GEN life.DAT
buru-z-ko zen-bait xehetasun ere.
head.ISDF.INS.ADN some detail also

b. Hori i-kus-i nahi d-u-en-a-k Aita Villasante-k iaz argitara
that see want.PPR TRA.NRE.ZEP.ERG Father Villasante.ERG last_year publish.PEF
z-u-e(n)-n liburuxk(a)-an i-kus de-za-ke.
TRA.PST.NRE booklet.LOC see.RAD TRA.POT

c. Ezkon-du berri-a n-a-iz eta ez n-a-i-te-ke j-oa-n.
marry.PEF new be.1.SYN and not 1.ITR.POT go.RAD

(4) a. Eser al n-a-i-te-ke zu-re ondo-an?
sit.RAD INT 1.ITR.POT you.GEN side.LOC

b. Nahi d-u-zu-n-e-an has z-a-i-tez-ke z-eu-re ipuin-a konta-tze-n.
want.PPR /2.TRA.NRE.LOC start.RAD 2.ITR.POT you.REF.GEN tale tell.VEN.LOC

c. Ja-ki-n al da-i-te-ke isileko hori?
know.RAD INT ITR.POT secret that

d. Ni-re-ga(i)-tik nahi d-u-en-a e-gi-n de-za-ke hon-e-k.
I.MOT want.PPR TRA.NRE.ZEP do.RAD TRA.POT this_one.ERG

(5) a. Orain aurke-z i-kus de-za-ke-zu.
now face.IDF.INS see.RAD /2.TRA.POT

b. Zer e-gi-n da-i-te-ke orain?
what do.RAD ITR.POT now

c. Beste film bat e-gi-te-n ari omen da Chaplin. Zer esa-n
other film a make.VEN.LOC be_busy.PPR REP ITR Chaplin what tell.RAD
d-ie-za-gu-ke, azken hitz-a esa-n ondo-an?
/1PLU/.DTR.POT last word say contiguity.LOC

d. Da-torr-en urte-an i-kus de-za-ke-gu.
come.SYN.NRE year.LOC see.RAD /1PLU.TRA

(6) a. Itxur(a)-a, orde-a, engainagarri-a iza-n da-i-te-ke.
appearance however deceptive be.RAD ITR.POT

b. Nor salba da-i-te-ke, orduan.
who save.RAD ITR.POT that_time.LOC

c. Ez g-a-i-tez-ke zu gabe salba.
not 1PLU.ITR.POT you without.PRE save.RAD

(7) a. Ilargi-tik hon-(r)a ba-li-tz, zer-bait esa-n n-e-za-ke.
moon.ELA here.ALL CDP.ITR.COD something say.RAD /1.TRA.POT.COD

b. Zu-k nahi ba-z-en-u, ber-e-ha(r-en)-la Amerik(a)-e-ta-ra j-oa-n
you.ERG want.PPR CDP./2.TRA.COD at_once America.PLU.ALL go.RAD
g-in-tez-ke.
1PLU.ITR.POT.COD

c. Onar n-e-za-ke oinaze-a, ba-n-e-ki no-n-dik
accept.RAD /1.TRA.POT.COD suffering CDP.know./1.SYT.COD where.ELA
da-torr-en.
come.SYN.NCZ

(8) a. Abiada hon-e-ta-n Cordoba-n iza-n g-in-tez-ke eguerdi alde-ra.
speed this.LOC Cordoba.LOC be.RAD 1PLU.ITR.POT.COD noon point.ALL

b. Ehun urte-an ere ezin ikas-i n-e-za-ke.
hundred year.LOC even NPP learn /1.TRA.POT.COD

(9) a. Horr-e(n)-la-ko-rik gerta al l-i-te-ke?
that_way.ADN.ZEP.PAR happen.RAD INT ITR.POT.COD

b. Edo-zein-i gerta le-ki-o-ke horr-e(n)-la-ko-rik.
anyone.DAT happen.RAD DIT.POT.COD that_way.ADN.ZEP.PAR

(10) a. Jan al n-e-za-ke zer-bait, mesede-z?
eat.RAD INT /1.TRA.POT.COD something favor.IDF.INS

b. Barru-ko jatetxe-an bazkal g-ene-za-ke, ez?
inside.ADN restaurant.LOC have_lunch.RAD /1PLU.TRA.POT.COD not

(11) a. Garbitasun horr-e-ta-z mintza g-in-tez-ke luzaro-an.
purity that.INS speak.RAD 1PLU.ITR.POT.COD long_time.LOC

b. Lekuko-rik aski aurki g-ene-za-ke neke-rik gabe.
witness.PAR plenty find.RAD /1PLU.TRA.POT.COD effort.PAR without.PRE

(12) a. No-la esa-n z-ene-za-ke-te gauza on-ik?
how say.RAD /2PLU.TRA.POT.COD thing good.PAR

b. Zer e-gi-n n-e-za-ke ni-re alab(a)-a-ren bizi-a zuzen-tze-ko?
what do.RAD /1.TRA.POT.COD I.GEN daughter.GEN life put_right.VEN.AND

(13) a. Margari-ren etxe-ko ate-a zabal-ik i-kus z-i-te-ke-en.
Margari.GEN house.ADN door wide_open.STA see.RAD ITR.POT.PST

b. Ez n-u-en uste gogo-z e-gi-te-n ari n-a-iz-en
not /1.TRA.PST think.PPR pleasure.IDF.INS do.VEN.LOC be_busy.PPR 1.ITR.NRE
egiteko hori gogo-z e-gi-n z-i-te-ke-e(n)-n-ik.
task that pleasure.IDF.INS do.RAD ITR.POT.PST.PCZ

c. Agi-an, orain-dik e-ma-n ze-za-ke-en buelta bat plaza-ra-ino.
perhaps still give.RAD TRA.POT.PST walk a town_square.TER

d. Inor-k ere ez ze-za-ke-en kantu hura ikas.
anybody.ERG even not TRA.POT.PST song that learn.RAD

(14) a. Huts hori-ek erraz osa z-i-tez-ke-en,
gap that.PLU easily fill.RAD PLU.ITR.POT.PST
euskaldun-ok nahi iza-n ba-g-en-u.
Basque.INC.ERG want have.PEF CDP./1PLU.TRA.COD

b. Indiarr-ek sor ze-za-ke-te-n gaur-ko
Indian.PLU.ERG create.RAD /PLU.TRA.POT.PST today.ADN
fisik(a)-a, bide horr-e-ta-tik abia-tu iza-n ba-l-ir-a.
physics trail that.PLU.ELA set_out.PEF be.PEF CDP.PLU.ITR.COD

c. Gizon hau aska z-i-te-ke-en, enperadore-a-gan-(r)a jo iza-n ez
man this free.RAD ITR.POT.PST emperor.ALL appeal.PEF have.PEF not
ba-l-u.
CDP.TRA.COD

d. Garesti asko sal z-i-te-ke-en eta diru-a behartsu-e-i e-ma-n.
expensively quite sell.RAD ITR.POT.PST and money poor.PLU.DAT give.RAD

(15) a. Eder-ki sal z-i-te-ke-en hori eta sari-a pobre-e-i e-ma-n.
nicely sell.RAD ITR.POT.PST that and proceeds poor.ZEP.PLU.DAT give.RAD

b. Errege-ren alab(a)-a eri ze-n, eta inor-k ez ze-za-ke-en
king.IDF.GEN daughter ill.IDF be.SYN.PST and anybody.ERG not TRA.POT.PST
senda.
cure.RAD

c. Eta irri e-gi-te-tik ez z-i-te-ke-en geldi gehi-ago.
and laughter.IDF make.VEN.ELA not ITR.POT.PST stop.RAD more.COP

(16) a. Barren-e-ko huts-a ez de-za-ke kanpo-ko ezer-k bete.
inside.ADN emptiness not TRA.POT exterior.ADN anything.ERG fill.RAD

b. Ez da-ki-o-ke horr-e(n)-la-ko-rik gerta euskaldun irakurle-a-ri.
not DIT.POT like_that.ADN.ZEP.PAR happen.RAD Basque reader.DAT

c. Ez de-za-ke beste inor-ekin e-gi-n.
not TRA.POT other somebody.SOC do.RAD

(17) a. Ezin de-za-ke-gu gehi-ago esa-n.
NPP /1PLU.TRA.POT more.COP say.RAD
b. Baroja-k Euskal Herri-a maite z-u-e(n)-n-ik ezin da-i-te-ke uka.
Baroja.ERG Basque Country love.PPR TRA.PST.PCZ NPP ITR.POT deny.RAD
c. Algeria-ko gerla hau ezin de-za-ke-t onar.
Algeria.ADN war this NPP /1.TRA.POT accept.RAD
d. Zu eta en-e buru-a ezin d-it-za-ke-t engaina.
you and I.GEN head NPP PLU/1.TRA.POT deceive-RAD

(18) a. Inor-k ezin bi nagusi zerbitza d-it-za-ke.
somebody.ERG NPP two boss.IDF serve.RAD PLU/.TRA.POT
b. Arbola on-a-k ezin fruitu gaizto-rik e-ma-n de-za-ke.
tree good.ERG NPP fruit bad.PAR give.RAD TRA.POT
c. Eta ezin inor-k han-dik atera de-za-ke.
and NPP someone.ERG over_there.ELA take_out.RAD TRA.POT

(19) a. Eta ezin alda da-i-te-ke jabe-a-ren baimen-ik gabe.
and NPP alter.RAD ITR.POT owner.GEN consent.PAR without.PRE
b. Ezin uka da-i-te-ke osasungarri-ak d-ir-en-ik.
NPP deny.RAD ITR.POT healthy.PLU be.PLU.SYN.PCZ
c. Ezin sinets de-za-ke-gu akaba-tu-ko g-a-r-ela.
NPP believe.RAD /1PLU.TRA.POT come_to_an_end.FUT 1PLU.ITR.LCZ

(20) a. Ben-e-ta-n, oso arriskutsu-a iza-n da-i-te-ke.
serious.IDF.LOC very dangerous be.RAD ITR.POT
For the meaning of 'benetan', see Spanish *y esto va en serio* 'and I really mean it'.
b. Ikastol(a)-e-ta-n e-ra-bil-tzen d-en euskar(a)-a ez da-i-te-ke iza-n,
Basque_school.PLU.LOC use.IPF ITR.NRE Basque not ITR.POT be.RAD
eta ez da, inor-en ama-ren hi(t)zkuntz(a)-a.
and not be.SYN anybody.IDF mother.IDF.GEN language
c. Biziklet(a)-a iza-n z-i-te-ke-en ni-re amona, bi gurpil iza-n
bicycle be.RAD ITR.POT.PST I.GEN grandmother two wheel.IDF have.PEF
ba-l-it-u.
CDP.PLU/.TRA.COD

(21) a. Ba-da-i-te-ke hori ere.
AFF.be.SYN.POT that too
b. Hori ezin da-i-te-ke.
that NPP be.SYN.POT

c. Ni-k uste d-u-t non-bait i-kus-i z-a-it-u-da-la zu— Ni?
I.ERG think.PPR /1.TRA somewhere.LOC see.PEF 2/1.TRA.LCZ you I
Ba-l-i-te-ke.
AFF.be.SYN.POT.COD

(22) a. Ba-da-i-te-ke zu-(e)-ekin geldi n-a-di-n.
AFF.be.SYN.POT you.PLU.SOC stay.RAD 1.ITR.SUJ.NCZ
b. Ba-da-i-te-ke zu-(e)-ekin geldi-tze-a.
AFF.be.SYN.POT you.PLU.SOC stay.VEN
c. Ba-da-i-te-ke ni-k gauz(a)-ak ilun i-kus-te-a.
AFF.be.SYN.POT I.ERG thing.PLU gloomy.IDF see.VEN
d. Ba-da-i-te-ke inoiz oker i-bil-tze-a Axular.
AFF.be.SYN.POT sometimes wrong.PRE go.VEN Axular
e. No-la da-i-te-ke, bada, gu-re-ta-ko bakoitz-a-k ber-e
how be.SYN.POT INF we.LOC.ADN each.ERG he_himself.GEN
jatorri-z-ko hi(t)zkuntz(a)-an hori-e-i e-ntzu-te-a?
origin.IDF.INS.ADN language.LOC that_one.PLU.DAT hear.VEN
f. Ba-l-i-te-ke zu bizi-rik u(t)z-te-a.
AFF.be.SYN.POT.COD you alive.STA leave.VEN
g. Ba-l-i-te-ke hurren-go-an zu-ri ere horr-e(n)-la-ko bitxi-ren
AFF.be.SYN.POT.COD next.ADN.ZEP.LOC you.DAT also like_that.ADN jewel.IDF.GEN
bat e-kar-tze-a.
a bring.VEN

(23) a. Apaiz-a-k ere ez de-za-ke deus asko-rik.
priest.ERG too not do.SYT.POT something much.PAR
b. Ba-da-ki-t den-a de-za-ke-zu-la zu-k.
AFF.know./1.SYT everything do./2.SYT.POT.LCZ you.ERG
c. N-e-za-ke-e(n)-n guzti-a e-gi-n d-u-t.
do./1.SYT.POT.PST.NRE all do.PEF /1.TRA
d. Jende hon-ekin ni-k bakarr-ik ezin de-za-ke-t.
people this.SOC I.ERG alone.STA NPP do./1.SYT.POT

(24) a. Gu-re gogo-a ezin da-go-ke gogoeta gabe.
we.GEN mind NPP stay.SYN.POT thought.IDF without.PRE
b. Ber-e larru-an ez da-go-ke.
he_himself.GEN skin.LOC not stay.SYN.POT
c. Inor ni-gan-(r)a ezin da-tor-ke, ni bidal-i
somebody I.ALL NPP come.1.SYN.POT I send.PEF
n-ind-u-e(n)-n ni-re aita-k ez ba-da-kar.
1/.TRA.PST.NRE I.GEN father.ERG not AFF.lead.SYT

d. Ezin ze-tor-ke-en bat, ber-a-z, Larramendi-rekin.
NPP come.SYN.POT.PST one therefore Larramendi.SOC

e. Ba-z-oa-z-ke z-eu-re etxe-ra, han-txe aurki-tu-ko d-u-zu
AFF.go.2.SYN.POT you.REF.GEN house.ALL over_there.LOC.EMP find.FUT /2.TRA
senarr-a.
husband

f. Ba-d-oa-z-ke lasai Josetxu eta Txantxo Miami-ra.
AFF.go.PLU.SYN.POT unworried.PRE Josetxu and Txantxo Miami.ALL

(25) a. E-tor ba-da-i-te-ke, da-torr-ela ber-e-ha(r-en)-la!
come.RAD CDP.ITR.POT come.SYN.LCZ at_once

b. Ordain ba-de-za-ke-zu, ordain e-za-zu.
pay.RAD CDP./2.TRA.POT pay.RAD /2.TRA.IMP

c. E-tor ba-z-i-te-ke-en, zer-ga(i)-tik ez ze-n e-torr-i?
come.RAD CDP.ITR.POT.PST what.MOT not ITR.PST come.PEF

(26) a. Aita-k esa-n d-u j-oa-n ba-da-di agur-tu-ko d-u-ela.
father.IDF.ERG say.PEF TRA go.RAD CDP.ITR.POT.COD greet.FUT TRA.LCZ

b. Predikari-ak bidal-i-a-ga(i)-tik, zer probetxu iza-n-en d-u-te, baldin
preacher.PLU send.PEF.SIN.MOT what use have.FUT /PLU.TRA CPC
elkar adi ez ba-de-za-te?
each_other understand.RAD not CDP./PLU.TRA.POT.COD

c. Nor-bait-e-k i-kus ez ba-de-za, argibide hau eskain-i-ko d-i-o-t.
someone.ERG see.RAD not CDP.TRA.POT.COD example this offer.FUT //1.DTR

d. Ni-re eske-a on-tzat har ba-de-za-zu-e, eskerr-ak
I.GEN request good.PRO take.RAD CDP./2PLU.TRA.POT.COD thank.PLU
aurre-z.
front_part.IDF.INS

(27) a. Egun edo bihar *eizan* ida(t)z-ten has ba-n-a-di,
today or tomorrow *eizan* write.VEN.LOC start.RAD CDP.1.ITR.POT
alde-z_______aurre-tik e-ma-ten d-i-o-t edo-zein-i esku ero=etxe
side.IDF.INS front_part.ELA give.IPF //1.DTR everybody.DAT right.IDF madhouse
bat-e-an sar n-a-za-n.
a.LOC put.RAD 1/.TRA.SUJ.NCZ

b. Ez d-u behin ere Jainko-a-k u(t)z-ten gizon-a, baldin gizon-a-k lehen-ik
not TRA once even God.ERG abandon.IPF man CDC man.ERG first.STA
utz ez ba-de-za Jainko-a.
abandon.RAD not CDP.TRA.POT.COD God

(28) a. Barre e-gi-n-go l-u-ke lasai jende-a-k horr-e(n)-la-ko-rik
laugh.IDF make.FUT TRA.COD carefree.PRE people.ERG like_that.ADN.ZEP.PAR

i-kus ba-le-za.
see.RAD CDP.TRA.POT.COD.PST

b. Zer edo zer gerta ba-le-di, ba-da-ki-n ni-re
what or what happen.RAD CDP.ITR.POT.COD.PST AFF.know./2SOL.FEM.SYT I.GEN
etxe-ko telefono___zenbaki-a.
house.ADN phone.IDF number

c. Zu-ta-z ahaz/ahaz-tu ba-n-en-di, Jerusalen, geldi be-ki-t
you.INS forget.RAD/forget CDP.1.ITR.POT.COD.PST Jerusalem remain.RAD 1/.DIT.JUS
esku-a elbarri.
hand.SIN crippled.PRE

(29) a. Nahi ez d-u-gu-la bekatu-rik e-gi-n ahal ba-g-ene-za,
want not /1PLU.LCI sin.PAR do PPP CDP./1PLU.TRA.POT.COD.PST
hamaik(a)-ek gal-du-ko g-en-u-ke zeru-a
a_lot(_of).PLU.ERG lose.FUT /1PLU.TRA.COD paradise

b. Zen-bait herritarr-en kezk(a)-ak arin-du nahi n-it-u-z-ke orain,
certain citizen.IDF.GEN worry.PLU alleviate want.PPR PLU/1.TRA.COD now
arin ahal ba-n-it-za.
alleviate.RAD PPP CDP.PLU/1.TRA.POT.COD.PST

(30) a. Ez da egi(a)-a bi eta bi bost iza-n da-i-tez-ke-ela.
not be.SYN truth two.IDF and two.IDF five.IDF be.RAD PLU.ITR.POT.LCZ

b. **Ez da egi(a)-a bi eta bi bost iza-n ahal d-ir-ela.
not be.SYN truth two.IDF and two.IDF five.IDF be PPP PLU.ITR.LCZ

(31) a. . . . eta gero lapur-tu ahal iza-n-go d-i-o etxe-a.
. . . and after_that rob PPP have.FUT DTR house

b. Eta ordu-an ahal iza-n-go d-i-o etxe-a os-tu.
and that_time.LOC PPP have.FUT DTR house rob

(32) a. Ea beste bat noiz bidal-i ahal d-i-da-zu-n.
WCC another one when send PPP /1/2.DTR.NCZ

b. E-zer e-gi-n ahal ba-d-u-zu, erruki z-a-i-tez gu-ta-z eta lagun
anything do PPP CDP./2.TRA take_pity.RAD 2.ITR.IMP we.INS and help.RAD
ie-za-gu-zu.
/1PLU/2.DTR.IMP

c. Baldin gizon-en bat-e-k konta-tu ahal ba-d-u lurr-e-ko hauts-a, zu-re
CDC person.IDF.GEN a.ERG count PPP CDP.TRA earth.ADN dust you.GEN
jatorri-a ere konta de-za-ke.
progeny too count.RAD TRA.POT

(33) a. Aski goiz e-torr-i ahal iza-n da.
quite early come PPP be.PEF ITR

b. Horr-e(n)-ga(i)-tik idatz-i ahal iza-n d-it-u-t.
that.MOT write PPP have.PEF PLU/1.TRA

(34) a. Lehen maitasun horr-en aztarn(a)-ak antzeman ahal iza-n z-it-u-en
first love that.GEN relic.PLU notice PPP have.PEF PLU/.TRA.PST
ber-e bait(a)-an.
he_himself.GEN inside.LOC

b. Bakar bat-e-an sar-tu ahal iza-n n-it-u-en gauza guzti-ak.
single.ZEP one.LOC put PPP have.PEF PLU/1.TRA.PST thing.PLU all.PLU

(35) a. Hemen ez d-it-u-gu-n esertoki-ak eskain-i ahal iza-n-go
here.LOC not have.PLU/1PLU.SYT.NRE seat.PLU offer PPP have.FUT
d-i-z-ki-zu-e-t.
PLU/2PLU/1.DTR

b. Noiz e-ntzu-n ahal iza-n-go d-u-gu "Illet(a)-a" Donostia-n?
when hear PPP have.FUT /1PLU.TRA "Illeta" San_Sebastian.LOC

(36) a. Egun hori-e-ta-n ez n-u-en i-kus-i ahal iza-n.
day that.PLU.LOC not /1.TRA.PST see PPP have.PEF

b. Ni-k ez n-u-ke-en aurki-tu ahal iza-n-go.
I.ERG not /1.TRA.COD.PST find PPP have.FUT

(37) a. Ni n-oa-n toki-ra zu-ek ezin z-a-r-e-te j-oa-n.
I go.1.SYN.NRE place.ALL you.PLU NPP 2PLU.ITR go

b. Ezin al d-u ber-a-k nahi d-u-en-a e-gi-n
NPP INT TRA he_himself.ERG want.PPR TRA.NRE.ZEP do
ber-e etxe-an, ezin al da nahi d-u-en-e-an sar-tu?
he_himself.GEN house.LOC NPP INT ITR want.PPR TRA.NRE.LOC come_in

(38) a. Ezin d-u-t e-ra-ma-n futbol-a.
NPP /1.TRA stand soccer

b. Ezin n-u-en ni-re maitale-a bazter-tu.
NPP /1.TRA.PST I.GEN lover turn_away

c. Ezin al d-it-u-gu hemen utz-i?
NPP INT PLU/1PLU.TRA here.LOC leave

d. Itziarr-e-k ezin iza-n z-u-en auker(a)-a pasa-tze-n utz-i.
Itziar.ERG NPP have.PEF TRA.PST opportunity pass.VEN.LOC let

(39) a. Ezin iza-n-go d-i-o-te gerta-tzen za-i-zu-n-a-ri izen-ik jarr-i.
NPP have.FUT //PLU.DTR happen.IPF 2/.DIT.NRE.ZEP.DAT name.PAR put

b. Ezin iza-n-go n-it-u-z-ke den-ak konta-tu.
NPP have.FUT PLU/1.COD all.ZEP.PLU tell

(40) a. Ezin-go n-a-iz mutilzahar geldi-tu.
NPP.FUT 1.ITR bachelor remain

b. Ezin-go z-a-it-u-t infernu-ra bota.
NPP.FUT 2/1.TRA hell.ALL throw

(41) a. Ezin asma-tu d-u-t haserre-tu gabe hitz bat esa(n)-ten.
NPP manage /1.TRA get_angry without.PRE word a say.VEN.LOC
b. Baina ezin senda-tu iza-n d-i-da-te.
but NPP cure have.PEF /1/PLU.DTR
c. Gu ezin j-oa-n iza-ten g-a-r-a oso maiz.
we NPP go be.IPF 1PLU.ITR very often

(42) a. Ni n-a-go-en toki-ra zu-ek ezin e-torr-i-ko z-a-r-e-te.
I be.1.SYN.LOC place.ALL you.PLU NPP come.FUT 2PLU.ITR
b. Izeb(a)-a i-kus-i gabe ezin atera-ko n-a-iz etxe hon-e-ta-tik.
aunt see without.PRE NPP go_out 1.ITR house this.ELA
c. Ezin ken-du-ko d-i-o-zu lege-z-ko d-u-en-a.
NPP take_away //2.DTR law.IDF.INS.ADN.IDF have.SYT.NRE.ZEP

(43) a. Ezin lo-rik e-gi-n-go d-u-t.
NPP sleep.PAR do.FUT /1.TRA
b. Ezin txartel-ik e-ma-n-go d-i-zu-t.
NPP certificate.PAR give.FUT /2/1.DTR
c. Ezin buru-tik ken-du d-u-t Eneko Amerik(a)-e-ta-ra di-h-oa-n-a.
NPP head.ELA put_out_of /1.TRA Eneko America.PLU.ALL go.SYN.NRE.ZEP

(44) a. Egi(a)-a e-zagu(t)-tzen ahal d-u.
truth know.IPF PPP TRA
b. Hilabete-ak e-go-ten ahal da nahi-rik gabe.
month.PLU stay.IPF PPP ITR volition.PAR without.PRE

(45) a. Ez d-u garai(t)-tzen ahal.
not TRA overcome.IPF PPP
b. E-zagu(t)-tzen ez d-en-a ez da mai-ta-tzen ahal.
know.IPF not ITR.NRE.ZEP not ITR love.IPF PPP

(46) a. Zer iharde(t)s-ten ere ahal n-u-en?
what answer.IPF indeed PPP /1.TRA.PST
b. Horr-i esker ikas-ten ahal iza-n d-u-t mundu-ko zen-bait berri.
that_one.DAT thanks.PRE learn.IPF PPP have.PEF /1.TRA world.ADN some news

(47) a. Ez d-u kordoka-tu ahal.
not TRA shake.PEF PPP
b. Ez d-u kordoka-tu ahal iza-n.
not TRA shake PPP have.PEF
c. No-la hon-en laster atzeman ahal iza-n d-u-zu?
how this.GEN quickly capture PPP have.PEF /2.TRA

d. Ez d-u-t idatz-i ahal iza-n fisiko-ki.
not /1.TRA write PPP have.PEF physically

(48) a. Nor da igurik-i-ren ahal d-u-en-a?
who be.SYN stand.FUT PPP TRA.NRE.ZEP

b. Nor-k irau-n-en ahal du?
who.ERG last.FUT PPP TRA

c. Diru-ta-n ere ez da eskura-tu-ko ahal.
money.IDF.LOC even not ITR obtain.FUT PPP

d. Ez d-u ber-e azken hats-a bota-ko ahal.
not TRA he_himself.GEN last breath throw_out PPP

e. Ez da-ki-t lo handi-rik e-gi-n-en ahal-ko d-u-da-n.
not know./1.SYT sleep long.PAR do.FUT PPP.FUT /1.TRA.NCZ

(49) a. Egun bat-e-z, ez d-it-u-t bazter-tzen ahal-ko egia-z-ko
day one.IDF.INS not PLU/1.TRA put_aside PPP.FUT truth.IDF.INS.ADN
galde eta erantzun-ak.
question.IDF and answer.PLU

b. Deus-e-k ez g-a-it-u bereiz-ten ahal-ko Jainko-a-ren maitasun-a-gan-ik.
anything.ERG not 1PLU/.TRA separate.IPF PPP.FUT God.GEN love.ELA

c. Zer e-gi-ten ahal-ko z-u-en hainbeste haurr-en aitzin-e-an?
what do.IPF PPP.FUT TRA.PST so_many child.GEN front.LOC

d. Ez-deus-e-k ez d-u aldara-tu ahal-ko ber-e sail-e-tik.
nothing.ERG not TRA keep_from PPP.FUT he_himself.GEN enterprise.ELA

(50) a. Ezin egun-da-ino garai(t)-tu z-u-te-n ber-e etsai-ek.
NPP today.TER overcome.PEF /PLU.TRA.PST he_himself.GEN enemy.PLU.ERG

b. Egun-da-ino ezin jasan d-u-t har-en ahalkesun-a-ren handi-a.
today.TER NPP bear.PEF /1.TRA he_himself.GEN majesty.GEN great.ZEP

c. Mediku-ek deus ezin e-gi-n d-u-te.
doctor.PLU.ERG anything NPP do.PEF /PLU.TRA

d. Ezin e-gi-n iza-n z-u-te-n.
NPP do have.PEF /PLU.TRA.PST

(51) a. Ezin mintza-tu-ren h-a-iz.
NPP speak.FUT 2SOL.ITR

b. Ezin mintza-tu-ko z-a-r-a.
NPP speak.FUT 2.ITR

(52) a. Eri bat da hospitale-an, inor-k ezin hurbil-du-a,
patient a be.SYN hospital.LOC anybody.ERG NPP approach.PTC.ZEP
inor-k ezin i-kus-i-a.
anybody.ERG NPP see.PTC.ZEP

b. Ez d-u-zu e-gi-n-en, inor-k ezin e-gi-n-a da eta!
not /2.TRA do.FUT anyone.ERG NPP do.PTC.ZEP ITR EEC

c. Oi, en-e maite ezin ukan-a, zein z-a-r-en xarmagarri-a!
O I.GEN love NPP have.PTC.ZEP how be.2.SYN.NCZ charming

d. Hau ezin e-ra-ma-n-a za-i-t.
this NPP bear.PTC.ZEP 1/.DIT

(53) a. Pentsa ahal-ak aurtiki arte-ino ez da isil-tzen.
conceive.RAD MOQ.PLU blurt_out until not ITR fall_silent.IPF

b. Izurde-ak sar-tzen d-ir-a arrain pilo-a-ren erdi-an, jan
dolphin.PLU get_into.IPF PLU.ITR fish.IDF school.GEN middle.LOC eat.(RAD)
ahal-ak ja(n)-te-n eta irents ahal-ak iren(t)s-te-n.
MOQ.PLU eat.VEN.LOC and swallow.RAD MOQ.PLU swallow.VEN.LOC

c. Hemen segi-tu behar-ko d-u-zu, ja-rrai-tu, kosta ahal-a kosta
here.LOC go_on have_to.FUT /2.TRA continue cost.RAD MOQ cost.RAD

d. Artale-a jan ahal-a bota-tzen ba-d-i-zu-e-te, ez da-go
grain_of_corn eat.(RAD) MOQ throw.IPF CDP./2PLU/PLU.DTR not be.SYN
problema-rik.
problem.PAR

(54) a. Hi-k jan behar d-u-k ni-k e-gi-n ahal-a talo!
you.SOL.ERG eat must.PPR /2SOL.TRA I.ERG make.(RAD) MOQ corncake.IDF

b. Eska ahal-a mesede e-gi-ten d-i-z-ki-gu.
ask_for MOQ favor.IDF do.IPF PLU/1PLU/.DTR

(55) a. Zorr-ak gehi-tu ahal-a, dirutz(a)-a urri-tze-n zi-h-oa-z-ki-gu-n.
debt.PLU increase GSC capital dwindle.VEN.LOC go.1PLU/.DYT.PST

b. Neb(a)-a, drog(a)-a har-tu ahal-a, petral-du-z j-oa-n ze-n.
brother drug take GSC become_mean.IDF.INS go.PEF ITR.PST

c. Urte-ek, j-oa-n ahal-a, i-ra-kats-i d-i-gu-te gauza ederr-ak
year.PLU.ERG go GSC teach.PEF /1PLU/PLU.DTR thing beautiful.PLU
aberats-en-tzat sor-tu z-it-u-e(n)-la Jainko-a-k.
rich.ZEP.PLU.BEN create.PEF PLU/.TRA.PST.LCZ God.ERG

(56) a. Andres-e-k, sar-tu ahal-a, lehen begiraldi-a-ren lehen segundo-an, i-kus-ten
Andrew.ERG come_in GSC first glance.GEN first second.LOC see.IPF
d-u zahar-tu e-gi-n z-a-r-ela.
TRA grow_old do.PEF 2.ITR.LCZ

b. Beste gaixo bat senda-tu ahal-a, neke madarikatu hura nagusi-tzen
other patient a cure GSC fatigue curse.PEF yonder overpower.IPF
zi-tza-i-o-n.
DIT.PST

(57) a. Alferr-ik d-u-zu, on Lander. Ez da-(d)uka-zu ihes egite-rik.
in_vain.STA have./2.SYT Don Lander not have./2.SYT escape.IDF do.VEN.PAR
b. Leize handi bat da-go zu-(e)-en eta gu-re arte-an; nahi-ta
chasm great a be.SYN you.PLU.GEN and we.GEN between.LOC want.PPR.PEC
ere, ez da-(d)uka inor-k hemen-dik zu-(e)-en-gan-(r)a igaro-tze-rik.
even not have.SYT anyone.ERG here.ELA you.PLU.ALL cross.VEN.PAR
c. Oso gazi-a da-go, ez da-go ja(n)-te-rik.
very salty be.SYT not be.SYT eat.VEN.PAR
d. Zu-rekin ez dago eztabaid(a)-an ari-tze-rik.
you.SOC not be.SYN dispute.LOC be_busy.VEN.PAR

(58) a. Ez d-u-t mendi-ra j-oa-te-rik, lan-a e-gi-n behar d-u-t.
not have./1.SYT mountain.ALL go.VEN.PAR work do have_to.PPR /1.TRA
b. Ez da-ki-t ezer e-gi-te-rik e-duki-ko d-u-da-n.
not know./1.SYT anything do.VEN.PAR have.FUT /1.TRA.NCZ
c. Berri-z eros-te-rik ez da iza-n-en gero-an.
new.IDF.INS buy.VEN.PAR not ITR be.FUT future.LOC

(59) a. Zu-re pentsu pixka bat ja(n)-te-rik ba al da-(d)uka-t?
you.GEN feed.IDF bit a eat.VEN.PAR AFF INT have./1.SYT
b. Gaur ez da-(d)uka-zu-e hemen-dik ino-ra j-oa-te-rik afal-du arte.
today not have./2PLU.SYT here.ELA anywhere.ALL go.VEN.PAR have_dinner until
Hau Joanito-ren enkargu-a da.
this Joanito.GEN order be.SYN
c. Nobela horr-en zati-ren bat irakur-tze-rik ba al da-go?
novel that part.IDF.GEN a read.VEN.PAR AFF INT be.SYN
d. Ez da-go gizon-a-z etsi-tze-rik.
not be.SYN man.INS despair.VEN.PAR

(60) a. I-kus-te-a da-(d)uka-k.
see.VEN have./2SOL.SYT
b. Hi-k i-kus-te-a ba-da-(d)uka-k, baina ni-k?
you.SOL.ERG see.VEN AFF.have./2SOL.SYT but I.ERG
c. E-tor-tze-a d-u.
come.VEN have.SYT
d. Ordu-an, no-la da-u-de gauz(a)-ak? Ja-ki-te-a
that_time.LOC how be.PLU.SYN thing.PLU know
da-(d)uka-da-n neurri-an, noski.
have./1.SYT.NRE extent.LOC of_course

(61) a. J-oa-te-a z-en-u-en.
go.VEN have./2.SYT.PST

b. Auto-(e)-en prezio-a-k go(i)-ra e-gi-n d-u: lehen-ago eros-te-a z-u-en.
car.PLU.GEN price.ERG top.ALL do.PEF TRA before.COP buy.VEN have.SYT.PST

c. Lehen-txe-ago e-tor-tze-a z-u-te-n, ez ze-n sarraski-a gerta-tu
before.DIM.COP come.VEN have./PLU.SYT.PST not ITR.PST massacre happen.PEF
iza-n-go.
be.FUT

(62) a. Harri-tze-ko gauza da.
get_amazed.VEN.ADN matter.IDF be.SYN

b. Ez da barre e-gi-te-ko gauza.
not be.SYN laugh.IDF make.VEN.ADN matter.IDF

(63) a. Ez n-a-iz i-bil-tze-ko gauza.
not be.1.SYN walk.VEN.ADN able.IDF

b. Bai, hori i-kus-te-ko gauza ba-n-a-iz ni ere.
yes that see.VEN.ADN able.IDF AFF.be.1.SYN I too

c. Ez da sekula arrautza bat friji-tze-ko gauza iza-n.
not be.SYN ever egg a fry.VEN.ADN able.IDF be.PEF

(64) a. Liburuxka bat beste-rik agerr-araz-te-ko ez ze-n gauza iza-n.
booklet a other.IDF.PAR appear.CAU.VEN.ADN not be.SYN.PST able.IDF be.PEF

b. Laguntz(a)-a eska-tze-ko ere ez z-a-r-a gauza.
help ask.VEN.ADN too not be.2.SYN able.IDF

(65) a. Gauza d-ela euskar(a)-a horr-e(n)-la-ko gai-ak
able.IDF be.SYN.LCZ Basque that_way.ADN topic.PLU
adi-eraz-te-ko?
understand.CAU.VEN.ADN

b. Gauza al z-a-r-e-te ni-k edan behar d-u-da-n edari samin-e-tik
able.IDF INT be.2.SYN I.ERG drink be_to.PPR /1.TRA.NRE potion bitter.ELA
eda(n)-te-ko?
drink.VEN.ADN

(66) a. Ez n-a-iz dantza-ra-ko gauza.
not be.1.SYN dancing.ALL.ADN fit.IDF

b. Lan-e-ra-ko gauza ez.
work.ALL.ADN fit.IDF not

c. Egun oso-an ez n-in-tz-e-n ezer-ta-ra-ko gauza iza-n.
day whole.LOC not be.1.SYN.PST anything.ALL.ADN fit.IDF be.PEF

(67) a. Ez da gai iza-ten beste euskalki-z mintza-tze-ko.
not ITR able.IDF be.IPF other Basque_dialect.IDF.INS speak.VEN.ADN

b. Asma-tu-ko d-u zer-bait. Asko-ta-n iza-n da gai.
think_up.FUT TRA something a_lot.IDF.INS be.PEF ITR able.IDF

c. Ber-a-k hai-e-i e-ra-kuts-i nahi z-i-e-n
he_himself.ERG yonder_one.PLU.DAT show want.PPR /PLU/.DTR.PST
euskar(a)-a gai ze(-n)-la edo-zer gauza esa-te-ko.
Basque suited be.SYN.PST.LCZ any thing say.VEN.ADN

(68) a. Elizatxo-a ez ze-n gai jende hura kabi-tze-ko.
little_church not be.SYN.PST suited.IDF mass_of_people yonder hold.VEN.ADN
b. Aipa-tze-ko gai l-i-te-ke-en jauregi-rik ez d-u-gu
mention.VEN.ADN worth.IDF be.SYN.POT.COD.NRE palace.PAR not /1PLU.TRA
i-kus-ten.
see.IPF
c. Izen eder horr-en gai ez g-a-r-a sendi (senti-tzen)
name beautiful that.GEN worthy not 1PLU.ITR feel.PPR feel.IPF
d. Ez n-a-iz gai sar z-a-i-tez-en ni-re aterpe-an.
not be.1.SYN worthy enter.RAD 2.ITR.SUJ.NCZ I.GEN shelter.LOC

Chapter 25

(1) a. Noemi Moab lurralde-tik e-torr-i-a da.
Naomi Moab region.ELA come.PEF.SIN be.SYN
b. Hemen-dik urruti-ra j-oa-n-a da.
here.ELA far away.ALL go.PEF.SIN be.SYN
c. Fortunato, aita ager-tu ze-(n)-n-e-an, etxe-ra sar-tu-a
Fortunato father.IDF appear.PEF ITR.PST.NRE.LOC house.ALL enter.PEF.SIN
ze-n.
be.SYN.PST
d. Hiru gerra haundi-ta-n eta lau txiki-ta-n i-bil-i-a n-a-iz.
three war big.IDF.LOC and four small.DEL.IDF.LOC walk.PEF.SIN be.1.SYN
e. Makina bat lehen-ago j-oa-n-ak ba-d-ir-a gu-re adineko-ak.
great_number a before.COP go.PEF.PLU AFF.be.PLU.SYN we.GEN peer.PLU
f. Itsasgizon-en andre asko da alargun geldi-tu-a.
seaman.PLU.GEN wife any be.SYN widow.IDF end_up.PEF.SIN

(2) a. Ni ere zer-bait sufri-tu-a n-a-iz.
I too some suffer.PEF.SIN be.1.SYN
b. Asko i-kus-i-a n-a-iz, gero-z-tik, ni-re bizitza luze-an.
a_lot see.PEF.SIN be.1.SYN since_then I.GEN life long.LOC
c. Zerbait ikas-i-a n-a-iz Xerapi kurander(a)-a-rekin.
something learn.PEF.SIN be.1.SYN Xerapi healing_lady.SOC
d. Hau ere ibilaldi luze-ak e-gi-n-a ze-n.
this_one too journey long.PLU make.PEF.SIN be.SYN.PST

(3) a. Hau ez da ni-k asma-tu-a.
this not be.SYN I.ERG invent.PEF.SIN
b. Kortatxo-ko baso-a Urruzula-k eros-i-a ze-n.
Kortatxo.ADN woods Urruzula.ERG buy.PEF.SIN be.SYN.PST
c. Ba-da-ki-t nor-k e-ma-n-ak d-ir-en.
AFF.know./1.SYT who.ERG give.PEF.SIN be.PLU.SYN.NCZ
d. Gizonezko-ren bat-e-k esku-z idatz-i-a ze-n.
male.IDF.GEN a.ERG hand.IDF.INS write.PEF.SIN be.SYN.PST

(4) a. Bertso hau-ek Asteasu-n kanta-tu-ak omen d-ir-a.
verse this.PLU Asteasu.LOC sing.PEF.PLU REP be.PLU.SYN
b. Noiz e-gi-n-a da argazki hau?
when make.PEF.SIN be.SYN photograph this
c. Den-ak d-ir-a dei-tu-ak, baina gutxi aukera-tu-ak.
all.PLU be.PLU.SYN call.PEF.PLU but few.IDF choose.PEF.PLU
d. Lan guzti-ak e-gi-n-ak d-ir-a.
job all.PLU do.PEF.PLU be.PLU.SYN

(5) a. Hi, Etxahun, non-go zori madarika-tu-a-z jo-a bizi
you.SOL Etxahun where.ADN fatality curse.PEF.INS strike.PEF.SIN live.PPR
h-a-iz ba mundu-an?
2SOL.ITR INF world.LOC
b. Satan-e-z tenta-tu-a ze-n.
Satan.INS tempt.PEF.SIN be.SYN.PST

(6) a. E-zagu-tzen d-it-u-t n-eu-re ardi-ak, eta e-zagu-tzen n-a-iz n-eu-re
know.IPF PLU/1.TRA I.REF.GEN sheep.PLU and know.IPF 1.ITR I.REF.GEN
ardi-e-z.
sheep.PLU.INS
b. . . . e-kar-tzen z-u-te(-n)-la laur-e-z e-ra-ma-ten ze(-n)-n paralitiko bat.
. . . bring.IPF /PLU.TRA.PST.LCI four.IDF.INS carry.IPF ITR.PST.NRE paralytic a
c. . . . zer-en egun ihardets-i behar bai(t)-t(<*d)-u-t Judu-e-z akusa-tzen
. . . CAC today answer be_to.PPR ACP./1.TRA Jew.PLU.INS accuse.IPF
n-a-iz-en gauza guzi-e-z.
1.ITR.NRE thing all.PLU.INS

(7) a. Bi-e-ta-ko bat ezkon-du-a da-go.
two.ZEP.PLU.ADN one marry.PEF.SIN be.SYN
b. Ia den-ek hil-a ze-go-e(n)-la z-io-te-n.
nearly everybody.PLU.ERG die.PEF.SIN be.SYN.PST.LCZ say./PLU.SYT.PST
c. Ibai bazterr-e-ta-n eser-i-ak g-e-u-n-de-n negarr-e-z.
river side.PLU.LOC sit.PEF.PLU be.1PLU.SYN.PST tear.IDF.INS

d. Herri hon-e-ta-z asper-tu-a ere ba-n-a-go.
village this.INS get_bored.PEF.SIN even AFF.be.1.SYN

(8) a. Zer da-go idatz-i-a Moises-en lege-an?
what be.SYN write.PEF.SIN Moses.GEN law.LOC
b. Zer-ta-z da-go e-gi-n-a buru-a?
what.INS be.SYN make.PEF.SIN head
c. Bazkari-a e-gi-n-a da-go.
lunch make.PEF.SIN be.SYN
d. Auker(a)-ak eskain-i-ak da-u-de.
choice.PLU offer.PEF.PLU be.PLU.SYN
e. Barka-tu-a da-go.
forgive.PEF.SYN be.SYN

(9) a. Aspaldi-danik hitz-a e-ma-n-a n-a-go.
long_ago.ELA word give.PEF.SIN be.1.SYN
b. Maiz elkarr-ekin lan e-gi-n-a g-e-u-n-de-n.
often each_other.SOC work.IDF do.PEF.SIN be.1PLU.SYN.PST
Instead of *egina*, we expect *eginak* according to the rule of number agreement (cf., e.g., example sentence [9d] with *gaude ... ikusiak*).
c. Hemen ostatu-an arrautza friji-tu pare bat har-tu-a n-a-go.
here.LOC inn.LOC egg fry.PEF couple a take.PEF.SIN be.1.SYN
d. Mudantza askotxo g-a-u-de g-eu-re begi-z i-kus-i-ak.
change quite_a_lot.IDF be.1PLU.SYN we.REF.GEN eye.IDF.INS see.PEF.PLU

(10) a. Sukalde-ko mahai-a pipi-a-k jo-a da-go.
kitchen.ADN table woodworm.ERG infest.PEF.SIN be.SYN
b. Gu-re hizkuntz(a)-a diglosi(a)-a-k jo-a da-go.
we.GEN language diglossia.ERG affect.PEF.SIN be.SYN
c. Ni-re gona gorri-a zerren-a-k zula-tu-a da-go.
I.GEN skirt red clothes_moth.ERG perforate.PEF.SIN be.SYN
d. Sagar hau-ek zu-re txerri-ek marruska-tu-ak da-u-de.
apple this.PLU you.GEN pig.PLU.ERG rub.PEF.PLU be.PLU.SYN
e. Hon-e(n)-la-xe bai(t)-t(<*d)a-go Profet(a)-a-k idatz-i-a: . . .
this_way.EMP ACP.be.SYN Prophet.ERG write.PEF.SIN
f. Mediku-ek esa-n-a ze-go-en ez z-u-e(n)-la haurr-ik iza-n-go.
doctor.PLU.ERG tell.PEF.SIN be.SYN.PST not TRA.PST.LCZ child.PAR have.FUT

(11) a. Nor d-u-t n-eu-re alde-ko?
who have./1.SYT I.REF.GEN side.ADN.IDF
b. Ni-re-a h-a-u-t!
I.GEN.ZEP have.2SOL/1.SYT

c. Ni-re irakaspen-a ez d-u-t n-eu-re-a.
I.GEN teaching not have./1.SYT I.REF.GEN.ZEP

(12) a. Nor z-a-it-u-gu, ba?
who have.2/1PLU.SYT INF
b. Zer d-u-gu, gazte?
what have./1PLU.SYT young_man.ZEP.IDF
c. Eta noiz d-u-gu, ba, egun hori?
and when have./1PLU.SYT INF day that

(13) a. Tori, ama.— Zer d-u-zu hau?
take.2 Mother what have./2.SYT this
b. Horr-e-ta-n Don Abraham ez d-u-zu batere zeken.
that.LOC Don Abraham not have./2.SYT at_all stingy.IDF

(14) a. Salome alab(a)-a d-u-t.
Salome daughter have./1.SYT
b. Gabriel n-u-en izen-a.
Gabriel have./1.SYT.PST name
c. Orain da-to(r)-z-en-ak adiskide-ak d-it-u-gu.
now come.PLU.SYN.NRE.PLU friend.PLU have.PLU/1PLU.SYT
d. Baina, Pernando, no-n d-u-zu seme-a?
but Pernando where.LOC have./2.SYT son
e. Andre-a leitzarr-a du.
wife.SIN from_Leitza.SIN have.SYT
f. Izpiritu-a goibel d-u eta bihotz-a eri.
spirit.SIN glum.IDF have.SYT and heart.SIN aching.IDF

(15) a. Publio-ren ait(a)-a aspaldi-an gaixo ze-go-en.
Publius.GEN father long_time.LOC sick.PRE be.SYN.PST
b. Bi gizon ze-u-de-n behe-an ber-e zain.
two man.IDF be.PLU.SYN.PST below.LOC she(_herself).GEN waiting.PRE

(16) a. Publio-k ait(a)-a aspaldi-an gaixo ze-uka-n.
Publius.ERG father long_time.LOC sick.PRE have.SYT.PST
b. Bi gizon ze-u-z-ka-n behe-an zain.
two man.IDF have.PLU/.SYT.PST below.LOC waiting.PRE

(17) a. Mende erdi-a j-oa-n-a d-u-gu.
century half.SIN go.PEF.SIN have./1PLU.SYT
b. Ama hil-a al d-u-zu?
mother.IDF die.PEF.SIN INT have./2.SYT
c. Begi-ak nahigabe-z lauso-tu-ak d-it-u-t.
eye.PLU grief.IDF.INS blur.PEF.PLU have.PLU/1.SYT

d. Gizon-a, barka-tu-ak d-it-u-zu bekatu-ak.
man forgive.PEF.PLU have.PLU/2/SYT sin.PLU

e. Buru oso-a zauri-tu-a d-u-zu-e, bihotz-a erabat eror-i-a.
head whole.SIN wound.PEF.SIN have./2PLU.SYT heart.SIN utterly sink.PEF.SIN

f. Denbora guzti-a har-tu-a iza-ten d-u-t.
time all.SIN take.PEF.SIN have.IPF /1.TRA

g. Aspaldi eska-tu-a n-u-en artikulu-ren bat *Jakin*-e-ra-ko, gai hon-e-ta-z.
long_ago request.PEF.SIN have./1.SYT.PST article.IDF a *Jakin*.DES subject this.INS

(18) Hau zu-re aita-k e-ma-n-a d-u-t.
this you.GEN father.IDF.ERG give.PEF.SIN have./1.SYT

(19) a. Auto-a konpon-du-a d-u-t.
car.SIN fix.PEF.SIN have./1.SYT

b. Garbi-tu-ak d-it-u-t oin-ak.
wash.PEF.PLU have.PLU/1.SYT foot.PLU

c. Txartel-a eska-tu-a d-u-t.
ticket.SIN request.PEF.SIN have./1.SYT

(20) a. Ni-k eraspen haundi-a d-i-o-t Santiago-ri. Lehen ere bi txango e-gi-n-ak ba-d-it-u-t.
I.ERG devotion great have.//1.DTR James.DAT before too two trip.IDF make.PEF.PLU AFF.have.PLU/1.SYT

b. Lehen-ago ere une ederr-ak ba-d-it-u gu-ri e-ma-n-ak.
before.COP too moment nice.PLU AFF.have.PLU/.SYT we.DAT give.PEF.PLU

c. Jose-k ere ba-d-it-u sos batzu-k bil-du-ak.
Joseph.ERG too AFF.have.PLU/.SYT penny a_few.PLU collect.PEF.PLU

d. Historia franko ba-d-it-u-zu zu-k mundu hon-e-ta-n i-kus-i-ak.
happening quite_a_few AFF.have.PLU/2.SYT you.ERG world this.LOC see.PEF.PLU

e. Zu-(e)-en lurr-a eta zu-(e)-en etxe-a pena-z z-en-u-te-n utz-i-a.
you.PLU.GEN land and you.PLU.GEN home sorrow.IDS.INS have./2PLU.SYT.PST leave.PEF.SIN

f. Zer d-u-zu i-kus-i-a? (*i-kus-i)
what have./2.SYT see.PEF.SIN see.PEF

(21) a. Horr-e(n)-ga(i)-tik nahigabe-tu-a da-uka-gu bihotz-a.
that.MOT sadden.PEF.SIN have./1PLU.SYT heart

b. Gauza hau-ek lehen seguru asko da-u-z-ka-zu irakurr-i-ak.
thing this.PLU before certainly quite have.PLU/2.SYT read.PEF.PLU

c. Eta zu-ri zer e-ra-ntzu-n ere pentsa-tu-a da-uka-t azkar.
and you.DAT what answer too think.PEF.SIN have./1.SYT quickly

(22) a. Esku-ak izo(t)z-tu-ak ze-u-z-ka-n.
hand.PLU freeze.PEF.PLU have.PLU/.SYT.PST

b. Elizabet(-)e-k ber-a-k Plentzia-ko etxe-a ere i-kus-i-a ze-uka-n.
Elisabeth.ERG she_herself.ERG Plencia.ADN house also see.PEF.SIN have.SYT.PST

c. Andoni-k hilabete buru-an lurr-a eros-i-a ze-uka-n eta
Anthony.ERG month.IDF head.LOC land.SIN buy.PEF.SIN have.SYT.PST and
makin(a)-ak eska-tu-ak ere bai.
machine.PLU order.PEF.PLU also yes

d. Ernio mendi-tik kable-a jarr-i-a ze-uka-te-n.
Ernio mount.ELA cable.SIN put_up.PEF.SIN have./PLU.SYT.PST

(23) a. Lehen-ago ere mila duro askotxo aurrera-tu-ak d-i-z-ki-zu.
before.COP too thousand duro quite_a_few.IDF lend.PEF.PLU have.PLU/2/.DYT

b. Hebron inguru-ko herrixk(a)-ak e-ma-n-ak z-i-z-ki-o-te-n
Hebron periphery.ADN village.PLU give.PEF.PLU have.PLU//PLU.DYT.PST
jabetz(a)-an Kaleb-i.
possession.LOC Caleb.DAT

(24) a. Kemen guzti-a gal-du-a d-u-t.
energy all.SIN lose.PEF.SIN have./1.SYT

In the case of forms like *dut*, I continue using the label SYT/DYT in characterizing the personal form of the verb as soon as we deal with the occurrence of the definite article on the participle, even if, in sentences like (24a) R. de Rijk starts talking about a "present perfect" in the case of the combination of those participles with a personal form of the verb **edun*.

b. Aha(t)z-tu-a d-u-t zer esa-n z-i-da(-n)-n Franzisko-k.
forget.PEF.SIN have./1.SYT what tell.PEF /1/.DTR.PST.NCZ Francisco.ERG

c. Zu-re eskutitz-a gogo-z irakurr-i-a d-u-t.
you.GEN letter.SIN pleasure.IDF.INS read.PEF.SIN have./1.SYT

d. Behin eta berri-ro irakurr-i-a d-u-t.
once and again read.PEF.SIN have./1.SYT

e. Gu-re banko-a-k agindu hori e-ma-n-a d-i-t.
we.GEN bank.ERG order that give.PEF.SIN have./1/.DYT

(25) a. Daniel-e-k ber-e indar guzti-a-z jo-a z-u-en.
Daniel.ERG he_himself.GEN strength all.INS strike.PEF.SIN have.SYT.PST

b. Jaun-a-ri eskain-i-a n-i-o-n zilar hau.
Lord.DAT dedicate.PEF.SIN have.//1.DYT silver this

c. Saltzaile-a-k seinale hau jarr-i-a z-i-e-n: . . .
betrayer.ERG signal this arrange.PEF.SIN have./PLU/.DYT.PST

d. Ni-k sermoi guzti-a perretxiko-e-z e-gi-n-a n-u-en.
I.ERG sermon whole.SIN mushroom.PLU.INS make.PEF.SIN have./1.SYT.PST

e. Josue-k agindu hau e-ma-n-a z-i-o-n herri-a-ri: . . .
Joshua.ERG command this give.PEF.SIN have.DYT.PST people.DAT

(26) a. Lantegi-tik e-torr-i berri da.
factory.ELA come.PEF recent.IDF be.SYN

Even in constructions of this type I've opted to label the personal forms of *izan*/**edun* as synthetic forms of these very verbs, considering the modified participles as instances of (in)transitive predication, for example, in line with the analysis of the example sentences in section 25.1.1, in order to preserve the focus on the origin of these constructions.

b. Inazio i-kus-i berri d-u-t.
Ignatius see.PEF recent.IDF have./1.SYT

c. I-kus-i berri d-u-gu-n-ez, . . .
see.PEF recent.IDF have./1PLU.SYT.NRE.ZEP.IDF.INS

d. Errege-ri e-gi-n berri d-i-o-da-n bisit(a)-a-k ez z-u-en
king.IDF make.PEF recent.IDF have.//1.DYT.NRE visit.ERG not have.SYT.PST
beste asmo-rik.
other purpose.PAR

(27) a. Ni-k ama hil berri-a n-u-en ordu-an.
I.ERG mother.IDF die.PEF recent.SIN have./1.SYT.PST that_time.LOC

b. Frantzia gud(a)-an sar-tu berri-a ze-n.
France.IDF war.LOC enter.PEF recent.SIN be.SYN.PST

c. I-kus-i berri-a n-u-en "Psychosis."
see.PEF recent.SIN have./1.SYT.PST "Psycho".IDF

d. Liburutegi-a-k eros-i berri-a d-u eskuizkribu bat.
library.ERG buy.PEF recent.SIN have.SYT manuscript a

e. Ez n-in-tz-e-n edan zaharr-a.
not be.1.SYN.PST drink.PEF old.SIN

(28) a. Albiste-a har-tu berri-an enparantza-ra irte(n)-te-ko
News receive.PEF recent.SIN.LOC village_square.ALL go_out.VEN.ADN
asmo-a ze-uka-n.
intention have.SYT.PST

b. Has-i berri-an nolanahi-ko paper-ak sorr-araz-i z-it-u-en
start.PEF recent.SIN.LOC in_any_way.ADN paper.PLU appear.CAU.PEF PLU/.TRA.PST
Iraultz(a)-a-k.
Revolution.ERG

(29) a. Nikanor, orde-a, gazte-rik hil-ko da.
Nicanor however young.STA die.FUT ITR
b. Ez n-a-iz ni lehen-ik has-i.
not 1.ITR I first.STA start.PEF
c. Den-ek beso zabalik har-tu-ko h-a-u-te.
everyone.PLU.ERG arm open.STA receive.FUT 2SOL/PLU.TRA
d. Biluz-ik irten n-in-tz-e-n ama-ren sabel-e-tik, biluz-ik
naked.STA come_out.PEF 1.ITR.PST mother.IDF.GEN womb.ELA naked.STA
itzul-i-ko n-a-iz lurr-a-ren sabel-e-ra.
return.FUT 1.ITR earth.GEN womb.ALL

(30) a. Ni-k gazte-rik gorde-tzen d-u-t bihotz-a.
I.ERG young.STA keep.IPF /1.TRA heart
b. Zu-k gordin-ik ere kilo pare bat jan-go z-en-it-u-z-ke.
you.ERG raw.STA even kilo.IDF couple a eat.FUT PLU/2.TRA.COD
c. Gu-re maizterr-ek mandio-ak huts-ik da-u-z-ka-te.
we.GEN tenant.PLU.ERG barn.PLU empty.STA have.PLU/PLU.SYT
d. Ezin harrapa-tu d-u-t bakarr-ik.
NPP catch.PTC /1.TRA alone.STA
e. Aita Uriarte-k ere oso-rik itzul-i z-u-en.
Father.IDF Uriarte.ERG too whole.STA translate.PEF TRA.PST

(31) a. Bakarr-ik e-go-n-go z-a-r-a.
alone.STA be.FUT 2.ITR
b. Poz-ik al z-a-u-de *Egan*-ekin?
joy.STA INT be.2.SYN *Egan*.SOC
c. Emakume-a urduri samar ze-go-en.
woman nervous.PRE rather.IDF be.SYN.PST
d. Ni on-ik n-a-go, ama.
I fine.STA be.1.SYN Mother.IDF
e. Gaixo-rik e-go-n n-in-tz-e-n ia hilabete-an.
sick.STA be.PEF 1.ITR.PST almost month.LOC
f. Egunero da-u-de zu-re-tza(t)-ko ate-ak zabal-ik.
every_day be.PLU.SYN you.BEN door.PLU open.STA

(32) a. Igel bat ze-go-en behin idi bat-i begira.
frog a be.SYN.PST once ox a.IDF.DAT looking.PRE
b. Ez n-a-bil erantzunbeharr-a-ri itzuri.
not walk.1.SYN responsibility.DAT shirking.PRE
c. Jende guzti-a zu-re bila da-bil.
people all you.GEN looking_for walk.SYN

d. Bihotz-bihotz-e-z n-a-bil-ki-zu bila.
heart heart.IDF.INS walk.2/1.DYN in_search_for.PRE

e. Zer-en zain z-a-u-de-te?
what.GEN waiting_for.PRE be.2PLU.SYN

(33) a. Bixenta asper-tu-rik ze-go-en.
Bixenta to_get_bored.PEF.STA be.SYN.PST

b. Gaur neka-tu-rik n-a-go.
today get_tired.PEF.STA be.1.SYN

(34) a. Ni sinets-i-rik n-a-go kartzela-tik laster atera-ko g-a-r-ela.
I believe.PEF.STA be.1.SYN prison.ELA soon come_out.FUT 1PLU.ITR.LCZ

b. Salome andregai-tzat har-tu-rik da-bil-ela ja-ki-n d-u-t.
Salome fiancée.PRO take.PEF/STA walk.SYN.LCZ find_out.PEF /1.TRA

c. Jesus zein ze(-n)-n i-kus-i nahi-rik ze-bil-en.
Jesus who be.SYN.PST.NCZ see want.PPR.STA be_busy.SYN.PST

(35) a. Barka-tu-rik z-a-u-de.
forgive.PEF.STA be.2.SYN

b. Gose-a-k hil-ik da-go.
hunger.ERG kill.PEF.STA be.SYN

c. Txakur bat i-bil-i ohi ze-n gose-a-k hil-ik.
dog a walk_around be_in_habit.PPR ITR.PST hunger.ERG kill.PEF.STA

d. Gu-re bihotz-ak da-u-de poz-a-k zabal-du-rik.
we.GEN heart.PLU be.PLU.SYN joy.ERG expand.PEF.STA

(36) a. E-ra-ntzu-n ezin-ik geldi-tu z-ir-e-n.
answer.PTC NPP.STA remain.PEF PLU.ITR.PST

b. Lo e-gi-n ezin-ik al h-a-go?
sleep.IDF do.PTC NPP.STA INT be.2SOL.SYN

c. Lo-a-k har-tu ezin-ik da-go.
sleep.ERG catch.PTC NPP.STA be.SYN

(37) a. Ez da-uka-t Oñatibia aha(t)z-tu-rik.
not have./1.SYT Oñatibia forget.PEF.STA

b. Rut-e-k ber-e erabaki-a har-tu-rik ze-uka-n.
Ruth.ERG she_herself.GEN decision take.PEF.STA have.SYT.PST

c. J-oa-n d-en urte-an eros-i-ta-ko-a ezin sal-du-rik da-uka-gu.
go.PEF ITR.NRE year.LOC buy.PEC.ADN.ZEP NPP sell.PTC.STA have./1PLU.SYT

d. Het-en alab(a)-ek bizitze-z asper-tu-rik n-a-uka-te.
Heth.GEN daughter.PLU.ERG living.IDF.INS bore.PEF.STA have.1/PLU.SYT

e. Bizitze-z asper-tu-rik n-a-go Het-en alab(a)-(e)-en-ga(i)-tik.
living.IDF.INS bore.PEF.STA be.1.SYN Heth.GEN daughter.PLU.MOT

(38) a. Landare hau ez da zu-k zain-du-rik haz-i.
plant this not ITR you.ERG tend.PEF.STA grow.PEF
b. Hai-ek ber-ta-n utz-i-rik, txalupa-ra igo ze-n.
yonder_one.PLU it_itself.LOC leave.PEF.STA boat.ALL go_up.PEF ITR.PST

(39) a. Oso gai(t)z-ki zauri-tu-rik atera d-u-te.
very badly wound.PEF.STA pull_out.PEF /PLU.TRA
b. Ni-k haurr-ak zil-a ebaki-rik u(t)z-ten d-it-u-t mundu-an.
I.ERG child.PLU navel_string.SIN cut.PEF.STA leave.IPF PLU/1.TRA world.LOC

(40) a. Harri-tu-rik utz-i z-it-u-en ikasle-ak esaldi hon-e-k.
turn_to_stone.PEF.STA leave.PEF PLU/.TRA.PST disciple.PLU saying this.ERG
b. Harri-tu-rik utz-i n-a-u ber-e aberastasun-a-k.
amaze.PEF.STA leave.PEF 1/.TRA he_himself.GEN richness.ERG

(41) a. Etxera-tu-rik emakume-ak ume-a-rekin, Porrot geldi-tu ze-n orain-dik
go_home.PEF.STA woman.PLU child.SOC Porrot remain.PEF ITR.PST still
atze-ra.
back_part.ALL
b. Herri-ko gizon-e-ta-rik zenbait-e-k ha(r-en)-la nahi-rik, eskola
village.ADN man.PLU.ELA some.ERG yonder_way.ALL want.PPR.STA school
berri-a e-gi-n z-u-te-n.
new make.PEF /PLU.TRA.PST
c. Zenbat zor d-i-zu-gu, horr-e(n)-la zu-k gu lagun-du-rik?
how_much debt.IDF have./2/1PLU.DYT that_way.ALL you.ERG we help.PTC.STA
d. Zu-e-ta-ko norbait-e-k, seme-a-k ogi-a eska-tu-rik, harri-a e-ma-n-go
you.PLU.ADN someone.ERG son.ERG bread ask_for.PTC.STA stone give.FUT
ote d-i-o?
DUB DTR
e. Ha(r-en)-la iza-n-ik ere, ez d-u-zu horr-e(n)-la mintza-tu behar.
yonder_way.ALL be.PTC.STA even not /2.TRA that_way.ALL talk must.PPR
f. Zenbait aldi-z, ber-a-k ez nahi-rik ere, negarr-a nagusi-tzen
some time.INS he_himself.ERG not want.PPR even weeping overwhelm.IPF
zi-tza-i-o-n.
DIT.PST

(42) a. Horr-e(n)-la-ko liburu lodixko-a irakur-tze-n has-te-ko beldurr-a-k dago.
that_way.ADN book rather_thick read.VEN.LOC start.VEN.ADN fear.ERG be.SYN
b. E-ma-da-zu eda(n)-te-n ur pittin bat, egarri-a-k n-a-go eta.
give./1/2/DYT.IMP drink.VEN.LOC water.IDF little a thirst.ERG be.1.SYN EEC
c. Horr-e(n)-la-ko zerbait-en egarri-a-k g-e-u-n-de-n aspaldi-an.
that_way.ADN something.GEN longing.ERG be.1PLU.SYN.PST while.LOC

d. Beste batzu-e-ta-n gose-a-k e-go-ten n-a-iz.
other some.PLU.LOC hunger.ERG be.IPF 1.ITR

e. Hotz-a-k ba-da-go edo ba-da-go gose-a-k, . . .
cold.ERG CDP.be.SYN or CDP.be.SYN hunger.ERG

(43) a. Hotz-a-k esna-tu ze-n.
cold.ERG wake_up.PEF ITR.PST

b. Noiz aurki-tu z-int-u-gu-n gose-a-k?
when find.PEF 2/1PLU.TRA.PST hunger.ERG

c. Ez da beldurr-a-k i-bil-i beharr-ik.
not be.SYN fear.ERG walk need.PAR

d. Gau guzti-an han-txe-n e-go-n g-in-e-n, euri-ta-n, hotz-a-k,
night all.LOC there.LOC.EMP stay.PEF 1PLU.ITR.PST rain.IDF.LOC cold.ERG
logale-a-k eta batere lo-rik e-gi-n gabe, estalpe bat ere ez
sleepiness.ERG and at_all sleep.PAR do without.PRE shelter one even not
ze-go-e(n)-la-ko, eta gose-a-k, zer jan-ik ez g-en-u-e(n)-la-ko.
be.SYN.PST.LCZ.ADN and hunger.ERG what eat.PAR not have/1PLU.SYT.PST.LCZ.ADN

(44) a. Bero-a-k erre-tze-n z-a-u-de.
heat.ERG burn.VEN.LOC be.2.SYN

b. Ni gose-a-k akaba-tze-n n-a-go.
I hunger.ERG kill.VEN.LOC be.1.SYN

(45) a. Oso kezka-tu-ta n-a-go.
very worry.PEC be.1.SYN

b. Zeharo maitemin-du-ta ze-go-en.
totally fall_in_love.PEC be.SYN.PST

c. Gabiria-n ere iza-n-da n-a-go.
Gabiria.LOC too be.PEC be.1.SYN

d. Ikasle-ak zeharo harri-tu-ta ze-u-de-n esan hon-ekin.
disciple.PLU greatly amaze.PEC be.PLU.SYN.PST saying this.SOC

e. Neskatx(a)-a ez da-go hil-da; lo da-go.
girl not be.SYN die.PEC sleep.IDF be.SYN

(46) a. Ez da-uka-t aha(t)z-tu-ta.
not have./1.SYT forget.PEC

b. Hi-re-tzat ere aukera-tu-ta n-e-uka-n norbait.
you.SOL.BEN too choose.PEC have./1.SYT.PST someone

(47) a. Harr-ek jan-da hil ze-n.
worm.PLU.ERG eat.PEC die.PEF ITR.PST

b. Beso-tik har-tu-ta ber-e-ga(n)-ra e-karr-i n-ind-u-en.
arm.ELA take.PEC she_herself.ALL bring.PEC 1/.TRA.PST

(48) a. Errota haundi-ko zubipe-an auto bat amil-du-ta i-kus-ten
mill great.ADN place_under_the_bridge.LOC car a fall_down.PEC see.IPF
d-u-gu.
/1PLU.TRA
b. Aurr(e-)en-a, e-tza-n-da ohe-an jar de-za-gu-n.
front_part.SUP lie_down.PEC bed.LOC put.RAD /1PLU.TRA.SUJ.NCZ

(49) a. Katalin hil-da, nola bizi-ko n-a-iz, ba?
Katalin die.PEC how live.FUT 1.ITR INF
b. Ait(a)-a-ren izen-a e-ntzu-n-da, begi-ak lauso-tu e-gi-n zi-tza-i-z-ki-o-n Ikerr-i.
father.GEN name hear.PEC eye.PLU blur do.PEF /PLU.DIT.PST Iker.DAT
c. Eser-i-ta, gauz(a)-ak lasai-ago e-sa(n)-ten d-ir-a.
sit_down.PEC thing.PLU comfortable.PRE.COP say.IPF PLU.ITR
d. Zu-e-ta-ko norbait-e-k, seme-a-k ogi-a eska-tu-ta, harri-a e-ma-n-go
you.PLU.ADN someone.ERG son.ERG bread ask_for.PEC stone give.FUT
ote d-i-o?
DUB DTR

Chapter 26

(1) a. Hitz e-gi-ten d-u-en beza-la ida(t)z-ten d-u.
word.IDF do.IPF TRA.NRE SIP write.IPF TRA
b. Barka ie-za-z-ki-gu gu-re zorr-ak, gu-k gu-re zordun-e-i
forgive.RAD PLU/1PLU/2.DTR.IMP we.GEN debt.PLU we.ERG we.GEN debtor.PLU.DAT
barka-tzen d-i-z-ki-e-gu-n beza-la.
forgive.IPF PLU/PLU/1PLU.DTR.NRE SIP
c. Ez z-it-u-en Bonaparte-k Eliz(a)-a-k agin-du beza-la argitara-tzen.
not PLU/.TRA.PST Bonaparte.ERG Church.ERG prescribe.PEF SIP publish.IPF

(2) a. Orain bihotz-a ur-tu-a da-uka-t gatz-a ur-e-an beza-la.
now heart melt.PEF.SIN have./1.SYT salt water.LOC SIP
b. Oinaze bizi-ta-n aurki-tu-ko z-a-r-a, emakume-a erdimin-e-ta-n beza-la.
pain sharp.IDF.LOC find.FUT 2.ITR woman labor_pain.IDF.LOC SIP

As for *erdiminetan*, graphemically speaking, we are not able to decide whether we are dealing here with the plural or with the indefinite; therefore, on the basis of parallelism between the two inessives (cf. *bizi-ta-n*), I opt for the indefinite reading. In spoken Souletin, moreover, contrastive accent is used in order to avoid ambiguity in dealing with number categories: proparoxytonic, in case of indefinite forms, (e.g., *erdimínetan*) versus paroxytonic, in case of plural forms (e.g., *erdiminétan*).

c. E-gi-n be-di zu-re nahi-a, zeru-an beza-la lurr-e-an ere.
do(.RAD) ITR.JUS you.GEN will heaven.LOC SIP earth.LOC also

d. Katu-a-k beza-la zazpi bizi ote da-u-z-ka-k?
cat.ERG SIP seven life.IDF DUB have.PLU/2SOL.SYT

e. E-ra-bak-i beza-la e-gi-n z-u-te-n.
decide.PEF SIP do.PEF /PLU.TRA.PST

(3) a. Ezer adi-tu ez ba-l-u beza-la, Luis-e-k ez d-u inon-go
anything hear.PEF not CDP.TRA.COD SIP Luis.ERG not TRA anywhere.ADN
seinale-rik e-ma-ten.
signal.PAR give.IPF

b. Buru-an mailu haundi bat-ekin jo ba-n-ind-u-te beza-la gera-tu
head.LOC hammer big a.SOC hit.PEF CDP.1/PLU.TRA.COD SIP end_up.PEF
n-a-iz.
1.ITR

c. Hasiera-tik aspaldi-ko lagun-ak ba-g-in-a beza-la, mintza-tu
beginning.ELA long_ago.ADN friend.PLU CDP.be.1PLU.SYN.COD SIP speak.PEF
g-in-tza-i-z-ki-o-n elkarr-i.
/1PLU.DIT.PST each_other.DAT

(4) a. Ni, Orixe ez beza-la, Galileo ondoko-a n-a-iz.
I Orixe not SIP Galileo heir be.1.SYN

b. Etxepare oso-rik har da-i-teke, Leizarraga ez beza-la.
Etxepare whole.STA take.RAD ITR.POT Leizarraga not SIP

(5) a. Beste asko beza-la-ko egun bat.
other many SIP.ADN day a

b. Ohi ez beza-la-ko zer-bait ba-d-u horr(-en-g)a(i)-tik film hon-e-k.
HAB not SIP.ADN something AFF.have.SYT nevertheless film this.ERG

c. Zu-ek beza-la-ko seme bat iza-n-go ba-n-u, . . .
you.PLU SIP.ADN son a have.FUT CDP./1.TRA.COD

(6) a. Den-ek da-ki-gu-n beza-la, Azkue iritzi horr-en etsai-a ze-n.
all.PLU.ERG know./1PLU.SYT.NRE SIP Azkue view that.GEN opponent be.SYN.PST

b. Batzar hon-e-ta-n esa-n d-en beza-la, batasun-a ez d-u
meeting this.LOC say.PEF ITR.NRE SIP unity not TRA
Euskaltzaindi-a-k e-gi-n-go.
Basque_Academy.ERG bring_about.FUT

(7) a. Esa-n beza-la gu-re saio-a arratsalde-an iza-ten ze-n.
say.PEF SIP we.GEN session afternoon.LOC be.IPF ITR.PST

b. Jesus-e-k aitzin-e-tik i-kus-i beza-la, has-i lan-a utz-i behar-tu zi-tza-i-o-n
Jesus.ERG before.ELA see.PEF SIP begin.PEF work abandon force.PEF DIT.PST

Jon__Doni Petri-ri.
Saint Peter.DAT

(8) a. Horr-(r)a e-torr-i ze-n lan-e-ra, ehule beza-la, gu-re aitona.
there.ALL come.PEF ITR.PST work.ALL weaver.IDF SIP we.GEN grandfather
b. Funts-e-z-ko zimentarri beza-la, hon-(r)a-ko puntu hau-ek
basis.IDF.INS.ADN foundation.IDF SIP here.ALL.ADN point this.PLU
azpimarra-tu-ko n-it-u-z-ke ni-k.
underline.FUT PLU/1.TRA.COD I.ERG
c. Ordu ber-e-an adiskide beza-la har-tu z-u-te-n.
moment same.LOC friend.IDF SIP accept.PEF /PLU.TRA.PST
d. Lege-z-ko seme-a beza-la jarr-i z-u-te-n bataio-ko liburu-an.
law.IDF.INS.ADN son SIP put.PEF /PLU.TRA.PST baptism.ADN book.LOC

(9) a. Har-en alde atera-tu d-ir-a laurehun gizon beza-la.
yonder.GEN side.IDF come_out.PEF PLU.ITR four_hundred man.IDF SIP
b. Zeru-a isiltasun-e-an geldi-tu ze-n oren erdi bat beza-la.
heaven silence.LOC remain.PEF ITR.PST hour.IDF half a SIP
c. Zen-bat urte beza-la?
how_many year SIP
d. Herri-tik kilometro bat beza-la da-go *La Fanderia* izen-e-ko
village.ELA kilometer a SIP be.SYN La Fanderia name.ADN
pentsu=fabrik(a)-a, eta hemen-dik
feed_plant and here.ELA
kilometro eta erdi beza-la da-go Sagasti baserri-a.
kilometer.IDF and half.IDF SIP be.SYN Sagasti.IDF farmhouse

(10) a. Ez da-go gaur Mundaka-n ni lege-z/ ni lege-z-ko neska-rik.
not be.SYN today Mundaca.LOC I SIP I SIP.ADN girl.PAR
b. Katu-a sagu-a-ren zain lege-z da-u-de.
cat mouse.GEN waiting_for.PRE SIP be.PLU.SYN
c. Emakume ero bat-e-k le(ge-)z e-gi-ten d-u-zu hitz.
woman crazy a.ERG SIP do.IPF /2.TRA word

(11) a. Hitz-en kontu-a-ri lo(t)-tu behar-ko n-a-tza-i-o, zor
word.PLU.GEN topic.DAT stick_to have_to.FUT /1.DIT debt.IDF
d-u-da-n lege-z.
have./1.SYT.NRE SIP
b. I-kus-ten d-u-en-a konta-tzen d-u, jakile lege-z.
see.IPF TRA.NRE.ZEP tell.IPF TRA witness SIP
c. Urtarril-e-an zen-bat lege-z ikasle gera-tu z-ir-e(-n)-la uste d-u-zu?
Januay.LOC how_many SIP student stay.PEF PLU.ITR.PST.LCZ think.PPR /2.TRA

(12) a. Gaur mediku-en pare g-a-r-a.
today doctor.PLU.GEN SIP be.1PLU.SYN

b. Ba-d-irudi ur garbi-a-ren pare behar d-u-ela iza-n behar beza-la-ko pros(a)-a-k.
AFF.seem.SYT water clean.GEN SIP must.PPR TRA.LCZ be need.IDF SIP.ADN prose.ERG

(13) a. Urre gorri-a-ren pare-ko d-ir-a utz-i z-i-z-ki-gu(-n)-n orrialde-ak.
gold red.GEN SIP.ADN be.PLU.SYN leave.PEF PLU/1PLU/.DTR.PST.NRE page.PLU

b. Ez da-go deus ere horr-en pare-ko-rik.
not be.SYN anything even that.GEN SIP.ADN.PAR

(14) a. Anttoni Edurne bezain polit-a da.
Tony Edurne ELP pretty be.SYN

b. **Anttoni Edurne polit-a d-en bezain polit-a da.
Tony Edurne pretty be.SYN.NRE ELP pretty be.SYN

c. Anttoni Edurne d-en bezain polit-a da.
Tony Edurne be.SYN.NRE ELP pretty be.SYN

(15) a. Lastim(a)-a da e-go-n ohi d-en bezain garesti e-go-te-a gatz-a.
pity be.SYN be be_in_habit.PPR ITR.NRE ELP expensive.IDF be.VEN salt

b. Eder-ki da-go hori; ez, orde-a, uste d-u-gu-n bezain eder-ki.
beautifully be.SYN that not however believe.PPR /1PLU.TRA.NRE ELP beautifully

c. Mug(a)-ak ez d-ir-a behar g-en-it-u-z-ke-en bezain zabal-ak.
limit.PLU not be.PLU.SYN need.PPR PLU/1PLU.TRA.COD.NRE ELP broad.PLU

d. D-io-te-n bezain gauza argi-a ote da hori?
say./PLU.SYT.NRE ELP matter clear DUB be.SYN that

(16) a. Ze(-n)-n bezain sutsu joka-tu ze-n.
be.SYN.PST.NRE ELP full_of_verve.IDF act.PEF ITR.PST

b. D-en bezain argi azal-du d-u guzti-a.
be.SYN.NRE ELP lucid.IDF explain.PEF TRA everything

(17) a. Baina zaharr-ak eroso-ak bezain nekagarri-ak gerta-tzen d-ir-a bide berri-ak.
but old.PLU.ZEP smooth.PLU ELP fatiguing.PLU turn_out_to-be.IPF PLU.ITR way new.PLU

b. Erdara-z ugari bezain euskara-z urri idatz-i z-u-en Larramendi-k.
Spanish.IDF.INS plentiful.IDF ELP Basque.IDF.INS sparse.IDF write.PEF TRA.PST Larramendi.ERG

(18) a. Hori ba-da-ki-zu-e hon-e-z-kero, ni-k bezain on-gi.
that AFF.know./2PLU.SYT by_now I.ERG ELP well
b. Non=nahi bezain on-do bizi-ko li-tza-te-ke Malentxo gu-re etxe-an.
anywhere.LOC ELP well live.FUT ITR.COD Maud we.GEN house.LOC

(19) a. Beste-la busti bezain laster lehor-tzen da.
otherwise moisten.PEF ELP soon dry_up.IPF ITR
b. Eliza-tik etxera-tu bezain laster, sukalde-an sar-tu ze-n Libe.
church.ELA come_home.PEF ELP soon kitchen.LOC go_into.PEF ITR.PST Libe
c. Zu-k alde e-gi-n bezain laster ida(t)z-ten d-u-t.
you.ERG distance.IDF make.PEF ELP soon write.IPF /1.TRA

(20) a. ... ez ote d-ir-a edo-zein Mikel Agirre edo Pedro Perez bezain
... not DUB be.PLU.SYN any Miguel Aguirre or Pedro Perez ELP
gizon?
human_being.IDF
b. Hor burdin gorri bezain bero-tu-ko eta bera-tu-ren n-a-iz.
there.LOC iron red.IDF ELP get_hot.FUT and get_soft.FUT 1.ITR

(21) a. Ugari bezain zorrotz ze-n hizket(a)-an, aberats bezain zehatz
copious.IDF ELP acute.IDF be.SYN.PST conversation.LOC rich.IDF ELP exact.IDF
eta doi.
and precise.IDF
b. Bi edo hiru lagun-en boz ozen bezain bakarr-a go-ra-behe-ra.
two or three person.IDF voice resounding.IDF ELP solitary despite
c. Euskar(a)-a-ren bide luze bezain malkarr-ak.
Basque_language.GEN way long.IDF ELP bumpy.PLU

(22) a. Ait(a)-a-k ezagu(t)-tzen d-u ber-e buru-a ezagut da-i-te-ke-en
Father.ERG know.IPF TRA He_himself.GEN head know.RAD ITR.POT.NRE
adina.
ENP
b. Ez n-a-u, ber-(h)orr-e-k uste d-u-en adina, aberats iza-te-a-k harro-tzen.
not 1/.TRA you.DFR.ERG think.PPR TRA.NRE ENP rich.IDF be.VEN.ERG gratify.IPF

(23) a. Oinaze eta min-ak e-ra-ma-te-ko adina indar eta bihotz
torment.IDF and pain.PLU bear.VEN.ADN ENP strength.IDF and heart.IDF
iza-n-go d-u-zu-e?
have.FUT /2PLU.TRA
b. Erregalo-ta-n ere, ba-z-u-en tren bat karga-tze-ko adina.
present.IDF.LOC too AFF.have.SYT.PST train a load.VEN.ADN ENP
c. Bizi-tze-ko adina ba-d-u gorputz-a-k.
live.VEN.ADN ENP AFF.have.SYT body.ERG

(24) a. Ardo-ta-n hi-re idi-a-k ur-e-ta-n adina eda(n)-ten d-u-k eta.
wine.IDF.LOC you.2SOL.GEN ox.ERG water.IDF.LOC ENP drink.IPF /2SOL.TRA EEC
b. Zu-ek adina edo-zein asto-k da-ki.
you.PLU ENP any ass.ERG know.SYT
c. Gizon-a-ren bizi-a-k ez z-u-en arkakuso bat-en-a-k adina balio.
man.GEN life.ERG not TRA.PST flea a.GEN.ZEP.ERG ENP be_worth
d. Ez da liburu-rik hiztegi bat-e-k adin-a huts bil
not be.SYN book.PAR dictionary a.ERG ENP mistake.IDF collect.RAD
de-za-ke-en-ik.
TRA.POT.NRE.ZEP.PAR

(25) a. Ber-e irakasle-a adin-a iza-n-go da.
he_himself.GEN teacher ENP be.FUT ITR
b. Orain-dik ez h-a-iz hi-re nagusi-a adin-a.
still not be.2SOL.SYN you.SOL.GEN master ENP

(26) a. Mostaza=hazi-a adin-a-ko fede-a iza-n-go ba-z-en-u-te, . . .
mustard_seed ENP.ADN faith have.FUT CDP./2PLU.TRA.COD
b. Sar-tzen d-ir-a itsas=barru-ra etxe-ak adin-a-ko baga zuri
enter.IPF PLU.ITR sea_interior.ALL house.PLU ENP.ADN wave white
sendo-en arte-tik.
strong.PLU.GEN gap.ELA

(27) a. Patrixi-ren-tzat ere, ez ze-n ber-e Xegundu adina-ko-rik.
Patricia.BEN too not be.SYN.PST she_herself.GEN Segundo ENP.ADN.ZEP.PAR
b. Zam(a)-a jaso-tze-n gu adina-ko-rik ba-da, be-tor
load lift.VEN.LOC we ENP.ADN.ZEP.PAR CDP.be.SYN come.SYN.JUS
bide=erdi-ra!
road_middle.ALL

(28) a. Har-tzen d-u-en hain-bat e-ma-ten d-u.
take.IPF TRA.NRE ENP give.IPF TRA
b. Zu-k maite z-en-u-e(n)-n hain-bat ber-a-k maite z-int-u-en.
you.ERG love.PPR /2.TRA.PST.NRE ENP he_himself.ERG love.PPR 2/.TRA.PST

(29) a. Ni-k bihotz-e-an atsegin hain-bat ur ez da-go itsaso-an.
I.ERG heart.LOC pleasure.IDF ENP water.IDF not be.SYN sea.LOC
b. Ni-k hon-i zur-i hain-bat e-ma-n nahi d-i-o-t.
I.ERG this_one.DAT you.DAT ENP give want.PPR //1.DTR
c. Inoiz, inor-k ez z-a-it-u ni-k hain-bat maita-tu-ko.
ever anybody.ERG not 2/.TRA I.ERG ENP love.FUT

(30) Aski d-u ikasle-a-k irakasle-a hain-bat iza-te-a, eta morroi-a-k nagusi-a
enough have.SYT pupil.ERG teacher ENP be.VEN and servant.ERG master

hain-bat.
ENP

(31) a. Har-tzen d-u-en bezain-bat e-ma-ten d-u.
take.IPF TRA.NRE ENP give.IPF TRA
b. Edan e-za-zu nahi bezain-bat.
drink.RAD /2.TRA.IMP want.IDF ENP
c. Eda(n)-ten d-u ahal bezain-bat.
drink.IPF TRA ability.IDF ENP
d. Giputz hauek, gain-e-ra, ez z-ir-e-n lapurtar hai-ek bezain-bat
Gipuzcoan this.PLU top.ALL not PLU.ITR.PST Labourdin yonder.PLU ENP
euskar(a)-a-ren alde ahalegin-du.
Basque_language.GEN side.IDF exert_oneself.PEF

(32) a. Behin ba-ze-n apaiz bat on-a bezain-bat bitxi.
once be.SYN.PST priest a good ENP eccentric
b. Logikazale bezain-bat musikazale-a bait-ze-n.
fond_of_logic.IDF ENP fond_of_music ACP.be.SYN.PST

(33) a. Mariño-k ez d-u inoiz e-du-ki orain da-uka-n beste diru.
Marino.ERG not TRA ever have.PEF now have.SYT.NRE ENP money
b. Esa-n-go z-en-u-ke abade iza-te-ko beste ba-da-ki-ela.
say.FUT /2.TRA.COD priest.IDF be.VEN.ADN ENP AFF.know.SYT.LCZ
c. No-n etxe-an beste babes?
where.LOC house.LOC ENP support.IDF
d. Ai! Ja-ki-n iza-n ba-n-u gaur beste!
ah know.PEF have.PEF CDP./1.TRA.COD today ENP

(34) a. Ez ze-n inor ber-(e)-en ait(a)-a iza-n ze(-n)-n beste.
not be.SYN.PST anybody he_himself.PLU.GEN father be.PEF ITR.PST ENP
b. Hamar emakume ere ez z-ir-e-n gizon bat beste.
ten woman.IDF even not be.PLU.SYN.PST man one.IDF ENP

(35) Zahar eta andre-ak ez omen z-ir-e-n ha-ra-ino igo-tze-ko
old.ZEP.IDF and lady.PLU not REP be.PLU.SYN.PST over_there.TER climb.VEN.ADN
beste.
ENP

(36) a. Gu-k baino asko-z gutxi-ago da-ki Ximon-e-k.
we.ERG SRP a_lot.INS few.COP.IDF know.SYT Simon.ERG
b. Aldizkari-ak asko-z hobe-ak d-ir-a egun-go egun-e-an.
magazine.PLU much.INS good.COP be.PLU.SYN today.ADN day.LOC
c. Hori baino ere txiro-ago ze-n gu-re Migel Permin. Asko-ta-z
that SRP even poor.COP.IDF be.SYN.PST we.GEN Miguel Fermin a_lot.INS

txiro-ago.
poor.COP.IDF

d. Herri hizker(a)-a asko-ta-z ere aska-tu-ago-a iza-ten da.
people.IDF speech much.INS even liberate.PEF.COP be.IPF ITR

(37) a. Zu orain z-a-r-en-a baino gazte-ago ze-n emakume hura.
you now be.2.SYN.NRE.ZEP SRP young.COP.IDF be.SYN.PST woman yonder

b. Ni-k uste n-u-e(n)-n baino luze-ago, mardul-ago eta
I.ERG think.PPR /1.TRA.PST.NRE SRP tall.COP.IDF robust.COP.IDF and
ederr-ago da.
handsome.COP.IDF be.SYN

(38) a. Gu-re bihotz-a baino haundi-ago-a da Jainko-a.
we.GEN heart SRP great.COP be.SYN God

b. Gu baino azkarr-ago i-bil-i ze-n Okerra.
we SRP fast.COP.IDF walk.PEF ITR.PST Okerra

In the case of Okerra, no hyphening is offered, since we are dealing here with a proper name.

(39) a. **Gu-re bihotz-a haundi-a d-en baino haundi-ago-a da Jainko-a.
we.GEN heart great be.SYN.NRE SRP great.COP be.SYN God

b. **Gu i-bil-i g-in-e(-n)-n modu-an baino azkarr-ago i-bil-i ze-n
we walk.PEF 1PLU.ITR.PST.NRE way.LOC SRP fast.COP.IDF walk.PEF ITR.PST
Okerra.
Okerra

(40) a. Ba-di-h-oa-z hon-e(n)-la-ko edo ha(r-en)-la-ko ume-ak gozotegi-ra
AFF.go.PLU.SYN this_way.ADN or yonder_way.ADN child.PLU candy_store.ALL
baino poz-ago.
SRP happy.COP.IDF

b. Joseba lan-e-an baino erne-ago i-bil-i ze-n mus-e-an Andoni.
Joseph work.LOC SRP alert.COP.IDF be_busy.PEF ITR.PST "mus".LOC Anthony

(41) a. Hori gaitz-a-ren orde-z gaitz-ago-a sar-tze-a da.
that ailment.GEN substitute.IDF.INS bad.COP.ZEP introduce.VEN be.SYN

b. Ni baino gizon-ago porta-tu h-a-iz.
I SRP man.COP.IDF behave.PEF 2SOL.ITR

c. Azeri-ak ber-ak baino azeri-ago-ak d-ir-a.
fox.PLU he_himself.PLU SRP fox.COP.PLU be.PLU.SYN

d. Abere-ak baino abere-ago e-gi-n n-a-iz!
beast.PLU SRP beast.COP.IDF become.PEF 1.ITR

e. Handi-a d-u-gu, ba, gau-a no-la ez d-en bihur-tu gau-ago.
strange.SIN have./1PLU.SYT INF night how not ITR.NCZ become.PEF night.COP.IDF

(42) a. Isaak-e-k maite-ago z-u-en Esau; Rebeka-k, aldi-z, Jakob
Isaac.ERG dear.COP.IDF have.SYT.PST Esau Rebecca.ERG turn.IDF.INS Jakob
z-u-en maite-ago.
have.SYT.PST dear.COP.IDF

The glossing of *maiteago* and of the other comparable comparatives in the following sentences is in line with the direct context of analysis offered by R. de Rijk in this paragraph, although, starting with sentence (9c) in Chapter 14, he has decided to analyze these kinds of constructions as preterito-present verbs (PPR in the glosses).

b. Ni-k zu z-a-it-u-t maite-ago arraintxo-ek ur-a baino.
I.ERG you have.2/1.SYT dear.COP.IDF little_fish.PLU.ERG water SRP

(43) a. Garai bat-e-an pilot(a)-a g-en-u-en ogi-a baino nahi-ago.
period a.SIN.LOC pilota_game have./1PLU.SYT.PST bread SRP will.COP.IDF

b. Har-k, egi(a)-a esa-n, nahi-ago z-u-en Leizarraga Axular
yonder_one.ERG truth tell will.COP.IDF have.SYT.PST Leizarraga Axular
baino.
SRP

(44) a. Itsasalde-ko-a baino beharrago za-i-n osasun-a-ren-tzat
seaside.ADN.ZEP SRP need.COP.IDF be.2SOL.FEM/.DYN health.BEN
lehorralde-ko haize-a.
land_side.ADN wind

b. Arnas(a)-a baino beharr-ago z-a-it-u-n NN.
breathing SRP need.COP.IDF have.2/.SYT.NRE NN

(45) a. Nahi-ago n-u-en hemen e-go-n ba-li-tz!
will.COP.IDF have./1.SYT.PST here.LOC stay.PEF CDP.ITR.COD

b. Iturri-tik baino zu-re suil-e-tik e-ma-n-go ba-z-en-i-t, nahi-ago
fountain.ELA SRP you.GEN pail.ELA give.FUT CDP./1/2.DTR.COD will.COP.IDF
n-u-ke.
have./1.SYT.COD

c. Nahi-ago n-u-ke, egi(a)-a esan, beste-la iza-n ba-li-tz.
will.COP.IDF have./1.SYT.COD truth tell otherwise be.PEF CDP.ITR.COD

(46) Lan-a baino alferkeri(a)-a maite-ago d-u-gu.
work SRP laziness dear.COP.IDF have./1PLU.SYT

(47) a. Oilarr-a-k jo baino lehen, hiru aldi-z uka-tu-ko n-a-u-zu.
cock.ERG crow SRP formerly.IDF three time.INS.IDF deny.FUT 1/2.TRA

b. Ni-k ez n-u-en ezagu(t)-tu eritegi-ra e-torr-i baino lehen.
I.ERG not /1.TRA.PST know.PEF hospital.ALL come SRP formerly.IDF

c. Zu-ek eska-tu baino lehen-ago ere ba-da-ki zu(-e)-en
you.PLU.ERG ask SRP formerly.COP.IDF even AFF.know.SYT you.PLU.GEN
Aita-k zer behar d-u-zu-e-n.
Father.ERG what need.PPR /2PLU.TRA.NCZ

d. Pentsa e-za-zu une bat-e-z lasai, e-ra-ntzun baino lehen-ago.
think.RAD /2.TRA.IMP moment a.INS calm.PRE answer SRP formerly.COP.IDF

There is no hyphen between the stem *-ntzu-* and participial *-n*, since the archaic causative *erantzun* never shows a synthetic conjugation, in contrast with its base verb *entzun* (cf. section 16.1).

(48) a. Ber-a ni baino lehen irits-i ze-n.
she_herself I SRP formerly.IDF arrive.PEF ITR.PST

b. Gipuzkoa-n hemezortzigarren mende-an ez d-ir-a hainbeste
Guipuzcoa.LOC eighteenth century.LOC not be.PLU.SYN so_many
Larramendi baino lehen-ago idatz-i z-u-te(-n)-n lekuko-ak.
Larramendi SRP formerly.COP.IDF write.PEF /PLU.TRA.PST.NRE witness.PLU

(49) a. Horr-e(n)-la uste ba-n-u, lehen-ago
that_way think.PPR CDP./1.TRA.COD formerly.COP.IDF
e-gi-n-go uko n-i-o-ke euskaltzaletasun-a-ri zentzu-a-ri baino.
do.FUT denial.IDF /1.DTR.COD bascophily.DAT common_sense.DAT SRP

b. Emakume egarri-a n-u-e(n)-la esa-n? Lehen-ago
woman.IDF thirst have./1/SYT.PST.LCZ say formerly.COP.IDF
lurpe-an sar-tu!
underground.LOC enter

(50) a. Alargun behartsu hon-e-k beste guzti-ek baino gehi-ago bota d-u
widow poor this.ERG other all.PLU.ERG SRP more.COP.IDF cast.PEF TRA
kutxa-ra.
box.ALL

b. Emakume-ek beti da-ki-gu gizon-ek uste baino
woman.PLU.ERG always know./1PLU.SYT man.PLU.ERG think.PPR SRP
gehi-ago.
more.COP.IDF

c. Inoiz baino gehi-ago jan___arazi z-i-da-n.
ever SRP more.COP.IDF eat.CAU.PEF /1/.DTR.PST

(51) a. Zu-k baino diru gehi-ago d-u-t.
you.ERG SRP money more.COP.IDF have./1.SYT

b. Hai-ek baino neke gehi-ago jasan d-u-t.
yonder_one.PLU.ERG SRP fatigue more.COP.IDF suffer.PEF /1.TRA

c. Jende gehi-ago hil z-u-en kazkabar=harri-a-k israeldarr-en
people more.COP.IDF kill.PEF TRA.PST hail(-)stone.ERG Israelite.PLU.GEN

ezpat(a)-a-k baino.
sword.ERG SRP

(52) a. Laudorio eta goramen baino kritika zorrotz gehi-ago e-gi-n omen
eulogy.IDF and praise.IDF SRP criticism sharp more.COP.IDF make.PEF REP
d-i-o-t Azkue-ren obra nagusi-a-ri.
//1.DTR Azkue.GEN work main.DAT

b. Diru baino amets gehi-ago z-u-en agure-ak.
money.IDF SRP dream more.COP.IDF have.SYT.PST old_man.ERG

c. Buru-an ile d-u-zu-n baino bekatu gehi-ago e-gi-n d-u-zu.
head.LOC hair.IDF have./2.SYT.NRE SRP sin more.COP do.PEF /2.TRA

(53) Ez ote da bizi-a janari-a baino gehi-ago?
not DUB be.SYN life food SRP more.COP.IDF

(54) a. Txori guzti-ek baino gehi-ago balio d-u-zu-e.
bird all.PLU.ERG SRP more.COP.IDF be_worth.PPR /2PLU.TRA

b. Odolki-a baino gehi-ago estima-tzen da odolki emaile-a.
blood_sausage SRP more.COP.IDF appreciate.IPF ITR blood_sausage.IDF giver

c. Jone ez zi-tza-i-o-n ber-a baino gehi-ago gusta-tzen.
Jone not DIT.PST she_herself SRP more.COP.IDF like.IPF

Gustatzen has here the same obsolete intransitive meaning as in English 'it likes me not'.

(55) a. Ni-rekin ez d-u-zu-e gehi-ago lan-ik iza-n-go.
I.SOC not /2PLU.TRA more.COP.IDF work.PAR have.FUT

b. Mutil-a ez ze-n sekula gehi-ago ohe-tik jaik-i.
boy not ITR.PST ever more.COP.IDF bed.ELA get_up.PEF

I have hyphenated the participle *jaiki*, not because we find *jaik* as a radical in the Souletin dialect, but by reason of the existence of traces of synthetic conjugation (cf. *DGV*, s.v.)

(56) a. Lehen baino pisu gutxi-ago ze-ra-ma(-n)-la laster antzeman
formerly.IDF SRP weight little.COP.IDF carry.SYT.PST.LCZ quickly notice.PEF
z-i-o-n asto-a-k.
DTR.PST donkey.ERG

b. Ez da guzti-a gu-re irispide-ra hel-du, gutun-ak
not ITR every.ZEP we.GEN reach.ALL arrive.PEF letter.PLU
eta antz-e-ko-ak beste-rik baino gutxi-ago.
and likeness.ADN.ZEP.PLU else.PAR SRP few.COP.IDF

c. Gutxi idatz-i z-u-en euskara-z, beste-ri e-ra-gi-n baino
little write.PEF TRA.PST Basque_language.IDF.INS other.IDF.DAT do.CAU.PEF SRP

gutxi-ago.
little.COP.IDF

d. Uste d-u-t ez n-a-iz-ela superapostolu hori-ek baino gutxi-ago.
believe.PPR /1.TRA not 1.ITR.LCZ superapostle that.PLU SRP little.COP.IDF

(57) a. Itziar zaharr-a da. Mikel, berri-z, are zaharr-ago-a.
Itziar old be.SYN Michael new.IDF.INS TOP old.COP

b. Mikel Itziar baino zaharr-ago-a da, Andoni are zaharr-ago-a.
Michael Itziar SRP old.COP be.SYN Tony TOP old.COP

c. Lur eder bat, Holanda, herri xarmangarri-ak eta hiri are
land beautiful a Holland village charming.PLU and city TOP
xarmangarri-ago-ak d-it-u-en-a.
charming.COP.PLU have.PLU/.SYT.NRE.ZEP

d. Eta hor geldi-tu-ko n-a-iz are istilu gorri-ago-e-ta-n ez
and there.LOC stop.FUT 1.ITR TOP problem red.COP.PLU.LOC not
murgil-tze-arren.
plunge.VEN.IDF.NPS

(58) a. Zu gaizto-a z-a-r-a eta hura are-ago.
you bad be.2.SYN and yonder_one TOP.COP.IDF

b. Zuhur joka-tu beharr-e-an g-a-u-de, are-ago ugal ez
shrewdly act need.LOC be.1PLU.SYN TOP.COP increase.RAD not
da-i-tez-en.
PLU.ITR.SUJ.NCZ

(59) a. Profet(a)-a baino ere handi-ago-a.
prophet SRP even great.COP.ZEP

b. Zu-re azken egintz(a)-ak lehen-en-go-ak baino ere
you.GEN latest deed.PLU formerly.SUP.ADN.ZEP.PLU SRP even
bikain-ago-ak d-ir-a.
excellent.COP.PLU be.PLU.SYN

(60) a. Ilun baino ilun-ago da-go ber-(h)o(r)i-(e)-en zentzu-a zer
obscure.IDF SRP obscure.COP.IDF be.SYN that_very_one.PLU.GEN sense what
d-en.
be.SYN.NCZ

b. Txukun baino txukun-ago ager-tzen d-ir-a beti.
neat SRP neat.COP.IDF appear.IPF PLU.ITR always

c. Ni-k on-do baino hobe-to gogora-tzen d-it-u-t Caulfield-en
I.ERG well SRP well.COP remember.IPF PLU/1.TRA Caulfield.GEN
gorabeher(a)-ak.
adventure.PLU

d. Musarro-k, noski, eder-ki baino eder-ki-ago ze-ki-en hau.
Musarro.ERG of_course well SRP well.COP know.SYT.PST this

e. Maiz baino maiz-ago e-ntzu-n-a d-u-te horr-en izen-a.
often SRP often.COP hear.PEF.SIN have./PLU.SYT that_one.GEN name

f. Argi baino garbi-ro-ago e-ra-ku(t)s-ten d-i-gu aurki-tze-a ez d-ela
clearly SRP clearly.COP show.IPF /1PLU/.DTR find.VEN not be.SYN.LCZ
aski.
enough

(61) a. Aurre-ra zi-h-oa-(n)-la, gero eta urduri-ago ze-go-en.
front.ALL go.SYN.PST.LCI afterward EXP nervous.COP.PRE be.SYN.PST

b. Gero eta azkarr-ago i-bil-tzen z-a-r-a.
afterward EXP fast.COP.IDF walk.IPF 2.ITR

c. Gero eta abil-ago h-a-iz lagun-ak engaina-tze-n.
afterward EXP skillful.COP.IDF be.2SOL.SYN companion.PLU deceive.VEN.LOC

(62) a. Jende-a gero-ago eta eder-ki-ago jan(t)z-ten da.
people afterward.COP EXP smartly.COP dress.IPF ITR

b. Gero-ago eta gorroto gehi-ago z-i-o-n.
afterward.COP EXP hate.PPR more.COP.IDF DTR.PST

c. Gero-ago eta okerr-ago zi-h-oa-n har-en osasun-a.
afterward.COP EXP wrong.COP.IDF go.SYN.PST yonder_one.GEN health

(63) a. Euskaldun e-go-n beti, beti eta gehi-ago euskaldun.
Basque.IDF stay always always EXP more.COP.IDF Basque.IDF

b. Baina, orro-a beti eta handi-ago, beti eta hurbil-ago e-ntzu-ten
but roar always EXP loud.COP.IDF always EXP near.COP.IDF hear.IPF
n-u-en.
/1.TRA.PST

c. I-kus-ten d-u-t beti eta hobe z-oa-z-ela.
see.IPF /1.TRA always EXP good.COP.IDF go.2.SYN.LCZ

(64) a. Zen-bat eta gehi-ago saia-tu egintza hori-(e)-en arrazoi
how_much EXP more.COP.IDF try work that.GEN reason.IDF
bila, hain-bat eta neke-z-ago aurki-tu-ko d-u-te.
looking_for.PRE so_much EXP hard.COP.IDF find.FUT. /PLU.TRA

b. Ba-d-irudi, ha(r-en)-la ere, zen-bat eta gehi-ago ni-k zu-ek
AFF.seem.SYT yonder_way even how_much EXP more.COP.IDF I.ERG you.PLU
maite iza-n, hain-bat eta gutxi-ago maite n-a-u-zu-e-la
love.PPR have so_much EXP little.COP.IDF love.PPR 1/2PLU.TRA.LCZ
zu-ek ni.
you.PLU.ERG I

c. Zen-bat eta urte gutxi-ago, hain-bat eta txiki-ago-a prezio-a.
how_much EXP year.IDF few.COP.IDF so_much EXP small.COP price

(65) a. Zen-bat eta gehi-ago agin-du, ordu-an eta are-ago
how_much EXP more.COP.IDF order that_time.LOC EXP TOP.COP.IDF
zabal-tzen z-u-te-n.
proclaim.IPF /PLU.TRA.PST

b. Baina zen-bat eta zanpa-tu-ago, ordu-an eta ugari-ago
but how_much EXP oppress.PEF.COP.IDF that_time.LOC and abundant.COP.IDF
eta heda-tu-ago e-gi-n z-ir-e-n.
and spread.PEF.COP.IDF become.PEF PLU.ITR.PST

c. Aspaldixko ikas-i g-en-u-en jende hori-ek zen-bat eta
a_long_while_ago learn.PEF /1PLU.TRA.PST people that.PLU how_much EXP
bakezale-ago, ordu-an eta beldurgarri-ago iza-ten d-ir-ela.
peace-loving.COP.IDF that_time.LOC EXP terrifying.COP.IDF be.IPF PLU.ITR.LCZ

(66) a. Hain-bat gaizto-ago e-gi-ten ez d-u-te-n-en-tzat.
so_much bad.COP.IDF do.IPF not /PLU.TRA.NRE.ZEP.BEN

b. Hain-bat hobe-to ni-re-tzat, horr-e(n)-la ba-li-tz.
so_much well.COP I.BEN that_way CDP.be.SYN.COD

c. Iza-n z-it-u-z-te(-n)-n nahigabe gogorr-ek hain-bat bero-ago
have.PEF PLU/PLU.TRA.PST.NRE sorrow harsh.PLU.ERG so_much warm.COP.IDF
jar-tzen z-it-u-z-te-n ber(-e)-en bihotz zintzo-ak.
get.IPF PLU/PLU.TRA.PST he_himself.PLU.GEN heart honest.PLU

(67) a. Den-ak zein baino zein ederr-ago-ak!
all.PLU which_one SRP which_one beautiful.COP.PLU

b. Den-ak zaunkaka ze-to(r)-z-en, zein baino zein
all.PLU barking.ADV come.PLU.SYN.PST which_one SRP which_one
amorratu-ago.
furious.COP.IDF

c. Bederatzi mahai-ko, eta zein-e-k baino zein-e-k
nine table.ADN.ZEP.IDF and which_one.ERG SRP which_one.ERG
ja(n)-te-ko gogo ederr-ago-a.
eat.VEN.ADN appetite great.COP

d. Hiru opari eskain-i z-i-z-ki-o-te-n, zein baino zein
three present.IDF offer.PEF PLU//PLU.DTR.PST which_one SRP which_one
galgarri-ago-ak.
pernicious.COP.PLU

(68) a. Ken-du behar-ko da maite-en d-u-gu-n-a ere.
remove have_to.FUT ITR dear.SUP.IDF have./1PLU.NRE.ZEP too

For the analysis of *maiteen* here and in the next sentence, see example (42a). The same remark holds for *nahien* and *beharren* in the following sentences.

b. Bi-e-ta-ko zein-e-k iza-n-go ote d-u maite-en?
two.PLU.ADN which_one.ERG have.FUT DUB TRA dear.SUP.IDF

(69) a. Ez alegi(a)-a, ber-a-k ame(t)s-tu eta nahi-en iza-n z-u-e(n)-n neskatil(a)-a.
not indeed he_himself.ERG dream_of.PEF and want.SUP.IDF have.PEF TRA.PST.NRE girl

b. Hori-xe d-u-t nahi-en.
that.EMP have./1/SYT want.SUP.IDF

(70) a. Zer da ni-k e-gi-n beharr-en n-u-ke-en-a?
what be.SYN I.ERG do need.SUP.IDF have./1.SYT.COD.NRE.ZEP

b. I-kus de-za-la ber-a-k zer d-en beharr-en d-u-gu-n-a.
see.RAD /1.TRA.SUJ.LCZ he_himself.ERG what be.SYN.NCZ need.SUP.IDF have./1PLU.SYT.NRE.ZEP

(71) a. Etxe hura da-go hurbil-en / hurbil-en-a / hurbil-en-ik.
house yonder be.SYN near.SUP.IDF near.SUP near.SUP.PAR

I adopt R. de Rijk's partitive reading despite the reservedness displayed (cf. "possibly identical with the partitive suffix").

b. Z-eu bizi z-a-r-a on-do-en / on-do-en-a / on-do-en-ik.
you.REF live.PPR 2.ITR well.SUP.IDF well.SUP well.SUP.PAR

c. Peru bizi da hobe-ki-en / hobe-ki-en-a / hobe-ki-en-ik.
Pete live.PPR ITR well.SUP.IDF well.SUP well.SUP.PAR

(72) a. Inoiz-ko soinu-rik gozo-en-ak jo-tze-n has-i ze-n.
ever.ADN melody.PAR sweet.SUP.ZEP.PLU play.VEN.LOC start.PEF ITR.PST

b. Inoiz-ko ipuin-ik poli-ten-a e-ntzu-n d-u-gu gaur.
ever.ADN tale.PAR pretty.SUP.ZEP hear.PEF /1PLU.TRA today

c. Senar hori laster iza-n-go d-u-zu inoiz-ko zoriontsu-en.
husband that soon have.FUT /2.TRA ever.ADN happy.SUP.IDF

(73) a. Igaro e-za-k denbora ahal-ik goxo-en-a.
spend(.RAD) /2SOL.TRA.IMP time possible.ZEP.PAR pleasant.SUP

b. Ahal-ik eta on-do-en-a itzul-tze-n saia-tu n-a-iz.
possible.ZEP.PAR EXP well.SUP translate.VEN.LOC try.PEF 1.ITR

c. Ahal-ik eta lasterr-en-a abia-tze-a komeni za-i-gu.
possible.ZEP.PAR EXP quickly.SUP start_out.VEN convenient.PRE be.1PLU/.DYN

(74) a. Etxe hori handi-egi da zu-re-tzat.
house that big.ECS.IDF be.SYN you.BEN

b. Berritsu-egi da langile on-a iza-te-ko.
garrulous.ECS.IDF be.SYN worker good be.VEN.ADN

(75) a. Jantzi ederr-egi-a da hau zu-re-tzat.
dress beautiful.ECS be.SYN this you.BEN
b. Ikusmin gehi-egi-a-k gal-tzen g-a-it-u.
curiosity too_much.ECS.ERG ruin.IPF 1PLU/.TRA

(76) a. Gazte-egi z-a-r-a hil-tze-ko.
young.ECS.IDF be.2.SYN die.VEN.ADN
b. Narras-egi n-a-go hon-e(n)-la-ko etxe txukun-e-an sar-tze-ko.
shabby.ECS.IDF be.1.SYN this_way.ADN house neat.LOC enter.VEN.ADN
c. Goiz-egi da igaro berri-a d-u-gu-n mende erdi-a
early.ECS.IDF be.SYN pass_through.PEF recent.SIN /1PLU.TRA.NRE century.IDF half
azter-tze-ko eta epai-tze-ko.
examine.VEN.ADN and judge.VEN.ADN

(77) a. Ez g-a-it-u gehi-egi maite euskaldun-ok.
not have.1PLU/.SYT too_much.ECS.IDF dear.IDF Basque.INC
For the analysis of *maite* and also *maiteegi* in the next sentence, see (42a).
b. Elizgizon-ek ez d-u-te maite-egi iza-n Euskar(a)-a
cleric.PLU.ERG not /PLU.TRA dear.ECS.IDF have.PEF Basque_language

(78) a. Oxalde: nor-tsu ze(-n)-n eta zer-tsu bizitza e-rama-n z-u-e(n)-n.
Oxalde: who.APP be.SYN.PST.NCZ and what.APP life lead.PEF TRA.PST.NCZ
For the sake of simplicity, I don't hyphenate *eraman* as an archaic causative of *joan*, as *DGV* proposes (cf. section 16.1).
b. Hon-(r)a zer-tsu z-io-e(n)-n.
here.ALL what.APP say.SYT.PST.NCZ
c. Lehen-dik ba omen ze-ki-en non-tsu e-go-ten z-ir-e(-n)-n
before.ELA AFF REP know.SYT.PST where.APP be.IPF PLU.ITR.PST.NCZ
karabinero-ak.
border_guard.PLU
d. Laborari-a-k aski d-u ja-ki-te-a noiz-tsu e-gi-ten d-ir-en lan-ak.
farmer.ERG enough have.SYT know.VEN when.APP do.IPF PLU.ITR.NCZ job.PLU
e. Zen-ba(t)-tsu urte d-it-u-zu?
how_many.APP year have.PLU/2.SYT

(79) a. Ha(r-en)-la-xe joka-tu-ko n-u-e(n)-la esa-n n-i-o-n n-eu-re
yonder_way.EMP act.FUT /1.TRA.PST.LCZ say.PEF //1.DTR.PST I.REF.GEN
buru-a-ri.
head.DAT

In the case of emphatics, the actual order of the symbols will follow the order of the morphemes concerned in the sentence at hand.

b. Hau-xe agin-tzen d-i-zu-e-t: maita de-za-zu-e-la elkar.
this.EMP command.IPF /2PL/1.DTR love.RAD /2PLU.TRA.SUJ.LCZ one_another

c. Eta Mitxelena-k ber-a-k ere hori-xe e-gi-n-go d-u.
and Mitxelena.ERG he_himself.ERG also that.EMP do.FUT TRA

d. Horr-e-txe-k ez d-u beharbada gehi-egi poz-tu-ko.
that.EMP.ERG not TRA perhaps too_much.ECS.IDF make_happy.FUT

e. Urte hori-e-xe-ta-n argitara ze-n Bilbo-n *Eguna* egunkari-a.
year that.PLU.EMP.LOC publish.PEF ITR.PST Bilbao.LOC *Eguna* daily

f. Gu-re ama-k ho(n-en)-la-ko-xe aldarte-ak
we.GEN mother.IDF.ERG this_way.ADN.EMP change_in_feelings.PLU
iza-ten z-it-u-en.
have.IPF PLU/.TRA.PST

g. Afal-du ordu-ko-xe ohera-tu z-ir-e-n gau har-ta-n
eat_supper time.ADN.EMP go_to_bed.PEF PLU.ITR.PST night yonder.LOC
guzti-ak.
everyone.ZEP.PLU

(80) a. Bada horr-e-txe-k hi-ri, seaska-ko-a h-in-tz-e(-n)-la,
INF that_one.EMP.ERG you.SOL.DAT cradle.ADN.ZEP be.2SOL.SYN.PST.LCI
hain-beste on e-gi-n z-i-a-n.
so_much good do.PEF /2SOL/.DTR.PST

b. Merezi l-u-ke, ba, horr-e-txe-k bertso bat.
deserve.PPR TRA.COD INF that_one.EMP.ERG verse a

(81) a. Zer modu da-go alab(a)-a?
what manner be.SYN daughter

b. Zer modu-z di-h-oa gerra hori?
what manner.INS go.SYN war that

(82) a. Abaltzisketa-n zer modu?
Abaltzisketa.LOC what manner

b. Zer modu-z, Angel?
what manner.INS Angel

Chapter 27

(1) a. Guraize zorrotz-e-z, trist, trast, mo(t)z-tu z-i-z-ki-o-n goi=ezpain-e-ko
scissors sharp.PLU.INS snip snap cut_off.PEF PLU//.DTR.PST above.IDF_lip.ADN
bizarr-ak.
beard.PLU

b. Burdina-z-ko makil(a)-a-z hauts-i-ko d-it-u-zu.
iron.IDF.ADN rod.INS break.FUT PLU/2.TRA

c. Txakurr-a-k e-gi-n-i(k)-ko zauri-a osa-tzen da txakurr-ar-en ile-a-z.
dog.ERG make.PEF.STA.ADN wound heal.IPF ITR dog.GEN hair.INS

d. Perla-z eta diamant-a-ren itxura-ko harri batzu-e-z apain-du.
pearl.IDF.INS and diamond.GEN appearance.ADN stone some.PLU.INS decorate

e. Lehor-tu gabe-ko zazpi soka berri-z lo(t)-tu-ko ba-n-ind-u-te,
dry.PEF without.PRE.ADN seven rope new.IDF.INS bind.FUT CDP.1/PLU.TRA.COD
ahul-du-a geldi-tu-ko n-in-tza-te-ke.
weaken.PEF.SIN end_up.FUT 1.ITR.COD

f. Ezer-ta-ra-ko e-ra-bil-i ez d-en sok(a)-a-z on-do lo(t)-tzen ba-n-a-u-te,
anything.DES use.PEF not ITR.NRE rope.INS well bind.IPF CDP.1/PLU.TRA
gal-du e-gi-n-go d-u-t indarr-a.
lose do.FUT /1.TRA strength

(2) a. Zazpi kriseilu e-gi-n z-it-u-en urre garbi-z.
seven lamp.IDF make.PEF PLU/.TRA.PST gold pure.IDF.INS

b. Ez da-ki-t zer e-gi-n n-eu-re haur gaixo-e-z.
not know./1/.SYT what do I.REF.GEN child poor.PLU.INS

c. Barbituriko pastila pilo-a irents-i-rik, ber-e buru-a-z
barbiturate.IDF tablet.IDF heap swallow.PEF.STA she_herself.GEN head.INS
beste e-gi-n d-u.
something_else.IDF make.PEF TRA

d. Jainko-a-k gizon-a-ri ken-du z-i-o(-n)-n zati-a-z emakume bat
God.ERG man.DAT take_from.PEF DTR.PST.NRE piece.INS woman a
era-tu z-u-en.
fashion.PEF TRA.PST

e. Jainko Jaun-a-k lur=hauts-e-z gizon-a molda-tu z-u-en.
God Lord.ERG earth.IDF_dust.IDF.INS man form.PEF TRA.PST

f. Inguru-ko erdar(a)-ek beste-ta-n-dik har-tu-ri(k)-ko
surroundings.ADN tongue.PLU.ERG else.IDF.LOC.ELA take.PEF.STA.ADN
gai-e-z osa-tzen
material.PLU.INS put_together.IPF
d-it-u-z-te ber-(e)-en hitz eskola-tu-ak.
PLU/PLU.TRA he_himself.PLU.GEN word instruct.PEF.PLU

(3) a. Eta Jainko Jaun-a-k Adam-i ken-du z-i-o(-n)-n saihets=hezurr-e-tik
and God Lord.ERG Adam.DAT take_from.PEF DTR.PST.NRE rib.IDF_bone.ELA
e-gi-n z-u-en emazteki-a.
make.PEF TRA.PST woman

b. Gizon-a-ri har-tu saihets=hezurr-e-tik Jainko Jaun-a-k emazte-a
man.DAT take_from.PEF rib.IDF_bone.ELA God Lord.ERG woman
e-ra-iki z-u-en.
build.PEF TRA.PST

According to section 16.1, this verb is an archaic causative built on the base verb *jaiki* 'to rise'; nevertheless, the gloss CAU will be omitted, since I consider its meaning sufficiently idiomatic at the synchronic level to deal with it as a proper base verb, notwithstanding the hyphenation used. The same remark holds for the treatment of the other archaic causatives listed in 16.1.

c. Hezur hon-ekin lehen-en-go emakume-a e-gi-n z-u-en.
bone this.SOC formerly.SUP.ADN woman make.PEF TRA.PST

(4) a. Hemen-txe ase-ko z-a-r-a ni-re maitasun-e-z; ber-ta-n apain-du-ko
here.LOC.EMP satiate.FUT 2.ITR I.GEN love.IDF.INS same.IDF.LOC adorn.FUT
z-a-it-u-t zeru-ko dohain-e-z.
2/1.TRA heaven.ADN gift.IDF.INS

b. Bete it-za-zu-e ontzi-ak ur-e-z.
fill(.RAD) PLU/2PLU.TRA.IMP vessel.PLU water.IDF.INS

c. Irin garbi-z, ezti-z eta olio-z elika-tzen z-in-e-n.
flour pure.IDF.INS honey.IDF.INS and oil.IDF.INS nourish.IPF 2.ITR.PST

d. Egipto guzti-a igel-e-z estal-i ze-n.
Egypt all frog.IDF.INS cover.PEF ITR.PST

e. Lanbro-a-k ber-e gandu-z estal-tzen z-it-u-en bazterr-ak.
mist.ERG he_himself.GEN haze.IDF.INS cover.IPF PLU/.TRA.PST surroundings.PLU

f. Hon-e-ta-ra-ko ingura da-i-te-ke hautserre bero-z.
this.DES border.RAD ITR.POT ashes hot.IDF.INS

g. Izotz-a-k arbol(a)-ak zilarr-e-z jantz-i z-it-u-en.
frost.ERG tree.PLU silver.IDF.INS clothe.PEF PLU/.TRA.PST

h. Abraham-e-k egurr-a-z karga-tu z-u-en Isaak.
Abraham.ERG wood.INS load.PEF TRA.PST Isaac

i. Ukabilkada-z jos-i z-u-te-n.
punch.IDF.INS overwhelm.PEF /PLU.TRA.PST

(5) Jainko Jaun-a-k gizon-a-ri ken-du-ri(k)-ko saihets=hezurr-e-z emakume-a
God Lord.ERG man.DAT take_from.PEF.STA.ADN rib.IDF_bone.IDF.INS woman
molda-tu eta gizon-a-ri e-ra-ma-n z-i-o-n.
fashion.PEF and man.DAT lead.PEF DTR.PST

(6) a. . . . esku-a-z lepo-a igur(t)z-ten z-i-o-(n)-la-rik.
. . . hand.INS neck pat.IPF DTR.PST.LCI

b. Esku-a-z har d-it-za-ke-zu-e galburu-ak.
hand.INS take.RAD PLU/2PLU.TRA.POT ear.PLU

(7) a. Horm(a)-a zula-tu n-u-en esku-z.
wall make_a_hole_through.PEF /1.TRA.PST hand.IDF.INS
b. Begi, oin eta esku-z keinu-ak e-gi-ten d-it-u engaina-tze-ko.
eye.IDF foot.IDF and hand.IDF.INS gesture.PLU make.IPF PLU/.TRA deceive.VEN.ADN

(8) a. ... begi-e-z no-la z-ene-kus-a(-n)-n zu-re jabe handi-a.
... eye.PLU.INS how see./2.SYT.PST.NCZ you.GEN master great
b. ... begi-e-z ez i-kus-te-ko, belarri-e-z ez e-ntzu-te-ko, buru-a-z ez
... eye.PLU.INS not see.VEN.ADN ear.PLU.INS not hear.VEN.ADN head.INS not
konpreni-tze-ko.
undertsand.VEN.ADN

(9) a. Ez d-it-u-t begi-z i-kus-i nahi.
not PLU/1.TRA eye.IDF.INS see want.PPR
b. ... begi-z ez i-kus-te-ko, eta belarri-z ez e-ntzu-te-ko; ...
... eye.IDF.INS not see.VEN.ADN and ear.IDF.INS not hear.VEN.ADN

(10) a. ... ber-e esku-e-z e-gi-n d-it-u-en ontzi-(e)-en
... he_himself.GEN hand.PLU.INS make.PEF PLU/.TRA.NRE ship.PLU.GEN
pe-an.
lower_part.LOC
b. ... ber-e esku-z desegin.
... she_herself.GEN hand.IDF.INS destroy

(11) a. Ber-e esku-z e-ra-ma-n-go d-u.
he_himself.GEN hand.IDF.INS carry.FUT TRA
b. N-eu-re esku-z ida(t)z-ten d-i-zu-e-t.
I.REF.GEN hand.IDF.INS write.IPF /2PLU/1.DTR

(12) a. Z-eu-re begi-e-z i-kus-i ba-d-u-zu ere, ...
you.REF.GEN eye.PLU.INS see.PEF CDP./2.TRA even
b. Ez be-za-te ber(-e)-en begi-e-z i-kus, ...
not /PLU.TRA.JUS he_himself.PLU.GEN eye.PLU.INS see.RAD

(13) a. Bakoitz-a-k ber-e begi-z i-kus-ten d-it-u gauz(a)-ak.
each.ZEP.ERG he_himself.GEN eye.IDF.INS see.IPF PLU/.TRA thing.PLU
b. Gauza harrigarri hai-ek egi(a)-ak z-ir-e(-n)-n ala ez,
thing amazing yonder.PLU truth.PLU be.PLU.SYN.PST.NCZ or not
ber-e begi-z egiazta-tze-ko gogo-a sor-tu zi-tza-i-o-n.
he_himself.GEN eye.IDF.INS verify.VEN.ADN desire arise.PEF DIT.PST

(14) H-eu-re mailu-a-z jo e-za-k etsai oro.
you.SOL.REF.GEN hammer.INS hit(.RAD) /2SOL.TRA.IMP enemy all.IDF

(15) a. Gauza hilkorr-ak bakarr-ik e-gi-n d-it-za-ke ber-e esku
thing mortal.PLU only.STA make(.RAD) PLU/.TRA.POT he_himself.GEN hand
gaizto-e-z.
evil.PLU.INS

b. Ber-e esku kutsa-tu-z har-tu z-it-u-en ontzi
he_himself.GEN hand pollute.IDF.INS take.PEF PLU/.TRA.PST vessel.PLU
sakra-tu-ak.
consecrate.PEF.PLU

c. Ber-(h)ai-ek ez d-it-u-z-te behatz bat-e-z ere mugi-tu
same.IDF_yonder_one.PLU.ERG not PLU/PLU.TRA finger a.IDF.INS even move
nahi.
want.PPR

d. En-e begi hau-e-ta-z berri-z i-kus-i-ko z-a-it-u-t.
I.GEN eye this.PLU.INS again see.FUT 2/1.TRA

(16) a. Musu bat-e-z sal-tzen al d-u-zu Gizon-a-ren Seme-a?
Kiss a.IDF.INS betray.IPF INT /2.TRA Man.GEN Son

b. Judas-en-ak nagusi-tu z-ir-e-n Jainko-a-ren laguntz(a)-a-z.
Judas.GEN.ZEP.PLU prevail.PEF PLU.ITR.PST God.GEN help.INS

c. Inor-k ber-e iritzi-z eta burubide-z lagun-du nahi
anyone.ERG he_himself.GEN opinion.IDF.INS and advice.IDF.INS help want.PPR
ba-d-i-gu, mila esker.
CDP./1PLU/.DTR thousand gratitude.IDF

(17) a. Poe-ren hitz-e-z azal de-za-ke-gu.
Poe.GEN word.PLU.INS explain.RAD /1PLU.TRA.POT

b. Herri hon-e-k ezpain-e-z ohora-tzen n-a-u.
people this.ERG lip.IDF.INS honor.IPF 1/.TRA

c. Hi(t)zkuntza arrotz-e-z hitzegin-go d-i-o-t herri hon-i.
language foreign.IDF.INS speak.FUT //1.DTR people this.DAT

d. Seta-z-ko ahots-e-z oso lasai mintza-tu zi-tza-i-da-n.
persistence.IDF.INS.ADN voice.IDF.INS very calm.PRE speak.PEF 1/.DIT.PST

e. Ez da gai iza-ten beste euskalki-z mintza-tze-ko,
not be.SYN able.IDF be.IPF other Basque_dialect.IDF.INS speak.VEN.ADN
aho-z nahi-z izkribu-z.
mouth.IDF.INS will.IDF.INS written_word.IDF.INS

(18) a. Autobus-e-z j-oa-te-a d-u-zu hobe-ren-a.
bus.IDF.INS go.VEN have./2.SYT good.SUP.ZEP.SIN

b. Han-dik hamabi ordu-an igo-ko z-ir-e-n Bogota-ra nahi-z
over_there.ELA twelve hour.LOC go_up.FUT PLU.ITR.PST Bogota.ALL will.IDF.INS

tren-e-z nahi-z beribil-e-z.
train.IDF.INS will.IDF.INS car.IDF.INS

c. Bide hura ez n-u-en ontzi-z, zaldi-z edo oin-e-z e-gi-n
way yonder not have./1.SYT.PST ship.IDF.INS horse.IDF.INS or foot.IDF.INS do
beharr-ik.
need.PAR

(19) a. Ama=alab(a)-ak azken-en-go tren-e-an ber(-e)-en herri-ra
mother_and_daughter.PLU last.SUP.ADN train.LOC she_herself.PLU.GEN village.ALL
j-oa-n z-ir-e-n.
go.PEF PLU.ITR.PST

b. Azken-e-ko tren-e-an ba-da-tor, garai hori behar d-u etxera-tze-ko.
last.ADN train.LOC CDP.come.SYN time that need.PPR TRA get_home.VEN.ADN

(20) a. Lagun zahar bat-en bide-z ikas-i z-u-en.
friend old a.IDF.INS way.IDF.INS learn.PEF TRA.PST

b. Hon-en bide-z bidal-tzen d-i-zu-e-t eskutitz hau.
this_one.GEN way.IDF.INS send.IPF /2PLU/1.DTR letter this

c. Jaun-a-k mirari bat-en bide-z gorde z-u-en.
Lord.ERG miracle a.IDF.INS way.IDF.INS protect.PEF TRA.PST

(21) a. E-gi-n d-u-t ni-re eskabide-a Antonio Done-a-ren bitarte-z.
make.PEF /1.TRA I.GEN petition Anthony Saint.GEN intervention.IDF.INS

b. Erantzun-ak musikalari(-e)-en bitarte-z e-torr-i-ko za-i-z-ki-gu.
answer.PLU musician.PLU.GEN intervention.IDF.INS come.FUT 1PLU/.DIT

c. Euskara ba(t)-tu-a-k, izkribu-z-ko batasun-a-ren
Basque_language unify.PEF.ERG written_word.IDF.INS.ADN unity.GEN
bitarte-z, judu(-e)-en-tzat adina jentil(-e)-en-tzat e-gi-n-a
intervention.IDF.INS Jew.PLU.BEN ENP Gentile.PLU.BEN make.PEF.SIN
behar d-u iza-n.
have_to.PPR TRA be

(22) a. Bekatu-a mundu-an sar-tu da gizon bakar bat-en medio-z.
sin world.LOC come_into.PEF man single one.IDF.GEN means.IDF.INS

b. Arim(a)-a-ren medio-z gizon-a-k egi(a)-a e-zagu-t de-za-ke.
soul.GEN means.IDF.INS man.ERG truth know.RAD TRA.POT

c. Gu-re hitz=altxorr-a ugari-tu beharr-e-an aurki-tzen g-a-r-a, d-ela
we.GEN word.IDF_stock increase need.LOC find.IPF 1PLU.ITR be.SYN.LCZ
hitz sor-tu(-e)-en medio-z, d-ela beste-ta-ri(k)-ko hitz
word invent.PEF.PLU.GEN means.IDF.INS be.SYN.LCZ else.IDF.ELA.ADN word
arrotz(-e)-en bitarte-z.
foreign.PLU.GEN intervention.IDF.INS

(23) a. Am(a)-a-ga(i)-tik andre oro behar l-u-ke gora-tu.
mother.MOT woman all.IDF ought_to.PPR TRA.COD praise
b. Hai-ek bi-ak gal-du d-it-u-t, amore-a, ni-k zu-ga(i)-tik.
yonder_one.PLU two.PLU lose.PEF PLU/1/TRA love I.ERG you.MOT

(24) a. Ez da gose-z hil-ko.
not ITR hunger.IDF.INS die.FUT
b. Begi-ak erre-ta d-it-u-t samin-e-z.
eye.PLU burn.PEC PLU/1.TRA bitterness.IDF.INS
c. Gaur egun-e-an ezin da-i-te-ke zigarro-rik pi(t)z-tu su-a sor-tu-ko d-en
today day.LOC NPP ITR.POT cigar.PAR light fire break_out.FUT ITR.NCZ
beldurr-e-z.
fear.IDF.INS
d. Mendi-ak mugi omen da-i-tez-ke fede-a-z.
mountain.PLU move REP PLU.ITR.POT faith.INS
e. G-eu-re erru-z gal-du g-en-u-en.
we.REF.GEN fault.IDF.INS lose.PEF /1PLU.TRA.PST
f. N-eu-re indarr-e-z libra-tu n-in-tz-e-n.
I.REF.GEN strength.IDF.INS free.PEF 1.ITR.PST
g. Hil n-a-di-la maitasun-e-z.
die(.RAD) 1.ITR.SUJ.LCZ love.IDF.INS
h. Hori(-e)-en erregu-z bigun-tzen d-ir-a Jaungoiko-a-ren
that_one.PLU.GEN prayer.IDF.INS soften.IPF PLU.ITR God.GEN
haserre-ak.
indignation.PLU

(25) a. Beldurr-a-ren beldurr-e-z ez ze-ki-en zer e-gi-n ere.
fear.GEN fear.IDF.INS not know.SYT.PST what do even
b. Anai(a)-ek, izu-a-ren izu-z, ez z-u-te-n e-ra-ntzu-te-n
brother.PLU.ERG fright.GEN fright.IDF.INS not /PLU.TRA.PST answer.VEN.LOC
asma-tzen.
manage.IPF
c. Ez zi-tza-i-o-n e-ma-n hizkuntz(a)-a, egi(a)-a, neke-a-ren neke-z
not DIT.PST give.PEF language truth effort.GEN effort.IDF.INS
beregana-tu z-u-en.
appropriate.PEF TRA.PST
d. Lo-rik e-gi-te-rik ez z-u-en iza-n-go, noski, urduritasun-a-ren
sleep.PAR do.VEN.PAR not TRA.PST have.FUT of_course nervousness.GEN
urduritasun-e-z.
nervousness.IDF.INS

e. Gogoet(a)-a-ren gogoeta-z gerta-tu-a desgert(a)-araz-te-ko
thinking.GEN thinking.IDF.INS happen.PEF.ZEP unhappen.CAU.VEN.ADN
modu-rik ba-le-go bezala.
possibility.PAR CDP.be.SYN.COD SIP
Even if the *DGV* does not mention a base verb *desgertatu*, I opt for a "causative" analysis of *desgertarazi*: the play with *gertatua* was simply too beautiful not to act in this way.

f. Hau-ek ez d-u-te fits-ik ere gal-du nahi
this_one.PLU.ERG not /PLU.TRA little_bit.PAR even lose want.PPR
indarkeri(a)-a-ren indarkeria-z sakelera-tu d-u-te-n-e-tik.
brutal_force.GEN brutal_force.IDF.INS pocket.PEF /PLU.NRE.ZEP.ELA

(26) a. Eda-n-a-ren eda-n-e-z, zabuka eta oin-ak loka-tu-ta d-i-h-oa-z
drink.PTC.GEN drink.PTC.IDF.INS reeling and foot.PLU dislocate.PEC go.PLU.SYN
etxe-ra.
house.ALL
In forms like *zihoan* I consider the *-i-* to be a product of raising (out of the past tense marker *ze-*) while analogically spreading over into the corresponding forms of the present tense (e.g., *dihoa*); an alternative hypothesis could be the interpretation of *-i-* as the initial prefix of the stem of the verb *joan* (personal communication from Bernard Oyharçabal).

b. Maiz gerta-tu ohi da idazle-a esa-n-a-ren esa-n-e-z
frequently happen be_in_habit.PPR ITR author say.PTC.GEN say.PTC.IDF.INS
asper-tu-rik bezala mintza-tzen za-i-gu-la.
get_bored.PEF.STA SIP speak.IPF PLU/.DIT.LCZ

(27) a. Kontu zaharr-a! Ja-ki-n-a-ren ja-ki-n-e-z aha(t)z-tu-rik
story old know.PTC.GEN know.PTC.IDF.INS forget.PEF.STA
da-uka-gu-n-a.
have./1PLU.SYT.NRE.ZEP

b. Zaldi-a-k ez z-i-o-n bide-tik behin-go-an alde e-gi-n, ezin
horse.ERG not DTR.PST road.ELA once.ADN.LOC side.IDF make.PEF NPP
z-u-e(n)-la-ko neka-tu-a-ren neka-tu-z.
TRA.PST.LCZ.ADN get_exhausted.PTC.GEN get_exhausted.PTC.IDF.INS

c. Neka-tu-a-ren neka-tu-z ezin ja-rraik z-i-tez-ke-en
get_exhausted.PTC.GEN get_exhausted.PTC.IDF.INS NPP chase.RAD PLU.ITR.POT.PST
ihestiarr(-e)-en ondo-tik.
fugitive.PLU.GEN side.ELA

(28) a. Ni negarr-e-z n-a-go.
I crying.IDF.INS be.1.SYN

b. Herrimin-e-z n-a-go Kalifornia-n.
homesickness.IDF.INS be.1.SYN California.LOC

c. Erdainkuntz(a)-a-ga(i)-tik min-e-z ze-u-de(-n)-la, . . .
circumcision.MOT pain.IDF.INS be.PLU.SYN.PST.LCI

d. Har-k ez d-u ezer e-ra-ntzu-n, baina lotsa-z e-go-n-go da.
yonder_one.ERG not TRA anything answer.PEF but shame.IDF.INS be.FUT ITR

e. Bihotz-a d-u-t samin-e-z, begi-ak negarr-e-z.
heart have./1.SYT bitterness.IDF.INS eye.PLU tear.IDF.INS

(29) a. Sekula-ko ikara-z eta dardara-z ze-bil-ki-o-n gorputz-a.
terrible.ADN shaking.IDF.INS and trembling.IDF.INS go_about.DYN.PST body

b. Zu-rekin hitz e-gi-te-ko beldurr-e-z i-bil-i-ko n-a-iz hemen-dik aurre-ra.
you.SOC word.IDF do.VEN.ADN fear.IDF.INS walk.FUT 1.ITR here.ELA front.ALL

c. Kale-ra atera-tze-ko lotsa-z n-en-go-en.
street.ALL go_out.VEN.ADN shame.IDF.INS be.1.SYN.PST

d. Dohatsu zuzenbide-a-ren gose-z eta egarri-z
blessed.IDF justice.GEN hunger.IDF.INS and thirst.IDF.INS
da-u-de-n-ak.
be.PLU.SYN.NRE.ZEP.PLU

e. Ez e-go-n har-en jaki gozo(-e)-en irrika-z.
not be(.RAD) yonder_one.GEN dish tasty.PLU.GEN longing.IDF.INS

(30) a. S. Franses Xavier oihu-z ze-go-en Jainko-a-ri:
St. Francis Xavier shout.IDF.INS be.SYN.PST God.DAT
"Aski, Jaun-a, aski!"
"enough, Lord enough!"

b. Ez bakarr-ik dei-e-z g-a-u-de, baizik deiadarr-e-z.
not only.STA call.PLU.INS be.1PLU.SYN but clamor.PLU.INS

c. Senar-tzat nahi al n-a-u-zu-n e-go-n n-a-iz galde-z.
husband.PRO want.PPR INT 1/2.TRA.NCZ be.PEF 1.ITR question.IDF.INS

d. Zu-re anai-a-ren odol-a lurr-e-tik oihu-z da-go-ki-t.
you.GEN brother.GEN blood ground.ELA shout.IDF.INS be.1/.DYN

(31) a. Gizarte-a-ri oihu-z ari n-a-iz zuzentasun-a-ren galde-z.
society.DAT shout.IDF.INS be_busy.PPR 1.ITR justice.GEN question.IDF.INS

b. Zu-re dei-e-z g-a-u-de Eba-ren ume herbeste-tu-ok.
you.GEN call.PLU.INS be.1PLU.SYN Eve.GEN child exile.PEF.INC

(32) a. Irribarre-z har-tu z-it-u-en Don Pedro-k.
smile.IDF.INS receive.PEF PLU/.TRA.PST Don Pedro.ERG

b. Neke-z e-gi-n n-u-en ni-re bide-a.
effort.IDF.INS make.PEF /1.TRA.PST I.GEN way

c. Beti ausardia-z joka-tu d-u-t.
always intrepidity.IDF.INS act.PEF /1.TRA

d. Guzti-ek begira-tzen z-i-da-te-n lotsa-z eta beldurr-e-z.
all.PLU.ERG look_at.IPF 1/PLU.DTR.PST respect.IDF.INS and fear.IDF.INS

(33) a. Plazer haundi-z hitzegin-go d-u-t zu-rekin.
pleasure great.IDF.INS speak.FUT /1.TRA you.SOC

b. Arreta haundi-z e-ntzu-ten g-en-i-o-n.
attention great.IDF.INS listen.IPF //1PLU.DTR.PST

c. Abots fin-e-z eta asti-ro irakurr-i d-u ber-e papertxo-a.
voice fine.IDF.INS and slowly read.PEF TRA he_himself.GEN little_paper

d. Andre Maria-k begi gozo-z eta hitz gozo-ago-z e-ra-ntzu-n
Lady Mary.ERG eye sweet.IDF.INS and word sweet.COP.IDF.INS answer.PEF
z-i-da-n.
/1/.DTR.PST

e. Ben-e-ta-ko-a z-irudi-e(n)-n irribarre bat-e-z agur-tu d-it-u-t
true.ZEP.PLU.ADN seem.SYT.PST.NRE smile a.IDF.INS greet.PEF PLU/1.TRA
den-ak.
everybody.PLU

(34) a. Osasun-e-z on-gi n-a-go.
health.IDF.INS well be.1.SYN

b. Martin Saldias ez ze-n lanbide-z zelatari.
Martin Saldias not be.SYN.PST profession.IDF.INS spy.IDF

c. Arrain-e-z ere gai(t)z-ki g-a-bil-tza.
fish.IDF.INS too badly walk.1PLU.SYN

d. Esku-z bezain-bat buru-z ere azkarr-a z-a-r-a.
hand.IDF.INS ENP head.IDF.INS too quick be.2.SYN

e. Ni-re anaia ze(-n)-n-a-k ondasun-e-z oso poli(t)-ki utz-i
I.GEN brother.IDF be.SYN.PST.NRE.ZEP.ERG goods.IDF.INS very nicely leave.PEF
z-u-en.
TRA.PST

f. Garai-z eta aldarte-z, zeharo ezberdin-ak d-ir-a.
period.IDF.INS and temperament.IDF.INS totally different.PLU be.PLU.SYN

(35) Eta alde-z damu d-u-t, eta alde-z atsegin.
and side.IDF.INS regret.IDF have./1.SYT and side.IDF.INS pleasure.IDF

(36) a. Beste hamabost urte-z luza-tu-ko d-i-zu-t bizi-a.
other fifteen year.IDF.INS lengthen.FUT /2/1.DTR life

b. Ez de-za-ke inor-k ber-e bizi-a luza-tu, ezta minutu
not TRA.POT anybody.ERG he_himself.GEN life lengthen not_either minute

bat-e-z ere.
one.IDF.INS even

(37) a. Eta zen-bat-e-z ez da gehi-ago gizaki-a ardi-a baino?
and how_much.INS not be.SYN more.COP.IDF human_being sheep SRP
b. Eta zen-bat-e-z z-a-r-e-te zu-ek gehiago, txori-ak baino!
and how_much.INS be.2PLU.SYN you.PLU more.COP.IDF bird.PLU SRP

(38) a. Eta egun hura hamar ordu-z luze-ago iza-n ze-n.
and day yonder ten hour.IDF.INS long.COP.IDF be.PEF ITR.PST
b. Gu-re euskar(a)-a, hura baino bi mila urte baino
we.GEN Basque_language yonder_one SRP two thousand year.IDF SRP
gehi-ago-z gazte-ago-a da.
more.COP.IDF.INS young.COP be.SYN
c. Homero Detxepare baino bi mila urte-z lehen-ago
Homer Detxepare SRP two thousand year.IDF.INS formerly.COP.IDF
jaio ze-n.
be_born.PEF ITR.PST
d. Buru-a-z handi-ago ze-n Edurne senarr-a baino.
head.INS tall.COP.IDF be.SYN.PST Edurne husband SRP
e. Ezkon-du ze-n ber-a baino lau urte-z gazte-ago-ko Marie
marry.PEF ITR.PST he_himself SRP four year.IDF.INS young.COP.ADN Marie
Peydouvan bat-ekin.
Peydouvan a.IDF.SOC

(39) a. Hiru egun-e-z atseden har-tu n-u-en.
three day.IDF.INS rest.IDF take.PEF /1.TRA.PST
b. Berrogei egun-e-z irau-n z-u-en uholde-a-k.
forty day.IDF.INS last.PEF TRA.PST flood.ERG
c. Une bat-e-z gurutza-tu d-ir-a bi(-e)-en begi-ak.
moment a.IDF.INS cross.PEF PLU.ITR two.ZEP.PLU.GEN eye.PLU

(40) Harri horr-e-k bost segundo-z lurr-a jo d-u.
stone that.ERG five second.IDF.INS ground hit.PEF TRA

(41) a. Ostegun-e-z Itziar-ko Ama Birjin(a)-a i-kus-te-ra igo
Thursday.IDF.INS Itziar.ADN Mother Virgin see.VEN.ALL go_up.PEF
g-in-e-n.
1PLU.ITR.PST
b. Jerusalen-(r)a abia-tu-ko da biharamun goiz-e-z.
Jerusalem.ALL start_out.FUT ITR next_day.IDF morning.IDF.INS
c. Beste egun-e-z ere e-tor g-in-tez-ke-en, ja-ki-n iza-n
other day.IDF.INS too come.RAD PLU.ITR.POT.PST know.PEF have.PEF

ba-g-en-u.
CDP./1PLU.TRA.COD

d. Negu-ko egun goibel bat-e-z hel-du n-in-tz-e-n Villamediana-ra.
winter.ADN day gloomy a.IDF.INS arrive.PEF 1.ITR.PST Villamediana.ALL

(42) a. Gauza hori(-e)-en gain-e-an mintza-tu za-i-gu.
thing that.PLU.GEN top.LOC talk.PEF 1PLU/.DIT

b. Aspaldi-an jende-a isil-ik da-go kontrabando-a-ren gain-e-an.
while.LOC people silent.STA be.SYN smuggling.GEN top.LOC

c. Nahi-ko n-u-ke zerbait ja-ki-n txindurri(-e)-en gain-e-an.
want.FUT /1.TRA.COD something know ant.PLU.GEN top.LOC

d. On-gi d-eritz-a-t Baiona-n izen-a-ren gain-e-an e-ra-baki
well deem.//1.DYT Bayonne.LOC noun.GEN top.LOC decide.PEF
z-u-te(-n)-n-a-ri.
/PLU.TRA.PST.NRE.ZEP.DAT

See (3b) for the analysis of 'erabaki'.

(43) a. En-e gain-e-an negarr-ik ez e-gi-n.
I.GEN top.LOC crying.PAR not do(.RAD)

In the case of *egin*, I gloss (.RAD), since we are dealing here with a verb form both analyses of which can be considered acceptable in Euskara Batua, though this sentence originates from a northern text by Duvoisin.

b. Ez ni-ta-z negar e-gi-n.
not I.INS crying.IDF do(.RAD)

c. Ez e-gi-n negarr-ik ni-re-ga(i)-tik.
not do(.RAD) crying.PAR I.MOT

(44) a. Fede-a-k e-ra-ku(t)s-ten d-i-gu zer eginbide d-u-gu-n gu-re
faith.ERG show.IPF /1PLU/.DTR what duty have./1PLU.SYT.NCZ we.GEN
kreatzaile-a-ri buru-z.
creator.DAT head.IDF.INS

For the analysis of *erakusten*, see example (3b).

b. Benveniste-k iker-tu z-u-en hiztun-a-k no-la joka-tzen d-u-en
Benveniste.ERG investigate.PEF TRA.PST speaker.ERG how behave.IPF TRA.NCZ
denbor(a)-a-ri buru-z.
time.DAT head.IDF.INS

c. Arana Goiri eta Azkue ez z-ir-e-n talde ber-e-ko-ak
Arana Goiri and Azkue not be.PLU.SYN.PST group same.ADN.ZEP.PLU
euskar(a)-a-ri buru-z.
Basque_language.DAT head.IDF.INS

(45) a. Hon-(r)a zer d-io-en hitz berri-e-i buru-z:
here.ALL what say.SYT.NCZ word new.PLU.DAT head.IDF.INS

b. Engaina-tu nahi z-a-it-u-z-te-n-e-i buru-z idatz-i
deceive want.PPR 2PLU/PLU.TRA.NRE.ZEP.PLU.DAT head.IDF.INS write.PEF
d-i-zu-e-t hau.
/2PLU/1.DTR this

c. Ben-e-ta-ko baldarkeri(a)-a orain-go garai-o-ta-n Kant-i buru-z
true.ZEP.PLU.ADN stupidity now.ADN time.INC.LOC Kant.DAT head.IDF.INS
hitzegi-te-a.
talk.VEN

(46) a. Zu(-e)-en baimen-a-rekin n-eu-re buru-a-z zerbait esa-n nahi
you.PLU.GEN permission.SOC I.REF.GEN head.INS something say want.PPR
n-u-ke.
/1.TRA.COD

b. Ait(a)-a-z mintza-tzen al ze-n?
father.INS talk.IPF INT ITR.PST

c. Bi-o-z mintza-tu-ko n-a-tza-i-zu-e orain, eta bat-e-z___ere
two.ZEP.INC.INS talk.FUT 2PLU/1.DIT now and especially
bigarren-a-z.
second.ZEP.INS

d. Egunero-ko bizitz(a)-a-z hitzegi-n g-en-u-en gosal-du bitarte-an.
every_day.ADN life.INS speak.PEF /1PLU.TRA.PST have_breakfast interval.LOC

e. Har-ta-z da-go idatz-i-a Liburu Santu-an:...
yonder_one.INS be.SYN write.PEF.SIN Book Holy.LOC

(47) a. Mundu zabal-a-ri galdegi-n n-i-o-n ene Jainko-a-z.
world wide.DAT ask.PEF //1.DTR.PST I.GEN God.INS

b. Norbait-e-k ni-ta-z galdegi-ten ba-d-u,...
someone.ERG I.INS ask.IPF CDP.TRA

c. Hor=hemen bil(a)-an ze-bil-e(n)-la, anai(a)-e-z galde-tu z-i-o-n
there.LOC-here.LOC search.LOC walk.SYN.PST.LCI brother.PLU.INS ask.PEF DTR.PST
gizon bat-i.
man a.IDF.DAT

(48) a. Beste bat-e-an e-ntzu-n-go d-i-zu-gu horr-e-ta-z.
other a.LOC hear.FUT /2/1PLU.DTR that.INS

b. Zer da zu-ta-z e-ntzu-n d-u-da-n hori?
what be.SYN you.INS hear.PEF /1.TRA.NRE that

c. Adi-tu al d-u-zu zerbait gerr(a)-a-z?
hear.PEF INT /2.TRA something war.INS

(49) a. Ea zer da-ki-zu-n hamabost eta hamaseigarren mende-a-z.
WCC what know./2.SYT.NCZ fifteen and sixteenth century.INS

b. Ni-ta-z ez da-ki-da-n zerbait Zu-ta-z ba-da-ki-t.
I.INS not know./1.SYT.NRE something You.INS AFF.know./1.SYT

(50) a. Ber-e egiteko(-e)-en gain-e-ko galde asko e-gi-n z-i-z-ki-o-n.
she_herself.GEN duty.PLU.GEN top.ADN question many make.PEF PLU//.DTR.PST
b. Arranondo-ko gauz(a)(-e)-en gain-e-ko jardun luze bat-e-an has-i
Arranondo.ADN matter.PLU.GEN top.ADN conversation long a.LOC begin.PEF
z-ir-e-n.
PLU.ITR.PST

(51) a. Humboldt e-torr-i zi-tza-i-gu-n gu-re-ra, gu-re gauz(a)-e-i
Humboldt come.PEF 1PLU/.ITR.PST we.GEN.ZEP.ALL we.GEN affair.PLU.DAT
buru-z-ko zenbait berri atzerri-an jaso ondo-an.
head.IDF.INS.ADN some news foreign_country.LOC get side.LOC
b. Sintaxi-a-ri buru-z-ko saio-ak inoiz baino ugari-ago
syntax.DAT head.IDF.INS.ADN essay.PLU ever SRP plentiful.COP.IDF
d-it-u-gu.
have.PLU/1PLU.SYT

(52) a. Ez d-u-gu hitz hori balia-tzen.
not /1PLU.TRA word that use.IPF
b. Ez g-a-r-a hitz horr-e-ta-z balia-tzen.
not 1PLU.ITR word that.INS use.IPF

(53) a. Aha(t)z-tu-ko g-a-it-u-z-te.
forget.FUT 1PLU/PLU.TRA
b. Ez d-ir-a gu-ta-z erabat aha(t)z-tu.
not PLU.ITR we.INS completely forget.PEF

(54) a. Gogora Lot-en emazte-a.
remember.RAD Lot.GEN wife
b. Gogora-tzen al z-a-r-a Andoni-z?
remember.IPF INT 2.ITR Anthony

(55) a. Orain ere urrun z-a-r-ela-r-ik oroi(t)-tu-ko z-a-it-u-t.
now even far_away.IDF be.2.SYN.LCI remember.FUT 2/1.TRA
b. Gu-re ama-z oroi(t)-tu n-in-tz-e-n.
we.GEN mother.IDF.INS remember.PEF 1.ITR.PST

(56) a. Iliad(a)-a zahar=gazte-ek goza de-za-ke-te-la
Iliad old.IDF_young.ZEP.PLU.ERG enjoy.RAD /PLU.TRA.POT.LCZ
ba-da-ki-t.
AFF.know./1/SYT

b. Maitasun horr-en berotasun-a-z luza-z de-za-te-la goza.
love that.GEN warmth.INS long(_time).INS /PLU.TRA.SUJ.LCZ enjoy.RAD

(57) a. Buruzagi-ek burla-tzen z-u-te-n Jesus.
ruler.PLU.ERG make_fun_of.IPF /PLU.TRA.PST Jesus

b. Ez n-a-iz zu-ta-z burla-tzen.
not 1.ITR you.INS make_fun_of.IPF

(58) a. Nor-k trufa-tu z-a-it-u berri-z ere?
who.ERG make_fun_of.PEF 2/.TRA new.IDF.INS too

b. Ez da Jainko-a-z trufa-tzen.
not ITR God.INS make_fun_of.IPF

(59) a. Z-eu-o-(e)n buru-ak erruki / erruki-tu it-za-zu-e.
you.REF.INC.GEN head.PLU have_pity_on.RAD have_pity_on PLU/2PLU.TRA.IMP

b. Erruki z-a-i-tez gu-ta-z.
have_pity_on.RAD 2.ITR.IMP we.INS

(60) a. Erdi-tu-ko d-u seme-a.
give_birth_to.FUT TRA son

b. Erdi-ko da seme bat-e-z.
give_birth_to.FUT ITR son a.IDF.INS

(61) a. Maiz nabari-tzen d-u-gu premia hori.
often sense.IPF /1PLU.TRA need that

b. On-gi nabari-tu ze-n Azkue horr-e-ta-z.
well sense.PEF ITR.PST Azkue that.INS

(62) a. Hiru-ek, bai am(a)-a-k, bai alab(a)-ek, mintza-tzen d-u-te euskar(a)-a.
three.ZEP.PLU.ERG both mother.ERG and daughter.PLU.ERG speak.IPF /PLU.TRA Basque_language

b. Hiru-ak mintza-tzen d-ir-a euskara-z.
three.ZEP.PLU speak.IPF PLU.ITR Basque_language.IDF.INS

(63) a. Une bat-e-tik beste-ra etxe eta ondasun-e-z jabe-tu-ko da.
moment one.ELA other.ZEP.ALL house and asset.PLU.INS take_over.FUT ITR

b. Egi(a)-a-z jabe-tu-ko z-a-r-a.
truth.INS get_to_know.FUT 2.ITR

c. Ez n-a-iz jabe-tzen d-io-zu-n-a-z.
not 1.ITR grasp.ITR say./2.SYT.NRE.ZEP.INS

(64) a. Zer pasione-k gu-re bihotz-a nagusi-tzen d-u-te?
what passion.ERG we.GEN heart dominate.IPF /PLU.TRA

b. Ez z-ir-e-n ber(-e)-en arm(a)-e-i esker nagusi-tu
not PLU.ITR.PST he_himself.PLU.GEN weapon.PLU.DAT thanks.IDF conquer.PEF
lurralde-a-z.
land.INS

(65) a. Beste zerbait-e-ta-z ohar-tu / ohar(t)-tu n-in-tz-e-n.
else something.INS notice.PEF notice.PEF 1.ITR.PST
b. Ohar(t)-tzen / ohar-tzen al n-in-tz-e-n gerta-tze-n ari
notice.IPF notice.IPF INT 1.ITR.PST happen.VEN.LOC be_busy.PPR
ze(-n)-n-a-z?
ITR.PST.NRE.ZEP.INS

(66) Kalte haundi-ak e-gi-n ondo-an kontura-tu z-ir-e-n horr-e-ta-z.
damage big.PLU do continuity.LOC realize.PEF PLU.ITR.PST that.INS

(67) Haurr-e-z ez ze-n deus ere ardura-tzen.
child.PLU.INS not ITR.PST anything even be_interested_in.IPF

(68) a. Ez l-u-ke inor-k erantzun hon-e-ta-z harri-tu behar.
not TRA.COD anybody.ERG answer this.INS be_surprised should.PPR
b. Txirrita sagardo-a-ren prezio-a-z kezka-tzen ze-n.
Txirrita cider.GEN price.INS be_worried.IPF ITR.PST
c. Ez ze-n ait(a)-a-z lotsa-tzen?
not ITR.PST father.INS be_ashamed.IPF
d. Ez n-a-iz etsai-a-ren hondamendi-a-z poz-tu
not 1.ITR enemy.GEN disaster.INS rejoice.PEF
e. Mutil-a-rekin gerta-tu za-i-zu-e-n-a-z, ni ere nahigabe-tzen n-a-iz.
boy.SOC happen.PEF 2PLU/.DIT.NRE.ZEP.INS I too be_grieved 1.ITR

(69) a. Gabe-tu nahi n-a-u-zu-e bizi-a-z.
deprive want.PPR 1/2PLU.TRA life.INS
b. Ez d-u-t esku-e-ta-n d-u-da-n-a-z gabe-tu nahi.
not /1.TRA hand.PLU.LOC have./1.SYT.NRE.ZEP.INS be_deprived want.PPR

(70) a. Ez=deus e-gi-te-a-z ber-a-z ikas-ten da gaizki e-gi-te-n.
nothing do.VEN.INS it_itself.ZEP.INS learn.IPF ITR evil.IDF do.VEN.LOC
b. Astakeria handi bat e-gi-n z-u-te-n haitz-e-ta-ra egun guzti-ra-ko
stupidity big a do.PEF /PLU.TRA.PST rock.PLU.ALL day whole.DES
j-oa-te-a-z.
go.VEN.INS
c. Ni-re seme=alab(a)-ek eta ni-k hutsune galant-a iza-n-go
I.GEN son.IDF_and_daughter.PLU.ERG and I.ERG emptiness great have.FUT
d-u-gu etxe-an har-en j-oa-te-a-z.
/1PLU.TRA house.LOC yonder_one.GEN go.VEN.INS

d. Etxe-an geldi e-go-te-a-z, bat asper-tzen da.
house.LOC idle.PRE stay.VEN.INS one get_bored.IPF ITR

(71) a. Arrain gordin-a jan-e-z irau-n n-u-en.
fish raw eat.PTC.IDF.INS endure.PEF 1.TRA.PST

b. Drog(a)-a eros-te-ko diru-a, gorputz-a sal-du-z irabaz-ten d-u-te.
drugs buy.VEN.ADN money body sell.PTC.IDF.INS earn.IPF /PLU.TRA

c. N-e(u)-r(e_h)on-e-k galaraz-i-ko d-u-t agintari(-e)-en-gan-(r)a j-oa-n-e-z eta
I_myself.ERG prevent.FUT /1.TRA authority.PLU.ALL go.PTC.IDF.INS and
sala-tu-a-z.
denounce.PTC.INS

Synchronically, I have *galarazi* not analyzed as a causative (separately lemmatized by I. Sarasola) despite its obvious link with *gal-du*.

d. Z-eu(-e)-en herri-a-ri su e-ma-n-a-z ager-tzen d-u-zu-e
you.REF.PLU.GEN village.DAT fire.IDF give.PTC.INS show.IPF /2PLU.TRA
zu(-e)-en bilaukeri(a)-a.
you.PLU.GEN villainy

e. Gero lo=kuluxka bat e-gi-n-e-z, buru-ko min-a j-oa-n-go
afterward sleep.IDF-short_nap.IDF a do.PTC.IDF.INS head.ADN ache go.FUT
za-i-t.
1/.DIT

(72) a. Bazter bat-e-an geldi-tzen da malko-ak xuka-tu-a-z.
corner a.LOC remain.IPF ITR tear.PLU dry.PTC.INS

b. —Antz e-ma-n-a n-en-go-en— musu bat e-ma-n-a-z esa-n z-i-o-n.
—likeness.IDF give.PEF.SIN be.1.SYN.PST— kiss a give.PTC.INS tell.PEF DTR.PST

c. Hon-e-k, haurr-e-i agur e-gi-n-a-z, har-tu d-u ber-e
this_one.ERG child.PLU.DAT goodbye.IDF do.PTC.INS take.PEF TRA he_himself.GEN
etxe-ra-ko bide-a.
house.ALL.ADN road

d. Inguru-ra begirada azkar bat bote-a-z presaka alde e-gi-n
surroundings.ALL glance quick a cast.PTC.INS in_a_hurry span.IDF make.PEF
d-u-t han-dik.
/1.TRA over_there.ELA

e. Hotzikara bat senti-tu d-u goi-tik behe-ra zeharka-tu-z.
cold_shiver a feel.PEF TRA top.ELA bottom.ALL pass_through.PTC.IDF.INS

(73) a. Adurr-a ze-ri-o-n ezpain-e-ta-tik gaztai-a jan nahi-a-z.
saliva drip.DYN.PST lip.PLU.ELA cheese eat want.PTC.INS

b. Aspaldi-danik da-bil hemen lantegi berri bat eraiki nahi-z.
while.ELA be_around.SYN here.LOC factory new a build want.PTC.IDF.INS

c. Eeeeep . . . !— oihu ze-gi-e-n hai(-e)-en gogo-a su-tu
"eeeeep . . . !"— shout.IDF do./PLU/.DYT yonder_one.PLU.GEN spirit fire_up
nahi-z.
want.PTC.IDF.INS

(74) a. Lan ederr-a jarr-i d-i-gu-zu-e horren-beste galtza txuri jos-i
job great impose.PEF /1PLU/2PLU.DTR so_many pants white sew
beharr-e-z.
need.PTC.IDF.INS

b. Atera ze-n jan beharr-e-z.
go-out.PEF ITR.PST eat need.PTC.IDF.INS

c. Egun bat-e-z abia-tzen da Haxko, basajaun-a no-ra j-oa-ten d-en
day a.IDF.INS set_off.IPF ITR Haxko sylvan_man where.ALL go.IPF ITR.NCZ
i-kus-i beharr-e-z.
see need.PTC.IDF.INS

(75) a. Jaun-a-ren hitz-a aitzina-tu-z eta heda-tu-z zi-h-oa-n.
Lord.GEN word advance.PTC.IDF.INS and spread.PTC.IDF.INS go.SYN.PST
For *zihoan* see example (26a).

b. Egun-e-tik egun-e-ra, ilun-du-z eta flaka-tu-z d-oa.
day.ELA day.ALL get_obscure.PTC.IDF.INS and get_weak.PTC.IDF.INS go.SYN

c. Orain behinola-ko giro hura alda-tu-z d-oa.
now once.ADN atmosphere yonder change.PTC.IDF.INS go.SYN

d. Eten-a da antzina-ko lokarri-a eta oroitzapen-a ber-a ere
break.PEF.SIN ITR long_ago.ADN bond and memory it_itself even
ezaba-tu-z d-oa.
disappear.PTC.IDF.INS go.SYN

e. Orde-a, horr-en parte-z, are-ago esna-tu-z j-oa-n
substitute that.GEN part.IDF.INS TOP.COP.IDF wake_up.PTC.IDF.INS go.PEF
n-in-tz-e-n.
1.ITR.PST

(76) Eta neurri-a ez d-oa urri-tze-n, haz-te-n eta ugari-tzen baizik.
and quantity not go.SYN diminish.IPF grow.IPF and increase.IPF but

(77) a. **Hitz-ik ez esa-n-e-z j-oa-n ze-n.
word.PAR not say.PTC.IDF.INS go.PEF ITR.PST

b. Hitz-ik esa-n gabe j-oa-n ze-n.
word.PAR say without.PRE go.PEF ITR.PST

(78) a. Beste-rik esa(n)-te-ke u(t)z-ten al g-a-it-u-zu?
else.ZEP.PAR say.VEN.PRI leave.IPF INT 1PLU/2.TRA

b. Hamar minutu inguru j-oa-n z-ir-e-n Mateo-k aho-rik
ten minute.IDF surroundings.IDF go.PEF PLU.ITR.PST Mateo.ERG mouth.PAR
zabal-tze-ke.
open.VEN.PRI

c. No-ra zi-h-oa(-n)-n ohar(t)-tze-ke / ohar-tze-ke, aurre-ra eta aurre-ra
where.ALL go.SYN.PST.NCZ notice.VEN.PRI notice.VEN.PRI front.ALL and front.ALL
jo z-u-en.
go_ahead.PEF TRA.PST

d. Lehen, egun bat elkar i-kus-te-ke ezin pasa; eta orain, egun oso
formerly day one each_other see.VEN.PRI NPP pass.RAD and now day whole
bat ezin pasa elkarr-ekin.
a NPP pass.RAD each_other.SOC

Chapter 28

(1) a. Nor d-ir-a hori-ek?
who be.PLU.SYN that_one.PLU

b. Nor d-ir-a hau-ek?
who be.PLU.SYN this_one.PLU

c. Nor-tzu-k d-ir-a hau-ek?
who.PLU be.PLU.SYN this_one.PLU

d. Eliz(a)-an nor-tzu-k bil-du-ko g-a-r-a?
church.LOC who.PLU get_together.FUT 1PLU.ITR

(2) a. Ez n-a-iz ni nor auzi hori e-ra-baki-tze-ko.
not be.1.SYN I who dispute that decide.VEN.ADN

b. Gu ez g-a-r-a nor galdera hau e-ra-ntzu-te-ko.
we not be.1PLU.SYN who question this answer.VEN.ADN

c. Jaun-a, ni ez n-a-iz nor zu n-eu-re aterpe-an sar z-a-i-tez-en.
Lord I not be.1.SYN who you I.REF.GEN roof.LOC enter.RAD 2.ITR.SUJ.NCZ

(3) a. Hai-e-ta-rik bi-e-ta-rik, zein-e-k i-ra-gan ote z-u-en
yonder_one.PLU.ELA two.ZEP.PLU.ELA which_one.ERG undergo.PEF DUB TRA.PST
mundu hon-e-ta-n pena eta trabailu gehi-ago?
world this.LOC pain and tribulation more.COP

b. Bi-e-ta-ko zein nahi d-u-zu-e aska-tze-a?
two.ZEP.PLU.ADN which_one want.PPR /2PLU.TRA release.VEN

c. Zein da gu-re helburu-a? G-eu-re buru-a-ren atsegin-a ala
which be.SYN we.GEN goal we.REF.GEN head.GEN pleasure or
euskar(a)-a-ren on-a eta bizi-a?
Basque_language.GEN welfare and existence

d. Zein ur, geldi-a ala lasterr-a?
which water stagnant.ZEP or running.ZEP

e. Ez al da-ki-zu-e gaur zein egun d-u-gu-n?
not INT know./2PLU.SYT today which day have./1PLU.SYT.NCZ

f. Zein leku ikaragarri-a hau!
which place awesome this_one

(4) a. Gero j-oa-n z-ir-e-n nor ber-e etxe-ra.
later go.PEF PLU.ITR.PST who he_hmself.GEN house.ALL

b. Nor-i ber-e-a da zuzenbide-a.
who.DAT he_himself.GEN.ZEP be.SYN right

c. Nor-k ber-e bide-a hauta-tu behar d-u.
who.ERG he_himself.GEN way choose must.PPR TRA

d. Jende-a-k, oinaze-a-ren oinaze-z, nor-k ber-e mihi-a-ri hozka
people.ERG pain.GEN pain.IDF.INS who.ERG he_himself.GEN tongue.DAT bite.IDF
e-gi-ten z-i-o-n.
do.IPF DTR.PST

(5) a. Gu-re semealab(a)-ek ba-da-uka-te zein-e-k
we.GEN son_and_daughter.PLU.ERG AFF.have./PLU.SYT which_one.ERG
ber-e etxe-a.
he_himself.GEN house

b. Beste nazione guzti-ek, zein-e-k ber-e lengoaje-an beza-la,...
other nation all.PLU.ERG which_one.ERG he_himself.GEN language.LOC SIP

c. Eta ba-zi-h-oa-z-e-n oro, zein ber-e hiri-ra, ber-e
and AFF.go.PLU.SYN.PST all which_one he_himself.GEN village.ALL he_himself.GEN
izen-a e-ma-te-ra.
name give.VEN.ALL

d. Soinulari hau-e-i zein-i ber-e tresn(a)-a-ren balio-a
musician this.PLU.DAT which_one.DAT he_himself.GEN instrument.GEN value
ordain-du behar-ko za-i-o.
compensate must.FUT DIT

(6) a. Nor-k ez d-u maite nor-ber-e sorleku-a?
who.ERG not TRA love.PPR who_he_himself.GEN birthplace

b. Norber-a-k ez d-u ber-e makarr-ik i-kus-ten.
who_he_himself.ERG not TRA he_himself.GEN speck.PAR see.IPF

c. Norber-a-k g-eu-re hutsegite-ak d-it-u-gu.
who_he_himself.ERG we.REF.GEN fault.PLU have.PLU/1PLU.SYT

(7) a. Zer-k d-irudi gezurr-a?
what.ERG seem.SYT lie

b. Zer-k ez z-a-it-u harri-tzen?
what.ERG not 2/.TRA surprise.IPF

c. Zer-k e-ra-kar-tzen g-a-it-u? Maite d-it-u-gu-n gauz(a)-(e)-ekin
what.ERG attract.IPF 1PLU/.TRA love.PPR PLU/1PLU.TRA.NRE thing.PLU.SOC
zer-k adiskide-tzen g-a-it-u?
what.ERG conciliate.IPF 1PLU/.TRA

(8) a. Etxe-an zer lan e-gi-ten d-u-zu?
house.LOC what work do.IPF /2.TRA

b. Zer berri da-kar-ki-gu-zu?
what news bring./1PLU/2.DYT

c. Zer oker e-gi-n d-u, bada, hon-e-k?
what evil do.PEF TRA INF this_one.ERG

d. Zer gogo-k e-ma-n z-i-o-n zerbait e-gi-te-a, lehen inoiz ezer
what desire.ERG give.PEF DTR.PST something do.VEN before ever anything
e-gi-n gabe?
do without.PRE

e. Ze(r) berri?
what news

f. Ba-da-ki-zu-e ze(r) ordu d-en:
AFF.know./2PLU.SYT what hour be.SYN.NCZ:
"later than you think."
"later than you think"

g. Ze(r) gai erabil-tzen da eta zein hiskuntza-ta-n?
what material use.IPF ITR and which language.LOC

(9) a. Ezer on-ik atera ote da-i-te-ke Nazaret-e-tik?
anything good.ZEP.PAR come_out(.RAD) DUB ITR.POT Nazareth.ELA

b. Zer-bait bero-a ere jan behar-ko d-u-gu.
something warm.ZEP.SIN also eat need.FUT /1PLU.TRA

c. Zer-nahi gauz(a)-a ikas-ten d-u.
what_you_want thing.SIN study.IPF TRA

d. Inor egoki-rik aurki-tu al d-u-zu lan har-ta-ra-ko?
someone suitable.ZEP.PAR find.PEF INT /2.TRA work yonder.DES

e. Norbait jakintsu-a behar d-u-gu.
someone wise.ZEP.SIN need.PPR /1PLU.TRA

(10) a. Ez da-uka-zu zer esa-n-ik?
not have./2.SYT what say.ZEP.PAR

b. Han-dik begira-tu-ta, ba-ze-go-en zer i-kus-i-a.
over_there.ELA look.PEC AFF.be.SYN.PST what see.ZEP

c. Bi-ak, elkarr-ekin zer i-kus-i pixka bat ba-d-u-te.
two.ZEP.PLU each_other.SOC what see.ZEP.IDF little_bit a AFF.have./PLU.SYT

(11) a. Moises-e-k e-ra-ntzu-n z-i-e-n ez z-u-te(-n)-la zer
Moses.ERG answer.PEF /PLU/.DTR.PST not have./PLU.SYT.PST.LCZ what
ikara-tu.
be_afraid.ZEP.IDF

b. Jainko-a-ri beldur d-i-o-n-a-k ezer-ga(i)-tik ez d-u zer
God.DAT fear.IDF have.DYT.NRE.ZEP.ERG anything.MOT not have.SYT what
beldur-tu.
be_frightened.ZEP.IDF

c. Zu-k horr-e(n)-la pentsa-tze-a ez da zer harri-tu.
you.ERG that_way think.VEN not be.SYN what be_surprised.ZEP.IDF

(12) a. Non-dik no-ra e-ki-n z-en-i-o-n euskar(a)-a-ri?
where.ELA where.ALL take_up.PEF //2.DTR.PST Basque.DAT

b. Ez n-e-ki-en non-dik no-ra has-i.
not know./1.SYT.PST where.ELA where.ALL begin

c. Non-dik no-ra h-a-bil hi egun guzti-an?
where.ELA where.ALL walk.2SOL.SYN you.SOL day all.LOC

d. Non-dik no-ra da-kar-k?
where.ELA where.ALL bring./2SOL.SYT

(13) a. Inon-dik ino-ra iza-n ezin l-i-te-ke-en gauz(a)-a, ez
somewhere.ELA somewhere.ALL be.RAD NPP ITR.POT.COD.NRE thing not
bat-e-ra eta ez beste-ra.
one.ZEP.ALL and not other.ZEP.ALL

b. Ez d-u-t e-gi-n-go inon-dik inor-a.
not /1.TRA do.FUT somewhere.ELA somewhere.ALL

(14) a. Ez da inon-dik ere aditz-a euskalki(-e)-en arte-ko
not be.SYN somewhere.ELA even verb Basque_dialect.PLU.GEN between.ADN
bereizkuntza-rik larri-en-a.
difference.PAR great.SUP

b. Beste-a, eri-a, ez da asma-tu-a inon-dik ere.
other.ZEP illness not ITR imagine.PEF.SIN somewhere.ELA even

(15) Gaur egun gauz(a)-ak zeharo alda-tu d-ir-a.
today today thing.PLU completely change PLU.ITR

(16) a. Ez da-ki-gu hori-e-ta-z deus.
not know./1PLU.SYT that_one.PLU.INS anything

b. Hil ondo-an ez da deus gehi-ago gu-ta-rik geldi-tzen.
death.IDF remains.LOC not ITR anything more.COP we.PAR remain.IPF

c. Ez da-go deus ere horr-en pare-ko-rik.
not be.SYN anything also that_one.GEN pair.ADN.ZEP.PAR

(17) a. Inor gutxi-k da-ki-z-ki gaur ber-e euskalki-a-ren lege-ak.
someone few.IDF.ERG know.PLU/.SYT today he_himself.GEN Basque_dialect.GEN rule.PLU

b. Orain, Hollywood-e-tik ere deus gutxi e-tor-tzen za-i-gu.
now Hollywood.ELA even something little come.IPF 1PLU/.DIT

c. Inoiz gutxi-ta-n e-tor-tzen da hon-(r)a.
ever few.LOC come.IPF ITR here.ALL

d. Bi gauza, inon gutxi-ta-n idoro da-i-te-z-ke-en-ak.
two thing.IDF somewhere few.LOC find.RAD PLU.ITR.POT.NRE.ZEP.PLU

e. Inor-k ezer gutxi da-ki emakume hon-e-ta-z.
someone.IDF.ERG something little know.SYT woman this.INS

(18) a. Ez da inor-txo ere plaz(a)-an.
not be.SYN someone.DIM even square.LOC

b. Ezer-txo ez n-e-ki-en.
anything.DIM not know./1.SYT.PST

c. Argitaratzaile-a ere, egi(a)-a e-sa-n behar ba-d-u-gu, mire(t)s-ten da zer-txo-bait.
publisher even truth say have_to.PPR CDP./1PLU.TRA be_surprised.IPF ITR something.DIM

(19) a. Aho isil-e-tik ez da ezer ja-ki-ten.
mouth silent.ELA not ITR anything learn.IPF

b. Ez al z-int-u-en atzo goiz-e-an inor-k hemen i-kus-i?
not INT 2/.TRA.PST yesterday morning.LOC anyone.ERG here.LOC see.PEF

c. Inor-k non ze(n)-n ez ze-ki-te-n.
anyone.ERG where.LOC be.SYN.PST.NCZ not know./PLU.SYT.PST

d. Ez z-i-o-te-n inor-k sinets-i nahi.
not //PLU.DTR.PST anyone.ERG believe want.PPR

(20) a. Inor-k i-kus-i al z-a-it-u?— Inor-k ez.
someone.ERG see.PEF INT 2/.TRA anyone.IDF.ERG not

b. Ezer gerta-tu al za-i-zu?— Ezer ez.
something happen INT 2/.DIT anything.IDF not

(21) a. Inor-txo-k ere ez d-i-zu-e poz hori ken-tze-rik iza-n-go.
anyone.DIM.ERG even not /2PLU/.DTR joy that take_from.VEN.PAR have.FUT

b. Inor-txo ere ez ze-n aurki-tzen ber-ta-n.
anyone.DIM even not ITR.PST find.IPF right_there.LOC

c. Ez d-u har-en aztarren-ik inon ere aurki-tzen.
not TRA yonder_one.GEN trace.PAR anywhere.LOC even find.IPF

d. Ez za-i-o inoiz ere damu-tu-ko.
not DIT ever even regret.FUT

e. Neska hori ez za-i-k ino-la ere komeni.
girl that not 2SOL/.DIT in_any_way even convenient.PRE

(22) a. Etxeko-ren bat hil-zori-an d-u-gu, ino-la-z ere.
member_of_the_family.IDF.GEN one.IDF about_to_die have./1PLU.SYT somehow even

b. Inon-dik ere, lapurr-a Txomin da.
somewhere.ELA even thief Txomin be.SYN

c. Deabru-a da-bil, inola-z ere, gu-re eliz(a)-an.
devil be_at_large.SYN somehow even we.GEN church.LOC

(23) a. Inor-k d-u beti erru-a.
someone.ERG. have.SYT always fault

b. Inor-en lepo-tik on-do eda(n)-ten d-u-te.
someone.GEN neck.ELA well drink.IPF /PLU.TRA

(24) a. Ezein jaun-e-k ez d-u nahi mutil gaixto-a e-duki.
any master.IDF.ERG not TRA want.PPR servant bad keep

b. O andere excelente, ezein pare gabe-a ...
O lady exalted any equal.IDF without

c. Hizkuntza integrakuntz(a)-a beste ezein bezain beharr-e-z-ko-a d-u-gu.
language.IDF integration else.IDF any ELP need.IDF.INS.ADN.ZEP have./1PLU.SYT

(25) a. Ez d-u euskar(a)-a-k egun-daino kalte-rik e-karr-i inon-go fede-a-ri.
not TRA Basque.ERG today.TER harm.PAR bring.PEF anywhere.ADN faith.DAT

b. Ez n-a-iz ino-la-ko ezkutapen(-e)-ekin i-bil-i.
not 1.ITR somehow.ADN mystery.PLU.SOC go_around.PEF

(26) a. Atzerri-ra ihes e-gi-te-ko inon-go arrazoi-rik ez da-uka-gu.
foreign_country.ALL escape.IDF make.VEN.ADN somewhere.ADN reason.PAR not have./1PLU.SYT

b. Baina gu-k ez d-u-gu inon-go zalantza-rik horr-e-ta-n.
but we.ERG not have./1PLU.SYT somewhere.ADN doubt.PAR that_one.LOC

(27) a. Zenbait ohoin-e-k ebats-i d-u-ke zu-re zaldi-a.
some thief.ERG steal.PEF TRA.FUT you.GEN horse

b. Gu-ta-rik zenbait hil-en g-a-r-a aurten.
we.PAR some die.FUT 1PLU.ITR this_year

c. Zenbait aipa-tu-ko d-it-u-t.
some mention.FUT PLU/1.TRA

d. Zenbait kritiko-k, berri-z, harrera uzkurr-a e-gi-n d-i-o-te.
some critical.ZEP.ERG however reception stubborn make.PEF //PLU.DTR

(28) a. Gu-re ait(a)-a ez da eliza-ra j-oa-ten, zerbait-en-ga(i)-tik da sozialist(a)-a.
we.GEN father not ITR church.ALL go.IPF something.MOT be.SYN socialist

b. Zer edo zer-ga(i)-tik iza-n-go da.
what or what.MOT be.FUT ITR

(29) a. Pello mozkor-tu-rik ze-go-en, non-bait.
Pello get_drunk.PEF.STA be.SYN.PST somewhere.LOC

b. Non-bait-en sor-tu ze-n euskar(a)-a.
somewhere.LOC originate.PEF ITR.PST Basque_language

(30) a. Lehendakari-a-k hiru-r-(h)ogei-(e)ta hamar urte d-it-u, hor non-bait / non-bait han.
president.ERG seventy year.IDF have.PLU/.SYT there.LOC somewhere.LOC somewhere.LOC over_there.LOC

b. Jainko-a-k mendi-a-ri e-ma-ten d-i-o-n belarr-a ardi-a-k non-bait han aski d-u.
God.ERG mountain.DAT give.IPF DYT.NRE grass sheep.ERG somewhere.LOC over_there.LOC enough.IDF have.SYT

(31) a. Kofesa-tze-ko manamendu hau konpli-tu behar da, noiz iza-n-en bai(t)-t(<*d)a ere, noiz-bait.
confess.VEN.ADN command this fulfill need.PPR ITR when be.FUT ACP.ITR even at_some_time

b. Noiz-bait ager-tu-ko n-a-iz herri-ra.
at_some_time show_up.FUT 1.ITR village.ALL

c. Noiz-bait-en, ez da-ki-t zein urte-ta-n, iza-n-da n-a-go har-en etxe-an.
at_some_time.LOC not know./1.SYT which year.LOC be.PEC be.1.SYN yonder_one.GEN house.LOC

d. Noiz-bait e-torr-i ze-n.
at_some_time come.PEF ITR.PST

(32) a. No-la-bait konpon-du ze-n inor neka-tu gabe.
somehow arrange.PEF ITR.PST anyone bother without.PRE

b. Aitor de-za-gu-n, luza-tu gabe, no-la-bait-e-ko-tzat ets-i
admit.RAD 1PLU.TRA.SUJ.NCZ delay without.PRE somehow.ADN.PRO consider.PEF
d-it-u-ela hon-e-k.
PLU/.TRA.LCZ this_one.ERG

(33) a. Zenbat=nahi arrain e-karr-i-ko d-u-t.
as_much_as_you_want fish bring.FUT /1.TRA
b. Bainan behar d-u-gu, zenbat=nahi dorpe
but must.PPR /1PLU.TRA as_much_as_you_want demanding.IDF
za-i-gu-n.
be.1PLU/.DYN.NCZ
c. Nahi hain-a diru irabaz de-za-ke-zu-e.
want ENP money.IDF earn.RAD /2PLU.TRA.POT
d. Nahi ahal-a e-duki g-en-u-en jan eta edan-a egun har-ta-n.
want MOQ have.PEF /1PLU.TRA.PST food.IDF and drink day yonder.LOC

(34) Ganibet ber bat-e-k de-bak-a ogi-a eta eri-a.
knife same a.ERG cut.SYT bread and finger

(35) a. Sorgin ber hori da-tor hon-(r)a.
witch same that come.SYN here.ALL
b. Sorgin ber-a-k esa-n d-u.
witch same.ERG say.PEF TRA
c. Sorgin ber-a-ren erratz-a-z balia-tu-ko n-a-iz.
witch same.GEN broom.INS make_use_of.FUT 1.ITR
d. Euskaldun ber-ek d-u-te falt(a)-a.
Basque same.PLU.ERG have./PLU.SYT fault

(36) a. Sorgin hori ber-a da-tor hon-(r)a.
witch that she_herself come.SYN here.ALL
b. Sorgin-a-k ber-a-k esa-n d-u.
witch.ERG she_herself.ERG say.PEF TRA
c. Sorgin-a-ren ber-a-ren erratz-a-z balia-tu-ko n-a-iz.
witch.GEN she_herself.GEN broom.INS make_use_of.FUT 1.ITR
d. Euskaldun-ek ber-ek d-u-te falt(a)-a.
Basque.PLU.ERG he_himself.PLU.ERG have./PLU.SYT fault

(37) a. Eta beti historia ber-ber-a.
and always story same_same
b. N-eu-re aberri-tik egotz-i n-a-u-te n-eu-re seme ber-ber-ak.
I.REF.GEN homeland.ELA expel.PEF 1/PLU.TRA I.REF.GEN son same_same.PLU.ERG

(38) a. Irakur-tze-n ari z-a-r-en liburu ber-a-xe irakurr-i d-u-t ni-k ere.
read.VEN.LOC be_busy.PPR 2.ITR.NRE book same.EMP read.PEF /1.TRA I.ERG also

b. Hon-(r)a hemen bila-tzen z-en-u-e(n)-n mutil-a ber-ber-a-xe.
here.ALL here.LOC look_for.IPF /2.TRA.PST.NRE boy he_himself.EMP

(39) a. Ber-a han ze-go-en.
he_himself over_there.LOC be.SYN.PST
b. Ber-a-k da-ki-ke on-gi-en zer e-gi-n.
he_himself.ERG know.SYT.FUT well.SUP what do
c. Zeregin hori e-gi-n de-za-la ber-a-k.
chore that do(.RAD) TRA.SUJ.LCZ he_himself.ERG
d. Ber-ek sine(t)s-ten ez d-u-te-n-a, gu-ri sinets-araz-i
he_himself.PLU.ERG believe.IPF not /PLU.TRA.NRE.ZEP we.DAT believe.CAU
nahi d-i-gu-te.
want.PPR /1PLU/PLU/DTR

(40) a. N-eu-re mutil-a bidal-i gabe, n-e(u)-r(e_h)au e-torr-i n-a-iz.
I.REF.GEN boy send instead.PRE I_myself come.PEF 1.ITR
b. . . . baldin z-e(u)-r(e_h)ori nor ba-z-a-r-a . . .
CDC you_yourself who CDP.be.2.SYN
c. N-e(u)-r(e_h)on-i, egi(a)-a esa-n, bat n-en-torr-e-n Txillardegi-rekin.
I_myself truth say one come.1.SYN.PST Txillardegi.SOC
This form also appears in absolutive function (cf. *DGV*, s.v. *Ni neroni naiz*).
d. Eta z-e(u)-r(e)-ok da-ki-zu-e n-eu-re indar guzi-a-rekin
and you_yourself.PLU.ERG know./2PLU.SYT I.REF.GEN strength all.SOC
serbi-tu d-u-da-la zu-(e)-en ait(a)-a.
serve.PEF /1.TRA.LCZ you.PLU.GEN father
e. H-e(u)-r(e_h)orr-e-k esa(n)-ten d-it-u-k den-ak.
you_yourself.SOL.ERG tell.IPF PLU/2SOL.TRA all.PLU
f. Baina orain-dik g-e(u)-r(e)-ok bakarr-ik da-ki-gu gerta-tu-a.
but still we_ourselves.ERG only.STA know./1PLU.SYT happen.PEF.SIN
g. Behartsu-ak z-e(u)-r(e)-o(-e)kin beti iza-n-go d-it-u-zu-e, ez orde-a
poor.PLU you_yourself.PLU.SOC always have.FUT PLU/2PLU.TRA not however
Ni.
I

(41) a. N-eu-k ere on-gi da-ki-t hori.
I.EMP.ERG also well know./1.SYT that
b. N-eu-k behin-tzat ez d-u-t horr-e(n-)la-ko-rik esa-n.
I.EMP.ERG at_least not /1.TRA that_way.ADN.ZEP.PAR say.PEF
c. Noiz jaik-i z-in-e-n bada z-eu?
when get_up.PEF 2.ITR.PST INF you.EMP

(42) E-karr-i giltz(a)-a, mesede-z. Ni-k da-uka-t, ala?— Bai, zu-k da-uka-zu.
bring key favor.IDF.INS I.ERG have./1.SYT or yes you.ERG have./2.SYT

(43) a. Baina ordu-an ni ez n-in-tz-e-n n-eu.
but time.LOC I not be.1.SYN.PST I.REF
b. N-eu-re on-ak n-eu-k nahi d-it-u-t goza-tu eta maneia-tu.
I.REF.GEN good.PLU I.EMP.ERG want.PPR PLU/1.TRA enjoy and manage
c. N-eu n-a-iz den-o-ta-tik zaharr-en-a.
I.EMP be.1.SYN all.INC.ELA old.SUP.ZEP
d. Ujentu! H-eu al h-a-iz?
Ujentu you.SOL.EMP INT be.2SOL.SYN
e. Ba, h-eu-k ere hori-xe e-gi-n d-u-k.
INF you.SOL.EMP also that.EMP do.PEF /2SOL.TRA
f. Paga e-za-zu z-e(u)-r(e_h)orr-e-k, z-eu-k zor d-u-zu-n-a-z
pay.RAD /2.TRA.IMP you_yourself.ERG you.EMP.ERG debt.IDF /2.TRA.NRE.ZEP.INS
gero-z-tik.
since
g. Gorputz eta arima n-a-iz z-eu-re-a.
body.IDF and soul.IDF be.1.SYN you.EMP.ZEP
h. Zer-en berdin ezin e-ra-ma-n z-en-it-za-ke-en z-eu-r(e)-ekin.
CAC equally NPP take_with.RAD PLU/2.TRA.POT.PST you.EMP.SOC
i. Igor de-za-gu-n aitzin-e-tik, eta da-ra-ma-gu-n
send.RAD /1PLU.TRA.SUJ.NCZ front_part.ELA and carry_off/1PLU.SYT.SUJ.NCZ
g-eu-r(e)-ekin ere.
we.EMP.SOC also
j. Gu g-a-r-a g-eu, ez hobe-ak eta ez txarr-ago-ak, baina g-eu.
we be.1PLU.SYN we.REF not good.COP.PLU and not bad.COP.PLU but we.REF
k. G-eu-k jaso d-u-gu etxe hau eta ez izerdi gutxi-rekin.
we.EMP.ERG build.PEF /1PLU.TRA house this and not sweat little.SOC
l. Z-eu-ek zenbat e-ma-n-go d-i-o-zu-e mutil-a-ri?
you.EMP.PLU.ERG how_much give.FUT //2PLU.DTR boy.DAT
m. Ez n-a-u-zu-e zu-ek aukera-tu, n-eu-k aukera-tu z-a-it-u-z-te-t
not 1/2PLU.TRA you.PLU.ERG choose.PEF I.EMP.ERG choose.PEF 2PLU/1.TRA
zu-ek.
you.PLU

(44) a. Ni-k n-eu-k ez n-it-u-en e-zagu(t)-tu.
I.ERG I_myself.ERG not PLU.1.TRA.PST know.PEF
b. Gu-k g-eu-k da-uka-gu inor-k baino gehi-ago.
we.ERG we_ourselves.ERG have./1PLU.SYT anyone.ERG SRP more.COP

(45) a. Ber(-e_h)on-e-k asma-tzen d-it-u galdera eta erantzun-ak.
he_himself.ERG think_up.IPF PLU/.TRA question.IDF and answer.PLU
b. Bitxi-ok eder, ber(-e_h)ori ez.
jewel.INC beautiful.IDF she_herself not

c. Ber(-e_h)au da interes-ik haundi-en-a e-duki behar l-u-ke-en-a.
he_himself be.SYN interest.PAR great.SUP.ZEP have should.PPR TRA.COD.NRE.ZEP

d. Bada arrazoi horr-en ber(-e_h)on-en-ga(i)-tik ez d-u-t i-kus-i nahi.
INF reason that he_himself.MOT not /1.TRA see want.PPR

e. Maisu, hori itsu jaio-tze-ko, zein-e-k bekatu e-gi-n
Master.IDF that_one blind.IDF be_born.VEN.ADN which_one.ERG sin.IDF do.PEF
z-u-en? Ber(-e_h)orr-e-k ala horr-en guraso-ek?
TRA.PST he_himself.ERG or that_one.GEN parent.PLU.ERG

(46) a. Patxi Zabaleta, Donostia-n jaio-a, eta ber-ta-n
Patxi Zabaleta San_Sebastian.LOC be_born.PEF.ZEP and it_itself.IDF.LOC
bizi d-en-a.
reside.PPR ITR.NRE.ZEP

b. Miren Igartea, hemen jaio-a, eta ber-to-n bizi
Miren Igartea here.LOC be_born.PEF.ZEP and it_itself.IDF.INC.LOC reside.PPR
d-en-a.
ITR.NRE.ZEP

c. Gaur, bakarr-ik bizi n-a-iz ni n-eu-re herri-an ber-ta-n arrotz!
today alone.STA live.PPR 1.ITR I I.REF.GEN land.LOC it_itself.IDF.LOC stranger.IDF

d. Ez z-a-r-a hemen etxe-on ber-to-n bizi ala?— Ez.
not 2.ITR here.LOC house.INC.LOC it_itself.IDF.INC.LOC live.PPR or— no
Goizueta-n ber-to-n baina n-eu-re etxe-an.
Goizueta.LOC it_itself.IDF.INC.LOC but I.REF.GEN house.LOC

(47) a. Orain-txe ber-to-n bidal-du behar d-u-t nor-bait
now.EMP it_itself.IDF.INC.LOC send need.PPR /1.TRA someone
Bizkarrondo(-re)n-e-ra.
Bizkarrondo.GEN.DEL.ALL

b. Orain-txe ber-to-n-txe hil behar ba-n-u ere, berdin
now.EMP it_itself.IDF.INC.EMP die have_to.PPR CDP./1.TRA.COD even equally
esa-n-go n-u-ke.
say.FUT /1.TRA.COD

c. Orain-txe ber-to-n n-oa-ki-o atze-tik.
now.EMP it_itself.IDF.INC.LOC go./1.DYN back_part.ELA

d. Eta gaur ber-ta-n al z-oa-z?
and today it_itself.IDF.LOC INT go.2.SYN

e. Bihar ber-ta-n-txe behar d-u-t zu-re erantzun-a.
tomorrow it_itself.IDF.LOC.EMP need.PPR /1.TRA you.GEN answer

(48) a. Artzain oro-k bil-tzen d-it-u ardi-ak arratsalde-an.
shepherd each.IDF.ERG gather.IPF PLU/.TRA sheep.PLU evening.LOC

b. Beste nazione oro-k uste d-u-te ezin deus ere skriba
other nation all.IDF.ERG think.PPR /PLU.TRA NPP anything even write.RAD
da-i-te(-ke)-ela lengoaje har-ta-n.
ITR.POT.LCZ language yonder.LOC

c. Justo oro igan-en da ber-ta-n goi-ti(k) aire-an.
just all.IDF rise.FUT ITR it_itself.IDF.LOC top.ELA air.LOC

d. ... egun oro mez(a)-a e-ntzu-te-a ...
day all.IDF mass hear.VEN

e. Lur oro-k ba-d-u buztin eta harea.
soil all.IDF.ERG AFF.have.SYT clay.IDF and sand.IDF

f. ... bai eta ere neska gazte oro-ri etsenplu e-ma-i-ten.
yes and also girl young all.IDF.DAT example.IDF give.IPF

(49) a. Gauza hai-ek oro ebats-i gauz(a)-ak d-ir-a, eta
thing yonder.PLU all.IDF steal.PEF thing.PLU be.PLU.SYN and
hai(-e)-en jabe-ak oro hil-ak.
yonder_one.PLU.GEN owner.PLU all.IDF dead.PLU

b. Ber-e bekatu-ak oro ba-d-it-u ere konfesa-tu, ...
he_himself.GEN sin.PLU all.IDF CDP.PLU/.TRA even confess.PEF

c. Berri hori(-e)-en oro-ren ja-ki-te-z ...
report that.PLU.GEN all.IDF.GEN know.VEN.IDF.INS

d. Hori(-e)-en-ga(i)-tik oro-ga(i)-tik zer da zu(-e)-en pagu-a?
that_one.PLU.MOT all.IDF.MOT what be.SYN you.PLU.GEN payment

e. N-eu-re bekatu-e-z oro-z d-u-da-n barkamendu-a.
I.REF.GEN sin.PLU.INS all.IDF.INS have./1.SYT.NCZ forgiveness

(50) a. En-e ongi=egin-ak ere orai(n) oro gaitz d-ir-a.
I.GEN good_deed.PLU even now all.IDF bad.IDF be.PLU.SYN

b. Saindu-ak ere ordu har-ta-n oro e-go-n-en isil-ik.
Saint.PLU even moment yonder.LOC all.IDF be.FUT silent.STA

c. Etxe-ko berri-ak kanpo-an oro sala-tzen d-i-z-ki-zu.
house.ADN news.PLU outside.LOC all.IDF disclose.IPF PLU/2/.DTR

d. Alab(a)-a d-u-te-n-e-i esa-n-en d-i-e-t oro-ri ...
daughter have./PLU.SYT.NRE.ZEP.PLU.DAT say.FUT /PLU/1.DTR all.IDF.DAT

(51) a. Ni baita-n d-u-ke-zu adiskide bat.
I in.LOC have./2.SYT.FUT friend a

b. Har-tu d-u-te-n plazer oro ordu-an i-ra-gan da-te.
take.PEF /PLU.TRA.NRE pleasure all.IDF that_time.LOC pass_by.PEF ITR.FUT

c. Eta ordu-an denbora on-a-ren seinale-a da-te-ke.
and that_time.LOC weather good.GEN sign be.SYN.FUT

d. Non-dik d-u-ke-zu ur bizi hura?
where.ELA have./2.SYT.FUT water living yonder

e. Gauza ber-a e-zagu(t)-tu d-u-ke-zu z-e(u)-r(e_h)orr-e-k ere.
thing same experience.PEF /2/TRA.FUT you_yourself.ERG also

f. Zer e-ma-n-en d-i-o-zu, edo zer on d-u-ke zu-re-gan-(d)ik?
what give.FUT //2.DTR or what good have.SYT.FUT you.ELA

g. Lan hori-ek ber(-e)-en sari on-a da-kar-ke-te.
work that.PLU.ERG it_itself.PLU.GEN reward good bring./PLU.SYT.FUT

h. Har-k ba-da-ki-ke zer e-gi-n.
yonder_one.ERG AFF.know.SYT.FUT what do

i. Ez d-u-ke hori nahi iza-n Jesu=Kristo-k.
not TRA.FUT that want have.PEF Jesus_Christ

j. Ni-re emazte-a-k amets e-gi-n d-u-ke.
I.GEN wife.ERG dream.IDF make.PEF TRA.FUT

k. I-kus-i d-u-ke bi aldi-z bizkitarte-an!
see.PEF TRA.FUT two time.IDF.INS meanwhile.LOC

l. Ber-e-ha(r-en)-la hemen d-u-ke-zu-e etxe-k(o)' andre-a.
right_away here.LOC have./2PLU.SYT.FUT house.ADN lady

m. Bai, bai, ber-e-a d-u-ke segur-ki.
yes yes she_herself.GEN.ZEP have.SYT.FUT surely

n. Zer d-u-ke-gu ja(n)-te-ko edo eda(n)-te-ko?
what have./1PLU.SYT.FUT eat.VEN.ADN or drink.VEN.ADN

o. Zer buruhauste berri d-u-ke-t?
what problem new have./1.SYT.FUT

p. Satan-e-k ifernu-tik e-gi-n d-u-ke burla.
Satan.ERG hell.ELA make.PEF TRA.FUT scoff.IDF

q. Han d-ir-a-te-ke erro-tik herritarr-ak harri-tu-rik.
over_there.LOC PLU.ITR.FUT root.ELA villager.PLU get_astonished.PEF.STA

r. Orai-ko-an zu-re aldi(a) ze-n, noiz da-te-ke gu-re-a?
now.ADN.LOC you.GEN turn be.SYN.PST when be.SYN.FUT we.GEN.ZEP

s. Ja-ki-n d-u-ke-zu orain d-u-ela hamar egun Hernandorena,
find_out.PEF /2.TRA.FUT now have.SYT.LCI ten day.IDF Hernandorena
Elizondo-ko alkate-a, Izpegi-n hil z-u-te(-n)-la.
Elizondo.ADN mayor Izpegi.LOC kill.PEF /PLU.TRA.PST.LCZ

Chapter 29

(1) a. Ba-da-tor zu-re am-a eta oso haserre da zu-rekin.
AFF.come.SYN you.GEN mother.IDF and very be_mad.PPR ITR you.SOC

b. Ba-ze-torr-e-k hi-re ama eta oso haserre d-u-k
AFF.come.SYN.ALC.SOL you.SOL.GEN mother.IDF and very be_mad.PPR ITR.ALC.SOL
hi-rekin.
you.SOL.SOC

c. Ba-ze-torr-e-n hi-re ama eta oso haserre
AFF.come.SYN.ALC.SOL.FEM you.SOL.GEN mother.IDF and very be_mad.PPR
d-u-n hi-rekin.
ITR.ALC.SOL.FEM you.SOL.SOC

(2) a. Zu-re ama-k irabaz-i d-u diru-a, baina zu-re aita-k ez
you.GEN mother.IDF.ERG earn.PEF TRA money but you.GEN father.IDF.ERG not
da-ki.
know.SYT

b. Hi-re ama-k irabaz-i d-i-k diru-a, baina hi-re
you.SOL.GEN mother.IDF.ERG earn.PEF TRA.ALC.SOL money but you.SOL.GEN
aita-k ez ze-ki-k.
father.IDF.ERG not know.SYT.ALC.SOL

c. Hi-re ama-k irabaz-i d-i-n diru-a, baina hi-re
you.SOL.GEN mother.IDF.ERG earn.PEF TRA.ALC.SOL.FEM money but you.SOL.GEN
aita-k ez ze-ki-n.
father.ERG not know.SYT.ALC.SOL.FEM

(3) a. Zu-re beldur n-a-iz eta inor-k ez d-i-t beldur hori
you.GEN be_afraid_of.PPR 1.ITR and anyone.ERG not /1/.DTR fear that
ken-du-ko.
take_away.FUT

b. Hi-re beldur n-a-u-k eta inor-k ez z-i-da-k beldur
you.SOL.GEN fear.PPR 1.ITR.ALC.SOL and anyone.ERG not /1/.DTR.ALC.SOL fear
hori ken-du-ko.
that take_away.FUT

c. Hi-re beldur n-a-u-n eta inor-k ez z-i-da-n
you.SOL.GEN fear.PPR 1.ITR.ALC.SOL.FEM and anyone.ERG not /1/DTR.ALC.SOL.FEM
beldur hori ken-du-ko.
fear that take_away.FUT

(4) a. Aita-k gona gorri-a eros-i d-i-o zu-re ama-ri, baina ez
father.IDF.ERG skirt red buy.PEF DTR you.GEN mother.DAT but not
da-ki-t zer-ga(i)-tik.
know./1.SYT what.MOT

b. Aita-k gona gorri-a eros-i z-i-o-k hi-re ama-ri,
father.IDF.ERG skirt red buy.PEF DTR.ALC.SOL you.SOL.GEN mother.IDF.DAT

baina ez ze-ki-a-t zer-ga(i)-tik.
but not know./1.SYT.ALC.SOL what.MOT

c. Aita-k gona gorri-a eros-i z-i-o-n hi-re ama-ri,
father.IDF.ERG skirt red buy.PEF DTR.ALC.SOL.FEM you.SOL.GEN mother.IDF.DAT
baina ez ze-ki-na-t zer-ga(i)-tik.
but not know./1.SYT.ALC.SOL.FEM what.MOT

(5) Nor ausar(t)-tu d-u-k hi zauri-tze-ra?
who dare.PEF ITR.ALC.SOL you.SOL injure.VEN.ALL

(6) a. Zer e-gi-n gogo d-u-zu?
what do intend.PPR /2.TRA

b. Zer uste z-en-u-en hemen aurki-tu?
what expect.PPR /2.TRA.PST here.LOC find

c. Hobe-ko d-u-zu jan.
do_better.FUT /2.TRA eat

(7) a. Nor-i e-ma-n nahi d-i-o-zu?
who.DAT give want.PPR //2.DTR

b. Ni-k nor-i e-ma-te-a nahi d-u-zu?
I.ERG who.DAT give.VEN want.PPR /2.TRA

(8) a. Ezin asma-tu d-u-t haserre-tu gabe hitz bat esa(n)-te-n.
NPP manage /1.TRA get_angry without.PRE word one say.VEN.LOC

b. ... e-ma-n nahi d-i-o-te-n-a eska-tze-n ohi-tu d-u-te-la
... give want.PPR //PLU.DTR.NRE.ZEP ask.VEN.LOC accustom.PEF /PLU.TRA.LCZ
jende-a.
people

c. Ez al z-a-r-e-te has-i euskar(a)-a-z ida(t)z-te-n?
not INT 2PLU.ITR start.PEF Basque_language.INS write.VEN.LOC

(9) a. Ba-n-oa zer-bait eros-te-ra.
AFF.go.1.SYN something buy.VEN.ALL

b. Permiti ie-za-gu-k urdalde har-ta-ra j-oa-te-ra.
allow.RAD /1PLU/2SOL.DTR.IMP herd_of_swine yonder.ALL go.VEN.ALL

c. Atzen-e-an ausar(t)-tu n-a-iz bertso-ak papel-e-an jar-tze-ra ere.
end.LOC dare.PEF 1.ITR verse.PLU paper.LOC put_down.VEN.ALL also

(10) Ber-e-ha(r-en)-la etxera-tze-ko agin-tzen d-i-zu-e aita-k.
immediately come_home.VEN.ADN order.IPF /2PLU/.DTR father.IDF.ERG

(11) Etxe-an e-go-te-a e-ra-baki d-u-gu.
house.LOC stay.VEN decide.PEF /1PLU.TRA

(12) Atzo e-ra-baki g-en-u-en zu e-tor-tze-a.
yesterday decide.PEF /1PLU.TRA.PST you come.VEN

(13) a. (. . .) eta kosta e-gi-ten zi-tza-i-da-n agerpen hura ain-tzat har-tze-a.
(. . .) and cost.PPR do.IPF 1/.DIT.PST appearance yonder serious.PRO take.VEN

b. Ez ze-n ha(r-en)-la-ko-a ni-k aurki-tze-a pentsa-tzen n-u-en
not be.SYN.PST that_way.ADN.ZEP I.ERG find.VEN think.IPF /1.TRA.PST
eguraldi-a.
weather

c. Zu-k eta ni-k ja-ki-te-a aski da.
you.ERG and I.ERG know.VEN sufficient.IDF be.SYN

d. Ez da on gizon-a bakarr-ik e-go-te-a.
not be.SYN good.IDF man alone.STA be.VEN

e. Zer-k e-ra-go(t)z-ten d-u ni bataia-tze-a?
what.ERG hinder.IPF TRA I baptize.VEN

f. Nahi=eta=nahiez-ko-a da zu hon-(r)a e-tor-tze-a.
want_and_not_want.ADN.ZEP be.SYN you here.ALL come.VEN

g. Ja(n)-te-a-k ez z-i-o-n hizket(a)-an e-gi-te-a gal-eraz-ten.
eat.VEN.ERG not DTR.PST talk.LOC do.VEN lose.CAU.IPF

h. Ba-z-i-te-ke-en den-a "happy end" bat-e-z buka-tze-a.
AFF.be.SYN.POT.PST everything "happy end" a.IDF.INS end.VEN

i. Kosta za-i-t ni-re laguntz(a)-a har-k on(h)ar-tze-a.
cost.PPR 1/.DIT I.GEN help yonder_one.ERG accept.VEN

(14) a. Hamaika bider damu-tu zi-tza-i-o-n etxe-tik irten-a.
eleven time.IDF regret.PEF DIT.PST house.ELA leave.PEF.ZEP

b. . . . damu d-u-t ez hemen geldi-tu-a.
. . . regret.PPR /1.TRA not here.LOC stay.PEF.ZEP

c. Gezurr-a d-irudi Xabier hain azkar ber-e on-e-ta-ra
lie seem.SYT Xabier so quickly he_himself.GEN good.ZEP.PLU.ALL
e-torr-i-a.
come.PEF.ZEP

d. Seme (h)on-e-k da-za(g)u ber-e donga-ro e-gi-n-a.
son this.ERG acknowledge.SYT he_himself.GEN wrongly do.PEF.ZEP

e. Asko senti-tzen d-u-t eguraldi tzar hon-e-ta-n zu hon(-r)a-ino e-karr-i
much regret.IPF /1.TRA weather bad this.LOC you here.TER bring.PEF
iza-n-a.
be/have.PEF.ZEP

(15) a. Asko poz-ten n-a-iz zu-ri atsegin e-ma-te-a.
much be_happy.IPF 1.ITR you.DAT pleasure.IDF give.VEN

b. Asko poz-ten n-a-iz zu-ri atsegin e-ma-te-a-z.
much be_happy.IPF 1.ITR you.DAT pleasure.IDF give.VEN.INS
c. Azko poz-ten n-a-u zu-ri atsegin e-ma-te-a-k.
much make_happy.IPF 1/.TRA you.DAT pleasure.IDF give.VEN.ERG

(16) a. Asko poz-ten n-a-iz zu-ri atsegin e-ma-n-a.
much be_happy.IPF 1.ITR you.DAT pleasure.IDF give.PEF.ZEP
b. Asko poz-ten n-a-iz zu-ri atsegin e-ma-n-a-z.
much be_happy.IPF 1.ITR you.DAT pleasure.IDF give.PEF.ZEP.INS
c. Asko poz-ten n-a-u zu-ri atsegin e-ma-n-a-k.
much make_happy.IPF 1/.TRA you.DAT pleasure give.PEF.ZEP.ERG

(17) a. Ez n-e-ki-en ohe-ra j-oa-n edo ber-ta-n gera.
not know./1.SYT.PST bed.ALL go.RAD or it_itself.LOC stay.RAD
b. Ez da-ki-gu no-la joka.
not know./1PLU.SYT how play.RAD
c. Ez da-ki-t aldizkari-ak nor-i e-ma-n.
not know./1.SYT magazine.PLU who.DAT give(.RAD)

Chapter 30

(1) a. Esne-a noiz da-kar-k baina?
milk when bring./2SOL.SYT but
b. Ez n-a-iz baina eztabaid(a)-e-ta-n has-i-ko.
not 1.ITR but argument.PLU.LOC start.FUT

(2) . . . erdi behar, edo hil.
. . . give_birth must.PPR or die

(3) a. Mixterio-ak, edo gu-k ezin konprenitu-z-ko gauz(a)-ak, ez ote
mystery.PLU or we.ERG NPP understand.PTC.IDF.INS.ADN thing.PLU not DUB
d-ir-a, bada, Erlijione-an baizik aurki-tzen?
be.PLU.SYN INF religion.LOC only find.IPF
b. Bat edo beste-a: edo gezurr-a z-io-te-n Apostolu-ek, edo
one.IDF or other.ZEP or lie tell./PLU.SYT.PST Apostle.PLU.ERG or
Judu-ak hobendun-ak z-ir-e-n.
Jew.PLU guilty.PLU be.PLU.SYN.PST

(4) a. Bihar edo etzi e-torr-i-ko (al) z-a-r-e-te?
tomorrow or the_day_after_tomorrow come.FUT INT 2PLU.ITR
b. Bihar ala etzi e-torr-i-ko z-a-r-e-te?
tomorrow or the_day_after_tomorrow come.FUT 2PLU.ITR

c. Bihar edo etzi e-torr-i-ko z-a-r-e-te?
tomorrow or the_day_after_tomorrow come.FUT 2PLU.ITR

(5) a. Hil-ak ala bizi-ak d-ir-a?
dead.PLU or alive.PLU be.PLU.SYN

b. Zein parte estima-tzen d-u-zu hobe, Jainko-a-ren-a ala Deabru-a-ren-a?
which share consider.IPF /2.TRA good.COP.IDF god.GEN.ZEP or devil.GEN.ZEP

c. Zein-e-k bekatu e-gi-n d-u, hon-e-k ala hon-en
which_one.ERG sin.IDF do.PEF TRA this_one.ERG or this_one.GEN
ait(a-)am(a)-ek ...?
father(_and)_mother.PLU.ERG

d. Mendi-ra j-oa-n-go z-a-r-a ala etxe-an geldi-tu-ko z-a-r-a?
mountain.ALL go.FUT 2.ITR or house.LOC stay.FUT 2.ITR

e. Ama emazte z-u-e(n)-n (in the manuscript: *luyen*) ala ez, nahi
mother.IDF woman.IDF have.SYT.PST.NCZ or not want.PPR
n-u-ke galde-tu.
/1.TRA.COD ask

f. Ez d-i-gu axol(a)-a Cayatte zuzen ala oker da-go-en
not have./1PLU.DYT interest Cayatte right.IDF or wrong.IDF be.SYN.NCZ
ja-ki-te-a-k.
know.VEN.ERG

g. Ez n-e-ki-en Euskal Herri-tik kanpo bizi nahi n-u-e(n)-n
not know./1.SYT.PST. Basque Country.ELA outside live want.PPR /1.TRA.PST.NCZ
ala ez.
or not

h. Joxe-k ez z-i-da-n esa-n e-torr-i-ko ze(-n)-n ala ez.
Joseph.ERG not /1/.DTR.PST tell.PEF come.FUT ITR.PST.NCZ or not

i. Bihar e-ra-baki-ko d-u-gu j-oan-go g-a-r-en ala gera-tu e-gi-n-go
tomorrow decide.FUT /1PLU.TRA go.FUT 1PLU.ITR.NCZ or stay do.FUT
g-a-r-en.
1PLU.ITR.NCZ

j. Bihar e-ra-baki-ko d-u-gu j-oa-n ala gera.
tomorrow decide.FUT /1PLU.TRA go.RAD or stay.RAD

(6) a. Andrea eder eta aberats-a, edo ero edo farat(a)-a.
woman beautiful.IDF and rich or crazy.IDF or conceited

b. Edo dantzari-a h-a-iz, edo ez h-a-iz dantzari-a. Beste aukera-rik ez
or dancer be.2SOL.SYN or not be.2SOL.SYN dancer other option.PAR not
da-go.
be.SYN

c. Bi-e-ta-tik bat: gu-rekin e-torr-i behar duk, edo etxe-an
two.ZEP.PLU.ELA one.IDF we.SOC come have_to.PPR /2SOL.TRA or house.LOC
bakarr-ik geldi-tu.
alone.STA stay

d. ... hil edo bizi-ko auzi-a d-u-gu-la ...
... death.IDF or life.ADN matter have./1.SYT.LCZ

(7) a. Zein nahi d-u-zu-e larga d-ie-za-zu-e-da-n? Barrabas,
which_one want.PPR /2PLU.TRA release.RAD /2PLU/1.DTR.SUJ.NCZ Barrabas
ala Iesus, dei-tzen d-en-a Christ?
or Jesus call.IPF ITR.NRE.ZEP Christ

b. Zein nahi d-u-zu-e libro igor de-za-da-n, Barrabas edo
which_one want.PPR /2PLU.TRA free.IDF remit.RAD /1.TRA.SUJ.NCZ Barrabas or
Jesus, Kristo dei-tu-a d-en-a?
Jesus Christ call.PEF.SIN ITR.NRE.ZEP

(8) a. Bai bat-a bai beste-a e-torr-i d-ir-a. (rarely also *e-torr-i da*)
yes one.ZEP yes other.ZEP come.PEF PLU.ITR come.PEF ITR

b. Bai bat-a eta bai beste-a e-torr-i d-ir-a. (also *e-torr-i da*)
yes one.ZEP and yes other.ZEP come.PEF PLU.ITR come.PEF ITR

c. Bai bat-a, bai eta beste-a e-torr-i d-ir-a. (also *e-torr-i da*)
yes one.ZEP yes and other.ZEP come.PEF PLU.ITR come.PEF ITR

(9) a. Bai zeru-an bai lurr-e-an ...
yes heaven.LOC yes earth.LOC

b. Bai Testamendu Zaharr-a, bai Berri-a Jainko-a-ren izen-a-z bete-ak d-ir-a.
yes Testament Old yes New.ZEP God.GEN name.INS full.PLU be.PLU.SYN

c. Hau (da) teatrogizon oso-a, bai antzezlari bai komeri=sortzaile
this_one be.SYN man_of_the_theater complete yes actor.IDF yes playwright.IDF
lege-z.
SIP

d. Eta desegi-n z-it-u-en lurr-a-ren gain-e-an bizi z-ir-e(-n)-n
and destroy.PEF PLU/.TRA.PST earth.GEN top.LOC live.PPR PLU.ITR.PST.NRE
guzti-ak, gizon-a-gan-dik abere-ra-ino, bai arrastakari-ak eta bai
all.PLU human_being.ELA animal.TER yes creeping_animal.PLU and yes
zeru-ko hegazti-ak.
sky.ADN bird.PLU

e. ... bai lehen, bai eta orai(n) ...
... yes before yes and now

f. ... beso-ak zabal-ik har-tu d-u-te kritiko-ek, bai beratxek
... arm.PLU open.STA receive.PEF /PLU.TRA critic.PLU.ERG yes mild.ZEP.PLU.ERG

eta bai xorrotz-ek.
and yes demanding.ZEP.PLU.ERG

(10) a. Ez apaiz-ik ez moja-rik e-torr-i da.
not priest.PAR not nun.PAR come.PEF ITR
b. Ez apaiz-ik eta ez moja-rik e-torr-i da.
not priest.PAR and not nun.PAR come.PEF ITR
c. Ez apaiz-ik ez eta moja-rik e-torr-i da.
not priest.PAR not and nun.PAR come.PEF ITR
d. Ez apaiz-ik ez moja-rik ez da e-torr-i.
not priest.PAR not nun.PAR not ITR come.PEF
e. Apaiz-ik ez moja-rik ez da e-torr-i.
priest.PAR not nun.PAR not ITR come.PEF

(11) a. Ez ber-a-k lan-ik e-gi-ten d-u, ez beste-ri e-gi-te-n utz-i.
not he_himself.ERG work.PAR do.IPF TRA not other.ZEP.IDF.DAT do.VEN.LOC let
b. Ez haragi-a-k, ez odol-a-k hori e-ra-kuts-i d-i-zu . . .
not flesh.ERG not blood.ERG that reveal.PEF /2/.DTR
c. Ez haragi-k ez odol-e-k, ez bai(t)-t(<*d)-i-zu adi-eraz-i hori
not flesh.IDF.ERG not blood.IDF.ERG not ACP./2/.DTR understand.CAU.PEF that
zu-ri . . .
you.DAT
d. Haragi-a-k ez odol-a-k ez d-i-k (for the original *eztrauc*)
flesh.ERG not blood.ERG not /2SOL/.DTR
hori revela-tu . . .
that reveal.PEF
e. Ez d-u-te jakitate-rik ez aberastasun-ik.
not have./PLU.SYT wisdom.PAR not wealth.PAR
f. Ez n-in-tz-e-n oroit, ez zenbat, ez nola-ko bertso-ak iza-n
not 1.ITR.PST remember.PPR not how_many not how.ADN verse.PLU be.PEF
z-ir-e-n.
PLU.ITR.PST
g. Ez z-it-u-en ez hitz-ak leun-du, ez gorroto-ak estal-i.
not PLU/.TRA.PST not word.PLU soften.PEF not hatred.PLU hide.PEF
h. Emazte-rik ez d-en leku-an ez da-kus-a-t plazer-ik, ez gizon-a
woman.PAR not be.SYN.NRE place.LOC not see./1.SYT pleasure.PAR not man
ez etxe-a behin ere xahu-rik.
not house once even clean.STA
i. Inor-en zilarr-ik, ez urre-rik, ez soineko-rik ez d-u-t nahi iza-n.
anyone.GEN silver.PAR not gold.PAR not apparel.PAR not /1.TRA want have.PEF

j. Gaur-ko "sasi=teatroan" ez gai ez hitz eta ez ipuin-ik
today.ADN "pseudo-theater".LOC not theme.IDF not word.IDF and not story.PAR
behar ez d-ela e-sa(n)-ten d-u-te-n-ak ba-d-ir-a.
need.PPR not ITR.LCZ say.IPF /PLU.TRA.NRE.ZEP.PLU AFF.be.PLU.SYN

(12) a. Gu-re euskaldun teatrogile-ak, nahi-z egile eta nahi-z
we.GEN Basque playwright.PLU.ERG want.IDF.INS writer.IDF and want.IDF.INS
itzultzaile, lan-e-an ja-rrai-tu-ko d-u-te-la ez d-u-gu batere
translator.IDF.INS work.LOC continue.FUT /PLU.TRA.LCZ not /1PLU.TRA at_all
zalantza-rik.
doubt.PAR

b. Orain, nahi-z bat-e-ra-ko eta nahi-z beste-ra-ko berandu da.
now want.IDF.INS one.ZEP.DES and want.IDF.INS other.ZEP.DES too_late be.SYN

c. Han beti zegoen ontzi-ren bat bete nahi-z hu(t)s-tu
over_there.LOC always be.SYN.PST ship.IDF.GEN one load want.IDF.INS unload
beharra
need

d. Nahi-z sinis-tu, nahi-z ez, esan behar dut, gazte-txo-a
want.IDF.INS believe want.IDF.INS not say have_to.PPR /1.TRA young.ZEP.DIM
n-in-tz-e(-n)-la, irakurr-i eta azal-du ohi n-it-u-e(-n)-la
be.1.SYN.PST.LCI read and interpret use_to.PPR PLU/1.TRA.PST.LCZ
Fedro-ren latin-e-z-ko ipuin-ak.
Phaedrus.GEN Latin.IDF.INS.ADN fable.PLU

e. Nahi-z d-ela zamari-a nahi-z gizon-a, ez da bizi-ko.
want.IDF.INS be.SYN.LCZ beast_of_burden want.IDF.INS man not ITR live.FUT

f. Nahi-z d-ela Italia, oro-bat Frantzia, bi-e-ta-n bila-tu
want.IDF.INS be.SYN.LCZ Italy all_one France two.ZEP.PLU.LOC encounter.PEF
d-u-t anitz malizia.
/1.TRA much malice

(13) a. Edo egi(a)-a-z nahi-z gezurr-a-z elika-tu-ko n-a-iz.
or truth.INS want.IDF.INS lie.INS take_nourishment.FUT 1.ITR

b. Nahi-z d-oa-n Frantzia-ra edo Espainia-ra . . .
want.IDF.INS go.SYN.NCZ France.ALL or Spain.ALL

c. . . . edo lehen edo gero . . .
. . . or before or later

d. Zer-en, nahi-z gizon-a, nahi-z emazteki-a, nahi-z noble-a,
CAC want.IDF.INS man want.IDF.INS woman want.IDF.INS nobleman
enperadore-a, edo errege-ren ume-a, edo har-en leinu-ko-a;
emperor or king.IDF.GEN son or yonder_one.GEN lineage.ADN.ZEP

nahi-z etorki-rik apal-en-e-tik, edo txiki-en-e-tik hel-du
want.IDF.INS origin.PAR low.SUP.ZEP.ELA or humble.SUP.ZEP.ELA arrive.PEF
d-en-a; nahi-z aberats-a, nahi-z probe-a, nahi-z gazte-a,
ITR.NRE.ZEP want.IDF.INS rich.ZEP want.IDF.INS poor.ZEP want.IDF.INS young.ZEP
nahi-z zaharr-a; baldin ugatz-e-an diti-a-rekin edan z-u-e(n)-n
want.IDF.INS old.ZEP CDP breast.LOC mother's_milk.SOC drink.PEF TRA.PST.NRE
hizkuntz(a)-a-z beste-rik ez ba-da-ki, gauza segur-a da, hogei
language.INS other.ZEP.PAR not CDP.know.SYN thing certain be.SYN twenty
egun-en bide-an beste herri-e-ta-ko hizkuntz(a)-ak behar-tu gabe,
day.IDF.GEN trip.LOC other country.PLU.ADN language.PLU need without.PRE
ezin d-oa-ke-la. (Batua: *d-oa-ke-ela*)
NPP go.SYN.POT.LCZ

(14) a. Zein organo-a, zein biolin(a)-a, zein kitarr(a)-a, zein danbolin(a)-a,
whether organ whether violin whether guitar whether drum
zein tronp(a)-a, zein zartagin zahar bat, guzti(-e)-ekin jo-tzen da
whether Jew's harp whether frying_pan old a.IDF all.ZEP.PLU.SOC play.IPF ITR
soinu-a.
music

b. Hil zein bizi, senarr-a ahal-ik arin-en i-kus-i nahi
dead.IDF whether alive.IDF husband possible.ZEP.PAR fast.SUP.IDF see want
iza-n d-u-da-la-ko.
have.PEF /1.TRA.LCZ.ADN

c. Idatz-i zein idatz-i ez, orde-a, ez d-u-t inoiz aha(t)z-tu-ko.
write whether write not however not /1.TRA ever forget.FUT

d. Berri-ta-n olio hau da on-en-a, bai gordin-ik ja(n)-te-ko
fresh.ZEP.IDF.LOC oil this be.SYN good.SUP yes uncooked.STA eat.VEN.ADN
zein lapiko-ra-ko.
whether pot.DES

(15) a. D-ela koinaka, d-ela bermut, d-ela chartreuse,
be.SYN.LCZ cognac.IDF be.SYN.LCZ vermouth.IDF be.SYN.LCZ chartreuse.IDF
zer-nahi izen-e-ta-ko edari guzti-e-ta-rik urrats guzti-e-z
what(_you)_want name.PLU.ADN drink all.PLU.ELA step all.PLU.INS
eda(n)-te-ko.
drink.VEN.ADN

b. . . . d-ela irakur-tze-an, d-ela mintza-tze-an . . .
. . . be.SYN.LCZ read.VEN.DEF.LOC be.SYN.LCZ speak.VEN.DEF.LOC

(16) a. Jende-a, nor zaldi-z, nor oin-e-z, e-torr-i ze-n.
people who horse.IDF.INS who foot.IDF.INS come.PEF ITR.PST

b. Alde guzti-e-ta-n, no-n gehi-ago no-n gutxi-ago . . .
area all.PLU.LOC where.LOC more.COP.IDF where.LOC few.COP.IDF . . .

c. Bi jokabide i-kus-ten d-it-u-t nagusi, noiz bat-a, noiz
two mode_of_conduct.IDF see.IPF PLU/1.TRA main.IDF when one.ZEP when
beste-a.
other.ZEP

d. Behin Donostia-ra j-oa-ten g-a-r-a, behin Bilbo-ra.
once San_Sebastian.ALL go.IPF 1PLU.ITR once Bilbao.ALL

(17) a. Bainan lur on-e-an erein-a iza-n d-en-a, hura da hitz-a
but soil good.LOC sow.PEF.SIN be.PEF ITR.NRE.ZEP yonder_one be.SYN word
e-ntzu-ten eta adi-tzen d-u-en-a, eta fruitu da-karr-en-a;
hear.IPF and understand.IPF TRA.NRE.ZEP and fruit.IDF bear.SYT.NRE.ZEP
zein-e-k bat-en-tzat ehun, zein-e-k hirur(h)ogei, zein-e-k
which_one.ERG one.IDF.BEN hundred which_one.ERG sixty which_one.ERG
hogei(-e)t(a-h)amar.
thirty

b. Eta e-ma-n z-u-te-n fruitu, no-n bat-a-rik ehun, no-n
and give.PEF /PLU.TRA.PST fruit.IDF where.LOC one.ZEP.ELA hundred where.LOC
hirur(h)ogei eta no-n hogei(-e)t(a-h)amar.
sixty and where.LOC thirty

c. Noiz bat-en-tzat ehun, noiz hirur(h)ogei, noiz hogei(e-)t(a-h)amar
when one.IDF.BEN hundred when sixty when thirty.

d. Hon-e(n-)la behin bat-e-k eta behin beste-a-k garai(t)-tzen z-u-en.
this_way once one.ZEP.IDF.ERG and once other.ZEP.ERG triumph.IPF TRA.PST

e. Hemen behin iparr-a-k eta behin hego-a-k jo-tzen d-u.
here.LOC once north_wind.ERG and once south_wind.ERG blow.IPF TRA

(18) a. Bada, edo ja(n)-ten ba-d-u-zu-e, edo eda(n)-ten ba-d-u-zu-e, edo zer-bait
INF or eat.IPF CDP./2PLU.TRA or drink.IPF CDP./2PLU.TRA or something
beste-rik e-gi-ten ba-d-u-zu-e, guzti-a Jainko-a-ren gloria-ta-n
else.PAR do.IPF CDP./2PLU.TRA all.ZEP God.GEN glory.IDF.LOC
e-gi-zu-e.
do.2PLU.SYT.IMP

b. Ber-a-z, edo engana-tu g-a-it-u Jainko-a-k, edo zorion hori non-bait
same.INS or betray.PEF 1PLU/.TRA God.ERG or happiness that somewhere
aurki da-i-te-ke.
find.RAD ITR.POT

c. Iza-n da-di-n edo abere-a edo gizon-a, ez da bizi-ko.
be.RAD ITR.SUJ.NCZ or beast or man not ITR live.FUT

d. Edo orain-txe, edo inoiz ez.
or now.EMP or ever not

(19) a. Ez da antsia, ala probe-a-ri ala Jesu Kristo ber-a-ri
not be.SYN concern.IDF or poor.ZEP.DAT or Jesus Christ.IDF he_himself.DAT
e-ma-n . . .
give . . .

b. Ala etxe-an geldi-tu, ala ahizp(a)-a-rekin j-oa-n, beste aukera-rik ez
or house.LOC stay or sister.SOC go other choice.PAR not
da-uka-zu.
have./2.SYT

(20) a. Ni-k higuin d-u-t baratxuri-a arrainzop(a)-an eta Miren-e-k maite d-u
I.ERG hate.PPR /1.TRA garlic fish_soup.LOC and Mary.ERG love.PPR TRA
baratxuri-a arrainzop(a)-an.
garlic fish_soup.LOC

b. Ni-k higuin d-u-t eta Miren-e-k maite d-u baratxuri-a arrainzop(a)-an.
I.ERG hate.PPR /1.TRA and Mary.ERG love.PPR TRA garlic fish_soup.LOC

c. Ni-k higuin d-u-t baratxuri-a arrainzop(a)-an eta Miren-e-k maite d-u
I.ERG hate.PPR /1.TRA garlic fish_soup.LOC and Mary.ERG love.PPR TRA
(ber-ta-n).
it_itself.LOC

(21) a. Egun-a-k gau-a da-kar gurpil ero-an eta goiz-a-k arratsalde-a
day.ERG night bring.SYT wheel crazy.LOC and morning.ERG afternoon
da-kar gurpil ero-an.
bring.SYT wheel crazy.LOC

b. Egun-a-k gau-a eta goiz-a-k arratsalde-a da-kar gurpil ero-an.
day.ERG night and morning.ERG afternoon bring.SYT wheel crazy.LOC

(22) a. Miren-e-k sagar bat eta Karmen-e-k udare bat jan-go d-u.
Mary.ERG apple a and Carmen.ERG pear a eat.FUT TRA

b. Jon-e-k bost sagar eta Patxi-k lau udare jan-go d-it-u.
John.ERG five apple.IDF and Frank.ERG four pear.IDF eat.FUT PLU/.TRA

(23) a. Miren-e-k sagar bat eta Karmen-e-k udare bat jan-go d-it-u-z-te.
Mary.ERG apple a and Carmen.ERG pear a eat.FUT PLU/PLU.TRA
(also *d-u-te*)
/PLU.TRA

b. Jon-e-k bost sagar eta Patxi-k lau udare jan-go d-it-u-z-te.
John.ERG five apple.IDF and Frank.ERG four pear.IDF eat.FUT PLU/PLU.TRA

(24) Abel artzain-a eta Kain nekazari-a z-ir-a-n. (Batua: *z-ir-e-n*)
Abel shepherd and Cain farmer be.PLU.SYN.PST

(25) a. Zu-re liburu-ak, ni-re liburu-ak eta ni-re emazte-a-ren liburu-ak hor
you.GEN book.PLU I.GEN book.PLU and I.GEN wife.GEN book.PLU there.LOC
da-u-de lurre-an.
be.PLU.SYN floor.LOC
b. Zu-re, ni-re eta ni-re emazte-a-ren liburu-ak hor da-u-de lurre-an.
you.GEN I.GEN and I.GEN wife.GEN book.PLU there.LOC be.PLU.SYN floor.LOC
c. Zu-re liburu-ak, ni-re-ak eta ni-re emazte-a-ren-ak hor
you.GEN book.PLU I.GEN.ZEP.PLU and I.GEN wife.GEN.ZEP.PLU there.LOC
da-u-de lurre-an.
be.PLU.SYN floor.LOC

(26) Etxe edo herri har-ta-tik.
house.IDF or city yonder.ELA
(Similarly in Lz: *etxe edo hiri hartarik.*)

(27) a. . . . bihotz eta arima gabe . . .
. . . heart.IDF and soul.IDF without.PRE
b. . . . Jainko-a-ren lege eta amorio gabe . . .
. . . God.GEN law.IDF and love.IDF without.PRE

(28) Ber-a-z, ait(a)-a ez da nihoiz iza-tu seme-a gabe eta Espiritu Saiñdu-a
same.INS father not ITR ever be.PEF son without.PRE and Spirit Holy
gabe?
without.PRE

(29) a. Etorki-a-ren aurka (e)ta o(h)itur(a-e-)en aurka . . .
nature.GEN against and custom.PLU.GEN against . . .
b. Jaun-a-ren aurka eta har-k aukera-tu-ri(k)-ko errege-a-ren aurka . . .
Lord.GEN against and yonder_one.ERG choose.PEF.STA.ADN king.GEN against

(30) a. . . . Jaun-a-ren eta On-e-k (Batua: *Honek*)
. . . Lord.GEN and this_one.ERG
Igurtzi-ta-ku-a-ren (Batua: *Igurtzitakoaren*) kontra . . .
Anoint.PEC.ADN.ZEP.GEN against
b. . . . Jaun-a-ren kontra eta Har-en Kristo-ren kontra.
. . . Lord.GEN against and Yonder_one.GEN Christ.GEN against
c. . . . har-en eta har-en(-e)-en kontra . . .
. . . yonder_one.GEN and yonder_one.GEN.ZEP.PLU.GEN against

(31) a. Adiskide on bat da-uka-gu zu-k eta ni-k.
friend good one.IDF have./1PLU.SYT you.ERG and I.ERG
b. **Adiskide on bat da-uka-gu zu eta ni-k.
friend good one.IDF have./1PLU.SYT you and I.ERG

(32) a. Patxi-k eta Pello-k atsegin-e-z irakurr-i d-u-te liburu hori.
Frank.ERG and Pete.ERG pleasure.IDF.INS read.PEF /PLU.TRA book this
b. Patxi eta Pello-k atsegin-e-z irakurr-i d-u-te liburu hori.
Frank.IDF and Pete.ERG pleasure.IDF.INS read.PEF /PLU.TRA book this

(33) Ber-ta-ko langille-ek (Batua: *langileek*)— Agirre-ren seme, alaba,
right_there.ADN worker.PLU.ERG Agirre.GEN son.IDF daughter.IDF
sui (Batua: *suhi*) (e)ta ilob(a)-ek— dan-ak (Batua: *denek*) ze-ki-te-n
son-in-law.IDF and nephew.PLU.ERG all.PLU.ERG know./PLU.SYT.PST
euskara-z.
Basque_language.IDF.INS

(34) Ez da orde-an ez bihi-rik, ez azienda-rik, ez arbola-rik, ez
not be.SYN compensation.LOC not grain.PAR not cattle.PAR not tree.PAR not
ba-da lan, artha eta buru-rik.
CDP.be.SYN work.IDF care.IDF and head.PAR

(35) a. N-eu-re morroi eta mirabe-e-i ere . . .
I.REF.GEN servant.IDF and handmaiden.PLU.DAT too
b. . . . har-en maxima gal-du (e)ta moda ergel-e-i ja-rrai-k-i
. . . yonder_one.GEN maxim lose.PEF.IDF and fashion silly.PLU.DAT follow.PEF
h-a-tza-i-e . . .
PLU/2SOL.DIT
c. . . . ingura-tzen z-it-u-e(n)-n onthasun (Batua: *ontasun*), ohore (e)ta
. . . surround.IPF PLU/.TRA.PST.NRE wealth.IDF honor.IDF and
atsegin-e-i . . . beha-tu-rik, . . .
pleasure.PLU.DAT . . . look.PEF.STA

(36) a. . . . Jesus-en ama Maria eta anai=arreb(a-e)-ekin . . .
. . . Jesus.GEN mother Maria.IDF and brother.IDF.(-and)-sister.PLU.SOC
b. . . . Maria Jesus-en am(a)-a-rekin, eta har-en
. . . Maria Jesus.GEN mother.SOC and yonder_one.GEN
anay(-e)-ekin (Batua: *anaiekin*).
brother.PLU.SOC

(37) a. Gain-e-ra-ko-ek behe-r(a)-ago-ko eta
top.ALL.ADN.ZEP.PLU.ERG lower_part.ALL.COP.ADN.IDF and
arrunt-ago-rekin kontent z-ir-e-n.
ordinary.COP.ZEP.IDF.SOC satisfied.IDF be.PLU.SYN.PST
b. Noe atzen-ean, ber-e hiru seme Sem, Kam eta Jafet eta
Noah end.LOC he_himself.GEN three son.IDF Shem.IDF Ham.IDF and Jafet and
lau-r-(e)-en emazte-a(-e-e)kin (Batua: *emazteekin*) kutx(a)-an sartu
four.ZEP.PLU.GEN wife.PLU.SOC ark.LOC go_into.PEF

ze-n.
ITR.PST
(Cf. Gn 7.13:
Egun har-ta-n ber-ta-n sar-tu ze-n Noe untzi-an
day yonder_one.LOC it_itself.IDF.LOC go_into.PEF ITR.PST Noah ark.LOC
ber-e seme Sem, Kam eta Jafet-ekin, ber-e
he_himself.GEN son.IDF Sem.IDF Ham.IDF and Japheth.IDF.SOC he_himself.GEN
emazte eta errain[-e]-ekin.)
wife.IDF and daughter-in-law.PLU.SOC

c. ... ber-e emazte, hiru seme eta hiru errañ-a(-e-e)kin
... he_himself.GEN wife.IDF three son.IDF and three daughter-in-law.PLU.SOC
irten zen.
come_out.PEF ITR.PST
(Cf. Gn 8.18:
Atera ze-n Noe ber-e emazte, seme eta
come_out.PEF ITR.PST Noah he_himself.GEN wife.IDF son.IDF and
errain[-e]-ekin.)
daughter-in-law.PLU.SOC

(38) a. Etxe bat eros-i dugu, eta ber-e-ha(r-en)-la sal-du.
house a buy.PEF /1PLU.TRA and immediately sell(.PEF)
b. Etxe bat eros-i, eta ber-e-ha(r-en)-la sal-du d-u-gu.
house a buy and immediately sell.PEF /1PLU.TRA

(39) a. Etxe bat eros-ten d-u-gu, eta ber-e-ha(r-en)-la saltzen.
house a buy.IPF /1PLU.TRA and immediately sell.IPF
b. Etxe bat eros-i, eta ber-e-ha(r-en)-la saltzen dugu.
house a buy and immediately sell.IPF /1PLU.TRA

(40) a. Etxe bat eros i-ko d-u-gu, eta ber-e-ha(r-en)-la sal-du-ko.
house a buy.FUT /1PLU.TRA and immediately sell.FUT
b. Etxe bat eros-i, eta ber-e-ha(r-en)-la salduko dugu.
house a buy and immediately sell.FUT /1PLU.TRA

(41) a. Etxe bat eros dezagun, eta ber-e-ha(r-en)-la sal.
house a buy.RAD /1PLU.TRA.SUJ.NCZ and immediately sell.RAD
b. Etxe bat eros-i, eta ber-e-ha(r-en)-la sal dezagun.
house a buy and immediately sell.RAD /1PLU.TRA.SUJ.NCZ

(42) Etxe bat eros-i eta, ber-e-ha(r-en)-la saldu dugu.
house a buy.PEF ENC immediately sell.PEF /1PLU.TRA

(43) a. Tresna hauek da-ka-tza-gu, eta ber-e-ha(r-en)-la e-ra-bil-tzen.
tool this.PLU bring.PLU/1PLU.SYT and immediately use.IPF

b. Tresna hauek ekarri, eta ber-e-ha(r-en)-la ba-da-ra-bil-tza-gu.
tool this.PLU bring and immediately AFF.use.PLU/1PLU.SYT

(44) a. Gu-k etxe bat eros-ten d-u-gu, eta zu-ek ber-e-ha(r-en)-la saltzen.
we.ERG house a buy.IPF /1TRA and you.PLU.ERG immediately sell.IPF
b. Gu-k etxe bat eros-i, eta zu-ek ber-e-ha(r-en)-la salt-zen d-u-zu-e.
we.ERG house a buy and you.PLU.ERG immediately sell.IPF /2PLU.TRA

(45) a. Pen(a)-ak oro ji-ten d-ir-a Jainko-a-ren nahi-tik, eta ber-a-k
suffering.PLU all.IDF come.IPF PLU.ITR God.GEN will.ELA and he_himself.ERG
permititzen oro hoben-a-ga(i)-tik.
allow.IPF all.IDF sin.MOT
b. Ni-k han da-kus-a-da-n zu-re begitarte-a, eta saindu(e)-ekin
I.ERG over_there.LOC see./1/SYT.NCZ you.GEN countenance and saint.PLU.SOC
lauda zu-re majestate-a.
praise.RAD you.GEN majesty
c. Zer-en hainbat bekatu-ta-n da-rama-gu bizia, eta g-e(u)-r(e)-ok gu-re
why so_much sin.LOC lead./1PLU.SYT life and we_ourselves.ERG we.GEN
falt(a)-a-z gal-tzen gu-re buru-a?
fault.INS lose.IPF we.GEN head
d. Zer-en ordu-an z-eu-re etsai-a, z-eu-re buru-a, eta deabru-a ere
CAC that_time.LOC you.REF.GEN enemy you.REF.GEN head and devil too
garai(t)-tzen bait-(d)-it-u-zu, eta arim(a)-a, eta gorputz-a ere bake-an,
defeat.IPF ACP.PLU/2.TRA and soul and body too peace.LOC
sosegu-an eta segur-e-an ipin-tzen.
calm.LOC and safety.LOC put.IPF
e. Eri-ak senda-tzen z-it-u-en, hil-ak pi(t)z-ten, haize-ak
sick.ZEP.PLU cure.IPF PLU/.TRA.PST dead.ZEP.PLU revive.IPF wind.PLU
jabal-tzen, itsaso-a ema-tzen.
pacify.IPF sea calm.IPF
f. Laster e-gi-ten d-u hilerri-ra, iriki-tzen d-u hobi-a eta ber-e
race.IDF do.IPF TRA cemetery.ALL open.IPF TRA grave and she_herself.GEN
alab(a)-a bizi eta azkar hatzema(n)-ten.
daughter alive.IDF_and_kicking.IDF find.IPF
g. Noizbait-e-an ere, bi zakurr-ak irits-i omen z-ir-e-n palazio-ko
sometime.LOC too two dog.PLU reach.PEF REP PLU.ITR.PST palace.ADN
ate-e-ta-ra, bai(-e)ta ber-ta-n txiki-tu deabrua, hauts-i
gate.PLU.ALL also it_itself.LOC tear_to_pieces devil break_down
hama(r)hiru ate-ak, eta ber(e)-en nagusi-a libra-tu ere.
thirteen door.PLU and he_himself.PLU.GEN master liberate too

h. Ber-a ez d-u-t i-kus-ten, bai botz-a e-ntzu-ten.
he_himself not /1.TRA see.IPF yes voice hear.IPF

(46) a. Eta ni-k gizon-a gal-du eta alab(a)-a aurki-tu n-u-en.
and I.ERG man lose.PEF and daughter find.PEF /1.TRA.PST

b. Bi-ok bat-e-ra bazkal-du eta afal-tzen z-u-te-n.
two.ZEP.INC.ERG one.ALL have_lunch.PEF and have_dinner.IPF /PLU.TRA.PST

c. Hau adi-tu z-u-e(n)-n-e-an neska hori beldur-tu, eta atezulo-tik
this hear.PEF TRA.PST.NRE.LOC girl that get_scared(.PEF) and doorway.ELA
luza-tu e-gi-n omen z-i-o-n behatz-a.
extend do.PEF REP DTR.PST finger

d. Eta ha(r-en)-la, ustegabe, erabat abera(t)s-tu, eta herri
and yonder_way unexpected.PRE very become_wealthy(.PEF) and village
bat-e-ra jaits-i, eta han anai(a-)arreb(a)-ak eta zakurr-ak
a.ALL go_down(.PEF) and over_there.LOC brother_and_sister.PLU and dog.PLU
on-do bizi iza-n omen z-ir-e-n.
well live be.PEF REP PLU.ITR.PST

e. Juan Martin aintzindari haundi-(e)-en-gan-(r)a j-oa-n eta Jose Larrekoa-ren
Juan Martin leader high.PLU.ALL go and Jose Larrekoa.GEN
hauzi-a konpon-du z-u-en.
case settle.PEF TRA.PST

f. Etxe-ra j-oa-n eta ohe-ra sar-tu n-in-tz-e-n.
house.ALL go.PEF and bed.ALL get_into.PEF 1.TR.PST

g. Ni mendi-tik e-torr-i eta Joxe-k etxe-tik aldegi-n z-u-en.
I mountain.ELA come and Joseph.ERG house.ELA leave.PEF TRA.PST

(47) a. Ordu-an libra-tu-ren d-u anai(a)-a-k anai(a)-a herio-ta-ra, eta ait(a)-a-k
that_time.LOC deliver.FUT TRA brother.ERG brother death.IDF.ALL and father.ERG
haurr-a.
child

b. Oin-a-k zerbitza-tzen d-u esku-a, eta esku-ak oin-a.
foot.ERG serve.IPF TRA hand and hand.ERG foot

c. Hil-ak pi(t)z-tu-ko d-ir-en-e-an, ez d-u-te har-tu-ko ez
dead.ZEP.PLU rise.FUT PLU.ITR.NRE.LOC not /PLU.TRA take.FUT not
gizon-ek emazte-rik, ez eta emazteki-ek senarr-ik.
man.PLU.ERG wife.PAR not and woman.PLU.ERG husband.PAR

d. Zu-k e-ma-n-go d-i-o-zu zuku-a, eta ni-k babarrun-ak.
you.ERG give.FUT //2.DTR soup and I.ERG bean.PLU

e. Hama(r)lau urte z-it-u-en ordu-an mutil-a-k, eta zu-k
fourteen year.IDF have.PLU/.SYT.PST that_time.LOC boy.ERG and you.ERG

hama(r)hiru.
thirteeen.IDF

(48) Zu-ek gu-re alab(a)-a-rekin gero zer e-gi-n-go d-u-zu-e?
you.PLU.ERG we.GEN daughter.SOC later what do.FUT /2PLU.TRA

(49) a. Alkate-a-k eta nor-k lapur-tu z-u-te-n artaldea?
mayor.ERG and who.ERG steal.PEF /PLU.TRA.PST flock_of_sheep
b. Ohe-an ber-e emazte-a eta nor i-kus-i z-it-u-en?
bed.LOC he_himself.GEN wife and who see.PEF PLU/PLU.TRA.PST
c. Ber-e izen-a eta zer aha(t)z-tu za-i-z-ki-o?
he_himself.GEN name and what forget.PEF /PLU.DIT
d. Madril-e-ra eta no-ra zi-h-oa-z-e-n?
Madrid.ALL and where.ALL go.PLU.SYN.PST
e. La(u)r(h)ogei eta zenbat urte d-it-u?
eighty and how_many year have.PLU/.SYT

(50) a. Nor-k eta alkate-a-k lapur-tu z-u-en artaldea!
who.ERG and mayor.ERG steal.PEF TRA.PST flock_of_sheep
b. Ohe-an nor eta ber-e emazte-a i-kus-i z-u-en!
bed.LOC who and he_himself.GEN wife see.PEF TRA.PST
c. Zer eta ber-e izen-a aha(t)z-tu za-i-o!
what and he_himself.GEN name forget.PEF DIT
d. No-ra eta Madril-e-ra zi-h-oa-z-en!
where.ALL and Madrid.ALL go.PLU.SYN.PST
e. Zenbat eta la(u)r(h)ogei urte d-it-u!
how_many and eighty year.IDF have.PLU/.SYT

(51) a. Zein-e-k (variant of *nor-k*) eta Odolki-k zirika-tu behar ber-a,
which_one.ERG who.ERG and Odolki.ERG prod need.PPR he_himself
Moxolo!
Moxolo
b. Nor-k eta Peru-k e-sa-n behar!
who.ERG and Peter.ERG say should.PPR
c. Nor-k, eta hi-k aukera-tu d-u-k, ber-a-z, Txanton alkate?
who.ERG and you.SOL.ERG elect.PEF /2SOL.TRA same.INS Txanton mayor.IDF
d. No-n gain-e-ra eta ber-e jaioterri-an!
where.LOC top.ALL and he_himself.GEN native_land.LOC
e. Ha(r-en)-la-ko eskeintz(a)-a … No-n eta New York-e-n!
yonder_way.ADN offer where.LOC and New York.LOC
f. Zahar-tu eta maskal-du-ta gero ezkon-tze-a! Nor-ekin eta
grow_old.(PEF) and grow_weak.PEC later get_married.VEN who.SOC and

asko-ta-z gazte-ago eta neskame etxe-an iza-n z-en-u-te(-n)-n
much.INS young.COP.IDF and maid.IDF house.LOC have.PEF /2PLU.TRA.PST.NRE
Agar emagaldu horr-ekin!
Agar whore that.SOC

g. Non-dik eta zerraldo-tik atera z-ir-e-n hitz hai-ek.
where.ELA and coffin.ELA come_out.PEF PLU.ITR.PST word yonder.PLU

(52) a. Zer e-gi-n eta zeru-ko giltz(a-)a puska-tu z-i-o-te-n aingeru
what do(.PEF) and heaven.ADN key break.PEF //PLU.DTR.PST angel
koskorr-ek San Pedro-ri!
little.PLU.ERG St. Peter.DAT

b. Nor harri-tu eta errege harri-tu.
who be_surprised and king be_surprised

c. Eta hori noiz gerta-tu-ko eta orain gerta-tzen.
and that when happen.FUT and now happen.IPF

d. Zer ken-du-ko mediku-a-k, eta gozo-a.
what take_away.FUT doctor.ERG and candy

(53) a. Zepai-k eta han-dik alde e-gi-n z-u-te-n.
Zepa.ERG ENC over_there.ELA place.IDF make.PEF /PLU.TRA.PST

b. Ama-txo-ri eta ez beldur-tze-ko e-sa-n.
Mother.DIM.IDF.DAT ENC not be_afraid.VEN.ADN tell(.RAD)

c. Nor bizi da etxe horr-e-ta-n?— Pello eta.
who live.PPR ITR house that.LOC Pello ENC

d. Joxepa-k eta barre e-gi-n z-u-te-n.
Joseph.ERG ENC laugh.IDF do.PEF /PLU.TRA.PST

(54) a. Sukalde-ko ontzi-ak, plater-ak eta, hauts-i z-it-u-en.
kitchen.ADN dish.PLU plate.PLU ENC break.PEF PLU/PLU.TRA.PST

b. Tabern(a-)a eta iza-n behar d-u-te.
tavern ENC have must.PPR /PLU.TRA

(55) a. Hamar urte edo n-it-u-en.
ten year.IDF ENC have.PLU/1.SYT.PST

b. . . . alab(a-)a berri-z haurtzain edo ze-(d)uka-n nonbait . . .
. . . daughter new.IDF.INS babysitter.IDF ENC have.SYT.PST somewhere.LOC

c. Hogei edo e-torr-i d-ir-a.
twenty.DEL.IDF ENC come.PEF PLU.ITR

d. Adimen kamuts-a d-u-da-la-ko edo ni-k ez di-o-t igar-tzen.
mind dull have/1.SYT.LCZ.ADN ENC I.ERG not //1.DTR notice.IPF

e. Ba-da-ki-zu non-dik da-torr-en?— Indi(a)-e-ta-tik edo.
AFF.know./2.SYT where.ELA come.SYN.NCZ America.PLU.ELA ENC

f. Losintxakeri(a-)an al z-a-to(r)-z edo?
flattery.LOC INT come.2.SYN ENC

g. Diru-rik edo al ze-go-en hemen?
money.PAR ENC INT be.SYN.PST here.LOC

h. Eta zenbat behar n-u-e(n)-n edo galdera e-gi-n z-i-da-n.
and how_much need.PPR /1.TRA.PST.NCZ ENC question.IDF do.PEF /1/.DTR.PST

(56) Errenteria-ko-a edo horr-e(n)-la iza-n behar z-u-en.
Errenteria.ADN.ZEP ENC that_way be must.PPR TRA.PST

(57) a. Zu(-e-)en Anton-e-k ber-e buru-a hil ote d-u-en edo,
you.PLU.GEN Tony.ERG he_himself.GEN head kill.PEF DUB TRA.NCZ ENC
d-io-te.
say./PLU.SYT

b. Itsaspeko-rik agiri ote ze(-n)-n edo beti itsaso-ra begi-ra.
submarine.PAR appear.PPR DUB ITR.PST.NCZ ENC always sea.ALL watching.PRE

(58) a. Loteri(a-)a eskain-tzen al d-i-o-zu ala?
lottery offer.IPF INT //2.DTR ENC

b. Lanpe-tu-a i-kus-ten h-a-u-t. Eskribi-tze-n, ala?
be_busy.PEF.SIN see.IPF 2SOL/1.TRA write.VEN.LOC ENC

c. Sal-du ordu-ko, ez z-en-u-en z-eu-re-a, ala?
sell time.ADN not have./2.SYT.PST you.REF.GEN.ZEP ENC

d. Gu-re hizkuntz(a)-a-ren egoera larri-a-k ez z-a-it-u-z-te nahigabe-tzen
we.GEN language.GEN status precarious.ERG not 2PLU/.TRA make_sad.IPF
ala?
ENC

e. Lo z-a-u-de ala?
asleep.PRE be.2.SYN ENC

(59) Ifernu-an sar-tu n-a-iz, ala zer?
hell.LOC enter.PEF 1.ITR or what

(60) Ez d-u-zu e zagu(t)-tu? Zu-re seme-a be-ra ze-n eta!
not /2.TRA recognize.PEF you.GEN son he_himself be.SYN.PST EEC

(61) a. Beste lagun bat eta bi-ak atze-ra j-oa-n z-ir-e-n.
other friend a and two.ZEP.PLU back.ALL go.PEF PLU.ITR.PST

b. Beste bertso asko, andre-a eta bi-ak elkarr-ekin kanta-tze-ko
other verse many wife.DEF and two.ZEP.ERG.PLU each_other.SOC sing.VEN.ADN
e-gi-n-ak d-ir-a.
make.PEF.PLU be.PLU.SYN

c. Zestua-ra j-oa-n g-in-e-n aita eta bi-ak.
Cestona.ALL go.PEF 1PLU.ITR.PST Father.IDF and two.ZEP.PLU

(62) a. Zepai eta bi-ok e-torr-i g-in-e-n ordu-an.
Zepai and two.ZEP.INC come.PEF 1PLU.ITR.PST that_time.LOC
b. Ni-k, nagusi-a-k eta bi-ok e-gi-ten g-en-it-u-e(n)-n lan-ak,
I.ERG boss.ERG and two.INC.ERG do.IPF PLU/1PLU.TRA.PST.NRE work.PLU
bakarr-ik erraz e-gi-n-go n-it-u-zke-en.
alone.STA easily do.FUT PLU/1.TRA.COD.PST
c. Aita eta bi-ok mendi-ra j-oa-n g-in-e-n.
Father.IDF and two.ZEP.INC mountain.ALL go.PEF 1PLU.ITR.PST

(63) a. Ama, Itziar eta hiru-r-ok geldi-tu g-in-e-n etxe-an.
Mother.IDF Itziar and three.INC stay.PEF 1PLU.ITR.PST house.LOC
b. Ba, g-oa-z-en ordu an, g-oa-z-en Teresa eta lau r-ok.
INF go.1PLU.SYN.NCZ that_time.LOC go.1PLU.ITR.SYN.NCZ Teresa and four.INC
c. Eta ho(n-en)-la-xe i-bil-i g-in-e-n azken ud(a)-an ere, Toby, Frankie,
and this_way.EMP walk.PEF 1PLU.ITR.PST last summer.LOC too Toby Frankie
Kent, aitona eta bost-ok . . .
Kent Grandfather.IDF and five.INC

(64) a. Nahi ba-d-u eta nahi ez ba-d-u ni-re Joxe-k ez d-u ile bat
want.PPR CDP.TRA and want.PPR not CDP.TRA I.GEN Joseph.ERG not TRA hair a
ere iku-tzen ni-re baimen-ik gabe.
even touch.IPF I.GEN permission.PAR without.PRE
b. Baina, nahi ba-z-u-en eta ez ba-z-u-en, zaku madarika-tu-an sar-tu
but want.PPR CDP.TRA.PST and not CDP.TRA.PST sack curse.PEF.LOC go_into
behar iza-n zi-tza-i-o-n.
have_to be.PEF DIT.PST
c. Nahi ba-d-u-zu eta ez ba-d-u-zu, ezkon-du beharr-a z-a-r-a.
want.PPR CDP./2.TRA and not CDP./2.TRA get_married need.PPR 2.ITR
d. Orain sendo-a n-a-iz, on ba-za-i-n eta ez ba-za-i-n.
now healthy be.1.SYN good.IDF CDP.2SOL.FEM/.DYN and not CDP.2SOL.FEM/.DYN
e. Ez da, orde-a, ez bihi-rik, ez azienda-rik, ez arbola-rik, ez
not be.SYN substitute not grain.PAR not cattle.PAR not tree.PAR not
ba-da lan, arta eta buru-rik.
CDP.be.SYN work.IDF care.IDF and head.PAR

(65) Kobratuko duk, bai, Jainko-a-k nahi ba-d-u zein ez ba-d-u!
receive.FUT /2SOL.TRA yes God.ERG want.PPR CDP.TRA or not CDP.TRA

(66) a. Botila ba(t)-na ardo edan de-za-gu-n.
bottle.IDF one.DIS wine.IDF drink(.RAD) /1PLU.TRA.SUJ.NCZ
b. Ha-n ba-z-ir-e-n sei ontzi harri-z-ko,
over_there.LOC AFF.be.PLU.SYN.PST six container.IDF stone.IDF.INS.ADN.IDF

bizpahiru-na metreta ze-(d)uka-te(-n)-n-ak.
two_or_three.DIS metreta.IDF hold./PLU.SYT.PST.NRE.ZEP.PLU

c. Bi-na arima d-it-u-gu gehi-en-ek.
two.DIS soul.IDF have.PLU/1PLU.SYT much.SUP.PLU.ERG

d. E-ma-n z-i-z-ki-gu-te-n bi-na gu-ri, lau-na beste-e-i.
give.PEF PLU/1PLU/PLU.DTR.PST two.DIS we.DAT four.DIS other.ZEP.PLU.DAT

e. Guzti-ak e-duki-ko d-it-u-z-te hamar-na beso luzer(a)-an, eta
all.ZEP.PLU.ERG have.FUT PLU/PLU.TRA ten.DIS yard.IDF length.LOC and
zabaler(a)-an ba(t)-na eta erdi.
breadth.LOC one.DIS and half.IDF

f. Gu-re etxe-an lau(r)-ren-tzako gaur sei sardina, baina ez d-u-te
we.GEN house.LOC four.DEL.IDF.BEN today six sardine.IDF but not /PLU.TRA
e-gi-n partizio berdin-a; gu-ri ba(t)-na eta ber-ak jan
do.PEF divison even we.DAT one.DIS and he_himself.PLU.ERG eat.PEF
d-i-gu-te bi-na zer-ga(i)-tikan ez parti-tu bat eta erdi-na?
/1PLU/PLU.DTR two.DIS what.MOT not divide one and half.DIS

g. Zenba(t)-na liburu eros-i d-u-zu-e?
how_much.DIS book buy.PEF /2PLU.TRA

h. Har-k bi-na liburu eros-i d-it-u liburudenda guzti-e-ta-n.
yonder_one.ERG two.DIS book.IDF buy.PEF PLU/.TRA bookstore all.PLU.LOC

i. Ohera-tu g-a-r-a bi-ok ohe ba(t)-na-ta-n.
go_to_sleep.PEF 1PLU.ITR two.ZEP.INC bed one.DIS.LOC

(67) a. Bos(t)-na gizon-e-k lagun-du d-i-gu-te.
five.DIS man.ERG help.PEF /1PLU/PLU.DTR

b. Gu-k hiru-na ikasle-ri lagun-tzen d-i-e-gu lan-ak e-gi-te-n.
we.ERG three.DIS student.DAT help.IPF /PLU/1PLU.DTR work.PLU do.VEN.LOC

c. Bi-na neska-k e-ma-n z-i-gu-te-n musu.
two.DIS girl.ERG give.PEF /1PLU/PLU.DTR.PST kiss.

d. Gu bizikleta ba(t)-na-ta-n e-torr-i g-a-r-a.
we bike one.DIS.LOC come.PEF 1PLU.ITR

e. Hiru-na neska-rekin i-kus-i n-i-tu-en.
three.DIS girl.SOC see.PEF PLU/1.TRA.PST

Chapter 31

(1) a. Gaur=biharr-e-ta-n buka-tu-ko d-u-gu lan hori.
today-tomorrow.PLU.LOC finish.FUT /1PLU.TRA work that

b. Ez al d-u-zu-e bihar=etzi-e-ta-ra-ko utz-i-ko?
not INT /2PLU.TRA tomorrow-the_day_after_tomorrow.PLU.DES leave.FUT

(2) a. Eta gain-e-ra abioitxo ba(t)-na, eskola-ra j-oa-n=e-tor-tze-ko.
and top.ALL airplane.DIM one.DIS school.ALL go-come.VEN.ADN

b. Isil=isil-ik jan-edan z-u-te-n.
quiet.IDF-quiet.STA eat-drink.PEF /PLU.TRA.PST

(3) a. ... Ni-k Aritz harrapa-tu-z gero ez d-u-t inon-go
... I.ERG Aritz arrest.PEF.IDF.INS since not have./1.SYT somewhere.ADN
zalantza-rik.— Zer ardura za-i-z-ki-gu hi-re zalantz(a)-ak eta
doubt.PAR what matter be.1PLU/PLU you.GEN.SOL doubt.PLU and
malantz(a)-ak?— oihu e-gi-n z-u-en Galarreta-k. Hemen
'doubt'.PLU shout.IDF make.PEF TRA.PST Galarreta.ERG here.LOC
froga hobe-ak behar d-i-z-ki-a-gu.
(piece_of_)evidence good.COP.PLU need.PPR PLU/1PLU.TRA.ALC.SOL

b. —Bai, baina ni oporr-e-ta-n n-a-go eta ...
yes but I vacation.PLU.LOC be.1.SYN and ...
—Zer oporr-ak eta moporr-ak! Batzu-e-ta-n ume bat baino
what vacation.PLU and 'shmacation'.PLU some.PLU.LOC child a SRP
okerr-ago h-a-iz.
wrong.COP.IDF be.2SOL.SYN

c. Hi-k uste baino amona bekatari-ago-a da-uka-k, Jon.
you.SOL.ERG think.PPR SRP grandmother.IDF sinful.COP have./2SOL.SYT Jon
—Zer bekatu eta mekatu, asti-rik ere ez bai(t)-t(<*d)-u-zu iza-n!
what sin.IDF and 'sin' free_time.PAR even not ACP./2.TRA have.PEF

d. —Gizon-a haserre-tzen za-i-gu. Haserre edo maserre ... aditu hitz-ak.
man get_mad.IPF 1PLU/.DYN mad.IDF or 'mad'.IDF listen_to word.PLU

e. —Ez n-e-ki-a-n hain sikologo on-a h-in-tz-e-(n)-n-ik—
not know./1SYT.PST.ALC.SOL so psychologist good be.2SOL.SYN.PST.PCZ
bota z-i-o-n alai detektibe-a-k.
throw.PEF DTR.PST cheerful.PRE detective.ERG
—Ze sikologo eta mikologo— e-ra-ntzu-n z-i-o-n
what psychologist.IDF and 'psychologist'.IDF answer.PEF DTR.PST
Rodriguez-e-k bero samar.
Rodriguez.ERG hot.PRE rather.ADV

(4) Pello-k hitzegi-n-go ba-l-u, moj(a)-ek aldegi-n-go l-u-ke-te.
Pello.ERG speak.FUT CDP.TRA.COD nun.PLU.ERG walk_out.FUT /PL.TRA.COD

(5) a. Hau d-ela eta, e-ra-baki n-u-en bi-ak eraberri-tze-a.
this be.SYN.LCZ EEC decide.PEF /1.TRA.PST two.ZEP.PLU revise.VEN

b. Ezkontz(a)-a-ren hauts-eraz-te-a hitz(h)ar-tu z-u-te-n.
matrimony.GEN break.CAU.VEN agree.PEF /PLU.TRA.PST

c. Gehi-en-ik irri e-gi-n araz-i-ko d-i-o-n-a-ri hitz-e-ma-ten d-i-o
much.SUP.STA laughter.IDF do CAU.FUT DTR.NRE.ZEP.DAT promise.IPF DTR
zinta zeta bat ederr-a.
ribbon silk.IDF a beautiful.ZEP.SIN

(6) a. Eta hau esa-n z-u-e(n)-n-e-an, lokar-tu ze-n.
and this say.PEF TRA.PST.NRE.LOC die.PEF ITR.PST

b. Una-tu-ak iza-n-ik bi-ak, laster lokar-tu z-ir-e-n.
get_exhausted.PEF.PLU be.PEF.STA two.ZEP.PLU quickly fall_asleep.PEF PLU.ITR.PST

c. Gu-re mutil-a sukar-tu ze-n, ja-ki-n z-u-e(n)-n-e-an soldadu
we.GEN boy flare_up.PEF ITR.PST find_out.PEF TRA.PST.NRE.LOC soldier.IDF
ze(-n)-la.
be.SYN.PST.LCZ

(7) a. Aitor de-za-gu-n nolabait-e-ko-tzat ets-i d-it-u-ela
acknowledge.RAD /1PLU.TRA.SUJ.NCZ somehow.ADN.PRO consider.PEF PLU/.TRA.LCZ
hon-e-k.
this_one.ERG

b. Zenbait adiskide-k ni-re aldegi-te-a koldarkeria-tzat ets-i d-u-te.
some friend.IDF.ERG I.GEN escape.VEN cowardice.PRO conside.PEF /PLU.TRA

(8) a. Eta guzti-z mirakulu e(t)s-ten z-u-te-n.
and all.IDF.INS wonder.IDF consider.IPF /PLU.TRA.PST

b. Aski e(t)s-ten d-u edo sobera e(t)s-ten d-u.
enough.IDF consider.IPF TRA or too_much.IDF consider.IPF TRA

(9) a. Arrain buruhandi, haginzorrotz, larrume(he)-a.
fish big_head.IDF sharp_teeth.IDF thin_skin

b. Bi idi handi, kopetazuri, bizkarbeltz, adarr(h)andi-ak.
two ox big.IDF white_forehead.IDF black_back.IDF big_horn.PLU

c. Gizon burusoil bizarzuri bat . . .
man bald_head white_beard a

d. Etxepila bat teilatu=zahar=(h)aundi, tximinia=ketsu,
couple_of_houses a big_old_roof.IDF smoked_chimney.IDF
(h)ormabeltz=sendo-ak.
firm_dark_wall.PLU

e. Nicolls jeneral-a begi eta izter eta beso=bakarr-a ze-n.
Nicolls General eye.IDF and thighbone.IDF and one_arm be.SYN.PST

Chapter 32

(1) a. Etxe hau zahar=zaharr-a da.
house this old.IDF-old be.SYN

b. Bero=bero ze-go-en bitarte-an.
warm.IDF-warm.IDF stay.SYN.PST interval.LOC

c. En-e lagun on=on-a.
I.GEN friend good.IDF-good.IDF

d. ... eliza oso-a zoko guzti-e-ta-n bete=bete-a.
church whole corner all.PLU.LOC full.IDF-full

e. Eska-tu eta har-tu-ko d-u-zu-e, zu(e)-en poz-a bete=bete-a iza-n
ask and receive.FUT /2PLU.TRA you.PLU.GEN joy full.IDF-full be(.RAD)
da-di-n.
ITR.SUJ.NCZ

(2) a. Ber-e ile gorri=gorri hori luzi-tze-a gusta-tzen za-i-o.
she_herself.GEN hair red.IDF-red.IDF that show.VEN like.IPF DIT

b. Ordu-an emakume eder=ederr-a i-kus-i z-u-en
that_time.LOC woman beautiful.IDF-beautiful see.PEF TRA.PST
beregana-tze-n.
come_at_herself.VEN.LOC

c. Lo gozo=gozo-an n-en-go-en.
sleep sweet.IDF-sweet.LOC be.1.SYN.PST

(3) a. Liburu guzti=guzti-a irakurr-i d-u-t.
book whole.IDF-whole read.PEF /1.TRA

b. Liburu guzti=guzti-ak irakurr-i d-it-u-t.
book all.IDF-all.PLU read.PEF PLU/1.TRA

c. Guzti=guzti-a esa-n-go d-i-o-t. (Also *den=den-a*)
everything.IDF-everything tell.FUT //1.DTR everything.IDF-everything

d. Guzti=guzti-ek z-it-u-z-te-n hil-da-ko-ak ugari.
all.IDF-all.PLU.ERG have.PLU/PLU.SYT.PST die.PEC.ADN.ZEP.PLU abundantly

(4) a. Z-a-r-en=z-a-r-en-a bait-z-a-r-a zu-ta-z pena d-i-zu-t ni-k.
be.2.SYN.NRE-be.2.SYN.NRE.ZEP ACP.be.2.SYN you.INS pain.IDF have./2/1/DYT I.ERG

b. Barka-tu, lagun, baina d-en=d-en-a ezin d-i-zu-t esa-n.
forgive friend.IDF but be.SYN.NRE-be.SYN.NRE.ZEP NPP /2/1.DTR tell

c. N-a-iz-en=n-a-iz-en-a zu-ri esker n-a-iz.
be.1.SYN.NRE-be.1.SYN.NRE.ZEP you.DAT thank.IDF be.1.SYN

(5) a. Araudi-a da-go-en=da-go-en-e-an utz-i-ko d-u-gu.
rule be.SYN.NRE-be.SYN.NRE.ZEP.LOC leave.FUT /1PLU.TRA

b. Ze-u-de(-n)-n=ze-u-de(-n)-n-e-an da-to(r)-z berri-z,
be.PLU.SYN.PST.NRE-be.PLU.SYN.PST.NRE.ZEP.LOC come.PLU.SYN new.IDF.INS
huts-ik ere zuzen-du gabe.
mistake.PAR even correct without.PRE

(6) a. Urte-an urte-an igaro-tzen d-u-te hemen-txe ud(a)-a.
year.LOC year.LOC spend.IPF /PLU.TRA here.LOC.EMP summer
b. Ud(a)-an ud(a)-an alde e-gi-ten d-u-te.
summer.LOC summer.LOC place.IDF make.IPF /PLU.TRA

(7) a. Ilunbe-a-k ez d-u konprehendi-tu.
darkness.ERG not TRA grasp.PEF
b. Urpe-a garbi-tu d-u-te.
underwater clean.PEF /PLU.TRA

Chapter 33

(1) a. Pitxerkada ardo-a edan z-u-en arnas(a)-a har-tu gabe.
jarful wine drink.PEF TRA.PST breath take without.PRE
b. Eskukada diru-a ba-d-u.
handful money AFF.have.SYT
c. Har e-za-zu golkokada bete intxaur.
take.RAD /2.TRA.IMP bosom_full full.IDF walnut.IDF
d. Bi platerkada tomate jan z-it-u-en.
two plateful tomato.IDF eat.PEF PLU/.TRA.PST

Index of Basque Words That Appear Only in the Example Sentences

The translations provided here are identical to those given in the grammar. Every translation is appropriate for the example sentence in which the word occurs; if the word were used in a different sentence, another translation might of course be called for. The number following the translation refers to the relevant chapter, and the number in parentheses identifies the example in which the word is used. Other words used in the examples are to be found in the Basque-English section of the Vocabulary at the end of Volume 1.

siriar	Syrian	16 (78a)
sistema	system	19 (6b)
soil	bald	31 (9c)
soilik	only	7 (25b)
solas	conversation	14 (13c); 20 (74)
sorleku	birthplace	23 (75b); 28 (6a)
soro	field	18 (37d)
sortalde	east	17 (35b); 18 (50c)
sos	penny/money	12 (23c); 25 (20c)/19 (62b)
sosegu	calm	30 (45d)
sostengatu	to support	13 (12c)
sozialista	socialist	28 (28a)
soziolinguistika	sociolinguistics	20 (6d)
su emaile	arsonist	23 (41b)
suhi	son-in-law	30 (33)
sumatu	to notice	16 (90a)
superapostolu	superapostle	26 (56d)
superbio	arrogance	20 (49a)
susmo	suspicion	8 (31)
sutu	to fire up	27 (73c)
tabako	tobacco	16 (10a)
tabernari	bartender	21 (8c)
talo	corncake	24 (54a)
tarta	pastry	24 (1c)
tarteko	all that is in the way	23 (69e)
tatxa	fault	23 (68a)
taula	wooden board	19 (80b)
taxi	taxi	19 (24a)
teatro	theater	23 (35a)
teatrogile	playwright	30 (12a)
teatrogizon	man of the theater	30 (9c)
telebista	television	16 (29b)
telefono	phone	24 (28b)
tenplu	temple	19 (23)
tentatu	to tempt	25 (5b)
Testamendu	Testament	30 (9b)
tira	come on	22 (11f)
tiratu	to shoot	22 (16a)
tiro	shot	23 (3d)

Tolstoizale	Tolstoi fan	19 (45a)
tomate	tomato	33 (1d)
topatu	to find	11 (20c); 20 (39j)
tortoka	turtle	9 (17b)
trabailu	tribulation	28 (3a)
trast	snap	27 (1a)
trinko	synthetic	23 (58b)
trist	snip	27 (1a)
triste	sad	17 (12b)
tronpa	Jew's harp	30 (14a)
trumoi	thunder	10 (5a)
txabola	hut	15 (14b); 23 (63b)
txalupa	boat	25 (38b)
txanda	time/turn	19 (27d)/20 (25b)
txango	trip	25 (20a)
txapel	beret	10 (11b)
tximinia	chimney	31 (9d)
tximista	lightning	18 (58b)
tximu	monkey	17 (46b)
txint	sound	20 (4a)
txipiroi	squid	20 (70a)
txorimalo	scarecrow	15 (38b)
txukatu	to dry	19 (2c)
udare	pear	30 (22b)
ugaldu	to increase	26 (58b)
ugaritu	to increase	16 (73d); 27 (22c)
ugatz	breast	30 (13d)
ugazaba	boss	19 (16a)
ugazaita	stepfather	20 (15a)
uholde	flood	27 (39b)
ukabilkada	punch	27 (4i)
ukatu	to deny	24 (17b)
ukitu	to touch	15 (54d)
unatu	to exhaust	31 (6b)
unibertsitate	university	15 (35a); 23 (14b)
urdalde	herd of swine	29 (9b)
urdindu	turn gray	16 (30b)
ur-ertze	edge of the water	12 (30c)
urkatu	to hang	17 (1a); 23 (48a)

urpe	underwater	32 (7b)
urririk	free of charge	22 (7e)
uzkur	stubborn	28 (27d)
uztazale	reaper	19 (57b)
xamar	jacket	23 (43d)
xarmagarri	charming	24 (52c)
xarmangarri	charming	26 (57c)
xerri	scrofula	11 (24d)
xorrotx	demanding	30 (9f)
zabalera	breadth	30 (66e)
zabuka	to reel	27 (26a)
zahar-gazte	young and old	20 (43a); 27 (56a)
zain	keeper	8 (10a)
zain	vein	16 (90c); 20 (21b, 55a)
zaku	bag/sack	22 (10f)/30 (64b)
zalaparta	disturbance	23 (27b)
zaldi irrintzi	neigh	22 (40e)
zama	burden/load	15 (27b, 28b)/26 (27b)
zamari	mule/beast of burden	20 (60a)/30 (12e)
zanpatu	to crush/to oppress	20 (25c)/26 (65b)
zapatari	cobbler	20 (39l)
zapi(ak)	linen	19 (85b)
zartagin	frying pan	30 (14a)
zatiño	little fragment	20 (75a)
zaunkaka	barking	26 (67b)
zeharkatu	to pass through	27 (72e)
zelatari	spy	27 (34b)
zen	late	27 (34e)
zendu	to pass away	20 (10a)
zentzatu	to come to one's senses	14 (35d)
zentzu	common sense/sense	26 (49a)/26 (60a)
zerbitzatu	to serve	24 (18a); 30 (47b)
zerga	tax	21 (9c)
zergati	reason	16 (49c)
zerraldo	coffin	30 (51g)
zerren	moth	25 (10c)
zertan	why	17 (11a)
zeru-lur	heaven and earth	20 (42a)
Zestua	Cestona	30 (61c)

Selected Index of Basque Formatives and Words

In addition to the formatives, a few words, expressions, and supplementary material have been added to those already given in the Basque-English vocabulary.

Index of Personal Names

Subject Index